State Immunity in International Law

The immunity or exemption enjoyed by States from legal proceedings before foreign national courts is a crucial area of international law. On the basis of an exhaustive analysis of judicial decisions, international treaties, national legislation, government statements, deliberations in international organizations as well as scholarly opinion, Xiaodong Yang traces the historical development of the relevant doctrine and practice, critically analyses the rationale for restrictive immunity and closely inspects such important exceptions to immunity as commercial transactions, contracts of employment, tortious liability, separate entities, enforcement of judgments, waiver of immunity, and the interplay between State immunity and human rights. The book draws a full picture of the law of State immunity as it currently stands, and endeavours to provide useful information and guidance for practitioners, academics and students alike.

XIAODONG YANG was a lecturer in law at the University of Aberdeen when he wrote this book. He now works as a legal officer for the Preparatory Commission for the Comprehensive Nuclear-Test-Ban Treaty Organization in Vienna.

CAMBRIDGE STUDIES IN INTERNATIONAL AND COMPARATIVE LAW

Established in 1946, this series produces high quality scholarship in the fields of public and private international law and comparative law. Although these are distinct legal sub-disciplines, developments since 1946 confirm their interrelations.

Comparative law is increasingly used as a tool in the making of law at national, regional and international levels. Private international law is now often affected by international conventions, and the issues faced by classical conflicts rules are frequently dealt with by substantive harmonization of law under international auspices. Mixed international arbitrations, especially those involving State economic activity, raise mixed questions of public and private international law, while in many fields (such as the protection of human rights and democratic standards, investment guarantees and international criminal law) international and national systems interact. National constitutional arrangements relating to 'foreign affairs', and to the implementation of international norms, are a focus of attention.

The Series welcomes works of a theoretical or interdisciplinary character, and those focusing on the new approaches to international or comparative law or conflicts of law. Studies of particular institutions or problems are equally welcome, as are translations of the best work published in other languages.

General Editors   James Crawford SC FBA
                       Whewell Professor of International Law, Faculty of Law,
                       University of Cambridge

                       John S. Bell FBA
                       Professor of Law, Faculty of Law, University of Cambridge

A list of books in the series can be found at the end of this volume.

State Immunity in International Law

Xiaodong Yang

CAMBRIDGE
UNIVERSITY PRESS

University Printing House, Cambridge CB2 8BS, United Kingdom

Cambridge University Press is part of the University of Cambridge.

It furthers the University's mission by disseminating knowledge in the pursuit of education, learning and research at the highest international levels of excellence.

www.cambridge.org
Information on this title: www.cambridge.org/9780521844017

© Xiaodong Yang 2012

This publication is in copyright. Subject to statutory exception and to the provisions of relevant collective licensing agreements, no reproduction of any part may take place without the written permission of Cambridge University Press.

First published 2012
Reprinted 2013

A catalogue record for this publication is available from the British Library

Library of Congress Cataloguing in Publication data

Yang, Xiaodong, 1965–
   State immunity in international law / Xiaodong Yang.
     p. cm. – (Cambridge studies in international and comparative law)
   ISBN 978-0-521-84401-7 (Hardback)
1. Immunities of foreign states.   2. Government liability (International law)   I. Title.
KZ4012.Y36 2012
342.08′8–dc23

2011041596

ISBN 978-0-521-84401-7 Hardback

Cambridge University Press has no responsibility for the persistence or accuracy of URLs for external or third-party internet websites referred to in this publication, and does not guarantee that any content on such websites is, or will remain, accurate or appropriate.

To my brothers and their families
For everything

Contents

Foreword by Professor James Crawford	*page* xvi
Preface and acknowledgements	xix
Abbreviations	xxiii
Table of cases	xxx
Legal instruments and codification documents	cliii
Introduction	1

1 The history of State immunity — 6
1. The age of absolute immunity — 7
2. Exceptions to absolute immunity — 10
3. The emergence of the doctrine of restrictive immunity — 11
4. The descent of the State — 19
5. The irrelevance of ideologies — 23
6. The defendant States — 25
7. The sources of the law of State immunity — 26
8. Cross-fertilization — 27
9. Terminology — 29
Conclusion — 31

2 General principles — 33
1. A general statement of principles — 34
2. State immunity as a principle of customary international law — 34
3. The presumption of immunity — 37
4. Immunity and municipal law — 42
5. The legal basis for immunity — 44

ix

5.1.	'Sovereignty' and the affiliated concepts	46
5.2.	*Par in parem non habet imperium?*	51
5.3.	What is the basis of immunity?	55
6.	The legal basis for denying immunity	58
6.1.	The 'private person' test	59
6.2.	The principle of territorial jurisdiction	64
6.3.	Private act plus territoriality – *Binnenbeziehung*	68
Conclusion		73

3 Commercial activity — 75

1.	What is a commercial activity?	76
2.	What is a non-commercial activity?	79
3.	Nature or purpose?	85
3.1.	The 'nature' approach	86
3.2.	The difficulties with the 'nature' approach	87
3.3.	The 'purpose' approach	98
3.4.	The 'context' approach	103
3.5.	A summary	108
4.	The jurisdictional nexus requirement under the US FSIA	108
4.1.	The first clause of section 1605(a)(2)	110
4.1.1.	'Based upon a commercial activity'	110
4.1.2.	'Substantial contact'	112
4.2.	The second clause of section 1605(a)(2)	113
4.3.	The third clause of section 1605(a)(2)	115
4.3.1.	The 'act'	116
4.3.2.	The 'direct effect'	124
4.3.3.	'An immediate consequence'	125
4.3.4.	The 'place of performance' test	127
4.3.5.	The 'legally significant act' test	129
Conclusion		129

4 Contracts of employment — 132

1.	Terminology	134
2.	The peculiar features of employment cases	136
2.1.	Specialized tribunals	136
2.2.	The inadequacy of the nature/private person test	137
3.	Two models	143
4.	The UK Model	144

	4.1.	The European Convention		144
		4.1.1.	The plaintiff	145
		4.1.2.	The place of performance	147
		4.1.3.	The choice of law	147
	4.2.	The UK SIA		148
		4.2.1.	Contracts of employment as a separate category	149
		4.2.2.	The plaintiff	149
		4.2.3.	The choice of law	149
	4.3.	The Australia FSIA		150
	4.4.	Other instruments		152
	4.5.	The importance of having a contract		154
5.	The US Model			157
	5.1.	The US FSIA		157
	5.2.	The plaintiff		162
		5.2.1.	Individuals: their nationality	162
		5.2.2.	Trade unions	162
6.	Diverse approaches			164
	6.1.	The employment relationship		165
	6.2.	The duties and functions of the employee		166
	6.3.	The status of the employer		170
	6.4.	The acts of the employer		171
	6.5.	The status of the employee		172
	6.6.	The nature of the particular activity		173
	6.7.	The territorial connection		173
	6.8.	The choice of law clause		174
	6.9.	The remedies sought		175
7.	The savings regime			179
	7.1.	Diplomatic and consular missions		179
		7.1.1.	Proceedings against the foreign State	181
		7.1.2.	'Institutional aims'	185
		7.1.3.	Proceedings against the diplomat personally	191
	7.2.	Foreign armed forces		193
	7.3.	Other public institutions		194
8.	Diversity and lack of uniform rules			194
	Conclusion			196
5	Non-commercial torts			199
1.	Terminology			199
2.	The targeted torts			200

2.1.	Physical injury and tangible property	200
2.2.	'Insurable risks'?	201
2.3.	'Discretionary function'	203

3. The *jure imperii / jure gestionis* distinction? 207
4. The territorial connection 215
    4.1. Tortious act/omission only 216
    4.2. Injury/damage only 218
    4.3. Both tortious act/omission and injury/damage 221
    4.4. A direct effect? 223
    4.5. States without immunity legislation 224
5. Attribution 224
6. The terrorism exception in US law: a departure 225
Conclusion 228

6 Separate entities 230
1. Terminology 231
2. Diverse approaches 232
    2.1. The UK Model 232
    2.2. The US Model 242
        2.2.1. The presumption of immunity 244
        2.2.2. A question of status 244
        2.2.3. 'A separate legal person' 247
        2.2.4. 'An organ of a foreign State' 249
        2.2.5. 'Pooling' 259
        2.2.6. 'Tiering' 264
        2.2.7. The question of timing 273
        2.2.8. Other uses of the instrumentality status 273
        2.2.9. The Canadian law 274
    2.3. Comparison and summary 277
    2.4. Somewhere in-between: the Australian law and others 280
    2.5. The practice of the States without immunity statutes 283
3. Piercing the corporate veil? 287
Conclusion 296

7 Expropriation 298
1. The general principle: immunity 299
2. Legality and immunity 301
3. The ILC's aborted provision 303

4.	The 'expropriation' provision in the US FSIA	303
	4.1. 'Rights in property'	305
	4.2. 'Taken in violation of international law'	307
	4.3. The territorial nexus requirement	311
5.	The Helms-Burton Act	313
	Conclusion	315

8	**Waiver of immunity**	**316**
1.	The US practice	317
	1.1. Who can waive immunity?	317
	1.2. Explicit or express waiver	319
	1.3. How explicit must an explicit waiver be?	322
	1.4. Implicit or implied waiver	324
	1.4.1. Arbitration	325
	1.4.2. The governing law of a contract	327
	1.4.3. Participation or involvement in litigation	329
	1.5. Implicit waiver as explicit waiver	333
	1.6. The specificity of waiver	333
	1.7. Counterclaims	334
2.	The UK practice	335
3.	The practice of other States	340
4.	Does a violation of human rights constitute an implied waiver?	340
	Conclusion	342

9	**Measures of constraint**	**343**
1.	Terminology	344
2.	Two distinct immunities: immunity from suit and immunity from execution	347
	2.1. The judicial power of the court	348
	2.2. The universal distinction between the two immunities	350
	2.2.1. The treaties	351
	2.2.2. The US FSIA	353
	2.2.3. The UK SIA and other national statutes	356
	2.2.4. The practice of other States	358
	2.2.5. Two distinct immunities: a universal rule	361
3.	The resurfacing of the 'purpose' test	362
	3.1. The treaties	363
	3.2. The US FSIA	363

xiv CONTENTS

| | 3.3. | The UK SIA and other national statutes | 367 |
| 3.4. | The practice of the States without immunity legislation | 369 |

4. Prejudgment measures 373
    4.1. Immunity as a preliminary issue 374
    4.2. The conditions for prejudgment measures 378
        4.2.1. Under the same conditions as execution 378
        4.2.2. Under more liberal conditions 383
        4.2.3. Under stricter conditions 383
5. The conditions for measures of constraint 390
    5.1. Waiver 390
    5.2. The 'purpose' test 392
    5.3. Separate entity ownership 394
        5.3.1. Legal instruments 394
        5.3.2. The practice of the States without immunity legislation 398
    5.4. The 'connection' requirement 399
        5.4.1. Subject-matter connection 399
        5.4.2. Territorial connection – *Binnenbeziehung* 399
        5.4.3. The entity connection 401
    5.5. The territorial presence requirement 402
    5.6. Executive oversight or authorization 404
6. Categories of property under special protection 404
    6.1. Diplomatic property 404
        6.1.1. Diplomatic premises 405
        6.1.2. Embassy bank accounts 407
    6.2. Central bank property 410
        6.2.1. The US FSIA 410
        6.2.2. The UK SIA 414
        6.2.3. The Australia FSIA 416
    6.3. Military property 417
    6.4. Other types of public property 418
7. Mixed accounts and accounts without definite destination 418
    7.1. Mixed accounts 418
    7.2. Accounts without definite destination 421
Conclusion 421

10 State immunity and human rights violations 423
1. Territorial jurisdiction 424
2. State immunity and criminal proceedings 426

	3.	State immunity and *jus cogens*	428
	4.	The assertion of extraterritorial jurisdiction	431
	5.	The State and its officials	432
	6.	The *Pinochet* case: a dissection	436
	7.	Immunity and legality	438
		Conclusion	440
11		The genesis of the UN Convention	441
	1.	Early efforts at codification	441
	2.	The work of the International Law Commission	446
	3.	The debate in the General Assembly Sixth Committee	447
	4.	Universal support for the UN Convention	454
	5.	What the UN Convention enshrines	455
	6.	What the UN Convention avoids	456
		Conclusion	457
		General conclusions	459
		Notes	466
		Bibliography	706
		Index	747

Foreword

State immunity is a rule of international law aimed at facilitating the performance of State functions by preventing the State from being sued in foreign courts. Aimed as it is at the conduct, specifically the abstention, of those courts, it depends substantially on their law and procedural rules conforming with international requirements. Correspondingly the law of State immunity developed primarily through domestic case law and legislation, with limited treaty practice. Only on 2 December 2004 did the General Assembly adopt the UN Convention on Jurisdictional Immunities of States and Their Property, based on the International Law Commission's lengthy work on the topic.[1] Xiaodong Yang underscores the importance of the Convention, referring to it as 'an epoch-making document' marking 'the final establishment of restrictive immunity as the prevailing doctrine in international law'.

The book presents a comprehensive overview of the development of the law and doctrine of State immunity, trying to 'delineate how the law of State immunity has come to be what it is, and what it is that it has become'. This is done through a systematic examination of over 2,000 cases decided over two centuries, combined with an analysis of treaties, national legislation, government statements, discussions in international organizations, and writings of scholars. The strength of the work is very much in the detailed analysis of the extensive caselaw, as well as of the literature, which he does with great vigour and capacity for legal analysis.

The book explores two principal themes – a critical analysis of the proposed rationales for State immunity and the gradual change to the restriction of the formerly monolithic principle of absolute immunity. In a systematic analysis of the different theories of State immunity Dr Yang demonstrates that it might not be possible to pin down an exact rationale for State immunity as between the various grounds currently advanced: sovereignty, independence, equality, dignity, comity, and the Latin maxim *par in parem non habet imperium*. He highlights the lack of reference to the legal basis of immunity in the practice of courts. With regard to restrictions on the principle of absolute immunity, Dr Yang correctly shows that '[w]hat is under debate is only the extent to which that immunity ought to be restricted'. He emphasizes that the true cause of the replacement of absolute immunity by restrictive immunity was not any theoretical breakthrough in the doctrine of international law, but the changed reality of international economic life: the dramatic increase of State trading and commercial activities in foreign territories.

As Dr Yang points out in this lucid work, State immunity 'is chiefly judge-made law, argued before and decided by numerous national courts that are above all limited by the territoriality of their jurisdiction'. He demonstrates how this leads to the rules deduced from State practice being replete with complexities and subtleties of various national laws. This he uses as a justification for the historical and comparative approach he adopts in conducting the study of State immunity. He aims to distill sound and reliable conclusions in this field and give an appropriate indication of the direction in which the law will evolve. Dr Yang observes two essentially opposing trends: *unification* in general principles and *fragmentation* in technical rules – while the courts have come to be increasingly unanimous on the general principles concerning the grant and denial of immunity, the law itself continues to differentiate, particularize and specialize, with progressively more refined domestic rules concerning the conditions for the grant of immunity.

Dr Yang provides new insight into the 'nature' and 'purpose' tests, showing how the so-called 'nature' test has repeatedly proved to be inadequate, especially in respect of contracts of employment, and how the 'purpose test', discredited in many courts at the adjudicative stage, re-emerges at the enforcement stage to be a determinative factor. He demonstrates how current case law suggests that courts often have to resort to a multifactor analysis, considering all the relevant factors of a case, including the purpose of the act in question.

Overall, the book is a vigorous, clear and detailed account of a subject-matter which will continue to play an important role in international life. Despite the extensive literature on this topic, this book manages to add original insights and its comprehensiveness has a value of its own.

James Crawford
Whewell Professor of International Law
Lauterpacht Centre for International Law
University of Cambridge

Preface and acknowledgements

This book grows out of part of my thesis submitted for the degree of Doctor of Philosophy at the Faculty of Law, University of Cambridge, in 2002. Unlike in the Ph.D. thesis, I have now, for the publication of the book, concentrated on the more 'traditional' aspects of State immunity, such as commercial transactions, non-commercial torts, contracts of employment and the enforcement of judgments, while giving issues of, say, the interplay of State immunity and human rights, and related subjects, no more than some very general remarks. I have considerably expanded my Ph.D. thesis and have thoroughly researched the whole area of State immunity, with a time span of two centuries.

The aim of the book is to state and expound the subject of State immunity in current international law, tracing its evolution and critically analysing various doctrinal intricacies and practical concerns. I have endeavoured to make my book three things at once: an interesting exposition of the subject for academics in the quiet of the study, a useful practical reference text for lawyers in the courtroom, and a friendly and accessible research guide for students in the classroom. To what extent I have succeeded I leave to the judgment of the reader; but I nonetheless wish to appeal to their favourable opinion by pointing out some of the delicate balancing acts that I have had to perform: being thorough without weighing down the narrative with tedious detail; providing necessary historical insights without burdening the reader with antiquated cases that are of limited value in today's court; and drawing general propositions that would serve as meaningful points of reference without making them too reductive and removed from reality. I cannot pretend to be completely exhaustive: new cases keep coming out even as I am putting the final punctuation mark to this book. Nor can I say that I have left no stone unturned; but what I can indeed say is that I have turned every known stone more than once. As far as possible, I have tried my best to bring the book up to date with the judicial practice. Insofar as the notion should apply to Public International Law at all, this book hopes to state the law as at 1 December 2011.

I am greatly and profoundly indebted to my supervisor, Professor Christine Gray at St John's College, University of Cambridge. She has been a most strict and responsible supervisor and a most considerate friend. She gave me meticulous advice at every stage and on every aspect of my research, never missing even the minutest of details, unfailingly encouraged me in my time of difficulty, and showed the kindest care for my career and my future. Without her guidance and support this book would not exist. I have always regarded and will continue to regard myself as a most fortunate student who has learned and has become confident in his trade under the ever-watchful eyes of a great teacher. More than that, for me her friendship has been a source of enduring inspiration, strength and hope. To her I owe an everlasting gratitude.

I am deeply grateful to my examiners, Professor James Crawford at Jesus College, University of Cambridge, and Professor Sir Christopher Greenwood at the London School of Economics, now Judge of the International Court of Justice at The Hague, who kindly approved my thesis without reservation, and whose good humour and graciousness made my viva a delightful and memorable experience.

I came to know Professor Crawford in 1995, when I first worked at the annual session of the UN International Law Commission as assistant to the Chinese member, the late Professor He Qizhi. Since then Professor Crawford has kindly helped me on many occasions. One of the earliest and most renowned authorities on State immunity, and originator and drafter of the Australian Foreign States Immunities Act of 1985, he has been most generous in sharing with me his expertise, insights and experience, for which I am wholeheartedly grateful. As General Editor of the Cambridge Studies in International and Comparative Law, of which my book is to form a part, he made the crucial suggestion that I concentrate on the traditional aspects of State immunity in my book, a suggestion the perceptiveness of which I came more and more to appreciate and admire the further I proceeded with the preparation for the publication of the book.

I should now record my blessings over the years across two careers when I have had the immense fortune and honour to be inspired, guided and helped by a great many people. Thus I owe an enormous debt of gratitude to Professor Li Peiying, for her unwavering confidence in me throughout all these years and for her tender care for myself and my family; to the late Professor Gong Xiangrui, for his teachings and friendship; to Professor Gong Renren, who first introduced me to the subject of State immunity while I was a student at the School of Law, Beijing University, and who has set me a shining example over these years with his deep sense of social responsibility; to Dr Zhang Kening, for helping me get my job with the Foreign Ministry and for his lasting friendship; to Judge Liu Daqun, for his care, help and mentoring when I first started my diplomatic career, and for his unstinting support at crucial junctures of my life; to Judge Xue Hanqin, for her friendship and advice; to the late Professor He Qizhi, for his good humour and teachings; to Dr Odette Jankowitsch-Prevor, for her enduring friendship, care and encouragement throughout all these years and for her continued support for my career aspirations; to Professor Akbar S. Ahmed, who encouraged me and gave me crucial help whenever I needed it, and who continues to inspire me with his vision, profound knowledge, penetrating insights, untiring spirit and deep sense of justice; to Mr Timothy J. Winter, whose encouragement and help came to me at each critical moment, and whose erudition, perspicacity and sense of humour demonstrate to me the possibility of living serenely in a hectic age; to Professor Paul Beaumont, who as Head of the School of Law, University of Aberdeen, kindly offered me the lectureship which gave me the time and resources to complete my research; to Professor Francis Lyall, for his invaluable guidance during my first years as a lecturer, and for his friendship, encouragement and help; to Professor Anthony Carty, who has been for me a critical teacher and a caring friend, and has given me invaluable advice and guidance in my work; to Professor Anthony Aust, who has introduced me to the wider community of international lawyers, has encouraged and supported me and has shared with me his vast experience and insights; to Sir Franklin Berman for his friendship and help; to the late Dr Geoffrey Marston of Sidney Sussex College, Cambridge, for supervising and guiding me during Professor Gray's sabbatical; to Professor Elihu Lauterpacht for his kind and timely help when I was a student at Cambridge; to Professor Bryan MacGregor, former Head of the College of Arts and Social Sciences, for his help at Aberdeen University; and to Ms Lisa Tabassi, for her friendship and advice, and her kind encouragement and support when I finally prepared the typescript for publication.

I am truly grateful to my editors at Cambridge University Press, Ms Finola O'Sullivan, Mr Richard Woodham, Ms Nienke van Schaverbeke, and Mr Ed W. Robinson, who have been most gracious and indulgent in allowing me the time to complete the book, and who have seen through its publication with dedication and professionalism. I am also most grateful to Ms Cheryl Prophett, whose careful reading of the typescript has yielded numerous refinements; and to Mr John Jeffries, for preparing a fine index for the book.

The British Council funded my studies for the Diploma in International Law at Cambridge in the academic year 1998–1999. That was the single most important opportunity I have ever had in my life. My special thanks to this great organization that has changed the lives of so many like me.

My special thanks also go to the staff at the Squire Law Library, Cambridge, and at the Taylor Library, Aberdeen, who are the most pleasant, helpful and competent librarians I have ever met.

I also wish to thank the editors of the *British Year Book of International Law* and of the *International Company and Commercial Law Review*, for their kind permission to use portions of my articles published in these journals.

I now wish to record my profound gratitude to the people to whom I owe my new life. Words fail me when I come to mention my brothers, to whom this book is gratefully dedicated. They loved me and trusted me, gave me hope and courage, and financially supported me through my PhD years at Cambridge and thus helped me realize a dream, which would otherwise have remained a dream, long lost and forgotten. Food in the desert, just as Moses and his people were given: such is the immensity of the debt I owe them, a debt which it will never be in my poor power to repay. I shall pray for them and for their families as long as I live.

This book then bears testimony to the most humbling experience in my life. I therefore attribute every single merit that may be found in this book to the guidance, encouragement, help, and support of these extraordinary people whom I have had the honour and privilege to call my friends and colleagues, and I reserve for myself the sole responsibility for all the defects and errors. E. M. Forster once said that the reason why he wrote was to win the respect of people whom he respected. For me with my humble abilities I would be quite content if my teachers and my friends could say that their trust and confidence in me has not been altogether misplaced.

Finally I wish to thank my wife Mina and my daughters Salwa and Sarah, and my extended families on both sides, for their love, trust and care, and for their patient forbearance of my unavoidable and yet unforgivable neglect.

Xiaodong Yang
Vienna

Abbreviations

AALCO	Asian-African Legal Consultative Organization
AALR	*Anglo-American Law Review*
ABA	American Bar Association
AD	Annual Digest of Public International Law Cases
AEDPA	Antiterrorism and Effective Death Penalty Act of 1996
AFDI	*Annuaire français de droit international*
African JICL	*African Journal of International and Comparative Law*
AI	*Arbitration International*
AIDI	*Annuaire de l'Institut de Droit international*
AJIL	*American Journal of International Law*
ALI	American Law Institute
ALRC	Australian Law Reform Commission
APLD	*All Pakistan Legal Decisions (Journal)*
Arizona LR	*Arizona Law Review*
ASDI	*Annuaire suisse de droit international*
Asian YIL	*Asian Yearbook of International Law*
ASIL Proceedings	*American Society of International Law Proceedings*
ATF	Arrêts du Tribunal Fédéral Suisse
AUILR	*American University International Law Review*
AUJILP	*American University Journal of International Law and Policy*
Australia FSIA	Australia Foreign States Immunities Act of 1985
Austrian JPIL	*Austrian Journal of Public and International Law*
Austrian RIEL	*Austrian Review of International and European Law*
AYIL	*Australian Yearbook of International Law*
Baltic YIL	*Baltic Yearbook of International Law*
BCICLR	*Boston College International and Comparative Law Review*
BCTWLJ	*Boston College Third World Law Journal*
Berkeley JIL	*Berkeley Journal of International Law*

xxiii

xxiv ABBREVIATIONS

BGE	Bundesgerichtsentscheide or Entscheidungen des Schweizerischen Bundesgerichts
Brooklyn JIL	*Brooklyn Journal of International Law*
BUILJ	*Boston University International Law Journal*
BVerfGE	Entscheidungen des Bundesverfassungsgerichts
BYBIL	*British Year Book of International Law*
BYULR	*Brigham Young University Law Review*
California LR	*California Law Review*
California WILJ	*California Western International Law Journal*
Cambridge YELS	*Cambridge Yearbook of European Legal Studies*
Canada SIA	Canada State Immunity Act of 1982
Cardozo LR	*Cardozo Law Review*
Chicago JIL	*Chicago Journal of International Law*
CJIL	*Chinese Journal of International Law*
CLF	*Criminal Law Forum*
CLJ	*Cambridge Law Journal*
Columbia JLA	*Columbia Journal of Law and the Arts*
Columbia JTL	*Columbia Journal of Transnational Law*
Columbia LR	*Columbia Law Review*
Connecticut JIL	*Connecticut Journal of International Law*
Cornell ILJ	*Cornell International Law Journal*
Creighton LR	*Creighton Law Review*
Criminal LR	*Criminal Law Review*
CWRLR	*Case Western Reserve Law Review*
CYIL	*Canadian Yearbook of International Law*
Dalloz	Jurisprudence Générale: Répertoire Méthodique et Alphabétique de Législation, de Doctrine et de Jurisprudence
Denver JILP	*Denver Journal of International Law and Policy*
DePaul LR	*DePaul Law Review*
Dickinson JIL	*Dickinson Journal of International Law*
DPCI	*Droit et pratique du commerce international*
Duke JCIL	*Duke Journal of Comparative and International Law*
Duke LJ	*Duke Law Journal*
ECHR	European Court of Human Rights
ECJ	European Court of Justice
EHRLR	*European Human Rights Law Review*
EJIL	*European Journal of International Law*
Emory ILR	*Emory International Law Review*
Emory JIDR	*Emory Journal of International Dispute Resolution*

Emory LJ	*Emory Law Journal*
Finnish YIL	*Finnish Yearbook of International Law*
Florida JIL	*Florida Journal of International Law*
Fordham ILJ	*Fordham International Law Journal*
Fordham LR	*Fordham Law Review*
GAOR	(United Nations) General Assembly Official Records
Georgetown LJ	*Georgetown Law Journal*
Georgia JICL	*Georgia Journal of International and Comparative Law*
Georgia LJ	*Georgia Law Journal*
Georgia LR	*Georgia Law Review*
German LJ	*German Law Journal*
German YIL	*German Yearbook of International Law*
GMULR	*George Mason University Law Review*
GWILR	*George Washington International Law Review*
GWJILE	*George Washington Journal of International Law and Economics*
GWLR	*George Washington Law Review*
Harvard HRJ	*Harvard Human Rights Journal*
Harvard ILCJ	*Harvard International Law Club Journal*
Harvard ILJ	*Harvard International Law Journal*
Harvard LR	*Harvard Law Review*
Hastings ICLR	*Hastings International and Comparative Law Review*
Hastings LJ	*Hastings Law Journal*
Hofstra LR	*Hofstra Law Review*
Houston JIL	*Houston Journal of International Law*
Houston LR	*Houston Law Review*
HRLR	*Human Rights Law Review*
HYIL	*Hague Yearbook of International Law*
IALR	*International Arbitration Law Review*
IBLJ	*International Business Law Journal*
ICCLR	*International Company and Commercial Law Review*
ICJ	International Court of Justice
ICLQ	*International and Comparative Law Quarterly*
ICSID	International Centre for the Settlement of Investment Disputes
ICTY	International Criminal Tribunal for the former Yugoslavia
IDI	Institut de Droit International
IL	*International Lawyer*
ILA	International Law Association

xxvi ABBREVIATIONS

ILC	(United Nations) International Law Commission
ILF	*International Law Forum*
ILM	International Legal Materials
ILR	International Law Reports
ILSA JICL	*ILSA Journal of International and Comparative Law*
ILT	*International Legal Theory*
Israel LR	*Israel Law Review*
Italian YIL	*Italian Yearbook of International Law*
ITBL	*International Tax and Business Lawyer*
ITLR	*International Trade Law & Regulation*
JAIL	*Japanese Annual of International Law*
JALC	*Journal of Air Law and Commerce*
JCL	*Journal of Chinese Law*
JCSL	*Journal of Conflict & Security Law*
JDI	*Journal du droit international*
JDIP	*Journal du droit international privé*
JIA	*Journal of International Arbitration*
JIBLR	*Journal of International Banking Law and Regulation*
JICJ	*Journal of International Criminal Justice*
JMLC	*Journal of Maritime Law and Commerce*
John Marshall LR	*John Marshall Law Review*
JTLP	*Journal of Transnational Law and Policy*
JWTL	*Journal of World Trade Law*
JYIL	*Japanese Yearbook of International Law*
LCP	*Law and Contemporary Problems*
LJIL	*Leiden Journal of International Law*
LNTS	League of Nations Treaty Series
Louisiana LR	*Louisiana Law Review*
Loyola LAICLJ	*Loyola of Los Angeles International and Comparative Law Journal*
Loyola LAICLR	*Loyola of Los Angeles International and Comparative Law Review*
LPIB	*Law and Policy in International Business*
LQR	*Law Quarterly Review*
LS	*Legal Studies*
Marquette LR	*Marquette Law Review*
Maryland JILT	*Maryland Journal of International Law and Trade*
McGill LJ	*McGill Law Journal*
Melbourne JIL	*Melbourne Journal of International Law*
Melbourne ULR	*Melbourne University Law Review*

Michigan JIL	Michigan Journal of International Law
Michigan LR	Michigan Law Review
Michigan YILS	Michigan Yearbook of International Legal Studies
Minnesota JGT	Minnesota Journal of Global Trade
Minnesota LR	Minnesota Law Review
MLR	Modern Law Review
Monash ULR	Monash University Law Review
MSJIL	Michigan State Journal of International Law
NATO	North Atlantic Treaty Organization
NDAA	National Defense Authorization Act for Fiscal Year of 2008
New England LR	New England Law Review
New York ILR	New York International Law Review
NILR	Netherlands International Law Review
Nordic JIL	Nordic Journal of International Law
North Car JILCR	North Carolina Journal of International Law and Commercial Regulation
Northwestern JILB	Northwestern Journal of International Law and Business
NYIL	Netherlands Yearbook of International Law
NYLSJICL	New York Law School Journal of International and Comparative Law
NYU JILP	New York University Journal of International Law and Politics
NYU JLPP	New York University Journal of Legislation and Public Policy
NYULR	New York University Law Review
NZYIL	New Zealand Yearbook of International Law
OAS	Organization of American States
OJLS	Oxford Journal of Legal Studies
Oregon LR	Oregon Law Review
Pakistan SIO	Pakistan State Immunity Ordinance of 1981
Polish YIL	Polish Yearbook of International Law
PSLR	Penn State Law Review
RBDI	Revue belge de droit international
RC	Recueil des Cours: Collected Courses of the Hague Academy of International Law
RCDIP	Revue critique de droit international privé
RDI	Rivista di diritto internazionale
RDILC	Revue de droit international et de législation comparée
RGDIP	Revue générale de droit international public
RHDI	Revue hellénique de droit international
RIAA	Reports of International Arbitral Awards

xxviii ABBREVIATIONS

RSDIE	*Revue suisse de droit international et de droit européen*
Rutgers LR	*Rutgers Law Review*
SAJHR	*South African Journal on Human Rights*
San Diego LR	*San Diego Law Review*
SAYIL	*South African Yearbook of International Law*
SI	(United Kingdom legislation) Statutory Instrument
Singapore SIA	Singapore State Immunity Act of 1979
South Africa FSIA	South Africa Foreign States Immunities Act of 1981
Southwestern JLTA	*Southwestern Journal of Law and Trade in the Americas*
Spanish YIL	*Spanish Yearbook of International Law*
Sri Lanka JIL	*Sri Lanka Journal of International Law*
SRSC	Summary Record of the (United Nations General Assembly) Sixth Committee
Stanford JIL	*Stanford Journal of International Law*
Temple ICLJ	*Temple International and Comparative Law Journal*
Texas ILJ	*Texas International Law Journal*
Texas LR	*Texas Law Review*
TJLR	*Thomas Jefferson Law Review*
TLCP	*Transnational Law and Contemporary Problems*
TMCLR	*Thomas M. Coolie Law Review*
Tulane JICL	*Tulane Journal of International and Comparative Law*
Tulane LR	*Tulane Law Review*
Tulane MLJ	*Tulane Maritime Law Journal*
Tulsa JCIL	*Tulsa Journal of Comparative and International Law*
TWLS	*Third World Legal Studies*
UCD JILP	*University of California Davis Journal of International Law and Policy*
UChLF	*University of Chicago Legal Forum*
UChLR	*University of Chicago Law Review*
UCinLR	*University of Cincinnati Law Review*
UCLA JILFA	*UCLA Journal of International Law and Foreign Affairs*
UILR	*University of Illinois Law Review*
UK SIA	United Kingdom State Immunity Act of 1978
UMiaIALR	*University of Miami Inter-American Law Review*
UNGA	United Nations General Assembly
UNTS	United Nations Treaty Series
UPennJIBL	*University of Pennsylvania Journal of International Business Law*

UPennLR	University of Pennsylvania Law Review
US FSIA	United States Foreign Sovereign Immunities Act of 1976
Valparaiso ULR	Valparaiso University Law Review
Vanderbilt JTL	Vanderbilt Journal of Transnational Law
Vanderbilt LR	Vanderbilt Law Review
Villanova LR	Villanova Law Review
Virginia JIL	Virginia Journal of International Law
Virginia LR	Virginia Law Review
VUWLR	Victoria University Wellington Law Review
Whittier LR	Whittier Law Review
Willamette JILDR	Willamette Journal of International Law and Dispute Resolution
Wisconsin ILJ	Wisconsin International Law Journal
WLLR	Washington and Lee Law Review
WMLR	William and Mary Law Review
Yale JIL	Yale Journal of International Law
Yale LJ	Yale Law Journal
YCA	Yearbook of Commercial Arbitration
YILC	Yearbook of the International Law Commission
ZaöRV	Zeitschrift für ausländisches öffentliches Recht und Völkerrecht

Table of cases

Decisions of International Courts and Tribunals

International Court of Justice

Armed Activities (Armed Activities on the Territory of the Congo (New Application: 2002) (Democratic Republic of the Congo v. Rwanda) (Request for the Indication of Provisional Measures)), International Court of Justice (ICJ), Order of 10 July 2002, *ICJ Reports* 2002, p. 219   430

Armed Activities (Case concerning Armed Activities on the Territory of the Congo: Jurisdiction of the Court and Admissibility of the Application (Democratic Republic of the Congo v. Rwanda)), ICJ, Judgment of 3 February 2006, *ICJ Reports* 2006, p. 6   430, 431

Arrest Warrant (Arrest Warrant of 11 April 2000 (Democratic Republic of the Congo v. Belgium)), ICJ, Judgment of 14 February 2002, *ICJ Reports* 2002, p. 3; 128 ILR 1   30, 35, 51, 54, 425, 429, 434, 436, 437

Barcelona Traction, Light and Power Company, Limited (Belgium v. Spain) (Second Phase), ICJ, Judgment of 5 February 1970, *ICJ Reports* 1970, p. 3   430

East Timor (Portugal v. Australia), ICJ, Judgment of 30 June 1995, *ICJ Reports* 1995, p. 90   425, 430, 431

Genocide Convention (Application of the Convention on the Prevention and Punishment of the Crime of Genocide (Bosnia and Herzegovina v. Yugoslavia) (Preliminary Objections)), ICJ, Judgment of 11 July 1996, *ICJ Reports* 1996, p. 595   430

Genocide Convention (Application of the Convention on the Prevention and Punishment of the Crime of Genocide (Bosnia and Herzegovina v. Serbia and Montenegro)) (Merits), ICJ, Judgment of 26 February 2007, *ICJ Reports* 2007, p. 43   427

Interhandel Case (Switzerland v. United States), ICJ, Judgment of 21
    March 1959, *ICJ Reports* 1959, p. 6 310
Military and Paramilitary Activities in and against Nicaragua (Nicaragua
    v. United States and America) (Merits), ICJ, Judgment of 27 June 1986,
    ICJ Reports 1986, p. 14 430
Nuclear Weapons (Legality of the Threat or Use of Nuclear Weapons), ICJ,
    Advisory Opinion of 8 July 1996, *ICJ Reports* 1996, p. 226 430
Wall (Legal Consequences of the Construction of a Wall in the Occupied
    Palestinian Territory), ICJ, Advisory Opinion of 9 July 2004, *ICJ Reports*
    2004, p. 136 430

European Court of Justice

Lechouritou v. Dimosio tis Omospondiakis Dimokratias tis Germanias,
    European Court of Justice (Second Chamber), Case C-292/05, 2007,
    [2007] 2 All ER (Comm) 57; [2007] ILPr 14, 216 51

European Court of Human Rights

Al-Adsani v. United Kingdom, Application No. 35763/97, European Court
    of Human Rights (ECHR) (Grand Chamber), 21 November 2001, (2002)
    34 EHRR 11; 123 ILR 24 35, 46, 51, 54, 216, 429
Association SOS Attentats and de Boëry v. France, Application No. 76642/
    01, ECHR (Grand Chamber): Decision of 4 October 2006 (Admissibility),
    unreported but noted in *European Human Rights Law Review* (2007-1)
    93 434
Fogarty v. United Kingdom, Application No. 37112/97, ECHR (Grand
    Chamber), 21 November 2001, (2002) 34 EHRR 12; 123 ILR 53 35, 46,
    51, 54, 156, 157
Kalogeropoulou v. Greece and Germany, Application No. 59021/00, ECHR
    (First Section), 12 December 2002, ECHR Reports 2002-X, p. 421; (2002)
    129 ILR 537 35, 51, 54, 214, 359, 429
McElhinney v. Ireland, Application No. 31253/96, ECHR (Grand
    Chamber), 21 November 2001, (2002) 34 EHRR 13; 123 ILR 73 35, 46,
    51, 54, 203, 212, 213

International Criminal Tribunal for the former Yugoslavia

Prosecutor v. Blăskić (Objection to the Issue of *Subpoenae Duces Tecum*),
    International Criminal Tribunal for the former Yugoslavia (ICTY), Trial
    Chamber II, 18 July 1997, Case IT-95-14-PT; Appeals Chamber, 29 July,
    12 August and 29 October 1997, Case IT-95-14-AR 108*bis*, 110 ILR
    607 51, 433

xxxii TABLE OF CASES

Prosecutor v. Furundzija, ICTY, Case IT-95-17/1, Trial Chamber II, Judgment of 10 December 1998, 121 ILR 213   430

Prosecutor v. Krstić, ICTY, Appeals Chamber, Decision on Application for Subpoenas, 1 July 2003, Case IT-98−33-A   51

Special Court for Sierra Leone

Prosecutor v. Taylor (Decision on Immunity from Jurisdiction), Special Court for Sierra Leone, Appeals Chamber, Case SCSL-2003-01-1, (2004) 128 ILR 239   46, 434

Arbitral Tribunals

Island of Palmas Case, Max Huber, Sole Arbitrator, (1928) 2 RIAA 829   48

LETCO (Liberian Eastern Timber Corporation) v. Government of the Republic of Liberia), International Centre for the Settlement of Investment Disputes, Arbitration Tribunal, (1986) 89 ILR 313   327

Rainbow Warrior (New Zealand v. France), France−New Zealand Arbitration Tribunal, (1990) 82 ILR 499   209, 439

Saudi Arabia v. Arabian American Oil Company (ARAMCO), Arbitration Tribunal, (1958) 27 ILR 117   35, 46, 54

Société Européenne d'Études et d'Entreprises v. People's Federal Republic of Yugoslavia, Arbitrators, (1956) 24 ILR 761   340

SPP (Middle East) Ltd and Southern Pacific Properties Ltd v. Arab Republic of Egypt and Egyptian General Company for Tourism and Hotels, International Chamber of Commerce, Court of Arbitration, ICC Arbitration No. YD/AS No. 3493, (1983) 86 ILR 434   35, 340

Texaco Overseas Petroleum Company and California Asiatic Oil Company v. Government of the Libyan Arab Republic, Dupuy, Sole Arbitrator, Award on the Merits, (1977) 53 ILR 389   35, 46, 54

Decisions of National Courts

Argentina

Gobierno de Italia en Suc v. Consejo Nacional de Educacion, Argentina, Camara Civil de la Capital, (1940) 10 AD 196   44

Ibarra y Cía v. Captain of the Spanish Steamer Ibaí, Argentina, Federal Supreme Court, (1937) 8 AD 247 and 9 AD 293 (reported twice by AD)   10, 18, 35, 46, 299

Manauta v. Embassy of Russian Federation, Argentina, Supreme Court, (1994) 113 ILR 429   18, 21, 28, 35, 46, 54, 137, 162, 176
National Sanitation Services v. Embassy of Cuba, Argentina, Supreme Court, (1992) 113 ILR 434   18, 77
Oppenlander de Soska v. Embassy of Ecuador, Argentina, Supreme Court, (1951) 65 ILR 2   10, 18
Peru (Government of Peru) v. SA Sociedad Industrial Financiera Argentina SIFAR, Argentina, Supreme Court, (1958) 26 ILR 195   10, 18
Townshend de Briochetto v. Office of the Department of Commerce of Canada, Argentina, Supreme Court, (1949) 65 ILR 1   10, 18

Australia

Adeang v. Nauru Phosphate Royalties Trust, Australia, Supreme Court of Victoria, 1992, 14 *Australian Yearbook of International Law* (1993) 340   77, 281
Australian Federation of Islamic Councils Inc. v. Westpac Banking Corporation, Australia, Supreme Court of New South Wales, Commercial Division, (1988) 17 NSWLR 623; 104 ILR 405   9, 28, 46
Chow Hung Ching and Si Pao Kung v. The King, Australia, High Court, 1948, [1949] ALR 29; (1948) 15 AD 147   28
Costa Vraca v. Bell Regal Pty Ltd, Australia, Federal Court of Australia, [2003] FCA 65, Transcript at LexisNexis   216
Garsec v. His Majesty the Sultan of Brunei, Australia, Supreme Court of New South Wales – Court of Appeal, [2008] NSWCA 211; (2008) 250 ALR 682   434
Garsec v. His Majesty the Sultan of Brunei, Australia, Supreme Court of New South Wales, [2007] NSWSC 882, (2007) 213 FLR 331   434
Grunfeld v. United States of America, Australia, New South Wales, Supreme Court, Sydney, [1968] 3 NSWR 36; 52 ILR 332   18
Kubacz v. Shah, Australia, Supreme Court of Western Australia, 1983, [1984] WAR 156; 118 ILR 293   28, 339, 434
Pan v. Bo, Australia, Supreme Court of New South Wales, [2008] NSWSC 961, (2008) 220 FLR 271   27, 40, 434
Reid v. Republic of Nauru, Australia, Supreme Court of Victoria, 1992, [1993] 1 VR 251; 101 ILR 193   21, 25, 28, 46, 47, 54, 55, 62, 77, 104, 106, 107, 138, 152, 162, 166
Robinson v. Kuwait Liaison Office, Australia, Industrial Relations Court, (1997) 145 ALR 68   339
Tasita Pty Ltd v. Sovereign State of Papua New Guinea, Australia, Supreme Court of New South Wales, [1991] 34 NSWLR 691   77

Thor Shipping A/S v. The Ship Al Duhail, Australia, Federal Court of Australia, Queensland District Registry, [2008] FCA 1842, [2008] 252 ALR 20; [2008] 173 FCR 524; 140 ILR 530   27

Tokic v. Yugoslavia, Australia, Supreme Court of New South Wales, 1991, 13 *Australian Yearbook of International Law (AYIL)* (1990–1991) 258 and 14 *AYIL* (1992) 335   216

USA (United States of America) v. Republic of China, Australia, Supreme Court of Queensland, (1950) 17 ILR 168   18, 28, 316

Victoria Aircraft Leasing Ltd v. United States, Australia, Court of Appeal of Victoria, [2005] VSCA 76, [2005] 218 ALR 640; [2005] 190 FLR 351   27, 28, 83

Wells Fargo Bank Northwest National Association v. Victoria Aircraft Leasing Ltd, Australia, Supreme Court of Victoria, [2004] VSC 262; 185 FLR 48   83, 106

Wells Fargo Bank Northwest National Association v. Victoria Aircraft Leasing Ltd (No. 2), Australia, Supreme Court of Victoria, Commercial and Equity Division, [2004] VSC 341   83, 106

Wright v. Cantrell, Australia, Supreme Court of New South Wales, (1943) ALR 427; (1943) 12 AD 133   28, 44

Zhang v. Jiang, Australia, Supreme Court of New South Wales, [2008] NSWSC 1296, (2008) 251 ALR 707   434

Austria

Airport Linz v. United States, Oberster Gerichtshof (Supreme Court of Austria), Decision No. 2 Ob 156/03k, 28 August 2003, noted by Stephan Wittich, 99 *AJIL* (2005) 248   214

Arrears of Rent Case, Austria, Regional Court for Civil Matters in Vienna (as Court of Appeal), Decision No. 4 OR 7/01b, 2001, 6 *Austrian Review of International and European Law* (2001) 313   21, 69, 77, 86

Austrian Bondholders v. Hungarian State, Austria, Supreme Court, (1930) 5 AD 120   10, 15

British Embassy Driver Case, Austria, Superior Provincial Court (Oberlandesgericht) of Vienna, Case No. E 630/78, (1978) 65 ILR 20   35, 165, 196, 359, 371

Case against the Foreign Minister of Belgium, Austria, Supreme Court (Oberster Gerichtshof), Decision 4 Ob 97/01w, 14 May 2001, 6 *Austrian Review of International and European Law* (2001) 288   35, 39, 83, 200, 201

Collision with Foreign Government-Owned Motor Car (Austria) Case, Austria, Supreme Court, (1961) 40 ILR 73   30, 69, 86, 211

Dralle v. Republic of Czechoslovakia, Austria, Supreme Court, (1950) 17 ILR 155   12, 15, 20, 21, 28, 35, 69, 359, 445

TABLE OF CASES   xxxv

Embassy Interpreter Dismissal Case, Austria, Administrative Court, Case
No. 04/01/0260-11, (1985) 77 ILR 485   35, 44, 137, 162, 186, 192, 196
Foreign State Bank Account Case, Austria, Supreme Court, (1986) 86 ILR
570 note   371, 381
Foreign States (Legation Buildings) Immunities Case, Austria, Supreme
Court in Civil Matters, (1928) 4 AD 178   10, 15, 35
French Consular Employee Claim Case, Austria, Supreme Court,
Case No. 9 Ob A 170/89, (1989) 86 ILR 583   25, 35, 69, 86, 162, 166,
174, 446
Garnishee Order against Occupant (Austria) Case, Austria, District Court
of Appeal of Vienna, (1952) 19 ILR 211   359
German Immunities in Austria Case, Austria, Supreme Court, (1935) 8
AD 246   15, 438, 439
Hunting Rights Contamination Claim Case, Austria, Supreme Court,
Case No. 3 Nd 511/87, (1987) 86 ILR 564   86, 210, 219, 224, 381
Immunities (Foreign State in Private Contracts) Case, Austria, Supreme
Court in Civil Matters, (1920) 1 AD 118   15, 46, 69
Leasing West GmbH v. People's Democratic Republic of Algeria,
Austria, Supreme Court (OGH), Case No. 3 Ob 38/86, (1986) 116
ILR 526; duplicate report *sub nom* Republic of 'A' Embassy Bank
Account Case, Austria, Supreme Court, Case No. 3 Ob 38/86,
(1986) 77 ILR 488   10, 25, 28, 30, 35, 77, 360, 370, 371, 404, 407,
408, 409, 420
Municipality of Salzburg v. Deutsche Bundesbahn, Austria, Supreme
Court, Case No. 1 Ob 41/80, (1981) 86 ILR 542   219
Neustein v. Republic of Indonesia, Austria, Supreme Court, Case No. 6 Ob
126/58, (1958) 65 ILR 3   10, 30, 135, 165, 196, 360, 371, 381, 404
Nuclear Power Plant Injunction Case (No. 1), Austria, Supreme Court,
Case No. 5 Nd 509/87, (1988) 86 ILR 575   35, 79, 210, 224, 382
Nuclear Power Plant Injunction Case (No. 2), Austria, Superior Provincial
Court (Oberlandesgericht) of Linz, Case No. 3 R 273/88, (1989) 86 ILR
578   224, 382
Payroll Taxes Case, Austria, Supreme Court, Decision 8 Ob A 201/00t,
2001, 6 *Austrian Review of International and European Law* (2001) 304   86
Prince of X Road Accident Case, Austria, Supreme Court, Case No. 2 Ob
1731/64, (1964) 65 ILR 13   434
Private Servant of Diplomat Case, Austria Supreme Court, Case No. 6 Ob
94/71, (1971) 71 ILR 546   30, 35, 376, 404
Radiation Contamination Claim Case, Austria, Supreme Court, (1988) 86
ILR 571   224, 371, 381, 404

xxxvi   TABLE OF CASES

Republic of 'A' Embassy Bank Account Case, Austria, Supreme Court, Case No. 3 Ob 38/86, (1986) 77 ILR 488; duplicate report *sub nom* Leasing West GmbH v. People's Democratic Republic of Algeria, Austria, Supreme Court (OGH), Case No. 3 Ob 38/86, (1986) 116 ILR 526   10, 28, 30, 360, 371, 404, 409, 420

Seidenschmidt v. United States of America, Austria, Supreme Court (OGH), Case No. 9 Ob A 116/92, (1992) 116 ILR 530   25, 69, 166, 174, 175, 177, 184, 446

Soviet Distillery in Austria Case, Austria, Administrative Court, (1954) 21 ILR 101   30, 35, 44, 46, 69

Steinmetz v. Hungarian People's Republic, Austria, Supreme Court, Case No. 5 Ob 56/70, (1970) 65 ILR 15   15, 46, 61, 305, 381

X v. Federal Republic of Germany, Austria, Supreme Court, Case No. SZ 36/26, (1963) 65 ILR 10   15, 27, 35, 46, 64, 69, 83

X v. Government of Czechoslovakia, Austria, Supreme Court, Case No. 23/143, 1950, *Materials on Jurisdictional Immunities*, 1982, p. 183   15

Belgium

Belgian State and Ministry for National Defence v. Dahlen and Luchte, Belgium, Court of Cassation (First Chamber), (1985) 91 ILR 239   210

Brasseur and Associates v. Republic of Greece, Belgium, Court of Appeal of Brussels, (1933) 6 AD 164   35, 46, 61, 299, 340, 358

Burundi v. Landau, Belgium, Court of Appeal of Brussels (Ninth Chamber), (2002) 127 ILR 98   340, 404

Castanheira v. Commercial Office of Portugal, Belgium, Labour Court of Brussels (Sixteenth Chamber), (1980) 82 ILR 100   46, 61, 162, 165, 295

Collée v. Gécamines Commerciale, Belgium, Labour Court of Brussels (Fourth Chamber), (1990) 115 ILR 435 note   137, 165

De Decker v. United States of America, Belgium, Court of Appeal of Léopoldville (Belgian Congo), (1956) 23 ILR 209   35, 46, 61, 162, 194, 196

De Queiroz v. State of Portugal, Belgium, Labour Court of Brussels (Fourth Chamber), (1992) 115 ILR 430   25, 40, 61, 86, 137, 162, 165, 196, 446

De Roover v. States of Belgium and France, Belgium, Civil Tribunal of Antwerp, (1920) 1 AD 120   46

Devos v. Supreme Headquarters Allied Powers Europe (SHAPE) and Belgium, Belgium, Court of Cassation (Third Chamber), (1985) 91 ILR 242   173

Époux Perevostchikoff-Germeau v. State of Canada, Belgium, Civil Tribunal of Antwerp, (1934) 9 AD 249   165, 194

François v. State of Canada, Belgium, Labour Court of Brussels (First Chamber), (1989) 115 ILR 418   25, 61, 137, 162, 165, 175, 178

TABLE OF CASES   xxxvii

Herbillon v. Lentz, Belgium, Civil Tribunal of Huy, (1920) 1 AD 120   438
Iraq v. Dumez, Belgium, Civil Court of Brussels (Attachment), (1995) 106
   ILR 284   25, 61, 404, 407, 408
Iraq v. Vinci Constructions, Belgium, Court of Appeal of Brussels (Ninth
   Chamber), (2002) 127 ILR 101   35, 39, 40, 41, 61, 372, 404, 407, 408
Mobutu v. SA Cotoni, Belgium, Civil Court of Brussels (Attachment
   Jurisdiction), (1988) 91 ILR 259   295, 434
Morocco (Kingdom of Morocco) v. DR, Belgium, Labour Court of Brussels
   (Sixth Chamber), (1989) 115 ILR 421   25, 61, 137, 162, 174, 178, 196, 446
NV Filmpartners, Belgium, Civil Tribunal of Brussels, (1971) 65 ILR 26   372, 374
Petroleum Companies Case, Belgium, Court of Antwerp, (1939) 8 AD
   239 note   299
Piha v. Belgium, Belgium, Labour Court of Mons (First Chamber), (1982)
   82 ILR 109   173, 196
Portugal (State of Portugal) v. Sauvage, Belgium, Court of Appeal of
   Brussels, (1921) 1 AD 154   46, 358
Rafidain Bank and Iraqi Ministry for Industry v. Consarc Corporation,
   Belgium, Court of Appeal of Brussels (Eighth Chamber), (1993) 106
   ILR 274   61, 77, 78, 86, 295, 344, 346
Rau, Vanden Abeele et Cie v. Duruty, Belgium, Cour d'appel, Gand, 1879,
   Pasicrisie Belge, 1879-II-175; 26 *AJIL Supplement* (1932) 612   13, 46
Re Pinochet, Belgium, Court of First Instance of Brussels, (1998) 119
   ILR 345   436
Re Sharon and Yaron, Belgium, Court of Appeal of Brussels (Chambre des
   mises en accusation), 2002; Court of Cassation (Second Chamber),
   (2003) 127 ILR 110   431, 434
Rousseau v. Republic of Upper Volta, Belgium, Labour Court of Brussels
   (Third Chamber), (1983) 82 ILR 118   35, 46, 48, 61, 86, 165, 186, 196, 340
SA Biocare v. Gécamines (Zaire) and Republic of Zaire, Belgium, Civil Court
   of Brussels (Second Chamber), (1989) 115 ILR 415   25, 61, 83, 300, 376
Saez Murua v. Pinillos and Garcia, Belgium, Court of Appeal of Brussels,
   1938; affirmed, Court of Cassation, 1939; 9 AD 289   31, 35, 46, 64, 299
Société Anonyme 'Dhlellemes et Masurel' v. Banque Centrale de la
   République de Turquie, Belgium, Court of Appeal of Brussels, (1963)
   45 ILR 85   80, 86, 134
Société anonyme Compagnie des chemins de fer Liégeois Limbourgeois
   v. Etat Néerlandais/Ministre du Waterstaat, Belgium, Cour de
   Cassation (1re ch.), 1903, Pasicrisie Belge, 1903-II-294; 31 *Journal du droit
   international privé* (1904) 417; 26 *AJIL Supplement* (1932) 613   13, 48,
   61, 86

xxxviii TABLE OF CASES

Société générale pour favoriser l'industrie nationale v. Syndicat d'amorissement, Gouvernment des Pays-Bas, et Gouvernement belge, Belgium, Appellate Court of Brussels, 1840, *Pasicrisie Belge* 1841-II-33 35

Société Lemoine & Co v. Belgian and British Governments, Belgium, Civil Court of Brussels, (1925) 3 AD 169 61

Société Monnoyer et Bernard v. France, Belgium, Charleroi Civil Court, (1927) 4 AD 177 14, 61

Société pour la Fabrication des Cartouches v. Ministre de la Guerre de Bulgaire, Belgium, Tribunal Civil de Bruxelles, 1888, *Pasicrisie Belge* 1889-III-62 13, 61, 77

Socobelge v. Greek State, Belgium, Tribunal Civil de Bruxelles, (1951) 18 ILR 3 21, 46, 47, 61, 358

Szczesniak v. Backer, Belgium, Court of Appeal of Brussels, (1955) 65 ILR 23 18, 344, 374

Urrutia and Amollobieta v. Martiarena, Belgium, Court of Brussels, (1937) 8 AD 237 46, 299

Vaessen v. American Battle Monuments Commission, Belgium, Labour Court of Verviers, (1997) 115 ILR 435 134, 137, 165, 286, 295

West Russian Steamship Company v. Captain Sucksdorff, Belgium, Commercial Tribunal of Antwerp, (1920) 1 AD 152 9, 46, 340, 358

Zaire v. D'Hoop, Belgium, Civil Court of Brussels (Attachments), (1995) 106 ILR 294 25, 77, 421

Brazil

Consulate General of Japan v. Ribeiro de Lima, Brazil, Labour Court of Pernambuco, 2002, noted in 24(12) *Journal of International Banking Law and Regulation* (2009), N102 18, 196

Représentation commerciale de RDA, Brésil, Tribunal Suprême Fédéral, 1989, noted in 126 *Journal du droit international* (1999) 451 (in French) 18, 63

Syria (Arab Republic of Syria) v. Arab Republic of Egypt, Brazil, Supreme Court (Plenary Session), Case No. 298-DF, (1982) 91 ILR 288 18, 35, 54

Canada

Amanat Khan v. Fredson Travel Inc. (No. 2), Canada, High Court of Ontario, (1982) 36 OR (2d) 17; 133 DLR (3d) 632; 64 ILR 733 18, 28, 30

Arar v. Syrian Arab Republic, Canada, Ontario Superior Court of Justice, [2005] OJ No. 752; [2005] 137 ACWS (3d) 823 39, 46, 429

TABLE OF CASES   xxxix

Aristocrat v. National Bank of the Republic of Kazakhstan, Canada, Ontario Superior Court of Justice, 15 June 2001, [2001] 107 ACWS (3d) 595; [2001] OTC 523   83

Bouchard v. JL Le Saux Ltée, Canada, Ontario Supreme Court (Master's Chambers), (1984) 45 OR (2d) 792; 92 ILR 658   31

Bouzari v. Islamic Republic of Iran, Canada, Ontario Court of Appeal, (2004) 243 DLR (4th) 406; 128 ILR 586   30, 35, 39, 43, 46, 81, 221, 429

Bouzari v. Islamic Republic of Iran, Canada, Ontario Superior Court of Justice, (2002) 124 ILR 427   21, 28, 35, 39, 43, 46, 62, 81, 215, 221, 429

Bouzari v. Islamic Republic of Iran, Canada, Supreme Court, (2005) 122 CRR (2d) 376 (note)   221, 429

Brown v. SS Indochine, Canada, Exchequer Court, Quebec, Admiralty Division, (1922) CLR, 21 Exchequer, 406; 1 AD 157   9, 18

Butcher v. Saint Lucia (Government), Canada, Ontario Court (General Division), [1998] 79 ACWS (3d) 815; [1998] 61 OTC 208   177

Butcher v. Saint Lucia (Government), Canada, Ontario Court of Appeal, [1999] 87 ACWS (3d) 800; 1999 OAC Lexis 99   177

Cantieri Riuniti dell'Adriatico v. Gdynia-Ameryka Linje Zeglugowe, Canada, Supreme Court of Nova Scotia, 1939, (1940) 1 DLR 102; 9 AD 282   299

Cargo ex the Ship Atra v. Lorac Transport Ltd, Canada, Federal Court of Appeal, (1986) 28 DLR (4th) 30; 84 ILR 700   18, 28, 30, 46, 86, 98, 219

Carrato v. United States of America, Canada, Ontario High Court, (1982) 141 DLR (3d) 456; [1982] 40 OR (2d) 459; 90 ILR 229   25, 81, 140, 219, 433, 439

Castle v. United States Department of Justice (Attorney General), Canada, Ontario Court of Appeal, [2006] OJ No. 4897   200, 219, 220, 221

Chateau-Gai Wines Ltd v. France (Le Gouvernement de la Republicque Française), Canada, Exchequer Court, (1967) 61 DLR (2d) 709; 53 ILR 284   10, 18, 35

City of Ottawa and Village of Rockcliffe Park, Reference re Power of Municipalities to Levy Rates on Foreign Legations and High Commissioners' Residences, Canada, Supreme Court, [1943] SCR 208; (1943) 2 DLR 481; 10 AD 337   35, 54, 55

Collavino Inc. v. Yemen (Tihama Development Authority), Canada, Alberta Court of Queen's Bench, [2007] AJ No. 531   78, 274, 275, 276, 277, 294, 336

Congo (Government of the Democratic Republic of the Congo) v. Venne, Canada, Supreme Court, (1971) 22 DLR (3d) 669; 64 ILR 24   18, 25, 28, 30, 47, 100, 140, 337

Corriveau v. Republic of Cuba, Canada, Ontario High Court, (1979) 103 DLR (3d) 520; 64 ILR 59   18

xl TABLE OF CASES

Croteau v. United States of America (Federal Trade Commission), Canada, Ontario Superior Court of Justice, [2005] OJ No. 6222   274

Croteau v. United States of America (Federal Trade Commission), Canada, Ontario Court of Appeal, [2006] OJ No. 158   274, 275

D & J Coustas Shipping Co SA v. Cia de Navegacao Lloyd Brasileiro, Canada, Federal Court, Trial Division, [1990] 48 FTR 161   274, 275

Davidson v. British Columbia (Attorney General), Canada, British Columbia Court of Appeal, [2006] 214 CCC (3d) 373   434

Dessaulles v. Republic of Poland, Canada, Court of King's Bench of Quebec; affirmed, Supreme Court; (1944) 4 DLR 1; 12 AD 92   10, 18, 28, 35, 46

Ferguson v. Arctic Transportation, Canada, Federal Court, Trial Division, [1995] 101 FTR 16; [1995] 3 FC 656   78, 276

Ferranti-Packard Ltd v. Cushman Rentals Ltd, Canada, Ontario Divisional Court, (1981) 30 OR (2d) 194 (Div. Ct.); affirmed, Ontario Court of Appeal (1981) 31 OR (2d) 799 (CA); 64 ILR 93   275

Flota Maritima Browning de Cuba SA v. The Steamship Canadian Conqueror and the Republic of Cuba, Canada, Supreme Court, (1962) 34 DLR (2d) 628; [1962] SCR 598; 42 ILR 125   18, 28

Fraser-Brace Overseas Corporation v. Municipality of the City and Country of Saint John, Canada, New Brunswick Supreme Court (Appeal Division), (1957) 9 DLR (2d) 391; 24 ILR 231   10, 44

Gascon Estate v. Paradis Estate, Canada, Ontario Court (General Division), [1991] 26 ACWS (3d) 722   200, 220

Jaffe v. Miller, Canada, High Court of Justice, Ontario, (1990) 73 DLR (4th) 420; [1990] 75 OR (2d) 133; 87 ILR 197   30, 81, 219, 337, 433, 439

Jaffe v. Miller, Canada, Ontario Court of Appeal, (1993) 103 DLR (4th) 315; 13 OR (3d) 745; 95 ILR 446   28, 30, 35, 39, 40, 46, 81, 215, 219, 337, 433, 439

JRS v. Glendinning, Canada, Ontario Superior Court of Justice, (2000) 191 DLR (4th) 750   31

Karabulut v. Allegro Airlines, Canada, Ontario Superior Court of Justice, 2003, [2003] OJ No. 5748; [2003] 130 ACWS (3d) 921   83, 294

Lab Chrysotile Inc. v. Rasheed Bank, Canada, Quebec Court of Appeal, [2003] 127 ACWS (3d) 757   406

Lorac Transport Ltd v. Owners and All Interested in Cargo ex the Ship Atra, Canada, Federal Court, Trial Division, (1984) 9 DLR (4th) 129   18

Lovell v. New Zealand Tourism Board, Canada, British Columbia Supreme Court, [1992] ACWSJ Lexis 38241   99, 177, 201

MacFarlane v. United States, Canada, Ontario District Court, 15 April 1987, Docket: 288267/87, 1987 CarswellOnt 2859   170, 196

Municipality of the City and County of Saint John, Logan and Clayton v. Fraser-Brace Overseas Corporation, Canada, Supreme Court, (1958) 13 DLR (2d) 177; 26 ILR 165   10, 18, 28, 44, 46, 48, 66

Novopharm Ltd v. Government of the United States of America, Canada, Commissioner of Patents, 18 CPR (3d) 26 (1987)   44, 78

Old HW-GW Ltd v. Minister of National Revenue, Canada, Federal Court of Appeal, [1993] 153 NR 136   16, 31

Old HW-GW Ltd v. Minister of National Revenue, Canada, Federal Court of Canada, [1991] 43 FTR 197   16, 31

P v. Westwood, Canada, British Columbia Supreme Court, [2003] BCJ N. 1944   221, 433

Parent v. Singapore Airlines Ltd and the Civil Aeronautics Administration, Canada, Quebec Supreme Court, (2003) 133 ILR 264   31

Penthouse Studios Inc. v. Government of the Sovereign Republic of Venezuela, Canada, Quebec Court of Appeal, (1969) 8 DLR (3d) 686; 64 ILR 20 18

Re Canada Labour Code (Unites States of America v. Public Service Alliance of Canada), Canada, Supreme Court, (1992) 91 DLR (4th) 449; [1992] 2 SCR 50; 94 ILR 264   18, 21, 25, 28, 30, 35, 46, 47, 77, 88, 99, 100, 105, 106, 158, 162, 164, 177, 193, 219

Re Canada Labour Code, Canada, Federal Court of Appeal, 1989, [1990] 1 FC 332; 86 ILR 626   21, 28, 30, 46, 47, 98, 140, 162, 163, 164

Re Royal Bank of Canada and Corriveau, Canada, Ontario High Court, (1980) 117 DLR (3d) 199; 64 ILR 69   18, 30, 410

Reference re Exemption of United States Forces from Canadian Criminal Law, Canada, Supreme Court, [1943] SCR 483; (1943) 4 DLR 11; 12 AD 124   28, 35

Ritter v. Donell, Canada, Alberta Court of Queen's Bench, Judicial District of Calgary, [2005] AJ No. 958   220, 433

Roxford Enterprises SA v. Cuba, Canada, Federal Court, Trial Division, (2003) 124 ACWS (3d) 294; [2003] 236 FTR 1, [2003] 2003 FCT 763; [2003] 4 FC 1182   28, 35, 276, 277, 288, 294

Sarafi v. Ship Iran Afzal, Canada, Federal Court, Trial Division, (1996) 111 FTR 256; [1996] 2 FC 954   18

Schreiber v. Attorney General of Canada, Canada, Ontario Superior Court of Justice, (2000) 187 DLR (4th) 146   39, 46, 220, 339, 439

Schreiber v. Federal Republic of Germany, Canada, Ontario Court of Appeal, (2001) 196 DLR (4th) 281   28, 39, 46, 215, 220, 332, 339, 376

Schreiber v. Federal Republic of Germany, Canada, Supreme Court, (2002) 216 DLR (4th) 513; [2002] 3 SCR 269   35, 39, 43, 46, 54, 55, 210, 215, 220, 221, 332, 339, 376, 429

xlii   TABLE OF CASES

Sieniecki v. Shea Construction Ltd, Canada, Ontario Supreme Court, 4
   ACWS (3d) 244 (1987)   78
Smith v. Canadian Javelin Ltd, Canada, Ontario High Court, (1976) 68
   DLR (3d) 428; 64 ILR 47   18, 433
Smith v. Chin, Canada, Ontario Superior Court of Justice, 2006, [2006] OJ
   No. 4091; 152 ACWS (3d) 149   99, 177, 433
Teitelbaum v. Israel, Canada, Quebec Superior Court, Docket: C.S. Qué.
   Montréal 500-17-043751-083, 26 November 2008, 2008 CarswellQue
   12119 83
TMR Energy Ltd v. State Property Fund of Ukraine, Canada, Federal
   Court, Trial Division, [2003] 244 FTR 1, 2003 FC 1517   275
Tritt v. United States of America, Canada, Ontario Court of Justice, (1994)
   45 ACWS (3d) 1140   81, 433, 439
Tritt v. United States of America, Canada, Ontario High Court, (1989) 68
   OR (2d) 284; 94 ILR 260   25, 81, 219, 433, 439
University of Calgary v. Colorado School of Mines, Canada, Alberta
   Court of Queen's Bench, Judicial District of Calgary, [1995]
   179 AR 81   220, 276
USA (United States of America) v. Friedland; Friedland v. United States
   of America, Canada, Ontario Court of Justice, General Division, (1998)
   40 OR (3d) 747; Ontario Court of Appeal, (1999) 182 DLR (4th) 614;
   120 ILR 417   25, 28, 39, 200, 220, 338, 339, 433
Venne v. Democratic Republic of the Congo, Canada, Quebec Court of
   Queen's Bench, Appeal Side, (1968) 5 DLR (3d) 128; 64 ILR 1   18, 21,
   30, 140
Walker v. Bank of New York Inc., Canada, Court of Appeal for Ontario,
   (1994) 111 DLR (4th) 186; 104 ILR 277   39, 46, 209, 215, 220, 274, 433,
   434
Walker v. Bank of New York Inc., Canada, Ontario Court (General
   Division), (1993) 15 OR (3d) 596   209, 215, 220
Western Surety Co. v. Elk Valley Logging Ltd; The Queen in Right of
   Alberta, Third Party, Canada, British Columbia Supreme Court, (1985)
   23 DLR (4th) 464   31
White v. The Ship Frank Dale, Canada, Nova Scotia (in Admiralty), (1946)
   13 AD 82   9, 28
Yin-Tso Hsiung v. Toronto, Canada, Ontario High Court, (1950) 4 DLR 209;
   17 ILR 153   54, 55
Zodiac International Products Inc. v. Polish People's Republic,
   Canada, Ontario Court of Appeal, (1977) 81 DLR (3d) 656; 64
   ILR 51   18, 21

Chile

Senerman Rapaport v. Republic of Cuba, Chile, Supreme Court, (1975) 65 ILR 29   13, 27, 35, 46, 445

X v. Embassy of Yugoslavia, Chile, Supreme Court, 1968; X v. Government of Bolivia, Chile, Supreme Court, 1969, Materials on Jurisdictional Immunities of States and Their Property, 1982, pp. 250–251   13

X v. Government of China, Chile, Supreme Court, (1969) 65 ILR 31 note   13, 35

China

Rizaeff Frères v. Soviet Mercantile Fleet, Republic of China, Provisional Court of Shanghai (Civil Division), (1927) 40 ILR 84   11, 35

Czechoslovakia

Enforcement of International Awards (Czechoslovakia), Czechoslovakia, Supreme Court of Justice, (1928) 4 AD 174   10

Immunity of Legation Buildings (Czechoslovakia) Case, Czechoslovakia, Supreme Court of Justice, (1929) 4 AD 370   10

Denmark

Den Franske Republik (France) v. Intra ApS (company), Denmark, Supreme Court (Højesteret), 9 March 1992, available from the Council of Europe Database on State practice regarding State Immunities: www.coe.int/t/dlapil/cahdi/State_Immunities/default_en.asp; also noted in 130 *JDI* (2003) 853   18, 35

Embassy of the Socialist Republic of Czechoslovakia v. Jens Nielsen Bygge-Enterpriser A/S, Denmark, Eastern Provincial Court (Fifteenth District); Supreme Court (Appeals Committee), (1982) 78 ILR 81   18, 25, 30, 35, 192, 340

Italien (The Italian Stat) v. Amaliegade 21 A-D (privately owned property company), Denmark, Eastern High Court (Østre Landsret), 19 May 1993, available from the Council of Europe Database   18, 35

Pakistans Ambassade (Pakistan) v. Shah Travel ved Hermunir Hussein Shah (private travel agency), Denmark, Supreme Court (Højesteret), 5 March 1999, available from the Council of Europe Database; also noted in 130 *JDI* (2003) 853   18, 35

State Immunity (Denmark) Case, Denmark, Supreme Court, 69 *NYIL* (2000) 338   78

xliv   TABLE OF CASES

Egypt

Manuel v. Ministère Public, Egypt, Mixed Court of Cassation, (1943) 12
    AD 154   28
Ministère Public v. Tsoukharis, Egypt, Mixed Court of Cassation, (1943)
    12 AD 150   46

Estonia

Pärtsel v. Tsentrosojuss (No. 1), Estonia, Court of Cassation, (1932)
    8 AD 242   13, 35
Pärtsel v. Tsentrosojuss (No. 2), Estonia, Court of Cassation, (1934) 8 AD
    244   10, 13
Soviet Trade Delegation in Estonia v. JV Paulin, Estonia, Court of
    Cassation, (1927) 8 AD 241   10, 13, 66

Finland

Hanna Heusala v. Turkish State, Finland, Supreme Court, Case No. S 92/
    44.3, 30 September 1993, noted by Ruth Donner, 5 *Finnish Yearbook of
    International Law* (1994) 408   40, 182, 196, 446

France

Administration des Chemins de Fer du Gouvernement Iranien v. Société
    Levant Express Transport, France, Court of Cassation, (1969) 52 ILR
    315   15, 103, 360
Agent judiciaire du Trésor v. Malta Maritime Authority et Carmel X, France,
    Cour de cassation (Ch. crim.), 23 novembre 2004, 94 *Revue critique de droit
    international privé* (2005) 469 (case note by Isabelle Pingel)   433
Aget v. French State and Spanish State, France, Tribunal Civil of
    Perpignan, (1939) 11 AD 144   15, 31
Allianz Via Insurance v. United States of America, France, Court of
    Appeal of Aix-en-Provence (Second Chamber), (1999) 127 ILR 148   83
AXA Courtage IARD v. Asecna, France, Cour de cassation (1re Ch. civ.), 14
    décembre 2004, 94 *Revue critique de droit international privé* (2005) 470
    (case note by Isabelle Pingel)   433
Barrandon v. United States of America, France, Court of Cassation (First
    Civil Chamber), 1992; Court of Appeal of Versailles (Social Chambers in
    Plenary Session), 1995; 123 *JDI* (1996) 102; 113 ILR 464   25, 30, 35, 40,
    137, 162, 191, 192, 194, 346
Barrandon v. United States of America, France, Court of Cassation (Social
    Chamber), (1998) 116 ILR 622   25, 195, 196

TABLE OF CASES xlv

Benvenuti and Bonfant Ltd v. Banque Commerciale Congolaise, *France*,
Court of Cassation, (1987) 82 ILR 91   295
Benvenuti et Bonfant SARL v. Government of the People's Republic of the
Congo, France, Court of Appeal of Paris, (1981) 65 ILR 88   346
Blagojevic v. Bank of Japan, France, Court of Cassation (First Civil
Chamber), (1976) 65 ILR 63   285
Blanchet v. Gouvernement d'Haïti, France, Tribunal Civil du Havre, 1827,
Dalloz, 1849-I-6; Sirey, 1849-I-83   35
Caisse centrale de co-opération économique v. Société Midland
International Service (France) and State of Senegal, France, Tribunal
de grande instance de Paris (summary jurisdiction), (1983) 77 ILR
524 note   374, 379
Caisse d'Assurance Vieillesse des Non-Salariés v. Caisse Nationale des
Barreaux Français, France, Court of Cassation (First Civil Chamber),
(1977) 65 ILR 70   285, 398
Cameroons Development Bank v. Société des Établissements
Robber, France, Court of Cassation (First Civil Chamber), (1986)
77 ILR 532   77, 376, 379
Ceara (State of Ceara) v. Dorr, France, Court of Appeal of Colmar
(First Chamber), (1928) 4 AD 39   31, 35, 46
Céara (State of) v. D'Archer de Montgascon, France, Court of Cassation,
(1932) 6 AD 162   31
Chaliapine v. Russian State and Librairie Brenner, France, Commercial
Tribunal of the Seine, (1930) 5 AD 19 note   15
Chaliapine v. Union of Socialist Soviet Republics, France, Court of
Cassation (Chambre des Requêtes), (1936) 8 AD 225   15
Chaussois v. La Tabacoop de Bône, France, Court of Appeal of Paris, (1966)
47 ILR 152   13, 46, 170, 285
Clerget v. Banque Commerciale pour l'Europe du Nord and Banque du
Commerce Extérieur du Vietnam, France, Court of Appeal of Paris,
(1969) 52 ILR 310   31, 35, 40, 46, 103, 134, 137, 360
Clerget v. Banque Commerciale pour l'Europe du Nord, France, Court of
Cassation (First Civil Chamber), (1971) 65 ILR 54   31, 35, 40, 46, 103,
134, 137, 360
Clerget v. Représentation Commerciale de la République Démocratique
du Viet-Nam, France, Tribunal de grande instance of the Seine, (1967)
48 ILR 145   30, 31, 40, 134, 137, 360
Coco v. State of Argentina, France, Court of Cassation (Social Chamber),
(1996) 113 ILR 491   103, 162, 167, 191, 195, 196

xlvi TABLE OF CASES

Congo (République démocratique du Congo) v. Syndicat des
propriétaires de l'immeuble Résidence Antony Châtenay, France, Cour
de cassation (1re Ch. civ.), 25 janvier 2005, 95 *Revue critique de droit
international privé* (2006) 123   10, 35, 44, 46, 63
Corporacion del Cobre v. Braden Copper Corporation and Société
Groupement d'Importation des Métaux, France, Tribunal de grande
instance of Paris (summary jurisdiction), (1972) 65 ILR 57   83, 301, 360
Cotigny and French Parachuting Federation v. Suarez and United States
of America, France, Court of Cassation (First Civil Chamber), 2004,
94 *RCDIP* (2005) 75; (2004) 127 ILR 168   30, 213, 346
Crédit Lyonnais, Banque de Paris et des Pays-Bas v. Viel and the State of
Finland, France, Court of Appeal of Paris, (1936) 8 AD 228   10, 340
Creighton Ltd v. Minister of Finance of Qatar, France, Court of Cassation
(First Civil Chamber), 127 *JDI* (2000) 1054; (2000) 127 ILR 154   25, 35,
340, 346, 379, 380
Dumez v. Iraq, France, Court of Cassation (First Civil Chamber), 1999, 127
JDI (2000) 45; (1999) 127 ILR 144   295, 346, 379, 399, 439
Dumont v. State of Amazonas, France, Tribunal Civil de la Seine, (1948)
15 AD 140   31, 48
Duvalier v. State of Haiti, France, Court of Cassation (First Civil
Chamber), 1990, 113 ILR 448   83, 434
Egypt (Arab Republic of Egypt) v. Southern Pacific Properties Ltd and
Southern Pacific Properties (Middle East) Ltd, France, Court of Appeal
of Paris (First Additional Chamber), 1984; affirmed, Court of Cassation
(First Civil Chamber), 1987; 86 ILR 474   295, 340
Englander v. Statni Banka Ceskoslovenska, France, Court of Cassation,
(1969) 52 ILR 335   15, 360, 420
Entreprise Pérignon v. Gouvernement des États-Unis, France, Court of
Cassation, (1964) 45 ILR 82   103
État d'Irak v. Société Dumez GTM, SA Vinci Construction Grands Projets,
France, Cour d'appel de Paris, 20 février 2002, 91 *Revue critique de droit
international privé* (2002) 746; 107 *Revue générale de droit international
public* (2003) 1008   439
État Irakien v. Société Dumez GTM, France, Cour de Cassation, Première
chambre civile, Arrêt n° 679 du 25 avril 2006, 110 *Revue générale de droit
international public* (2006) 950; also available at www.courdecassation.
fr   439
Euroéquipement SA v. Centre Européen de la Caisse de Stabilisation et
de Soutien des Productions Agricoles de la Côte d'Ivoire, France,

TABLE OF CASES xlvii

Tribunal d'Instance of Paris (Second District), (1991) 89 ILR 37 77, 103, 286

Ex-King Farouk of Egypt v. Christian Dior, SARL, France, Court of Appeal of Paris, (1957) 24 ILR 228 434

Federal Republic and National Bank of Yugoslavia v. Republics of Croatia, Slovenia, Macedonia and Bosnia-Herzegovina, France, Court of Cassation (First Civil Chamber), 1999, 127 *JDI* (2000) 1036; (1999) 128 ILR 627 346

Gaddafi, France, Court of Appeal of Paris (Chambre d'accusation), 2000; Court of Cassation, 2001, 125 ILR 490 434

General National Maritime Transport Company v. Société Marseille Fret, France, Court of Cassation (First Civil Chamber), (1986) 77 ILR 530 35, 40, 299, 379

Gouvernement espagnol v. Cassaux, France, Cour de Cassation, 22 janvier 1849, Sirey, 1849-I-81; Dalloz, 1849-I-5 15, 30, 35, 46, 77

Gouvernement espagnol v. Veuve Aguado, France, Court of Appeal of Paris, Dalloz, Pér., 1867-II-49, case note by Charles Royer 19, 60

Guggenheim v. State of Vietnam, France, Court of Appeal of Paris, (1955) 22 ILR 224 15, 46, 77

Guggenheim v. State of Vietnam, France, Court of Cassation, (1961) 44 ILR 74 15, 77

Guinea (Popular Revolutionary Republic of Guinea) v. Atlantic Triton Co., France, Court of Appeal of Rennes (Second Chamber), 1984; Court of Cassation (First Civil Chamber), 1986; 114 *JDI* (1987) 125; 82 ILR 75 340, 344, 374, 379

Hertzfeld v. Union of Soviet Socialist Republics, France, Court of Appeal of Paris, (1938) 9 AD 243 299

Hertzfeld v. USSR, France, Civil Tribunal of the Seine, (1933) 7 AD 184 15, 35, 46, 299

Huttinger v. Upper Congo–Great African Lakes Railway Co., The Independent State of the Congo, and the Belgian Minister for the Colonies, France, Civil Tribunal of the Seine, (1934) 7 AD 172 15, 46

In re Commercial Representation in France of the Union of Socialist Soviet Republics, France, Commercial Tribunal of the Seine, (1927) 4 AD 30 15, 44

In re D, France, Conseil d'État, (1966) 47 ILR 57 44, 83

In re Hanukiew, France, Court of Cassation (Chambre des Requêtes), (1933) 7 AD 174 10, 15, 46

Iran (Islamic Republic of Iran) v. Société Eurodif, France, Court of Cassation (Civil Chamber), 79 *RCDIP* (1990) 346; (1989) 89 ILR 31 25, 79, 103, 340, 344, 372, 374, 376, 379, 380

xlviii   TABLE OF CASES

Iran (Islamic Republic of Iran) v. Société Eurodif, France, Court of Cassation (First Civil Chamber), (1984) 77 ILR 513   27, 103, 340, 372, 374, 379

Iran (Republic of Iran) v. Société Eurodif and Sofidif and Commissariat à l'Énergie Atomique, France, Court of Appeal of Paris, (1982) 65 ILR 93   340, 360, 372

Kuwait News Agency v. Parrott, France, Court of Cassation (First Civil Chamber), 1990, 80 *RCDIP* (1991) 142; (1990) 113 ILR 457   30, 137, 167, 171, 285, 346

Lakhowsky v. Swiss Federal Government and Colonel de Reynier, France, Tribunal de Commerce of the Seine (Eighth Chamber), 1919; Court of Appeal of Paris (First Chamber), 1921; 1 AD 122   15, 46, 433

Larrasquitu and the Spanish State v. Société Cementos Rezola, France, Court of Appeal of Poitiers, (1937) 8 AD 196   15, 299

Laurans and Société Marseillaise de Crédit v. Government of Morocco and Maspéro, France, Court of Cassation (Chambre des Requêtes), (1934) 7 AD 171   10, 15, 31

Malagasy Republic v. Société Bruynzeel (Netherlands), France, Tribunal de grande instance of Paris (summary jurisdiction), (1971) 65 ILR 51   340, 360

Minister of Foreign Affairs v. Burgat, France, Conseil d'Etat, (1976) 74 ILR 277   44

Ministry for Economic and Financial Affairs of the Islamic Republic of Iran v. Société Framatome, France, Court of Cassation (First Civil Chamber), (1990) 113 ILR 452   25, 79, 295, 340, 372, 374, 379

Mobutu and Republic of Zaire v. Société Logrine, France, Court of Appeal of Paris (First Chamber), 1994, 122 *JDI* (1995) 641; (1994) 113 ILR 481   30, 346, 434

Montefiore and Association Nationale des Porteurs de Valeurs Mobilières v. Colony of the Belgian Congo and Belgian State, France, Court of Cassation, (1961) 44 ILR 72   31

Montefiore v. The Belgian Congo, France, Tribunal Civil de la Seine, (1955) 22 ILR 226   103

Morocco (Government of Morocco and Maspero) v. Laurens, Société Marseillaise de Crédit, France, Court of Aix, (1930) 5 AD 116   10, 15, 31, 46

Mouracade v. Arab Republic of Yemen, France, Tribunal de grande instance of Paris (First Chamber), 1991, 119 *JDI* (1992) 398; (1991) 113 ILR 462   25, 30, 63, 103, 346

National Iranian Gas Corporation v. Pipeline Services, France, Court of Cassation (First Civil Chamber), 1990, 80 *RCDIP* (1991) 140; (1990) 113 ILR 446   30, 40, 83, 285, 346

Neger v. État de Hesse, France, Tribunal de grande instance de Paris and affirmed by Paris Court of Appeal, (1969) 52 ILR 329   31

Office for Cereals of Tunisia v. Société Bec Frères, France, Court of Cassation (First Civil Chamber), (1995) 113 ILR 485   285, 295, 379, 399

Officina del Aceite v. Domenech, France, Court of Appeal of Aix, (1938) 9 AD 239   10, 15, 46, 63

Passelaigues v. Mortgage Bank of Norway, France, Tribunal Civil de la Seine, (1955) 22 ILR 227   35

Petrococchino v. Swedish State, France, Civil Tribunal of the Seine, (1929) 5 AD 306   10, 15, 30, 63

Procureur de la République v. LIAMCO, France, Tribunal de grande instance of Paris, (1979) 65 ILR 78   46, 379, 408, 420

Procureur de la République v. SA Ipitrade International, France, Tribunal de grande instance of Paris, (1978) 65 ILR 75   46, 340, 360, 379, 408

Procureur Général près la Cour de Cassation v. Vestwig, France, Court of Cassation (Chambre des Requêtes), (1946) 13 AD 78   15, 46

Red Nacional de Ferrocariles Espanoles v. Mrs Cavaillé, France, Court of Appeal of Montpellier, (1968) 65 ILR 41   46, 224, 285

Robert v. Procureur de la République, France, Court of Cassation (First Civil Chamber), (1990) 113 ILR 450   137, 167, 191

Rossignol v. State of Czechoslovakia, France, Tribunal Civil de la Seine, (1949) 16 AD 140   15, 46

Roumania (State of Roumania) v. Aricastre, France, Court of Appeal of Poitiers (Joint Session of all Divisions), (1949) 16 AD 138   10, 15, 31, 35, 46

Roumania (State of) v. Pascalet, France, Commercial Tribunal of Marseilles, (1924) 2 AD 132   15, 35, 46, 48

Roumanian State v. Arricastre, France, Court of Appeal of Bordeaux, (1937) 8 AD 232   10, 15, 46, 48

Russian Federation v. Noga Import/Export Company, France, Court of Appeal of Paris (First Chamber), 2000, 128 *JDI* (2001) 116; (2000) 127 ILR 156   35, 340, 346, 360, 381, 404, 405, 407

Russian Trade Delegation v. Sakharoff, France, Court of Appeal of Paris, (1933) 7 AD 170   165

Russian Trade Delegation v. Société Française Industrielle et Commerciale des Pétroles (Groupe Malopolska), France, Civil Tribunal of the Seine (Référés), (1940) 9 AD 245   15, 301

Saignie v. Embassy of Japan, France, Court of Cassation (First Civil Chamber), 1997, 86 *RCDIP* (1997) 332; (1997) 113 ILR 492   30, 162, 167, 191, 195, 196, 346

TABLE OF CASES

Salabert v. Government of the United States of America, France, Tribunal Civil de la Seine, (1956) 23 ILR 192   35, 63

Senghor v. International Bank for West Africa and Republic of Senegal, France, Court of Cassation (First Civil Chamber), 1990, 80 *RCDIP* (1991) 341; (1990) 113 ILR 460   25, 30, 83, 295, 346

Société Air Zaire v. Gauthier and Van Impe, France, Court of Appeal of Paris (First Chambre), (1984) 77 ILR 510   103, 166, 177, 372, 374, 379, 398

Société Algérienne de Commerce Alco v. Sempac, France, Court of Cassation (First Civil Chamber), (1978) 65 ILR 73   83, 295, 301

Société Bauer-Marchal et Cie v. Gouvernment Turc, France, Court of Appeal of Rouen, (1965) 47 ILR 155   15, 63, 77, 103, 360

Société Bauer-Marchal v. Ministre des Finances de Turquie, France, Court of Paris, (1957) 24 ILR 204   35, 46

Société Européenne d'Études et d'Entreprises and International Bank for Reconstruction and Development v. France and Socialist Federal Republic of Yugoslavia, France, Court of Cassation (First Civil Chamber), (1986) 82 ILR 58   340, 372, 379

Société Européenne d'Études et d'Entreprises v. World Bank, Yugoslavia and France, France, Court of Appeal of Rouen (Combined First and Second Civil Chambers), (1984) 82 ILR 58   63, 104, 340

Société Française Industrielle et Commerciale des Pétroles v. Russian Trade Delegation, France, Court of Appeal of Paris, (1941) 11 AD 145   15

Société Immobilière des Cités Fleuries Lafayette v. United States of America, France, Court of Appeal of Paris, First Chamber, (1960) 42 ILR 123   15, 63

Société Internationale de Plantations d'Hévéas v. Lao Import Export Company, France, Court of Cassation (First Civil Chamber), (1987) 80 ILR 688   35, 40, 83, 301

Société Internationale de Plantations d'Hévéas v. Lao Import Export Company, Popular Democratic Republic of Laos, France, Court of Appeal of Paris (First Chamber), (1983) 80 ILR 430   40, 83, 300

Société Jean Dessès v. Prince Farouk and Mrs Sadek, France, Tribunal de grande instance of the Seine, (1963) 65 ILR 37   434

Société le Gostrog et Union des Républiques Socialistes Soviétiques v. Association France-Export, France, First Chamber of the Cour de Paris, (1926) 3 AD 174   15, 46, 398

Société Nationale des Tabacs et Allumettes v. Chaussois, France, Court of Cassation (First Civil Chamber), (1969) 65 ILR 44   13, 15, 46, 170, 285

TABLE OF CASES   li

Société Nationale des Transports Routiers v. Compagnie Algérienne de Transit et d'Affrètement Serres et Pilaire, France, Court of Cassation (Commercial and Financial Chamber), (1979) 65 ILR 83   285, 301

Société Ouest Africaine des Bétons Industriels (SOABI) v. State of Senegal, France, Court of Appeal of Paris (First Chamber), 1989; Court of Cassation, 1991; 117 *JDI* (1990) 141; 118 *JDI* (1991) 1005; 113 ILR 440   25, 340, 346, 379, 380

Société Paul Liegard v. Captain Serdjuk and Magne, France, Tribunal de Commerce of La Rochelle (summary jurisdiction), (1964) 65 ILR 38   18, 360

Société Prony habitations v. Guinée Bissau et Mme Marie Genia Da Costa Gomez, France, Cour de cassation, civ. 1ère, 20 septembre 2006, 110 *RGDIP* (2006) 971   77

Société Sonatrach v. Migeon, France, Court of Cassation (First Civil Chamber), (1985) 77 ILR 525   27, 177, 285, 372, 374, 398, 399

Société Transshipping v. Federation of Pakistan, France, Court of Cassation, (1966) 47 ILR 150   77, 340

Société Viajes v. Office National du Tourisme Espagnol, France, Tribunal Civil de la Seine, (1936) 8 AD 227   15

Socifros v. USSR (Union of Socialist Soviet Republics), France, Civil Tribunal of Toulon; Court of Appeal of Aix, (1938) 9 AD 236   15, 31, 35, 46

Solon v. Gouvernement égyptien, France, Tribunal Civil de la Seine, 16 avril 1847, Dalloz, 1849-I-7   10

Spanish State and the Bank of Spain v. Banco de Bilbao, France, Court of Appeal of Rouen, (1937) 8 AD 229   15

Spanish State v. Société Anonyme de l'Hôtel George V, France, Court of Cassation (First Civil Chamber), (1973) 65 ILR 61   63, 103

Statni Banka and Banque d'État Tchécoslovaque v. Englander, France, Court of Appeal of Aix-en-Provence, (1966) 47 ILR 157   35, 46, 360, 420

Syndicat des Copropriétaires du 14/16 Boulevard Flandrin, France, Administrative Court of Appeal of Paris (Third Chamber), (1992) 113 ILR 470   44, 191

USA (United States of America (Director of the United States Foreign Service)) v. Perignon, France, Court of Appeal of Paris (1st Chamber), (1962) 44 ILR 76   46

USA (United States of America) v. Perières, France, Court of Appeal of Montpellier (Social Chamber), (1997) 113 ILR 494   25, 137, 165, 174

USSR (Union of Socialist Soviet Republics) v. Association France Export, France, Court of Cassation, (1929) 5 AD 18   15, 23, 398

lii   TABLE OF CASES

X v. Saudi School in Paris and Kingdom of Saudi Arabia, France, Court of
Cassation (Mixed Chamber), 2003, 130 *JDI* (2003) 1124; 92 *RCDIP* (2003)
647; (2003) 127 ILR 163   30, 35, 103, 195, 196, 346

Yugoslavia (Socialist Federal Republic of Yugoslavia) v. Société
Européenne d'Études et d'Entreprises, Crédit Lyonnais, Air France and
Others, France, Tribunal de grande instance of Paris (Summary
proceedings), (1985) 82 ILR 58   46, 83, 372, 374, 418

Yugoslavia (Socialist Federal Republic of Yugoslavia) v. Société Européenne
d'Études et d'Entreprises, France, Tribunal de grande instance of Paris
(summary jurisdiction), (1970) 65 ILR 46   340, 346, 360

Gabon

Nkoghe Martin v. Embassy of the Central African Republic, Gabon,
Supreme Court, (1989) 89 ILR 43   13, 77

Germany

Arms Sales Commission Agreement Case, Federal Republic of Germany,
Superior Provincial Court (Oberlandesgericht) of Coblenz, Case No. 6
U 520/68, (1972) 65 ILR 119   86

Border Guards Prosecution Case, Federal Republic of Germany, Federal
Supreme Court (BGH), Case No. 5 StR 370/92, (1992) 100 ILR 364   439

Center for Constitutional Rights v. Donald Rumsfeld, Germany, Decision
of the General Federal Prosecutor at the Federal Court of Justice, 10
February 2005, 45 ILM 119 (2006)   434

Center for Constitutional Rights v. Rumsfeld *et al.*, Germany,
Oberlandesgericht Stuttgart, 13 September 2005, 45 ILM 122 (2006)   434

Central Bank of Nigeria Case, Federal Republic of Germany, Provincial
Court (Landgericht) of Frankfurt, 1975 (Case No. 3/8 O 186/75) and 1976
(Case No. 3/8 O 14/76), 65 ILR 131   35, 46, 57, 77, 87, 284, 349, 361, 379

Church of Scientology Case, Federal Republic of Germany, Federal
Supreme Court, Case No. VI ZR 267/76, (1978) 65 ILR 193   35, 340, 433

Claim against the Kenyan Embassy Case, Germany, Bundesgerichtshof
(Federal Court of Justice), (2003) IXa ZB 19/03, available at: www.
bundesgerichtshof.de   30

Conrades v. United Kingdom of Great Britain and Northern Ireland,
Federal Republic of Germany, Hanover Labour Court, Case No. 2 Ca. 20/
80, (1981) 65 ILR 205   30, 35, 61, 86, 137, 183, 196

Distomo Massacre Case (Greek Citizens v. Federal Republic of Germany),
Federal Republic of Germany, Federal Supreme Court (BGH), 2003,

Case No. III ZR 245/98 (available at: www.bundesgerichtshof.de), (2003) 129 ILR 556 30, 35, 203, 214, 429, 446

Distomo Massacre Case (Greek Citizens v. Federal Republic of Germany), Federal Republic of Germany, Federal Constitutional Court (BVerfG) (Second Chamber, First Section), Case No. 2 BvR 1476/03, (2006) 135 ILR 186 429

Economic Agreement Case, Germany, Court of the Reich in Labour Matters, (1933) 7 AD 175 35

Empire of Iran Case (Claim against the Empire of Iran Case), Federal Republic of Germany, Federal Constitutional Court, (1963) BVerfGE 16, 27; 45 ILR 57 12, 13, 15, 17, 21, 28, 30, 35, 61, 68, 77, 79, 80, 86, 360, 370, 445, 454

Foreign State Garnishment Case, Federal Republic of Germany, Provincial Court of Bonn, (1966) 57 ILR 152 30

Foreign Trade Institute Bank Account Case, Federal Republic of Germany, Provincial Court (Landgericht) of Hamburg, Case No. 18 T 13/81, (1981) 65 ILR 209 78, 86, 284, 398

Former Syrian Ambassador to the German Democratic Republic, Federal Republic of Germany, Federal Constitutional Court, Case No. 2 BvR 1516/96, (1997) BVerfGE 96, 68; 115 ILR 595 30

French Consulate Disabled Employee Case, Federal Republic of Germany, Administrative Court (VG) of Mainz, Case No. AZ 1K 4/88, (1988) 114 ILR 507 44, 46, 141, 162, 183, 184, 316

French Shares (Cross-Suit) Case, Germany, Prussian Tribunal for Conflicts of Jurisdiction (Kompetenzkonflikts-Gerichtshof), (1928) 4 AD 163 10, 17

Garden Contamination Case (1), Federal Republic of Germany, Provincial Court (Landgericht) of Bonn, Case No. 5 T 151/86; affirmed, Superior Provincial Court (Oberlandesgericht) of Cologne, Case No. 1 W 14/87, (1987) 80 ILR 367 35, 218

Garden Contamination Case (2), Federal Republic of Germany, District Court (Amtsgericht) of Bonn, Case No. 9 C 362/86; affirmed, Provincial Court (Landgericht) of Bonn, Case No. 5 T 184/87, (1987) 80 ILR 377 21, 210, 218, 219, 284, 295, 382

Halig Ltd v. Polish State, Germany, Prussian Tribunal for Conflicts of Jurisdiction (Kompetenzkonflikts-Gerichtshof), (1928) 4 AD 164 10, 17, 35

Honecker Prosecution Case, Federal Republic of Germany, Supreme Constitution Court (VerfGH) of Berlin, Case No. VerfGH 55/92, (1993) 100 ILR 393 434

Hungarian Embassy Case, Federal Republic of Germany, Federal Supreme Court, Case No. VZR 122/65, (1969) 65 ILR 110 10, 30, 406

liv   TABLE OF CASES

Immunity of United Kingdom from Jurisdiction (Germany) Case, Federal
  Republic of Germany, Court of Appeal of Schleswig, (1957) 24 ILR
  207   17, 46
Import of American Cigarettes (Germany) Case, German Federal
  Republic, District Court of Bremen, (1955) 22 ILR 233   30, 44
In re Danish State Railways in Germany, German Federal Republic,
  District Court of Kiel, (1953) 20 ILR 178   17, 21, 35, 46, 61
In re The Charkow, Federal Republic of Germany, Provincial Court
  (Landgericht) of Bremen, Case No. Q 50/1959, (1959) 65 ILR 100   17, 21,
  35, 361
Indian Foreign Minister Judicial Assistance Case, Federal Republic of
  Germany, Federal Administrative Court (BVerwG), Case No. 9 CB 47.88,
  (1988) 90 ILR 408   44, 83, 433
Jurisdiction over Yugoslav Military Mission (Germany) Case, Federal
  Republic of Germany, Federal Constitutional Court, (1962) BVerfGE 15,
  25; 38 ILR 162   10, 17, 30, 35, 44
Kenyan Diplomatic Residence Case, Federal Republic of Germany,
  Federal Supreme Court (BGH), Case No. IXa ZB 19/03, (2003) 128 ILR
  632   35, 134, 137, 162, 176, 361, 370, 404, 407, 408, 409, 420
L'Affaire du Département des chemins de fer de l'Etat belge,
  L'Allemagne, Arrêt de révision (Cassation) du Tribunal d'Empire
  (Reichsgericht) à Leipzig du 12 Décembre 1905, RGZ 62, 165; 34 *Journal
  du droit international privé (Clunet)* (1907) 166   10, 17, 35, 46, 429, 437
Land Purchase Broker's Commission Case, Federal Republic of Germany,
  Superior Provincial Court (Oberlandesgericht) of Munich, Case No. 1
  U 3951/74, (1974) 65 ILR 125   10, 77
Land Sale Authorisation Case, Federal Republic of Germany, Superior
  Court (Kammergericht) of West Berlin, Case No. 1 W 744/73, (1973) 65
  ILR 122   10
Latvia (Republic of Latvia) Case, German Federal Republic, Higher Court of
  Appeal (Kammergericht) of Berlin, (1955) 22 ILR 230   17, 21, 30, 35, 46, 61
Latvia (Republic of Latvia) Case, German Federal Republic, Restitution
  Chamber of Berlin, (1953) 20 ILR 180   17, 35, 46
Muller v. United States of America, Federal Republic of Germany,
  Regional Labour Court (LAG) of Hesse, Case No. 10 Sa 1506/97, (1998)
  114 ILR 512   25, 35, 86, 137, 141, 184, 446
NIOC (National Iranian Oil Company) Legal Status Case, Federal
  Republic of Germany, Superior Provincial Court (Oberlandesgericht)
  of Frankfurt, Case No. 5 W 24/80, (1980) 65 ILR 199   35, 284,
  295, 361

NIOC (National Iranian Oil Company) Pipeline Contracts Case, Federal Republic of Germany, Superior Provincial Court (Oberlandesgericht) of Frankfurt am Main, Case No. 5 U 202/81, (1982) 65 ILR 212   35, 78, 284, 285, 295, 361, 398

NIOC (National Iranian Oil Company) Revenues from Oil Sales Case, Federal Republic of Germany, Federal Constitutional Court, Case No. 2 BvR 678, 679, 680, 681, 683/81, (1983) BVerfGE 64, 1; 65 ILR 215   28, 30, 35, 284, 295, 344, 348, 361, 370, 371, 379, 398, 399, 421

Oder-Neisse Property Expropriation Case, Federal Republic of Germany, Superior Provincial Court (Oberlandesgericht) of Munich, Case No. 1 W 1347/75, (1975) 65 ILR 127   83, 299

Philippine Embassy Bank Account Case, Federal Republic of Germany, Federal Constitutional Court, Case No. 2 BvM 1/76, (1977) BVerfGE 46, 342; 65 ILR 146   28, 30, 35, 40, 54, 77, 344, 348, 361, 362, 370, 371, 378, 404, 407, 408, 420, 454

Polish Loan Bank Case, Germany, Prussian Tribunal for Conflicts of Jurisdiction, (1921) 1 AD 116   10, 17, 35

Re Honecker, Federal Republic of Germany, Federal Supreme Court (Second Criminal Chamber), Case No. 2 ARs 252/84, (1984) 80 ILR 365   31, 35, 46, 434

Re Treaty on the Basis of Relations between the Federal Republic of Germany and the German Democratic Republic, 1972, Federal Republic of Germany, Federal Constitutional Court, Case No. 2 BvF 1/73, 36 BVerfGE 1, 22; (1973) 78 ILR 149   31

Restitution of Property (Republic of Italy) Case, German Federal Republic, Court of Appeal of Hamm, (1951) 18 ILR 221   10, 30, 35, 66, 67

Russian Federation Payment Case, Germany, Bundesgerichtshof (Federal Court of Justice), (2005) VII ZB 9/05, available at: www. bundesgerichtshof.de   30

Shooting Range Extension Case, Federal Republic of Germany, Supreme Administrative Court (Verwaltungsgerichtshof) of Kassel, Case No. 9 TG 198/83, (1984) 86 ILR 532   35, 44

Spanish Consular Bank Accounts Case, Federal Republic of Germany, Provincial Court (Landgericht) of Stuttgart, Case No. 2 T 536/71, (1971) 65 ILR 114   28, 35, 361, 370, 371, 408, 421

Spanish State Tourist Office Case, Federal Republic of Germany, Superior Provincial Court (Oberlandesgericht) of Frankfurt, Case No. 6 U 184/74, (1977) 65 ILR 140   35, 46, 47, 57, 86, 284

The Cumene, Germany, Reichsgericht, (1925) 3 AD 175   10

The Ice King, Germany, Reichsgericht in Civil Matters, (1921) 1 AD 150   10, 17

lvi TABLE OF CASES

The Visurgis and The Siena, Germany, Court of Appeal of Hamburg, 1937; Supreme Court of the Reich (in Civil Matters), 1938, RGZ 157, 389; 9 AD 284   17, 445

Turkish Purchases Commission Case, Germany, Prussian Tribunal for Conflicts of Jurisdiction, (1920) 1 AD 114   10

X v. Argentina, Federal Republic of Germany, Federal Labour Court (BAG), Case No. 2 AZR 513/95, (1996) 114 ILR 502   25, 35, 46, 86, 137, 141, 162, 166, 183, 184

Yugoslav Military Mission Case, Federal Republic of Germany, Federal Supreme Court, Case No. V ZR 22/67, (1969) 65 ILR 108   10

Greece

Distomo Massacre Case (Prefecture of Voiotia v. Federal Republic of Germany), Greece, Court of Cassation (Areios Pagos), Case No. 11/ 2000, (2000) 129 ILR 513, noted by Maria Gavouneli and Ilias Bantekas, 95 *AJIL* (2001) 198   28, 30, 35, 47, 63, 87, 213, 359, 429, 446

Embassy Eviction Case, Greece, Tribunal of First Instance of Athens, Judgment No. 2626/1965, (1965) 65 ILR 248   99, 340, 359, 362, 371, 372, 407

Margellos v. Federal Republic of Germany, Greece, Special Supreme Court (Anotato Eidiko Dikastirio), Case No. 6/2002, (2002) 129 ILR 525   35, 46, 48, 54, 203, 214, 429

Prefecture of Voiotia v. Federal Republic of Germany, Case No. 137/1997, Court of First Instance of Leivadia, Greece, 1997, noted by Ilias Bantekas, 92 *AJIL* (1998) 765   429

Purchase of Embassy Staff Residence Case, Greece, Tribunal of First Instance of Athens, Judgment No. 26534/1967, (1967) 65 ILR 255   35, 46, 47, 63, 77, 359

Roumanian Legation (Greece) Case, Greece, Court of Appeal of Athens, (1949) 16 AD 291   15, 35, 46

Sale of British Embassy Building Case, Greece, Court of Cassation (First Chamber), Judgment No. 460/1962, (1962) 65 ILR 247   359

Soviet Republic (Immunity in Greece) Case, Greece, Civil Court of Athens, (1935) 8 AD 30   13

Soviet Republic (Immunity in Greece) Case, Greece, Court of Athens, (1928) 4 AD 172, affirmed by the Areopagus (Supreme Court) on appeal: Areopagus, No. 29, Themis, Vol. 40, p. 842   10, 15, 63, 359

India

Agarwala v. Union of India, India, Supreme Court, 1980, AIR 1980 Sikkim 22; 118 ILR 421   18, 35

Colonel HH Raja Sir Harinder Singh Barar Bans Bahandur v. Commissioner of Income Tax, Punjab, India, Supreme Court, 1971, [1972] 2 SCR 16; 64 ILR 523   31, 44

Commissioner of Income Tax, Andhra Pradesh v. HEH Mir Osman Ali Bahadur, India, Supreme Court, 1965, AIR 1966 SC 1260; [1966] 2 SCR 296; 64 ILR 482   31, 44

German Democratic Republic v. Dynamic Industrial Undertaking Ltd, India, High Court at Bombay, 1970, AIR 1972 Bombay 27; 64 ILR 504   18, 21, 31, 35, 46, 376

Harbhajan Singh Dhalla v. Union of India, India, Supreme Court, 1986, AIR 1987 SC 9; 92 ILR 530   18, 28, 46, 54, 55

Indian National Steamship Co. v. Maux Faulbaum, India, High Court of Calcutta, (1955) 22 ILR 248   10, 18, 28, 316

Institute Indo-Portuguese v. Borges, India, High Court of Bombay, (1958) 27 ILR 111   10

Maharaja Bikram Kishore of Tripura v. Province of Assam, India, High Court of Calcutta, (1948) 22 ILR 64   31, 44

Mirza Ali Akbar Kashani v. UAR (United Arab Republic), India, Supreme Court, 1965, [1966] 1 SCR 319; 64 ILR 489   18, 35

New Central Jute Mills Co. Ltd v. VEB Deutfracht Seereederei Rostock, India, Calcutta High Court, 1983, AIR 1983 Calcutta 225; 92 ILR 509 (The Supreme Court did not challenge the restrictive immunity point on appeal in 1993, 5 *Asian Yearbook of International Law* (1995))   18, 21, 28, 35, 376

Royal Nepal Airline Corporation v. Monorama Meher Singh Legha, India, High Court at Calcutta, 1964, AIR 1966 Calcutta 319; 64 ILR 430   18, 28, 30

Syrian Arab Republic v. Jajodia, India, High Court of Delhi, Case No. R.F.A. (OS) No. 30/2003, 2004   25

UAR (United Arab Republic) v. Mirza Ali Akbar Kashani, India, High Court at Calcutta, 1961, AIR 1962 Calcutta 387; 64 ILR 394   18, 27, 28, 35, 46, 47, 48, 54, 55, 64, 66

Union of India v. Chinoy Chablani and Co, India, High Court at Calcutta, AIR 1976 Calcutta 467; 64 ILR 534   18

Ireland

Canada (Government of Canada) v. Employment Appeals Tribunal and Burke, Ireland, High Court, 1991; Supreme Court, 1992; [1992] 2 IR 484; 95 ILR 467   9, 18, 21, 25, 28, 30, 35, 40, 54, 55, 106, 182, 195, 196

lviii   TABLE OF CASES

Fusco v. O'Dea, Ireland, Supreme Court, [1994] 2 ILRM 389; 103 ILR
    318   28, 44, 46, 346
Herron v. Ireland, Ireland, Supreme Court, Case No. 242/1997 (1997)
    (Transcript)   433, 439
McElhinney v. Williams and Her Majesty's Secretary of State for
    Northern Ireland, Ireland, High Court, [1994] 2 ILRM 115; 103 ILR
    311   35, 203, 212, 439
McElhinney v. Williams and Her Majesty's Secretary of State for
    Northern Ireland, Ireland, Supreme Court, 1995, [1996] 1 ILRM 276;
    104 ILR 691   28, 35, 47, 57, 106, 203, 212, 439, 446
Saorstat and Continental Steamship Company Ltd v. Rafael de las Morenas,
    Ireland, Supreme Court, 1944, [1945] IR 291; 12 AD 97   10, 18, 28, 35
Schmidt v. Home Secretary of the Government of the United Kingdom,
    the Commissioner of the Metropolitan Police and Jones, Ireland, High
    Court, 1994, [1995] ILRM 301; 103 ILR 322   84, 212, 433
Schmidt v. Home Secretary of the Government of the United Kingdom,
    the Commissioner of the Metropolitan Police and Jones, Ireland,
    Supreme Court, [1997] 2 IR 121   30, 84, 212, 433
The Ramava, Ireland, High Court, 1941, [1942] IR 148; 10 AD 91   11, 28, 35, 46

Israel

Attorney-General of the Government of Israel v. Adolf Eichmann, Israel,
    District Court of Jerusalem, (1961) 36 ILR 5   53
Her Majesty the Queen in Right of Canada v. Edelson, Israel, Supreme
    Court, Case No. PLA 7092/94, [1997] IsrLR 403; 131 ILR 279   18, 28, 35,
    47, 63, 77, 86, 99, 106
Reinhold v. HM The Queen in Right of Canada, Israel, 1991; Rina Navot v.
    South African Airways, Israel, 1992, noted in 26 *Israel Law Review*
    (1992) 559   18

Italy

Association of Italian Knights of the Order of Malta v. Piccoli, Italy, Court
    of Cassation (Joint Session), Case No. 1653, (1974) 65 ILR 308   31, 35,
    54, 69, 101, 139, 162, 185, 186, 194, 196, 376
Association of Italian Knights of the Sovereign Military Order of Malta v.
    Guidetti, Italy, Court of Cassation (Joint Session), Case No. 150/1999, 9
    Italian Yearbook of International Law (1999) 154   31
Bacchelli v. Comune di Bologna, Italy, Court of Cassation, Case No. 804,
    (1978) 77 ILR 621   31

TABLE OF CASES   lix

Banamar-Capizzi v. Embassy of the Popular Democratic Republic of Algeria, Italy, Court of Cassation (Plenary Session), Case No. 2085, (1989) 87 ILR 56   21, 25, 35, 134, 137, 176, 349, 359, 371, 376, 409, 421

Banco de la Nación v. Credito Varesino SpA, Italy, Court of Cassation (Plenary Session), Case No. 5275, (1984) 87 ILR 15   35, 69, 77, 376

Bari Institute of the International Centre for Advanced Mediterranean Agronomic Studies v. Chirico, Italy, Tribunal of Bari (Labour), (1985) 87 ILR 19   190, 196, 219, 337, 433, 439

Bari Institute of the International Centre for Advanced Mediterranean Agronomic Studies v. Jasbez, Italy, Court of Cassation (Joint Session), Case No. 4502, (1977) 77 ILR 602   35, 54, 162, 196, 376, 446

Baronci v. Ospedale del Bambino Gesù, Italy, Tribunal of Rome, (1956) 24 ILR 215   31, 69, 139

Bayerischer Rundfunk v. Schiavetti Magnani, Italy, Court of Cassation (Plenary Session), Case No. 110, (1987) 87 ILR 38   174, 177, 376

Bolivia (Government of Bolivia) v. Italian Association for Aeronautical Exports, Italy, Court of Cassation (United Sections), (1948) 15 AD 133   14, 35, 54, 55, 68

Borga v. Russian Trade Delegation, Italy, Court of Cassation (United Chambers), (1953) 22 ILR 235   46, 47, 69

Borri v. Repubblica Argentina, Italia, Cassazione (Sez. un.), 27 maggio 2005, n. 6532 (ord.), 88 Rivista di diritto internazionale (2005) 856   35, 54, 60, 102

British Consulate-General in Naples v. Toglia, Italy, Court of Cassation (Plenary Session), Case No. 2329, (1989) 101 ILR 379   35, 76, 137, 176, 177, 186, 187, 188, 190, 196, 376, 446

British Government and the Municipality of Venice v. Guerrato, Italy, Tribunal of Venice, (1959) 28 ILR 156   359

Bruno v. United States, Italy, Court of Cassation (Joint Session), Case No. 355, (1977) 65 ILR 316   35, 54, 172

Bulli v. Foreign and Commonwealth Office of the United Kingdom of Great Britain and Northern Ireland, Italy, Examining Magistrate (Pretore) of Venice, (1981) 65 ILR 343   25, 101, 182, 186

Camera Confederale del Lavoro CGIL v. Bari Institute of the International Centre for Advanced Mediterranean Agronomic Studies, Italy, Court of Cassation (Joint Session), Case No. 2425, (1979) 78 ILR 86   165

Campione v. Peti-Nitrogenmuvek NV and Hungarian Republic, Italy, Court of Cassation (Joint Session), Case No. 3368, (1972) 65 ILR 287   14, 35, 69, 299, 300, 302, 359

lx TABLE OF CASES

Canada v. Cargnello, Italy, Court of Cassation (Plenary Session), Decision
No. 4017/1998, (1998) 114 ILR 559   25, 35, 40, 54, 101, 137, 141, 177, 190

Carbonar v. Magurno, Italy, Court of Cassation (Plenary Session),
Decision No. 9675/1993, (1993) 114 ILR 534   25, 35, 137, 162, 166, 176,
192, 196, 376

Castiglioni v. Federal People's Republic of Yugoslavia, Italy, Tribunal of
Rome, (1952) 19 ILR 203   21, 35, 54, 55, 68

Cavallucci v. Hungarian Embassy, Italy, Tribunal of Rome, (1967) 71
ILR 238   192

Church v. Ferraino, Italy, Court of Cassation (Plenary Session), Case No.
283, (1986) 101 ILR 370   101, 139, 162, 185, 194, 376

Ciniglio v. Indonesian Embassy and Compagnia di Assicurazioni
Intercontinentali, Italy, Examining Magistrate (Pretore) of Rome,
(1966) 65 ILR 268   35, 60, 211

Condor and Filvem v. Minister of Justice, Italy, Constitutional Court,
Case No. 329, (1992) 101 ILR 394   28, 35, 78, 102, 349, 359, 371, 379,
409, 421

Consorzio Agrario dell Tripolitania v. Federazione Italiana Consorzi
Agrari and Cassa di Risparmio della Libia, Italy, Court of Cassation
(Joint Session), Case No. 2830, (1966) 65 ILR 265   31, 46, 100, 286

Consul-General of Belgium in Naples v. Esposito, Italy, Court of Cassation
(Plenary Session), Case No. 666, (1986) 101 ILR 376   186, 196

Cristiani v. Italian Latin-American Institute, Italy, Court of Cassation
(Plenary Session), Case No. 5819, (1985) 87 ILR 20   35, 54, 194, 446

Danish Cultural Institute and Krogh v. Hansen, Italy, Court of Cassation
(Joint Session), Case No. 979, (1979) 65 ILR 325   35, 54, 55, 101, 137,
162, 185, 190, 194, 196

De Ritis v. United States, Italy, Court of Cassation (Joint Session), Case No.
3441, (1971) 65 ILR 283   101, 185, 186, 194, 196

De Semenoff v. Railway Administration of the Norwegian State, Italy,
Court of Appeal of Rome, (1936) 8 AD 234   68, 165

Department of the Army of the United States of America v. Savellini, Italy,
Court of Cassation (United Civil Chamber), (1955) 23 ILR 201   172

Ecole française de Rome v. Guadagnino, Italy, Court of Cassation (Joint
Session), Case No. 8768, 9 September 1997, 9 *Italian Yearbook of
International Law* (1999) 152   35, 194

Embassy of the Kingdom of Morocco v. Società Immobiliare Forte
Barchetto, Italy, Court of Appeal of Rome, (1979) 65 ILR 331   77, 102

European University v. Piette, Italy, Court of Cassation (Joint Session), Case
No. 149/1999, 9 *Italian Yearbook of International Law* (1999) 155   31, 54

TABLE OF CASES   lxi

Ferrini v. Federal Republic of Germany, Italy, Court of Cassation
    (Plenary Session), Decision No. 5044/2004, (2004) 128 ILR 658   28, 35,
    210, 344, 429
FILT-CGIL Trento v. United States of America, Italy, Court of Cassation
    (Plenary Session), Decision No. 530/2000, (2000) 128 ILR 644   35, 54,
    214, 376
Food and Agriculture Organization v. INPDAI, Italy, Court of Cassation
    (Plenary Session), Case No. 5399, (1982) 87 ILR 1   54
France (Republic of France, French Embassy in Italy and Lycée Chateaubriand)
    v. Jacuzio, Italy, Court of Cassation (Plenary Session), Case No. 9322, (1987)
    87 ILR 53   21, 25, 35, 46, 54, 55, 101, 177, 187, 190, 194, 196, 376
Francischiello v. Government of the United States of America, Italy,
    Tribunal of Naples, (1959) 28 ILR 158   35, 46, 54, 55, 68, 101, 137, 172,
    185, 196
French Government v. Serra & Co., Italy, Court of Appeal of Genoa, (1925)
    3 AD 178   68
French Ministry of Finance v. Banca Italiana di Sconto in Liquidation,
    Italy, Court of Cassation, (1932) 6 AD 36   68
Galasso v. Italian Latin-American Institute, Italy, Court of Cassation, Case
    No. 667, (1986) 87 ILR 28 note   194
Germany v. Mantelli, Italy, Court of Cassation, Case No. 14201/2008, 29
    May 2008, noted by Carlo Focarelli, 103 *AJIL* (2009) 122   429
Giaffreda v. French Republic, Italy, Court of Cassation (Plenary Session),
    Decision No. 12315/1992, (1992) 114 ILR 558 note   25, 177, 190, 196, 376
Giamahiria araba libica v. Condor s.r.l., Italy, Cassazione (Sez. un.), 23
    agosto 1990, n. 8568, 74 *Rivista di diritto internazionale* (1991) 679   35
Giamahiria araba libica socialista v. Riunione Adriatica di Sicurtà s.p.a.,
    Italy, Cassazione (Sez. un.), 30 maggio 1990, n. 5091, 74 *Rivista di diritto
    internazionale* (1991) 990   35
Greece (Kingdom of Greece) v. Gamet, Italy, Court of Cassation, (1957) 24
    ILR 209   35, 54, 55, 69, 299, 376, 439
Greece (Kingdom of Greece) v. Gamet, Italy, Court of Cassation, (1959) 28
    ILR 153   21, 35, 46, 69, 299, 376, 439
Guttieres v. Elmilik, Italy, Corte di Cassazione, Firenze, 1886, Foro
    Italiano 1886-I-913; Giurisprudenza Italiana, 1886-I-1-486; 26 *AJIL
    Supplement* (1932) 622   14, 19, 46, 60, 68
HAFSE v. Sindicato FILTAT-CISL Vicenza, Italy, Court of Cassation, Case
    No. 3368, (1978) 77 ILR 630   54
Hamspohn v. Bey di Tunisi, Italy, Corte d'Appello, Lucca, 1887, Foro
    Italiano 1887-I-474, 26 *AJIL Supplement* (1932) 480 and 713   14, 371

lxii TABLE OF CASES

Harrie Lurie v. Steinmann, Italy, Court of Rome, (1927) 4 AD 364   30, 35, 46, 54, 55

Hungarian Papal Institute v. Hungarian Institute (Academy) in Rome, Italy, Court of Cassation (United Chambers), (1960) 40 ILR 59   35, 54, 55, 69

Hungarian Papal Institute v. Hungarian Institute in Rome, Italy, Tribunal of Rome, (1957) 24 ILR 218   35

Hungarian People's Republic v. Onori, Italy, Court of Cassation (United Chamber), (1956) 23 ILR 203   69, 162, 194, 196

Hurwitz v. Consul of the Republic of Panama, Italy, Court of Cassation (Joint Session), (1977) 77 ILR 598 note   186

In re Polimeni, Italy, Military Court of Rome, (1935) 8 AD 248   30

In re Savini, Italy, Court of Appeal of Rome, (1927) 4 AD 166   30, 31

Italian Trade Union for Embassy and Consular Staff v. United States, Italy, Examining Magistrate (Pretore) of Milan, (1981) 65 ILR 338   35, 46, 54, 55, 137, 162, 165

La Mercantile v. Kingdom of Greece, Italy, Tribunal of Rome, (1955) 22 ILR 240   69

Libya (Arab Republic of Libya) v. SpA Imprese Marittime Frassinetti and SpA Italiana Lavori Marittimi e Terrestri, Italy, Court of Cassation, Case No. 3062, (1979) 78 ILR 90   35, 46, 54, 55, 83, 102, 103, 299, 376, 439

Libya (Libyan Arab Jamahiriya) v. Trobbiani, Italy, Court of Cassation (Plenary Session), Decision No. 145/1990, (1990) 114 ILR 520   25, 35, 101, 137, 162, 170, 176, 188, 189, 194, 196, 376

Libya (Libyan Arab Socialist People's Jamahiriya) v. Rossbeton SRL, Italy, Court of Cassation (Plenary Session), Case No. 2502, (1989) 87 ILR 63   21, 25, 28, 35, 137, 349, 359, 371, 376, 379, 409, 421

Libya (Libyan Arab Socialist People's Jamahiriya) v. SPA Records and Civil Tribunal of Rome, Italy, Court of Cassation (Plenary Session), Case No. 7076, (1983) 87 ILR 11   25, 69, 376

Little v. Riccio and Fischer, Italy, Court of Appeal of Naples, 1933; affirmed by the Court of Cassation, 1934, 7 AD 177   46, 165

Luna v. Socialist Republic of Romania, Italy, Court of Cassation (Joint Session), Case No. 3803, (1974) 65 ILR 313   35, 60, 101, 184, 185, 196

Mallaval v. French Ministry of Foreign Affairs, Italy, Examining Magistrate (Pretore) of Rome, (1974) 65 ILR 303   35, 46, 54, 55, 68, 69, 162, 177, 187, 192, 194, 196, 376

Milde v. Italy, Italy, Court of Cassation, Case No. 1072, 21 October 2008, noted by Annalisa Ciampi, 7 *Journal of International Criminal Justice* (2009) 597   429

TABLE OF CASES   lxiii

Mininni v. Bari Institute of the International Centre for Advanced Mediterranean Agronomic Studies, Italy, Court of Cassation (Plenary Session), Case No. 2317, (1986) 87 ILR 28   21, 46, 54, 55, 194

Mininni v. Bari Institute of the International Centre for Advanced Mediterranean Agronomic Studies, Italy, Tribunal of Bari (Labour Chamber), (1981) 78 ILR 112   359

Ministry of Finance v. Association of Italian Knights of the Order of Malta, Italy, Court of Cassation, Case No. 2051, (1978) 65 ILR 320   31, 35, 44, 46, 54, 55, 69, 102

Ministry of Foreign Affairs v. Federici and Japanese State, Italy, Tribunal of Rome, (1968) 65 ILR 275   60, 212

Morellet v. Governo Danese, Italy, Corte di Cassazione di Torino, 10 novembre 1882, Giurisprudenza Italiana, 1883-I-125, 130; 26 *AJIL Supplement* (1932) 481 and 595   14, 60

Nacci v. Bari Institute of the International Centre for Advanced Mediterranean Agronomic Studies, Italy, Court of Cassation (Plenary Session), Decision No. 5565/1994, (1994) 114 ILR 539   35, 54, 177, 194

Nanni v. Pace and the Sovereign Order of Malta, Italy Court of Cassation, (1935) 8 AD 2   31, 35, 44, 102

Nobili v. Emperor Charles I of Austria, Italy, Court of Cassation of Rome, (1921) 1 AD 36   14, 68, 434

Norwegian Embassy v. Quattri, Italy, Court of Cassation (Plenary Session), Decision No. 12771/1991, (1991) 114 ILR 525   25, 35, 54, 69, 101, 137, 162, 170, 176, 177, 185, 186, 188, 189, 190, 196, 376, 446

Novaco v. United States Navy, Italy, Tribunal of Naples, (1957) 24 ILR 219   69, 171, 196

Padri Benedettini della Basilica di S Paolo v. Nunzi, Italy, Court of Cassation, (1957) 24 ILR 214   21, 35, 60

Panattoni v. Federal Republic of Germany, Italy, Court of Cassation (Plenary Session), Case No. 6172, (1987) 87 ILR 42   25, 35, 69, 101, 137, 186, 190, 196

Paradiso v. Bari Institute of the International Centre for Advanced Mediterranean Agronomic Studies, Italy, Court of Cassation, Case No. 2316, (1986) 87 ILR 37 note   194, 421

Paradiso v. Bari Institute of the International Centre for Advanced Mediterranean Agronomic Studies, Italy, Court of Cassation (Plenary Session), Case No. 3733, (1986) 87 ILR 38 note   177, 194

Parravincini v. Commercial Bureau of the People's Republic of Bulgaria, Italy, Tribunal of Milan, (1969) 65 ILR 282   101, 162, 166, 185, 376

Pauer v. Hungarian People's Republic, Italy, Court of Cassation, (1956) 24 ILR 211   35, 46, 299

Perrini v. Académie de France, Italy, Court of Cassation (Plenary Session), Decision No. 5126/1994, (1994) 114 ILR 536   35, 54, 101, 137, 162, 170, 177, 189, 190, 194, 196, 376

Perrucchetti v. Puig y Cassauro, Italy, Court of Rome, (1928) 4 AD 365   68

Pontificia Opera di Assistenza v. Inps and Smith, Italy, Court of Cassation (Joint Session), Case No. 6569, (1979) 65 ILR 333   31, 101, 162, 186, 190, 194, 196

Prefect of Milan v. Federici and Savoldi, Italy, Court of Cassation, Case No. 3032, (1968) 65 ILR 270   359

Presidenza Consiglio ministri v. Federazione italiana lavoratori trasporti; Stati Uniti d'America v. Federazione italiana lavoratori trasporti, Italy, Corte di cassazione (Sezioni unite civili), Sentenza 3 agosto 2000, n. 530, *RDI* 2000, p. 1155   30

Re Arafat and Salah, Italy, Court of Cassation, 28 June 1985, 7 *Italian Yearbook of International Law* (1986–87) 287 (case note by Francesco Salerno)   31, 434

Re Marcinkus, Mennini and De Strobel, Italy, Court of Cassation (Criminal Division), Case No. 3932, (1987) 87 ILR 48   31, 433

Regno di Spagna v. Chiesa di San Pietro in Montorio, Italy, Cassazione (Sez. un.), 6 maggio 1997, n. 3957, 80 *Rivista di diritto internazionale* (1997) 1163   35

Rubin v. Consul of the Republic of Panama, Italy, Court of Cassation (Joint Session), Case No. 3007, (1977) 77 ILR 593   101, 137, 177, 186, 188, 190, 196, 376

Rumania (Stato di Rumania) v. Trutta, Italy, Corte di Cassazione del Regno, Sezioni unite, 1926, 1926 Giurisprudenza Italiana 774; *Foro Italiano*, 1926-I-584; 26 *AJIL Supplement* (1932) 626 and 711; 3 AD 179 note   14, 43, 60, 77, 100, 371

Russian Commercial Representation v. Tesini and Malvezzi, Italy, Court of Cassation (Combined Divisions), (1925) 3 AD 176   10, 68

Russian Trade Delegation in Italy v. De Castro, Italy, Court of Appeal of Genoa, 1934; Court of Cassation, 1935, 7 AD 179   68, 398

Russian Trade Delegation in Italy v. Kazmann, Italy, Court of Cassation, (1933) 7 AD 178   60, 165

Scarfò v. Sovereign Order of Malta, Italy, Tribunal of Rome, (1957) 24 ILR 1   31, 54, 55, 100, 139, 162, 185

Sindacato UIL (Bari Branch) v. Bari Institute of the International Centre for Advanced Mediterranean Agronomic Studies, Italy, Court of Cassation (Plenary Session), Case No. 3732, (1986) 87 ILR 37   162, 194, 376

TABLE OF CASES   lxv

Slomnitzky v. Trade Delegation of the USSR in Italy, Italy, Court of
Appeal of Milan, (1932) 6 AD 169   54, 55, 68, 165
Società di Navigazione Generale 'Gerolimich' v. Russian Trade
Delegation in Italy, Italy, Court of Cassation, (1938) 9 AD 247   398
Società Riunite di Assicurazione e Riassicurazione v. United States Shipping
Board, Italy, Court of Appeal of Naples, (1925) 3 AD 179 note   68
Sovereign Order of Malta v. Soc An Commerciale, Italy, Tribunal of
Rome, (1954) 22 ILR 1   31, 35, 46, 69
Special Representative of State of the City of the Vatican v. Pieciukiewicz,
Italy, Court of Cassation (Joint Session), Case No. 4005, (1982) 78
ILR 120   31, 35, 54, 102, 162, 191, 194, 196, 376
Storelli v. French Republic (Government of), Italy, Court of Rome, (1924)
2 AD 129   10, 46, 68
Tani v. Russian Trade Delegation in Italy, Italy, Court of Cassation
(United Sections), (1947) 15 AD 141   54, 60, 68, 165, 376
The Ditta Pomante v. Federal Republic of Germany, Italy, Civil Court of
L'Aquila, (1960) 40 ILR 64   21, 25, 35, 54, 55, 69
Typaldos, Console di Gregia v. Manicomio di Aversa, Italy, Corte di
Cassazione di Napoli, Giurisprudenza Italiana, 1886-I-1-228; 26 *AJIL*
Supplement (1932) 623   14, 19, 35, 46
US (United States Government) v. Bracale Bicchierai, Italy, Court of
Appeal of Naples, (1968) 65 ILR 273   35, 54, 69, 77, 100
US (United States Government) v. IRSA, Italy, Court of Cassation, Case No.
1178, (1963) 65 ILR 262   69, 77, 100
US (United States) v. Gereschi, Italy, Court of Cassation (Joint Session),
Case No. 4372, (1977) 77 ILR 598   172, 376
USA (United States of America) v. Lo Gatto, Italy, Court of Cassation
(Plenary Session), Decision No. 4483/1995, (1995) 114 ILR 555   25, 35,
46, 54, 55, 137, 177, 190, 196, 376
Velloso v. Borla, Italy, Court of Cassation (Joint Session), Case No. 3063,
(1979) 65 ILR 328   101, 162, 186, 196
Zambian Embassy v. Sendanayake, Italy, Court of Cassation (Plenary
Session), Decision No. 5941/1992, (1992) 114 ILR 532   35, 137, 162, 166,
176, 196, 376
Zucca v. Fondazione Internazionale Premio Balzan and Swiss
Confederation, Italy, Court of Appeal of Milan, (1969) 65 ILR 280   54, 83

Japan

Case No. 1231 [2003], Japan, Supreme Court, 1416 Saibansho Jihō 8 (Sup.
Ct. Jul. 21, 2006), noted by Colin P. A. Jones, 100 *AJIL* (2006) 908   13

lxvi   TABLE OF CASES

In re Hoover, Japan, District Court of Aomori, (1956) 23 ILR 265   10, 35

Limbin Hteik Tin Lat v. Union of Burma, Japan, District Court of Tokyo, (1954) 32 ILR 124   10, 31, 35, 66, 67

Masatoshi Suzuki v. Tokyo Civilian Open Mess, Japan, District Court of Tokyo, (1957) 24 ILR 226   10, 46

Matsuyama and Sano v. Republic of China, Japan, Supreme Court, (1928) 4 AD 168   10, 13, 35

Republic of China v. Chuka Newspaper Co Ltd, Japan, District Court of Tokyo, (1955) 23 ILR 210   10, 35, 316

Ryuichi Shimoda v. The State, Japan, District Court of Tokyo, (1963) 32 ILR 626; 8 *Japanese Annual of International Law* (1964) 212   35, 438

X v. Republic of the Marshall Islands, Japan, Tokyo District Court, 2000, 45 *Japanese Annual of International Law* (2002) 146   13

X v. State of Georgia of the United States of America, Japan, Tokyo High Court, 2008, Case No. HJ (1997) 155 [2008]; judgment quashed by the Supreme Court, 2009, 52 *Japanese Yearbook of International Law* (2009) 658   13

X v. The Mayor of Shibuya Ward; X v. The Building Manager of Shibuya Ward, Japan, Tokyo District Court, 2007, 51 *Japanese Yearbook of International Law* (2008) 533   13

X v. United States of America, Japan, Supreme Court, 2002, 46 *Japanese Annual of International Law* (2003) 161   13, 21, 35, 214

X v. United States of America, Japan, Tokyo District Court, Hachioji Branch, 1997, 41 *Japanese Annual of International Law* (1998) 91   13, 35

X v. United States of America, Japan, Tokyo High Court, 1998, 42 *Japanese Annual of International Law* (1999) 138   13, 21

X v. Y1 and Y2, Japan, Tokyo District Court, 1990, 35 *Japanese Annual of International Law* (1992) 151   134, 173

Yamaguchi v. United States, 56 Minshū 729, Japan, Supreme Court, 12 April 2002, noted by Mizushima Tomonori, 97 *AJIL* (2003) 406   214

Jordan

Nashashibi v. Consul-General of France in Jerusalem, Jordan, Supreme Court of Cassation, (1958) 26 ILR 190   10, 77

Kenya

UK (Ministry of Defence of the Government of the United Kingdom) v. Joel Ndegwa, Kenya, Court of Appeal, 1983, (1982–88) KAR 135; (1983) 103 ILR 235   13, 25, 28, 87

Lebanon

Lebanon Expropriation Case, Lebanon, Court of Cassation, (1926) 3 AD
  44   10

Lithuania

Cudak (Senkevič) v. Embassy of the Republic of Poland, Lithuania, Supreme
  Court, Case No. 3K-3-203/2001 (2001), noted by Michail Cvelich, 3 *Baltic
  Yearbook of International Law* (2003) 320   18, 35, 46, 196, 446
Norwegian Enterprise Vilnius Property AS v. Embassy of Russian Federation,
  Lithuania, Supreme Court, Case No. 3K-3–566/2003 (2003), noted by
  Laima Masalaite, 4 *Baltic Yearbook of International Law* (2004) 351   18
Stukonis v. Embassy of the USA in the Republic of Lithuania, Lithuania,
  Supreme Court, Case No. 3K-1 (1998), noted by Michail Cvelich, 2 *Baltic
  Yearbook of International Law* (2002) 270   18, 46, 446

Malaysia

Australia (Commonwealth of Australia) v. Midford (Malaysia) Sdn Bhd,
  Malaysia, Supreme Court, [1990] 1 Curr LJ 878; 86 ILR 640   18, 25, 28,
  30, 46, 83, 106, 439
Village Holdings Sdn Bhd v. Her Majesty the Queen in Right of Canada,
  Malaysia, High Court (Malaya), 1987, [1988] 2 MLJ 656; (1987) 87 ILR
  223   18, 28, 30, 46, 434

The Netherlands

Advokaat v. Schuddinck and the Belgian State, The Netherlands, District
  Court of Dordrecht, (1923) 2 AD 133   35, 46, 66
Arias v. Venezuela, The Netherlands, District Court of The Hague, (1998)
  128 ILR 684   25, 35, 162, 182, 196, 446
'Atlantic' Algemene Verzekering Maatschappij NV v. USSR (Union of
  Soviet Socialist Republics), The Netherlands, District Court of
  Rotterdam, (1979) 65 ILR 377   340
Belgium (State of Belgium) v. EAG de Badts, The Netherlands, District
  Court of Rotterdam, (1922) 1 AD 129   10
Bergverksaktiebolaget Kosmai v. Militär-Liquidierungsamt, of Vienna,
  The Netherlands, Court of Appeal of Amsterdam, First Chamber, (1921)
  1 AD 130   10, 35
Brinkhof NV v. NV Nederlandse Spoorwegen and Deutsche Bundesbahn,
  The Netherlands, District Court of Utrecht, (1969) 65 ILR 354   286, 295

lxviii   TABLE OF CASES

BV v. Instituto Italiano di Cultura per i Paesi Bassi and the Republic of Italy, The Netherlands, District Court of Amsterdam, 1990, 23 *NYIL* (1992) 447   162, 174, 178, 195

BV v. Instituto Italiano di Cultura per i Paesi Bassi and the Republic of Italy, The Netherlands, Sub-District Court of Amsterdam, 1991, 24 *NYIL* (1993) 341   162, 178, 195

Church of Scientology in the Netherlands Foundation v. (1) Herold and (2) Heinrich Bauer Verlag, The Netherlands, District Court of Amsterdam, (1980) 65 ILR 380   212

Consulate-General of Italy Case, The Netherlands, Local Court of Rotterdam, (1979) 65 ILR 380 note   174, 196

De Booy v. German Reich (Government of Holland Intervening), The Netherlands, Supreme Court, (1924) 1 AD 124   10, 35

De Froe v. The Russian State, Now Styled 'The Union of Soviet Socialist Republics', The Netherlands, District Court of Amsterdam, (1932) 6 AD 170   10, 40

De Sousa v. Republic of Portugal, The Netherlands, Local Court of Amsterdam, (1979) 65 ILR 378   63, 134, 162, 165, 166, 174, 178, 196

Edwards v. BV Bureau Wijsmuller Scheepvaart Transport-en-Zeesleepvaart-Maatschappij, The Netherlands, Court of Appeal of Amsterdam, (1987) 94 ILR 361   35, 79

FLM v. The Public Prosecutions Department, The Netherlands, Supreme Court, 1993, 25 *NYIL* (1994) 527   162

G v. United States of America and L, The Netherlands, District Court of Utrecht, 1992, 27 *NYIL* (1996) 320   162, 193

Gootjes v. Kingdom of Belgium, The Netherlands, Local Court of Rotterdam, (1978) 65 ILR 372   182, 184, 196

H. 't Hooft v. Republic of France, The Netherlands, Sub-District Court of The Hague, 1986, 19 *NYIL* (1988) 438, note 27   174

ICC Handel Maatschappij v. Union of Soviet Socialist Republics, The Netherlands, District Court of Amsterdam, (1976) 65 ILR 368   63, 77

Indonesia (Republic of Indonesia) v. Van der Haas, The Netherlands, President of the District Court of The Hague in Summary Proceedings, (1958) 26 ILR 181   18, 54, 299, 439

Italy (Republic of Italy) v. BV, The Netherlands, District Court of Amsterdam, 1993, 26 *NYIL* (1995) 338   134, 162, 178, 195

JPH v. Indonesian State, The Netherlands, Local Court of The Hague, (1979) 65 ILR 379 note   40, 63, 174

Krol v. Bank Indonesia, The Netherlands, Court of Appeal of Amsterdam, (1958) 26 ILR 180   18, 46

LF and HMHK v. Federal Republic of Germany, The Netherlands, District
Court of Haarlem, (1986) 94 ILR 342   25, 35, 40, 63, 84, 439, 446
LFLM v. The Public Prosecutions Department, The Netherlands, Supreme
Court, 1993, 25 *NYIL* (1994) 527   182
LM v. Netherlands, Minister for Netherlands Antilles Affairs and Aruban
Affairs, The Netherlands, Court of Appeal of the Netherlands Antilles
and Aruba, (1998) 128 ILR 681   31, 446
MDDA v. Australian Embassy, The Netherlands, Sub-District Court of The
Hague, 1986, 19 *NYIL* (1988) 438, note 27   162, 191
MHC v. Republic of Cuba, The Netherlands, Sub-District Court of The
Hague, 1992, 27 *NYIL* (1996) 319   162, 174, 175, 177
MK v. Republic of Turkey, The Netherlands, Sub-District Court of The
Hague, (1985) 94 ILR 350   25, 35, 63, 166, 174, 175, 177, 196
MK v. State Secretary for Justice, The Netherlands, Council of State,
(1986) 94 ILR 357   35, 44, 134, 177, 372, 404, 408, 419
Morocco (Kingdom of Morocco) v. Stichting Revalidatiecentrum 'De
Trappenberg', The Netherlands, District Court of Amsterdam
(Summary Proceedings), (1978) 65 ILR 375   63, 134, 162, 166, 212, 421
Morocco (Kingdom of Morocco) v. Stichting Revalidatiecentrum 'De
Trappenberg', The Netherlands, Supreme Court, 1994, 128 ILR
676   162, 166
Nederlandse Rijnbank, Amsterdam v. Mühlig Union, Teplitz-Schönau,
The Netherlands, Council for the Restoration of Legal Rights, Division
for Judicial Settlement, (1947) 14 AD 77   35
Netherlands v. Azeta BV, The Netherlands, District Court of Rotterdam,
(1998) 128 ILR 688   35, 372, 408
NV Cabolent v. National Iranian Oil Company, The Netherlands, Court
of Appeal at The Hague, (1968) 47 ILR 138   18, 35, 72, 340, 349,
372, 398
NV Exploitatie-Maatschappij Bengkalis v. Bank Indonesia, The Netherlands,
Court of Appeal of Amsterdam, (1963) 65 ILR 348   35, 83, 231, 286
NV Limburgsch Landbouw-Syndicaat, of Wijk-Maastricht v. German
Reich, The Netherlands, District Court of Maastricht, (1916) 1 AD 129
note   10, 35, 40
Oltmans v. Republic of Surinam, The Netherlands, Supreme Court, 1990,
23 *NYIL* (1992) 442   346
Parsons v. Republic of Malta, The Netherlands, District Court of Alkmaar,
(1977) 65 ILR 371   63
PAvH v. United States of America, The Netherlands, Rotterdam Local
Court, 65 ILR 374 note   176, 182

lxx   TABLE OF CASES

Poortensdijk Ltd v. Soviet Republic of Latvia, The Netherlands, District
Court of Amsterdam, 1941; affirmed, Court of Appeal of Amsterdam,
1942; 11 AD 142   30, 35, 46, 299
Portugal (Republic of Portugal) v. Algemene Oliehandel International,
The Netherlands, District Court of Rotterdam, (1982) 94 ILR 315   25,
35, 340
Portugal (Republic of Portugal) v. De Sousa, The Netherlands, District Court
of Amsterdam, (1981) 94 ILR 314   25, 35, 63, 87, 134, 162, 165, 166, 174, 196
Russian Federation v. Pied-Rich BV, The Netherlands, Court of Appeal of
The Hague, 5 August 1992, 24 *NYIL* (1993) 346   63
Russian Federation v. Pied-Rich, The Netherlands, Supreme Court, 28
May 1993, 41 *NILR* (1994) 116   87
Société Européenne d'Études et d'Entreprises en Liquidité Volontaire v.
Socialist Federal Republic of Yugoslavia, The Netherlands, Court of
Appeal of The Hague, 1972; Supreme Court, 1973, 65 ILR 356; Supreme
Court, 1975, 1 *Yearbook of Commercial Arbitration* (1976) 198   18, 21, 35,
63, 87, 418
South Africa (Union of South Africa) v. Herman Grote, The Netherlands,
District Court of Amsterdam, in Summary Procedure, (1921) 1 AD
22   31, 438, 439
South Moluccas (Republic of the South Moluccas) v. Royal Packet Shipping
Company, The Netherlands, District Court of Amsterdam, 1950; Court of
Appeal of Amsterdam, 1951, 17 ILR 143   18, 31, 35, 46, 438
Stichting Revalidatiecentrum 'De Trappenberg' v. Kingdom of Morocco,
The Netherlands, Court of Appeal of Amsterdam, 1991; Kingdom of
Morocco v. Stichting Revalidatiecentrum 'De Trappenberg', The
Netherlands, Supreme Court, 1994, 128 ILR 676   134, 212
Stichting Revalidatiecentrum 'De Trappenberg' v. Kingdom of Morocco, The
Netherlands, District Court of Amsterdam, (1984 and 1986) 94 ILR
355   25, 134, 162, 166, 212
Ter K v. State of the Netherlands, Surinam and Indonesia, The
Netherlands, District Court of The Hague, (1951) 18 ILR 223   31
The Garbi, Holland, District Court of Middelburg, (1938) 11 AD 155   35, 299
USA (United States of America) v. Eemshaven Port Authority, The
Netherlands, Supreme Court, (1999) 127 ILR 225   214
USA (United States of America) v. FEWH, The Netherlands, District Court
of The Hague, 2002, 35 *NYIL* (2004) 447   175, 184
USA (United States of America) v. Havenschap Delfzijl/Eemshaven (Delfzijl/
Eemshaven Port Authority), The Netherlands, Court of Appeal of
Arnhem, 2003, noted by L. A. N. M. Barnhoorn, 36 *NYIL* (2005) 436   214

USSR (Union of Soviet Socialist Republics) v. ICC Handel Maatschappij, The Netherlands, Court of Appeal of Amsterdam, (1981 and 1987) 87 ILR 103   25, 295

Van der Hulst v. United States, The Netherlands, Supreme Court, (1989) 94 ILR 373   25, 162, 184, 196

Weber v. Union of Soviet Socialist Republics, Holland, Court of Appeal of Amsterdam, (1942) 11 AD 140   31, 46, 445

Zaire (Republic of Zaire) v. Duclaux, The Netherlands, Court of Appeal of The Hague, (1988) 94 ILR 368   25, 35, 134, 196, 346

New Zealand

Air New Zealand Ltd v. Director of Civil Aviation, New Zealand, High Court, Auckland, [2002] 3 NZLR 796   54, 55

Buckingham v. Aircraft Hughes 500D Helicopter, Registration Mark C-GPNN, New Zealand, High Court (in Admiralty), [1982] 2 NZLR 738; 64 ILR 551   18, 21, 28, 30, 47, 63, 106

Controller and Auditor-General v. Davison, New Zealand, Court of Appeal, [1996] 2 NZLR 278; 104 ILR 526   18, 21, 22, 28, 30, 35, 46, 47, 62, 67, 83, 106, 107, 137

Governor of Pitcairn and Associated Islands v. Sutton, New Zealand, Court of Appeal, 1994, [1995] 1 NZLR 426; 104 ILR 508   18, 21, 28, 30, 31, 35, 39, 46, 47, 62, 106, 138, 170, 190, 195, 196, 376, 446

KPMG Peat Marwick v. Davison; Controller and Auditor-General v. Davison; Brannigan v. Davison, New Zealand, Court of Appeal, 16 February 1996, [1996] 2 NZLR 278; 104 ILR 526   31

Li v. Jiang, New Zealand, High Court of Auckland, CIV 2004-404-5843, Judgment of 21 December 2006   434

Marine Steel Ltd v. Government of the Marshall Islands (No. 1), New Zealand, High Court, [1981] 2 NZLR 1; 64 ILR 539   18, 21, 25, 28, 30, 31

Marine Steel Ltd v. Government of the Marshall Islands (No. 2), New Zealand, High Court, (1982) 64 ILR 562   18, 25, 28, 30, 31

Reef Shipping Co Ltd v. The Ship Fua Kavenga, New Zealand, Auckland High Court (in Admiralty), [1987] 1 NZLR 550; 90 ILR 556   18, 21, 25, 28, 30, 47, 54, 55, 77, 104, 106, 339

Sam Fang v. Zemin Jiang, New Zealand, High Court, Auckland Registry, CIV 2004-404-5843, 11 December 2006   429, 434, 456

The Rainbow Warrior Case: R v. Mafart and Prieur, New Zealand, High Court, Auckland Registry, 1985; Rainbow Warrior (New Zealand v. France), United Nations, Secretary-General, 1986; 74 ILR 241   209, 439

lxxii   TABLE OF CASES

Nigeria

Kramer Italo Ltd v. Government of the Kingdom of Belgium; Embassy of
Belgium, Nigeria, Nigeria, Court of Appeal, 1988, (1989) 1 CLRQ 126;
103 ILR 299   13, 25, 28, 87

Norway

Campuzano v. Spanish Government, Norway, Supreme Court, (1938) 11
AD 68   18, 31
Case against South Africa, Norway, Eidsivating Court of Appeal
(*Eidsivating Lagmannsrett*), Case No. 92-00339K (February 1992); Case
against the USA, Norway, Oslo City Court (*Oslo Byrett*), Case No. 92-
01176 A/56 (June 1992); Case against the USA, Norway, Borgarting
Court of Appeal (*Borgarting Lagmannsrett*), Case No. 00-02837 K/04
(January 2001), noted by Fife and Jervell, 70 *Nordic Journal of
International Law* (2001) 547, 550–551   18, 446
Fredrikstad Havnevesen v. A/S Bertelsens Mek Verksted, Norway,
Supreme Court, (1949) 17 ILR 167   11, 18
The Guernica, Norway, Supreme Court (Appellate Division), (1938) 11
AD 139   18, 35, 299
The Hanna I, Norway, Supreme Court, (1948) 15 AD 146   11, 18

Pakistan

Qureshi v. USSR (Union of Soviet Socialist Republics), Pakistan, Supreme
Court, 1981, PLD 1981 SCt 377; 64 ILR 585   18, 21, 28, 30, 35
Secretary of State of the United States of America v. Gammon-Layton,
Pakistan, High Court of West Pakistan, 1970, 23 PLD 1971 Karachi 315;
64 ILR 567   18, 21, 27, 28

The Philippines

Carried Lumber Company v. United States of America (Directorate of
Procurement of the Philippine Air Force Depot (Secondary) Clark Air
Force Base), The Philippines, Court of Appeals, Seventh Division, (1974)
64 ILR 661   18, 63
Harry Lyons Inc. v. United States of America, The Philippines, Supreme
Court, 1958, 104 Phil. 593; 55 Philippines Official Gazette 1364 (1959);
88 ILR 711   18, 25, 46, 63, 134
Johnson v. Major-General Howard M. Turner, Philippines, Supreme
Court, (1954) 21 ILR 103   18

TABLE OF CASES   lxxiii

Larkins v. National Labor Relations Commission, The Philippines,
Supreme Court, Case No. 92432, (1995) 102 ILR 148 note   193, 340
Parreño v. McGranery, The Philippines, Supreme Court, 12 March 1953,
Materials on Jurisdictional Immunities of States and Their Property, 1982,
p. 367   35
Philippine Alien Property Administration v. Castelo, Philippines,
Supreme Court, 1951; Parreño v. McGranery, Philippines, Supreme
Court, 1953; Baer v. Tizon, The Philippines, Supreme Court, 1974,
Materials on Jurisdictional Immunities, 1982, pp. 364, 367, 370   18
Sanders and Moreau v. Veridiano, Rossi and Wyers, The Philippines,
Supreme Court, Case No. L-46930, (1988) 102 ILR 148 note   193
Syquia v. López, The Philippines, Supreme Court, 1949, 47 Philippines
Official Gazette 665 (1951); 18 ILR 228   18, 66
The Holy See v. Starbright Sales Enterprises Inc., The Philippines,
Supreme Court (en banc), (1994) 102 ILR 163   21, 25, 31, 98, 376
USA (United States of America) v. Guinto, Valencia and Others, Case No.
76607; USA (United States of America) v. Ceballos and Bautista, Case
No. 80018; USA (United States of America, Lamachia and Others) v.
Rodrigo and Genove, Case No. 79470, The Philippines, Supreme Court,
(1990) 182 Supreme Court Reports Annotated 644; 102 ILR 132   25, 35,
54, 55, 78, 134, 162, 170, 193
USA (United States of America) v. Ruiz and De Guzman and Co., The
Philippines, Supreme Court (en banc), Case No. L-35645, (1985) 136
Supreme Court Reports Annotated 487; 102 ILR 122   21, 25, 46, 47, 62,
63, 83, 98

Poland

Czechoslovak Republic (Responsibility in Tort) Case, Poland, Supreme
Court, (1926) 3 AD 180   13, 46
French Consulate in Cracow Case, Poland, Supreme Court, (1958) 26
ILR 178   10, 35, 46
German Immunities in Poland Case, Poland, Supreme Court, (1937) 8
AD 239   13, 35, 46
Maria B v. Austrian Cultural Institute in Warsaw, Poland, Supreme Court
(Labour and Social Insurance Chamber), (1987) 82 ILR 1   10, 40, 46, 194, 196
S v. British Treasury, Poland, Supreme Court, (1948) 24 ILR 223   10, 11,
46, 54, 55, 67
Trade Delegation at Warsaw of USSR v. Maurycy Fajans (Commercial and
Industrial Joint Stock Co.), Poland, Supreme Court, First Division
(Plenary Session), (1928) 4 AD 170   10, 13, 46

lxxiv TABLE OF CASES

Portugal

Brazilian Embassy Employee Case, Portugal, Supreme Court, Case No.
706, (1984) 116 ILR 625   10, 18, 25, 28, 35, 54, 55, 87, 137, 173
Ramos v. United States of America, Portugal, High Court of Lisbon, (1994)
116 ILR 634   10, 18, 25, 35, 137, 173, 340
X v. Israel, Portugal, Supreme Court, (2002) 127 ILR 310   18, 28, 35, 87,
162, 167, 173, 192, 195, 196

Singapore

Civil Aeronautics Administration v. Singapore Airlines Ltd, Singapore,
Court of Appeal, [2004] 1 SLR 570; 133 ILR 371   31
Olofsen v. Government of Malaysia, Singapore, High Court, [1966] 2 MLJ
300; (1966) 55 ILR 409   18, 27, 31, 64
The Hai Hsuan, Singapore, High Court, (1950) 17 ILR 170   18

South Africa

Banco de Moçambique v. Inter-Science Research and Development
Services (Pty) Ltd, South Africa, Supreme Court, Transvaal Provincial
Division, 1982, 1982 (3) SA 330; 87 ILR 239   28, 295
Ex parte Sulman, South Africa, Supreme Court, Cape of Good Hope
Provisional Division, [1942] SALR (CPD) 407; 10 AD 247   18
Inter-Science Research and Development Services (Pty) Ltd v. Republica
Popular de Moçambique, South Africa, Supreme Court, Transvaal
Provincial Division, 1979, 1980 (2) SA 111; 64 ILR 689   18, 21, 22, 25,
28, 30, 35, 76, 83, 295
Jose Baldo v. Government of the Republic of Namibia, South Africa,
noted by D. J. Devine, 19 South African Yearbook of International Law
(1993–94) 157   40
Kaffraria Property Co (Pty) Ltd v. Government of the Republic of Zambia,
South Africa, Supreme Court, Eastern Cape Division, 1980 (2) SA 709;
64 ILR 708   18, 22, 25, 28, 30, 35, 40, 77
Kavouklis v. Bulgaris, South Africa, Supreme Court (Natal Provincial
Division), Durban and Coast Local Division, (1943) 12 AD 113   18
KJ International v. MV Oscar Jupiter (Compania de Navigatie
Maritime 'Romline' SA and Others Intervening), South Africa,
Supreme Court, Durban and Coast Local Division, 1997, 1998 (2) SA
130; 131 ILR 529   87, 367
Leibowitz v. Schwartz, South Africa, Supreme Court, Transvaal
Provincial Division, 1973, 1974 (2) SA 661; 64 ILR 672   18, 28, 35, 46

Lendalease Finance Co (Pty) Ltd v. Corporacion de Mercadeo
Agricola, South Africa, Supreme Court, Cape Provincial Division,
1975 (4) SA 397; Appellate Division, 1976 (4) SA 464; 64 ILR 675   18,
28, 35
Parkin v. Government of the Republique Democratique du Congo, South
Africa, Supreme Court, Witwatersrand Local Division, 1970, 1971 (1)
SA 259; 64 ILR 668   18, 28, 35
Prentice, Shaw and Schiess Inc.orporated v. Government of the Republic
of Bolivia, South Africa, Supreme Court, Transvaal Provincial Division,
1978 (3) SA 938; 64 ILR 685   18, 28, 135, 136, 182
South Atlantic Islands Development Corporation Ltd v. Buchan, South
Africa, Supreme Court, Cape Provincial Division, 4 November 1970,
1971 (1) SA 234; 55 ILR 1   35
The Akademik Fyodorov (Government of the Russian Federation v.
Marine Expeditions Inc.), South Africa, Supreme Court, Cape
Provincial Division, 1996, 1996 (4) SA 422; 131 ILR 460   18, 28,
87, 367
The India (De Howorth v. The SS India; Mann, George & Co. (Delagoa) Ltd
v. The SS India), Union of South Africa, Supreme Court (Cape
Provincial Division), [1921] SALR 451; 1 AD 156   9, 10, 18

Spain

Abbott v. Republic of South Africa, Spain, Constitutional Court (Second
Chamber), Decision No. 107/92, (1992) 113 ILR 411   28, 35, 46, 54, 55,
63, 134, 180, 349, 361, 372, 399, 404, 407, 409, 420, 446
Attorney-General v. Federal Republic of Germany, Spain, Supreme Court,
Case No. 2497, (1983) 88 ILR 679   25, 44
Diana A v. Republic of South Africa, Spain, Supreme Court, Case No.
7231, (1986) 86 ILR 512   18, 25, 35, 46, 57, 63, 134, 162, 165, 174, 177,
191, 196, 361, 446
Emilio BM v. Embassy of Equatorial Guinea, Spain, Supreme Court,
Case No. 727, (1986) 86 ILR 508   18, 25, 35, 57, 162, 165, 174, 177, 191,
196, 361, 404
Leon P v. Federal Electric International Inc., Spain, Supreme Court,
Case No. 1365, (1982) 88 ILR 687   18
Pinochet, Spain, National Court (Criminal Division) (Plenary Session),
(1998) 119 ILR 331   436
State Marine Corporation and Currence v. United States of America,
Spain, Provincial Court of Cadiz, (1999) 128 ILR 701   417

Sweden

Backman v. Chinese People's Republic, Sweden, Supreme Court, (1957)
24 ILR 221 13

Erixon v. Bulgarian People's Republic, Sweden, Court of Appeal of Svea,
(1949) 16 AD 141 13

In re Bolin, Sweden, Supreme Court, (1934) 7 AD 186 13, 30, 31, 35, 40,
46, 299

Russian Trade Delegation v. Carlbom (No. 1), Sweden, Supreme Court,
(1944) 12 AD 61 299

Russian Trade Delegation v. Carlbom (No. 2), Sweden, Supreme Court,
(1944) 12 AD 112 13, 299, 445

The Rigmor, Sweden, Supreme Court, (1942) 10 AD 240 13, 18, 46, 299,
445

The Solgry, Sweden, Supreme Court, (1942) 11 AD 153 13, 299

Västerås (Municipality of Västerås) v. Iceland, Sweden, Supreme Court,
(1999) 128 ILR 705 13, 35, 46, 83, 107, 340, 376

Switzerland

A v. B, Switzerland, Tribunal fédéral, (2003) ATF 130 III 136, available at:
www.bger.ch/fr/index.htm 30

Arab Organization for Industrialization, Arab British Helicopter
Company and Arab Republic of Egypt v. Westland Helicopters Ltd,
United Arab Emirates, Kingdom of Saudi Arabia and State of Qatar,
Switzerland, Court of Justice of Geneva, Judgment No. 443, 1987;
affirmed, Federal Supreme Court (First Civil Court), 1988, 80
ILR 622 340

B v. Autorité de Surveillance des Offices de Poursuite pour Dettes
et de Faillite du Canton de Genève, Switzerland, Tribunal fédéral,
1990, 2 *Revue suisse de droit international et de droit européen* (1992)
585 410

Banco de la Nacion Lima v. Banco Cattolica del Veneto, Switzerland,
Federal Tribunal, (1984) BGE 110 Ia 43; 82 ILR 10 72, 286, 401, 446

Banque Bruxelles Lambert (Suisse) SA v. République du Paraguay,
Switzerland, Tribunal fédéral, 20 août 1998, (1998) ATF 124 III 382,
available at: www.bger.ch/fr/index.htm 31, 71, 72

Banque Centrale de la République de Turquie v. Weston Compagnie de
Finance et d'Investissement SA, Switzerland, Federal Tribunal, (1978)
BGE 104 Ia 367; 65 ILR 417 28, 30, 35, 69, 72, 73, 76, 87, 286, 349, 379,
401, 414, 446

TABLE OF CASES   lxxvii

Banque Commerciale Arabe SA Case, Switzerland, Federal Tribunal, (1977) ATF 103 III 1; 65 ILR 412   349, 371

Banque du Gothard v. Chambre des Recours en Matière Pénale du Tribunal d'Appel du Canton du Tessin, Switzerland, Federal Tribunal, (1987) ATF 113 Ib 157; 82 ILR 50   31, 421

Champel Bellevue SA v. State of Geneva, Switzerland, Court of Justice of Geneva, (1984) 102 ILR 180   40, 407

Dreyfus (K. k. Oesterreich. Finanzministerium gegen Dreyfus), Switzerland, Bundesgericht, (1918) BGE 44 I 49   14, 28, 30, 35, 46, 70, 349, 400

Egypt (Arab Republic of Egypt) v. Cinetelevision International Registered Trust, Switzerland, Federal Tribunal, (1979) 65 ILR 425   69, 72, 78, 87, 349, 370, 371, 401, 446

État C v. Dame X, Switzerland, Cour d'Appel du Canton de Berne, 8 *Revue suisse de droit international et de droit européen* (1998) 643   371, 420

État du Koweit v. X.S.A., Switzerland, Tribunal fédéral, 24 janvier 1994, 5 *Revue suisse de droit international et de droit européen* (1995) 593   71, 72

Greece (Kingdom of Greece) v. Julius Bär & Co., Switzerland, Federal Tribunal, (1956) ATF 82 I 75; 23 ILR 195   14, 30, 70, 71, 286, 349, 371, 400

Greek Republic v. Walder, Switzerland, Federal Tribunal, (1930) BGE 56 I 237; 5 AD 121   14, 70, 286, 299, 349, 359, 400, 404

Griessen, Switzerland, Federal Tribunal, (1982) ATF 108 III 107; 82 ILR 5   371, 404, 420

Guinée (République de Guinée) v. M, Switzerland, Tribunal fédéral, 1985, 42 *Annuaire suisse de droit international* (1986) 69   371, 421

Italian Republic, Italian Ministry of Transport and Italian State Railways v. Beta Holding SA, Switzerland, Federal Tribunal, (1966) 65 ILR 394   28, 35, 69, 72, 87, 349, 370, 371, 401, 404

Italian State v. X and Court of Appeal of the Canton of the City of Basle, Switzerland, Federal Tribunal, (1985) BGE 111 Ia 52; 82 ILR 23   35, 69, 72, 83, 87, 349, 376, 446

K v. Socialist Republic of Vietnam, Switzerland, Court of Appeal of the Canton of Berne, (1981) 75 ILR 122   40, 77

Landano v. United States of America, Switzerland, Labour Court (TPH) of Geneva, (1987) 116 ILR 636   25, 28, 35, 69, 72, 137, 143, 167, 173, 175, 196, 349

Libya (Libyan Arab Socialist People's Jamahiriya) v. Actimon SA, Switzerland, Federal Tribunal, (1985) BGE 111 Ia 62; 82 ILR 30   35, 69, 72, 78, 87, 349, 370, 371, 401, 421, 446

lxxviii   TABLE OF CASES

Libya (Socialist Libyan Arab Popular Jamahiriya) v. Libyan American Oil Company (LIAMCO), Switzerland, Federal Supreme Court, First Public Law Department, (1980) BGE 106 Ia 142; 62 ILR 228   28, 35, 54, 69, 72, 73, 286, 340, 349, 401, 402

M v. Arab Republic of Egypt, Switzerland, Federal Tribunal, (1994) ATF 120 II 400; 116 ILR 656   25, 28, 35, 69, 71, 72, 87, 137, 143, 162, 167, 173, 196, 446

Marcos and Associates v. Chambre d'Accusation, Geneva, Switzerland, Federal Tribunal, (1987) ATF 113 Ib 257; 82 ILR 53   436

Marcos and Marcos v. Federal Department of Police, Switzerland, Federal Tribunal, (1989) ATF 115 Ib 496; 102 ILR 198   340, 434, 437

Nicoud v. United States of America, Switzerland, Labour Court of Geneva (TPH), (1994) 116 ILR 650   28, 40, 72, 134, 137, 162, 173, 175, 178, 183, 196

R v. Republic of Iraq, Switzerland, Federal Tribunal, (1994) ATF 120 II 408; 116 ILR 664   25, 69, 71, 72, 87, 137, 143, 162, 167, 173, 195, 196

Republic of Ghana Case, Switzerland, Superior Cantonal Court (Obergericht) of Zurich, (1973) 65 ILR 404   346

République de Y v. Office fédérale de la justice du DFJP, Switzerland, Tribunal fédérale, 25 juin 2001, 12 *Revue suisse de droit international et de droit européen* (2002) 607   70, 71, 73, 80, 87

République X v. A, Switzerland, Tribunal fédéral, 1re cour civile, 17 janvier 2003, 130 *Journal du droit international* (2003) 1125   70, 71, 72, 162, 167, 173, 196

République Y v. X Ltd, Switzerland, Tribunal fédéral, 8 décembre 2000, 11 *Revue suisse de droit international et de droit européen* (2001) 589   70, 73, 80, 87, 349, 371

S v. India, Switzerland, Federal Tribunal, (1984) BGE 110 II 255; 82 ILR 13   28, 46, 69, 72, 73, 87, 137, 162, 167, 173, 186, 196, 446

S v. Socialist Republic of Romania, Switzerland, Federal Tribunal, (1987) ATF 113 Ia 172; 82 ILR 45   35, 69, 72, 73, 83, 87, 137, 299, 300, 349, 401, 446

Société générale de surveillance Holding SA v. République Islamique du Pakistan, Switzerland, Tribunal fédéral, 23 novembre 2000, 11 *Revue suisse de droit international et de droit européen* (2001) 587   70, 71

Sogerfin SA v. State of Yugoslavia, Switzerland, Federal Tribunal, (1938) 10 AD 232   340

Spain (Kingdom of Spain) v. Company X SA, Switzerland, Federal Tribunal, (1986) BGE 112 Ia 148; 82 ILR 38   28, 35, 69, 72, 77, 78, 349, 371, 401, 404, 407, 408, 446

State Immunity (Switzerland) (No. 1) Case, Switzerland, Superior Court
of Zürich (VerwaltungsKommission [Administrative Branch]), (1937) 10
AD 230   14, 71, 400
State Immunity (Switzerland) (No. 2) Case, Switzerland, Superior Court
of Zürich, 1939; affirmed, Federal Tribunal, 1940, 10 AD 235   71, 134,
340, 359, 400, 404
Swissair v. X, Switzerland, Federal Tribunal, (1985) 82 ILR 36   35, 54, 55,
69, 72, 349, 401
Tsakos v. Government of the United States of America, Switzerland,
Labour Tribunal of Geneva, (1972) 75 ILR 78   40, 72, 136, 137,
162, 173
UAR (United Arab Republic) v. Mrs X, Switzerland, Federal Tribunal,
(1960) ATF 86 I 23; 65 ILR 385   28, 30, 69, 72, 73, 77, 153, 286, 349, 371,
374, 379, 401, 404, 421
Universal Oil Trade Inc. v. Islamic Republic of Iran, Switzerland, Federal
Tribunal (Second Civil Chamber), (1981) ATF 107 Ia 171; 65 ILR
436   35, 340
X v. United States of America, Switzerland, Labour Court (TPH) of
Geneva, (1995) 116 ILR 668   25, 28, 40, 72, 134, 137, 162, 167, 173, 178,
183, 196, 446
Z v. Geneva Supervisory Authority for the Enforcement of Debts and
Bankruptcy, Switzerland, Federal Tribunal, (1990) 102 ILR 205   35, 77,
371, 410

Trust Territory of the Pacific Islands

Alig v. Trust Territory of the Pacific Islands, Trust Territory of the Pacific
Islands, High Court, Appellate Division, (1967) 3 Trust Territory
Reports 603; 61 ILR 88   31

United Kingdom

A Company Ltd v. Republic of X, England, High Court, Queen's Bench
Division, 1989, [1990] 2 Lloyd's Rep 520; 87 ILR 412   62, 76, 337, 376,
377, 385, 409
A Limited v. B Bank and Bank of X, England, Court of Appeal, 1996, [1997]
FSR 165; 111 ILR 590   62, 67, 77
ABCI (Formerly Arab Business Consortium International Finance and
Investment Co.) v. Banque Franco-Tunisienne, England, High Court,
Queen's Bench Division (Commercial Court), 2001, [2002] 1 Lloyd's
Rep 511   274

lxxx TABLE OF CASES

ABCI (Formerly Arab Business Consortium International Finance and Investment Co.) v. Banque Franco-Tunisienne, England, Court of Appeal, [2003] 2 Lloyd's Rep 146   274

Addiscombe Garden Estates Ltd v. Crabbe, England, Court of Appeal, 1957, [1958] 1 QB 513   136

Advocate v. Abdelbaset Ali Mohmed Al Megrahi and Al Amin Khalifa Fhimah, Scotland, High Court of Justiciary at Camp Zeist, Case No. 1475/99, 2001, 2001 WL 14966   80

Ahmed v. Government of the Kingdom of Saudi Arabia, England, Court of Appeal, Civil Division, 1995, [1996] 2 All ER 248; [1996] ICR 25; 104 ILR 629   39, 181, 182, 339, 376

AIC Ltd v. Federal Government of Nigeria, England, High Court, Queen's Bench Division, [2003] EWHC 1357 (QB); (2003) 129 ILR 571   18, 25, 67, 346, 356, 357, 358, 369, 416

AIG Capital Partners Inc. v. Republic of Kazakhstan (National Bank of Kazakhstan Intervening), England, High Court, Queen's Bench Division, 2005, [2006] 1 WLR 1420; [2006] 1 All ER 284; 129 ILR 589   18, 25, 39, 356, 415, 416, 454

Al-Adsani v. Government of Kuwait, England, Court of Appeal, (1994) 100 ILR 465   25

Al-Adsani v. Government of Kuwait, England, Court of Appeal, (1996) 107 ILR 536   25, 28, 43, 216, 225, 356, 429

Al-Adsani v. Government of Kuwait, England, High Court, Queen's Bench Division, (1995) 103 ILR 420   25, 28, 216, 225, 429

Alcom Ltd v. Republic of Colombia, England, Court of Appeal, Civil Division, 1983, [1983] 3 WLR 906; [1984] 1 AC 580; 74 ILR 170   409

Alcom Ltd v. Republic of Colombia, England, High Court, Queen's Bench Division, 1983, [1984] 2 Lloyd's Rep 31   409

Alcom Ltd v. Republic of Colombia, England, House of Lords, 1984, [1984] 1 AC 580; 74 ILR 170   18, 21, 25, 28, 30, 35, 39, 40, 43, 47, 62, 83, 278, 356, 369, 370, 374, 404, 407, 408, 409, 410, 419

An International Bank Plc v. Republic of Zambia, England, High Court, Queen's Bench Division (Commercial Court) (1997) 118 ILR 602   25, 39, 46

Anonymous, 3 H 7 (1487), England, Exchequer-Chamber, Jenk. 174–5; 145 ER 115   53

Anton Piller KG v. Manufacturing Processes Ltd, England, Court of Appeal, [1976] Ch 55   385

Arab Monetary Fund v. Hashim (No. 3), England, House of Lords, 1991, [1991] 2 AC 114   232

TABLE OF CASES   lxxxi

Argentina (Republic of Argentina) v. NML Capital Ltd, England, Court of
    Appeal, [2010] EWCA Civ 41; [2010] 3 WLR 874   18, 25, 39, 336, 337,
    346, 356, 357, 358, 376
Aziz v. Aziz (HM the Sultan of Brunei intervening), England, Court of
    Appeal, 2007, [2008] 2 All ER 501; 136 ILR 587   434
Aziz v. Embassy of Republic of Yemen, England, Employment Appeal
    Tribunal, [2004] All ER (D) 347   339
Baccus SRL v. Servicio Nacional del Trigo, England, Court of Appeal,
    1956, [1957] 1 QB 438; 23 ILR 160   9, 232
Banai v. Canadian High Commission, England, Employment Appeal
    Tribunal, (1990) 107 ILR 600   40, 154
Banco Nacional de Cuba v. Cosmos Trading Corporation, England, Court
    of Appeal, 1999, [2000] BCC 910   416
Bank of Credit and Commerce International (Overseas) Ltd (In
    Liquidation) v. Price Waterhouse (A Firm), England, High Court,
    Chancery Division, 1996, [1997] 4 All ER 108; 111 ILR 604   31,
    234, 434
Buck v. Attorney-General, England, Court of Appeal, 1964, [1965] Ch 745;
    42 ILR 11   46
Bunce v. Postworth Ltd t/a Skyblue, England, Court of Appeal, [2005]
    IRLR 557   136
Buttes Gas and Oil Company v. Hammer (No. 2); Occidental Petroleum
    Corporation v. Buttes Gas and Oil Company, England, Court of Appeal,
    1974, [1975] QB 557; 57 ILR 33; House of Lords, 1981, [1982] AC 888; 641
    ILR 331   46, 80
C. Czarnikow Ltd v. Centrala Handlu Zagranicznego Rolimpex, England,
    Court of Appeal, 1977, [1978] QB 176; House of Lords, 1978, [1979] AC
    351; 64 ILR 195   233, 295
Camdex International Ltd v. Bank of Zambia (No. 2), England, Court of
    Appeal, [1997] 1 WLR 632   77
Cardinal Financial Investment Corporation v. Central Bank of Yemen,
    England, High Court, 13 April 2000, 2000 WL 699384   77, 415
Central Bank of Yemen v. Cardinal Financial Investments Corporation,
    England, Court of Appeal (Civil Division), 2000, [2001] Lloyd's
    Rep Bank 1   77, 415
Chung Chi Cheung v. The King, England, Judicial Committee of the Privy
    Council, 1938, [1939] AC 160; 9 AD 264   10, 28, 35, 40, 44, 66
Civil Air Transport Inc. v. Central Air Transport Corporation, England,
    Judicial Committee of the Privy Council, 1952, [1953] AC 70;
    19 ILR 85   10

lxxxii   TABLE OF CASES

Compania Mercantil Argentina v. United States Shipping Board, England, Court of Appeal, [1924] All ER 186; [1924] 18 Lloyd's Rep 369; [1924] 131 LT 388; 2 AD 138   9, 11

Coreck Maritime GmbH v. Sevrybokholodflot, Scotland, Court of Session, Outer House, 1993, [1994] SLT 893; 107 ILR 658   18, 233, 243

Cretanor Maritime Co. Ltd v. Irish Marine Management Ltd, England, Court of Appeal, [1978] 1 WLR 966   385

Dacas v. Brook Street Bureau (UK) Ltd, England, Court of Appeal, [2004] IRLR 358; [2004] ICR 1437   136

De Haber v. The Queen of Portugal, England, (1851) 17 QB 171/204   35

Derby & Co. Ltd v. Weldon (Nos. 3 and 4), England, Court of Appeal, [1989] 2 WLR 412; [1990] Ch 65   385

Diepreye Solomon Peter Alamieyeseigha v. The Crown Prosecution Service, England, High Court, Queen's Bench Division (Administrative Court), 2005, No. CO/9133/2005, [2005] EWHC 2704 (Admin)   31

Donegal International Ltd v. Zambia, England, High Court, Queen's Bench Division (Commercial Court), [2007] EWHC 197 (Comm), [2007] 1 Lloyd's Rep 397   25, 337

Duff Development Company Ltd v. Government of Kelantan, England, House of Lords, [1924] AC 797; 2 AD 124   9, 10, 16, 31, 40, 46, 48, 337, 349

Duke of Brunswick v. King of Hanover, England, Court of Chancery, (1848) 6 Beav. 1   46

Egypt (Arab Republic of Egypt) v. Gamal-Eldin, England, Employment Appeal Tribunal, 1995, [1996] 2 All ER 237; [1996] ICR 13; 104 ILR 673   28, 40, 149, 181, 182, 196, 339, 376

Empresa Exportadora de Azucar (Cubazucar) v. Industria Azucarera Nacional S. A. (IANSA), England, Court of Appeal, (1982) 64 ILR 368   295

ETI Euro Telecom International NV v. Republic of Bolivia, Empresa Nacionale de Telecomunicaciones Entel SA, England, High Court, Queen's Bench Division (Commercial Court), [2008] EWHC 1689 (Comm), 2008 WL 2697081   25, 358

ETI Euro Telecom International NV v. Republic of Bolivia, England, Court of Appeal, 2008, [2008] EWCA Civ 880, [2009] 1 WLR 665   25, 39, 356, 358, 375, 376

Ferguson v. John Dawson & Partners (Contractors) Ltd, England, Court of Appeal, [1976] 1 WLR 1213   136

Forth Tugs Ltd v. Wilmington Trust Co, Scotland, Court of Session, Inner House (First Division), 1985, 1985 SC 317; 1987 SLT 153; 107 ILR 641   18, 21, 25, 30, 39, 43, 46, 47, 356, 376

TABLE OF CASES   lxxxiii

Gerber Products Co. v. Gerber Foods International Ltd, England, High Court (Chancery Division), [2002] EWHC 428, [2002] ETMR 77   77

Ghosh v. D'Rozario, England, Court of Appeal, 1962, [1963] 1 QB 106; 33 ILR 361   54, 55

Grovit v. De Nederlandsche Bank NV, England, Court of Appeal, 2007, [2007] EWCA Civ 953, [2008] 1 WLR 51   433

Grovit v. De Nederlandsche Bank NV, England, High Court, Queen's Bench Division, 2005, [2005] EWHC 2944 (QB), [2006] 1 WLR 3323   433

Haile Selassie v. Cable and Wireless Ltd (No. 1), England, Court of Appeal, [1938] Ch 839; 9 AD 171   9, 46, 66

Haiti (Republic of Haiti) v. Duvalier, England, Court of Appeal, 1988, [1990] QB 202; 107 ILR 490   316, 434

Harb v. His Majesty King Fahd bin Abdul Aziz, England, Court of Appeal, [2005] EWCA Civ 632, [2005] Fam Law 778; 136 ILR 574   434

Hicks v. United States of America, England, Employment Appeal Tribunal, (1995) 120 ILR 606   25, 106, 138, 193

Hispano Americana Mercantil SA v. Central Bank of Nigeria, England, Court of Appeal, Civil Division, [1979] 2 Lloyd's Rep 277; 64 ILR 221   18, 77, 349, 385, 414

Holland v. Lampen-Wolfe, England, House of Lords, [2000] 1 WLR 1573; 119 ILR 367   17, 29, 35, 40, 46, 47, 54, 55, 62, 106, 213, 433, 446

I Congreso del Partido, England, Court of Appeal, Civil Division, 1979, [1981] 1 All ER 1092; [1980] 1 Lloyd's Rep 23; 64 ILR 227   18, 28, 66, 86, 104, 310, 439

I Congreso del Partido, England, High Court, Queen's Bench Division, 1977, [1978] 1 QB 500; 64 ILR 154   18, 28, 46, 62, 86, 104, 439

I Congreso del Partido, England, House of Lords, 1981, [1983] 1 AC 244; 64 ILR 307   17, 18, 21, 25, 28, 30, 35, 39, 40, 46, 47, 54, 55, 62, 67, 79, 86, 104, 105, 137, 233, 240, 439, 446

In re Banco Nacional de Cuba (Banca Carige SpA Cassa di Risparmio Genova e Imperia v. Banco Nacional de Cuba), England, Chancery Division, Companies Court, [2001] 3 All ER 923; [2001] 1 WLR 2039; 124 ILR 550   18, 62, 78, 104, 105, 277, 376, 416

Intpro Properties (UK) Ltd v. Sauvel, England, Court of Appeal, [1983] QB 1019; [1983] 2 WLR 908; 64 ILR 384   406

Intpro Properties (UK) Ltd v. Sauvel, England, High Court, Queen's Bench Division, [1983] QB 1019; [1983] 2 WLR 1; [1983] 1 All ER 658; 64 ILR 363   406

Iraqi Ministry of Defence v. Arcepey Shipping Co. SA, England, High Court, Queen's Bench Division, [1980] 1 All ER 480   385

Jayetilleke v. High Commission of the Bahamas, England, Employment
Appeal Tribunal, (1994) 107 ILR 622 25, 182

JH Rayner (Mincing Lane) Ltd v. Department of Trade and Industry;
Maclaine Watson & Co. Ltd v. Department of Trade and Industry;
Maclaine Watson & Co. Ltd v. International Tin Council, England,
House of Lords, 1989, [1990] 2 AC 418; [1989] 3 WLR 969;
81 ILR 670 376

Johnson v. Unisys Ltd, England, House of Lords, [2003] 1 AC 518; [2001]
ICR 480; [2001] IRLR 279 10

Jones v. Saudi Arabia (Jones v. Ministry of the Interior of the Kingdom
of Saudi Arabia and Another (Secretary of State for Constitutional
Affairs and Another Intervening); Mitchell and Others v. Al-Dali and
Others), England, High Court, Queen's Bench Division, 2003,
Transcript; 2003 WL 22187644; Court of Appeal, 2004, [2005] QB 699;
[2005] 2 WLR 808; House of Lords, 2006, [2007] 1 AC 270; [2006] 2 WLR
1424; 129 ILR 629 25, 28, 29, 35, 46, 54, 216, 344, 427, 429, 433, 440,
454, 456

Juan Ysmael & Co. Inc. v. Government of the Republic of Indonesia,
England, Judicial Committee of the Privy Council, 1954, [1955] AC 72;
21 ILR 95 35, 46

Kahan v. Pakistan Federation, England, Court of Appeal, [1951] 2 KB 1003;
18 ILR 210 9, 46, 337

Ketchum v. Group Public Relations Ltd, England, Court of Appeal, [1997]
1 WLR 4 385

Kingdom of Spain v. Augusto Pinochet Ugarte, England, Bow Street
Magistrates' Court, (1999) 119 ILR 253 436

Koo Golden East Mongolia v. Bank of Nova Scotia, England, Court
of Appeal, 2007, [2007] EWCA Civ 1443, [2008] QB 717 415,
433, 454

Krajina v. Tass Agency (of Moscow), England, Court of Appeal, [1949] 2 All
ER 274; 16 AD 129 9

Kuwait Airways Corporation v. Iraqi Airways Co. ('Perjury Action'),
England, High Court, Queen's Bench Division (Commercial Court),
[2003] EWHC 31 (Comm); [2003] 1 Lloyd's Rep 448; 126 ILR 758 62,
105, 239, 303, 376

Kuwait Airways Corporation v. Iraqi Airways Company (No. 2), England,
House of Lords, 2000, [2001] 1 WLR 429 239

Kuwait Airways Corporation v. Iraqi Airways Company (Nos. 4 and 5),
England, Court of Appeal, 2000, [2001] 3 WLR 1117; [2002] 2
AC 883 303

TABLE OF CASES lxxxv

Kuwait Airways Corporation v. Iraqi Airways Company (Nos. 4 and 5), England, House of Lords, 2002, [2002] 2 AC 883   303

Kuwait Airways Corporation v. Iraqi Airways Company and the Republic of Iraq, England, High Court, Queen's Bench Division, 1992, unreported; Court of Appeal, 1993, [1995] 1 Lloyd's Rep 25; House of Lords, [1995] 1 WLR 1147; 103 ILR 340   18, 21, 28, 35, 39, 47, 62, 86, 104, 105, 231, 236, 237, 238, 239, 240, 241, 277, 301, 302, 339

Kuwait Airways Corporation v. Iraqi Airways Company, England, High Court, Queen's Bench Division (Commercial Court), 1998, [1999] CLC 31; 116 ILR 534   303

Kuwait v. Fevzi, England, Employment Appeal Tribunal, 1999, 1999 WL 1425695   182, 196

Lariviere v. Morgan, England, Court of Appeal in Chancery, (1872) LR 7 Ch 550   10

Littrell v. United States of America (No. 2), England, High Court, Queen's Bench Division, 1992, unpublished; Court of Appeal, 1993, [1994] 4 All ER 203; [1995] 1 WLR 82; 100 ILR 438   21, 25, 105, 213

London Branch of the Nigerian Universities Commission v. Bastians, England, Employment Appeal Tribunal, 1994, [1995] ICR 358; 107 ILR 613   339, 376

Maclaine Watson & Co. Ltd v. Department of Trade and Industry; JH Rayner (Mincing Lane) Ltd v. Department of Trade and Industry, England, Court of Appeal, 1988, [1989] Ch 72; [1988] 3 WLR 1033; 80 ILR 47   30, 31, 54, 55, 76, 376, 377

Malaysian Industrial Development Authority v. Jeyasingham, England, Employment Appeal Tribunal, 1997, [1998] ICR 307   40, 339

Mareva Compania Naviera SA v. International Bulkcarriers SA, England, Court of Appeal, [1975] 2 Lloyd's Rep 509   385

Mariam Aziz v. Aziz & Ors, HM the Sultan of Brunei, England, Court of Appeal (Civil Division), [2007] EWCA Civ 712; [2007] Fam Law 1047   47

Market Investigations v. Minister of Social Security, England, High Court, Queen's Bench Division, [1969] 2 QB 173   136

Massey v. Crown Life Insurance Co., England, Court of Appeal, 1977, [1978] ICR 590   136

Matthews v. Ministry of Defence, UK, House of Lords, [2003] 1 AC 1163   35, 46, 54, 55

Mauritius Tourism Promotion Authority v. Wong Min, England, Employment Appeal Tribunal, 2008, 2008 WL 4963091   40, 376

Megrahi v. Advocate, Scotland, Appeal Court, High Court of Justiciary at Camp Zeist, Case No. 14 and Appeal No. C104/01, 2002, 2002 JC 99   80

lxxxvi TABLE OF CASES

Mellenger v. New Brunswick Development Corporation, England, Court of Appeal, [1971] 1 WLR 604; 52 ILR 322   9, 232

Mighell v. Sultan of Johore, England, Court of Appeal, 1893, [1894] 1 QB 149   9, 30, 434

Military Affairs Office of the Embassy of the State of Kuwait v. Caramba-Coker, England, Employment Appeal Tribunal, 2003, 2003 WL 1610407   182, 200

Mills v. United States of America, England, Employment Appeal Tribunal, (2000) 120 ILR 612; affirmed, Mills v. Embassy of the United States of America, England, Court of Appeal (Civil Division), 9 May 2000, Transcript   25, 39, 181, 196, 338, 376

Ministry of Trade of the Republic of Iraq v. Tsavliris Salvage (International) Ltd (The 'Altair'), England, High Court, Queen's Bench Division (Commercial Court), [2008] EWHC 612 (Comm), [2008] 2 Lloyd's Rep. 90   30, 39, 62, 104, 234, 236, 239, 338

Mitchell v. Al-Dali, England, Court of Appeal (Civil Division), [2005] EWCA Civ 720   358

Montgomery v. Johnson Underwood Ltd, England, Court of Appeal, [2001] ICR 819   136

Morgan v. Lariviére, England, House of Lords, (1875) LR 7 HL 423   10

Nippon Yusen Kaisha v. Karageorgis, England, Court of Appeal, [1975] 1 WLR 1093   385

NML Capital Ltd v. Republic of Argentina, England, High Court, Queen's Bench Division (Commercial Court), [2009] QB 579   25, 337

NML Capital Ltd v. Republic of Argentina, England, Supreme Court, [2011] UKSC 31; [2011] 2 AC 495   337

O'Kelly v. Trusthouse, England, Court of Appeal, [1984] QB 90   136

Orascom Telecom Holding SAE v. Republic of Chad, Citibank NA (Third Party) International Bank for Reconstruction and Development and Another (Intervening), England, High Court, Queen's Bench Division (Commercial Court), [2008] EWHC 1841 (Comm), [2008] 2 Lloyd's Rep 396   25, 28, 76, 369

Owners of SS Victoria v. Owners of SS Quillwark, Scotland, Court of Session, Outer House, 1921, (1922) SLT 68; 11 AD 149   9, 35, 46

Paprocki v. German State (Bonn), England, Court of Appeal, (1995) 104 ILR 684   25, 40, 339, 376

Philipp Brothers v. Sierra Leone and Commission of the European Communities, England, High Court, Queen's Bench Division, 1993, [1994] 1 Lloyd's Rep 111; affirmed, Court of Appeal, [1995] 1 Lloyd's Rep 289; 107 ILR 517   25, 337, 374, 377

TABLE OF CASES lxxxvii

Pinochet No. 3 (Regina v. Bow Street Metropolitan Stipendiary
Magistrate, *ex parte* Pinochet Ugarte (No. 3)), England, House of Lords,
1999, [2000] 1 AC 147; 119 ILR 135   29, 30, 35, 43, 46, 54, 55, 429, 433,
434, 436, 437

Planmount Ltd v. Republic of Zaire, England, High Court, Queen's Bench
Division (Commercial Court), 1980, [1980] 2 Lloyd's Rep 393; [1981] 1
All ER 1110; 64 ILR 268   18, 25, 28, 62, 77

Pocket Kings Ltd v. Safenames Ltd, Commonwealth of Kentucky,
England, High Court of Justice Chancery Division, [2009] EWHC 2529
(Ch)   31

President of India v. Metcalfe Shipping Co. Ltd, England, Court of Appeal,
[1970] 1 QB 289   338

Propend Finance Pty Limited v. Sing, England, High Court, Queen's
Bench Division, 1996; Court of Appeal, 1997, 111 ILR 611   21, 28, 35,
46, 62, 80, 81, 86, 237, 339, 433

R v. Inland Revenue Commissioners, *ex parte* Camacq Corporation,
England, Court of Appeal, 1989, [1990] 1 WLR 191; 103 ILR 327   28, 44

R v. Secretary of State for the Home Department, *ex parte* Amnesty
International / R v. Secretary of State for the Home Department,
ex parte Kingdom of Belgium, England, High Court, Queen's
Bench Division; Divisional Court, Queen's Bench Division, (2000) 119
ILR 261   436

Radwan v. Radwan, England, High Court, Family Division, 1972, [1973]
Fam 24; 55 ILR 579   54

Rahimtoola v. Nizam of Hyderabad, England, House of Lords, 1957, [1958]
AC 379; 24 ILR 175   10, 17, 19, 22, 30, 46, 47, 60, 66, 67, 80, 82, 104

Re Bo Xilai, England, Bow Street Magistrates' Court, (2005) 128
ILR 713   434

Re Mofaz, England, Bow Street Magistrates' Court, (2004) 128
ILR 709   434

Re P (No. 2), England, High Court, Family Division, 1998; Court of Appeal,
Civil Division, 1998, [1998] 1 FLR 1027; 114 ILR 485   376

Re Rafidain Bank, England, High Court, Chancery Division, (1991) 101
ILR 332   238

Ready Mixed Concrete (South East) Ltd v. Minister of Pensions and
National Insurance, England, High Court, Queen's Bench Division,
[1968] 2 QB 497   136

Sabah Shipyard (Pakistan) Ltd v. Islamic Republic of Pakistan, England,
Court of Appeal, [2002] EWCA Civ 1643, [2003] 2 Lloyd's Rep 571   25,
30, 338, 385

lxxxviii TABLE OF CASES

Sarrio SA v. Kuwait Investment Authority, England, Court of Appeal, 1996, [1997] 1 Lloyd's Rep 113   274

Sarrio SA v. Kuwait Investment Authority, England, High Court, Queen's Bench Division (Commercial Court), 1995, [1996] 1 Lloyd's Rep 650   274

Saudi Arabia (Government of the Kingdom of Saudi Arabia) v. Ahmed, England, Employment Appeal Tribunal, 1993, Transcript; affirmed, Ahmed v. Government of the Kingdom of Saudi Arabia, England, Court of Appeal, Civil Division, 1995, [1996] 2 All ER 248; [1996] ICR 25; 104 ILR 629   39, 134, 182, 196, 339

Saudi Arabia v. Nasser, England, Employment Appeal Tribunal and affirmed by Court of Appeal, (2000) Transcript at LexisNexis   162, 182, 196

Sayce v. Ameer Ruler Sadig Mohammad Abbasi Bahawalpur State, England, Court of Appeal, [1952] 2 QB 390; 19 ILR 212   16, 434

Sengupta v. Republic of India, England, Employment Appeal Tribunal, 1982, [1983] ICR 221; 64 ILR 352   21, 28, 35, 40, 138, 148, 155, 162, 181, 196, 446

Short v. J & W Henderson Ltd, UK, House of Lords, [1946] SC (HL) 24; [1946] SLT 230   136

Spain (Government of the Republic of Spain) v. National Bank of Scotland, Scotland, Court of Session, Inner House, Second Division, 1939 SC 413   30, 80, 299

Stephenson v. Delphi Diesel Systems Ltd, England, Employment Appeal Tribunal, 2002, [2003] ICR 471   136

Strousberg v. Republic of Costa Rica, England, Court of Appeal, (1881) 44 LT 199   10

Sultan of Johore v. Abubakar Tunku Aris Bendahar, England, Judicial Committee of the Privy Council, [1952] AC 318; 19 ILR 182   9, 10, 16, 17, 35, 46

Svenska Petroleum Exploration AB v. Government of the Republic of Lithuania (No. 2), England, Court of Appeal, 2006, [2006] EWCA Civ 1529, [2007] QB 886   25, 30, 39, 62, 104, 336, 337, 338, 356, 358, 454

Svenska Petroleum Exploration AB v. Government of the Republic of Lithuania (No. 2), England, Queen's Bench Division (Commercial Court), 2005, [2005] EWHC 2437 (Comm), [2006] 1 Lloyd's Rep. 181   25, 39, 336, 337, 338, 358

Swiss Israel Trade Bank v. Government of Salta and Banco Provincial de Salta, England, High Court, Queen's Bench Division, [1972] 1 Lloyd's Rep. 497; 55 ILR 411   9

TABLE OF CASES   lxxxix

Taff Vale Railway Company v. Amalgamated Society of Railway Servants, England, House of Lords, [1901] AC 426   243

Tatchell v. Mugabe, England, Bow Street Magistrates' Court, (2004) 136 ILR 572   434

Thai-Europe Tapioca Service Ltd v. Government of Pakistan, Ministry of Food and Agriculture Directorate of Agricultural Supplies (Import and Shipping Wing) (The Harmattan), England, Court of Appeal, Civil Division, [1975] 1 WLR 1485; 64 ILR 81   18, 28, 30, 66, 338

The Arantzazu Mendi, England, High Court (Probate Division), [1938] P 233; Court of Appeal, 1938, [1939] P 37; House of Lords, [1939] AC 256; 9 AD 60   16, 35, 46, 48, 299

The Arraiz, England, High Court (Admiralty Division), (1938) 61 Ll L Rep 39; 9 AD 273   31, 299

The Broadmayne, England, Court of Appeal, [1916] P 64   9

The Charkieh, England, High Court of Admiralty, PDAD, (1873) LR 4 A & E 59   10, 11, 17, 19, 46, 66

The Condado (No. 2), Scotland, Court of Session (Outer House), (1939) 63 Ll L Rep 83; Court of Session (Inner House), (1939) 63 Ll L Rep 330; 9 AD 225   31, 80, 299

The Cristina (Compania Naviera Vascongado v. Steamship 'Cristina'), England, House of Lords, [1938] AC 485; 9 AD 250   9, 10, 11, 17, 21, 22, 28, 31, 35, 46, 54, 55, 66, 299, 439

The El Condado (No. 1), Scotland, Greenock Sheriff Court, (1937) 59 Ll L Rep 119; 9 AD 277   80, 299

The El Condado, Scotland, Court of Session, (1939) 63 Lloyd's Rep 330   30

The El Neptuno, England, High Court (Admiralty Division), (1938) 62 Ll L Rep 7; 9 AD 279   46, 299

The Eschersheim (The Eschersheim, The Jade, Erkowit (Owners) v. Jade (Owners); Erkowit (Owners of Cargo Lately Laden on Board) v. Eschersheim (Owners)), England, House of Lords, [1976] 1 WLR 430; 72 ILR 1   18

The Gagara, England, Court of Appeal, [1919] P 95   9, 11

The Jassy, England, Probate Divorce and Admiralty Division, [1906] P 270   9, 11

The Jupiter, England, Court of Appeal, [1924] P 236   9, 11

The Jupiter (No. 3), England, Admiralty, [1927] P 122   299

The Kabalo, England, High Court (Admiralty Division), (1940) 67 Ll L Rep 572; 9 AD 281   299

The Parlement Belge, England, Court of Appeal, (1880) 5 PD 197   9, 17, 28, 35, 46, 48, 66

The Parlement Belge, England, Probate Divorce and Admiralty Division, (1879) 4 PD 129   9, 17

The Philippine Admiral (Philippine Admiral (Owners) v. Wallem Shipping (Hong Kong) Ltd), England, Judicial Committee of the Privy Council, 1975, [1977] AC 373; 64 ILR 90   9, 10, 11, 12, 18, 21, 28, 30, 35, 278

The Porto Alexandre, England, Court of Appeal, 1919, [1920] P 30   9, 11, 21, 46

The Prins Frederik, England, (1820) 2 Dods. 451   17

The Rita Garcia, England, High Court (Admiralty Division), (1937) 59 Ll L Rep 140; 9 AD 272   31, 299

The Tervaete, England, Court of Appeal, [1922] P 259; 1 AD 148   9, 46

Third Chandris Shipping Corporation v. Unimarine SA, England, Court of Appeal, [1979] QB 645   385

Trendtex Trading Corporation v. Central Bank of Nigeria, England, Court of Appeal, Civil Division, [1977] QB 529; 64 ILR 111   18, 21, 25, 28, 30, 35, 46, 47, 67, 77, 104, 233, 278, 349, 374, 376, 385, 414

Trendtex Trading Corporation v. Central Bank of Nigeria, England, High Court, Queen's Bench Division, [1976] 1 WLR 868; 64 ILR 111   18, 414

UAE (United Arab Emirates) v. Abdelghafar, England, Court of Appeal and Employment Appeal Tribunal, (1995) 107 ILR 626   25, 40, 138, 162, 181, 182, 196, 376

UAE (United Arab Emirates) v. Abdelghafar, England, Employment Appeal Tribunal, 1994, [1995] ICR 65; 104 ILR 647   35, 40

Uganda Co (Holdings) Ltd v. Government of Uganda, England, High Court, Queen's Bench Division (Commercial Court), 1978, [1979] 1 Lloyd's Rep 481; 64 ILR 209   18, 25

USA (United States of America and Republic of France) v. Dollfus Mieg et Cie SA and Bank of England, England, House of Lords, [1952] AC 582; 19 ILR 163   9, 17, 30, 35, 46, 47, 57, 66

USSR (Union of Soviet Socialist Republics) v. Belaiew, England, High Court, King's Bench Division, (1925) 42 TLR 21; 3 AD 172   10, 335

Westland Helicopters Ltd v. Arab Organization for Industrialization, England, High Court, Queen's Bench Division, 1994, [1995] QB 282; 108 ILR 564   46

Westminster City Council v. Government of the Islamic Republic of Iran, England, High Court, Chancery Division, [1986] 1 WLR 979; [1986] 3 All ER 284; 108 ILR 557   339, 406

Wilhelm Finance Inc. v. Ente Administrador del Astillero Rio Santiago, England, High Court, Queen's Bench Division (Commercial Court), [2009] EWHC 1074 (Comm), [2009] 1 CLC 867   236

Yemen (Republic of Yemen) v. Aziz, England, Court of Appeal, [2005] ICR 1391   40, 339

Yendall v. Commonwealth of Australia, England, Employment Appeal Tribunal, (1984) 107 ILR 590   25, 134, 162, 184, 196, 339

United States

767 Third Avenue Associates v. Consulate General of Socialist Federal Republic of Yugoslavia, US, Court of Appeals, 218 F.3d 152 (2nd Cir. 2000)   10

767 Third Avenue Associates v. Permanent Mission of the Republic of Zaire to the United Nations, US, Court of Appeals, 988 F.2d 295 (2nd Cir. 1993); 99 ILR 194   77

767 Third Avenue Associates v. Permanent Mission of the Republic of Zaire to the United Nations, US, District Court, 787 F.Supp. 389 (S.D. N.Y. 1992)   77

Abbott v. A-Best Prods Co., 122 F.Supp.2d 688 (N.D.W.V. 2000)   245

Abiola v. Abubakar, US, District Court, 267 F.Supp.2d 907 (N.D.Ill. 2003)   16, 46, 434, 435

Aboujdid v. Singapore Airlines, Ltd and Gulf Aviation Ltd, US, Supreme Court of New York, 18 Avi.Cas. (CCH) No. 18,059, No. 18,060 (N.Y.Sup.Ct. June 11, 1984); reversed in part on other grounds, Aboujdid v. Singapore Airlines, Ltd and Gulf Aviation Ltd, US, Court of Appeals of New York, 67 N.Y.2d 450, 503 N.Y.S.2d 555, 494 N.E.2d 1055 (N.Y.Ct.App. 1986)   260

Abrams v. Société Nationale des Chemins de Fer Français, US, Court of Appeals, 332 F.3d 173 (2nd Cir. 2003)   127, 223, 227, 245

Abrams v. Société Nationale des Chemins de Fer Français, US, Court of Appeals, 389 F.3d 61 (2nd Cir. 2004)   25, 244, 245

Abrams v. Société Nationale des Chemins de Fer Français, US, District Court, 175 F.Supp.2d 423 (E.D.N.Y. 2001)   127, 223, 227, 244, 245, 324, 325

Abur v. Republic of Sudan, US, District Court, 437 F.Supp.2d 166 (D.D.C. 2006)   223, 227, 324

Acosta v. Islamic Republic of Iran, US, District Court, 574 F.Supp.2d 15 (D. D.C. 2008)   225, 227

Acree v. Republic of Iraq, US, Court of Appeals, 370 F.3d 41 (D.C.Cir. 2004)   225, 226, 227

xcii TABLE OF CASES

Acree v. Republic of Iraq, US, District Court, 271 F.Supp.2d 179 (D.D.C. 2003)   225, 226, 227

Acree v. Republic of Iraq, US, District Court, 661 F.Supp.2d 1 (D.D.C. 2009)   225

Adler v. Federal Republic of Nigeria, US, Court of Appeals, 107 F.3d 720 (9th Cir. 1997)   25, 39, 115, 126, 128, 129, 244

Adler v. Federal Republic of Nigeria, US, Court of Appeals, 219 F.3d 869 (9th Cir. 2000)   25, 39, 76, 79, 128, 201

ADM Milling Co. v. Republic of Bolivia, US, District Court, 63 ILR 56 (D. D.C. 1975)   16

Aerotrade, Inc. and Aerotrade International, Inc. v. Republic of Haiti, US, District Court, 376 F.Supp. 1281 (S.D.N.Y. 1974); 63 ILR 41   16

Af-Cap, Inc. v. Chevron Overseas (Congo) Ltd, US, Court of Appeals, 475 F.3d 1080 (9th Cir. 2007)   320, 364, 365, 366, 396

Af-Cap, Inc. v. Republic of Congo (Af-Cap II), US, Court of Appeals, 383 F.3d 361 (5th Cir. 2004)   364, 366, 402, 403

Af-Cap, Inc. v. Republic of Congo, US, Court of Appeals, 462 F.3d 417 (5th Cir. 2006)   43, 324, 325, 364, 389, 403

Af-Cap, Inc. v. Republic of Congo, US, District Court, 326 F.Supp.2d 128 (D.D.C. 2004)   407

AGIP, USA, Inc., US, National Labor Relations Board, 196 NLRB 1144 (1972); 63 ILR 18   137, 162

Agrocomplect, AD v. Republic of Iraq, US, District Court, 524 F.Supp.2d 16 (D.D.C. 2007)   25, 128

Aguasviva v. Iberia Lineas Aereas de Espana, US, District Court, 937 F.Supp. 141 (D.P.R. 1996)   81

Agudas Chasidei Chabad of United States v. Russian Federation, US, Court of Appeals, 528 F.3d 934 (D.C.Cir. 2008)   76

Aguinda v. Texaco, Inc., US, District Court, 175 F.R.D. 50 (S.D.N.Y. 1997)   319, 333

Alberti v. Empresa Nicaraguense de la Carne, US, Court of Appeals, 705 F.2d 250 (7th Cir. 1983); 92 ILR 392   38, 40, 41, 83, 304, 309

Aldy v. Valmet Paper Machinery, US, Court of Appeals, 74 F.3d 72 (5th Cir. 1996)   123, 126, 245

Alejandre v. Republic of Cuba, US, District Court, 42 F.Supp.2d 1317 (S.D. Fla. 1999)   225, 227, 268, 291

Alejandre v. Republic of Cuba, US, District Court, 996 F.Supp. 1239 (S.D. Fla. 1997); 121 ILR 603   225, 227, 291

Alejandre v. Telefonica Larga Distancia de Puerto Rico, Inc., US, Court of Appeals, 183 F.3d 1277 (11th Cir. 1999)   225, 226, 245, 268, 287, 289, 291

TABLE OF CASES xciii

Alfred Dunhill of London, Inc. v. Republic of Cuba, US, Supreme Court, 425 US 682 (1976); 66 ILR 212   16, 20, 62, 95, 301

Alicog v. Kingdom of Saudi Arabia, US, Court of Appeals, 79 F.3d 1145 (5th Cir. 1996) (Table)   435

Alicog v. Kingdom of Saudi Arabia, US, District Court, 860 F.Supp. 379 (S.D.Tex. 1994); 113 ILR 509   204, 435

Alifieris v. American Airlines, Inc., US, District Court, 523 F.Supp. 1189 (E.D.N.Y. 1981)   245, 274

All American Trading Corporation v. Cuartel General Fuerza Aerea Guardia Nacional de Nicaragua, US, District Court, 818 F.Supp. 1552 (S.D.Fla. 1993)   56, 417

Allen v. Gold Country Casino, US, Court of Appeals, 464 F.3d 1044 (9th Cir. 2006)   31

Allen v. Russian Federation, US, District Court, 522 F.Supp.2d 167 (D.D.C. 2007)   25, 127, 272, 304, 305

Allendale Mutual Insurance Co. v. Bull Data Systems, Inc., US, Court of Appeals, 10 F.3d 425 (7th Cir. 1993)   268, 335

Allied Bank International v. Banco Credito Agricola de Cartago, US, Court of Appeals, 757 F.2d 516 (2nd Cir. 1985)   77

Allied Bank International v. Banco Credito Agricola de Cartago, US, District Court, 566 F.Supp. 1440 (S.D.N.Y. 1983)   77

Alperin v. Vatican Bank, US, Court of Appeals, 410 F.3d 532 (9th Cir. 2005)   304

Alpha Therapeutic Corporation v. Nippon Hoso Kyokai, US, Court of Appeals, 199 F.3d 1078 (9th Cir. 1999)   126, 127, 129, 201, 223, 249, 252, 254, 324, 325, 333

Alpha Therapeutic Corporation v. Nippon Hoso Kyokai, US, Court of Appeals, 237 F.3d 1007 (9th Cir. 2001)   254

Altmann v. Republic of Austria, US, Court of Appeals, 317 F.3d 954 (9th Cir. 2002)   43, 78, 304, 305, 306, 307, 310, 311, 312

Altmann v. Republic of Austria, US, District Court, 142 F.Supp.2d 1187 (C.D.Cal. 2001)   43, 78, 273, 304, 305, 307, 311, 312

Aluminum Distributors, Inc. v. Gulf Aluminum Rolling Mill Co., US, District Court, No. 87-C-6477, 1989 WL 64174 (N.D.Ill. 1989)   265, 266, 274

Amerada Hess Shipping Corporation v. Argentine Republic, US, Court of Appeals, 830 F.2d 421 (2nd Cir. 1987); 79 ILR 1   223, 224, 438

America West Airlines, Inc. v. GPA Group, Ltd, US, Court of Appeals, 877 F.2d 793 (9th Cir. 1989); 92 ILR 454   109, 110, 118, 125, 126, 244, 245, 268

xciv TABLE OF CASES

American Bonded Warehouse Corporation v. Compagnie Nationale Air France, US, District Court, 653 F.Supp. 861 (N.D.Ill. 1987) 79, 435

American International Group, Inc. v. Islamic Republic of Iran and Central Insurance of Iran, US, District Court, 493 F.Supp. 522 (D.D.C. 1980); 63 ILR 452 245, 311, 390

American International Group, Inc. v. Islamic Republic of Iran, US, Court of Appeals, 657 F.2d 430 (D.C.Cir. 1981) 17, 227

American Telecom Co., LLC v. Republic of Lebanon, US, Court of Appeals, 501 F.3d 534 (6th Cir. 2007) 25, 43, 78, 127

American Telecom Co., LLC v. Republic of Lebanon, US, District Court, 408 F.Supp.2d 409 (E.D.Mich. 2005) 25, 78, 127

Amkor Corporation v. Bank of Korea, US, District Court, 298 F.Supp. 143 (S.D.N.Y. 1969); 53 ILR 291 16

Amorrortu v. Republic of Peru, US, District Court, 570 F.Supp.2d 916 (S.D. Tex. 2008) 25, 223

Ampac Group, Inc. v. Republic of Honduras, US, District Court, 797 F. Supp. 973 (S.D.Fla. 1992) 78, 127

Anderman v. Federal Republic of Austria, US, District Court, 256 F. Supp.2d 1098 (C.D.Cal. 2003) 83, 88, 108, 304, 311, 312, 320, 324, 333

Anderson v. Islamic Republic of Iran, US, District Court, 90 F.Supp.2d 107 (D.D.C. 2000) 225, 228

Anglo-Iberia Underwriting Management Company v. PT Jamsostek, US, Court of Appeals, 600 F.3d 171 (2nd Cir. 2010) 43, 83

Antares Aircraft, LP v. Federal Republic of Nigeria and Nigerian Airports Authority, US, Court of Appeals, 948 F.2d 90 (2nd Cir. 1991); 107 ILR 225 79, 129, 304, 313

Antares Aircraft, LP v. Federal Republic of Nigeria and Nigerian Airports Authority, US, Court of Appeals, 999 F.2d 33 (2nd Cir. 1993); 107 ILR 225 25, 79, 126, 127, 128, 129, 304, 313

Antares Aircraft, LP v. Federal Republic of Nigeria, US, Supreme Court, 505 US 1215 (1992) 304, 313

Antoine v. Atlas Turner, Inc., US, Court of Appeals, 66 F.3d 105 (6th Cir. 1995) 268, 274

Aquamar SA v. Del Monte Fresh Produce NA, Inc., US, Court of Appeals, 179 F.3d 1279 (11th Cir. 1999) 41, 245, 317, 318, 319, 320, 324

Arango v. Guzman Travel Advisors Corporation, US, Court of Appeals, 621 F.2d 1371 (5th Cir. 1980); 63 ILR 467 41, 110, 111, 231, 244, 245

Arango v. Guzman Travel Advisors, US, Court of Appeals, 761 F.2d 1527 (11th Cir. 1985) 46, 231, 244, 245, 262, 274

TABLE OF CASES XCV

Argentina (Republic of Argentina) v. City of New York, US, New York
Court of Appeals, 25 N.Y.2d 252 (1969); 53 ILR 544   316
Argentina (Republic of Argentina) v. Weltover, Inc., US, Supreme
Court, 504 US 607 (1992); 119 L.Ed.2d 394 (1992); 100 ILR 509   25,
42, 43, 62, 77, 78, 88, 89, 90, 95, 96, 102, 110, 116, 124, 125, 128,
129, 244, 245
Argentine Airlines v. Ross, US, New York Supreme Court, Appellate
Division, Third Department, 408 N.Y.S.2d 831 (1978); 63 ILR 195   137,
176, 322
Argentine Republic v. Amerada Hess Shipping Corporation, US,
Supreme Court, 488 US 428 (1989); 102 L.Ed.2d 818 (1989); 81
ILR 658   25, 38, 40, 42, 43, 203, 223, 224, 314, 319, 341, 438
Arriba Ltd v. Petroleos Mexicanos, US, Court of Appeals, 962 F.2d 528 (5th
Cir. 1992); 103 ILR 490   108, 109, 111, 293, 329
Art Metal-USA, Inc. v. United States, US, Court of Appeals, 753 F.2d 1151
(D.C.Cir. 1985)   201
Aschenbrenner v. Conseil Regional de Haute-Normandie, 851 F.Supp. 580
(S.D.N.Y. 1994)   84
Asemani v. Islamic Republic of Iran, US, District Court, 266 F.Supp.2d 24
(D.D.C. 2003)   227
Asociacion de Reclamantes v. United Mexican States, US, Court of
Appeals, 735 F.2d 1517 (D.C.Cir. 1984); 84 ILR 87   10, 25, 42, 222,
223, 304
Asociacion de Reclamantes v. United Mexican States, US, District Court,
561 F.Supp. 1190 (D.D.C. 1983)   10, 25, 223, 304
Atlantic Tele-Network, Inc. v. Inter-American Development Bank, US,
District Court, 251 F.Supp.2d 126 (D.D.C. 2003)   123, 128, 320, 328, 341
Atwood Turnkey Drilling, Inc. v. Petroleo Brasileiro, SA, US, Court of
Appeals, 875 F.2d 1174 (5th Cir. 1989)   245, 321, 365, 374, 388,
390, 403
Australian Government Aircraft Factories v. Lynne, 743 F.2d 672 (9th Cir.
1984); 98 ILR 22   127
Austria (Republic of Austria) v. Altmann, US, Supreme Court, 541 US 677
(2004)   17, 24, 25, 38, 40, 42, 43, 46, 78, 304, 306, 310
Autotech Technologies LP v. Integral Research & Development
Corporation, US, Court of Appeals, 499 F.3d 737 (7th Cir. 2007)   333
Baglab Ltd v. Johnson Matthey Bankers Ltd, US, District Court, 665
F.Supp. 289 (S.D.N.Y. 1987)   39, 41, 83, 289, 290, 293, 304
Bahsoon v. Pezetel, Ltd, US, District Court, 768 F.Supp. 507 (E.D.N.C.
1991)   38, 109, 123, 242, 245

xcvi TABLE OF CASES

Bailey v. Grand Trunk Lines New England, US, Court of Appeals, 805 F.2d 1097 (2nd Cir. 1986)   160, 245, 274

Bailey v. Grand Trunk Lines New England, US, District Court, 609 F.Supp. 48 (D.C.Vt. 1984)   160

Baker v. Hanvit Bank, US, District Court, No. 02 Civ. 8251, 2003 WL 21729962, 2003 U.S.Dist.Lexis 12837 (S.D.N.Y. 2003)   272

Bakhtiar v. Islamic Republic of Iran, US, District Court, 571 F.Supp.2d 27 (D.D.C. 2008)   225, 226, 227, 228

Balentine v. Union Mortgage Co., US, District Court, 795 F.Supp. 266 (N.D. Ill. 1992)   243, 274

Banco Central de Reserva del Peru v. Riggs National Bank of Washington, DC, US, District Court, 919 F.Supp. 13 (D.D.C. 1994)   293, 387, 411, 413

Banco de Seguros del Estado v. Mutual Marine Office, Inc., US, Court of Appeals, 344 F.3d 255 (2nd Cir. 2003)   319, 323, 387, 388, 389, 390

Banco de Seguros del Estado v. Mutual Marine Offices, Inc., US, District Court, 230 F.Supp.2d 362 (S.D.N.Y. 2002)   327, 389

Banco de Seguros del Estado v. Mutual Marine Office, Inc., US, District Court, 230 F.Supp.2d 427 (S.D.N.Y. 2002)   389

Banco Nacional de Cuba v. Chase Manhattan Bank, US, Court of Appeals, 658 F.2d 875 (2nd Cir. 1981)   309, 413

Banco Nacional de Cuba v. Chase Manhattan Bank, US, District Court, 505 F.Supp. 412 (S.D.N.Y. 1980)   413

Banco Nacional de Cuba v. Chemical Bank New York Trust Co., US, Court of Appeals, 782 F.2d 377 (2nd Cir. 1986)   292

Banco Nacional de Cuba v. First National City Bank of New York, US, Court of Appeals, 442 F.2d 530 (2nd Cir. 1971)   302

Banco Nacional de Cuba v. First National City Bank, US, Court of Appeals, 431 F.2d 394 (2nd Cir. 1970); 42 ILR 45   301

Banco Nacional de Cuba v. Sabbatino, US, Supreme Court, 376 US 398 (1964); 35 ILR 2   301, 316

Banco para el Comercio Exterior de Cuba v. First National City Bank, US, Court of Appeals, 658 F.2d 913 (2nd Cir. 1981)   287

Banco para el Comercio Exterior de Cuba v. First National City Bank, US, District Court, 505 F.Supp. 412 (S.D.N.Y. 1980)   287, 289

Bank of China v. NBM, US, District Court, 2002 WL 1072235 (S.D.N.Y. 2002)   266, 268, 274

Bank of Credit and Commerce International (Overseas) Ltd v. State Bank of Pakistan, US, District Court, 46 F.Supp.2d 231 (S.D.N.Y. 1999)   245, 330, 413

TABLE OF CASES xcvii

Banque Compafina v. Banco de Guatemala, US, District Court, 583
 F.Supp. 320 (S.D.N.Y. 1984); 92 ILR 399   245, 389, 411, 412, 413
Bao Ge v. Li Peng, US, District Court, 201 F.Supp.2d 14 (D.D.C. 2000)   81,
 126, 129, 434
Barapind v. Reno, US, Court of Appeals, 225 F.3d 1100 (9th Cir. 2000)
 332
Barkanic v. General Administration of Civil Aviation of Peoples Republic
 of China, US, Court of Appeals, 822 F.2d 11 (2nd Cir. 1987); 98 ILR
 44   109, 110, 128, 245, 322
Barnett v. Iberia Air Lines of Spain, US, District Court, 660 F.Supp. 1148
 (N.D.Ill. 1987)   109, 110, 114
Barragan v. Banco BCH, US, Court of Appeals, 188 Cal.App.3d 283; 232
 Cal.Rptr. 758 (1986)   244
Baumel v. Syrian Arab Republic, US, District Court, 550 F.Supp.2d 110 (D.
 D.C. 2008)   248, 274, 435
Baumel v. Syrian Arab Republic, US, District Court, 667 F.Supp.2d 39 (D.
 D.C. 2009)   226
Bayer & Willis Inc. v. Republic of Gambia, US, District Court, 283
 F.Supp.2d 1 (D.D.C. 2003)   245, 287, 289, 293, 396
Beaty v. Republic of Iraq, US, District Court, 480 F.Supp.2d 60 (D.D.C.
 2007)   226
Beecham v. Socialist People's Libyan Arab Jamahiriya, US, Court of
 Appeals, 424 F.3d 1109 (D.C.Cir. 2005)   225
Beecham v. Socialist People's Libyan Arab Jamahiriya, US, District Court,
 245 F.R.D. 1 (D.D.C. 2007)   225
Beer v. Islamic Republic of Iran, US, District Court, 574 F.Supp.2d 1 (D.
 D.C. 2008)   226, 227, 228
Beg v. Islamic Republic of Pakistan, US, Court of Appeals, 353 F.3d 1323
 (11th Cir. 2003)   83, 121, 122, 304, 310
Behring International, Inc. v. Imperial Iranian Air Force, US, District
 Court, 475 F.Supp. 383 (D.N.J. 1979) and 475 F.Supp. 396 (D.N.J. 1979);
 63 ILR 261   245, 323, 389
Belgrade v. Sidex International Furniture Corporation, US, District
 Court, 2 F.Supp.2d 407 (S.D.N.Y. 1998)   46, 273, 274, 329
Belhas v. Ya'alon, US, Court of Appeals, 515 F.3d 1279 (D.C.Cir. 2008)
 429, 435
Belhas v. Ya'alon, US, District Court, 466 F.Supp.2d 127 (D.D.C. 2006)
 435
Belkin v. Islamic Republic of Iran, US, District Court, 667 F.Supp.2d 8 (D.
 D.C. 2009)   227

xcviii TABLE OF CASES

Bennett v. Islamic Republic of Iran, US, District Court, 507 F.Supp.2d 117 (D.D.C. 2007) 227, 228

Bennett v. Islamic Republic of Iran, US, District Court, 604 F.Supp.2d 152 (D.D.C. 2009) 406

Ben-Rafael v. Islamic Republic of Iran, US, District Court, 540 F.Supp.2d 39 (D.D.C. 2008) 225, 227, 228

Berdakin v. Consulado de la Republica de El Salvador, US, District Court, 912 F.Supp. 458 (C.D.Cal. 1995) 77, 88, 244, 328

Bergesen v. Joseph Muller Corporation, US, Court of Appeals, 710 F.2d 928 (2nd Cir. 1983) 327

Bergesen v. Joseph Muller Corporation, US, District Court, 548 F.Supp. 650 (S.D.N.Y. 1982) 327

Berkovitz v. Islamic Republic of Iran, US, Court of Appeals, 735 F.2d 329 (9th Cir. 1984); 81 ILR 552 125, 127, 223, 318

Berkovitz v. United States, US, Supreme Court, 486 US 531 (1988) 204

Bettis v. Islamic Republic of Iran, US, Court of Appeals, 315 F.3d 325 (D.C. Cir. 2003) 227

Big Sky Network Canada, Ltd v. Sichuan Provincial Government, US, Court of Appeals, 533 F.3d 1183 (10th Cir. 2008) 126

Birch Shipping Corporation v. Embassy of the United Republic of Tanzania, US, District Court, 507 F.Supp. 311 (D.D.C. 1980); 63 ILR 524 325, 420

Biton v. Palestinian Interim Self-Government Authority, US, District Court, 412 F.Supp.2d 1 (D.D.C. 2005) 31

Biton v. Palestinian Interim Self-Government Authority, US, District Court, 510 F.Supp.2d 144 (D.D.C. 2007) 31

Blais v. Islamic Republic of Iran, US, District Court, 459 F.Supp.2d 40 (D.D.C. 2006) 225, 227, 228

Blaxland v. Commonwealth Director of Public Prosecutions, US, Court of Appeals, 323 F.3d 1198 (9th Cir. 2003) 201, 224, 324, 332

Board of Regents of the University of Texas System v. Nippon Telephone and Telegraph Corporation, US, Court of Appeals, 478 F.3d 274 (5th Cir. 2007) 254, 274

Bodoff v. Islamic Republic of Iran, US, District Court, 424 F.Supp.2d 74 (D. D.C. 2006) 225, 227

Bodoff v. Islamic Republic of Iran, US, District Court, 567 F.Supp.2d 141 (D.D.C. 2008) 226

Borgships Inc. v. M/V Macarena, US, District Court, 1993 WL 408342 (E.D. La. 1993) 329

Borgships Inc. v. M/V Macarena, US, District Court, 1993 WL 278453 (E.D. La. 1993) 35, 44, 46, 242, 268

Bosco v. US Army Corps of Engineers, Fort Worth District, US, District Court, 611 F.Supp. 449 (D.C.Tex. 1985) 201

Boshnjaku v. Federal Republic of Yugoslavia, US District Court, 2002 WL 1575067 (N.D.Ill. 2002) 341, 435

Bowers v. Transportes Navieros Ecuadorianos (Transnave), US, District Court, 719 F.Supp. 166 (S.D.N.Y. 1989) 77, 245, 247, 274, 390

Boykin v. Bergesen DY A/S, US, District Court, 835 F.Supp. 274 (E.D.Va. 1993) 123

BP Chemicals Ltd v. Jiangsu SOPO Corporation (Group) Ltd, US, Court of Appeals, 285 F.3d 677 (8th Cir. 2002) 38, 112, 245

BP Chemicals Ltd v. Jiangsu SOPO Corporation (Group) Ltd, US, Court of Appeals, 420 F.3d 810 (8th Cir. 2005) 38, 112, 245

BP Chemicals Ltd v. Jiangsu SOPO Corporation, Ltd, US, District Court, 144 F.Supp.2d 1140 (E.D.Mo. 2001) 112

BPA International, Inc. v. Kingdom of Sweden, US, District Court, 281 F.Supp.2d 73 (D.D.C. 2003) 110, 123, 126

Braka v. Bancomer, US, Court of Appeals, 762 F.2d 222 (2nd Cir. 1985) 77, 82

Braka v. Bancomer, US, District Court, 589 F.Supp. 1465 (S.D.N.Y. 1984) 77

Branko International v. Saudi Arabian Airlines, US, Court of Appeals, 880 F.2d 1318 (2nd Cir. 1989) (Table) 245

Branko International, Inc. v. Saudi Arabian Airlines, US, District Court, 704 F.Supp. 386 (S.D.N.Y. 1989) 245

Brenntag International Chemicals, Inc. v. Bank of India, US, Court of Appeals, 175 F.3d 245 (2nd Cir. 1999) 374, 388

Brenntag International Chemicals, Inc.. v. Norddeutsche Landesbank GZ, US, District Court, 9 F.Supp.2d 331 (S.D.N.Y. 1998) 245, 374, 388

Brewer v. Islamic Republic of Iran, US, District Court, 664 F.Supp.2d 43 (D.D.C. 2009) 225, 227

Brewer v. Socialist People's Republic of Iraq, US, Court of Appeals, 890 F.2d 97 (8th Cir. 1989) 166, 304, 306

Bridas S.A.P.I.C. v. Government of Turkmenistan ('Bridas I'), US, Court of Appeals, 345 F.3d 347 (5th Cir. 2003) 292

Bridas S.A.P.I.C. v. Government of Turkmenistan, US, Court of Appeals, 447 F.3d 411 (5th Cir. 2006) 277, 292

Brink's Ltd v. South African Airways, US, Court of Appeals, 93 F.3d 1022 (2nd Cir. 1996) 244, 245

British Rail International, Inc., US, National Labor Relations Board, 163 NLRB 721 (1967); 63 ILR 5 137, 162

c   TABLE OF CASES

Broadbent v. Organization of American States, US, Court of Appeals, 628 F.2d 27 (D.C.Cir. 1980); 63 ILR 337   137, 158

Broadfield Finance, Inc. v. Ministry of Finance of Slovak Republic, US, District Court, 99 F.Supp.2d 403 (S.D.N.Y. 2000)   128, 245

Brown v. Valmet-Appleton, US, Court of Appeals, 77 F.3d 860 (5th Cir. 1996)   38

Bryks v. Canadian Broadcasting Corporation, US, District Court, 906 F.Supp. 204 (S.D.N.Y. 1995)   79, 89, 201, 245, 435

Burke v. Compagnie Nationale Air France, US, District Court, 699 F.Supp. 1016 (D.P.R. 1988)   78, 245, 274

Burnett v. Al Baraka Investment and Development Corporation, US, District Court, 292 F.Supp.2d 9 (D.D.C. 2003)   89, 204, 222, 224, 227

Butters v. Vance International, Inc., US, Court of Appeals, 225 F.3d 462 (4th Cir. 2000)   83, 137, 435

Bybee v. Oper der Standt Bonn, US, District Court, 899 F.Supp. 1217 (S.D. N.Y. 1995)   245

Byrd v. Corporacion Forestal y Industrial de Olancho SA, US, Court of Appeals, 182 F.3d 380 (5th Cir. 1999)   109, 110, 115, 123, 245, 435

C & L Enterprises, Inc.. v. Citizen Band Potawatomi Indian Tribe of Oklahoma, US, Supreme Court, 532 US 411 (2001)   31

Cabiri v. Assasie-Gyimah, US, District Court, 921 F.Supp. 1189 (S.D.N.Y. 1996)   435

Cabiri v. Government of the Republic of Ghana, US, Court of Appeals, 165 F.3d 193 (2nd Cir. 1999)   201, 223, 324, 325, 330, 333, 335, 341

Cabiri v. Government of the Republic of Ghana, US, District Court, 981 F.Supp. 129 (E.D.N.Y. 1997)   223, 325, 333, 335, 341

California Department of Water Resources v. Powerex Corporation, US, Court of Appeals, 533 F.3d 1087 (9th Cir. 2008)   244

California v. NRG Energy Inc., US, Court of Appeals, 391 F.3d 1011 (9th Cir. 2004)   125, 252, 258, 270, 274, 287

Callejo v. Bancomer SA, US, Court of Appeals, 764 F.2d 1101 (5th Cir. 1985); 84 ILR 106   46, 61, 90, 110, 111, 123, 127

Calzadilla v. Banco Latino Internacional, US, Court of Appeals, 413 F.3d 1285 (11th Cir. 2005)   43, 201, 324

Campbell v. Canadian National Railway, US, District Court, 684 F.Supp. 14 (D.Me. 1988)   245, 274

Campuzano v. Islamic Republic of Iran, US, District Court, 281 F.Supp.2d 258 (D.D.C. 2003)   227

Canadian Overseas Ores Ltd v. Compania de Acero del Pacifico SA, US, Court of Appeals, 727 F.2d 274 (2nd Cir. 1984); 101 ILR 470   243, 306, 329, 330

Canadian Overseas Ores Ltd v. Compania de Acero del Pacifico SA, US, District Court, 528 F.Supp. 1337 (S.D.N.Y. 1982)   243, 306, 329, 330

Capital Ventures International v. Republic of Argentina, US, Court of Appeals, 552 F.3d 289 (2nd Cir. 2009)   319, 321

Carey and New England Petroleum Corporation v. National Oil Corporation and the Libyan Arab Republic, US, Court of Appeals, 592 F.2d 673 (1979); 63 ILR 232   83, 200, 310

Carey and New England Petroleum Corporation v. National Oil Corporation and the Libyan Arab Republic, US, District Court, 453 F.Supp. 1097 (S.D.N.Y. 1978); 63 ILR 164   83, 200, 310

Cargill International SA v. M/T Pavel Dybenko, US, Court of Appeals, 991 F.2d 1012 (2nd Cir. 1993); 103 ILR 572   40, 227, 273, 320, 324, 325, 327

Caribbean Trading and Fidelity Corporation v. Nigerian National Petroleum Company, US, District Court, No. 90 Civ. 4169, 1993 WL 541236 (S.D.N.Y. 1993)   78, 89, 123, 127

Caribbean Trading and Fidelity Corporation v. Nigerian National Petroleum Corporation, US, Court of Appeals, 948 F.2d 111 (2nd Cir. 1991)   390

Carl Marks & Co. Inc. v. Union of Soviet Socialist Republics, US, Court of Appeals, 841 F.2d 26 (2nd Cir. 1988)   24, 77

Carl Marks & Co. Inc. v. Union of Soviet Socialist Republics, US, District Court, 665 F.Supp. 323 (S.D.N.Y. 1987); 84 ILR 158   24, 25, 38, 42

Carl Zeiss Stiftung v. VEB Carl Zeiss Jena, US, District Court, 293 F.Supp. 892 (S.D.N.Y. 1968); affirmed, Carl Zeiss Stiftung v. VEB Carl Zeiss Jena, US, Court of Appeals, 433 F.2d 686 (2nd Cir. 1970); 61 ILR 35   301

Carnival Cruise Lines, Inc. v. Oy Wartsila Ab, US, District Court, 159 B.R. 984 (S.D.Fla. 1993)   201, 245

Casalino v. Ente Ferrovie dello Stato, US, District Court, 779 F.Supp. 338 (S.D.N.Y. 1991)   109, 112, 114, 127, 245

Cassirer v. Kingdom of Spain, US, Court of Appeals, 580 F.3d 1048 (9th Cir. 2009)   25, 43, 304, 307

Cassirer v. Kingdom of Spain, US, District Court, 461 F.Supp.2d 1157 (C.D. Cal. 2006)   25, 307

Castillo v. Shipping Corporation of India, US, District Court, 606 F.Supp. 497 (S.D.N.Y. 1985)   110, 245

Castro v. Saudi Arabia, US, District Court, 510 F.Supp. 309 (W.D.Tex. 1980); 63 ILR 419   225, 319, 324

Certain Underwriters at Lloyds London v. Great Socialist People's Libyan Arab Jamahiriya, US, District Court, 677 F.Supp.2d 270 (D.D.C. 2010)   226

cii   TABLE OF CASES

Chalabi v. Hashemite Kingdom of Jordan, US, Court of Appeals, 543 F.3d
725 (D.C.Cir. 2008)   25, 77

Chalabi v. Hashemite Kingdom of Jordan, US, District Court, 503
F.Supp.2d 267 (D.D.C. 2007)   25, 77, 244, 304, 435

Chicago Bridge & Iron Company v. Islamic Republic of Iran, US, District
Court, 506 F.Supp. 981 (N.D.Ill. 1980); 63 ILR 511   223, 245, 388, 389

Chisholm & Co. v. Bank of Jamaica, US, District Court, 643 F.Supp. 1393
(S.D.Fla. 1986); 121 ILR 487   78, 83

Chong Boon Kim v. Kim Yong Shik and David Kim, US, Civil Action No.
12565, 81 ILR 604 (Hawaii Cir.Ct. 1963); 58 *AJIL* (1964) 186   434

Chromalloy (In the Matter of the Arbitration of Certain Controversies
between Chromalloy Aeroservices and Arab Republic of Egypt), US,
District Court, 939 F.Supp. 907 (D.D.C. 1996)   327

Chuidian v. Philippine National Bank, US, Court of Appeals, 912 F.2d
1095 (9th Cir. 1990); 92 ILR 480   16, 42, 201, 245, 274, 304, 310, 318,
434, 435

Chukwu v. Air France, US, District Court, 218 F.Supp.2d 979 (N.D.Ill.
2002)   245

Cicippio v. Islamic Republic of Iran, US, Court of Appeals, 30 F.3d 164 (D.C.
Cir. 1994); 107 ILR 296   25, 82, 84, 85, 223

Cicippio v. Islamic Republic of Iran, US, District Court, 18 F.Supp.2d 62
(D.D.C. 1998)   225, 227

Cicippio-Puleo v. Islamic Republic of Iran, US, Court of Appeals, 353 F.3d
1024 (D.C.Cir. 2004)   225, 227

Cimino v. Raymark Industries, Inc., US, District Court, 751 F.Supp. 649 (E.D.
Tex. 1990)   245, 274

City of Englewood v. Socialist People's Libyan Arab Jamahiriya, US, Court
of Appeals, 773 F.2d 31 (3rd Cir. 1985)   10, 364

City of New Rochelle v. Republic of Ghana, US, Westchester County
Court, 255 N.Y.S.2d 178 (1964); 35 ILR 129   353

City of Sherrill, N.Y. v. Oneida Indian Nation of New York, US, Supreme
Court, 125 S.Ct. 1478 (2005)   31

Clay v. Socialist People's Libyan Arab Jamahiriya, US, District Court, 614
F.Supp.2d 21 (D.D.C. 2009)   226

Close v. American Airlines, Inc., US, District Court, 587 F.Supp. 1062 (S.D.
N.Y. 1984)   127

Coastal Cargo Co., Inc. v. M/V Gustav Sule, US, District Court, 942 F.Supp.
1082 (E.D.La. 1996)   242, 324, 325, 329

Coleman v. Alcolac, Inc., US, District Court, 888 F.Supp. 1388 (S.D.Tex.
1995)   109, 111, 123, 127, 223, 245, 318, 324, 325

College Savings Bank v. Florida Prepaid Postsecondary Education
Expense Board, US, Supreme Court, 527 US 666 (1999)   31
Collett v. Libya (Socialist Peoples' Libyan Arab Jamahiriya), US, District
Court, 362 F.Supp.2d 230 (D.D.C. 2005)   225, 227, 434, 435
Colonial Bank v. Compagnie Générale Maritime et Financière, US,
District Court, 645 F.Supp. 1457 (S.D.N.Y. 1986); 98 ILR 26   110, 126,
245, 319, 324, 328, 334
Commercial Bank of Kuwait v. Rafidain Bank and Central Bank of Iraq,
US, Court of Appeals, 15 F.3d 238 (2nd Cir. 1994); 107 ILR 261   76, 125,
128, 244, 245, 411
Commercial Corporation Sovrybflot v. Corporacion de Fomento de la
Produccion, US, District Court, 980 F.Supp. 710 (S.D.N.Y. 1997)   245,
319, 324, 335
Commonwealth of Virginia *ex rel.* Kilgore v. Bulgartabac Holding Group,
US, District Court, 360 F.Supp.2d 791 (E.D.Va. 2005)   245, 274
Compagnie Noga d'Importation et d'Exportation SA v. Russian
Federation, US, Court of Appeals, 361 F.3d 676 (2nd Cir. 2004)
248, 328
Compania Mexicana de Aviacion, SA v. United States District Court for
the Central District of California, US, Court of Appeals, 859 F.2d 1354
(9th Cir. 1988); 98 ILR 69   109, 110, 115, 127, 244, 245, 322
Concepcion v. VEB Backereimaschenbau Halle, US, District Court, 120
F.R.D. 482 (D.N.J. 1988)   42
Concesionaria DHM, SA v. International Finance Corporation, US,
District Court, 307 F.Supp.2d 553 (S.D.N.Y. 2004)   245
Concord Reinsurance Co. v. Caja Nacional de Ahorro y Seguro, US,
District Court, No. 93 Civ. 6606, 1994 WL 86401 (S.D.N.Y. 1994)
411, 412
Connecticut Bank of Commerce v. Republic of Congo (Af-Cap I), US, Court
of Appeals, 309 F.3d 240 (5th Cir. 2002)   46, 123, 355, 364, 365, 366,
367, 396, 402, 403
Consarc Corporation v. Iraqi Ministry, US, Court of Appeals, 27 F.3d 695
(D.C.Cir. 1994); 106 ILR 408   346
Continental Transfer Technique Ltd v. Federal Government of Nigeria,
US, District Court, 697 F.Supp.2d 46 (D.D.C. 2010)   327
Corporacion Mexicana de Servicios Maritimos, SA de CV v. M/T Respect,
US, Court of Appeals, 89 F.3d 650 (9th Cir. 1996)   251, 252, 253, 258,
268, 324, 325, 335
Corporacion Venezolana de Fomento v. Vintero Sales Corporation, US,
District Court, 477 F.Supp. 615 (S.D.N.Y. 1979); 63 ILR 299   245

civ TABLE OF CASES

Corzo v. Banco Central de Reserva del Peru, US, Court of Appeals, 243 F.3d 519 (9th Cir. 2001)   38, 43, 46, 111, 122, 245, 324, 333, 341

Coyle v. PT Garuda Indonesia, US, Court of Appeals, 363 F.3d 979 (9th Cir. 2004)   112, 244, 245, 322

Coyle v. PT Garuda Indonesia, US, District Court, 180 F.Supp.2d 1160 (D.Or. 2001)   112, 322

Crédit Lyonnais v. Getty Square Associates, US, District Court, 876 F.Supp. 517 (S.D.N.Y. 1995)   243, 265, 266, 268

Creighton Ltd v. Government of State of Qatar, US, Court of Appeals, 181 F.3d 118 (D.C.Cir. 1999)   25, 324, 325, 327

Crimson Semiconductor, Inc. v. Electronum, US, District Court, 629 F.Supp. 903 (S.D.N.Y. 1986)   127, 245, 310

Crist v. Republic of Turkey, US, District Court, 995 F.Supp. 5 (D.D.C. 1998)   307, 309, 311, 312

Croesus EMTR Master Fund LP v. Federal Republic of Brazil, US, District Court, 212 F.Supp.2d 30 (D.D.C. 2002)   111, 126, 128

Cronin v. Islamic Republic of Iran, US, District Court, 238 F.Supp.2d 222 (D.D.C. 2002)   225, 227, 228

Cruise Connections Charter Management 1, LP v. Attorney General of Canada, US, Court of Appeals, 600 F.3d 661 (D.C.Cir. 2010)   127

Cruise Connections Charter Management 1, LP v. Attorney General of Canada, US, District Court, 634 F.Supp.2d 86 (D.D.C. 2009)   127

Crum v. Kingdom of Saudi Arabia, US, District Court, No. Civ.A.05–275, 2005 WL 3752271 (E.D.Va. 2005)   196

Cruz v. United States, US, District Court, 387 F.Supp.2d 1057 (N.D.Cal. 2005)   25, 88, 96

Dale v. Colagiovanni, US, Court of Appeals, 443 F.3d 425 (5th Cir. 2006)   31, 43, 79, 89, 109, 287

Dale v. Colagiovanni, US, District Court, 337 F.Supp.2d 825 (S.D.Miss. 2004)   31, 79, 89, 109, 201

Dalehite v. United States, US, Supreme Court, 346 US 15 (1953)   203

Daliberti v. Republic of Iraq, US, District Court, 97 F.Supp.2d 38 (D.D.C. 2000)   41, 81, 122, 225, 227, 324, 341

Daliberti v. Republic of Iraq, US, District Court, 146 F.Supp.2d 19 (D.D.C. 2001)   227

Daly v. Castro Llanes, US, District Court, 30 F.Supp.2d 407 (S.D.N.Y. 1998)   77, 245, 268, 274

Dames and Moore v. Regan, US, Supreme Court, 453 US 654 (1981); 72 ILR 270   17, 227, 404

Dammarell v. Islamic Republic of Iran, US, District Court, 281 F.Supp.2d 105 (D.D.C. 2003)   227, 248

Dammarell v. Islamic Republic of Iran, US, District Court, 404 F.Supp.2d 261 (D.D.C. 2005)   225, 227, 248

Dar El-Bina Engineering & Contracting Co. v. Republic of Iraq, US, District Court, 79 F.Supp.2d 374 (S.D.N.Y. 2000)   128

Darby v. Compagnie Nationale Air France, US, District Court, 769 F.Supp. 1255 (S.D.N.Y. 1991)   110, 114, 127, 245

Daventree Ltd v. Republic of Azerbaijan, US, District Court, 349 F.Supp.2d 736 (S.D.N.Y. 2004)   25, 78, 110, 127, 304, 305, 306

Dayton v. Czechoslovak Socialist Republic, US, District Court, 672 F.Supp. 7 (D.D.C. 1986); affirmed, Dayton v. Czechoslovak Socialist Republic, US, Court of Appeals, 834 F.2d 203 (D.C.Cir. 1987); 79 ILR 590   293, 312, 329

De Sanchez v. Banco Central de Nicaragua, US, Court of Appeals, 770 F.2d 1385 (5th Cir. 1985); 88 ILR 75   61, 88, 110, 137, 201, 305, 306, 310

De Sanchez v. Banco Central de Nicaragua, US, District Court, 515 F.Supp. 900 (E.D.La. 1981); 63 ILR 584   309, 310, 312

Decor by Nikkei International, Inc. v. Federal Republic of Nigeria, US, District Court, 497 F.Supp. 893 (S.D.N.Y. 1980); 63 ILR 480   125, 245

Delgado v. Shell Oil Company, US, Court of Appeals, 231 F.3d 165 (5th Cir. 2000)   269, 274

Delgado v. Shell Oil Company, US, District Court, 322 F.Supp.2d 798 (S.D. Tex. 2004)   271

Delgado v. Shell Oil Company, US, District Court, 890 F.Supp. 1315 (S.D. Tex. 1994)   269, 274

Delgado v. Shell Oil Company, US, District Court, 890 F.Supp. 1324 (S.D. Tex. 1995)   273

Dewhurst v. Telenor Invest AS, US, District Court, 83 F.Supp.2d 577 (D. Md. 2000)   114, 128, 268, 274, 311, 435

Dexter and Carpenter v. Kunglig Jarnvägsstyrelsen, US, Court of Appeals, 43 F.2d 705 (2nd Cir. 1930); 5 AD 109   353, 356

Diaz-Aguasviva v. Iberia Lineas Aereas de Espana, US, District Court, 902 F.Supp. 314 (D.P.R. 1995)   78, 81, 245

Djordjevich v. Bundesminister der Finanzen, Federal Republic of Germany, US, District Court, 827 F.Supp. 814 (D.D.C. 1993)   24, 127

Doe I v. State of Israel, US, District Court, 400 F.Supp.2d 86 (D.D.C. 2005)   82, 126, 127, 128, 223, 324, 325, 341, 344, 434, 435

Doe I v. Unocal Corporation, US, Court of Appeals, 395 F.3d 932 (9th Cir. 2002)   117, 127

cvi   TABLE OF CASES

Doe v. Bolkiah, US, District Court, 74 F.Supp.2d 969 (D.Hawaii 1998) 274, 435

Doe v. Holy See, US, Court of Appeals, 557 F.3d 1066 (9th Cir. 2009)   25, 31, 204

Doe v. Holy See, US, District Court, 434 F.Supp.2d 925 (D.Or. 2006)   25, 31, 92, 110, 111, 204, 225

Doe v. Karadzic, US, District Court, 866 F.Supp. 734 (S.D.N.Y. 1994)   434

Doe v. Liu Qi, US, District Court, 349 F.Supp.2d 1258 (N.D.Cal. 2004)   341, 429, 434, 435

Doe v. Roman Catholic Diocese of Galveston-Houston, US, District Court, 408 F.Supp.2d 272 (S.D. Tex. 2005)   435

Doe v. Unocal Corporation, US, District Court, 963 F.Supp. 880 (C.D.Cal. 1997)   117, 129

Dole Food Company v. Patrickson, US, Supreme Court, 538 US 468 (2003)   46, 252, 261, 269, 270, 271, 273, 274, 287, 290, 293

Dominican Energy Ltd, Inc. v. Dominican Republic, US, District Court, 903 F.Supp. 1507 (M.C.Fla. 1995)   78, 94, 124, 126, 128

Doty v. Magnum Research, Inc., US, District Court, 994 F.Supp. 894 (N.D. Ohio 1997)   245, 274

Drexel Burnham Lambert Group Inc. v. Committee of Receivers for AW Galadari, US, Court of Appeals, 12 F.3d 317 (2nd Cir. 1993)   40, 122, 245, 324, 329, 333

Drexel Burnham Lambert Group Inc. v. Committee of Receivers for AW Galadari, US, District Court, 810 F.Supp. 1375 (S.D.N.Y. 1993); 103 ILR 532   41, 122, 329

Driscoll v. United States, US, Court of Appeals, 525 F.2d 136 (9th Cir. 1975)   206

Dumont v. Saskatchewan Government Insurance (SGI), US, Court of Appeals, 258 F.3d 880 (8th Cir. 2001)   124, 127

Eaglet Corporation Ltd v. Banco Central de Nicaragua, US, Court of Appeals, 23 F.3d 641 (2nd Cir. 1994)   320

Eaglet Corporation Ltd v. Banco Central de Nicaragua, US, District Court, 839 F.Supp. 232 (S.D.N.Y. 1993)   245, 319, 320, 324, 328

EAL (Delaware) Corporation, Electra Aviation Inc. *et al*. v. European Organization for the Safety of Air Navigation and English Civil Aviation Authority, US, District Court, 1994 U.S.Dist.Lexis 20528 (D. Del. 1994); 107 ILR 318 (D.Del. 1994)   82, 232

Ebrahim v. Shell Oil Co., US, District Court, 847 F.Supp. 65 (S.D.Tex. 1994)   254

Eckert International, Inc. v. Government of the Sovereign Democratic Republic of Fiji, US, Court of Appeals, 32 F.3d 77 (4th Cir. 1994); 107 ILR 347   25, 324, 328

Eckert International, Inc. v. Government of the Sovereign Democratic Republic of Fiji, US, District Court, 834 F.Supp. 167 (E.D.Va. 1993)   76, 328

Ecuador (Republic of Ecuador) v. ChevronTexaco Corporation, US, District Court, 376 F.Supp.2d 334 (S.D.N.Y. 2005)   25, 274

Edlow International Co. v. Nuklearna Elektrarna Krsko, US, District Court, 441 F.Supp. 827 (D.D.C. 1977); 63 ILR 100   258

EIE Guam Corporation v. Long Term Credit Bank of Japan, Ltd, US, Court of Appeals, 322 F.3d 635 (9th Cir. 2003)   43, 244, 251, 256, 258, 274

Eisenfeld v. Islamic Republic of Iran, US, District Court, 172 F.Supp.2d 1 (D.D.C. 2000)   225, 227, 228

Elahi v. Islamic Republic of Iran, US, District Court, 124 F.Supp.2d 97 (D. D.C. 2000)   225, 227, 228, 248

Elbasir v. Kingdom of Saudi Arabia, US, District Court, 468 F.Supp.2d 155 (D.D.C. 2007)   41, 82

El-Fadl v. Central Bank of Jordan, US, Court of Appeals, 75 F.3d 668 (D.C. Cir. 1996)   435

El-Hadad v. Embassy of the United Arab Emirates, US, District Court, 69 F.Supp.2d 69 (D.D.C. 1999)   41, 158, 201

El-Hadad v. Embassy of the United Arab Emirates, US, District Court, No. 96-1943, 2006 WL 826098 (D.D.C. 2006)   90, 159, 168, 201

El-Hadad v. Embassy of UAE, US, District Court, No. 96-1943 (D.D.C. July 16, 2001)   158

El-Hadad v. United Arab Emirates, US, Court of Appeals, 216 F.3d 29 (D.C. Cir. 2000)   90, 158, 159, 160, 201

El-Hadad v. United Arab Emirates, US, Court of Appeals, 496 F.3d 658 (D. C.Cir. 2007)   89, 110, 159, 168, 201

Elixir Shipping SA v. Perusahaan Pertambangan Minyak Dan Gas Bumi Negara, US, District Court, 267 F.Supp.2d 659 (S.D.Tex. 2003)   109, 127, 245, 324, 325, 334

Elliott v. British Tourist Authority, US, Court of Appeals, 172 F.3d 37 (2nd Cir. 1999) (Table)   110, 158, 169

Elliott v. British Tourist Authority, US, District Court, 986 F.Supp. 189 (S.D.N.Y. 1997)   90, 110, 158, 169, 245

EM Ltd v. Republic of Argentina, US, Court of Appeals, 382 F.3d 291 (2nd Cir. 2004)   414

EM Ltd v. Republic of Argentina, US, Court of Appeals, 473 F.3d 463 (2nd Cir. 2007)   83, 97, 287, 319, 396, 412, 413, 414

EM Ltd v. Republic of Argentina, US, District Court, No. 03 Civ. 2507 (TPG), 2003 WL 22120745 (S.D.N.Y. 2003)   414

cviii   TABLE OF CASES

EM Ltd v. Republic of Argentina, US, District Court, No. 03 Civ. 2507 (TPG), 2003 WL 22454934 (S.D.N.Y. 2003)   414

Embassy of the Arab Republic of Egypt v. Lasheen, US, Court of Appeals, 603 F.3d 1166 (9th Cir. 2010)   25, 79

Employers Insurance of Wausau v. Banco de Seguros del Estado, US, Court of Appeals, 199 F.3d 937 (7th Cir. 1999)   327

Employers Insurance of Wausau v. Banco de Seguros del Estado, US, District Court, 34 F.Supp.2d 1115 (E.D.Wis. 1999)   327

Empresa Cubana del Tabaco v. Culbro Corporation, US, District Court, 123 F.Supp.2d 203 (S.D.N.Y. 2000)   245

Enahoro v. Abubakar, US, Court of Appeals, 408 F.3d 877 (7th Cir. 2005)   435

English v. Thorne, US, District Court, 676 F.Supp. 761 (S.D.Miss. 1987)   42, 204, 223

Enron Equipment Procurement Company v. M/V Titan 2, US, District Court, 82 F.Supp.2d 602 (W.D.La. 1999)   76, 245, 319, 324, 325, 387

Enron Oil Trading & Transportation Co. v. Walbrook Insurance Co., US, Court of Appeals, 132 F.3d 526 (9th Cir. 1997)   252

EOTT Energy Operating Limited Partnership v. Winterthur Swiss Insurance Company, US, Court of Appeals, 257 F.3d 992 (9th Cir. 2001)   244, 252, 257, 268, 274

Ervin v. Quintanilla, US, Court of Appeals, 99 F. 935 (5th Cir. 1938); 9 AD 219   299

Estate of Bayani v. Islamic Republic of Iran, US, District Court, 530 F.Supp.2d 40 (D.D.C. 2007)   225, 227, 228

Estate of Botvin v. Islamic Republic of Iran, US, District Court, 684 F.Supp.2d 34 (D.D.C. 2010)   227

Estate of Heiser v. Islamic Republic of Iran, US, District Court, 466 F.Supp.2d 229 (D.D.C. 2006)   225, 227, 228

Estate of Heiser v. Islamic Republic of Iran, US, District Court, 605 F.Supp.2d 248 (D.D.C. 2009)   225, 227

Estate of Heiser v. Islamic Republic of Iran, US, District Court, 659 F.Supp.2d 20 (D.D.C. 2009)   225, 227

Estates of Yaron Ungar & Efrat Ungar v. Palestinian Authority, US, District Court, 153 F.Supp.2d 76 (D.R.I. 2001)   227

E-Systems, Inc. v. Islamic Republic of Iran, US, District Court, 491 F.Supp. 1294 (N.D.Tex. 1980); 63 ILR 424   323

Evans v. Pemex, US, District Court, 390 F.Supp.2d 587 (S.D.Tex. 2005)   108

Ex parte Peru (Ex parte Republic of Peru (The Ucayali)), US, Supreme Court, 318 US 578 (1943); 10 AD 199   16, 46

Exchange National Bank of Chicago v. Empresa Minera del Centro del Peru SA, US, District Court, 595 F.Supp. 502 (S.D.N.Y. 1984)   245

Export Group v. Reef Industries Inc. and Mexican Coffee Institute, US, Court of Appeals, 54 F.3d 1466 (9th Cir. 1995); 107 ILR 393   201

Fabe v. Aneco Reinsurance Underwriting Ltd, US, District Court, 784 F.Supp. 448 (S.D.Ohio 1991)   244, 274

Fagan v. Deutsche Bundesbank, US, District Court, 438 F.Supp.2d 376 (S.D.N.Y. 2006)   201

Fagot Rodriguez v. Republic of Costa Rica, US, Court of Appeals, 297 F.3d 1 (1st Cir. 2002)   10, 77, 204

Fagot Rodriguez v. Republic of Costa Rica, US, District Court, 139 F.Supp.2d 173 (D.P.R. 2001)   10, 77, 204

Fagot Rodriguez v. Republic of Costa Rica, US, District Court, 934 F.Supp. 493 (D.P.R. 1996)   10, 83, 304, 311

Falcoal, Inc. v. Turkiye Komur Isletmeleri Kurumu, US, District Court, 660 F.Supp. 1536 (S.D.Tex. 1987)   113, 114, 127, 329

Falcon Investments, Inc. v. Republic of Venezuela, US, District Court, 2001 WL 584346 (D.Kan. 2001)   77, 126, 128, 129

Fargo Weite Reisen GmbH v. Jamaica Vacations Ltd, Inc., US, District Court, 790 F.Supp. 272 (S.D.Fla. 1992)   113, 329

Federal Insurance Co. v. Richard I Rubin & Co., Inc., US, Court of Appeals, 12 F.3d 1270 (3rd Cir. 1993)   38, 109, 115

Ferrostaal Metals Corporation v. SS Lash Pacifico, US, District Court, 652 F.Supp. 420 (S.D.N.Y. 1987)   244, 245, 318, 321

FG Hemisphere Associates v. Democratic Republic of Congo, US, Court of Appeals, 447 F.3d 835 (D.C.Cir. 2006)   41

FG Hemisphere Associates, LLC v. Democratic Republic of Congo, US, District Court, 603 F.Supp.2d 1 (D.D.C. 2009)   389

FG Hemisphere Associates, LLC v. République du Congo, US, Court of Appeals, 455 F.3d 575 (5th Cir. 2006)   43, 402, 403

Fickling v. Commonwealth of Australia, US, District Court, 775 F.Supp. 66 (E.D.N.Y. 1991); 103 ILR 447   10, 25, 83, 123, 127, 223, 245, 312, 320, 324, 325, 333, 341

Fidelity Partners, Inc. v. First Trust Company of New York, US, District Court, 58 F.Supp.2d 52 (S.D.N.Y. 1997)   403

Fidelity Partners, Inc.. v. Philippine Export and Foreign Loan Guarantee Corporation, US, District Court, 921 F.Supp. 1113 (S.D.N.Y. 1996)   245, 403

Filartiga v. Pena-Irala, US, Court of Appeals, 630 F.2d 876 (2nd Cir. 1980); 77 ILR 169   35

TABLE OF CASES

Filetech SA v. France Telecom SA, US, Court of Appeals, 157 F.3d 922 (2nd Cir. 1998) 110, 129

Filetech SA v. France Telecom SA, US, Court of Appeals, 304 F.3d 180 (2nd Cir. 2002) 110, 126, 128

Filetech SA v. France Telecom, SA, US, District Court, 212 F.Supp.2d 183 (S.D.N.Y. 2001) 110, 126, 128

Filetech SARL v. France Telecom, US, District Court, 978 F.Supp. 464 (S.D. N.Y. 1997) 110

Filler v. Hanvit Bank, US, Court of Appeals, 378 F.3d 213 (2nd Cir. 2004) 43, 253, 255, 266, 272

Filler v. Hanvit Bank, US, District Court, 247 F.Supp.2d 425 (S.D.N.Y. 2003) 41, 123, 126, 255, 272

Filler v. Hanvit Bank, US, District Court, No. 01 Civ. 9510, 2003 WL 21729978, 2003 U.S.Dist.Lexis 12836 (S.D.N.Y. 2003) 272

Filus v. Lot Polish Airlines, US, Court of Appeals, 907 F.2d 1328 (2nd Cir. 1990) 109

First American Corporation v. Al-Nahyan, US District Court, 948 F.Supp. 1107 (D.D.C. 1996); 121 ILR 577 435

First City, Texas-Houston, NA v. Rafidain Bank, US, Court of Appeals, 150 F.3d 172 (2nd Cir. 1998) 245, 293, 414

First Fidelity Bank, NA v. Government of Antigua and Barbuda– Permanent Mission, US, Court of Appeals, 877 F.2d 189 (2nd Cir. 1989); 99 ILR 125 25, 308, 318

First Merchants Collection Corporation v. Republic of Argentina, US, District Court, 190 F.Supp.2d 1336 (S.D.Fla. 2002) 82, 83, 88, 89

First National Bank of Mobile v. Kaufman, US, District Court, 593 F.Supp. 1189 (N.D.Ala. 1984) 42

First National City Bank v. Banco Nacional de Cuba, US, Supreme Court, 406 US 759 (1972); 66 ILR 102 46, 302

First National City Bank v. Banco Nacional de Cuba, US, Supreme Court, 400 US 1019 (1971) 302

First National City Bank v. Banco para el Comercio Exterior de Cuba (Bancec), US, Supreme Court, 462 US 611 (1983); 80 ILR 566 226, 245, 277, 287, 288, 289, 293, 319

Fisher v. Great Socialist People's Libyan Arab Jamahiriya, US, District Court, 541 F.Supp.2d 46 (D.D.C. 2008) 225, 227

Flatow v. Alavi Foundation, US, Court of Appeals, 225 F.3d 653 (4th Cir. 2000) (Table) 290

Flatow v. Islamic Republic of Iran, US, Court of Appeals, 305 F.3d 1249 (D.C. Cir. 2002) 228

TABLE OF CASES   cxi

Flatow v. Islamic Republic of Iran, US, Court of Appeals, 308 F.3d 1065 (9th Cir. 2002)   43, 225, 228, 287, 289, 293

Flatow v. Islamic Republic of Iran, US, District Court, 67 F.Supp.2d 535 (D.Md. 1999)   242, 287, 290

Flatow v. Islamic Republic of Iran, US, District Court, 74 F.Supp.2d 18 (D.D.C. 1999)   31, 228

Flatow v. Islamic Republic of Iran, US, District Court, 76 F.Supp.2d 16 (D.D.C. 1999)   226, 227, 228, 366, 367, 406, 407, 410

Flatow v. Islamic Republic of Iran, US, District Court, 76 F.Supp.2d 28 (D.D.C. 1999)   228

Flatow v. Islamic Republic of Iran, US, District Court, 999 F.Supp. 1 (D. D.C. 1998); 121 ILR 618   225, 227, 228

Flota Maritima Browning de Cuba, SA v. Motor Vessel Ciudad de la Habana, US, Court of Appeals, 335 F.2d 619 (4th Cir. 1964); 35 ILR 122   16, 356

Fogade v. ENB Revocable Trust, US, Court of Appeals, 263 F.3d 1274 (11th Cir. 2001)   310

Ford v. Johns-Manville Sales Corporation, US, District Court, 662 F.Supp. 930 (S.D.Ind. 1987)   268

Foremost-McKesson, Inc. v. Islamic Republic of Iran, US, Court of Appeals, 905 F.2d 438 (D.C.Cir. 1990); 101 ILR 536   25, 111, 115, 122, 125, 287, 289, 293, 309, 318, 324, 325, 330, 333

Foremost-McKesson, Inc. v. Islamic Republic of Iran, US, District Court, 759 F.Supp. 855 (D.D.C. 1991)   201

Forsythe v. Saudi Arabian Airlines Corporation, US, Court of Appeals, 885 F.2d 285 (5th Cir. 1989)   41, 244, 245, 274

Four Corners Helicopters, Inc. v. Turbomeca SA, US, District Court, 677 F.Supp. 1096 (D.Colo. 1988)   110, 114, 123, 125, 126, 223, 245

Foxworth v. Permanent Mission of the Republic of Uganda to the United Nations, US, District Court, 796 F.Supp. 761 (S.D.N.Y. 1992); 99 ILR 138   407, 410

French Republic v. Inland Nav. Co., US, District Court, 263 F. 410 (E.D.Mo. 1920)   335

French v. Banco Nacional de Cuba, US, Court of Appeals of New York, 23 N.Y.2d 46 (1968)   302

French v. Banco Nacional de Cuba, US, Court of Appeals of New York, 295 N.Y.S. 433 (1968); 66 ILR 6   16

Freund v. Republic of France, US, District Court, 592 F.Supp.2d 540 (S.D. N.Y. 2008)   245, 304

cxii   TABLE OF CASES

Friedar v. Government of Israel, US, District Court, 614 F.Supp. 395 (S.D. N.Y. 1985)   304, 306, 334

Frolova v. USSR (Union of Soviet Socialist Republics), US, Court of Appeals, 761 F.2d 370 (7th Cir. 1985); 85 ILR 236   40, 42, 223, 319, 324, 325, 329, 333

Frolova v. USSR (Union of Soviet Socialist Republics), US, District Court, 558 F.Supp. 358 (N.D.Ill. 1983)   223, 319

Frontera Resources Azerbaijan Corporation v. State Oil Company of Azerbaijan Republic, US, Court of Appeals, 582 F.3d 393 (2nd Cir. 2009)   25

Frontera Resources Azerbaijan Corporation v. State Oil Company of Azerbaijan Republic, US, District Court, 479 F.Supp.2d 376 (S.D.N.Y. 2007)   25, 326

Gabay v. Mostazafan Foundation of Iran and Mostazafan Foundation of New York (Gabay I), US, District Court, 151 F.R.D. 250 (S.D.N.Y. 1993); 107 ILR 242   126, 129, 245, 274, 290, 304, 311, 313

Gabay v. Mostazafan Foundation of Iran (Gabay II), US, District Court, 968 F.Supp. 895 (S.D.N.Y. 1997)   290, 293, 304, 313

Gabay v. Mostazafan Foundation of Iran, US, Court of Appeals, 152 F.3d 918 (2nd Cir. 1998) (Table)   290, 293, 313

Gadsby & Hannah v. Socialist Republic of Romania, US, District Court, 698 F.Supp. 483 (S.D.N.Y. 1988)   244, 245, 318, 321

Gang Chen v. China Central Television, US, Court of Appeals, 320 Fed. Appx. 71, 73, 2009 WL 932578, April 08, 2009 (No. 07-3882-CV)   244

Garb v. Republic of Poland, US, Court of Appeals, 440 F.3d 579 (2nd Cir. 2006)   25, 46, 83, 118, 122, 248, 304, 305, 312

Garb v. Republic of Poland, US, District Court, 207 F.Supp.2d 16 (E.D.N.Y. 2002)   25, 83, 248, 304, 312, 341, 429

Gardiner Stone Hunter International v. Iberia Lineas Aereas de Espana, SA, US, District Court, 896 F.Supp. 125 (S.D.N.Y. 1995)   259, 262, 263, 264, 268, 273

Gates v. Syrian Arab Republic, US, District Court, 580 F.Supp.2d 53 (D. D.C. 2008)   25, 225, 227

Gates v. Syrian Arab Republic, US, District Court, 646 F.Supp.2d 79 (D. D.C. 2009)   226

Gates v. Victor Fine Foods, US, Court of Appeals, 54 F.3d 1457 (9th Cir. 1995); 107 ILR 371   38, 41, 46, 109, 110, 161, 162, 244, 247, 251, 258, 264, 268, 293, 324, 332, 333, 334

GE Transport SpA v. Republic of Albania, US, District Court, 693 F.Supp.2d 132 (D.D.C. 2010)   25, 327

General Electric Capital Corporation v. Grossman, US, Court of Appeals, 991 F.2d 1376 (8th Cir. 1993)   41, 46, 125, 129, 273, 274, 333

Gerding v. Republic of France, US, Court of Appeals, 943 F.2d 521 (4th Cir. 1991); 98 ILR 159   25, 40, 108, 109, 110

German School Society, Washington, US, National Labor Relations Board, 260 NLRB 1250 (1982)   137, 162

Germany (Federal Republic of Germany) v. Elicofon, US, District Court, 536 F.Supp. 813 (E.D.N.Y. 1978); affirmed, Kunstsammlungen zu Weimar v. Elicofon, US, Court of Appeals, 678 F.2d 1150 (2nd Cir. 1982); 94 ILR 133   299, 316, 335

Gerritsen v. Escobar y Cordova, US, District Court, 688 F.Supp. 556 (C.D. Cal. 1988)   406, 407

Gerritsen v. Miguel de la Madrid Hurtado, US, Court of Appeals, 819 F.2d 1511 (9th Cir. 1987); 101 ILR 476   204, 244

Ghawanmeh v. Islamic Saudi Academy, US, District Court, 672 F.Supp.2d 3 (D.D.C. 2009)   134, 175, 196, 328

Gibbons and Beiseigel v. Republic of Ireland, US, District Court, 532 F.Supp. 668 (D.D.C. 1982); 86 ILR 75   25, 43, 293, 318

Gibbons and Beiseigel v. Udaras na Gaeltachta and the Industrial Development Authority of Ireland, US, District Court, 549 F.Supp. 1094 (S.D.N.Y. 1982); 86 ILR 81   38, 111, 309, 312, 318

Gilmore v. Palestinian Interim Self-Government Authority, US, District Court, 422 F.Supp.2d 96 (D.D.C. 2006)   31

Gilson v. Republic of Ireland, US, Court of Appeals, 682 F.2d 1022 (D.C. Cir. 1982); 92 ILR 374   25, 201, 268, 293

Gittler v. German Information Center, US, New York County, Supreme Court, Special Term, Part 1, 408 N.Y.S.2d 600 (N.Y.S.C. 1978); 63 ILR 170

Glencore, Ltd v. Chase Manhattan Bank, NA, US, District Court, 1998 WL 74294 (S.D.N.Y. 1998)   253

Global Index, Inc. v. Mkapa, US, District Court, 290 F.Supp.2d 108 (D.D.C. 2003)   77, 126, 128

Globe Nuclear Services and Supply (GNSS), Ltd v. AO Techsnabexport, US, Court of Appeals, 376 F.3d 282 (4th Cir. 2004)   38, 77, 89, 96, 110, 113, 244, 245, 266

Goar v. Compania Peruana de Vapores, US, Court of Appeals, 688 F.2d 417 (5th Cir. 1982)   42, 245, 262, 274

Goar v. Compania Peruana de Vapores, US, District Court, 510 F.Supp. 737 (E.D.La. 1981)   274

Goethe House New York, German Cultural Center, US, National Labor Relations Board, 288 NLRB 257 (1988)   137, 163, 245

cxiv TABLE OF CASES

Goethe v. NLRB (Goethe House New York, German Cultural Center v. National Labor Relations Board), US, Court of Appeals, 869 F.2d 75 (2nd Cir. 1989)   163

Goethe v. NLRB (Goethe House New York, German Cultural Center v. National Labor Relations Board), US, District Court, 685 F.Supp. 427 (S.D. N.Y. 1988)   163, 245

Gomez-Perez v. Potter, US, Supreme Court, 128 S.Ct. 1931 (2008)   31

Gonzalez Paredes v. Vila, US, District Court, 479 F.Supp.2d 187 (D.D.C. 2007)   191

Gonzalez v. Industrial Bank, US, New York Supreme Court, Special Term, Part I, 227 N.Y.S.2d 456 (1961); 63 ILR 1   16

Good v. Aramco Services Co., US, District Court, 971 F.Supp. 254 (S.D.Tex. 1997)   108, 109, 127, 166, 245, 319, 324, 329

Goodman Holdings v. Rafidain Bank, US, Court of Appeals, 26 F.3d 1143 (D.C.Cir. 1994)   110, 112, 128

Gosain v. State Bank of India, US, District Court, 689 F.Supp.2d 571 (S.D. N.Y. 2010)   126, 129

Gould, Inc. v. Mitsui Mining & Smelting Co., US, Court of Appeals, 947 F.2d 218 (6th Cir. 1991); 98 ILR 136   78, 110

Gould, Inc. v. Pechiney Ugine Kuhlmann and Trefimetaux, US, Court of Appeals, 853 F.2d 445 (6th Cir. 1988); 98 ILR 136   40, 61, 78, 90, 110, 111, 127, 268, 273

Gould v. Aerospatiale Helicopter Corporation, US, Court of Appeals, 40 F.3d 1033 (9th Cir. 1994)   242, 274

Granfinanciera, SA v. Nordberg, US, Supreme Court, 492 US 33 (1989)   273, 274

Grass v. Credito Mexicano, SA, US, Court of Appeals, 797 F.2d 220 (5th Cir. 1986)   127

Gray v. Permanent Mission of People's Republic of Congo to United Nations, US, Court of Appeals, 580 F.2d 1044 (2nd Cir. 1978) (Table)   244

Gray v. Permanent Mission of People's Republic of Congo to United Nations, US, District Court, 443 F.Supp. 816 (S.D.N.Y. 1978); 63 ILR 121   244, 407

Great American Boat Co. v. Alsthom Atlantic, Inc., US, District Court, Nos. 84-0105, 84-5442, 1987 WL 4766 (E.D.La. 1987)   268, 274

Greenbaum v. Islamic Republic of Iran, US, District Court, 451 F.Supp.2d 90 (D.D.C. 2006)   225, 227, 228

Greenpeace, Inc. (USA) v. State of France, US, District Court, 946 F.Supp. 773 (C.D.Cal. 1996)   223, 304, 305, 308, 309, 310, 311, 312, 319, 324, 331

Greenspan v. Crosbie, US, District Court, 90 Federal Securities Law Reports 826 (S.D.N.Y. 1976); 63 ILR 67 (S.D.N.Y. 1976)   16

Gregorian v. Izvestia, US, Court of Appeals, 871 F.2d 1515 (9th Cir. 1989); 98 ILR 76   38, 125, 126, 128, 201, 293

Gregorian v. Izvestia, US, District Court, 658 F.Supp. 1224 (C.D.Cal. 1987)   201

Guaranty Trust Company of New York v. United States, US, Supreme Court, 304 US 126 (1938); 9 AD 184   16, 31, 46, 316

Guevara v. Republic of Peru, US, Court of Appeals, 468 F.3d 1289 (11th Cir. 2006)   77, 93, 95, 112

Guevara v. Republic of Peru, US, Court of Appeals, 608 F.3d 1297 (11th Cir. 2010)   112

Guirlando v. TC Ziraat Bankasi AS, US, Court of Appeals, 602 F.3d 69 (2nd Cir. 2010)   43, 129, 245

Gulf Resources America, Inc. v. Republic of Congo, US, Court of Appeals, 370 F.3d 65 (D.C.Cir. 2004)   43, 320

Gulf Resources America v. Republic of Congo, US, District Court, 276 F.Supp.2d 20 (D.D.C. 2003)   76, 123, 126, 127, 129, 320

Gupta v. Thai Airways International, Ltd, US, Court of Appeals, 487 F.3d 759 (9th Cir. 2007)   43, 243, 245, 329

Gutch v. Federal Republic of Germany, US, District Court, 444 F.Supp.2d 1 (D.D.C. 2006)   10, 201, 223, 304, 306, 319, 320, 324, 325, 329

Guzel v. State of Kuwait, US, District Court, US, District Court, 818 F.Supp. 7 (D.D.C. 1993)   225

Haim v. Islamic Republic of Iran, US, District Court, 425 F.Supp.2d 56 (D.D.C. 2006)   225, 227

Haim v. Islamic Republic of Iran, US, District Court, 567 F.Supp.2d 146 (D.D.C. 2008)   226

Hanil Bank v. PT Bank Negara Indonesia (Persero), US, Court of Appeals, 148 F.3d 127 (2nd Cir. 1998)   77, 115, 125, 128, 129, 245

Hanil Bank v. PT Bank Negara Indonesia (Persero), US, District Court, 1997 U.S.Dist.Lexis 10450 (S.D.N.Y. 1997)   77, 115, 128, 129

Hannes v. Kingdom of Roumania Monopolies Institute, US, Supreme Court of New York, Appellate Division, First Department, 20 N.Y.S.2d 825 (1940); 9 AD 198   21

Hansen v. Danish Tourist Board, US, District Court, 147 F.Supp.2d 142 (E.D. N.Y. 2001)   90, 110, 160, 172, 245

Harris Corporation v. National Iranian Radio and Television and Bank Melli Iran, US, Court of Appeals, 691 F.2d 1344 (11th Cir. 1982); 72 ILR 172   123, 128, 318, 390

Harris v. Boreham, US, Court of Appeals, 233 F.2d 110 (3rd Cir. 1956)   31

Harris v. Municipality of St Thomas and St John, US, Court of Appeals, 212 F.2d 323 (3rd Cir. 1954)   31

Harris v. Socialist People's Libyan Arab Jamahiriya, US, District Court, 620 F.Supp.2d 1 (D.D.C. 2009)   226

Harris v. VAO Intourist, Moscow, US, District Court, 481 F.Supp. 1056 (E.D.N.Y. 1979); 63 ILR 318   110, 114, 127, 324

Hashemite Kingdom of Jordan v. Layale Enterprises, SA (In re B-727 Aircraft Serial No. 21010), US, Court of Appeals, 272 F.3d 264 (5th Cir. 2001)   43

Hatzlachh Supply Inc. v. Savannah Bank of Nigeria, US, District Court, 649 F.Supp. 688 (S.D.N.Y. 1986)   123, 127

Haven v. Rzeczpospolita Polska (Republic of Poland), US, Court of Appeals, 215 F.3d 727 (7th Cir. 2000)   83, 108, 110, 304, 319, 329, 333

Haven v. Rzeczpospolita Polska (Republic of Poland), US, District Court, 68 F.Supp.2d 947 (N.D.Ill. 1999)   83, 108, 304, 311, 312, 319, 329

Heaney v. Government of Spain and Adolpho Gomero, US, Court of Appeals, 445 F.2d 501 (2nd Cir. 1971); 57 ILR 153   16, 46

Hegna v. Islamic Republic of Iran, US, Court of Appeals, 376 F.3d 226 (4th Cir. 2004)   226, 228, 407

Hegna v. Islamic Republic of Iran, US, Court of Appeals, 402 F.3d 97 (2nd Cir. 2005)   225, 227

Hegna v. Islamic Republic of Iran, US, District Court, 287 F.Supp.2d 608 (D.Md. 2003)   226, 407

Hegna v. Islamic Republic of Iran, US, District Court, 299 F.Supp.2d 229 (S.D.N.Y. 2004)   228

Hellenic Lines, Ltd v. South Viet Nam, US, District Court, 275 F.Supp. 860 (S.D.N.Y. 1967); 63 ILR 16   16

Herbage v. Meese, US, Court of Appeals, 946 F.2d 1564 (D.C.Cir. 1991) (Table)   81, 433, 439

Herbage v. Meese, US, District Court, 747 F.Supp. 60 (D.D.C. 1990); 98 ILR 101   81, 433, 439

Hercaire International, Inc. v. Argentina, US, Court of Appeals, 821 F.2d 559 (11th Cir. 1987); 98 ILR 48   277, 287, 289, 290, 293, 318, 396

Hercaire International, Inc. v. Argentina, US, District Court, 642 F.Supp. 126 (S.D.Fla. 1986)   289, 290, 318, 396

Hester International Corporation v. Federal Republic of Nigeria, US, Court of Appeals, 879 F.2d 170 (5th Cir. 1989); 90 ILR 604   78, 245, 287, 289, 290, 293

TABLE OF CASES   cxvii

Hester International Corporation v. Federal Republic of Nigeria, US, District Court, 681 F.Supp. 371 (N.D.Miss. 1988)   78, 113, 289, 290

Higgins v. Islamic Republic of Iran, US, District Court, 2000 WL 33674311 (D.D.C. 2000)   225

Higgins v. Islamic Republic of Iran, US, District Court, 545 F.Supp.2d 122 (D.D.C. 2008)   226

Hijazi v. Permanent Mission of Saudi Arabia to United Nations, US, District Court, 689 F.Supp.2d 669 (S.D.N.Y. 2010)   160, 161, 196, 244

Hilao v. Marcos (In re Estate of Ferdinand Marcos Human Rights Litigation (Hilao v. Estate of Marcos)), US, Court of Appeals, 94 F.3d 539 (9th Cir. 1996)   83, 324, 330, 332, 333, 436

Hilao v. Marcos (In re Estate of Ferdinand Marcos, Human Rights Litigation (Hilao v. Estate of Marcos)), US, Court of Appeals, 25 F.3d 1467 (9th Cir. 1994); 104 ILR 119   434, 435, 436

Hilaturas Miel, SL v. Republic of Iraq, US, District Court, 573 F.Supp.2d 781 (S.D.N.Y. 2008)   76, 128

Hill v. Republic of Iraq, US, Court of Appeals, 328 F.3d 680 (D.C.Cir. 2003)   225, 227

Hill v. Republic of Iraq, US, District Court, 175 F.Supp.2d 36 (D.D.C. 2001)   225, 227

Hill v. Republic of Iraq, US, District Court, 2003 WL 21057173 (D.D.C. 2003)   293

Hirsh v. State of Israel and State of Germany, US, Court of Appeals, 133 F.3d 907 (2nd Cir. 1997)   83

Hirsh v. State of Israel and State of Germany, US, District Court, 962 F.Supp. 377 (S.D.N.Y. 1997); 113 ILR 543   82, 83, 223, 306, 312, 324, 327, 329, 333, 341

Hoesl v. United States, US, Court of Appeals, 629 F.2d 586 (9th Cir. 1980)   201

Hoesl v. United States, US, District Court, 451 F.Supp. 1170 (N.D.Cal. 1978)   201

Holden v. Canadian Consulate, US, Court of Appeals, 92 F.3d 918 (9th Cir. 1996)   38, 109, 158, 168

Holland v. Islamic Republic of Iran, US, District Court, 545 F.Supp.2d 120 (D.D.C. 2008)   226

Honduras Aircraft Registry, Ltd v. Government of Honduras, US, Court of Appeals, 119 F.3d 1530 (11th Cir. 1997)   76, 111

Honduras Aircraft Registry, Ltd v. Government of Honduras, US, Court of Appeals, 129 F.3d 543 (11th Cir. 1997)   76

cxviii TABLE OF CASES

Honduras Aircraft Registry Ltd v. Government of Honduras, US, District Court, 883 F.Supp. 685 (S.D.Fla. 1995) 76, 111

Howland v. Hertz Corporation, US, District Court, 431 F.Supp.2d 1238 (M.D. Fla. 2006) 225, 245

HSMV Corporation v. ADI Ltd, US, District Court, 72 F.Supp.2d 1122 (C.D. Cal. 1999) 245, 324, 325, 327, 330

Hungarian People's Republic v. Cecil Associates, Inc., US, District Court, 118 F.Supp. 954 (S.D.N.Y. 1953); 20 ILR 176 335

Hunt v. Mobil Oil Corporation, US, Court of Appeals, 550 F.2d 68 (2nd Cir. 1977); 66 ILR 288 299

Hurst v. Socialist People's Libyan Arab Jamahiriya, US, District Court, 474 F.Supp.2d 19 (D.D.C. 2007) 225, 227

Hwang Geum Joo v. Japan, US, Court of Appeals, 332 F.3d 679 (D.C.Cir. 2003) 24, 43, 84, 319, 341, 429

Hwang Geum Joo v. Japan, US, Court of Appeals, 413 F.3d 45 (D.C.Cir. 2005) 24, 84, 341, 429

Hwang Geum Joo v. Japan, US, District Court, 172 F.Supp.2d 52 (D.D.C. 2001) 24, 84, 319, 341, 429

Hwang Geum Joo v. Japan, US, Supreme Court, 542 US 901 (2004) 24, 84, 341, 429

Hyatt Corporation v. Stanton, US, District Court, 945 F.Supp. 675 (S.D. N.Y. 1996) 247, 268, 274

ICC Chemical Corporation v. Industrial and Commercial Bank of China, US, District Court, 886 F.Supp. 1 (S.D.N.Y. 1995) 245, 324

In re Air Crash Disaster near Roselawn, Indiana on October 31, 1994, US, Court of Appeals, 96 F.3d 932 (7th Cir. 1996) 232, 242, 243, 245, 259, 261, 262, 263, 266, 267, 268, 274

In re Air Crash Disaster near Roselawn, Indiana on October 31, 1994, US, District Court, 909 F.Supp. 1083 (N.D.Ill. 1995) 245, 261, 266, 268, 274

In re Air Crash Disaster near Warsaw, Poland on May 9, 1987, US, District Court, 716 F.Supp. 84 (E.D.N.Y. 1989) 78, 112, 114

In re Air Crash near Nantucket Island, Massachusetts, on Oct. 31, 1999, US, District Court, 392 F.Supp.2d 461 (E.D.N.Y. 2005) 124, 127, 245, 322

In re Aircrash Disaster near Monroe, Michigan on January 9, 1997, US, District Court, 987 F.Supp. 975 (E.D.Mich. 1997) 243, 245, 273, 274

In re Asemani, US, Court of Appeal, 455 F.3d 296 (D.C.Cir. 2006) 227

In re Chase & Sanborn Corporation, US, Court of Appeals, 835 F.2d 1341 (11th Cir. 1988) 273

TABLE OF CASES   cxix

In re Clearsky Shipping Corporation, US, District Court, 1999 WL
    1021825 (E.D.La. 1999)   268, 274
In re Delta American Re Insurance Co., US, Court of Appeals, 900 F.2d 890
    (6th Cir. 1990)   389
In re Disaster at Riyadh Airport, US, District Court, 540 F.Supp. 1141 (D.
    D.C. 1982)   245
In re Doe, US, Court of Appeals, 860 F.2d 40 (2nd Cir. 1988); 121 ILR
    567   16, 434, 435
In re Grand Jury Proceedings Doe No. 700, US, Court of Appeals, 817 F.2d
    1108 (4th Cir. 1987); 81 ILR 599   434
In re Hashim, US, Bankruptcy Court, 188 B.R. 633 (D.Arizona. 1995); 107
    ILR 405   232, 274
In re Iran (In re Islamic Republic of Iran Terrorism Litigation), US,
    District Court, 659 F.Supp.2d 31 (D.D.C. 2009)   228
In re Linee Aeree Italiane (Alitalia), US, Court of Appeals, 469 F.3d 638
    (7th Cir. 2006)   274
In re Muir, US, Supreme Court, 254 US 522 (1921); 1 AD 143   16, 28,
    31, 46
In re Multiponics, Inc., US, Court of Appeals, 622 F.2d 709 (5th Cir.
    1980)   292
In re Oil Spill by the Amoco Cadiz off the Coast of France, US, District
    Court, 491 F.Supp. 161 (N.D.Ill. 1979); 63 ILR 310   335
In re Papandreou, 139 F.3d 247 (D.C.Cir. 1998)   113
In re Philippines (In re Republic of the Philippines), US, Court of Appeals,
    309 F.3d 1143 (9th Cir. 2002)   324
In re Potash Antitrust Litigation, US, District Court, 686 F.Supp.2d 816 (N.D.
    Ill. 2010)   245
In re Ski Train Fire in Kaprun, Austria on November 11, 2000,
    US, District Court, 198 F.Supp.2d 420 (S.D.N.Y. 2002)   46, 243, 245,
    268, 273
In re Surinam Airways Holding Co., US, Court of Appeals, 974 F.2d 1255
    (11th Cir. 1992)   245, 274
In re Tamimi, US, Court of Appeals, 176 F.3d 274 (4th Cir. 1999)   110,
    244, 245, 324, 325, 333, 334
In re Terrorist Attacks on September 11, 2001, US, Court of Appeals, 538
    F.3d 71 (2nd Cir. 2008)   43, 204, 206, 227, 435
In re Terrorist Attacks on September 11, 2001, US, District Court, 349
    F.Supp.2d 765 (S.D.N.Y. 2005)   84, 89, 204, 206, 227, 253, 272, 435
In re Terrorist Attacks on September 11, 2001, US, District Court, 392
    F.Supp.2d 539 (S.D.N.Y. 2005)   204, 206, 253, 258, 334, 435

In re Texas Eastern Transmission PCB Contamination Litigation, US, Court of Appeals, 15 F.3d 1230 (3rd Cir. 1994)   46

Ingrassia v. Chicken Ranch Bingo and Casino, US, District Court, 676 F.Supp.2d 953 (E.D.Cal. 2009)   31

Intel Corporation and Dell Inc. v. Commonwealth Scientific and Industrial Research Organisation, US, Court of Appeals, 455 F.3d 1364 (Fed.Cir. (Cal.) 2006)   78

Intercontinental Dictionary Series v. De Gruyter, US, District Court, 822 F.Supp. 662 (C.D.Cal. 1993)   84, 90, 97, 201, 223, 247, 252, 253, 258, 304, 306, 311, 312, 329, 435

Intercontinental Resources, NA v. Federal Republic of Nigeria, US, District Court, No. 98-CIV-5114, 1999 WL 219909 (S.D.N.Y. 1999)   79

International Association of Machinists and Aerospace Workers v. OPEC, US, Court of Appeals, 649 F.2d 1354 (9th Cir. 1981); 66 ILR 413   61, 90, 260

International Association of Machinists and Aerospace Workers v. OPEC, US, District Court, 477 F.Supp. 553 (C.D.Cal. 1979); 63 ILR 284   35, 44, 260

International Housing Ltd v. Rafidain Bank Iraq, US, Court of Appeals, 893 F.2d 8 (2nd Cir. 1989); 98 ILR 93   125, 126, 129

International Insurance Company v. Caja Nacional de Ahorro y Seguro, US, Court of Appeals, 293 F.3d 392 (7th Cir. 2002)   41, 243, 319, 327, 390

International Road Federation v. Embassy of the Democratic Republic of the Congo, US, District Court, 131 F.Supp.2d 248 (D.D.C. 2001)   321

International Schools Service v. Government of Iran, US, District Court, 505 F.Supp. 178 (D.N.J. 1981); 63 ILR 550   274

Iran (Islamic Republic of Iran) v. Pahlavi, US, Supreme Court of New York, Appellate Division (First Department), 464 N.Y.S.2d 487 (1983); Court of Appeals of New York, 478 N.Y.S.2d 597 (1984); 81 ILR 557   316, 434

Iraq (Republic of Iraq) v. Beaty, US, Supreme Court, 129 S.Ct. 2183, 173 L.Ed.2d 1193 (2009)   226

Isbrandtsen Tankers v. President of India, US, Court of Appeals, 446 F.2d 1198 (2nd Cir. 1971); 57 ILR 147   16, 46

IT Consultants, Inc. v. Republic of Pakistan, US, Court of Appeals, 351 F.3d 1184 (D.C.Cir. 2003)   123, 128

Jackson v. People's Republic of China, US, Court of Appeals, 794 F.2d 1490 (11th Cir. 1986); 84 ILR 132   23, 42

Jackson v. People's Republic of China, US, District Court, 23 ILM 402 (N.D. Ala. 1984); 84 ILR 132   23

Jackson v. People's Republic of China, US, District Court, 550 F.Supp. 869 (N.D.Ala. 1982); 84 ILR 132   23, 25

Jackson v. People's Republic of China, US, District Court, 596 F.Supp. 386 (N.D.Ala. 1984); 84 ILR 132   23, 42

Jackson v. Resolution GGF Oy, US, Court of Appeals, 136 F.3d 1130 (7th Cir. 1998)   268, 274

Jafari v. Islamic Republic of Iran, US, District Court, 539 F.Supp. 209 (N.D. Ill. 1982); 72 ILR 124   311, 318

Janini v. Kuwait University, US, Court of Appeals, 43 F.3d 1534 (D.C.Cir. 1995); 107 ILR 367   113, 162, 171

Jenco v. Islamic Republic of Iran, US, District Court, 154 F.Supp.2d 27 (D.D.C. 2001)   225, 227, 228

Jet Line Services Inc. v. M/V Marsa el Hariga, US, District Court, 462 F.Supp. 1165 (D.Md. 1978); 63 ILR 214   35, 44

JJ Ryan & Sons, Inc. v. Rhone Poulenc Textile, SA, US, Court of Appeals, 863 F.2d 315 (4th Cir. 1988)   268

Jones v. Petty-Ray Geophysical Geosource, Inc., US, Court of Appeals, 954 F.2d 1061 (5th Cir. 1992)   223, 273, 274

Joseph v. Office of the Consulate General of Nigeria, US, Court of Appeals, 830 F.2d 1018 (9th Cir. 1987); 101 ILR 485   38, 41, 61, 76, 77, 88, 92, 109, 110, 111, 204, 225, 324, 328, 330, 333

Jota v. Texaco, Inc., US, Court of Appeals, 157 F.3d 153 (2nd Cir. 1998)   319, 333

Jungquist v. Sheikh Sultan bin Khalifa al Nahyan, US, Court of Appeals, 115 F.3d 1020 (D.C.Cir. 1997)   435

Jungquist v. Sheikh Sultan bin Khalifa al Nahyan, US, District Court, 940 F.Supp. 312 (D.D.C. 1996); 113 ILR 522   435

Kadic v. Karadzic, US, Court of Appeals, 70 F.3d 232 (2nd Cir. 1995)   434

Kalamazoo Spice Extraction Company v. Provisional Military Government of Socialist Ethiopia, US, District Court, 616 F.Supp. 660 (W.D.Mich. 1985); 90 ILR 596   245, 289

Kalasho v. Iraqi Government, US, District Court, 2001 U.S.Dist.Lexis 7504 (W.D.Mich. 2001)   227

Kao Hwa Shipping Co., SA v. China Steel Corporation, US, District Court, 816 F.Supp. 910 (S.D.N.Y. 1993)   324, 328, 329

Karaha Bodas Company, LLC v. Perusahaan Pertambangan Minyak Dan Gas Bumi Negara (Pertamina), US, Court of Appeals, 313 F.3d 70 (2nd Cir. 2002)   244, 245, 248, 293, 321, 396

Kato v. Ishihara, US, Court of Appeals, 360 F.3d 106 (2nd Cir. 2004)   83, 141, 158, 161, 245, 435

cxxii TABLE OF CASES

Kato v. Ishihara, US, District Court, 239 F.Supp.2d 359 (S.D.N.Y. 2002)
141, 158, 245, 435
Keene Corporation v. US, US, Supreme Court, 508 US 200 (1993) 273
Keller v. Central Bank of Nigeria, US, Court of Appeals, 277 F.3d 811 (6th
Cir. 2002) 79, 128, 129, 435
Keller v. Transportes Aereos Militares Ecuadorianos, US, District Court,
601 F.Supp. 787 (D.D.C. 1985) 127, 245, 332, 333, 334
Kelly v. Syria Shell Petroleum Development BV, US, Court of Appeals, 213
F.3d 841 (5th Cir. 2000) 43, 111, 247, 254, 269
Kensington International Ltd v. Itoua, US, Court of Appeals, 505 F.3d 147
(2nd Cir. 2007) 126, 245, 266
Kensington International Ltd v. Republic of Congo, US, Court of
Appeals, 461 F.3d 238 (2nd Cir. 2006) 319, 321, 323, 388, 389,
390, 402
Kensington International Ltd v. Republic of Congo, US, District Court,
2005 WL 646086 (S.D.N.Y. 2005) 388
Kensington International Ltd v. Société Nationale des Pétroles du Congo,
US, District Court, 2006 WL 846351 (S.D.N.Y. 2006) 245
Kern v. Jeppesen Sanderson, Inc., US, District Court, 867 F.Supp. 525 (S.D.
Tex. 1994) 243, 245, 261, 262, 269, 273, 274
Kern v. Oesterreichische Elektrizitaetswirtschaft AG, US, District Court,
178 F.Supp.2d 367 (S.D.N.Y. 2001) 115, 243, 245, 266, 320, 324
Kerr v. Islamic Republic of Iran, US, District Court, 245 F.Supp.2d 59 (D.
D.C. 2003) 225, 227
Kilburn v. Republic of Iran, US, District Court, 277 F.Supp.2d 24 (D.D.C.
2003) 225, 227, 248
Kilburn v. Socialist People's Libyan Arab Jamahiriya, US, Court of
Appeals, 376 F.3d 1123 (D.C.Cir. 2004) 41, 225, 227
Kilroy v. Windsor (Prince Charles, the Prince of Wales), US, District
Court, Civil Action No. C-78-291, 81 ILR 605 (N.D.Ohio 1978) 434
Kiowa Tribe of Oklahoma v. Manufacturing Technologies, Inc., US,
Supreme Court, 523 US 751 (1998) 31
Kirkham v. Société Air France, US, Court of Appeals, 429 F.3d 288 (D.C.
Cir. 2005) 112
Kirkpatrick Inc. v. Environmental Tectonics Corporation International,
US, Supreme Court, 493 US 400 (1990); 88 ILR 93 301
Kirschenbaum v. Islamic Republic of Iran, US, District Court, 572
F.Supp.2d 200 (D.D.C. 2008) 226, 227, 228
Kline v. Kaneko, US, District Court, 685 F.Supp. 386 (S.D.N.Y. 1988); 101
ILR 497 82, 84, 90, 109, 223, 304, 311, 312, 433, 435

TABLE OF CASES   cxxiii

Kline v. Kaneko, US, Supreme Court of New York, 535 N.Y.S.2d 303 (N.Y. Sup.Ct. 1988)   435

Kline v. Republic of El Salvador, US, District Court, 603 F.Supp. 1313 (D. D.C. 1985)   223

Klinghoffer v. SNC Achille Lauro, US, Court of Appeals, 937 F.2d 44 (2nd Cir. 1991); 96 ILR 68   31, 316

Knox v. Palestine Liberation Organization, US, District Court, 306 F.Supp.2d 424 (S.D.N.Y. 2004)   31

Koirala v. Thai Airways International, Ltd, US, Court of Appeals, 126 F.3d 1205 (9th Cir. 1997)   245

Kramer v. Boeing Company, US, District Court, 705 F.Supp. 1392 (D.Minn. 1989)   109, 110, 123, 127, 243, 245, 328

Kully v. Aircraft Service International Group, Inc., US, District Court, 662 F.Supp.2d 259 (E.D.N.Y. 2009)   274

La Reunion Aerienne v. Libya (Socialist People's Libyan Arab Jamahiriya), US, Court of Appeals, 533 F.3d 837 (D.C.Cir. 2008)   225, 226

La Reunion Aerienne v. Libya (Socialist People's Libyan Arab Jamahiriya), US, District Court, 477 F.Supp.2d 131 (D.D.C. 2007)   225, 226, 435

Lafontant v. Aristide, US District Court, 844 F.Supp. 128 (E.D.N.Y. 1994); 103 ILR 581   434, 435

Lapides v. Board of Regents of the University System of Georgia, US, Supreme Court, 535 US 613 (2002)   31

Laroque v. Qantas Airways, Ltd, US, Court of Appeals, 900 F.2d 263 (9th Cir. 1990)   38

Lasagne v. Divi Hotels, US, District Court, 685 F.Supp. 88 (S.D.N.Y. 1988)   109, 113, 126, 127

Ledgerwood v. State of Iran, US, District Court, 617 F.Supp. 311 (D.D.C. 1985)   223

LeDonne v. Gulf Air, Inc., US, District Court, 700 F.Supp. 1400 (E.D.Va. 1988)   90, 201, 232, 242, 260, 263, 273, 274

Lee v. China Airlines, Ltd, US, District Court, 669 F.Supp.979 (C.D.Cal. 1987)   322

Lehman Brothers Commercial Corporation v. Minmetals International Non-Ferrous Metals Trading Company, US, District Court, 169 F.Supp.2d 186 (S.D.N.Y. 2001)   266, 268, 274

Lempert v. Republic of Kazakstan, US, District Court, 223 F.Supp.2d 200 (D.D.C. 2002)   113, 114, 128

LETCO (In the Matter of the Application of Liberian Eastern Timber Corporation v. Government of the Republic of Liberia), US, District Court, 650 F.Supp. 73 (S.D.N.Y. 1986); 89 ILR 355   25, 327, 418

cxxiv TABLE OF CASES

LETCO (In the Matter of the Application of Liberian Eastern
Timber Corporation v. Government of the Republic of Liberia), US,
District Court, 659 F.Supp. 606 (D.D.C. 1987); 89 ILR 360   25, 402, 407,
410, 420
Letelier v. Republic of Chile and Linea Aerea Nacional-Chile, US, Court of
Appeals, 748 F.2d 790 (2nd Cir. 1984); 79 ILR 561   41, 61, 84, 90, 93,
201, 287, 289, 293, 355, 396, 397, 399
Letelier v. Republic of Chile, US, District Court, 488 F.Supp. 665 (D.D.C.
1980); 63 ILR 378   202, 206, 209, 222, 399
Letelier v. Republic of Chile, US, District Court, 502 F.Supp. 259 (D.D.C.
1980)   248, 274
Letelier v. Republic of Chile, US, District Court, 567 F.Supp. 1490 (S.D.N.Y.
1983)   293, 355
Letelier v. Republic of Chile, US, District Court, 575 F.Supp. 1217 (S.D.N.Y.
1983)   293, 355, 397
L'Europeenne de Banque v. Republica de Venezuela, US, District Court,
700 F.Supp. 114 (S.D.N.Y. 1988); 98 ILR 100 Note   77, 128, 324, 325
Leutwyler v. Office of Her Majesty Queen Rania Al-Abdullah, US, District
Court, 184 F.Supp.2d 277 (S.D.N.Y. 2001)   78, 91, 110, 111, 201,
306, 435
Levin v. Islamic Republic of Iran, US, District Court, 529 F.Supp.2d 1 (D.
D.C. 2007)   225, 227, 228
Li Weixum v. Bo Xilai, US, District Court, 568 F.Supp.2d 35 (D.D.C.
2008)   435
Liberia (Republic of Liberia) v. Bickford, US, District Court, 787 F.Supp.
397 (S.D.N.Y. 1992); 96 ILR 90   316
Libra Bank Ltd v. Banco Nacional de Costa Rica, SA, US, Court of Appeals,
676 F.2d 47 (2nd Cir. 1982); 72 ILR 119   245, 319, 323, 333, 388, 389
Libya (Great Socialist People's Libyan Arab Jamahiriya) v. Miski, US,
District Court, 683 F.Supp.2d 1 (D.D.C. 2010)   335
Lin v. Japan, US, District Court, 1994 WL 193948, 1994 U.S.Dist.Lexis 6061
(D.D.C. 1994)   24
Lindgren v. United States, US, Court of Appeals, 665 F.2d 978 (9th Cir.
1982)   206
Linton v. Airbus Industrie, US, Court of Appeals, 30 F.3d 592 (5th Cir.
1994)   243, 260, 263, 269, 274
Linton v. Airbus Industrie, US, District Court, 794 F.Supp. 650 (S.D.Tex.
1992)   243, 259, 260, 262, 263, 265, 269, 274
Liu v. Republic of China, US, Court of Appeals, 892 F.2d 1419 (9th Cir.
1989); 101 ILR 519   204, 206, 209, 225

TABLE OF CASES   CXXV

LNC Investments, Inc. v. Banco Central de Nicaragua, US, Court of
   Appeals, 228 F.3d 423 (2nd Cir. 2000)   244, 245, 287, 289, 290, 293, 319,
   411, 413, 414
LNC Investments, Inc. v. Republic of Nicaragua, US, District Court, 115
   F.Supp.2d 358 (S.D.N.Y. 2000)   244, 245, 287, 289, 290, 293, 319, 411,
   413, 414
Logan v. Secretary of State, US, Court of Appeals, 553 F 2d 107 (D.C.Cir.
   1976); 63 ILR 70   16
Lonon v. Companhia de Navegacao Lloyd Basileiro, US, District Court, 85
   F.R.D. 71 (E.D.Pa. 1979); 63 ILR 329   245, 274
Lopez-Smith v. Hood, US, Court of Appeals, 121 F.3d 1322 (9th Cir.
   1997)   332
Lord Day & Lord v. Socialist Republic of Vietnam, US, District Court,
   134 F.Supp.2d 549 (S.D.N.Y. 2001)   78, 112, 304, 305, 306, 312, 324,
   330, 335
Los Angeles News Service v. Conus Communications Co. Ltd Partnership,
   US, District Court, 969 F.Supp. 579 (C.D.Cal. 1997)   79, 89, 115, 123,
   244, 245, 328
Lyon v. Agusta SpA, US, Court of Appeals, 252 F.3d 1078 (9th Cir. 2001)
   115, 126, 129
MacArthur Area Citizens Association v. Republic of Peru, US, Court of
   Appeals, 809 F.2d 918 (D.C.Cir. 1987); 107 ILR 196   10, 25, 43, 83, 204
MacArthur Area Citizens Association v. Republic of Peru, US, Court of
   Appeals, 823 F.2d 606 (D.C.Cir. 1987)   204
Magness v. Russian Federation, US, Court of Appeals, 247 F.3d 609 (5th
   Cir. 2001)   248, 274
Magness v. Russian Federation, US, District Court, 54 F.Supp.2d 700 (S.D.
   Tex. 1999)   123
Magnus Electronics, Inc. v. Argentine Republic, 637 F.Supp. 487 (N.D.Ill.
   1986)   109
Maizus v. Weldor Trust Reg, US, District Court, 820 F.Supp. 101 (S.D.N.Y.
   1993)   126, 245
Malewicz v. City of Amsterdam, US, District Court, 362 F.Supp.2d 298 (D.
   D.C. 2005)   46, 78, 91, 245, 305, 310, 312
Malewicz v. City of Amsterdam, US, District Court, 517 F.Supp.2d 322 (D.
   D.C. 2007)   91
Mangattu v. M/V Ibn Hayyan, US, Court of Appeals, 35 F.3d 205 (5th Cir.
   1994)   232, 242, 245, 259, 261, 263, 266, 388, 390
Mann v. Hanil Bank, US, District Court, 900 F.Supp. 1077 (E.D.Wis.
   1995)   109, 268

cxxvi   TABLE OF CASES

Marchisella v. Government of Japan, US, District Court, No. 02 Civ. 10023 (DC), 2004 WL 307248 (S.D.N.Y. 2004)   206

Maritime International Nominees Establishment v. Republic of Guinea, US, Court of Appeals, 693 F.2d 1094 (D.C.Cir. 1982); 72 ILR 152   108, 125, 319, 324, 325, 333

Maritime International Nominees Establishment v. Republic of Guinea, US, District Court, 505 F.Supp. 141 (D.D.C. 1981); 63 ILR 535   319, 325, 333

Maritime Ventures International, Inc. v. Caribbean Trading & Fidelity, Ltd, US, District Court, 689 F.Supp. 1340 (S.D.N.Y. 1988)   317, 325

Maritime Ventures International, Inc. v. Caribbean Trading & Fidelity, Ltd, US, District Court, 722 F.Supp. 1032 (S.D.N.Y. 1989)   318

Marlowe v. Argentine Naval Commission, US, District Court, 604 F.Supp. 703 (D.D.C. 1985)   328

Martin v. Republic of South Africa, US, Court of Appeals, 836 F.2d 91 (2nd Cir. 1987); 92 ILR 448   25, 127

Martin v. Warden, US, Court of Appeals, 993 F.2d 824 (11th Cir. 1993)   332

Martinez v. Dow Chemical Co., US, District Court, Nos. 95-3212, 95-3214, 1996 WL 502461 (E.D.La. 1996)   268, 274

Mashayekhi v. Iran, US, District Court, 515 F.Supp. 41 (D.D.C. 1981)   318

Massie v. Government of Democratic People's Republic of Korea, US, District Court, 592 F.Supp.2d 57 (D.D.C. 2008)   225, 227

Matar v. Dichter, US, Court of Appeals, 563 F.3d 9 (2nd Cir. 2009)   43, 435

Matar v. Dichter, US, District Court, 500 F.Supp.2d 284 (S.D.N.Y. 2007)   435

Matter of Rimsat, Ltd, US, Court of Appeals, 98 F.3d 956 (7th Cir. 1996)   242

Matter of Sedco, Inc., US, District Court, 543 F.Supp. 561 (S.D.Tex. 1982); 72 ILR 110   204, 223

MBL International Contractors, Inc. v. Republic of Trinidad and Tobago, US, District Court, 725 F.Supp. 52 (D.D.C. 1989)   326

McDonald v. Socialist People's Libyan Arab Jamahiriya, US, District Court, 666 F.Supp.2d 50 (D.D.C. 2009)   226

McDonnell Douglas Corporation v. Islamic Republic of Iran, US, Court of Appeals, 758 F.2d 341 (8th Cir. 1985)   77

MCI Telecommunications Corporation v. Alhadhood, US, Court of Appeals, 82 F.3d 658 (5th Cir. 1996)   79, 90, 93, 225

McKeel v. Islamic Republic of Iran, US, Court of Appeals, 722 F.2d 582 (9th Cir. 1983); 81 ILR 543   42, 223

TABLE OF CASES   cxxvii

McKesson Corporation v. Islamic Republic of Iran, US, Court of Appeals, 52 F.3d 346 (D.C.Cir. 1995)   111, 125, 289, 290

McKesson Corporation v. Islamic Republic of Iran, US, District Court, 1997 WL 361177 (D.D.C. 1997)   310

McKesson HBOC, Inc. v. Islamic Republic of Iran, US, Court of Appeals, 271 F.3d 1101 (D.C.Cir. 2001)   43, 111, 125

Meadows v. Dominican Republic, US, Court of Appeals, 817 F.2d 517 (9th Cir. 1987); 98 ILR 37   25, 38, 40, 61, 76, 125, 128

Meadows v. Dominican Republic, US, District Court, 628 F.Supp. 599 (N.D. Cal. 1986)   76, 125, 128

Mendenhall v. Saudi Aramco, US, District Court, 991 F.Supp. 856 (S.D.Tex. 1998)   245, 324

Menendez v. Saks & Co., US, Court of Appeals, 485 F.2d 1355 (2nd Cir. 1973)   301

Mexico (Republic of Mexico) v. Hoffman, US, Supreme Court, 324 US 30 (1945); 12 AD 143   9, 16, 21, 28, 46

Mexico (United Mexican States) v. Ashley, US, Supreme Court of Texas, 556 S.W.2d 784 (1977); 63 ILR 95   83, 299, 301

Millen Industries, Inc. v. Coordination Council for North American Affairs, US, Court of Appeals, 855 F.2d 879 (D.C.Cir. 1988); 98 ILR 61   31, 110, 111, 115

Millicom International Cellular v. Republic of Costa Rica, US, District Court, 995 F.Supp. 14 (D.D.C. 1998)   128, 245, 266, 268, 304, 309, 310

Mills v. Aetna Fire Underwriters Insurance Company, US, Court of Appeals, 511 A.2d 8, 13 (D.C.App. 1986)   310

Ministry of Defence of the Islamic Republic of Iran v. Gould Inc., US, Court of Appeals, 887 F.2d 1357 (9th Cir. 1989); 969 F.2d 764 (9th Cir. 1992); 96 ILR 1   316, 327

Ministry of Defense and Support for Armed Forces of Islamic Republic of Iran v. Cubic Defense Systems, Inc., US, Court of Appeals, 385 F.3d 1206 (9th Cir. 2004)   43, 77, 88, 228, 245, 248, 249, 274, 316, 356, 366

Ministry of Defense and Support for Armed Forces of Islamic Republic of Iran v. Cubic Defense Systems, Inc., US, Court of Appeals, 495 F.3d 1024 (9th Cir. 2007)   228, 249, 366

Ministry of Defense and Support for Armed Forces of Islamic Republic of Iran v. Cubic Defense Systems, Inc., US, District Court, 29 F.Supp.2d 1168 (S.D.Cal. 1998)   248, 316

Ministry of Defense and Support for Armed Forces of Islamic Republic of Iran v. Cubic Defense Systems, Inc., US, District Court, 236 F.Supp.2d 1140 (S.D.Cal. 2002)   228, 248, 249, 274, 366

cxxviii TABLE OF CASES

Ministry of Defense and Support for Armed Forces of Islamic Republic of Iran v. Elahi, US, Supreme Court, 129 S.Ct. 1732 (2009) 249

Ministry of Defense and Support for Armed Forces of Islamic Republic of Iran v. Elahi, US, Supreme Court, 546 US 450 (2006) 249, 274, 366, 396

Ministry of Supply v. Universe Tankships, Inc.., 708 F.2d 80 (2nd Cir. 1983); 98 ILR 13 110

Minpeco, SA v. Hunt, US, District Court, 686 F.Supp. 427 (S.D.N.Y. 1988) 289, 292

Mobil Corporation v. Abeille General Insurance Co., US, Court of Appeals, 984 F.2d 664 (5th Cir. 1993) 242, 274

MOL, Inc. v. Peoples Republic of Bangladesh, US, Court of Appeals, 736 F.2d 1326 (9th Cir. 1984); 80 ILR 583 40, 117

Monegasque de Reassurances SAM (Monde Re) v. Nak Naftogaz of Ukraine, US, Court of Appeals, 311 F.3d 488 (2nd Cir. 2002) 326

Montanez Miranda v. Banco Progreso SACA, US, District Court, 973 F.Supp. 89 (D.P.R. 1997) 83

Moore v. National Distillers and Chemical Corporation, US, District Court, 143 F.R.D. 526 (S.D.N.Y. 1992) 388, 389, 390

Moore v. United Kingdom, US, Court of Appeals, 384 F.3d 1079 (9th Cir. 2004) 25

Moran v. Kingdom of Saudi Arabia, US, Court of Appeals, 27 F.3d 169 (5th Cir. 1994); 107 ILR 303 25, 41, 225

Morgan Equipment Co. v. Novokrivorogsky State Ore Mining and Processing Enterprise, US, District Court, 57 F.Supp.2d 863 (N.D.Cal. 1998) 113, 114, 129, 245

Morgan Guaranty Trust Company of New York v. Republic of Palau, US, Court of Appeals, 924 F.2d 1237 (2nd Cir. 1991); 87 ILR 590 31, 273

Morgan Guaranty Trust Company of New York v. Republic of Palau, US, District Court, 639 F.Supp. 706 (S.D.N.Y. 1986); 87 ILR 590 31, 273

Morgan Guaranty Trust Company of New York v. Republic of Palau, US, District Court, 693 F.Supp. 1479 (S.D.N.Y. 1988); 87 ILR 590 76

Morris v. People's Republic of China, US, District Court, 478 F.Supp.2d 561 (S.D.N.Y. 2007) 24, 25, 77, 124, 128, 129

Moses v. Air Afrique, US, District Court, No. 99-CV-541, 2000 WL 306853 (E.D.N.Y. 2000) 227, 232, 245, 262

Mousa v. Islamic Republic of Iran, US, District Court, 238 F.Supp.2d 1 (D. D.C. 2001) 225

Mukaddam v. Permanent Mission of Saudi Arabia to the United Nations, US, District Court, 111 F.Supp.2d 457 (S.D.N.Y. 2000) 88, 91, 123, 158, 160, 165, 166, 171, 201, 245

TABLE OF CASES   cxxix

Murphy v. Korea Asset Management Corporation, US, District Court, 421 F.Supp.2d 627 (S.D.N.Y. 2005)   46, 78, 109, 128, 253, 256, 258, 272

Musopole v. South African Airways (Pty) Ltd, US, District Court, 172 F.Supp.2d 443 (S.D.N.Y. 2001)   266, 268, 274

Mwani v. bin Laden and Afghanistan, US, Court of Appeals, 417 F.3d 1 (D.C. Cir. 2005)   25, 43, 84, 227

Napolitano v. Tishman Construction Corporation, US, District Court, No. 96 Civ. 4402(SJ), 1998 WL 102789 (E.D.N.Y. 1998)   206

National American Corporation v. Federal Republic of Nigeria and the Central Bank of Nigeria, US, District Court, 420 F.Supp. 954 (S.D.N.Y. 1976); 63 ILR 63   16

National City Bank of New York v. Republic of China, US, Supreme Court, 348 US 356 (1955); 22 ILR 210   10, 16, 46, 65, 335

National Expositions, Inc. v. DuBois, US, District Court, 605 F.Supp. 1206 (W.D.Pa. 1985)   245, 305, 311

National Iranian Oil Co v. Ashland Oil, Inc., US, District Court, 716 F.Supp. 268 (S.D.Miss. 1989)   245

National Petrochemical Company of Iran v. M/T Stolt Sheaf, US, Court of Appeals, 860 F.2d 551 (2nd Cir. 1988); 87 ILR 583   316

National Petrochemical Company of Iran v. M/T Stolt Sheaf, US, District Court, 671 F.Supp. 1009 (S.D.N.Y. 1987)   316

National Union Fire Insurance Co. of Pittsburgh, PA v. BP Amoco PLC, US, District Court, 319 F.Supp.2d 352 (S.D.N.Y. 2004)   78, 245

National Union Fire Insurance Company of Pittsburgh, PA v. People's Republic of the Congo, US, District Court, 729 F.Supp. 936 (S.D.N.Y. 1989)   321

Nationsbank of Florida v. Banco Exterior de Espana, US, District Court, 867 F.Supp. 167 (S.D.N.Y. 1994)   245

Nazarian v. Compagnie Nationale Air France, US, District Court, 989 F.Supp. 504 (S.D.N.Y. 1998)   111, 112, 245

Nelson v. Saudi Arabia, US, Court of Appeals, 923 F.2d 1528 (11th Cir. 1991); 88 ILR 189   81

Nemariam v. Federal Democratic Republic of Ethiopia, US, Court of Appeals, 491 F.3d 470 (D.C.Cir. 2007); 135 ILR 679   43, 304, 305, 307, 312

Nemariam v. Federal Democratic Republic of Ethiopia, US, District Court, 400 F.Supp.2d 76 (D.D.C. 2005)   304, 305, 306, 307, 312

Nevada v. Hall, US, Supreme Court, 440 US 410 (1979)   46

New England Merchants National Bank v. Iran Power Generation and Transmission Company, US, Court of Appeals, 646 F.2d 779 (2nd Cir. 1981)   323, 387, 389

CXXX   TABLE OF CASES

New England Merchants National Bank v. Iran Power Generation and Transmission Company, US, District Court, 502 F.Supp. 120 (S.D.N.Y. 1980); 63 ILR 497   323, 387, 388, 389

New York and Cuba Mail Steamship Co. v. Republic of Korea, US, District Court, 132 F.Supp. 684 (S.D.N.Y. 1955); 22 ILR 220   16, 353, 374

New York Bay Co. v. State Bank of Patiala, US, District Court, No. 93 Civ. 6075, 1994 WL 369406 (S.D.N.Y. 1994)   268

New York (City of New York) v. Permanent Mission of India to the United Nations, US, Court of Appeals, 446 F.3d 365 (2nd Cir. 2006)   10, 38, 43, 407

New York (City of New York) v. Permanent Mission of India to the United Nations, US, District Court, 376 F.Supp.2d 429 (S.D.N.Y. 2005)   10, 38, 407

Nexhat Boshnjaku v. Federal Republic of Yugoslavia, US, District Court, 2002 U.S.Dist.Lexis 13763 (N.D.Ill. 2002)   429

Nikbin v. Islamic Republic of Iran, US, District Court, 471 F.Supp.2d 53 (D.D.C. 2007)   225, 227

Nikbin v. Islamic Republic of Iran, US, District Court, 517 F.Supp.2d 416 (D.D.C. 2007)   225, 227, 228

Nordmann v. Thai Airways International, US, Court of Appeals, 112 F.3d 517 (9th Cir. 1997) (Table); 1997 WL 199971 (9th Cir. 1997)   125, 127

North East Shipping Corporation v. Government of Pakistan, US, District Court, (S.D.N.Y. 1975); 63 ILR 52   16

NYSA-ILA Pension Trust Fund v. Garuda Indonesia, US, Court of Appeals, 7 F.3d 35 (2nd Cir. 1993)   110, 245, 293

Obenchain Corporation v. Corporation Nacionale de Inversiones, US, District Court, 656 F.Supp. 435 (W.D.Pa. 1987)   109, 113, 127

O'Bryan v. Holy See, US, Court of Appeals, 556 F.3d 361 (6th Cir. 2009) 25, 31, 43, 205

O'Bryan v. Holy See, US, District Court, 471 F.Supp.2d 784 (W.D.Ky. 2007) 25, 31, 205

Ocasek v. Flintkote Company, US, District Court, 796 F.Supp. 362 (N.D.Ill. 1992)   266, 268, 273

Ocean Line Holdings Ltd v. China National Chartering Corporation, US, District Court, 578 F.Supp.2d 621 (S.D.N.Y. 2008)   272

Ocean Transport Co. v. Government of the Republic of the Ivory Coast, US, District Court, 269 F.Supp. 703 (E.D. Louis. 1967); 63 ILR 9   16, 387

O'Connell Machinery Company, Inc. v. M/V Americana and Italia di Navigazione SpA, US, Court of Appeals, 734 F.2d 115 (2nd Cir. 1984); 81 ILR 539   268, 389

O'Connell Machinery Company, Inc. v. M/V Americana and Italia di Navigazione SpA, US, District Court, 566 F.Supp. 1381 (S.D.N.Y. 1983) 268, 389

Odyssey Marine Exploration, Inc. v. Unidentified, Shipwrecked Vessel, US, District Court, 675 F.Supp.2d 1126 (M.D.Fla. 2009) 445

O'Hair v. Andrus, Civil Action No. 79-2462; Wojtyla, Civil Action No. 79-2463, US, District Court, 81 ILR 607 (D.D.C. 1979) 434

Ohntrup v. Firearms Center Inc., US, Court of Appeals, 760 F.2d 259 (3rd Cir. 1985) (Table) 123, 125, 324, 325, 334

Ohntrup v. Firearms Center Inc., US, District Court, 516 F.Supp. 1281 (E. D.Pa. 1981); 63 ILR 632 123, 125, 324, 325, 334

Olsen, by Sheldon v. Government of Mexico; Sanchez, by Cernie v. Republic of Mexico, US Court of Appeals, 729 F.2d 641 (9th Cir. 1984); 84 ILR 96 25, 205, 206, 223

Olson v. Republic of Singapore, US, District Court, 636 F.Supp. 885 (D.D.C. 1986) 206

Olympia Express, Inc. v. Linee Aeree Italiane SpA, US, District Court, 437 F.Supp.2d 780 (N.D.Ill. 2006) 274

Olympic Chartering SA v. Ministry of Industry and Trade of Jordan, US, District Court, 134 F.Supp.2d 528 (S.D.N.Y. 2001) 244, 411, 413, 414

ONE Shipping Ltd v. Flota Mercante Grancolombiana, SA, US, Court of Appeals, 830 F.2d 449 (2nd Cir. 1987) 268

Orient Mineral Co. v. Bank of China, US, Court of Appeals, 506 F.3d 980 (10th Cir. 2007) 38, 109, 125, 244, 245

Ortega Trujillo v. Banco Central del Ecuador, US, District Court, 17 F.Supp.2d 1340 (S.D.Fla. 1998) 201, 245

Oster v. Republic of South Africa, US, District Court, 530 F.Supp.2d 92 (D. D.C. 2007) 25

Oveissi v. Islamic Republic of Iran, US, Court of Appeals, 573 F.3d 835 (D.C. Cir. 2009) 225, 227

Oveissi v. Islamic Republic of Iran, US, District Court, 498 F.Supp.2d 268 (D.D.C. 2007) 225, 227

Owens v. Republic of Sudan (Owens I), US, District Court, 374 F.Supp.2d 1 (D.D.C. 2006) 227

Owens v. Republic of Sudan (Owens II), US, District Court, 412 F.Supp.2d 99 (D.D.C. 2006) 227

Owens v. Republic of Sudan, US, Court of Appeals, 531 F.3d 884 (D.C.Cir. 2008) 227

Palicio y Compania, SA v. Brush, US, District Court, 256 F.Supp. 481 (S.D. N.Y. 1966) 310

cxxxii TABLE OF CASES

Panama (Republic of Panama) v. Air Panama Internacional SA, US, District Court, (S.D.Fla. 1988); 96 ILR 43   316

Parex Bank v. Russian Savings Bank, US, District Court, 81 F.Supp.2d 506 (S.D.N.Y. 2000)   264, 266, 268, 274

Parex Bank v. Russian Savings Bank, US, District Court, 116 F.Supp.2d 415 (S.D.N.Y. 2000)   115, 123, 128, 129

Park v. Shin, US, Court of Appeals, 313 F.3d 1138 (9th Cir. 2002)   77, 192, 434, 435

Paterson, Zochonis (UK) Ltd v. Compania United Arrow, SA, US, District Court, 493 F.Supp. 621 (S.D.N.Y. 1980); 63 ILR 354   334

Patrickson v. Dole Food Company, Inc., US, Court of Appeals, 251 F.3d 795 (9th Cir. 2001)   244, 252, 258, 268, 269, 271, 273, 274

Paul v. Avril, US, District Court, 812 F.Supp. 207 (S.D. Fla. 1993); 103 ILR 553   434

Pena-Perez v. Procuraduria General de Justicia of Nicaragua, US, District Court, No. 96 Civ. 0168, 1997 WL 122823 (S.D.N.Y. 1997)   83

Peninsula Asset Management (Cayman) Ltd v. Hankook Tire Co., Ltd, US, Court of Appeals, 476 F.3d 140 (2nd Cir. 2007)   253, 255, 274

Peninsula Asset Management (Cayman) Ltd v. Hankook Tire Co., Ltd, US, District Court, 2005 WL 3046284 (S.D.N.Y. 2005)   255, 274

People of Puerto Rico v. Shell Co., US, Supreme Court, 302 US 253 (1952)   31

People of Saipan v. United States Department of the Interior, US, Court of Appeals, 502 F.2d 90 (9th Cir. 1974); 61 ILR 113   31, 324

People of Saipan v. United States Department of the Interior, US, District Court, 356 F.Supp. 645 (D.Haw. 1973)   31

Pere v. Nuovo Pignone, Inc., US, Court of Appeals, 150 F.3d 477 (5th Cir. 1998)   46, 115, 273, 320, 324, 328, 333

Perez v. The Bahamas, US, Court of Appeals, 652 F.2d 186 (D.C. Cir 1981); 63 ILR 601   223

Perez v. The Bahamas, US, District Court, 482 F.Supp. 1208 (D.D.C. 1980); 63 ILR 350   223, 341

Permanent Mission of India to the United Nations v. City of New York, US, Supreme Court, 551 US 193; 127 S.Ct. 2352 (2007)   10, 38, 43

Persinger v. Islamic Republic of Iran (No. 2), US, Court of Appeals, 729 F.2d 835 (D.C.Cir. 1984); 90 ILR 586   222, 223

Persinger v. Islamic Republic of Iran, US, Court of Appeals, 72 ILR 132 (D.C. Cir. 1982)   223

Peterson v. Islamic Republic of Iran, US, District Court, 264 F.Supp.2d 46 (D.D.C. 2003)   225, 227

TABLE OF CASES cxxxiii

Peterson v. Islamic Republic of Iran, US, District Court, 515 F.Supp.2d 25 (D.D.C. 2007)   225, 227, 228

Peterson v. Islamic Republic of Iran, US, District Court, 563 F.Supp.2d 268 (D.D.C. 2008)   244

Peterson v. Royal Kingdom of Saudi Arabia, US, Court of Appeals, 416 F.3d 83 (D.C.Cir. 2005)   43, 82, 128, 245, 289, 304, 305, 306

Peterson v. Royal Kingdom of Saudi Arabia, US, District Court, 332 F.Supp.2d 189 (D.D.C. 2004)   82, 128, 245, 289, 304, 305, 306

Petroleos Mexicanos v. Crawford Enterprises, Inc., US, District Court, 643 F.Supp. 370 (S.D.Tex. 1986)   403

Phaneuf v. Republic of Indonesia, US, Court of Appeals, 106 F.3d 302 (9th Cir. 1997)   25, 38, 109, 245, 435

Philippine Export and Foreign Loan Guarantee Corporation v. Chuidian, US, Court of Appeal, Sixth District, California, 218 Cal.App.3d 1058; 267 Cal.Rptr. 457 (1990)   402, 403

Philippines (Republic of the Philippines) v. Marcos (No. 1), US, Court of Appeals, 806 F.2d 344 (2nd Cir. 1986); 81 ILR 581   316, 436

Philippines (Republic of the Philippines) v. Marcos (No. 2), US, Court of Appeals, 818 F.2d 1473 (9th Cir. 1987); reheard en banc, Republic of the Philippines v. Marcos, US, Court of Appeals, 862 F.2d 1355 (9th Cir. 1988); 81 ILR 608   316, 436

Philippines (Republic of the Philippines) v. Marcos, US, District Court, 665 F.Supp. 793 (N.D.Cal. 1987)   434, 435

Philippines (Republic of the Philippines) v. Pimentel, US, Supreme Court, 128 S.Ct. 2180 (2008)   46

Philippines (Republic of the Philippines) v. Westinghouse Electric Corporation, US, Court of Appeals, 43 F.3d 65 (3rd Cir. 1994/95)   316

Phillips Plastics Corporation v. Hatsujou Kabushiki Kaisha, 57 F.3d 1051 (Fed.Cir. (Wis.) 1995)   78

Phoenix Consulting Inc. v. Republic of Angola, US, Court of Appeals, 216 F.3d 36 (D.C.Cir. 2000)   41, 43

Plaintiffs A, B, C, D, E, F v. Jiang Zemin, US, District Court, 282 F.Supp.2d 875 (N.D.Ill. 2003)   341, 429, 434, 435

Poddar v. State Bank of India, US, District Court, 235 F.R.D. 592 (S.D.N.Y. 2006)   123, 128, 245, 274, 324

Polhill v. Islamic Republic of Iran, US, District Court, 2001 U.S.Dist.Lexis 15322 (D.D.C. 2001)   225, 227

Pons v. People's Republic of China, US, District Court, 666 F.Supp.2d 406 (S.D.N.Y. 2009)   128

Porto Rico v. Rosaly y Castillo, US, Supreme Court, 227 US 270 (1913)   31

cxxxiv TABLE OF CASES

Powerex Corporation v. Reliant Energy Services, Inc., US, Supreme Court, 551 US 224; 127 S.Ct. 2411 (2007)   245, 274

Practical Concepts, Inc. v. Republic of Bolivia, US, Court of Appeals, 811 F.2d 1543 (D.C.Cir. 1987); 92 ILR 420   25, 40, 61, 76, 85, 90

Practical Concepts, Inc.. v. Republic of Bolivia, US, District Court, 613 F.Supp. 863 (D.D.C. 1985)   85

Practical Concepts, Inc.. v. Republic of Bolivia, US, District Court, 615 F.Supp. 92 (D.D.C. 1985)   85

Pradhan v. Al-Sabah, US, District Court, 299 F.Supp.2d 493 (D.Md. 2004)   77, 435

Pravin Banker Associates, Ltd v. Banco Popular del Peru, US, District Court, 9 F.Supp.2d 300 (S.D.N.Y. 1998)   245, 289, 292, 293

Premier Steamship Corporation v. Embassy of Algeria, US, District Court, 336 F.Supp. 507 (S.D.N.Y. 1971); 57 ILR 328   325

Prevatt v. Islamic Republic of Iran, US, District Court, 421 F.Supp.2d 152 (D.D.C. 2006)   225, 227

Prevatt v. Islamic Republic of Iran, US, District Court, 567 F.Supp.2d 144 (D.D.C. 2008)   226

Price v. Socialist People's Libyan Arab Jamahiriya, US, Court of Appeals, 294 F.3d 82 (D.C.Cir. 2002)   38, 225, 226, 227

Price v. Socialist People's Libyan Arab Jamahiriya, US, Court of Appeals, 389 F.3d 192 (D.C.Cir. 2004)   225, 227

Price v. Socialist People's Libyan Arab Jamahiriya, US, District Court, 110 F.Supp.2d 10 (D.D.C. 2000)   227

Price v. Socialist People's Libyan Arab Jamahiriya, US, District Court, 274 F.Supp.2d 20 (D.D.C. 2003)   227

Price v. Socialist People's Libyan Arab Jamahiriya, US, District Court, 384 F.Supp.2d 120 (D.D.C. 2005)   227

Princz v. Federal Republic of Germany, US, District Court, 813 F.Supp. 22 (D.D.C. 1992); reversed, Princz v. Federal Republic of Germany, US, Court of Appeals, 26 F.3d 1166 (D.C.Cir. 1994); 103 ILR 594   41, 125, 126, 127, 324, 325, 333, 341, 429

Procter & Gamble Cellulose Co. v. Viskoza-Loznica, US, District Court, 33 F.Supp.2d 644 (W.D.Tenn. 1998)   258, 274

Proyecfin de Venezuela, SA v. Banco Industrial de Venezuela, SA, US, Court of Appeals, 760 F.2d 390 (2nd Cir. 1985); 87 ILR 538   322

Psinakis v. Marcos, US, District Court, Civil Action No. C-75-1725-RHS, 81 ILR 605 (N.D.Cal. 1975)   434

Pugh v. Socialist People's Libyan Arab Jamahiriya, US, District Court, 530 F.Supp.2d 216 (D.D.C. 2008)   225, 227, 228

TABLE OF CASES CXXXV

Pulaski v. Republic of India, US, District Court, 212 F.Supp.2d 653 (S.D. Tex. 2002) 10, 206

Pullman Construction Industries, Inc. v. United States, US, Court of Appeals, 23 F.3d 1166 (7th Cir. 1994) 46

Raccoon Recovery, LLC v. Navoi Mining and Metallurgical Kombinat, US, District Court, 244 F.Supp.2d 1130 (D.Colo. 2002) 109, 244, 245, 320, 324

Randolph v. Budget Rent-A-Car, US, Court of Appeals, 97 F.3d 319 (9th Cir. 1996) 41, 111, 225, 244, 245

Randolph v. Budget Rent-A-Car, US, District Court, 878 F.Supp. 162 (C.D. Cal. 1995) 111, 225, 245

Ratnaswamy v. Air Afrique, US, District Court, No. 95-CV-7670, 1996 WL 507267 (N.D.Ill. 1996) 223, 262

Reading & Bates Corporation v. National Iranian Oil Company, US, District Court, 478 F.Supp. 724 (S.D.N.Y. 1979); 63 ILR 305 323, 388, 389

Reed International Trading Corporation v. Donau Bank AG, US, District Court, 866 F.Supp. 750 (S.D.N.Y. 1994) 123, 128, 245

Reed v. Islamic Republic of Iran, US, District Court, 242 F.R.D. 125 (D.D.C. 2007) 225

Reed v. Islamic Republic of Iran, US, District Court, 439 F.Supp.2d 53 (D. D.C. 2006) 225

Reers v. Deutsche Bahn AG, US, District Court, 320 F.Supp.2d 140 (S.D. N.Y. 2004) 127, 245, 271, 320

Regier v. Islamic Republic of Iran, US, District Court, 281 F.Supp.2d 87 (D. D.C. 2003) 225, 227, 248, 274

Reichler, Milton & Medel v. Republic of Liberia, US, District Court, 484 F.Supp.2d 1 (D.D.C. 2007) 76, 123

Rein v. Socialist People's Libyan Arab Jamahiriya, US, Court of Appeals, 162 F.3d 748 (2nd Cir. 1998) 227

Rein v. Socialist People's Libyan Arab Jamahiriya, US, District Court, 995 F.Supp. 325 (E.D.N.Y. 1998) 227

Reiss v. Société Centrale du Groupe des Assurances Nationales, US, Court of Appeals, 235 F.3d 738 (2nd Cir. 2000) 43, 78, 110

Renchard v. Humphreys and Harding, Inc. (2), US, District Court, 381 F.Supp. 382 (D.D.C. 1974); 63 ILR 33 16

Rendall-Speranza v. Nassim, US, Court of Appeals, 107 F.3d 913 (D.C.Cir. 1997) 204

Rendall-Speranza v. Nassim, US, District Court, 932 F.Supp. 19 (D.D.C. 1996) 204

cxxxvi TABLE OF CASES

Rendall-Speranza v. Nassim, US, District Court, 942 F.Supp. 621 (D.D.C. 1996   204

Republic of China v. American Express Co., US, Court of Appeals, 195 F.2d 230 (2nd Cir. 1952); 19 ILR 192   335

Resource Dynamics International, Ltd v. General People's Committee for Communications and Maritime Transport in the Socialist People's Libyan Arab Jamahiriya, US, District Court, 593 F.Supp. 572 (N.D.Ga. 1984)   328

Rex v. Compania Pervana de Vapores, SA, US, Court of Appeals, 660 F.2d 61 (3rd Cir. 1981); 72 ILR 93   38, 42, 274

Rex v. Compania Pervana De Vapores, SA, US, District Court, 493 F.Supp. 459 (E.D.Pa. 1980); 63 ILR 435   274

Rich v. Naviera Vacuba SA, US, District Court, 197 F.Supp.710 (E.D.Va. 1961); affirmed, Court of Appeals, 295 F.2d 24 (4th Cir. 1961); 32 ILR 127   356

Richards v. United States, US, Supreme Court 369 US 1 (1962)   31

Richmark Corporation v. Timber Falling Consultants, Inc., US, District Court, 747 F.Supp. 1409 (D.Or. 1990)   247

Richmark Corporation v. Timber Falling Consultants, US, Court of Appeals, 959 F.2d 1468 (9th Cir. 1992)   403

Rimkus v. Islamic Republic of Iran, US, District Court, 575 F.Supp.2d 181 (D.D.C. 2008)   225, 227

Rimsat, Ltd v. Hilliard, US, District Court, 207 B.R. 964 (D.D.C. 1997)   242

Rio Grande (In the Matter of the Complaint of Rio Grande Transport Inc.), US, District Court, 516 F.Supp. 1155 (S.D.N.Y. 1981); 63 ILR 604   245, 329

Rios v. Marshall, US, District Court, 530 F.Supp. 351 (S.D.N.Y. 1981)   232, 258, 260, 435

Risk v. Halvorsen, US, Court of Appeals, 936 F.2d 393 (9th Cir. 1991); 98 ILR 125   25, 204

Risk v. Kingdom of Norway, US, District Court, 707 F.Supp. 1159 (N.D.Cal. 1989)   204, 244

Robert Bosch Corporation v. Air France, US, District Court, 712 F.Supp. 688 (N.D.Ill. 1989)   77, 109, 245

Robinson v. Government of Malaysia, US, Court of Appeals, 269 F.3d 133 (2nd Cir. 2001)   41, 43, 224

Rodriguez v. Republic of Costa Rica, US, District Court, 934 F.Supp. 493 (D. Puerto Rico 1996)   83, 304, 311

Rodriguez v. Transnave, Inc., US, Court of Appeals, 8 F.3d 284 (5th Cir. 1993)   324, 325, 329, 330, 333

Rodriguez v. Transnave, Inc., US, District Court, 810 F.Supp. 194 (S.D.Tex. 1993)   325, 329, 330

Roeder v. Islamic Republic of Iran, US, Court of Appeals, 333 F.3d 228 (D.C. Cir. 2003)   225, 248

Roeder v. Islamic Republic of Iran, US, District Court, 195 F.Supp.2d 140 (D.D.C. 2002)   225, 227

Romania (Kingdom of Romania) v. Guaranty Trust Co. of New York, US, Court of Appeals, 250 F. 341 (2nd Cir. 1918)   77

Rosner v. Bank of China, US, District Court, 528 F.Supp.2d 419 (S.D.N.Y. 2007)   79

RSM Production Corporation v. Fridman, US, District Court, 643 F.Supp.2d 382 (S.D.N.Y. 2009)   434

RSM Production Corporation v. Petroleos de Venezuela Societa Anonima (PDVSA), US, District Court, 338 F.Supp.2d 1208 (D.Colo. 2004)   128, 257, 258

Rubin v. Islamic Republic of Iran, US, District Court, 281 F.Supp.2d 258 (D.D.C. 2003)   228

Rubin v. Islamic Republic of Iran, US, District Court, 349 F.Supp.2d 1108 (N.D.Ill. 2004)   228

Rubin v. Islamic Republic of Iran, US, District Court, 408 F.Supp.2d 549 (N.D.Ill. 2005)   228

Rubin v. Islamic Republic of Iran, US, District Court, 456 F.Supp.2d 228 (D.Mass. 2006)   109, 226, 228, 418

Ruggiero v. Compania Peruana de Vapores Inc.a Capac Yupanqui, US, Court of Appeals, 639 F.2d 872 (2nd Cir. 1981); 63 ILR 540   42, 46, 274

Rush v. Savchuk, US, Supreme Court, 444 US 320 (1980)   387, 403

Rush-Presbyterian-St. Luke's Medical Center v. Hellenic Republic, US, Court of Appeals, 877 F.2d 574 (7th Cir. 1989); 101 ILR 509   25, 62, 76, 78, 88, 90, 93, 94, 109, 110, 126, 129

Rush-Presbyterian-St. Luke's Medical Center v. Hellenic Republic, US, District Court, 690 F.Supp. 682 (N.D.Ill, 1988)   78

Rutkowski v. Occidental Chemical Corporation, US, District Court, No. 83 C 2339, 1988 WL 107342 (N.D.Ill. 1988)   268

Rux v. Republic of Sudan, US, Court of Appeals, 461 F.3d 461 (4th Cir. 2006)   227

Rux v. Republic of Sudan, US, Court of Appeals, No. 07-1835 (4th Cir. 2009)   226

Rux v. Republic of Sudan, US, District Court, 495 F.Supp.2d 541 (E.D.Va. 2007)   227, 228

cxxxviii TABLE OF CASES

Rux v. Republic of Sudan, US, District Court, 672 F.Supp.2d 726 (E.D.Va. 2009)   226

Rux v. Republic of Sudan, US, District Court, 2005 WL 2086202 (E.D.Va. 2005)   227

S & Davis International, Inc. v. Republic of Yemen, US, Court of Appeals, 218 F.3d 1292 (11th Cir. 2000)   25, 38, 43, 76, 277, 287, 290, 324, 326, 327

S & S Machinery Co. v. Masinexportimport and Romanian Bank for Foreign Trade, US, Court of Appeals, 706 F.2d 411 (2nd Cir. 1983); 72 ILR 183   244, 245, 318, 319, 323, 387, 388, 389, 390

S & S Machinery Co. v. Masinexportimport, US, District Court, 802 F. Supp. 1109 (S.D.N.Y. 1992); 107 ILR 239   90, 244, 245, 406, 407

Sabbithi v. KH N.S. Al Saleh, US, District Court, 605 F.Supp.2d 122 (D.D.C. 2009)   191

Sablan Construction Company v. Government of the Trust Territory of the Pacific Islands, US, District Court, Northern Mariana Islands, Appellate Division, 526 F.Supp. 135 (1981); 87 ILR 546   31

Salazar v. Islamic Republic of Iran, US, District Court, 370 F.Supp.2d 105 (D.D.C. 2005)   225, 227

Saltany v. Reagan, US, Court of Appeals, 886 F.2d 438 (D.C.Cir. 1989); 87 ILR 679   16, 31, 434, 435

Saltany v. Reagan, US, District Court, 702 F.Supp. 319 (D.D.C. 1988); 80 ILR 19   16, 31, 434, 435

Saludes v. Republica de Cuba, US, District Court, 577 F.Supp.2d 1243 (S.D. Fla. 2008)   227

Saludes v. Republica de Cuba, US, District Court, 655 F.Supp.2d 1290 (S.D. Fla. 2009)   226, 227

Samantar v. Yousuf, US, Supreme Court, 130 S.Ct. 2278 (2010)   42, 43, 435

Samco Global Arms, Inc. v. Arita, US, Court of Appeals, 395 F.3d 1212 (11th Cir. 2005)   76, 77, 126, 128

Sampson v. Federal Republic of Germany, US, Court of Appeals, 250 F.3d 1145 (7th Cir. 2001)   46, 83, 306, 324, 325, 332, 333, 341, 429

Sampson v. Federal Republic of Germany, US, District Court, 975 F.Supp. 1108 (N.D.Ill. 1997)   83, 223, 306, 325, 341

Sanchez-Espinoza v. Reagan, US, Court of Appeals, 770 F.2d 202 (D.C.Cir. 1985); 80 ILR 586   31, 435

Santos v. Compagnie Nationale Air France, US, Court of Appeals, 934 F.2d 890 (7th Cir. 1991); 98 ILR 131   110, 112, 114, 245

TABLE OF CASES cxxxix

Saudi Arabia v. Nelson, US, Supreme Court, 507 US 349 (1993); 123 L.Ed.2d 47 (1993); 100 ILR 544   25, 38, 43, 62, 81, 88, 89, 90, 95, 109, 110, 111, 112, 115, 161, 168, 201, 244, 245, 439

Saudi Basic Industries Corporation v. Exxonmobil Corporation, US, District Court, 194 F.Supp.2d 378 (D.N.J. 2002)   124, 127, 129, 245, 266, 319, 324, 329, 334

Saunders Real Estate Corp. v. Consulate General of Greece, 1995 U.S.Dist. Lexis 14893 (D.Mass. 1995)   77

Scarborough v. Principi, US, Supreme Court 541 US 401 (2004)   31

Schmidt v. Polish People's Republic, US, Court of Appeals, 742 F.2d 67 (2nd Cir. 1984)   24

Schmidt v. Polish People's Republic, US, District Court, 579 F.Supp. 23 (S.D. N.Y. 1984)   24, 114

Schoenberg v. Exportadora de Sal, SA de CV, US, Court of Appeals, 930 F.2d 777 (9th Cir. 1991); 98 ILR 118   78, 90, 243, 245

Sea Transport Contractors, Ltd v. Industries Chemiques du Sénégal, US, District Court, 411 F.Supp.2d 386 (S.D.N.Y. 2006)   262, 263, 268, 387

Sea Transport Corporation v. The S/T Manhattan, US, District Court, 405 F.Supp. 1244 (S.D.N.Y. 1975); 63 ILR 49   16

Sealift Bulkers, Inc. v. Republic of Armenia, US, District Court, 965 F.Supp. 81 (D.D.C. 1997)   76

Security Pacific National Bank v. Derderian, US, Court of Appeals, 872 F.2d 281 (9th Cir. 1989)   38, 125, 126, 223, 311

Security Pacific National Bank v. Government and State of Iran, US, District Court, 513 F.Supp. 864 (C.D.Cal. 1981)   318, 323, 389

Seetransport Wiking Trader Schiffahrtsgesellschaft MBH & Co., Kommanditgesellschaft v. Navimpex Centrala Navala, US, Court of Appeals, 989 F.2d 572 (2nd Cir. 1993); 103 ILR 559   324, 325, 326

Seetransport Wiking Trader Schiffarhtsgesellschaft MBH & Co., Kommanditgesellschaft v. Navimpex Centrala Navala, US, District Court, 793 F.Supp. 444 (S.D.N.Y. 1992)   326

Segni v. Commercial Office of Spain, US, Court of Appeals, 835 F.2d 160 (7th Cir. 1987); 98 ILR 55   46, 61, 76, 87, 88, 90, 135, 158, 160, 162, 168

Segni v. Commercial Office of Spain, US, District Court, 650 F.Supp. 1042 (N.D.Ill. 1986)   76, 135, 162

Segni v. Commercial Office of Spain, US, District Court, 650 F.Supp. 1040 (N.D.Ill. 1986)   247, 274

Seisay v. Air France, US, District Court, 1997 WL 431084 (S.D.N.Y. 1997) 112, 245

cxl TABLE OF CASES

Seramur v. Saudi Arabian Airlines, US, District Court, 934 F.Supp. 48 (E.D. N.Y. 1996) 245, 274

Servaas Inc. v. Republic of Iraq, US, District Court, 686 F.Supp.2d 346 (S.D. N.Y. 2010) 76

Sesostris, SAE v. Transportes Navales, SA, US, District Court, 727 F.Supp. 737 (D.Mass. 1989) 403

Shaffer v. Heitner, US, Supreme Court, 433 US 186 (1977) 364, 387

Shakour v. Federal Republic of Germany, US, District Court, 199 F.Supp.2d 8 (E.D.N.Y. 2002) 83

Shapiro v. Republic of Bolivia, US, Court of Appeals, 930 F.2d 1013 (2nd Cir. 1991); 98 ILR 109 25, 77, 109, 110, 113, 125, 324, 333, 335

Sherer v. Construcciones Aeronauticas, SA, US, Court of Appeals, 987 F.2d 1246 (6th Cir. 1993) 274

Shih v. Taipei Economic and Cultural Representative Office, US, District Court, 693 F.Supp.2d 805 (N.D.Ill. 2010) 169, 196

Shirobokova v. CSA Czech Airlines, Inc., US, District Court, 335 F.Supp.2d 989 (D.Minn. 2004) 256, 274

Siderman de Blake v. Republic of Argentina, US, Court of Appeals, 965 F.2d 699 (9th Cir. 1992); 103 ILR 454 25, 35, 38, 44, 78, 83, 92, 110, 112, 115, 123, 124, 125, 126, 128, 223, 258, 304, 305, 307, 309, 310, 311, 324, 330, 331, 332, 333, 341, 429

Simon v. Republic of Iraq, US, Court of Appeals, 529 F.3d 1187 (D.C.Cir. 2008) 226

Simpson v. Socialist People's Libyan Arab Jamahiriya, US, Court of Appeals, 326 F.3d 230 (D.C.Cir. 2003) 227

Simpson v. Socialist People's Libyan Arab Jamahiriya, US, Court of Appeals, 470 F.3d 356 (D.C.Cir. 2006) 227

Simpson v. Socialist People's Libyan Arab Jamahiriya, US, District Court, 180 F.Supp.2d 78 (D.D.C. 2001) 227

Simpson v. Socialist People's Libyan Arab Jamahiriya, US, District Court, 362 F.Supp.2d 168 (D.D.C. 2005) 225, 227

Singh v. Commonwealth of Australia, US, District Court, 521 F.Supp.2d 91 (D.D.C. 2007) 25, 227

Sisso v. Islamic Republic of Iran, US, District Court, 448 F.Supp.2d 76 (D.D.C. 2006) 227

SK Products Corporation Case, US, National Labor Relations Board, 230 NLRB 1211 (1977); 63 ILR 647 137, 162

Skeen v. Federative Republic of Brazil, US, District Court, 566 F.Supp. 1414 (D.D.C. 1983); 121 ILR 481 225

TABLE OF CASES cxli

Slade v. United States of Mexico, US, Court of Appeals, 790 F.2d 163 (1986) (Table)   24

Slade v. United States of Mexico, US, District Court, 617 F.Supp. 351 (D. D.C. 1985)   24, 42

Smith v. Federal Reserve Bank of New York, US, Court of Appeals, 346 F.3d 264 (2nd Cir. 2003)   293

Smith v. Federal Reserve Bank of New York, US, District Court, 280 F.Supp.2d 314 (S.D.N.Y. 2003)   228, 293

Smith v. Islamic Emirate of Afghanistan, US, District Court, 262 F.Supp.2d 217 (S.D.N.Y. 2003)   25, 227, 228

Smith v. Libya (Socialist People's Libyan Arab Jamahiriya), US, Court of Appeals, 101 F.3d 239 (2nd Cir. 1996); 113 ILR 534   25, 223, 320, 324, 325, 330, 333, 341, 429

Smith v. Libya (Socialist People's Libyan Arab Jamahiriya), US, District Court, 886 F.Supp. 306 (E.D.N.Y. 1995); 107 ILR 382   223, 341, 429

Société Nationale des Chemins de Fer Français v. Abrams, US, Supreme Court, 124 S.Ct. 2834 (2004); 542 US 901 (2004)   245

Sokolow v. PLO (Palestine Liberation Organization), US, District Court, 583 F.Supp.2d 451 (S.D.N.Y. 2008)   31

Sosa v. Alvarez-Machain, US, Supreme Court, 542 US 692 (2004); 159 L.Ed.2d 718 (2004); 127 ILR 691   31

Sotheby's, Inc. v. Garcia, US, District Court, 802 F.Supp. 1058 (S.D.N.Y. 1992)   330

Soudavar v. Islamic Republic of Iran, US, Court of Appeals, 186 F.3d 671 (5th Cir. 1999)   108, 111, 113, 127

Southeastern Leasing Corporation v. Stern Dragger Belogorsk, US, Court of Appeals, 493 F.2d 1223 (1st Cir. 1974); 63 ILR 39   16

Southern Seafood Co. v. Holt Cargo Systems, Inc., US, District Court, 1997 WL 539763 (E.D.Pa. 1997)   268

Southway v. Central Bank of Nigeria, US, Court of Appeals, 198 F.3d 1210 (10th Cir. 1999)   79, 201

Southway v. Central Bank of Nigeria, US, Court of Appeals, 328 F.3d 1267 (10th Cir. 2003)   38, 43, 79

Southway v. Central Bank of Nigeria, US, District Court, 149 F.Supp.2d 1268 (D.Colo. 2001)   79

Southway v. Central Bank of Nigeria, US, District Court, 994 F.Supp. 1299 (D.Colo. 1998)   79, 201

Space Systems (In the Matter of the Arbitration between Space Systems/ Loral, Inc. v. Yuzhnoye Design Office), US, District Court, 164 F.Supp.2d 397 (S.D.N.Y. 2001)   245

cxlii   TABLE OF CASES

Spacil v. Crowe, US, Court of Appeals, 489 F.2d 614 (5th Cir. 1974); 63
ILR 24   16

Sperry International Trade, Inc. v. Government of Israel, US, District
Court, 532 F.Supp. 901 (S.D.N.Y. 1982)   388

Starrett v. Iberia Airlines of Spain, US, District Court, 756 F.Supp. 292
(S.D.Tex. 1989)   169, 245

State Bank of India Case, US, National Labor Relations Board, 229 NLRB
838 (1977); 63 ILR 81   137, 162

State Bank of India Case, US, National Labor Relations Board, 273 NLRB
264 (1984) and 273 NLRB 267 (1984)   162

State Bank of India v. NLRB (National Labor Relations Board), US, Court of
Appeals, 808 F.2d 526 (7th Cir. 1986)   162, 268

State *ex rel*. National Institute of Agrarian Reform v. Dekle, US, District
Court of Appeal of Florida, Third District, 137 So.2d 581 (Fla. 1962); 33
ILR 181   353

Stena Rederi AB v. Comision de Contratos del Comite Ejecutivo General
del Sindicato Revolucionario de Trabajadores Petroleros de la
Republica Mexicana, SC, US, Court of Appeals, 923 F.2d 380 (5th Cir.
1991); 103 ILR 433   41, 78, 90, 108, 109, 111, 113, 115, 123, 125, 127,
128, 245, 364, 388

Stephen v. Zivnostenska Banka, US, Supreme Court of New
York, Appellate Division, First Department, 222 N.Y.S.2d 128 (1961)
387

Stephens v. National Distillers & Chemical Corporation, US, Court of
Appeals, 69 F.3d 1226 (2nd Cir. 1995)   388, 389, 390

Stephens v. National Distillers & Chemical Corporation, US, District
Court, 1993 WL 228851 (S.D.N.Y. 1993)   390

Stern v. Islamic Republic of Iran, US, District Court, 271 F.Supp.2d 286 (D.
D.C. 2003)   225, 227, 228

Stethem v. Islamic Republic of Iran, US, District Court, 201 F.Supp.2d 78
(D.D.C. 2002)   225, 227

Stethem v. Islamic Republic of Iran, US, District Court, 568 F.Supp.2d 1
(D.D.C. 2008)   226

Storr v. National Defense Security Council of the Republic of Indonesia,
US, District Court, 1997 WL 633405 (S.D.N.Y. 1997)   109

Strach v. Casino Windsor, US, District Court, 351 F.Supp.2d 641 (E.D.
Mich. 2004)   125, 127

Straub v. AP Green, Inc., US, Court of Appeals, 38 F.3d 448 (9th Cir. 1994);
107 ILR 359   268, 273, 274

TABLE OF CASES   cxliii

Street v. Quebec Provincial Agency for the Indemnification of Victims of Criminal Acts, US, Court of Appeals, 1992 U.S. App. LEXIS 5591 (1st Cir. 1992)   223

Sudano v. Federal Airports Corporation, US, District Court, 699 F.Supp. 824 (D.Haw. 1988)   123, 125, 126, 127, 245

Sugarman v. Aeromexico, Inc., US, Court of Appeals, 626 F.2d 270 (3rd Cir. 1980); 63 ILR 446   109, 127, 245, 247

Sugimoto v. Exportadora de Sal, SA de CV, US, Court of Appeals, 19 F.3d 1309 (9th Cir. 1994)   112, 113

Sun v. Taipei Economic and Cultural Representative Office, US, Court of Appeals, 34 Fed.Appx. 529 (9th Cir. 2002)   112

Sun v. Taiwan, US, Court of Appeals, 201 F.3d 1105 (9th Cir. 2000)   43, 84, 90, 91, 112, 113

Supra Medical Corporation v. McGonigle, US, District Court, 955 F.Supp. 374 (E.D.Pa. 1997)   78, 89, 109, 115, 123, 249, 253, 254, 435

Surette v. Islamic Republic of Iran, US, District Court, 231 F.Supp.2d 260 (D.D.C. 2002)   225, 227

Sutherland v. Islamic Republic of Iran, US, District Court, 151 F.Supp.2d 27 (D.D.C. 2001)   225, 227, 228

Swarna v. Al-Awadi, US, District Court, 607 F.Supp.2d 509 (S.D.N.Y. 2009)   192, 204

Tabion v. Mufti, US, Court of Appeals, 73 F.3d 535 (4th Cir. 1996); 107 ILR 452   191

Tabion v. Mufti, US, District Court, 877 F.Supp. 285 (E.D.Va. 1995)   191

Tachiona v. Mugabe, US, District Court, 169 F.Supp.2d 259 (S.D.N.Y. 2001)   227, 434, 435

Tachiona v. Mugabe, US, District Court, 186 F.Supp.2d 383 (S.D.N.Y. 2002)   434

Tachiona v. Mugabe, US, District Court, 216 F.Supp.2d 262 (S.D.N.Y. 2002)   434

Tachiona v. Mugabe, US, District Court, 234 F.Supp.2d 401 (S.D.N.Y. 2002)   434

Tachiona v. United States, US, Court of Appeals, 386 F.3d 205 (2nd Cir. 2004)   434

Talbot v. Saipem AG, US, District Court, 835 F.Supp. 352 (S.D.Tex. 1993) 268, 274, 330

Tannenbaum v. Rabin, US, District Court, 1996 WL 75283 (E.D.N.Y. 1996)   435

Taylor v. Standard Gas Co., US, Supreme Court, 306 US 307 (1939)   288

cxliv TABLE OF CASES

Telcordia Tech Inc. v. Telkom SA Ltd, US, Court of Appeals, 458 F.3d 172 (3rd Cir. 2006)   245, 273

Teledyne, Inc. v. Kone Corporation, US, Court of Appeals, 892 F.2d 1404 (9th Cir. 1989)   109

Tel-Oren v. Libyan Arab Republic, US, District Court, 517 F.Supp. 542 (D. D.C. 1981); affirmed, Tel-Oren v. Libyan Arab Republic, US, Court of Appeals, 726 F.2d 774 (D.C.Cir. 1984); 77 ILR 192   31, 223

Temengil v. Trust Territory of the Pacific Islands, US, Court of Appeal, 881 F.2d 647 (9th Cir. 1989); 96 ILR 32   31

Tennessee Gas Pipeline Co. v. Continental Casualty Co., US, District Court, 814 F.Supp. 1302 (M.D.La. 1993)   245

Tennessee Student Assistance Corp. v. Hood, US, Supreme Court, 541 US 440 (2004)   31

Tennessee v. Lane, US, Supreme Court, 541 US 509 (2004)   31

TermoRio SA ESP v. Electranta SP, US, Court of Appeals, 487 F.3d 928 (D.C. Cir. 2007)   245, 327

TermoRio SA ESP v. Electrificadora del Atlantico SA ESP, US, District Court, 421 F.Supp.2d 87 (D.D.C. 2006)   112, 128, 245, 327

Texas Trading & Milling Corporation v. Federal Republic of Nigeria, US, Court of Appeals, 647 F.2d 300 (2nd Cir. 1981); 63 ILR 552   25, 53, 55, 61, 76, 77, 90, 110, 111, 114, 125, 127, 128

Texas Trading & Milling Corporation v. Federal Republic of Nigeria, US, District Court, 500 F.Supp. 320 (S.D.N.Y. 1980); 63 ILR 459   125

The Navemar, US, District Court, 18 F.Supp. 153 (E.D.N.Y. 1937); Court of Appeals, 90 F. 673 (2nd Cir. 1937); Supreme Court, 303 US 68 (1938); District Court, 24 F.Supp. 495 (E.D.N.Y. 1938); Court of Appeals; 102 F. 444 (2nd Cir. 1939); 9 AD 176   9, 16, 299

The Nereide, US, Supreme Court, 13 US (9 Cranch) 388 (1815)   35

The Paquete Habana, US, Supreme Court, 175 US 677 (1900)   35

The Pesaro (Berizzi Bros Co. v. The Pesaro), US, Supreme Court, 271 US 562 (1926); 3 AD 186   9, 10

The Schooner Exchange v. McFaddon, US, Supreme Court, 11 US (7 Cranch) 116 (1812)   8, 35, 44, 60, 65, 68

Theo H Davies & Co., Ltd v. Republic of the Marshall Islands, US, Court of Appeals, 161 F.3d 550 (9th Cir. 1998)   78

Theo H Davies & Co., Ltd v. Republic of the Marshall Islands, US, Court of Appeals, 174 F.3d 969 (9th Cir. 1998)   78, 113

Thompson v. United States, US, Court of Appeals, 592 F.2d 1104 (9th Cir. 1979)   206

TABLE OF CASES cxlv

Tifa Ltd v. Republic of Ghana, US, District Court, 692 F.Supp. 393 (D.N.J. 1988) 78, 90, 109, 123, 127, 201, 245

TMR Energy Ltd v. State Property Fund of Ukraine, US, Court of Appeals, 411 F.3d 296 (D.C.Cir. 2005) 248, 327

Tolliver v. Federal Republic of Nigeria, US, District Court, 265 F.Supp.2d 873 (W.D.Mich. 2003) 79, 90, 109

Tonoga, Ltd v. Ministry of Public Works and Housing of Kingdom of Saudi Arabia, US, District Court, 135 F.Supp.2d 350 (N.D.N.Y. 2001) 78, 110, 111

Tote v. Iberia International Airlines, US, District Court, 649 F.Supp. 41 (E.D. Pa. 1986) 42, 109, 112, 245

Tracy v. Islamic Republic of Iran, US, District Court, Civ. No. 01-2517, slip op. (D.D.C. 2003) 225, 227, 248

Trajano v. Marcos (In re Estate of Ferdinand E. Marcos Human Rights Litigation (Trajano v. Marcos)), US, Court of Appeals, 978 F.2d 493 (9th Cir. 1992); 103 ILR 521 322, 435, 436

Trajano v. Marcos, US, Court of Appeals, 878 F.2d 1439 (9th Cir. 1989) (Table) 436

Trans Chemical (In the Matter of the Arbitration between Trans Chemical Ltd and China National Machinery Import and Export Corporation), US, District Court, 978 F.Supp. 266 (S.D.Tex. 1997) 247, 273, 290, 324, 325, 327

Trans Chemical Ltd v. China National Machinery Import and Export Corporation, US, Court of Appeals, 161 F.3d 314 (5th Cir. 1998) 247, 273, 324, 325, 327

Transaero, Inc. v. La Fuerza Aerea Boliviana, US, Court of Appeals, 30 F.3d 148 (D.C.Cir. 1994); 107 ILR 308 247, 248, 249, 274

Transamerica Leasing, Inc. v. Republica de Venezuela, US, Court of Appeals, 200 F.3d 843 (D.C.Cir. 2000) 109, 289, 292, 293

Transamerica Leasing, Inc. v. Republica de Venezuela, US, District Court, 21 F.Supp.2d 47 (D.D.C. 1998) 289, 292

Transamerican Steamship Corporation v. Somali Democratic Republic and Somali Shipping Agency, US, District Court, 590 F.Supp. 968 (D. D.C. 1984); affirmed in part and reversed in part, and remanded, Transamerican Steamship Corporation v. Somali Democratic Republic and Somali Shipping Agency, US, Court of Appeals, 767 F.2d 998 (D.C. Cir. 1985); 86 ILR 55 25, 125

Transatlantic Shiffahrtskontor GmbH v. Shanghai Foreign Trade Corporation, US, Court of Appeals, 204 F.3d 384 (2nd Cir. 2000) 38, 109, 324, 327

cxlvi   TABLE OF CASES

Transatlantic Shiffahrtskontor GmbH v. Shanghai Foreign Trade
  Corporation, US, District Court, 1998 WL 799671 (S.D.N.Y. 1998)   327
Trans-Orient Marine Corporation v. Star Trading & Marine, Inc., US,
  District Court, 736 F.Supp. 1281 (S.D.N.Y. 1990)   78
Travel Associates Inc. v. Kingdom of Swaziland, US, District Court, 107
  ILR 219 (D.D.C. 1990)   25, 201, 204, 319
Trump Taj Mahal Associates v. Costruzioni Aeronautiche Giovanni
  Agusta, SpA, US, Court of Appeals, 958 F.2d 365 (3rd Cir. 1992) (Table)
  268, 274
Trump Taj Mahal Associates v. Costruzioni Aeronautiche Giovanni
  Agusta, SpA, US, District Court, 761 F.Supp. 1143 (D.N.J. 1991)   268,
  274
Tubular Inspectors, Inc. v. Petroleos Mexicanos, US, Court of Appeals, 977
  F.2d 180 (5th Cir. 1992)   108, 109, 251
Tucker v. Whitaker Travel, Ltd, US, Court of Appeals, 800 F.2d 1140 (3rd
  Cir. 1986) (Table)   114, 127
Tucker v. Whitaker Travel, Ltd, US, District Court, 620 F.Supp. 578 (E.D.
  Pa. 1985)   114, 127, 223
Turkmani v. Republic of Bolivia, US, District Court, 193 F.Supp.2d 165 (D.
  D.C. 2002)   77, 113
Turner v. Islamic Republic of Iran, US, District Court, 2002 U.S.Dist.Lexis
  26730 (D.D.C. 2002)   227
Ulen & Co. v. Bank Gospodarstwa Krajowego (National Economic Bank),
  US, Supreme Court of New York, Appellate Division, Second
  Department, 24 N.Y.S.2d 201 (1940); 9 AD 213   46
UNC Lear Services, Inc. v. Kingdom of Saudi Arabia, US, Court of Appeals,
  581 F.3d 210 (5th Cir. 2009)   25, 43, 193
Underhill v. Hernandez, US, Supreme Court, 168 US 250 (1897)   299
Ungar (Estates of Ungar) v. Palestinian Authority, US, District Court, 153
  F.Supp.2d 76 (D.R.I. 2001)   31
Ungar (Estates of Ungar) v. Palestinian Authority, US District Court, 304
  F.Supp.2d 232 (D.R.I. 2004)   293
Ungar (Estates of Ungar) v. Palestinian Authority, US, District Court, 315
  F.Supp.2d 164 (D.R.I. 2004)   31, 35, 44, 329
Ungar (Estates of Ungar) v. Palestinian Authority, US, District Court, 325
  F.Supp.2d 15 (D.R.I. 2004)   31, 319, 320, 333
Ungar (Estates of Ungar) v. Palestinian Authority, US, District Court, 613
  F.Supp.2d 219 (D.R.I. 2009)   31
Ungar v. Islamic Republic of Iran, US, District Court, 211 F.Supp.2d 91
  (D.D.C. 2002)   225, 227

TABLE OF CASES   cxlvii

Ungar v. PLO (Palestine Liberation Organization), US, Court of Appeals, 402 F.3d 274 (1st Cir. 2005)   31

Unidyne Corporation v. Aerolineas Argentinas, US, District court, 590 F.Supp. 398 (E.D.Va. 1984)   247

United Euram Corporation v. Union of Soviet Socialist Republics, US, District Court, 461 F.Supp. 609 (S.D.N.Y. 1978); 63 ILR 228   201

United World Trade, Inc. v. Mangyshlakneft Oil Production Association, US, Court of Appeals, 33 F.3d 1232 (10th Cir. 1994)   125, 126, 127, 128, 129

United World Trade, Inc. v. Mangyshlakneft Oil Production Association, US, District Court, 821 F.Supp. 1405 (D.Colo. 1993)   126, 127, 129

Upton v. Empire of Iran, US, District Court, 459 F.Supp. 264 (D.D.C. 1978); 63 ILR 211   125, 127

URS Corporation v. Lebanese Company for the Development and Reconstruction of Beirut Central District SAL, US, District Court, 512 F.Supp.2d 199 (D.Del. 2007)   257

US Fidelity (United States Fidelity & Guaranty Co.) v. Braspetro Oil Services Co., US, Court of Appeals, 199 F.3d 94 (2nd Cir. 1999)   77, 78, 113, 115, 124, 125, 128, 129, 250

US Fidelity (United States Fidelity and Guaranty Co.) v. Braspetro Oil Services Co., US, District Court, 219 F.Supp.2d 403 (S.D.N.Y. 2002)   243, 245, 250, 293

US Fidelity (United States Fidelity & Guaranty Co.) v. Braspetro Oil Services Co., US, District Court, 1999 U.S.Dist.Lexis 7236 (S.D.N.Y. 1999)   77, 78, 113, 128, 129, 293

US Fidelity (United States Fidelity & Guaranty Co.) v. Braspetro Oil Services Co., US, District Court, No. 97 CIV. 6124 (JGK), 1999 WL 307666 (S.D.N.Y. 1999)   250, 253, 268, 293

US Fidelity (United States Fidelity & Guaranty Co.) v. Braspetro Oil, US, District Court, 379 F.Supp.2d 487 (S.D.N.Y. 2005)   77

US Fidelity (United States Fidelity & Guaranty Co.) v. Petroleo Brasileiro SA, US, District Court, 1999 U.S.Dist.Lexis 7235 (S.D.N.Y. 1999)   77, 115, 128

US Titan, Inc. v. Guangzhou Zhen Hua Shipping Co., Ltd, US, Court of Appeals, 241 F.3d 135 (2nd Cir. 2001)   124, 244, 245, 327

US Titan, Inc. v. Guangzhou Zhen Hua Shipping Co., Ltd, US, District Court, 16 F.Supp.2d 326 (S.D.N.Y. 1998)   124, 244, 245, 327

US (United States) v. Belmont, US, Supreme Court, 301 US 324 (1937)   310

US (United States) v. County of Arlington, Virginia, US, Court of Appeals, 669 F.2d 925 (4th Cir. 1982); 72 ILR 652 (also reported at 98 ILR 1)   44, 406

cxlviii   TABLE OF CASES

US (United States) v. County of Arlington, Virginia, US, Court of Appeals, 702 F.2d 485 (4th Cir. 1983)   90, 406

US (United States) v. Hendron, US, District Court, 813 F.Supp. 973 (E.D.N.Y. 1993)   427

US (United States) v. Holy Land Foundation for Relief & Development, US, Court of Appeals, 445 F.3d 771 (5th Cir. 2006)   293

US (United States) v. Kostadinov, US, Court of Appeals, 734 F.2d 905 (2nd Cir. 1984)   406

US (United States) v. Lee, US, Supreme Court, 106 US 196 (1882)   16

US (United States) v. Lumumba, US, Court of Appeals, 741 F.2d 12 (2nd Cir. 1984); 88 ILR 37   31

US (United States) v. Moats, US, Court of Appeals, 961 F.2d 1198 (5th Cir. 1992); 103 ILR 480   90, 108, 109, 111

US (United States) v. Mora, US, Court of Appeals, 821 F.2d 860 (1st Cir. 1987)   53, 55

US (United States) v. Noriega, US, Court of Appeals, 117 F.3d 1206, 1212 (11th Cir. 1997); 121 ILR 591   434, 435

US (United States) v. Noriega, US, District Court, 746 F.Supp 1506 (S.D.Fla. 1990); 808 F.Supp. 791 (S.D.Fla. 1992); 99 ILR 143   434, 435

US (United States) v. SA Empresa de Viacao Aerea Rio Grandense (Varig Airlines), US, Supreme Court, 467 US 797 (1984)   204

US (United States) v. Scott-Emuakpor, US, District Court, 2000 WL 288443 (W.D.Mich. 2000)   79

USX Corporation v. Adriatic Insurance Company, US, Court of Appeals, 345 F.3d 190 (3rd Cir. 2003)   46, 244, 252, 254, 256, 257, 273, 274

Valore v. Islamic Republic of Iran, US, District Court, 478 F.Supp.2d 101 (D.D.C. 2007)   225, 227

Velasco v. Government of Indonesia, US, Court of Appeals, 370 F.3d 392 (4th Cir. 2004)   43, 77, 109, 123, 248, 434, 435

Velidor v. L/P/G Benghazi, US, Court of Appeals, 653 F.2d 812 (3rd Cir. 1981); 63 ILR 622   61, 90, 109

Vencedora Oceanica Navigacion, SA v. Compagnie Nationale Algérienne de Navigation, US, Court of Appeals, 730 F.2d 195 (5th Cir. 1984); 87 ILR 520   41, 109, 110, 111, 304, 312

Venus Lines Agency v. CVG Industria Venezolana de Aluminio, CA, US, Court of Appeals, 210 F.3d 1309 (11th Cir. 2000)   245, 388, 389

Verlinden BV v. Central Bank of Nigeria, US, Court of Appeals, 647 F.2d 320 (2nd Cir. 1981); 63 ILR 573   77

Verlinden BV v. Central Bank of Nigeria, US, District Court, 488 F.Supp. 1284 (S.D.N.Y. 1980); 63 ILR 390   77, 325

TABLE OF CASES   cxlix

Verlinden BV v. Central Bank of Nigeria, US, Supreme Court, 461 US 480 (1983); 79 ILR 548   38, 40, 42, 46, 62, 77, 110, 160, 244

Vermeulen v. Renault, USA, Inc., US, Court of Appeals, 985 F.2d 1534 (11th Cir. 1993)   76, 125, 126, 244, 245

Victory Transport Inc. v. Comisaría General de Abastecimientos y Transportes, US, Court of Appeals, 336 F.2d 354 (2nd Cir. 1964); 35 ILR 110   16, 19, 21, 46, 65, 77, 80, 137, 299

Vietnam (Republic of Vietnam) v. Pfizer, Inc., US, Court of Appeals, 556 F.2d 892 (8th Cir. 1977); 94 ILR 199   316

Vine v. Republic of Iraq, US, District Court, 459 F.Supp.2d 10 (D.D.C. 2006)   226

Virtual Countries, Inc. v. Republic of South Africa, US, Court of Appeals, 300 F.3d 230 (2nd Cir. 2002)   40, 41, 84, 125, 126, 127, 128, 129

Virtual Countries, Inc. v. Republic of South Africa, US, District Court, 148 F.Supp.2d 256 (S.D.N.Y. 2001)   84, 125

Virtual Defense & Development International, Inc. v. Republic of Moldova, US, District Court, 133 F.Supp.2d 1 (D.D.C. 1999)   77

Voest-Alpine Trading USA Corporation v. Bank of China, US, Court of Appeals, 142 F.3d 887 (5th Cir. 1998)   88, 109, 111, 115, 123, 125, 126, 127, 128, 129, 244, 245

Von Dardel v. USSR (Union of Soviet Socialist Republics), US, District Court, 623 F.Supp. 246 (D.D.C. 1985); 77 ILR 258   23, 25, 38, 40, 319, 325, 333

Von Dardel v. USSR (Union of Soviet Socialist Republics), US, District Court, 736 F.Supp. 1 (D.D.C. 1990)   23, 25, 40, 201, 223, 319, 324, 325, 333

Wachsman v. Islamic Republic of Iran, US, District Court, 537 F.Supp.2d 85 (D.D.C. 2008)   225, 227

Wachsman v. Islamic Republic of Iran, US, District Court, 603 F.Supp.2d 148 (D.D.C. 2009)   225, 227

Wagner v. Islamic Republic of Iran, US, District Court, 172 F.Supp.2d 128 (D.D.C. 2001)   225, 227, 228

Wahba v. National Bank of Egypt, US, District Court, 457 F.Supp.2d 721 (E.D.Tex. 2006)   46, 127, 245, 304, 307, 310

Walker International Holdings Ltd v. Republic of Congo, US, Court of Appeals, 395 F.3d 229 (5th Cir. 2004)   319, 321, 365, 396, 402, 403

Walpex Trading Co. v. Yacimientos Petroliferos Fiscales Bolivianos, US, District Court, 109 F.R.D. 692 (S.D.N.Y. 1986)   245

Walpex Trading Co. v. Yacimientos Petroliferos Fiscales Bolivianos, US, District Court, 712 F.Supp. 383 (S.D.N.Y. 1989)   127

cl TABLE OF CASES

Walter Fuller Aircraft Sales, Inc. v. Republic of the Philippines, US, Court of Appeals, 965 F.2d 1375 (5th Cir. 1992); 103 ILR 503   25, 38, 41, 76, 78, 90, 109, 111, 123, 127, 128, 129

Walters v. People's Republic of China, US, District Court, 672 F.Supp.2d 573 (S.D.N.Y. 2009)   403

Wasserstein Perella Emerging Markets Finance, LP v. Province of Formosa, US, District Court, 2000 U.S.Dist.Lexis 6416 (S.D.N.Y. 2000); 2000 WL 573231 (S.D.N.Y. 2000)   125, 319

Wasserstein Perella Emerging Markets Finance, LP v. Province of Formosa, US, District Court, 2002 U.S.Dist.Lexis 12012 (S.D.N.Y. 2002); 2002 WL 1453831 (S.D.N.Y. 2002)   76, 115, 127

Wei Ye v. Jiang Zemin, US, Court of Appeals, 383 F.3d 620 (7th Cir. 2004)   341, 429, 434, 435

Weilamann v. Chase Manhattan Bank, US, Supreme Court of New York, Special Term, 192 N.Y.S.2d 469 (1959); 28 ILR 165   353

Weininger v. Castro, US, District Court, 462 F.Supp.2d 457 (S.D.N.Y. 2006)   226, 293

Weinstein v. Islamic Republic of Iran, US, District Court, 184 F.Supp.2d 13 (D.D.C. 2002)   225, 227, 228, 274

Weinstein v. Islamic Republic of Iran, US, District Court, 274 F.Supp.2d 53 (D.D.C. 2003)   228

Weinstein v. Islamic Republic of Iran, US, District Court, 299 F.Supp.2d 63 (E.D.N.Y. 2004)   228

Welch v. Islamic Republic of Iran, US, District Court, 545 F.Supp.2d 118 (D.D.C. 2008)   226

Weltover, Inc. v. Republic of Argentina, US, Court of Appeals, 941 F.2d 145 (2nd Cir. 1991)   78, 102, 110, 124, 125, 129

Weltover, Inc. v. Republic of Argentina, US, District Court, 753 F.Supp. 1201 (S.D.N.Y. 1991)   102, 124

West v. Multibanco Comermex, SA, US, Court of Appeals, 807 F.2d 820 (9th Cir. 1987); 84 ILR 187   38, 46, 61, 77, 245, 273, 304, 305, 306, 307, 308, 309, 311

Westex (In the Matter of TB Westex Foods, Inc.), US, Court of Appeals, 950 F.2d 1187 (5th Cir. 1992)   364

Weston Compagnie de Finance et d'Investissement, SA v. La Republica del Ecuador, US, District Court, 823 F.Supp. 1106 (S.D.N.Y. 1993)   25, 387, 412, 413

Whitehead v. Grand Duchy of Luxembourg, 1998 U.S. App. LEXIS 22307 (4th Cir. 1998)   201

TABLE OF CASES   cli

Whiteman v. Dorotheum GmbH & Co. KG, US, Court of Appeals, 431 F.3d 57 (2nd Cir. 2005)   25

Wilk v. Creditanstalt Bankverein, US, District Court, 1993 WL 97259 (S.D. N.Y. 1993)   123, 243, 245

Willamette Transport, Inc. v. Compania Anonima Venezolana de Navegacion, US, District Court, 491 F.Supp. 442 (E.D.La. 1980); 63 ILR 416   390

Williams v. Shipping Corporation of India, US, Court of Appeals, 653 F.2d 875 (4th Cir. 1981); 63 ILR 639   42, 274

WMW Machinery, Inc. v. Werkzeugmaschinenhandel GmbH IM Aufbau, US, District Court, 960 F.Supp. 734 (S.D.N.Y. 1997)   78, 201

Wolf v. Banco Nacional de Mexico, SA, US, Court of Appeals, 739 F.2d 1458 (9th Cir. 1984); 92 ILR 413   77, 273

Wolf v. Federal Republic of Germany, US, Court of Appeals, 95 F.3d 536 (7th Cir. 1996)   82, 83, 223

World Wide Demil, LLC v. Nammo, AS, US, Court of Appeals, 51 Fed. Appx. 403 (4th Cir. 2002)   78, 90, 111, 127, 268, 324, 328, 329

World Wide Demil, LLC v. Nammo, AS, US, District Court, No. 00-1992-A, Mem. Op. (E.D.Va. Jan. 18, 2002)   90

World Wide Minerals, Ltd v. Republic of Kazakhstan, US, Court of Appeals, 296 F.3d 1154 (D.C.Cir. 2002)   43, 244, 245, 319, 320, 324, 325

World Wide Minerals, Ltd v. Republic of Kazakhstan, US, District Court, 116 F.Supp.2d 98 (D.D.C. 2000)   245, 320

Wyatt v. Syrian Arab Republic, US, District Court, 362 F.Supp.2d 103 (D. D.C. 2005)   25, 225, 227

Wyle v. Bank Melli of Tehran, Iran, US, District Court, 577 F.Supp. 1148 (N.D.Cal. 1983)   245

Xuncax v. Gramajo, US, District Court, 886 F.Supp. 162 (D.Mass. 1995); 104 ILR 165   435

Yang Rong v. Liaoning Province Government, US, Court of Appeals, 452 F.3d 883 (D.C.Cir. 2006)   83, 119, 120, 122, 304, 305, 306, 310

Yang Rong v. Liaoning Provincial Government, US, District Court, 362 F.Supp.2d 83 (D.D.C. 2005)   83, 120, 122, 304, 305, 306, 310

Yessenin-Volpin v. Novosti Press Agency, TASS, US, District Court, 443 F.Supp. 849 (S.D.N.Y. 1978); 63 ILR 127   201, 258

Youming Jin v. Ministry of State Security, US, District Court, 475 F.Supp.2d 54 (D.D.C. 2007)   41, 82

Youming Jin v. Ministry of State Security, US, District Court, 557 F.Supp.2d 131 (D.D.C. 2008)   82

clii   TABLE OF CASES

Yousuf v. Samantar, US, Court of Appeals, 552 F.3d 371 (4th Cir. 2009)
   43, 435
Yucyco, Ltd v. Republic of Slovenia, US, District Court, 984 F.Supp. 209 (S.D.
   N.Y. 1997)   201
Zappia Middle East Construction Company Ltd v. Emirate of Abu Dhabi,
   US, Court of Appeals, 215 F.3d 247 (2nd Cir. 2000)   122, 304, 305, 306,
   308, 309
Zappia Middle East Construction Company Ltd v. Emirate of Abu Dhabi,
   US, District Court, No. 94 Civ. 1942 (KMW) (AJP), 1996 WL 413680 (S.D.
   N.Y. 1996)   304, 306
Zedan v. Kingdom of Saudi Arabia, US, Court of Appeals, 849 F.2d 1511
   (D.C.Cir. 1988); 92 ILR 462   25, 113, 114, 125, 126, 127, 128, 129, 161
Zernicek v. Brown & Root, Inc., US, Court of Appeals, 826 F.2d 415 (5th
   Cir. 1987); 92 ILR 442   125, 127, 320, 324, 325, 328
Zernicek v. Petroleos Mexicanos (Pemex), US, District Court, 614 F.Supp.
   407 (S.D.Tex. 1985)   320, 324, 325, 328
Zhou v. Li Peng, US, District Court, 286 F.Supp.2d 255 (S.D.N.Y. 2003)
   434
Zveiter v. Brazilian National Superintendency of Merchant Marine, US,
   District Court, 833 F.Supp. 1089 (S.D.N.Y. 1993)   90, 158, 171, 196, 243,
   245
Zveiter v. Brazilian National Superintendency of Merchant Marine, US,
   District Court, 841 F.Supp. 111 (S.D.N.Y. 1993)   171

Vatican City

Re Marcinkus, De Strobel and Mennini, Vatican City, Court of First
   Instance, (1987) 100 ILR 603   31, 433

Zimbabwe

Barker McCormac (Pvt) Ltd v. Government of Kenya, Zimbabwe, Supreme
   Court, (1983) (4) SA 817; High Court, (1985) (4) SA 197; 84 ILR 18   18,
   21, 25, 28, 30, 35, 47, 82, 87, 100, 140, 376

Legal instruments and codification documents

Treaties

1919 Treaty of Peace between the Allied and Associated Powers and Germany, signed at Versailles, 28 June 1919 (Treaty of Versailles); Treaty of Peace between the Allied and Associated Powers and Austria, signed at Saint-Germain-en-Laye, 10 September 1919 (Treaty of Saint-Germain); Treaty of Peace between the Allied and Associated Powers and Hungary, signed at Trianon, 4 June 1920 (Treaty of Trianon); Treaty of Peace between the Allied and Associated Powers and Bulgaria, signed at Neuilly-sur-Seine, 27 November 1919 (Treaty of Neuilly); Treaty of Peace between the Allied and Associated Powers and Turkey, signed at Sèvres, 10 August 1920 (Treaty of Sèvres). Carnegie Endowment for International Peace, *The Treaties of Peace 1919–1923*, New York, 1924 (in two volumes), Vol. I, pp. 3, 267 and 461; Vol. II, pp. 653 and 789

1926 Brussels Convention: International Convention for the Unification of Certain Rules relating to the Immunity of State-owned Vessels, signed at Brussels, 10 April 1926, and Additional Protocol, signed at Brussels, 24 May 1934, 176 LNTS 199 and 214, entry into force: 8 January 1936; Current status: thirty parties (see www.diplomatie.be/fr/pdf/treaties/i6.pdf)

1928 Bustamante Code: Convention on Private International Law, signed at Habana, 20 February 1928, 86 LNTS 111 (English text on p. 246), Annex: Bustamante Code (Code of Private International Law); entry into force: 25 November 1928

1929 Warsaw Convention (Convention for the Unification of Certain Rules Relating to International Transportation by Air), 12 October 1929, 137 LNTS 11, entry into force: 13 February 1933

cliii

cliv LEGAL INSTRUMENTS AND CODIFICATION DOCUMENTS

1945 Nuremberg Charter: Charter of the International Military Tribunal – Annex to the Agreement for the Prosecution and Punishment of the Major War Criminals of the European Axis, signed at London on 8 August 1945, 82 UNTS 279

1948 Convention on the Prevention and Punishment of the Crime of Genocide, 78 UNTS 277, entry into force: 12 January 1951

1950 US–Ireland Treaty of Friendship, Commerce and Navigation, 1 UST 785; TIAS No. 2155

1951 NATO Status of Forces Agreement (Agreement between the Parties to the North Atlantic Treaty Regarding the Status of their Forces), 199 UNTS 67, entry into force: 23 August 1953

1952 International Convention relating to the Arrest of Seagoing Ships, signed at Brussels, 439 UNTS 193, entry into force: 1956

1955 US–Iran Treaty of Amity, Economic Relations and Consular Rights, 8 UST 899; 284 UNTS 93

1958 New York Convention on the Recognition and Enforcement of Foreign Arbitral Awards, 330 UNTS 3, entry into force: 7 June 1959

1958 Convention on the High Seas, 450 UNTS 11, entry into force: 30 September 1962

1958 Convention on the Territorial Sea and the Contiguous Zone, 516 UNTS 205, entry into force: 10 September 1964

1960 Paris Convention on Third Party Liability in the Field of Nuclear Energy, 956 UNTS 264, entry into force: 1 April 1968, amended in 1964, 1982 and 2004

1961 Vienna Convention on Diplomatic Relations, 500 UNTS 95, entry into force: 24 April 1964

1963 Vienna Convention on Consular Relations, 596 UNTS 261, entry into force: 19 March 1967

1963 Brussels Convention Supplementary to the 1960 Paris Convention on Third Party Liability in the Field of Nuclear Energy, 1041 UNTS 358, entry into force: 4 December 1974, amended in 1964, 1982 and 2004

1963 Vienna Convention on Civil Liability for Nuclear Damage, 1063 UNTS 266, entry into force: 12 November 1977

1965 ICSID Convention (Convention on the Settlement of Investment Disputes between States and Nationals of Other States), 575 UNTS 159, entry into force: 14 October 1966

1965	International Convention on the Elimination of All Forms of Racial Discrimination, 660 UNTS 195, entry into force: 4 January 1969
1969	International Convention on Civil Liability for Oil Pollution Damage, 973 UNTS 3, entry into force: 19 June 1975
1969	Vienna Convention on the Law of Treaties, 1155 UNTS 331, entry into force: 27 January 1980
1972	European Convention on State Immunity, European Treaty Series No. 74, 1495 UNTS 182; 11 ILM 470 (1972); entry into force: 11 June 1976; it has now been ratified by eight States: Austria, Belgium, Cyprus, Germany, Luxembourg, the Netherlands, Switzerland, and the UK. Portugal has signed but not ratified it
1973	International Convention on the Suppression and Punishment of the Crime of Apartheid, 1015 UNTS 243, entry into force: 18 July 1976
1973	International Convention for the Prevention of Pollution from Ships, 1340 UNTS 184, entry into force: 2 October 1983
1975	Agreement on Trade Relations between the United States and the Romanian Government, 2 April 1975, 26 UST 2305, 2308–2309, TIAS No. 8159
1980	Convention concerning International Carriage by Rail (COTIF), 1397 UNTS 76, entry into force: 1 May 1985; Appendix A to the Convention is entitled 'Uniform Rules concerning the Contract for International Carriage of Passengers and Luggage by Rail (CIV)'
1980	Rome Convention (EC Convention on the Law Applicable to Contractual Obligations), Convention 80/934/EEC, OJ L 266 of 9 October 1980, entry into force: 1 April 1991; now replaced by Regulation (EC) No. 593/2008 of the European Parliament and of the Council of 17 June 2008 on the Law Applicable to Contractual Obligations (Rome I), OJ L 177/6 of 4 July 2008, entry into force: 17 December 2009
1982	UN Convention on the Law of the Sea, 1833 UNTS 3, entry into force: 16 November 1994
1983	Treaty between the United States of America and the Republic of Haiti concerning the Reciprocal Encouragement and Protection of Investment, available from the OAS 'Bilateral Investment Treaties' webpage at: www.sice.oas.org/investment/bitindex_e.asp

clvi LEGAL INSTRUMENTS AND CODIFICATION DOCUMENTS

1984 Convention against Torture and Other Cruel, Inhuman or Degrading Treatment or Punishment, 1465 UNTS 85, entry into force: 26 June 1987

1988 Agreement concerning the Encouragement and Reciprocal Protection of Investment between China and Japan, 1555 UNTS 237, entry into force: 14 May 1989

1988 Joint Protocol relating to the Application of the Vienna Convention on Civil Liability for Nuclear Damage and the Paris Convention on Third Party Liability in the Field of Nuclear Energy, 1672 UNTS 302, entry into force: 27 April 1992

1997 Treaty for the Encouragement and Reciprocal Protection of Investment between the US and Estonia, 1997, 1987 UNTS 145, entry into force: 16 February 1997

1997 Protocol to Amend the Vienna Convention on Civil Liability for Nuclear Damage, 2241 UNTS 270/302; entry into force: 4 October 2003

1997 Convention on Supplementary Compensation for Nuclear Damage, not yet in force, text available at: http://ola.iaea.org/OLA/treaties/multi.asp

1998 Rome Statute of the International Criminal Court, 2187 UNTS 3, entry into force: 1 July 2002

1999 International Convention on the Arrest of Ships, not yet in force, United Nations / International Maritime Organization, Diplomatic Conference on Arrest of Ships, A/CONF.188/6, 19 March 1999, text available at: www.unctad.org/en/docs/imo99d6.pdf

2004 United Nations Convention on Jurisdictional Immunities of States and Their Property, text appearing as Annex to the United Nations General Assembly Resolution A/RES/59/38 of 2 December 2004; 44 ILM 803 (2005); opened for signature by all States from 17 January 2005 until 17 January 2007, not yet in force

Other International Documents

1945 Charter of the International Military Tribunal for the Far East (Tokyo Charter), promulgated by General Douglas MacArthur, as Supreme Commander of the Allied Powers in Japan

National Legislation

Argentina	Decree Law No. 9015/63, 1963 Immunity of Foreign States from the Jurisdiction of Argentinian Courts, 1995 (Law No. 24,488)
Australia	Foreign States Immunities Act, 1985
	Foreign States Immunities Amendment Act, 2009
Austria	Introductory Act to the Jurisdictional Statute
Belgium	Law of 16 June 1993 concerning the Punishment of Grave Breaches of the Geneva Conventions of 12 August 1949 and Their Additional Protocols I and II of 8 June 1977
	Law of 10 February 1999 concerning the Punishment of Grave Breaches of International Humanitarian Law
	Law Amending the Law of June 16, 1993, 23 April 2003
	Law on Grave Breaches of International Humanitarian Law (Law Amending the Laws of 1993, 1999 and 2003), 5 August 2003, entered into force on 7 August 2003
Canada	State Immunity Act, 1982 (as amended)
	Federal Courts Act, 1985
	Order Restricting Certain Immunity in Relation to the United States, SOR/97–121, P.C. 1997-242, 1997
China	Law of Immunity of the Property of Foreign Central Banks from Judicial Compulsory Measures, 2005
France	Loi n° 91-650 du 9 juillet 1991 portant Réforme des Procédures civiles d'exécution (NOR: JUSX8900065L)
Germany	Act to Introduce the Code of Crimes against International Law of 26 June 2002
Israel	Foreign States Immunity Law 5769-2008
New Zealand	Admiralty Act, 1973
Pakistan	State Immunity Ordinance, 1981
Singapore	State Immunity Act, 1979
South Africa	Foreign States Immunities Act, 1981
	Admiralty Jurisdiction Regulation Act 105, 1983
Spain	Royal Decree No. 1654/1980 of 11 June 1980 (R. 1856 and 2119)
United Kingdom	Health and Safety at Work etc. Act, 1974
	State Immunity Act, 1978
	State Immunity (Federal States) Order, 1979 (SI 1979/457)
	Supreme Court Act, 1981, as amended by the Constitutional Reform Act, 2005 (now Senior Courts Act, 1981)
	Criminal Justice Act, 1988
	Trade Union and Labour Relations (Consolidation) Act, 1992
	Social Security Contributions and Benefits Act, 1992
	State Immunity (Federal States) Order, 1993 (SI 1993/2809)
	Employment Rights Act, 1996

clviii LEGAL INSTRUMENTS AND CODIFICATION DOCUMENTS

	Employment Tribunals Act, 1996 (initially known as the 'Industrial Tribunals Act')
	Civil Procedure Act, 1997
	Employment Rights (Dispute Resolution) Act, 1998
	Civil Procedure Rules, 1998 (SI 1998/3132) (came into force on 29 April 1999)
	Employment Tribunals (Constitution and Rules of Procedure) Regulations, 2004 (SI 2004/1861)
United States	Federal Tort Claims Act, 1946/1948
	Immigration and Nationality Act, 1952
	Second Hickenlooper Amendment, 1964
	Foreign Sovereign Immunities Act, 1976
	Taiwan Relations Act, 1979
	Antiterrorism and Effective Death Penalty Act, 1996
	Cuban Liberty and Democratic Solidarity (Libertad) Act (Helms-Burton Act), 1996
	Civil Liability for Acts of State Sponsored Terrorism, 1996, enacted as part of the Omnibus Consolidated Appropriations Act, 1997
	Omnibus Consolidated and Emergency Supplemental Appropriations Act, 1999
	Victims of Trafficking and Violence Protection Act, 2000
	Terrorism Risk Insurance Act, 2002
	National Defense Authorization Act for Fiscal Year 2008, 2008
	Libyan Claims Resolution Act, 2008

The Argentina immunity statute, Inmunidad Jurisdiccional de los Estados Extranjeros ante los Tribunales Argentinos ('Immunity of Foreign States from the Jurisdiction of Argentinian Courts'), (both the Spanish and the English texts) can be found in Dickinson *et al.*, *State Immunity*, pp. 461 (Spanish text) and 465 (English translation); for the Spanish text see also the official website: http://infoleg.mecon.gov.ar/infolegInternet/anexos/20000-24999/22523/norma.htm.

The Australia FSIA is reproduced at 25 ILM 715 (1986), but the most up-to-date text (with amendments) can easily be downloaded from the publicly accessible official website: www.comlaw.gov.au.

A translation of the Austria Introductory Act can be found in Seidl-Hohenveldern, State Immunity, 97.

The Canada SIA is reproduced at 21 ILM 798 (1982), but the most up-to-date bilingual (English–French) text of both the SIA (with amendments) and the Federal Courts Act can easily be downloaded from the publicly accessible official website: http://laws-lois.justice.gc.ca/eng/index.html.

The French Loi n° 91-650 du 9 juillet 1991 portant Réforme des Procédures civiles d'exécution (NOR: JUSX8900065L) is available from the official website of French legislation: www.legifrance.gouv.fr. Under 'Les autres textes législatifs et réglementaires' type '91-650' in 'Numéro du texte'.

The Israeli immunity statute is available on the Council of Europe's official website 'Data Base on State Practice regarding State Immunities': www.coe.int/t/dlapil/cahdi/State_Immunities/default_en.asp.

The Pakistan, Singapore and South Africa immunity statutes are reproduced in a UN official compilation entitled United Nations Legislative Series, ST/LEG/SER.B/20, *Materials on Jurisdictional Immunities of States and their Property*, New York, 1982, pp. 20, 28, 34.

The UK SIA came into force on 22 November 1978: SI 1978/1572; it is reproduced at 17 ILM 1123 (1978); more conveniently, the UK SIA and other UK statutes can be found at Westlaw or at the publicly accessible official websites: www.legislation.gov.uk/ or www.opsi.gov.uk/legislation/about_legislation.

The US FSIA was officially reported at 90 Stat. 2891; the text is reproduced at 15 ILM 1388 (1976), but the most up-to-date text (with amendments) can easily be downloaded from the publicly accessible official website: http://uscode.house.gov/download/pls/28C97.txt (US Code, Title 28, Chapter 97).

United Nations Documents

UN General Assembly Resolutions

> UNGA Resolution 174 (II), 21 November 1947
> UNGA Resolution 373 (IV), 6 December 1949
> UNGA Resolution 2625 (XXV), 24 October 1970
> UNGA Resolution 32/151, 19 December 1977
> UNGA Resolution 33/139, 19 December 1978
> UNGA Resolution 34/141, 17 December 1979
> UNGA Resolution 35/163, 15 December 1980
> UNGA Resolution 36/114, 10 December 1981
> UNGA Resolution 37/111, 16 December 1982
> UNGA Resolution 38/138, 19 December 1983
> UNGA Resolution 39/85, 13 December 1984
> UNGA Resolution 40/75, 11 December 1985
> UNGA Resolution 41/81, 3 December 1986
> UNGA Resolution 42/156, 7 December 1987

clx LEGAL INSTRUMENTS AND CODIFICATION DOCUMENTS

UNGA Resolution 43/169, 9 December 1988
UNGA Resolution 44/35, 4 December 1989
UNGA Resolution 45/41, 28 November 1990
UNGA Resolution 46/54, 9 December 1991
UNGA Resolution 46/55, 9 December 1991
UNGA Resolution A/RES/49/61, 9 December 1994
UNGA Resolution A/RES/52/151, 15 December 1997
UNGA Resolution A/RES/53/98, 8 December 1998
UNGA Resolution A/RES/54/101, 9 December 1999
UNGA Resolution A/RES/55/150, 12 December 2000
UNGA Resolution A/RES/56/78, 12 December 2001
UNGA Resolution A/RES/57/16, 19 November 2002
UNGA Resolution A/RES/58/74, 9 December 2003
UNGA Resolution A/RES/59/38, 2 December 2004

UN General Assembly decisions

UNGA Decision 47/414 of 25 November 1992
UNGA Decision 48/413 of 9 December 1993

Reports of the Secretary-General

Report of the Secretary-General, 20 August 1997, A/52/294
Report of the Secretary-General, 24 August 1998, A/53/274
Report of the Secretary-General, 14 September 1998, A/53/274/Add.1
Report of the Secretary-General, 19 August 1999, A/54/266
Report of the Secretary-General, 17 August 2000, A/55/298
Report of the Secretary-General, 14 August 2001, A/56/291
Report of the Secretary-General, 24 October 2001, A/56/291/Add.1
Report of the Secretary-General, 5 November 2001, A/56/291/Add.2

Reports of the International Law Commission

International Law Commission, Report to the General Assembly on
the Work of the First Session, also known as 'Official Records of
the General Assembly, Fourth Session, Supplement No. 10 (A/925)',
A/4/10, *Yearbook of the International Law Commission (YILC)*, 1949,
p. 277

Report of the International Law Commission Covering its Second
Session, 5 June–29 July 1950, Document A/1316, *YILC*, 1950-II, p. 364
(containing the Principles of International Law Recognized in the
Charter of the Nürnberg Tribunal and in the Judgment of the Tribunal
(Nuremberg Principles)

Report of the International Law Commission on the Work of its Twenty-eighth Session, A/31/10, *YILC*, 1976-II-2, p. 69

Report of the International Law Commission on the Work of its Twenty-ninth Session, A/32/10, *YILC*, 1977-II-2, p. 130

Report of the International Law Commission on the Work of its Thirtieth Session, A/33/10, Chapter VIII-D, 'Jurisdictional Immunities of States and their Property', and Annex to Chapter VIII-D, Report of the Working Group on Jurisdictional Immunities of States and their Property, A/CN.4/L.279/Rev.1, *YILC*, 1978-II-2, p. 152

Report of the International Law Commission on the Work of its Thirty-first Session, A/34/10, Chapter VII, 'Jurisdictional Immunities of States and their Property', *YILC*, 1979-II-2, p. 185

Report of the International Law Commission on the Work of its Thirty-second Session, A/35/10, Chapter VI, 'Jurisdictional Immunities of States and their Property', *YILC*, 1980-II-2, p. 137

Report of the International Law Commission on the Work of its Thirty-third Session, A/36/10, Chapter VI, 'Jurisdictional Immunities of States and their Property', *YILC*, 1981-II-2, p. 153

Report of the International Law Commission on the Work of its Thirty-fourth Session, A/37/10, Chapter V, 'Jurisdictional Immunities of States and their Property', *YILC*, 1982-II-2, p. 93

Report of the International Law Commission on the Work of its Thirty-fifth Session, A/38/10, Chapter III, 'Jurisdictional Immunities of States and their Property', *YILC*, 1983-II-2, p. 17

Report of the International Law Commission on the Work of its Thirty-sixth Session, A/39/10, Chapter IV, 'Jurisdictional Immunities of States and their Property', *YILC*, 1984-II-2, p. 58

Report of the International Law Commission on the Work of its Thirty-seventh Session, A/40/10, Chapter V, 'Jurisdictional Immunities of States and their Property', *YILC*, 1985-II-2, p. 51

Report of the International Law Commission on the Work of its Thirty-eighth Session, A/41/10, Chapter II, 'Jurisdictional Immunities of States and their Property', *YILC*, 1986-II-2, p. 7

Report of the International Law Commission on the Work of its Thirty-ninth Session, A/42/10, Chapter VI (B), 'Other Decisions and Conclusions of the Commission', *YILC*, 1987-II-2, p. 53

Comments and observations received from Governments, A/CN.4/410 and Add.1–5, *YILC*, 1988-II-1, p. 45

Report of the International Law Commission on the Work of its Fortieth Session, A/43/10, Chapter VI, 'Jurisdictional Immunities of States and their Property', *YILC*, 1988-II-2, p. 98

Report of the International Law Commission on the Work of its Forty-first Session, A/44/10, Chapter VI, 'Jurisdictional Immunities of States and their Property', *YILC*, 1989-II-2, p. 97

Report of the International Law Commission on the Work of its Forty-second Session, A/45/10, Chapter III, 'Jurisdictional Immunities of States and their Property', *YILC*, 1990-II-2, p. 31

Report of the International Law Commission on the Work of its Forty-third Session, A/46/10, Chapter II, 'Jurisdictional Immunities of States and their Property' (containing Draft Articles on the Jurisdictional Immunities of States and their Property and commentaries thereto), *YILC*, 1991-II-2, p. 12

Report of the International Law Commission on the Work of its Fifty-first Session, A/54/10, Chapter VII, 'Jurisdictional Immunities of States and their Property', and Annex, 'Report of the Working Group on Jurisdictional Immunities of States and their Property', *YILC*, 1999-II-2, pp. 127 and 149

Report of the International Law Commission on the Work of its Fifty-third Session, A/56/10, Chapter IV, 'State Responsibility' (containing Draft Articles on Responsibility of States for Internationally Wrongful Acts and commentaries thereto), *YILC*, 2001-II-2, p. 20

Report of the International Law Commission on the Work of its Fifty-eighth Session (1 May–9 June and 3 July–11 August 2006), United Nations General Assembly Official Records (GAOR), Sixty-first Session, Supplement No. 10 (A/61/10)

Report of the International Law Commission on the Work of its Fifty-ninth Session (7 May–5 June and 9 July–10 August 2007), GAOR, Sixty-second Session, Supplement No. 10 (A/62/10)

Report of the International Law Commission on the Work of its Sixtieth Session (5 May–6 June and 7 July–8 August 2008), GAOR, Sixty-third Session, Supplement No. 10 (A/63/10)

Report of the International Law Commission on the Work of its Sixty-first Session (4 May–5 June and 6 July–7 August 2009), GAOR, Sixty-fourth Session, Supplement No. 10 (A/64/10)

Report of the International Law Commission on the Work of its Sixty-second Session (3 May–4 June and 5 July–6 August 2010), GAOR, Sixty-fifth Session, Supplement No. 10 (A/65/10)

Reports of the ILC Special Rapporteurs on Jurisdictional Immunities

Eleven reports in total, eight by Sompong Sucharitkul and three by Motoo Ogiso:

Sompong Sucharitkul, Preliminary Report on Jurisdictional Immunities of States and their Property, A/CN.4/323, *Yearbook of the International Law Commission (YILC)*, 1979-II-1, p. 227

Sompong Sucharitkul, Second Report on Jurisdictional Immunities of States and their Property, A/CN.4/331 and Add.1, *YILC*, 1980-II-1, p. 199

Sompong Sucharitkul, Third Report on Jurisdictional Immunities of States and their Property, A/CN.4/340 & Corr.1 and Add.1 & Corr.1, *YILC*, 1981-II-1, p. 125

Sompong Sucharitkul, Fourth Report on Jurisdictional Immunities of States and their Property, A/CN.4/357 and Corr.1, *YILC*, 1982-II-1, p. 199

Sompong Sucharitkul, Fifth Report on Jurisdictional Immunities of States and their Property, A/CN.4/363 & Corr.1 and Add.1 & Corr.1, *YILC*, 1983-II-1, p. 25

Sompong Sucharitkul, Sixth Report on Jurisdictional Immunities of States and their Property, A/CN.4/376 and Add.1 and 2, *YILC*, 1984-II-1, p. 5

Sompong Sucharitkul, Seventh Report on Jurisdictional Immunities of States and their Property, A/CN.4/388 and Corr.1 & Corr.2, *YILC*, 1985-II-1, p. 21

Sompong Sucharitkul, Eighth Report on Jurisdictional Immunities of States and their Property, A/CN.4/396 and Corr.1, *YILC*, 1986-II-1, p. 21

Motoo Ogiso, Preliminary Report on Jurisdictional Immunities of States and their Property, A/CN.4/415 and Corr.1, *YILC*, 1988-II-1, p. 96

Motoo Ogiso, Second Report on Jurisdictional Immunities of States and their Property, A/CN.4/422 & Corr.1 and Add.1 & Corr.1, *YILC*, 1989-II-1, p. 59

Motoo Ogiso, Third Report on Jurisdictional Immunities of States and their Property, A/CN.4/431 and Corr.1, *YILC*, 1990-II-1, p. 3

Reports of the ILC Working Group

Report of the Working Group on Jurisdictional Immunities of States and their Property, 1978, Document A/CN.4/L.279/Rev.1, in Report of the International Law Commission on the Work of its Thirtieth Session, A/33/10, Chapter VIII (D), Annex, *YILC*, 1978-II-2, p. 153

Report of the Working Group on Jurisdictional Immunities of States and their Property, 1999, Document A/CN.4/L.576, in Report of the International Law Commission on the Work of its Fifty-first Session, A/54/10, Annex, *YILC*, 1999-II-2, p. 149

Other ILC Documents

Survey of International Law in Relation to the Work of Codification of the International Law Commission, Memorandum submitted by the Secretary-General, UN General Assembly, A/CN.4/1/Rev.1, Sales No. 1948.V.1(1), New York, 1949

Future Work in the Field of the Codification and Progressive Development of International Law, Working paper prepared by the Secretariat, A/CN.4/145, *YILC*, 1962-II, p. 84

Organization of Future Work, Working paper prepared by the Secretariat, A/CN.4/L.119, *YILC*, 1967-II, p. 337

Review of the Commission's Programme and Methods of Work, Working paper prepared by the Secretariat, annexed to the Report of the International Law Commission on the Work of its Twentieth Session, A/7209/Rev.1, *YILC*, 1968-II, p. 226

Review of the Commission's Programme of Work and of the Topics Recommended or Suggested for Inc.lusion in the Programme, Working paper prepared by the Secretariat, A/CN.4/230, *YILC*, 1970-II, p. 247

Survey of International Law, Working paper prepared by the Secretary-General, A/CN.4/245, *YILC*, 1971-II-2, p. 1

Documents of the UN General Assembly Sixth Committee

UN General Assembly, Forty-eighth Session, Agenda Item 147, 'Convention on Jurisdictional Immunities of States and Their Property', Report of the Sixth Committee, A/48/616 (1993)

UN General Assembly, Forty-ninth Session, Agenda Item 143, 'Convention on Jurisdictional Immunities of States and Their Property', Report of the Sixth Committee, A/49/744 (1994)

UN General Assembly, Fifty-second Session, Agenda Item 144, 'Convention on Jurisdictional Immunities of States and Their Property', Report of the Sixth Committee, A/52/645 (1997)

UN General Assembly, Fifty-third Session, Agenda Item 148, 'Convention on Jurisdictional Immunities of States and their Property', Report of the Sixth Committee, A/53/629 (1998)

UN General Assembly, Fifty-fourth Session, Agenda Item 152, 'Convention on Jurisdictional Immunities of States and Their Property', Report of the Sixth Committee, A/54/607 (1999)

UN General Assembly, Fifty-fifth Session, Agenda Item 157, 'Convention on Jurisdictional Immunities of States and Their Property', Report of the Sixth Committee, A/55/607 (2000)

UN General Assembly, Fifty-sixth Session, Agenda Item 160, 'Convention on Jurisdictional Immunities of States and Their Property', Report of the Sixth Committee, A/56/587 & Corr.1 (2001)

UN General Assembly, Fifty-seventh Session, Agenda Item 154, 'Convention on Jurisdictional Immunities of States and Their Property', Report of the Sixth Committee, A/57/561 (2002)

UN General Assembly, Fifty-eighth Session, Agenda Item 150, 'Convention on Jurisdictional Immunities of States and Their Property', Report of the Sixth Committee, A/58/512 (2003)

UN General Assembly, Fifty-ninth Session, Agenda Item 142, 'Convention on Jurisdictional Immunities of States and Their Property', Report of the Sixth Committee, A/59/508 (2004)

United Nations General Assembly Official Records (GAOR), Forty-sixth Session, Summary Record of the 22nd Meeting of the Sixth Committee, 28 October 1991, A/C.6/46/SR.22

GAOR, Forty-sixth Session, Summary Record of the Sixth Committee (SRSC), 29 October 1991, A/C.6/46/SR.23

GAOR, Forty-sixth Session, SRSC, 30 October 1991, A/C.6/46/SR.24

GAOR, Forty-sixth Session, SRSC, 30 October 1991, A/C.6/46/SR.25

GAOR, Forty-sixth Session, SRSC, 1 November 1991, A/C.6/46/SR.27

GAOR, Forty-sixth Session, SRSC, 6 November 1991, A/C.6/46/SR.30

GAOR, Forty-sixth Session, SRSC, 7 November 1991, A/C.6/46/SR.32

GAOR, Forty-sixth Session, SRSC, 7 November 1991, A/C.6/46/SR.33

GAOR, Forty-sixth Session, SRSC, 11 November 1991, A/C.6/46/SR.34

GAOR, Forty-sixth Session, SRSC, 12 November 1991, A/C.6/46/SR.35

GAOR, Forty-sixth Session, SRSC, 13 November 1991, A/C.6/46/SR.36

GAOR, Forty-sixth Session, SRSC, 13 November 1991, A/C.6/46/SR.37

GAOR, Forty-sixth Session, SRSC, 10 November 1992, A/C.6/47/SR.32

GAOR, Forty-eighth Session, SRSC, 15 November 1993, A/C.6/48/SR.29

GAOR, Forty-ninth Session, SRSC, 6 October 1994, A/C.6/49/SR.7

GAOR, Forty-ninth Session, SRSC, 11 November 1994, A/C.6/49/SR.32

GAOR, Forty-ninth Session, SRSC, 14 November 1994, A/C.6/49/SR.33

GAOR, Forty-ninth Session, SRSC, 17 November 1994, A/C.6/49/SR.37
GAOR, Forty-ninth Session, SRSC, 18 November 1994, A/C.6/49/SR.38
GAOR, Fifty-second Session, SRSC, 11 November 1997, A/C.6/52/SR.26
GAOR, Fifty-third Session, SRSC, 9 November 1998, A/C.6/53/SR.23
GAOR, Fifty-third Session, SRSC, 24 November 1998, A/C.6/53/SR.35
GAOR, Fifty-fourth Session, SRSC, 25 October 1999, A/C.6/54/SR.15
GAOR, Fifty-fourth Session, SRSC, 26 October 1999, A/C.6/54/SR.16
GAOR, Fifty-fourth Session, SRSC, 27 October 1999, A/C.6/54/SR.17
GAOR, Fifty-fourth Session, SRSC, 27 October 1999, A/C.6/54/SR.18
GAOR, Fifty-fourth Session, SRSC, 28 October 1999, A/C.6/54/SR.19
GAOR, Fifty-fourth Session, SRSC, 28 October 1999, A/C.6/54/SR.20
GAOR, Fifty-fourth Session, SRSC, 29 October 1999, A/C.6/54/SR.21
GAOR, Fifty-fourth Session, SRSC, 1 November 1999, A/C.6/54/SR.22
GAOR, Fifty-fourth Session, SRSC, 2 November 1999, A/C.6/54/SR.23
GAOR, Fifty-fourth Session, SRSC, 4 November 1999, A/C.6/54/SR.26
GAOR, Fifty-fourth Session, SRSC, 4 November 1999, A/C.6/54/SR.27
GAOR, Fifty-fourth Session, SRSC, 5 November 1999, A/C.6/54/SR.28
GAOR, Fifty-fourth Session, SRSC, 19 November 1999, A/C.6/54/SR.36
GAOR, Fifty-fifth Session, SRSC, 16 November 2000, A/C.6/55/SR.31
GAOR, Fifty-seventh Session, SRSC, 22 October 2002, A/C.6/57/SR.18
GAOR, Fifty-seventh Session, SRSC, 24 October 2002, A/C.6/57/SR.19
GAOR, Fifty-seventh Session, SRSC, 21 October 2003, A/C.6/58/SR.12
GAOR, Fifty-seventh Session, SRSC, 25 October 2004, A/C.6/59/SR.13
GAOR, Fifty-seventh Session, SRSC, 26 October 2004, A/C.6/59/SR.14

Reports of the UN Sixth Committee Working Group

UN General Assembly, Forty-seventh Session, Agenda Item 130,
Convention on Jurisdictional Immunities of States and Their
Property, Report of the Working Group, 3 November 1992,
A/C.6/47/L.10
Report of the Working Group, 11 November 1993, A/C.6/48/L.4 and 15
November 1993, A/C.6/48/L.4/Corr.2
Report of the Chairman of the informal consultations held in the Sixth
Committee, 4 October 1994, A/C.6/49/L.2
UN General Assembly, Fifty-fourth Session, Sixth Committee, Agenda
Item 152, Convention on Jurisdictional Immunities of States and Their
Property, Report of the Chairman of the Working Group, 12 November
1999, A/C.6/54/L.12
Report of the Chairman of the Working Group, 10 November 2000,
A/C.6/55/L.12

Reports of the General Assembly Ad Hoc Committee

Report of the Ad Hoc Committee on Jurisdictional Immunities of States and Their Property, 4–15 February 2002, United Nations General Assembly Official Records (GAOR), Fifty-seventh Session, Supplement No. 22 (A/57/22)

Report of the Ad Hoc Committee on Jurisdictional Immunities of States and Their Property, 24–28 February 2003, GAOR, Fifty-eighth Session, Supplement No. 22 (A/58/22)

Report of the Ad Hoc Committee on Jurisdictional Immunities of States and Their Property, 1–5 March 2004, GAOR, Fifty-ninth Session, Supplement No. 22 (A/59/22)

The Ad Hoc Committee's website: www.un.org/law/jurisdictionalimmunities/index.html

Comments by Governments and Compilations of Materials

United Nations Legislative Series, ST/LEG/SER.B/20, *Materials on Jurisdictional Immunities of States and Their Property*, Sales No. E/F 81.V.10, New York: United Nations, 1982 (reproducing materials received from the Member States in 1981)

Comments and Observations Received from Governments, 1988, Document A/CN.4/410 and Add.1–5, *YILC*, 1988-II-1, p. 45

Comments received after 1991 are reproduced in reports by the UN Secretary-General, see especially A/52/294 (1997); A/53/274 (1998); A/53/274/Add.1 (1998); A/54/266 (1999); A/55/298 (2000); A/56/291 (2001); A/56/291/Add.1 (2001); A/56/291/Add.2 (2001)

Note verbale dated 12 August 1993 from the Permanent Representative of Belgium to the United Nations addressed to the Secretary-General, A/48/313

Note verbale dated 30 September 1993 from the Permanent Representative of Japan to the United Nations addressed to the Secretary-General, A/48/464

Note verbale dated 6 October 1993 from the Permanent Mission of the Republic of Bulgaria to the United Nations addressed to the Secretary-General, A/C.6/48/3

Documents of Other International Organizations

Asian-African Legal Consultative Organization (AALCO)

AALCO's resolutions on the Jurisdictional Immunities of States and their Property at its annual sessions

        RES/39/10 (2000)
        RES/40/6 (2001)

clxviii LEGAL INSTRUMENTS AND CODIFICATION DOCUMENTS

> RES/41/7 (2002)
> RES/42/7 (2003)
> RES/43/S7 (2004)
> RES/44/S7 (2005)
> RES/45/S7 (2006)

Reports prepared by the AALCO Secretariat to the annual sessions

> Report to the Forty-second Session (2003), AALCO/XLII/SEOUL/2003/S.7
> Report to the Forty-third Session (2004), AALCO/43/BALI/2004/SD/S 7
> Report to the Forty-fourth Session (2005), AALCO/44/NAIROBI/2005/SD/S 7
> Report to the Forty-fifth Session (2006), AALCO/45/HEADQUARTERS
> SESSION (NEW DELHI)/2006/SD/S 7

All these documents are available from the AALCO's official website: www.aalco.int

Council of Europe

Council of Europe, *Explanatory Reports on the European Convention on State Immunity and the Additional Protocol*, Strasbourg, 1972, also available at: http://conventions.coe.int/ (Full list – Nos. 74 and 74A)

Council of Europe, Data base on State Practice regarding State Immunities: www.coe.int/t/dlapil/cahdi/State_Immunities/default_en. asp and its companion volume, Hafner *et al.*, *State Practice*

Organization of American States (OAS)

OAS Draft, 1983: The Inter-American Judicial Committee of the Organization of American States, Inter-American Draft Convention on Jurisdictional Immunity of States, approved on 21 January 1983, 22 ILM 292 (1983)

National Documents

ALRC (Australian Law Reform Commission), Report No. 24, *Foreign State Immunity*, Canberra: Australian Government Publishing Service, 1984, also available at: www.alrc.gov.au/report-24

Elsea, Jennifer K., *Suits against Terrorist States by Victims of Terrorism*, as a Congressional Research Service report for US Congress, updated on 8 August 2008, Order Code RL 31258, available at: www.fas.org/sgp/crs/ terror/RL31258.pdf

Leigh Letter, Letter of November 2, 1976 from Monroe Leigh, Legal Adviser, Department of State, to Edward H. Levi, Attorney General, Department of Justice, reprinted in 75 *Department of State Bulletin* 649 (1976); *US Federal Register*, Vol. 41, No. 224 (18 November 1976), pp. 50883–50884; 15 ILM 1437 (1976)

LEGAL INSTRUMENTS AND CODIFICATION DOCUMENTS   clxix

Lord Woolf, Report of July 1996, *Access to Justice*, London: HMSO, 1996; also available at: www.dca.gov.uk/civil/final/index.htm

Switzerland: Circulaire du Département fédéral de justice et police, du 8 juillet 1986, 43 *Annuaire suisse de droit international* (1987) 162

Switzerland: Note de la Direction du droit international public du Département fédéral des affaires étrangères, du 28 août 1990, 1 *Revue suisse de droit international et de droit européen* (1991) 519

Tate Letter, Letter of May 19, 1952 from Jack B. Tate, Acting Legal Adviser, Department of State, to Philip B. Perlman, Acting Attorney General, Department of Justice, reprinted in 26 *Department of State Bulletin* 984 (1952); reproduced in *Alfred Dunhill of London Inc.* v. *Republic of Cuba*, US, Supreme Court, 425 US 682, 711 (1976), Appendix 2; 66 ILR 212, 229

UK, Hansard, *Parliamentary Debates*, Series 5, House of Lords, 16 March 1978, Vol. 389, cols. 1527–1528

UK, Hansard, *Parliamentary Debates*, Series 5, House of Commons Debates, 13 June 1978, Vol. 951, col. 844

US Department of Justice, Suggestion of Immunity for Pope Benedict XVI (Sept. 19, 2005), *Doe 1* v. *Archdiocese of Galveston-Houston*, Civ. Action No. H-05-1047 (S.D. Tex.), 100 *AJIL* (2006) 219

US House of Representatives, Report No. 94-1487, 1976: United States House of Representatives, Legislative History, Foreign Sovereign Immunities Act of 1976, US House of Representatives, Report (Judiciary Committee) No. 94-1487, September 9, 1976; 1976 USCCAN 6604; 15 ILM 1398 (1976)

US Secretary of State, *Country Reports on Terrorism 2004*, submitted 27 April 2005: www.state.gov/s/ct/rls/crt/c14818.htm

US Secretary of State, *Country Reports on Terrorism 2006*, submitted 30 April 2007: www.state.gov/s/ct/rls/crt/2006/index.htm

US Secretary of State, *Country Reports on Terrorism 2008*, submitted 30 April 2009: www.state.gov/s/ct/rls/crt/2008/index.htm

Documents of International Learned Bodies

Harvard Research

Harvard Research, 1932: Harvard Law School, Research in International Law: Competence of Courts in Regard to Foreign States, 26 *American Journal of International Law Supplement* (1932) 451–738 (containing 'Draft Convention on Competence of Courts in regard to Foreign States, with Comment')

clxx LEGAL INSTRUMENTS AND CODIFICATION DOCUMENTS

Institut de Droit International (IDI)

IDI, Projet, 1891: Institut de Droit International, Projet de règlement international sur la compétence des tribunaux dans les procès contre les États, souverains ou chefs d'État étrangers (Rapporteurs: L. von Bar and J. Westlake), adopté en séance plénière du 11 septembre 1891, *Annuaire de l'Institut de Droit International*, Vol. 11, Session de Hambourg, septembre 1891, pp. 436–438; a slightly different version can be found on the IDI's official website: www.idi-iil.org; see also Quinzième commission d'étude, Compétence des tribunaux dans les procès contre les États ou souverains étrangers, Rapport par de Bar, *Annuaire de l'Institut de Droit International*, Vol. 11, 1891, p. 414

IDI, Draft, 1991: L'Institut de Droit International, Contemporary Problems concerning the Immunity of States in Relation to Questions of Jurisdiction and Enforcement, 1991, *Annuaire de l'Institut de Droit International*, Vol. 64-II, Session de Bâle, 1991, pp. 388/389 (parallel French and English texts, with the English text being authentic)

IDI, Draft, 2001: L'Institut de Droit International, Les immunités de juridiction et d'exécution du chef d'Etat et de gouvernement en droit international / Immunities from Jurisdiction and Execution of Heads of State and of Government in International Law, *Annuaire de l'Institut de Droit International*, Vol. 69 (2000–2001), Session de Vancouver, 2001, pp. 742/743 (parallel French and English texts)

IDI, *Tableau Général pendant la période décennale 1904 à 1914*, La Haye/Paris, 1919, pp. 344–346

Annuaire de l'Institut de Droit International, Vol. 10 (Session de Lausanne, septembre 1888), pp. 16 and 295 ('Compétence des tribunaux dans les procès contre les États ou souverains étrangers', with von Bar and Westlake as Rapporteurs)

Annuaire de l'Institut de Droit International, Vol. 44-I, Session de Sienne, 1952, L'immunité de juridiction et d'exécution forcée des Etats étrangers (Première Commission), Rapport et projet de Résolutions définitifs, présentés par M. Ernest Lémonon, p. 5 at 5–7; p. 36 ('Projet définitif' (containing nine articles)) and p. 39 ('Projet provisoire de convention sur l'immunité de juridiction et d'exécution forcée des Etats étrangers' (23 juin 1951) (containing seventeen articles)

Annuaire de l'Institut de Droit International, Vol. 45-II, Session d'Aix-en-Provence, 1954, p. 293, Résolution III, L'immunité de juridiction et d'exécution forcée des Etats étrangers' (1re Commission) (containing five articles) (English translation on p. 301)

Annuaire de l'Institut de Droit International, Vol. 62-I, Session du Caire, 1987,
  p. 13, Ian Brownlie, Contemporary Problems concerning the
  Jurisdictional Immunity of States: Preliminary Report; p. 45, Ian
  Brownlie, Contemporary Problems concerning the Jurisdictional
  Immunity of States: Definitive Report and Draft Set of Resolutions
Annuaire de l'Institut de Droit International, Vol. 63-I, Session de Saint-
  Jacques-de-Compestelle, 1989, p. 13, Ian Brownlie, Contemporary
  Problems concerning the Jurisdictional Immunity of States:
  Supplementary Report
Annuaire de l'Institut de Droit International, Vol. 64-I, Session de Bâle, 1991,
  p. 80, Ian Brownlie, Contemporary Problems concerning the
  Jurisdictional Immunity of States: Memorandum

International Law Association (ILA)

ILA, Drafts (1982 and 1994): International Law Association, Montreal
  Draft Articles for a Convention on State Immunity, *Report of the Sixtieth
  Conference (Montreal)*, 1982, pp. 5 and 325; Revised Buenos Aires Draft
  Articles for a Convention on State Immunity, *Report of the Sixty-Sixth
  Conference (Buenos Aires)*, 1994, pp. 21 and 452
ILA, Final Report, 1982, Final Report of the Committee on State
  Immunity, *Report of the Sixtieth Conference Held at Montreal*, 1982, p. 325
ILA, Final Report, 1994: Final Report on Developments in the Field of
  State Immunity and Proposal for a Revised Draft Convention on State
  Immunity, *Report of the Sixty-Sixth Conference (Buenos Aires)*, 1994, p. 452
ILA, *Report of the Thirty-Fourth Conference (Vienna)*, 1926 (containing Karl
  Strupp, 'Réforme et codification du droit international – Projet d'une
  convention sur l'immunité en droit international' (in French), at
  p. 426)
ILA, *Report of the Forty-Fourth Conference (Copenhagen)*, 1950
ILA, *Report of the Forty-Fifth Conference (Lucerne)*, 1952
ILA, *Report of the Forty-Sixth Conference (Edinburgh)*, 1954
ILA, *Report of the Forty-Seventh Conference (Dubrovnik)*, 1956
ILA, *Report of the Forty-Eighth Conference (New York)*, 1958
ILA, *Report of the Fifth-Eighth Conference (Manila)*, 1978
ILA, *Report of the Fifth-Ninth Conference (Belgrade)*, 1980 (containing 'State
  Immunity: Preliminary Report of the Working Group', at p. 208)
ILA, *Report of the Sixtieth Conference (Montreal)*, 1982 (containing Resolution
  on State immunity with nine draft articles to be designated as 'The ILA
  Montreal Draft Convention on State Immunity', at p. 5; and 'State

clxxii   LEGAL INSTRUMENTS AND CODIFICATION DOCUMENTS

Immunity: Final Report of the Committee', with a section-by-section analysis of the Draft Convention on State Immunity, at p. 325)

ILA, *Report of the Sixty-Third Conference (Warsaw)*, 1988 (containing 'Interim Report of the Committee on State Immunity', at p. 973)

ILA, *Report of the Sixty-Fourth Conference (Broadbeach)*, 1990 (containing 'International Committee on State Immunity, First Report on Developments in the Field of State Immunity since 1982', at p. 393)

ILA, *Report of the Sixty-Fifth Conference (Cairo)*, 1992 (containing 'International Committee on State Immunity, Second Report on Developments in the Field of State Immunity since 1982', at p. 290)

ILA, *Report of the Sixty-Sixth Conference (Buenos Aires)*, 1994 (containing Resolution on State Immunity, with 'Annex: Revised Draft Articles for a Convention on State Immunity' (nine articles)), at p. 21; and 'International Committee on State Immunity, Final Report on Developments in the Field of State Immunity and Proposal for a Revised Draft Convention on State Immunity', with a section-by-section analysis of the Revised Draft Convention on State Immunity', at p. 452)

ILA, Second Report, 1992: Second Report on Developments in the Field of State Immunity since 1982, *Report of the Sixty-Fifth Conference (Cairo)*, 1992, p. 290

Introduction

The aim of this book is to delineate how the law of State immunity has come to be what it is, and what it is that it has become. Before turning grandiloquent with legalese so as to lend this book some measure of respectability, I wish to confess to the reader that the study of the law of State immunity is far from an exact science and that they are well advised in particular to take all the technical terms used in this book not as terms of art but as terms of convenience, for these denote nothing more than just common factors that run through the myriad legal systems and their varied approaches to the subject of State immunity.

State immunity is a principle of customary international law. Barring a satisfactory explanation as to the meaning of 'State' and 'immunity', which would generate still more questions, this statement encompasses two propositions: first, that State immunity is a principle of international, as opposed to national or municipal, law; and secondly, that the relevant rules, insofar as can be reasonably demonstrated, are customary in nature; that is, they have come into existence without the aid of international treaties of relatively universal applicability.

State immunity has both a broad and a narrow meaning. In its broad sense, State immunity is capable of covering every situation in which a State (together with its various emanations) enjoys exemption from or non-amenability to any outside authority, be it national or international, and whether legislative, administrative or judicial. Thus, generally speaking, in the absence of its consent a State cannot be made accountable for its actions within its own borders before an international body, or before a foreign court or administrative authority; and, unless it submits to the local jurisdiction, a State is normally exempt from the proceedings of foreign national courts and tribunals, even for the acts performed

2   INTRODUCTION

within the territory of the forum State, the immunity of diplomatic and consular missions or other types of envoys being an obvious example. Naturally, if we move our gaze onto the internal constitutional arrangements of a State, we shall find that under certain circumstances a State is even exempt from legal proceedings from its own courts or tribunals. Indeed, to the extent that the existence of individual States must pre-date that of international intercourse among them, there is good reason, though this can at best be regarded as academic, to believe that the international law principle of State immunity owes its origin to the notion of immunity in domestic law.

Over the years immunity in its broad sense has been further compartmentalized into various branches of international law. The law of international organizations addresses the dynamics between such organizations and their member States (and, in the case of the United Nations, non-member States as well – see, for example, Article 2(6) of the Charter of the United Nations). The accountability of States for their actions in their own territory is dealt with either by international treaties (such as those for the protection of human rights, which would contain a mechanism of reporting and monitoring, including the lodging of complaints and the conduct of investigations) or by such rules as the 'act of State' doctrine (as with the US courts) or 'non-justiciability' (as in the UK). In this connection, it must be noted that the issue of accountability of a State for its actions in its own territory before a foreign judicial authority, so far as international law is concerned, remains fraught with uncertainties and confusions. Needless to say, the immunity of diplomatic and consular missions and other types of envoys of a similar status is now the subject of an entirely separate body of legal rules. Moreover, an attempt to bring a State to account for its actions in its own territory before a foreign administrative authority, though logically possible, has not yet been made.

It must be pointed out from the outset that, in using words such as 'accountable', 'amenable' and their derivatives, or even such simple phrases as 'brought before a foreign court', we are using them, in the context of State immunity, as terms shorn of all substantive connotations and overtones. They indicate purely procedural rules governing the forum where a dispute is to be settled, and by no means address either the merits of the dispute or any issue of liability or substantive responsibility.

Then, 'State immunity', as currently understood to be a distinct branch of international law and as used in this book, means what it does in its narrow sense: immunity from, or non-amenability to, foreign judicial proceedings; that is, a State cannot be sued without its consent before a foreign national court or tribunal. In saying this we normally exclude diplomatic and consular missions unless they are sued as representatives of their sending States (such as in the cases concerning contracts of employment). However, it must be borne in mind that this is too simplistic a statement; for we ought to attach different qualifications depending on what timeframe we have in mind. During the nineteenth century, the predominant position, dubbed as the 'absolute immunity' doctrine, was that a State could not be brought before a foreign domestic court under *any* circumstance; the twentieth century, especially the latter half of it, saw the emergence of a 'restrictive or relative immunity' doctrine, which made significant inroads into the absolutist position. As a consequence, when discussing the rule of State immunity during the twentieth century, one should always describe the situation in terms of two opposing practices: some courts would grant absolute immunity to foreign States whereas others would limit that immunity to a greater or lesser degree.

All this, however, is now a thing of the past. The law of State immunity now allows only limited, restrictive or relative immunity. The antagonism or antinomy between the doctrine of absolute immunity and that of restrictive immunity has long ceased to exist, thanks to a rapid dwindling of the number of States adhering to the absolute doctrine, especially following the collapse of the Soviet Union and the regimes under its tutelage. Some isolated States may or may not still stick to the traditional absolutist position but their views are largely irrelevant, either because they have hardly more than minimum contact with and presence in foreign States (such as North Korea), or because they are regularly sued in foreign courts anyway (such as Cuba in the US courts). Apart from this, no State of any international standing and whose position is known advocates absolute immunity. After all, it is the national courts that determine the theory and practice of State immunity; and at present it is their unanimous position that foreign States only enjoy limited or restricted immunity. What is under debate is only the extent to which that immunity ought to be restricted. That is, a State enjoys immunity from legal proceedings before foreign national courts in some cases but not in others; what matters now is not *whether* State immunity should be limited, but *when* and *how*.

A distinctive characteristic of the law of State immunity is its astonishing diversity and variedness – and the concomitant fragmentation – a consequence of the vagaries of the times and the idiosyncrasies of the

4 INTRODUCTION

judges. It is chiefly judge-made law, argued before and decided by numerous national courts that are above all limited by the territoriality of their jurisdiction. These courts are bound by all manner of domestic procedural rules. They constantly refer to foreign cases; and indeed such references constitute a persistent feature in cases of State immunity, so numerous are they as to render any referential list unnecessary. This will mean that the rules deducible from State practice are replete with complexities and subtleties of various national laws. Considering the present source of rules in this field, a historical and comparative approach is both necessary and inevitable. It is the only sensible way of gaining a full appreciation of the scope and content of the law of State immunity. Only an exhaustive study of relevant national legislation and decisions of national courts as well as treaty provisions can lead to sound and reliable conclusions in this field and give an appropriate indication of the direction in which the law will evolve. What is more, in stating any rule of a purportedly general character, one should be well-advised to remain confined to those 'lowest common denominators' of the multitude of approaches developed by national courts, marked by nuances peculiar to individual national judicial systems.

These features of the law itself determine the structure of this book, which will consist of a brief history of the law; a statement of general principles and a comparative study of State practice regarding such exceptions to immunity as commercial transactions, contracts of employment, tortious liability, separate entities, enforcement of judgments and other measures of constraint, waiver of immunity; and, last but not least, an assessment of the 2004 UN Convention on State Immunity.

The historical development has been well documented by previous writers. Partly because of this and partly because of my resolve not to rest contented simply with repeating or summarizing what others have said, I have set out to delve deeper into past materials, including those cases which have been well discussed by my predecessors. This involves, in particular, going through the field already trodden by others, and hence extra time, but it has yielded extremely rewarding results. I have had a number of exciting revelations and discoveries, and these have led to conclusions that so far have eluded commentators (including myself). My wish is to present these conclusions in as convincing a manner as possible. In order to achieve this, I have endeavoured, so far as humanly possible, to provide a preponderance of evidence, gathered from a large number of cases. Also, in stating anything now considered as established position, my idea is to tell the reader, as accurately as I possibly can, where and when this position *first* appeared. And for this I have been constantly checking and cross-checking historical sources. I have not done this merely to satisfy an antiquarian curiosity of mine; for I wish to show that, traced to its very source, the received wisdom appears largely a result of repetition only, rather than of any mysterious principles. Moreover, each re-reading of a case would lead to some new discoveries and insights, and would prompt me to look at the case in a fresh light, and that would lead to further adjustments in doctrinal reasoning. Despite the extraordinary amount of time and energy devoted to this exercise, I believe that the result can prove it worthwhile; and I shall now lay before the reader the result of my enquiries.

1   The history of State immunity

The history of the law of State immunity is the history of the triumph of
the doctrine of restrictive immunity over that of absolute immunity. The
accomplishment of that triumph, on the plane of international law, has
been a slow, gradual and incremental process and has taken more than a
century. This history is also one of specialization and particularization.
The current law of State immunity has developed predominantly as a
result of cases decided by national courts in legal proceedings against
foreign States. Courts across the world have started with very little in
their aid and have over the years developed a fully grown branch of the
law, with diverse yet often detailed and elaborate principles and rules
regarding various restrictions to be placed on the immunity enjoyed by
foreign States from judicial proceedings; and around this vast body of
case law has evolved an increasingly sophisticated academic discourse.
As a matter of historical fact, judicial decisions have played a pivotal role
in the evolution of the law, while doctrinal debates among the scholars
are of much later occurrence and are generally of an exegetical nature in
relation to the case law. That is to say, the literature in this field consists
largely of comments on decided cases. However, one important contribution of academic disputation has been the refinement of the techniques adopted by the courts in characterizing and categorizing the
functions and activities of the State, and in pigeonholing any particular
act of a State for the purposes of granting or denying immunity; and
with this refinement came the maturation of the necessary language for
describing such a process. The practice concerning State immunity,
comprising numerous otherwise disparate decisions by judicial and
other authorities of various countries, has been endowed with necessary
order and inner logic, and can now be assessed, analysed and debated
within a generally accepted frame of reference. Simply put, the study of

State immunity, thanks to the efforts of generations of great legal minds, has now become a worthy discipline. This has also facilitated the process of cross-fertilization, a defining feature of the law of State immunity, for the shared, common theoretical framework has truly transcended the differences of legal system and judicial culture, and judges across the world now find it not only possible, but also imperative, to refer to the judicial decisions of other countries in order to deduce applicable rules, to derive guidance, or simply to shed light on the case at hand.

The point of departure for an examination of the history of development of the doctrine and practice of State immunity, both logically and in the sequence of time, is absolute immunity.

1. The age of absolute immunity

Basically, 'absolute immunity' means that States enjoyed immunity before foreign courts with regard to any subject matter; that is to say, in the past, a State could not without its consent be made a defendant before a foreign court. One can see at once from this statement that there could not have been, as there has never been, a truly 'absolute' immunity; for it could have been and has always been possible for a State to *consent* to be sued. Whereas it has always been agreed that a State should enjoy immunity for activities in the exercise of sovereign authority – and this indeed remains the core of the principle of immunity during the periods of both absolute and restrictive immunity – the controversy has revolved around whether immunity could be claimed with regard to non-sovereign or commercial activities as well. Generally speaking, absolute immunity was the prevailing position of international law during the nineteenth century. It means that a sovereign or sovereign State was absolutely immune from legal proceedings in foreign national courts, whatever the character of the legal relationship involved, and whatever the type and nature of the legal proceedings. That is to say, States enjoyed immunity even in respect of commercial or other private law dealings, and their property, even if used exclusively for commercial purposes, was not subject to judicial enforcement measures. This may sound outrageous in today's globalized world, where States and their entities and enterprises routinely engage in commercial, trading, and other private law activities, and commonly own, possess or dispose of commercial property, in foreign countries. However, at a time when State trading activities were rare and State presence in

8   THE HISTORY OF STATE IMMUNITY

foreign countries limited to a few diplomatic or military missions, that was a natural response in view of the fact that a State would normally be engaged in nothing but public or governmental activity in the territory of another State. Besides, absolute immunity was never truly absolute: it could be waived by the defendant State, and courts regularly did assume jurisdiction in cases involving local immovable property pursuant to the ancient principle of *lex rei sitae*.

Absolute immunity was granted in an age when the distinction between sovereign and non-sovereign activities was less manifest, given that State functions were at that time confined to the traditional spheres of, say, legislation, administration, national defence, and the conduct of State-to-State political relations and that, as a result, it was possible and natural to regard 'State' activities as synonymous with 'sovereign' activities. The growing participation of States in international economic activities fundamentally transformed the functions of State and that transformation resulted in a vastly different conception of the State. With the steadily increasing volume of commercial and other dealings between States and foreign private persons on an equal footing, came the gradually diminishing justifiability of a State's assertion of immunity vis-à-vis a valid claim based on such dealings in a foreign court. In this sense, the evolution of the doctrine of restrictive immunity has witnessed and to a significant extent contributed to a redefinition of sovereign activities and therefore of sovereignty, and has ultimately even led to an encroachment of the area traditionally regarded as typically sovereign.

The early history and evolution of State immunity are well documented.[1] The first case on State immunity is universally agreed to be *The Schooner Exchange*, in which Chief Justice Marshall of the US Supreme Court upheld immunity as claimed by the French emperor in an action for repossession of a ship which had been captured and converted into a man-of-war by the French Navy.[2]

However, because *The Schooner Exchange* involved a foreign warship, that is to say, because it impinged on something that is quintessentially sovereign, it cannot furnish conclusive evidence that Chief Justice Marshall was holding foreign States immune from all claims, regardless of whether such claims involved the foreign States' public or private/commercial dealings.[3] In this sense, *The Schooner Exchange* has been rightly perceived as ambiguous, since one would wonder what Justice Marshall might have decided if the ship had been a merchant vessel,[4] just as the members of the English Privy Council wondered how the previous cases that followed the reasoning of *The Schooner Exchange* would have been decided if relationships of a more private law nature had been involved.[5] In any case, such a hypothetical reasoning is at best an ingenious way around an otherwise solid jurisprudence which was accustomed to state the principle of immunity in absolute and the broadest terms, without bothering about a purported public/private distinction.[6] In *The Cristina*, the leading UK case on absolute immunity, Lord Atkin referred to:

two propositions of international law engrafted into our domestic law which seem to me to be well established and to be beyond dispute. The first is that the courts of a country will not implead a foreign sovereign, that is, they will not by their process make him against his will a party to legal proceedings whether the proceedings involve process against his person or seek to recover from him specific property or damages.

The second is that they will not by their process, whether the sovereign is a party to the proceedings or not, seize or detain property which is his or of which he is in possession or control. There has been some difference in the practice of nations as to possible limitations of this second principle as to whether it extends to property only used for the commercial purposes of the sovereign or to personal private property. In this country it is in my opinion well settled that it applies to *both*.[7]

This leaves little room for imagining that the judges would *not* have granted immunity with respect to commercial activities. In the case of the US, such a reinterpretation of past jurisprudence was clearly foreclosed by *The Pesaro*, where the Supreme Court declared unequivocally that:

The decision in *The Exchange* therefore cannot be taken as excluding merchant ships held and used by a government from the principles there announced. On the contrary, if such ships come within those principles, they must be held to have the same immunity as war ships.[8]

Any remaining doubt should have been dispelled by *The Navemar*, in which the Supreme Court again declared:

Admittedly a vessel of a friendly government in its possession and service is a public vessel, even though engaged in the carriage of merchandise for hire, and as such is immune from suit.[9]

Although early cases might contain much that can be converted into material in support of a restrictive immunity doctrine, the public/private dichotomy seems nonetheless to be a treacherous guide, if only because the word 'public' can be construed to cover virtually anything

10 THE HISTORY OF STATE IMMUNITY

and everything that a State does.[10] Thus, recasting past decisions as ambiguous in respect of immunity for commercial activities is nothing but a rationalization of a new doctrine by reference to an alleged *absence* of rules directly to the contrary. Such rationalization, otherwise ahistorical, was made possible, and indeed compelling, only when changes previously unknown – and therefore unaddressed by courts – took place, whereby the forms and nature of State activity had undergone a fundamental transformation, making it harder, and then impossible, for the defendant foreign State still to claim an immunity that distinctly belonged to the past. Before dwelling on that transformation, it is necessary briefly to address the limited exceptions to immunity in the era of absolutism.

2. Exceptions to absolute immunity

'Absolute immunity' has never been truly 'absolute'. It has actually been subject to certain exceptions from the very beginning. First, it has always been possible for a State to submit to the local jurisdiction or otherwise to waive its immunity, either by invoking the jurisdiction of the court as a plaintiff,[11] or by simply waiving it in a prior agreement or appearing as a defendant without objection.[12] It was also stated that a State could not be made a defendant unless it voluntarily submitted to the jurisdiction.[13] The correlative rule is that once a State itself brings an action then it cannot claim immunity from a counterclaim directly related to the principal claim.[14] Secondly, immovable property has always been regarded as forming an integral part of the territory of the forum State and therefore is subject to no other law than that of the territory where it is situated (*lex rei sitae*). For this reason, territorial jurisdiction has been asserted over immovable property without interruption during the whole history of State immunity;[15] and the immovable property exception to immunity has been preserved in current law on State immunity.[16] Thirdly, there might also have been other instances in which a foreign State could not claim immunity.[17] On the whole, immovable property and submission/waiver have been two main exceptions to absolute immunity from the start.[18] While there have been debates as to the true meaning, scope and significance of submission and/or waiver (such as whether the conduct of commercial activity constituted a waiver, properly so called[19]), cases involving immovable/real property have been accepted by proponents of both the absolute and the restrictive doctrine to give rise to a valid exception to immunity.[20] Surprisingly, there has also been confusion over the two, in that the acquisition of immovable property in the territorial State might be regarded as an *implied waiver* of immunity.[21]

Given the limited nature of State trading activities at that time, it is hardly surprising that early cases of State immunity mainly involved State-owned vessels.[22] What is significant is that, at a very early stage, especially with the conclusion of the 1926 Brussels Convention, the immunity of State-owned merchant vessels, which were now 'subject to the same rules of liability and to the same obligations as those applicable to private vessels', was relinquished, even by those States who otherwise still adhered to an absolute immunity doctrine.[23]

3. The emergence of the doctrine of restrictive immunity

To say that the history of State immunity is one of movement from absolute to restrictive immunity does not mean that there is a sharply defined point of time at which international practice as a whole made such a shift. For there is no such point: except for the first few decades following *The Schooner Exchange*, in which States were markedly unanimous in adhering to the doctrine of absolute immunity, at any given time there were always the States that asserted absolute immunity and those that advocated restrictive immunity. Nevertheless, two things can be noted to provide a convenient guide to that history: first, both the doctrine and jurisprudence on State immunity, whether in a particular State or as general international practice, *started* with absolute immunity; secondly, it is still possible, by a simple statistical majority of States, to tell whether it is absolute or restrictive immunity that seems to have been the dominant doctrine in a given period.

It remains difficult, indeed impossible, to draw a sharp line as to exactly when the prevailing doctrine in international law moved from absolute to restrictive immunity; for that movement has been a gradual and long-drawn-out process.[24] Whereas attempts have always been made to assert jurisdiction over foreign States, the most far-reaching changes occurred after the Second World War:

There is no doubt ... that since the Second World War there has been ... a movement away from the absolute theory of sovereign immunity ... towards a more restrictive theory. This restrictive theory seeks to draw a distinction between acts of a state which are done jure imperii and acts done by it jure gestionis and accords the foreign state no immunity either in actions in personam or in actions in rem in respect of transactions falling under the second head.[25]

The middle point in time seems to be marked by the 'Tate Letter' of 1952, so named after its addresser, which at that time noted the 'existence of two conflicting concepts of sovereign immunity, each widely held and firmly established', namely, 'the classical or absolute theory of sovereign immunity' and 'the newer or restrictive theory of sovereign immunity'.[26] In other words, in 1952, States were 'fairly evenly divided between those whose courts adhered to the absolute theory and those which adopted the restrictive'.[27] Since then the doctrine of absolute immunity has been steadily on the decline. In 1963, when the German Constitutional Court decided to adopt restrictive immunity, it observed that, since the First World War:

State immunity has been involved in a process of contraction; its history has become the history of the struggle over the number, nature and extent of the exceptions.[28]

Later on, the number of States adhering to absolute immunity shrank still further. While in 1972, the framers of the European Convention on State Immunity still had to concede that the Convention 'represents a compromise between the doctrines of absolute and relative State immunity',[29] in 1975, when the landmark English case *The Philippine Admiral* was decided, the Privy Council pointed out that, ever since the Tate Letter:

there is no doubt that in the last 20 years the restrictive theory has steadily gained ground ... there are now comparatively few countries outside the Commonwealth which can be counted adherents of the absolute theory.[30]

Allowing perhaps for some minor deviations,[31] it can be safely asserted that restrictive immunity has now completely replaced absolute immunity with the conclusion of the UN Convention on State Immunity in 2004. In the same year, the editors of the *International Law Reports* declared confidently that:

With the restrictive doctrine now long established, it seems inappropriate to continue to index material under the subheadings 'absolute' and 'restrictive' immunity.[32]

It must be borne in mind that, at any given point in time (especially prior to the culmination in 2004), there have always been those States that advocated absolute immunity and those that adhered to restrictive immunity. So the best that can be said about any period is that at that time, absolute or restrictive immunity was the predominant position

EMERGENCE OF THE DOCTRINE OF RESTRICTIVE IMMUNITY 13

practised by a majority of States. For even now, when restrictive immunity is firmly established as *the* law of State immunity, there are still traces of the old doctrine in certain countries, albeit less pronounced than before. What is interesting, however, is that even those States having an absolutist inclination appear unmistakably supportive of the restrictive doctrine.[33]

As will be seen, the transition from absolute to restrictive immunity has taken many years to accomplish. The following is a discussion of when the courts of major jurisdictions made the transitional move. It is hard to delineate an exact timeline for each and every State and, in any case, such a timeline is of secondary importance to what we shall be focusing on here, namely that immunity has been denied not simply on the ground of a sovereign/commercial (*jure imperii / jure gestionis*) distinction, but at the same time on the basis of a connection with the territory of the forum State.[34]

The Belgian and the Italian courts were the first to adopt restrictive immunity.[35] The earliest recorded case of restrictive immunity is perhaps *Rau v. Duruty*, decided in 1879 by the Belgian Court of Appeal of Ghent, which involved a suit for freight of guano shipped to Ostend Port, Belgium. The court assumed jurisdiction on the ground that, when a State sold guano and entered into contracts that were universally considered as commercial, it submitted to the jurisdiction of commercial tribunals.[36] What is of crucial importance, for our purposes, is that both the cargo and the defendant were in a Belgian port and therefore subject to the territorial jurisdiction of Belgium. The factor of territorial connection is also manifest in a case concerning a contract for the purchase of bullets, which was held to be a private law activity. It should be noted that the plaintiff was a Belgian company and, in all probability, the bullets had been delivered from Belgium.[37]

The doctrine of restrictive immunity received its final approval in Belgium in 1903 by the Court of Cassation in the case of *Compagnie des chemins de fer Liégeois Limbourgeois*. In that case the plaintiff company sued for reimbursement of sums advanced by it to the Netherlands government under a contract for the enlargement of a railway station in the Netherlands. The Court of Cassation held that, when a State was not exercising public power (*puissance publique*) but was acting like a private person (*personne civile ou privée*) pursuant to private law (*droit privé*), then it could not enjoy immunity; and the competence of the court derived from the *nature* of the act (*nature de l'acte*) in question. It is clear that, although the enlargement project took place in the Netherlands, it was a joint project between a *Belgian company* and the Netherlands; and the Court of Cassation invoked the Belgian *Code civil*, which allowed suit brought by a Belgian national against a foreigner (including a foreign State).[38] The public power / private law distinction was closely followed in *Monnoyer*, which concerned a French government agency's purchase of raw materials and equipment *from Belgium*.[39]

The Italian practice made the transition in 1882–1886. In the 1882 case of *Morellet*, which involved Denmark's succession to real property in Italy, the Court of Cassation opined that the State existed both as a 'political entity' (*ente politico*) and as a 'legal person in the limited sense of the private law' (*persona giuridica nel senso ristretto del diritto privato*) and must, if need be, 'exercise civil rights in like manner as any other juristic person [*corpo morale*] or private individual'. Where a foreign State acted in the latter capacity in the Italian territory, the Italian courts could assert jurisdiction.[40] In *Typaldos*, the Court of Cassation assumed jurisdiction in an action against Greece for the expenses of maintenance of a Greek subject sheltered in an asylum in Aversa, *Italy*. Although the court's decision seems to have been mainly based on a purported dual personality of the foreign State as both a 'political entity' (*ente politico*) and a 'civil entity' (*ente civile*) (that is, a private law entity),[41] the territorial link is undeniable. The same *ente politico / ente civile* distinction was maintained in *Guttieres*,[42] which concerned a suit brought by an interpreter against the Bey of Tunis for translation services rendered in judicial proceedings *in Italy*. The court declared, in particular, that a foreign State, acting as a private person, could be 'sued before the judicial authorities thereof in cases involving obligations arising out of contracts or transactions concluded or to be performed *therein* [that is, in Italy]'.[43]

The Swiss practice shifted to restrictive immunity in 1918, when the Federal Tribunal (Bundesgericht) in the *Dreyfus* case upheld the validity of an attachment order against assets of Austria with regard to a claim for the return of Austrian State treasury notes circulated in Switzerland. The Federal Tribunal drew a distinction between acts arising from the exercise of sovereign power (*jure imperii*), for which States enjoyed immunity, and acts performed by a State as a subject of private law (*jure gestionis*), for which immunity was unavailable.[44] What is significant is that the Tribunal at the same time stressed that the relevant event had taken place in Switzerland.[45] The *jure imperii / jure gestionis* distinction and the territorial nexus requirement have since constituted two pillars of Swiss jurisprudence on State immunity.[46]

The Greek courts have practised restrictive immunity since 1928, when immunity was denied in a case involving the selling and delivery of cattle by the Soviet Union to a Greek national.[47]

The Austrian courts had followed the absolute immunity doctrine (subject only to real action and voluntary submission) until 1907, when a judgment declared that a foreign State, like the home State, could be sued 'in the ordinary courts in all matters concerning private law'.[48] This restrictive immunity principle was affirmed by the Supreme Court in 1920, in a case involving defaulted payments for works executed in an Embassy building in Vienna; and the Court made it clear that it asserted jurisdiction because the foreign State had concluded a contract to be fulfilled *in Austria*.[49] Afterwards the Austrian practice strangely reverted to absolute immunity,[50] until 1950, when the Supreme Court in the *Dralle* case resumed its restrictive stand, finding that the so-called *acta gestionis* were no longer exempt from municipal jurisdiction, and denied immunity to Czechoslovakia in a case concerning prohibited uses of trade marks in the territory of Austria.[51] From then on, Austrian practice has remained in the line of restrictive immunity.

The French courts were among the first to adhere to the doctrine of absolute immunity.[52] Indeed, the earliest pronouncement on absolute immunity can be traced to the year 1849.[53] It was only at the beginning of the twentieth century that some measure of ambivalence started to be discernible in the French practice.[54] Sometimes confusing statements can be found in French cases.[55] Even when the public/private law distinction was already accepted in the French jurisprudence, there were still courts which held that immunity covered 'commercial interests' of a foreign State.[56] At any rate, it was the local and lower courts that first adopted a more stringent position on foreign State immunity. The 1924 case of *Roumania* v. *Pascalet*, the first case clearly decided on the basis of restrictive immunity because the act in question did not 'possess the character of acts of public authority',[57] concerned a foreign State's purchase of goods *from a French company*. From then on, where immunity was indeed denied regarding commercial activity, the cases invariably concerned acts connected with the French territory.[58] On the other hand, cases granting absolute or unqualified immunity were far from rare.[59] The French Court of Cassation seems to have been seized with this confusion; for it in the main continued to adhere to an absolute stand,[60] but occasionally decided cases on a distinctly restrictive reasoning.[61] However, when the doctrine of restrictive immunity was finally adopted by the Court of Cassation in 1969, the territorial connection was obvious.[62]

16   THE HISTORY OF STATE IMMUNITY

The US practice veered towards the restrictive doctrine in 1952 with the celebrated 'Tate Letter', an official communication nicknamed after its addresser, in which the State Department declared that it would from then on 'follow the restrictive theory of sovereign immunity in the consideration of requests of foreign governments for a grant of sovereign immunity'.

It must be noted that the Tate Letter was primarily a statement of policy of the State Department itself, and was not meant to provide guidance for the courts;[63] but then it was in fact the State Department that at that time decided, upon the 'requests' of foreign States, whether to grant or deny immunity;[64] and it has been a long-standing US practice that the courts regularly deferred to the State Department's 'suggestions' to deny[65] or grant[66] immunity, and asserted some autonomy only where the State Department declined to act or was silent on the matter.[67] Such deference to the Executive has been considered a 'guiding principle' by the US Supreme Court, in whose opinion:

It is ... not for the courts to deny an immunity which our government has seen fit to allow, or to allow an immunity on new grounds which the government has not seen fit to recognize.[68]

As described in *Chuidian*:

Typically, a foreign state or instrumentality faced with a suit in a court in our country would apply to the State Department for a finding of immunity. The State Department would make a determination ... and would convey the finding to the relevant court by filing a 'suggestion'. In fact ... the courts treated such 'suggestions' as binding determinations, and would invoke or deny immunity based upon the decision of the State Department.[69]

For our purposes it is important to note that *Victory Transport*, the first leading authority in which the court took the initiative to apply restrictive immunity on the basis of the *jure imperii / jure gestionis* distinction, was decided on the ground that, by agreeing to arbitrate in *New York*, i.e. in the territory of the forum State, the foreign State must be deemed to have consented to the court's jurisdiction in an action to compel arbitration.[70]

But precisely because the State Department was first of all a political organ dealing with foreign relations, the entanglement of political and legal issues began to make it hard to keep its decisions free of pressure from foreign governments. This was among the chief reasons for the enactment of the US Foreign Sovereign Immunities Act in 1976,[71] a principal purpose of which was declared by the legislators to be 'to transfer the determination of sovereign immunity from the executive branch to the judicial branch, thereby reducing the foreign policy implications of immunity determinations'.[72] One of the defining features of the US FSIA is a strict requirement of territorial nexus together with other jurisdictional contacts.[73]

The most remarkable case in the history of the law of State immunity is undoubtedly the *Empire of Iran Case*, decided by the German Federal Constitutional Court in 1963.[74] Until 1945, Germany had been among those States whose courts granted unlimited immunity, even with regard to private law claims.[75] In 1953, a local German court took the lead in denying immunity in a case against Denmark for damages for personal injuries sustained as a result of the alleged negligence of the driver of a bus which was owned by the Danish State Railways and operated in Germany.[76] The *Empire of Iran Case* concerned a claim for payment for repairs carried out to the heating system at the Iranian Embassy in Cologne, Germany. Upon a careful survey of international practice with regard to State immunity, as evidenced by foreign municipal court decisions, treaties and attempts at codification by international bodies,[77] the Court made the important declaration that 'unrestricted immunity can no longer be regarded as a rule of customary international law'.[78] The case thus not only furnishes valuable documentation of the development and transformation of the law of State immunity but also remains one of the most prominent cases in which the judicial practice of other countries is considered in order to shed light on the issue at hand, a method so characteristic of the law and practice on State immunity. Moreover, in three other respects the case erected what may be regarded as the pillars of the law on State immunity. First, it reaffirmed the crucial distinction between sovereign and non-sovereign activities, or between acts *jure imperii* and acts *jure gestionis*, a distinction that has underlain the restrictive doctrine of State immunity ever since the Belgian, Italian and Swiss courts first invented it.[79] Secondly, it laid down the basic test for making that distinction.[80] Thirdly, it asserted that '[t]he qualification of State activity as sovereign or non-sovereign must in principle be made by national (municipal) law'.[81]

Apart from some isolated and sporadic notes of discordance,[82] the UK courts generally remained curiously unperturbed by the fundamental changes taking place in the world and, until 1975, 'continued to adhere to a pure, absolute, doctrine of state immunity in all cases'.[83] Such an unswervingly absolutist position was so deeply entrenched that,

18   THE HISTORY OF STATE IMMUNITY

even in 1984, Lord Diplock still used the phrase 'absolute sovereign immunity' to refer to the immunity under section 1 of the UK State Immunity Act of 1978,[84] which is manifestly restrictive, being subject to a number of exceptions in that statute. In 1972, however, the UK signed the European Convention on State Immunity. Though the UK did not ratify the Convention until 1979,[85] it gave significant impetus to the establishment of restrictive immunity in the UK courts, and led to the enactment of the UK SIA, which superseded the common law on the topic and gave effect to the 1972 European Convention.[86] At common law it 'took three actions for English law finally to escape from the unsatisfactory corner in which it had boxed itself'.[87] The two landmark cases in which the English common law turned to restrictive immunity, *The Philippine Admiral*, decided in 1975, and *Trendtex*, decided in 1977, both referred to the Convention for support.[88] The facts of these cases were closely connected with the UK territory. *The Philippine Admiral* involved a claim for payment for the repairs of a ship and damages for breach of contract. At all material times the ship remained at the port of Hong Kong, then under British rule. *Trendtex* concerned an irrevocable letter of credit issued by the Central Bank of Nigeria in London for the purchase of cement. Lord Denning pointed out, in particular, that:

The letter of credit was issued in London through a London bank in the ordinary course of commercial dealings. It is completely within the *territorial jurisdiction* of our courts.[89]

The celebrated case of *I Congreso del Partido*, decided in 1981, in which the UK House of Lords first endorsed the doctrine of restrictive immunity at common law, involved facts taking place entirely outside the UK territory, but was based on the 'sister ship' principle, well established in international maritime law, whereby the plaintiff caused the arrest of a Cuban State trading ship in Sunderland, UK, to establish jurisdiction over a claim of breach of contract regarding the cargoes of two other Cuban State-owned ships.[90]

Exactly the same phenomenon can be observed in other countries. When the Philippines in 1958,[91] the Netherlands in 1968[92] to 1973,[93] South Africa[94] and Singapore[95] in 1979, Pakistan in 1981,[96] New Zealand in 1981,[97] Canada[98] and Denmark in 1982,[99] Zimbabwe in 1983,[100] Australia in 1985,[101] India[102] and Spain[103] in 1986, Brazil in 1989,[104] Malaysia in 1990,[105] Ireland in 1991–1992,[106] Norway in 1992,[107] Argentina in 1992 to 1994,[108] Israel in 1997,[109] Lithuania in 1998,[110] and Portugal in 2002,[111] moved over to restrictive immunity by adopting the distinction between *acta jure imperii* and *acta jure gestionis*, they invariably did so in cases having a territorial connection with the forum State.

A parallel development to what has taken place in court is the practice of limiting, through bilateral treaties, the immunity of State-owned enterprises *within the territory of the other party*.[112]

4. The descent of the State

What caused the significant shift from absolute to restrictive immunity was not some revolutionary breakthrough in the theory of international law. In fact, historically, the theory of State immunity grew only subsequently to the judicial practice of municipal courts.[113] The doctrine of restrictive immunity has been formulated and developed as a response to a new development in the international community, that is, the phenomenal increase of State trading, commercial and other activities in foreign countries. With the descent of the State into the arena of private rights and obligations,[114] courts gradually accepted the argument that it was no longer in keeping with justice that immunity should be retained in the case of a foreign State acting, not as a sovereign entity, but as a trader.

Thus, Sir Robert Phillimore asserted, as early as 1873, that:

No principle of international law, and no decided case, and no dictum of jurists ... has gone so far as to authorize a sovereign prince to assume the character of a trader, when it is for his benefit; and when he incurs an obligation to a private subject to throw off ... his disguise, and appear as a sovereign, claiming for his own benefit, and to the injury of a private person ... all the attributes of his character.[115]

In 1886, the Italian Court of Cassation, in asserting jurisdiction, noted 'the twofold function of the State, as head of political and of economic activity'.[116] Similarly, the *Guttieres* case drew attention to the 'varied political, civil and economic conditions of the modern States'.[117] In general, however, the nineteenth and the early-twentieth century up to the First World War saw no large scale State trading activity and therefore was marked by absolute immunity simply because courts did not have much occasion to deal with the problem and related issues.[118] After the two world wars, especially with the ascendancy of the Soviet Union and its type of States, State trading activities became an ever-growing international phenomenon: States

20 THE HISTORY OF STATE IMMUNITY

frequently and on an increasing scale participated in various commercial activities that had previously remained the preserve of private persons, entered into various contracts, and owned and disposed of property. With the rapid growth of trading activities came an unprecedented increase in the number of disputes between States and their private business partners. When more and more private businesses took the initiative to bring foreign States to courts for breach of contract and other matters, courts began to deal with State immunity on a regular basis. The previous practice of treating the position of foreign States before the authorities of the territorial State as a matter of foreign relations, and consequently the previous unavailability of judicial recourse to private litigants, came to be regarded as inadequate and unjust.

In the *Dralle* case of 1950, the Austrian Supreme Court said:

The classic doctrine of immunity arose at a time when all the commercial activities of States in foreign countries were connected with the political activities, either by the purchase of commodities for their diplomatic representatives abroad, or by the purchase of war material for war purposes, etc. Therefore there was no justification for any distinction between private transactions and acts of sovereignty. Today the position is entirely different; States engage in commercial activities and, as the present case shows, enter into competition with their own nationals and with foreigners. Accordingly, the classic doctrine of immunity has lost its meaning and, *ratione cessante*, can no longer be recognised as a rule of international law.[119]

When the US Department of State decided to follow the doctrine of restrictive immunity, it reasoned that:

the widespread and increasing practice on the part of governments of engaging in commercial activities makes necessary a practice which will enable persons doing business with them to have their rights determined in the courts.[120]

The US Supreme Court agreed in *Alfred Dunhill*:

Participation by foreign sovereigns in the international commercial market has increased substantially in recent years. The potential injury to private businessmen and ultimately to international trade itself from a system in which some of the participants in the international market are not subject to the rule of law has therefore increased correspondingly.[121]

In *Empire of Iran*, the leading case marking Germany's move towards restrictive immunity, the German Constitutional Court remarked:

The increase in State activity in the economic field, in particular the expansion of State trading, made it seem necessary to exclude *acta jure gestionis* from State immunity. It was felt necessary to grant to a greater degree than before the legal protection of the courts to individuals, not only against their own State but also against foreign States ... This trend in the jurisprudence of many States is connected with the increase in the various activities of States in spheres which were formerly reserved to private persons.[122]

In *Victory Transport*, a case that marked the change from absolute to restrictive immunity in the common law of the US, the Second Circuit said:

because of the *dramatic changes in the nature and functioning of sovereigns*, particularly in the last half century, the wisdom of retaining the doctrine has been cogently questioned. Growing concern for individual rights and public morality, coupled with the increasing entry of governments into what had previously been regarded as private pursuits, has led a substantial number of nations to abandon the absolute theory of sovereign immunity in favor of a restrictive theory.[123]

Lord Denning was of the same opinion in *Trendtex*, the landmark English case:

A century ago no sovereign state engaged in commercial activities. It kept to the traditional functions of a sovereign ... In the last 50 years there has been a complete transformation in the functions of a sovereign state. Nearly every country now engages in commercial activities. It has its departments of state – or creates its own legal entities – which go into the market places of the world. They charter ships. They buy commodities. They issue letters of credit. This transformation has changed the rules of international law relating to sovereign immunity.[124]

In numberless cases the States' growing participation in international trade and commerce was noted and identified as the primary cause for the adoption of restrictive immunity;[125] and the same awareness can even be discovered in some otherwise absolutist judgments.[126]

Seen against this backdrop, absolute immunity seems to have obtained only at a time when State activities were confined primarily to what today would be regarded as sovereign activities par excellence. Thus Badr is quite right when he suggests that early cases on absolute immunity could not preclude the exercise of jurisdiction.[127] It is then precisely because of the changed realities that the English judges, in justifying their abandonment of the absolute immunity doctrine, were able to declare that restrictive immunity was 'more consonant with justice'.[128]

The following statement of the South African Supreme Court can serve as a good summary:

22   THE HISTORY OF STATE IMMUNITY

The justification for the modern rejection of absolute immunity is two-fold. Firstly, the old-style sovereigns wielding power by acts of States, and but rarely descending into commercial intercourse in foreign lands, enjoyed absolute immunity because what they did was regarded as *acta jure imperii*; but they have given way to modern governments, regularly contracting at home and abroad, and often engaged in international trading through state-owned or state-controlled corporations. Secondly, justice to the other parties involved demands that the sovereign who chooses to enter the market-places and to engage in trading operations in other countries should be held to his bargains and to his obligations.[129]

The fact that restrictive immunity emerged largely because of a fundamental change in the realities of the international community attests the responsive or reactive nature of current law on State immunity. This means that underlying the law of State immunity is not some deeply entrenched and fervently held philosophy but practical considerations. This also explains why, with the deepening of development of State immunity law, courts have become less and less interested in the origin and basis, or any other theoretical underpinnings, of State immunity, and have tended more frequently to focus their attention on highly technical matters concerning the application of specific exceptions to immunity. Because courts have to deal with such technical matters primarily in the context of their respective national legal and judicial systems, the law on State immunity now consists mainly of a vast body of case law decided by various courts whose guiding principles, rules, criteria and *rationes decidendi* (if this term can be borrowed), though broadly consistent (which is the very *raison d'être* of this book), display an astonishing degree of diversity, divergence and, at times, incompatibility. Fragmentation seems to be the right word to describe this still unfolding feature of the law.

More importantly, the responsive or reactive nature of the law also indicates that the law of State immunity tends to lag behind factual developments in the international community, and behind developments in other branches of the law, for that matter. The leaps and bounds achieved in recent decades in the area of international protection of human rights have already exposed, at least from the perspective of a human rights advocate, a conspicuous defect in international law in this respect. On the one hand, the individual has emerged as the ultimate repository of values accepted as universal by international law, which lays down myriad rules as to how a State, as a *public* entity, ought to treat individuals; on the other hand, current law on State immunity is firmly rooted in the *jure imperii / jure gestionis* distinction, a distinction that was developed in the context of trading and commercial activities and vis-à-vis the State as a trader, i.e. a *private* entity. Current law on State immunity, therefore, is by its nature inimical to a legal action against a State as an actor in the sovereign or governmental or public sphere. Thus, when a State breaches a contract for the sale of, say, cigarettes, it can be held accountable before a foreign court; but it cannot be made answerable for acts of arbitrary imprisonment, torture, murder or disappearance, purportedly committed by its police force, a typical apparatus of sovereign power. The law has no rules for such things, simply because the law was evolved in another era and in another area.

5. The irrelevance of ideologies

It is doubtful whether ideological differences played any significant part in the evolution of State immunity rules.[130] Even the Soviet Union and China, at the time both fiercely and ruthlessly ideological and politicized within their own borders, would all of a sudden become perfectly intelligible before, say, a US court. Thus, in *Von Dardel*, a case for alleged unlawful arrest and subsequent imprisonment and possible death of Raoul Wallenberg, a Swedish diplomat, the Soviet Union first defaulted[131] and then entered a special appearance for the purpose of contesting jurisdiction and, invoking US procedural rules, moved for relief from the default judgment and for dismissal for lack of subject matter jurisdiction.[132] In *Jackson*, involving an action against China for defaulted payment of bearer bonds issued by the Imperial Chinese Government in 1911, China first defaulted and then appeared to claim immunity:

> Thus, according to China, restrictive sovereign immunity is applicable only within the group of nations that have adopted it and is not applicable to China, which continues to adhere to the principle of absolute sovereign immunity. Finally, China contends that even if sovereign immunity can be changed by the United States, to apply the change retroactively would violate international law.[133]

Because of a strong intervention by the US government, the default judgment was set aside and later the action dismissed on the ground that the US FSIA did not apply retroactively to bonds issued in 1911 and maturing in 1951, well before the US government announced its shift from absolute to restrictive immunity in the Tate Letter in 1952.[134]

If, in *Jackson*, China still resorted to the phraseology of absolute immunity, then, as time went on, it came to argue for immunity more and more within the general frame of reference of restrictive immunity. Thus, in *Morris*, a similar action was brought against China by US citizens to collect almost US$90 billion on defaulted bonds issued in 1913 by the then Chinese central government. Instead of arguing for a blanket absolute immunity, China moved, and was granted the motion, to dismiss the action on the rather technical grounds, in particular, that (1) none of the exceptions under the FSIA were applicable; and (2) the statute of limitations had long since expired.[135]

Likewise, in the case of *Carl Marks*, after default judgments had been entered against it in actions to recover on debt instruments issued by the Imperial Russian government in 1916, the Soviet Union moved to vacate the judgment in reliance on, inter alia, highly technical points like the statute of limitations and the non-retroactivity of statutes, which would render the 1976 US FSIA inapplicable to pre-1952 claims.[136]

Such reasoning and language were a far cry from what would otherwise be adopted by the Soviet and the Chinese governments in their own countries. The references to the internal rules of procedure of the State of the forum, to rules and principles of international law (such as that a rule of customary international law does not bind a State that persistently objects to it), and to general principles of law (such as the non-retroactivity of statutes), show that these States must have been aware that political doctrines, Marxist or otherwise, were useless for the purposes of claiming immunity in a foreign court and would indeed be incomprehensible to the judge who was to hear the case. What really mattered were *legal* rules binding on the court. And such rules would naturally come from two sources: international law, whose customary rules are binding on all States and their courts; and domestic rules of procedure of the forum State, which bind the court in question.

Thus, using mutually, nay, universally understandable legal terms to contend for both absolute and restrictive immunity has been a defining feature of the whole history of evolution of the law on State immunity. States, however variegated their legal and political systems and however divergent their philosophies that inform such systems, have now found a common language. And this feature has also run through the debates within the International Law Commission, a body purposely designed to represent and reflect such diversity, in drafting an international convention on State immunity. Seen in this light, the development of the law of

State immunity has an undeniably unifying effect. It is a subject on which States can in fact *agree* to disagree.

6. The defendant States

Nor can it be supposed that the so-called 'developed countries / developing countries' division has been seriously determinative of the shaping of the rules of State immunity.[137] Over the years a great number of States have been sued in foreign courts. These include, without exhaustively listing all the countries sued and all the cases, Afghanistan,[138] Albania,[139] Algeria,[140] Antigua and Barbuda,[141] Argentina,[142] Australia,[143] Austria,[144] Azerbaijan,[145] the Bahamas,[146] Belgium,[147] Bolivia,[148] Brazil,[149] Canada,[150] Chad,[151] China,[152] Colombia,[153] the Congo/Zaire,[154] Cuba,[155] Czechoslovakia,[156] the Dominican Republic,[157] Ecuador,[158] Egypt,[159] Equatorial Guinea,[160] Fiji,[161] France,[162] Germany,[163] Greece,[164] the Holy See,[165] Indonesia,[166] Iran,[167] Iraq,[168] Ireland,[169] Jordan,[170] Kazakhstan,[171] Kenya,[172] Kuwait,[173] Lebanon,[174] Liberia,[175] Libya,[176] Lithuania,[177] Marshall Islands,[178] Mexico,[179] Morocco,[180] Mozambique,[181] Nauru,[182] Nigeria,[183] Norway,[184] Pakistan,[185] Peru,[186] the Philippines,[187] Poland,[188] Portugal,[189] Qatar,[190] Saudi Arabia,[191] Senegal,[192] Sierra Leone,[193] Somalia,[194] South Africa,[195] Soviet Union[196] and then the Russian Federation,[197] Spain,[198] Swaziland,[199] Syria,[200] Tonga,[201] Turkey,[202] Uganda,[203] United Arab Emirates,[204] the United Kingdom,[205] the United States,[206] Venezuela,[207] Yemen[208] and Zambia.[209]

Ironically, the US, whose courts have decided more State immunity cases than the rest of the world put together, is also the State sued most. This common experience – if not empathy – may have in some measure contributed to the convergence of views which finally led to the conclusion of the UN Convention on State Immunity.

Thus State immunity is not a particularly developing-countries problem, nor a problem that can be reasonably assigned to any artificial category of States. It can be seen that the defendants include States of varying degrees of development, of diverse political persuasions and quite dissimilar legal and economic systems, and can thus be regarded as broadly representative of the international community as a whole. Such a broad spectrum of the family of nations cannot be divided into convenient groupings such as 'developed' or 'developing' countries, the 'Soviet bloc', the 'West', or the 'East'. The fact that these States, including some of the staunchest adherents of restrictive immunity – Belgium, France, Germany, the UK and the US – have all claimed immunity, wherever possible, either by doing it directly before the court or simply by refusing to appear in court, shows that State immunity has been universally accepted as a general principle of international law. And the fact that States of various stripes have felt the need to claim immunity must also mean that the urge to claim immunity may not be rooted in some mystic ideology but may lie in practical necessity shared by all States. Putting these facts together, one sees a prime exemplar of *opinio juris sive necessitatis*, so essential an element for a rule of customary international law. What has lost favour with the States, therefore, is only absolute or unlimited immunity, but not immunity itself. In this respect the law of State immunity, because of the necessity of finding a common language whereby a State can claim immunity in whichever court it is sued, has a uniquely equalizing and harmonizing effect on the development of international law.

7. The sources of the law of State immunity

The law of State immunity has developed chiefly from case law, together with other sources such as national legislation, treaties, both bilateral and multilateral, statements made by governments and scholarly opinions including particularly the codification efforts by learned bodies. The diversity of the sources is a fact well observed and documented by authorities of international repute.[210] This makes it necessary to collect relevant materials both within and without the remit of the judicial authorities, and these materials would include court cases, national legislation, government statements and deliberations of international organizations. Indeed, repeated compilations of cases and other materials over the years[211] constitute the hallmark of the general endeavour to impose some order on this otherwise chaotic branch of the law.

The rules and principles regarding State immunity have evolved chiefly *from within* the States, not *between* them; that is, such rules are primarily the result of hundreds of cases decided by various domestic courts in their handling of claims brought against (and, in rare cases, by) foreign States. In this respect such rules very much resemble those conflict of law rules in the field of private international law. Indeed, if one accepts that a foreign State, when sued before and denied immunity by a domestic court, can be regarded as assimilated to a private individual, there is no reason why such rules cannot be considered as forming part of private international law as well. This has been acknowledged by case law[212] and treaty law,[213] as well as by academic works on private international law.[214] Article 10(1) of the 2004 UN Convention thus stipulates:

If a State engages in a commercial transaction with a foreign natural or juridical person and, by virtue of the applicable rules of *private international law*, differences relating to the commercial transaction fall within the jurisdiction of a court of another State, the State cannot invoke immunity from that jurisdiction in a proceeding arising out of that commercial transaction. (Emphasis added)

8. Cross-fertilization

A recurrent phenomenon in the historical development of State immunity is cross-fertilization in the judicial practice across the world, marked by constant references to cases decided by foreign national courts, arbitral tribunals or other authorities. This is certainly what is most interesting about the law of State immunity and can most assuredly be regarded as a (if not *the*) defining feature of that law. On the one hand, whatever rules and principles can be said to exist as a matter of customary international law have been enunciated mainly by domestic courts in their separate decisions; on the other hand, these courts invariably justify their decisions in terms of international, rather than domestic, law. This in itself entails a regular recourse to foreign domestic judicial decisions, which are now of necessity regarded as evidence, not merely of how judicial procedural laws in various countries operate in cases involving foreign States as actual or potential litigants, but, more importantly, of how rules of customary international law concerning foreign State immunity emerge, crystallize and consolidate. Thus the survey of foreign domestic court cases is now more than a comparative law exercise for information purposes only: it forms the very essence of the process of identifying the binding legal rules to be applied to the issues at hand. These cases are no longer just raw materials of foreign *national* laws, which can never be binding and in which one may or may not wish to find inspiration, but instances of *international* law, which contain or embody rules one *must* apply. To put it crudely, foreign domestic cases are now considered not merely as facts, but also as law. Whereas more often a court has to rely upon the absence of a prohibitive

28 THE HISTORY OF STATE IMMUNITY

rule against, rather than the existence of a permissive rule authorizing, the denial of immunity, the frequent examination of the practice of other States every time the court hears a case contributes to a 'snow-balling' growth of the restrictive immunity doctrine: one State copies the practice of other States and, meanwhile, also pushes some steps forward, which in turn adds to the overall accumulation of practice for other States to draw from, and so on ad infinitum. This has been the case especially during the early stages, when it was necessary to have recourse to foreign decisions in order to clarify a point, to reinforce the court's position, or more importantly, to justify a hitherto unattempted shift from absolute to restrictive immunity. Indeed, if one accepts that State immunity is a principle of international law that has been developed primarily through domestic court decisions, then it becomes necessary and inevitable that courts should refer to foreign judicial practice. And they have done so on a regular basis and on an astonishingly large scale,[215] and have often expressly declared this as a standard judicial policy.[216] Rules are now directly derived from judicial decisions. The fact that the law of State immunity is mainly judge-made law gives judicial decisions a prominent position within the genealogy of sources of international law. This has profound consequences for international law itself. For among the sources of international law as envisaged by Article 38(1) of the Statute of the International Court of Justice, judicial decisions are regarded only as a 'subsidiary means for the determination of rules of law'. As far as State immunity is concerned, however, judicial decisions are now not a *subsidiary* but a *principal* means for the determination of rules of law; one might even say that judicial decisions constitute the very *source* of international law on State immunity. Moreover, generally speaking, rules deduced from foreign judicial decisions are directly applied to the case at hand, indicating a universal *opinio juris* that, at least where State immunity is concerned, international law rules are directly applicable on the national plane. There is no longer, and cannot be, any artificial dividing line between what is international and what is national. This demands nothing less than a reconceptualization of what is international law and how it evolves and operates; one must look afresh at the sources of international law, and at the relationship and interaction between international law and national legal systems.

On the other hand, the endeavour to search for international law rules is more characteristic of the earlier stages of the restrictive immunity doctrine. With the advent of national statutes and the steady accumulation of case law, national courts can now apply more concrete rules and workable criteria which clearly circumscribe the nature and extent of foreign State immunity. As a consequence, they are now for the most part freed from the agonizing process of doctrinal argumentation and are in a much better position to adopt a more practical and workable approach towards State immunity. There emerges a tendency to move away from general principles governing State immunity towards more specifically individualized situations for immunity or non-immunity and this tendency is becoming more and more manifest. State immunity, for all its international dimensions, has on the technical level become the subject of a body of national procedural rules, and consequently assumes the colour and texture of the particular judicial system in which it operates. *International law is now nationalized.* This interweaving of international and national law would have significant and interesting implications for our idea of what international law is or ought to be, which regrettably it is not within the remit of this book to explore. As the courts grow ever more confident, foreign case law begins to decline in importance. However, cross-referencing has not ceased in recent times. Wherever necessary, courts seem never to have hesitated to refer to foreign cases.[217]

9. Terminology

It must be stated at the outset that, because of the imprecise nature of the terms adopted in the discourse on State immunity, the various terms used throughout this book are to be treated as terms of convenience rather than strict terms of art. An attempt to understand the issues of State immunity simply through a literal reading of the terms would lead to treacherous pitfalls the danger of which cannot be over-stressed. The discussion at this juncture will be devoted to an explanation of the term 'State immunity'; whereas other terms will be discussed in the particular contexts in which they appear.

Both the singular and plural forms of the word 'immunity' are used in actual practice, to all intents and purposes interchangeably. Thus, on the one hand one finds the 1972 European Convention on State *Immunity* and the 1978 UK State *Immunity* Act; while, on the other, one finds the 1976 US Foreign Sovereign *Immunities* Act and the 2004 UN Convention on Jurisdictional *Immunities* of States and Their Property. There is reason to think that 'immunities' rather than 'immunity' should be used; for, in a sense, there are more sorts of immunity than one (as there are different sorts of legal proceedings). The ICJ, for example, contrasted 'immunities from jurisdiction in other States, both civil and criminal' with 'the immunity from criminal jurisdiction'.[218] But then there are many who would find no problem with using the word 'immunity' in the singular form to cover those 'immunities' as the ICJ would see them.[219] At any rate, the word 'immunity' in the singular form has both an abstract and a concrete connotation; for it can both signify the non-amenability of a State to the jurisdiction of another State, thereby embracing all the 'immunities' collectively; and it can refer to a particular 'immunity' from a particular proceeding. In other words, 'immunity' in the singular form is capable of covering the situations denoted by both its singular and plural forms. For this reason, the word 'immunity' is used in this book. There is also a practical consideration: if the word 'immunities' were used, then both 'immunities' and 'immunity' would have to be used, as the case might require, and this might cause further confusion.

Still more problems arise from the fact that there is no uniform reference in current State practice. The courts of the UK (and other common law countries) traditionally adopted the expression 'sovereign immunity',[220] but switched mainly to 'State immunity' after the enactment of the 1978 UK State Immunity Act while still retaining the term 'sovereign immunity'. This has resulted in a mixed use of both terms.[221] Such a mixture is also characteristic of US courts despite the 1976 US Foreign Sovereign Immunities Act. In a similar vein, courts within the common law family also use a mixture of 'sovereign immunity' and 'State immunity'.[222] In Germany, 'State immunity' (Staatenimmunität)[223] and sometimes 'foreign State immunity' (Immunität des fremden Staates)[224] are used. The French courts use 'immunity from jurisdiction' (immunité de juridiction) and sometimes the longer version 'immunity from jurisdiction of foreign States' (immunité de juridiction des Etats étrangers).[225] In line with both the German and the French predilections, the Swiss Federal Tribunal employs 'immunity from jurisdiction' (immunité de juridiction) when it renders its judgment in the French language,[226] but resorts to 'State immunity' (Staatsimmunität) and its variants when conducting its proceedings in German.[227] Historically, the word 'exterritoriality'[228] or 'extraterritoriality'[229] has sometimes been used to describe immunity.[230] Thus it is also possible that in some places the word 'immunity' may not have appeared at all.[231]

This book adopts the term 'State immunity' (or 'immunity' for short) instead of 'sovereign immunity' in order to avoid any confusion that might arise from the versatile and multifarious nature of the word 'sovereign'. In the US domestic law,[232] for example, 'sovereign immunity' refers to at least three types of 'internal' immunity enjoyed by various entities: (1) immunity enjoyed by the US government (and its officials) and federal agencies before the US courts;[233] (2) immunity enjoyed by a constituent State of the United States before the US courts by virtue of the Eleventh Amendment to the US Constitution;[234] and (3) immunity enjoyed by the American Indian tribes.[235] Furthermore, the notion of 'sovereign immunity' was also applied to the Trust Territory of the Pacific Islands, of which the US was the 'administering authority' under the UN trusteeship system.[236] No less confusing will be the notion of 'sovereign immunity' granted by courts to domestic organizations.[237] The term 'State immunity', on the other hand, would at least circumvent this quagmire. Besides, it finds favour with a number of authorities as well.[238]

Needless to say, an entity has to be a State in order to enjoy *State* immunity. State immunity, to the extent that it is 'State' immunity, does not apply to an entity that is not considered a 'State',[239] or 'sovereign'[240] or 'independent'[241] by the forum State. Conversely, immunity can be granted to an entity which is considered a 'State'[242] or 'sovereign/independent'[243] in the opinion of the court/forum State. For this purpose, complete sovereignty or independence does not seem to be necessary.[244] What is more, a State does not *ipso facto* enjoy immunity before a foreign domestic court; in order to do so it has to be officially recognized by the forum State.[245]

Conclusion

The trajectory of the law of State immunity starts from absolute immunity and then finally culminates in restrictive immunity. The history of that evolution shows that absolute immunity as a doctrine and a practice was finally ousted, not necessarily because it was inherently illogical or indefensible – in fact in its own time it was part and parcel of the international legal order and well served its purpose. The true cause for the passing of absolute immunity is that international economic life, and with it the very conceptualization of the State itself, had undergone so phenomenal a change that the law inevitably and inexorably became out of step with the reality, and thus had to be discarded as a thing of the past. It is only for this reason – and not because of any philosophical breakthrough, that the doctrine of absolute immunity finally appeared so anachronistic and untenable: *cessante ratione legis cessat ipsa lex*. As international law currently stands, States no longer enjoy absolute immunity; they enjoy immunity only with regard to sovereign or governmental acts (*acta jure imperii*), but have no immunity with respect to commercial or private acts (*acta jure gestionis*). The transition from absolute to restrictive immunity has been a slow, gradual and yet irreversible process. All the States that have now accomplished the transition from absolute to restrictive immunity have stayed restrictive in their outlook, and so far none has reverted to the practice of the absolute doctrine. As the most important legal basis of jurisdiction, the principle of territoriality has played a crucial role in the transition and has provided the strongest rationale for the denial of immunity. The fundamental change in the overall approach to the issue of immunity has been due chiefly to the practical necessity to reconsider the position of foreign States before national courts, presented to lawyers and judges alike by the growing participation of States in commercial and trading activities abroad. The theory of State immunity, though it may have played some role in boosting the change of attitude towards immunity, has been, still is, and will most probably remain, an outgrowth and, to all intents and purposes, but a poor reflection of the unequalled richness, diversity and charm of the voluminous judicial practice entailed by a transformed conception of the State on the international plane.

2 General principles

Apart from a few generalized statements concerning the manner in which immunity is granted or denied to foreign States, we know very little about the origin and the legal basis of State immunity. Owing to the unique features of the law of State immunity, a statement of principles is either a list of the lowest common denominators or simply a rationalization. We shall find that these principles are, and should not be considered as anything more than, signposts that point in the right direction, but contain little information as to the condition of the terrain ahead. In other words, even though we know that, broadly speaking, immunity might be granted or denied in certain types of cases, the actual handling of any particular case, from the initiation of the judicial proceedings, to the service of process, the examination of evidence, the characterization of the specific conduct in question, the assessment of facts, and finally to the passing of judgment and the oversight of its execution, etc., lies primarily – or, one may even assert, exclusively – with the court whose function it is simply to interpret and apply the law of the forum State. Under such circumstances it is only natural to conclude that the international law of State immunity is the result of a confluence of domestic judicial practice of all and sundry States; and it would be equally valid to describe the situation as one in which international law delegates to domestic courts an unparalleled discretion, to such an extent that the rules and principles of international law on State immunity would not and could not meaningfully exist without reference to domestic laws and judicial practice. It is not surprising then that one should find a most voluminous, complex and diverse jurisprudence on immunity, hardly observable anywhere else in international law. Such a situation, ironically, makes it all the more necessary to suggest some guidelines, in the broadest possible terms, if

34 GENERAL PRINCIPLES

only for the purpose of putting the law of State immunity, this most diversified branch of international law, in a proper perspective, and, more importantly, in a serviceable frame of reference.

1. A general statement of principles

Here is a short list of principles on which a broad consensus can be asserted to exist, both in jurisprudence and in doctrine.

1. States enjoy immunity before foreign national courts as a principle of customary international law.
2. International law prescribes a presumption of immunity; that is, first, immunity is the norm rather than the exception, and it can be denied only when one or more exceptions allowed by international law are present; and, secondly, immunity must be given due effect even if the defendant State does not appear before the court.
3. States enjoy immunity for sovereign, or public, or governmental acts (*acta jure imperii*) but not for commercial, or private, or non-governmental acts (*acta jure gestionis*).
4. The characterization of and distinction between these two types of acts are performed primarily by reference to domestic law, i.e. the law of the forum State.
5. The exceptions to immunity are almost exclusively based on territorial jurisdiction; and the restrictions on territorial jurisdiction become more stringent and extensive where attachment or other enforcement measures against foreign State property are involved.
6. The immunity enjoyed by a foreign State encompasses two distinct immunities in connection with the two distinct stages of the judicial process: immunity from adjudication and immunity from execution; loss of immunity from adjudication does not automatically lead to a loss of immunity from execution.
7. Immunity can be waived by the defendant State either expressly or impliedly. Two separate waivers are needed for the adjudicatory and the executory stages, unless the defendant State has made a clear and unmistakable indication of a combined waiver.

2. State immunity as a principle of customary international law

It is now universally recognized and accepted that States enjoy immunity by virtue of international law. Since the earliest times courts have been aware that in granting immunity to foreign States they were applying a principle of international law, even though the scope of such immunity has always been in dispute.[1] This has now been confirmed by the highest judicial authorities of various countries,[2] various lower courts,[3] international conventions,[4] international tribunals and other international institutions,[5] national legislative bodies,[6] and accepted by scholarly opinion.[7]

Because the law of State immunity has developed largely through domestic judicial decisions and because so far there has been no international treaty of universal participation dealing with the matter, it is more accurate to say that State immunity is a principle of *customary* international law. Indeed in numerous cases the courts specifically emphasized the customary nature of State immunity by declaring either that State immunity is a principle of customary international law or that it is, in the absence of treaties, a principle of general international law.[8] As the culmination of over a century's practice, the 2004 UN Convention on Jurisdictional Immunities of States and Their Property states in its first preambular paragraph that 'the jurisdictional immunities of States and their property are generally accepted as a principle of customary international law'.

As a matter of constitutional principle, in a number of countries rules and principles of customary international law form part of the domestic law that must be cognized and applied by the courts, and the courts have taken the position that State immunity is such a rule.[9] However, the implications of State immunity being a rule of customary international law are yet to be fully appreciated and worked out. For one thing, if immunity is required by international law, then a failure to grant immunity where due would theoretically be a breach of international law that would incur State responsibility. However, how true this is remains to be seen. All that is certain is that courts have been aware that, in granting or denying immunity, they are obliged by *international law* to act in conformity with certain minimum standards, but not as a matter simply of domestic rules of procedure or out of considerations of expediency. Beyond that international law allows States (that is, their legislatures, courts and tribunals) a vast measure of discretion in deciding on the concrete rules whereby questions of immunity are to be settled. Admittedly, though rare, there remain cases where States tend to react strongly to a denial of immunity as an unfriendly act bearing serious repercussions.[10] On the whole, however, States are becoming more and more inclined to view the issue of immunity with equanimity, as something that belongs in a different, more mundane, realm.

36   GENERAL PRINCIPLES

Immunity being a rule of international law means that a State enjoys immunity from the courts of another State by virtue of international law, not pursuant to national law; thus the grant or denial of immunity is pre-determined by a legal system that is extraneous to national law. This means not only that the law of State immunity always retains a constant core of general principles despite the great variety of national legal systems in which the issue of immunity has been and is being decided, but also that the absence of national legislation on immunity does not in principle affect the immunity of the defendant State; on the contrary, where national legislation is lacking, courts can, and are indeed under an international legal obligation to, work out the parameters of immunity by referring to a variety of *international* sources, such as cases decided by foreign courts, treaties and other international instruments, government statements, and scholarly writings. At a more technical level, this entails that, insofar as immunity is concerned, certain rules and principles are and ought to be accepted as givens, necessary premises upon which a court has to proceed, so that a court is not entirely free to formulate its own rules with regard to the immunity of a foreign State. The grant and denial of immunity have thus been placed within bounds – shifting though they are – imposed by international law binding upon all States and their courts.

Nor can the law of State immunity be simply regarded as the sum total of State practice, an offshoot of domestic procedural rules applied to cases where foreign States are sued, without regard to how international law views the subject. To say that before national courts started to decide cases on immunity, international law knew no rules on State immunity, and therefore the law of State immunity is a new creature brought forth entirely by national courts, is only partially true. International law knows abundant instances where new rules have had to be fashioned to accommodate new realities; but then such rules became rules of international law precisely because they were formulated in accordance with existing rules of international law and in pursuance of normal procedures generally accepted by States as capable of endowing new rules with an international legal validity. Crucially, to make principles and rules regarding State immunity those of international law will require that the courts have had to be aware from the start that they were not entirely free to do whatever they might regard as appropriate under their national laws, but were obliged by a legal regime over and above their respective systems to follow a certain course of action.

There is no denying that the rules and principles of the current law of State immunity have, both in point of time and in substance, grown out of the judicial practice of various courts, but the important fact still remains that since the very beginning, it has been a standard pronouncement by the courts to the effect that they were not creating new rules out of nothing, but were applying the general principles of *public international law* to a novel problem. Whether they were granting or denying immunity, they always declared that they were doing so in strict conformity with international law, that is, they were doing this not as an instance of a simple application of domestic procedural rules to domestic cases, but within boundaries set by public international law, over and above their respective domestic legal systems. This gives the law of State immunity a degree of predictability, from which one can also deduce an increasing uniformity of practice and thence the logical possibility of an international instrument, such as an international convention of a universal character, which would at least serve as a guide to general practice, if not as a binding document laying down uniform rules. This also shows that, from the very beginning, foreign States as litigants have been treated *differently* from private participants in litigation, and this is precisely what international law has done: giving States a presumption of immunity before foreign courts.

3. The presumption of immunity

The fact that State immunity is a principle of international law gives rise to, and is closely bound up with, the principle that a State is presumptively immune under international law. The most obvious implication of this principle is that a State does not lose immunity simply because it chooses not to appear before a foreign court to defend that immunity: immunity shall be granted insofar as circumstances require, even if the State refuses to appear before the foreign court. On the other hand, immunity shall be denied if an exception to immunity as set forth by international law is established in a case, despite vigorous defence by the defendant State. That is, active defence, just like default, is in principle irrelevant to, and undeterminative of, the question of immunity. What determines whether or not a State should enjoy immunity is whether that State engages in certain activities that are regarded by international law as unprotected by immunity.

All current State immunity instruments follow the pattern of a general principle of State immunity qualified by a number of specified

38   GENERAL PRINCIPLES

exceptions to that immunity allowing the exercise of forum jurisdiction.[11] By way of example, section 1604 of the US FSIA provides:

Subject to existing international agreements to which the United States is a party at the time of enactment of this Act a foreign state shall be immune from the jurisdiction of the courts of the United States and of the States except as provided in sections 1605 to 1607 of this chapter.

And section 1 ('General immunity from jurisdiction') of the UK SIA stipulates:

(1) A State is immune from the jurisdiction of the courts of the United Kingdom except as provided in the following provisions of this Part of this Act.
(2) A court shall give effect to the immunity conferred by this section even though the State does not appear in the proceedings in question.

Such a uniform pattern of general immunity qualified by particular exceptions can only mean one thing, namely, that the starting premise is always that a foreign State is presumed immune unless and until proven otherwise. The US practice is especially prominent in enunciating this presumption of immunity. According to the legislators, the US FSIA:

starts from a premise of immunity and then creates exceptions to the general principle. [It] is thus cast in a manner consistent with the way in which the law of sovereign immunity has developed.[12]

It was the Court of Appeals for the Third Circuit that first used the phrases 'presumptive immunity from suit' and 'presumption of immunity'.[13] Then, for the first time, in *Gibbons*, a district court pronounced that:

Under the FSIA, an entity having the status of a foreign state is entitled to a presumption of immunity, which presumption can be rebutted if the plaintiff shows that an exception to the general rule of immunity is available.[14]

Other courts quickly followed the suit;[15] and the notion finally received the stamp of authority from the Supreme Court in *Saudi Arabia* v. *Nelson*:

Under the [FSIA], a foreign state is *presumptively immune* from the jurisdiction of United States courts; unless a specified exception applies, a federal court lacks subject-matter jurisdiction over a claim against a foreign state.[16]

Since the endorsement by the Supreme Court, the expression 'presumption of immunity', together with its variants like 'presumptively immune' and 'presumed to be immune', have been consistently applied by the US courts.[17]

Courts in other countries adhere to the same principle of 'general immunity subject to exceptions' or 'presumption of immunity' without necessarily resorting to the same expressions.[18] In some cases, the expression 'presumption of immunity' was indeed adopted.[19]

It is safe to assert that the presumption of immunity has now been established as a principle of universal validity. Thus the court is required *ex proprio motu* to give effect to immunity even though the defendant foreign State does not appear before the court; and no default judgment can be entered until the court has satisfied itself that the foreign State is not entitled to immunity. That the failure to appear before the court does not in any way prejudice the enjoyment of immunity is made abundantly clear by the 2004 UN Convention, which provides that:

A State shall give effect to State immunity ... by refraining from exercising jurisdiction in a proceeding before its courts against another State and to that end shall ensure that its courts determine on their own initiative that the immunity of that other State ... is respected. (Article 6(1))

Failure on the part of a State to enter an appearance in a proceeding before a court of another State shall not be interpreted as consent by the former State to the exercise of jurisdiction by the court. (Article 8(4))

And that:

A default judgment shall not be rendered against a State unless the court has found that ... the present Convention does not preclude it from exercising jurisdiction. (Article 23(1)(c))[20]

This is also the rule adopted by the 1972 European Convention[21] and national statutes.[22] The combined effect of the above provisions is that a failure to appear does not automatically lead to a loss of immunity and should not be treated as a waiver of immunity, and that a default judgment against a foreign State can only be entered when one or more of the exceptions to immunity as envisaged by the Convention apply to the case. If none of the exceptions to immunity is applicable, immunity must be upheld. In this connection it must be understood that 'giving effect to State immunity' does not mean granting immunity; it simply means that the court will of its own motion consider the issue of immunity, even though the issue has not been raised in the proceedings, and then decide whether to grant *or* deny immunity. On the other hand, provided ample opportunity is given to it to defend its immunity, a foreign State (or its entity) should not, so to speak, 'sit idly by and wait'

40 GENERAL PRINCIPLES

until it is too late, say, five months after the close of the relevant proceedings, to claim immunity.[23]

As the US Supreme Court pointed out in *Verlinden*:

Under the [FSIA] ... subject matter jurisdiction turns on the existence of an exception to foreign sovereign immunity. Accordingly, even if the foreign state does not enter an appearance to assert an immunity defense, a district court still must determine that immunity is unavailable under the [FSIA].[24]

This principle has likewise been adhered to by the UK courts,[25] other courts with immunity legislation,[26] and the courts of those States without immunity legislation.[27]

To repeat, under current international law, a State's failure to appear before a foreign court does not automatically lead to a loss of immunity and shall not be treated as a waiver of immunity, and a default judgment (indeed any judgment) against a foreign State can only be entered when one or more of the generally recognized exceptions to immunity apply to the case.

Apart from the proscription on default judgment in the absence of a valid exception to immunity, a direct and immediate effect of the presumption of immunity on the judicial procedure concerns the burden of proof. Because a foreign State is presumptively immune, where there is a prima facie case that the defendant is, or can be assimilated to or otherwise regarded as, a foreign State, then it is immune from the proceedings of the court unless one or more exceptions, as permitted by international law, apply to the case, even though, as in the nature of judicial proceedings, it is ultimately the defendant's job to defend itself. As enunciated by a US circuit court:

Once the defendant presents a prima facie case that it is a foreign sovereign, the plaintiff has the burden of going forward with evidence showing that, under exceptions to the FSIA, immunity should not be granted, although the ultimate burden of persuasion remains with the alleged foreign sovereign.[28]

And as more clearly delineated by a US district court:

The basic premise of FSIA is that foreign sovereigns are immune from suit in the United States unless the action falls under one or more of the nine specific exceptions enumerated in the statute ... The plaintiff bears the burden of producing evidence to show that the foreign sovereign defendant does not enjoy immunity and that one or more of the nine exemptions to FSIA constitutes a waiver of the defendant's sovereign immunity thereby conferring federal court jurisdiction over the plaintiff's claims. Once the plaintiff has shown that the foreign sovereign defendant is not immune from suit, the burden shifts to the defendant to prove that the plaintiff's allegations do not bring the case within one of the statutory exceptions to immunity. A court may dismiss a complaint brought under FSIA only if it appears beyond doubt that the plaintiff can prove no set of facts that would entitle him to relief.[29]

In a case upholding immunity of embassy bank accounts from attachment, a Belgian court said:

> To require proof of the allocation of funds to be the responsibility of the State against which attachment is sought would be contrary to the very principle of immunity that, by definition, establishes a presumption in favour of the State that enjoys immunity. The imposition of a duty on a State to prove systematically and at any moment that it is indeed entitled to rely on its immunity would in practice exclude reliance on its immunity.[30]

Thus the burden of proof resides primarily with the plaintiff to rebut the presumption of immunity; only then will it become incumbent upon the defendant to persuade the court that the exception(s) in question should not apply. Also, because immunity is presumed (i.e. no proof is needed), even if a foreign State does not appear before the court to defend itself, the plaintiff still bears the burden of proving that that presumption ought to be overcome in the particular case. Therefore, immunity shall be denied only when two conditions are fulfilled: first, that the plaintiff has discharged his burden of proving the existence of one or more exceptions to immunity; and secondly, that the foreign State has not appeared and therefore provided no defence whatsoever, or has appeared but failed to persuade the court why those exceptions do not apply. In either case, the plaintiff's burden of proof is an essential and characteristic stage of any procedure against a foreign State; and the fact that this burden of proof may be relatively easy to discharge in certain circumstances does not eliminate the requirement. In this respect international law confers upon the defendant State a rather privileged position, one that is normally not available to a private person. For better or for worse, States are indeed treated differently by international law with respect to foreign domestic judicial proceedings. This is something worthy of remembering when one embarks upon a consideration of issues of foreign State immunity; and, as we shall see, it has significant implications for the most important criterion for the determination of acts *jure imperii* and acts *jure gestionis*, that is, the 'private person' test.

42 GENERAL PRINCIPLES

4. Immunity and municipal law

Parallel and correlative to the presumption of immunity is the decision, especially in UK and US case law, that the national immunity statute is the 'sole' or 'exclusive' basis for deciding cases against foreign States and their emanations. Thus a legal action against a foreign State can only be brought under such statutes.

The legislators explained that the US FSIA, as a *comprehensive* jurisdictional scheme', lays down 'comprehensive rules', whereby 'jurisdiction in actions against foreign states is comprehensively treated'; that is, it 'sets forth the *sole and exclusive* standards to be used in resolving questions of sovereign immunity raised by foreign states before [the US courts]'.[31] It was again the lower courts that took the initiative in pronouncing that the FSIA provides the *sole or exclusive basis* for obtaining jurisdiction over foreign States. In *Ruggiero*, it was held that the FSIA was 'the exclusive means whereby a plaintiff may sue any foreign state', and that it provided 'a single vehicle for actions against foreign states'.[32] In *Williams*, the court opined that the FSIA established 'comprehensive and exclusive standards' for the question of foreign State immunity.[33] Then, in *Rex*, it was declared that the FSIA constituted 'the sole basis for federal subject matter jurisdiction in civil actions against agencies or instrumentalities of foreign sovereigns'.[34]

It took the Supreme Court some years to warm up to this obvious conclusion. In *Verlinden*, the Court declared that the FSIA 'contains a comprehensive set of legal standards governing claims of immunity in every civil action against a foreign state or its political subdivisions, agencies or instrumentalities',[35] and that:

[The FSIA is] a statute comprehensively regulating the amenability of foreign nations to suit in the United States. The statute must be applied by the district courts in every action against a foreign sovereign, since subject matter jurisdiction in any such action depends on the existence of one of the specified exceptions to foreign sovereign immunity. At the threshold of every action in a district court against a foreign state, therefore, the court must satisfy itself that one of the exceptions applies ...[36]

If one of the specified exceptions to sovereign immunity applies, a federal district court may exercise subject matter jurisdiction ... but if the claim does not fall within one of the exceptions, federal courts lack subject matter jurisdiction.[37]

Finally, in *Amerada Hess*, the Supreme Court, stressing the 'comprehensiveness of the statutory scheme in the FSIA',[38] concluded that the FSIA provides 'the sole basis for obtaining jurisdiction over a foreign state' in the US courts.[39] Since then this has been religiously intoned and consistently applied by the lower courts.[40] Thus no suit can be brought against a foreign State and its agencies and instrumentalities unless one of the exceptions contained in the FSIA applies. And the same also applies to other national statutes.

According to English case law, the UK SIA is designed to 'deal comprehensively with the jurisdiction of courts of law in the United Kingdom both ... to adjudicate upon claims against foreign states ... and ... to enforce by legal process ... judgments pronounced and orders made in the exercise of their adjudicative jurisdiction',[41] and is 'intended to provide the sole source of English law on this topic'.[42] As a 'comprehensive code', therefore, the SIA 'is not subject to overriding considerations', such as, for example, the prohibition of torture.[43] Where no statutory exception to immunity can be established, immunity remains unaffected, even in a case of torture. The Canadian courts have the same view on the Canada SIA; that is, '[e]ssentially, foreign states are immune from civil suits in Canadian courts, unless one of the exceptions in the Act applies, or the state waives its immunity'.[44]

We are then faced with two apparently irreconcilable propositions. On the one hand, State immunity is a principle of international law, to which a national court must have reference in a case against a foreign State; on the other hand, a domestic court by its very nature applies ultimately nothing but domestic legal rules.[45] One is compelled to conceive of an absence of conflict and inconsistency between national and international law on the issue of immunity; in other words, one must either regard national law and international law as identical on this point, or else find that international law in this connection is so lax and uncommitted that, so long as immunity is ensured under certain circumstances, any manner of doing so would be in conformity with, or rather not prohibited by, international law. Since the international law on State immunity has evolved as a result of domestic judicial practice, it may not be unwarrantable to think either way. In any case, the most intelligible and workable theorization would perhaps be that, at the practical level, international law leaves national law (and judicial practice) a wide measure of discretion as to the specific circumstances in which foreign State immunity is to be given effect. No better enunciation can be found than that made by the US legislators:

44   GENERAL PRINCIPLES

Sovereign immunity is a doctrine of international law under which domestic courts, in appropriate cases, relinquish jurisdiction over a foreign state ... In virtually every country ... sovereign immunity is a question of international law to be determined by the courts ... [T]he central premise of the [FSIA is that] decisions on claims by foreign states to sovereign immunity are best made by the judiciary on the basis of a statutory regime which incorporates standards recognized under international law.

Although the general concept of sovereign immunity appears to be recognized in international law, its specific content and application have generally been left to the courts of individual nations.[46]

5. The legal basis for immunity

To start with, exactly why States should enjoy immunity in the courts of other States has never been satisfactorily explained.[47]

The *locus classicus* of the doctrine of State immunity is *The Schooner Exchange*, 'a judgment which has illumined the jurisprudence of the world'.[48] Chief Justice Marshall, in rejecting a claim by the former owners to regain possession of a vessel which had been seized by the French navy and converted into a warship, made the following pronouncements:

The world being composed of distinct sovereignties, possessing equal rights and equal independence, whose mutual benefit is promoted by intercourse with each other, and by an interchange of those good offices which humanity dictates and its wants require, all sovereigns have consented to a relaxation in practice, in cases under certain peculiar circumstances, of that absolute and complete jurisdiction within their respective territories which sovereignty confers ...

This full and absolute territorial jurisdiction being alike the attribute of every sovereign, and being incapable of conferring extraterritorial power, would not seem to contemplate foreign sovereigns nor their sovereign rights as its objects. One sovereign being in no respect amenable to another; and being bound by obligations of the highest character not to degrade the dignity of his nation, by placing himself or its sovereign rights within the jurisdiction of another, can be supposed to enter a foreign territory only under an express license, or in the confidence that the immunities belonging to his independent sovereign station, though not expressly stipulated, are reserved by implication, and will be extended to him.

This perfect equality and absolute independence of sovereigns, and this common interest impelling them to mutual intercourse, and an interchange of good offices with each other, have given rise to a class of cases in which every sovereign is understood to waive the exercise of a part of that complete exclusive territorial jurisdiction, which has been stated to be the attribute of every nation.[49]

What is striking is that Chief Justice Marshall referred to no pre-existing rule or principle of international law, be it customary or conventional, which specifically obligated the courts to grant immunity to a foreign State. Immunity was seen purely as a matter of natural reason, logic and practical considerations regarding international intercourse, rather than an interpretation and application of existing legal rules. That a State ought to be exempt from the jurisdiction of another State was deduced from the perceived attributes of Statehood and the necessity of maintaining friendly international relations. Thus, for Chief Justice Marshall, immunity was called for, not because the US courts were under a specific international legal obligation – whether that obligation emanated from a treaty or a custom – to grant immunity to the French emperor in respect of the ship, but because reason, common sense and logic together compelled such a result. It is then not very far from reality to say that immunity was, at least in its inception, a matter of grace and comity, and that a State enjoyed immunity, not as a right, but as a privilege. It is equally noteworthy that Chief Justice Marshall did not refer to any previous judicial decision on State immunity, be it American or foreign; and he did not, and could not, find any specific legal rules on the matter. His opinion that a foreign sovereign should be exempt from local jurisdiction was the consequence of a logical deduction from such properties as are normally associated with a sovereign being a sovereign (such as 'perfect equality and absolute independence'). Remarkably forceful as far as logic goes, this says nothing about the *legal* basis for immunity. Not that he did not wish to state any: there was simply no legal basis, because there was not yet any legal rule. This is the situation that must have confronted many a lawgiver in prehistoric times: no principles, no rules, no judicial precedents; all they had was an uncannily perceptive intuition that enabled them to pronounce on the rules that ought to exist, to make the law from scratch. Now, if Chief Justice Marshall found it necessary to lump together various attributes of Statehood (sovereignty, independence, equality and dignity, etc.), the implication is clearly that none of these attributes alone could singlehandedly provide a sufficient basis for granting (and claiming) immunity. So a foreign sovereign enjoyed immunity because of all those qualities that made a sovereign a sovereign. In other words, a sovereign enjoys immunity because he is a sovereign; and a State enjoys immunity because it is a State.

What we have found here will have profound implications for the doctrine of State immunity. First, any pronouncement of the *legal* basis of State immunity is, in essence, only a rationalization; secondly, it is for this reason unnecessary, doctrinally, to probe into the possible legal basis (or bases) of immunity; and, thirdly, it will not be profitable to make such a probe: one will gain nothing by doing it. This will be fully demonstrated by an exhaustive survey of case law, out of which there will emerge a scene of utter confusion as to the legal basis/bases of State immunity.

5.1. 'Sovereignty' and the affiliated concepts

A close inspection of the judicial decisions over the span of two centuries reveals a truly kaleidoscopic picture regarding the perceived bases of State immunity, running the whole gamut of 'sovereignty' (and its variants, such as 'sovereign capacity' or simply being a sovereign),[50] 'independence',[51] 'equality',[52] 'dignity',[53] 'comity/courtesy',[54] 'reciprocity',[55] foreign policy/relations considerations,[56] and their various permutations and combinations.[57] A convenient reference inventory can be found in *Halsbury's Laws of England*, which states that:

> An *independent sovereign* state may not be sued in the English courts against its will and without its consent. This immunity ... is accorded upon the grounds that the exercise of jurisdiction would be incompatible with the *dignity* and *independence* of any superior authority enjoyed by every sovereign state. The principle involved is not founded upon any technical rules of law, but upon broad considerations of *public policy*, international law and *comity*.[58]

These and kindred notions regarded as forming the basis of immunity are even more exhaustively enumerated in *Davison*, where it was declared that:

> *Public policy justifications* for allowing a degree of immunity for foreign states and their agencies from the jurisdiction of domestic Courts derive from general principles of *territorial sovereignty*, the *equality* and *independence* of states, notions of *comity and reciprocity* and an assessment of the *risk to foreign relations* of excessive claims to jurisdiction.

And that the following are:

> the established theories which have been advanced to rationalise the immunity: the *equality and independence* of states, the avoidance of *indignity* for a state in subjecting it to municipal jurisdiction, the conferment of immunity as a matter of *comity and goodwill* or because of notions of *reciprocity*, the maintenance of international order, or the adoption of an approach based largely on *expediency* exempting a foreign government from the local jurisdiction where the *interests of diplomacy* so require.[59]

In a similar vein, the Greek Court of Cassation said:

> In its contemporary version, the institution of sovereign immunity constitutes a consequence of the *sovereignty, independence* and *equality* of nations, whilst its aim is to *avoid the disturbance of international relations.*[60]

On the other hand, opposite pronouncements have also been made, to the effect that such notions as sovereignty, equality, independence, dignity and international comity do not necessarily prevent courts from exercising jurisdiction under appropriate circumstances.[61] Thus:

> as far as the principle of equality and independence of States is concerned, that principle would not be violated by submitting a foreign State to the jurisdiction of our courts so long as we make the distinction between those activities of the foreign State which involve the exercise of public power, on the one hand, and mere private law activities, on the other.[62]

> It is more in keeping with the dignity of a foreign sovereign to submit himself to the rule of law than to claim to be above it, and his independence is better ensured by accepting the decisions of courts of acknowledged impartiality than by arbitrarily rejecting their jurisdiction.[63]

> To require a state to answer a claim based upon such [commercial, or other private law] transactions does not involve a challenge to or inquiry into any act of sovereignty or governmental act of that state. It is, in accepted phrases, neither a threat to the dignity of that state, nor any interference with its sovereign functions.[64]

Thus:

> The immunity does not derive from the authority or dignity of sovereign states or the need to protect the integrity of their governmental functions.[65]

More than that:

> Constant resort by a foreign State or its agents to the doctrine of State immunity in this jurisdiction impinges unduly upon our sovereignty and dignity as a nation.[66]

Therefore:

> Each of these theories – independence, dignity and comity – can be shown to be unsatisfactory as a basis for immunity.[67]

No general pattern can be discerned from the ways in which courts refer to these bases; in fact, one finds a highly haphazard, even whimsical lumping-together of them. The casualness and carelessness with which the judges refer to such purported bases serves as a telling indication of

48   GENERAL PRINCIPLES

a general lack of confidence as to what the real bases of immunity are or should be; and that might be why sometimes several bases are suggested at one time – just to make sure that one of them hits the mark. Added to the perplexity is the fact that in the vast majority of cases State immunity is simply referred to as a principle of international law without any specification of its origin. What is also remarkable is that such a multitude of beliefs frequently occurs in the courts of one and the same country, while even the same court in one and the same case would subscribe to different rationales/grounds for immunity.

From the relevant pronouncements made by courts, other institutions and scholars regarding the various attributes of Statehood, such as 'sovereignty', 'independence', 'equality' and 'dignity', one will see that there can be no sharp distinction between these attributes. Thus, for example, 'sovereign equality' includes 'political independence';[68] 'equality' is a consequence or corollary of 'sovereignty';[69] 'sovereignty' signifies, or is, 'independence',[70] while 'independence' may either rightfully flow from,[71] or be a precondition for,[72] 'sovereignty'; but then, 'sovereignty' and 'independence' may even be the one and the same thing;[73] and 'respect [for "the sovereignty of foreign States"] is the foundation of the equality of States';[74] simpler still, 'sovereignty' leads to both 'equality and independence';[75] and 'dignity' is but another name for 'independence'.[76] By a parity of reasoning, 'sovereignty' should also mean 'dignity' or vice versa, and so on and so forth, ad infinitum. Put crudely in a formulaic fashion:

Sovereignty = Independence = Equality = Dignity = Sovereignty

Or:

Sovereignty is independence is equality is dignity is sovereignty.

To the extent that these qualities of Statehood are conveniently interchangeable and mutually replaceable, 'sovereignty', 'independence', 'equality' and 'dignity' are, theoretically, but different aspects of the same Statehood and cannot be sharply and finely distinguished. That being the case, one cannot convincingly argue that immunity is derived from any *one* of these qualities or aspects. It will be difficult, indeed impossible, to assert that immunity stems from sovereignty, but not from independence, or equality, or dignity, and so forth. For if sovereignty denotes complete autonomy and supremacy of one's own will, a State cannot, without its consent, be subject to the will of another State; then independence must be accepted as a given. In a community of

States all of which are sovereign and independent, one must assume that they are endowed with the same quantity and quality of sovereignty and independence, then equality must also be accepted as a given. Because equal autonomy and supremacy logically preclude any overlap of authority, in order for equally sovereign and independent States to coexist, the notion of territory, being the ultimate extent and measure of sovereign authority, must be accepted as a primary legal concept. If that is the case, sovereignty must not mean any more than territorial sovereignty. Equal sovereignty or sovereign equality will then mean that the will of a State – and hence the implementation of that will – reigns supreme within its own territory and that any restriction on that will must spring from that will itself, not from without.[77] From this it must be concluded that being sovereign means that a State enjoys and exercises territorial jurisdiction with complete autonomy, subject only to principles of natural justice, principles that must pre-date, and therefore logically cannot form part of, the law unless deliberately incorporated; and to those restrictive rules and principles accepted by the State as *legally* binding; then it is purely a matter of choice whether or not the territorial State decides to exercise its jurisdiction; that is to say, whether or not a State chooses to exercise its jurisdiction within its own territory is entirely a matter of discretion. Jurisdiction, being a direct consequence and a primary manifestation of territorial sovereignty, cannot but be endued with the same quality, i.e. supremacy and autonomy, and the absence of restrictions except those, in the ultimate analysis, self-imposed by the State itself. If no State has a natural right to restrict the territorial sovereignty of another State, it follows that no State has an inherent right to demand exemption from another State's jurisdiction within the latter's territory. Thus immunity, in the sense that a foreign State cannot be made a defendant before the local court, is only a matter of grace, i.e. comity. Seen in this light, immunity rests only on the sufferance and good will of the territorial sovereign; it is only a privilege and can be withdrawn by the territorial sovereign when and where the latter sees fit. If immunity resides only in the will of the territorial State, it then follows that the grant of immunity is, ultimately, irrespective of the foreign State's status or conduct. Because States have no natural or inherent right to immunity, merely being a sovereign State cannot of itself lead to immunity in the territory of another State; in other words, immunity, in the final analysis, cannot be derived from sovereignty, or from a State being a State.

50   GENERAL PRINCIPLES

Moreover, if territorial sovereignty is accepted as a given, the very notion that a foreign State can, on the basis of sovereignty, be immune for acts *jure imperii* is a paradox. On the one hand, if a State has sovereignty within its own territory, then no other State is free logically and justifiably to exercise sovereign authority (*jus imperii*) within such territory. On the other hand, if any State is free to exercise sovereign authority (*jus imperii*) in the territory of any other State, the word 'sovereignty' will become nonsensical. Thus the idea that a State can exercise sovereign authority in the territory of another is antithetical to the idea of sovereignty; it follows that the exercise of sovereign authority in the territory of another State can only be the result of a concession or indulgence on the part of the territorial State. To the extent that the exercise of sovereign authority (*jus imperii*) in the territory of another is ultimately repugnant to the notion of territorial sovereignty, no State has the inherent right to exercise sovereign authority in foreign territory without the consent of the territorial State. It then follows that being *jure imperii* alone does not give any act a primordial claim to immunity; immunity is again shown to be a matter of grace and cannot be a corollary of sovereignty.

In short, 'sovereignty' is a dubious concept to serve as the basis of immunity. The simple fact is that both the defendant State and the forum State have sovereignty. If the defendant State has reason to claim immunity, the forum State has even more reason to demand submission to jurisdiction. That is to say, sovereignty can serve equally forcefully as the basis for immunity and the denial of immunity, depending on from whose perspective the matter is approached. Thus, the idea that immunity derives from sovereignty is doctrinally self-contradictory and self-defeating. And, because of the interchangeability discussed above, this conclusion with regard to sovereignty also applies to independence, equality, dignity or any other attribute of Statehood.

One way to avoid such difficulty, and apparently to be always on the safe side, is to assert that all these qualities or attributes of Statehood *collectively* serve as the basis for State immunity, as has been done by a number of authorities quoted above. This amounts to saying that a State enjoys immunity because of the sum total of all its attributes in the eyes of international law, because it stands as an amalgam of such attributes. Stated plainly, this is saying that:

A State enjoys immunity because it is a State.

This is both circular and tautological. We are back at the starting point. Moreover, if none of these attributes of Statehood can serve *singly* as the basis for immunity because of an inherent logical impasse, and if any one of them can be identified with practically any other one of them, so that they all suffer from the same illogicality, it is difficult to imagine how they can *collectively* perform the task.

It then seems far more advisable to accept immunity as a creature of long-standing State practice growing out of practical necessity, or to say that immunity is purely a matter of grace and comity; but this cannot explain the painstaking effort of the courts in search of rules of international *law* regarding immunity. In other words, the repeated declarations to the effect that State immunity is a principle of, and must therefore be decided in a manner consistent with, international law suggests the universal recognition that immunity is not, or is not entirely, a matter of complete discretion based on practical considerations.

Perhaps it is now the time for us to admit that any doctrinal inquiry into the legal basis of immunity will lead to a dead end.

5.2. Par in parem non habet imperium?

It is tempting to think that the basis of State immunity is to be found in the Latin maxim *par in parem non habet imperium* (literally, an equal has no power or authority over another equal) and, admittedly, there is nothing wrong in remaining contented with such a notion. As the Council of Europe stated in its explanatory report for the 1972 European Convention:

'State immunity' is a concept of international law, which has developed out of the principle *par in parem non habet imperium*, by virtue of which one State is not subject to the jurisdiction of another State.[78]

Some thirty years later, this was repeated verbatim by the European Court of Human Rights:

sovereign immunity is a concept of international law, developed out of the principle *par in parem non habet imperium*, by virtue of which one State shall not be subject to the jurisdiction of another State.[79]

The idea seems to be entertained by other prominent international judges as well,[80] and by the International Law Commission.[81] Indeed, that State immunity owes its origin to, or is derived from, this Latin maxim seems to be an almost universally held belief within the circles of

52 GENERAL PRINCIPLES

international law and beyond, as can be seen from repeated references in national court decisions and in scholarly writings.

It will be disheartening, then, to point out from the outset that the origin of the *par in parem* maxim itself has nothing to do with State immunity or even with international law. According to Dinstein,[82] this epigram is derived from canon law and can be traced to a ruling of Pope Innocent III, delivered in the year 1199, to the effect that one Pope could not impinge upon the right of his successors to exercise their respective powers, for the authority of the predecessor would be no more than that of those who followed (*cum non habeat imperium par in parem*). Obviously the rule in its original conception only concerned the relationship of *successive* rulers at different times. The axiom was first stated as *par in parem non habet imperium* by Dante Alighieri (1265–1321), the poet who composed *The Divine Comedy*, in *De Monarchia* (composed circa 1309–1313),[83] where he applied it to *contemporary* rulers, the context of the maxim having been converted from a vertical line to a horizontal plane. According to him:

> It is clear that a dispute may arise between two princes ... therefore a judgment between them is indispensable. However, since neither can take cognizance over the other (neither being subject to the other – and equals do not rule over equals (*par in parem non habet imperium*)), there needs to be a third person enjoying wider jurisdiction who by right rules over both of them. This person ... eventually ... will be the Monarch, or Emperor. Therefore monarchy is necessary to the world.[84]

With Dante, the maxim is one of the grounds on which he argues that the rule (Monarchy or Empire) by a single person (Monarch or Emperor) is necessary for the well-being of mankind.[85] Thus *par in parem* envisions a scenario more akin to what we now would view as the relationship between the component parts of a unitary State (that is, internal relationship within the State) than to what takes place between and among a group of States, each having full authority/sovereignty within its own borders and with no super-State authority over and above them. In a more metaphysical sense, the *par* maxim can with perfect felicity be used to describe the relationship of human beings living as individuals in a purported state of nature, a primeval condition prior to the birth of organized institutions, including the State.[86] Hence this maxim, being a general proposition applicable to all, is of particular pertinence to none. While it is interesting to note that the popularity of this alleged epigram of *international law* should owe much to a poet,[87] it must also be realized that *par in parem* with Dante is a far cry from what we take it to mean today.

As regards State immunity itself, the earliest reference to the *par in parem* adage seems to have been made by Hartmann in 1890,[88] seventy-eight years after *The Schooner Exchange*. Von Bar also spoke of the maxim *par in parem non habet jurisdictionem* in 1891, listing it as one of four possible grounds for immunity;[89] but he then hastened to add that the *par* maxim was nothing but a rule of domestic criminal law in feudal times:

Le viel adage cité: *Par in parem non habet jurisdictionem* n'appartenait en vérité qu'au droit interne ... au temps féodal, et ne s'appliquait qu'à la juridiction pénale.[90]

The invocation of the maxim (variously phrased) by courts is of much later occurrence. If we take *The Schooner Exchange* decided by the US Supreme Court in 1812 as the earliest case on State immunity, then it is something of a surprise that this maxim, believed to lie at the fountainhead of immunity, was not mentioned in the US courts until some 170 years later, in the 1981 case of *Texas Trading*. The US Supreme Court, with which the doctrine of State immunity originated, has never referred to the *par* principle as the basis of immunity, whether in *The Schooner Exchange* or in any other case thereafter. In fact, the US courts do not seem to have a high regard for the epigram so popular with other, especially the Italian, courts. Up to now the saying has been mentioned in only two US decisions: one did not concern State immunity at all;[91] and the other quoted the maxim only to disparage Latin phrases in general as speaking 'with a hoary simplicity inappropriate to the modern financial world'.[92] At any rate, in point of time, the *par* maxim did not gain popularity with courts, nor with scholars, until after the late 1920s.[93] In other words, the *par* principle obtained currency over a century after the seminal case of *The Schooner Exchange* and at a time when the doctrine of State immunity, with or without restrictions, had already become firmly entrenched in international law and practice. If the maxim was virtually unknown during the early development of the doctrine and practice of State immunity, and if it entered into general discourse only at a much later stage, when the principle of immunity had already been established and widely accepted as a principle of international law without any reference to it, then it cannot possibly and reasonably have served as the basis of immunity. Thus the *par* principle appears to have been more of a summarization, or rather *post factum* rationalization, of the position adopted by the courts, rather than a guiding principle informing from the start how the issue of immunity was to be resolved.

54   GENERAL PRINCIPLES

A closer examination of the ways in which the *par* maxim has been intoned in State immunity cases not only shows that the earliest references to the maxim were made only in the 1920s but also reveals that courts in various countries have never been unanimous on the exact wording of this aphorism: they use a number of variants: '*par in parem non habet imperium*',[94] '*par in parem non habet jurisdictionem*',[95] '*par in parem non habet judicium*',[96] '*par in parem non habet imperium nec judicium*',[97] or simply a cryptic '*par in parem*'.[98] Sometimes the court itself would appear unsure as to which one of them is better worded or more controlling.[99] It is more important to note that, statistically, the two most popular formulations, *par in parem non habet imperium* and *par in parem non habet jurisdictionem* have approximately the same number of occurrences. Thus, if it is to be asserted that immunity derives from *par in parem non habet imperium*, it will be equally justifiable to claim that immunity emanates instead from *par in parem non habet jurisdictionem*. Moreover, from a longer, but less well-known, version: *Jurisdictio inhaeret, cohaeret, adhaeret imperio; par in parem non habet judicium*[100] (literally, 'jurisdiction/ judicial authority inheres in, coheres with and adheres to sovereign power/authority; one equal does not have judicial competence to sit in judgment upon another equal'), it can be deduced that *jurisdictio, imperium*, and *judicium* are practically one and the same thing.

If the courts cannot agree on the exact wording of the maxim, it becomes difficult and unwarrantable to point to any particular *one* of these several formulations as *the basis* of immunity. For statistically any one of them can fulfil, and has fulfilled, that function; which of course means that none of them can be said to be the only one from which State immunity has derived. We are thus either faced with a number of different axioms, each having its particular connotations, or, perhaps more accurately, compelled to regard these as variants of a proto- or meta-maxim, the more so when these high-sounding terms (*jurisdictio, imperium* and *judicium*) appear to be freely interchangeable. Whereas such a proto-/meta-maxim is nowhere to be found in the history of State immunity, it is more reasonable to view these different formulations as different expressions of the same *notion* or *idea*. That is to say, if the *par* maxim were to be regarded as the basis of immunity, it would be more appropriate to postulate that what constitutes the basis of immunity is not any particularly worded maxim (because, whatever formulation you choose, there is always another formulation that is equally entitled to be chosen), but the notion to which these different sayings – or different variants of the same saying – give expression. This is tantamount to

THE LEGAL BASIS FOR IMMUNITY   55

saying that the maxim itself, however worded, cannot, *physically as an idiomatic expression*, serve as the basis of State immunity.

The question is, if the *par* aphorism cannot *physically*, but can only *notionally*, serve as the basis for State immunity, what is precisely the notion that is embodied in it? Since the axiom literally means 'one equal does not have sovereign power/authority (*imperium*) or jurisdiction/judicial authority (*jurisdictionem*) over, or judicial competence to sit in judgment (*judicium*) upon, another equal', one would naturally regard it as simply a seemingly more venerable way of expressing the *equality* of States. A closer look at the case law, however, reveals a much more mottled picture: the *par in parem* adage has been construed to mean, or associated with, a whole spectrum of attributes of the State, such as sovereignty (or sovereign authority),[101] equality,[102] independence,[103] 'rights of liberty',[104] and, unsurprisingly, various combinations of these and others.[105] The converse position has also been expressed that the adage *par in parem non habet jurisdictionem* is itself 'deduced' from 'the principle of the equality and independence of States one from the other'.[106] And scholars display the same diversity of opinion in citing the adage as denoting equality (or 'sovereign equality'),[107] sovereignty,[108] independence,[109] a combination of several attributes of Statehood,[110] or simply as a free-standing expression without any particular connotation specified.[111]

Whereas the case law more often associates *par in parem* with sovereignty, the scholarly opinion more frequently links it with equality. Moreover, the same court may think differently at different times;[112] and judges in the same case may not necessarily give the same interpretation.[113] Thus, whereas Lord Wilberforce[114] and Lord Goff[115] would see *par in parem* as connected with sovereignty, Lord Millett regarded it as linked to both sovereignty and equality.[116]

We are back at the original question: which one of those vague concepts such as sovereignty, independence and equality is the basis of State immunity? This in its turn means that we are also back at the answer to that question: none of them can singly be the basis of State immunity, and none of them has ever done so.

5.3. *What is the basis of immunity?*

This demonstrates that it is really a barren exercise trying to pin down the exact basis of State immunity to any of those vague notions of sovereignty, independence, equality and dignity, or trying to argue against any one of them: for they collectively have served that purpose,

56 GENERAL PRINCIPLES

and it is a matter of little practical import for us to be absolutely clear what the basis of immunity is or ought to be.

There is a notable paucity of discussion of the basis of immunity in later cases after the 1970s. This shows that it is possible to solve the practical issues of State immunity without reference to the doctrinal intricacies regarding the origin and basis of immunity itself. Indeed the modern law of State immunity seems to have largely evolved through designing concrete methods for solving concrete, real-life issues. The fact that courts have to apply existing domestic rules of procedure means that they have little need to probe into such metaphysical issues as the origin and basis of State immunity. This has in large measure contributed to the general process whereby purely theoretical issues have been relegated to the background, with the result that such issues are now only of academic interest: that present schemes of State immunity, be they domestic statutes or international conventions, concentrate rather on concrete rules than generalized principles, bears full testimony to this.

If what constitutes the basis of immunity is the sum total of the attributes of Statehood, then we are saying nothing but that a State enjoys immunity because it is a State. But why should a State qua State enjoy immunity? Other things apart, their Statehood seems to be the only denominator whereby all the States in the world become comparable to one another. That being the case, a remark on the nature and prerogative of Statehood is not only a perception of others, but will necessarily be a self-perception. Thus when a court holds that the defendant State shall not enjoy immunity under certain circumstances, that will be the same as saying that the court's own State shall not enjoy immunity under these or similar circumstances, and the forum State will be estopped from asserting a wider immunity should it become a defendant itself in a foreign court. The US legislators were fully aware of this when they observed, with regard to more extensive protection of foreign States' military property from execution, that the purpose of such protection was to:

avoid the possibility that a foreign state might permit execution on military property of the United States abroad under a reciprocal application of the [FSIA].[117]

Such a consideration of reciprocity has also found its way into national legislation. Section 15 of the Canada SIA of 1982, for example, stipulates:

The Governor in Council may, on the recommendation of the Minister of Foreign Affairs, by order restrict any immunity or privileges under this Act in relation to a foreign state where, in the opinion of the Governor in Council, the immunity or privileges exceed those accorded by the law of that state.[118]

The problem with reciprocity is that, in practice, very few courts have expressly referred to it as the basis of immunity.[119] To be sure, there are even statements dismissing it as having any bearing on the question of immunity.[120] In the absence of empirical evidence, any suggestion that reciprocity should be *the* basis is highly speculative; but at least the following observation ought to be undeniable. Since immunity is an important issue faced by all the States, including in particular those whose courts regularly deal with immunity cases, and since even the staunchest adherents of restrictive immunity (such as Belgium and Italy) do themselves claim immunity, it seems highly unlikely that immunity can be completely abolished, or otherwise restricted to a significantly greater extent than it has already been. Indeed the significance of the 2004 UN Convention on Jurisdictional Immunities, the conclusion of which was blessed with universal support evidenced by favourable official statements and a swift reaching of consensus, lies not in suggesting that immunity should be restricted: so far as international law is concerned, restrictive immunity is already *the* principle, with or without the Convention. Rather, its significance resides in the fact that it seeks to establish a *treaty regime* of State immunity, that is, a regime that shall obtain and prevail as between States accepting the same legal obligations towards one another. As far as the States parties to the Convention are concerned, immunity shall be granted or denied on a *reciprocal* basis.

Thus such notions as sovereignty, equality, independence, dignity and reciprocity are but items on a random list, to be chosen à la carte, according to the predilections of whoever is making the choice, but cannot be seriously identified as the theoretical underpinnings of State immunity. Ultimately, the discussion of the doctrinal basis or bases of immunity is neither profitable nor even necessary, and is at best of academic interest only, for courts regularly deal with the issue of State immunity without regard to any doctrinal consideration and this tendency is becoming more and more manifest.

Whatever its perception of State immunity, a defendant State always has to defend its position in the terms and provisions peculiar to the particular court in which it is sued. As soon as a State becomes a party to the litigation, the underlying legal relationship ceases to be that of a

State-to-State nature but proceeds more in the way of a dispute between private parties. Time-honoured notions such as sovereignty, independence, equality and dignity, etc., are becoming increasingly insufficient in defending immunity of the State either from suit or from execution. As their practice accrues, national courts are developing ever more sophisticated legal regimes comprising various criteria for granting or denying immunity. With this there grows a 'checklist' of situations both in favour of and against immunity. Defendant States are obliged to look for defences only from such a list of concrete instances. The whole process now departs from the arena of international law and becomes more of a matter of domestic procedural rules.

Thanks to the rapidly growing body of case law, the courts are now able to decide their cases with absolutely no need to discuss the legal basis of immunity. Because of the increasingly concretized and refined procedural rules concerning the circumstances in which immunity is to be granted or denied, cases of immunity can now be decided with clinical detachment, disinterest, and (one hopes) ease. From the Olympian heights of sovereignty and independence in the era of *The Schooner Exchange* State immunity has finally descended to the ground, to the world of mundane technicalities. The judge is no longer concerned about where immunity comes from: it is already there. All that matters, in a particular case, is whether the defendant foreign State's act, measured by the benchmarks of domestic procedural rules, ought or ought not to be immune. The more important and pressing issue, therefore, is to know the basis on which immunity is *denied* by the courts.

6. The legal basis for denying immunity

It is now universally accepted that States enjoy immunity only with regard to sovereign, public, governmental, or non-commercial acts (*acta jure imperii*), but not in respect of non-sovereign, private, non-governmental, or commercial acts (*acta jure gestionis*). However, scant attention has been paid to the other important ground – mostly taken for granted – for the courts to deny immunity, namely that the acts in question were performed in the territory of the forum State. In fact, as the discussion will show, the twin rules of (a) a private act and (b) performed in the territory of the forum State are both equally crucial to the doctrine and practice of restrictive immunity, so equally crucial that they must be regarded as the two pillars of restrictive immunity.

It must be pointed out at once that the phrase 'in the territory of the forum State' is intended to be only a shorthand for various situations where an act has a jurisdictional connection with the territory of the forum State: performed in the territory, performed outside, but having some link with, the territory, or performed broadly within the jurisdiction of the forum State. Empirically, at any rate, the expression 'in the territory of the forum State' ought not to cause any misunderstanding. The vast majority of the cases reported so far actually involve acts performed *within* the territory of the forum State, so much so that the phrase 'in the territory of the forum State' will be quite sufficient in describing the normal situation. Besides, in the final analysis, other jurisdictional links than the territory itself cannot but be regarded as extensions of territorial jurisdiction, and must accordingly operate on the basis of and subject to the territorial principle.

6.1. The 'private person' test

How can one tell whether a particular act is a commercial or private act? This is the single most important theme that runs through the whole history of State immunity, and, naturally, throughout this book. What will be discussed here is the overall, universal rule of thumb adopted by all the courts in the world; that is, if an act is one that a private individual can perform, then this is a commercial or private act. In other words, an analogy is drawn between the defendant State and a private individual. From the beginning this was but a natural response on the part of the courts to the ever-increasing State participation in international trade and other commercial activities. Over the years this has proved to be the most viable, the most versatile, and the most easily operable test for the judges. On the other hand, it is becoming increasingly obvious that this analogy should not be pushed too far under current circumstances. If the evolution of restrictive immunity has been the result of an expansion of *State* activities into formerly commercial and private areas, and with it a redefinition of the sovereign functions of a State, then an equally powerful trend that is unfolding before our very eyes at this very moment must compel a fresh look at the law itself. And that trend is globalization. Globalization has seen, among other things, an unprecedented expansion of *private* activities, especially over the past decade, into the formerly sovereign or public sphere. When private companies are now rendering logistical support for military operations, running prisons and conducting interrogations, providing armed escort for personnel and convoys, doing general policing work,

60   GENERAL PRINCIPLES

and carrying out surveillance, it is becoming more and more difficult, without offending either logic or common sense, to insist on maintaining that a particular activity is 'quintessentially sovereign' or 'typically private'. The boundary between *jus imperii* and *jus gestionis* has never been so elusive and treacherous. Only time will show how the law of State immunity will be transformed yet again by this new reality, just as time has done over the past hundred years. To be better prepared for what will happen in the future, it is now necessary to take stock of what has happened in the past.

The 'private person' test was put forward at the very beginning of the evolution of State immunity. In *The Schooner Exchange*, the US government submitted that:

So if a sovereign descend from the throne and become a merchant, he submits to the laws of the country. If he contract private debts, his private funds are liable. So if he charter a vessel, the cargo is liable for the freight.[121]

Royer wrote in 1867:

Quand un gouvernement fait acte d'autorité, quant il exerce l'*imperium*, nous admettons qu'il repousse fièrement toute ingérence étrangère, qu'il maintienne son indépendance à l'abri de toute atteinte. C'est son droit et c'est son devoir. Mais s'il descend dans l'arène où s'agitent les intérêts privés, non pour les soumettre à son action régulatrice, mais pour traiter avec eux; s'il achète, s'il emprunte, s'il contracte, en un mot, il se place, par cela même, dans la situation d'un simple particulier.[122]

Unsurprisingly, it was the Belgian and the Italian courts that first adopted the notion. In 1882, the Italian Corte di Cassazione di Torino said, in *Morellet*:

it being incumbent upon [the State] to provide for the administration of the public body and for the material interests of the individual citizens, it must acquire and own property, it must contract, it must sue and be sued, and, in a word, it must exercise civil rights in like manner as any other juristic person or private individual.[123]

In 1886, the Italian Corte di Cassazione di Firenze made this declaration in *Guttieres*:

when the Government, as a civil body (*ente civile*), descends into the sphere of contracts and transactions so as to acquire rights and to assume obligations like any private person, then its independence is not pertinent. The State, when dealing solely with private transactions and obligations, must follow the rules of the common law.[124]

In the earliest 'purchase of bullets case' in 1888, a Belgian court held that, in making a contract with a Belgian company for the purchase of bullets, Bulgaria acted as a *private person*, and submitted itself to all the civil consequences of the contract, including the rules governing judicial competence.[125]

In the landmark 1903 case of *Compagnie des chemins de fer Liégeois Limbourgeois*, the Belgian Cour de Cassation denied immunity on the following reasoning:

Mais attendu que l'État ne doit pas se confiner dans son rôle politique; qu'en vue des besoins de la collectivité, il peut acquérir et posséder des biens, contracter, devenir créancier et débiteur; qu'il peut même faire le commerce, se réserver des monopoles ou la direction de services d'utilité générale;

Que, dans la gestion de ce domaine ou de ces services, l'Etat ne met pas en oeuvre la puissance publique, mais fait ce que *des particuliers* peuvent faire et, partant, n'agit que comme *personne civile ou privée*.[126]

In the well-known *Empire of Iran Case*, the German Constitutional Court, after an exhaustive survey of cases German and foreign, declared:

As a means for determining the distinction between acts *jure imperii* and *jure gestionis* one should rather refer to the nature of the State transaction or the resulting legal relationships, and not to the motive or purpose of the State activity. It thus depends on whether the foreign State has acted in exercise of its sovereign authority, that is in public law, or *like a private person*, that is in private law.[127]

The Austrian Supreme Court said, in *Steinmetz*:

As soon as a foreign State acts in the capacity of a contractual partner in commercial transactions, for example as the owner of a nationalized undertaking, it thereby descends to the level of subjects of private law and is as much amenable to domestic jurisdiction as any other foreigner.[128]

In the US, the drafters of the US FSIA explained:

the sovereign immunity of foreign states should be 'restricted' to cases involving acts of a foreign state which are sovereign or governmental in nature, as opposed to acts which are either commercial in nature or those which private persons normally perform.[129]

Applying the FSIA, the Second Circuit said in *Texas Trading*:

if the activity is one in which a private person could engage, it is not entitled to immunity.[130]

62 GENERAL PRINCIPLES

Then in *Rush-Presbyterian*, the Seventh Circuit said:

In determining the nature of the foreign state's action, an important inquiry is whether a private person could have engaged in similar conduct. If a private person could have engaged in the same *type* of activity, then the sovereign has presumptively engaged in 'commercial activity' within the meaning of the FSIA; however, if no private party could have engaged in the challenged conduct, then the conduct is a sovereign act, and the foreign state is immune from suit.[131]

Even before the enactment of the FSIA, the US Supreme Court opined, in *Alfred Dunhill*, that:

In their commercial capacities, foreign governments do not exercise powers peculiar to sovereigns. Instead, they exercise only those powers that can also be exercised by private citizens.[132]

Citing *Alfred Dunhill* and *Rush-Presbyterian*, the Supreme Court in *Weltover* concluded that:

when a foreign government acts, not as regulator of a market, but in the manner of a private player within it, the foreign sovereign's actions are 'commercial' within the meaning of the FSIA ... the issue is whether the particular actions that the foreign state performs (whatever the motive behind them) are the *type* of actions by which a private party engages in 'trade and traffic or commerce'.[133]

The English courts also embrace the 'private person' test. In *I Congreso del Partido*, Justice Robert Goff (as he then was) said that a non-immune act was 'an act any private citizen can perform', and that a foreign State did not enjoy immunity where it acted 'as any private citizen may act'.[134] Expressly endorsing this reasoning, Lord Wilberforce said:

When therefore a claim is brought against a state ... and state immunity is claimed, it is necessary to consider what is the relevant act which forms the basis of the claim: is this ... an act 'jure gestionis' or is it an act 'jure imperii': is it ... a 'private act' or is it a 'sovereign or public act', a private act meaning in this context an act of a private law character such as a private citizen might have entered into?[135]

Lord Goff, speaking for the majority in *Kuwait Airways*, said:

It is apparent from Lord Wilberforce's statement of principle that the ultimate test of what constitutes an act jure imperii is whether the act in question is of its own character a governmental act, as opposed to an act which any private citizen can perform.[136]

Such a 'private person' formula has run through the whole modern history of the law of State immunity, has been endorsed by the highest judicial authorities in other countries and has been closely followed by various lower courts as well.[137] It has even been written into the only international convention currently in force, the 1972 European Convention:

A Contracting State cannot claim immunity from the jurisdiction of a court of another Contracting State if it has on the territory of the State of the forum an office, agency or other establishment through which it engages, *in the same manner as a private person*, in an industrial, commercial or financial activity, and the proceedings relate to that activity of the office, agency or establishment.[138]

Over the years the 'private person' test has been variously expressed as 'on an equal footing with a private person/individual'; 'as possessor of private rights and duties'; 'in the same manner as an ordinary private individual'; 'in a private capacity'; 'in the realm/sphere of private law'; and so on; but the essence and tenor remains constant: the analogy of the foreign State to a private individual. We shall see later in this book that a pure and over-simplistic 'private person' test has on many occasions proved inadequate and unworkable, especially with regard to employment contracts and foreign armed forces, so that it often becomes necessary to resort to other tests, including, in particular, the status of the defendant and the purpose of the act in question. More importantly, at the same time that States are venturing into the private sector, thereby causing a reconceptualization of the role and function of the State and its position before foreign courts, the general trend of democratization and privatization in the domestic sphere has witnessed a parallel expansion of activities that can be pursued by private persons, natural or juristic/corporate; and, with the advent of multinational corporations, the scope of activities of private persons has been revolutionized. In many cases it has become increasingly difficult to tell which activities can only be performed by a private person and which are the preserve of the exalted power of the State. As pointed out earlier, little attention has been paid to the rapid expansion of private persons (both natural and legal persons) into areas formally reserved exclusively to States. If war activities can be 'outsourced' to private companies, then there is almost nothing that cannot be delegated to a private entity that happens to be the highest bidder, or has the best connections. In this light, the difference between a State and a private person is more and more blurred and should now be regarded as one of degree, rather than of kind. If almost any and everything can be engaged in by a private

64   GENERAL PRINCIPLES

person and is therefore a private activity, then what distinguishes a private person from a State is nothing but a name. Consequently, the 'private person' test can no longer be sufficient or reliable in distinguishing between an immune and a non-immune act. This is the new challenge for the State immunity doctrine at present and for the future. Unless States would wish to see their various acts, previously perceived as quintessentially sovereign, now indifferently canvassed, assessed and maybe arraigned in foreign courts, then something must be done in order at least to supply for the inherent inadequacy of the private person test. More factors have to be brought in than a simplistic dichotomy between a State and a private person, as such dichotomy has been and continues to be diminished to vanishing point in real life. If the current trend of globalization and extreme privatization continues, it will not be long before the 'private person test' loses even its semblance of a viable or even valid criterion: *cessante ratione legis cessat ipsa lex*.

6.2. The principle of territorial jurisdiction

The most important principle for the denial of immunity is actually not a *jure imperii / jure gestionis* distinction, but territorial jurisdiction. Indeed, the very term 'immunity', meaning exemption from jurisdiction, by definition presupposes the existence of that jurisdiction. If jurisdiction itself does not exist in the first place, then no issue of immunity arises, because the absence of jurisdiction means that the court is not competent to hear and decide the case, whoever happens to be the defendant, be it a State or a private person. Because the establishment of jurisdiction involves various connecting factors, chief among which is territoriality, the law of State immunity forms a legitimate concern for private international law as well.[139]

The traditional law of State immunity has developed out of cases decided on matters taking place within the territorial limits of the forum State, hence the realization from the very inception of the law of State immunity that immunity constituted a derogation from the territorial jurisdiction of the forum State. Indeed, that the relevant transaction or act in question had taken place in the territory of the forum State was the primary reason why the courts felt justified that immunity should be denied. In fact, when one goes back in history, one finds that the territoriality principle has always assumed a prominent position in cases concerning State immunity. It was only when the court was confident that it had jurisdiction that it began to formulate rules whereby exemption from that jurisdiction was to be permitted. Since the issue of immunity is first of all an issue of jurisdiction, the principle of territorial jurisdiction has remained a common feature of cases of immunity, whatever doctrine (absolute or restrictive) was followed by the court. Thus in cases of absolute immunity, the courts made it quite clear that that they were dealing with *exemption* from the fundamental principle of territorial jurisdiction. In the very first case on State immunity, *The Schooner Exchange*, a trading vessel originally belonging to US citizens had been seized on the high seas by the French navy and later converted into a warship, and in the instant case had been driven by stress of weather into the port of Philadelphia, US, whereupon the original owners sought to repossess the ship. Chief Justice Marshall characterized the case in the following terms:

This case involves the very delicate and important inquiry, whether an American citizen can assert, in an American court, a title to an armed national vessel, found *within the waters of the United States*.[140]

He then made this pronouncement:

The jurisdiction of the nation within its own *territory* is necessarily exclusive and absolute. It is susceptible of no limitation not imposed by itself ... All exceptions, therefore, to the full and complete power of a nation within its own *territories*, must be traced up to the consent of the nation itself. They can flow from no other legitimate source ... [For the sake of international intercourse,] all sovereigns have consented to a relaxation in practice, in cases under certain peculiar circumstances, of that absolute and complete jurisdiction within their respective *territories* ... This full and absolute *territorial* jurisdiction [is] the attribute of every sovereign ... One sovereign ... can be supposed to enter a foreign *territory* only under an express license ... [This situation has] given rise to a class of cases in which every sovereign is understood to waive the exercise of a part of that complete exclusive *territorial jurisdiction*, which has been stated to be the attribute of every nation.[141]

Clearly, from the very beginning immunity was conceived as a relaxation of, or exemption from, the 'full, complete, exclusive and absolute' *territorial* jurisdiction,[142] an ultimately self-imposed diminution of the jurisdiction each State exercises within its own territory. And such exemption could be withdrawn by the territorial State as it deemed appropriate.[143]

Territorial jurisdiction has been invoked as the strongest reason why immunity of a foreign State should be denied, especially at those critical moments when the judicial authorities of a State first decided to shift from absolute to restrictive immunity, or even earlier, when some dissident voice called for restrictive immunity within an absolute immunity

66   GENERAL PRINCIPLES

jurisprudence. Thus, in *Charkieh*, a foreign ship was arrested in the port of London for damage caused as a result of a collision in the Thames. Deciding the case at a time when the UK jurisprudence favoured the absolute immunity doctrine, Sir Robert Phillimore opined that '[u]pon principles of general jurisprudence the presence of a person or of property within the limits of a state founds the jurisdiction of the tribunals of that state' and that an absolute right of exemption would be 'incompatible with the right of the territorial sovereign'.[144]

In *The Parlement Belge*, one of the earliest English cases establishing absolute immunity, Brett LJ explained:

The principle [of immunity] is that ... each and every [State] declines to exercise by means of its Courts any of its *territorial jurisdiction* over the person of any sovereign or ambassador of any other state, or over the public property of any state which is destined to public use, or over the property of any ambassador, though such sovereign, ambassador, or property be *within its territory*, and, therefore, but for the common agreement, subject to its jurisdiction.[145]

Lord Denning was a staunch advocate of restrictive immunity even before UK courts adopted that position. In *Rahimtoola*, he said:

There is no reason why we should grant to the departments or agencies of foreign Governments an immunity which we do not grant our own, provided always that the matter in dispute arises within the jurisdiction of our courts and is properly cognizable by them.[146]

... sovereign immunity should not depend on whether a foreign government is impleaded, directly or indirectly, but rather on the nature of the dispute ... if the dispute concerns, for instance, the commercial transactions of a foreign government (whether carried on by its own departments or agencies or by setting up separate legal entities), and it arises properly within the territorial jurisdiction of our courts, there is no ground for granting immunity.[147]

He further clarified the rule in *Thai-Europe*:

a foreign sovereign has no immunity when it enters into a commercial transaction with a trader *here* and a dispute arises which is properly within the *territorial jurisdiction* of our courts ... This test would apply to all the exceptions which I have stated. I would stress particularly the necessity that the dispute should 'arise properly within the territorial jurisdiction of our courts'. By this ... I mean that the dispute should be concerned with property actually situate within the jurisdiction of our courts or with commercial transactions having a most close connection with England, such that, by the presence of parties or the nature of the dispute, it is more properly cognisable here than elsewhere.[148]

Finally, in the landmark case of *Trendtex*, which concerned a letter of credit opened by the Nigerian Government for the purchase of cement, Lord Denning based the denial of immunity squarely on the territoriality principle:

Trendtex here are not suing on the contracts of purchase. They are claiming on the letter of credit which is an entirely separate contract. It was a straightforward commercial transaction. The letter of credit was issued in London through a London bank in the ordinary course of commercial dealings. It is completely within the territorial jurisdiction of our courts. I do not think it is open to the Government of Nigeria to claim sovereign immunity in respect of it.[149]

Thomas J expressed much the same sentiment in *Controller*:

I regard territorial sovereignty as the starting point. Practice and reality demand no less. This being the case, state immunity is to be seen as a derogation from territorial sovereignty and the exclusive jurisdiction which that sovereignty confers.[150]

In this connection, it must be recalled that one of the exceptions to absolute immunity, which involved immovable property, was firmly rooted in the territoriality principle. Because immovable property has always been considered inseparable from the territory, it has never been suggested that immovable property should be subject to any other law than that of the territory in which the property is located (*lex situs* and *forum rei sitae*). Thus, even at a time when absolute immunity was the prevailing doctrine, jurisdiction was unswervingly upheld where territorial jurisdiction was at its most manifest, i.e. with regard to immovable property.[151]

In 1891, when the Institut de Droit International proposed its draft articles on State immunity, these were explicitly predicated on territoriality:

Article II (1)

   1. Les seules actions recevables contre un État étranger sont:
   (1) les actions réelles, y compris les actions possessoires, se rapportant à une chose, immeuble ou meuble, qui se trouve sur le *territoire*;
   (2) les actions fondées sur la qualité de l'État étranger comme héritier ou légataire d'un ressortissant du *territoire*, ou comme ayant droit à une succession ouverte sur le *territoire*;
   (3) les actions qui se rapportent à un établissement de commerce ou industriel ou à un chemin de fer exploités par l'État étranger dans le *territoire*;
   (4) les actions pour lesquelles l'État étranger a expressément reconnu la compétence du tribunal ...

68   GENERAL PRINCIPLES

   (5) les actions fondées sur des contrats conclus par l'État étranger dans le *territoire*, si l'exécution complète dans ce même *territoire* en peut être demandée d'après une clause expresse ou d'après la nature même de l'action;

   (6) les actions en dommages-intérêts nées d'un délit ou quasi-délit, qui a eu lieu sur le *territoire*.[152]

As the law developed and as the number of cases grew, it became so commonplace for courts to assert their jurisdiction in cases involving matters territorially connected with the forum State that the territorial connection, this most crucial requirement for the assertion of jurisdiction, tended to fade into the background and, in most cases, to be completely forgotten. This tendency has continued to this day and will have serious consequences for the law under current circumstances, as the exercise of *extraterritorial* jurisdiction is becoming more and more a feature of international practice. Where the jurisdiction of the court is not based on territoriality but on some other ground permitted by international law (such as universal jurisdiction in international human rights law), it will be highly questionable to decide the issue of immunity, i.e. exemption from jurisdiction, without determining whether the court should have jurisdiction in the first place.

6.3.   *Private act plus territoriality* – Binnenbeziehung

In a number of major jurisdictions the courts have made it clear that the reason for the denial of immunity was twofold: the foreign State has performed a *private act* in the *territory* of the forum State.

For the Italian courts, *princeps in alterius territorio privatus* (literally 'A prince becomes a private person in another prince's territory').[153] They have consistently referred to the 'private person' test combined with the territorial connection as a single measure for non-immunity. In *Guttieres*, the Italian Court of Cassation held that foreign States, once they descended 'into the sphere of contracts and transactions so as to acquire rights and to assume obligations like any private person', could not enjoy immunity 'in cases involving obligations arising out of contracts or transactions concluded or to be performed therein [i.e. in Italian territory]'.[154] In *Borga*, the Court of Cassation clearly declared:

when a foreign State carries out, in the territory of another State, an economic activity which could be performed by a private person, it thereby divests itself of its public law personality and it cannot claim immunity from the jurisdiction of that other State.[155]

And this has remained the Italian position ever since.[156]

The Austrian practice adopts the same approach. In *Dralle*, the Austrian Supreme Court said:

Where ... the foreign State conducts itself as the holder of ordinary private rights and enters into contracts to be performed within the territory (i.e. Austria), it enters the confines of the legal system of that territory and cannot therefore remain entirely independent thereof; in such cases the foreign State too must be subject to the jurisdiction of the State in whose territory the business enterprise is domiciled.[157]

In the US, this 'double test' of 'private act plus territoriality' was the position taken by scholars long before the US practice shifted to restrictive immunity. The Harvard Law School research programme on 'Competence of Courts in regard to Foreign States', headed by Jessup, declared in 1932:

A State may be made a respondent in a proceeding in a court of another State when, *in the territory of such other State*, it engages in an industrial, commercial, financial or other business enterprise in which *private persons* may there engage, or does an act there in connection with such an enterprise wherever conducted, and the proceeding is based upon the conduct of such enterprise or upon such act.[158]

The US FSIA has a built-in territorial connection requirement for exceptions to immunity of foreign States.[159]

The most prominent example of strict adherence to the 'private act plus territoriality' test as justification for denying immunity is the Swiss jurisprudence. Like the courts in other countries, the Swiss courts use the private person test as an important yardstick for determining that a particular act is *de jure gestionis*. Thus:

a foreign State cannot rely on immunity if it descends to the same level as a private individual, in particular when it acts as the holder of a private right (*jure gestionis*).[160]

However, the Swiss Federal Tribunal has consistently held that the mere fact that the foreign State has acted like a private person is not enough for the assertion of Swiss jurisdiction: there must at the same time be a sufficient connection with the Swiss territory. As early as 1918, when it first adopted the doctrine of restrictive immunity in the *Dreyfus* case, the

70   GENERAL PRINCIPLES

Tribunal in upholding an attachment based on a claim for the return of Austrian State treasury notes circulated in Switzerland made it clear that immunity was denied not only because the case involved a private law relationship (*Privatrechtsverhältnis* or *jure gestionis*), but also because the relevant act had occurred in Switzerland.[161] This was reaffirmed in *Walder*, where, in the absence of a territorial connection, the Tribunal vacated a writ of attachment obtained in Zurich by some Swiss nationals who were owners of bonds against Greece as successor to a loan issued by a railway company which had subsequently been nationalized. The Tribunal stated that, although the *Dreyfus* case involved acts of private law, the Tribunal:

upheld the order of arrest against the Austrian State not for this reason alone. For in that case the claim arose from a debt-relationship established within Swiss territory ... In order to consider the debt out of which arose the claims for attachment as one established in Swiss territory, it should have been either originated, concluded, or performed here by the debtor, or there should have been at least such acts performed by the debtor for which he must have designated a place of performance in Switzerland [*in der Schweiz*].[162]

Since none of these occurred in this case, immunity from attachment had to be preserved; this even though the original debtor, the railway company, would have been subjected to the arrest of alien property pursuant to Swiss law concerning bankruptcy. This also clearly shows that the Federal Tribunal applied a different, stricter territorial connection requirement to a foreign State than to a private individual.

The territorial connection requirement was first fully articulated by the Tribunal in *Julius Bär*, in which an attachment order against Greece was vacated for lack of such a connection. The Tribunal said:

A distinction must be made according to whether the foreign State acts in the exercise of its sovereignty (*jure imperii*) or in a private law capacity (*jure gestionis*). Only in the former case is it completely covered by the principle of immunity from jurisdiction. In the latter case it may be sued before the courts of another State, and may be subjected to measures of forced execution. However, even in the last named case the Federal Tribunal does not recognize the jurisdiction of Swiss courts without further condition; on the contrary, it requires some connecting factor [*une circonstance de rattachement*]. Not every private law relationship entered into by a foreign State can give rise to proceedings in Switzerland. That relationship must at least have some links [*certains liens*] with Swiss territory.[163]

Thus the fact that a foreign State had engaged in some act *jure gestionis* could not of itself lead to a loss of immunity. According to the Tribunal:

THE LEGAL BASIS FOR DENYING IMMUNITY 71

The fundamental reason for [the *Dreyfus*] decision was that the loan had been raised in Switzerland, that Austria had undertaken to reimburse it in Switzerland in Swiss currency, and that Switzerland was as it were the theatre of all the operations. There was thus a clear link [*manifestement un lien de rattachement*] between the legal relationship which had given rise to dispute and Swiss territory.[164]

Obviously, it was the territorial connection rather than the private law nature of the act in question that decided the issue of immunity. In the instant case, the Tribunal declined even to consider whether a loan raised by a State from a private company in connection with a contract for the supply of goods was an act of public authority or an act of private law, because the condition that the act should have some connection (*rattachement*) with Swiss territory, was not satisfied. What was decisive was not the nature of the act of raising a loan, private or otherwise, but that:

The loan in dispute was not raised in Switzerland but in Sweden, and from a Swedish company, and the sum loaned was paid to the Greek Government by an English bank ... the legal relationship in dispute does not, in view of its substance and the circumstances of its origin, have any connection (*lien*) with Swiss territory.[165]

Thus, in the Swiss practice, it is not enough that the defendant foreign State has engaged in a commercial or private-law activity; in order for the Swiss courts to assert jurisdiction, there must be a connection between the act in question and the Swiss territory. Such total and thorough embracement of the territoriality principle has been reiterated in a great number of subsequent cases. Owing to the peculiar system of law reporting in Switzerland, this territorial nexus, termed '*rattachement*' or '*lien*'[166] in cases reported in the French language, has been given the famous appellation of '*Binnenbeziehung*' (literally, 'internal/domestic relationship/connection') in cases reported in German. As a matter of fact, the Swiss Federal Tribunal seems to favour the German term so much that it uses it even in French reports as well.[167]

In *UAR v. Mrs X*, the Federal Tribunal more precisely stated the territorial connection for exercising Swiss jurisdiction:

A distinction must be made according to whether the foreign State acts in the exercise of its sovereignty (*iure imperii*) or in a private law capacity (*iure gestionis*) ... In the latter case ... a foreign State may be sued before the Swiss courts and may be subjected in Switzerland to enforcement measures, on condition that the legal relationship to which it is a party is connected with Swiss territory [*rattaché au territoire de ce pays*]. This condition requires that the relationship has its origin in Switzerland, falls to be performed there, or at least that the debtor has taken certain steps capable of making Switzerland a place of performance.[168]

The German term *Binnenbeziehung* seems to have been first used in connection with foreign State immunity in a 1978 case, where the Federal Tribunal, in upholding attachment orders in connection with a failure to repay a loan which was to have been repaid in Swiss francs at a Swiss bank, said that:

Two questions remain to be decided in this case. Did the obligation which the attachment under appeal was intended to enforce have its basis in an exercise of public power by the Turkish State (*ius imperii*) or did it have a different basis making it analogous to a private law relationship (*ius gestionis*)? If the latter was the case, did the obligation have the necessary connection with Swiss territory [*Binnenbeziehung zur Schweiz*]?[169]

The Tribunal then reiterated the formula for the territorial connection as:

Such a connection was present if the debtor's obligation arose from a legal relationship which had its origin in Switzerland or fell to be performed in Switzerland, or where the debtor had at least taken certain steps making Switzerland a place of performance.[170]

More recently, in *M* v. *Egypt*, the Federal Tribunal, finding that hiring a chauffeur for an embassy did not involve the exercise of sovereign powers, went on to say:

However, this circumstance alone is insufficient to justify Switzerland exercising jurisdiction over the dispute. It is not every relationship under private law entered into by a foreign State which gives rise to jurisdiction in Switzerland. It is also necessary to establish that the relationship in question has certain links with Swiss territory (*Binnenbeziehung*), that is to say that it arose there, must be performed there, or at least that the debtor performed certain acts such as to make it a place of performance of the contract.[171]

For the Swiss Federal Tribunal, the territorial nexus even serves as an indicator of the *jure gestionis* nature of the act in question:

In order to distinguish between acts *iure gestionis* and acts *iure imperii*, the judge must base himself not on the purpose of the acts but on their nature and examine whether, in this regard, the act is an act of public power or whether it is similar to an act which *any private individual* could perform ... In applying this distinction based on the nature of the act the judge may also make use of criteria which are extraneous to the act itself. From this point of view the place where the act was performed by the foreign State may sometimes furnish certain indications. Where a State enters into a relationship with a private individual beyond its own frontiers and *on the territory of another State* without involving in any way its (diplomatic) relations with that other State, this is a good indication that the State is performing an act *iure gestionis*.[172]

Conversely, '[i]f a domestic relationship is lacking, nor does it need to be decided whether the legal dispute between the parties is caused by the [defendant's] sovereign or non-sovereign action'.[173]

Whatever practical reasons for such a strict criterion in Swiss courts,[174] for our purposes this practice affirms the crucial importance of territorial jurisdiction in cases of foreign State immunity.

Conclusion

Immunity constitutes a derogation from the territorial jurisdiction of the forum State. In this sense, immunity grew out of a conscious balancing of the interests of the territorial sovereign and the foreign sovereign admitted into the territory. The principle of territoriality lies at the root of the issue of State immunity. Indeed, the most important rationale for denying immunity, seen in this light, is not the *jure imperii / jure gestionis* distinction, but the territoriality principle.

Immunity is not synonymous with the lack of jurisdiction. On the contrary, immunity presupposes jurisdiction. Because immunity signifies the suspension, rather than negation, of jurisdiction, there is no primordial reason why a court should not exercise jurisdiction and deny immunity to foreign States in any and all cases. Since the jurisdiction of a State within its own territory is necessarily complete and exclusive, there is nothing against the exercise of territorial jurisdiction in all the matters arising within the territory of the forum State, or against a complete elimination of the notion of immunity. On the other hand, since States regularly do have to discharge functions of a sovereign nature in foreign States with the consent of the territorial State, a complete disappearance of immunity would mean that every sovereign act performed in a foreign State could potentially be challenged, in court or elsewhere, thereby severely hampering the ability of a State to fulfil its functions in foreign territories. Thus the grant of immunity to foreign States must have emanated from an awareness on the part of the forum State that such an unrestricted exercise of jurisdiction will ultimately work against itself. The distinction between acts *jure imperii* and acts *jure gestionis*, seen in this light, apart from serving as the working basis for deciding the issue of immunity, also fulfils the objective of protecting the forum State from undue harassment in foreign courts. In this sense immunity is certainly reciprocal; and the conclusion of an international convention, whereby contracting States accept to grant and deny immunity under clearly defined circumstances, is designed precisely on this basis.

We can see that the determination of a particular act as one of commercial or private-law nature depends on whether that act can also be performed by a private individual, but not on whether that act is in conformity with or in violation of international law: if it is an essentially public act then foreign courts have no jurisdiction, whether or not that act violates international law. This conclusion has a significant bearing on human rights litigation, as we shall see later.

The legal basis on which States enjoy immunity before foreign domestic courts has never been satisfactorily specified or identified, and perhaps never will. Empirical evidence indicates that State immunity cannot be based on any one of the grounds suggested from various quarters, such as sovereignty, independence, equality, dignity, comity, and the Latin maxim *par in parem non habet imperium*. They may or may not have collectively served as the legal basis for immunity; but this is unimportant and beside the point. In the vast majority of cases, the issue of immunity has been decided without any reference to the legal basis of immunity at all. As the cases accrue and the jurisprudence grows more sophisticated, there will be even less need for a court to worry about such metaphysical issues. The courts, if only for their own convenience, increasingly come to formulate the issues of State immunity as procedural matters of purely technical significance. State immunity has now become a highly specialized branch of the law, with complicated technicalities peculiar to each and every national legal system in which immunity cases are decided and as such cannot but be a boon for those lawyers in possession of the relevant expertise.

3 Commercial activity

The expression 'commercial activity' is a term of convenience. In its broad sense, used alongside and synonymously with such other terms as 'private/private-law act' and '*actum jure gestionis*', as opposed to 'sovereign/public act' or '*actum jure imperii*', it denotes both the totality of the situations where a State is not immune from the jurisdiction of a foreign domestic court and the general criterion for identifying and establishing such situations. In its narrow sense, it refers to a specific exception to immunity, to be distinguished from other exceptions which may not be strictly 'commercial', such as that of personal injury or damage to property, or which may be statutorily stipulated as separate exceptions, such as that of contracts of employment. For this reason, and because current law treats the adjudication of a case and the execution of the judgment as two distinct stages, 'commercial activity' serves a dual purpose in the law of State immunity. First, it underlies the decision whether a State is immune from adjudicative proceedings in a foreign national court; and, secondly, it provides the yardstick for deciding whether the property of a State is immune from enforcement measures. To put it succinctly, a State is not immune, in respect of a commercial or private-law activity, from the (adjudicative) jurisdiction of a foreign court; and the property of a State, used for commercial purposes, is not immune from attachment or execution in a foreign national court.

At the heart of the debate, since the inception of the law of State immunity, is the criterion for deciding what constitutes a commercial activity. Some courts assert that it is the nature of a particular act that is decisive. That is, if an act is by its nature a commercial, or private, act, then it is a commercial act; and it makes no difference if that act serves some sovereign or public purpose, since every act of a State, by definition, serves a public purpose. Other courts are of the opinion that the

76   COMMERCIAL ACTIVITY

sovereign or public purpose served by the act in question should also be taken into account: a sovereign purpose may immunize an act; indeed, it would not be possible in some cases to talk about the nature of an act without considering its purpose. Before entering this still raging debate, it is worthwhile to start with concrete examples of commercial activity in actual practice.

1.   What is a commercial activity?

All the current legal instruments on State immunity provide that a foreign State is not immune from the jurisdiction of the forum State with respect to a 'commercial activity' or 'commercial transaction';[1] but the definition of this term is far from settled or uniform.

Some instruments only contain a very broad reference to commercial activity or transactions, leaving it entirely to the court to work out what such an activity or transaction is. As far as the present discussion is concerned, not much guidance can be derived from such references as 'an industrial, commercial or financial activity' engaged in by the foreign State 'in the same manner as a private person',[2] 'a regular course of commercial conduct or a particular commercial transaction or act',[3] 'any particular transaction, act or conduct or any regular course of conduct that by reason of its nature is of a commercial character',[4] or 'a particular transaction or commercial or trading act'.[5]

Other instruments adopt an approach of combining a broad reference with a list of specific commercial activities. However, such an approach does not seem to be any more helpful, for what is listed boils down to no more than two types of commercial activity, namely (variations among different instruments notwithstanding):

(1)   a contract for the sale/supply of goods or services;[6] and
(2)   a contract for a loan or other transaction for the provision of finance, including any obligation of guarantee or indemnity in respect of such loan or transaction.[7]

Contracts for the purchase and sale of goods,[8] contracts for services,[9] and loan and guaranty agreements[10] are proverbial exemplars of a commercial activity. More significantly, it is now part of the received wisdom that such an activity becomes no less commercial when conducted by, for, with participation of, or in connection with, the armed forces.[11] 'Thus, a contract by a foreign government to buy provisions or equipment for its armed forces or to construct a government building constitutes a commercial activity.'[12] As the US Supreme Court pointed out, 'a contract to buy army boots or even bullets is a "commercial" activity, because private companies can similarly use sales contracts to acquire goods'.[13] Thus, both the purchase and sale of weapons, ammunition, military equipment and supplies, and related services are commercial activities.[14]

Apart from these relatively straightforward cases, all other types of commercial activity will have to be determined under either a reference to 'any other transaction or activity/contract'[15] or a broad rubric (which is supposed to subsume the above-listed two types of commercial activity) of 'relationships of a private law character',[16] 'a commercial, trading, business, professional or industrial or like transaction ... or a like activity'[17] or of 'a regular course of commercial conduct or a particular commercial transaction or act'.[18] Some instruments set forth an additional test, namely, that a commercial activity should be the type of activity in which a State engages 'otherwise than in the exercise of sovereign authority'.[19]

Except the aforementioned two broad categories of commercial activity (contracts for the sale/supply of goods and services, and contracts for loans), all that the current instruments on State immunity say is, in essence, that 'a commercial activity is a commercial activity'. This is pure tautology.[20] In most cases, therefore, the courts are left to their own devices; and an examination of the relevant case law reveals a picture of great variety and complexity. Most cases would match the description of 'commercial activity' in the ordinary sense of the term:

- leasing (or purchasing) of immovable property/premises and related services such as repairs, even if the property is used by diplomatic, consular, or other missions,[21] or by cultural institutions.[22] This is of course the oldest exception to immunity, even in the era of absolute immunity;
- issuance of government bonds, public debt, and promissory notes;[23] procurement of performance guarantee bonds and use of bank accounts to conduct financial transactions;[24] acting as guarantor of bonds;[25]
- banking activities, such as accepting bank deposits;[26] issuance of and failure to honour letters of credit;[27] guarantee of bills of exchange;[28] manufacture (not issuance), keeping and disposal of bank notes in the forum State;[29] sale of certificate of deposits;[30]
- carriage of goods;[31] sailing a ship and discharging or receiving cargo;[32] guarantee under a charterparty for the charter of a ship to a governmental corporation;[33] hiring a ship for commercial trading;[34]

78 COMMERCIAL ACTIVITY

- operation of an airline;[35] air transport of passengers;[36] purchase of air tickets (even if by an embassy);[37] arranging air transportation for business partners;[38]
- ownership of patents in the forum State;[39] patent licensing negotiations, even when unsuccessful;[40] in this regard, even a patentee's *attempt* to conduct licence negotiations may also qualify as a 'commercial activity';[41] acquisition and utilization of trade secrets;[42]
- construction of oil production platforms;[43] building of oil and natural gas pipelines;[44] construction of other works;[45] implementing a rice farm project;[46] supply and assembly of a milk pasteurizing plant;[47] supply and installation of electrical materials;[48] transformation works on buildings;[49] agreement relating to the overhaul of an electric generator;[50]
- engagement of a marketing agent;[51] contracts for management of cellular phone networks;[52] execution of contract to reimburse physicians and organ bank for kidney transplants performed in the US;[53] arrangement for a photographer to photograph a royal family and then publication of some of the photographs in breach of copyright;[54]
- privatization of government companies, such as conversion of former State-owned businesses into free market enterprises,[55] sale of shares of government company to a private corporation,[56] and offering of vouchers to private purchasers;[57]
- contract negotiations and contractual obligations;[58] negotiation and execution of insurance contracts;[59] negotiations culminating in an oral contract;[60] guarantee of a commercial contract;[61] promises and guarantee of payment;[62] breach of a commercial contract[63] or a promise;[64]
- purchase of medical and scientific materials as well as the provision of services intended to render the materials operational;[65] testing of medical equipment;[66]
- sale of bankrupt company's assets at international auction;[67]
- management of an expropriated business, operation of a hotel, and receipt of profits from the company's operations;[68]
- initiation and settlement of commercial litigation;[69] and
- public relations and advertising.[70]

However, there are still a number of cases where the commerciality of the activity in question may not be immediately obvious. These include:

- publicizing an art exhibition;[71] loaning of pieces of art for exhibition;[72] leasing of films;[73]
- solicitation of bids to build electrical generation facilities, even when no contract was finally concluded;[74]
- contracts of concession for barbers' shops at a military base;[75]
- the operation, management and maintenance of the Panama Canal by the Panama Canal Commission;[76]

- contracting with a company to manage a health benefits plan and agreeing to indemnify that company;[77]
- TV news broadcasting, even if no commercial advertising is involved;[78]
- signing of a standard form for the salvage of a warship;[79]
- construction and operation of a nuclear power plant;[80] construction of nuclear reactors and enrichment of uranium;[81] and
- detention of aircraft and collection of outstanding parking and landing fee.[82]

At any rate, these examples show that it is impossible for any legislator or judge to provide an all-encompassing list of commercial activities. It seems far more preferable to have no list at all, or to have an open-ended list coupled with the broadest guidelines, thereby leaving the matter largely to the discretion of the judge, who can then decide the issue on a case-by-case basis. This is precisely what current State practice has done.

Incidentally, according to the US courts, the illegality of an act does not necessarily negate its commercial character. Thus a financial scam was held to be a commercial activity because the purported act was a deal to license and sell medical equipment.[83] The same was said of fraudulent purchase of insurance companies, which was regarded as 'clearly commercial in nature, although performed in an illegal manner'.[84]

2. What is a non-commercial activity?

Over the years it has proven equally elusive to grasp what is a sovereign, governmental, or non-commercial activity. Such convenient labels as *acta jure imperii* and *acta jure gestionis* are of little assistance since they are normally attached to an activity only after that activity has already been classified as sovereign or private. In the opinion of the German Constitutional Court in the time-honoured *Empire of Iran* case, the ultimate test is to see whether the act in question falls 'within the essential sphere of State authority'.[85] This is not so helpful as it may first appear, not least because different countries may have vastly different notions of what constitutes 'the essential sphere of State authority'. Besides, we have already seen how our new age of globalization and privatization has brought unprecedented shifts and changes along the traditional interface between the public sector and the private sector. The boundary line between the two has never been so treacherous. Nevertheless, it might still be worthwhile to go back to the misty realm of past judicial decisions and thence to glean whatever we can. In *Rahimtoola*, Lord

Denning propounded the then unorthodox view of restrictive immunity in the House of Lords, saying:

If the dispute brings into question, for instance, the legislative or international transactions of a foreign government, or the policy of its executive, the court should grant immunity.[86]

In *Empire of Iran*, the German Federal Constitutional Court stated:

In this generally recognizable field of sovereign activity are included transactions relating to foreign affairs and military authority, the legislature, the exercise of police authority, and the administration of justice.[87]

In the same year, a Belgian court said:

Regulating external trade, decreeing measures for the protection of the currency, concluding trade or payments agreements with foreign countries, ordering or forbidding transfers of currency – all these constitute acts of executive power, since, in such cases, the State ... is exercising its governmental authority.[88]

Along a similar line, a US court referred to certain 'categories of strictly political or public acts'; these include:

(1) internal administrative acts, such as expulsion of an alien. (2) legislative acts, such as nationalization. (3) acts concerning the armed forces. (4) acts concerning diplomatic activity. (5) public loans.[89]

In the opinion of the Swiss Federal Tribunal, acts accomplished *jure imperii* include 'les activités militaires et les actes analogues à une expropriation ou une nationalisation'.[90]

According to the IDI's 1991 Draft, the 'criteria indicative of the incompetence of the organs of the forum State to determine the substance of the claim' would cover such matters as 'the validity of the internal administrative and legislative acts', and 'the foreign defence and security policies', of the defendant State (Article 2(3)(b) and (d)).

The greatest common defect of these lists is that they fail to draw the obviously necessary distinction between what is done in the territory of the foreign State itself and what is done in the territory of the forum State. 'Expulsion of an alien' can only take place in the territory of the State which expels the alien. The same can also be said of 'the administration of justice' and of expropriation or nationalization.[91] The legislature of a State normally legislates for the territory of the State, unless it intends its laws to have extraterritorial effects, in which case such laws would have to be recognized by other States in order to have such effects

WHAT IS A NON-COMMERCIAL ACTIVITY? 81

or, as the case might be, they would be resisted as encroachments upon the sovereignty of other States. Again it is impossible to see how the police from one State can exercise 'police authority' in the territory of another State other than with the latter's consent and collaboration. Only if an act is committed in the territory of the forum State, thus falling properly within the territorial jurisdiction of the forum State, will the question of immunity arise. On the other hand, if the act took place in the territory of the foreign State, then the question confronting the court is not immunity, but whether the court has jurisdiction in the first place. In other words, these lists conflate, or confuse, the issue of immunity with lack of jurisdiction. This is a significant question, in both a doctrinal and a practical sense, but its exploration in the context of this book, whose ambit is fixed within the confines of the issue of immunity itself, will be an unnecessary digression. So we leave it at that.

In any case, providing a list can never be a satisfactory way of dealing with the problem. Realities are far more complex than can be reflected by any list, however exhaustive. Will it then be possible to have some kind of essentialist generalization, a yardstick, a test, whereby the diverse acts of States can be characterized and pigeonholed? It must at once be observed that an all-encompassing and all-useful test has not yet been found; and courts decide their cases in a very much ad hoc, haphazard fashion.

For a starter, a convenient test might be the opposite of the 'private-person' rule, and this has indeed been adopted by some courts. For example, in *Nelson*, the plaintiff worked as a monitoring systems engineer in Saudi Arabia at a hospital owned and operated by the Saudi government. After he reported a number of safety defects, he was arrested by Saudi government officials, jailed, tortured, and beaten. He subsequently sued in a US federal court, alleging various intentional torts. The US Supreme Court found that the alleged conduct (wrongful arrest, imprisonment, and torture) could not qualify as a commercial activity because the conduct amounted to abuse of police powers by the Saudi government. According to the Court:

> however monstrous such abuse undoubtedly may be, a foreign state's exercise of the power of its police has long been understood ... as peculiarly sovereign in nature ... Exercise of the powers of police and penal officers is not the sort of action by which private parties can engage in commerce.[92]

In *Jin*, practitioners of Falun Gong (a form of meditation) alleged that various Chinese Government ministries had hired local 'thugs' in various

82   COMMERCIAL ACTIVITY

US cities to intimidate them. The court held that the 'hiring of thugs', even if taken as true, was not a commercial activity, 'considering the broader political context of these allegations':

The defendant ministries are the alleged perpetrators responsible for hiring 'thugs' to implement China's policy of eradicating Falun Gong ... The defendant ministries' mandate to implement China's policy and its authority to hire 'thugs' is not of the nature that may be exercised by private citizens participating in the marketplace ... This is the exercise of the quintessential police power ... This conduct, therefore, is akin to claims involving abuses of state power, subsumed under sovereign immunity.[93]

Thus when Israel was sued for activities connected with the Jewish settlements in the West Bank, the court found that the plaintiffs were challenging actions that were taken pursuant to Israeli national policy:

Whether territorial expansion or national defense, the settlement activities are only possible by virtue of the fact that the actors are infused with the force and power of the Israeli government. Private entities cannot engage in these activities. The complaint may allege that the Israeli government has taken actions akin to 'sovereign expropriation', but such actions neither constitute the type of actions in which private actors engage nor amount to market transactions.[94]

By the same token, the seizure of goods by the police force 'is not the type of action by which a private party engages in trade, traffic or commerce. Rather, such an action is quintessentially sovereign in nature';[95] the issuance of exchange controls 'could not be engaged in for profit by a private citizen and, therefore, not commercial in nature';[96] the expulsion of foreign nationals 'is not an activity customarily carried out for profit by private persons';[97] the imposition and collection of navigation charges for flights through national and international airspace were sovereign activities which were 'not among the powers exercised by private parties';[98] and the termination of foreign workers' social insurance benefits is 'an act that is distinctly sovereign, rather than commercial, in nature' because 'a private player in the market certainly could not engage in the 'particular actions' of initiating, administering, and ending a scheme of mandatory social insurance'.[99]

Generally speaking, legislative acts, international transactions of foreign governments and government policies have been declared off limits to jurisdiction.[100] The administration of a health/medical care system or a similar government health and welfare benefit programme was 'uniquely sovereign in nature';[101] the acceptance of and subsequent refusal to remove caveats on the property of a corporation was 'intrinsic-ally governmental in nature';[102] the operation of a tax system was a 'quintessential example of governmental activity';[103] and a foreign State's decision as to how best to secure the safety of its leaders was 'quintessentially an act peculiar to sovereigns'.[104]

Among sovereign, governmental and non-commercial activities are included expropriation/nationalization[105] or confiscation,[106] regulation of imports and exports,[107] maintenance of the monetary position of the country,[108] regulation and monitoring of commercial banks,[109] provi-sion and administration of a national health insurance programme;[110] deployment of troops in military operations,[111] acts of a warship, even if causing civilian damage;[112] repair of shore installations at a naval base;[113] installation of a protection system for an oil pipeline;[114] regula-tion of overflight and levying of overflight charges;[115] acquisition and management of assets of liquidated companies pursuant to special legislation;[116] failure to return historic stone tablets in reliance on public law legislation protecting objects of historical and archaeological value;[117] failure to pay war reparations as required by a treaty;[118] oper-ation of a diplomatic mission,[119] a consulate[120] or a chancery for the Naval Attaché;[121] establishment of security measures at an embassy or a consulate;[122] seizure of documents by foreign customs officers in the territory of the forum State;[123] an order for the payment of income tax;[124] using administrative power to freeze funds[125] or to intervene in the performance of a contract;[126] conclusion[127] and performance[128] of a treaty; a promise of a financial assistance package by one State to another, even though it may serve as inducement of a commercial transaction;[129] recovery of money allegedly unlawfully appropriated by a former head of a foreign State in his own country;[130] and borrowing from the International Monetary Fund and repayment of such a debt.[131]

Surprisingly, the promotion of commerce, including business devel-opment assistance, participation in trade shows and leasing of office space, was held to be a 'quintessential' 'governmental function', on the (somewhat flimsy) ground that, although private businesses may also engage in promotional activities on their own behalf, they do not nor-mally promote the products of *other* businesses.[132]

In *Virtual Countries*, the court found that the issuance by South Africa of a press release claiming its right to own the southafrica. com domain name, and to take the matter up in international forums, was not a commercial activity, for South Africa's activity arose from its role as policymaker within, and, indirectly, regulator

84   COMMERCIAL ACTIVITY

of, the market of internet domain names, rather than its role as a participant in such market.[133]

In some cases the courts found that the mere opposite of a 'private person' test may not be enough. A more contextual approach is called for. Thus, an exhibition of glasswork, even if having features of both a non-profit museum exhibition and a for-profit art gallery show, was not a commercial activity because, 'taken as a whole', the activity in question was not 'of a type that a private entity would carry on for profit' and the exhibition was thus '*more* closely analogous to a publicly-sponsored, not-for-profit art exhibition *than* to a private, for-profit gallery show or auction'.[134]

The compilation of a dictionary falls outside 'the more routine classifications assigned to activities as either "commercial" or "non-commercial"'. On the one hand, 'the compilation of a linguistic treatise ... is not one that only a sovereign can perform'; on the other hand, 'the compilation of a linguistic treatise spanning decades and the lifetimes of many scholars is not "of the type an individual would customarily carry on for profit"'. For this reason, '[t]he creation of massive, scholarly texts are not normally undertaken by "private players in the market" of trade or commerce, and the acts of the ... defendants are collaborative, academic, and non-profit in nature'.[135]

Japan's use of its wartime military to impose sexual slavery upon the women of occupied Asian countries was not a commercial activity but might be characterized properly as a war crime or a crime against humanity.[136] Kidnapping is not a commercial activity, not because it is an activity that cannot be carried out by private persons, but because kidnapping by itself is not something that private persons can *lawfully* engage in,[137] and because it cannot be described as an act 'typically performed by participants *in the market*'.[138] Money laundering[139] and political assassination[140] have been likewise excluded. In a Dutch case, where a Dutch national challenged his arrest in Germany in the course of delivering narcotic drugs under an agreement concluded in the Netherlands between him and an undercover police officer of Germany, the court rejected the claim, holding that the German criminal investigation officials, even if 'disguised as individuals', could not be regarded as entering into a legal relationship on an equal footing with individuals, because private individuals could not 'enter into a similar legal relationship in a similar way with similar consequences'.[141]

This seems to suggest that a 'commercial activity' must be truly 'commercial':

Unless an act takes place *in a commercial context* it would be impossible to determine whether it is conducted in the manner of a private player in the market. Otherwise, any act directed by a foreign government and carried out by irregular operatives in whatever circumstances could be thought commercial including isolated acts of assassination, extortion, blackmail, and kidnapping.[142]

If this is not enough to show the complexity and elusiveness of the characterization of commercial activity, one can perhaps refer to the fact that often conflicting decisions would be given on the same facts. In *Practical Concepts*, a US corporation sued Bolivia for breach of a technical assistance and consulting services contract. The district court granted immunity on the ground that the contract contained 'numerous terms which only a sovereign state could perform, and which no private firm or individual going into the market place could ever offer'.[143] Denying the corporation's motion for reconsideration, the district court stated: 'Where, as here, a state exempts a private party from taxation, grants preferential bureaucratic treatment, and diplomatic privileges, it is acting in a sovereign capacity.'[144] The circuit court, however, denied immunity on the basis of a distinction between 'auxiliary provisions' and the 'agreement's core':

The essence of the ... contract plainly was the exchange of money for advice on the development of rural areas. Prompt provision of documents to facilitate entry of material and personnel and tax exemptions to simplify [the plaintiff's] receipt of payments from Bolivia, just as plainly, were auxiliary to the basic exchange.[145]

In short, much remains uncertain. It would be wishful thinking to imagine that the problem of commercial activity can be solved by some uniform, clear-cut rules. It is not surprising that in discussing this matter scholars usually propose a *whole set of guidelines* rather than attempt any specific definition.[146] In the words of Crawford:

The better approach is to deal with the specific categories or classes of case that have arisen in practice and to elaborate specific rules for each such category, taking into account the reasons for extending immunity or asserting jurisdiction in that context.[147]

3. Nature or purpose?

The nature/purpose debate is almost as old as the restrictive doctrine of State immunity. Three positions have emerged over the years, which can for the sake of convenience be dubbed as the 'nature' approach, the 'purpose' approach, and the 'context' approach.

3.1. The 'nature' approach

The predominant position in the current law and practice on State immunity is that the decisive factor for the question of immunity is the nature, not the purpose, of the particular act of the foreign State. If the act is by its nature a commercial or private-law act, then there is no immunity regarding that act, even if that act might have served some sovereign or public purpose. In the earliest Belgian case on restrictive immunity, the Belgian Cour de Cassation declared that the competence of the court 'dérive, non du consentement du justiciable, mais de la nature de l'acte'.[148] More recently, a Belgian court declared:

> The character of the act as having been performed *jure gestionis* ... is determined by the nature of the act and is not influenced by the real purpose being pursued ... The fact that the material ordered was allegedly intended for the production of nuclear arms supposedly destined to secure the defence of the national sovereignty of Iraq is irrelevant to the categorization of the act performed and therefore to the delimitation of the jurisdictional immunity of the State of Iraq.[149]

In the *Collision Case*, the Austrian Supreme Court opined that:

> we must always look at the act itself which is performed by State organs, and not at its motive or purpose ... Whether an act is of a private or sovereign nature must always be deduced from the nature of the legal transaction, *viz.* the nature of the action taken or the legal relationship arising ... in determining whether an action may be brought, it is the act from which the claim is derived which is decisive, and not the object or purpose of the act.[150]

The German Constitutional Court expressed the same view in the *Empire of Iran Case*:

> The distinction between sovereign and non-sovereign State activities cannot be drawn according to the purpose of the State transaction and whether it stands in a recognizable relation to the sovereign duties of the State. For, ultimately, activities of State, if not wholly then to the widest degree, serve sovereign purposes and duties, and stand in a still recognizable relationship to them ... As a means for determining the distinction between acts *jure imperii* and *jure gestionis* one should rather refer to the nature of the State transaction or the resulting legal relationships, and not to the motive or purpose of the State activity. It thus depends on whether the foreign State has acted in exercise of its sovereign authority, that is in public law, or like a private person, that is in private law.[151]

A German provincial court thus reasoned:

> the difference between governmental and non-governmental activity cannot be determined by a reference to the purpose of the activity or whether the activity is

connected with a recognizable sovereign business. Since every activity conducted by a state ... serves largely sovereign purposes and has a direct connection with such purposes, the purpose test cannot be used in distinguishing between activities *iure imperii* and activities *iure gestionis*.[152]

The Swiss judicial practice has maintained consistently that the distinction between acts *jure gestionis* and acts *jure imperii* should be based on the nature of the act or legal relationship rather than its purpose.[153] In particular, the Swiss Federal Tribunal pointed out:

In distinguishing official acts from unofficial private acts, the purpose underlying the acts is of little or no importance since all State activity is directed in the last analysis towards the public interest ... it is the nature of the act which the State performs which is decisive.[154]

The 'nature' approach has also been adopted by the Dutch,[155] Greek,[156] Kenyan,[157] Nigerian,[158] Portuguese,[159] South African,[160] and Zimbabwean[161] courts.

3.2. The difficulties with the 'nature' approach

The US practice serves to highlight the difficulties associated with the 'nature' test. Section 1603(d) of the US FSIA provides:

The commercial character of an activity shall be determined by reference to the nature of the course of conduct or particular transaction or act, rather than by reference to its purpose.

According to the draftsmen:

the fact that goods or services to be procured through a contract are to be used for a public purpose is irrelevant; it is the essentially commercial nature of an activity or transaction that is critical.[162]

The case law, however, has shown that the drafters' paradigm may not be practicable under all circumstances, and that the purpose of an act may just sneak into the picture in one guise or another. Indeed, it seems to be the subconscious belief of the legislators themselves that the purpose of an act should also be relevant to the determination of its nature, when they say that:

Certainly, if an activity is customarily carried on *for profit*, its commercial nature could readily be assumed.[163]

In other words, the commercial *nature* of an act is determined precisely by its profit-seeking *motive* or *purpose*. This has not escaped the notice of

88   COMMERCIAL ACTIVITY

the courts. In *De Sanchez* the Fifth Circuit held that, in light of its purpose of controlling foreign currency reserves, Nicaragua's refusal to honour a cheque it had issued to cover a private bank debt was a sovereign act entitled to immunity. In the opinion of the court:

> We do not interpret [s. 1603(d)] ... to bar us totally from considering the purposes of different types of activities. Indeed, we do not believe that an absolute separation is always possible between the ontology and the teleology of an act. Often, the essence of an act is defined by its purpose – gift-giving, for example. Unless we can inquire into the purposes of such acts, we cannot determine their nature. Indeed, commercial acts themselves are defined largely by reference to their purpose. What makes these acts commercial is not some ethereal essence inhering in the conduct itself; instead, as Congress recognized, acts are commercial because they are generally engaged in for profit.[164]

The Seventh Circuit agreed:

> Certainly, 'nature' and 'purpose' do not demark hermetically sealed, separate domains.[165]

In *Segni*, where an Argentine national had been employed by the Commercial Office of Spain for the promotion of sales of Spanish wine, the Seventh Circuit pointed to the 'problems involved in determining where nature ends and purpose begins', saying:

> In the case now before us, the nature/purpose distinction is further muddied by the fact that the public purpose behind Segni's hiring ... is itself related to commerce ... Thus, confusingly enough, we must decide whether the *nature* of Segni's hiring is commercial, conscious of the fact that the underlying *purpose* is both commercial *and* public. In doing so we are sympathetic to the concerns expressed by the *De Sanchez* court ... about the difficulty in separating these concepts. Nevertheless, the command of Congress ... requires that we confine any consideration of purpose as closely as we can, considering that purpose only so far as is absolutely necessary to define the nature of the act in question.[166]

However, this line of reasoning was overruled by the US Supreme Court in the *Weltover* case:

> because the Act provides that the commercial character of an act is to be determined by reference to its 'nature' rather than its 'purpose', the question is not whether the foreign government is acting with a profit motive or instead with the aim of fulfilling uniquely sovereign objectives. Rather, the issue is whether the particular actions that the foreign state performs (whatever the motive behind them) are the *type* of actions by which a private party engages in 'trade and traffic or commerce'.[167]

Expressly referring to *De Sanchez*, the Court held that the fact that Argentina issued government bonds (called 'Bonods') to help stabilize its currency was not a valid basis for distinguishing these bonds from ordinary debt instruments:

> The commercial character of the Bonods is confirmed by the fact that they are in almost all respects garden-variety debt instruments: They may be held by private parties; they are negotiable and may be traded on the international market (except in Argentina); and they promise a future stream of cash income ... private parties regularly issue bonds, not just to raise capital or to finance purchases, but also to refinance debt. That is what Argentina did here ...[168]

> However difficult it may be in some cases to separate 'purpose' (i.e., the *reason* why the foreign state engages in the activity) from 'nature' (i.e., the outward form of the conduct that the foreign state performs or agrees to perform), the statute unmistakably commands that to be done ... it is irrelevant *why* Argentina participated in the bond market in the manner of a private actor; it matters only that it did so.[169]

This 'in practice means rejecting any argument that rests on the foreign state's *reasons* for undertaking the activity alleged to be commercial'.[170] That is to say, 'whether a state acts in the manner of a private party is a question of behavior, not motivation'.[171]

The explicit disavowal of a 'profit motive', contrary to the legislative report, in identifying a 'commercial activity', pronounced by the Supreme Court in its eagerness to stress the decisive importance of 'nature' over 'purpose', has led to the curious decision in the *Dale* case that the creation of a charitable foundation was 'the type of activity by which a private party could participate in "trade and traffic or commerce"'.[172] The use of the expression 'trade and traffic or commerce',[173] which also resulted in TV news broadcasting being held a commercial activity,[174] is significant. Both the words 'trade' and 'traffic', as signifying business dealings, are absent from the US FSIA and the accompanying legislative report, which only talk about a '*commercial* activity'; and the word 'traffic', when it means the use of public roads by vehicles, appears only in the legislative report (not in the FSIA itself) in the context of non-commercial torts under section 1605(a)(5).[175] Seen in this light, what was said in the *Dale* case is actually that setting up a charity is a 'commercial activity'. The classification of some activity devoid of commercial interest as an activity within the meaning of section 1605(a)(2) is baffling. For one thing, the term 'commercial activity' does not appear so elastic under the US FSIA, for section 1603(d) defines a 'commercial activity' as 'either a regular course of *commercial* conduct or a particular *commercial* transaction or act' (emphasis added). Such a definition relies essentially on the *commerciality* of the act as the determining factor: in other words, an act is a 'commercial activity' if it is a 'commercial' activity. This is a prime example of a circular definition, and worse, for it leaves the crucial term 'commercial' undefined.[176]

According to the US Congress, the omission of a definition of 'commercial' is deliberate:

The courts would have a great deal of latitude in determining what is a 'commercial activity' ... It has seemed unwise to attempt an excessively precise definition of this term, even if that were practicable.[177]

The Supreme Court thus opined that the meaning of 'commercial' must be the meaning generally required by the restrictive theory of immunity at the time the FSIA was enacted.[178] But then, '[u]nder the restrictive, as opposed to the "absolute", theory of foreign sovereign immunity, a state is immune from the jurisdiction of foreign courts as to its sovereign or public acts (*jure imperii*), but not as to those that are private or commercial in character (*jure gestionis*)'.[179] One is back at the starting point. The above-quoted pronouncement of the Supreme Court therefore has the effect – intended or otherwise – of extending the scope of section 1605(a)(2) beyond its boundaries as envisaged by the legislators. The fact that such effect actually materialized in the *Dale* case throws into sharp relief the inconsistency that may result from a complete renunciation of 'purpose' or 'motive'. This is aptly shown by the *Dale* Court's choice of the vague expression 'trade and traffic or commerce', rather than a straightforward 'commercial activity', indicating the awareness of the difficulty of linking a charity with the word 'commercial' under section 1605(a)(2). The approach more in line with the FSIA itself, coupled with the legislative report, seems to be that adopted by the Fifth Circuit, in whose opinion:

an activity has a commercial nature for purposes of FSIA immunity if it is of a type that a private person would customarily engage in *for profit*.[180]

Framed in a highly teleological vein, this is unmistakably a 'purpose' test. Heretical as it may sound, it owes its origin to none other than the legislators themselves, who, it will be recalled, state in their report that:

Certainly, if an activity is customarily carried on *for profit*, its commercial nature could readily be assumed.[181]

However, there is a subtle but crucial difference between the Fifth Circuit's opinion and the legislative report. According to the Fifth

Circuit, an activity will be commercial if it is customarily engaged in (1) *by a private person* and (2) *for profit*, whereas the legislative report only requires profit without specifying the actor. The question then arises how to characterize an act that a State has performed without any profit in view but which if done by a private person may definitely have a profit motive. If one follows the legislators' instructions, one may hesitate to characterize this act as 'commercial activity', because there is no profit motive on the part of the foreign State; on the other hand, the formula suggested by the First Circuit would certainly see this act as 'commercial': if it is something a *private person* ordinarily does *for profit*, then it is a 'commercial activity', even if the State in question did it for no profit at all. Thus, sponsoring and operating a cultural tour, even without charging the participants and for the sole purpose of fostering closer cultural ties between peoples, was construed as a 'commercial activity', because the foreign government's 'actions as a promoter, organizer and guide are undoubtedly acts of a kind that are undertaken regularly by private parties'.[182] And the City of Amsterdam engaged in 'commercial activities' when it loaned works of art to museums in the US, despite the City's argument that the exchange of artworks between not-for-profit organizations in different countries did not constitute 'trade and traffic or commerce'. Even though the particular loan in question was for purely educational and cultural purposes without any intention of offering the works for sale, such 'purposes' could not remove this kind of sovereign loan from 'commerce' because the court was not to consider the purpose of an activity. According to the court, '[t]here is nothing "sovereign" about the act of lending art pieces, even though the pieces themselves might belong to a sovereign. Loans between and among museums (both public and private) occur around the world regularly'. Besides, 'the international loan of artworks between museums can and does occur with *potential* sales of the works contemplated by the parties'.[183]

Pushed to its extreme, such an overstretched reconstruction of the relevant facts would leave precious little that is done by a State, short of an all-out war, outside the scope of a 'commercial activity'. Diplomatic negotiations, for example, could be 'commercial activity', because private persons regularly engage in negotiations for profit. This is precisely the quandary that confronted a district court in a case involving an unusual sovereign, the Holy See. As soon as the court removed the word 'religious' – which would indicate a 'purpose' – from its inquiry, it found that:

92 COMMERCIAL ACTIVITY

the Holy See's provision of 'religious and pastoral guidance, education and counseling services' should be broadly categorized as providing guidance, education and counseling services in general. Clearly, private actors *can* provide counseling services, education and guidance. These are not the kinds of activities in which only government actors may engage.[184]

Then the court came to the realization that:

Under the above analysis, with purpose and motive deleted from the evaluation, the alleged activities of the Holy See might be characterized as commercial. This would be, to say the least, ironic ... To describe core religious duties as the equivalent of private commercial activity may superficially apply existing precedent, but ultimately results in a transmogrification of the facts.[185]

In the court's opinion:

It might be possible, under existing precedent, to say that a priest administering communion to a supplicant who makes donations to the church is like a private actor selling bread.[186]

Fortunately, the court discovered that it was rescued from this predicament by the simple fact that it did not have to tackle it, since the 'true essence of the complaint' was not 'property damage, breach of contract, product liability, copyright infringement', etc., but 'the injury inflicted by a sexually abusive priest at [the] plaintiff's church', a claim that did not concern any commercial activity at all.[187]

In brief, insofar as 'profit' is concerned, the legislative instructions are ambiguous and misleading, while the case law appears unsettled at best. Besides, there have also been attempts to discard the 'for profit' test altogether. In *Joseph*, which involved a lease of residence for the employees of the Consulate General of Nigeria, the district court concluded that the commercial activity exception did not apply because the Consulate did not contract to be a lessee of the residential property for profit. The Ninth Circuit, however, found the reasoning to be flawed. According to the latter:

there is no indication that Congress intended the presence of a profit motive on the part of the sovereign to be a *threshold requirement* for applying the commercial activity exception ... Moreover, the use of profit motive as a threshold requirement for applying the commercial activity exception would be inconsistent with the FSIA's focus on the nature of the transaction at issue rather than its purpose ... we conclude that, although the lease agreement at issue was not undertaken by the Consulate for profit, it nevertheless was a commercial transaction.[188]

The Seventh Circuit agreed:

> since foreign sovereigns often enter the commercial marketplace with no intention of making a profit thereby (for example, to purchase supplies to outfit the nation's military), [the] suggestion [of a profit motive] would virtually eliminate the 'commercial activity' exception to sovereign immunity.[189]

Nonetheless, it can be seen that two criteria have emerged in practice: (1) that the activity is engaged in 'for profit' and (2) that the activity is capable of being carried out by a 'private person'. Both criteria can in fact be found in the legislative report, but with an important nuance:

> Certainly, if an activity is customarily carried on *for profit*, its commercial nature could readily be assumed. At the other end of the spectrum, a single contract, if of the same character as a contract which might be made by a *private person*, could constitute a 'particular transaction or act'.[190]

This is of course a comment on section 1603(d), which provides:

> A 'commercial activity' means either a regular course of commercial conduct or *a particular commercial transaction or act*. The commercial character of an activity shall be determined by reference to the nature of the course of conduct or *particular transaction or act*, rather than by reference to its purpose. (Emphases added)

Clearly, 'a particular commercial transaction or act' is to be distinguished from 'a particular transaction or act', for the simple reason that 'a particular transaction or act' may or may not be 'commercial': the 'character' of the 'particular transaction or act' has to be 'determined' before one can be sure that it is indeed 'commercial'. That is to say, of the two criteria proposed in the legislative report as quoted above, while 'for profit' would 'certainly' decide the 'commercial nature' of an activity, the 'private person' criterion appears 'neutral', for it addresses only what constitutes a 'particular transaction or act', but not what should be a 'particular *commercial* transaction or act'. In other words, the 'private person' criterion does not necessarily prejudge the *nature* of a particular transaction or act, commercial or otherwise. To rely on a test of 'private person' for the *commerciality* of an activity thus not only marks a departure from, or at least a skewed construction of, the legislative intent, but is also to have faith in a false guide. In reality, 'not every act of a foreign state that could be done by a private citizen ... is "commercial activity"':[191] 'Private parties may engage in talks, negotiations, and may even make promises to resolve disputes, but not all such activity will be deemed "commercial".'[192] As more fully put by the Seventh Circuit:

94   COMMERCIAL ACTIVITY

certain contracts, although generally of a type in which a private person could enter, are by their nature governmental, since only a sovereign entity deals in the particular kind of goods or services. For example, although a private party could allow another to exploit the animal or mineral resources on the former's land (to the extent permitted by local law), a contract whereby a foreign state grants a private party a license to exploit the state's natural resources is *not* a commercial activity, since natural resources, to the extent they are 'affected with a public interest', are goods in which only the sovereign may deal. Further, while private persons routinely enter employment agreements, employment contracts between a foreign state and its civil servants, diplomats or military personnel are not 'commercial' transactions, since the employment of such personnel is intimately connected with the foreign state's formulation and execution of government policy.[193]

All considered, the 'private person' test itself seems to need something more than a simple 'private person'. To the extent that no private individual will maintain a regular air force, or buy, say, large quantities of supersonic fighter jets or long-range missiles, to construe contracts for the purchase of weapons as 'commercial' will involve a shift of focus from such factors as 'weapons', 'the air force' and (further removed) 'national defence' to 'purchase' only. Thus, a contract to purchase fighter jets will only be a 'contract to purchase'. The same is true when a court holds that 'any private person may enter the marketplace and solicit bids and proposals from contractors', while finding that 'private individuals do not customarily solicit proposals to build electrical generation facilities'.[194] In both cases, what the court does is a deliberate disregard of some unique features of such contracts (misleadingly referred to as the 'purpose') and to characterize them in the most generic terms possible. Such a reductionist and eviscerating reconstruction of a particular activity is, admittedly, of great value to courts, as can be demonstrated by the long-standing popularity of the 'private person' test; but precisely because of its reductionism it cannot be good at all times and in all places: it is obviously inadequate for the issue of contracts of employment (in that private persons regularly engage in 'employment'); the diversity of approaches (amounting in effect to almost a complete abandonment of the 'private person' test) and, above all, the purposive construction the courts are prone to give to certain employment relationships, bear eloquent testimony to the deficiencies of the 'private person' test under certain circumstances. Nor does this test play any significant role in the face of the exalted position granted to foreign armed forces.

Thus the only viable criterion for the commercial nature of an activity, as suggested by the legislators, would be a motive 'for profit'. This understanding, however, would at once place the legislators and the Supreme Court at variance, for the Supreme Court declared in *Weltover* that the question was not whether there was 'a profit motive' but whether the actions of the foreign State were those of 'a private party'.[195] Indeed, the Court said that '[e]ngaging in a commercial act does not require the receipt of fair value, or even compliance with the common-law requirements of consideration'.[196] Later, the Supreme Court reaffirmed that a State:

engages in commercial activity ... where it exercises only those powers that can also be exercised by private citizens, as distinct from those powers peculiar to sovereigns. Put differently, a foreign state engages in commercial activity for purposes of the restrictive theory only where it acts in the manner of a private player within the market.[197]

In other words, the Supreme Court explicitly discarded the 'for profit' criterion, which the legislators would regard as decisive on the commerciality of the activity in question, and opted for the more hazy test of a 'private person', which as we can see may or may not be concerned with whether a transaction or act is commercial. On the other hand, the legislators, it will again be recalled, hastened to add the following in their report, for good measure:

As the definition indicates, the fact that goods or services to be procured through a contract are to be used for a public purpose is irrelevant; it is the essentially commercial nature of an activity or transaction that is critical. Thus, a contract by a foreign government to buy provisions or equipment for its armed forces or to construct a government building constitutes a commercial activity. The same would be true of a contract to make repairs on an embassy building. Such contracts should be considered to be commercial contracts, even if their ultimate object is to further a public function.[198]

This departs from the legislators' own suggestion that a commercial activity is an activity engaged in 'for profit'; nor is it clear whether the activities mentioned here are categorized as 'commercial' because they are the type of activities in which a private person normally engages, or in which a private person normally engages *for profit*. Insofar as 'purpose' is concerned, the legislators seem to be insisting that there ought to be a distinction between two types of purpose: a profit-seeking purpose, which is to be accepted as a valid test that definitely clinches a commercial activity; and a not-for-profit or sovereign/public purpose, which is to be rejected as argument for a non-commercial activity. In other words, a 'profit purpose' would be decisive, whereas a 'public purpose' is irrelevant. Such a split attitude towards the 'purpose' of an activity logically suggests that the 'purpose' test can, and must, be retained in those cases where there is a clear motive 'for profit'; but then that will run counter to section 1603(d), which expressly disavows the reference to 'purpose'. Ultimately and as a matter of logic, if purpose per se cannot be a criterion, then 'for profit' cannot be a criterion; for if purpose cannot render an act sovereign, then it should not make it private either. In this regard, the legislators themselves seem to be confused, for they on the one hand instruct that no resort whatever should be had to the 'purpose' of an act, whether it is for profit or otherwise, but on the other hand suggest that a profit-seeking purpose or motive can be decisive of the commercial character of an activity.

The ineluctable result is that, as far as US law is concerned, authorities are inconsistent, indeed self-contradictory, about whether 'purpose' should as a matter of principle be considered in deciding whether a particular act is a commercial activity. This is further compounded by the Supreme Court's advice according to which one should turn to the whole body of heterogeneous and diverse international practice of restrictive State immunity for guidance:

The meaning of 'commercial' is the meaning generally attached to that term under the restrictive theory at the time the [FSIA] was enacted.[199]

Furthermore, if one accepts that both 'for profit' and 'private person' can be viable tests, they still seem questionable, if carried to extremes. We have already discovered that the expression 'for profit' presents a curious dilemma for the court: if the court follows it strictly, the court will be adopting a 'purpose' test; on the other hand, a complete disregard of profit would result in a charity being considered as a 'commercial activity'. The 'private person' test will appear even more problematic and ultimately unhelpful in relation to contracts of employment.

However, it would be mistaken to think that this 'nature' approach is monolithic and admits of no other considerations. In *Weltover*, Argentina contended that, although the FSIA bars consideration of purpose, a court must nonetheless fully consider the *context* of a transaction in order to determine whether it is commercial. On this point, the Supreme Court did not say that context *should not* be considered, but instead said that, 'even in full context', there was nothing about the issuance of those bonds that was 'not analogous to a private commercial transaction'.[200] So it would seem that the Supreme Court did not completely rule out a contextual approach. In *Intercontinental Dictionary Series*, the court said:

although the absence of a profit motive is generally irrelevant because it focuses on a particular activity's purpose, the Court notes that the absence of profit motive may be relevant in this instance. Research toward the compilation of a technical, linguistic treatise constitutes an academic or scholarly endeavor, and the lack of a profit motive is characteristic of that very nature; in other words, the nature and purpose of the activity coincide.[201]

In *EM*, the Second Circuit held that Argentina's borrowing from, and repayment to, the IMF did not constitute 'commercial activity'. The court relied on a number of considerations for its decision, and these include: (1) only sovereign States can become members of the IMF and make use of its financing; (2) Argentina's borrowing programme is 'part of a larger regulatory enterprise intended to preserve stability in the international monetary system and foster orderly economic growth'; (3) the terms and conditions of the borrowing relationship are not governed by a 'garden-variety debt instrument', but by treaty obligations; and (4) 'IMF loans are structured in a manner unique to the international organization, and are not available in the commercial market'.[202]

In other words, Argentina did not engage in commercial activity when it borrowed funds from the IMF as a sovereign State, in a unique, international/governmental context outside the commercial market-place, and for a regulatory, i.e. sovereign, purpose. This ruling not only shows that the 'nature' approach is inadequate and that the context approach is more useful, but it also affords a vindication of the 'purpose' test. The court must have been keenly aware that the determination of a commercial activity is not a straightforward exercise, and that a simple answer by reference to the nature of the transaction would not suffice; for otherwise the court would not have found it necessary to go into such detailed analysis of every circumstance surrounding the IMF loan. Every private person can borrow money; what distinguishes the IMF loan from a private loan is not its nature, but its purpose, and the accompanying circumstances. The loan itself, an act of borrowing regularly engaged in by private persons, natural and corporate, is not sufficient to decide its commercial or non-commercial character; the answer must be sought outside the loan. What matters is not only 'what' has been done, but also 'by whom' and 'how' and 'for what'.

The Philippine practice closely follows that of the US. In *Ruiz*, the Philippine Supreme Court, though expressly stating that 'the correct test for the application of State immunity is not the conclusion of a contract by a State but the *legal nature* of the act', allowed immunity for the conduct of public bidding for the repair of various shore installations at a US naval base because the projects were an integral part of the naval base devoted to the defence of both the US and the Philippines, 'indisputably a function of the government of the highest order' and were 'not utilized for nor dedicated to *commercial or business purposes*'.[203] In a dispute concerning the sale of certain land in Manila by the Holy See, the Philippine Supreme Court, while again affirming the nature test, granted immunity on the ground that the land was acquired by the Holy See through donation and was not intended 'for commercial purpose', but for constructing thereon the official place of residence of the Papal Nuncio.[204]

3.3. The 'purpose' approach

The 'purpose' test, to the effect that an act is to be classified as a 'sovereign' act if it serves a sovereign 'purpose', although much discredited over the years, has survived to this day and features in a drastically reduced form in the UN Convention. It is one of the earliest possible arguments in favour of State immunity and would sound especially plausible at a time when the functions of a State were limited to such exalted matters as keeping public order and maintaining sufficient armed force for the defence of the country. It naturally lost much of its validity when States, in particular the Soviet-type States in the twentieth century, increasingly engaged in all manner of activities formerly conducted only by private individuals or companies. In fact, the whole doctrine of restrictive immunity, throughout its history of evolution, has been predicated on the abandonment or rejection of the 'public purpose' argument in favour of a 'private nature' test.

Despite a clear (and circular) provision in the Canada SIA that '"commercial activity" means any particular transaction, act or conduct or any regular course of conduct that *by reason of its nature* is of a commercial character' (section 2, emphasis added),[205] the Canadian Supreme Court explicitly adopted a 'purpose' approach in the case of *Re Canada Labour Code*, where a Canadian trade union applied for certification as bargaining agent for the Canadian civilians employed at a US naval base at Argentia, Newfoundland. The lower court denied immunity on the ground that the certification proceedings related to the employment of members of the proposed bargaining unit under contracts of service, entry into which was conduct of a commercial character. The court expressly refused to consider the purpose of the employment relationship.[206]

Obviously, this reasoning treated the question of employment contracts (which could be concluded between two private parties) quite in isolation from the broader context, namely the management of the naval base to serve US defence, i.e. sovereign or public, purposes. The Supreme Court rejected this approach and reversed the decision on three interrelated propositions; first, that the court must ask not only whether the activity in question was of a commercial nature, but also whether the proceedings in the instant case related to that activity; second, that the *purpose* of an activity was highly relevant to the determination of the *nature* of that activity; and, third, that the employment relationship at the naval base, being multi-faceted, had both sovereign and commercial aspects, and that, because the action in the instant case related to the sovereign aspects of the employment relationship, it must be dismissed.[207]

La Forest J, speaking for the majority, said:

I find it difficult if not impossible to distinguish in a principled manner between the nature and purpose of employment relationships, and I would thus decline to follow this approach. Nature and purpose are interrelated, and it is impossible to determine the former without considering the latter. I do not accept that the definition of 'commercial activity' in the [State Immunity] Act precludes consideration of its purpose ... In many cases, it may be unnecessary to delve into metaphysical distinctions between the ontology and teleology of the activity in question. However, if consideration of purpose is helpful in determining the nature of an activity, then such considerations should be and are allowed under the Act. Further, when an activity is multifaceted in nature (as in the instant case) consideration of its purpose will assist in determining which facets are truly 'related' to the proceedings in issue.[208]

... state activity can be characterized only after appreciating its entire context. Rigid dichotomies between the 'nature' and 'purpose' of state activity are not helpful in this analysis ... The entire context includes both the nature and purpose of the act.[209]

It seems to me that a contextual approach is the only reasonable basis of applying the doctrine of restrictive immunity. The alternative is to attempt the impossible – an antiseptic distillation of a 'once-and-for-all' characterization of the activity in question, entirely divorced from its purpose. It is true that purpose should not predominate, as this approach would convert virtually every act by commercial agents of the state into an act *jure imperii*. However, the converse is also true. Rigid adherence to the 'nature' of an act to the exclusion of purpose would render innumerable government activities *jure gestionis*. Neither of these extremes offers an appropriate resolution of the problem.[210]

100 COMMERCIAL ACTIVITY

Even the dissenting judge agreed with this approach:

Sometimes, the nature of the act itself may only become evident when it is viewed in light of the purpose for which it was undertaken.[211]

Thus, although the employment contracts themselves carried rights and obligations similar to those in the commercial realm, the management and operation of a military base was undoubtedly a sovereign activity, because the sovereign *purpose* of the military base could not be denied. Since the union certification procedure sought to impose a statutory scheme of collective bargaining upon the management of the base, it related directly to the sovereign attributes of a foreign State, which must remain immune from such proceedings. This reasoning had its forerunner in the case of *Congo* v. *Venne*, involving the commissioning of an architect to draw plans for the construction of the Congo's national pavilion at 'Expo 67' in Montreal. The Supreme Court of Canada held that this involved a public sovereign act of State on behalf of the Congo and that the commissioning of the architect was a step taken in the performance of that sovereign act. Ritchie J, delivering the judgment of the majority, stated:

Considered from the point of view of the architect, it may well be that the contract was a purely commercial one, but, even if the theory of restrictive sovereign immunity were applicable, the question to be determined would not be whether the contractor was engaged in a private act of commerce, but whether or not the Government of the Congo ... was engaged in the performance of a public sovereign act of State.[212]

The Italian practice provides another example of the 'purpose' approach. Apart from – and in spite of – a few scattered declarations that the private law nature of a particular transaction cannot be altered by the public purpose it serves,[213] the Italian courts generally adopt an almost undisguised purpose test, in that a particular act will be considered as having a sovereign nature if it purportedly fulfils the 'institutional aims' or 'public purposes' of the foreign State. This is especially manifest in cases concerning contracts of employment.

Thus, even though health and care services could also be performed by private individuals, the employment of a medical doctor was a sovereign activity, because his job was part of a general arrangement that served 'public purposes'.[214] In rejecting the claim by an Italian citizen who had been employed as a lift attendant and messenger of a US naval base in Italy, the Tribunal explicitly declared:

The nature of the work performed by the employees is irrelevant – it may be purely manual work – because what matters is the person who provides the work and the purpose it serves.[215]

The Italian Court of Cassation soon offered its stamp of approval and in a string of cases upheld the immunity of the foreign States on the basis of the perceived public purposes, variously termed (at least in the English translations of the case reports) as 'public aims', 'institutional aims', 'institutional ends', 'institutional objectives', 'institutional purposes', 'public objectives' or simply 'public purposes', served by the legal relationships in question. These cover the employment of an assistant librarian in the US Information Office,[216] an administrative secretary at a hospital operated by the Order of Malta,[217] an administrative clerk in the Romanian Commercial Agency,[218] a secretary working for the cultural representative of the Danish Institute,[219] an 'assistant' in the Brazilian Embassy,[220] a commercial officer at the British Consulate in Venice,[221] a chancery usher at the German Embassy to the Holy See,[222] an Italian elementary school teacher at the Lycée Chateaubriand in Rome,[223] a secretary and telephonist employed by the Libyan State at the Jana Information Agency,[224] a secretary and administrative officer at the Commercial Office of the Royal Norwegian Embassy,[225] an administrator in the *Académie de France* in Rome,[226] and a commercial officer by the General Consulate of Canada in Milan.[227]

In the case of *Pontificia Opera*, brought by a warehouse worker for damages for failure to establish an insurance and social security plan, the Court of Cassation specifically pointed out that, while the practice of restricting foreign State immunity is predicated on 'the distinction between *iure imperii* and *iure gestionis* acts', it is impossible to place employment relations within the classification scheme of such a 'dichotomy of the acts', and that the duties of a warehouse worker amounted to 'an essential and indispensable instrument for the very performance of the public function fulfilled by the Opera'.[228] In dismissing the claim of a typist and translator in the Consul-General of Panama in Venice the Court declared that:

The question to be resolved here, therefore, is whether the relations of employment or of work which are entered into in order to satisfy the requirements of the consular office can be considered as falling outside the jurisdiction of our State, quite irrespective of the *nature* or content of the tasks actually performed by the employee.[229]

In upholding immunity in a case brought by an announcer and translator employed by Vatican Radio, the Court of Cassation further stated that:

The only decisive element is the worker's continuous participation in activities intended to achieve the State's public *purposes*.[230]

The purpose test is not confined to employment cases, but applies to other matters as well.[231] The generality of the test in the Italian practice can be demonstrated by the *Borri* case. In this connection it may be recalled that, in the *Weltover* case, the US Supreme Court held that, since the issuance of bonds was a commercial activity, the plaintiffs could sue for breach of contract when Argentina unilaterally extended the time for payment on the bonds, because the rescheduling of the maturity dates on the bonds had a 'direct effect' in the US.[232] By contrast, in *Borri* v. *Argentina*, an analogous case, similarly involving Argentina's extension of the term of payment on bonds issued in New York, the Italian Court of Cassation upheld immunity and denied injunctive relief to the plaintiff. The Court drew a line between the issuance of the bonds and the subsequent extension.

Ciò perché, mentre natura innegabilmente privatistica hanno gli atti di emissione e di collocazione sul mercato internazionale delle obbligazioni di che trattasi, non analoga natura paritetica hanno i successivi provvedimenti di moratoria, adottati dal Governo argentine ... ed il conseguente inadempimento di quello Stato.[233]

Referring to the Argentine laws of 2002 and 2003 extending the term of payment, the Court said:

Tali provvedimenti ... manifestano, evidentemente, la potestà sovrana dello Stato. E ciò ... soprattutto, per le ... *finalità, eminentemente pubbliche*, perseguite, di governo della finanza in funzione della tutela di bisogni primari di sopravvivenza economica della popolazione in un contesto storico di grave emergenza nazionale.[234]

That is, even though the issuance of bonds was a private law activity, the subsequent rescheduling and the consequent failure of Argentina to fulfil its obligations *served sovereign purposes* and therefore had a sovereign character.

Moreover, it would seem that, in the opinion of the Italian Court of Cassation, the 'nature' test is in essence a 'purpose' test:

Foreign States do not enjoy State immunity in cases of acts of a merely private nature, which are not intended to achieve public ends. Thus it is essential, in deciding the question of immunity, to determine the *nature* of the activities of the foreign State, that is whether these were intended to achieve public, institutional *ends*.[235]

The French position is proverbially ambivalent. Thus, on the one hand, it is pronounced that immunity is based on 'the nature of the activity';[236] on the other hand, it is also said that 'an act is ... regarded as an act of public power if its purpose is the performance of a public service'.[237] It is further declared that both the *nature* and the *purpose* of the transaction should be considered.[238] To add to the confusion, in *Euroéquipement*, which concerned a contract for a commercial lease of premises, immunity was denied because the defendant State entity in question pursued a 'purely commercial objective' in using the building, even though the question of immunity must be examined 'in relation to the nature of the activity performed'.[239] Then, finally, the Court of Cassation stated that:

Foreign States ... enjoy jurisdictional immunity in so far as the act giving rise to the dispute between the parties, by its *nature or purpose*, is an exercise of the sovereignty of such States and is therefore not a normal act of administrative management.[240]

In line with such practice, the 2004 UN Convention retains a limited role for 'purpose'. Article 2(2) provides:

In determining whether a contract or transaction is a 'commercial transaction' ... reference should be made primarily to the nature of the contract or transaction, but its purpose should also be taken into account if the parties to the contract or transaction have so agreed, or if, in the practice of the State of the forum, that purpose is relevant to determining the non-commercial character of the contract or transaction.

3.4. The 'context' approach

The UK SIA says nothing, nature or purpose, about the criterion for the determination of a commercial activity. The case law, at first blush, seems in favour of the 'nature' approach. In *Trendtex*, Lord Denning MR declared:

It was suggested that the original contracts for cement were made by the Ministry of Defence of Nigeria: and that the cement was for the building of barracks for the army. On this account it was said that the contracts of purchase were acts of a governmental nature, jure imperii, and not of a commercial nature, jure gestionis. They were like a contract of purchase of boots for the army. But I do not think this should affect the question of immunity. If a

104 COMMERCIAL ACTIVITY

government department goes into the market places of the world and buys boots or cement – as a commercial transaction – that government department should be subject to all the rules of the market place. The seller is not concerned with the *purpose* to which the purchaser intends to put the goods.[241]

Then Justice Robert Goff said in *I Congreso*:

it is not just that the purpose or motive of the act is to serve the purposes of the state, but that the act is of its own character a governmental act, as opposed to an act which any private citizen can perform.[242]

Lord Denning agreed:

Immunity depends on the nature of the act and not on its purpose ... Sovereign immunity depends on the nature of that action: not on the purpose or intent or motive – use whichever word you like – with which it is done. To prove this I would take the old chestnut. All the pundits say that when a government department places an order for boots for the army, it is acting jure gestionis, not jure imperii: but when it places an order for guns it is jure imperii. I cannot accept that distinction. Suppose the Navy Department of a foreign government orders a helicopter for military purposes, and its Agriculture Department orders a like helicopter for surveying the fields. In neither case is the foreign government entitled to sovereign immunity. The seller is not concerned with the purpose for which the helicopter is required. Likewise with a gun. The seller is not concerned whether the foreign government wants it to kill an enemy or to fire a salute or to train recruits. Whenever a foreign government orders goods or services of a trader, it ought to pay for them, no matter for what purpose it intends to use them.[243]

Lord Goff later repeated his proposition in *Kuwait Airways*:

the ultimate test of what constitutes an act jure imperii is whether the act in question is of its own character a governmental act, as opposed to an act which any private citizen can perform ... To attract immunity ... what is done ... must be something which possesses that character ... in the absence of such character, the mere fact that the purpose or motive of the act was to serve the purposes of the state will not be sufficient.[244]

Expressly endorsing this line of reasoning, Lord Wilberforce observed, in *I Congreso del Partido*:

Its [Trendtex's] value in the present case lies in the reasoning that if the act in question is of a commercial nature, the fact that it was done for governmental or political reasons does not attract sovereign immunity.[245]

However, quoting with approval the passages on the 'nature' test in the German *Empire of Iran* case and praising that case as 'one of great clarity',[246] Lord Wilberforce nevertheless noted that 'beyond this proposition (which is not decisive here) [the German cases] do not give direct guidance upon the questions we have to consider'.[247]

He then made his own proposition, which later was to assume biblical prominence in the common law jurisprudence:

> The conclusion which emerges is that in considering, under the 'restrictive theory', whether state immunity should be granted or not, the court must consider *the whole context* in which the claim against the state is made, with a view to deciding whether the relevant act(s) upon which the claim is based, should, in that context, be considered as fairly within an area of activity, trading or commercial, or otherwise of a private law character, in which the state has chosen to engage, or whether the relevant act(s) should be considered as having been done outside that area, and within the sphere of governmental or sovereign activity.[248]

Such an approach that considers 'the whole context' of a case naturally takes into account all the circumstances of the case and would therefore give relevance to the *purpose* of the act. Lord Wilberforce soon added:

> I agree that the purpose ... is not decisive but it may throw some light upon the nature of what was done.[249]

In the sense that all the surrounding circumstances should be considered, this might prove to be, in effect, the 'purpose' approach in disguise, even though 'purpose' as a test may be explicitly dismissed. In *Littrell* v. *USA (No. 2)*, where the English Court of Appeal dismissed an action against the US claiming damages for personal injuries allegedly resulting from medical treatment at a US Air Force hospital in England, the Court held that, viewed in its *context*, namely the maintenance of armed forces by the US in the UK, the operation of a military hospital, although no doubt requiring much the same skills as the operation of a civilian hospital, was a recognized military activity. The standard of medical care that the US afforded its own servicemen was thus a matter within its own sovereign authority.[250] In other words, running a hospital may be a private act, but running a hospital for a military or sovereign *purpose* is not.

The disguised 'purpose' test is aptly illustrated by *Holland*, which involved a claim for defamation against the education officer at a US military base in England, who had written a memorandum questioning the plaintiff's professional competence as a professor. The overall *context* was held to be that of the provision of educational services to military personnel and their families at the military base, the maintenance of which was plainly a sovereign activity. Though the writing of a memorandum by a civilian education officer in relation to an educational programme provided by civilian staff employed by a university, or the educational programme itself for that matter, hardly seemed an act *jure imperii*,[251] the provision of education, which was designed to strengthen the quality and efficiency of the armed forces or to ease their transition to civilian life on retirement from active service, was part of the process of maintaining forces and associated civilians on the base to serve the needs of the US military authorities and this was enough to make the disputed acts sovereign.[252]

Therefore the standard of education that the US afforded its servicemen and their families was a matter within its own sovereign authority and so accordingly was the act of writing the memorandum in the course of the supervision of the education programme. In other words, because the provision of education served a military/sovereign purpose, it and related acts assumed a sovereign character. Thus, despite their declared intention that only the *nature* of the activity in question should be considered, their Lordships actually adopted in essence a *purpose* test.[253]

The cases of *Littrell* and *Holland* thus indicate that the consideration of the 'overall context' will embrace what can be rightfully called a sovereign purpose of the act in question. Even if the courts may ostensibly express a great aversion to the invocation of a sovereign 'purpose', the net result is that the 'context' can and does serve as a cloak under which 'purpose' may sneak into the courtroom. In this regard, the 'purpose' test adopted by the Canadian courts can be seen as a more radical form of the 'contextual' approach.

'Purpose' was even expressly considered in *Hicks*, where a US citizen, who had been employed as an equipment repairer at a bowling alley at a US air base in England, brought proceedings for unfair dismissal and redundancy payments. The Employment Appeal Tribunal, while holding that the 'primary *purpose* of providing recreational facilities' at an air base was to 'sustain the effectiveness of its central military activity or capability', especially criticized the tribunal of the first instance for focusing on 'the *nature* of the contract of employment ... without being asked to consider fully what was involved in investigating the acts relied on as giving rise to the claims'.[254]

The 'context' approach is also followed by courts in Australia, Ireland, Israel, Malaysia and New Zealand.[255] In the *Davison* case, for example, the plaintiff, as Government Auditor of the Cook Islands, applied for judicial review to challenge the right of the Commissioner in the well-known 'Winebox Inquiry' to require the giving of evidence or the production of documents, in connection with a scheme wherein the Cook Islands Government issued (for a pecuniary consideration) tax payment/credit certificates which could then be used to set off against (and thus evade) income tax in New Zealand. The central issue with regard to the immunity of the Cook Islands Government and its auditor was whether issuing of tax credit certificates was a commercial activity. The court found it to be a commercial activity in this case. In the court's opinion, imposing taxes, collecting taxes, and issuing tax credit certificates were certainly functions of a sovereign State, but the Cook Islands Government did far more than engage in a tax regime. In view of the whole *context*, including the nature and *purpose*, of its act, the Cook Islands Government was actually engaged in a commercial transaction in which the tax credit certificates were used as a medium for financial gain. In other words, it was a sale, rather than issuance, of tax credits.[256]

The full extent and implications of the contextual approach were succinctly brought out by Vincent J in *Reid*, where he said:

> In some situations, for example, the divorcement of act, motive, or purpose may not be possible. In other words, the motive or purpose underlying particular conduct may constitute part of the definition of the act itself, while in others the nature or quality of the act performed may not be ascertainable without reference to the context within which it is carried out. Further, even if the 'relevant act' can be isolated, a plethora of possible relationships to the exercise of sovereign power can exist, the character and proximity of which would be dependent upon the perception held or policy adopted within the jurisdiction in which the matter arises as to attributes of sovereignty itself.[257]

The contextual approach was also adopted by the Swedish Supreme Court in *Västerås*, where the Court found that it was difficult to formulate a distinction simply on a nature–purpose basis, since '[i]n practice, it seems that the judge will often need to make an overall assessment of the circumstances'. Thus the Court concluded that a contract between the Icelandic Ministry of Education and Culture and the Swedish Local Authority of Västerås for the purposes of providing flight-technician education to Icelandic students in Sweden, even though containing a clause whereby disputes concerning its implementation were to be settled according to Swedish law, was a public act.[258]

108   COMMERCIAL ACTIVITY

3.5. A summary

The upshot is that the 'purpose' of a particular activity, though roundly denounced, may become relevant in some situations and even prove decisive in others. The haunting spectre of 'purpose' shows no sign of being dissipated, since 'purpose' is always one aspect of the multi-faceted reality daily confronting the judges.

However that may be, the nature/purpose debate may not be terribly crucial in practice. In the vast majority of cases, the nature test is either mentioned only in passing or not mentioned at all. Whatever the test, the courts tend to look into all the relevant circumstances. What is more, for many courts, finding an activity commercial represents only one initial step towards the actual assertion of jurisdiction over a foreign State: other conditions must also be satisfied. We next turn to examine the decisive role played by the requirement of a territorial connection in the US practice. Compared with this requirement, the nature or purpose of the particular act often occupies a secondary place.

4. The jurisdictional nexus requirement under the US FSIA

As a matter of fact, in the overwhelming majority of US cases, the courts' attention was focused, not on the nature or purpose of the act in question, but on whether there existed a connection between the US territory and the act upon which the claim was based. Absence of such a connection would lead to a rejection of the claim. For example, in *Stena*, the court granted immunity even though there existed undisputed commercial activity between the parties. Since all the commercial activity relevant to the plaintiff's claims for breach of contract and negligent misrepresentation had occurred within the territorial boundaries of Sweden and Mexico, the defendant company's commercial acts did not form the basis for the plaintiff's complaints and so the commercial activities exception did not apply. In the words of the court: 'The commercial activities exception to sovereign immunity applies *only if* the sovereign's commercial activity has a sufficient connection – a "jurisdictional nexus" – with the United States.'[259] In *Soudavar*, the court even refused to consider whether the acts complained of were sovereign or commercial, because the requisite jurisdictional nexus with the US was found to be lacking.[260]

This is because, under the US FSIA, it is not enough for the foreign State merely to have engaged in a commercial activity; the plaintiff's action must be 'based upon'[261] any of the three types of acts prescribed in section 1605(a)(2) of the FSIA, which provides:

A foreign state shall not be immune from the jurisdiction of courts of the United States or of the States in any case – in which the action is based upon a commercial activity carried on in the United States by the foreign state; or upon an act performed in the United States in connection with a commercial activity of the foreign state elsewhere; or upon an act outside the territory of the United States in connection with a commercial activity of the foreign state elsewhere and that act causes a direct effect in the United States.[262]

Obviously, the FSIA requires a 'double connection' before immunity can be denied: a territorial connection and a subject-matter connection. As the Fifth Circuit pointed out:

A foreign sovereign ... does not abrogate its sovereign immunity simply because it conducts commercial operations that have a connection with the United States. Not only must there be a jurisdictional nexus between the United States and the commercial acts of the foreign sovereign, there must be a connection between the plaintiff's cause of action and the commercial acts of the foreign sovereign.[263]

In the words of the Third Circuit:

We adopt a two-part test when determining whether a foreign state's commercial activities are sufficient to deprive it of sovereign immunity under the FSIA commercial activity exception. Under this test, the initial inquiry is whether there is a sufficient jurisdictional connection or nexus between the commercial activity and the United States. The second inquiry is whether there exists a substantive connection or nexus between the commercial activity and the subject matter of the cause of action.[264]

This jurisdictional nexus requirement will in general mean that if the material facts as alleged in a claim occurred abroad, then it becomes difficult for the plaintiff to invoke the commercial activity exception. In particular, the plaintiff cannot rely on the commercial activity exception in the hope of overcoming the strict territorial requirement contained in the tortious activity exception. For example, if the facts alleged as the basis of the claim happen to be torture by police officers in a foreign country, it will not be open to the plaintiff to argue the case by saying that the plaintiff had been recruited and hired in the US.[265] In most cases, the US courts tend to occupy themselves with looking for one of the connecting factors in section 1605(a)(2), rather than ascertaining the 'nature' or the more mystic 'purpose' of the act or transaction. Surprisingly, out of a vast body of case law on the issue of territorial

110   COMMERCIAL ACTIVITY

connection no uniform or even generally applicable rules can be distilled. What is available is a matrix of pointers or indicators, now concurring, now conflicting. This is the most diversified, the most fluid, the most confusing and hence the most fascinating part of the US judicial practice on State immunity.

4.1.   The first clause of section 1605(a)(2)

The first clause of section 1605(a)(2) provides that a foreign State shall not be immune 'in any case in which the action is based upon a commercial activity carried on in the United States by the foreign state'. Section 1603(e) defines a 'commercial activity carried on in the United States by a foreign state' as 'commercial activity carried on by such state and having substantial contact with the United States'.[266] In other words, for the first clause of section 1605(a)(2) to apply, a plaintiff's 'action must be "based upon" some "commercial activity" by [a defendant foreign State] that had "substantial contact" with the United States'.[267] It is immediately obvious that a territorial connection is built into the very definition of 'commercial activity'. According to the case law, the first clause focuses 'not on whether the foreign state generally engages in commercial activity in the United States, but on whether the particular conduct giving rise to the claim is a part of commercial activity having substantial contact with the United States'.[268]

4.1.1.   'Based upon a commercial activity'

According to the US Supreme Court, the phrase 'based upon' denotes 'those elements of a claim that, if proven, would entitle a plaintiff to relief under his theory of the case'.[269] This means that a suit 'based upon a commercial activity' 'calls for something more than a mere connection with, or relation to, commercial activity'.[270] Thus, to sustain jurisdiction on this basis, there must be 'a *significant nexus* between the commercial activity in this country upon which the exception is based and a plaintiff's cause of action'.[271] Obviously, personal injury suffered (or death that occurred) in a foreign country cannot provide the plaintiff with a cause of action.[272] In a case involving a plane crash in Mexico, the only nexus alleged by the plaintiffs in this case, however, was that the aeroplane had been in Chicago (where it had received routine servicing) the day prior to the crash and ultimately was due to land in Los Angeles. The court found this to be insufficient.[273]

In deciding on the 'nexus' issue, courts must focus on the 'gravamen of the complaint'.[274] That is:

it would not be sufficient for the plaintiff to demonstrate merely that the defendants undertook their objectionable conduct in furtherance of the commercial activity, or that the conduct was somehow incidental to a commercial transaction. Rather, for jurisdictional purposes, he would have to prove that the commercial activity itself gave rise to the particular cause of action.[275]

The fact that the foreign State or its agency carries out commercial operations in the US is inadequate in itself to support a finding of subject matter jurisdiction under section 1605(a)(2), as the only relevant acts for the purposes of jurisdiction under the FSIA are those acts that *form the basis of the plaintiff's complaint*.[276] Even if the defendant State conducted commercial activities in the US, immunity would still be granted if there is no adequate connection between the plaintiff's cause of action and the defendant's commercial activities in the US.[277] When 'the commercial activity in question centers on the formation of a contract, the United States will be found to have had a substantial contact with that activity if ... substantial aspects of the contract were to be performed here'.[278] Similarly, a foreign State does not lose immunity simply because it owns assets in the US that the plaintiff seeks to attach.[279]

When a transaction consists of both commercial and sovereign elements, jurisdiction will turn on which element the cause of action is based on.[280] Jurisdiction will not be available if the cause of action is based on a sovereign activity,[281] but will obtain where the cause of action is based on the commercial element. Thus, in *Honduras Aircraft Registry*, where the Honduran Government contracted two private companies to provide technical expertise for aircraft inspections and staff training in order to set up an aircraft registry, the court found that the case involved both commercial and sovereign rights. In the court's opinion, whereas registering aircraft under the Honduras flag was an act peculiar to sovereignty, contracting for services was a commercial act. Since the plaintiffs were not contending for the right to register aircraft but were merely seeking to enforce the contract, under which they had provided goods and services to Honduras by inspecting and certifying aircraft airworthiness for the registration, Honduras could not enjoy immunity.[282]

Following the same logic, the Eleventh Circuit in *Guevara* held that a foreign State's offer of a reward in return for information enabling it to locate and capture a fugitive was a 'commercial activity'. Peru had offered US$5 million for the information. The court pointed out that the location and capture of a fugitive by law enforcement officials of a country might be a sovereign act, but that was not what this case was about; the question before the court was whether Guevara could use US courts to compel Peru to keep its contractual promise to pay him the money it had offered. What was at issue was simply a contract to purchase information, a common staple of the private sector.[283]

Therefore, for a suit to be 'based on a commercial activity in the US' does not mean that every relevant act or element has to be commercial in nature;[284] nor does it mean that all the relevant facts must take place in the US. According to the Seventh Circuit in *Santos*:

> We conclude that a claim is 'based upon' events in the United States if those events establish a legal element of the claim ... An action is based upon the elements that prove the claim, no more and no less. If one of those elements consists of commercial activity within the United States or other conduct specified in the Act, this country's courts have jurisdiction.[285]

On the other hand, 'a claim cannot be "based upon" a commercial activity that forms no part of the proof of that claim'.[286] Thus it was not possible for an action to be brought against Air France for injuries caused by negligent driving of an Air France employee in a Paris airport, because none of the elements of the claim concerned acts of Air France in the US, nor could the plaintiff establish a duty of care on Air France towards him.[287] In contrast, it was allowable for a passenger who had sustained foot injuries in a Paris airport to sue for negligence against Air France on the basis of ticket sale (which constituted a commercial activity) in Washington DC.[288]

In *Nelson*, an employee of a Saudi government-run hospital brought an action against Saudi Arabia and the hospital for injuries arising from his alleged detention and torture in Saudi Arabia. In an obvious attempt to overcome the difficulty that his injuries had been sustained in Saudi Arabia, not in the US, the plaintiff relied on the first clause of section 1605(a)(2) and pointed to the fact that the defendants had recruited him and signed the contract of employment with him in the US. The Supreme Court, however, found that the plaintiff was not alleging breach of contract, but personal injuries. It was those torts, not the commercial activities that preceded their commission, that formed the basis of the suit.[289] Therefore, his claim was rejected.

4.1.2. 'Substantial contact'

The FSIA requires 'substantial contact with the United States' for a commercial activity to be one 'carried on in the United States' (section 1603(e)) but does not define 'substantial contact'. In many cases the courts often have to conduct a careful consideration of the relevant circumstances. Thus 'substantial contact' could be established where a Russian corporation concluded a contract with a US corporation transferring title to commercial nuclear material located in the US.[290] In *Shapiro*, the court held that the issuance by a foreign State of negotiable promissory notes, some of which were sent to the US and which were to pay for the purchase of aircraft, amounted to 'a commercial activity having substantial contact with the United States'.[291] In *Braspetro*, a Brazilian State entity's negotiation and procurement of performance bonds in New York that were understood to be (although not contractually obliged to be) payable in New York and the entity's actual payment from its New York bank account were considered as constituting 'substantial contact' with the US.[292] Of course, if the defendant State issued bonds in, say, New York City, a 'sufficient nexus' can easily be established.[293]

More attenuated contact with the US territory, such as mere recruitment efforts, solicitation of customers and preliminary negotiations, if not resulting in a contract being concluded in the US, cannot itself be deemed a substantial contact,[294] nor can 'post-contract execution communications'.[295]

Furthermore, even if the entire case need not be based on the commercial activity of the defendant, at least one element of the plaintiff's claim should consist in conduct that occurred in commercial activity carried on in the US. So the family of a US student drowned while participating in a cultural tour could not sue Taiwan or its entities for wrongful death because the specific conduct, i.e. failure to take reasonable care in allowing the students to swim, had occurred in Taiwan. The defendants' promotion and application process in the US was not conduct capable of proving any of the elements of the plaintiffs' action.[296]

It seems that the word 'substantial' is only a matter of appreciation. For example, the conclusion in the US of an agreement relating to the overhaul of an electric generator, though a single transaction, was held sufficient to found jurisdiction, even though the overhaul took place in the Marshall Islands.[297] However, a single visit to the US, without more, clearly does not constitute a substantial contact.[298]

4.2. The second clause of section 1605(a)(2)

Under the second clause, a foreign State is not immune in a case where the action is 'based upon an act performed in the United States in connection with a commercial activity of the foreign state elsewhere'.

114   COMMERCIAL ACTIVITY

Needless to say, if the suit is not based upon an act performed in the US,[299] or if the act cannot be attributed to the foreign State,[300] there is no jurisdiction under this clause. There is nothing here to indicate what nature – commercial or otherwise – the 'act performed in the United States' must have; the legislative report, however, enunciates that:

Examples of this type of situation might include: a representation in the United States by an agent of a foreign state that leads to an action for restitution based on unjust enrichment; an act in the United States that violates U.S. securities laws or regulations; the wrongful discharge in the United States of an employee of the foreign state who has been employed in connection with a commercial activity carried on in some third country.

Although *some or all* of these acts might also be considered to be a 'commercial activity carried on in the United States' ... it has seemed advisable to provide expressly for the case where a claim arises out of a specific act in the United States which is *commercial or private in nature* and which relates to a commercial activity abroad. It should be noted that the acts (or omissions) encompassed in this category are *limited* to those which in and of themselves are sufficient to form the basis of a cause of action.[301]

Apart from acknowledging a high degree of overlap between the first and the second clauses of section 1605(a)(2), in that 'some or all' of the acts covered by the second clause may also come within the first clause,[302] the whole statement is particularly puzzling with regard to the nature of the 'act' in question. While declaring that 'some or all' of the 'examples' they had in mind might be commercial activities, implying that 'some' of those acts might not necessarily be commercial,[303] the legislators nonetheless narrowed down the scope of the 'act' in the second clause to 'a specific act ... which is commercial or private in nature'. This leaves the reader at a loss as to whether those 'examples' should be treated as illustrations of the subject matter of the second clause, or whether they are simply representative of a vast range of possibilities out of which only those 'commercial or private' acts shall be covered by the second clause. The latter seems more to be the case since the acts (or omissions) as contemplated by the legislators are 'limited' to those capable of providing a cause of action against a foreign State; and it is difficult to imagine how that can be possible without the acts themselves being commercial or private in character. Therefore, allowing some variation in the interpretation of the word 'private' (which variation may not make much difference in view of the way 'private' is used as a test for commercial activity, as discussed above), the legislators' statement in effect introduces a 'double commerciality' rule; that is, immunity shall be denied under the second clause only if the case is one in which the foreign State performs a *commercial* (or private for that matter) act in the US that has some connection with a *commercial* activity elsewhere. A district court understood this clause precisely in this manner when it commented on the fact that the defendants, British medical schools, were contemplating the establishment of wound treatment centres in the US:

This is a commercial activity carried on in the United States and in connection with a commercial activity performed elsewhere.[304]

This 'double commerciality' would mean that a claim based upon a sovereign (or public) act is bound to fail, however strong a connection can be established between that act and a commercial activity. Considering this, the following pronouncement, although made by the Supreme Court in reference to the first clause, would apply with particular force to the second clause:

where a claim rests entirely upon activities sovereign in character ... jurisdiction will not exist ... regardless of any connection the sovereign acts may have with commercial activity.[305]

Next, on 'connection', the guidance provided by the case law appears haphazard and inadequate. Thus, while some courts would require a 'substantive connection' or 'causal link' between the act and the commercial activity,[306] others demand a 'material connection ... between the act performed in the United States and plaintiff's cause of action',[307] or a 'significant nexus'.[308] There should also exist a 'material connection' between the plaintiff's cause of action and the 'act performed in the United States'.[309]

Negotiation in the US of indemnity agreements regarding the construction of oil platforms in Brazil, which contained payment obligations in the US, and subsequent breach of those obligations by failing to make payment in the US, were held to be such acts.[310]

4.3. The third clause of section 1605(a)(2)

Dubbed a 'rather enigmatic proposition',[311] the third clause has so far proved to be the most problematic of the three clauses of section 1605(a)(2). It provides that a foreign State shall not enjoy immunity in any case 'in which the action is based ... upon an act outside the territory of the United States in connection with a commercial activity of the foreign state elsewhere and that act causes a direct effect in the United States'.

116   COMMERCIAL ACTIVITY

Obviously, this provision speaks of three things: (1) an 'act'; (2) a 'commercial activity'; and (3) a 'direct effect'. What is crucial here is that the 'direct effect' has to be caused by the 'act', not the 'commercial activity'. Indeed, the Supreme Court understood as much when it said in *Weltover* that, in order to establish jurisdiction under the third clause:

our analysis is therefore limited to considering whether this lawsuit is (1) 'based ... upon an act outside the territory of the United States'; (2) that was taken 'in connection with a commercial activity' of Argentina outside this country; and (3) that 'cause[d] a direct effect in the United States'.[312]

And the Court followed exactly this three-part test. It identified (1) the 'act outside the territory of the United States' (Argentina's unilateral rescheduling of the maturity dates on the Bonods); (2) the 'commercial activity' (Argentina's issuance of the Bonods); and (3) the 'direct effect in the United States' (New York being the place of payment).[313]

4.3.1.   The 'act'

It may be asked whether the 'act' outside the US territory that is required to be 'in connection with a commercial activity' should itself be a commercial activity as well. The FSIA is silent on this point and *Weltover* is not of much help. True, in identifying Argentina's rescheduling of the bonds as the 'act', the Supreme Court did not specify whether the rescheduling of bonds was itself a commercial activity; however, since the Court also found that 'private parties regularly issue bonds',[314] then conceivably private parties regularly reschedule bonds too. There then is nothing inherently governmental about Argentina's rescheduling of the bonds, which would also be a commercial act. Thus *Weltover* still does not answer the question whether jurisdiction can also be available under the FSIA in an action based upon a *governmental or noncommercial* act outside the US (e.g. revocation of a business licence) in connection with a commercial activity and that act causes a direct effect in the US. In all probability, the issue of jurisdiction in such a case would be decided in the negative. In a case concerning the revocation by Bangladesh of a business licence to capture and export rhesus monkeys, the Ninth Circuit stated that the case fell under the third clause of section 1605(a)(2) but considered only two points: (1) commercial activity; and (2) direct effect, and decided that a negative finding on commercial activity dispensed with any consideration on direct effect:

Bangladesh was terminating an agreement that only a sovereign could have made. This was not just a contract for trade of monkeys. It concerned

Bangladesh's right to regulate imports and exports, a sovereign prerogative. It concerned Bangladesh's right to regulate its natural resources, also a uniquely sovereign function. A private party could not have made such an agreement ... In short, the licensing agreement was a sovereign act, not just a commercial transaction. Its revocation was sovereign by nature, not commercial.[315]

More importantly for our purposes:

Because the act complained of was not a commercial activity and Bangladesh has sovereign immunity, effect in the United States is irrelevant.[316]

Besides showing a foreshortened vision of the third clause, this is a resounding affirmation that a claim based upon a sovereign act will fail, whether or not that act happens to be connected with a commercial activity, or have any 'direct effect' in the US. Perplexingly, the Ninth Circuit apparently had a change of heart eighteen years later, when it declared that there was nothing in the case law or the legislative report to suggest 'that a foreign state's conduct "*in connection with* a commercial activity" must itself be a commercial activity to fall within the third exception to foreign sovereign immunity'.[317] The exact opposite, however, seems to be the case. According to the legislative report, the third clause:

would embrace *commercial conduct abroad having direct effects within the United States* which would subject such conduct to the exercise of jurisdiction by the United States consistent with principles set forth in section 18, Restatement of the Law, Second, Foreign Relations Law of the United States (1965).[318]

When one collates the expressions 'that act causes a direct effect in the United States' in the third clause and 'commercial conduct abroad having direct effects within the United States' in the legislative report, the inescapable conclusion is that, for the legislators, the 'act' actually means 'commercial conduct', i.e. a commercial activity, and that, therefore, the third clause, according to the authoritative interpretation given by its drafters, ought to be read as that a foreign State shall not enjoy immunity in any case 'in which the action is based ... upon a *commercial activity* outside the territory of the United States in connection with a commercial activity of the foreign state elsewhere and *the former commercial activity* causes a direct effect in the United States'. This is nothing if not an undisguised 'double commerciality' rule. Section 18 of the Second Restatement, invoked by the legislative report as providing the guiding principles, corroborates this conclusion, for it refers to such 'conduct and its effect' as are 'generally recognized as constituent elements of a crime or tort',[319] thereby precluding prima facie any governmental or sovereign character of the conduct in question.

This, however, is not even the real problem. What is even more obfuscating – and, in a crooked sense, telling – is that, instead of the trio of 'act' plus 'commercial activity' plus 'direct effect' in the third clause, the legislative report actually mentions only a duo, that is, 'commercial conduct' plus 'direct effects'. In other words, in the minds of the legislators, the 'act' and the 'commercial activity' were one and the same thing: 'commercial conduct'. So what the legislators really meant was actually 'a commercial activity outside the US that has caused a direct effect in the US'. This equation and conflation of the 'act' and the 'commercial activity', besides further underscoring the point of 'double commerciality', has been the root cause of a muddled and blurry jurisprudence on the third clause.

In *Garb*, where the plaintiffs sued Poland for expropriation of real property from Jews in Poland following the Second World War under, among others, the third clause of section 1605(a)(2), the Second Circuit upheld immunity on the ground that expropriation, upon which the claims were based, was a decidedly sovereign activity. In this connection, 'subsequent commercial transactions involving expropriated property do not give rise to subject matter jurisdiction over claims arising from the original expropriation', since Congress's intention was to 'deny sovereign immunity to foreign States only with respect to *commercial, and not sovereign, acts*'.[320]

The court said nothing about the issue of 'direct effect'. Translated in the terms of the third clause, the court's decision boils down to this: because expropriation, that is, the 'act outside the territory of the United States' upon which the action was based, was a sovereign activity, that 'act' could not possibly have been done 'in connection with a (subsequent) commercial activity', and then it became unnecessary to consider whether 'that act cause[d] a direct effect in the United States'. In brief, once the 'act' is found to be sovereign and non-commercial, it is dispositive of an action under the third clause. Conversely, jurisdiction can only be exercised under the third clause in a case where there is 'a *commercial* act outside the US in connection with a *commercial* activity'. This is unmistakably a 'double commerciality' rule. This conclusion is further supported by the court's repeated emphasis on the sovereign nature of the 'act' upon which the plaintiffs' claims were based: for if it was irrelevant whether the 'act' was commercial or non-commercial, there should have been no need for the *Garb* court to discuss the sovereign nature of the act of expropriation at all, and it would be difficult to explain why the court should have said that Congress's intention was to deny immunity only with respect to *commercial* acts.

The *Yang Rong* case provides another apt illustration. In that case, the plaintiff had entered into a business partnership with the City of Shenyang, Liaoning Province, China. To expand the venture through access to American capital, the partners had decided to list the joint venture on the New York Stock Exchange. Upon the request of Chinese government officials, the plaintiff had joined a number of Chinese governmental entities in creating the Chinese Financial Educational Development Foundation, an entity which was to be the majority shareholder of Brilliance Holdings Ltd, the 'financing vehicle' incorporated by Yang Rong for the purposes of listing in New York. In 2002, a 'Working Committee' headed by the Assistant Governor of Liaoning Province declared that all equity interests held in the name of the Foundation, including Yang Rong's interest in Brilliance Holdings, were State assets. At the direction of the Province, the Brilliance Holdings board dismissed Yang Rong as President, CEO and Director and placed Working Committee members in those and other management positions. When Yang Rong sued the Liaoning Provincial Government under the third clause of section 1605(a)(2), the DC Circuit recounted the plaintiffs' claim in the following terms:

Here Rong claims that the Province's 'implementation of the scheme to take Plaintiff's shares, other equity interests, and other property and then to maintain control thereof for its own commercial benefit', was 'commercial activity' under the third clause of 28 U.S.C. § 1605(a)(2), that is, an act 'outside the territory of the United States in connection with a commercial activity of the foreign state elsewhere and that act causes a direct effect in the United States'.[321]

The only thing that is clear is that the action was brought under the third clause; everything else remains hazy at best. According to this statement, the defendant Province's conduct was a 'commercial activity' and therefore an 'act in connection with a commercial activity'. What is most revealing is that the DC Circuit uncritically restated the plaintiff's claim without any indication that such a formulation was improper. In other words, both the plaintiffs and the court failed to appreciate that they were telescoping the three-item analysis in the third clause into a two-item analysis.

Our criticism is buttressed by a careful reading of the case. The court noted that the parties did not agree on the conduct of the Province that formed the basis of the plaintiff's suit; but it did not express its own opinion as to what was that conduct. In other words, neither the parties themselves nor the court knew exactly what was the 'act' upon which the plaintiff's claim was based; but the court nonetheless proceeded to consider various actions of the Province, and said:

> The Province did not assume control over Brilliance Holdings by purchasing the majority of Brilliance Holdings' stock ... as a private party would; instead, it declared the Brilliance Holdings shares held by the Foundation to be state assets and claimed them as does a sovereign. A private party in the market could not have done what the Province did here ... These acts ... constituted a quintessentially sovereign act, not a corporate takeover.[322]

No trouble was taken to specify, as is required by the third clause, what was the 'act' and what was the 'commercial activity' in connection with which the 'act' has to be taken outside the US. All one hears from the court is that, because no commercial activity was involved, the court found it unnecessary to consider the 'direct effect' requirement.[323] One is left to wonder what the court meant when it denied jurisdiction because there was no commercial activity. Did it mean that the 'act outside the US' was a sovereign act, and therefore, even if it might be connected with a *subsequent* commercial activity, the court still did not have jurisdiction? Or did it mean that, whatever the 'act', it had not been done 'in connection with a commercial activity'? Or did it simply mean that the third clause only requires a commercial activity that causes a direct effect in the US, without it being necessary to isolate any particular (whatever its nature) 'act' for the purposes of jurisdiction? The first possibility harks back to the 'double commerciality' rule in the context of the second clause, making it extremely tempting to think that the 'act ... in connection with a commercial activity of the foreign state elsewhere' ought itself to be a commercial activity as well; the second possibility seems to fall squarely within the third clause but the question remains how one can be sure of the 'connection' without knowing the 'act'; the third possibility would be in agreement with what is declared by the drafters in their report but would run afoul of the three-part test in *Weltover*.

In *Beg*, where the plaintiff sued Pakistan for expropriation of land in Pakistan, the Eleventh Circuit seems to have been utterly oblivious to the 'act' requirement. Noting that the plaintiff relied exclusively on the third clause of section 1605(a)(2), the court said:

The key issue we address is whether the Pakistani government was engaged in commercial activity.[324]

Here are the court's findings:

Here, we conclude that the Pakistani government's actions involve the power of eminent domain and, therefore, are not commercial. The power of eminent domain is a sovereign power ... Confiscation of real property is a public act because private actors are not allowed to engage in 'takings' in the manner that governments are ... Consequently, the Pakistani government's actions do not fall under the commercial exception to the FSIA.[325]

No attempt was made to isolate an 'act' and a 'commercial activity'; nothing was said about the 'direct effect'; and the conclusion was deceptively simple:

Because we conclude that the defendants did not engage in commercial activity, this suit does not fall under the § 1605(a)(2) exception to foreign government immunity.[326]

The result is again a much telescoped view of the third clause. It is not clear whether, by 'commercial activity' the court meant that the 'act' was not a 'commercial activity', or that the 'act' was not taken 'in connection with a commercial activity'. Because the court in its conclusion said that 'the defendants *did not engage in* commercial activity', without any reference to a 'connection', there is good reason to infer that, in the opinion of the court, the third clause involves only a simplistic discovery as to whether any commercial activity is alleged. Where there is no commercial activity, there is immunity. This is either a 'single commerciality' rule (where the 'act' and the 'commercial activity' are merged), or a reductivist 'double commerciality' rule (where the 'act' has also to be a commercial activity). In either case, it confirms the impression that, where the 'act' is sovereign or governmental, the claim will in all likelihood fail. The point that the 'act' itself should also be a commercial activity was unambiguously underlined by the case of *Drexel*, in which the Second Circuit held that the 'acts' upon which the plaintiffs' claims were based were various decisions made by a government committee regarding, inter alia, the security interests of the company and therefore could not have been performed by private parties. The court especially pointed out that the 'connection' requirement in the third clause did not 'include tangential commercial activities to which the "acts" forming the basis of the claim have only an attenuated connection', for otherwise 'the "commercial activity" exception would effectively be rewritten to authorize the exercise of jurisdiction over acts that are essentially sovereign in nature'.[327]

One thing that these cases[328] have in common is that they concerned claims of expropriation (or a vaguer 'taking'). There might be some doubt as to whether expropriation claims should be brought under the expropriation exception contained in section 1605(a)(3) of the FSIA, but not the commercial activity exception in section 1605(a)(2);[329] but that doubt can be dispelled by the very fact that expropriation claims have indeed been pleaded, entertained and decided either solely under section 1605(a)(2),[330] or simultaneously under both section 1605(a)(2) and (3),[331] which shows that there is nothing to preclude a claim of expropriation being brought under the commercial activity exception. The conclusions drawn from the above cases, despite the subject matter being claims of expropriation, thus hold good for the issue of the 'act' under the third clause. At any rate, there are still further cases in which the 'act' of the foreign State outside the US was not 'expropriation' (or 'taking' or 'confiscation') (and therefore cannot be said to fall only under the expropriation exception) but in which the courts nonetheless followed exactly the same reasoning.

In *Corzo*, the assignee of a judgment creditor sought to 'domesticate' a Peruvian judgment against the monetary authority of Peru and to attach its assets in the US. The court conducted only a two-part analysis: 'a. Commercial Activity' and 'b. Direct Effect'.[332] Again in this case, the parties disagreed on 'what activity gave rise to the present suit', but this did not deter the court from 'assum[ing] for the sake of argument' that the 'the relevant ... activity is that which gave rise to the original lawsuit in Peru'.[333] The court then found that the 'relevant activity', i.e. 'the denial of the exchange-rate application', was 'not commercial activity, but a sovereign act'. Then:

> Because we have concluded that the relevant activity was not commercial in nature, a determination of whether that activity had a 'direct effect' in the United States is not critical to the outcome of this case.[334]

There was again no mention of separate analyses of such elements as the 'act' which should have taken in 'connection' with a 'commercial activity'. Once the (even though only assumed) 'act' or 'activity' was held not to be a 'commercial activity', that was the end of the matter.

The same truncated application of the third clause can also be observed in *Aldy*, where survivors of workers killed while working with a paper machine at a paper mill in Louisiana, US, brought product liability action against Valmet, the Finnish company (which was held by the court to qualify as a foreign sovereign) that designed and manufactured the machine. The court held that the plaintiffs' suits were 'based upon the *commercial acts* of Valmet outside the US' and were therefore 'classic design and manufacturing defect suits, which the third clause of the commercial activities exception is broad enough to cover'.[335]

Again, in *Poddar*, where bondholders sued the State Bank of India for delay in making payment following their redemption of development bonds issued by the Bank, the court found that:

> the action is based upon defendant's activities, acts, and failures to act that occurred in India, specifically defendant's failure to send plaintiffs their redemption payments before February 15, 1997 so that plaintiffs could receive payment on the bond redemption date, February 15, 1997. Only the third clause of Section 1605(a)(2) might apply in this case to provide jurisdiction over plaintiffs' claims. However, this clause allows for jurisdiction over this action only if defendant's *commercial acts in India*, upon which this action is based, caused a 'direct effect' in the United States.[336]

Of some interest is the *Magness* case, where Russia was sued by the owners of a piano factory in Russia for expropriation. The court, opining that section 1605(a)(2) applied to the case, said:

> [Russia's] seizure and sale, for continuing operation and lease, of plaintiffs' property constitute acts ... performed outside the United States territory and in connection with the commercial activities [i.e. running paid exhibitions, etc.] of operating the properties and managing of Plaintiffs' real estate in Russia. These activities are 'of a kind in which a private party might engage', and such acts cause a direct effect in the United States in that Plaintiffs were to accept delivery of their pianos in Houston, Texas, U.S.A.[337]

This would have been a complete three-part analysis comprising an 'act'/ 'acts', a 'commercial activity' and a 'direct effect' had the court not made it clear beforehand that:

> The Russian Federations' seizure of personal and real property with subsequent leasing, operation, or sale similarly constitutes commercial activity.[338]

Thus ultimately this case amounts to just another instance of the 'commercial activity + direct effect' format. In fact, such a two-part, abridged approach is so pervasive in cases concerning the third clause[339] that it would not be very far from reality to conclude that the pattern of 'commercial activity + direct effect' seems rather to be the norm in the US courts, despite the wording of the third clause itself.

124   COMMERCIAL ACTIVITY

In those cases where the courts indeed proposed a three-part analysis, the evidence is inconclusive of the 'act' issue. *Weltover*, as discussed above, is a germane example, so are a number of other cases. Thus one finds the following activities identified as the 'act(s) taken outside the US' under the third clause: default on bonds (breach of the terms of the bonds) in connection with the commercial activity of issuance of bonds;[340] incorporation of the terms of a commercial agreement into an insurance policy;[341] default on performance guarantee bonds;[342] attempt to extort bribes as a condition for the award of government contracts;[343] conclusion and breach of joint venture agreements;[344] negotiating a charter party by correspondence,[345] and continued management of and profiting from expropriated property.[346] These are all acts that are not uniquely governmental, sovereign, public, or non-commercial in nature, but which are regularly engaged in by private persons.

4.3.2.   The 'direct effect'

More often, the case turns on the 'direct effect', that is, a direct, territorial connection between the act of the defendant foreign State and the US. In fact, in a typical third clause case, this is by the very terms of that clause the only jurisdictional link. In *Weltover*, for example, none of the parties was of US nationality and the transaction that formed the basis of the claim had taken place outside the US: the plaintiffs/respondents were two Panamanian corporations and a Swiss bank, the defendants/ petitioners were Argentina and its central bank, and the disputed bonds (called 'Bonods' in this case) had apparently been issued in Argentina. The only connection with the US was that the 'Bonods' provided for payment of interest and principal in US dollars on the London, Frankfurt, Zurich, or New York market, at the election of the creditor, and that, when Argentina unilaterally extended the time for payment and offered bondholders substitute instruments as a means of rescheduling the debts, the plaintiffs/respondents refused to accept the rescheduling and insisted on full payment, specifying New York as the place where payment should be made. It was this 'place of payment' that secured jurisdiction and denial of Argentina's immunity.[347] In other words, once the commerciality of a transaction can be established, what causes the immunity to be denied is the territorial link with the US. In the absence of such a link, it will not be possible to sue a foreign State for an act or transaction that took place entirely outside the US, however commercial the transaction may be. In actual practice, the determination of a direct effect 'generally admits of no easy, clear-cut answer' and is 'fraught with artifice'.[348]

4.3.3. 'An immediate consequence'

The central phrase 'direct effect' is not defined. Since the legislative report refers to section 18 of the Second Restatement of the Foreign Relations Law of the United States (1965),[349] many courts, looking to section 18 for guidance, concluded that a 'direct effect' must be 'substantial and foreseeable'.[350] However, in *Texas Trading*, the Second Circuit rejected the reference to section 18 of the Second Restatement as 'a bit of a *non sequitur*', because section 18 concerns the application of substantive US law to conduct abroad, not principles of extraterritorial jurisdiction. Thus, the court found that 'certain limitations built into the text of s. 18, such as the requirement that the "direct effect" be "substantial" or "foreseeable", are not necessarily apposite to the direct effect clause of s. 1605(a)(2)'.[351] The reasoning in *Texas Trading* obviously struck a chord with the Supreme Court, which, in *Weltover*, while accepting that 'jurisdiction may not be predicated on purely trivial effects in the United States', explicitly rejected the suggestion that section 1605(a)(2) contained 'any unexpressed requirement of "substantiality" or "foreseeability"' and held that an effect was 'direct' if it followed as 'an immediate consequence' of the defendant's activity.[352] Thus Argentina's unilateral rescheduling of the maturity dates on its government bonds had a 'direct effect' in the US because New York was 'the place of performance for Argentina's ultimate contractual obligations', even if 'the plaintiffs were all foreign corporations with no other connections to the United States'.[353]

In *Virtual Countries*, the court held that a press release issued by South Africa challenging the ownership of an Internet domain name (www. southafrica.com) by Virtual Countries, a US corporation, had no direct effect in the US. Virtual Countries argued that the press release had a devastating and direct effect on its business operations by, in particular, damaging its ability to raise capital. The court reasoned that the press release's effect fell 'at the end of a long chain of causation' and was 'mediated by numerous actions by third parties'. According to the court, such a 'tangled causal web does not provide the requisite immediacy to establish jurisdiction'; and a '"speculative" injury ... does not suffice to satisfy s. 1605(a)(2)'s third clause'.[354] Similarly, in *Lyon*, where survivors of the victims of an airplane crash brought an action against the designers of the aircraft, the court, while 'eschew[ing] both substantiality and foreseeability', opined that, 'where failure of a manufactured product is concerned, a more appropriate reading of the phrase ["immediate consequence"] should focus on whether some intervening act broke the chain of causation leading from the asserted wrongful act to its impact in the United States'.[355] So the claim was dismissed where it involved only 'speculative, generalized, immeasurable, and ultimately unverifiable effects in the United States',[356] or where the effect was 'dependent on an intervening factor'.[357] Moreover, such 'injuries' as expenditures for judicial proceedings, lost profits from future sales and harm to business reputation would be 'too indirect and speculative' to constitute 'immediate consequences'.[358] Most significantly for our purposes, the court in *Virtual Countries* found that the absence of a direct effect in the US was 'dispositive' of the claim in question.[359] Similarly, in *Security Pacific*, the Ninth Circuit declared that the 'dispositive question' was whether the effect was 'sufficiently direct and sufficiently in the United States'. Thus, even though one of the defendants, Banco BCH, a bank owned by the Government of Mexico, was engaged in commercial activity by allegedly accepting for deposit gold coins derived from proceeds of a stolen cheque, such deposit caused no injury in the US; rather, the injury to the plaintiff had actually been caused by the theft of the cheque:

The commercial activity of Banco BCH was subsequent to and relatively remote from the direct injury and as such is insufficient to bring Banco BCH before United States courts. Otherwise, all foreign sovereign banking institutions would be subject to United States jurisdiction if they merely accepted funds for deposit by account holders, when, unknown to the bank, those funds were obtained wrongfully or illegally in the United States.[360]

There is still controversy as to whether financial loss suffered in the US by a US national can be regarded as a direct effect for the purposes of section 1605(a)(2). Some courts have held that mere financial loss cannot be a direct effect.[361] In *Virtual Countries*, when the plaintiff contended that a substantial financial loss on the part of a US corporation should be regarded as occurring within the US, the court held that the plaintiff's expansive theory, that any US corporation's financial loss constituted a direct effect in the US, was 'plainly flawed', because the endorsement of that view would 'render superfluous the analysis', generally followed by US courts, 'of the locus of contractual obligation when deciding whether a direct effect occurred in the United States'.[362] By the same token, financial loss sustained outside the US is even less of a direct effect.[363] Conversely, so it seems, *financial gain* cannot be a direct effect either. In a case where citizens of Myanmar sued the Myanmar Government and Unocal, a US corporation, for alleged torture, murder and forced labour in Myanmar, they could not rely on the defendant corporation's profits in the US as a 'direct effect'.[364] Future financial gain (and potential taxes to the US Government) cannot be an 'immediate consequence' of a failed bid in a foreign country.[365] On the other hand, the opposite view has been taken that financial loss can indeed be regarded as a direct effect, provided that it is an immediate and direct consequence of the defendant's activity.[366] This is held to be especially the case with corporate entities, which 'can only suffer financial loss'.[367] Thus, 'wrongfully obtaining and utilizing plaintiff's trade secrets', which would inevitably cause financial loss for a corporation domiciled in the US, is conduct that has a direct effect upon the plaintiff.[368] And the same applied where the termination of a contract thwarted the performance of further contracts, resulting in tremendous losses.[369]

A 'ripple-effect' is not a direct effect; that is, the plaintiff cannot sue on the basis of a mere *continuation* of harms suffered in a foreign country before returning to the US, regardless of how quickly he returned.[370] Injuries suffered outside the US and/or the lingering effects thereof,[371] effects of death in a foreign country on the surviving relatives,[372] emotional distress[373] or injury to feelings suffered in the US because of a wrongful act in a foreign country[374] falls squarely within this category and therefore cannot be a 'direct effect'.

The attempts to retain a US corporation and its affiliates to arrange a $40 million loan by selling debt securities in US capital markets to American institutional investors was held to be a commercial activity having direct effects in the US.[375] The provision of extraterritorial automobile liability and family security insurance coverage while travelling in the US was also held to be a direct effect in the US.[376]

Thus it seems that a decision on 'direct effect' really depends on a careful analysis of the facts in a case rather than on any a priori principle. In practice, courts have developed certain tests but again these tests are no more than rules of thumb.

4.3.4. The 'place of performance' test

Exactly what a 'direct effect' should be seems more often to turn on the cause of action or the subject matter of the claim. If it is a claim of breach of contract, for example, the 'direct effect' should be 'nontrivial' and must follow as an immediate consequence of the defendant's activity; that is, there would be no 'direct effect' if 'there was no contractual obligation in the United States, the breach of which had an effect here'.[377] In such a case the court will look for 'a clause in a contract mandating the fulfillment of contractual obligations *in the United States*'.[378] It now seems to be established law that the place of performance of the contract is a decisive factor.[379] Where there is no contract,[380] or where no part of the contract is to be performed in the US,[381] there is no direct effect.

Thus the Supreme Court had 'little difficulty concluding that Argentina's unilateral rescheduling of the maturity dates on the [government bonds] had a "direct effect" in the United States', because the defendants/respondents 'had designated their accounts in New York as the place of payment'.[382] In many cases, an obligation upon the defendant to make a payment to a bank account in the US has been held sufficient to satisfy the 'direct effect' clause, even if this account might not be directly held by the plaintiff.[383] Even if the original agreement did not specify the US as the place of payment, so long as it allowed the plaintiff to designate a place and a US location was designated,[384] or if such a possibility can be reasonably inferred from the contract,[385] the requirement of direct effect would be satisfied. Pre-default payments are not necessary for the requirement of a direct effect based on a default to pay; that is, whether, in the days leading up to a default, payments were or were not made in a certain location is not a significant factor. It is sufficient if the default itself necessarily results in the non-appearance of monies intended for deposit at a location in the US.[386] Sometimes it seems that, if the place of payment is the US, the court would decline to take any other factors into consideration. Thus, in *Barkanic*, the court found that the Chinese General Administration of Civil Aviation (CAAC), an agent of China providing domestic and international air services to passengers travelling in, to, and from China, was liable for the deaths of two US businessmen who had died in a plane crash during an internal flight within China, because CAAC had accepted payment for the transportation in the US.[387] The place of performance is not necessarily limited to the performance by the defendant. In *Braspetro*, for example, immunity was denied because the plaintiffs, rather than the defendant, had to make payment in the US.[388]

Naturally, on the other hand, where the US was not designated as the place of performance, the claim would fail.[389] In this respect, the designation of payment in US currency does not satisfy the direct effect requirement.[390]

4.3.5. The 'legally significant act' test

A number of courts have been looking for the so-called 'legally significant act(s)' when deciding on the issue of direct effect. However, this
seems to be a treacherous test; for it has never been made clear whether
the 'legally significant act' ought to be the act causing the direct effect
(in which case it should have taken place *outside* the US), or the direct
effect itself (in which case it should have taken place *within* the US).[391]
Besides, there are some courts that refuse point blank to adopt it.[392]

Conclusion

The discussion of commercial activity addresses both a specific exception to immunity and the general criteria for determining non-immune
acts (*acta jure gestionis*). The term 'commercial activity' may mean two
things in practice: first, it refers to a commercial activity in the proper
sense of the term; and, secondly, it may be used as a shorthand term for
any activity for which a foreign State does not enjoy immunity; that is, it
may refer to an activity that is not necessarily 'commercial' *stricto sensu*
but may nonetheless be a private law activity not protected by immunity, in which case it is synonymous with such terms as 'non-sovereign
activity', 'non-governmental activity', or '*actum jure gestionis*'. While it is
commonly agreed that a contract for the sale/supply of goods or services,
and a contract for a loan or other transaction for the provision of
finance, including any obligation of guarantee or indemnity in respect
of such loan or transaction, are the two most obvious examples of
commercial activity, State practice remains unsettled as to what constitutes a commercial activity.

The central issue in deciding whether a particular act is a commercial
activity or *actum jure gestionis* is whether the character or nature of that
act should be decisive in determining that it is a commercial activity, or
whether the purpose of the act should also be taken into consideration.
If nature alone is to be considered, then if an act can also be engaged in
by a private individual, it must be a commercial act, whatever the
motive of the State in entering into the act, and whatever purpose or
objective that that act may serve. On the other hand, if the purpose of
the act should also be considered, this means that a particular act, even
though it can also be performed by a private individual, can still be
regarded as a sovereign or public act if it serves a sovereign or public
purpose. In other words, if some act is by its nature a commercial

activity, should that act be straightforwardly held to be a commercial activity, or should it matter if that act was done for some public objective? For example, private parties regularly buy and sell grains; so if a State buys grains on the international market, this must be a commercial activity. But what if the State bought the grains not for resale to make a profit, but to relieve an ongoing famine in the country? If this public purpose can be taken into account, then the act of buying grains assumes a distinctly sovereign or public character. But then it can be countered that every act of a State must serve some public purpose and, as a consequence, all the acts of a State must be immune. This is still a hotly debated issue in current law and three major positions have emerged: (1) that the court should only consider the nature of the activity; (2) that the court should consider the whole context of the activity (including the purpose of the act); and (3) that in some cases the purpose may be decisive. While the 'nature-only' position seems ostensibly to enjoy a greater prominence, it is not possible under current circumstances to adopt any simplistic solution, given the complicated situations the courts have to deal with.

Perhaps the most important requirement and the most fundamental rule in a case against a foreign State is that the act or legal relationship in question must have some connection with the territory of the forum State. Though sometimes elided or unstated, a territorial connection gives the court a firm ground for asserting jurisdiction. For this reason, territorial connection has played a significant role during the transition from absolute to restrictive immunity and has always underlain the decisions asserting jurisdiction over foreign States. This requirement has been codified in a number of legal instruments, chief among which is the US FSIA, and has been repeatedly confirmed in case law, especially in the Swiss practice. For a US court to deny immunity to a foreign State, the commercial activity must have occurred in the US, or be closely connected with US territory. For the Swiss courts, it is not enough that a foreign State has engaged in a commercial activity; there must at the same time be a connection between such activity and the Swiss territory. This is often referred to as *Binnenbeziehung*, a 'domestic connection'.

Much still remains uncertain and chaotic about the crucial concept of commercial activity. Judicial practice in this area consists mainly of an intuitive appreciation of the factual situations. Basically, an activity is a commercial activity because the judge thinks that it is a commercial activity. It is not possible to deduce uniform criteria from the divergent court findings due to complicated real-life cases; and it may be asked whether any universal, a priori definition can be practicable or even doctrinally tenable. The age-old debate on the nature/purpose dichotomy seems to be highly academic since in actuality courts usually consider all the relevant factors (the 'purpose' of the particular act included) in order to reach a sensible conclusion. More importantly, the issue of immunity is not determined by the subject matter alone. It is not enough to say that a State is immune for sovereign acts but not for commercial activities. The complete statement should be that a State is not immune for commercial activities carried out in the State of the forum or having a connection therewith. In other words, the restrictive immunity doctrine is actually based on two premises: first, that the activity in question is of a commercial or private law character, and, secondly, that this activity has a connection with the territory of the State of the forum. The territorial element is so often taken for granted that it is generally omitted in the statements of the restrictive doctrine. It must always be remembered, however, that it is this territoriality that truly confers the jurisdiction on the court. Immunity from jurisdiction becomes meaningful only when jurisdiction itself is beyond doubt.

4 Contracts of employment

Contracts of employment constitute the most complicated area in the field of State immunity, not only because they involve a myriad of procedural problems, but also because, in many cases, various substantive rules of labour law will come into play. Typically, the question of State immunity with regard to contracts of employment covers the situation where an individual as employee sues a foreign State that has employed the individual to exercise certain functions or to conduct certain activities within the territory or jurisdiction of the State of the forum. Thus a tort claim for vicarious liability of the State for acts of its employees is excluded from the purview of this discussion, though the claim may also be based on a contract of employment. However, in some cases a third party may indeed come onto the scene. A trade union would institute proceedings regarding representation in collective bargaining or other industry- or company-related matters; and a dependant of the employee may also bring an action for benefits due under the contract of employment. All the cases in this connection concern contracts of employment within the territory of the forum State.

We shall see that immunity with regard to employment contracts is one based chiefly on status; that is, because of the privileged status of the defendant State, jurisdiction cannot be exercised. This runs counter to the elementary rule developed in the context of commercial transactions whereby it is the *nature of the act*, rather than the *status of the actor*, that is decisive. The mere fact that a State performed an act cannot automatically immunize that act; for if that is the case, then all acts of a State should be immune. Such an absolutist attitude towards immunity has long been abandoned in favour of a more restrictive construction of a State's activities: some acts are done *jure imperii* while others are done *jure gestionis*. *Acta jure imperii* enjoy immunity, while *acta jure gestionis* do not. Then how can these two types of act be distinguished? The answer is, as we have seen, by using the litmus test of a 'private person': if something can also be done by a private person (with or without economic or financial gain in view), then it is a commercial or private act unprotected by immunity. But then this will mean that all and every employment contract entered into by a State with a private individual in the territory of another State, including the local employment of, say, a consular officer, is a private and non-immune act, because it is not the *employment of a consular officer*, but *employment, tout court*, that matters, and any private person can *employ* another private person. The courts will either have to deny immunity altogether, which will have disastrous consequences for the forum State itself, given that such denial will surely be reciprocated by foreign national courts; or they will somehow have to find a way to exclude certain types of employment relationship from their jurisdiction. Because private persons regularly hire other private persons, there can be nothing particularly elevated about employment by a State: the *nature* of an employment relationship is that a private person can also create it. What is the difference between being employed as an accountant by an embassy and being employed as an accountant by a supermarket? Can there be a difference between chauffeuring an ambassador and chauffeuring a film star? By *nature* such accountancy and chauffeuring cannot possibly be different; it is only *for whom* you are working that distinguishes them. In other words, the *purpose* of the employment relationship has all of a sudden become crucial. Not surprisingly, we shall find two different answers in actual practice. Some courts think that embassy drivers are no different from other drivers, while others may hold that an embassy driver has an important position which precludes him from suing the embassy. The court wishing to retain immunity for certain State employment relationships cannot but construe such relationships as necessary for the State as a political entity; that is, serving a higher, sovereign or governmental *purpose*. Thus, in the context of employment contracts one observes the exact reverse of the general trend of the development of State immunity law. While the general law of State immunity has rejected the absolutist view of treating the mere status of being a State as dispositive of the issue of immunity and has instead focused on the nature of the conduct in question, the practice surrounding contracts of employment has reverted to the proposition that an act should be immune simply because it serves the State or the public aims of a State. In brief, while the general law of State immunity has completed the transition from status to conduct, the particular law on contracts of employment is returning from conduct to status; while the general law has relied on the 'nature', the particular law has resorted to the 'purpose', of an act.

It must also be pointed out that a decision against immunity from jurisdiction is quite distinct from an eventual judgment in favour of the individual plaintiff. Since the question of immunity is only a preliminary matter of procedure, the loss of immunity only makes possible, but does not prejudge, a consideration of the merits. Therefore, it is not rare to find cases where, after assuming jurisdiction over the foreign State, the court decided that the plaintiff failed on the merits of the case.[1] Thus, for example, it is perfectly conceivable that a court, upon holding that it has jurisdiction over a case of unfair dismissal, decides that the dismissal is nonetheless fair.[2] Moreover, even though a plaintiff may successfully obtain a judgment against a foreign State, there is still the possibility that he or she may not be able to execute the judgment owing to the operation of immunity from execution,[3] which is a further separate issue under current international law.

1. Terminology

The phrase 'contract of employment' used in this chapter is only a term of convenience. In the first place, such a contract can take many forms: it can be either express or implied and, when express, either written or oral.[4] Occasionally, the court has to assume the existence of a contract in a de facto employment relationship in which no such contract has been concluded or the contract of employment is concluded only after the employee has worked for the employer for a considerable period of time.[5] In this latter situation the contract has to be construed as applicable retrospectively to cover the period before the conclusion of the contract. Strictly speaking, for such a special period, the term 'contract of employment' is no more than a judicial construct. Secondly, in many countries, the term 'employment' itself remains a matter of great controversy and in need of more precise legislative and judicial definition.

No guidance on the definition of a 'contract of employment' can be derived from the relevant practice on State immunity. The US and Canadian statutes on State immunity do not even contain a separate provision on contracts of employment. The same is true of the practice of those States that do not have a specific statute on State immunity. Even in those statutes that do contain provisions on contracts of employment, these likewise offer no definition of the term but instead merely enumerate various connecting factors between such a contract and the forum State for the purposes of establishing jurisdiction.

Thus the current law of State immunity leaves the meaning of 'contract of employment' to common understanding. This means that various difficulties surrounding the definition of contract of employment, which bedevil labour law in many countries, have potentially been introduced lock, stock and barrel into the law of State immunity. This can sometimes cause complicated problems. In the UK, for example, whether or not there exists a contract of employment in a particular case often does not have a straightforward answer.[6] Section 230(2) of the Employment Rights Act 1996 (ERA) defines 'contract of employment' as 'contract of service',[7] which amounts to no definition at all, since 'contract of service' has been the traditional term for contract of employment. By defining 'contract of employment' as 'contract of service' the ERA simply leaves the matter to the common law, which is notoriously convoluted and confusing as far as a contract of employment is concerned, not to mention the fact that the common law definition of 'contract of service' evolved before the advent of modern employment law and in contexts other than that of the employment relationship as properly understood now.[8] This means that the criteria used in the past differ from those used in modern employment law and that, accordingly, a 'contract of service' in the past may not be seen as a 'contract of employment' now, and vice versa.

In the UK, there has been a long-standing (and often confusing to the layman) distinction between a contract *of service* (i.e. a contract of employment) and a contract *for services*; and the workers who work under these two types of contract are referred to as *employees* and *self-employed* or *independent contractors*, respectively.[9] This distinction between an employee and an independent contractor is essential to the UK labour law and, in this sense, to our present discussion. For one thing, certain labour rights are reserved exclusively to employees.[10] Such rights, such as the right not to be unfairly dismissed (section 94(1) of the ERA), often form the subject matter of labour disputes between the individual employee and the foreign employer State. However, in practice, the boundary line between an employee and an independent contractor might be blurred, since current UK labour law, for various purposes, often extends the definition of 'employee' to cover other types of workers.[11] What is more, such a distinction, where it exists in other jurisdictions, might be different from the UK one.[12]

For the purposes of ascertaining whether there is a contract of employment the UK courts and tribunals have developed a so-called 'multiple-factor test', which requires a consideration of all the circumstances of a case, including such factors as control, remuneration, personal service, tools and equipment, delegation of authority, investment and management, and risk and profit,[13] none of which is decisive.

Moreover, how the parties may view their contract is irrelevant: even if the parties themselves call it a contract of employment, it may not be one in the opinion of the judge;[14] on the other hand, even if both parties think that the contract is not a contract of employment, it may still be regarded as one by the court.[15] The difficulties become especially exacerbated for 'agency workers', i.e. workers who render services through employment agencies. Such workers, owing to the complicated triangular relationship (worker – agency – 'end-user' of services), are dubbed as 'in limbo'[16] and are often regarded as not having a contract of *employment*.[17]

For the courts of some countries permanency might not be a decisive factor in defining the term 'employment', since they would classify the engagement of workers for a single short-term task as a relationship of employment.[18] By the same token, while in the courts of some States the nationality of the employing State is certainly a jurisdictional bar, in others an individual is allowed to sue his or her national State.

Such intricacies, however, do not directly impinge on the issue of State immunity, which does not arise until there is held to be a contract of employment. They nonetheless have to be noted because they form part of the complexity of the question of employment contracts in general. In sum, the term 'contracts of employment' in the present discussion should be broadly understood as including all aspects of an employment relationship, including the terms and conditions of the contract as well as any rights or duties imposed by law on an employer or employee in respect of the employment relationship. In other words, this term can only serve as a signpost for the various legal and factual factors that will be the subject of the present study.

2. The peculiar features of employment cases

2.1. *Specialized tribunals*

Whereas other aspects of State immunity are normally dealt with by ordinary courts, the handling of employment disputes is characterized by the variety of forums. While ordinary courts and judges play a significant role in settling labour disputes,[19] in many countries employment cases are heard, especially at first instance, by specialized labour/employment tribunals – although further appeals normally lie before the ordinary chain of appellate courts dealing with civil matters.[20] The composition of such tribunals varies from country to country but they are all organized in such a way as to ensure that the interests of both the employer and the employee are reflected by their membership. What is more important, legal qualifications play at most only a secondary role, or no role at all.[21] This makes an employment or labour tribunal a unique creature. Quasi- or semi-judicial in nature, they are concerned more with fact-finding, balancing of interests and mediation, and their procedures are more informal and flexible though in many respects analogous to those followed by ordinary courts. In an indirect way, this compounds the issue of State immunity in that political issues tend to be brought into the consideration of immunity, especially given the fact that employment disputes often involve complicated substantive issues, many of which have serious social implications, such as equality of pay, discrimination, recognition of trade unions and collective bargaining.

Cases concerning employment relationships are particularly complicated and often involve elaborate enquiries into every circumstance of the case and a delicate balance of various interests.[22] This is an area of law that cannot be compartmentalized comfortably into any traditional notion of legal discipline and which is best described in terms normally associated with institutions of fact-finding and conciliation. Experience, sophistication in human affairs, and intuitive understanding are more important than legal training. The three-part structure of the British employment tribunals (a chairman with legal background and two 'lay members' representing the employer and the employee respectively) bears vivid testimony to this peculiar feature of employment law. By virtue of a procedure based on majority vote, the two lay members may outvote the legally qualified chairman.

2.2. The inadequacy of the nature/private person test

The issue of employment contracts, for which the courts have had to resort to a multiple-factor test, presents by far the most serious challenge to the 'private-law activity carried out as a private person' theory. It will be recalled that, in the context of commercial transactions, the dominant opinion is that it is the nature, not the purpose, of a particular act that is decisive of whether that act is *jure imperii* or *jure gestionis*. When one transposes this rule to contracts of employment, however, one immediately enters into treacherous terrain. If only the *nature*, rather than the *purpose*, of the employment relationship can serve as the criterion for immunity, then, given the fact that a private individual or entity can and does regularly act as the employer, there will be nothing inherently sovereign about an employment relationship. This means that the 'private person' test is ultimately unworkable so far as contracts of employment are concerned; for either all employment relationships, in that they can be engaged in by private persons, should be private and therefore non-immune, or, as it actually happens, courts and tribunals would have to give a *purposive* interpretation to the employment relationship. One cannot express this difficult situation better than did Browne-Wilkinson J (as he then was) in *Sengupta*, in which immunity was granted with regard to a claim for unfair dismissal brought by a low-grade clerk at the Indian High Commission in London, who was not a member of the Indian diplomatic or civil service:

It is true that any private individual can employ another, i.e. can enter into a contract of employment. Therefore in that sense the entry into a contract of employment is a private act. But when one looks to see what is involved in the performance of the applicant's contract, it is clear that the performance of the contract is part of the discharge by the foreign state of its sovereign functions in which the applicant himself, at however lowly a level, is under the terms of his contract of employment necessarily engaged ... A contract to work at a diplomatic mission in the work of that mission is a contract to participate in the public acts of the foreign sovereign. The dismissal of the applicant was an act done in pursuance of that public function, i.e. the running of the mission. As a consequence, the fairness of any dismissal from such employment is very likely to involve an investigation by the industrial tribunal into the internal management of the diplomatic representation in the United Kingdom ... an investigation wholly inconsistent with the dignity of the foreign state and an interference with its sovereign functions.[23]

Obviously, Browne-Wilkinson J regarded the 'private person' test as far from sufficient, for he proposed four questions to be considered:

(a) Was the contract of a kind which a private individual could enter into? (b) Did the performance of the contract involve the participation of both parties in the public functions of the foreign state, or was it purely collateral to such functions? (c) What was the nature of the breach of contract or other act of the sovereign state giving rise to the proceedings? (d) Will the investigation of the claim by the tribunal involve an investigation into the public or sovereign acts of the foreign state?[24]

The 'private person' test features only as one of the four questions to be asked. Briefly put, in order to preserve immunity at least for some employment relationships, courts and tribunals are compelled to hold that the relationship in question should be immune *because it serves a sovereign purpose*. This is the essence of the whole current legal regime regarding contracts of employment.

Earlier, an Italian court made the same remark when a medical doctor employed by the Sovereign Order of Malta sued his employer for breach of contract. Upon ascertaining that the medical services performed by the plaintiff under his contract of employment were connected with the activities performed by the Order in accordance with the objects for which it had been established, including the care of the sick, the court granted immunity, saying:

> It is true that work in the fields of health and care need not, as such, be of a public nature since that work *can be performed by private individuals*. However, this is irrelevant in the present case because it is quite clear that the public character of such work always predominates where the work ... is performed ... by a sovereign entity ... whose essential characteristic is the performance of precisely this activity ... Thus there can be no doubt that everything concerning the organization of these activities, including the employment of medical personnel, must form part of the public function of the sovereign entity, because it is to serve its *public purposes*. By reason of its direct connection with these *purposes*, therefore, the contract of employment ... falls within the framework of the activities of the organization and enables it to carry out its *public objects* ... the courts cannot interfere in relations which ... are regarded by the Order of Malta as being within its own sovereign sphere because they directly *serve its constitutional objects*.[25]

This reasoning was endorsed by the Italian Court of Cassation in *Piccoli*, where an administrative secretary at a hospital operated by the Order of Malta in Salerno, Italy, sued the Order for failure to pay a fair salary. In granting immunity, the Court declared:

> Therefore even if, as often happens, the right is of a private nature, the said activity may well be public if, as in this instance, it fulfils an institutional aim of the international public subject ... In the case under consideration ... there has instead been a private law transaction ... and through which the appellant Association has solely procured the necessary means to exercise its institutional functions.[26]

In other words, a public purpose can turn an otherwise private law transaction into a sovereign activity covered by immunity.

In *Canada Labour Code*, a Canadian judge, while finding that the provisions of the Canadian SIA 'do not countenance the purpose or object of

140   CONTRACTS OF EMPLOYMENT

the state's activity but rather compel us to focus on the nature of the alleged commercial activity in issue',[27] put forward much the same view regarding the 'nature/private person' test:

> I would not put so great an emphasis on the question whether the contract of employment could have been entered into by a private party ... To give an example, it may well be that the function of a computer programmer in a foreign state's military base could well be carried out by a private party, but if the work of the programmer were in relation to highly confidential and sensitive information gathering and analysis, I doubt whether such duties would constitute commercial activity ... so as to repel state immunity.[28]

This echoes an observation made by Ritchie J, for the majority of the Canadian Supreme Court, in *Venne*, where an architect engaged by the Congo to prepare plans for the construction of the national pavilion of the Congo at an international exhibition in Canada (Expo '67) claimed fees for the services he had rendered:

> Considered from the point of view of the architect, it may well be that the contract was a purely commercial one, but, even if the theory of restrictive sovereign immunity were applicable, the question to be determined would not be whether the contractor was engaged in a private act of commerce, but whether or not the Government of the Congo, acting as a visiting sovereign State through its duly accredited diplomatic representatives, was engaged in the performance of a public sovereign act of State.[29]

This prompted the remark that 'acts that some persons might normally consider to be commercial are not so when they are done in the performance of a sovereign act of State'.[30]

According to the German courts, if the employment relationship happens to be connected with the 'core sphere of sovereign activity', such as consular functions, then such employment relationship would be tinted and imbued with sovereignty, even if that relationship would normally be regarded as of a private law nature:

> If the content of the employment relationship was the direct fulfilment of tasks which fall within the sphere of State authority ... questions in dispute which are connected with the establishment and termination of the employment relationship must be excluded from German jurisdiction, because the connection with the fulfilment of sovereign tasks of the foreign State outweighs the ... private law character of the establishment and termination of an employment relationship.
>
> ... it may be necessary under public international law to classify the activity of a foreign State as an act performed *jure imperii* because it is to be attributed to the

core sphere of State authority, although under national law it would be viewed as private law activity and not public law activity.

It is unimportant whether the legal relationship in dispute was established by a private law declaration of intent, as would automatically be the case where an employment relationship under German law was concerned, or by an act of sovereignty ... A legal relationship which imposes an obligation to perform tasks which are to be attributed to the activity of the foreign power, police power or the administration of justice normally cannot be the subject-matter of a dispute ... before German courts, without breaching the immunity of the foreign State concerned, irrespective of how the relationship was formed.[31]

Thus, activities regarded as falling within the private-law sphere under national law must be viewed as sovereign if they are attributable to the core area of State authority ... It is beyond doubt that the formation, alteration and termination of an employment relationship take place in private-law form under national law. It is likewise beyond doubt that this fact alone is not decisive ... If the core area of State authority is affected, the private-law character of the relationship takes on secondary importance.[32]

According to the Italian Court of Cassation:

[The] principle [of equality], which requires similar treatment of similar situations, is not applicable here since the functions, guarantees and rights/duties of an employee are different depending on whether he is employed by a consulate or a company of the same foreign State.[33]

These clear and unequivocal statements indicate that, though the courts concede that an employment relationship is of a private law *nature*, in that such a relationship is what private persons regularly engage in, there is more to such a relationship than a mere private law nature. If the employment relationship serves a sovereign purpose or is connected with the exercise of sovereign functions, then the court must hold it immune. Simply put, in the context of contracts of employment, the *purpose* test assumes the predominant position.

The fact that the employment relationship often cannot be straightforwardly characterized as a downright commercial/private activity is indicative of both the complex nature of such a relationship and the courts'/tribunals' difficulty in attaching an exact label to it. The result is a diversity of methods adopted by different courts and tribunals in trying to fit the employment relationship into the overall framework of the public/private dichotomy. That courts and tribunals have had to resort to such complicated mechanisms bears resounding testimony to the inadequacy of the nature/private person test.

142   CONTRACTS OF EMPLOYMENT

Contracts of employment thus present a curious phenomenon. For one thing, they demonstrate the makeshift and limited nature of the rules developed in the course of the evolution of the doctrine and practice of State immunity. The inadequacy of the commonly accepted formula of a State 'acting as a private individual' becomes manifest, because any private business can hire someone to do something. The 'nature' test, therefore, proves unworkable, since there is nothing inherently different between employment by a foreign State and that by a private business. The only way a court can uphold immunity for a foreign State is by applying some sort of a purposive test, i.e. by construing the employment relationship as closely connected with the exercise of sovereign power. It is only by reading something extraneous into the employment relationship, thereby elevating it above the common run of everyday commercial business, that a court can, if it so wishes, preserve immunity for a foreign State. A court has frequently to ascertain whether the employer is a foreign State itself, or whether the act of employment can in any case be attributed to it. In contrast to the cases concerning commercial activities, where the nature of the *act* itself determines the issue of immunity, in cases involving contracts of employment, the identity and status of the *actor* become decisive.

Apart from the difficulty associated with such identification, the court has to consider all the surrounding circumstances, including, almost invariably, connecting factors in private international law. Besides, distinguishing between immune and non-immune contracts is closely connected with, and in most cases entails resort to, the criteria for distinguishing between commercial and non-commercial activities. It would be quite mistaken to assume that every contract of employment is a private law relationship that could therefore be subjected to local jurisdiction. The frequent references to substantive rules of labour law only add to the complexity.

It is precisely because the employer is a foreign State that such a contract of employment cannot be entirely assimilated to one between private parties. In some cases the foreign State might employ an individual to carry out purely commercial activities, in others purely sovereign functions and in still others activities which might not be so clear-cut, thereby necessitating an examination of all the relevant circumstances by the court. Even though the employment itself and all related acts – recruitment, supervision, disciplinary measures, remuneration and other benefits, dismissal[34] and so on – are no different from those performed by private individuals and companies, the purpose of the employment and the functions exercised by the employee might be so closely connected with the organization and administration of the foreign State that it is impossible for a local court to investigate the employment relationship without infringing upon the sovereignty and independence of the foreign State concerned. Therefore, in cases concerning contracts of employment:

In order to classify a particular act, the court may also have regard to criteria which are external to the act in question. In each case, the court should also weigh up the interest of the foreign State in enjoying immunity with the interest of the State of the forum in exercising its jurisdictional sovereignty and the interest of the plaintiff in obtaining the judicial protection of his rights.[35]

3. Two models

There are two distinct models in current State practice concerning contracts of employment in the context of State immunity: one regards the contract of employment as a separate exception to State immunity; the other considers the contract of employment as a category of commercial activity. The first model is adopted by the European Convention, the UK SIA, the Australia FISA, the Argentina Law of 1995, the Israeli Law of 2008, and drafts prepared by IDI, ILA, ILC and the UN Convention; the second model by the US FSIA, the Canadian SIA and those States that do not have immunity legislation. For convenience, these two models are referred to as the UK Model and the US Model, respectively.

By treating contracts of employment as a separate exception to immunity, the UK Model has the advantage of freeing the court from the problem of having to decide whether a contract of employment belongs to the realm of commercial activities for which immunity will not be available for the foreign State, since the contract of employment is, by virtue of statutory provision, explicitly not immune from local jurisdiction. The foreign State will thus automatically be denied immunity unless certain exceptions can be established. The difficulty with this approach is that, apart from the intricate circumstances surrounding the existence and operation of a contract of employment, which, as has been shown above, often make it difficult for the court to decide whether there is indeed a contract of employment in its proper sense, a number of other statutory qualifications, in particular connecting factors, have to be satisfied before the court is really in a position to exercise its jurisdiction.

144 CONTRACTS OF EMPLOYMENT

The US Model views the contract of employment not as a separate exception to State immunity but as one of many categories of commercial activity. Here the emphasis is placed on the contract. What matters is not that the foreign State has entered into an *employment* contract, but that the foreign State has entered into a *contract* with a private individual. In fact any dealing between a foreign State and a private individual on the basis of private law will be prima facie evidence that the State has acted not as a subject of international law but on the same footing as a private person, and this is what precludes it from claiming immunity from local jurisdiction. This approach sidesteps the difficulties associated with the identification of a proper employment relationship, since the court has to care less about the content of the contract than about the manner in which the contract was concluded, i.e. whether under international or municipal law. Its difficulty, however, lies in that the court is faced with all the problems involved in distinguishing between commercial activities, for which the foreign State enjoys no immunity, and non-commercial activities, for which immunity will be granted, while the criteria for such a distinction are well known for their complexity and elusiveness. Obviously the two models can be seen as two sides of the same coin: one's advantage is precisely the other's disadvantage and vice versa.

4. The UK Model

4.1. *The European Convention*

Article 5 of the 1972 European Convention provides:

1. A Contracting State cannot claim immunity from the jurisdiction of a court of another Contracting State if the proceedings relate to a contract of employment between the State and an individual where the work has to be performed on the territory of the State of the forum.
2. Paragraph 1 shall not apply where:
    (a) the individual is a national of the employing State at the time when the proceedings are brought;
    (b) at the time when the contract was entered into the individual was neither a national of the State of the forum nor habitually resident in that State; or
    (c) the parties to the contract have otherwise agreed in writing, unless, in accordance with the law of the State of the forum, the courts of that State have exclusive jurisdiction by reason of the subject-matter.

3. Where the work is done for an office, agency or other establishment referred to in Article 7, paragraphs 2.a and b of the present article apply only if, at the time the contract was entered into, the individual had his habitual residence in the Contracting State which employs him.

Under Article 7(1), such an 'office, agency or other establishment' means one which a foreign State maintains 'on the territory of the State of the forum ... through which it engages, in the same manner as a private person, in an industrial, commercial or financial activity'.

4.1.1. The plaintiff

Article 5(2) provides that Article 5(1) shall not apply (i.e. the defendant State shall enjoy immunity) where (a) 'the individual is a national of the employing State at the time when the proceedings are brought' or (b) 'at the time when the contract was entered into the individual was neither a national of the State of the forum nor habitually resident in that State'. Two inferences can be drawn here: first, that Article 5(2)(a) would also preclude an individual with dual or multiple nationality from suing the employer State, if one of his nationalities is that of the employer State; secondly, that under Article 5(2)(b), if the individual was *either* a national *or* a habitual resident of the forum State at the time when the contract was entered into, he[36] would be able to sue the employer State, so long as he does not have the nationality of the employer State at the time when the proceedings are brought. Thus the following types of individual can bring an action: (1) a national of the forum State at all relevant times, regardless of his habitual residence;[37] (2) an individual having the nationality of both the forum State and the employer State at the time when the contract was entered into but relinquishing the nationality of the employer State before bringing the claim; (3) a national of the employer State but habitually resident in the forum State at the time when the contract was entered into and later relinquishing the nationality of the employer State before bringing the claim; (4) an individual having the nationality of both the forum State and a third State at the time when the contract was entered into, wherever his habitual residence; and (5) a national of a third State but habitually resident in the forum State at the time when the contract was entered into.

The common thread that runs through all these categories is a connection with the forum State, whether in the form of nationality or habitual residence. This should not be surprising given the long-standing bases for jurisdiction in general international law, i.e. territoriality and nationality.

146   CONTRACTS OF EMPLOYMENT

Article 5(3), read with Article 7(1), provides that, '[w]here the work is done for an office, agency or other establishment' on the territory of the State of the forum, through which the employer State 'engages, in the same manner as a private person, in an industrial, commercial or financial activity', Article 5(2)(a) and (b) 'apply only if, at the time the contract was entered into, the individual had his habitual residence in the Contracting State which employs him'. Thus, where the work is done for a commercial establishment of a foreign State, provided he *did not* have his habitual residence in the employer State at the time the contract was entered into, *any individual* can sue the employer State, *whatever his nationality or wherever his habitual residence.*

Thus under Article 5 of the European Convention it is possible for nationals of either the forum, the employer, or the third State to sue the employer State, provided certain conditions are met. This conclusion is contrary to that of some scholars, who think that Article 5 discriminates against third State nationals by denying them the right to initiate lawsuits.[38] The language of Article 5 seems only to bar an individual without any connection whatsoever with the forum State from bringing proceedings but not an individual who has a connection with both the third and the forum State; for what is decisive is a link with the forum State, not the link with a third State.

Regrettably, the explanatory report on the European Convention is confusing on this point. Commenting on Article 5(2)(b), it states that immunity should be available to the employer State 'when the employee is a national neither of the State for whom he works, nor of the State where he works, and where the contract of employment was not concluded on the territory of the latter State – namely where the employee is a foreign worker who has not been locally recruited'.[39] Such a comment totally ignores the possibility that a person's State of nationality and State of habitual residence may be different and that the place of conclusion of a contract and the place of performance may not be the same. Thus, it is quite conceivable for, say, a national of State A, with habitual residence in State B, to enter into a contract, in State C, with the government of State D, to work in a State D government agency in State B. By the terms of Article 5, he can sue State D for employment disputes in the courts of State B; but, (wrongly) according to the explanatory report, he cannot.

Additionally, Article 5 does not seem to prevent dependants of the employer, a trade union or other third parties to the contract of employment from instituting proceedings, provided the proceedings are related to the contract.

4.1.2. The place of performance

Typically, as is the case with all national statutes in the UK Model, Article 5 does not offer a further definition of the contract of employment but instead lays down a number of qualifying circumstances and connecting factors for a contract of employment to be subjected to local jurisdiction. Apart from the status of the employee as discussed above, a contract of employment has also to be one 'where the work has to be performed on the territory of the State of the forum' (Article 5(1)). In this way the place of performance serves as a connecting factor common in private international law for activating local jurisdiction. However, it is not clear whether Article 5(1) is limited to the situation where the work is to be performed *wholly* on the territory of the forum State or it is also intended to cover one where the contract is to be performed only *partly* on that territory. The language itself may be open to both interpretations while the explanatory report is silent on this point.[40]

Moreover, Article 5 does not specify the place where the contract of employment was concluded. As a consequence, it is uncertain whether relevant provisions would be applicable only to locally recruited employees or also to an employee who entered into a contract of employment in a place other than the forum State and was then dispatched to work in that State. The absence of a specific provision would ordinarily render all sorts of contract coverable, wherever concluded, but controversy might nonetheless arise where the place of recruitment operates as a decisive factor in identifying the governing law of the contract, as is increasingly the case in international labour law, especially within the framework of the EU law.

Both points are clarified in the UK SIA which provides that the contract has to be one *made in the UK* or that the work has to be *wholly or partly* performed there (section 4(1)). Such a provision would cover those employees recruited in the UK but dispatched to work in another country.

4.1.3. The choice of law

It is also possible for the employer State to enjoy immunity where 'the parties to the [employment] contract have otherwise agreed in writing, unless, in accordance with the law of the State of the forum, the courts of that State have exclusive jurisdiction by reason of the subject-matter' (Article 5(2)(c)). Such written agreement would be that which stipulates, for example, settlement of disputes by a court of the employing State or

148   CONTRACTS OF EMPLOYMENT

an arbitral tribunal. According to the explanatory report on the European Convention, jurisdiction will not be regarded as exclusive for this purpose if resort may be had to arbitration.[41]

Article 5(2)(c) thereby establishes the principle that party autonomy shall not displace the application of mandatory forum law. As a consequence employment becomes something more than a mere contractual relationship and the employer will not be in a position to dictate whatever terms suit him. This principle is enshrined in Regulation (EC) No. 593/2008, Article 8 of which provides that a choice of law clause 'may not ... have the result of depriving the employee of the protection afforded to him by provisions that cannot be derogated from by agreement'.[42] Seen in this light, such a provision is significant not only in procedural matters concerning the jurisdiction of the local courts, but also in substantive matters such as statutory protection of employees, who are perceived as having a weaker bargaining position.

4.2. The UK SIA

Section 4 of the UK SIA provides:

(1) A State is not immune as respects proceedings relating to a contract of employment between the State and an individual where the contract was made in the United Kingdom or the work is to be wholly or partly performed there.

(2) Subject to subsection (3) and (4) below, this section does not apply if –
  (a) at the time when the proceedings are brought the individual is a national of the State concerned; or
  (b) at the time when the contract was made the individual was neither a national of the United Kingdom nor habitually resident there; or
  (c) the parties to the contract have otherwise agreed in writing.

(3) Where the work is for an office, agency or establishment maintained by the State in the United Kingdom for commercial purposes, subsection (2)(a) and (b) above do not exclude the application of this section unless the individual was, at the time when the contract was made, habitually resident in that State.

(4) Subsection (2)(c) above does not exclude the application of this section where the law of the United Kingdom requires the proceedings to be brought before a court of the United Kingdom.
  . . .

(6) In this section 'proceedings relating to a contract of employment' includes proceedings between the parties to such a contract in respect of any statutory rights or duties to which they are entitled or subject as employer or employee.[43]

Since the relevant provisions of the UK SIA are almost identical with those of the European Convention, many of the comments on the Convention are also applicable here. The discussion will focus on those aspects particular to the SIA.

4.2.1. Contracts of employment as a separate category

Section 3 of the UK SIA provides that the provision of non-immunity regarding 'commercial transactions' does not apply to a contract of employment. This makes it clear that contracts of employment are separate and distinct from 'commercial transactions' and therefore subject to different rules. Such separation has been copied by other national statutes.[44]

4.2.2. The plaintiff

Section 4(3) sets forth the rule that, if an individual has worked for 'an office, agency or establishment maintained by the [employer] State in the United Kingdom for commercial purposes', even if he is a national of the employer State, he will not be precluded from suing that State unless he was, 'at the time when the contract was made, habitually resident in that State'. Obviously, commercial purposes and habitual residence are two decisive factors. However, the SIA gives a rather circular definition of 'commercial purposes'. According to section 17, 'commercial purposes' means 'purposes of such transactions or activities as are mentioned in s. 3(3)', which, in its turn, enumerates a number of 'commercial transactions' without defining the word 'commercial'. Habitual residence, despite its significance in private international law, has never been precisely defined.[45] Therefore, much would turn upon how the court considers all the relevant factors. Sometimes it takes a great deal of fact-finding to ascertain whether the establishment in question serves commercial purposes or otherwise. In this connection, the medical office of the Egyptian Embassy in London, for example, could not be regarded as being 'maintained for commercial purposes'.[46] What is noteworthy here is that, under the UK law, 'purpose' becomes a decisive criterion in determining the question of immunity in the case of a foreign national suing his own State provided he is habitually resident in the UK.

4.2.3. The choice of law

Unlike Article 5(2)(c) of the European Convention, section 4(4) of the UK SIA provides that party autonomy shall be overridden 'where the law of the United Kingdom requires the proceedings to be brought before a court of the United Kingdom'.[47] Here it seems that the term 'exclusive jurisdiction' is deliberately avoided. It is not clear why this avoidance was made. At any rate, it seems reasonable to infer that the language of the SIA broadens its scope of application beyond what can be achieved by an express 'exclusive jurisdiction' formula, in that it contemplates *concurrent jurisdiction*: it applies so long as the UK law requires the proceedings to be brought before a UK court, quite irrespective of whether the proceedings should also be brought before a court of another State. In other words, the SIA will apply whether or not the UK court has *exclusive* jurisdiction.

In the final analysis the question becomes one of relationship between a choice of law clause and the local mandatory rules. This relationship can be broadly stated as this: the courts will generally respect a formal choice of law made by the parties to the contract, but they will uphold the overriding rules of employment protection law and will disregard a choice of law clause which established as the proper law one with which the contract had no real connection, and which was manifestly to the employee's disadvantage. As a rule, the UK law prevents employees working in the UK for foreign employers from contracting out of the jurisdiction of employment tribunals.[48]

4.3. *The Australia FSIA*

For lack of space, to the extent that the Australia FSIA resembles the UK SIA, the relevant Australian provisions will not be reproduced word for word here. A number of unique features of the Australia FSIA can be observed.

First, a proceeding concerning a contract of employment includes '(a) a right or obligation conferred or imposed by a law of Australia on a person as employer or employee; or (b) a payment the entitlement to which arises under a contract of employment' (section 12(2)). In this way, statutory provisions and other rights *outside* the contract itself are expressly taken into account. According to the draftsmen's explanation:

The 'contract of employment' should not be interpreted narrowly. The whole of the proposed section should apply to all relations between employer and employee as such. The employee should be able, where the foreign state employer is not immune on the contract, to sue not only on the contents of the contract but also over any rights or duties imposed by law on an employer or employee in respect of the employment relationship, including pension rights arising under such a contract.[49]

However, as shown above, the European Convention and the UK SIA, despite an absence of such express provisions, can also be interpreted as covering such a proceeding.

Secondly, the Australia FSIA does not make a distinction between employment by the foreign State in connection with an office, agency or establishment maintained for commercial purposes and other sorts of employment.[50]

Thirdly, the Australia FSIA omits any requirement as to the status of the plaintiff at the time when the proceedings are brought but keeps only the requirements at the time when the contract was made.[51] Under section 12(3), the employer State shall enjoy immunity where 'at the time when the contract of employment was made, the person employed was (a) a national of the foreign State but not a permanent resident of Australia; or (b) an habitual resident of the foreign State'. In this regard, the Australia FSIA, in addition to the term 'habitual resident', introduces a new term 'permanent resident of Australia', which is defined as '(a) an Australian citizen; or (b) a person resident in Australia whose continued presence in Australia is not subject to a limitation as to time imposed by or under a law of Australia' (section 12(7)). As a matter of principle, 'no general distinction should be drawn between Australian and third state nationals with respect to local employment'.[52]

It is worthwhile to make a comparison between these provisions and those of the UK SIA. Under the UK SIA, the following individuals will be able to bring a legal action: (1) a national of the employer State but not a habitual resident of the UK at the time when the contract was made, provided that he was not a habitual resident of the employer State (that is, if he was a habitual resident of a third State) at the time when the contract was made, and that he sues in relation to work done for a commercial establishment; (2) a habitual resident of the employer State but a UK national at the time when the contract was made; and (3) a national of the employer State but a habitual resident of the UK at the time when the contract was made, if he changes his nationality into that of the UK before bringing the proceedings.

Under the Australia FSIA, which makes no provision for allowing law-suits regarding commercial establishments, gives Australian nationals no special position, and which dispenses with the time slot when the proceedings are brought, the first two of the above-mentioned categories of individual are effectively prevented from initiating judicial procedures, while the status of the third category becomes uncertain. Having only to apply a single set of criteria, the court is spared the troublesome task of

152 CONTRACTS OF EMPLOYMENT

investigating whether the establishment concerned is for commercial purposes or otherwise. However, this is done at the expense of depriving certain individuals of access to the judicial process. In this sense the scope of application of the Australia FSIA is more restricted than that of the UK SIA.

Finally, as far as the choice of law clause is concerned, the foreign State shall enjoy immunity if two conditions are satisfied: '(a) an inconsistent provision is included in the contract of employment; and (b) a law of Australia does not avoid the operation of, or prohibit or render unlawful the inclusion of, the provision' (section 12(4)). The particular 'inconsistent provision' targeted here, according to the draftsmen, is one 'ousting the jurisdiction of the courts in a contract of employment'.[53]

It must be borne in mind that the issues of nationality or habitual residence, the place of conclusion and performance of the contract are only 'threshold requirements'. Having satisfied itself that all these requirements are met, the court will then proceed to examine the employment relationship itself, so as to determine whether the public functions of the foreign State are actually involved. Sometimes the court will set about scrutinizing the nature of the employment and the relationship between the role performed by the employee and the sovereign functions of the State, without even mentioning these threshold requirements. In such cases, one has to assume that the threshold requirements have been met.[54]

4.4. Other instruments

The Argentina Law of 1995 provides in Article 2(d) that a foreign State shall not enjoy immunity with regard to a claim brought 'by Argentinians or residents of Argentina, relating to a contract of employment executed in Argentina or abroad with effects in Argentina'. This allows a much narrower range of plaintiffs and sets forth a territorial nexus requirement. Likewise, the Israeli Law of 2008 in section 4 denies immunity to a foreign State where all three conditions are fulfilled: (1) the cause of action is within the exclusive jurisdiction of a Regional Labour Court; (2) the subject matter is labour partly or wholly performed or to be performed in Israel; and (3) when the cause of action arose, the employee was an Israeli citizen or habitually resident in Israel; however, where the cause of action is a commercial transaction, immunity will be denied even if the three conditions are not satisfied.

The IDI 1991 Draft simply states that '[t]he organs of the forum State are competent in respect of proceedings concerning contracts of employment and contracts for professional services to which a foreign State (or its agent) is a party' (Article 2(c)), without giving any further guidance as to the manner and circumstances in which this provision is to be applied.

The ILA Draft closely follows the European Convention and the UK SIA but has two notable characteristics: (1) as to the time of the conclusion of the contract, the Draft uses the term 'permanent resident' instead of 'habitual resident' (Article III(C)(2)); (2) the Draft contains no limitation on an agreement between the employer and employee ousting the local jurisdiction (Article III (C)(3)).[55]

Article 11 of the 2004 UN Convention, entitled 'Contracts of employment', provides:

1. Unless otherwise agreed between the States concerned, a State cannot invoke immunity from jurisdiction before a court of another State which is otherwise competent in a proceeding which relates to a contract of employment between the State and an individual for work performed or to be performed, in whole or in part, in the territory of that other State.
2. Paragraph 1 does not apply if:
    (a) the employee has been recruited to perform particular functions in the exercise of governmental authority;
    (b) the employee is:
        (i) a diplomatic agent, as defined in the Vienna Convention on Diplomatic Relations of 1961;
        (ii) a consular officer, as defined in the Vienna Convention on Consular Relations of 1963;
        (iii) a member of the diplomatic staff of a permanent mission to an international organization or of a special mission, or is recruited to represent a State at an international conference; or
        (iv) any other person enjoying diplomatic immunity;
    (c) the subject-matter of the proceeding is the recruitment, renewal of employment or reinstatement of an individual;
    (d) the subject-matter of the proceeding is the dismissal or termination of employment of an individual and, as determined by the head of State, the head of Government or the Minister for Foreign Affairs of the employer State, such a proceeding would interfere with the security interests of that State;
    (e) the employee is a national of the employer State at the time when the proceeding is instituted, unless this person has the permanent residence in the State of the forum; or
    (f) the employer State and the employee have otherwise agreed in writing, subject to any considerations of public policy conferring on the courts of the State of the forum exclusive jurisdiction by reason of the subject-matter of the proceeding.

154   CONTRACTS OF EMPLOYMENT

Article 11 of the UN Convention generally reproduces ILC 1991 Draft Article 11 but introduces a number of changes in paragraph (2). First, the words 'perform functions closely related to the exercise' have been changed into 'perform particular functions in the exercise', thereby further restricting the scope of the subparagraph; secondly, paragraph 2(c) in the 1991 Draft Article, which grants immunity where 'the employee was neither a national nor a habitual resident of the State of the forum at the time when the contract of employment was concluded', is deleted;[56] thirdly, ILC Draft Article 11(2)(d) (now Article 11(2)(e)) is given a new proviso, namely, 'unless this person has the permanent residence in the State of the forum', thereby relaxing the rule prohibiting legal action by an employee against his national State; and, finally, new savings clauses have been inserted (now Article 11(2)(b) and (d), which will be discussed later).

The place of the conclusion of the contract is not specified, so that the provision would cover contracts made either within or outside the forum State. The work is such that is 'performed or to be performed'. The word 'performed' seems to suggest that a contract might be concluded post hoc to cover some work that had already been done before the contract was made.

Article 11(2)(c) is unusual, for, except for the case of recruitment, it invalidates an employee's claim by reason of the remedies sought. According to the ILC, this is 'in support of the rule of immunity in the exercise of the discretionary power of appointment or non-appointment by the State of an individual to any official post or employment position';[57] and 'the immunity does not exclude jurisdiction for unpaid salaries or, in certain cases, damages for dismissal'.[58]

As to the potential plaintiff, the ILC states in its commentary that the 'employees' include 'both regular employees and short-term independent contractors'.[59] This will be problematic at least in the context of the UK labour law, which does not regard independent contractors as 'employees'.

4.5.   The importance of having a contract

An action under the UK SIA has to be based upon an actual *contract* of employment. Thus a claim for racial discrimination based on job advertisements was rejected because no contract of employment had actually been concluded.[60] Nor is the UK SIA applicable to contracts of employment concluded before its entry into force on 22 November

1978 (section 23(3)(b)), even where the alleged breach of contract took place after that date.[61]

In this connection it bears remarking that all the relevant provisions in current legal instruments governing State immunity in respect of employment matters are predicated on the existence of an *actual, existing contract of employment*.[62] This precludes claims based on any pre-employment or pre-contract acts (such as recruitment advertisements, interviews, negotiations, and expressions of intent, etc.) in contemplation of a possible future employment relationship. In *Fogarty*, for example, the plaintiff, who had worked as an administrative assistant at the US Embassy in London, instituted proceedings against the US Government, claiming that her dismissal had been the result of sex discrimination. The US Government appeared in court and did not claim State immunity. The employment tribunal upheld the applicant's complaint and compensation was agreed between the parties. Later, while her first claim was still pending, the applicant obtained a twelve-month fixed term contract as an administrative assistant again at the US Embassy. Upon the expiry of the contract, she applied for two secretarial posts at the US Embassy but was unsuccessful. She then brought fresh proceedings, claiming that the Embassy's refusal to re-employ her was a consequence of her previous successful sex discrimination claim, and accordingly constituted victimization and discrimination under the 1975 UK Sex Discrimination Act.[63] The US Government indicated its intention to claim State immunity from the jurisdiction of the tribunal, pointing out, in particular, that each of the posts for which the applicant had applied were part of the administrative and technical staff of the Embassy, and accordingly fell within the ambit of the immunity granted by section 16(1)(a) of the UK SIA.[64]

Fogarty then instituted proceedings in the European Court of Human Rights (ECHR) against the UK for denial of access to court because of the immunity granted to the US by the SIA. The ECHR upheld immunity, observing that, even though there appeared to be a trend in international and comparative law towards limiting State immunity in respect of employment-related disputes, where the proceedings related to employment in a foreign mission or embassy, international practice was divided on the question whether State immunity continued to apply and, if it did, whether it covered disputes relating to the contracts of all staff or only more senior members of the mission. It could not be said that the UK was alone in holding that immunity attached to suits by employees at diplomatic missions or that, in affording such immunity

156 CONTRACTS OF EMPLOYMENT

the UK fell outside any currently accepted international standards. The ECHR found that:

the proceedings which the applicant wished to bring did not concern the contractual rights of a current embassy employee, but instead related to alleged discrimination in the recruitment process. Questions relating to the recruitment of staff to missions and embassies may by their very nature involve sensitive and confidential issues, related, *inter alia*, to the diplomatic and organisational policy of a foreign State. The Court is not aware of any trend in international law towards a relaxation of the rule of State immunity as regards issues of recruitment to foreign missions.[65]

It can be seen that the ECHR's decision in *Fogarty* relied on the importance of recruitment to diplomatic missions, but the word 'recruitment' does not appear in the UK SIA. In fact, with the exception of the UN Convention, none of the current legal instruments, whether national or international, contains the word 'recruitment'. All the relevant provisions in these documents require an *existing contract of employment*. Since the present rules on State immunity with regard to contracts of employment are predicated on an already existent employment relationship (there has to be a 'contract of employment'), recruitment to whatever institution (not limited to a diplomatic or consular mission) never emerges as a valid cause of action. As far as those States without immunity legislation are concerned, a survey of case law will show that, in the cases where jurisdiction was asserted, it was likewise done over existing, as opposed to prospective, contracts of employment. As a matter of fact, so far no case has been decided in a claimant's favour on the sole basis of recruitment prior to the conclusion of a contract.

As noted earlier, the only place where the word 'recruitment' does appear is the UN Convention. Article 11(2)(c) provides that a State shall enjoy immunity where 'the subject-matter of the proceeding is the recruitment, renewal of employment or reinstatement of an individual'. Note that here no mention is made of diplomatic or consular missions in the context of recruitment. In the commentary to this provision (then Article 11(2)(b)), the ILC does not refer to diplomatic or consular missions either; instead, it finds that:

The employer State has an interest in the application of its laws in regard to the selection, *recruitment* and appointment of an employee by *the State or one of its organs, agencies or instrumentalities* acting in the exercise of governmental authority.[66]

Evidently, when it speaks of 'recruitment', the ILC has in mind, not recruitment to a diplomatic or consular mission, as the ECHR understood it, but recruitment to *any institution*. Therefore, when the ECHR reasoned that, had Fogarty taken her case to an English court, immunity could have been justifiably granted because the intended proceedings concerned *recruitment to a diplomatic mission*, it was asserting something totally absent from current State practice.

In its commentary to Article 11 the ILC makes it clear that this sub-paragraph does not 'prevent an employee from bringing action against the employer State in the State of the forum to seek redress for damage arising from recruitment'.[67] Note that here the ILC talks about *damage* arising from recruitment rather than recruitment itself. Presumably, sex discrimination in the course of recruitment may be regarded as distinct from the recruitment itself. Here it would be interesting to speculate what the ECHR would have said if the applicant had insisted that her intention was not to bring an action based upon the employment relationship itself (since there was no contract of employment yet) or, for that matter, upon the recruitment process, but to sue for sex discrimination[68] by a potential employer. But then a simple answer would have sufficed: Ms Fogarty could not sue either for sex discrimination or for a prospective employment relationship because the UK SIA does not contain an exception to State immunity for sex discrimination and it requires an *existing contract* in order to establish jurisdiction regarding an employment relationship.

Fortunately, the situation has been salvaged somewhat by the normal practice of concluding a written contract when a foreign State is the employer. The discussion in this chapter will proceed on the assumption that a contract exists in the cases considered.

5. The US Model

The US Model encompasses the practice of both the US and Canada, which have State immunity legislation, and of those States that do not have such legislation. In contrast to the UK Model, which makes specific provision for contracts of employment, the US Model does not have such a provision and analyses the contract of employment in the light of a commercial or private law act. In addition, the UK case law before the entry into force of the UK SIA also falls within this model.

5.1. The US FSIA

Under the US FSIA, cases relating to contracts of employment have to be brought within the commercial activity exception to State immunity

158 CONTRACTS OF EMPLOYMENT

(section 1605(a)(2) and section 1603(e)).[69] Presumably, the jurisdictional links in these provisions also apply to employment contracts.

According to the legislative report:

Also public or governmental and not commercial in nature, would be the employment of diplomatic, civil service, or military personnel, but not the employment of American citizens or third country nationals by the foreign state in the United States . . . Activities such as a foreign government's . . . employment or engagement of laborers, clerical staff or public relations or marketing agents . . . would be among those included within the definition [of a commercial activity].[70]

Clearly, employment by a foreign State can be characterized as either commercial or governmental, depending on the job description and nationality of the person employed.[71] An 'act performed in the United States in connection with a commercial activity of the foreign state elsewhere' includes, inter alia, 'the wrongful discharge in the United States of an employee of the foreign state who has been employed in connection with a commercial activity carried on in some third country'.[72]

The phrase 'third country nationals' has been regarded by some courts as highly relevant when determining the private nature of the employment relationship, so that the employment of US or third country nationals is considered as prima facie commercial.[73] Hence it will be interesting to ask what nature is to be ascribed to the employment by a foreign State of a third country national for its diplomatic service in the US, since, according to the legislative report, such an employment relationship would be simultaneously of a public (employment of diplomatic personnel) and a private (employment of a third country national) nature.

In *El-Hadad*, an Egyptian citizen employed as an auditor and supervising accountant in the Cultural Attaché's Office at the Embassy of the United Arab Emirates in Washington brought an action for breach of employment contract and defamation, having been dismissed on the basis of allegedly trumped-up charges of dishonest behaviour. The district court denied immunity on the ground of third country nationality.[74] The circuit court remanded the case for further inquiry, concluding that 'a per se rule of non-immunity for a foreign state's employment of third country nationals is inconsistent with Congress' intent to immunize foreign governmental activity from suit in American courts'.[75] Immunity was again denied on remand[76] and the denial of immunity reaffirmed (without discussing the issue of third country nationality) after a bench trial by the district court, with damages awarded.[77] Upon further appeal, the DC Circuit concluded that El-Hadad was not a civil servant, and his work did not involve the exercise of distinctively governmental powers, thus affirming the district court in applying the commercial activity exception and denying immunity.[78]

In its own consideration of the case, the DC Circuit proposed what it termed a 'multi-factor inquiry', enumerating a number of questions for the trial court to consider, and these were:

First, how do the U.A.E.'s own laws define its civil service, and do El-Hadad's job title and duties come within that definition? Second, what was the nature of El-Hadad's employment relationship with the U.A.E.? Did he have a true contractual arrangement ... ? Third, what was the nature of El-Hadad's employment relationship when he worked in the U.A.E., and how did his subsequent employment at the Embassy relate to that prior tenure? ... Fourth, what was the nature of El-Hadad's work? Fifth, what is the relevance of El-Hadad's Egyptian nationality on the facts of this case? Is the U.A.E. a country in which, as the House Report assumed, non-nationals are unlikely to be employed as governmental officers? Or does the U.A.E. often employ non-nationals in governmental positions?[79]

Apparently the nationality of the employee had little or no impact upon the final determination of the nature of the employment relationship, since the court turned mainly to the job title and the duties performed by the employee. The factor of third country nationality comes at the very end of the list and, whatever it might have done for the case, it is obvious that it cannot, contrary to the legislators' suggestion, automatically render an employment relationship non-immune.

The multi-factor test in *El-Hadad* was further applied in *Mukaddam*, where a former employee of the Permanent Mission of Saudi Arabia to the UN in New York sued for wrongful termination, sexual harassment and discrimination. The plaintiff's duties included writing speeches that Saudi government officials delivered to the UN and were published in local newspapers, establishing and maintaining a data bank classification system, establishing a system for registering and responding to correspondence to and from the Mission, drafting correspondence and public statements, writing memos, letters, faxes and reports to the Ministry of Foreign Affairs in Saudi Arabia and, on one occasion, speaking with students concerning Saudi Arabia's public positions on international issues. The question turned on whether such duties could be characterized as those of a 'civil servant'. The court found that, in deciding whether an individual's employment by a foreign State

160   CONTRACTS OF EMPLOYMENT

constitutes civil service, the US courts had considered whether the employee competed for an examination prior to being hired, was entitled to tenure, was provided the same benefits as foreign service officers, or received civil service protections from the hiring government.[80] Since such conditions were lacking in the present case, the plaintiff was only a 'contract employee hired to conduct research and perform other clerical duties', and her employment could not be properly categorized as civil service.[81]

The court added that the fact that the plaintiff was an American and not a Saudi Arabian citizen was but one factor to be considered in determining the nature of her employment. That fact, however, gave 'additional weight' to the conclusion that her employment was a commercial activity.[82]

It is not clear whether a national of the employer State may sue his own State. A national of a foreign State employed by that State for governmental service will certainly be precluded.[83] However, in such a case, what precludes the individual from legal action seems to be the governmental service rather than his nationality. Beyond that the provision does not seem to rule out the possibility of a foreign national suing his own State, especially where the foreign State employs its own nationals for commercial purposes. The Supreme Court is specifically of the opinion that:

The [FSIA] contains no indication of any limitation based on the citizenship of the plaintiff ... we conclude that, when considered as a whole, the legislative history reveals an intent not to limit jurisdiction under the [FSIA] to actions brought by American citizens ... If an action satisfies the substantive standards of the [FSIA], it may be brought ... regardless of the citizenship of the plaintiff.[84]

Nor is any distinction made between nationality and habitual residence, between the time of the conclusion of the contract and that of the bringing of the proceedings, or between a US citizen and a national of the employer or third State. Evidently, so long as the proceedings relate to a commercial activity which is either carried out in or in any way connected with US territory, they will prima facie be admitted.[85] Moreover, third parties to the contract of employment, such as the dependants of the employee or trade unions, also seem to be allowed to sue if the action is 'based upon' a commercial activity as defined above.[86]

In *Hijazi*, a Jordanian citizen residing in New York and employed as an 'advisor' by the Permanent Mission of Saudi Arabia to the UN, filed suit against her employer alleging gender discrimination, sexual harassment, hostile work environment, national origin discrimination, and retaliation. The district court took the view that:

whether a sovereign's employment of an individual in the United States is commercial in nature depends both on the nature of the sovereign's activities in the United States of which the plaintiff's employment is a part and the extent to which the plaintiff's individual duties are themselves either integral or incidental to any governmental function.[87]

The court then proposed a two-step inquiry:

the first inquiry is whether the activity to which the plaintiff's employment was directed is governmental ... In this case the ultimate activity to which the plaintiff's employment is directed is plainly diplomatic, and therefore governmental.[88]

The second inquiry is whether the plaintiff's employment relationship was sufficiently intertwined with that activity to provide that the employment relationship itself was part of the governmental function ... In this case, the plaintiff's activities are sufficiently intertwined with the defendant's governmental function to fall outside the commercial activities exception. The plaintiff was an Advisor, the number two employee in both departments in which she worked, just below the diplomatic level. It is clear from the facts put forth by the defendant, without contradiction, that the plaintiff performed significant duties in that position, including speaking on one occasion on behalf of Saudi Arabia at a United Nations conference. Therefore, the plaintiff's employment relationship with the defendant is governmental in nature and the commercial activity exception to the FSIA does not apply.[89]

Obviously the court did not regard the nationality of the plaintiff as of much relevance. As a matter of fact, section 1605(a)(2) says nothing about the nationality of the plaintiff; instead, its language suggests that what is decisive is a territorial connection with the US. For an employment contract to fall within the provisions of the US FSIA, it must be a commercial activity or a related act with a jurisdictional connection with the US territory. This is broad enough to cover claims arising out of employment by a foreign State where the contract of employment was concluded elsewhere or where the work is to be performed outside the US. The place of conclusion or performance of the contract becomes immaterial if a territorial connection can otherwise be established. In brief, three factors are important: (1) the employment must be a commercial activity or a related act; (2) the action must be based on such an activity or act;[90] and (3) there must be a territorial connection with the US.[91]

5.2. The plaintiff

5.2.1. Individuals: their nationality

In the US Model, the nationality of the plaintiff rarely constitutes a jurisdictional bar so long as the act on which the claim is based is proved to be commercial or private. It is common under this model for the court to allow the claim by a national of the employer State at the time of bringing the proceedings,[92] or at least not to deny jurisdiction on the basis of the nationality of the plaintiff.[93] In proceedings brought by nationals of the third State, jurisdiction was either asserted[94] or declared to be lacking on other grounds.[95] In fact, in a great number of cases, the nationality of the plaintiff was not even mentioned by the courts.[96] Nor does one find any reference to habitual residence as a factor to be taken into account, which means that a residential connection between the plaintiff and the forum State is not a condition for the admissibility of a claim. The employer State may also be sued by a third party to the employment contract, such as by a dependant of the employee for benefits or other compensation,[97] or by a hospital for medical expenses pursuant to an alleged liability on the employer State to ensure that one of its employees and his dependants are insured against medical expenses.[98]

In *M* v. *Egypt*, the Swiss Federal Tribunal declared that the fact that the plaintiff was a national of the sending State, to which he returned occasionally on holiday, was not sufficient to prevent subjecting the dispute to Swiss jurisdiction. Such a fact constituted 'merely one factor, amongst others, which should be taken into consideration within the framework of the total examination of the situation'.[99]

5.2.2. Trade unions

Claims brought by trade unions normally concern collective issues such as representation of employees, collective bargaining and other industrial matters.[100] Insofar as a claim does not concern the public aspects of the employer (be it a foreign State or a State entity), the court would affirm jurisdiction. This is especially true when the proceedings relate to a separate State entity engaged in commercial activities.[101]

Sometimes a complex situation would arise where the targeted institution engages largely in less commercially oriented activities. In *Goethe House*, for example, a trade union filed a petition for representation, seeking to represent certain employees of Goethe House New York, a branch of the celebrated Goethe Institute of Germany. Goethe House, funded directly by the Government of Germany, was a non-profit institution for cultural, educational, and informational exchange and was not incorporated or licensed to do business in New York. The National Labor Relations Board asserted jurisdiction and, upon finding that the relevant employees of Goethe House constituted an appropriate collective bargaining unit, directed that an election be held to determine whether those employees wished to be represented by the union.[102] The Board opined that, since the unit petitioned for covered only those employees, most of whom were in clerical or maintenance positions and who were either 'American citizens or third country nationals', the employees for whom the Petitioner had filed a representation petition fitted almost exactly within these examples of non-exempt 'commercial activity' under the FSIA.[103]

Generally speaking, courts tend to become very cautious where claims brought by trade unions may affect the organization and exercise of public functions of the foreign State. More importantly, unlike the proceedings brought by individuals, those brought by trade unions to enforce trade union rights often require changes in the whole system of employment or seek to impose mandatory orders on the employer to take or refrain from taking certain measures of a general nature.[104] This would inevitably result in an unwarranted intrusion into the internal administrative arrangement of the foreign State. In such a case, the claim would be rejected. Thus, in a case brought by an Italian trade union for the staff of foreign consulates in Italy alleging 'anti-trade union behaviour' in the procedures followed for hiring the consular staff, the Italian Court of Cassation conceded that the employment relationships with Italian members of the staff of a consulate (whose functions were administrative and clerical) were essentially of a private nature within the sphere of *jure gestionis* and could not be exempt from Italian civil jurisdiction; but the Court nonetheless upheld immunity on the ground that the case involved 'special proceedings' initiated by trade unions for the protection of collective interests:

In order to protect these interests [i.e. collective interests in relation to trade unions] effectively, the judge is called upon to interfere considerably in all the various powers of the employer (organisational, managerial and disciplinary powers, etc.) and impart direct 'orders' to put an end to the offending behaviour and to rectify the situation and he has to apply repressive measures which do not only affect this or that relationship of employment but also impinge upon the employer's prerogatives in their entirety. Now it is obvious that if a Court were to interfere in the organisational power of a foreign State (for

164   CONTRACTS OF EMPLOYMENT

example in its power to organise Consular offices) it would upset a whole set of acts performed *jure imperii*.[105]

The caution concerning trade union claims is well illustrated by the case of *Re Canada Labour Code*, where a Canadian trade union, the Public Service Alliance of Canada, applied to the Canada Labour Relations Board for certification under the Canada Labour Code 1985 as bargaining agent for the Canadian civilians employed as fire-fighters and maintenance workers, such as plumbers, carpenters and electricians, at a US naval base at Argentia, Newfoundland. The function of the base was to support anti-submarine warfare command and tactical forces through the operation of a communications centre. The Labour Relations Board and, upon appeal, the Federal Court of Appeal held that, since the certification proceedings related to the employment of members of the proposed bargaining unit under contracts of service, entry into which was conduct of a commercial character, the US was not entitled to immunity.[106] The Supreme Court reversed, finding that:

the application seeks to supplant the private contractual relationship between the employees and employer with a statutory scheme of collective bargaining which by definition regulates the management of the base. The union certification procedure relates most obviously and directly to the sovereign attributes of a foreign state, which must remain immune from such proceedings.[107]

6. Diverse approaches

This section discusses the factors usually considered by various courts within both models examined above. As a general rule, in handling cases concerning contracts of employment, courts usually conduct a multi-factor inquiry. Indeed, in employment disputes courts often consider far more factors than in any other type of State immunity case. These include, but are not confined to, the characterization of the employment relationship; the status and acts of the employer, the status, duties and functions of the employee; the nature of the particular activity for which the employee was engaged; the territorial connection; whether there is a choice of law clause in the contract; and whether the remedies sought affect the sovereign or public functions of the defendant State. It should be noted that the factors enumerated here should be understood as references to various points on which courts usually lay emphasis in their reasoning, in a manner that varies with time, case and court, but not as clear-cut criteria. Often – and this is most important – the court in a case may refer to several of the factors listed here, without specifying which one of them is decisive or controlling. Indeed one will find that the factors considered by the courts may not be neatly separable in all cases. Therefore, it should always be remembered that the factors as discussed hereinafter under the separate headings are only *artificially isolated* for the sake of convenience. All said, a multi-factor test, namely that a court needs to examine all the relevant circumstances of a case, still remains the generic term closest to reality.

6.1. The employment relationship

In some cases jurisdiction was asserted on the ground that the employment relationship between the foreign State and the individual was governed by private law. Thus, in a case for damages for wrongful dismissal brought by a Portuguese national employed as a language teacher by the consular section of the Portuguese Embassy, a Belgian court held that, in hiring an individual by means of a contract of employment, which established relations governed by private law, to teach Portuguese language and culture in Belgium, Portugal had not behaved as a public authority in the exercise of its political sovereignty.[108] Termination of a private law employment relationship would also be an ordinary commercial act.[109] So, in concluding and terminating, without notice or payment of compensation, a contract of employment which did not contain any aspect of an appointment to a public function, the Commercial Office of Portugal in Brussels (which, as an emanation of the Portuguese State, was in principle entitled to jurisdictional immunity) performed a private commercial act in respect of which immunity could not be invoked.[110] Of course telltale signs indicating that the employment relationship was subject to local law were discovered by the court in the contract of employment, which provided that the employee enjoyed benefits and assumed obligations under the provisions of 'Belgian social legislation and the collective bargaining agreements applicable in Belgium', which the employer undertook to respect.[111] The contract between an Embassy and its chauffeur was considered as a contract of manual employment, whereby the bond between the parties was one of private law and the defendant had not performed any public act.[112] The employment contract of a laboratory technician was a contract governed by private law since that had no connection with political, diplomatic or public functions.[113] Similarly, a Dutch court held that the conclusion of a contract of employment with a Dutch clerical worker (a secretary) who had no diplomatic or civil service status was an act which the defendant performed on the same footing as a natural or legal person under private law and that there was therefore no question of a purely governmental act in the instant case.[114] The Austrian Supreme Court held that a foreign State, when concluding a contract in respect of work to be performed on the receiving State's territory, acted as a private law entity, and could not be entitled to terminate such an employment relationship merely 'on security grounds' by having recourse to an act of sovereignty.[115] Even the head of the visa section of a foreign consulate (and a national of the employer State at that) had her claim allowed because the court held that the foreign State had acted as a holder of private rights and concluded a contract of employment for work to be performed on the territory of the State of the forum.[116]

Immunity may also be denied on the ground that the employment relationship in question is something that private entities and individuals engage in. In *De Sousa*, a Portuguese national employed by the Portuguese Ministry of Education as a teacher at the Portuguese School of Amsterdam brought a claim for unlawful dismissal. The Dutch courts denied immunity on the ground that, since the provision of education was something that could also be done by a private entity, Portugal, in hiring a teacher in the Netherlands, had entered into a legal relationship on an equal footing with a private person.[117] Engagement of a researcher to perform research, writing, and clerical duties is likewise a commercial activity because private parties enter into such contracts routinely.[118] So is the hiring of a pilot.[119]

6.2. The duties and functions of the employee

It is normal for a court to look into the duties and functions of the employee in order to decide whether a particular employment relationship is commercial or not. Senior employees with responsibilities closely connected with the sovereign power of the foreign State will be precluded from suing. By contrast, employees with only secondary, auxiliary or menial duties are permitted to sue. According to the Italian Court of Cassation, the fact that the duties carried out by the plaintiff were of a secondary, auxiliary nature in relation to the purposes and functions of a foreign embassy in Rome brought the dispute within the scope of the jurisdiction of the Italian courts.[120]

In *R* v. *Iraq*, the Swiss Federal Tribunal closely examined the duties of the plaintiff, a Moroccan national employed as an interpreter/translator by the Permanent Mission of Iraq to the United Nations in Geneva. According to the Tribunal:

> In practice, a translator/interpreter does not normally participate in the formation of the policies of his employer, but is exclusively responsible for rendering as faithfully as possible the meaning of what he reads or hears. It is certainly true that such an activity may be of a markedly confidential nature, depending on the content of the written documents for translation or the sentiments requiring interpretation. Nevertheless, this is not a decisive element in the classification of the activity in question, because many other persons working in the service of the sending State are required to perform confidential tasks or to take account of information of that nature, even though they occupy subordinate posts such as secretaries, typists, archivists, drivers, members of the security service, etc. ... In these circumstances, the activity at issue cannot be regarded as other than involving the exercise of a subordinate function.[121]

Similarly, in *M* v. *Egypt*, the Federal Tribunal found that the plaintiff, an Egyptian national employed as a chauffeur at the Permanent Mission of Egypt to the UN in Geneva, performed a subordinate function that did not involve the exercise of sovereign powers; and that the situation of a chauffeur was 'equivalent to that of porters, gardeners and kitchen workers'.[122]

In *Coco*, the French Court of Cassation based its decision to deny immunity on a similar analysis of the duties of the plaintiff, who had been employed by the Embassy of Argentina in Paris as an assistant in the press section, with the task of collecting, ordering and transmitting information of interest to Argentina. His tasks were such that he had not been charged with any special responsibility for the exercise of a public service and his dismissal therefore constituted an ordinary act of administration (*acte de gestion*).[123]

In *X* v. *Israel*, a catering assistant/cleaner at the residence of the Israeli Ambassador in Lisbon brought proceedings for unlawful dismissal. The Portuguese Supreme Court, in denying immunity, found that:

> In these proceedings, the functions performed by the claimant were clearly of a subordinate character and she obviously did not hold any position of authority within the organization of the public service of the defendant State and did not perform any representative functions ... [T]he function performed by the claimant, essentially cleaning and the preparation of meals, cannot be considered as forming part of the 'public administration' of the defendant.[124]

The US courts consistently approach an employment case from the standpoint of the employee's duties and functions. In *Segni*, an Argentine citizen and a permanent resident of the US brought an action to

168   CONTRACTS OF EMPLOYMENT

challenge his dismissal by the Commercial Office of Spain, which had employed him to develop a market for Spanish wines in the US. The Office described Segni's work as 'diplomatic activity', the direct execution of a policy designed to increase exports of Spanish wines and thereby reduce unemployment in Spain, but the court thought that his employment was simply the 'hiring of a marketing agent', a commercial activity:

> An examination of the nature of his activities indicates that he cannot be considered either as a civil servant or a diplomatic officer. He had no role in the creation of the government policy or its administration; rather, he simply carried it out. There is no indication in the record that he was so supervised or monitored by the Commercial Office, or so privy to its political deliberations, as to be considered a part of the Spanish government, as a civil servant or diplomat would be ... For purposes of this case, Segni's employment by the Commercial Office is best described as a contract under which he would provide services in the area of product marketing.[125]

In *Holden*, a former commercial officer sued the Canadian Consulate in San Francisco for wrongful termination alleging, among others, sex and age discrimination. The court first held that she was not a 'civil servant' since she 'did not compete for any examination prior to being hired, was not entitled to tenure, was not provided the same benefits as foreign service officers and did not receive any civil service protections from the Canadian government';[126] it went on to find that the employee's duties 'were primarily promoting and marketing and she was not involved in any policy-making and was not privy to any governmental policy deliberations. She did not engage in any lobbying activity or legislative work for Canada, and she could not speak for the government'. Thus, as in *Segni*, her employment was 'more analogous to a marketing agent'.[127]

The cases of *Segni* and *Holden* provided the necessary benchmarks for subsequent cases. Of course, under the US FSIA, the mere fact that a foreign State has been engaged in a commercial activity does not automatically deprive that State of immunity; for the claim must also be 'based upon' that commercial activity.[128] In *Elliott*, a marketing executive at the New York office of the British Tourist Authority (BTA), a British government agency chartered to promote tourism to the UK, sued that agency for wrongful dismissal due to age discrimination. The court noted that the plaintiff was characterized as a marketing executive and his last job title was 'Manager of Industry Relations'. From that characterization and the nature of BTA's mission, the court found that the plaintiff fitted squarely within the decisions of *Segni* and *Holden*, namely that the hiring of a marketing agent was certainly a commercial activity. Furthermore, the plaintiff, a resident of New York, was assumed to be a US citizen, and his lack of British citizenship would place his employment beyond the scope of immunized 'non-commercial' employment of civil servants. Since there was clearly a significant nexus between the commercial activity of employment and the plaintiff's claim of age discrimination, immunity was displaced.[129]

The fact that the employee performed menial duties would make it easier for the court to reach a decision in his favour. In *Shih*, three former employees of Taipei Economic and Cultural Representative Office (TECRO) in the US, who had performed secretarial or clerical tasks, sued their employer, alleging that they had suffered age discrimination under a document entitled 'Guideline for Local Employees Hired by ROC Embassies, Consulates and Offices Abroad', which stated that 'a person who is qualified for a local employee position must be over 18 years old and must not exceed 45 years old'. The court had no trouble finding that:

Making decisions about what tasks employees perform, how much they are paid, or how they are treated in the workplace does not implicate concerns 'peculiar to sovereigns.' These are decisions that parties in the private sector make every day.[130]

As is characteristic of the case law on State immunity, contrary rulings can also be found. In *Sutton*, a New Zealand citizen had been employed as a typist/clerk in the Auckland Office (which was located within the British Consulate-General) of the Governor of Pitcairn, which post was held simultaneously by the British High Commissioner in New Zealand. Her duties comprised the provision of all typing and secretarial services and registering all mail going into and out of the Office of the Governor. In her proceedings seeking compensation for unjustifiable dismissal, the Court of Appeal unanimously reversed the first instance decision denying immunity and held that a typist/clerk's duties were so important as to justify immunity. According to the court:

Mrs Sutton's duties did not entail any significant responsibility for decision-making, but they were close to the heart of the administrative process. She was an important cog in the administrative wheel. It cannot be right for a New Zealand Court to inquire into and adjudicate on how well or how badly the British overseas administrative machine dealt with her ... Mrs Sutton was directly involved in the production, recording and communication of decisions affecting the administration of Pitcairn including the Governor's official

170 CONTRACTS OF EMPLOYMENT

instructions. She was in a position of trust and confidentiality. It was highly likely that confidential official matters would come to her notice in the ordinary course of her work.[131]

It is difficult to see how a typist can be 'in a position of trust and confidentiality' and, even if that be the case, how that fact can significantly impinge on the case, which is only about the dismissal, and not about the confidentiality agreement. If the employer should have found no qualms in dismissing a typist regardless of certain 'confidential official matters' which may have come to her notice, then surely it cannot be altogether impossible for a tribunal to pass an opinion on the dismissal itself without touching on such 'confidential matters'?

6.3. The status of the employer

A finding that the actual employer is not the foreign State itself but an agency or instrumentality of the foreign State (such as a foreign State-owned school or trading corporation), engaged in commercial or private activities, will easily render the employment relationship non-immune, since in such a case the exercise of jurisdiction will not affect the sovereignty of the foreign State. Thus, when a cook employed at a US Air Force recreation centre restaurant claimed unfair dismissal, the Philippine Supreme Court rejected the plea of the club manager that he was entitled to immunity as an officer of the US Air Force. According to the Court's analysis, the restaurant services offered at the recreation centre were a business enterprise undertaken by the US Government in its proprietary capacity. They were not free services extended exclusively to US servicemen but were available to the general public, who paid for the facility, which was undoubtedly operated for profit as a commercial and not a governmental activity.[132] The same reasoning had been applied by an Italian court in a case where an Italian citizen had been employed as an interpreter and cashier at a recreation and rest centre in Naples established by the US Navy for US Navy personnel stationed or on leave in that city. The court opined that, in setting up the recreation centre, the US 'did not intend to carry out an act of sovereignty appurtenant to its essentially military activity, but to engage in activities which have an essentially private purpose'; besides, the plaintiff was not entrusted with any functions which served military ends; on the contrary, she did work of a nature accessory to the internal services of the club, performing the duties of cashier, interpreter, clerk at the information desk and bookkeeper. Thus the employment relationship could not be regarded as one for the performance of sovereign functions.[133]

In *Kuwait News Agency*, the French Court of Cassation decided against the immunity of the Kuwait News Agency on the basis of its separate legal entity. The Court held that the Kuwait News Agency had its own legal personality and independent budget. The protected interests of the State of Kuwait justifying jurisdictional immunity could not be infringed by the act of administration whereby a press agency, even if it was an emanation of the State, dismissed a journalist appointed within the framework of its activities, where that person had no special responsibilities.[134]

6.4. The acts of the employer

On the other hand, under US law, because of a presumption of immunity for foreign State entities,[135] the mere fact that the employer happens to be an entity rather than the foreign State is not enough, for an 'agency or instrumentality' of a foreign State enjoys the same immunity as does its national State. Also, even the fact that the entity in question is a commercial institution may not be sufficient, for US law also requires the claim to be based upon a 'commercial activity' of the foreign State before immunity can be denied. Thus, in *Zveiter*, even though the employment of a secretary by a foreign State entity was a commercial activity, the court denied immunity only when it was also satisfied that the plaintiff's allegations of sexual harassment concerned the terms and conditions of her employment and raised questions concerning her discharge and were therefore 'based upon' her employment.[136] In *Janini*, former employees of Kuwait University brought an action for damages for the termination of their employment contracts by the university. The court held that the applicability of immunity depended upon the characterization of the action upon which the claim was based. In the present matter, the action was based upon the unilateral termination of the contracts of employment, about which there could be nothing peculiarly sovereign.[137]

In *Hansen*, a Danish citizen employed by the Danish Tourist Board in New York sued the Board for age and sex discrimination. In particular, the plaintiff alleged that after she rejected the sexual advances of her supervisor, her salary increases were not as large as those of similarly situated employees, her workload was increased, her responsibilities were changed, she had been passed over for promotion in favour of a younger, less qualified and less experienced person for the position, and

172 CONTRACTS OF EMPLOYMENT

that her supervisor had forced her to travel extensively, falsely accused her of refusing to perform work, and ridiculed her for wishing to spend time with her ailing husband. The plaintiff contended that such conduct constituted harassment in retaliation for her confronting her supervisor about his allegedly unlawful conduct, was directed at her because of her age and gender, and continued until she was dismissed. The court found that the actions that formed the basis of Hansen's complaint did not reflect the exercise of sovereign power; rather, the Tourist Board's activities, as alleged by the plaintiff, were basic employment decisions akin to those made by many small businesses. As such, they reflected an exercise of powers that could also be exercised by private citizens and qualified as commercial activity under the FSIA. Therefore the Board could not claim immunity.[138]

6.5. The status of the employee

The status of the employee was taken as a standard for classifying the employment relationship in two Italian cases concerning employment of civilian staff by NATO forces, where the Court of Cassation denied immunity by relying on the 1951 NATO Status of Forces Agreement, which divided civilian personnel employed by an armed force into two distinct categories: (1) the 'civilian component' (Article I(1)(b)), who were normally subject to the jurisdiction of the sending State or 'State of origin'; and (2) locally employed civilian workers, who were the subjects of a local private law relationship and consequently subject to Italian jurisdiction (Article IX(4)). Immunity was denied because the plaintiff did not form part of the 'civilian component'.[139]

In so deciding the Italian Court of Cassation seems to have tacitly overruled earlier Italian practice of erring on the side of immunity where US military bases were concerned. In *Savellini*, the Italian Court of Cassation rejected a claim for unpaid wages by a 'civilian employee' of the US military base at Livorno, Italy, on the ground that the activity of the US base fell within the framework of the North Atlantic Treaty, which served the sovereign purpose of mutual assistance in the event of aggression.[140]

In *Piha*, a case brought by an Italian national employed first as a warehouse keeper and then as a 'contract specialist' by NATO, a Belgian labour court drew a similar distinction between the 'civilian component', non-Belgian personnel in the employ of a NATO member State; and 'civilian workers', recruited locally, without consideration of nationality. The 'civilian component' enjoyed a privileged status and immunity from jurisdiction so long as they were in the employ of the sending State. The employment of such individuals could not be governed by Belgian law. By contrast, Piha was 'a worker under a private law contract ... In this case his employer is subject to Belgian social security legislation and ... his right to a pension has been governed ... by the Belgian Law on the pensions of salaried employees.'[141]

6.6. The nature of the particular activity

This happens where the foreign State engages someone for a particular task. In *Tsakos*, a Swiss court took the view that, as the plaintiff was engaged by the US Permanent Mission to the UN in Geneva specifically for the purpose of organizing an exhibition and his duties were clearly specified, the US Government had not acted in its capacity as a public power but rather as a private person, and could not claim immunity.[142]

6.7. The territorial connection

Many courts refer to a territorial connection between the contract of employment and the forum State as a ground for asserting jurisdiction. Swiss courts are the foremost and the strictest in adhering to this requirement, normally referred as *Binnenbeziehung* (internal/domestic relationship/connection). According to the Swiss Federal Tribunal, it is not enough that the employment relationship has already been characterized as private or commercial, since:

this circumstance alone is insufficient to justify Switzerland exercising jurisdiction over the dispute. It is not every relationship under private law entered into by a foreign State which gives rise to jurisdiction in Switzerland. It is also necessary to establish that the relationship in question has certain links with Swiss territory [*Encore faut-il que le rapport de droit en cause ait certains liens avec le territoire suisse ('Binnenbeziehung')*], that is to say that it arose there, must be performed there, or at least that the debtor performed certain acts such as to make it a place of performance of the contract.[143]

For this reason, Swiss judicial practice regards contracts of employment concluded in Switzerland between a sending State and locally recruited staff, especially those who are not nationals of the sending State and who perform a subordinate function with no diplomatic status, as contracts concluded *jure gestionis*, in the same category as a commercial contract.[144]

Similarly, the Dutch courts have consistently held that, where the contract of employment was concluded in the Netherlands, and the

174   CONTRACTS OF EMPLOYMENT

agreed work was to be performed in the Netherlands, the employment relationship should in principle be governed by Dutch law, even if the plaintiff might not be a Dutch national and even if the plaintiff is a national of the employer State.[145] The Spanish Supreme Court held that the Spanish law conferred jurisdiction on Spanish courts over matters of rights and obligations derived from contracts of employment where the contract provided for performance of services in Spain, or where the contract was concluded on Spanish territory.[146] The Austrian Supreme Court likewise held that, where a foreign State acted as the holder of private rights and concluded a contract of employment for work to be performed in the territory of the State of the forum, that foreign State could also be subjected to proceedings concerning the employment relationship. What must be examined is not the purpose of the work but the nature of the employment obligations.[147] A French court expressed the opinion that, in concluding an employment contract on French soil, with a French employee hired to perform activities in a research laboratory having no connection with political, diplomatic or public functions, the defendant State had behaved as an employer entering into a contract governed by private law.[148] A Belgian court specifically stated that: 'The nationality of the employee has no bearing on the laws applicable to contracts of employment executed in Belgium.'[149]

6.8. The choice of law clause

A court will assume jurisdiction by virtue of a choice of law clause in the contract, which either designates the forum court or provides the application of the law of the forum.

Thus, the Italian Court of Cassation found that the Italian courts had jurisdiction in a case where the contract of employment declared that the parties 'willingly and clearly accepted the jurisdiction of the Italian courts over any claim arising in relation to the interpretation of all the different aspects of the contract', that they 'agreed on the point that the labour laws in force in Italy were to have effect, if applicable', and that 'the procedures laid down in the provisions of Italian legal and judicial orders would be complied with'. Moreover, the plaintiff was covered by the Italian social security provisions.[150] The Spanish Supreme Court held that the Spanish courts had jurisdiction in a case where the employment was covered by Spanish social security provisions and subjected to applicable Spanish labour laws.[151] A Belgian court assumed jurisdiction in a case where, in terminating the contract, the defendant State had allocated an indemnity in lieu of notice, making express reference to Belgian law.[152] A Swiss labour court also found the payment of social security contributions and the affiliation of the employee to a professional provident fund to be 'additional indications in favour of the existence of an employment relationship concluded and performed *jure gestionis*'.[153] A US court held that a clause in an employment contract to the effect that '[a]ll disputes under this Agreement and in the interpretation or validity of any provision, shall be governed by the laws of the Commonwealth of Virginia', constituted an implicit waiver of immunity.[154]

Interestingly, the absence of a choice of law clause has also been relied upon as a basis for jurisdiction. In *MHC*, a Dutch court held that Dutch law – i.e. the law of the country where the plaintiff performed her work – was applicable since there was no evidence of any other choice of law.[155] In *MK*, the same court, having found that the parties had not made any choice regarding the system of law applicable to the agreement, nevertheless founded its jurisdiction on the following facts: that the work was performed by an employee of Dutch nationality in the Netherlands; that the plaintiff received her salary in Dutch currency and that the defendant paid the contributions owing under the Dutch social security legislation. Accordingly, the court said, this was clearly a case in which the interests of the Dutch labour market were very closely involved and the links with Dutch law were therefore sufficient to make Dutch law applicable.[156] The same connecting factors were also accepted in another Dutch case as calling for the application of Dutch law in the absence of a clear and unambiguous choice of law clause, even though the employment contract expressly provided that the local laws did not apply.[157] In *Seidenschmidt*, the Austrian Supreme Court found that the employment relationship in question and its termination were governed by Austrian law because the parties had not made any specific choice of the applicable law.[158] A Swiss court even took the position that a contract of employment internal to Switzerland was governed, in an obligatory manner, by Swiss employment law and the parties were not free to derogate from that rule by the choice of the law of a third State.[159]

6.9. *The remedies sought*

In some cases the remedies sought are also stressed so as to bring the case under the jurisdiction of the forum court, if those remedies do not affect the sovereign or public functions of the defendant State. Thus, in a series of cases, the Italian Court of Cassation established that, in the case of contracts of employment, the jurisdiction of the Italian courts applies not only where the employment is merely auxiliary to the institutional or public functions of the defendant State or entity, but also to those cases where the employee performs duties closely bound up with public functions but the claim and the related judgment which upholds it concern *purely financial aspects* of the employment relationship[160] because such a claim, being of a *purely financial nature*, is not liable to affect or interfere with those institutional or public functions.[161]

In *Manauta*, decided by the Argentine Supreme Court, the plaintiffs, who had been employed by the Press Office of the Embassy of the Soviet Union in Argentina, claimed damages, from the Russian Federation as the successor, for non-payment of social security contributions, union contributions and family allowances, which their employer should have paid on their behalf. The Court held that what was at issue was not a governmental act since the dispute submitted to the Court related to the performance of obligations concerning employment and welfare contributions, so that the normal activity of a diplomatic representation was in no way involved.[162]

Although courts themselves may not have explicitly stated or even been aware, the denial of immunity in respect of the *financial aspects* of the employment relationship implies that an employment relationship may simultaneously have both sovereign and financial, i.e. private, aspects. It then becomes the court's role to ensure that immunity is unavailable only if the proceedings touch exclusively on the private aspects. This confirms the multi-faceted nature of an employment relationship with a foreign State and further exposes the simplicity – and impracticality and inadequacy – of a mere 'private person' test while underscoring the necessity of a more contextual approach that takes into consideration all the relevant circumstances of the case. By extension, a more rounded, contextual view of any relationship between an individual and a foreign State will be necessary for handling immunity cases; for, in the nature of things, it would be inconceivable if the jurisprudence of any court regularly applies a sovereign/financial dichotomy in a case involving a contract of employment without that analysis being recognized as useful, demanded and utilized in other types of cases as well. Thus, a finding that the employment relationship at issue has both sovereign and financial or commercial aspects may precisely stem from a general conception that any particular relationship between a foreign State and an individual may have both aspects to it, and that immunity may only be denied when the proceedings relate to the commercial aspects. This is what the Canadian Supreme Court established in the case of *Canada Labour Code*, where the Court held that the 'activity' at the Argentia US Naval Base, Newfoundland, had a 'double aspect' in that it was 'at once sovereign and commercial'. Because the proceedings for the representation of certain employees on that base related to the management and operation of the base itself, they touched on the sovereign aspect of the activity, for which the US must enjoy immunity.[163] The reasoning was followed in *Lovell*, where a former marketing officer of the New Zealand Tourism Board challenged the severance package offered him upon his being made redundant. The court found that the plaintiff's employment with the Board had both commercial and sovereign aspects. However, because the proceedings only related to the commercial aspects, namely the alleged failure of the defendant to pay the plaintiff a redundancy severance package in accordance with the terms of the employment contract, immunity was not available.[164] Sure enough, the 'double aspects' analysis appeared in other cases which may or may not concern employment relations.[165]

In *Air Zaire*, two former Air Zaire pilots, in claiming for compensation following their allegedly wrongful dismissal, applied successfully for orders allowing them to obtain the attachment of Air Zaire's aircraft landing at Roissy airport in France. Air Zaire argued that it was entitled to immunity from the proceedings as a State public service since the property at issue was in use for that service. The court rejected the plea of immunity and confirmed the attachment orders with regard to one pilot (the other pilot having been adequately compensated by the company).[166]

While some courts tend to be unfavourable to remedies such as reinstatement,[167] others would not hesitate to grant them.[168] In a case heard by a Dutch court, termination of the contract of employment together with compensation of five months' salary was ordered.[169] In *MK*, the same court declared the disputed dismissal void because the defendant had dismissed the plaintiff without the consent of the Director of the competent Regional Employment Office, without the consent of the plaintiff and without any urgent reason.[170]

Sometimes, whether reinstatement can be ordered seems to depend on how one views the context of the employment relationship. In *BV*, for example, an employee at the Italian Cultural Institute in Amsterdam, which was dependent on the Italian Embassy in The Hague, claimed that the termination of her contract was null and void because the contract had been terminated without the consent of the director of the Regional Employment Office as required by Dutch law. The District Court of Amsterdam, after finding that the act occasioning the proceedings was not a typical governmental act but a contract of employment under Dutch civil law, held that, since the prior consent of the director of the Local Employment Office was not required for the termination of the employment of foreign embassy and consulate staff, the contract of employment in this case was lawfully terminated. Therefore, the claim for reinstatement was rejected.[171] The plaintiff subsequently disputed the validity of the termination before the Sub-District Court and applied to be reinstated. The Sub-District Court held the termination to be null and void and ordered reinstatement.[172] Upon appeal by Italy, the District Court held that the relevant labour law provisions did not apply to the present employment relationship and that the contract of employment between the parties was validly terminated.[173]

In *François*, the plaintiff, who had been employed as a technician at the Cultural and Information Centre of the Canadian Embassy in Brussels, claimed, following his dismissal, that the indemnity offered to him in lieu of notice was inadequate. The Labour Court of Brussels, after determining the employment contract as a private act, went on to say that, taking account of the seniority of the claimant, his function as a technician, his annual salary and his age, the period of notice given to him should have been ten months. Since an indemnity of only nine months was paid, an additional indemnity of one month was due.[174] In *Morocco v. DR*, where a chauffeur of the Embassy of Morocco brought proceedings claiming compensation for unjustifiable/wrongful dismissal, the same court held that, in accordance with Belgian labour law, an employer was liable to pay special compensation if he could not prove that he had dismissed his employee for reasons inherent in his aptitude for the job, or his conduct, or service requirements. Since the defendant State had failed to justify the dismissal, special compensation was payable.[175] The Swiss courts, while refusing to examine the sending State's reasons for dismissal, assert local jurisdiction over the *financial consequences of a summary dismissal*. The refusal by the employer State to communicate justifiable reasons for dismissal would mean that the State should be ordered to pay salary in lieu of notice, or the amount of salary due for the remaining period of a fixed-term contract.[176] Equally, the courts of the forum have jurisdiction over any financial claim which does not require an intrusion into the internal life of a diplomatic or consular mission or an examination of its staff policy.[177] This seems to restrict a claim of dismissal to what is *contractually* due to the employee (such as arrears of salary, overtime and holiday pay, etc.) to the exclusion of statutory compensation schemes that would be available under the labour laws of many countries.[178]

The UK and Australian courts will not grant reinstatement if the employer is a foreign State. While the UK SIA provides that 'relief shall not be given against a State by way of injunction or order for specific performance' (section 13(2)(a)),[179] the Australia FSIA expressly stipulates that 'a court may not make an order that a foreign state employ a person or re-instate a person in employment' (section 29(2)). As laid down in the 1991 ILC Draft (Article 11(2)(b)), the 2004 UN Convention provides that the employer State shall enjoy immunity if 'the subject-matter of the proceeding is the recruitment, renewal of employment or reinstatement of an individual' (now Article 11(2)(c)).

7. The savings regime

In current State practice there is a savings regime, which excludes certain institutions of foreign States from the sphere of local jurisdiction with regard to contracts of employment. Diplomatic and consular missions and foreign armed forces are prime examples. However, these institutions are not monolithically sovereign in all circumstances. First, according to long-established international practice, diplomatic and consular personnel have been graded and accorded different treatment, including privileges and immunities, by reference to their ranks, functions, and closeness to the core of State authority. Secondly, foreign armed forces stationed in the receiving State often employ local workers to perform supporting duties. These workers might be covered by local labour laws and social security systems. Criteria are therefore needed for distinguishing among a variety of foreign State employees, ranging from diplomatic and consular representatives to manual labourers. As a general rule, those with senior ranks, closely linked to essential administration, involved in the decision-making process or privy to certain restricted information are treated as integrated into the overall public apparatus of the foreign State. Their employment is thus outside the scope of local jurisdiction.

7.1. *Diplomatic and consular missions*

All the current legal instruments on State immunity contain savings clauses to the effect that provisions on State immunity shall not affect

180 CONTRACTS OF EMPLOYMENT

the privileges and immunities under the two Vienna Conventions on diplomatic and consular relations.[180] However, in affirming the two Vienna Conventions, these provisions focus on the personal immunities and privileges of diplomatic and consular staff but do not relate these immunities and privileges to the issue of employment contracts,[181] nor do they envisage the situation of diplomatic or consular personnel or similar persons suing the employer State.

As aforementioned, there is no specific provision in the US FSIA on contracts of employment. Such cases therefore have to be brought under the commercial activity exception to State immunity (section 1605(a)(2)). However, the legislative report does state that 'the employment of diplomatic, civil service, or military personnel' would be 'public or governmental and not commercial in nature'.[182] The Canadian SIA likewise contains no specific provision on contracts of employment but gives even less guidance.

The UK SIA, on the other hand, clarifies in section 16(1)(a) that section 4 (on contracts of employment) 'does not apply to proceedings concerning the employment of the members of a mission ... or of the members of a consular post' within the meaning of the two Vienna Conventions.[183] The Australia FSIA goes a step further and attempts to solve this problem by a two-pronged approach. Besides affirming the two Vienna Conventions (section 6), it makes detailed provisions on State immunity with respect to different categories of diplomatic and consular employees. In accordance with section 12(5) and (6), the foreign State shall enjoy immunity in relation to the employment of (1) a member of the diplomatic staff of a mission or a consular officer and (2) a member of the administrative and technical staff of a mission or a consular employee, unless the member or employee was, at the time when the contract of employment was made, a permanent resident of Australia. To date the Australia FSIA is the only national statute that specifically addresses the relationship between diplomatic and consular immunity and State immunity in respect of employment contracts.

The ILA Draft imitates this approach. While affirming the diplomatic and consular immunities (Article IX), the draft contains a proviso to the effect that the foreign State shall enjoy immunity 'in respect of employees appointed under the public (administrative) law of the foreign State' (Article III of the 1982 Draft). This was later clarified as: 'The employee was appointed under the public (administrative) law of the foreign State, such as, inter alia, members of the mission, diplomatic, consular or military staff' (Article III(C)(4) of the 1994 Draft).

As proposed by the ILC,[184] the 2004 UN Convention now provides that immunity shall remain intact where the employee is 'a diplomatic agent', 'a consular officer', 'a member of the diplomatic staff of a permanent mission to an international organization or of a special mission, or is recruited to represent a State at an international conference', or 'any other person enjoying diplomatic immunity' (Article 11(2)(b)). According to the understanding in the Annex to the Convention, 'the receiving State has a duty to exercise its jurisdiction in such a manner as not to interfere unduly with the performance of the functions of the mission or the consular post'.

7.1.1. Proceedings against the foreign State

Many courts display great caution in respect of matters of embassy/consular employment. The UK courts and tribunals have maintained an absolute immunity in cases concerning employment at a diplomatic mission. In *Sengupta*, the tribunal rejected the claim for unfair dismissal by an Indian national who had been employed at the Indian High Commission in London as a low-level clerk, with duties like receiving and circulating newspapers, and selecting and making press cuttings, and without access to any confidential information, and who was not a member either of the Indian Foreign Service or of the Indian Civil Service, and enjoyed no diplomatic privileges. The tribunal held that employment, at however lowly a level, in a diplomatic mission necessarily involved the employee in the public acts of the foreign State and the dismissal of such an employee was an act done in pursuance of the public function of running that mission.[185] Thus there can be no jurisdiction over claims of unfair dismissal 'by those engaged in carrying out the work of the mission in however humble a role' since admitting such a claim 'would or might involve an investigation into the public acts of the foreign state'.[186] Although the case was decided at common law since the employment relationship had been entered into before the coming into force of the UK SIA, the tribunal nonetheless examined section 16(1)(a) of the UK SIA and found that it 'operates to exclude jurisdiction over claims relating to the employment not only of diplomatic staff but also of lower grade administrative, technical and domestic staff irrespective of their nationality'.[187]

The application of section 16(1)(a) resulted in immunity being upheld in cases brought by a British national employed as an administrative assistant in the consular section of the US Embassy in London,[188] by a British national employed as a bilingual secretary in the Defence Office of the Embassy of Saudi Arabia in London,[189] by two Egyptian nationals employed as drivers at the medical office of the Egyptian Embassy in London,[190] by a British national employed as a senior accounts clerk at the Bahamas High Commission in London,[191] by a Chief Accountant and a medical interpreter of the Medical Office of the Embassy of the United Arab Emirates in London,[192] and by a shipping clerk at the Kuwaiti Embassy in London.[193] In all these cases the plaintiffs were considered 'members of the mission', and the fact that the plaintiffs did not enjoy diplomatic immunities or privileges was specifically held to be irrelevant.[194]

Following the same line, the Irish Supreme Court held immune the employment of a chauffeur of the ambassador's car at the Canadian Embassy in Dublin, on the ground that the element of trust and confidentiality placed in the driver of an embassy car created a bond with his employers that had the effect of involving him in the employing government's public business organization and interests. The Court thus reversed the lower court's decision that driving of an embassy car was an act of a commercial nature.[195] In a Dutch case, even though the work of the plaintiff, who had been employed in the administrative service of a Belgian consulate-general, consisted of typing and filing, she was held to have been employed to render services to a public body by the defendant State acting in a public capacity.[196] In a similar vein, the Finnish Supreme Court held that a contract of employment concluded between the embassy of a foreign State and one of its employees, even where that employee was a national of the forum State and the contract was of a private law nature, remained immune from the jurisdiction of the courts of the host State.[197]

Some courts even consider employment *in connection with* an embassy as protected by immunity. The South African Supreme Court held that the employment of quantity surveyors by the duly appointed representatives of a foreign government in South Africa in relation to the erection of an embassy was an act *jure imperii*.[198] A US court held that employment related to the making of some documentary films for the Information Centre of a German consulate-general was a public act.[199]

It is also common for courts to rely on the duties and functions of the employee and the principle of *ne impediatur legatio* (the functions of a mission shall not be impeded) in granting immunity (especially when courts are called upon to examine the circumstances surrounding the dismissal of an embassy employee). Swiss courts would not examine the *reasons* which led the sending State to terminate its relationship with a locally recruited employee of its diplomatic mission and neither would they summons the employer State to justify such termination. The decision to terminate such an employment relationship is regarded as a sovereign activity (*acte de gouvernement*) and is therefore not subject to the jurisdiction of the courts of the receiving State, in accordance with the rule *ne impediatur legatio*.[200]

In an earlier German case, a German citizen had been employed at the UK Consulate at Hanover, Germany, for such activities as receiving visitors, general secretarial duties, visiting British subjects and acting as interpreter. In the court's opinion, the performance of consular duties was an activity of a sovereign nature, and the legal relationship between the State and its employees in the consulate was one of public law, even where German citizens were employed.[201] By the same token, in *X v. Argentina*, the court stated that, where an employment relationship with a foreign State involved the performance of consular functions, including the issue and extension of passports and the processing of visas, even though the employee had a subordinate role in the performance of those functions, the employment belonged to the 'core sphere of sovereign activity' of the State concerned and was exempt from German jurisdiction so far as the legal relationship in dispute and its termination were concerned. Any examination of the dismissal of such an employee would conflict with the principle that diplomatic or consular relations should not be impeded (*ne impediatur legatio*).[202] The same decision can also be found in a case brought by a caretaker at a French consulate in Germany challenging his dismissal on the ground that the consent of the local Welfare Office, which was required under German law because he was disabled, had not been obtained,[203] and in one brought by a German national employed as a financial assistant responsible for financial analysis and budgetary preparation at the US Consulate General in Frankfurt, after his employment had been terminated for reasons of 'organisational restructuring' and he had been offered new employment at a lower grade. In this latter case, the court held that the preparation and drafting of budget plans for the financing of the work of a consulate fell within the 'core area of consular activity' and that the manner in which a foreign State provided for the fulfilment of consular tasks from an organizational standpoint was a matter for sovereign decision. Any examination into the plausibility of business reorganization of a consulate would therefore necessarily involve the danger that the labour courts would exercise review powers with regard to the internal administration and organizational structure of the consulate and would

184   CONTRACTS OF EMPLOYMENT

adversely affect the guarantee under international law of the unimpeded fulfilment of the tasks of the consulate.[204]

It is noteworthy that, in these cases, the German courts indicated in one way or another that, had the employer not been a foreign State acting in its public capacity or carrying out sovereign activities, the employment would have been regarded as a private law activity and so rightly amenable to German jurisdiction; and conversely, if the core area of State authority was affected, the private law character of the relationship took on secondary importance.[205] In other words, because the relevant institutions/agencies are pursuing sovereign objectives or because the relevant acts serve sovereign aims, the court of the forum cannot exercise jurisdiction. This is nothing but a 'purpose' test in disguise, the same test observed in cases involving foreign armed forces, where it has been applied to the fullest extent by the English courts.

A related ground for immunity is that the employment relationship has been terminated for purported 'security reasons'. In *Seidenschmidt*, in which an Austrian citizen had been dismissed as an official at the US Information Service within the US Embassy in Vienna on unspecified security grounds, the Austrian Supreme Court denied immunity on the ground that there was no principle in international law whereby a State was entitled to terminate an employment relationship, concluded under private law, on the grounds of security by recourse to an act of sovereignty; however, the court nonetheless stated that the question as to which security requirements the US should have relied upon for dismissal was not to be examined by an Austrian court, as each State retained the right to determine for itself the standard of security for its diplomatic representatives abroad, and to impose corresponding obligations in the service contracts of the personnel which it employed.[206] In an English case the plaintiff's claim failed because she had been employed as a machine operator in the Communications Section of the Australian High Commission in London and later dismissed because, for security reasons, jobs in the Communications Section should be held only by Australian citizens.[207] Likewise, the Dutch Supreme Court also refused to investigate the termination of the employment of a secretary in the Foreign Commercial Service Department of the US Embassy in The Hague for security reasons.[208] An embassy could not be obliged to be completely open about the modernized computer network which led to the dismissal of its former computer management assistant.[209] In this respect, it must be observed that the 2004 UN Convention provides that immunity shall remain intact where 'the subject-matter of the proceeding is the dismissal or termination of employment of an individual and ... such a proceeding would interfere with the security interests of that State' (Article 11(2)(d)).[210]

7.1.2. 'Institutional aims'

The Italian courts have consistently maintained a criterion of 'institutional aims' of the foreign State. In *Scarfò*, where a medical doctor employed by the Sovereign Order of Malta sued the Order for breach of contract of employment, the Tribunal dismissed the claim on the ground that the courts could not interfere in relations which directly served 'constitutional objects'.[211] This reasoning was soon fully embraced by the Court of Cassation, which further delineated it in subsequent cases. Thus the employment of an assistant librarian in the US Information Office was a public law relationship because the activities of the Office abroad were directed towards the attainment of certain sovereign public aims.[212] In *Piccoli*, the Court held that the employment of an administrative secretary at a hospital operated by the Order of Malta was a sovereign activity, because it fulfilled 'an institutional aim' and constituted a means necessary for the exercise of 'institutional functions'.[213]

In *Luna*, the Court of Cassation held that the plaintiff, who had worked for eighteen years as a secretary, telephone operator, accountant and administrator at the Romanian Commercial Agency in Italy, which was an integral part of the Romanian Embassy, had been firmly established with the organization concerned. The employment relationship then fell within the framework of activities of a public nature of a foreign State which were correlated to the *institutional (i.e. public) ends* of the State itself, in this case to the promotion and control of commercial activities in which the State in question had a collective interest. Moreover, it was irrelevant, on the question of jurisdiction, that the relationship had also been governed by provisions of private employment in force in Italy.[214] A secretary working for the cultural representative of the Danish Institute was employed 'for the attainment of the institutional aims which the Danish State pursues through its activity in Italy', and under a contract which provided for the inclusion of the plaintiff in the organization of the Institute which allowed her also to manage the Institute's affairs for a considerable period of time.[215] The contract of employment of an 'assistant' at the Brazilian Embassy in Italy was held to have involved the running of the embassy offices 'in furtherance of *institutional aims* of a public nature', the employment being of a permanent

186   CONTRACTS OF EMPLOYMENT

nature (over fifteen years) within the administration of the embassy.[216] The job of a warehouse worker amounted to 'an essential and indispensable instrument for the very performance of the public function'.[217] The duties performed by a marketing officer at the British Consulate in Venice, who had been in charge of promoting the sale of British goods in Italy and who had been responsible to the British Embassy and ultimately to the Foreign Office, were held to be correlated with the *institutional aims* of the Foreign Office, with the result that he had participated in the public activity of the foreign State which had employed him. As a commercial officer he had furthered the public interest of the British Government in encouraging British exports rather than the private interests of British firms in exporting their products, which could be served by local commercial agents appointed by the firms themselves.[218]

In *Rubin*, a typist and translator of the Consul General of Panama in Venice, who had been responsible for drafting, typing and translating letters and drawing up ships' licences and other documents, had her claim rejected because, in the opinion of the court:

it is clear that, in the first place, the claimant was inserted into the organizational structure of the consular office and that her work was used to further the very ends for which the office was set up. Secondly, it is clear that the tasks which were entrusted to the claimant involved a certain measure of responsibility.[219]

In *Panattoni*, a chancery usher at the Embassy of Germany to the Holy See claimed that his pension entitlement was lower than it should have been, because his employers had failed to pay national insurance contributions. The court held that he had been a permanent employee with a stable position within the organization of the embassy, and had taken part in functions through which that State pursued its *public purposes*. The Court of Cassation stated, in particular, that:

clerical employment relationships which involve a stable position within the structure of a diplomatic mission constitute part of the activities which a foreign State performs, represented by its embassy, in order to carry out its public functions ... [I]mmunity is only excluded in relation to claims concerning the performance of those manual or temporary duties which are extraneous to the organization of an embassy.[220]

In *Jacuzio*, an Italian elementary school teacher at the Lycée Chateaubriand in Rome sued for reinstatement following her dismissal. The Court rejected her claim, finding that the activity of the Lycée was 'directly connected with the French State', since the Lycée, despite its receiving fee-paying pupils, was administratively controlled by the French Ministry of Foreign Affairs and financially controlled by the French Treasury, such control being exercised locally by the French Embassy in Rome. For this reason, 'the Lycée Chateaubriand clearly exercises functions of a public character and is an expression of the sovereign power of the French State in Italy'.[221]

Now if a school directly funded by a foreign State and managed by the embassy is beyond the reach of the local courts in employment matters, it is difficult to imagine anything, however remotely connected with an embassy, over which a local judge can exercise jurisdiction. This rigid position was somewhat relaxed, albeit momentarily in the light of the Court's subsequent jurisprudence, in *Toglia*, where an Italian national employed by the British Consulate General in Naples brought an action, upon her retirement, claiming arrears of salary and additional national insurance contributions allegedly payable under Italian law because she should have had a higher grade. The Court of Cassation, while stressing 'the necessity to proceed cautiously where there is a possibility of interference from local judicial authorities' as such interference 'impinges upon the essential core of consular activity *stricto sensu*', made the following qualified finding:

Consular immunity was therefore recognized only in respect of disputes involving the Consul or those employees who, by reason of their specific tasks, appeared to be properly inserted into the organizational structure of the consular office, and whose work served to further the aims for which the office had been established, involving collaboration in the performance of consular functions.[222]

The court then proposed two criteria whereby immunity could be excluded. First, employment disputes concerning employees who perform merely auxiliary duties, not concerned with consular functions *stricto sensu*, should be allowed to proceed; secondly and more importantly, where there is unlikely to be interference with the performance of consular functions, then immunity ought to be excluded, even though the employee might carry out high-level tasks and directly collaborate in the performance of consular functions *stricto sensu*. In the light of this criterion:

Immunity should be excluded whenever a claim, and the related judgment which upholds it, concern purely financial aspects of the employment relationship which gave rise to the dispute brought before the Italian courts.[223]

188 CONTRACTS OF EMPLOYMENT

In this case the plaintiff, who had retired from the British Consulate General in Naples, was already outside the organization of the Consulate General when she lodged her claim. Besides, she did not request reinstatement in her post but instead claimed only a higher grade and payment of arrears, on the basis of the duties which she used to perform while in the employment of the Consulate. Therefore Italian courts were competent to exercise jurisdiction over the claim.[224]

The Court of Cassation apparently changed its mind a year later in *Trobbiani*, where the plaintiff had been employed by the Libyan diplomatic mission, or People's Office, working for the Jana Information Agency as a secretary and telephonist. She brought exactly the same claim as did the *Togila* plaintiff, i.e. for arrears of salary allegedly payable under Italian law because she had been wrongly graded. This time the Court was unwilling to affirm the jurisdiction of the Italian courts. It started by observing that the activities of the Jana Agency were 'directly referable to [the Libyan] State', which, like other States, attaches much importance to information policy and 'may well insist on exercising absolute control over the means [for] projecting their image abroad'. It went on to find that the duties of the plaintiff as a secretary and telephonist:

clearly denote a position of trust within the organization, inasmuch as they are directly bound up with the work of its officials and also inevitably involve access in practice to information concerning the agency's official activities and business. It may accordingly be concluded that there was an objective internal link, both immediate and direct, between the employment relationship and the institutional aims of the Jana Agency, and hence that the applicant was fully integrated into the public-law organizational structure of the foreign State, which conducted its information policy through that Agency.[225]

More significant, the Court in this case redefined what constituted a 'purely financial aspect of the employment relationship':

where it is impossible to evaluate the financial consequences of a matter ... without at the same time adjudicating ... upon the relationship out of which the claim is alleged to arise, then in effect the relationship itself becomes the subject of the court's enquiry. The court examines what the relationship actually involves and should involve and passes judgment on both aspects. In such circumstances the subject-matter of the dispute passes out of the realm of the merely financial.[226]

On the other hand, a purely 'pecuniary'/'financial' case would be 'where the claim is for payment of sums due in respect of remuneration whose amounts are not in dispute, or for additional amounts on account of late payment of sums whose exact amounts are known'.[227]

Such an incredibly fine line was reaffirmed and adopted in *Quattri*, where a former secretary and technical-administrative officer of the Commercial Office of the Royal Norwegian Embassy had been dismissed without notice for unspecified 'organizational reasons' and was now claiming reinstatement, damages and various allowances payable under Italian law. The Court of Cassation held that Italian courts lacked jurisdiction over the claims for reinstatement and damages but they were competent to exercise jurisdiction over the claim for unpaid allowances. The Court reached its decision irrespective of the fact that the contract of employment expressly referred to the laws and regulations currently in force in Italy, particularly as regards the notice period, pregnancy and maternity. According to the Court, a foreign State was immune from the jurisdiction of other States in respect of employment relationships created 'for *purposes* of the achievement of its *institutional aims*', and no intervention should be allowed which touched on 'the essential core of [the foreign] State's activities and functions'.[228]

Following its *Trobbiani* decision, the Court said:

Clearly, even where the content of a claim is purely financial, the source of the disputed obligation is always the employment relationship between the foreign State and its employee ... This Court accordingly takes the view that it is important to avoid a situation where (with the exception of cases where the employee's duties are of a merely auxiliary character) every claim, even those of a purely financial character, ends up falling outside the jurisdiction of the Italian courts, to an extent going beyond the reasonable limits imposed by the need to respect the essential core of the foreign State's functions.

... any enquiry into the lawfulness of the dismissal constitutes a direct interference with the public-law powers of the foreign State with regard to the manner in which it organises its ambassadorial offices and services, which are matters not susceptible of examination by the Italian courts. This lack of jurisdiction (i.e. as to the lawfulness of the dismissal) accordingly extends to those claims those acceptance would imply a declaration that the dismissal was invalid, namely the claims for reinstatement, consequential loss, and payment of salary from the date of dismissal until reinstatement.[229]

In the same vein, the Court rejected claims for reinstatement and damages brought by a former clerk, telephone operator and receptionist at the US Consulate in Palermo, Italy, on the ground that the duties of a telephone operator, who was seen as 'inserted into the organization' of the consulate, fell within those tasks which were based on trust and belonged to the public organization of the office itself, and that any examination of the reasons for, or lawfulness of, the dismissal would directly interfere with the exercise of the sovereign powers of a foreign State in relation to the organization of its representative offices.[230]

This tripartite criterion, comprising (1) the insertion/integration of the employee into the organizational structure of the diplomatic or consular mission,[231] (2) institutional aims of the foreign State, and (3) non-interference in the organization of the foreign State and its performance of public functions, was definitively enunciated in its entirety by the Italian Court of Cassation in *Cargello*. In that case, an Italian citizen formerly employed as a commercial officer by the General Consulate of Canada in Milan instituted proceedings for a declaration that his dismissal was unlawful and for compensation in lieu of reinstatement. The Court held that the duties of a commercial officer, which fell completely within consular functions, entailed the plaintiff's integration into the institutional structure of the consulate with the result that he participated in the public functions of the foreign State. The immunity of a foreign State from the jurisdiction of another State is recognized in relationships established for the achievement of the foreign State's institutional aims and where the exercise of jurisdiction would interfere with the essential core of sovereign functions. Thus jurisdiction was certainly excluded where reinstatement in an employment position was sought. It was also consistent with the jurisprudence to exclude jurisdiction where, as here, a purely monetary claim for compensation would nonetheless require an investigation into the behaviour of the foreign State as employer and would thus directly interfere with the exercise of public-law powers related to the organization of the administration of the foreign State and the management of its employment relationships.[232]

There can be no doubt that the formulation 'institutional aims' is but another name for the 'purpose' test; and the Italian Court of Cassation further confirms this by expressly using the phrase 'public purposes(s)' in its judgments.[233] More than that, the Court of Cassation extends this purpose test to other public institutions of a foreign State as well, and would not shrink from stretching the job description of the employee to the point of amazing hyperbole, should it appear necessary to defend the perceived 'public purposes' of the institution in question. In *Pieciukiewicz*, a former announcer and translator of Vatican Radio instituted proceedings against the State of Vatican City for payment of salary arrears and insurance contributions. The Court of Cassation first declared that:

when a person is formally designated as an employee, because the job is permanent, and takes part in activities through which the foreign State pursues its *public purposes*, the only necessary and sufficient elements for removing that relationship from the jurisdiction of Italian courts are present ... The only decisive element is the worker's continuous participation in activities intended to achieve the State's *public purposes*.[234]

The Court then found that the plaintiff's job had provided services that helped to achieve the purposes of the Vatican City. While conceding that, 'in Italian Law translating is not in itself an activity which would confer a public nature to the job', since it 'consists in the mechanical repetition of things said or written by others in another language', the Court nonetheless found that the plaintiff, as an 'announcer in Russian', had performed a function that was directly and closely linked to the public activities of the Vatican City and the Church's 'mission in the world'. A radio announcer's job then assumed magical proportions:

Indeed one cannot consider the function of an announcer, whether or not this includes the translation and writing of texts read over the air, as a merely mechanical activity. Even in the case of the announcer only reading texts, voice inflexion, pauses and other technical details making the presentation of the programme effective all affect the persuasive force of the medium, especially in view of the aims of the broadcasts and the nature of the State making them. Thus the job obviously requires a culture of both a specific and general nature, a knowledge of psychology and broadcasting techniques, the need to make choices and adaptations, and cannot constitute a merely mechanical activity.[235]

Naturally, immunity must be upheld.

7.1.3. Proceedings against the diplomat personally

Ironically, however lowly their position and however menial their duties, home servants or other employees *personally* engaged by diplomats will not be able to sue owing to the immunities granted to diplomats *ratione personae*. Thus, a butler in the Australian Embassy in the Netherlands,[236] a security officer at the US Embassy in Paris[237] and a domestic servant in the home of the First Secretary and later Counsellor of the Jordanian Embassy in Washington[238] had their claims rejected because they had been employed not by the embassy but by the respective ambassadors personally. Under Article 31(1) of the 1961 Vienna Convention diplomats enjoy immunity from civil jurisdiction except where, among others, a commercial activity is involved;[239] the hiring of a domestic servant, etc. is, according to the courts, incidental to a diplomat's life and not a commercial activity. Of course a *former* diplomat can be sued for various claims lodged by a personally hired domestic servant, but then the State of the diplomat cannot be sued for the same claims, simply because the State is not the employer in such a case.[240]

Therefore locally recruited domestic servants for an embassy or a diplomat, and those in like position, might not be able to make use of the local judicial system for labour protection simply because they happened to have signed their employment contract with a nominally different employer. In this connection a home servant has a puzzle to solve when he attempts to sue a diplomat: was the contract concluded by the diplomat in a personal capacity or as a representative of the State? In other words, should the servant sue the foreign State[241] or the diplomat? These questions have not been satisfactorily answered but, in principle, those immunities are enjoyed by diplomatic agents only in their personal capacity. They cannot be extended to cover the State that those diplomatic agents represent. This can be seen in a case at the Italian Court of Cassation, which upheld a claim by an employee at the Brazilian Consulate against the Brazilian Ambassador, not personally but as representative of Brazil, for losses arising from the non-payment of social security contributions.[242] Similarly, a catering assistant and cleaner employed at the residence of the Israeli Ambassador in Lisbon successfully instituted proceedings for unlawful dismissal because, noted the court, 'these proceedings were brought against the State of Israel, and not against the ambassador in his personal capacity'.[243]

The fickleness of the law of State immunity seems to be everywhere. In *Park*, a former *personal* domestic servant sued the Deputy Consul General of the Korean Consulate in San Francisco, and his wife, alleging several employment-related claims, including the failure to pay the minimum wage or overtime pay. The plaintiff made clear that she was suing the Deputy Consul *personally*. The court found that, in hiring a personal family employee and paying her with family funds, the defendant was not acting exclusively or even primarily as an agent of Korea. He could not have acted within the scope of his official duties when he committed the acts alleged. Therefore, he could not qualify as a foreign State and could not enjoy immunity. Even if, the court added for good measure, he could be characterized as a foreign State, he still would not be entitled to immunity, because the act of hiring a domestic servant was not an inherently public act; to the contrary, private actors commonly employ domestic servants.[244]

7.2. Foreign armed forces

Some international instruments and national statutes contain specific provisions to the effect that the position of foreign armed forces shall remain unaffected.[245] As with diplomatic missions and consular posts, the compelling reason for granting immunity with respect to foreign military institutions is their inherent sovereign character.[246]

The status of visiting forces and foreign military establishments, such as military bases, is usually regulated by international agreements,[247] which must be taken into account when a court considers a case in this respect. Generally speaking, courts usually stay away from the internal administration of foreign military establishments,[248] and therefore will not seek to exercise jurisdiction over military personnel. However, the position with respect to civilian employees of a military establishment, particularly where they are nationals or residents of the forum, is unclear.[249]

In *Hicks*, the tribunal rejected the claim for unfair dismissal of an equipment repairer at a bowling alley because the bowling alley was located at a US air base in England and therefore partook of a military, that is, sovereign character. According to the Tribunal:

Of course any private individual can enter into a contract of employment. And there is nothing exceptional about a contract of employment to repair bowling alley equipment. But here, as the contract was between the United States Airforce and a US national, it was subject to the airforce regulations and other US labour laws. To this extent the position of the US Airforce is different from any private contractor.[250]

In *UNC*, Saudi Arabia awarded Lear a service contract under which Lear sent hundreds of personnel to Saudi Arabia to provide training and support services to the Royal Saudi Air Force (RSAF). These employees were integrated with RSAF personnel, and provided training and support in post-ejection survival, photo reconnaissance, flight operations, tactics and weapons to the RSAF. They worked directly for and under the control of the RSAF and were responsible for developing and coordinating emergency action procedures for the pilots of the F-5 aircraft. When Lear sued Saudi Arabia for breach of contract, the court found that the contract was not a commercial activity, and that those employees were integrated into the RSAF and could be considered military personnel.[251]

194   CONTRACTS OF EMPLOYMENT

7.3. Other public institutions

Apart from embassies and consulates, courts often grant immunity to other institutions established by foreign States with analogous functions. Not surprisingly, one often finds that courts apply similar tests to those evolved in the context of embassies and consulates and their dependent institutions, such as the duties and functions of the employee,[252] the status and functions of the employer office,[253] insertion/integration of the employee into the relevant organization,[254] 'institutional aims',[255] and non-interference in the internal organization of an institution.[256]

Article 11(2)(a) of the 2004 UN Convention provides that the employer State shall enjoy immunity if 'the employee has been recruited to perform particular functions in the exercise of governmental authority'.[257] This provision appears to be sufficiently broad to cover the employment in diplomatic and consular missions and military establishments, as well as in other public institutions.[258]

8. Diversity and lack of uniform rules

This odyssey through a voluminous yet chaotic body of case law that defies any effort to make the broadest of generalizations yields a picture of enormous diversity. The fact that courts normally consider many and sundry factors within and surrounding the employment relationship has led to a great variety of approaches and a multiplicity of often conflicting results. Contradictory decisions regarding the same facts can be given by different courts in the same country, such as happened in the *Barrandon* case. Madame Barrandon, who had been employed by the US Embassy in Paris as a nurse and medical secretary, brought an action for wrongful dismissal. At first instance her claim was allowed in part, and, on her appeal, the Court of Appeal of Paris even increased the award of damages. The *Procureur Général* intervened to appeal to the Court of Cassation, asserting that the US should be granted immunity. The Court of Cassation remitted the case to the Court of Appeal of Versailles.[259] The Court of Appeal of Versailles held that the US enjoyed immunity since:

Madame Barrandon performed her functions for the benefit of American and non-American civil and military personnel posted in Paris, as well as visitors to the Embassy, in the interests of the public service organized by the United States of America for the benefit of its agents, its nationals and foreign citizens subject to its authority or for whom it was responsible.[260]

Upon appeal by Barrandon, the Court of Cassation quashed this judgment, finding that 'the tasks performed by Madame Barrandon did not give her any special responsibility for the performance of the public service of the Embassy, so that her dismissal constituted an ordinary act of administration (*acte de gestion*)'.[261]

In *Burke*, an Irish citizen employed as a chauffeur in the Canadian Embassy in Dublin, who was not a member of the Canadian foreign service and enjoyed no diplomatic privileges, brought a claim for unfair dismissal. The High Court of Ireland held that the driving of an embassy car was an act of a commercial nature.[262] The Supreme Court, however, upheld Canada's immunity. According to O'Flaherty J:

> The employment of a chauffeur at the Canadian Embassy is clearly not a commercial contract in the ordinary sense of the word ... the element of trust and confidentiality that is reposed in the driver of an embassy car creates a bond with his employers that has the effect of involving him in the employing government's public business organisation and interests.[263]

Thus the same duties, tasks and functions might be perceived and characterized in diametrically opposed ways, so that the same employment relationship (or some crucial aspects of it) might be characterized as either *de jure imperii* or *de jure gestionis*. This remarkable phenomenon has recurred in the courts of other countries.[264] In *Sutton*, for another example, where a typist/clerk in the Auckland office of the Governor of Pitcairn sued to challenge her summary dismissal, the judge at the employment court who first heard the case opined that her work did not amount to the carrying on of the work of the mission:

> The work was mechanical. She worked apparently without exercising any discretions. She simply typed what she was told to type, and so on. To impart to her work the same lofty character and responsibility that attended the decisions and actions of her employer is in my view to go beyond the reality ... To impart that character to the acts of selecting, employing and dismissing her is likewise insupportable.[265]

Yet, in the Court of Appeal, Mrs Sutton was regarded as discharging duties 'close to the heart of the administrative process', with the result that she became 'an important cog in the administrative wheel'; she was then 'in a position of trust and confidentiality', involved 'in the public acts of the British Crown'. Consequently, to allow consideration of a claim of unjustifiable dismissal would intrude on the foreign State's exercise of sovereign functions.[266]

196 CONTRACTS OF EMPLOYMENT

In this respect, the law of State immunity now becomes inconsistent, confusing and self-contradictory. Similar facts may get different results at different times,[267] while employees in identical or near identical situations may be given vastly different judgments in different countries. Thus, drivers/chauffeurs,[268] interpreters/translators,[269] secretaries,[270] receptionists/telephonists/assistants,[271] warehouse workers,[272] as well as other workers with similarly menial duties,[273] have found the immunity of the employer foreign States either upheld (and hence their claims rejected) or denied (and their claims allowed), depending on which court heard the case. In one court, 'porters, gardeners, kitchen workers, etc' would be regarded as performing tasks not involving the exercise of sovereign functions,[274] but, in another court, 'cleaners' and 'domestic staff' may be viewed as having 'a sufficient association with the sovereign functioning of the office'.[275] One court would think that 'hiring purely clerical staff, even clerical staff that types diplomatic speeches, comes within the commercial activity exception',[276] whereas another court would hold that employment as 'typist, receptionist, secretary, record clerk and general office work in the consulate office' does not relate to any commercial activity of the foreign State.[277] Teachers and professors face the same situation.[278] Such a chasmic divergence of opinion makes it impossible to deduce any uniform rules[279] and creates the irresistible impression that the case law as a whole tends to be rather capricious as regards contracts of employment.

Conclusion

This is by far the fastest-growing part of the law of State immunity, and the most diverse and complicated. It is closely connected to the issue of commercial activity. Indeed, in those States without immunity legislation or without a specific provision on contracts of employment in their immunity statutes (such as the US FSIA), the issue of contracts of employment, like everything else, is decided under the rubric of commercial activity or activity *jure gestionis*. What is particularly notable is that there is no standard uniform test whereby an employment relationship can be categorized as *de jure imperii* or *de jure gestionis*. A great diversity of approaches, unobservable in any other area of the law of State immunity, can be found in the case of contracts of employment. Some courts, like the US and the Swiss courts, would emphasize the requirement of a territorial connection between the employment relationship and the forum State, while others, like the Italian courts, would consider whether the employee can be regarded as fully integrated into the general State apparatus of the employer State. While State practice is generally unanimous that the employment within foreign diplomatic missions must be subject to some special considerations and protection, there is no agreement as to how far such protection should reach. Some States, like the UK, would be willing to immunize almost any employment relationship in an embassy, whilst others, like Switzerland, would deny immunity in cases of employment of manual workers such as drivers and gardeners.

In contrast to a simple, albeit vague and sometimes unpractical, nature/private person test, all the courts in their decisions on contracts of employment have chosen to consider all the relevant circumstances of the case. Indeed, courts in dealing with employment disputes have to, and do, consider far more factors than in any other kind of State immunity cases, and these include, but are not confined to, the characterization of the employment relationship; the status and functions of the employer; the status, duties and functions of the employee; the activity on which the claim is based; the choice of law clause in the contract; and the remedies sought by the plaintiff. Apart from procedural rules, courts frequently have to consider substantive rules of local labour protection as well.

Such an inevitable multi-factor analysis applied by courts has led to a diversity of approaches and a multiplicity of results. In some States an individual is barred from suing his State of nationality, while in other States he is not; some States consider employees with minor duties such as interpreters, typists and drivers as occupying very important positions, while others do not; some States treat foreign diplomatic and consular missions as almost sacrosanct, while others have no misgivings about exercising jurisdiction over certain employment contracts entered into by embassies; some courts would reject the claim on the basis of the remedies, while others may not do so. It is impossible to make any generalization out of current State practice, much less to distil any uniform rule, and litigation experience gained in one country may not be of much use in another.

The recurrent theme, which is rendered even more pronounced by the universal resort to the multi-factor analysis, is that the nature/private person test is inadequate, and that, therefore, the purpose of the employment relationship should also be considered. To a large extent, this places contracts of employment in a *sui generis* category, different from other areas of State immunity, as is confirmed by the fact that in some national statutes separate provisions have been made for contracts of employment. The debate as to whether the nature or the purpose should be the decisive factor loses all its significance here: nature and purpose may be equally useful in characterizing an employment relationship.

5　Non-commercial torts

In certain circumstances, courts also assert jurisdiction over cases of tortious conduct that has resulted in injury to the person or damage to property in the territory of the forum State. A tort exception to foreign State immunity, in varying forms and phraseology, has thus also been written into all the current legal instruments in this field. The tort exception does not turn on whether the tortious act/omission in question can be characterized as *actum jure imperii* or *actum jure gestionis*, but rather on whether actual harm has been caused. With the *jure imperii / jure gestionis* distinction sidelined and the concomitant nature/purpose debate effectively circumvented, the tort exception in this sense is a new development from the traditional doctrine of State immunity. On the other hand, it is not something entirely novel and unexpected; for it is both a rightful offshoot from and an eloquent affirmation of the territorial jurisdiction of the forum court, from which foreign State immunity constitutes an exception. That is why the requirement of a territorial nexus between the tort and the forum State, rather than the *jure imperii / jure gestionis* distinction, plays so pivotal a role in the cases discussed in this chapter.

1.　Terminology

It must be noted at the outset that the word 'tort' is not the term actually employed in any of the various legal instruments discussed in this chapter.[1] Therefore, the term 'non-commercial torts'[2] serves only as a convenient generic term for personal injury or death or loss of or damage to property covered by various national statutes and other instruments on State immunity.[3] Apart from the fact that the *jure imperii / jure gestionis* distinction has lost much of its relevance in State

200 NON-COMMERCIAL TORTS

practice with regard to tortious liabilities, it is very difficult to draw generalizations about either the scope of this exception to State immunity or the application of a territorial connection requirement, because current doctrine and practice remain unsettled in many respects.

2. The targeted torts

The foremost question is what torts are actually addressed by current statutes on State immunity.[4] It appears that personal safety and property are two areas envisaged by all the national statutes on State immunity as well as by various drafts proposed by international bodies. These use diverse formulations:

(1) as for personal safety: (a) personal injury only;[5] (b) personal injury or death (variously worded as: 'personal injury or death';[6] 'death or personal injury';[7] 'any death or personal or bodily injury';[8] 'death or injury to the person';[9] 'the death of, or personal injury to, a person';[10] and 'death or injury of any person'[11]);

(2) as for property: (a) damage to or loss of property;[12] (b) damage to or loss of *tangible* property (phrased either as 'damage to or loss of tangible property'[13] or 'loss of or damage to tangible property'[14]); and (c) damage to tangible property only.[15]

2.1. *Physical injury and tangible property*

The reference to *tangible* property will exclude torts committed against *intangible* property such as certain contractual rights. The problem arises, however, where the word 'property' has no qualifier in a statute, resulting in an ambiguity that makes it difficult to assert for certain that intangible property is not envisaged. For example, section 6(b) of the Canada SIA refers to 'any damage to or loss of property' but does not clarify whether the word 'property' means only tangible property or includes intangible property as well. According to the case law, however, section 6(b) 'applies only to physical harm to or destruction of property and does not extend to pure economic loss';[16] and it does not address 'losses such as interference with contractual relations, employment and punitive damages'.[17] The US FSIA, on the other hand, also uses only 'property', but it expressly excludes 'any claim arising out of ... interference with contract rights' (section 1605(a)(5)(B)).[18]

In practice, the term 'personal injury' has been generally understood to refer only to '*physical* injury', thus precluding, for example, claims based on mental injury, hurt feelings,[19] psychological injury,[20] damage to reputation, libel or defamation, while only damage to or loss of *tangible* property will result in a loss of immunity, excluding, for example, unfair competition, pure economic loss,[21] infringements of property rights, or interference with contract rights.[22]

Section 1605(a)(5)(B) of the US FSIA expressly excludes 'any claim arising out of malicious prosecution, abuse of process, libel, slander, misrepresentation, deceit' from the scope of the tort exception to immunity.[23] This provision has created a curious situation. Because the preclusion of claims of misrepresentation, and so on, is found only in section 1605(a)(5), one wonders if tortious activities such as commercially motivated fraud or misrepresentation can nevertheless be actionable under section 1605(a)(2) (the commercial activity exception), which does not contain a like restriction based on physical injury. The case law of a great majority of the US courts seems to have answered this question in the affirmative. On the basis of the words 'not otherwise encompassed in paragraph (2) above' at the beginning of section 1605(a)(5), these courts have reasoned that section 1605(a)(2) and (5) are mutually exclusive, and, therefore, that the specific preclusion in section 1605(a)(5)(B) does not necessarily rule out the possibility of bringing these and similar claims against a foreign State under the commercial activity provision in section 1605(a)(2), provided that the claim is reformulated as based on, or closely connected with,[24] a commercial activity.[25] This judicial practice at once contrasts sharply with the full immunity enjoyed by the US Government itself from such claims under section 2680(h) of the Federal Tort Claims Act,[26] the purported model of section 1605(a)(5)(B),[27] which provides, unambiguously, that the US Government shall be immune from '[a]ny claim arising out of ... malicious prosecution, abuse of process, libel, slander, misrepresentation, deceit, or interference with contract rights'.[28] It does seem strange that the legislators 'wished to create a double standard under which foreign sovereigns could be sued in United States courts on tort claims, such as libel, for which the United States Government itself is immune'.[29] In this respect, section 1605(a)(5)(B) provides a good example of muddled draftsmanship.

2.2. 'Insurable risks'?

One is still left with the question as to which particular tortious acts or omissions are actually contemplated by the above instruments. In the commentary to its draft Article 12 (now Article 12 of the 2004 UN Convention) on tortious liability, the ILC first declares that the torts covered by Article 12 are 'confined principally to *insurable risks*', namely:

202 NON-COMMERCIAL TORTS

accidental death or physical injuries to persons or damage to tangible property involved in traffic accidents, such as moving vehicles, motor cycles, locomotives or speedboats. In other words, the article covers most areas of accidents involved in the transport of goods and passengers by rail, road, air or waterways. Essentially, the rule of non-immunity will preclude the possibility of the *insurance company* hiding behind the cloak of State immunity and evading its liability to the injured individuals.

But then:

In addition, the scope of article 12 is wide enough to cover also intentional physical harm such as assault and battery, malicious damage to property, arson or even homicide, *including political assassination.*[30]

This is self-contradictory at best, for if the provision, as the commentary suggests, should be confined to 'insurable risks', then it is hard to imagine how it can also cover 'political assassination'. The contradiction can only be resolved if one interprets the commentary as indicating that Article 12 is confined only 'principally', but not *exclusively*, to 'insurable risks'. After all, the above quotation shows that the ILC used the word 'insurable' only in the particular context of traffic accidents, which would normally involve insurance companies. Nonetheless, the limiting effect – most probably unintended by the ILC – has not escaped notice. The Australian Law Reform Commission, which drafted the Australia FSIA, expressly disfavours the term 'insurable' and finds the limitation unnecessary.[31]

Be that as it may, the word 'insurable', which is misleading and highly questionable, cannot be found in any of the current legal instruments on State immunity, be they national statutes, international conventions, or various drafts prepared by learned bodies. It does not even appear in the ILC's own Draft Article 12. First and foremost, therefore, the notion of 'insurable risks' cannot, and in practice does not, exist as a limitation on jurisdiction over tortious conduct.

The tort exception to State immunity in current State practice, even if perhaps addressing primarily 'insurable risks', is definitely not limited to them. The ILC's inclusion of political assassination within the purview of the provision on non-commercial torts is obviously prompted by the US law and practice, especially the *Letelier* case.[32] In fact, the preceding ILC statement sounds remarkably similar to that contained in the US legislative report on FSIA, according to which section 1605(a)(5) of the FSIA on tortious liability 'is directed primarily at the problem of traffic accidents but is cast in general terms as applying to all tort actions for money damages'; and the purpose of the provision is 'to permit the victim of a traffic accident or *other non-commercial tort* to maintain an action against the foreign state to the extent otherwise provided by law'.[33]

More recently, however, there has emerged a separate tendency to excuse foreign armed forces from the tort exception to immunity by resorting to the 'insurable risk' limitation. Quoting the pronouncement of the ILC (but omitting the crucial reference to 'intentional physical harm'), the European Court of Human Rights in the *McElhinney* case said:

> there appears to be a trend ... towards limiting State immunity in respect of personal injury caused by an act or omission within the forum State, but ... the trend may primarily refer to 'insurable' personal injury, that is incidents arising out of ordinary road traffic accidents, rather than matters relating to the core area of State sovereignty such as the acts of a soldier on foreign territory which, of their very nature, may involve sensitive issues affecting diplomatic relations between States and national security.[34]

This was relied upon by the Greek Special Supreme Court[35] and the German Federal Supreme Court[36] in their decision that the massacre of civilians in Greek villages by German occupation forces during the Second World War was a sovereign act attracting immunity.

2.3. 'Discretionary function'

Section 1605(a)(5)(A) of the US FSIA adds a further limitation to the tort exception to immunity: the foreign State shall be immune with regard to 'any claim based upon the exercise or performance [of] or the failure to exercise or perform a discretionary function regardless of whether the discretion be abused'. A great deal of debate has taken place as to the definition and scope of this 'discretionary function'. The legislative report explains this as due to the enjoyment of immunity by the US Government in similar context in domestic proceedings under the Federal Tort Claims Act (FTCA), which has identical provisions.[37] In the leading case of *Dalehite*, the US Supreme Court regarded 'policy judgment and decision' as essential to a discretionary function.[38] Basically, a two-pronged test has to be carried out to determine whether a particular government action is 'discretionary' in the meaning of the FTCA. First, a court must consider whether the conduct in question 'is a matter of choice for the acting employee', since 'conduct cannot be discretionary unless it involves an element of judgment or choice'. Secondly, 'assuming the challenged conduct involves an element of judgment, a court must determine whether that judgment is of the kind that the discretionary function exception was designed to shield'.[39] The purpose of the exception is to 'prevent judicial "second-guessing" of legislative and administrative decisions grounded in social, economic, and political policy through the medium of an action in tort'.[40] Thus, it 'protects only governmental actions and decisions based on considerations of public policy' and 'insulates the Government from liability if the action challenged in the case involves the permissible exercise of policy judgment'.[41]

Abiding by the same reasoning in cases against foreign States, the US courts usually determine whether an act is discretionary by asking whether there is a choice of conduct that is grounded in social, economic, or political policy.[42] The following acts have been considered as among the discretionary functions: the alleged misuse of its funds and/or inadequate recordkeeping by a Saudi government organ (even if resulting in the funds going to terrorists);[43] Saudi Arabian consular officers' retention of the travel papers of Saudi nationals;[44] Norwegian consular officers' assistance of a Norwegian citizen and her children in leaving the US;[45] a foreign State's training and supervision of its ambassador;[46] and exploration of natural resources.[47] Besides, the discretionary function exception also covers *abuses* of that discretion. Thus a foreign State could not be sued for trespass on immovable property when the Consuls of that State had installed the Consulate on the property in violation of the terms of the lease agreement, because the setting up and operating of a Consulate involved policy issues and therefore discretion. A wrongful act was not necessarily a non-discretionary act.[48]

On the other hand, where personal injury or death or damage to or loss of property has occurred in the US, US courts would not hesitate to dismiss the defence of discretionary function. Thus, pure vandalism is not a discretionary function, even though this was committed in the course of acquisition and operation of a consular residence,[49] nor are alleged acts of kidnapping or assault with a deadly weapon, even if these were committed on behalf of a foreign consulate.[50] In a case brought against the Holy See by an alleged victim of sexual abuse by a Catholic priest, the court held that the Holy See's failure to warn parishioners, after notice of the priest's illegal conduct in sexually molesting four minors, 'was not a choice based on plausible policy considerations for which the Holy See is entitled to immunity under the discretionary function exception'.[51] In a similar case against the Holy See for alleged sexual abuse, the court held that the supervision of the allegedly abusive clergy did not implicate the discretionary function exception to the tortious act exception.[52]

It is hard to resist the impression that the discretionary function requirement reintroduces the distinction between *jure imperii* and *jure gestionis*.[53] However, the opposite conclusion seems to be the case. First, in none of the above cases where a discretionary function was acknowledged did the court ever mention such a distinction. Secondly and more importantly, these cases either did not involve 'personal injury or death' as provided in section 1605(a)(5), or they simply concerned some accident occurring in a foreign State. Where actual injury or damage has indeed occurred, the US courts would usually reject the defence of discretionary function. Moreover, one can find in the case law unequivocal statements to the contrary. For example, in *Olsen*, the court expressly rejected an argument to the effect that 'foreign states would be immune from jurisdiction for those torts which otherwise come within the bounds of section 1065(a)(5) but which are *public in nature*'. According to the court, Mexico's position that 'governmental acts are automatically read out of section 1605(a)(5)' was 'untenable', since it 'would render section 1605(a)(5)(A) superfluous'.[54]

But it must immediately be conceded that the spectre of *jus imperii* may not be easily dispelled out of hand by a simple recourse to section 1605(a)(5)(A). Indeed, in order effectively to be able to sue a foreign State, the plaintiff must show that the tortious act or omission can somehow be attributable to that State, that is, the act or omission must of necessity be *governmental* in character; but then it is impossible to banish the element of discretion from any governmental act: one cannot conceive of any governmental act that does not involve some measure of discretion. Once it is accepted that a particular act involves discretion then it becomes difficult, by the very terms of section 1605(a)(5)(A), not to allow immunity. To put it simplistically, an act or omission has to be *governmental* before it can be actionable as against a foreign State, but by being governmental it must be *discretionary*, and therefore prima facie non-actionable. This paradox seems to have been what the *Olsen* court had in mind when it proposed a distinction between acts at the 'planning level' of governmental activity and those at the 'operational level', i.e. 'acts designed to carry out policy'. In the words of the Court:

Because decisions at the planning level establish governmental policy, they are not actionable. But where decisions occur at the operational level, the discretionary function exemption provides no protection from liability even though such decisions or acts may involve elements of discretion.[55]

Thus, though Mexico's decision to enter into the Prisoner Exchange Treaty with the US or to transfer particular prisoners to US custody might well be deemed discretionary (an act at the planning level), Mexico's failure to maintain and pilot the aircraft with sufficient safety and care, which resulted in a crash causing the deaths of the prisoners in the course of the transfer, was an operational level act, and could not be immune, though 'the pilot and air controllers had considerable discretion in carrying out their assigned tasks'.[56] By following such a line of reasoning, as we can see, the court pushed itself to a curious juncture where it was compelled to hold an act not discretionary within the meaning of section 1605(a)(5)(A), even though it might involve 'considerable discretion'.[57]

This is plainly an undisguised effort to rescue the discretion provision in section 1605(a)(5)(A) by reconfiguring the parameters of its application. To what extent such a contortionist approach is doctrinally viable may be an interesting subject for academic speculation; in practice it seems to have been favoured by courts from other circuits as well.[58] More importantly for our discussion here, the case law tends to show that the decision on the discretionary function in the US courts does not follow any mechanical pattern or criterion but instead involves a pragmatic appreciation of all the relevant factors. Thus, 'there is no discretion to commit, or to have one's officers or agents commit, an illegal act. Whatever policy options may exist for a foreign country, it has no "discretion" to perpetrate conduct designed to result in the assassination of an individual or individuals.'[59] Similarly, a foreign official had no discretion to order gunmen to murder a journalist in the US, when murder was prohibited by the law in his own place,[60] nor did a foreign consulate carry out an act of discretion when it diverted water onto its neighbour's property, resulting in land erosion.[61]

In brief, the tort exception to State immunity in current State practice, even if perhaps addressing primarily 'insurable' risks, is definitely not limited to them. Nothing in current instruments on State immunity ever indicates that this exception is limited to traffic accidents. The US courts at least have applied this exception to political assassination[62] and murder.[63] As pointed out by Fox, provided the attribution and the territorial nexus are satisfied, section 5 of the UK SIA can be extended to State-backed acts of terrorism.[64]

Tort provisions in various instruments are also subject to other restrictions, such as proceedings concerning foreign armed forces,[65] diplomatic and consular immunities,[66] special agreements,[67] as well as other matters.[68] Some instruments also restrict the remedies.[69]

3. The *jure imperii* / *jure gestionis* distinction?

It remains to consider the relationship between the non-commercial torts exception to immunity and the time-honoured distinction between *acta jure imperii* and *acta jure gestionis*. The prevailing opinion holds that the distinction is irrelevant. The drafters of the 1972 European Convention would see tort proceedings simply as 'private law' disputes between individuals and States.[70] In the opinion of Sucharitkul, the ILC Special Rapporteur on State immunity, jurisdiction over tortious liability is:

based on the *locus delicti commissi* and the eventual and justifiable exercise of such jurisdiction, even in respect of damage resulting from activities normally categorized as *acta jure imperii*, and also, in any event, from activities of a non-commercial character, whether or not classified as *acta jure gestionis*. The distinction between *jus imperii* and *jus gestionis*, or the two types of activities attributable to the State, appears to have little or no bearing in regard to this exception ... Whatever the activities of a State giving rise to personal injuries or damage to property within the territory of another State, whether in connection with *acta jure imperii* or *acta jure gestionis*, the fact remains that injuries have been inflicted upon and suffered by innocent persons ... The exercise of jurisdiction by the court of the place where the damage has occurred is probably the best guarantee of sound and swift justice.[71]

The Australian Law Reform Commission agreed:

Where a foreign state wrongfully causes death or personal injury or damages property within the forum state, the forum's interest in asserting jurisdiction over the wrongful act seems clear. There is no merit in such cases in requiring the plaintiff to litigate in the defendant state's courts when the forum's courts provide the obvious and convenient local remedy. This argument applies to *all* torts properly within the jurisdiction irrespective of whether they originate in an act which might be described as 'sovereign', 'governmental' or *jure imperii*.[72]

It thus recommended 'a provision removing immunity for actions in tort without reference to any governmental/commercial distinction', since 'the reason for allowing immunity in the overall provision on torts is not based on any governmental/commercial distinction'.[73]

In current State practice, the *jure imperii* / *jure gestionis* dichotomy seems rather out of place with regard to jurisdiction over tortious conduct in the territory of the forum State. A number of States, chief among them the US and the UK, have abandoned the test altogether in the case of torts. All the current legal instruments on State immunity, whether national statutes or international treaties, provide for jurisdiction in terms of personal injury or death, or damage to or loss of property caused by an act or omission in the territory of the forum State, quite irrespective of the nature or purpose of the act or omission in question. All these provisions found jurisdiction on the actual injury, death, damage or loss the cause of which can be attributed to the defendant foreign State while none contains any indication that the act or omission in question has to be committed *jure gestionis*.

What is striking here is the shift of focus from the philosophical speculation about the nature or the purpose of the act or omission causing injury or damage, to purely clinical technicalities concerning the *assessment of liability* for the injury or damage caused. In other words, the court is now authorized to proceed directly to the *merits* of the case, without it at all being necessary to consider whether the defendant foreign State has any defence *in limine*, such as that of immunity. The notion of immunity is negated in the very conceptualization of tortious liability in terms of injury or damage caused: where there is injury or damage, there is jurisdiction. If the character of the act or omission has no relevance whatsoever, then there is no reason why a provision denying immunity with regard to tortious liability should be confined to a particular species of act or omission, or why the question of species should arise at all.

The current injury/damage-oriented provision has the effect therefore of truly placing the foreign State on the same footing with the private individual. According to the American Law Institute:

a diplomatic courier carrying confidential dispatches in an automobile may be engaged in a governmental function, but if the vehicle injures a pedestrian or another vehicle, the state will be subject to suit based on the injury.

Since the rationale of the restrictive theory is to assimilate liability of foreign states to that of private entities, the standard of liability in a claim against the state is the same as if the defendant were a private entity – whether for negligence, liability without fault, or intentional wrongs; the same principle applies to such issues as contribution among tortfeasors and indemnification.[74]

The celebrated case of *Letelier* v. *Chile* serves to bring out the potential of section 1605(a)(5) of the US FSIA in that the effects of the provision extend beyond traffic accidents to cover political assassinations. In that case, the relatives and representatives of the former Chilean Ambassador and Foreign Minister Orlando Letelier and another official, who had been killed in the US by a car bomb allegedly placed by Chilean intelligence agents, sought damages for tortious injuries connected with their deaths. The court held that the *jure imperii / jure gestionis* distinction was neither necessary nor warrantable:

Nowhere is there an indication that the tortious acts ... are to only be those formerly classified as 'private', thereby engrafting onto the statute, as the Republic of Chile would have the Court do, the requirement that the character of a given tortious act be judicially analysed to determine whether it was of the type heretofore denoted as *jure gestionis*, or should be classified as *jure imperii*.[75]

Crawford comments:

The basis for the assertion of jurisdiction over 'governmental torts' such as these is ... plainly not a distinction between 'governmental' and 'non-governmental' acts, but an assertion of local control over (i.e. jurisdiction over) obvious forms of harm or damage. Deliberately to cause harm or damage on the territory of another State by an act of 'public power' is, in the absence of some special exception, a plain violation of international law, whether the harm is caused by assassination or invasion. The exercise of local jurisdiction in such cases is an assertion of the forum's right, acknowledged by international law, to deal with the consequences of unlawful acts on its territory.[76]

In *Walker*, a Canadian court declared that:

The personal injury exemption to immunity under the State Immunity Act replaces the common law rule which distinguished between public and private acts of foreign states. Section 6 of the State Immunity Act permits a right of action against foreign states for torts even if committed in the exercise of governmental function or authority, provided the injury occurred in Canada.[77]

The appellate court, while reversing the lower court's decision on other grounds, nonetheless endorsed the above reasoning.[78]

Interestingly, the US, in whose courts the *jure imperii / jure gestionis* contention was rejected in relation to torts, brought up the ill-fated argument as an intervener in the Canadian case of *Schreiber*, in which the tort exception under section 6 of the Canada SIA was discussed. The US asserted that a distinction must be made between *acta jure imperii* and *acta jure gestionis* in determining whether any of the exceptions to immunity under the Canada SIA were applicable because each of the exceptions to immunity depended, it was submitted, on the nature of commercial or other private law conduct underlying the claim, with the consequence that the *jure imperii / jure gestionis* distinction which underlies the theory of restrictive immunity applies to the entire SIA. The Canadian Supreme Court rejected the argument and stressed the irrelevance of the *jure imperii* / *jure gestionis* distinction. According to the Court, the express wording of section 6(a) clearly states that this exception applies to all torts committed by a foreign State which cause death or personal injury.[79]

The Italian Court of Cassation expressed the same opinion in *Ferrini* by pointing out that 'the general approach to responsibility for illegal acts is evolving through the adoption of a different test from that based on acts *jure imperii* and *jure gestionis*, the inadequacy of which is well documented with regard to this type of dispute', so that 'it is certain that the test based on the nature of the harmful act can no longer be considered generally applicable'.[80]

Essentially, it is the tortious result, not the nature of the tortious act/ omission that gives the forum court its jurisdiction. One might argue that a State that causes injury is assimilated to a private person (and therefore the act or omission is rendered 'private') since a private person can also cause injury, but that is not the decisive factor, since jurisdiction will be exercised whether or not this argument is put forward. Thus, the legislation makes the distinction between acts *jure imperii* and *jure gestionis* irrelevant.

On the other hand, it is not uncommon for the courts in the States without immunity legislation to adopt a public/private law (*acta jure imperii* / *acta jure gestionis*) analysis, since that is the criterion they apply to virtually any and all actions against a foreign State.[81] Presumably, in these States, where the *jure imperii* / *jure gestionis* test serves as the overall criterion, it is still possible for a foreign State to argue for immunity on the ground that the act in question has been committed *jure imperii*. One would then expect the jurisdiction of the court to be restricted to a greater extent than in the States with immunity legislation. However, from the sparse case law on State immunity in tort, one observes a great measure of flexibility in the application of this test, so that it becomes a mere stamp of validity to justify the exercise of jurisdiction rather than an a priori principle upon which the jurisdiction hinges. Much depends on which aspect of the facts (the act/omission or the injury) the court sees as the core element of the tort. Thus, even if delivering an embassy's diplomatic bags may be a sovereign act, the delivery car's causing injury is not. In a case in which damages were sought for alleged damage to a motor car by the negligent driving of a car owned by the US Government, the Austrian Supreme Court held that, in determining whether an act performed by a foreign government was *jure imperii* or *jure gestionis*, the Court must consider only the act itself, and not the purpose for which it was performed. It then becomes a question of what 'act' one has in mind. The Court concluded that the fact that the car had carried mail for the US Embassy was irrelevant, since:

the act from which the plaintiff derives his claim for damages against the defendant is not the collection of mail but the operation of the motor car by the defendant and the latter's action as a road user ... [T]he operation of a motor vehicle by a foreign State and the use of public roads ... belong to the sphere of the private activities of that State even if ... such operation and use have occurred in the performance of official functions, and ... accordingly the foreign State can be sued for damages in a local court ... A traffic accident creates private legal relations between the foreign State and the private individual, on a basis of equal rights between them.[82]

Here one sees not so much a nature/purpose dichotomy as a different characterization of the act in question; that is, instead of viewing the act as delivery of mail for the embassy, the court projected it into the more general scenario of operation of motor vehicles and use of public roads, thereby effectively stripping the act of any colour of governmental authority, and then fitted it into the nature/purpose (and public/private) framework. In so doing the Court ignored the fact that both characterizations would be equally tenable.

Thus a distinction was drawn between the immediate act (causing injury) and the 'purported' act (the act in the course of which injury was caused, in this case carrying mail for the embassy). In other words, the jurisdiction of the court was based not so much on the nature of the act of mail delivery (whatever its characterization) as on the occurrence of a traffic accident. Where there is injury, there is jurisdiction. In this way a court without immunity legislation would reach the same result as one with such legislation, albeit from a different starting point.

In a similar case involving an embassy car, an Italian court held that, in matters regarding road traffic and civil responsibility for related matters, foreign States – and their legitimate representatives – acted *jure privatorum*. It was impossible, according to the court, 'to invest the use of a means of transport with the character of a public act or the exercise of the power of supremacy'.[83]

In *Morocco* v. *De Trappenberg*, a rehabilitation centre, after finding that one of its patients, the daughter of the caretaker of the Moroccan Consulate General at Amsterdam, who had been seriously injured in

212   NON-COMMERCIAL TORTS

an accident, was not covered by insurance for part of the costs for her medical treatment, applied for a garnishee order to secure the debt on funds held by Morocco, alleging that Morocco was liable in tort for failure to ensure that the caretaker and his family were adequately insured. The court held that, where a State became involved in a legal situation not as a public authority but in a private capacity it could be subjected to the jurisdiction of another State. Such a situation arose not only where a State undertook an obligation by entering into a legal relationship in the sphere of private law but also where such an obligation arose out of the law itself, for instance as a result of a tort committed by the State concerned acting as an employer in the same capacity as a private person. Therefore the court had jurisdiction to decide where a tort had been committed.[84]

However, there are cases where immunity was granted on the basis of a characterization of the conduct in question as 'sovereign' or 'governmental'. For example, jurisdiction was denied by an Italian court in a case for requisition of property seized by the Japanese occupying troops in Shanghai, China, during the Second World War,[85] by a Dutch court in a case against the Chief of the German Federal Police with regard to a police report that was alleged to have led to an insulting magazine article,[86] and by an Irish court in a case claiming damages for alleged torts including, inter alia, breach of constitutional rights and conspiracy to deny the right to free movement.[87] It should be noted that, had the last two cases been brought in a court of one of those States with immunity legislation, jurisdiction would most probably have been denied since they involved only non-physical injury torts.

The above-cited case against Japan has one thing in common with the Irish case of *McElhinney*, in that they both involved acts of foreign armed forces. In *McElhinney*, the plaintiff alleged that, following an incident at the Northern Ireland border, a British soldier on duty at the border checkpoint had assaulted him in Ireland. The Irish courts granted immunity on the ground that the soldier, in carrying out his duties, was performing governmental activities when the acts complained of occurred. These were therefore *acta jure imperii*, or sovereign acts, even if committed within the jurisdiction of Ireland, and were therefore covered by immunity.[88] When the case reached the European Court of Human Rights (ECHR), the Court held that a grant of immunity in this case was justified on two grounds: that the current tortious liability exception to immunity primarily concerned 'insurable' personal injury and that the tort in question had been committed *jure imperii*.[89]

THE 'JURE IMPERII / JURE GESTIONIS' DISTINCTION?   213

Besides erroneously relying on the rather dubious word 'insurable', which does not exist in any of the current instruments on State immunity and therefore cannot possibly serve to limit the scope of application of the tort exception to immunity, and resorting to a purported *jure imperii / jure gestionis* dichotomy, which has been discarded altogether by some States or adopted only at face value by others, the ECHR failed to notice two prominent features of the *McElhinney* case: that no *physical* injury had actually been caused and that the case concerned acts committed by a member of a foreign armed force.

As previously pointed out, in current State practice, where no physical injury has been incurred, courts would normally reject the claim. The position of foreign armed forces with regard to tortious liability, however, is somewhat uncertain. While some of the current legal instruments expressly preclude their application to the immunity of a foreign State in respect of its armed forces in the territory of the forum State,[90] others remain silent on this matter. The US FSIA contains no specific provision on foreign armed forces but its legislative report states that the FSIA 'would not alter the rights or duties of the United States under the NATO Status of Forces Agreement or similar agreements with other countries'.[91]

Generally speaking, State practice at present seems to be inclined towards treating the immunity of a foreign State with regard to its armed forces quite separately from immunity in other contexts. Some courts even display considerable readiness to grant immunity where foreign armed forces are concerned. In *Holland*, which involved a claim for defamation against the education officer at a US military base in England, the English House of Lords held that the provision of education and training to military personnel at a US military base was part of a State's sovereign function of maintaining its armed forces and so accordingly was the act of writing a memorandum in the course of the supervision of the education programme.[92] The House of Lords thus confirmed the reasoning in *Littrell (No. 2)*, where the English Court of Appeal held that the operation of a military hospital, although no doubt requiring much the same skills as the operation of a civilian hospital, was a recognized military activity. The standard of medical care that the US afforded its own servicemen was thus a matter within its own sovereign authority.[93]

In the *Distomo* case, the Greek courts denied immunity to Germany for atrocities (massacre and destruction of private property) committed by the German occupation forces in a Greek village in 1944;[94] but the

214 NON-COMMERCIAL TORTS

Special Supreme Court held that, under current international law, a foreign State continued to enjoy immunity in respect of a tort committed in the forum State in which its armed forces had participated.[95] This is of course a complete volte-face in Greek practice, which now seems to be no different from that of the UK regarding foreign armed forces.

In other States it may still remain a matter of conjecture how a court would resolve a situation where, for example, a foreign air force plane, on military operations, crashes in the forum State, killing persons on the ground.[96] Recent case law, however, seems to favour immunity for foreign armed forces where tort actions are concerned.[97]

In *McElhinney*, the assault was committed by a British soldier in the course of carrying out his duties; so it is conceivable that, had a similar act been committed by an Irish soldier in the performance of his duties in the UK, the UK courts might likewise have regarded the act as *jure imperii* and held him immune. But even if this were the case, it would not mean that an English court would be deciding the case solely in reliance on a *jure imperii / jure gestionis* distinction. To start with, section 16(2) of the UK SIA provides:

> This Part of this Act does not apply to proceedings relating to anything done by or in relation to the armed forces of a State while present in the United Kingdom and, in particular, has effect subject to the Visiting Forces Act 1952.

Applying this provision, an English court in a case against foreign armed forces would have to perform two tests, just as the House of Lords did in *Holland*: first, it must ascertain whether the act in question has been 'done by or in relation to' foreign armed forces; and (if that test has been satisfied and therefore the relevant part of the UK SIA does not apply), secondly, whether the act in dispute is to be characterized as *jure imperii* or *jure gestionis* at common law. That is to say, in such a hypothetical case, the *jure imperii / jure gestionis* distinction, which is the benchmark for foreign State immunity at common law, enters into the picture only when the application of the UK SIA is suspended in the limited context of foreign armed forces. Thus, where an act apparently attributable to foreign armed forces is at issue, an English court has to apply first of all a test that looks at the *status of the actor* rather than the *nature of the act*. If a *McElhinney*-type act is committed by someone unrelated to foreign armed forces, e.g. by a foreign *civilian policeman* instead of a *soldier*, the case will fall squarely within the tort exception to immunity contained in section 5 of the UK SIA and the whole issue will turn only on whether any injury has resulted from the act. The *jure imperii / jure gestionis* distinction will then become utterly irrelevant.

It might thus be surmised that the crux of the matter in the *McElhinney* case is that no actual injury had resulted from the alleged assault. Otherwise things might have been different. One might also speculate whether Irish courts would have decided differently on different facts from those in *McElhinney*, for example where physical injury had actually been caused, not by a soldier performing his duties, but by a policeman, in whatever capacity at the relevant time.

In fact, as far as tortious conduct committed within the forum State is concerned, the most important requirement in current State practice is not that the conduct be *jure gestionis*, but that it has some connection with the territory of the forum State. In the words of the ILC:

> The basis for the assumption and exercise of jurisdiction in cases covered by this exception is territoriality. The *locus delicti commissi* offers a substantial territorial connection regardless of the motivation of the act or omission, whether intentional or even malicious, or whether accidental, negligent, inadvertent, reckless or careless, and indeed irrespective of the nature of the activities involved, whether *jure imperii* or *jure gestionis*.[98]

4. The territorial connection

The non-commercial tort exception, though perhaps previously unknown to the law on State immunity,[99] is not entirely novel, since it is no more than an offshoot of territorial jurisdiction, from which State immunity constitutes an exception. The requirement that the tortious act/omission or the injury/damage be somehow connected with the territory of the forum State is common to all the statutes, though differences exist as to how and to what extent that requirement should be satisfied. As the tort exception authorizes the court to adjudicate upon certain acts of foreign States that may be governmental or sovereign in nature, the territorial connection emerges as an indispensable ground for jurisdiction. Unlike in some other areas of State immunity, such as that of contracts of employment, the status of the plaintiff is unimportant so long as the territorial nexus can be established. This means that a foreign national can be allowed to sue his own State of nationality if the tort occurs within the territory of the forum State. Although criticized as 'rigid' and 'limiting',[100] the requirement of a territorial nexus both fits in with the general principle of territoriality

216 NON-COMMERCIAL TORTS

as a basis of domestic jurisdiction under international law and helps advance the strong argument that the forum courts provide the most convenient local remedy.[101] The formulations of this requirement are as many as the instruments: jurisdiction can be established when either (1) the tortious act/omission (the UK SIA, the Australia FSIA, the IDI Draft, the European Convention, the ILC Draft and the UN Convention); (2) the injury/damage (the Canada SIA); (3) both the tortious act/omission and the injury/damage (the US FSIA); or (4) a direct effect (the ILA Draft) occurs in the forum State.

4.1. Tortious act/omission only

Section 5 of the UK SIA requires that the injurious consequences be 'caused by an act or omission in the United Kingdom'.[102] Applying this requirement, the UK courts in *Al-Adsani*[103] and *Jones*[104] declined to exercise jurisdiction over acts of torture committed in foreign countries. Section 13 of the Australia FSIA 1985 follows the UK SIA in providing that the injurious consequences must be 'caused by an act or omission done or omitted to be done in Australia'.[105] According to the drafters:

It is clear that where all the actions making up the tort including the resulting damage occur within the jurisdiction the local courts should have jurisdiction. Difficulties occur where some acts occur in one jurisdiction, some in another or where the acts occur in one jurisdiction and the damage in another ... Since the primary justification for asserting jurisdiction in this case is that the foreign state has no privilege to commit local physical injury or property damage, and since determining the place where the wrongful act or omission occurred is usually simpler than determining where damage occurred or the cause of action arose, it is recommended that Australian legislation follow the United Kingdom provision to this effect.[106]

Thus, if a tortfeasor sends a letter-bomb from the territory of the forum State to a person (whether or not he is a national of the forum State) in another State and that person suffers injury or death from the bomb, or if a tortfeasor constructs a timed car bomb in the territory of the forum State which later explodes in the territory of another State, the courts of the forum State will have jurisdiction.

Article 2(2)(e) of the 1991 IDI Draft affirms jurisdiction if the damage is 'attributable to activities of a foreign State and its agents within the national jurisdiction of the forum State'. This provision expands the jurisdiction of the forum State in two ways. First, by requiring that the damage be attributable to activities of a foreign State and its agents, it shifts the emphasis from the act or omission that constitutes the immediate cause of the injury/damage (the immediate act) to any activity in relation to which some injury/damage has been caused (the 'purported' act). That is, if the injury can be in any way linked to the activities of a foreign State or its agents (be they commercial or non-commercial, sovereign or private), the court will exercise jurisdiction. Where injury has been incurred, attribution becomes more important than the act itself. In this way the *jure imperii / jure gestionis* test is effectively discarded. Secondly, instead of 'territory' it speaks of 'national jurisdiction'. Under modern international law, national jurisdiction extends far beyond the proper territory to such areas as the contiguous zone and the exclusive economic zone or to such objects as ships on the high seas and aircraft in flight over areas beyond national jurisdiction. The term 'national jurisdiction' therefore gives the forum State a much wider jurisdiction than does mere 'territory'. The problem of overlapping jurisdictions seems to be inevitable, but the drafters give no indication how this is to be resolved.

Article 12 of the 1991 ILC Draft and of the 2004 UN Convention adopts another flexible formula by allowing jurisdiction 'if the act or omission occurred in whole or in part in the territory' of the forum State. Only part of the tortious act/omission occurring in the territory of the forum State will be sufficient to activate jurisdiction; but this is subject to a further limitation, namely 'if the author of the act or omission was present in that territory at the time of the act or omission'. This latter 'presence in the territory' requirement, the ILC explains, is designed to serve the dual purpose of demanding a closer territorial connection between the State of the forum and the author or individual whose act or omission is the cause of the damage in the State of the forum,[107] and of excluding from the application of Article 12 'cases of transboundary injuries or trans-frontier torts or damage, such as export of explosives, fireworks or dangerous substances which could explode or cause damage through negligence, inadvertence or accident' and 'cases of shooting or firing across a boundary or of spill-over across the border of shelling as a result of an armed conflict'. In a word, the Article is 'primarily concerned with accidents occurring *routinely* within the territory of the State of the forum'.[108]

Thus if the tortfeasor remains all the time outside the territory of the forum State, such as shooting across a boundary, the forum State has no jurisdiction. On the other hand, it is to be questioned whether this requirement will preclude transboundary torts altogether; for it must be noted that the material time for the restriction is when the act or omission was committed but not when the proceedings are instituted. Thus if a tortfeasor commits part of the tort within the territory of the forum State and then leaves there to carry out the other part, such as constructing a car bomb in the forum State and then enters another State and detonates the bomb by remote control or so detonates it while the car is travelling in another State, the court still has jurisdiction even if, at the time the proceedings are brought, the tortfeasor is outside the territory of the forum State, because at least part of the tortious act was committed in the territory of the forum State while he was there.

Article 11 of the European Convention allows jurisdiction where 'the facts which occasioned the injury or damage occurred in the territory of the State of the forum' and contains a similar limitation; i.e. 'if the author of the injury or damage was present in that territory at the time when those facts occurred'.[109]

German courts, even without the benefit of a State immunity statute, seem also to adopt the 'act/omission' rule. In the *Garden Contamination Case*, where a claim was lodged against the Soviet Union for damage to crops in a garden in Berlin, caused by radioactive contamination arising from the accident at the Chernobyl nuclear reactor in April 1986, the court held that the *situs* of 'prohibited acts' subject to 'international jurisdiction' should be:

in the place where the acts occurred. It is irrelevant where the damage occurred. It is true that an act 'takes place' not only where the perpetrator has carried it out but also where the consequences of his action occur. However, that is the case only where, without those consequences, the act would not be completed.[110]

It is difficult to draw a uniform picture as to the extent and scope of the territorial requirement: whether it covers the whole act or omission or only part of it or whether it extends only to the 'territory' in its proper sense or to other areas within the 'jurisdiction' of the forum State such as the contiguous zone and the exclusive economic zone or even to ships on the high seas and aircraft while in flight over the high seas. One might also find it hard to make sense of a 'presence of the tortfeasor' requirement.[111]

4.2. Injury/damage only

The regime under section 6 of the Canada SIA seems to be the obverse of the tortious act/omission-only pattern. Section 6, as later amended, provides: 'A foreign State is not immune from the jurisdiction of a court in any proceedings that relate to (a) any death or personal or bodily injury,[112] or (b) any damage to or loss of property, that occurs in Canada.' That is, no matter where the tortious act/omission occurs, the court has jurisdiction so long as the injurious consequences are suffered in the territory of the forum State. Such a formulation can be very advantageous to the plaintiff in the case of a tort with what one might call 'lingering' effects, that is, a tort that spans a considerable period of time or has some lapse of time between the tortious act/omission and the injurious consequences (so-called 'split tort'[113] or 'long-range tort'[114]). This can be demonstrated by an Austrian case, where the owner of fishing reserves over Austrian waters of the River Saalach brought an action against the operator of a hydro-electric power plant situated on the upper reaches of the same river in Germany, for damage caused to the fishing reserves in a storm, when an incorrectly opened lock-gate had been torn off its hinges and waters had burst out. The Austrian Supreme Court upheld jurisdiction, even though the plant was operated outside Austria:

> In such a case it is the law of the place where the effects of the act are produced which is to be applied, wherever it is clear that the author of the damage must ... have foreseen that his behaviour would have repercussions at the place in question. Anyone who performs acts producing effects abroad must take account of their consequences, that is to say the violation of rights protected abroad ... The victim of the damage ... must therefore be protected according to the law of the place where he is situated ... even if the operation of the damage-causing installation was authorized under foreign public law.[115]

But as long as 'instant' torts (the tortious conduct and the injury/damage occurring at the same time) are concerned, this pattern might not prove as liberal as it appears to be, and may have approximately the same effect as the one that requires the tortious act/omission to have occurred in the territory of the forum State.

In *Jaffe* v. *Miller*, where the plaintiff alleged that he had been kidnapped by US officials from Canada and taken to Florida, US, to face false criminal charges, the court granted immunity on the ground that the alleged tortious acts (malicious prosecution and kidnapping) were outside the scope of the SIA in that they had occurred either prior to the entry into force of the SIA or in the US, that is, outside the Canadian territory.[116] Though nowhere stated, the court obviously did not consider as a valid cause of action lingering mental distress that might have resulted from the alleged tortious acts and might continue to be felt even after the victim's return to Canada.

220   NON-COMMERCIAL TORTS

It then falls to be decided whether mental distress can be claimed as 'injury'; for if this is the case, then a claim might conceivably be brought under section 6 for, say, mental distress or psychological injury which may allegedly arise from physical injury inflicted abroad. To the extent that physical injury, occurring abroad, falls outside the scope of section 6, psychological injury, on the other hand, may give the plaintiff a cause of action, because such injury, by definition, would presumably continue to be suffered long after the victim of the tortious conduct returns to Canada.

The Canadian case law, however, has foreclosed such a possibility by construing the word 'injury' in section 6 as meaning only *physical* injury. In *Walker*, a Canadian citizen sued the US Government for unlawful imprisonment, conspiracy, misrepresentation and fraud in relation to an undercover operation in which US customs officers had used false identities to mislead the plaintiff into activities prohibited by US law, which resulted in his arrest and guilty plea in the US. He did not allege any physical injury. The court interpreted section 6 as encompassing 'mental distress, emotional upset, and restriction of liberty' (false imprisonment in this case) as well as physical injury. However, as he had suffered all this not in Canada, but in the US, section 6 did not apply.[117]

Walker remains the only case with an extended interpretation of the word 'injury'. Subsequent cases evince a clear intention to minimize the implications of the *Walker* ruling, if not to repeal it outright. In *Friedland*, the court took the view that:

the 'personal injury' exception refers primarily to physical injury and ... s. 6(a) extends to mental distress and emotional upset only insofar as such harm arises from or is linked to a physical injury.[118]

The issue of mental injury was finally settled in *Schreiber*, which involved the arrest and detention of a Canadian citizen in Toronto, Canada, upon an extradition request by Germany in relation to tax evasion and other offences. Schreiber brought an action against Germany, claiming personal injury, including mental distress, emotional upset, denial and restriction of liberty and damage to reputation. He did not allege, however, that he had suffered any physical injury. In affirming the lower courts' decisions, the Supreme Court agreed that 'personal injury' meant only 'physical injury'.[119] The Court further clarified that:

Friedland established that the scope of the exception in s. 6(a) is limited to instances where mental distress and emotional upset were linked to a physical injury. For example, psychological distress may fall within the exception where such distress is manifested physically, such as in the case of nervous shock.[120]

The Court pointed to 'the presence of a legislative intent to create an exception to state immunity which would be restricted to a class of claims arising out of a physical breach of personal integrity'.[121]

The case of *Bouzari* destroyed the last vestige of hope of bringing a claim under section 6 on the basis of emotional after-effects of physical injury suffered abroad. When the plaintiff argued that his suffering as a result of torture inflicted in Iran continued in Canada and that this constituted injury occurring in Canada, the court responded:

Section 6 only permits a Canadian court to take jurisdiction if the injury occurs in Canada. The Ontario Court of Appeal has held that this provision can apply to psychological injury or mental distress, but only if that injury arises from or is linked to a physical injury as well, and that injury must occur in Canada. In this case, the physical injury, as well as the related psychological injury, occurred in Iran because of acts of torture there. While Mr. Bouzari continues to suffer from those injuries in Canada, both physically and mentally, that does not change the fact that the injury occurred in Iran.[122]

It has further been held that harm suffered in Canada will not be sufficient for jurisdictional purposes if such harm derives only incidentally from events that occurred abroad.[123]

By declining to consider mental injury as within the scope of s. 6 the Canadian case law firmly brings the tort exception within the territorial limits of the forum State and precludes the possibility of suing for lingering mental or psychological effects of torts committed abroad. The resulting jurisdiction appears little different from one that emanates from a provision, such as that in the UK SIA, that requires the tortious conduct to have occurred within the forum State.

4.3. Both tortious act/omission and injury/damage

At first sight, the US FSIA seems also to adopt an 'injury/damage' pattern but there is some confusion regarding the interpretation of the relevant provisions and the court practice favours a stricter requirement, namely, that both the tortious act/omission and the injury/damage must occur in the US. Section 1605(a)(5) of the US FSIA denies immunity where an action is brought against a foreign State:

for personal injury or death, or damage to or loss of property, occurring in the United States and caused by the tortious act or omission of that foreign state or

222   NON-COMMERCIAL TORTS

of any official or employee of that foreign state while acting within the scope of his office or employment.

Doubtless, the injury/damage has to occur in the US; but it is not altogether clear where the act or omission should take place. The legislative report provides an important clue by stating plainly that 'the tortious act or omission must occur within the jurisdiction of the United States'.[124] However, it does seem odd that the drafters should have added this statement as an afterthought instead of including it in the statutory provision, for failing such a statement one might naturally reach quite the opposite conclusion that the place where the act or omission occurred is irrelevant. The American Law Institute is of the opinion that, under section 1605(a)(5):

courts in the United States have jurisdiction over tort claims against a foreign state only if the injury took place in the United States, *regardless of where the act or omission causing the injury took place.*

And that:

Thus, a claim arising from an injury in the United States caused by the malfunction of a defective product manufactured abroad by a foreign state instrumentality would be subject to jurisdiction in the United States under the FSIA; under the European Convention and the British Act, the court apparently would have jurisdiction of an action in tort only if the product had been manufactured in the forum state.[125]

This seems to be a correct interpretation of the language of the provision itself but is definitely at odds with the statement given by the drafters in the legislative report. If one follows the instruction of the drafters, one will demand both the act/omission and the injury/damage to occur in the forum State; on the other hand, if one ignores this instruction and follows the language of the provision itself, one will only require the injury/damage to take place in the forum State.

In *Letelier*, the district court obviously required only the injury to occur in the US when it rejected the reliance on the act of State doctrine by the Chilean Government:

Although the acts allegedly undertaken directly by the Republic of Chile to obtain the death of Orlando Letelier may well have been carried out entirely within that country, that circumstance alone will not allow it to absolve itself under the act of state doctrine *if the actions of its alleged agents resulted in tortious injury in this country.*[126]

But so far this remains the only case with such reasoning, and it has been rejected by the Court of Appeals for that circuit.[127] Thus, even though the statutory language is susceptible of the interpretation that only the injury/damage has to occur in the US, the case law definitely requires *both the tortious act/omission and the injury/damage* to occur in the US. Thus immunity was upheld for Argentina for destruction of an oil tanker on the high seas.[128] Where the acts or omissions causing the injury/damage took place in a foreign country, the US courts invariably denied jurisdiction.[129]

On the other hand, the US courts do not require that *all* the events happen in the US. In *Olsen*, for example, where the plaintiffs brought an action against the Government of Mexico in respect of the deaths of their parents who had been killed in a plane crash inside US territory when being transferred from Mexico to the US as prisoners, the court rejected Mexico's argument that the events at issue should have occurred wholly within the territory of the US. According to the court, if the plaintiffs could allege 'at least one entire tort' (in that case the negligent piloting of the aircraft) occurring in the US, they might claim under section 1605(a)(5).[130]

4.4.   *A direct effect?*

The most radical position so far is that taken by the International Law Association (ILA). Article III(F) of the 1982 ILA Draft grants jurisdiction if 'the act or omission which caused the death, injury or damage occurred *wholly or partly* in the forum State' (emphasis added). This follows the 'tortious act/omission-only' pattern. But the ILA later modified this provision in 1994 by adding 'or if that act or omission had a direct effect in the forum State', thereby putting forward a more liberal pattern in which a direct effect in the territory of the forum State is sufficient to justify a denial of immunity, regardless of where the tortious act/omission or the injury/damage itself has occurred. According to the drafters, the aim of such a modification is to cover transboundary torts.[131] One might be led to believe that only such a 'direct effect' pattern allows jurisdiction over transboundary torts.[132] But this is a misconception. As shown above, other patterns (including that followed by the 1982 ILA Draft) only exclude certain transboundary torts, not all of them.

The 'direct effect' proposition seems to have been inspired by section 1605(a)(2) of the US FSIA, but that provision applies in the entirely different context of commercial activity, not of tortious liability, and even in that context it still remains subject to a territorial nexus requirement.[133] Moreover, the US Supreme Court has already held that the requirements for tortious liability under section 1605(a)(5) were not satisfied by a showing that a tort had 'direct effects' in the US.[134] In view of the strict interpretation of the territorial requirement by various national courts, including those of the US, in relation to non-commercial torts, it seems unlikely that a very flimsy territorial connection, such as that of a mere 'direct effect' suggested by the ILA, may gain wide support.

4.5. States without immunity legislation

The same territorial connection requirement is also manifest in those States without immunity legislation. Where a territorial link remains unsatisfied or doubtful, immunity is affirmed.[135]

5. Attribution

The exception to immunity based on non-commercial torts covers only injury, death, damage or loss sustained by individuals as a result of conduct attributable to foreign States or their agents.[136] In practice, where the injury cannot be attributed to the foreign State defendant,[137] or if a direct causation cannot be established between the tort and the foreign State in question,[138] jurisdiction is usually denied.

In the US jurisprudence, the requirement contained in section 1605(a)(5), namely, that the injury/damage must be caused by a tortious act or omission 'of any official or employee of that foreign state while acting within the scope of his office or employment', has in a number of cases turned out to be a decisive factor for the issue of attribution. Where an employment relationship cannot be demonstrated between the tortfeasor and the foreign State in question, the claim is rejected. In *Robinson*, a security guard at a building owned by the Malaysian Government in New York sued Malaysia for negligence after being injured when he, while on duty, had slipped and fallen on a 'white substance'. The court found that there was no evidence to suggest that the Malaysian Government or any of its employees or agents had left the 'white substance'. While both parties assumed that one of the construction workers had left the substance, the complaint did not allege that the Malaysian Government in any relevant sense 'employed' those workers. Therefore the court held that Robinson had failed to show that his claim was for a 'tortious act or omission' caused by the Malaysian Government.[139] Similarly, in *Randolph*, the court found that Saudi Arabia was not liable for injuries caused by careless driving of a Saudi student who was studying in the US on a Saudi government scholarship, because he was not an employee of Saudi Arabia and, even if he could be regarded as a Saudi employee, his trip was outside the scope of that employment.[140] Bodily assault provides another example of an act unrelated to the course of employment.[141] Thus courts would only exercise jurisdiction when the officer or employee of the foreign State was acting within the scope of his employment at the time he committed the tortious act or omission.[142]

In *Al-Adsani*, the plaintiff alleged that he had been tortured in Kuwait by an influential member of the Kuwaiti royal family in retaliation for his disclosure of videotapes embarrassing the latter and that, upon his return to England, he had received death threats from agents of the Kuwaiti Government, especially those from the Kuwaiti Embassy in London. The courts, however, were not satisfied that the threats made in England had emanated from a person or persons acting at the behest of the Government of Kuwait, or for whom Kuwait was otherwise vicariously responsible. As a result, immunity could not be denied.[143]

6. The terrorism exception in US law: a departure

In contrast to the strict territorial requirement of section 1605(a)(5) of the US FSIA, the terrorism exception to immunity in US law, originally enacted as the US Antiterrorism and Effective Death Penalty Act of 1996 (AEDPA),[144] confers *extra-territorial* jurisdiction on the US courts over certain acts of terrorism committed *abroad*. The AEDPA adds several new provisions to the US FSIA: section 1605(a)(7) stipulates that a foreign State shall not be immune from the jurisdiction of the US courts in any case 'for personal injury or death that was caused by an act of torture, extrajudicial killing, aircraft sabotage, hostage taking, or the provision of material support or resources ... for such an act'.[145] These amendments to the US FSIA 'shall apply to any cause of action arising before, on, or after the date of the enactment of this Act' (AEDPA, section 221(c)). That is, they apply retroactively.[146]

In addition to the denial of immunity by the AEDPA, a statutory note entitled 'Civil Liability for Acts of State Sponsored Terrorism (1996)',[147] commonly referred to as the 'Flatow Amendment',[148] was enacted to create a cause of action for any act which would give a court jurisdiction under the newly enacted section 1605(a)(7) of the US FSIA. Under this note, 'an official, employee, or agent of a foreign state designated as a state sponsor of terrorism ... shall be liable ... for personal injury or death caused by acts of that official, employee, or agent ... for money damages which may include economic damages, solatium, pain, and suffering, and punitive damages'.[149]

226   NON-COMMERCIAL TORTS

These enactments have now been incorporated into and replaced by section 1083 of the National Defense Authorization Act for Fiscal Year 2008 (NDAA).[150] The 'terrorism exception to the jurisdictional immunity of a foreign state', now listed as section 1605A of the FSIA, provides:

A foreign state shall not be immune from the jurisdiction of courts of the United States or of the States in any case not otherwise covered by this chapter in which money damages are sought against a foreign state for personal injury or death that was caused by an act of torture, extrajudicial killing, aircraft sabotage, hostage taking, or the provision of material support or resources for such an act if such act or provision of material support or resources is engaged in by an official, employee, or agent of such foreign state while acting within the scope of his or her office, employment, or agency.[151]

Of especial significance is the total absence of any territorial requirement for the exercise of jurisdiction under this provision. This means that the US courts will sit in judgment over alleged tortious conduct occurring anywhere in the world. It must be noted, however, that the territorial link is indeed preserved as far as enforcement is concerned. Under section 1610(a)(7), where a foreign State is not immune under section 1605(a)(7), then its property 'used for a commercial activity in the United States, shall not be immune from attachment in aid of execution, or from execution, upon a judgment ... regardless of whether the property is or was involved with the act upon which the claim is based'.[152] The property of an agency or instrumentality of a foreign State shall be denied immunity in the same way (section 1610(b)(2) as amended). A new provision, section 1610(g)(1), positively overrides the separate status of agencies or instrumentalities with regard to enforcement measures.[153]

Thus, a foreign State is denied immunity, both from adjudication and enforcement, for personal injury or death caused by torture or certain other acts committed *outside the US*. A territorial connection with the US territory, as contemplated in the original US FSIA, has been dispensed with.[154] This amounts to a fundamental change to the immunity regime as demarcated by the US FSIA. However, this exception is subject to an important qualification, namely, that it shall only apply if the defendant foreign State 'was designated as a state sponsor of terrorism at the time the act [of terrorism] occurred, or was so designated as a result of such act' (section 1605A(a)(2)(A)(i)(I)). So far only seven States have been so designated by the US Department of State: Cuba, Iran, Iraq, Libya, North Korea, Sudan and Syria; but Iraq,[155] Libya[156] and North Korea[157] have now been removed from the list, reducing the total number of suable States to four: Cuba, Iran, Sudan and Syria.[158] Cases have been decided against Cuba,[159] Iran,[160] Iraq,[161] Libya,[162] North Korea,[163] Sudan[164] and Syria.[165] As can be expected, in most such cases the defendants did not enter an appearance.[166] This list seems to be an open-ended one and more foreign States might be designated as 'State sponsors of terrorism' and be subjected to the jurisdiction of the US courts;[167] but, at least for the time being, other States, not being designated, still enjoy immunity in respect of the terrorism exception.[168] Furthermore, it seems that even those designated States still enjoy immunity for alleged acts occurring *prior to their designation.*[169] Besides, only US nationals or employees can have recourse to the terrorism exception.[170]

The fact that the AEDPA is limited to certain acts and to specifically designated States has caused dissatisfaction among a number of scholars.[171] Some are also concerned about the difficulty of enforcement either in the US or abroad of judgments rendered under this Act.[172] However, the designation by the State Department of 'State sponsors of terrorism' will remain the defining feature of the terrorism exception. In short, if the terrorism exception is a judicial sword, this sword has to be drawn by an executive hand in the first place. Such an executive-decided non-immunity is certainly tantamount to a reversion to the pre-US FSIA mechanism of executive suggestion of immunity or non-immunity and is therefore not free from criticism of re-politicization of the question of State immunity.[173] For one moment the US legislature seems to have forgotten that the declared objective of the FSIA was to leave 'sovereign immunity decisions exclusively to the courts' and to 'depoliticize litigation against foreign states'.[174]

Ironically, as conceded by a Circuit Court, the enactment of the AEDPA had actually been 'consistently resisted by the executive branch' for fear 'that the proposed amendment to FSIA might cause other nations to respond in kind, thus potentially subjecting the American government to suits in foreign countries for actions taken in the United States'.[175] At present, the terrorism exception remains unique to the US and, as an outgrowth of the peculiar political relations between the US and those States specifically designated as 'State sponsors of terrorism', seems unlikely to have many followers outside the US. More importantly, whether the terrorism exception has achieved its policy objectives even within the US still remains a matter of doubt.[176] Most notably, colossal sums of damages (often in the region of hundreds of millions of US dollars[177]) have been awarded but remain largely uncollected, leading to the poignant remark that a judgment under the terrorism exception epitomizes a 'Pyrrhic victory'.[178]

The most telling assessment so far has come from the bench. In a massive, 110-page long omnibus opinion in 2009, which thoroughly chronicled and meticulously analysed the discouraging history, together with its host of difficulties, of the terrorism exception with regard to Iran, the DC District Court obviously felt no need to conceal its deep sense of frustration:

Today, the Court also reaches an even more fundamental conclusion: Civil litigation against Iran under the FSIA state sponsor of terrorism exception represents a failed policy. After more than a decade spent presiding over these difficult cases, this Court now sees that these cases do not achieve justice for victims, are not sustainable, and threaten to undermine the President's foreign policy initiatives during a particularly critical time in our Nation's history. The truth is that the prospects for recovery upon judgments entered in these cases are extremely remote.[179]

... the Court will respectfully urge the President and Congress to seek meaningful reforms in this area of law in the form of a viable alternative to private litigation as the means of redress for the countless deaths and injuries caused by acts of terrorism ... If the decade-long history of these FSIA terrorism actions has revealed anything, it is that the Judiciary cannot resolve the intractable political dilemmas that frustrate these lawsuits; only Congress and the President can.[180]

Conclusion

In view of the long-established *acta jure imperii / acta jure gestionis* distinction, the statutory authorization to exercise jurisdiction over acts or omissions attributable to foreign States causing personal injury or death or damage to or loss of property is a new development since it negates the above distinction by rendering it irrelevant and unnecessary. Provided the territorial connection can be established, jurisdiction is based on the fact that some act/omission of a foreign State has resulted in injury/damage, but not on the nature of the act or omission. This now seems to be a widely accepted rule. While it remains to be clarified what acts or omissions precisely are targeted by such a provision, the underlying rationale would defeat the commonplace argument that immunity should be granted because the act or omission in question has been committed in the course of activities of a sovereign nature, such as an embassy errand. In particular, such an exception to immunity would deal effectively with traffic accidents caused by diplomatic or consular

CONCLUSION 229

personnel/vehicles, or other types of personnel/vehicles enjoying various degrees of immunity. Meanwhile, court practice has shown that this exception to immunity is potentially extendable to a wider range of activities, including those bearing a manifest sovereign attribute, such as political assassination.

The most important requirement in the context of tort is a territorial connection between either the tortious act/omission or the resultant injury/damage, or both, and the forum State. In short, when torts committed in the forum State are concerned, the overriding consideration for a court is neither a *jure imperii* / *jure gestionis* test nor whether 'insurable' personal injury is at issue, but whether the tortious act or omission has a connection with the territory of the forum State. The *jure imperii* / *jure gestionis* distinction has been discarded altogether in some States and is followed by others only to the extent that, when injury has been caused, *causing injury* will be regarded as *jure gestionis*, regardless of whether the act in the course of which injury has been caused is *jure imperii* or *jure gestionis*. Except where foreign armed forces are involved, it is rather doubtful if, in the event of actual injury being caused in the State of the forum, a court will deny jurisdiction on the sole ground that the act in question is *jure imperii*.

The new 'terrorism provision' in the US FSIA, which completely abolishes the territorial connection requirement, marks a departure from the general practice. It remains unique to the US and, because of the difficulties that beset its application, has been considered a failed judicial policy.

6 Separate entities

States do not exist or function in the abstract. They operate through a variety of organs, agencies and other instrumentalities and entities. Of these some lie at the heart of the State apparatus, such as the legislature, the judiciary, and the executive, which are, naturally, identified with the State itself; others bear a more or less close relationship with the core organs of the State; and still others are deliberately set up to be remote from the centre. Many of these would be endowed with a separate personality, subject to principles and rules other than those applicable to governmental departments, can own and dispose of property in their own name, and have the capacity of suing and being sued. Besides, even private and commercial entities would sometimes be charged with and actually exercise sovereign, governmental or public functions. Our question here is in what circumstances immunity should be available to these myriad entities that have a distinct and separate personality from the State. This question now assumes a growing significance with the new surge of nationalization necessitated by the current financial and economic crisis, which has led to a proliferation of entities owned or controlled by the State.

It must be observed from the outset that jurisdictional immunity under international law remains strictly an attribute or prerogative of the State; it belongs to the State itself. In this sense, the availability of immunity turns on the identification or connection with the State: only the State itself, or an organ or individual identified or connected with the State, can be entitled to immunity. One can at once see that immunity becomes more derivative in nature, the further away one moves from the State proper. Seen in this light, it is not difficult to conclude that an entity separate from the State itself enjoys immunity only when it is, or can be considered as being, endowed with certain attributes of the State, such as structurally forming part of the State apparatus and/or exercising certain functions normally entrusted only to a governmental department of the State. This is by no means a radical approach. In fact, it is in line with one of the oldest exceptions to immunity, one dating back to the earliest times of restrictive immunity, whereby a foreign State enjoyed no immunity with regard to its commercial undertakings in the State of the forum.

There are then three major issues to be considered. First, whether and under what circumstances can entities separate and distinct from the State be regarded as assimilated to the State; secondly, whether, under what circumstances and to what extent such entities enjoy immunity; and, thirdly, under what circumstances the separate personality of such entities should be disregarded, so that a separate entity and the State can be held mutually liable for each other's debts. As will be seen, there are widely divergent approaches to these issues.

1. Terminology

As in other areas of State immunity, only a generic term can be used here to describe various entities distinct and separate from the State. 'State entities' might be a very convenient term but it cannot cover all aspects of the phenomenon. Such a term postulates an intimate relationship between the State and the entity by stressing the 'State-ness' of the entity in question, whereas, in practice, many entities might be licensed or authorized by the State to perform some sort of public function, but are in every other respect a private entity.[1] 'State enterprises' is an even narrower term, since not all State entities are enterprises. What is more, sometimes commercial entities, whether or not they are owned or controlled by the State, may be endowed with certain public functions. Thus, an otherwise commercial bank could act 'as a bank of issue and/or administrator of the foreign exchange reserves',[2] as could a commercial airline be 'impressed into service' to perform functions in connection with the immigration laws of the country.[3]

Different terms have been employed by national legislation and various multilateral treaties or drafts by international learned bodies, and they reflect quite divergent ways of legal reasoning. For example, section 1603 of the US FSIA uses 'agency or instrumentality of a foreign State', while section 14 of the UK SIA adopts the term 'separate entity'. Apparently, the US FSIA stresses the 'State-ness' of the entity and therefore presumes immunity for the entity unless the opposite can be proven.

The UK SIA, on the other hand, emphasizes the 'separateness' of the entity and hence presumes non-immunity for the entity unless they can be shown to be part of the State structure. Therefore these two terms actually emphasize two different aspects of the definition of entity connected with the State: State-ness and separateness. Occasionally, courts have to pass judgments on entities jointly established by several States; and this is normally done by analogy to entities set up by one single State.[4]

This chapter adopts the term 'separate entities' so as to cover, as far as possible, the subject matter to be examined herein and, at the same time, not to prejudge the discussion. That is, the term here is merely intended to capture the separate personality of these various entities, and not to pass any judgment on their relationship with the State or their entitlement to immunity.

2. Diverse approaches

Diverse approaches have been adopted with regard to the issue of immunity of entities having a separate personality from the State. These approaches follow divergent, even opposing, lines of reasoning. The UK practice, for example, sets forth a presumption of non-immunity for separate entities, whereas the US practice contemplates the exact opposite: a presumption of immunity. Still others try to steer a middle course. In the final analysis, however, there does not seem to be too much difference; for in all cases involving separate entities the courts must, and in practice do, consider all the relevant circumstances of the case before a sensible decision can be reached. A multi-factor analysis thus seems to be the only viable test, regardless of the approaches purportedly taken in the practice of individual States.

2.1. The UK Model

At common law, the only workable test for the judges was to see whether a particular entity could be treated as an 'alter ego or organ' of the foreign State. If an entity was or could be considered as an emanation, arm, alter ego, organ or department of the foreign State, then it was entitled to immunity from suit; otherwise not.[5] In the leading case of *Trendtex*, it was held that the Central Bank of Nigeria, which had been created as a separate legal entity with no clear expression of intent that it should have governmental status, was not an emanation or alter ego of Nigeria. The judges went to enormous lengths in examining all the relevant documents and circumstances regarding the status and functions of the bank. Lord Denning said:

> I confess that I can think of no satisfactory test except that of looking to the *functions and control* of the organisation ... I would look to *all the evidence* to see whether the organisation was under government control and exercised governmental functions.[6]

He then summed up the factors considered:

> At the hearing we were taken through the Act of 1958 under which the Central Bank of Nigeria was established, and of the amendments to it by later decrees. All the relevant provisions were closely examined: and we had the benefit of expert evidence on affidavit which was most helpful. The upshot of it all may be summarised as follows. (i) The Central Bank of Nigeria is a central bank modelled on the Bank of England. (ii) It has governmental functions in that it issues legal tender; it safeguards the international value of the currency; and it acts as banker and financial adviser to the government. (iii) Its affairs are under a great deal of government control in that the Federal Executive Council may overrule the board on monetary and banking policy and on internal administrative policy. (iv) It acts as banker for other banks in Nigeria and abroad, and maintains accounts with other banks. It acts as banker for the states within the federation: but has few, if any, private customers.[7]

The other two judges went through exactly the same process. Stephenson LJ conducted a meticulous examination of the status of the Nigerian Central Bank, its powers and duties, its separate personality, its capability of suing and being sued, and the degree of government control.[8] In the same vein, Shaw LJ declared:

> Whether a particular organisation is to be accorded the status of a department of government or not must depend on its constitution, its powers and duties and its activities. These are the basic factors to be considered ... [A] court before which the issue of sovereign immunity arises [has] the responsibility of examining *all the relevant circumstances*.[9]

He then carefully went through the Central Bank of Nigeria Act 1958 and the amending enactments, considering such factors as the status, personality, powers, legal attributes, structure, designated functions of the bank, and its control and supervision by the Nigerian Government. According to his finding, the bank had 'a status outside the government and separate from it', and was a mere agent for the government in certain matters and not vested with any executive power.[10]

234　SEPARATE ENTITIES

The UK practice is concisely summarized as follows:

(a) The characterisation of a party to proceedings as department of the government of a foreign sovereign State depends not on any single factor, but on a consideration of all relevant circumstances.
(b) The status of the party under the law of its home state is one relevant factor but is not decisive. Nor is the presence of separate legal personality itself decisive against characterising a party as a department of government.
(c) A detailed analysis of the constitution, function, powers and activities of the party of its relationship with the state is likely to be essential. The existence of State control is not, however, a sufficient criterion.
(d) The courts are likely to exercise caution before treating a party having separate legal personality as a department of government ...

As for the requirement that the entity be distinct from the executive organs of government, this would appear to require a careful examination of the entity's constitution, functions, powers and activities and its relationship with the State in order to determine whether the required degree of separation exists.[11]

Moorthy lists the following factors:

(1) Whether the body has any discretion of its own; if it has, what is the degree of control by the Executive over the exercise of that discretion; (2) Whether the property vested in the corporation is held by it for and on behalf of the Government; (3) Whether the corporation has any financial autonomy; (4) Whether the functions of the corporation are Governmental functions.[12]

This multifactor test has been preserved in the case law decided under the UK SIA. Section 14 provides:

(1) The immunities and privileges conferred by this Part of this Act apply to any foreign or commonwealth State other than the United Kingdom; and references to a State include references to –
(a) the sovereign or other head of that State in his public capacity;
(b) the government of that State; and
(c) any department of that government,

but not to any entity (hereafter referred to as a 'separate entity') which is distinct from the executive organs of the government of the State and capable of suing or being sued.

(2) A separate entity is immune from the jurisdiction of the courts of the United Kingdom if, and only if –
(a) the proceedings relate to anything done by it in the exercise of sovereign authority; and
(b) the circumstances are such that a State ... would have been so immune.[13]

By excluding 'separate entities' from the definition of the State, the UK SIA creates what may be conveniently termed as a 'presumption of non-immunity' for them; that is, such entities would normally be denied immunity and would be granted immunity only in the exceptional case where they have acted in the exercise of sovereign authority.

A two-step analysis emerges for the court from this provision, the first step being a determination of the *status* of the entity in question and the second a characterization of the particular *act* of that entity on which the claim is based. First, the court has to ascertain whether an entity is truly 'separate' from the State, meaning in particular that it possesses a separate legal personality or identity and enjoys financial and administrative independence. To do this the court has to conduct an investigation into the entity's incorporation, separate personality, status and its relationship with the State. Certainly, if the entity has no separate personality, it will be included in the definition of the State and its immunity has to be decided in the same terms as the State. Secondly, once the entity is found to be separate from the State, the court has to decide whether the entity would nonetheless be immune if certain conditions are fulfilled. The task is by no means an easy one, especially in view of the enormous variety of the entities having different relationships with the State, and the difficulty in defining the phrase 'the exercise of sovereign authority'. The section does not make it clear whether an entity that is separate but entrusted with public functions could be regarded as included in the term 'State', but the language of the provision seems strongly to suggest non-inclusion.

In *Tsavliris*, the court had to decide whether the Grain Board of Iraq (GBI), an entity with a separate legal personality which owned a cargo of wheat on board a ship involved in an arbitration award for salvage services, was a department of the Iraqi Ministry of Trade (MOT) and hence of the Iraqi Government, or a separate entity from the Iraqi Government. If the former, it would be entitled to rely on State immunity; if the latter, it would be amenable to the enforcement of the arbitral award and a freezing injunction.

Clearly, the central issue was the status of the GBI under section 14(1). Cross J examined an abundance of evidence, including:

(1) that the GBI is a public, State-owned, company incorporated pursuant to Article 1 of Law No. 22, which provides that a public company is '[a] self-financing economic unit which is fully owned by the State, has a juristic person[ality] and financial and administrative independence, and operates in accordance with economic principles'. More

236 SEPARATE ENTITIES

specifically, it was owned by the MOT, and its capital was determined by the Council of Ministers;

(2) that the Board of Directors of the GBI, chaired by a General Manager, enjoyed the widest powers in formulating the administrative, financial and regulatory policies and plans necessary to perform the duties of the company and achieve its objectives and to supervise and follow up the implementation thereof, and was free to set the budget of the GBI;

(3) that the main function and purpose of the GBI was to purchase grain, both in Iraq and abroad, for Iraqi citizens;

(4) that the GBI enjoyed separate legal personality and was entitled to enter into contracts in its own name;

(5) that, despite its government ownership, provided that it acted within the powers given to it, and performed the functions assigned to it, the GBI was controlled by the General Manager and not the Iraqi Government;

(6) that, in sum, although State established, capitalized and owned and although its employees were hired in accordance with the law governing the civil service, the GBI possessed a separate identity, together with financial and administrative independence, and had control over its own day-to-day business activities.

Cross J thus concluded that the GBI was a separate entity.[14] He pointed out, in particular, that the views of the 'home' State of the entity were not and could not be decisive.[15]

He then proceeded to consider the issue of immunity under section 14(2) and held that the entry into a salvage agreement on a Lloyd's Standard Form of Salvage Agreement, 2000 edition (LOF) was not a governmental activity.[16]

In *Wilhelm Finance*, the judge said:

Having considered ... the *constitution, function, powers and activities* of the Defendant and of its relationship with the state I have concluded that the Defendant is a separate entity.[17]

According to the UK SIA, one of the criteria for a separate entity is that it must be 'distinct from the executive organs of the government of the State'. Mann explains that this distinctness is 'a question of fact and depends on foreign law, viz., the status which the foreign law confers upon the entity rather than the factual situation' and that such distinctness 'must be of an organisational character in the sense that the test is provided by the existence of the right of executive organs to give directions about the conduct of the entity's daily business'.[18]

It is precisely this 'distinctness from executive organs' that later proved to be a problem. In *Propend*, the issue whether the particular act in question could be characterized as sovereign or non-sovereign depended on how the question of status was solved. The High Court held that the Australian Federal Police (AFP) was not part of, and therefore distinct from, the executive government of Australia and, therefore, its acts in question were not in the exercise of sovereign authority.[19] The Court of Appeal reversed the decision by giving a broader definition to the term 'government', thereby treating the performance of police functions as 'essentially a part of governmental activity'.[20]

It can be seen that separateness is a very important factor. Now that a 'separate entity' will not be included in the reference to the State, it naturally follows that a 'non-separate entity' will be included. However, it must be noted that, though separateness prima facie militates against immunity, it does not necessarily preclude immunity, just as non-separateness does not necessarily lead to immunity, because what then comes into operation is the rule regarding whether the entity has been engaging in the exercise of sovereign authority. If it has, it is immune. It is obviously insufficient if the court contents itself with the findings of separateness or non-separateness. It has to be further decided whether the particular act or transaction falls into the category that would make the State immune under similar circumstances. On the other hand, the question of status is still of great moment. Sometimes even the characterization of the act itself depends on whether the entity in question is distinct from or identifiable with the State. In a word, to be able to solve any practical problem it might encounter, the court often has to look at both the structure of a particular entity and the act or transaction giving rise to the claim.

Where the separateness of an entity is not in dispute, the focus will naturally be shifted to the question whether that entity has acted in the exercise of sovereign authority. In *Kuwait Airways*,[21] the Kuwait Airways Corporation (KAC) brought an action against the Iraqi Airways Company (IAC), claiming delivery up and/or damages (US $630 million) for the value of ten civilian aircraft belonging to KAC seized by Iraq during the Iraqi invasion of Kuwait in August 1990. The aircraft were used (though in an extremely limited fashion given the near-complete cessation of international flights to and from Iraq) by the IAC as part of its own fleet after 17 September 1990, when the Revolutionary Command Council Resolution 369, which purported to dissolve KAC and transfer all its assets to IAC, came into effect. Shortly before the invasion of Iraq by the coalition forces in 1991, six aircraft were flown to Iran, where they were impounded by the Iranian Government and were later

238   SEPARATE ENTITIES

returned to KAC. Four remaining aircraft were destroyed in air raids by the coalition forces.

Pursuant to section 14, two issues needed to be addressed: (1) whether the IAC was a 'separate entity'; (2) whether the particular act done by the IAC would warrant immunity. It was not doubted that IAC was a 'separate entity' within the meaning of section 14(1).[22] The essential facts on which a decision was needed under section 14(2) were the removal of the aircraft from Kuwait Airport to Iraq, and the treatment of the aircraft by IAC as part of its fleet after 17 September 1990. Different decisions made in this case reflect a lack of certainty.

The High Court held that the IAC was not entitled to immunity because the acts which it had performed in relation to the aircraft were not done in the exercise of sovereign authority. Although the invasion and occupation of Kuwait, including Kuwait airport, were clearly acts *jure imperii*, the removal of the aircraft and their subsequent use by IAC *for commercial purposes* were separate acts which were commercial and non-sovereign in character.[23]

The Court of Appeal held that the IAC was entitled to immunity. In the court's opinion, the dominant circumstance was the very act of appropriation itself. Iraq had invaded and occupied Kuwait by force of arms, and the subsequent expropriation of Kuwaiti assets was the action of a victorious military power exercising rights of conquest. The expropriation of foreign assets by a victorious power is an act *jure imperii*. The aircraft had been subjected to forcible confiscation or expropriation which, like the invasion itself, could only have been carried out by or at the behest of a sovereign State in exercise of its sovereign authority. The IAC had been simply an accomplice or a tool in the act of Iraq in confiscating the aircraft. The acts of seizing and 'looking after' the aircraft were done *jure imperii*: they had been done, and could only have been done, by the exercise of sovereign powers, since no civil airline could have commandeered the aircraft of another civil airline without invoking governmental authority. But for the seizure and removal of the aircraft, which indisputably were neither commercial acts nor such as might have been done by a private person, the aircraft could not have been 'looked after' by IAC as agent for Iraq. The IAC's ability to treat the aircraft as part of its civil airline fleet stemmed solely from Iraq's exercise of sovereign authority in the passing of Resolution 369. The fact that the IAC's purpose was to operate the aircraft as part of a commercial air service was immaterial, because it was the nature, not the purpose, of the act which was decisive.[24]

Most importantly, the court found it impossible to detach the IAC's acts over the different periods. In the words of Simon Brown LJ:

on the particular facts of this case, it is unreal and impermissible to seek to separate out IAC's eventual use of the disputed aircraft pursuant to the State's Decree from the circumstances of their initial acquisition. The reality is . . . that IAC was intimately involved throughout the entire expropriatory process: the planes were spoils of war and IAC was party to their taking. In the result IAC cannot now be impleaded: having acted in concert with the State in what was par excellence an act of sovereign authority – the exercise of militaristic power – it too is entitled to immunity from the jurisdiction of domestic Courts.[25]

The decision by the House of Lords is interesting. Their Lordships held unanimously that the acts of the IAC prior to 17 September 1990 were inseparable from the initial seizure of the aircraft by Iraq and thus attracted immunity.[26] But they were divided (by three to two) on the characterization of the IAC's acts *after* 17 September 1990. The majority held that, once the Revolutionary Command Council Resolution 369 came into effect on 17 September 1990, the IAC's position altered. From that moment, it acted as the owner of commercial property, title to which had been vested in it by the Resolution. The fact that the initial seizure of the aircraft was a sovereign act could not mean that all subsequent dealings with them by the IAC also possessed a sovereign character.[27]

In the leading opinion of the majority, Lord Goff, citing Lord Wilberforce's statement of the 'context' principle in *I Congreso del Partido*, declared:

It is apparent from Lord Wilberforce's statement of principle that the ultimate test of what constitutes an act jure imperii is whether the act in question is of its own character a governmental act, as opposed to an act which any private citizen can perform. It follows that, in the case of acts done by a separate entity, it is not enough that the entity should have acted on the directions of the state, because such an act need not possess the character of a governmental act. To attract immunity under section 14(2), therefore, what is done by the separate entity must be something which possesses that character . . . But where an act done by a separate entity of the state on the directions of the state does not possess the character of a governmental act, the entity will not be entitled to state immunity . . . Likewise, in the absence of such character, the mere fact that the purpose or motive of the act was to serve the purposes of the state will not be sufficient to enable the separate entity to claim immunity under section 14(2) of the Act.[28]

In other words, in order to attract immunity, what is done by a separate entity must, *standing alone and considered in its own right*, be

240 SEPARATE ENTITIES

a sovereign or governmental act. This marks a clear departure from Lord Wilberforce's *I Congreso* proposition that, in deciding whether there is a commercial activity, the court must consider the *whole context* of the claim, including the *purpose* of the act in question.[29] For what is implied in Lord Wilberforce's statement is precisely the opposite, that is, the possibility that, in some cases, the act in question, standing alone and viewed *outside its context* and solely in the light of its character, may not be straightforwardly a governmental act; hence it becomes necessary in such a situation to consider other factors beyond the mere character of the act itself. We shall see that Lord Goff's stringent test is not an easy one to apply under the circumstances.

As for the acts of the IAC prior to 17 September 1990, Lord Goff made the following finding:

> the taking of the aircraft and their removal from Kuwait Airport to Iraq constituted an exercise of governmental power by the State of Iraq. [It was] submitted that the participation of I.A.C. in that action, by supplying engineers and pilots who performed the mundane task of preparing the aircraft for flying and then flying them from Kuwait to Iraq, was not that of a sovereign but of a carrier. There is force in this argument; but I am satisfied that, in so acting, I.A.C. was not just doing a job of work, but was closely involved with the State of Iraq in the last stage of an enterprise which entailed both the seizure of the aircraft and their removal to Iraq to be used for such purposes as the Government of Iraq should direct, which in point of fact was to be their incorporation into I.A.C.'s fleet. On this basis I am of the opinion that I.A.C., in so acting, was acting in the exercise of sovereign authority.[30]

It is difficult to see how 'supplying engineers and pilots who performed the mundane task of preparing the aircraft for flying and then flying them', something regularly and routinely performed by private and commercial airlines every day, can be an act 'in the exercise of sovereign authority', an act '*of its own character* a governmental act, as opposed to an act which any private citizen can perform', unless one holds that, in checking, preparing and flying the aircraft, an activity which is by no means peculiarly sovereign in character, the IAC was acting within the *context* of a general scheme of expropriation of foreign assets by military force, 'on the directions of the State', and 'serving the *purposes* of the State'. Only then can it be fully and more clearly appreciated why Lord Goff said this:

> in so acting, I.A.C. was not just doing *a job of work* [that is, an ordinary commercial activity], but was *closely involved with the State of Iraq* in the last stage of an

enterprise which entailed both the seizure of the aircraft and their removal to Iraq to be used for such *purposes* as the Government of Iraq should direct. (Emphases added)

Stated generally and in the language of Lord Goff's declared principle, it boils down to this:

Even if what is done by a separate entity does not possess the character of a sovereign act, the separate entity can still claim immunity if that act was done on the directions of the State and served the purposes of the State.

Thus the decision of the majority in *Kuwait Airways* is manifestly inconsistent. It must be recalled that the KAC's legal action was basically one of conversion, that is, the KAC was claiming delivery up and/or damages for the forcible seizure of its aircraft. In other words, this action was based on the *confiscation*, not the *operation*, of the aircraft; and the confiscation was done by the IAC under orders from the Iraqi Government. The whole case thereby hinges on how one characterizes the IAC's *taking possession of* the aircraft. One either views the activity of the IAC solely in the light of its character and outside its context, in which case the acts of the IAC (checking, preparing and flying the aircraft), both before and after 17 September 1990, would constitute commercial or private activity. Or one considers what was done by the IAC within the whole context of the claim, in which case one has to hold, as did the Court of Appeal and the dissenting judges in the House of Lords,[31] that the acts of the IAC, both before and after 17 September 1990, were done pursuant to the actions of Iraq in its sovereign capacity; such acts were so closely connected with sovereign authority as to partake of the sovereign character of the acts of the Iraqi Government. Either way, there should not, and cannot, be a fine distinction between what was done before 17 September 1990 and what was done after that. If anything, this case further highlights the difficulty and impracticability of a 'nature-only' test in determining the existence of a commercial activity. It must also be remembered that the question of immunity is one of procedure only; it concerns the *forum* for the settlement of a dispute but has nothing directly to do with substantive responsibility or guilt. To say that a defendant is immune from current proceedings is not to say that it/he is not guilty or not responsible for the wrong committed; it is simply saying that this court or tribunal is, in the eyes of international law, not the right place to settle that dispute.

242   SEPARATE ENTITIES

2.2. The US Model

Unlike the UK SIA, which excludes 'separate entities' from the references to a 'State', the US FSIA includes separate entities in the definition of 'foreign State'. Section 1603 stipulates:

For purposes of this chapter –

(a) A 'foreign state' ... includes a political subdivision of a foreign state or an agency or instrumentality of a foreign state as defined in subsection (b).
(b) An 'agency or instrumentality of a foreign state' means any entity –
  (1) which is a separate legal person, corporate or otherwise, and
  (2) which is an organ of a foreign state or political subdivision thereof, or a majority of whose shares or other ownership interest is owned by a foreign state or political subdivision thereof, and
  (3) which is neither a citizen of a State of the United States[32] ... nor created under the laws of any third country.[33]

One can see that a 'separate entity' under the UK SIA and an 'agency or instrumentality' under the US FSIA are not exactly the same thing. First, a 'separate entity' must be 'distinct from the executive organs of the government of the State', whereas an 'agency or instrumentality', despite being 'a separate legal person', can be 'an organ of a foreign state or political subdivision thereof'. That is to say, the term 'agency or instrumentality' under the US FSIA includes both those entities that are 'distinct from the executive organs of the government' and those which, being 'organs' of a foreign State, are *indistinct* from or form part of the executive organs of the government. Thus, if a 'separate entity' is to be defined only in terms of its distinctness from the executive organs of the government, then the definition of an 'agency or instrumentality' under the US FSIA will include both 'separate' and 'non-separate' entities. Secondly, by defining a 'separate entity' as one 'distinct from the executive organs of the government of the State and capable of suing or being sued', and laying down a scheme whereby a separate entity can enjoy immunity for 'anything done by it in the exercise of sovereign authority', the UK SIA envisages the possibility of a wholly private-owned company being entitled to immunity; whereas the US FSIA, by requiring a close relationship between the 'agency or instrumentality' and the State (the agency having to be either an 'organ' of the State or majority-owned by it), precludes such possibility. Moreover, being 'a separate legal person' is not the same as being 'capable of suing or being sued'. Whereas being 'a separate legal person' would normally have the capability of suing and being sued, being 'capable of suing or being sued' does not necessarily presuppose a separate legal personality in the usual sense of the term. Trade unions in the UK, for example, have just such a curious legal status: a trade union is capable of suing or being sued in its own name, but does not have a separate legal personality.[34] Be that as it may, to the extent that a 'non-separate entity' (meaning non-separate or indistinct from the government/State) would at any rate be included in the definition of a 'State' under both the UK SIA and the US FSIA, we shall, for convenience's sake, from time to time in our discussion regard an 'agency or instrumentality of a foreign State' as equivalent to a 'separate entity', particularly when comparing the UK SIA and the US FSIA. Yet the distinction is worth remembering for the avoidance of confusion.

A brief word should be said here about the requirement of majority ownership in section 1603(b)(2). The legislative report merely states that:

> If such entities are entirely owned by a foreign state, they would of course be included within the definition. Where ownership is divided between a foreign state and private interests, the entity will be deemed to be an agency or instrumentality of a foreign state only if a majority of the ownership interests (shares of stock or otherwise) is owned by a foreign state or by a foreign state's political subdivision.[35]

But neither the US FSIA nor the legislative report defines 'majority'. The case law sets the threshold at 50 per cent, so that a 51 per cent[36] or even a 50.01 per cent,[37] or a vague 'more than 50 per cent'[38] ownership will be considered 'majority ownership', whereas 49.9 per cent or 'less than 50 per cent' will not. Interestingly, 'at least 50 per cent'[39] (which would logically include an exact 50 per cent share) has also been treated as a majority. In a few cases, even though the foreign State owned less than 50 per cent of the *total stock*, the entity in question was still regarded as majority-owned by the State on the ground that the State owned a majority of the *voting stock*.[40]

The legislative report offers, by way of example, a rather expansive list of entities that could be regarded as 'agencies or instrumentalities' of foreign States. Such entities:

> could assume a variety of forms, including a state trading corporation, a mining enterprise, a transport organization such as a shipping line or airline, a steel company, a central bank, an export association, a governmental procurement agency or a department or ministry which acts and is suable in its own name.[41]

Over the years, the assimilation of the State and its entity has led to a proliferation, in the eyes of US case law, of 'agencies and

244　SEPARATE ENTITIES

instrumentalities'. These multifarious entities include national air-lines,[42] central banks,[43] commercial banks,[44] broadcasting corpor-ations,[45] television stations,[46] oil and gas companies,[47] nuclear energy companies,[48] import–export companies,[49] mining companies,[50] shipping companies,[51] railway companies,[52] liquidators,[53] and car manufactur-ers.[54] Moreover, apart from various diplomatic and consular missions, which are considered to be either agencies or instrumentalities, or simply organs,[55] quasi-public entities such as national banks, state uni-versities, public television networks and others (such as the Norwegian Seaman's Mission), and an electric power corporation have been con-sidered 'organs' of foreign States.[56] By virtue of section 1603(a), they are all 'foreign States'. This is not surprising, since the legislative intent seems to be that the terms 'organ' and 'agency or instrumentality' are to be construed broadly.[57]

2.2.1.　The presumption of immunity

Under the US FSIA, as a matter of principle, 'a foreign state shall be immune from the jurisdiction of the courts of the United States' unless one of the exceptions applies (section 1604); and a 'foreign State', as defined by section 1603(a) 'includes a political subdivision of a foreign state or an agency or instrumentality of a foreign state'. Thus, in con-trast to the UK Model, the US Model accords an 'agency or instrumental-ity of a foreign State', which is a 'separate legal person', the same presumption of immunity as enjoyed by the foreign State itself; that is, an 'agency or instrumentality of a foreign State' or in other words a separate entity, being included in the definition of the State, is, like the State itself, presumptively immune from the jurisdiction of the US courts unless one of the statutory exceptions under the FSIA applies.

2.2.2.　A question of status

Since a foreign State or its agency or instrumentality is presumptively immune,[58] the first thing a court must do is to consider, not whether the particular entity has engaged in commercial activity, but whether that entity is an 'agency or instrumentality' and can therefore be assimilated to the foreign State. Thus, the question of immunity starts as and often becomes a question of *status*. The court is first of all concerned with the status of the defendant rather than its acts. The court must look into, among other things, the objectives of the entity, its structure and consti-tution, its proximity to and relationship with the State apparatus, its designed functions, obligations and privileges, and its budgetary arrangement, in order to determine whether the entity in question is an 'agency or instrumentality' of the State. Such a multifactor analysis was already implicit in the Supreme Court's description of separate entities set up by foreign States. In *Bancec*, the US Supreme Court said:

> Increasingly during this century, governments throughout the world have established separately constituted legal entities to perform a variety of tasks. The organization and control of these entities vary considerably, but many possess a number of common features. A typical government instrumentality, if one can be said to exist, is created by an enabling statute that prescribes the powers and duties of the instrumentality, and specifies that it is to be managed by a board selected by the government in a manner consistent with the enabling law. The instrumentality is typically established as a separate juridical entity, with the powers to hold and sell property and to sue and be sued. Except for appropriations to provide capital or to cover losses, the instrumentality is primarily responsible for its own finances. The instrumentality is run as a distinct economic enterprise; often it is not subject to the same budgetary and personnel requirements with which government agencies must comply.[59]

Because the presumption of immunity primarily turns on an entity being a State entity, then a finding that it is not such an entity should be dispositive of the issue of immunity. On the other hand, once an entity is found to be a State entity, it becomes necessary to see if its conduct triggers the application of any of the statutory exceptions to immunity. Clearly, in the US practice, an examination of the status of the entity precedes a determination of the alleged conduct which gives rise to the claim.

In many cases, an entity was found to be a State entity simply because it was wholly[60] or majority[61] owned by the foreign State or, even more simply, because the State entity status was assumed, conceded, or otherwise undisputed.[62] An entity whose status has been so established becomes – or 'is', in the language of the US courts, a 'foreign State',[63] entitled to a presumption of immunity. Only then will the court consider, for example, whether the State entity has engaged in commercial activity, thereby relinquishing its immunity.

In a sense, the US Model seems to be the exact obverse of the UK Model. The UK SIA includes non-separate entities in the definition of State but excludes separate ones, and applies a rule of presumption of non-immunity to separate entities. The UK SIA is thus preoccupied with the separateness of an entity in that, in every case, the court must ascertain whether the entity in question is indeed separate from the State; and this would often entail a toilsome examination of all the circumstances of the case while considering a multitude of factors including the constitution, powers and functions, government control, autonomy, and so on, of the entity. Once found to be distinct from the State, an entity can no longer enjoy immunity. By contrast, the US FSIA includes both separate and non-separate entities. The inclusion of such entities in the definition of the State places these entities under the same rules as the State itself. Immunity is thus presumed for these entities, separate or otherwise, unless certain exceptions can be proved. Since the separateness of an entity no longer appears to be an issue, one would expect the task of the US courts to be lighter, as they apparently only have to consider the activity of the entity in question to see if that falls within one of the exceptions to immunity under the US FSIA.

But the question is not that simple. Where the status of the entity is not in dispute, the court can of course proceed to consider the acts of the entity straightaway. However, when the status of the entity is not clear or is disputed, the court will be faced with no less arduous a task. For the US FSIA does not really eliminate the problem of separate personality but instead transforms it into one of 'State-ness'; that is, the question now becomes whether a particular entity can indeed be included in the definition of the State. In order to be included in that definition, the entity first has to fit into the definition of 'agency or instrumentality'. As section 1603(b) defines an 'agency or instrumentality' by reference to its separate legal personality, its position within the State apparatus or its ownership, together with its citizenship and place of incorporation, the court would now have to conduct an investigation into the overall system of the foreign State as well as the position, structure and functions of the entity, so as to determine if it indeed fits the description of section 1603(b). If the entity is as described by section 1603(b), then it is an 'agency or instrumentality of a foreign State', entitled to immunity; otherwise not.

Sometimes the ascertainment of State ownership can be complicated and time-consuming. In *Trans Chemical*, the court examined a considerable amount of evidence, including expert testimonies and various Chinese laws and regulations in order to decide whether the China National Machinery Import and Export Corporation (CNMC) was owned by China and therefore could be considered an 'agency or instrumentality' of the Chinese State. Based upon an analysis of the evolution of State-owned industrial enterprises in China and the CNMC's own documents (in which CNMC consistently held itself out to potential clients and creditors as a State-owned enterprise), the court concluded that the

CNMC, being one of the Chinese industrial enterprises 'owned by the whole people', was State-owned, with proprietary rights exercised by the State Council on behalf of the State. It was an agency or instrumentality of China.[64]

2.2.3. 'A separate legal person'

Since, under section 1603(b), an 'agency or instrumentality of a foreign state' must be 'a separate legal person', the question has arisen whether various government departments, to the extent that they may be given some separate personality, are to be treated as the foreign State itself, or as agencies or instrumentalities. This question is of critical practical importance as the FSIA does draw a distinction between the State proper and an agency or instrumentality, especially with respect to measures of constraint.

Some courts used to apply a 'legal characteristics' test, which relied on the following statement in the legislative report:

The first criterion, that the entity be a separate legal person, is intended to include a corporation, association, foundation, or any other entity which, under the law of the foreign state where it was created, can sue or be sued in its own name, contract in its own name or hold property in its own name.[65]

However, the more reliable and now the established test looks at the 'core functions' of an entity and distinguishes between 'an entity that is an integral part of a foreign state's political structure, and an entity whose structure and function is predominantly commercial'.[66] That is, an entity is a political subdivision if its 'core functions' are governmental in nature, but is an agency or instrumentality if its 'core functions' are commercial. In *Transaero*, the DC Circuit had to consider whether the Bolivian Air Force counted as a 'foreign State' or rather as an 'agency or instrumentality' for the purposes of service of process under section 1608 of the US FSIA. The court found fault with the 'legal characteristics test'. In its opinion, 'any nation may well find it convenient ... to give powers of contract and litigation to entities that on any reasonable view must count as part of the state itself'; under such a 'characteristics test', therefore, the US Departments of State and of Defense would count as 'instrumentalities'.[67]

The court proposed a so-called 'categorical approach'. It held that the distinction between foreign States and their instrumentalities established two categories of actors that corresponded to the restrictive theory's two categories of acts, and that such a distinction should be determined by ascertaining 'whether the core functions of the foreign entity are predominantly governmental or commercial'.[68] Applying this framework, the court held that the Bolivian Air Force was a 'foreign state or political subdivision' within the meaning of section 1608:

> armed forces are as a rule so closely bound up with the structure of the state that they must in all cases be considered as the 'foreign state' itself, rather than a separate 'agency or instrumentality' of the state. The 'powers to declare and wage war' are among the 'necessary concomitants' of sovereignty ... [I]t is hard to see what would count as the 'foreign state' if its armed forces do not.[69]

The DC Circuit further elaborated on the 'categorical approach' in *Roeder*, in which US citizens taken hostage in Iran in 1979 brought a class action against Iran and its Ministry of Foreign Affairs. The court had to consider whether Iran's Ministry of Foreign Affairs was an 'agent' of Iran for purposes of the Flatow Amendment, which provided a cause of action against officials, employees, and *agents* of foreign States. The court thus explicated the

> categorical approach: if the core functions of the entity are governmental, it is considered the foreign state itself; if commercial, the entity is an agency or instrumentality of the foreign state. A nation's armed forces are clearly on the governmental side. For similar reasons, the Ministry of Foreign Affairs must be treated as the state of Iran itself rather than as its agent. The conduct of foreign affairs is an important and 'indispensable' governmental function.[70]

Under section 1606 of the US FSIA, 'a foreign state except for an agency or instrumentality thereof shall not be liable for punitive damages'. Thus, the cases of *Transaero* and *Roeder*, even though not directly impinging on the issue, effectively foreclosed the possibility of awarding punitive damages against foreign governmental departments, which have come to be identified with the State and not regarded as 'agencies or instrumentalities'.[71]

The 'categorical approach' or the 'core functions' test received authoritative approval from the Supreme Court in *Ministry of Defense of Iran*, where a private citizen sought to attach, by imposing a lien upon, an International Chamber of Commerce arbitration award which the Iranian Ministry of Defence (MOD) had obtained in Switzerland and confirmed in a US court against Cubic Defense Systems, a military supplier,[72] in order to help satisfy a judgment against Iran for money damages for the assassination of his brother.[73] The district court allowed the attachment[74] and the Court of Appeals confirmed.[75] Upon appeal by the MOD, the Supreme Court vacated the judgment and remanded the case for reconsideration, stressing the different regimes under the FSIA of attachment against the 'property of a *foreign state*', *stricto sensu*, and the 'property of an *agency or instrumentality* of a foreign state'.[76] According to the Supreme Court, the Ninth Circuit did not explain what in the record might demonstrate that the Ministry was an 'agency or instrumentality' of the State rather than an integral part of the State itself and had therefore committed an error that was essential to its judgment.[77]

On remand, the Ninth Circuit opined that the answer turned on whether the entity, here the MOD, was a 'separate legal person'. Agreeing with the DC Circuit in *Transaero*, the Ninth Circuit said:

A foreign state is nothing more than the sum of its parts; in other words, like the United States, the state of Iran exists only through its head of state, its ministries, and the myriad administrative offices that collectively embody a sovereign state. More importantly, the foreign state can act only through these entities. We add that it is illogical to distinguish between a 'foreign state' and 'agency and instrumentality' on the basis that the latter is a 'separate legal person' while the former is not ... We adopt the 'core functions' test as the appropriate benchmark for deciding whether an entity should be viewed as a 'foreign state' or as an 'agency or instrumentality' ... The question thus becomes whether MOD is inherently a part of the political state or a commercial actor ... [W]e adopt a strong presumption that the armed forces constitute a part of the foreign state itself, and that presumption has not been rebutted here.[78]

2.2.4. 'An organ of a foreign State'

As noted by the US courts, there is no 'clear test' for determining whether or not an entity qualifies as an 'organ' of a foreign State.[79] It seems that an 'organ of a foreign State' is a very extensive concept and covers in particular State enterprises and other commercial institutions. And, even though section 1603(b) of the FSIA defines an 'agency or instrumentality' as an 'organ of a foreign state', the courts in practice do seem to maintain a distinction between an 'organ' and an 'agency or instrumentality', and adopt different criteria for them. In *Braspetro*, the court had to consider the status of Brasoil, a Cayman Islands corporation engaged in the oil business and a wholly owned subsidiary of Braspetro, which in turn was a fully owned subsidiary of Petrobras whose principal shareholder was the Brazilian Government. As Brasoil was not owned by Brazil or a political subdivision thereof; the Brazilian Government did not actively supervise Brasoil; Brasoil's employees were not civil servants; and Brasoil did not hold exclusive oil-related rights in Brazil, the court concluded that Brasoil was not an 'organ' of the Brazilian

250   SEPARATE ENTITIES

Government. And, because Brasoil was not owned by the Brazilian Government, but rather by another corporation, it could not qualify as an 'agency or instrumentality' either.[80] Petrobras was held to be 'an entity the majority of whose shares are owned by a foreign state or an organ of a foreign state', since it 'was created for a national purpose, was actively supervised by the Brazilian Government, and was granted a monopoly over the national oil industry'.[81] Somewhat confusingly, the court found that Braspetro qualified as an 'organ' of Brazil, even though it was *indirectly owned* by Brazil through the majority ownership and comprehensive control of Petrobras.[82] Once these two entities were determined to be 'organs', then:

> Petrobras, directly and indirectly through Braspetro employees who serve as Brasoil's officers, controlled the day-to-day operations of Brasoil to such an extent that Brasoil is the alter ego of Petrobras ... As the alter ego of Petrobras with respect to the Bonds, Brasoil is also entitled to foreign sovereign immunity under the FSIA unless one of the statutory exceptions to immunity applies.[83]

One is thus vividly acquainted with the usefulness of the term 'organ', which not only suppresses the application of the requirement of majority ownership (although such ownership may serve to reinforce the 'organ' status, as shown above), but also allows the defendant State entity to argue for immunity on the basis of a public purpose. The purpose test, much discredited at a later stage of deciding whether an act constitutes a 'commercial activity', is now secretly treated as a crucial criterion. Moreover, the catenation of a 'patronage effect', that is, the State entity status of one entity helps secure the State entity status of another entity, leaves much room for criticism, as will be discussed in the context of 'tiering'.

In *Gates*, a group of former employees who were dismissed by a California pork processing plant upon closedown sued the plant's parent company, Fletcher's Fine Foods (FFF), a pork processing plant headquartered in British Columbia, Canada, and FFF's own parent, Alberta Pork Producers Development Corporation (Alberta Pork), a Canadian entity established for the purposes of effective marketing and promotion of hogs produced in the Canadian Province of Alberta. Both Alberta Pork and FFF claimed that they were 'agencies or instrumentalities of a foreign state' and hence immune from the court's jurisdiction under the FSIA. The court held that Alberta Pork was an 'agency or instrumentality' of a foreign State even though the government did not exercise day-to-day management over the entity, for the following reasons: the government played an active supervisory role; Alberta Pork could only act on matters the government authorized; the government could order it to change its regulations; producers who were dissatisfied with a decision by Alberta Pork could appeal to an appellate body appointed by the government; and members of Alberta Pork's board were given immunity from liability similar to that given to government actors.[84] Although the court used only the broader term of 'agency or instrumentality' without specifying whether Alberta Pork was an 'organ' of the provincial government, it is obvious that the decision was based on the administrative structure and functions, rather than on ownership.[85] By contrast, FFF could not be considered an 'organ' of the Province of Alberta because it was only 'an ordinary pork processing plant', and was wholly owned by Alberta Pork, an agency or instrumentality of a foreign State, but not by 'a foreign state or political subdivision thereof', as required by the FSIA.[86]

In *Mexicana*, the court found that Pemex-Refinacion (Pemex-Refining), a Mexican oil refinery, constituted an 'organ' under the US FSIA. What is notable in this case is that Pemex-Refining was a subsidiary of Petroleos Mexicanos (Pemex), itself an 'agency or instrumentality' of the Mexican State.[87] In other words, one finds in this case an entity owned by another entity. Indeed, this fact was used in *Mexicana* to argue against the instrumentality status of Pemex-Refining. The main task for the Ninth Circuit was therefore to distinguish the instant case from its earlier decision in *Gates*, in which it held that a subsidiary of a foreign State instrumentality was not an instrumentality of that State. The Ninth Circuit first declared:

there are two ways in which an entity can fulfill the requirements of § 1603(b)(2). *Either* the entity can be an 'organ of a foreign state', *or* the entity can have a majority of its shares or other ownership interest owned by 'a foreign state or a political subdivision thereof'.[88]

What the Ninth Circuit was saying here is basically that, apart from an 'ownership test', which would exclude an entity owned by another entity but not by the foreign State itself from the term 'instrumentality', there was also an 'organ' test, which might allow an entity's entity to be regarded as an 'instrumentality'. Thus a subsidiary of an instrumentality 'could be an "organ of a foreign state" and therefore fulfill §1603(b)(2)'s requirements *by a different route*',[89] namely, not by resorting to a majority ownership by a foreign State, but by relying on its special relationship with the foreign State. Thus, despite its being a subsidiary, Pemex-

Refining was an 'organ', and therefore an 'instrumentality', of the Mexican State, because of its peculiar pedigree:

[Pemex-Refining] is an integral part of the United Mexican States. Pemex [-Refining] was created by the Mexican Constitution, Federal Organic Law, and Presidential Proclamation; it is entirely owned by the Mexican Government; is controlled entirely by government appointees; employs only public servants; and is charged with the exclusive responsibility of refining and distributing Mexican government property. Thus Pemex-[Refining] is a subdivision of the United Mexican States and therefore qualifies for foreign sovereign immunity under FSIA.[90]

This alternative route of becoming a 'foreign State' by being its 'organ' was further elaborated by the Ninth Circuit in *Patrickson*, where the court said:

In defining whether an entity is an organ, courts consider whether the entity engages in a public activity on behalf of the foreign government. In making this determination, courts examine the circumstances surrounding the entity's creation, the purpose of its activities, its independence from the government, the level of government financial support, its employment policies, and its obligations and privileges under state law ... The entity may be an organ even if it has some autonomy from the foreign government.[91]

In *Intercontinental Dictionary Series*, a private unincorporated affiliation of linguistic scholars brought an action against the Australian National University (ANU), its employees, and its Research School of Pacific Studies (RSPS), alleging copyright infringement with respect to treatises on Austronesian languages. As a preliminary matter, in the court's opinion, 'the fact that the ANU and RSPS are capable of suing and being sued, of holding property, and of contracting strongly militates in favor of a finding of agency or instrumentality status'.[92] When the plaintiff contended that the ANU and RSPS were not entities where a majority of shares or other ownership interest was owned by a foreign State, the court responded:

§ 1603(b)(2) is framed in the alternative. Under this section, an entity may be considered an agency or instrumentality of a foreign state if it is either an 'organ' of that state or if a majority of its shares are owned by a foreign state. This case presents the scenario where a defendant falls under the rubric of an 'organ of a foreign state' rather than under the corporate context defined by a majority ownership of shares. For example, the ANU and the RSPS were formed by the Australian government to further academic interests of national importance; the salaries of its employees (including the named individual Australian defendants) are paid by the Australian government; the ANU must submit

Annual Reports and is subject to funding by the Australian government; and the ANU and RSPS are treated as 'agencies' in other legislation. Despite their relative academic independence, the ANU defendants should be considered 'organs' of the Australian government.[93]

In *Supra Medical*, where a Pennsylvania corporation brought a suit against various parties, including British medical and dental schools, for misappropriation of trade secrets and confidential information, the defendants contended that they qualified as an 'organ of a foreign State'. The court considered several factors:

(1) whether the foreign state created the entity for a national purpose; (2) whether the foreign state actively supervises the entity; (3) whether the foreign state requires the hiring of public employees and pays their salaries; (4) whether the entity holds exclusive rights to some right in the country; and (5) how the entity is treated under foreign state law.[94]

Applying these factors, the court concluded that the medical schools were not an 'organ' of the British government because:

First ... the purpose of the Schools is to teach and train medical practitioners and dental surgeons and promote research in these disciplines ... The ... Defendants have supplied no evidence that these goals serve any peculiar national or governmental purpose in Great Britain. Second, there is no evidence that the government actively supervises the Schools or requires them to hire public employees. Third, the Schools serve as only one source of medical and dental education in the United Kingdom; they hold no exclusive rights. Finally, and most importantly, British law apparently treats the Schools as independent from the British government ... Moreover, under British law, the Schools' 'Council of Governors' is selected by private officials within the Schools and is responsible for the Schools' debts, contractual obligations, and lawsuits. The British government has no apparent control over or responsibility for these affairs.[95]

In *Alpha*, Nippon Hoso Kyokai (NHK), the public television broadcasting corporation of Japan, was held to be an 'organ' of Japan. The court considered 'the totality of the circumstances', including: (1) NHK was created by the Japanese Broadcast Law, which required it to broadcast for the 'public welfare'; (2) NHK's programming must satisfy government-mandated goals; (3) the management of NHK consists of a twelve-member Board of Governors, all of whom are appointed by the Japanese Prime Minister with consent of the Diet (the Japanese Parliament); (4) the Minister of Posts and Telecommunications supervised the Board and must review NHK's annual budget, which must be approved by the Diet; (5) NHK's funding was derived from a government-mandated fee on all

254   SEPARATE ENTITIES

Japanese television owners; (6) any amendment to the Articles of Corporation that governed NHK's operations must be adopted and approved by the Minister; (7) NHK could not earn profits and carried no commercial advertisements; and (8) NHK was the only broadcaster termed a 'designated public institution' by the Japanese Prime Minister. These factors proved that Japan had considerable control over the content of NHK's programming, budget, and operations, making NHK an organ of Japan despite a measure of autonomy it maintained from the Japanese government.[96]

In *Kelly*, the Fifth Circuit went into a similarly lengthy analysis of the status, structure and functions of a Syrian petroleum company, Al Furat, an 'entity's entity', 50 per cent of whose shares were owned by a Syrian Petroleum Company which was wholly owned by the Syrian Government. It was found to be an 'organ' of Syria because it was created by a Syrian government decree for a national purpose: the development and exploration of Syria's mineral resources; its board members, including the chairman, were invariably high-level Syrian government officials; it had the exclusive right to explore and develop Syria's identified petroleum reserves, which are the property of the Syrian Government.[97] The five *Supra Medical* factors were applied but with an important caveat, namely, 'although the *Supra* factors provide a helpful framework, we will *not* apply them mechanically or require that all five support an organ-determination'.[98]

Following the same reasoning, the Fifth Circuit in *Board of Regents* held that, under the *Kelly* factors, Nippon Telegraph & Telephone Corporation (NTT), Japan's largest telecommunications company, did not qualify as an 'organ' of the Japanese Government because: (1) NTT was not created for a national purpose but for the commercial purpose of privatizing what had been a government-controlled monopoly; (2) the Japanese Government did not actively supervise NTT; (3) NTT was not required to hire pubic employees; (4) it did not hold exclusive rights to some right in Japan; and (5) it was not treated as a governmental organ under Japanese law.[99]

In *Filler*, the Second Circuit, adopting the test in *Kelly*, held that the Korean Deposit Insurance Corporation (KDIC), a Korean governmental institution created by Korea's Depositor Protection Act and a presidential decree, was an 'organ' of the Korean State. Under its enabling statute, the KDIC existed as a 'special legal entity' for the purpose of operating a deposit insurance system, and was run by the Korean Ministry of Finance and the Economy. According to the findings of the circuit court, the KDIC was formed by statute (the Korea Depositors Protection Act) and presidential decree, it performed functions traditionally performed by the government (protecting depositors and promoting financial stability), its directors were appointed by the Ministry of Finance and Economy; its president appointed by the President of the Republic of Korea; and many of its operations overseen by the Ministry of Finance and Economy.[100] The court pointed out:

Although there is no specific test for 'organ' status under the FSIA, various factors are relevant:

    (1)   whether the foreign state created the entity for a national purpose;
    (2)   whether the foreign state actively supervises the entity;
    (3)   whether the foreign state requires the hiring of public employees and pays their salaries;
    (4)   whether the entity holds exclusive rights to some right in the [foreign] country; and
    (5)   how the entity is treated under foreign state law.[101]

In *Peninsula*, the Second Circuit held that, like the Korean Deposit Insurance Corporation in *Filler*, the Financial Supervisory Service of the Republic of Korea (FSS) was an organ of a foreign State because it: (1) was formed by statute and presidential decree; (2) performed traditional government functions and oversaw banks, securities companies, investment trust companies, insurers, and merchant banking corporations; (3) had directors appointed by the Korean Government; and (4) had many of its operations overseen by the Korean Government.[102] In particular, the court said:

We find that FSS provided sufficient evidence to satisfy four of the *Filler* factors, thereby establishing a prima facie case for foreign sovereign immunity. First, Korea created FSS for the national purpose of examining, supervising, and investigating Korean financial institutions. Second, the Korean government actively supervises FSS … Third, FSS has the exclusive right to receive monthly business reports from the solvent financial institutions it oversees. Finally, the Korean government informed the State Department and the district court that it treats FSS as a government entity.

Only one factor weighs against finding sovereign immunity: the Korean government neither requires the hiring of public employees for FSS positions, nor directly pays the salaries of FSS employees. Nonetheless, in light of the four other factors, this is insufficient to deny FSS sovereign immunity.[103]

The 'organ' issue assumes particular significance after *Dole Food* (see below), whose effect seems to impinge on the 'ownership' prong but

256   SEPARATE ENTITIES

not to the 'organ' prong of section 1603(b)(2). Indeed, as was made clear in *Murphy*, for a corporation which is neither a 'political subdivision', nor an entity the majority of whose stock was *directly* owned by a State, the only way to qualify as a 'foreign State' is to prove itself to be an 'organ' of a foreign State.[104] In other words, an entity indirectly owned by a foreign State can still qualify as an 'agency or instrumentality' provided that it can be shown to be an 'organ' of that State. It has been rightly conceded that to do this would entail a broadening of the term 'organ'.[105] In this respect, complexities are bound to occur:

because entities that are within reach of 1603(b)(2) are likely to be quasi-governmental in character – in other words, they are likely to share characteristics both with governments or their agencies and non-governmental entities – the analysis is necessarily *ad hoc*.[106]

Such a dichotomy between an 'organ' and a 'majority-owned entity' seems to underlie the understanding of the Third Circuit in *USX*, a case involving ICAROM, an insurance company indirectly owned by the Irish Government:

inasmuch as the statute and legislative history are silent as to a definition of the term 'organ', and that term inherently is vague and does not have a well-established common law meaning, Congress's inclusion of the term within the definition of 'agency or instrumentality' of a foreign state suggests the need for a more flexible approach under the *organ prong* of section 1603(b)(2) than the Court adopted in *Dole* with respect to the *ownership prong* of that section.

A flexible approach is particularly appropriate after *Dole*, inasmuch as courts likely now will be asked to evaluate the possible organ status of a wide variety of entities controlled by foreign states through tiering arrangements and because of the widely differing forms of ownership or control foreign states may exert over entities.[107]

The Third Circuit stressed that 'for an entity to be an organ of a foreign state it must engage in a public activity on behalf of the foreign government'.[108] The court then provided a list of factors to be considered:

In making this assessment, factors employed by both the Courts of Appeals for the Ninth and Fifth Circuits are relevant, although no one is determinative: (1) the circumstances surrounding the entity's creation; (2) the purpose of its activities; (3) the degree of supervision by the government; (4) the level of government financial support; (5) the entity's employment policies, particularly regarding whether the foreign state requires the hiring of public employees and pays their salaries; and (6) the entity's obligations and privileges under the foreign state's laws. To this list, we should add an additional factor: (7) the ownership structure of the entity. Under the organ prong, as opposed to the majority ownership prong of section 1603(b)(2), a foreign state might own only 10% of an entity; it might own directly 50% of the entity; or it might own even 100% of a holding company that owns 100% of the entity. On the other hand it is possible that a foreign state might not own any portion of any entity that nevertheless is its organ as section 1603(b)(2) does not require a foreign state to have any ownership interest in an entity for it to be its organ. Courts should consider how these different ownership structures might influence the degree to which an entity is performing a function 'on behalf of the foreign government'.[109]

The court added:

It is important to note with respect to the sixth factor that characteristics such as the entity's ability to sue and be sued in its own name, to contract in its own name, and to own property in its own name are not particularly significant with respect to a finding of organ status, given that all entities claiming agency or instrumentality status must, under 28 U.S.C. § 1603(b)(1), be a 'separate legal person'.[110]

It then conducted an elaborate analysis in line with the seven factors and found that five factors were in favour of an organ status: (1) the Irish Government indirectly acquired ICAROM, not to seek any profit-making opportunity, but to serve the important national interest of protecting the Irish insurance and banking industries from financial disaster, which in turn helped to maintain stability in the Irish economy; (2) the purpose of the company's activities was to serve the abovementioned national interest; (3) the company operated under substantial government supervision, though the latter does not control the operations on a day-to-day basis; (4) the government provides the company with significant financial support; and (5) Ireland had complete control over all shares of ICAROM, albeit through a tiered arrangement. Only two factors weighed against an organ status: (1) the employees were not civil servants; and (2) ICAROM had no obligations or privileges under Irish law. On balance, the court held that ICAROM was an organ of Ireland for purposes of section 1603(b)(2).[111]

Similarly, the court in *Murphy* held that the Korea Asset Management Corporation (KAMCO) was an 'organ' of the Korean State. The court weighed five factors and found three in favour of an 'organ' status: that the corporation served a public (national) purpose (for the preservation and development of the financial industry and financial markets), that it was under direct control and active supervision of the Korean Government; and that it had the exclusive right to use a special government fund. One factor was against such status, that is, the corporation was not required to hire employees who were paid by the government. Interestingly, one factor was found to be neutral: that the corporation was treated as both a public and a private entity under Korean law.[112]

Such a weighing and balancing exercise seems to have originated with the Ninth Circuit in *EIE*, in which the court held, on balance of relevant factors, that the Resolution and Collection Corporation, a Japanese corporation in the business of purchasing, administering, collecting, and disposing of non-performing loans purchased from failing institutions, was an organ of the Japanese Government. Among the factors contributing to the organ status were 'the circumstances of its founding; its funding and financial connection to the government and taxpayers of Japan; its mission; and its purpose'.[113]

A number of diverse entities, whether governmental, quasi-governmental or outright commercial in nature, have been considered 'organs' of foreign States on the basis of such a multiple-factor and balancing analysis.[114] Unsurprisingly, it has been found that an 'organ' could 'loosely be defined as an entity that either performs a government function or which is ultimately controlled by the state'.[115] If an entity is not run by government appointees, not staffed with civil servants, nor wholly owned by the government, enjoys no privileges, and does not exercise any regulatory authority, it cannot be an 'organ' of a foreign State.[116]

One thus again and again finds a mottled picture of a multitude of factors being painstakingly examined by the US courts in their effort to assess the legal status of a particular foreign entity. The lengthy, elaborate and assiduous exercise, typically with voluminous documentary and factual evidence, makes the reading of cases concerning separate entities extremely tedious and tiresome. However, I have still enumerated at length the various factors considered by the US courts, in order to drive home the message that the US courts frequently have to conduct a multifactor, structural analysis in order to determine the status of a particular foreign entity before they embark upon the question whether what was done by that entity warrants immunity. In this respect the US practice becomes no different from that of other countries, especially the UK. It can then be concluded with good reason that a multifactor analysis is a defining feature of that part of the law of State immunity regarding separate entities. Particularly important for our discussion, we find that the *purpose* of the establishment and of the activities of the entity in question has been considered a relevant factor, as have foreign laws and the views of foreign governments. What is more, the constantly growing, and in all likelihood open-ended, list of factors, none of which is singly determinative, provides ample indication that the practice concerning separate entities will remain a fertile ground for uncertainties and inconsistencies.

2.2.5. 'Pooling'

The requirement of majority ownership under section 1603(b)(2) led to the problem of 'pooling', namely, whether the minority shares or other ownership interests of two or more States can be 'pooled' so as cumulatively to produce a majority ownership, albeit by several States. In other words, the question is whether a company jointly owned by several States, none of which singly owns the majority shares of the company, can be regarded as a State-owned company.[117] A close look at section 1603(b)(2) of the US FSIA, which speaks of the majority owner as one single foreign State ('a majority of whose shares or other ownership interest is owned by *a* foreign state'), indicates that, apparently, the issue of pooling may not have occurred to the legislators of the FSIA.[118]

The formulation of section 1603(b)(2) thus makes it doubtful whether pooling is allowed under the FSIA, for it leaves open the question whether an entity 'a majority of whose shares or other ownership interest is owned by *two or more foreign states*' is also an 'agency or instrumentality'. 'Arguably,' said a district court:

had Congress wished to permit pooling, it could have easily defined a foreign state as an entity 50% or more of whose shares are owned by a foreign state or *states*. Because Congress did not so define foreign state, it is not for the courts to substitute this definition for the one provided.[119]

Thus:

Read literally, if two countries each own a 50-percent interest in a corporation and each exercise[s] equal control, the entity does not qualify as an agency or instrumentality of either state ... If the corporation is owned by three or more countries with each having less than a 50-percent interest, the situation is even more clearly not included within the literal provisions of the statute.[120]

Such a literal and formalistic interpretation of section 1603(b)(2) would, according to the Seventh Circuit, lead to an absurd result, that is:

A company owned 50.01% by one foreign state and the remainder by private interests would be entitled to the FSIA's protections, but an entity owned 50% each by two foreign states with no private ownership would not.[121]

260   SEPARATE ENTITIES

Besides, commentators are also of the opinion that disallowing pooling would 'frustrate the [FSIA's] purpose of maintaining good foreign relations with trading partners', since 'a suit against a corporation directly and completely owned by two foreign states likely will have as great or greater foreign policy consequences as a suit against a corporation 51 percent owned by one foreign state';[122] allowing pooling, on the other hand, would facilitate the FSIA's purpose of 'addressing the potential sensitivity of actions against foreign states'.[123]

In practice, therefore, the US courts have generally rejected too narrow a reading of the statutory provision and have in most cases allowed pooling. As the court reasoned in *Linton*:

In the Court's view, although reasonable minds could disagree, it does not do too much violence to either the plain language or the spirit of FSIA to hold that foreign states may pool their interests in an entity for purposes of determining whether that entity is a foreign state under FSIA. FSIA would unquestionably apply if any owner were a party or if more than 50% of the entity in question were owned by any single foreign state. It is not, therefore, too much of a stretch to assume that Congress intended FSIA to apply to an entity owned by several foreign states, even if no single foreign state owns a majority: a majority of the entity's stock or other ownership interest is still owned by foreign states to which Congress clearly intended FSIA to apply.[124]

The Fifth Circuit agreed:

This reasoning probably should be examined in light of the rules of statutory construction, *e.g.*, 1 U.S.C. § 1 (providing that 'words importing the singular include and apply to several persons, parties, or things' unless the context indicates otherwise), and in light of the cases in which the pooling issue has been considered.[125]

Thus in *LeDonne*, the court held that Gulf Air, Inc., an airline created as a joint stock company by a treaty among four Persian Gulf States (Abu Dhabi, Bahrain, Qatar and Oman), which jointly and equally owned 100 per cent of its stock, was an 'instrumentality of a foreign State', even though no single State owned a majority of the airline's shares. In the court's opinion, the view that the FSIA does not apply unless majority ownership vests in a single foreign State was:

an unnecessary literalism that runs counter to the Act's purpose and ignores the well-established international practice of states acting jointly through treaty-created entities for public or sovereign purposes. If the policies that animate the FSIA are to be given their full range, it must, therefore, apply to treaty-created instrumentalities jointly owned by foreign states.[126]

In *Mangattu*, a case where some seamen brought an action against a vessel and its owner for unpaid wages and other damages, the Fifth Circuit held that foreign States could pool their ownership interests and that the United Arab Shipping Co., a Kuwaiti corporation wholly owned by six States (Saudi Arabia, Kuwait, Qatar, United Arab Emirates, and Iraq each owned 19.33 per cent, and Bahrain owned 3.335 per cent), was an 'agency or instrumentality'.[127] In the court's opinion, 'an entity 100% owned by foreign states, created by an agreement of all the participating states, satisfies the requirements of § 1603(b)(2)'.[128]

In the case of *Air Crash Disaster*, representatives of the victims of an air crash, while bringing an action for wrongful death, named Avions de Transport Régional, GIE (ATR), a one-half French, one-half Italian aircraft manufacturer, as a defendant or third-party defendant. The court found that ATR was the product of an international joint commercial venture between France and Italy which acted together to develop their civil aeronautic industry within the framework of European cooperation. The two countries indirectly owned approximately three-quarters of ATR, and controlled and managed it by retaining approval authority over its actions and by appointing the officials who monitored and managed it. The court attached crucial importance to the existence of an intergovernmental agreement, because of which, in the court's opinion, the venture became 'a joint sovereign act by Italy and France', rendering ATR 'an agency or instrumentality'.[129]

The problem with this case, however, is that ATR was only *indirectly* owned by the two States through two aerospace companies, and this means that the court had to allow a pooling to be done where there existed one or more intermediaries – or 'tiers' – between the entity in question and its purported State owners. As will be seen, even though the court's reasoning in *Air Crash Disaster* on pooling in general remains unassailable, the holding that an 'entities' entity', i.e. a subsidiary entity of entities owned by States, is also a State entity has for all practical purposes been overruled by the Supreme Court in the case of *Dole Food*.[130]

The necessity of allowing such a 'tiered pooling' might be the reason why the court in *Air Crash Disaster* also relied on governmental 'control' in its decision (because the court could not rely fully on governmental *ownership*). It is difficult, however, to pin down the exact role assigned by the court to this factor. First, in some places the court mentioned the factor of control only after it had satisfied itself that the French and Italian Governments had a majority ownership of ATR (which is dubious, as we have seen); that is, in the opinion of the court, besides majority-owning ATR, the French and Italian Governments '*also* exercise substantial control over ATR by retaining approval authority and by appointing the officials who manage it'.[131] Secondly, while fully aware that ATR was 'indirectly' owned by the two governments,[132] the court asserted that the FSIA contemplated 'suits against commercial entities *controlled* by foreign governments (such as ATR)', and indicated that what it had in mind was 'an entity owned 50% each by two foreign states'.[133] One is at a loss as to whether, in the opinion of the court, 'control' was a factor distinct from but secondary or incidental to 'ownership' (in that 'control' was mentioned only when ownership was established), or synonymous with 'indirect ownership' (in that an indirectly owned ATR was an entity 'controlled by foreign governments'), or even the same as 'direct ownership' (in that an entity 'controlled by foreign governments' might mean 'an entity owned 50% each by two foreign States'). Whatever significance might have been attached by the court in *Air Crash Disaster* to the factor of control, it is no longer possible, under US case law, to rely on mere 'control' or 'influence' of a foreign State, in the absence of *direct majority ownership*, to press for a status of 'agency or instrumentality of a foreign state'.

Unsurprisingly, pooling was also allowed in cases involving Air Afrique, an airline jointly owned by a dozen African States.[134]

It can be seen from these cases that the determinative criterion is State ownership, as explicitly required by section 1603(b)(2), while the case law seems to have formulated a rather strict definition of that term. In those cases where pooling was disallowed, the rationale was either that the entities participating in the pooling must themselves be foreign States, thereby ruling out the possibility that an entity owned by two or more other entities (as opposed to foreign States themselves) can be regarded as an 'agency or instrumentality of a foreign state',[135] or that the entity in question was 'not a multinational joint venture or a treaty created entity'.[136] This practice of *restricted pooling* effectively precludes from the purview of section 1603(b) those entities one or more tiers removed from the State, or those whose coming into being has more to do with private business processes than with a direct and conscious State involvement, and keeps the enlarged application of section 1603(b) within manageable bounds.

A correlative issue arises as regards section 1603(b)(3), that is, in order to enjoy immunity, the entity in question must not have been 'created under the laws of any third country'. Since two or more foreign States are involved in a typical case of pooling, it has been pleaded that the entity in question must be treated as created under the laws of a third country. The courts have given short shrift to this assertion, holding that by 'third country' it is meant 'a country different from the owner nation'.[137] Thus, if the entity is 'created by an agreement that was given the force of law in all member nations, and incorporated under the laws of one of its members',[138] or even vaguely 'created under the laws of the owner nations',[139] the entity is not created under the laws of a third country.

Thus, even though the FSIA speaks of ownership by '*a* foreign State', the case law has expanded the term to cover also ownership by 'foreign States'. Through an innovative interpretation of the statutory provision, the courts have allowed the interests of foreign States to be 'pooled' where direct ownership by foreign States can be established. The reasons offered for the extension of the application of section 1603(b) seem varied and range from logical deduction[140] or the avoidance of absurdity,[141] to overall policy considerations associated with the language, structure and purpose of the FSIA.[142] Generally speaking, this seems to suggest a purposive interpretation of a statutory provision to accommodate a situation previously not envisaged by that provision. In other words, this is what courts do whenever an apparent lacuna in legislation is discovered. It must be noted that such allowance falls within the reasonable boundaries of the FSIA, as demonstrated by courts in cases both allowing and disallowing pooling.[143]

Allowing the interests of foreign States to be 'pooled' under certain circumstances has proved workable and viable in practice, has broadly served the legislative purposes of the FSIA, and, insofar as immunity is granted where there is a close connection between the entity and the State, is in line with how international law views State immunity. After all, strictly speaking, jurisdictional immunity under international law is a prerogative of the State, and the immunity enjoyed by a separate entity is only derivative; that is to say, a separate entity enjoys immunity only when it has, or is considered as having, certain attributes of the State, such as structurally forming part of the State mechanism and/or exercising certain functions normally entrusted only to a governmental department of the State. The 'majority ownership' requirement under the FSIA appears designed to ensure sufficient presence of a State within a company before immunity can be granted. This also explains why US case law tends to be averse to the claim of immunity by those entities further removed from the State itself, that is, entities not *directly owned* by a State. Nothing short of a direct State (whether singular or plural) ownership is permitted if an entity desires to claim immunity as an agency or instrumentality of a foreign State. If a State cannot endow the entity with its spirit by having a direct presence within the entity, then it cannot do so by telepathy. And that brings us to the associated issue of 'tiering'.

2.2.6. 'Tiering'

In some cases pooling has come to be closely entwined with another problem: 'tiering', that is, whether an entity majority-owned by an agency or instrumentality of a foreign State, thus only *indirectly* owned by the State itself through one or more intermediaries, is also an agency or instrumentality of that foreign State. This seems allowable, if not expressly allowed, by the wording of section 1603. For if the term 'foreign State' includes an 'agency or instrumentality of a foreign State', then an entity 'a majority of whose shares or other ownership interest is owned by an agency or instrumentality of a foreign State' will be synonymous with an entity 'a majority of whose shares or other ownership interest is owned by a foreign State', and such an entity will thus itself become an 'agency or instrumentality of a foreign State' and therefore enjoy jurisdictional immunities. Plainly put, this reasoning will place a company owned by a State-owned company in the category of State-owned companies, even though it might be one or more corporate 'tiers' away from the State itself. If such 'tiering' is permitted, it will then mean that:

a corporation many stages removed from direct control by a foreign government could still be considered a foreign state so long as majority ownership could be traced back to the government through majority ownership at each corporate level.[144]

In the opinion of the Ninth Circuit, this would result in a considerable expansion of the list of the beneficiaries of immunity:

To add to that list entities that are owned by an agency or instrumentality would expand the potential immunity considerably because it would provide potential immunity for every subsidiary in a corporate chain, no matter how far down the line, so long as the first corporation is an organ of the foreign state or political subdivision or has a majority of its shares owned by the foreign state or political subdivision.[145]

In the case of *Aluminum Distributors*, for example, the defendant corporation, the Gulf Aluminum Rolling Mill Company (GARMCO), was a

Bahrainian corporation jointly owned by Bahrain (25.47 per cent), Iraq (11.32 per cent), Oman (5.66 per cent) and Qatar (5.55 per cent). The rest of its shares were owned by three other companies: 14.15 per cent by the Gulf Investment Corporation, a Kuwait shareholding company owned by Bahrain, Saudi Arabia, Oman, Qatar, Kuwait and the United Arab Emirates; 20.75 per cent by the Saudi Basic Industries Corporation, which was 70 per cent owned by Saudi Arabia; and 16.98 per cent by the Industrial Bank of Kuwait, which was 31.4 per cent owned by Kuwait.[146] Evidently, the combined direct State ownership by Bahrain, Iraq, Oman and Qatar in GARMCO amounted only to 48 per cent, short of the 'majority' ownership as required by section 1603(b)(2), which is understood to be over 50 per cent; but the court nonetheless held that GARMCO was a 'foreign State',[147] though it gave no reason as to how a 48 per cent ownership could be considered a 'majority' ownership. However, at the start of its judgment, the court, while describing the ownership of GARMCO, stated that 'a majority of GARMCO's stock is currently owned by Bahrain, Iraq, Oman, Qatar, the United Arab Emirates, Saudi Arabia and Kuwait'.[148] Since, of the seven States considered by the court to be the owners of GARMCO, only four (Bahrain, Iraq, Oman and Qatar) had direct ownership, the only reasonable surmise is that the court must have pooled the shares of GARMCO (14.15 per cent) owned by the Gulf Investment Corporation, itself a State-owned company owned by, among others, the United Arab Emirates, Saudi Arabia and Kuwait, thus including these latter three States in the list of owner States. The Saudi Basic Industries Corporation, majority-owned by Saudi Arabia, may or may not have been included by the court, while the Industrial Bank of Kuwait, not being majority-owned by Kuwait, should have been left out of the picture, because it could not be considered as a State-owned entity anyway. In allowing pooling to take place one tier down, the court must have implicitly treated an entity owned by a group of States (the Gulf Investment Corporation) or majority-owned by a foreign State (the Saudi Basic Industries Corporation) as a 'foreign State'.[149]

Crucially, as has already been pointed out, allowing the pooling of *indirect* State ownership through State-owned companies so as to achieve a majority *direct* State ownership does not seem to be prohibited by section 1603. In fact, such an approach is perfectly in accord with the language of the provision: the expansive definition of 'foreign State' in section 1603(a) readily induces and leaves ample wiggle room for what has been dubbed in *Air Crash Disaster* as the 'infinite loop reasoning', namely:

266   SEPARATE ENTITIES

If 'foreign state' under the Act 'includes ... an agency or instrumentality of a foreign state' (*see* § 1603(a)), which in turn includes a separate corporation 'which is an organ of a foreign state or political subdivision thereof, or a majority of whose shares or other ownership interest is *owned by* a foreign state or political subdivision thereof' (sec. 1603(b)), then a corporation which is directly majority-owned by a foreign state constitutes a 'foreign state' itself. Thus ... a corporation which is owned by a corporation which in turn is owned by a foreign state is both *owned by* a foreign state and *is* a foreign state. Under this reading of the FSIA, so long as the corporate intermediaries standing between a foreign state and a defendant seeking to invoke foreign-state status are themselves majority-owned by a statutorily-defined 'foreign state' (which, to be explicit, includes an agency or instrumentality of a foreign state), such tiering of ownership interests will not deprive the defendant of foreign state status.[150]

A good example of an 'infinite loop' can be found in *Ocasek*, where the court found that the defendant Asbestos Corporation Ltd (ACL) was an agency or instrumentality of Canada, based on the following reasoning:

There is no question that the Province of Quebec is a political subdivision of the foreign state of Canada. Quebec owned all of SNA. Therefore, SNA was an entity 'a majority of whose shares or other ownership interest is owned by a foreign state'. SNA was accordingly an 'agency or instrumentality of a foreign state or a political subdivision thereof', and therefore was included in the term 'foreign state'. SNA owned 51.2 percent of Mines-S.N.A. Therefore, Mines-S.N.A. was an entity 'a majority of whose shares or other ownership interest is owned by a foreign state'. Mines-S.N.A. was accordingly an 'agency or instrumentality of a foreign state', and therefore was included in the term 'foreign state'. Mines-S.N.A. owned 54.6 percent of ACL. Therefore, ACL was an entity 'a majority of whose shares or other ownership interest is owned by a foreign state'. ACL was accordingly an 'agency or instrumentality of a foreign state', and therefore was included in the term 'foreign state'.[151]

Such reasoning is buttressed, so it seems, by the normal practice of the US courts, which, instead of employing the more cumbersome – but more accurate and correct – term of 'agency or instrumentality of a foreign State', are apt to describe a State-owned company or other State entity as a 'foreign State'.[152]

In the *Air Crash Disaster* case, the defendant company, ATR, was not owned directly by the French and Italian Governments, but only *indirectly* through two European commercial aerospace companies, each of which owned 50 per cent of ATR's shares: a French company, Aerospatiale, Société Nationale Industrielle SA (SNIA), and an Italian company, Alenia. The SNIA was 91.42 per cent owned by the French Government, with the remainder in private hands. Of the shares owned by the French Government, 62.16 per cent were owned directly, and 20 per cent more through a company named Sogepa. The remaining 17.81 per cent was owned by Crédit Lyonnais Industria, which in turn was owned by Crédit Lyonnais, 52 per cent of which was owned by the French Government. Alenia was a division of Finmeccanica SpA, which was 62.14 per cent owned by the Italian Instituto per la Riconstruzione Industriale (Institute for Industrial Reconstruction), which in its turn was a holding company wholly owned by the Italian Government through its treasury ministry. Through these intermediaries, France and Italy retained *indirect ownership* of approximately 75 per cent of ATR.[153] In short, ATR was directly owned, not by two *States*, but by two *companies*; it was, so to speak, only 'controlled' by the French and Italian Governments. Because section 1603(b)(2) provides that an 'agency or instrumentality' has to be an entity 'a majority of whose shares or other ownership interest is owned by a *foreign state*', and because ATR was majority-owned only by two *companies*, then, in order to hold ATR to be an 'agency or instrumentality of a foreign state', it was necessary to hold that the two companies were themselves 'foreign States'.

Given such a convoluted, multi-layered/tiered corporate structure, pooling, if allowed, would certainly result in an entity not directly owned by any foreign State being treated as an 'agency or instrumentality'. This can only be achieved by regarding a foreign State-owned company as nothing less than the foreign State itself. That is, because the reference to 'foreign State' includes an 'agency or instrumentality of a foreign State' (section 1603(a)), it requires but a little stretch of the imagination to hold that, since an 'agency or instrumentality of a foreign State' is also a 'foreign State', then an entity owned by an 'agency or instrumentality of a foreign State' is also one owned by a 'foreign State', and so on and so forth. The court, however, was undaunted by the prospect of stretching the wording of the FSIA:

The Act does not expressly require direct ownership, nor does it exclude the form in which France and Italy hold ATR as an instrumentality. SNIA is an 'agency or instrumentality of a foreign state' because it is more than 90% owned by France and meets the other requirements of § 1603(b). Likewise, Alenia is an 'agency or instrumentality of a foreign state' because it is a division of Finmeccanica SpA, which is 62% owned by I.R.I., which is a holding company 100% owned by Italy.

Although France and Italy controlled ATR through intervening entities, the language and legislative history consistent with the language of the FSIA

268   SEPARATE ENTITIES

demonstrate that ATR is the type of corporation included within the statutory definition of 'foreign state'.[154]

The problem of tiering has caused great confusion among the US courts. In *Gates*, the Ninth Circuit held that a corporation, a majority of whose shares were owned by an agency or instrumentality of a foreign State rather than by the foreign State itself, was not an agency or instrumentality of that foreign State.[155] Basically, the Ninth Circuit read section 1603(b)(2) as limiting an instrumentality of a foreign State to the *first tier* of ownership, namely, those entities owned directly by the foreign State itself (or by a political subdivision). An entity wholly owned by 'an agency or instrumentality of a foreign State' is thus not a foreign instrumentality under the FSIA.[156]

Other courts have taken an opposite view. The Seventh Circuit has been consistent in its view that an entity owned by a State entity is also a State entity.[157] The Second, the Third, the Fourth, the Sixth, the Eleventh, and the DC Circuits have taken a like position.[158] Interestingly, even the Ninth Circuit seems to have been on this side of the fence prior to *Gates*.[159] The district courts have been similarly divided.[160]

In *Delgado*, the Fifth Circuit held that indirect ownership was sufficient to qualify an entity as an agency or instrumentality of a foreign State. That case involved a State-court class action against many multinational fruit and chemical companies, alleging injuries from exposure to dibromochloropropane (DBCP), a harmful pesticide. As a litigation strategy to send these suits back to their countries of origin, the defendants sought to remove the action to a federal court, where the defence of *forum non conveniens* would be available. In the process, the Dead Sea Bromine Co. Ltd, an Israeli company, was also impleaded and attempted to remove the action in reliance on section 1441(d) of the FSIA, which provides:

Any civil action brought in a State court against a foreign state as defined in section 1603(a) of this title may be removed by the foreign state to the district court of the United States for the district and division embracing the place where such action is pending.

Obviously, whether or not Dead Sea Bromine was entitled to remove the action under this provision turned on whether it was a 'foreign State', or, more exactly, whether it was an 'agency or instrumentality' of Israel under section 1603(b). The Fifth Circuit noted that the State of Israel owned 75.3 per cent of Israel Chemicals Ltd, an entity which owned 88.2 per cent of Dead Sea Works Ltd, which in turn owned 100 per cent of

Dead Sea Bromine Co. Ltd. Through such a tiered structure, Israel indirectly owned a majority interest in Dead Sea Bromine.[161] The question thus was whether that indirect ownership was sufficient to satisfy section 1603. The court said:

> The plain language of the statute simply requires 'ownership' by a foreign state. It draws no distinction between direct and indirect ownership; neither does it expressly impose a requirement of direct ownership. Indeed, we have previously indicated that indirect ownership is sufficient to confer foreign state status ... Should any doubt remain concerning this Circuit's position on tiering or indirect ownership, we squarely hold today that indirect or tiered majority ownership is sufficient to qualify an entity as a foreign state, assuming that all other requirements are met.[162]

This controversy over 'tiered' or indirect ownership was finally settled by the US Supreme Court in *Dole Food*, an action involving the same facts as *Delgado* and this time impleading Dead Sea Bromine Co. Ltd, and Bromine Compounds, Ltd, collectively referred to as the Dead Sea Companies, which again sought removal of the action under section 1441(d). The Ninth Circuit characterized the status of the Dead Sea Companies in the following terms:

> In contrast to the oil refinery in *Corporacion Mexicana*, the Dead Sea Companies were not run by government appointees; their employees were not treated as civil servants; nor were the Companies wholly owned by the government of Israel. The Companies could sue and be sued, and could in fact sue the government of Israel (although official Israeli documents describe such disputes as between 'a government company and another government body'). Nor did the Companies exercise any regulatory authority ... These factors support the ... view of the Companies as independent commercial enterprises, heavily regulated, but acting to maximize profits rather than pursue public objectives. Although the question is close, we hold that the Dead Sea Companies were not organs of the Israeli government, but indirectly owned commercial operations, which do not qualify as instrumentalities under the FSIA.[163]

The Supreme Court dealt specifically with 'tiered ownership', that is:

> whether a corporate subsidiary can claim instrumentality status where the foreign State does not own a majority of its shares but does own a majority of the shares of a corporate parent one or more tiers above the subsidiary.[164]

The Supreme Court agreed with the Ninth Circuit that a subsidiary of an instrumentality was not itself entitled to instrumentality status.[165] According to the Supreme Court, the State of Israel did not have direct ownership of shares in either of the Dead Sea Companies at any time pertinent to this suit. Rather, these companies were, at various times, *separated from the State of Israel by one or more intermediate corporate tiers*. For example, from 1984 to 1985, Israel wholly owned a company called Israeli Chemicals, Ltd, which owned a majority of shares in another company called Dead Sea Works, Ltd, which owned a majority of shares in Dead Sea Bromine Co. Ltd, which owned a majority of shares in Bromine Compounds, Ltd.[166] Given such a tortuously tiered relationship, the Supreme Court found that the Dead Sea Companies, as *indirect subsidiaries* of the State of Israel, were not instrumentalities of Israel under the FSIA at any time, because 'only direct ownership of a majority of shares by the foreign state satisfies the statutory requirement'.[167]

The Supreme Court explained that, where section 1603(b) speaks of ownership, such a term should not be understood simply in its 'colloquial sense', but should be approached in terms of 'corporate formalities' and 'structure':

The language of § 1603(b)(2) refers to ownership of 'shares', showing that Congress intended statutory coverage to turn on formal corporate ownership. Likewise, § 1603(b)(1), another component of the definition of instrumentality, refers to a 'separate legal person, corporate or otherwise'. In light of these indicia that Congress had corporate formalities in mind, we assess whether Israel *owned shares* in the Dead Sea Companies *as a matter of corporate law*, irrespective of whether Israel could be said to have owned the Dead Sea Companies in everyday parlance.[168]

'A basic tenet of American corporate law', according to the Supreme Court, was that 'the corporation and its shareholders are distinct entities'.[169] Thus:

An individual shareholder, by virtue of his ownership of shares, does not own the corporation's assets and, as a result, does not own subsidiary corporations in which the corporation holds an interest. A corporate parent which owns the shares of a subsidiary does not, for that reason alone, own or have legal title to the assets of the subsidiary; and, it follows with even greater force, the parent does not own or have legal title to the subsidiaries of the subsidiary. The fact that the shareholder is a foreign state does not change the analysis.[170]

In the light of these principles, the relationship between Israel and the companies was characterized as follows:

Israel did not own a majority of shares in the Dead Sea Companies. The State of Israel owned a majority of shares, at various times, in companies one or more corporate tiers above the Dead Sea Companies, but at no time did Israel own a majority of shares in the Dead Sea Companies. Those companies were subsidiaries of other corporations.[171]

Thus, by adhering to 'the statutory text and elementary principles of corporate law', the Supreme Court found that the Dead Sea Companies were not instrumentalities of Israel:

A corporation is an instrumentality of a foreign state under the FSIA only if the foreign state itself owns a majority of the corporation's shares.[172]

That is, an entity which is majority-owned by another entity (or other entities, such as State-owned or -controlled companies) cannot be considered an 'agency or instrumentality'. This decision squarely rejected the Fifth Circuit's *Delgado* holding[173] and naturally decided the results of other cases as well. In *Filler*, for example, while holding that the Korean Deposit Insurance Corporation (KDIC), a Korean governmental institution run by the Ministry of Finance and Economy of the Republic of Korea, was an 'organ' of the Korean State, the Second Circuit also considered the status of two defendant Korean commercial banks, Chohung Bank and Hanvit Bank. At the time of the case, the KDIC directly owned 80 per cent of the shares of Chohung Bank and 100 per cent of the shares of Woori Finance Holdings Co., Ltd, which in turn owned 100 per cent of the shares of Hanvit Bank. In other words, at the material time, Chohung Bank was a second-tier subsidiary, and Hanvit a third-tier subsidiary, of the Korean Ministry of Finance and Economy.

The banks contended that once it was determined that the KDIC was an organ of the Government of South Korea, they would automatically become agencies or instrumentalities of the Korean State because the majority of their stock was owned by the KDIC. In other words, the banks argued that since the KDIC was an organ and therefore an agency or instrumentality of a foreign State, it was also a 'foreign State' by virtue of section 1603(a)'s definition of a foreign State as including its agencies or instrumentalities. And because the KDIC owned the majority of their shares, the two banks contended that they were agencies or instrumentalities of a 'foreign State' by virtue of section 1603(b)'s ownership prong. Put another way, the banks argued 'the transitive: (1) foreign state means agency or instrumentality; (2) agency or instrumentality means organ or majority-owned corporation; (3) therefore foreign state means organ or majority-owned corporation; and (4) therefore, majority-owned corporations of an organ are majority-owned corporations of a foreign state'.[174]

'Accepting their analysis', said the Second Circuit:

would permit an *infinite* number of subsidiaries to enjoy sovereign immunity. Each subsidiary becomes an agency or instrumentality, and therefore the

272   SEPARATE ENTITIES

'foreign state', for purposes of assessing its majority ownership of the next subsidiary in line.[175]

However, the owner of the two banks in this case was an 'organ' of the Korean State. The banks thus argued that an 'organ' under the first half of section 1603(b)(2) was also, by definition, a 'foreign State' under section 1603(a) and that a subsidiary owned by such an 'organ' was therefore *directly* owned by a 'foreign State' and entitled to immunity. The Second Circuit rejected this argument, saying:

> Such a result is incompatible with *Dole Food*. The Supreme Court made it unmistakably clear that 'a subsidiary of an instrumentality is not itself entitled to instrumentality status', and that 'only *direct* ownership of a majority of shares by the foreign state satisfies the statutory requirement'.

> The Banks' argument fails for a number of other reasons as well. First, the statutory language of § 1603(a) makes clear that a 'foreign state ... *includes* a political subdivision of a foreign state or an agency or instrumentality of a foreign state ...' This statement is not equivalent to saying that a foreign state *is* or *is defined as* an agency or instrumentality. While these latter terms would suggest equivalency between the foreign state and the agencies and instrumentalities, the use of the term 'includes' implies that agencies and instrumentalities, as well as political subdivisions, are subsumed within the 'foreign state'. Thus, a proper understanding of the term 'includes' does not support the notion of recursive tiering. Once an entity is determined to be an agency or instrumentality, it is deemed *part of* the foreign state but it does not *become* the foreign state and, therefore, cannot confer agency or instrumentality status on corporate entities further down the chain of ownership.[176]

In sum, the problem of tiering arose as a consequence of the muddled draftsmanship in section 1603 regarding the definition of a 'foreign State' and only after much confusion – and judicial juggling, as vividly shown by the above-quoted passage in *Filler* – came to be settled by way of a purposively narrow construction of section 1603 combined with the rejection of a literal reading which is not entirely unwarranted by the text of the statutory provision itself. The truth is that tiering was not anticipated at all by the legislators, who drafted a statutory provision that is capable of encompassing entities indirectly owned or controlled by a foreign State further down the corporate tier. To say that an entity can only be a State entity if it is *directly* owned by the foreign State itself, without more, only conceals but does not solve the problem, because the problem inheres in the statutory provision itself, and its real solution, therefore, lies in a new, amended provision by Congress to the effect that, so far as multi-tiered entities are concerned, the term 'foreign

State' is subject to a more restrictive definition. Until that happens, the stock formula in the US courts to the effect that a particular foreign entity 'is a foreign State', when they actually mean that it is an 'agency or instrumentality of a foreign State', cannot really be taken at face value, because it is so abundantly misleading and confusing. The answer to the question of tiering is already, at it were, hidden in this formula; for if an entity 'is a foreign State', then control or ownership by that entity is of course control or ownership by a 'foreign State', so that an entity owned by another entity can properly be characterized as a State entity as well, and so on and so forth. The problem lies with the definition of 'foreign State' in section 1603(a) and in the usual shorthand used by the courts when they describe a foreign State entity as a 'foreign State'.

2.2.7. The question of timing

The Supreme Court in *Dole Food* also dealt specifically with the question of timing, that is, 'whether a corporation's instrumentality status is defined as of the time an alleged tort or other actionable wrong occurred or, on the other hand, at the time suit is filed'.[177] The Supreme Court held that, since section 1603(b) speaks of the instrumentality status in the present tense, that status should be determined at the time the suit is filed, in the light of the long-standing principle that the jurisdiction of the court depends upon the state of things at the time of the action brought.[178] As any relationship recognized under the FSIA between the Dead Sea Companies and Israel had been severed before the suit was commenced, the Dead Sea Companies would not be entitled to instrumentality status.[179]

This means that a State entity may lose its immunity in the course of a business reorganization that results in its majority shares being owned privately; and that its being a State entity at the time of the wrongdoing will cease to be a useful argument for immunity. On the other hand, the reverse is also true, as a private entity may acquire a privileged position upon coming into the possession of a State. Thus the plaintiff against such an entity cannot argue that it does not enjoy immunity because it was not a State entity when the facts giving rise to the claim occurred.

2.2.8. Other uses of the instrumentality status

As a matter of fact, a number of issues are decided solely by reference to the status/structure of the entity. In the US, because of the different treatments of the foreign State itself and its entities, the courts have to

274   SEPARATE ENTITIES

decide upon the status of a foreign State entity for a variety of purposes apart from adjudicatory jurisdiction over a claim;[180] these include: entitlement to a non-jury trial (section 1330);[181] determination of 'diversity jurisdiction' (section 1332);[182] venue (section 1391(f));[183] removal of a case from a State to a federal court (section 1441(d));[184] punitive damages (sections 1605(a)(7) and 1606);[185] service of process (section 1608 (b));[186] subpoena and contempt sanctions,[187] and attachment and execution (section 1610(b)(2)).[188] These matters, especially the process of removal, are of a highly preliminary nature. Since removal is only available to a 'foreign State', the issue of status – hence the structural analysis – is of crucial importance to a corporation or other type of separate entity in obtaining a favourable position even before the claim itself is decided to determine the preliminary issue of immunity. In the sense that a motion to remove comes before the issue of immunity, which is itself a preliminary issue, a motion to remove is a preliminary step to a preliminary step. In a typical removal case, the issue of immunity does not even arise.[189]

2.2.9. The Canadian law

The Canada SIA falls within the US Model. Section 2 provides that the term 'foreign state' includes 'any agency of the foreign state', which is defined as 'any legal entity that is an organ of the foreign state but that is separate from the foreign state'.[190] The chief difference between the US and the Canadian practice is that, whereas a majority ownership by the State will make an entity an 'agency or instrumentality' of the foreign State entitled to the same immunity as the State under the US FSIA, the Canadian law and jurisprudence require a closer relationship between the entity and the government. Mere majority ownership of the State is not enough: the entity has to be 'an organ or alter ego' of the State.[191]

  In practice, it has been opined that:

The alter ego test involves the consideration of whether the entity performs functions associated with governmental authority and the effectiveness of the control exercised over it by the state. The alter ego test attaches little significance to whether the particular entity is endowed with a separate juridical personality; it determines the issue with regard to the foreign law under which the entity is created and controlled, but in accordance with domestic law.[192]

There have been conflicting decisions regarding the role of the capacity of suing and being sued.[193] In D&J, the court cited with approval the statement in a textbook:

If an agency is the alter ego of the foreign state and is 'an integral part of the state and its machinery of government it may be said the acts of the instrumentality are those of the state', the state is the only entity that could be sued. However, if an agency is not simply an emanation of the state but has a separate existence the Act recognizes that it may be sued in its own right.[194]

However, in *Croteau*, the court said:

In any event, in our view, the fact that the appellant may be able to sue and be sued in its own name is not conclusive on the central issue of whether the appellant is a 'legal entity that is an organ of the foreign state but that is separate from the foreign state'.[195]

But of course the 'alter ego or agent' test is directly derived from the UK jurisprudence, especially the case of *Trendtex*. As noted in *TMR*:

It must be remembered that the alter ego test was developed at a time when the *State Immunity Act* had not yet been enacted. At that time, the common law recognized the principle of immunity of foreign governments and extended that immunity to 'its department of state or any body which can be regarded as an alter ego or organ of the government'. The alter ego test was therefore a means of determining whether an entity was an 'organ' of the foreign state for the purpose of benefiting from state immunity. It had no use or application to the determination of whether the entity had a distinct legal existence.[196]

Seen in this light, the Canadian jurisprudence closely follows, or rather defers to, the US and the UK practice. This can be illustrated by two points.

First, the Canadian courts are likewise prepared to conduct a laborious multifactor analysis of the status of a particular entity to see whether it is an 'alter ego' of the foreign State. If it is, then it enjoys immunity, otherwise not.

In *Ferranti-Packard*, the court found that the New York State Thruway Authority was not the alter ego of the State of New York, since the Authority had the power to borrow money, could assume jurisdiction over State property, had the power to acquire real property, was a public corporation, could sue and be sued and was obliged to pay judgments out of its own monies.[197]

In *Ferguson*, the issue was whether the Panama Canal Commission was separate from the US Government for purposes of service of process. The court held that the Commission was not separate from the US, on the basis of the following factors: the Commission did not have a general right to sue and be sued; it had only a limited right to settle claims on behalf of the US Government; it had no general right to borrow money;

276   SEPARATE ENTITIES

its employees were subject to the duties and responsibilities imposed on US employees; the president retained extensive control; and the activities of the commission were undertaken by way of an international treaty that imposed responsibilities on the government.[198]

In the case of *University of Calgary*, the court had to decide whether the Colorado School of Mines (CSM) could be seen as a department of the local US Government. The court said:

It is clear that the important consideration is who has day to day control and management of the institution. For educational institutions, some of the indicia considered by the court are financial accountability, appointment of board members and whether the government has any direct role in the daily, routine governance of the institution. With those factors in mind, I turn to the constitutional and administrative make-up of CSM.[199]

The judge then considered various factors such as statutes governing CSM, structure, functions, control of management, appointments, decision-making power and process, and concluded that CSM was not an arm or agency of the State of Colorado but had independent status. Therefore CSM was not immune pursuant to the SIA.[200]

In *Roxford*, the judge likewise carefully examined Cubana's articles of incorporation and by-laws, its employment of personnel, management of financial affairs, powers of the board of directors, control of income, undertaking and assets, and, on the basis of this multifactor analysis, concluded that Cubana, Cuba's national airline, could not be considered an 'alter ego or agent' of Cuba, and therefore Cubana's assets could not be seized to satisfy a judgment against Cuba.[201] This was determined notwithstanding that under the Cuban constitution, transportation was deemed socialist State property; the right to the assets had been transferred from the former State-owned airline without significant consideration; the President of the airline's parent company was a longtime military leader in the Cuban revolution and that it was a consistent practice to set up State enterprises headed by high-ranking military officers.

In *Collavino*, there was again a multifactor analysis. The court considered such factors as autonomy, independent financial existence, initiation of its own budget process, capacity of suing and being sued, employment and payment of personnel, ownership of its own assets, and acting and being treated separately in legal proceedings.[202]

The second point is intimately linked with the first one. For if the Canadian law requires that an entity be an 'arm or alter ego' of the

State before it can be entitled to immunity, then once an entity is held to be an 'arm or alter ego' of a foreign State, and immunity from adjudication can be denied under the circumstances, the question immediately arises whether that entity can be held liable for the debts of the State; that is, whether the assets of that entity can be attached or seized to satisfy a debt owed by the State but not by that entity itself. Of course the matter would also arise in a case where an entity is *not* a party to the proceedings (and therefore there is no decision regarding its immunity from suit) but its assets are nonetheless targeted. On this issue, the Canadian courts accord a similar respect for the separate legal personality of an entity in that the assets of a separate entity cannot normally be attached to satisfy a debt of the State itself.[203]

2.3. Comparison and summary

As noted earlier, the US Model adopts a 'presumption of immunity' for foreign States and their agencies and instrumentalities. Under US law, the question of immunity of a foreign State entity is thus primarily one of *status*, which is then followed by an examination of the conduct or transaction of the entity that has given rise to the lawsuit, in order to determine whether the conduct or transaction falls within one or more of the exceptions to immunity under the US FSIA. A foreign State enjoys a presumptive immunity under the FSIA from the jurisdiction of the US courts, which imposes a heavy burden of proof on the plaintiff to show that one of the exceptions as stipulated by the FSIA applies in the case; at the same time, because the concept of 'foreign state' includes an 'agency or instrumentality of a foreign state' (section 1603(a)), it becomes imperative for the foreign State entity to prove that it is indeed an 'agency or instrumentality of a foreign state'.

The exalted position given to separate entities under the US FSIA is in stark contrast with that which obtains under the UK SIA. Here a reverse presumption, i.e. 'presumption of non-immunity', is stipulated by the UK SIA. Once the separate status becomes clear, the foreign entity in question will be denied immunity unless it can somehow justify immunity by producing evidence of the required circumstances.[204] Under UK law, therefore, the question of immunity of a foreign separate entity turns primarily on its *act*, rather than its status. In this respect, the notion of 'sovereign authority' (section 14(2)(a)) plays a crucial role in deciding immunity. According to Sucharitkul:

Unlike the sovereign or other heads of State and the central Government and its various organs or departments, which can be presumed to be acting for the State and in the exercise of its sovereign authority, agencies and instrumentalities of a State are not always so empowered. Immunity appears to be based on the attribution of activities to the State and on the fact that the act was done in the exercise of the sovereign authority of the State. Once these two qualifications are fulfilled, the agencies or instrumentalities of a foreign Government would in all likelihood be accorded the same immunity as that granted to the foreign State within whatever limits are recognized in prevailing State practice.[205]

However, there will inevitably be difficulties regarding the exact definition and delimitation of these circumstances, especially as regards the notion of 'sovereign authority'.[206] Nevertheless, the UK Model would be capable of drastically reducing the amount of work facing a UK court, as compared with the unenviable task for a US court, which often has to take great pains, routinely going into excruciating detail, to ascertain whether a particular entity qualifies as an 'agency or instrumentality' of a foreign State.

The exact rationale behind either the US or the UK approach remains obscure, especially given that both the US and the UK statutes were enacted against a background of a general absence of rules concerning foreign State immunity; that is, both statutes were meant to lay down *new* rules in this area.[207] In any case, the term 'separate entity' under the UK SIA appears much narrower than the 'agency and instrumentality' under the US FSIA. While the definition of 'State' under the UK SIA includes 'the government of that State and any department of that government', and a 'separate entity' must be 'distinct from the *executive organs* of the government of the State' (section 14(1)(b) and (c), emphasis added), the 'agency and instrumentality' under the US FSIA includes 'an organ of a foreign state or political subdivision thereof' (section 1603(b)(2)). Thus, as regards various governmental departments and other agencies established by the State for prima facie non-commercial purposes, there will not be much difference between the UK and the US approaches, whose main point of dissimilarity – to put it simplistically – occurs with regard to entities for non-governmental or commercial purposes, such as State companies and enterprises. So far as commercial entities are concerned, what the two approaches have in common is that they both look for a connection between the entity in question and its State: immunity is granted to a State entity if it is either *structurally* (US FSIA) or *functionally* (UK SIA) assimilated to that State, to which all immunity rightfully belongs in international law. It must, however, be borne in mind that this is an over-simplistic statement, for a US court will also have to consider whether the particular conduct of the defendant entity fits into one of the statutory exceptions to immunity (a functional assessment), while a UK court must also first make sure that the entity is indeed a 'separate' entity (a structural analysis). In view of the multitude of entities and agencies that States regularly bring into existence, with varying degrees of closeness to the State itself and different levels of authority to exercise governmental functions, it is not surprising that a court has often to consider all the relevant circumstances in a given case. At any rate, international law in this respect leaves a wide measure of discretion to national laws. Insofar as the immunity to be granted to a State entity or enterprise is ultimately attributable to the State itself, both the US and the UK approaches are in line with the general principles of international law relating to State immunity.

All the cases show that it is often necessary for the court to look into the structure of an entity and its relationship with the State even before considering whether that entity has engaged in any commercial activity. This certainly goes far beyond what can reasonably be expected under a narrowly defined 'functional' test, namely, whether or not the entity in question is engaging in a commercial activity. Indeed, as we can see, in many cases, before the issue of status is settled, the issue of commercial activity does not even arise. Moreover, these cases not only testify to the diverse types of entities that have been regarded as State entities but also bear witness to the often excruciating task of ascertaining the existence of an agency or instrumentality of a foreign State.

The purpose of the detailed and inevitably wearisome account of the factors considered by various courts is to show that, in deciding cases involving foreign entities, courts often have to look at the structures and functions of these entities even before they pass a judgment on the particular acts or transactions that have given rise to the claim. In order to solve the problem of immunity, the court first has to find out whether the entity is separate or not. To do this, the court must carry out an analysis of the structure and functions of the entity. Once that is done, it then becomes necessary to look at the particular act or transaction in order to decide whether certain exceptions to immunity apply. After all, who the defendant is and what he/it has done are two issues neither of which can be evaded if a court is to reach a sensible decision on any case. This is especially so in the field of State immunity where a prima facie identity with the State might cast serious doubt on the competence of the court. If the analysis of the structure, personality and status of an

280 SEPARATE ENTITIES

entity were really eliminated, the court would find itself at a loss in deciding many cases. In sum, the court has to consider all relevant factors, including both the structure and the acts of an entity.

2.4. Somewhere in-between: the Australian law and others

The drafters of the Australia FSIA were not impressed by either the UK model or the US model. In their view:

To deny state immunity to an entity simply because it has legal personality distinct from the state would be unacceptable to many states (including Australia, if such a rule were to be applied to it on a reciprocal basis). On the other hand it would clearly be unacceptable to go to the opposite extreme and let any foreign entity claim the protection of state immunity, however vaguely associated with the state. What is required is a test which discriminates, among entities with separate legal personality, between those entitled to claim immunity and those not so entitled.[208]

Thus section 3(3) of the Australia FSIA provides that the reference to a foreign State 'does not include a reference to a separate entity of a foreign State'. Under section 3(1) the term 'separate entity':

in relation to a foreign State, means a natural person (other than an Australian citizen), or a body corporate or corporation sole (other than a body corporate or corporation sole that has been established by or under a law of Australia), who or that:

(a) is an agency or instrumentality of the foreign State; and
(b) is not a department or organ of the executive government of the foreign State.

Section 3(2) further provides:

For the purposes of the definition of separate entity in subsection (1), a natural person who is, or a body corporate or a corporation sole that is, an agency of more than one foreign State shall be taken to be a separate entity of each of the foreign States.

The Australia FSIA then applies the rules concerning immunity of foreign States to separate entities. Under section 22, the rules concerning 'immunity from jurisdiction', i.e. immunity from adjudication, 'apply in relation to a separate entity of a foreign State as they apply in relation to the foreign State'.

Section 35, the rules concerning 'enforcement', states:

(1) This Part applies in relation to a separate entity of a foreign State that is the central bank or monetary authority of the foreign State as it applies in relation to the foreign State.

(2) Subject to subsection (1), this Part applies in relation to a separate entity of the foreign State as it applies in relation to the foreign State if, in the proceeding concerned:

 (a) the separate entity would, apart from the operation of section 10 ['Submission to jurisdiction'], have been immune from the jurisdiction; and

 (b) it has submitted to the jurisdiction.

The Australia FSIA thus attempts to steer a middle course between the US and the UK statutes. First, the Australia FSIA excludes separate entities, including agencies and instrumentalities, from the term 'State'. In this it resembles the UK Model but differs from the US Model. Secondly, it applies the provisions on immunity to separate entities in the same way as to foreign States themselves. In this it resembles the US Model but differs from the UK Model.

Like the UK and the US statutes, the Australia FSIA merely transposes the problem of separate entities onto a different plane but does not completely eliminate it. First, the Australia FSIA does not make it clear why, even if they are not included in the definition of the State, separate entities should nonetheless be subjected to the same rules concerning the immunity of the State itself. Upon closer inspection one finds a significant difference in the references to a separate entity in the UK SIA and the Australia FSIA. While the UK SIA speaks of a 'separate entity', the Australia FSIA speaks of a 'separate entity *of a foreign State*'. Maybe that is where the rub is: because the Australia FSIA prejudges a 'separate entity' to be that 'of a foreign State', it finds no difficulty in applying the same rules regarding the immunity of the State to the separate entity. But the court then has to decide whether a particular separate entity is indeed an entity that is both 'separate' and 'of a foreign State'. That is to say, the court must not only examine the status of the entity to verify its separate personality, it must also look into the relationship of the entity with the State to see if that entity is indeed one 'of a foreign State'. It can never achieve this without examining all the available and relevant evidence, including the structure and functions of the entity.[209] Secondly, whereas the US FSIA defines the 'agency or instrumentality of a foreign State' as any entity which is, inter alia, 'an organ of a foreign State or political subdivision thereof', section 3(1) of the Australia FSIA defines the term 'separate entity' in relation to a foreign State as 'a natural person ... or a body corporate or corporation sole ... who or that (a) is an agency or instrumentality of the foreign State; and (b) is not a department or organ of the executive government of the foreign State'. Therefore, according to the Australia FSIA, 'an agency or instrumentality of the foreign State' may not be 'a department or organ of the executive government of the foreign State'. The court is then faced with the task of deciding whether a separate entity is only an agency or instrumentality of the foreign State but not a department or organ of the executive government of the foreign State, or whether it is *both* an agency or instrumentality of the foreign State *and* a department or organ of the executive government of the foreign State. This is again impossible to achieve without considering all the circumstances of the case. Whichever angle one may choose to view the operation of the Australia FSIA, a multifactor analysis seems inevitable.

Article 2(1)(b)(iii) of the UN Convention provides that the term 'State' includes 'agencies or instrumentalities of the State or other entities, to the extent that they are entitled to perform and are actually performing acts in the exercise of sovereign authority of the State'. In including 'agencies or instrumentalities' in the definition of the State, it resembles the US model, but in *excluding* them when they are not exercising sovereign authority, it is akin to the UK model. Besides, it introduces more confusion. It not only leaves such crucial terms as 'agencies or instrumentalities' and 'entities' undefined, but it also states in the Annex, which under Article 25 'forms an integral part of the Convention', that:

The expression 'entity' [used in Article 19(c)] means the State as an independent legal personality, a constituent unit of a federal State, a subdivision of a State, an agency or instrumentality of a State or other entity, which enjoys independent legal personality.

Now the term 'entity' in the UN Convention becomes a virtual chameleon. One moment it is something other than the State, one moment it is *the* State, and then it can be both. It can be anything and everything: it can be a State, or a department of a State, or a province of a State, or an agency of a State, or a State-owned enterprise or company, or a private company working for or on behalf of the State. Such an inordinately loose conception incorporates all the evils we have so far discussed under various models and is destined to be unworkable in practice.

The IDI Draft 1991 presents another interesting case. Article 3(1) applies the same criteria of immunity to both foreign States and 'agencies of foreign States', 'whatever their formal designation or constitutional status in the State concerned'. Article 3(2) adds that 'the fact that an agency or political subdivision of a foreign State possesses a separate legal personality as a consequence of incorporation or otherwise under the law of the foreign State does not in itself preclude immunity in respect of its activities'.

On the surface, all the court has to do under Article 3 is apply the same set of rules equally to the State and its entities. But, upon careful examination, three problems arise. First, if the court is called upon to apply exactly the same rules to the State and State entities without discrimination, the question of the immunity of an entity will be automatically decided according to those rules regardless of whether the entity has a separate legal personality or not. It then seems redundant further to state that a separate legal personality does not preclude immunity, since the question of legal personality does not arise in any case in such a formula. Secondly, such a formula would be very effective in the event of an obviously commercial activity, but, in actual life, some acts are not so clear-cut and sometimes the issue of immunity with respect to certain acts depends precisely upon the status of the actor. Certain acts are treated as of a government character if carried out by a State organ but will be regarded as ordinary business activity if performed by a private enterprise. This is especially so in the field of contracts of employment. In such a case, it would be very important to know the status and structure of the entity in question. Thirdly, the draft fails to give a definition of State agency. The court always has to assume that an entity is a State entity and handle the case as if the State itself has been sued, while it is possible that the degree of State ownership or control of an entity is so low that the entity is an ordinary private enterprise rather than a State entity, in which case ordinary rules of civil procedure would apply, thereby rendering the rules of State immunity totally unnecessary. In sum, such a provision only conceals the problem of structure rather than addressing or dispensing with it.

The point is that, whatever legislative technique is employed, the same set of practical difficulties will always confront the court, which will always have to consider all the circumstances of the case before any sensible decision can be taken.

2.5. The practice of the States without immunity statutes

A survey of the case law developed by the courts of those States without immunity statutes reveals the same multifactor analysis. The common feature of the practice of these States is that entities with their own separate and independent personalities do not enjoy immunity, which is

284 SEPARATE ENTITIES

normally available only to States. On the other hand, if an entity can be considered an 'emanation of the State', then it can be entitled to immunity. In both situations, the control of the State has been held to be an important but insufficient factor. Only *extensive* control would render an entity an emanation of the State.

In German practice, it has been pronounced that 'separate legal entities of a foreign state enjoy no immunity'.[210] Since the decisive factor here is the separateness of an entity from a foreign State,[211] it would then become necessary for the court to conduct an examination of the structure of an entity, its *designated* functions, and the activities it normally engages in, quite apart from any consideration of the particular activity upon which the claim is based.[212] In other words, it is obvious that the matter of immunity, first of all, turns on the *status* of the entity in question rather than on its actual activities. Once it is satisfied that the entity (1) has been established as a juristic person; (2) can sue and be sued in its own name; and (3) can acquire and dispose of movable and immovable property, a German court would find it quite unnecessary even to consider whether the entity is also designed to exercise (as opposed to actually exercising) certain governmental functions.[213] In deciding upon the independence of the entity, the control of the State has been held to be an important but insufficient factor.[214]

Only if the entity is so closely connected with the foreign State that it could be regarded as an 'integral instrumentality' of that State would a German court then proceed to the act in question, i.e. whether the act upon which the claim is based is to be held as *acta jure imperii* or *acta jure gestionis*.[215] Given such a manifest bias against separate legal personality, it is tempting to think that the German practice goes even one step further from the UK approach, which allows a separate entity to enjoy immunity under certain circumstances. However, it seems safer to view the UK and the German practice as not substantially different. Notably, the rule in Germany has more often been stated in the following terms:

Commercial undertakings of a foreign State which have been endowed with their own independent legal personality do not enjoy any immunity.[216]

Here the 'undertakings' are not merely characterized by an 'independent legal personality': they are also qualified by the word 'commercial'. Thus it seems more accurate to say that the German courts would positively deny immunity only when a separate entity happens at the same time also to be a commercial enterprise, and would think twice when the entity appears of a somewhat non-commercial, i.e. public or sovereign, nature. This impression is in some measure strengthened by the above-mentioned practice of making a further distinction between sovereign and non-sovereign activities once it becomes evident that the entity is closely connected with the foreign State. Furthermore, it has been unambiguously declared that:

A foreign State – or a State enterprise or quasi-State enterprise – only enjoys freedom from German jurisdiction in relation to its sovereign activity (*acta iure imperii*), but not in relation to its non-sovereign activity (*acta iure gestionis*). If [the defendant] was acting on a sovereign basis, State immunity could in principle also be claimed by a legal person acting for the State.[217]

Insofar as a separate entity can indeed enjoy immunity when acting *jure imperii*, the German practice converges with that of the UK. In any case, it is abundantly clear that, in the German courts, a simple test, focusing solely upon the actual activity upon which the claim is based, is relegated to a much diminished state. The persistent preoccupation with the separate personality of the entity means that such a 'particular activity' criterion is deemed unnecessary and dispensable, to say the least, and then, when the circumstances indeed necessitate its application, it features as only a small part of the whole scenario to be taken into account.

In *National Iranian Gas Corporation*, where the commercial functions of a separate entity were not disputed, the French Court of Cassation held that foreign States, as well as the entities acting under their instructions or on their behalf, enjoy jurisdictional immunity only for acts of sovereign power or for acts performed in the interests of a public service.[218] But it would be mistaken to say that the French courts have totally discarded the analysis of the legal personality of the entity concerned. In fact, the courts are always ready to resort to such an analysis wherever necessary. In *Kuwait News Agency*, the French Court of Cassation decided against the immunity of the Kuwait News Agency on the basis of its separate legal entity. The Court held that the Kuwait News Agency had its own legal personality and independent budget. The protected interests of the State of Kuwait justifying jurisdictional immunity could not be infringed by the act of administration (*acte de gestion*) whereby a press agency, even if it were an emanation of the State, dismissed a journalist appointed within the framework of its activities, where that person had no special responsibilities.[219] In another case, a local French court found that the entity in question normally acted on behalf of a sovereign State. But the instant case involved a contract for a commercial lease, which

286 SEPARATE ENTITIES

the court held was not an act of public power and involved the exercise of rights governed by private law which were not covered by jurisdictional immunity.[220]

In a case concerning the Central Bank of Turkey, the Swiss Federal Tribunal first considered the following facts: the bank was a limited company with its own legal personality governed by Turkish private law; at least 51 per cent of its shares were required to be held by the Turkish State; it fulfilled the functions of a bank of issue and a central bank and its governor was appointed by the Council of Ministers on the recommendation of the Board of Directors. It was accordingly not legally identifiable with the Republic of Turkey. The Tribunal, however, left open whether the Central Bank as a separate entity could claim immunity (and, under the 'old case law' of the Federal Tribunal, it could not), since immunity was denied on other grounds.[221] In *Banco de la Nacion Lima*, however, the Tribunal finally formulated its position as:

> It appears from the jurisprudence that entities which, according to the law of the State in which they have their seat, possess their own distinct legal personality cannot take refuge behind the immunity of the State from which they emanate ... [T]he only possible exceptions being cases where such entities acted in the exercise of sovereign authority.[222]

It is clear that both the structure and the particular act should be taken into account. The Italian Court of Cassation also considers both the legal personality and the particular acts. Thus the fact that the entity might be considered as a public body in its own State was not decisive since, in order to be exempt from Italian jurisdiction, it must have acted as a sovereign power.[223] A Belgian court decided the question of immunity on the basis of both the legal personality of the entity and the particular act giving rise to the claim.[224] The opinions of the Dutch courts are few and unclear but at least seem to suggest the idea that all relevant factors should be considered.[225]

In sum, one finds the same multifactor analysis that takes into account both the status of the entity and its acts in the case. The court usually considers both the structure of the entity and the particular act or transaction leading to the claim. As has been said, who the defendant is and what he/it has done are always twin issues facing the court. Sometimes who the defendant is actually determines the characterization of the particular act in question. Therefore, the analysis of the status or personality of the entity is indispensable.

3. Piercing the corporate veil?

The question has arisen from time to time whether and under what circumstances the separate and independent personality of a State entity can be disregarded. That is, where an entity is so closely bound up with the State that it can be regarded as an 'alter ego', another self, of the State and therefore indistinguishable and inseparable from the latter, the entity and the State may be sued for each other's debts and held jointly liable, so that the assets held in the name of the State can be seized to satisfy a debt owed by the entity, and vice versa. This is usually referred to as 'piercing/lifting the corporate veil', namely to lift the facade of separate legal personality of an entity to reveal that the entity and the State are actually the one and the same. The case law, however, has generally accorded a high degree of respect for the separate legal personality of an entity and has only in exceptional cases allowed the 'corporate veil' to be 'pierced'.

In the leading US case of *Bancec*, the Banco para el Comercio Exterior de Cuba (Bancec), a Cuban State-owned bank, brought a suit against the First National City Bank (subsequently known as Citibank), a US bank, to recover an unpaid letter of credit. Citibank counterclaimed, asserting a right to set off the value of its Cuban assets expropriated by the Cuban Government. Before the filing of the counterclaim Bancec was dissolved and its capital was split between Banco Nacional, Cuba's central bank, and certain foreign trade enterprises of the Cuban Ministry of Foreign Trade. The question before the court was whether Citibank could obtain such a set-off, notwithstanding the fact that Bancec was established as a separate juridical entity. The district court allowed the set-off on the ground that Bancec was an alter ego of the Cuban Government; but the Circuit Court reversed.[226] The Supreme Court held that Bancec was not an entity independent from the Cuban Government, and therefore Citibank could set off the value of its assets seized by the Cuban Government against the amount sought by Bancec.

As a matter of general principle, the Supreme Court in *Bancec* declared that 'government instrumentalities established as juridical entities distinct and independent from their sovereign should normally be treated as such';[227] that is, 'duly created instrumentalities of a foreign state are to be accorded a *presumption of independent status*'.[228] This means that, even if an entity or instrumentality is wholly owned by a foreign State, it can still be treated as having an independent and separate legal status.

288 SEPARATE ENTITIES

As noted by the Supreme Court, this presumption was directly motivated by a concern for US corporations abroad. The legislative report of the US FSIA pronounced emphatically that:

The courts will have to determine whether property 'in the custody of' an agency or instrumentality is property 'of' the agency or instrumentality, whether property held by one agency should be deemed to be property of another, whether property held by an agency is property of the foreign state . . . Section 1610(b) will not permit execution against the property of one agency or instrumentality to satisfy a judgment against another, unrelated agency or instrumentality. There are compelling reasons for this. If U.S. law did not respect the separate juridical identities of different agencies or instrumentalities, it might encourage foreign jurisdictions to disregard the juridical divisions between different U.S. corporations or between a U.S. corporation and its independent subsidiary. However, a court might find that property held by one agency is really the property of another.[229]

Thus, the presumption that a foreign government's determination that its instrumentality is to be accorded separate legal status is buttressed by this congressional determination.[230]

The Court then declared that the presumption of independent status might be overcome in certain exceptional circumstances:

Thus, where a corporate entity is so extensively controlled by its owner that a relationship of principal and agent is created, we have held that one may be held liable for the actions of the other. In addition, our cases have long recognised the broader equitable principle that the doctrine of corporate entity, recognised generally and for most purposes, will not be regarded when to do so would work fraud or injustice.[231]

The Supreme Court decided that the presumption of independent status was indeed overcome in this case. In making this determination, the Court conducted a detailed structural analysis of Bancec and found that Bancec was empowered to act as the Cuban Government's exclusive agent in foreign trade, that the government supplied all of Bancec's capital and owned all of its stock, that all of Bancec's profits were deposited in the General Treasury, that Bancec's Governing Board consisted of delegates from Cuban government ministries and that the president of Bancec was the Minister of State.[232] Thus:

Bancec lacked an independent existence, and was a mere arm of the Cuban Government, performing a purely governmental function. The control of Bancec was exclusively in the hands of the Government, and Bancec was established solely to further Governmental purposes. Moreover, Bancec was totally dependent on the Government for financing and required to remit all of its profits to the Government.[233]

The Supreme Court declined 'to adhere blindly to the corporate form where doing so would cause ... an injustice':[234]

Having dissolved Bancec and transferred its assets to entities that may be held liable on Citibank's counterclaim, Cuba cannot escape liability for acts in violation of international law simply by retransferring the assets to separate juridical entities. To hold otherwise would permit governments to avoid the requirements of international law simply by creating juridical entities whenever the need arises ... Our decision today announces no mechanical formula for determining the circumstances under which the normally separate juridical status of a government instrumentality is to be disregarded. Instead, it is the product of the application of internationally recognized equitable principles to avoid the injustice that would result from permitting a foreign state to reap the benefits of our courts while avoiding the obligations of international law.[235]

As the Supreme Court refrained from articulating any 'mechanical formula', the courts usually would have to examine all the relevant factors, including majority ownership, appointment of the administrative staff and day-to-day decision-making, and would require a very high standard of proof. Such factors as majority ownership (even if this may be a 100 per cent ownership) and the appointment and majority control of the board of directors have been held as insufficient by themselves to establish a principal–agent relationship,[236] for which *substantial or extensive* State control over an entity's management and activities is required before the presumption can be overcome.[237] Mere oversight and participation in some decision-making, the type of activity akin to that of a majority shareholder, is not enough.[238]

In *Transamerica*, the DC Circuit stated that, in deciding on the 'agency' point, control is the central factor:

First, control is relevant when it significantly exceeds the normal supervisory control exercised by any corporate parent over its subsidiary and, indeed, amounts to complete domination of the subsidiary. A sovereign is amenable to suit based upon the actions of an instrumentality it dominates because the sovereign and the instrumentality are in those circumstances not meaningfully distinct entities; they act as one ... Second, control is relevant when the sovereign exercises its control in such a way as to make the instrumentality its agent; in that case control renders the sovereign amenable to suit under ordinary agency principles ... A sovereign does not create an agency relationship merely by owning a majority of a corporation's stock or by appointing its Board of Directors.[239]

290 SEPARATE ENTITIES

Thus, in *Hercaire*, even though Argentina expressly waived 'its sovereign immunity and that of its agencies', that waiver was insufficient to subject a Boeing 727 aeroplane, owned by Aerolineas Argentinas, Argentina's wholly owned national airline, to execution for a judgment against Argentina, since the airline, as an independent juridical entity, was neither a party to the litigation nor was in any way connected with the underlying transaction giving rise to the suit. Declaring that 'the presumption of independent status is not to be lightly overcome', the Eleventh Circuit held that the 100 per cent ownership of Aerolineas by Argentina was not sufficient to overcome this presumption, where there was no showing that Argentina exercised such *extensive control* over Aerolineas as to warrant a finding of principal and agent. The court also stated, in passing, that no 'fraud or injustice' would result from such a decision.[240]

By contrast, in *S & Davis*, a US corporation attempted to enforce an arbitration award against a Yemeni entity called the General Corporation for Foreign Trade and Grains. The court held that the award could be enforced against Yemen as a principal of its agent, the General Corporation. The Court of Appeals found that the Minister of Trade had given direct orders to terminate the contract on behalf of General Corporation, that Yemen had more than a regulatory role in the affairs of Public Corporations, that there was rebuttable evidence that the General Corporation was an agent of Yemen such that under the ordinary principles of agency, Yemen could be sued, and that Yemen failed to rebut that evidence.[241] The court noted, in particular, that, in applying the agency exception to the rule of immunity, it reviewed 'how much control the sovereign exercised over the instrumentality'.[242]

The catchphrase seems to be 'day-to-day control';[243] that is, a principal–agent relationship can be established, and therefore the corporate veil can be lifted, when the foreign State exercises extensive day-to-day control over the activities of the entity in question. However, according to the Supreme Court, the control test comes into play only when majority ownership by a foreign State, as required by section 1603(b)(2), can be established.[244]

The *Bancec* case in effect put forward a two-pronged test: principal–agent relationship (or an 'alter ego relationship' or 'agency relationship'[245]) and the prevention of fraud or injustice. Little discussion, however, has been devoted in the US courts to what constitutes 'fraud or injustice', despite that being an important prong of the *Bancec* test. The case law tends to construe the 'fraud or injustice' part of the test narrowly and treat it as only secondary or supplementary. That is to say, if a 'principal–agent' relationship cannot be established, the mere fact that some injustice might ensue is not by itself sufficient to overcome the presumption of separateness.

In *Alejandre*, the families of the American victims whose planes had been shot down by the Cuban Air Force in 1996[246] moved to enforce writs of execution and garnishment. The question before the court was whether it was permissible for the plaintiffs to collect a portion of their judgment against the Cuban Government and the Cuban Air Force[247] by garnishing certain debts owed to Empresa de Telecomunicaciones de Cuba, SA (ETECSA), a Cuban telecommunications company a majority of whose stock was held by three Cuban companies owned or controlled by the Cuban Government. In other words, the question was whether ETECSA, if it could be regarded as an instrumentality of Cuba,[248] must be held as separate from the Cuban Government, and therefore not responsible for the Government's debt to the plaintiffs. The district court held that the ETECSA was responsible for the Cuban Government's debt to the plaintiffs. While noting that a principal–agent relationship between Cuba and the ETECSA could not be established, the court disregarded the presumptively separate juridical status of the ETECSA by relying on the 'injustice' point in the second prong of the *Bancec* test, saying that the contrary solution would prevent the plaintiffs from collecting their final judgment for the victims of a terrorist attack.[249] The Eleventh Circuit vacated, holding that injustice alone was *not* a sufficient basis for overcoming the presumption of separate juridical status. The court said:

While the district court's concern about the injustice of preventing plaintiffs from collecting their judgment is understandable, this concern is present in every case in which a plaintiff seeks to hold an instrumentality responsible for the debts of its related government. Allowing the *Bancec* presumption of separate juridical status to be so easily overcome would effectively render it a nullity.[250]

In *Bridas*, an Argentine corporation had entered into a joint venture agreement (JVA) with an entity wholly owned by the Government of Turkmenistan to exploit oil and gas resources in Turkmenistan. When a dispute arose concerning the sharing of future proceeds the Turkmenistan Government ordered the corporation to halt operations, whereupon Bridas commenced an arbitration proceeding, as provided in the JVA, against the Government and Turkmenneft under the auspices of the International Chamber of Commerce. After Bridas filed its arbitration

292   SEPARATE ENTITIES

complaint, the Government dissolved the 'Turkmenian Party' in the JVA, replacing it with an entity called Turkmenneft, and decreed that all proceeds from oil and gas exports in the country were to be directed to a special State Oil and Gas Development Fund, whose assets were declared immune from seizure. Even though the Turkmenistan Government was not a party to the JVA, the arbitral panel held both Turkmenneft and the Government liable for repudiating the JVA, and awarded $495 million in damages to Bridas. The Fifth Circuit court gave judgment for the plaintiff to enforce the arbitration award against Turkmenistan on the 'alter ego' doctrine. The court first commented:

> The alter ego doctrine, like all variations of piercing the corporate veil doctrine, is reserved for exceptional cases. The doctrine applies only if (1) the owner exercised complete control over the corporation with respect to the transaction at issue and (2) such control was used to commit a fraud or wrong that injured the party seeking to pierce the veil.[251]

The court found that, by deliberately keeping Turkmenneft grossly undercapitalized, so that it had to rely exclusively upon another entity to service its debts, and by changing the law to prevent Turkmenneft's assets from being seized by a creditor such as Bridas, the Turkmenistan Government manipulated Turkmenneft legally and economically to repudiate the contract with Bridas and then render it impossible for Bridas to collect damages. Thus Turkmenneft was not financially independent from the government and the government used the lack of financial separateness to commit a fraud or another wrong on the plaintiffs. The government exercised such complete control over the oil company as to be its alter ego.[252] In the words of the court:

> Despite some indicia of separateness, the reality was that when the Government's export ban forced Bridas out of the joint venture, the Government then exercised its power as a parent entity to deprive Bridas of a contractual remedy. Intentionally bleeding a subsidiary to thwart creditors is a classic ground for piercing the corporate veil.[253]

Similarly, manipulating the agency or instrumentality in order to obtain a financial benefit is committing injustice,[254] but a simple failure to provide a shipping company with adequate financial resources so as to save it from bankruptcy is not.[255] Nor is it enough simply to argue that anything done (such as recovering a debt) by the entity in question will ultimately benefit the government.[256] In *LNC*, the court simply stated that no 'fraud or injustice' would result from insulating the Central Bank of Nicaragua's property from attachment in aid of execution of the judgment against Nicaragua, it being hearsay that Nicaragua would ultimately benefit from such a decision.[257]

Although *Bancec* addressed the relationship between a foreign State and an agency or instrumentality of the foreign State, *Bancec*'s principal–agent analysis has also been applied to the relationship between agencies or instrumentalities of a foreign State themselves.[258] One entity cannot be sued for the acts of another entity unless there exists such a relationship. Thus the Central Bank of Iraq (CBI), as an agency of Iraq, was immune from a suit against Rafidain, a commercial bank wholly owned by Iraq, unless it could be shown that the CBI's alleged control over Rafidain was sufficient to attribute Rafidain's acts or activities to the CBI under the alter ego theory.[259] Thus, once the principle of respect for the separate personality of the entity is established, it is but a small step to the conclusion that the State should not be held liable for its entities (and vice versa) and that an entity should not be held liable for another entity.[260] On the other hand, where a principal–agent relationship exists so that one entity can be regarded as the alter ego of another, then if one is immune, the other is also immune, unless one of the FSIA exceptions applies.[261]

The presumption of juridical separateness of entities covers both the adjudicatory and the executory stages. That is, absent an agency relationship, where a State entity is not immune, the claim is ordinarily to be brought only against the entity itself;[262] the property of a State cannot be attached to execute a judgment against a State entity;[263] conversely, the property of a State entity (even if it is wholly owned by the State) cannot be executed to satisfy a judgment against the State[264] or a judgment against another, unrelated entity.[265] More importantly, 'piercing the corporate veil' is only an extraordinary measure. In *Dole Food*, the Supreme Court, while reiterating the *Bancec* ruling, declared:

> The doctrine of piercing the corporate veil ... is the rare exception, applied in the case of fraud or certain other exceptional circumstances ... and usually determined on a case-by-case basis.[266]

In most cases, *Bancec* has been cited, not as authority on when and how to disregard separate personality, but as establishing the principle of respect for the separate personality.[267]

The Canadian practice closely follows that of the US. In *Roxford*, the judge had to decide whether the assets of Cubana, Cuba's national airline, could be seized to satisfy a judgment against Cuba. Cubana was not named in that action, nor did it take part in the proceedings.

Finding no Canadian case law on the issue, the judge turned to US jurisprudence for guidance.

The judge first referred to the decision of the US Supreme Court in *Bancec* that a duly created instrumentality of a foreign State should be presumed to possess independent status unless it is so extensively controlled as to create a principal and agent relationship, in which case one may be held liable for the other's actions. The judge found that the principle was 'both logical and sound and should be applied to the present case'. The judge then noted that in *Hercaire*, the US Circuit Court put forward the proposition that the presumption of independent status is not to be lightly overcome. Even 100 per cent ownership of an airline by Argentina was held insufficient to overcome the presumption.[268] The judge found that the decision 'would require delving into the complex factual and legal issues of ownership of the assets of Cubana, and its relationship to Cuba'.[269]

Upon examining all the available evidence, the judge found that the plaintiff had failed to dislodge the presumption that Cubana was a separate juridical entity. The facts did not support the conclusion that Cubana's business, income, undertaking and assets are controlled or even 'owned' by Cuba. Cubana carried on its own business and hired its own employees, who were not civil servants. It had its own banking facilities and prepared annual financial statements. Its board had all of the usual powers of a corporate board of directors. Although some of the facts were inconsistent with independent status, these were to be viewed from the perspective of a communist regime. The factors establishing effective control by Cubana of its business and assets supported the conclusion that it was an independent corporation, and not an agent of Cuba in respect of its business; and it was not sufficient to show that the State owned 100 per cent of the shares. The evidence fell short of demonstrating that Cuba exerted a controlling influence over Cubana. The plaintiff had failed to establish, on the balance of probabilities, that Cubana was the *alter ego* or agent of Cuba.[270]

The judge proposed a two-part test:

> To conclude that in its activities, business and use of its assets [Cubana] is an *alter ego* of Cuba would require both compelling evidence of a *de facto* assimilation of it, or of its business and property, to Cuba and a clear legal basis of a *de jure* assimilation to Cuba.[271]

The same elaborate examination of documentary and factual evidence can be found in the case of *Banco de Moçambique*, where the South African

Supreme Court enunciated the principle that the separate legal personality of a State entity should be respected, so that the monies to the credit of the Banco de Moçambique, the central bank of Mozambique, could not be attached to found jurisdiction in an action against the Government of Mozambique.[272]

In two UK cases related to this issue, the courts held that the entities in question were justified in relying on the governmental intervention as a *force majeure*. The separate personalities of the entities were to be respected.[273]

In the States without immunity legislation, one finds the same rules. Thus, if an entity can be seen as an 'emanation' or 'instrument' of a foreign State, then the two can be identified, with the result that the entity can enjoy the immunity available to the State.[274] If not, then the distinct and separate identity of the entity is to be respected.[275] In either case, the fact that the shares of the separate entity may be owned by the foreign State, or that the foreign State exercises supervision or control over the entity, or that the entity performs a devolved public service function, is insufficient to overcome the separate and independent status.[276]

The 2004 UN Convention leaves the question of 'piercing the corporate veil' open. Article 10(3) provides:

Where a State enterprise or other entity established by a State which has an independent legal personality and is capable of:

(a) suing or being sued; and
(b) acquiring, owning or possessing and disposing of property, including property which that State has authorized it to operate or manage,

is involved in a proceeding which relates to a commercial transaction in which that entity is engaged, the immunity from jurisdiction enjoyed by that State shall not be affected.

However, the Annex, which under Article 25 'forms an integral part of the Convention', adds the following understanding:

Article 10, paragraph 3, does not prejudge the question of 'piercing the corporate veil', questions relating to a situation where a State entity has deliberately misrepresented its financial position or subsequently reduced its assets to avoid satisfying a claim, or other related issues.

Nevertheless, it appears still safe to conclude that current law embraces a general principle of respect for the separate legal personality of State entities and such separate personality is disregarded only under exceptional circumstances.

Conclusion

Unless State immunity is completely abolished, there is always some area in which a State can enjoy immunity and, as a consequence, identification with the State can bring immunity to a particular entity. Supposing a purely functionalist approach is adopted, so that the immunity of an entity is determined by the act or transaction giving rise to the claim, the question of immunity can be decided regardless of whether the entity is separate from the State. If the entity is performing acts of a governmental character, it will enjoy immunity even if it has separate legal status; conversely, if it engages in non-governmental activities, it will not be granted immunity even if it is merely an organ or alter ego of the State without separate legal status. But the question of separate legal personality cannot be disposed of altogether. When an entity is sued, the first thing the court has to ascertain is whether there is an entity and whether that entity is linked in any manner with the State itself. If it is neither owned nor controlled by the State nor linked with it in any other way, the case falls into the category of ordinary civil litigation. On the other hand, if it is indeed a State entity, the question then turns on whether it has a legal personality independent of the State. If it is a State entity but operates entirely in its own name in the act or transaction in question, the proceedings should be directed at the entity itself. If, however, the entity has no independent legal personality or is controlled by the State to such an extent that it is just a facade through which the State engages in commercial dealings, the proceedings must be directed against the State itself or be seen as so directed. The question actually becomes one of the immunity of the State, not of the entity. It is here that the rules concerning foreign State immunity come into play. In fact, the question of immunity of entities other than the State arose precisely because these entities could be so closely linked with the State that they could be considered as partaking of a certain measure of the character, and therefore immunity, of the State itself. It would be quite impossible for the court to clarify such a relationship without looking into the laws and practices surrounding a particular entity and its overall structure, functions and the degree of State ownership or control.

What is more, even if the principle is that sovereign acts are immune and non-sovereign acts are not immune, in some cases it is not enough only to look at the acts in isolation from the actual circumstances and to disregard the actor. Some acts are immune precisely because they are carried out by the State. If carried out by a private individual or company they are regarded as only ordinary business dealings. This is especially so in the area of contracts of employment. In such cases, if the particular act can be attributed to the State, the entity should enjoy immunity with respect to this act. And the attribution cannot be clarified without an investigation into the relationship between the State and the entity.

In a word, there can be no purely structural or functional approach. Neither of the approaches alone is capable of solving the practical problems. Consequently, neither of them can be discarded in favour of the other. A court often has to resort to both approaches simultaneously so as to reach a sensible solution in a case concerning a separate entity. Also, the use of words such as 'structural' and 'functional' is not only of little help; it also serves to muddle the matter. In this connection a distinction is especially necessary between the designed functions of an entity and the actual activities: what activities/functions the entity in question normally engages in, and what activity it was that gave rise to and forms the basis of the claim. In fact one would be hard pressed to find a case in which the court did not approach the case by reference to these two types of activities.

The crux of the matter is whether the entity is indistinct from the State (an alter ego) or distinct from it (a separate entity), since the distinctness or otherwise between the State and entity is considered the first and the pivotal issue in the practice of all States. An indistinct entity will most probably be regarded as endowed with sovereign attributes and therefore entitled to immunity, whereas a distinct entity may or may not be granted immunity depending on the particular pattern of practice. And the question of distinctness runs through both the adjudicative and the executory stages of a judicial proceeding. In order to decide whether there does exist a State entity courts often have to make laborious efforts to examine such factors as the constitution and the by-laws of the entity; the foreign law under which the entity is constituted or incorporated; the legal personality of the entity (separate or otherwise); the capacity to hold property and capacity to sue and be sued; the financial and budgetary autonomy; the degree and nature of government control; the ownership and control of the entity; the relationship between the entity and the government; the appointment and dismissal of administrative personnel; and the decision-making process of the entity and its accountability. A multifactor analysis seems to be the only viable and workable approach.

7 Expropriation

It is difficult to imagine that expropriation can become the subject of proceedings before foreign domestic courts and therefore of the regime of State immunity. Measures of expropriation normally take place within the territorial limits of a State. The right to expropriate has long been regarded as part of territorial sovereignty. The taking of property of foreign nationals within the territory of a State is always a sovereign activity even if it violates international law. Therefore, it meets the requirements of both the act of State doctrine and State immunity principles so as to be outside the jurisdiction of foreign municipal courts and thus more fittingly falls to be governed by procedures under public international law, on the State-to-State level. Diplomatic negotiations, international agreements and compensation commissions are the usual vehicles for settling disputes relating to expropriation.

Courts rarely, if ever, assume jurisdiction over claims concerning measures of expropriation by and in foreign States. The chief reason seems to be that such expropriation usually takes place within the territory of foreign States and has no connection with the territory of the forum State. Since the jurisdiction of a court is in principle territorial, a court cannot but find itself handicapped in the absence of connecting factors that normally undergird the existence of judicial competence. So far, the US remains the only country whose courts are empowered by legislation to exercise some degree of jurisdiction over claims concerning expropriation in foreign countries. Such jurisdiction, upon closer inspection, is still territorial, not extraterritorial, for it requires a connection with US territory before the claim can be entertained.

1. The general principle: immunity

Over the years, courts have routinely declined to exercise jurisdiction over cases immediately arising out of, or otherwise linked with, acts of expropriation carried out by foreign States in their own territories. The reason given for such denial has been twofold: first, that expropriation was a sovereign, rather than commercial, activity; secondly, that the expropriation in question took place in the foreign State's own territory, having no connection with the State of the forum.[1]

Such widespread and uniform practice suggests that, in the law of State immunity, the rationale for denying immunity consists not only in the relevant act being *jure gestionis*, but also, more importantly, in the overriding principle of territorial jurisdiction. Moreover, during the time when the doctrine of absolute immunity prevailed, such expropriation measures, even if occurring within the territory of the forum State, often had their validity tacitly accepted by the court.[2] In the rare cases where expropriation was indeed challenged because it had taken place within the territory of the forum State, immunity was nonetheless upheld on the ground that the act of expropriation was taken peaceably and without compromising the sovereignty of the territorial/forum State.[3]

However, such abstention from jurisdiction seems rather to have arisen out of a sense of courtesy; for, if it wished, the forum State could still exercise jurisdiction. In *The El Condado*, for example, which involved requisition of a ship in the harbour of Greenock, Scotland, by the Spanish Consul at Glasgow, acting under instructions from the Republican Government of Spain, immunity was initially granted when Spain was sued against its will, but was denied when Spain itself brought an action in the court. According to the court, having invoked the jurisdiction of the court, Spain now had to establish its claim to possession of the ship. Since the requisition decree was ineffectual to attach a vessel which at the date of the decree was in Scotland and outwith Spanish territory or territorial waters, Spain had not established its title to take possession of the vessel.[4] In *Carlbom*, the Swedish Supreme Court declined to acknowledge the applicability of a nationalization decree by Estonia (which later became part of the Soviet Union) to a ship which at the material time lay in Stockholm harbour.[5]

The strict observance of the territoriality principle shows no signs of relaxation in more recent cases. In the Belgian case of *Biocare*, the plaintiff company brought a claim against a Zairian State-owned

300   EXPROPRIATION

company for compensation payable under the law of Zaire for the loss of its shareholding in a company incorporated in Zaire, which had been expropriated and transferred to the defendant company pursuant to the so-called 'Zairianization' (expropriation) decree, adopted by the President of Zaire in 1973. The plaintiff company argued that, since the defendant company had an office in Belgium, the debt could be claimed there. The court, while conceding that proceedings could be instituted against foreign companies in Belgium if they had established a registered office or subsidiary there, such proceedings could not be brought in this case because the debt claimed and the policy of Zairianization had no *connection* with the operation of the defendant company's office established in Belgium.[6]

It is obvious that the court circumvented the issue of expropriation and did not attempt to question its validity as a sovereign act. On the other hand, had the proceedings had any connection with the defendant company, the court would not have hesitated to exercise jurisdiction on the basis of a commercial/private activity exception to immunity, regardless of the link between the proceedings and the expropriation measures, so long as the court did not have to pass a direct decision on the expropriation measures. Apparently, whether or not the expropriation measures in question were in conformity with international law was regarded as a matter beyond the scope of the court's power to judge and therefore better to be avoided. One should note that this case has all the ingredients of the 'expropriation exception' in section 1605(a)(3) of the US FSIA: the plaintiff could have alleged that the expropriation was in violation of international law because no compensation had yet been paid; the shareholding had been transferred to (and was therefore 'owned or operated by') the defendant company and that company was engaged in commercial activities in Belgium. Thus, while a Belgian court denied jurisdiction in such a case, a US court would have assumed jurisdiction.

When a Romanian emigrant brought an action in Switzerland for compensation for the compulsory purchase of his immovable property in Romania by the Romanian State upon his leaving the country, the Swiss Federal Tribunal found that the case involved an act of expropriation; as such it was an act of sovereignty performed *jure imperii* by virtue of foreign public law and not an act which a private individual could have equally well performed *jure gestionis* following procedures under private law. Moreover, the Tribunal made it clear that, even in a case concerning an act *jure gestionis*, it was possible to sue a foreign State only if the underlying legal relationship had a connection with Swiss territory.[7]

Apparently, the immunity enjoyed by a State can also be made available to a company. Upon achieving independence, Algeria nationalized, without compensation, undertakings operated in Algeria by two French companies which manufactured foodstuffs. The French companies brought an action for compensation against the Algerian company to which the Algerian authorities had transferred the undertakings in question. The French Court of Cassation granted immunity to the Algerian company on the ground that the Algerian company had come into possession of the undertakings by virtue of a sovereign act of the Algerian State, so that the action was in reality directed against the Algerian State itself.[8] Strangely, a year later, the same Court (but a different chamber) denied immunity in a case against another Algerian company on almost identical subject matter, on the ground that a dispossession carried out by a foreign State could not be recognized in France as having legal effect if equitable compensation had not been paid.[9] At any rate, it would seem that, although the French courts sometimes assume jurisdiction over disputes arising out of expropriation by foreign States, they do not seek to question the legality of the expropriation under international law but instead adopt a rationale of non-recognition of legal effects of foreign expropriation within the territory of France.

Notably, it is possible to sue a foreign commercial entity that engages in commercial activities in the forum State allegedly by using expropriated property, even though the expropriation had taken place abroad. Thus a French company was held to be entitled to an order of seizure of property against the Soviet Russian Trade Delegation in France, as one of the organs of the Soviet Russian commercial organization that had deprived the French company of its property in the Soviet Union.[10] This decision, as we shall see, very much resembles the expropriation provision under the US FSIA.

2. Legality and immunity

Respect for the sovereign nature of nationalization or expropriation measures leads to the refusal to examine the lawfulness, under international law, of such measures for the purposes of deciding the issue of immunity. In the words of the US Supreme Court, a court 'will not examine the validity of a taking of property within its own territory by a foreign sovereign government . . . even if the complaint alleges that the taking violates customary international law'.[11] Similarly, the Italian Court of Cassation stated:

302   EXPROPRIATION

We see that the judges in the various States have constantly refused, by rejecting compensation and restitution claims, to hold foreign States liable for nationalization measures. It has been made clear, in fact, that these measures are to be recognised in the state and to the extent of their execution and are to be assessed as *faits accomplis* and as the exercise of effective sovereignty. The judge of the forum is thus obliged to refrain from checking in any way on the lawfulness, as to form and as to substance, of such measures, whether by reference to the rules in force in the State which has carried out nationalization, or by reference to international law, or even ... by reference to those fundamental values of the legal system of the forum that are safeguarded by public policy.[12]

That is to say (obnoxious though this may sound), immunity remains intact even though the expropriation measures in question are manifestly illegal. This can be amply demonstrated by the case of *Kuwait Airways*. In August 1990 Iraq invaded and occupied Kuwait. Under orders from the Iraqi Government, the Iraqi Airways Company (IAC) flew ten civilian aircraft belonging to Kuwait Airways Corporation (KAC), from Kuwait to Iraq. On 17 September 1990, the Iraqi Revolutionary Command Council passed Resolution 369, purportedly transferring all the assets of KAC to IAC. Thereupon IAC incorporated the ten aircraft into its own fleet. When KAC, after the Gulf War of 1991, sued IAC and Iraq for damages, both the English Court of Appeal, in reversing the decision of the High Court, and the House of Lords held that the seizure of the aircraft amounted to expropriation of foreign assets by a victorious State in a war. In other words, it was an act of sovereign authority or *de jure imperii*, and therefore attracted immunity.[13] Whether the evident unlawfulness of the seizure in question should have any impact on the decision on immunity was not even considered by the judges. However, in partly reversing the decision of the Court of Appeal, the House of Lords held that, once Revolutionary Command Council Resolution 369 came into force on 17 September 1990, IAC turned from an accomplice in the confiscation into an owner of commercial property. Its acts then assumed the character of a commercial activity, despite the sovereign nature of the initial seizure of the aircraft. As such, IAC could not be entitled to immunity for its acts subsequent to 17 September 1990.[14] Obviously, the House of Lords contented itself with putting a different gloss on the acts of IAC in maintaining and using the aircraft, but did not challenge the sovereign or *jure imperii* character of the seizure itself. The matter did not end there. In further actions the KAC successfully persuaded the English courts that the IAC's acts with regard to the aircraft *prior to* 17 September 1990 were far more extensive in a commercial sense than merely carrying out the confiscatory orders of the Iraqi Government. While declaring that patently unlawful expropriation, such as the seizure of Kuwaiti aircraft by Iraq following its invasion of Kuwait and the Iraqi Government resolution vesting the property rights over the aircraft in the IAC, was not to be recognized, the English courts held that, given the commercial nature of its activities throughout the period, the IAC had no immunity, either before or after 17 September 1990.[15] Clearly, the effect of not recognizing the expropriation on account of its illegality was simply that the previous House of Lords decision, denying the IAC immunity only with regard to the period after 17 September 1990, be disregarded, since now the IAC could not pray in aid any shred of government authority and its acts in the whole relevant period would amount to wrongful interference and conversion, that is, of a purely private and commercial nature. Thus the issue of illegality only serves to deprive the acts of the IAC of its colour of sovereignty, but does not in any way deny the sovereign nature of the expropriation itself. This means that the Iraqi Government, whose role was only that of the expropriating power, would remain, in all probability, immune.

3. The ILC's aborted provision

In 1986, the ILC provisionally adopted draft Article 20, which provided:

The provisions of the present articles shall not prejudge any question that may arise in regard to extraterritorial effects of measures of nationalization taken by a State with regard to property, movable or immovable, industrial or intellectual.[16]

The reaction from the governments was, however, less than enthusiastic;[17] so was the response of the ILC itself, with the result that draft Article 20 was deleted altogether. The members of the ILC were agreed that measures of nationalization, as sovereign acts, were not subject to the jurisdiction of another State and could not be considered as representing an exception to the principle of State immunity.[18]

4. The 'expropriation' provision in the US FSIA

At present, the US FSIA is the only statute that provides jurisdiction over claims concerning expropriation by foreign States. Insofar as the territorial nexus is concerned, the provision of the third clause of section

1605(a)(2), to the effect that immunity shall be denied in the case of an act outside the US in connection with a commercial activity carried out elsewhere having a 'direct effect' in the US, is closely connected with section 1605(a)(3) of the FSIA, which provides that a foreign State shall not be immune in any case:

in which rights in property taken in violation of international law are in issue and that property or any property exchanged for such property is present in the United States in connection with a commercial activity carried on in the United States by the foreign state; or that property or any property exchanged for such property is owned or operated by an agency or instrumentality of the foreign state and that agency or instrumentality is engaged in a commercial activity in the United States.[19]

This provision, according to the legislative history, was intended to cover 'nationalization or expropriation of property';[20] and it has thus come to be commonly referred to by the US courts as the 'expropriation exception'[21] or the 'takings exception'[22] to immunity.

Under a parallel provision of section 1610(a)(3):

The property in the United States of a foreign state ... used for a commercial activity in the United States, shall not be immune from attachment in aid of execution, or from execution ... if the execution relates to a judgment establishing rights in property which has been taken in violation of international law or which has been exchanged for property taken in violation of international law.

It must be noted that, in such a case, there does not have to be a connection between the executed property and the property in dispute. But this point has to be pursued in the discussion of measures of constraint.

Evidently, two conditions have to be satisfied before a US court can assume jurisdiction over proceedings involving foreign expropriation: a territorial connection and a violation of international law. A commercial activity lies at the heart of the territorial connection, for in its absence the expropriation exception to immunity cannot be activated. Where no commercial activity in the US can be shown, the action will fail.[23] This has the effect of narrowing down the scope of the jurisdiction of the US courts over claims concerning expropriation measures by presuming immunity when the property in question has been used in connection with a *sovereign activity*. However, such a presumption of immunity is undercut in two ways. First, the notion of 'property exchanged for the expropriated property' makes it unnecessary for the originally expropriated property to be present in the US: the presence of some secondary property suffices. Secondly, in the case of the property being owned or operated by a foreign State agency or instrumentality, the sovereign purpose of the property becomes irrelevant; in other words, even if the property itself is used for a sovereign activity, the mere fact that it is owned or otherwise operated by an agency or instrumentality, not the State itself, disallows the protection of immunity: the disputed property does not have to be connected with a commercial activity, nor does it have to be physically present in US territory. Although the whole matter seems to hinge on the narrowness or broadness of the definition of 'commercial activity', the general impression is that a US court will assume jurisdiction over an expropriation claim with only a minimal territorial connection. But of course it must be borne in mind that such a relatively liberal position only has to do with the establishment of adjudicative jurisdiction; separate consideration is needed for the taking of execution measures against the property of a foreign State. In particular, only commercial property can be executed upon.

As is made clear by the terms of the provision, to establish jurisdiction pursuant to this exception to immunity, a plaintiff must demonstrate each of four elements: (1) that rights in property are at issue; (2) that the property was 'taken'; (3) that the taking was in violation of international law; and (4) either of two territorial nexus requirements, namely that the property at issue or any property exchanged for it is either: (a) 'present in the United States in connection with a commercial activity carried on in the United States by the foreign state'; or (b) 'owned or operated by an agency or instrumentality of the foreign state and that agency or instrumentality is engaged in a commercial activity in the United States'.[24] The absence of any one of the four elements will defeat a claim under section 1605(a)(3).[25] Moreover, a claim of expropriation in the US should be brought within six years, under the statute of limitations.[26] The 'commercial activity' element means that expropriation claims fall simultaneously within the commercial activity and expropriation exceptions under the FSIA.[27]

4.1. 'Rights in property'

The first question is what is meant by 'property'. While neither the FSIA nor the legislative history provides any clue, it is established case law in the US that the word 'property' under section 1605(a)(3) means only 'tangible' or 'physical' property, i.e. property that can be touched and seen, and does not include 'intangible property' that lacks a physical existence, such as bank accounts, shares held in trust, contractual rights to exercise options to purchase shares, the right to receive payments, and intellectual property rights. Accordingly, such acts as repudiation of contract, infringement of copyright, or failure to make payments will not trigger the application of this exception.[28] The fact that the property in question is not tangible property has been treated as dispositive of the question whether the expropriation exception of the FSIA can apply.[29]

Thus the confiscation of paintings fell 'squarely within the expropriation exception to sovereign immunity' because 'rights in property' were in issue.[30] Stocks are not tangible property but can occasionally be treated as such under certain circumstances. In *Kalamazoo*, the court, while recognizing that the FSIA applied only to tangible property, held that the FSIA applied to the governmental seizure of some 'property interest', such as 51 per cent of a company's stock. The Court concluded that:

It would not make sense to distinguish between the expropriation of the physical assets of a company, which would clearly fall within section 1605(a)(3), and expropriation of a controlling interest in the stock of the company. In either case, the foreign state has expropriated control of the assets and profits of the corporation.[31]

In *Intercontinental Dictionary Series (IDS)*, the IDS, a private unincorporated affiliation of linguistic scholars, had compiled an unpublished manuscript entitled 'Intercontinental Dictionary Series, Volume II: Austronesian Languages' ('the IDS volume'). Meanwhile, a government-funded project by the Australian National University resulted in a so-called *Comparative Austronesian Dictionary* (CAD), with accompanying computer databases and word lists, likewise unpublished. The IDS alleged that the CAD pirated and was an infringing 'spin-off' of the IDS volume. In order for section 1605(a)(3) to apply, the plaintiffs maintained that the word lists, disks, and manuscripts associated with the IDS volume and the CAD were *tangible* forms of property. Since the disputed CAD manuscript and the related computer materials were located, not in the US but in Canberra, Australia, the court held that what was in issue was actually 'intangible intellectual property rights' in those materials or 'the right to receive payment on a contract', outside the scope of section 1605(a)(3) and therefore the plaintiffs could not bring a claim under this section.[32]

A breakthrough seems to be on the way with the case of *Nemariam*, in which individuals of Eritrean origin, descent or nationality filed a class action against Ethiopia and the Commercial Bank of Ethiopia, claiming that Ethiopia had, while expelling them from Ethiopia upon the eruption of armed conflict between Eritrea and Ethiopia, seized their bank accounts and other property. Specifically, they asserted that Ethiopia issued an order freezing their bank accounts, preventing any access to or withdrawal of funds. The district court dismissed the plaintiffs' bank account claims on the ground that they failed to satisfy both the 'rights in property' and the 'owned or operated' requirements of section 1605(a)(3). With regard to 'rights in property', the court held that it did not have subject-matter jurisdiction under the expropriation exception because that exception did not apply to intangible property, and that bank accounts constituted precisely a form of intangible property since 'once funds are deposited into a holders' account, the holder simply has a contractual right to receive the funds upon request, not physical possession or even control of the actual funds'.[33]

The circuit court disagreed with the district court's interpretation of the 'rights in property', saying that:

The plain language of section 1605(a)(3) – as well as its legislative history – does not limit its application to tangible property. Moreover, there seems to us to be no reason to distinguish between tangible and intangible property when the operative phrase is 'rights in property'. We therefore conclude that the expropriation exception applies to the appellants' bank accounts.[34]

So far, this is the only case that applies the expropriation exception to bank accounts.

4.2. 'Taken in violation of international law'

The first thing to note is that the FSIA provision on expropriation (section 1605(a)(3)) 'uses the passive voice' and therefore 'does not require that the foreign state (against whom the claim is made) be the entity who expropriated the property in violation of international law'.[35]

As for 'taking', according to the *Third Restatement*:

A state is responsible under international law for injury resulting from ... a taking by the state of the property of a national of another state that (a) is not for a public purpose, or (b) is discriminatory, or (c) is not accompanied by provision for just compensation.[36]

The concept of 'taking' was discussed in the case of *West*, brought by US nationals who suffered substantial losses when their certificates of

308 EXPROPRIATION

deposit denominated in US dollars were decreed by the Mexican Government to be repaid in Mexican pesos. The court first stated that:

Valid expropriations must always serve a public purpose; that public purpose in some cases may be so strong as to render lawful what otherwise might constitute a 'taking'.[37]

The court found that the introduction of controls by Mexico was an exercise of its basic authority to regulate economic affairs, which had been done non-discriminately and for a public purpose. Losses suffered as a result of Mexico's institution of exchange controls had not been occasioned by a 'taking' of property but had been one of the foreseeable risks involved in making overseas investments in order to secure extraordinary returns. Since there had been no 'taking' the question of adequate compensation did not arise.[38] Also, breach of a commercial contract is not a 'taking' of property.[39]

In *Greenpeace*, a case concerning France's arrest of certain employees and/or volunteers and seizure of vessels of Greenpeace, the well-known environmental activist organization which was protesting against France's resumed nuclear testing in 1995, the court found that the impounded Greenpeace vessels had been held at the direction of the Public Prosecutor as part of the criminal investigation of Greenpeace's own 'numerous violations of international law'. Thus, the seizure of the vessels served a public purpose that would render an otherwise unlawful taking lawful. Because the plaintiffs had failed to establish that a 'taking' occurred, there was no need to consider the question of just compensation.[40]

The question of violation of international law needs some further clarification. According to the legislative history:

The term 'taken in violation of international law' would include the nationalization or expropriation of property without payment of the prompt, adequate and effective compensation required by international law. It would also include takings which are arbitrary or discriminatory in nature.[41]

This seems to imply that the formula 'prompt, adequate and effective' is the standard of compensation under current international law. However, authoritative scholarly opinion in the US holds otherwise. According to the American Law Institute, the formulation of 'prompt, adequate and effective compensation', though incorporated in the US legislation and consistently adopted as an official position by the US government in diplomatic exchanges and in international forums, 'has met strong resistance from developing states and has not made its way into multilateral agreements or declarations or been universally utilized by international tribunals', and therefore remains largely the subject of bilateral agreements. On the other hand, there are 'authoritative declarations that under international law the compensation to be paid must be "appropriate"'. In addition, the ALI maintains that the compensation must also be 'just', while conceding that the 'elements constituting just compensation are not fixed or precise'.[42]

In practice, the US courts do not evince much confidence in the 'prompt, adequate and effective' formula. They rarely, if ever, refer to this formula.[43] Usually the courts require the compensation to be 'just', 'fair', 'appropriate', or 'proper'.[44] In the leading case of *Banco Nacional de Cuba*, after a detailed analysis of various positions regarding the standard of compensation, the Second Circuit declared that '"appropriate compensation", even considering the lack of precise definition of that term, would come closest to reflecting what international law requires'.[45] Little wonder that the Ninth Circuit should have found it advisable to juxtapose, without expressing any preference, 'prompt, adequate and effective compensation', 'just compensation' and 'appropriate compensation'.[46]

On the international plane, although the formula has been a consistent feature of bilateral investment treaties concluded by the US,[47] other States have adhered to different formulations.[48] In 1992, the World Bank issued 'Guidelines on the Treatment of Foreign Direct Investment'. Section VI(2) of the 'Guidelines' stated that 'Compensation for a specific investment taken by the State will ... be deemed "appropriate" if it is adequate, effective and prompt.' However, the Report was careful to add in its Preamble that 'these guidelines are not ultimate standards but an important step in the *evolution* of generally acceptable international standards which complement, but do not substitute for, bilateral investment treaties'.[49] It is thus safe to say that there is currently no accepted international standard of compensation for expropriation. Such issues are normally settled through bilateral investment treaties (BITs), which contain a variety of ways of settling related disputes.

As for the nationality of the plaintiff, the provision remains silent. The wording of the provision seems to suggest that the party affected by the expropriation, being a national of the expropriating State, does not preclude jurisdiction. So ostensibly it seems possible for a foreign national to sue his State of nationality in a US court for expropriation that took place in that foreign State, provided, of course, that the other

310 EXPROPRIATION

conditions of section 1605(a)(3) are satisfied. However, this inference seems to have been rejected by the US courts, so that a State's taking of property of its own nationals does not constitute a 'violation of international law'.[50] Thus, in practice, section 1605(a)(3) is strictly confined to claims by US nationals.[51] Logically, of course, this would require that the person whose property was expropriated be a national of the expropriating State at the time of the expropriation, for the expropriating State to enjoy immunity.[52] The plaintiff is also required to fulfil other conditions imposed by international law, such as the exhaustion of local remedies.[53]

On the whole, section 1605(a)(3) is unusual from the point of view of international law, since expropriation, even if against international law, is a highly sovereign act carried out by a foreign State in its own territory. Under the traditional distinction between public and private acts, expropriation easily falls within the category of *acta jure imperii* and therefore attracts immunity.[54] Thus a provision seeking to establish jurisdiction over expropriation that took place on foreign territory clearly constitutes a departure from the well-established *jure imperii / jure gestionis* distinction. But then it should be recalled that, in order to establish jurisdiction under the expropriation exception, the expropriated property must be present in the US, and there must be a connection between that property, or property exchanged for it, and a commercial activity in the US. As we shall see, it is this dual test of commerciality plus territoriality that is really the decisive factor in this type of case. In other words, what actually gives the US courts their jurisdiction over matters concerning expropriation in a foreign State is not the fact that that foreign State has carried out any unacceptable or illegal expropriation, but that that foreign State later engages in a commercial activity in the US using the expropriated property. The focus is subtly shifted from the act of expropriation to the engagement in a commercial activity in the US. The requirement of a connection between the expropriated property and a commercial activity in the US closely resembles the requirement in the commercial activity exception that the plaintiff's action must be 'based upon a commercial activity carried on in the United States'. This is the true reason why there is such an intimate relationship between the expropriation exception (section 1605(a)(3)) and the commercial activity exception (section 1605(a)(2)).[55]

United States judicial practice shows that the clause on the violation of international law does not actually entail a full court investigation into the legality of the expropriation, but instead amounts to no more than a prima facie ground for the plaintiff to bring the case before the court. It has been declared that, at the jurisdictional stage, the court 'need not decide whether the taking actually violated international law; as long as a 'claim is substantial and non-frivolous, it provides a sufficient basis for the exercise of ... jurisdiction'.[56] Compensation seems to be the sole consideration for the court. If the plaintiff can show that no compensation has been paid to him, then there is a violation of international law,[57] and the court will go no further. In some cases the violation of international law was simply assumed or found not in dispute.[58] We now turn our attention to the truly crucial requirement: the territorial nexus requirement.

4.3. The territorial nexus requirement

In order for section 1605(a)(3) to apply, a court must find that one of two territorial nexus requirements is satisfied, namely, that the expropriated property or its substitute is present in the US in connection with a commercial activity *in the US* by the foreign State, or that the expropriated property or its substitute is owned or operated by an 'agency or instrumentality of the foreign state' engaged in a commercial activity *in the US*. This requirement is much more important than the provision that the taking must be in violation of international law: it is dispositive of the case: where the seized property is not present in the US and is not owned or operated by a foreign State agency or instrumentality engaged in commercial activity in the US, there is immunity.[59] That is, even if property has been taken in violation of international law, the foreign State is still immune where the territorial nexus requirement is not satisfied.[60]

A commercial activity in the US is the common requirement for both a foreign State and a foreign State entity. If the plaintiff cannot point to any commercial activity having a substantial contact with the US, then section 1605(a)(3) does not apply.[61] The commercial activity requirement certainly helps satisfy the principle of general international law that expropriation taking place within the territory of one State cannot be the subject of court proceedings in another State. It can then be argued that section 1605(a)(3) applies not so much to foreign expropriation per se as to a commercial activity carried out in the US territory. If the exercise of jurisdiction under this provision impinges on a quintessentially sovereign act by a foreign State in its own territory, it does so only tangentially. If the foreign State in question has no presence at all within the US, then this provision cannot bite in that State. In asserting an indirect jurisdiction over foreign States with regard to their expropriation measures, the US law provides US nationals with a remedy that is unavailable in other States to their nationals. On the other hand, in restricting such a remedy on the basis of nationality, territoriality and commerciality, thereby limiting the number of cases to a minimum, the US position seems no different from that of any other State.

There is a subtle difference between the position of a foreign State and that of its agencies or instrumentalities. Where a foreign State itself is sued, the property in question has to be 'present in the United States', and the claim will be rejected if the plaintiff fails to identify any expropriated property (or the property exchanged for it) that is present in the US.[62] Here it must be noted that, for this prong of section 1605(a)(3) to apply, mere physical presence in the US is sufficient; the plaintiff does not have to seize the property, which may otherwise enjoy immunity from seizure and other forms of judicial process, such as the immunity enjoyed by imported artworks and cultural objects under the Mutual Educational and Cultural Exchange Program, administered by the US Department of State.[63]

By contrast, in the case of an agency or instrumentality, the property does not have to be present in the US, since mere ownership or operation will suffice.[64] In fact, this second prong of the provision is what is normally invoked by plaintiffs where the disputed property is clearly located in a foreign country.[65] Needless to say, if the entity in question, even if engaging in a commercial activity in the US, does not *own* the expropriated property or its substitute, jurisdiction cannot be established.[66]

Much turns on the meaning of 'owned or operated'. It appears that the exhibition of paintings falls within the term 'owned or operated'.[67] Further than that, the scanty case law is inconclusive. On the one hand, the opinion is expressed that, if a foreign State or a State entity has assumed control of the expropriated property (such as a vessel) and then used it for the benefit of the foreign State, that amounts to ownership or operation;[68] on the other hand, there is the view that the phrase 'owned or operated' 'does not include a benefit requirement', but simply means 'possessed or exerted control or influence over the property at issue'.[69]

Even if ownership can be established, if the State entity in question is not engaged in a commercial activity in the US, there is still immunity.[70] In this connection, the commercial activity of one State entity must not be assigned to another State entity for the purpose of establishing jurisdiction under section 1605(a)(3); that is, the commercial activity must be the activity of *the* State entity sued in a particular case.[71] However, assignation might be possible if an 'alter ego' relationship can be established between two State entities;[72] where such a relationship cannot be established, the expropriation exception does not apply.[73]

5. The Helms-Burton Act

Title III of the Helms-Burton Act[74] seeks to establish the most sweeping extraterritorial jurisdiction ever known to international law. Section 301(2) makes it clear that the Act was intended to be a response to the 'wrongful confiscation or taking of property belonging to United States nationals by the Cuban Government'. Section 302(a)(1)(A) provides that:

> any person that ... traffics in property which was confiscated by the Cuban Government on or after January 1, 1959, shall be liable to any United States national who owns the claim to such property for money damages.

By virtue of section 301(4)(A), the Act applies retroactively, as 'actions may be brought ... with respect to property confiscated before, on, or after the date of the enactment of this Act'. Under section 4(13)(A), 'a person "traffics" in confiscated property if that person knowingly and intentionally (i) sells, transfers, distributes, dispenses, brokers, manages, or otherwise disposes of confiscated property, or purchases, leases, receives, possesses, obtains control of, manages, uses, or otherwise acquires or holds an interest in confiscated property, (ii) engages in a commercial activity using or otherwise benefiting from confiscated property, or (iii) causes, directs, participates in, or profits from, trafficking ... by another person, or otherwise engages in trafficking ... through another person, without the authorization of any United States national who holds a claim to the property'.

In creating a right of action for US nationals, Title III places no limitations on the nationality of the potential defendant, nor does it specify where the targeted 'trafficking' ought to have taken place. Given the broad sweep of the definition of 'trafficking', any foreign national, in particular a foreign State entity, would be made a defendant if he/it happens in any way to be connected, however remotely and wherever in the world, with any 'confiscated property'. In other words, the Helms-Burton Act gives US courts jurisdiction over any foreign national with regard to business dealings that may have no connection whatever with US territory. Of course the Helms-Burton Act cannot bite any entity that has absolutely no presence within US territory; but for those corporations, especially multinational corporations, which regularly conduct their business on a global scale, the Act posed a real and serious threat. As could be expected, the Act provoked angry responses from various governments, including some of the most powerful in the world. Thus the EU presented two demarches to the US Department of State protesting against the 'extraterritorial applications of US jurisdiction', saying that the EU could not 'accept that the US unilaterally determine and restrict EU economic and commercial relations with third countries'. In particular, the EU objected, 'as a matter of principle, to those provisions that seek to assert extraterritorial jurisdiction of US Federal courts over disputes between the US and foreign companies regarding expropriated property located overseas'.[75] As a more concrete measure, the EU adopted a special Council Regulation designed to 'counteract the effects of the extra-territorial application of', among others, the Helms-Burton Act. The Regulation demanded non-recognition of judgments and non-compliance with orders (that might be rendered thereunder), provided for an entitlement to recover damages in the form of seizure and sale of assets from any person who may have caused such damages under the Helms-Burton Act, and threatened EU joint action.[76] Similar countermeasures were also contemplated by other States.[77]

In the face of such decidedly hostile reaction, the US Government saw it advisable to suspend the 'right to bring an action' created by Title III, and it has done so ever since the coming into force of the Helms-Burton Act in July 1996.[78] The suspension has been welcomed by other States.[79]

Because Title III has been in a state of dormancy since its inception, its exact impact on the issue of immunity remains a matter of speculation. Section 302(c)(1) provides that 'the provisions of title 28, United States Code ... apply to actions under this section'. Since the FSIA forms part of Title 28 of the US Code, this means that actions brought under the Helms-Burton Act shall also be governed by the provisions of FSIA. As the FSIA is the 'sole basis' on which to determine the question of immunity of foreign States and their entities,[80] one would expect the situation of immunity to remain very much the same. Furthermore, section 302(e) modifies the FSIA by adding a new paragraph (c) to section 1611:

Notwithstanding the provisions of section 1610 of this chapter, the property of a foreign state shall be immune from attachment and from execution in an action brought under section 302 of the Cuban Liberty and Democratic Solidarity (LIBERTAD) Act of 1996 to the extent that the property is a facility or installation used by an accredited diplomatic mission for official purposes.

In adding a new category of property specifically excluded from enforcement, this provision seems even to extend the scope of immunity afforded by section 1611. On the other hand, however, the real danger lies in the very broad definition of 'trafficking', which both covers and enlarges the concept of 'commercial activity' otherwise actionable under the FSIA. Provided some territorial connection with the US could be established, there would be no escape for foreign States and their entities from the teeth of the Helms-Burton Act.

Conclusion

At present the US FSIA remains the only instrument that provides jurisdiction over expropriation by foreign States in their own territories. It departs from the general practice whereby expropriation is treated as a highly sovereign act and immune from the scrutiny of the national courts of foreign States. The implication of section 1605(a)(3) seems to be that, even if the disputed expropriation is sovereign in nature, the foreign State is still not immune because it has violated international law. However, section 1605(a)(3) requires more than just a violation of international law; for even if the foreign State's act of expropriation has indeed violated international law, it is still immune if the territorial nexus requirement is not satisfied. As far as the violation of international law is concerned, a mere allegation by the plaintiff that the foreign State failed to compensate will be sufficient; what is decisive on the issue of immunity, however, is whether there is a connection between the expropriated property and a commercial activity in the US. In the absence of such a connection, the remedy for the affected person seems to lie elsewhere than in a court.

8   Waiver of immunity

Waiver of immunity or consent to jurisdiction or voluntary submission[1] denotes a conscious act on the part of a State to renounce its immunity before foreign national courts. The term 'waiver' has different meanings during the different periods of history. In the past, when absolute immunity prevailed, 'waiver' was used to cover both voluntary submission and other cases such as owning and possessing real property in the forum State and, later during the transitional period, engaging in commercial and other activities. Now the term 'waiver' is much narrower and refers only to the case of voluntary submission.

'Waiver of immunity' encompasses two things. First, there must be 'immunity' to waive; for if the State otherwise does not enjoy immunity it will be unnecessary to speak of a waiver. Secondly, the State must have expressed its wish, so clear and explicit as to be unmistakable, that it intends not to retain its immunity; or it must have taken some action which indubitably signals that the State will not claim immunity. In short, 'waiver of immunity' means both the existence of immunity and the volition of the defendant State not to claim it. Such volition can either be evidenced by an express declaration or inferred from certain types of action. It is the objective of this chapter to discuss what types of declaration and action are needed for the ascertainment of waiver.

There is no dispute that, when a State itself institutes proceedings before a foreign national court, it relinquishes its immunity.[2] Our main concern here, however, is under what circumstances a State that is made a *defendant* in a foreign court can be regarded as having waived its immunity. Broadly speaking, a State can waive its immunity either explicitly or by implication.

316

1. The US practice

We start by analysing the judicial practice in the US, where all aspects of the issue of waiver of immunity have been examined to the fullest extent possible. An account of the US practice will therefore provide a convenient template as well as necessary benchmarks for the assessment of the practice in other countries. This will also be the most economical way of treating this subject: after a careful analysis of the US practice, one will need but a very brief account of what is taking place elsewhere in the world.

The US FSIA of 1976 contains a very simple provision on waiver. Section 1605(a)(1) provides:

> A foreign state shall not be immune from the jurisdiction of courts of the United States or of the States in any case in which the foreign state has waived its immunity either explicitly or by implication, notwithstanding any withdrawal of the waiver which the foreign state may purport to effect except in accordance with the terms of the waiver.

The formula 'notwithstanding any withdrawal of the waiver which the foreign state may purport to effect except in accordance with the terms of the waiver'[3] is designed to preclude 'unilateral rescissions of waivers by foreign states'.[4] This is in line with the principle that a waiver of immunity may not be withdrawn except by consent of all parties concerned.[5] Stated conversely, 'sovereign immunity, once waived, cannot be reasserted'.[6]

1.1. Who can waive immunity?

Neither the FSIA nor the legislative report contains any reference to the person who can waive immunity on behalf of a State. However, it is commonly accepted that:

> when ... a duly accredited head of a diplomatic mission (such as an ambassador) files a waiver of his or her sovereign's immunity in a judicial proceeding, the court should assume that the sovereign has authorized the waiver absent extraordinary circumstances.[7]

It has also been held that lawyers of a foreign State,[8] or other private individuals acting as agents for a foreign State,[9] can waive immunity on that State's behalf.

On the other hand, even an ambassador should not be deemed to be authorized to waive his State's immunity under all circumstances; for it is conceivable that in some cases an ambassador may lack the authority

318   WAIVER OF IMMUNITY

to do so,[10] such as where the defendant foreign State contends that its ambassador exceeded his authority in signing a loan agreement and later a consent order for settlement that included a complete waiver of the immunity of his sending State.[11]

As to the waiver of immunity of a foreign State entity, the legislative report states:

Since the sovereign immunity of a political subdivision, agency or instrumentality of a foreign state derives from the foreign state itself, the foreign state may waive the immunity of its political subdivisions, agencies or instrumentalities.[12]

In practice, however, courts tend to adopt a more rigid and narrow approach. Owing to the respect for the separateness of foreign State entities, one State entity cannot waive the immunity of another State entity,[13] nor can a State implicitly waive the immunity of an entity having a separate status, even if the waiver states that the State 'hereby waives its sovereign immunity and that of its agencies'.[14]

Everything depends on the actual terms of the waiver; and normally such terms are narrowly construed. For example, Article XI(4) of the 1955 US–Iran Treaty of Amity provides:

No enterprise of either High Contracting Party, including corporations, associations, and government agencies and instrumentalities, which is publicly owned or controlled shall, if it engages in commercial, industrial, shipping or other business activities within the territories of the other High Contracting Party, claim or enjoy, either for itself or for its property, immunity therein from taxation, suit, execution of judgment or other liability to which privately owned and controlled enterprises are subject therein.

It has been held that this limited waiver extended only to the *enterprises* of Iran, not Iran itself, and that it extended only to those enterprises 'doing business' in the US.[15] Of course, this clearly shows that the immunity of State enterprises can be waived by the State, as the immunity of a State entity derives from the State itself.[16]

However, the fact that a State may waive the immunity of a State entity does not mean that that entity can necessarily be held liable for a debt of the State. In *LNC*, the waiver clause in a Loan Agreement stipulated:

To the extent that the Republic [of Nicaragua] or *any Governmental Agency* has or hereafter may acquire any immunity from jurisdiction of any court or from any legal process under any laws ... whether through service or notice, attachment prior to judgment, attachment in aid of execution, execution or otherwise, with respect to itself or its property, the Republic hereby irrevocably waives such immunity in respect of the Republic's obligations under this Agreement and the Notes.[17]

Even though Nicaragua had purportedly waived its own immunity and that of 'any Governmental Agency', the court still found that such a clause was insufficient to make the property of the Central Bank of Nicaragua available to satisfy a judgment against Nicaragua. According to the court, the waiver clause in the Loan Agreement solely affected the jurisdictional powers of the court and had absolutely no effect on the substantive issue of whether the Central Bank was responsible for the judgment against Nicaragua.[18]

1.2. Explicit or express waiver

There is no further definition of an explicit waiver in the FSIA. According to the legislative report:

> With respect to explicit waivers, a foreign state may renounce its immunity by treaty, as has been done by the United States with respect to commercial and other activities in a series of treaties of friendship, commerce, and navigation, or a foreign state may waive its immunity in a contract with a private party.[19]

Thus the two most common modes of explicitly waiving immunity are by treaty (as between/among States with regard to legal proceedings)[20] and by contract (as between a State and a private party). Three things must be noted about explicit waivers.

First, an explicit waiver, though it does not always have to be in writing,[21] must be explicit, specific[22] and intentional;[23] that is, an explicit waiver must give a clear, complete, unambiguous, unequivocal and unmistakable manifestation of the foreign State's intention to waive its immunity.[24] In a word, explicit waiver is made only when the defendant State (or the State entity) plainly says so.

Thus, Germany did not explicitly waive its immunity by unconditionally surrendering to the Allies in 1945, as the act of surrendering did not evince 'a clear and unambiguous intent to subject itself to legal proceedings'.[25] Where an international instrument (e.g. a treaty) does not explicitly provide for a waiver of immunity, then no immunity is waived.[26] According to the US Supreme Court, a foreign State does not waive its immunity 'by signing an international agreement that contains no mention of a waiver of immunity to suit'.[27]

In *Reers*, a suit was brought against French and German corporations arising from the death of US passengers in a train accident in France.

The plaintiffs relied on the 1980 Convention concerning International Carriage by Rail, which provides for a limited waiver of immunity before 'the competent court of the State in whose territory the accident to the passenger happened' (Appendix A, Article 52(1)). The plaintiffs recognized that the US was not a signatory of this treaty, but argued that this explicit waiver of immunity from suit in signatory countries was an implied waiver of immunity from suit in the US. The court upheld immunity, finding that Germany and its instrumentalities, through such a limited waiver, could not have impliedly waived immunity for lawsuits arising in non-signatory jurisdictions and in countries other than the country in which the injury giving rise to the suits occurred.[28]

Naturally, the same can also be said of contracts and other documents. Where a letter concerning a guaranty of payment contains no express or indirect reference to a waiver of immunity, there is no waiver.[29] When an agreement provides that it is governed by *English* law, there is no explicit waiver of immunity in the US courts, since 'there is no language clearly evincing the parties' intent to waive immunity and adjudicate matters in the United States'.[30] Understandably, a third party cannot benefit from a waiver of immunity in a contract unless that party is later incorporated into and becomes a beneficiary of and participant in the original agreement/ contract.[31]

If immunity has allegedly been waived explicitly by a document, it can be done only by the text of that document itself. If it is necessary to refer to the 'structure and history' of that document, then the waiver is not explicit.[32] In a case concerning four agreements entered into by a foreign State, only two of which contained a clause that 'irrevocably' waived immunity 'to the full extent permitted by the laws', the court found that immunity had been expressly waived only with regard to these two agreements but not to the other two, which had no waiver clause, and that that express waiver only covered an action for the breach of the two agreements and did not extend to any other claim.[33] Where the duly accredited ambassador of a foreign State filed an affidavit to the court saying that his government waived immunity 'for the purposes of these litigations only', the court found that the affidavit waived immunity 'completely and unambiguously, if somewhat awkwardly'.[34]

Secondly, in general, explicit waivers are narrowly construed in favour of the foreign State and are not enlarged beyond what the language of the waiver requires.[35]

Finally, it is always necessary for the court to examine the actual terms of the waiver before reaching a conclusion. In many cases, this tends to be a relatively straightforward exercise because of the clear and categorical language used by the waiver clause. For instance, explicit waivers are made when a foreign State 'agrees not to claim and waives' 'immunity from suit, execution, attachment (whether in aid of execution, before judgment or otherwise) or other legal process ... to the full extent permitted by the laws';[36] when a foreign State 'irrevocably waives' 'any immunity (sovereign or otherwise) from jurisdiction of any court or from any legal process';[37] when a foreign State 'irrevocably agrees not to claim and hereby irrevocably waives such sovereign immunity in respect of suit [and] jurisdiction of any court';[38] when a foreign embassy in a sublease agreement 'waives and relinquishes any and all rights to immunity';[39] when a foreign State signs a trade agreement with the US, under which '[n]ationals, firms, companies and economic organizations of either Party ... shall not claim or enjoy immunities from suit or execution of judgment or other liability in the territory of the other Party';[40] when a foreign State-owned company waives 'any ... right of immunity (sovereign or otherwise) which it or its assets now has or may have in the future';[41] and, in a fuller version, when a foreign State-owned company 'expressly and irrevocably waives any such right of immunity (including any immunity from the jurisdiction of any court or *from any execution or attachment in aid of execution prior to judgment or otherwise*) or claim thereto which may now or hereafter exist, and agrees not to assert any such right or claim in any such action or proceeding, whether in the United States or otherwise'.[42]

In some cases, a more complex, contextual approach may be needed to determine the existence of a waiver. In *Walker*, the Congo had signed a contract which stated that the Congo 'hereby irrevocably renounces to claim any immunity during any procedure relating to any arbitration decision handed down by an Arbitration Court'. In addition, the Congo also agreed to abide by the rules of the International Chamber of Commerce, Rule 28(6) of which states: 'By submitting the dispute to arbitration under these Rules, the parties undertake to carry out any Award without delay and shall be deemed to have waived their right to any form of recourse insofar as such waiver can validly be made.' So the court held that the Congo had explicitly waived its immunity in a procedure that related to the 'arbitration decision'.[43]

Where a loan agreement stated that the 'Borrower or the Guarantor' would waive 'immunity to the full extent permitted by the laws',

322 WAIVER OF IMMUNITY

immunity was explicitly waived under a separate 'supervisor agreement', which provided that the loan agreement was 'totally reproduced herein', as such language was 'so broad, unqualified and unambiguous as to require the conclusion that *all* of the provisions, including the waiver of immunity, are carried over to the Supervisory Agreement'.[44]

In *Coyle*, an action was brought against the Indonesian national airline for the deaths of two US nationals in a crash in Indonesia. The plaintiff contended that the airline had waived its immunity under a US Department of Transportation foreign air carrier operating permit at the time of the accident. In relevant part, the permit provided:

(3) The holder agrees that operations under this permit constitute a waiver of sovereign immunity ... but only with respect to proceedings instituted against it in any Court or Tribunal in the United States that are:

(a) Based upon its operations in international air transportation that, according to the contract of carriage, include a point in the United States as a point of origin, point of destination, or agreed stopping place, or for which the contract of carriage was purchased in the United States.[45]

The court held that immunity had not been waived with regard to the trip during which the accident had taken place. As the trip was one between two cities in Indonesia and for which the tickets had been purchased in Indonesia, it was a purely domestic flight and did not constitute 'international transportation'.[46]

It is not certain whether a State's expression of non-objection to suit amounts to a waiver of immunity.[47]

1.3. How explicit must an explicit waiver be?

An explicit waiver has to be clear and unambiguous but does not have to enumerate exhaustively all the proceedings from which immunity is waived. For example, section 1610(d)(1) of the FSIA provides that:

The property of a foreign state ... used for a commercial activity in the United States, shall not be immune from attachment prior to the entry of judgment ... if ... the foreign state has explicitly waived its immunity from attachment prior to judgment.

According to case law, provided that the waiver is sufficiently plain and unmistakable, immunity from prejudgment attachment can be waived under section 1610(d)(1) without necessarily using the words 'prejudgment attachment'. In *Libra Bank*, the defendant had made promissory notes which provided:

The Borrower hereby irrevocably and unconditionally waives any right or immunity from legal proceedings including suit judgment and execution ... which it or its property may now or hereafter enjoy.

Even though the promissory clause made no mention of the words 'prejudgment attachment', the court still found an explicit waiver of immunity under section 1610(d)(1). In the view of the court, section 1610(d)(1) is designed to prevent 'unintended', 'inadvertent, implied, or constructive waiver in cases where the intent of the foreign state is equivocal or ambiguous', but 'does not require verbatim recitation or express enumeration of immunity from prejudgment attachment as one of the waived immunities'. Where, as here, the waiver clause uses categorical language and 'evinces a clear and unambiguous intent to waive *all* claims of immunity in *all* legal proceedings', there can be no doubt as to the intent explicitly to waive immunity from prejudgment attachment, which is 'a form of "legal proceedings"'.[48]

The same court, however, grew more cautious in *S & S Machinery*, where it said:

We do not take lightly the congressional demand for explicitness. It would be improper for a court to subvert this directive by substituting a judicially reconstituted gloss on a facially unclear document for an unequivocal waiver by the foreign state.[49]

In this case, the court had to interpret Article IV(2) of the 1975 US–Romanian Agreement on Trade Relations, which provided:

Nationals, firms, companies and economic organizations of either Party ... shall not claim or enjoy immunities from suit or execution of judgment or other liability in the territory of the other Party with respect to commercial or financial transactions.

The court held that there was no explicit waiver of immunity from prejudgment attachment. In the court's opinion, 'waivers of immunity from suit or from execution of judgment have no bearing upon the question of immunity from prejudgment attachment', while the phrase 'other liability' 'is ill-suited to encompass prejudgment attachments' and 'does not unequivocally express the will of the parties to waive immunity from prejudgment attachment'.[50]

324   WAIVER OF IMMUNITY

If one compares the cases of *Libra Bank* and *S & S Machinery*, the waiver clauses do not appear to be terribly different. Whereas the defendant in *Libra Bank* waived 'immunity from legal proceedings including suit judgment and execution', the treaty in *S & S Machinery* waived 'immunities from suit or execution of judgment or other liability'. One is compelled to conclude that the decisive factor must have been the use of the phrase 'legal proceedings' in *Libra Bank*, which would be wide enough to encompass 'prejudgment attachment', with 'suit judgment and execution' only serving as illustrative examples. By contrast, in *S & S Machinery* the waiver was made only with regard to 'suit or execution of judgment' which, on a narrow construction, may not include 'prejudgment attachment'. In other words, even though an exhaustive enumeration of all the legal proceedings, or an express mention of 'prejudgment attachment' in particular, is not required, the language of the waiver must still be *broad* enough to cover prejudgment attachment in a plain and unquestionable manner. If a waiver of 'immunities from suit or execution of judgment' is incapable of waiving immunity from prejudgment attachment, much less can a document that does not even mention the word 'immunity'.[51]

1.4.   Implicit or implied waiver

The FSIA does not provide a further definition of an 'implicit waiver' either. The legislative report identifies three situations in which implicit waivers are to be found, namely:

(1) 'where a foreign state has agreed to arbitration in another country';
(2) 'where a foreign state has agreed that the law of a particular country should govern a contract'; and
(3) 'where a foreign state has filed a responsive pleading in an action without raising the defense of sovereign immunity'.[52]

'Waiver under the FSIA is rarely accomplished by implication.'[53] In applying the provision on implicit waiver the US courts have displayed a remarkable tendency to confine it within the narrowest possible limits. This is manifested through three interrelated aspects of the US practice on implied waiver:

(1) unanimous and persistent adherence to the general principle that the implicit waiver provision must be very narrowly construed;[54]
(2) unswerving reluctance to go beyond the three examples of implicit waiver suggested by the legislative report;[55] and

(3) adamant refusal to find an implicit waiver without strong evidence that waiver is clearly intended by the defendant State.[56] This is sometimes termed as the 'intentionality requirement'; that is, the foreign State must have 'at some point indicated its amenability to suit' or 'a willingness to waive immunity'.[57]

As declared by the leading case of *Frolova* and religiously repeated in a great number of US cases:

> Since the FSIA became law, courts have been reluctant to stray beyond these examples when considering claims that a nation has implicitly waived its defense of sovereign immunity ... [T]he implicit waiver clause of § 1605(a)(1) is narrowly construed ... Thus, courts rarely find that a nation has waived its sovereign immunity, particularly with respect to suits brought by third parties, without strong evidence that this is what the foreign state intended.[58]

Thus a State does not implicitly waive its immunity by signing a treaty unless there is convincing evidence that the treaty is intended to waive immunity.[59]

We shall now consider the three examples one by one.

1.4.1. Arbitration

According to the legislative report, an implied waiver can be established 'where a foreign state has agreed to arbitration in another country'. A literal interpretation of the words 'in another country' would naturally 'subject a foreign government to jurisdiction in the United States whenever it agreed to be governed by the laws or to arbitrate in the forum of any country other than its own, even when the contract makes no mention of the United States'.[60] The awareness of the undesirability of such a result has led to the general principle that an implicit waiver exists only when the foreign State contracts to arbitrate in the US,[61] but does not exist when the contract provides for arbitration in another country.[62]

However, the position seems to be different once an arbitration award has already been obtained, even though elsewhere than in the US, and the other party seeks to have that award enforced under an international convention to which the foreign State defendant is a party. But then it must be noted that this applies only if the States concerned are parties to the convention in question. In this connection two conventions deserve particular notice: the 1958 New York Convention on the Recognition and Enforcement of Foreign Arbitral Awards and the 1965 Convention on the Settlement of Investment Disputes between States and Nationals of Other States (hereinafter 'the ICSID Convention').

326   WAIVER OF IMMUNITY

In *Seetransport*, a German corporation sued a Romanian State-owned shipbuilding company to enforce an arbitration award issued by the International Chamber of Commerce (ICC) in France. The court agreed that the implicit waiver exception must be construed narrowly but observed that the defining feature of the instant case was that the plaintiff was seeking to have an already obtained ICC arbitral award recognized and enforced in the US courts, pursuant to the 1958 New York Convention, to which Romania, France and the US are all parties. Article I(1) of the Convention provides:

This Convention shall apply to the recognition and enforcement of arbitral awards made in the territory of a State other than the State where the recognition and enforcement of such awards are sought, and arising out of differences between persons, whether physical or legal. It shall also apply to arbitral awards not considered as domestic awards in the State where their recognition and enforcement are sought.

Under Article III '[e]ach Contracting State shall recognize arbitral awards as binding and enforce them in accordance with the rules of procedure of the territory where the award is relied upon'. Obviously, the recognition and enforcement as envisaged by the New York Convention is a reciprocal obligation assumed between the States parties to the Convention. Thus immunity was waived owing to the combined effect of section 1605(a)(1) of the FSIA and the New York Convention.[63]

Nevertheless, jurisdiction over a State that is not a party to the New York Convention can be achieved via a different route. In *S & Davis*, a US corporation had entered into a contract with Yemen for the sale of wheat. The contract was negotiated and signed in Yemen, but contained an arbitration clause providing that any dispute was to be arbitrated by the Grain and Feed Trade Association (GAFTA) in London, UK. The plaintiff sought to have the arbitral award issued by GAFTA recognized and enforced in the US courts, pursuant to the New York Convention. Since Yemen was not a party to the New York Convention, there was no waiver of immunity under section 1605(a)(1).[64] However, jurisdiction was nonetheless established under the much broader terms of section 1605(a)(6) of the FSIA,[65] which provides that a foreign State shall not enjoy immunity in any case:

in which the action is brought, either to enforce an agreement made by the foreign state with or for the benefit of a private party to submit to arbitration ... or to confirm an award made pursuant to such an agreement to arbitrate, if (A) the arbitration takes place or is intended to take place in the United States, [or]

(B) the agreement or award is or may be governed by a treaty or other international agreement in force for the United States calling for the recognition and enforcement of arbitral awards.[66]

Because section 1605(a)(6)(B) only required the US to be a party to the Convention, the court reasoned, Yemen had no immunity from a proceeding 'to confirm an award' that 'may be governed by a treaty ... calling for the recognition and enforcement of arbitral awards'.[67] Indeed, it seems to be established case law that 'the [New York] Convention is exactly the sort of treaty Congress intended to include in the arbitration exception'.[68]

On the other hand, even if the defendant State is a party to the New York Convention, immunity remains intact if the suit in question is not one 'to confirm an award' but for some other matter, say, indemnification.[69]

The question arises whether an arbitral award rendered in the US can also be recognized and enforced in the US courts under the New York Convention. Article I(1) of that Convention allows the possibility to the extent that the arbitral award at issue is not considered a 'domestic award' in the US. It has been held that an arbitral award involving two foreign parties, even though rendered in the US, is a 'non-domestic' award, and therefore can be confirmed under section 1605(a)(6)(B) of the FSIA.[70] In any case, such an arbitral award would fall under section 1605(a)(6)(A), which envisages confirmation where 'the arbitration takes place or is intended to take place in the United States'.[71] In general, three basic requirements must be met for a US court to find jurisdiction under the New York Convention, namely, 'the award (1) must arise out of a legal relationship (2) which is commercial in nature and (3) which is not entirely domestic in scope'.[72]

The 1965 ICSID Convention is another treaty under which immunity can be waived by implication. In *LETCO*, Liberia had entered into a concession agreement with a French corporation with a specific provision that any dispute shall be settled by arbitration under the rules of ICSID and its enforcement provision. The court held that Liberia, as a signatory to the ICSID Convention, had impliedly waived its immunity in the US, another signatory State, with respect to the enforcement of any arbitration award entered pursuant to that Convention.[73]

1.4.2. The governing law of a contract

In contrast to an express waiver by contract, an implied waiver by contract normally arises from a provision that specifies the governing law of the contract. Thus, implicit waiver was found in the following situations: where a lease provided that it 'shall be governed by the laws of the state where the Premises are located';[74] where a contract provided that it 'shall be governed by and construed in accordance with the laws of the District of Columbia';[75] or that '[t]his Agreement and the performance or breach hereof shall be governed by the procedural and substantive laws in effect in the State of Virginia';[76] or that the parties' 'obligations under this agreement will be governed by the laws of the State of Virginia';[77] or that '[a]ll disputes under this Agreement and in the interpretation or validity of any provision, shall be governed by the laws of the Commonwealth of Virginia';[78] or similarly that the parties agree to 'resolve disputes in accordance with Connecticut or New York law';[79] or where the parties to a loan agreement consented to suit in the State and federal courts of, inter alia, New York.[80]

The standard position is that an implied waiver can be accomplished 'where a contract *specifically* states that the laws of a jurisdiction within the United States are to govern the transaction'.[81] As is the case with the other types of implied waiver, 'when courts analyze whether a contract's choice of law provision constitutes implicit waiver, they look to the implied intent of the parties'.[82] In *Eckert*, a choice of law provision in a contract for consultant services stipulated that '[i]n the event of any controversy, this Agreement shall be construed and interpreted according to the laws of the state of Virginia in the United States'. The court found that this provision constituted an implied waiver by virtue of 'the implied intent of the parties', as evinced by the agreement to look to Virginia law.[83] Of special significance is the fact that the contract did not use the formula that it shall be 'governed' by the law of a particular jurisdiction or that the parties shall be 'bound' by that law, but instead stated that the law of a particular jurisdiction shall be the source for construction and interpretation. The court opined, however, that there was no 'substantial difference between a concept that Virginia law will "govern" a dispute between the parties and the concept that, in the event of controversy when legal interpretation is needed, the agreement shall be construed and interpreted according to Virginia law'.[84]

Naturally, there is no implied waiver of immunity where a contract specifies that it shall be governed or construed by the law, or subject to the jurisdiction of the courts, of a country other than the US.[85] Even if the contract is indeed governed by US law, this does not benefit a third party.[86] Where a purchaser–supplier contract provides that the jurisdiction for the settlement of disputes shall lie with a US court only in the case of the purchaser submitting a claim, then there is no US jurisdiction in a claim brought by the supplier.[87]

Nor can immunity be implicitly waived by a provision in the founding instrument of a State entity which provides for exclusive jurisdiction of the courts of the entity's own State,[88] or endows the entity with the capacity to sue and be sued,[89] or simply states that the entity in question 'shall conduct its activities on a commercial basis and for the purpose of profit as is done by private commercial companies'.[90]

1.4.3. Participation or involvement in litigation

Of particular interest is how deeply a State must be involved in litigation in order for an implied waiver to be established. The legislative report contemplates an implied waiver of immunity where 'a foreign state has filed a responsive pleading in an action without raising the defense of sovereign immunity'. The case law appears to demand a literal and narrow reading of the term 'responsive pleading'. That is to say, generally speaking, there must be a 'responsive pleading', called by that very name, which does not raise the defence of immunity, for immunity to be impliedly waived.[91]

Anything else that does not go by the name of a 'responsive pleading' does not constitute an implicit waiver, unless there is strong, irrefutable evidence to the contrary. In particular, 'motions' are distinguished from 'pleadings';[92] so a 'motion to dismiss', even if it may sometimes be called a 'responsive motion',[93] is not a 'responsive pleading', and filing a motion to dismiss does not constitute an implicit waiver of immunity.[94] The list of motions and other documents that are not considered 'responsive pleadings' includes a notice of removal,[95] a letter objecting to the service of process,[96] a claim to vessel and a motion for release of security in an *in rem* action against a ship,[97] a conditional claim together with a limitation complaint, both purportedly to be considered only in the event of a denial of immunity,[98] and communications with the plaintiff regarding the suit while not responding to the service of the complaint.[99] A foreign State does not implicitly waive its immunity by filing these documents. In such cases the foreign State does not even have to make an express assertion of the defence of immunity. But if the defence of immunity is indeed asserted while filing such documents, then perforce there is no implied waiver.[100] Needless to say, if the foreign State or State entity neither appears before the court nor files any responsive pleading, there cannot be an implied waiver.[101]

330   WAIVER OF IMMUNITY

No matter how many documents are filed, so long as a 'responsive pleading' is not among them, immunity remains intact. In *Canadian Overseas*, the defendant filed a variety of documents, including a petition for removal, a memorandum in opposition to remand, a stipulation concerning the amended complaint, and a motion to dismiss, but on the other hand never filed a 'responsive pleading', the court found that no immunity was lost.[102]

Of a relatively dubious status is a document called an 'answer to complaint'. Whether such an 'answer' is a 'responsive pleading' depends on the circumstances of the case. In *Foremost-McKesson*, a so-called 'Answer to Complaint' filed by Iran neither denied the allegations of the complaint nor asserted immunity, but contended that the lawsuit was barred by the Algiers Accords of 1981. In the court's opinion, such an 'answer', because of its limited nature, did not constitute an implied waiver.[103] On the other hand, a State entity implicitly waived its immunity 'by filing both an answer and amended answer to this lawsuit in state court and opposing this motion to remand without asserting the defense of sovereign immunity'.[104] Where the defendant 'filed a notice of removal which asserted that this Court had jurisdiction over this dispute pursuant to the FSIA, an answer which listed ten affirmative defenses, and this motion to dismiss without once raising the defense of sovereign immunity', the immunity was held to have been implicitly waived.[105] Filing an 'answer' without claiming immunity, coupled with an agreement to arbitrate in Los Angeles would definitely waive immunity.[106]

This is to say that if a foreign State is deeply involved in a proceeding, then immunity is implicitly waived. Appearing in an interpleader action,[107] for example, is treated as an implied waiver; while engaging in pre-trial discovery is not, even though the discovery may last for two years.[108] At any rate, it is also agreed that the legislative report 'does not purport to provide an exclusive list of the circumstances giving rise to implied waivers'.[109] In *Joseph*, the Nigerian Consulate General had signed a lease agreement that provided:

In the event that any action shall be commenced by either party hereto arising out of, or concerning this lease or any right or obligation derived therefrom, then in addition to all other relief at law or equity, the prevailing party shall be entitled to recover attorney's fees as fixed by the court.[110]

The provision nowhere specified the governing law of the agreement, nor did it even provide specifically for the adjudication of disputes in the US; however, the court held that it constituted an implied waiver of immunity. The court reasoned that, because the lease at issue concerned a house in San Francisco that Nigeria had rented, Nigeria must have had US courts in mind when it agreed to its adjudicatory provisions:

> Indeed, there appears to be no justification for requiring a contract to specifically state the governing law in order for there to be a waiver of immunity. Waiver by contract is premised on an agreement by the parties that the United States courts may become involved in disputes arising pursuant to the contract. Where an agreement contemplates adjudication of a dispute by the United States courts, the waiver exception should be applied, regardless of whether the governing law is explicitly identified. Because the lease at issue provides for adjudication of landlord–tenant disputes in court, we conclude that the lease contemplates participation of the United States courts in disputes between Joseph and her tenants. In light of the wholly local nature of the transaction, it is virtually inconceivable that the Consulate contemplated that adjudication of disputes would occur in a court outside of the United States.[111]

This decision, based on the involvement of the US courts, was reaffirmed in *Siderman*. According to the plaintiffs, the Argentine military junta imprisoned and tortured Siderman, and brought criminal proceedings against him in an Argentine court on trumped-up charges. As Siderman had fled Argentina and was now resident in Los Angeles, Argentina filed a letter rogatory with the Los Angeles Superior Court to request assistance in serving him with documents relating to the criminal action in Argentina. That letter rogatory, according to the court, constituted an implied waiver of immunity. Referring to its decision in *Joseph*, the Ninth Circuit said:

> Thus, the essential inquiry ... is whether a sovereign contemplated the involvement of United States courts in the affair in issue. Here, we confront a situation where Argentina apparently not only envisioned United States court participation in its persecution of the Sidermans, but by its actions deliberately implicated our courts in that persecution ... The evidence indicates that Argentina deliberately involved United States courts in its efforts to persecute Jose Siderman. If Argentina has engaged our courts in the very course of activity for which the Sidermans seek redress, it has waived its immunity as to that redress.[112]

Particular attention must be paid to the pronouncement that immunity can be waived only as regards the redress that is connected with the specific activity for which the foreign State is contemplating the involvement of the US courts. The court went on to enunciate such a claim-connection requirement not dissimilar to that in the context of commercial activities:

332   WAIVER OF IMMUNITY

To support a finding of implied waiver, there must exist a direct connection between the sovereign's activities in our courts and the plaintiff's claims for relief. Only because the Sidermans have presented evidence indicating that Argentina's invocation of United States judicial authority was part and parcel of its efforts to torture and persecute Jose Siderman have they advanced a sufficient basis for invoking that same authority with respect to their causes of action for torture.[113]

The requirement that there be a direct connection between the alleged waiver and the proceedings at hand was strictly applied by the Ninth Circuit in *Hilao* v. *Marcos*, where the court found that the Philippines did not implicitly waive its immunity in the instant case by either filing an amicus curiae brief or bringing lawsuits against the Estate of Marcos. In the amicus curiae brief, the Philippine Government expressed its support for the plaintiffs' human rights claims against Marcos:

The Government of the Philippines can state without hesitation or reservation that its foreign relations with the United States will *not* be adversely affected if these human rights claims against Ferdinand Marcos are heard in U.S. courts; and, in fact, relations may well be improved if Filipino citizens see that justice is available in U.S. courts.[114]

According to the court, the brief related to damages claims against the Estate rather than to potential relief from the Philippine Government and was *unrelated* to the Philippines' own actions to recover assets held by the Estate, and the plaintiffs failed to demonstrate a direct connection between their action for human rights abuses and the Philippines' pursuit of the Estate's assets.[115] Similarly, the Ninth Circuit held in *Gates* that, upon a narrow construction of the implied waiver exception, the fact that a foreign State entity had agreed to submit to the jurisdiction of US courts in connection with a loan collection action by a bank in Washington State did not in any way mean that it had also agreed to submit to the jurisdiction of US courts with regard to an action for statutory breaches brought by certain employees in California.[116]

By contrast, the involvement of the *executive branch* does not constitute an implied waiver before the *courts*. Thus, making a request to the Department of State for the extradition of an individual, which request is then handled by the Department of Justice, does not constitute an implied waiver of immunity.[117]

As a good summary on implicit waiver, in *Autotech* v. *Integral*, the defendant 'never raised an immunity defense' – 'not in a responsive pleading, not in any other motion, and not in the Agreed Order'; it then

THE US PRACTICE   333

participated fully in the court proceedings. What is more, it had 'signaled a waiver of its immunity by agreeing in its original contract ... to arbitrate in the United States and by agreeing to a contract governed by Illinois law'.[118] Of course it waived its immunity.

1.5. Implicit waiver as explicit waiver

In the end, under current US judicial practice, implicit waiver has come to partake of so many features of explicit waiver, and resembles the latter to such an extent, that the two can be regarded as almost indistinguishable in many important respects. Thus, like an explicit waiver, an implicit waiver must be 'clear, complete, unambiguous, and unmistakable',[119] and must be 'narrowly construed'. Indeed, sometimes the courts would declare that a waiver of immunity should be 'unambiguous' or 'narrowly construed' while discussing both explicit and implicit waivers.[120] Also, like an explicit waiver, an implicit waiver must be an *intentional* act; it must come from a *conscious* decision on the part of a State *knowingly and intentionally* to relinquish its immunity. And no implicit waiver exists in the absence of strong evidence of a State's intent to waive its immunity.[121]

Moreover, explicit waiver and implicit waiver share one important feature: the specificity of waiver.

1.6. The specificity of waiver

The 'specificity' here contains five layers of meaning.

First, a waiver can only be established where the defendant State has made a specific indication to that effect. For example, the State has made a 'specific and explicit' waiver,[122] or 'specifically contemplates the United States as a possible forum';[123] or 'where a contract *specifically* states that the laws of a jurisdiction within the United States are to govern the transaction'.[124]

Secondly, the waiver, especially an implicit waiver, must be closely related to the litigation process at hand.[125] In *Tamimi*, the ex-wife of an employee of the Saudi Arabian Airlines Corporation brought a garnishment action against the Corporation as employer, seeking to recover child support arrears. As evidence of an implied waiver the plaintiff relied on a letter sent to her by the Corporation, which stated that the husband had authorized the Corporation to deduct, from that date forward, $500 from his salary each month for child support payments. The court found that the letter, which had been sent in February 1996 and did not address any amounts in arrears, was insufficient to qualify as an implicit waiver in this garnishment action, which sought to recover child support payments that were *in arrears prior to* February 1996.[126] In other words, a purported waiver has to relate specifically to the proceeding in question in order to be effective; otherwise there can be no waiver. This can also be seen from the *Colonial Bank* case, where the court found that, even though a French State corporation had obtained a judgment confirming an arbitration award, thereby waiving its immunity, that corporation could not be considered as having waived its immunity in a separate action before the same court, which had a distinct subject matter and involved a different party.[127] That is to say, waiver with regard to one claim or action does not mean waiver for another, separate and distinct, claim or action.[128] Representations or promises made *before* the lawsuit was even contemplated do not constitute an implied waiver regarding that suit either.[129]

Thirdly, a waiver of immunity only takes place as between the parties to a contract or to a lawsuit, to the exclusion of third parties.

Fourthly, waiver of immunity before one court or in one jurisdiction does not mean waiver before another court or in another jurisdiction.[130] Thus, filing a suit in Singapore was not an implied waiver of immunity before a US court.[131] On the other hand, filing a suit in one court may lead to an implied waiver of immunity before another court in the same country, if the claims in both courts concern the same agreements and the same parties.[132]

Finally, a general intimation of readiness to waive immunity cannot be converted into a waiver of immunity before a particular foreign court absent a definite manifestation of intention to do so.[133]

In short, a waiver is a jurisdiction-specific, court-specific and action/claim-specific undertaking not to assert the defence of immunity.

1.7. Counterclaims

The central factor in denying immunity with regard to a counterclaim is the close relationship between the counterclaim and the principal claim. Section 1607(b) of the FSIA provides:

In any action brought by a foreign state, or in which a foreign state intervenes ... the foreign state shall not be accorded immunity with respect to any counterclaim ... arising out of the transaction or occurrence that is the subject matter of the claim of the foreign state.

The application of this provision has seen little difficulty. Thus immunity was denied where the counterclaim was related to the subject matter of the claim of the foreign State,[134] but was upheld where it was not so.[135] Of course, a foreign State loses its immunity when it itself brings a counterclaim without at the same time challenging the jurisdiction of the court.[136]

In *Cabiri*, Ghana started proceedings in a US court to evict Cabiri, a former Ghanaian trade representative to the US, and his family from a house owned by Ghana in New York. Cabiri brought counterclaims for breach of contract, false imprisonment, torture and intentional infliction of emotional distress. Since the possession of the property was an incident of Cabiri's contract of employment, the court allowed the counterclaim for breach of contract on the ground that the eviction proceeding and the breach of contract claim concerned the same transactions, namely, Cabiri's employment contract and its termination;[137] however, the court rejected the other counterclaims since they did not arise out of the same transaction as the eviction proceeding.[138]

2. The UK practice

The practice of the UK and other States with immunity legislation can broadly be approached in the light of the voluminous case law from the US, which covers all the essential issues and lays down the general pattern concerning the waiver of immunity. Nevertheless some peculiar points can be noted by reference to the sparse jurisprudence that is available.

Apart from 'the written consent of the State concerned' in section 13(3) with regard to enforcement measures, the UK SIA of 1978 contains two provisions on the waiver of immunity:

> 2. Submission to jurisdiction
> (1) A State is not immune as respects proceedings in respect of which it has submitted to the jurisdiction of the courts of the United Kingdom.
> (2) A State may submit after the dispute giving rise to the proceedings has arisen or by a prior written agreement; but a provision in any agreement that it is to be governed by the law of the United Kingdom is not to be regarded as a submission.
> (3) A State is deemed to have submitted –
>   (a) if it has instituted the proceedings; or
>   (b) subject to subsections (4) and (5) below, if it has intervened or taken any step in the proceedings.
> (4) Subsection (3)(b) above does not apply to intervention or any step taken for the purpose only of –
>   (a) claiming immunity; or

336   WAIVER OF IMMUNITY

    (b) asserting an interest in property in circumstances such that the State would have been entitled to immunity if the proceedings had been brought against it.

(5) Subsection (3)(b) above does not apply to any step taken by the State in ignorance of facts entitling it to immunity if those facts could not reasonably have been ascertained and immunity is claimed as soon as reasonably practicable.

(6) A submission in respect of any proceedings extends to any appeal but not to any counter-claim unless it arises out of the same legal relationship or facts as the claim.

(7) The head of a State's diplomatic mission in the United Kingdom, or the person for the time being performing his functions, shall be deemed to have authority to submit on behalf of the State in respect of any proceedings; and any person who has entered into a contract on behalf of and with the authority of a State shall be deemed to have authority to submit on its behalf in respect of proceedings arising out of the contract.

    . . .

9. Arbitrations

    (1) Where a State has agreed in writing to submit a dispute which has arisen, or may arise, to arbitration, the State is not immune as respects proceedings in the courts of the United Kingdom which relate to the arbitration.

    (2) This section has effect subject to any contrary provision in the arbitration agreement and does not apply to any arbitration agreement between States.[139]

This scheme is of course an adaptation of what is to be found under Articles 1 (institution of or intervention in proceedings), 2 (submission to jurisdiction), 3 (taking any step in the proceedings relating to the merits) and 12 (arbitration) of the 1972 European Convention, to which the UK SIA gives effect. Since there is not much judicial practice regarding the application and interpretation of the European Convention provisions in this respect, an understanding of the UK practice is all the more important in facilitating a better appreciation of the implications of such provisions.

In the English courts, it is sometimes stated that 'a clause which amounts to a waiver of immunity of a state will not necessarily constitute a submission to the jurisdiction of a court'.[140] This may sound Delphic to an outsider but makes perfect sense in the context of the UK system. First, for better or for worse, the English common law has been consistent in requiring a waiver or submission to jurisdiction on the part of a foreign sovereign State, to be effective, to be made in the face of the court and at the time the court is asked to exercise its jurisdiction;[141] secondly, the UK SIA uses the word 'submit' or 'submission' rather than 'waive' or 'waiver'; and, finally, as is made clear by section 2(1), 'submission to jurisdiction', is actually shorthand for 'submission to the jurisdiction of the courts of the United Kingdom'.[142] What is then meant by the above statement, with the commonly understood but here unexpressed parts supplied, is that 'a clause which amounts to a waiver of immunity of a state [*before the courts of a State/ States other than the United Kingdom*] will not necessarily constitute a submission to the jurisdiction of a court [*of the United Kingdom*]'. That is to say, in normal circumstances, if the UK courts are not expressly mentioned in a clause, then that is prima facie not a waiver of immunity for the purposes of the UK SIA.

Thus, Argentina did not waive its immunity before the English courts by agreeing to submit to 'the jurisdiction of any New York state or federal court sitting in the Borough of Manhattan';[143] whereas Zambia did so by virtue of a provision in a debt settlement agreement under which '[t]he Republic of Zambia agrees that the courts of England have jurisdiction to settle any disputes in connection with this Agreement and the Debt and accordingly submits to the jurisdiction of the English courts'.[144]

In *Svenska*, even though the Government of Lithuania was not named as a party to an agreement between two oil companies, Article 35.1 of the agreement nonetheless states that the Lithuanian 'Government hereby irrevocably waives all rights to sovereign immunity'. The trial judge refused to consider Article 35.1, 'which is purely a waiver of the State's immunity, as a written submission to the jurisdiction of the English court within sections 2(1) and (2) of the Act'.[145] The Court of Appeal agreed, finding Article 35.1 to be 'too imprecise'.[146] Obviously, by 'too imprecise', the court meant that 'the UK courts' were not specified in the waiver; for the *Svenska* courts distinguished their case from the case of *A Company Ltd* v. *Republic of X*, where the defendant State had agreed not only to waive 'whatever defence it may have of sovereign immunity for itself or its property' but also to 'submit to the jurisdiction of the English courts', and that the 'agreement shall be governed and construed in accordance with the laws of England'. The judge thereby had no difficulty in finding that that clearly amounted to an 'agreement and consent of the State that its property can be made the subject of a *Mareva* injunction',[147] that is, a waiver of immunity from injunctive relief. Similarly, an 'anti-suit injunction' (restraining a party from continuing with proceedings) was granted in *Sabah* against Pakistan, which had entered into a guarantee which provided that: 'Each Party consents to the jurisdiction of the Courts of England for any action filed by the other Party under this agreement to resolve any dispute between the Parties and may be enforced in England.'[148]

The above discussion serves to put in context the UK practice regarding waiver of immunity, which is generally a straightforward exercise consisting of a careful examination of the agreement in the light of the provisions of the SIA. In *Svenska*, a Swedish oil company entered into a joint venture agreement with a Lithuanian State-owned oil company for the exploitation of oil reserves in Lithuania. The Government of Lithuania was not a party to the agreement, but the agreement contained terms dealing expressly with the government's rights and obligations and over the signatures there appeared a rubric stating that the government acknowledged itself to be legally and contractually bound as if it were a signatory to the agreement. The agreement also contained an arbitration clause referring disputes to International Chamber of Commerce arbitration in Denmark. It was held that these terms amounted to an 'agreement in writing to submit to arbitration' and that Lithuania was therefore not immune from the proceeding for leave to enforce the arbitral award in the English courts, i.e. a proceeding 'which relate[d] to the arbitration' (section 9(1), SIA), even though this ruling had no bearing on the question of immunity enjoyed by State property from actual execution (section 13, SIA).[149] As far as arbitration is concerned, it was held in *Tsavliris* that the signing of a Lloyd's Standard Form of Salvage Agreement, 2000 edition (LOF), constituted a submission to arbitration under section 9(1) of the SIA.[150]

The rest of the UK practice is just an uneventful, mundane application of the statutory provisions. Thus submission to the jurisdiction by prior written agreement must be express, clear and unequivocal, and does not arise by implication. An Embassy employee's handbook, which formed part of the applicant's contract of employment, even if it stated that 'where the United Kingdom law affecting contracts of employment applies, that law shall take precedence', did not constitute such an agreement to submit to jurisdiction.[151] A solicitor's letter, addressed to the military attaché at the Embassy of Saudi Arabia in London and advising on the legal position of Embassy staff under English law, did not constitute a 'prior written agreement' between the Embassy and its employees within the meaning of section 2(2); such an 'agreement', in light of Article 2 of the European

Convention, has to be 'a prior contractual written agreement, or a prior written agreement in the nature of a contract', and it must be a whole agreement in writing, not something that had to be supplemented by further evidence.[152]

As regards participation in litigation, when a defendant asserts that the court has no jurisdiction, this is not 'taking a step in the proceedings';[153] writing a letter to the Industrial Tribunal clarifying the nationality of the claimant could not be considered as 'taking a step in the proceedings' either.[154] In the opinion of the Court of Appeal, it is a question of construing in every case what the application made or summons issued by a foreign State is intended to accomplish. If the intervention by a foreign State is only for the purpose of claiming immunity, then there is no submission.[155]

A note sent by the diplomatic mission of a foreign State to the Foreign and Commonwealth Office, even though it contained comments on the allegations in an originating application before an employment tribunal, was essentially a diplomatic communication and constituted neither a 'notice of appearance', for which there are strict formal and substantial requirements, nor 'taking a step in the proceedings'; nor did letters from the diplomatic mission directly to the employment tribunal, whose sole purpose was to challenge the tribunal's jurisdiction on immunity grounds, amount to any submission.[156]

Immunity can only be waived by the head of the diplomatic mission or someone acting on behalf of and with the authority of the foreign State.[157] In *Gamal-eldin*, where two drivers brought claims for unfair dismissal from the medical office of the Egyptian Embassy in London, the director of the medical office wrote two letters to the industrial tribunal concerning the applications. According to the Employment Appeal Tribunal, these letters could not be taken as constituting a submission to the jurisdiction since their author at the time did not occupy the position of the head of the diplomatic mission of Egypt in the UK and therefore did not have authority to submit to the jurisdiction on behalf of his State, nor was there any evidence that he had express authority to submit to the jurisdiction.[158]

A waiver of immunity, once given, cannot be withdrawn, but such a waiver only covers the original claim, and the claimant will not be allowed to amend their application so as to include another, fresh claim, since the new claim, had it been made in the original application, would have been met with a plea of immunity.[159]

3. The practice of other States

The practice of those States without immunity legislation can be even more briefly stated. Thus waiver, whether express or tacit, must be clear, specific, certain, indisputable, and unequivocal;[160] immunity can only be waived by competent authorities;[161] immunity can be waived implicitly but such waiver cannot be presumed;[162] where a State appears or otherwise arranges to be represented in court only in order to assert immunity, it does not waive immunity;[163] conversely, appearing in court without invoking immunity amounts to waiver;[164] an arbitration clause would waive the immunity from proceedings related to the recognition and enforcement of the arbitral award;[165] a contractual clause stating that any dispute shall be settled in local courts amounts to a waiver;[166] instituting proceedings before a court of another State means that the plaintiff State submits to counterclaims related to the principal claim;[167] and, occasionally, failure to lodge a timely objection to jurisdiction is treated as waiver of immunity.[168]

4. Does a violation of human rights constitute an implied waiver?

The answer given by current law is in the negative. This is yet another indicator of the firm rootedness of the current law of State immunity in traditional principles. What one can deduce from the discussion of implied waiver is that such a waiver must be intentional and specific. In other words, an implied waiver cannot simply be inferred from the surrounding circumstances; there must be a clear manifestation of intention to be subjected to jurisdiction, and that intention must at the same time be unambiguously directed to the proceedings at hand. There must be a close connection between the purported waiver and the plaintiff's claim. This means that an implied waiver cannot be construed from acts that display no willingness to be sued in a court of law, and that an implied waiver with regard to one claim cannot be extended to a different claim. In this sense, an implied waiver is not radically different from an express waiver; what distinguishes the two appears merely to be the presence or absence of the word 'waive' or 'waiver': if the foreign State says 'I hereby waive my immunity', that is an express waiver; while if it does not use the word 'waive/r' but nonetheless participates in litigation or declares itself prepared to do so in the future without saying that it ought to be immune, then it is an implied waiver. Moreover, a preparedness to be sued cannot simply be substituted by a mere awareness of a possibility of legal action against the foreign State in the future; much less can the possibility that a State might be sued in its own courts be translated into amenability to suit in a foreign court.[169] Thus, even if a State might have been engaged in illegal activities and therefore ought to have been aware that such activities would normally lead to court proceedings for remedies domestically, or even abroad,[170] this knowledge alone is insufficient to make that State suable before a foreign court. In other words, what is of decisive importance is not that a State knowingly broke the law, but that that State knowingly appears before, or knowingly allows itself to be haled into, a foreign court. Seen in this light, the difference between express and implied waivers lies in form, not in substance. This being the case, the conditions and requirements, such as intentionality, clarity and unambiguity, specificity, and close connection with the claim, are substantially the same for both.

It then follows that a violation of human rights does not by itself automatically constitute a waiver of immunity: a State must at some stage indicate that it can be sued before a foreign court for that violation. Since the violation itself is insufficient to subject a State to foreign jurisdiction, then the seriousness of that violation is irrelevant to the issue of immunity. Thus a State does not lose immunity before a foreign domestic court simply because it has violated a fundamental human right or some other peremptory norm of international law (*jus cogens*). Deplorable as this would certainly sound to human rights advocates, who would be perfectly justified to regard this as an abominable defect in the law, this is how international law currently stands with regard to State immunity.

It has been argued that a State loses its immunity with regard to a violation of a *jus cogens* norm, but the argument has been rejected by the courts. As far as US case law is concerned, the possibility of a loss of immunity with respect to human rights violations was foreclosed by the case of *Amerada Hess*, in which the Supreme Court, finding that the FSIA was 'the sole basis for obtaining jurisdiction over a foreign state in our courts', reached the broad conclusion that 'immunity is granted in those cases involving alleged violations of international law that do not come within one of the FSIA's exceptions'.[171]

The obvious consequence of this case is that, even if a foreign State has violated a fundamental human right, one protected by a norm of *jus cogens*, it is still immune from proceedings in the US courts, if that violation does not fall within one of the exceptions to immunity under the FSIA.[172] In particular, the violation of a *jus cogens* norm, without more, cannot be considered an implicit waiver under section 1605(a)(1).[173]

Conclusion

Over the years a number of rules and principles have developed with regard to waiver. In actual practice, what distinguishes an explicit waiver from an implicit waiver is only whether a State uses the word 'waive/waiver'. If, for example, the defendant State says, 'I waive my immunity', that is an express waiver. On the other hand, if it does not say so but simply goes to the court and starts defending itself on the merits without mentioning its immunity, that is an implied waiver. In other words, if the defendant State acts as if immunity had already been waived, it waives its immunity implicitly. Other than that, there is not much difference between the two; and almost identical requirements have been formulated for the determination of their existence. Thus, whether explicit or implicit, a waiver must be intentional, displaying a willingness on the part of the defendant foreign State to submit to the jurisdiction; it must be clear, unambiguous and unmistakable; and it must be specific, in that it must be directly related to the proceedings at hand. Clarity, intentionality and specificity are the three most important requirements for a waiver, whether explicit or implicit. As a result, cases in which a State can be held to have implicitly waived its immunity are strictly and narrowly defined and are very few in number.

9   Measures of constraint

'Measures of constraint' is a generic term covering both interlocutory, interim or pre-trial measures prior to final judgments and the execution or enforcement of judgments. In the context of State immunity, these are coercive or enforcement measures taken by the court either to restrain the foreign State in the disposition of its property, normally in the form of interlocutory injunctions, or otherwise to attach, arrest or seize the property of the foreign State. Such measures serve the purposes of either guaranteeing payment of debt, which may be the subject of an eventual judgment, or of satisfying a final judgment rendered by the competent court.

An examination of relevant State practice shows that, even though, as a general rule, preventive measures and measures of forced execution against foreign States and their property are permitted, such measures are subject to a number of conditions and limitations. First, a clear distinction has been drawn between immunity from the adjudicative process and immunity from measures of constraint, and hence the dichotomous distinction between adjudicative jurisdiction and enforcement jurisdiction (though logically the issue of jurisdiction precedes that of immunity). Secondly, the 'purpose' test, much discredited in the context of adjudicative jurisdiction, resurfaces as a determinative factor in the context of measures of constraint. Generally speaking, the property of a foreign State enjoys immunity from attachment, arrest and execution when it is used for sovereign or public purposes, but not when it is used for commercial purposes. Thirdly, the territorial nexus requirement is adhered to even more strictly in the process of enforcement and execution of judgments against foreign State property. Finally, certain categories of property still enjoy absolute immunity, even where the foreign State has expressly waived its immunity from execution. Overall, to the extent that it is the plaintiff who first must show the commercial use of particular foreign State property before the levy of execution can be possible, the same presumption of immunity as prevails at the adjudicatory stage for the foreign State now operates even more rigorously at the executory stage for the property of the foreign State. On these points at least, State practice is remarkably uniform, so that one would be justified to treat the aforegoing points not only as constituting a broad description of current practice, but also as a statement of general rules of current law.

There is no exaggerating the practical significance of measures of constraint. On the one hand, they are the concrete means whereby a court demonstrates in a material sense, or rather vindicates, its competence to deal with the proceedings; otherwise, as has been famously put by the Swiss Federal Tribunal, a judgment of the court would become a mere legal opinion without binding force. Moreover, from the plaintiff's viewpoint it would be senseless to sue a foreign State, in many cases at considerable expense, without any realistic prospect of having the orders and the final judgment of the court enforced, if necessary through coercive means. On the other hand, as these measures directly affect a foreign State's rights and interests in property, they are bound to cause serious foreign relations problems. For these reasons, they are rightly viewed as the most sensitive part of the question of State immunity.

1. Terminology

National courts use a variety of terms peculiar to their respective legal systems. For instance, the French courts use '*saisie conservatoire*' (conservatory seizure/attachment) or '*mesure conservatoire*' (conservatory measure), for prejudgment measures, and '*execution forcée*' (forced execution), for execution of judgment;[1] the Belgian courts use 'safeguarding measure',[2] 'conservatory attachment' and 'attachment in execution';[3] the German courts use '*vorläufiger Rechtsschutz*' (interim protection or relief),[4] '*Sicherungsmaßnahmen*' (protective, preventive or safeguarding measures) and '*Vollstreckungsmaßnahmen*' (measures of execution) or '*Zwangsvollstreckungsmaßnahmen*' (measures of forced execution).[5] The US FSIA envisages 'attachment prior to the entry of judgment', 'attachment in aid of execution' and 'execution',[6] whereas the UK SIA speaks of 'injunction' and 'enforcement of judgment'.[7] In some countries, notably France, the word 'execution' may also be used to cover prejudgment measures.

The list would grow if one were to examine exhaustively all the terms used by different domestic courts. However, whatever terms might be used, the coercive or enforcement measures fall broadly within two time slots: that prior to or pending the final judgment and that following it, and they can generally be covered by such terms as 'prejudgment/interim/provisional measures' and 'execution' or 'forcible execution'.

A more general term is needed to accommodate the differences pertaining to divergent judicial systems. Consequently, the ILC suggested the term 'measures of constraint' because:

> That general reference ... would also include all other measures of judicial constraint under domestic law, including certain types of interlocutory injunctions that might not be strictly considered as attachment, arrest or execution.[8]

For convenience of discussion, the term 'enforcement' will be used interchangeably with 'measures of constraint'. The terms 'prejudgment attachment' or 'prejudgment measures' and 'execution' will be used to denote measures taken against the property of a foreign State, depending on whether such measures are taken before or after the judgment; whereas the term 'injunction' will refer to measures operating against the foreign State *in personam*. It must particularly be remembered that measures of constraint can operate either *in personam* (enjoining the foreign State to act or refrain from acting in a certain way) or *in rem* (attaching or seizing the property of a foreign State).

In discussing the two distinct forms of immunity, 'immunity from suit', 'immunity from adjudication' and 'immunity from the adjudicative process' will be used to denote the exemption from the power of a court to hear and adjudge a case; and 'immunity from enforcement/execution' will be used, in place of the longer and more precise term 'immunity from measures of constraint', to signify the exemption from the enforcement of court orders and actual execution of judgments. In this respect, it must be noted in particular that the English term 'immunity from jurisdiction' has been used in two senses, which may easily lead to confusion. In its narrow sense the term 'immunity from jurisdiction' refers to immunity from the adjudicative process, without regard to the execution of judgment, and for this purpose it is to be distinguished from a separate term, 'immunity from execution'. In its broad sense, the term 'immunity from jurisdiction' signifies general jurisdictional immunity enjoyed by States in respect of the entirety of the judicial process, including both the adjudicatory and the executory stages; that is, it covers both immunity from suit and immunity from execution. Exactly the same situation is found in the French usage. Whereas the expression '*immunité de juridiction*' ('immunity from jurisdiction' or 'jurisdictional immunity') is capable of denoting either the general immunity or simply immunity from the adjudicative process,[9] the term '*immunité d'exécution*' ('immunity from enforcement/execution') is used where only enforcement measures are involved or where a distinction becomes necessary between the two immunities.[10] In what sense the phrase 'immunity from jurisdiction' ('*immunité de juridiction*') is used always depends on the context. In this connection it bears emphasizing that, in respect of State immunity, the judicial proceedings can normally be divided into two stages: the stage of adjudication and that of the execution of judgment. Measures of constraint can take place at both the adjudicatory and the executory stages, that is, they can be taken as interim measures pending the judgment and as full execution after the final judgment has been rendered. Because of this straddling nature of enforcement measures, it becomes difficult to insist on a sharp dividing line between the terms 'immunity from jurisdiction/adjudication' and 'immunity from execution'. It is important not to be misled by the terms used; and it is more than idle to be too preoccupied with them. It is necessary, rather, always to be clear about what stage of the litigation and what concrete judicial measure one has in mind.

There are some measures which cannot be comfortably pigeonholed along the above lines of pre- and post-judgment measures. An *exequatur* for the enforcement of either a foreign judgment[11] or an arbitral award[12] has been held not to be a measure of execution and therefore not to engage immunity from enforcement/execution, though the very purpose of an *exequatur* is precisely to allow execution to go ahead. The English courts also held that the process for the recognition and enforcement of foreign judgments lies at the adjudicative stage.[13] An order for security for costs has also been held not to be a measure of execution.[14] Naturally, certain measures are generally considered prohibited vis-à-vis a foreign State, such as a declaration of bankruptcy[15] or an order of discovery.[16] Under section 13(1) of the UK SIA: 'No penalty by way of committal or fine shall be imposed in respect of any failure or refusal by or on behalf of a State to disclose or produce any document or other information for the purposes of proceedings to which it is a party.'[17] Under section 1606 of the US FSIA, 'a foreign State except for an agency or instrumentality thereof shall not be liable for punitive damages'.[18]

2. Two distinct immunities: immunity from suit and immunity from execution

Once it is established that a court is competent to adjudicate on the proceedings involving a foreign State, there arises the question whether the orders and decisions of the court can be automatically enforced. From the viewpoint of the defendant State, the question becomes whether, after its claim of immunity from suit has failed, it is still left with the possibility of claiming immunity from enforcement. In other words, does the process of restricting foreign State immunity consist of only one stage, so that a State losing immunity from suit loses any further claim of immunity and becomes exposed to all kinds of measures of constraint just as a private litigant? Or does that process consist of two stages, in that a court will have to consider the issue of immunity afresh upon finding that the defendant foreign State is not immune from the trial proceedings? Moreover, the question also arises where the foreign State has waived its immunity and voluntarily submitted to the jurisdiction of the local courts. Then the question becomes whether such a waiver of immunity automatically renders measures of constraint permissible. This has led some scholars to ask whether one ought to speak of two separate immunities or two aspects of the same immunity.[19] Such is of course a highly academic point, since the two conceptualizations are equally warrantable theoretically and therefore it will be idle to attempt a definitive preference for either. That said, the parallel use of the two terms, 'immunity from suit' and 'immunity from execution', together with their variants (such as 'immunity from adjudication', 'immunity from enforcement' and 'immunity from measures of constraint'), is now a universal feature of the law of State immunity. For this reason it seems more convenient and less misleading to speak of two immunities, rather than two aspects of the same immunity.

The earlier pronouncements of the courts seem to be divided as to whether loss of immunity from suit automatically led to loss of immunity from enforcement. Some declared that immunity from enforcement was inseparable from immunity from suit while others seemed to maintain a distinction between the two. According to the former, if immunity from suit was denied, there would be no immunity from enforcement; for the latter, separate conditions for enforcement must be fulfilled. However, in the light of the present law of State immunity, this question is more of historical and theoretical than of current practical significance. First, this question emerged and was discussed largely against the backdrop of the coexistence of two conflicting doctrines, one absolute and the other restrictive, the former claiming either a blanket immunity from all court procedures or, in case of a voluntary waiver, an absolute immunity from execution.[20] Many apparently negative responses to assertions of immunity from execution were actually made to rebut the claim of *absolute* immunity and therefore should not be counted towards a total negation of immunity per se. In other words, at that time the debate was in fact not about whether the loss of immunity from suit should automatically lead to enforcement measures but about whether enforcement measures could be taken *at all*, even in the event of a successful judgment. Secondly, as can be seen through court practice, there have always been varying degrees of judicial self-restraint on the part of the courts while they pronounced against absolute immunity from execution, so that certain conditions and limitations have always had to be satisfied before execution could take place. Thus, however diverse the practice in various States, the issue of enforcement has been and continues to be considered *separately* from the adjudicatory phase; and courts, having denied immunity from suit, always pause to consider the permissibility of measures of constraint. This is perhaps the single most important aspect of the law of State immunity that makes judicial proceedings against a foreign State so undeniably different from those against a private individual, and it above all shows that a foreign State can never be fully assimilated to a private person.

2.1. The judicial power of the court

If a court is competent to sit in judgment on a case, it should naturally follow that the court must be empowered to enforce any order or decision it may see fit to render. Therefore, immunity enjoyed by a foreign State is, so to speak, indivisible. If, for one reason or another, a foreign State is immune from the judicial competence to adjudicate, there will be no question of execution since the State will at any rate not be haled into court. If, however, the foreign State, either through a waiver or voluntary submission (be it explicit or by implication) or through the operation of some pre-existing rules compelling non-immunity, enters into the judicial process, then it will be legitimately expected that the State should also obey the orders and decisions of the court. Such has been the expectation since ancient times. In the words of Blackstone, 'the sentence of a court would be contemptible, unless that court had power to command the execution of it'.[21] The law of State immunity, however, has come to hold otherwise.

IMMUNITY FROM SUIT AND IMMUNITY FROM EXECUTION   349

The Swiss courts have since earliest times maintained that, where a foreign State has acted in a private law capacity (*jure gestionis*), it can then be sued before the Swiss courts and may be subjected in Switzerland to enforcement measures, provided that the legal relationship to which it is a party is connected with Swiss territory.[22] The strict territorial nexus requirement, as will be discussed in more detail later, considerably limits the effects of the Swiss practice of merging or conflating the two stages of adjudication and execution. For our present purposes, the Swiss courts have been the foremost champion of the notion that execution is a logical consequence of adjudication. In the words of the Federal Tribunal:

> As soon as one admits that in certain cases a foreign State may be a party before Swiss courts to an action designed to determine its rights and obligations ... one must admit also that that foreign State may in Switzerland be subjected to measures intended to ensure the forced execution of a judgment against it. If that were not so, the judgment would lack its most essential attribute, namely, that it will be executed even against the will of the party against which it is rendered. It would become a mere legal opinion.[23]

Thus, 'the power of enforcement flows from the jurisdictional power',[24] that is:

> immunity from execution [is] simply the consequence of jurisdictional immunity. A foreign State which in a particular case does not enjoy jurisdictional immunity is not entitled to immunity from execution either, unless the measures of execution concern assets allocated for the performance of acts of sovereignty.[25]

Pronouncements to the same effect can be found in Dutch,[26] English,[27] German,[28] Italian[29] and Spanish[30] cases. Such pronouncements might imply that once immunity from adjudication is denied, then measures of constraint can be taken without any further and separate conditions. However, both as a matter of historical fact and under current law, this is not the case at all, since measures of constraint have always been considered separately from adjudication, with even more caution, and with further conditions and qualifications. It must then be noted that, historically, the reasoning ostensibly against a separate immunity from execution was actually designed to combat an *absolute* immunity from execution. That is to say, the above pronouncements meant no more than that, if a State did not enjoy *absolute* immunity from adjudication, then that State should not enjoy *absolute* immunity from execution either. It would make no sense to allow the court to pass a judgment

350 MEASURES OF CONSTRAINT

against a foreign State that could never be executed. In other words, in declaring that they had the power to enforce their orders and decisions these courts were simply asserting that judgments against foreign States were *in principle executable*, not that *all* judgments could and must, *equally and without restrictions*, be *executed*. Current law on State immunity holds that, even though, as a matter of principle, the judicial power of a court must be regarded as an integral whole, so that the competence of a court to hear the case is logically followed by the competence to enforce its orders and decisions regarding that case, that power may not be exercised to force a defendant foreign State to obey those orders and decisions unless a number of restrictions, conditions and qualifications are fulfilled. It is these restrictions, conditions and qualifications imposed on the taking of measures of constraint that form the central concern of this chapter. The starting point is that current law draws a firm and sharp distinction between two immunities: immunity from adjudication and immunity from execution or measures of constraint.

2.2. *The universal distinction between the two immunities*

A State can never be entirely assimilated to a private litigant. If it can be accepted that a State, even though it may occasionally engage in trading, commercial and other private-law activities, is first and foremost an institution whose very *raison d'être* is the running of public affairs, it then must be conceded that the property of a State can never be treated in exactly the same way as that of a private individual. At any given time the property of a State is always allocated to different departments and entities that perform different functions. Indeed, the most important element of statecraft, from time immemorial, is precisely a well-balanced distribution of public funds and other types of State property among the myriad bodies set up to perform a multitude of interrelated but distinct functions and activities of the State. That some segments of the property of the State may be used for private law activities at the moment in no way changes the fact that other segments are involved in distinctly sovereign functions. This natural and necessary differentiation, within each State, between different parts of the property of the State will inevitably project itself onto the judicial proceedings implicating foreign States. Interference with the property of a foreign State currently destined to perform sovereign or public functions will undoubtedly hinder the performance of such functions and will surely set off a strong reaction from the State concerned, thereby putting State-to-State relations in peril. For this reason, the fact that the court can sit in judgment on a case against a foreign State does not necessarily mean that the court will be in a good position to exercise its power to take enforcement measures against the property of that State. This does not negate the jurisdiction, or judicial power, or competence, of the court. Jurisdiction being in principle territorial in international law, a court always has jurisdiction over persons, things and acts in the territory of the forum State. The issue, now, is that the law may stipulate that, in certain circumstances, that jurisdiction should not be *exercised*. Thus, even though a court rightfully has the power to deal with any property situated in the territory of the forum State, whether that property belongs to a private individual or to a foreign State, mere prudence, if nothing else, dictates that the court exercise some degree of caution and judicial self-restraint when the property of a foreign State is targeted for measures of enforcement. If the property in question happens to be in use for a public or sovereign function, it will be better not to take any forcible measure against it, since such measure will no doubt be regarded as an unfriendly act by the foreign State, to say the least. Once a court decides that it will refrain from taking forcible enforcement measures against the foreign State property in question, there will be no better description than that the property is *immune* from forcible enforcement measures. In this regard, immunity is nothing but prudence translated into judicial terms. That is, having decided that the foreign State does not enjoy immunity from the adjudicative process, and having rendered a judgment in favour of the plaintiff, the court must now, out of practical necessity, consider whether the specific property of that State, which the plaintiff is seeking to attach or seize, should be immune from enforcement measures designed to execute the judgment. In other words, there is always the need to reconsider and re-examine the issue of immunity at the enforcement stage. It then becomes desirable, if only for the sake of convenience, to draw a distinction between immunity from adjudication and immunity from measures of constraint. This is precisely what the courts have done. The distinction between immunity from suit and immunity from enforcement/execution is now universally accepted as part and parcel of the law of State immunity. More than that: it is the defining feature of the judicial process against a foreign State.

2.2.1. The treaties

The 1972 European Convention clearly envisages two immunities. While Article 15 provides that:

352 MEASURES OF CONSTRAINT

A Contracting State shall be entitled to immunity from the jurisdiction of the courts of another Contracting State if the proceedings do not fall within Articles 1 to 14.

Article 23 further provides that:

No measures of execution or preventive measures against the property of a Contracting State may be taken in the territory of another Contracting State except where and to the extent that the State has expressly consented thereto in writing in any particular case.

Such immunity from execution or preventive measures would almost be absolute, but for the provisions in Articles 20–22 and 24–26, together with the Additional Protocol to the Convention, which set forth a contractual regime whereby the States parties to the Convention accept the *treaty obligation* to give effect to judgments against them by courts of other contracting States or, as between the contracting States which have voluntarily accepted what the framers called the 'optional regime', to allow the enforcement of a judgment against property of the defendant State in the State of the forum, used exclusively in connection with an industrial or commercial activity.[31] This evinces a clear intention not to apply the execution scheme under the Convention – already much limited – to non-States parties. Even among the parties to the Convention, according to the framers, this regime represents 'a compromise in that it combines an obligation on States to give effect to judgments (the obligation being controlled by judicial safeguards) with a rule permitting no execution'.[32]

The 2004 UN Convention moves some steps forward in allowing measures of constraint under certain limited circumstances without it being necessary to secure the consent of the defendant State. On the matter of the distinction between the two immunities, it is as exacting as the European Convention, if not more so. On top of a general 'immunity from the jurisdiction of the courts of another State' in Article 5, subject to a number of exceptions including 'express consent to exercise of jurisdiction' (Article 7), the Convention further provides that:

No pre-judgment measures of constraint, such as attachment or arrest, against property of a State may be taken in connection with a proceeding before a court of another State unless and except to the extent that the State has expressly consented to the taking of such measures. (Article 18(a))

And that:

No post-judgment measures of constraint, such as attachment, arrest or execution, against property of a State may be taken in connection with a proceeding before a court of another State unless and except to the extent that the State has expressly consented to the taking of such measures. (Article 19(a))

And, in particular, that:

Where consent to the measures of constraint is required under articles 18 and 19, consent to the exercise of jurisdiction under article 7 shall not imply consent to the taking of measures of constraint. (Article 20)

Article 20 of the UN Convention appears as Article 18(2) in the ILC's 1991 Draft Articles, which reads:

Consent to the exercise of jurisdiction under article 7 shall not imply consent to the taking of measures of constraint . . . for which separate consent shall be necessary.[33]

Article 20 of the UN Convention drops the words 'for which separate consent shall be necessary', but then it can be seen that the UN Convention, in addition to the caveat of Article 20, assiduously repeats the requirement of consent in Article 7 (concerning the adjudicative process), in Article 18 (concerning prejudgment measures) and in Article 19 (concerning post-judgment measures). The effect is nothing less than that separate consent is needed for the adjudicatory stage and then for the enforcement stage (which is further divided into the pre- and the post-judgment periods). It can then be concluded, so far as the UN Convention is concerned, first, that States enjoy both immunity from adjudication and immunity from enforcement before foreign courts; and, secondly, that a waiver/loss of immunity from adjudication does not mean a waiver/loss of immunity from enforcement, for which a separate waiver/determination has to be made. Current national statutes, as will be seen, follow exactly the same format.

2.2.2. The US FSIA

The US FSIA refers to two distinct immunities: 'immunity from jurisdiction' (section 1604) and 'immunity from attachment and execution' (section 1609),[34] together with two distinct waivers of these immunities.

The two immunities are dealt with by two separate groups of provisions. Section 1604, entitled 'Immunity of a foreign state from jurisdiction', stipulates:

a foreign state shall be immune from the jurisdiction of the courts of the United States and of the States except as provided in sections 1605 to 1607.

Section 1609, entitled 'Immunity from attachment and execution of property of a foreign state', stipulates:

354   MEASURES OF CONSTRAINT

the property in the United States of a foreign state shall be immune from attachment arrest and execution except as provided in sections 1610 and 1611.

Thus sections 1604–1607 deal with immunity from adjudication and exceptions to it, and sections 1609–1611 immunity from attachment and execution and its exceptions. The waiving of these immunities is likewise addressed separately in respect of the adjudicatory and the executional processes, for which two separate waivers are contemplated. In fact, as if to make the immunity of foreign States absolutely secure, the FSIA does not shrink from being overly repetitive:

A foreign state shall not be immune from the jurisdiction of courts of the United States or of the States in any case in which the foreign state has waived its immunity either explicitly or by implication. (section 1605(a)(1))

. . .

The property in the United States of a foreign state ... used for a commercial activity in the United States, shall not be immune from attachment in aid of execution, or from execution ... if the foreign state has waived its immunity from attachment in aid of execution or from execution either explicitly or by implication. (section 1610(a)(1))

... any property in the United States of an agency or instrumentality of a foreign state engaged in commercial activity in the United States shall not be immune from attachment in aid of execution, or from execution ... if the agency or instrumentality has waived its immunity from attachment in aid of execution or from execution either explicitly or implicitly ... (section 1610(b)(1))

. . .

The property of a foreign state ... used for a commercial activity in the United States, shall not be immune from attachment prior to the entry of judgment ... if the foreign state has explicitly waived its immunity from attachment prior to judgment. (section 1610(d)(1))

The legislators must have treated section 1604 as insufficient for the issue of exemption of foreign State property from enforcement and have therefore felt the necessity to create a separate section. The need to do so would become particularly manifest if one were to construe the word 'jurisdiction' in section 1604 expansively as including both the adjudicatory and the enforcement processes, and then view the enforcement measures as constituting an exception to immunity from jurisdiction. In that case, no property of a foreign State could be immune from execution once adjudicative jurisdiction could be established. The repetition in sections 1604 and 1609, and in sections 1605(a)(1) and

1610(a)(1), which otherwise would appear awkward, is therefore a deliberate policy announcement, making it unmistakable that the legislators considered the two immunities as distinct and hence spared no effort in eliminating any misunderstanding of their intention.

In *FG Hemisphere*, the Fifth Circuit declared:

Although jurisdiction over the parties does not change after the action commences or after the party submits to the court's jurisdiction, immunity from execution is nevertheless narrower than jurisdictional immunity ... We reject [the plaintiff's] argument because it conflates the considerations and effects attendant to commencement and/or notice of a suit seeking to execute upon the foreign sovereign's property with those attendant to deciding whether to authorize execution upon that property.[35]

In highlighting the distinction between 'commencement of a suit' and 'execution', the court reaffirmed the distinction between immunity from adjudication and immunity from execution. However, a most crucial part of the above statement needs some deciphering; for by saying 'immunity from execution is nevertheless narrower than jurisdictional immunity' the court did not mean that a foreign State enjoyed *less* ('narrower') immunity with regard to execution; quite the reverse: the court actually meant that a foreign State enjoyed *more* (broader) immunity in respect of execution. This is because the FSIA only *partially* lifts the immunity of a foreign State regarding execution. In the legislative report, the legislators explained that the FSIA:

would remedy, *in part*, the present predicament of a plaintiff who has obtained a judgment against a foreign state. Under existing law, a foreign state in our courts enjoys absolute immunity from execution, even in ordinary commercial litigation where commercial assets are available for the satisfaction of a judgment. [The FSIA] seeks to restrict this broad immunity from execution ... by *partially* lowering the barrier of immunity from execution.[36]

As understood by the courts, 'it was not Congress' purpose to lift execution immunity wholly and completely'.[37] Thus, by saying that 'immunity from execution is narrower than jurisdictional immunity', what was really meant was that the *restrictions* on a foreign State's immunity from execution are narrower (or less) than those on immunity from adjudication; or, in other words, that a foreign State enjoys a *broader* immunity with respect to execution. Moreover, even though not expressly stated in the same words in the FSIA (though the above-noted repetition makes it clear enough), it is an established principle (itself of a similarly long standing) in the US practice that waiver of immunity from jurisdiction is

356   MEASURES OF CONSTRAINT

separate from and does not automatically lead to a waiver of immunity from enforcement;[38] and that, conversely, a waiver of immunity from enforcement does not mean a waiver of immunity from suit either.[39]

2.2.3. The UK SIA and other national statutes

Section 1(1) of the UK SIA, entitled 'General immunity from jurisdiction', provides:

A State is immune from the jurisdiction of the courts of the United Kingdom except as provided in the following provisions of this Part of this Act.

And section 13(2) provides that:

   (a) relief shall not be given against a State by way of injunction or order for specific performance or for the recovery of land or other property; and
   (b) the property of a State shall not be subject to any process for the enforcement of a judgment or arbitration award or, in an action *in rem*, for its arrest, detention or sale.

As an exception to this general prohibition, section 13(3) provides:

Subsection (2) above does not prevent the giving of any relief or the issue of any process with the written consent of the State concerned; and any such consent (which may be contained in a prior agreement) may be expressed so as to apply to a limited extent or generally; but *a provision merely submitting to the jurisdiction of the courts is not to be regarded as a consent for the purposes of this subsection.*[40]

According to Lord Diplock, the UK SIA, like the US FSIA, deals with immunity from adjudication and immunity from execution separately, and in two distinct groups of provisions as well:

The [SIA] ... purports ... to deal comprehensively with the jurisdiction of courts of law in the United Kingdom both (1) to adjudicate upon claims against foreign states ('adjudicative jurisdiction'); and (2) to enforce by legal process ('enforcement jurisdiction') judgments pronounced and orders made in the exercise of their adjudicative jurisdiction ... [T]he Act ... draws a clear distinction between the adjudicative jurisdiction and the enforcement jurisdiction of courts of law in the United Kingdom. Sections 2 to 11 deal with adjudicative jurisdiction. Sections 12 to 14 deal with procedure and of these, sections 13(2) to (6) and 14(3) and (4) deal in particular with enforcement jurisdiction. Section 13(3) ... makes it clear that such submission does not of itself imply any submission to the enforcement jurisdiction of the courts. Separate consent to that is needed.[41]

Stanley Burnton J further commented:

> In *Alcom*, Lord Diplock used the terms 'adjudicative jurisdiction' and 'enforcement jurisdiction' as convenient shorthand references. Those expressions do not appear in the Act itself. Section 1 refers to an immunity not from the 'adjudicative and enforcement jurisdictions' of the court, but from 'the jurisdiction' *simpliciter*. It is noteworthy that Lord Diplock did not suggest that section 1 was concerned only with adjudicative jurisdiction. It clearly relates to the entirety of the jurisdiction of the court.[42]

So the expression 'immunity from jurisdiction' in the title of section 1(1) becomes ambiguous; for it can either signify a general, overarching immunity that covers the two stages of adjudication and enforcement, in that the provisions on both stages are to be found in 'this Part of this Act', namely, Part I of SIA, which includes, in particular, sections 2 to 11 and section 13; or it can mean only a narrowly defined immunity from the adjudicatory process, without impinging on the issue of enforcement, since the exemption of a State's property from enforcement is termed, not as 'immunity', but as 'privilege' (section 13 is entitled 'Other procedural *privileges*') under the general heading 'Procedure' (general heading for sections 12 to 13), and is prima facie unrelated to the issues of '*Immunity* from jurisdiction' (general heading for section 1) and 'Exceptions from *immunity*' (general heading for sections 2 to 11)(emphases added). This convoluted style of draftsmanship notwithstanding, the arrangement of these provisions into two different groups, at any rate, seems strongly to indicate that whether or not the property of a foreign State can be subjected to enforcement measures is treated by the legislators as not falling under – and therefore separate from – the issue of exceptions to immunity from adjudication.

The UK courts carefully follow the adjudication/enforcement distinction especially when dealing with borderline issues.[43] Thus the recognition and registration of a foreign judgment, in that it requires bringing an action before a UK court to convert the foreign judgment into a UK judgment, is an exercise of adjudicative jurisdiction, so that 'the court must be satisfied that there is a good arguable case that the proceedings fall within one of the exceptions to immunity set out in sections 2–11 of the SIA'.[44] (NB: section 13, which deals with measures of constraint, is not mentioned here.) Because the registration of a foreign judgment is not listed in sections 2 to 11 as one of the statutory exceptions to immunity, the applicant, apart from proving the regularity of the foreign judgment for registration purposes, must also show that one or more exceptions under the SIA apply to the case as well. The consequence is that, even if what underlies the foreign

358   MEASURES OF CONSTRAINT

judgment is indeed a commercial transaction, a foreign State is still immune from a proceeding for the registration and conversion of such a foreign judgment, where section 3(1)(a) ('commercial transaction') of the SIA, whose applicability must be separately considered pursuant to the UK civil procedural rules concerning the establishment of jurisdiction, does not apply, and where no other exception to immunity under the SIA can be engaged.[45] This makes the enforcement of a foreign judgment against a foreign State in the UK courts, in the absence of a treaty for the mutual recognition and enforcement of judgments, an impossible affair.

An application for *leave* to enforce an arbitration award as a judgment (i.e. a proceeding which relates to arbitration under section 9) is distinguished from enforcement *by execution* on property belonging to the State (section 13).[46] That is to say, the action to seek *permission* for the recognition and enforcement of an arbitral award engages the adjudicative jurisdiction while the actual *execution* upon the property of a foreign State belongs to the enforcement stage. By the same token, nothing in section 9 overrides the restrictions on proceedings for a freezing order to preserve the position pending execution of an award, which are within section 13 and are not 'proceedings which relate to the arbitration' for the purposes of section 9.[47] An undertaking not to appeal an order for costs is not a waiver of immunity from enforcement to be levied on property;[48] while a submission to enforcement jurisdiction is not a submission to adjudicative jurisdiction.[49]

2.2.4.   The practice of other States

The same situation can again be observed in the practice of those States without immunity legislation. Historically, for many courts the issue of enforcement/execution was not discussed or even contemplated until long after their practice had shifted from absolute to restrictive immunity with regard to the adjudicatory stage. Nowhere is such a dichotomous attitude more markedly displayed than in those courts which were the very initiators of the doctrine of restrictive immunity.

In Belgium, even though the restrictive doctrine was embraced in the late nineteenth century, the Belgian courts granted near-absolute immunity from measures of forceful execution, regardless of the distinction between public and private acts of the debtor State,[50] up to the 1950s, when exemption from execution was held no longer available with regard to economic activities.[51]

In Italy, jurisdictional immunity of foreign States was denied in the 1880s, but the general prohibition of execution on foreign State property has persisted up to this day. Law No. 1263 of 15 July 1926 banned execution on the property of a foreign State except by express authorization of the Minister of Justice;[52] and this law has been held to be 'still in force', though now subject to the limitation that it does not apply to property used for non-sovereign purposes.[53] Even in 1989, a century after its adoption of the restrictive doctrine, the Court of Cassation was still of the opinion that:

Undoubtedly there is a general rule of customary international law forbidding the forum State from instituting execution proceedings on the assets of foreign States.[54]

The Greek courts have since 1928 granted immunity to foreign States only with regard to acts of sovereignty,[55] but then the Emergency Law No. 15/1938 (now Article 923, Code of Civil Procedure) prohibited execution against foreign State property without the prior authorization of the Minister of Justice.[56] The standard position is as follows:

Where a State has given its consent for the resolution of a dispute by renouncing its immunity from jurisdiction this is not considered as consent for the taking of a provisional measure or for forcible execution of the subsequent judgment ... The power to exercise jurisdiction over a foreign State and the power to take measures of constraint against that State are two entirely separate powers and require separate manifestations of consent on the part of the State concerned.[57]

The Swiss courts were among the early adherents of the restrictive doctrine, and yet the Swiss government policy has been opposed to the taking of executionary measures against foreign State property.[58] Moreover, Switzerland has, ever since 1982, been a party to the 1972 European Convention on State Immunity, Article 23 of which confers a blanket immunity from execution upon a defendant State, subject only to certain conditions allowing execution as between and among the contracting States (Articles 20 and 21), especially in pursuance of the Additional Protocol to the Convention.

The Austrian Supreme Court adopted the restrictive approach in *Dralle* in 1950;[59] but absolute immunity from execution was soon declared,[60] and the denial of immunity from execution only came many years afterwards.[61] Now the established position of the Supreme Court is that, even though the underlying claim may involve a private law relationship, execution may still be denied if the property attached serves sovereign purposes. Therefore, even though adjudicative jurisdiction could be established in a case brought by a university professor against

360 MEASURES OF CONSTRAINT

his employer State, since an employment relationship was of a private-law nature:

No execution may be levied on extraterritorial property. A freezing order or a garnishee order may only be granted against persons outside the jurisdiction, including foreign States, under the conditions stated in Article IX(2) of the Introductory Act to the Jurisdictional Statute.[62]

That is to say, the loss of immunity from adjudication does not mean the loss of immunity from execution, for which separate and distinct conditions are required; but the conditions for execution are actually those that prevailed at the time of absolute immunity, namely voluntary submission and immovable property, as Article IX(2) of the Introductory Act to the Jurisdictional Statute (*EGJN*) provides:

Persons who enjoy exterritoriality according to principles of public international law shall be subject to domestic jurisdiction if and insofar as they submit voluntarily to the jurisdiction of domestic courts, or if the litigation concerned relates to their immovable assets located in Austria or to their vested rights in respect of domestic immovables belonging to other persons.[63]

Thus an embassy bank account could not be attached to pay for outstanding amounts due under a leasing agreement, even though a default judgment could be obtained against the foreign State, which did not dispute the ordinary commercial nature of the lease itself.[64]

The French practice steered towards restrictive immunity in the early twentieth century, and then definitively in the 1960s;[65] but the French courts continued to grant absolute immunity from execution.[66] Even in 1978, there was still the assertion of 'the absolute nature of the immunity from execution'.[67] Since the 1970s, the French courts have consistently treated immunity from adjudication and immunity from execution as distinct and dealt with them separately. This means two things: first, a denial/loss of immunity from adjudication does not automatically lead to a denial/loss of immunity from execution;[68] and, secondly, a waiver of immunity from adjudication does not automatically involve a waiver of immunity from execution.[69]

In Germany, the Federal Constitutional Court (FCC) decided to adopt the restrictive rule in the *Empire of Iran Case* in 1963;[70] but that case marked only the *initial* establishment of the restrictive doctrine in Germany. While declaring the German courts competent to adjudicate upon claims concerning *acta jure gestionis* of a foreign State, the Court said nothing about whether or how a judgment thus obtained could be executed against the defendant State. As a matter of fact, it was fourteen years later, in 1977, that the FCC discussed the issue of execution in the *Philippine Embassy Bank Account Case*, and decided that forced execution was not allowed on foreign State property destined for sovereign purposes.[71] This of course left open the criteria whereby property used for *private* purposes could be identified;[72] and it was another six years before the FCC decided, in the *NIOC Revenues Case* in 1983, that it was permissible to execute upon the property of a separate legal entity.[73] Meanwhile, it was the standard position of the German judicial authorities that a waiver or loss of immunity at the adjudicatory stage, even where a default judgment could be or had been entered against the foreign State, could not imply a loss of immunity from execution.[74]

In two cases in 1986, the Spanish Supreme Court embraced the restrictive doctrine, referring to a 1980 Royal Decree (the Royal Decree No. 1654/1980 of 11 June (R. 1856 and 2119)) concerning Legal Disputes involving the State Abroad, which stated in its preamble that 'the doctrine of absolute immunity from jurisdiction must be considered as having reached its final stage'.[75] Nevertheless, upon denying immunity to the foreign States in the cases, the Supreme Court went on to hold that immunity from execution still remained and that the trial judge must obtain a legal opinion from the government in laying down a separate procedure for execution 'in conformity with bilateral agreements and the applicable usages and practices of international law'.[76] The power of the judge to apply a rule of restrictive immunity from execution was recognized only in 1992.[77]

2.2.5. Two distinct immunities: a universal rule

Based on the above examination of State practice it now appears safe to state that current State practice – and therefore the law of State immunity – universally treats immunity from measures of constraint as distinct from immunity from adjudication; and this is also the common position held by scholars across the world.[78]

This means that, even when a court decides that a defendant foreign State does not enjoy immunity from adjudication and even though the court then decides that that foreign State must pay a sum of money to the plaintiff, the court must still satisfy itself that certain conditions, which are separate and wholly distinct from those pertaining to the adjudicative stage, are satisfied before the assets of that State can be forcibly attached or seized to satisfy the judgment. Consequently, the fact that a court may be competent to exercise jurisdiction with regard to the non-immune activities (*acta jure gestionis*) of a foreign State does not automatically imply that it can authorize measures of constraint against the defendant State or any property of that State situated in the territory of the State of the forum. In this connection even those States which have accepted the restrictive principle since earliest times, and which have been consistent and unwavering in their assertion of jurisdiction at the stage of adjudication, would display considerable caution and circumspection with regard to measures of constraint against the defendant foreign State. Immunity from execution remains, so to speak, 'the last bastion of State immunity'.[79]

At the same time, courts have been remarkably reticent as to why this should be so. The prevailing opinion, at present, is that such a cautious approach is adopted out of practical considerations; that is, in order to avoid friction and damage to friendly relations between the State of the forum and the defendant State. In the landmark *Philippine Embassy Case*, the German Federal Constitutional Court said:

> preventive measures and measures of forced execution generally have a much more direct and drastic impact on the exercise of sovereignty by the foreign State than do judicial judgments. It is therefore necessary to consider separately whether and to what extent general rules of international law preclude forced execution.[80]

3. The resurfacing of the 'purpose' test

The most prominent feature of the current law of State immunity with regard to enforcement is the coming back of the 'purpose' test – with a vengeance. Without exception current State practice grants immunity to foreign State property that is used for sovereign or governmental purposes and allows enforcement and execution only in respect of property used for commercial purposes. Thus the 'purpose' test, much discredited at the stage where the court decides whether it has adjudicatory power over a foreign State, now becomes the decisive criterion for the enforcement of the court's decisions, orders, rulings and judgments. The same court that vehemently rejects the argument of purpose at the adjudicative stage now unabashedly and unapologetically adheres to the 'purpose' test, allowing or disallowing execution upon foreign State property on the basis of the purpose or use of the property in question. The 'purpose' test in this regard has two formulas: an explicit, 'purpose' formula, in which the word 'purpose' is actually used; and an implicit, 'used for' formula, which does not employ the word 'purpose' itself, but holds that foreign State property

THE RESURFACING OF THE 'PURPOSE' TEST   363

can be subjected to execution if it is 'used for' a commercial activity but not if it is 'used for' a sovereign activity.

3.1. The treaties

Under Article 26 of the 1972 European Convention, subject to other conditions which it is not necessary to discuss here:

a judgment rendered against a Contracting State in proceedings relating to an industrial or commercial activity ... may be enforced in the State of the forum against property of the State against which judgment has been given, *used exclusively in connection with such an activity*. (Emphasis added.)

Article 19(c) of the 2004 UN Convention permits post-judgment measures of constraint against the property of a foreign State where:

the property is specifically in use or intended for use by the State for other than government non-commercial *purposes* and is in the territory of the State of the forum, provided that post-judgment measures of constraint may only be taken against property that has a connection with the entity against which the proceeding was directed. (Emphasis added.)

It should be noted that the word 'is' in this provision is deliberately intended to confine the measures of execution to a limited time frame, that is, 'at the time the proceeding for attachment or execution is instituted'.[81]

3.2. The US FSIA

Section 1610(a) allows attachment or execution against foreign State property under certain circumstances. It contains several references to the purpose test. Thus:

(a) The property in the United States of a foreign state ... *used for* a commercial activity in the United States, shall not be immune from attachment in aid of execution, or from execution ... if –

...

(2) the property is or was *used for* the commercial activity upon which the claim is based, or

...

(4) the execution relates to a judgment establishing rights in property –
  (A) which is acquired by succession or gift, or
  (B) which is immovable and situated in the United States:

364   MEASURES OF CONSTRAINT

> Provided, That such property is not *used for purposes of* maintaining a diplomatic or consular mission or the residence of the Chief of such mission. (Emphases added.)

In order for particular foreign State property to be attachable, it must be 'used for a commercial activity'. In fact, the expression 'used for commercial purposes' has been used extensively by courts in discussing this provision.[82]

A notable contrast between the US FSIA and the UN Convention (and the UK SIA and its progeny below) is that the US FSIA, by using the phrase 'is or was used', allows enforcement measures regardless of the *current* use of the property of a foreign State: so long as the property has at some point in the past been used for the commercial activity, then it will be subject to execution. The legislative report explains:

> The language 'is or was used' ... contemplates a situation where property may be transferred from the commercial activity which is the subject of the suit in an effort to avoid the process of the court.[83]

The phrase 'used for' has turned out to be a central element in the US jurisprudence; and it has been subjected to a strict and narrow reading. To start with, the property in question must be 'used for', and not merely 'acquired through' a commercial activity. In *City of Englewood*, the Third Circuit rejected an attempt to attach, for tax assessment purposes, real property used as a residence for Libya's Head of Mission to the UN, holding that it was irrelevant that the property had been acquired by Libya in a commercial transaction between a seller and a buyer. The court noted, in particular:

> If acquisition of property in a particular commercial transaction or act indelibly stamped the property as used for commercial activity, even foreign embassies and chancelleries would be subject to execution. Plainly Congress did not intend a result so inconsistent with recognized principles of international law ... The determinative issue is whether it is *currently* being used in a 'regular course of commercial conduct'.[84]

This reasoning was developed to the full in *Af-Cap*, a series of cases involving an action of garnishment[85] against the property of the Congo in execution of a judgment for a defaulted US$ 6.5 million loan made to the Congo by Af-Cap's predecessor, Equator Bank. The targeted property consisted of royalties payable to the Congo by certain Texas oil companies.[86] Pursuant to the loan agreement signed in 1984, the Congo had explicitly waived its immunity from execution.[87]

The Firth Circuit first declared that, as a general principle, even when a foreign State completely waived its immunity from execution, the US courts should still only execute against property that met the two statutory criteria in section 1610(a)(1), namely, 'property in the United States ... used for a commercial activity in the United States'.[88] The court then held that, in determining the amenability of the royalties and tax obligations to garnishment, the focus should not be on how the royalties and taxes were generated, but on what they were 'used for':

> What matters under the statute is what the property is 'used for', not how it was generated or produced. If property in the United States is used for a commercial purpose here, that property is subject to attachment and execution even if it was purchased with tax revenues or some other noncommercial source of government income. Conversely, even if a foreign state's property has been generated by commercial activity in the United States, that property is not thereby subject to execution or attachment if it is not 'used for' a commercial activity within our borders ... What matters under the statute is not how the Congo made its money, but how it spends it. The amenability of these royalties and taxes to garnishment depends on what they are 'used for', not on how they were raised.[89]

> The phrase 'used for' in § 1610(a) is not a mere syntactical infelicity that permits courts to look beyond the 'use' of property, and instead try to find any kind of nexus or connection to a commercial activity in the United States. The statute means what it says: property of a foreign sovereign, unlike property belonging to a mere agency or instrumentality, may be executed against only if it is 'used for' a commercial activity. That the property is revenue from or otherwise generated by commercial activity in the United States does not thereby render the property amenable to execution ... To use property for a commercial activity, within the ordinary meaning of 'use', would be to put the property in the service of the commercial activity, to carry out the activity by means of the property ... The revenue from a commercial transaction does not have the instrumental relationship to the commercial activity denoted by the phrase 'used for'; it is not put in service of that activity, instead it is the end result or income from the activity.[90]

> In this case, for example, the royalty and tax obligations would be used for a commercial activity in the United States if the Congo used them as collateral for loans obtained from United States banks.[91]

Following this logic, the court later considered whether *past* commercial use was sufficient to render these obligations property used for commercial purposes in the meaning of the FSIA. Agreeing that a single commercial use in the past was insufficient, the court opined that:

> determining the commercial (or non-commercial) status of a property's use requires a more holistic approach. Specifically, we think that an analysis applied

366   MEASURES OF CONSTRAINT

to such a question should examine the totality of the circumstances surrounding the property. This analysis should include an examination of the uses of the property in the past as well as all facts related to its present use, with an eye toward determining whether the commercial use of the property, if any, is so exceptional that it is 'an out of character' use for that particular property ... [U]nder the FSIA, foreign property retains its immunity protection where its commercial uses, considered holistically and in context, are bona fide exceptions to its otherwise noncommercial use.[92]

The test for 'used for' was further elaborated by the Ninth Circuit in the following terms:

Like the Fifth Circuit, we conclude that property is 'used for a commercial activity in the United States' when the property in question is put into action, put into service, availed or employed *for* a commercial activity, not *in connection* with a commercial activity or *in relation* to a commercial activity. The FSIA does not contemplate a strained analysis of the words 'used for' and 'commercial activity', and neither do we. Rather, we anticipate that this determination will be made by considering the use of the property in question in a straight-forward manner, with a proper appreciation of the fact that the further removed the property is from the referenced commercial transaction, the less likely it is that the property was used *for* that transaction ... [I]n order to satisfy § 1610(a), the property must have been 'used'; the mere fact that the property has a 'nexus or connection to a commercial activity in the United States' is insufficient.[93]

The use of the phrase 'used for a commercial activity' in section 1610 (concerning immunity from execution), in contrast to a broader 'in connection with a commercial activity' in section 1605(a)(2) (concerning immunity from adjudication), suggests that attachment or execution, as distinguished from adjudication, requires more than that the property in question be 'related', 'necessary' or 'integral' to a commercial activity in the US: 'used for' demands a particular kind of relationship and is intended to have a more specific and narrower meaning.[94] Besides, the term 'used for' also requires that the property be used by the *foreign State* itself; and the fact that, before selling particular property to a foreign State, private parties may have used that property in the past for commercial purposes is irrelevant.[95]

Thus the origin or source of the property is not important; what is important is its current use for a commercial activity. The threshold requirement that the property of a foreign State be used for a commercial activity in order for it to be attachable or executable means that the court, in deciding whether to order attachment or execution, must verify that the activity for which the property in question is used is a 'commercial activity'. If we regard the adjudicatory stage and the execution as forming a continuous process, then we find a broad 'double commerciality' rule: in order for the court to exercise adjudicative jurisdiction, the foreign State must have been engaged in a commercial activity; and then, for the execution to go ahead, the property of the foreign State must be used for a commercial activity. That is, the plaintiff must first show the existence of a commercial activity to obtain a judgment; and then, in order to execute that judgment, the plaintiff must further demonstrate that the activity for which the targeted property is used is commercial as well. In the opinion of the Fifth Circuit:

For both immunity from jurisdiction and immunity from attachment, 'commercial activity' generally constitutes the touchstone of the immunity determination.[96]

This is going through exactly the same exercise twice. Such a repetitive process might be simplified if, fortunately for the plaintiff, the targeted property is used for the same commercial activity for which immunity has been denied, as is indeed contemplated by section 1610(a)(2); but repetition will be unavoidable where there is no connection between the targeted property and the claim itself. Even if immunity from suit is denied for some other reason, the court still has to consider the issue of a 'commercial activity' in a decision on execution.[97] In other words, the concept of a commercial activity, with all its inherent and attendant difficulties and intricacies, is bound to beset the court and the plaintiff at both the adjudicative and the executional stages. Apart from making suing a foreign State a cumbersome affair, this ultimately serves to limit the extent to which immunity is restricted.

3.3. The UK SIA and other national statutes

Section 13(4) of the UK SIA stipulates that the property of a foreign State shall not be immune from enforcement if the property 'is for the time being in use or intended for use *for commercial purposes*' (emphasis added).[98] One can see that the use of the word 'is' in this provision brings the UK SIA closer to the UN Convention but sets it far apart from the US FSIA. As for what is meant by 'commercial purposes', the SIA does not contain a proper definition but instead refers back to the definition of 'commercial transaction' in section 3(3) for the purposes of divining 'commercial purposes'. Under section 17(1) of the SIA, '"commercial purposes" means purposes of such transactions or activities as are

368   MEASURES OF CONSTRAINT

mentioned in section 3(3)'; and section 3(3) defines 'commercial transaction' as meaning:

(a)   any contract for the supply of goods or services;
(b)   any loan or other transaction for the provision of finance and any guarantee or indemnity in respect of any such transaction or of any other financial obligation; and
(c)   any other transaction or activity (whether of a commercial, industrial, financial, professional or other similar character) into which a State enters or in which it engages otherwise than in the exercise of sovereign authority.

The category contained in section 3(3)(c) is of an obviously residual nature, and does not apply to 'a transaction or activity into which a State enters or in which it engages in the exercise of sovereign authority'.

Notably, under the UK SIA, the phrase 'commercial purposes' denotes purposes of narrowly defined 'commercial transactions' in section 3(3) but may not cover other types of transactions that may not be 'commercial' *stricto sensu* but which may otherwise be considered 'private' and therefore non-immune. For section 3(1) of the SIA states that:

A State is not immune as respects proceedings relating to –

(a)   a commercial transaction entered into by the State; or
(b)   an obligation of the State which by virtue of a contract (whether a commercial transaction *or not*) falls to be performed wholly or partly in the United Kingdom. (Emphasis added.)

And section 3 further provides that section 3(1) does not apply to 'a contract of employment between a State and an individual'; whereas, under section 4, a foreign State may not be immune 'as respects proceedings relating to a contract of employment between the State and an individual' under certain circumstances.

Here it is plain that a foreign State will not be immune from the adjudicatory process with regard to:

(1)   a 'commercial transaction' (section 3(1)(a), and section 3(1)(b) when it covers a commercial transaction, the term 'commercial transaction' in both these provisions as defined by section 3(3));
(2)   a transaction that is not commercial but which might nonetheless be regarded as 'private' and therefore not immune (section 3(1)(b) when it applies to a non-commercial transaction); and
(3)   a contract of employment (section 4).

And yet the property of a foreign State shall be levied upon only when it is used for the purposes of the first type of transaction, i.e. a narrowly defined 'commercial transaction' in section 3(3), or perhaps for even less.[99] This arrangement, coupled with other provisions, especially section 14(4) ('Property of a State's central bank or other monetary authority shall not be regarded for the purposes of [section 13(4)] as in use or intended for use for commercial purposes') and section 16(1) (which provides that even adjudicatory immunity is not lost with regard to a State's 'title to or its possession of property used for the purposes of a diplomatic mission'), means that only a specific, much reduced, portion of the property of a foreign State can be subjected to enforcement. And even this might prove illusory; for by virtue of section 13(5), a certificate by the head of the diplomatic mission of a foreign State 'to the effect that any property is not in use or intended for use by or on behalf of the State for commercial purposes shall be accepted as sufficient evidence of that fact unless the contrary is proved'.[100] If the court can exercise its adjudicative jurisdiction in three or more categories of transaction but can only execute its judgment with regard to one category or even less, the obvious conclusion is that, in a case against a foreign State, the scope of the court's enforcement jurisdiction is much narrower than that of its adjudicative jurisdiction. Such an unnatural disparity or discrepancy in a court's judicial power at two different stages of the judicial proceedings, expressed in practical terms, means that the court will render more judgments than it can possibly execute. In other words, it is highly possible, under the UK SIA, to have judgments against foreign States with little or no prospect of execution.

The Australia FSIA 1985 attempts to resolve the characterization problem by defining 'commercial property' for the purposes of execution. Commercial property means 'property, other than diplomatic property or military property, that is in use by the foreign State concerned substantially for commercial purposes' (section 32(3)(a)) and, uniquely, 'property that is apparently vacant or apparently not in use shall be taken to be being used for commercial purposes' (section 32(3)(b)). The term 'commercial purpose' is defined in section 3(5) as including 'a reference to a trading, a business, a professional and an industrial purpose'.[101]

3.4. *The practice of the States without immunity legislation*

One faces the same phenomenon in the practice of those States without immunity legislation. The question of forced execution was most

370   MEASURES OF CONSTRAINT

thoroughly examined by the German Constitutional Court in two well-known cases. In the *Philippine Embassy Case*, the Constitution Court found that:

There exists the following general rule of international law: Forced execution of judgment by the State of the forum under a writ of execution against a foreign State which has been issued in respect of non-sovereign acts (*acta iure gestionis*) of that State, on property of that State which is present or situated in the territory of the State of the forum is inadmissible without the consent of the foreign State if, at the time of the initiation of the measure of execution, such property serves *sovereign purposes* of the foreign State.[102]

It must be noted that this pronouncement of the 'purpose' test with respect to enforcement was made in 1977, fourteen years after the German jurisprudence definitively moved from absolute to restrictive immunity in the 1963 *Empire of Iran* case, in which the Federal Constitutional Court expressly adopted the 'nature' test.[103]

Next, in the *NIOC Revenues Case*, the Federal Constitutional Court held that this 'purpose' test also applies to safeguarding (i.e. prejudgment) measures:

According to established general State practice supported by cogent legal arguments, assets of a foreign State situated or present within the State of the forum cannot be subjected to measures of enforcement *or even safeguarding measures* without the consent of the foreign State concerned, so long as they serve *sovereign purposes* of that State.[104]

Even before these cases, a local German court expressly declared:

there is a rule of customary international law under which execution against the property of a foreign State which is devoted to sovereign *purposes* is not admissible ... [W]hat matters here ... is the *purpose* to which the property against which execution is to be levied is devoted.[105]

For the Swiss Federal Tribunal, 'in certain circumstances the purpose for which assets belonging to a foreign State are allocated may render such assets exempt from enforcement'.[106] That is:

Die Zwangsvollstreckung in Vermögenswerte des ausländischen Staates, die hoheitlichen Zwecken dienen, ist unzulässig. [Forced execution on the assets of a foreign State which serve sovereign purposes is inadmissible.][107]

... the levying of execution against the assets of a foreign State is only admissible in principle against those assets which are not allocated for the performance of sovereign functions. Having regard to the nature of the assets subjected to attachment, immunity under public international law can be claimed ... so long as the assets have been allocated in a recognizable manner for an identifiable purpose related to the exercise of State sovereignty.[108]

Along these lines, the Federal Tribunal has also applied to cases involving foreign States the Swiss domestic law distinction between two categories of property, namely patrimonial assets (*biens patrimoniaux*) and administrative assets (*biens administratifs*), the latter being immune from seizure because they are assets of the authority 'directly allocated for the performance of public law functions'. Additionally, the Tribunal has held that immunity from enforcement also applied to other assets allocated for the performance of public functions.[109] Due to the peculiar feature of Swiss multilingual law reporting, the distinction has been stated as one between *Verwaltungsvermögen* ('administrative assets') and *Finanzvermögen* ('financial assets'), the latter being 'comparable to property owned by natural or legal persons under private law'.[110]

The Austrian practice relies on the same 'purpose' assessment. The starting principle is a general ban on enforcement measures against foreign State property as stated in *Neustein*.[111] In *Leasing West*, the Supreme Court declared that:

> assets of foreign States serving sovereign functions [are] not subject to domestic jurisdiction. Consequently a bank account of a foreign State could not be subjected to an interim attachment even where the claim against the foreign State was admissible ... Whether the particular assets at issue are to be categorized as sovereign assets is dependent upon the *allocated purpose* of the assets concerned ... [T]here is a general rule of international law that an order for attachment in execution made by the forum State under a writ of execution against a foreign State, issued in respect of non-sovereign acts (*acta jure gestionis*) of that State, on property of that State which is present or situated in the territory of the forum State, is inadmissible without the consent of the foreign State concerned if, at the time of the initiation of the measure of execution, such property serves sovereign purposes of the foreign State.[112]

In Italy, the distinction between property destined for public purposes and that for private ones was established very early.[113] In the words of the Court of Cassation:

> the prevailing tendency is to consider the assets used for a public function or power, or indeed for sovereign purposes, as immune ... Execution against assets used for sovereign or public purposes is therefore forbidden.[114]

The now standard position of the French Court of Cassation is an affirmation of a general immunity from execution qualified by allowance for execution upon property used for commercial activities. In *Société Eurodif*, the Court said:

Foreign States enjoy immunity from execution as a matter of principle. Nevertheless this immunity can be set aside in exceptional cases such as where the assets attached have been allocated for an economic or commercial activity of a private law nature, which has given rise to the claim at issue.[115]

Again in *Société Sonatrach*, the Court said:

The assets of a foreign State are, in principle, not subject to seizure, subject to exceptions in particular where they have been allocated for an economic or commercial activity under private law which is at the origin of the title of the attaching debtor.[116]

In *Abbott*, the Spanish Supreme Court said:

It is considered beyond dispute that a domestic court cannot take measures of execution (or preventive measures [*medidas cautelares*]) against property held by a foreign State on the territory of the forum state where such property is intended for the purpose of supporting sovereign activities or activities carried on *jure imperii* ... [I]nternational law bars forced execution on property of the foreign State used or intended to be used in activities of a sovereign or *de imperio* nature, permitting it only in respect of property intended for the purposes of economic activities.[117]

In *NV Filmpartners*, a Belgian court said:

the solution to the problem must be sought in the light of the purpose for which the State against which the attachment is directed allocates or intends to allocate the articles in question. If the articles are allocated or in use for a purpose which concerns the *ius imperii* any attachment, even conservatory, is excluded.[118]

The 'purpose' test with regard to enforcement/execution can also be found in cases from Greece,[119] and the Netherlands.[120]

It still remains to assess the impact of the return of the 'purpose' test in the context of enforcement and execution measures on the overall doctrine of State immunity. One is tempted to regard this as but an extension of the *jure imperii / jure gestionis* dichotomy, which is the only test available especially to the courts without the blessing of an immunity statute; that is, property in connection with acts/functions *jure imperii* is immune from execution, just as acts performed *de jure imperii* themselves are immune from adjudication. However, at the adjudicative stage, what is decisive is held by most courts to be the nature, rather than the purpose, of the act: if the act is by its nature capable of being performed by a private individual, then that act is an act *de jure gestionis*, a private act unprotected by immunity; whether or not that act serves a sovereign or governmental purpose is to be generally disregarded. We have already seen that a pure 'nature test', according to which the purpose of the relevant act should not be taken into account at all, has repeatedly been found inadequate by a number of influential courts and judges, so that the 'nature test' itself should better be understood as something that only generally captures the overall sentiment towards the amenability of foreign States and their agencies, but can never be seen as representing the whole picture. Be that as it may, one still marvels at the drastic change of attitude of courts at the enforcement stage, where the 'nature test' is simply forgotten and replaced by an openly declared 'purpose' test. After all, there cannot be any difference between the *nature* of a bank account kept by a private individual and that of one maintained by a foreign State; and for this reason there is nothing that makes a bank account of a foreign State *by nature* un-executable. The only thing that does make a difference, so it seems, is the *use* to which a bank account maintained by a State can be put: it can be used to pay for cement purchased for construction works, or it can be used to ensure the functioning of an embassy or a military base; in other words, it can be used to serve either a commercial or a sovereign *purpose*. Either all bank accounts of a foreign State can be subjected to enforcement and execution, because any private individual can keep a bank account, or some of the accounts must be protected because they are there for a *purpose* that is normally not within the contemplation of a private individual. In an age of growing interdependence of States, an insistence on executing on any foreign State property regardless of its purpose will surely incur retaliatory measures from the targeted State. It is this practical calculation, this fear of retaliation, one suspects, that is the real motivation for the reassertion of the purpose test at the enforcement stage. No mystical doctrinal imperative is involved here. In fact, the whole body of purported rules of law on State immunity is nothing but a collection of practical considerations clothed in legal terminology.

4. Prejudgment measures

Prejudgment measures, variously termed as 'interim measures', 'interim relief', 'provisional measures', 'preventive measures', 'conservatory measures', 'interlocutory measures' or 'safeguarding measures', fall into two broad categories: those that operate *in rem* and those that operate *in personam*. Measures *in rem* would include the so-called 'conservatory attachment', which can be directed either against the assets held by the defendant or against those held by a third party;[121] and 'garnishee orders', which are directed specifically against assets held by third parties.[122] Measures *in personam* normally take the form of an injunction (or 'injunctive relief'), a judicial order compelling a person to perform a certain act, or restraining them from certain action.[123] Also, an injunction can be directed against either the defendant or a third party.[124]

What distinguishes such measures from actual execution is their timing, rather than the inherent nature of the measures themselves: many of these measures, such as garnishment, arrest and attachment, are also commonly taken at the execution stage.

4.1. *Immunity as a preliminary issue*

It might be said that the best illustration of the interaction between immunity from suit and immunity from enforcement is the taking of prejudgment measures. On the one hand, it is understandable that a plaintiff would have no incentive to expend time and money to pursue a claim against a foreign State if, in the end, no property could be available to satisfy a judgment. Therefore, the plaintiff would be much better secured if some measures, before and during the judicial proceedings, could be utilized to attach or arrest the property of the defendant State so as to prevent otherwise available assets from being removed from the jurisdiction of the court or dissipated. On the other hand, it is in the nature of prejudgment measures that only a prima facie argument can be made by the plaintiff to justify the application of such measures well before the time when the court can pass any definitive decision on the merits, i.e. before the question whether or not the defendant State enjoys immunity from suit is finally resolved. This can lead to an anomalous situation where, after attaching the assets of the defendant State, the court discovers that, from the very start of the proceedings, it lacks competence to adjudicate on the case, so that the order of attachment has to be vacated. This is especially true in the case of attachment as a means of establishing jurisdiction. That is perhaps the reason why attachment for the sole purpose of obtaining jurisdiction (commonly referred to as attachment *ad fundandam jurisdictionem*) is expressly prohibited by, say, the US FSIA (section 1610(d)(2)).[125]

Prejudgment measures are closely linked with immunity from suit. By definition, such measures are requested or taken either at the very start or right in the middle of the litigation against a foreign State; that is to say, they are normally contemplated at a time when the question of immunity from suit is not finally settled or simply has not yet been considered. It follows that, whenever prejudgment measures are invoked, immunity from suit should be decided as a preliminary question before the court can grant such measures. More than that, since the taking of prejudgment measures, whose purpose is in most cases to secure payment for an eventual judgment, not only directly engages the court's power to order or take forcible judicial measures, but also requires a decision, albeit preliminary, on the merits. Consequently, the court must not only ascertain that the plaintiff indeed has a case against the defendant foreign State, but also that the property of the foreign State, against which the plaintiff is seeking to obtain prejudgment measures, is not immune from enforcement/execution. For this reason prejudgment measures can be rightly seen as straddling pre- and post-judgment stages and triggering issues of both immunity from adjudication and immunity from enforcement/execution. This is precisely the reason (even though undeclared) behind this statement of Stanley Burnton LJ in *ETI*:

Where injunctive relief is sought, the claimant must deal both with the immunity from the adjudicative jurisdiction of the court and with the immunity from enforcement . . . In a case such as the present, the court must consider and decide the question of state immunity at as early a stage of the proceedings as practicable.[126]

This is in tune with the general consensus among the courts that, in principle, immunity should always be decided as a preliminary issue, that is, before a court enters into substantive proceedings against a foreign State, it must determine whether it is competent to adjudicate upon the case in the first place: it must decide whether the defendant foreign State enjoys immunity. If there is immunity, then the court cannot exercise its jurisdiction and should forthwith terminate the judicial process, and any coercive measure that has already been taken must be vacated. This is the paradox of State immunity: in order to ascertain whether it has jurisdiction, the court must undertake the judicial process, hearing arguments and considering evidence; but if immunity is indeed found to be warranted in the case, then, at least in logic, the judicial process should not have been undertaken. Immunity is a preliminary issue the determination of which nevertheless requires in many cases an examination of the merits, but then immunity, if upheld, means that the court lacks the very competence to consider the merits.

376   MEASURES OF CONSTRAINT

Thus the Italian Court of Cassation said:

> For reasons of logic and legal precedence we should first examine the case for State immunity, since immunity would exclude the need for further enquiry into the merits of this case and, in particular, into the connecting factors ... which would allow a foreigner to be summonsed to appear before an Italian judge.[127]

The same realization can be observed in English jurisprudence. In *Maclaine Watson*, for example, the English Court of Appeal held that, whenever the question arises under the UK SIA whether a defendant State is immune by virtue of section 1 or not immune by virtue of one of the exceptions, then that question must be decided as a preliminary issue in favour of the plaintiff before the substantive action can proceed, that is, before the court can try the proceedings.[128]

To the extent that immunity is a preliminary issue that logically precedes the consideration of the merits, the taking of conservatory or interlocutory measures, being even preliminary to the decision on immunity, is, so to speak, a preliminary to a preliminary. One may wish to split the hair further, but one thing is certain, that is, an affirmation of the existence of immunity would also dispense with the court's power to grant interlocutory relief. Thus, to view the issue of immunity in its entirety, including the part concerning interlocutory measures, the preliminary nature of this issue makes it unique within the whole scheme of the judicial process. For technically speaking, this means that the issue of immunity must be settled once and for all at the very start of any lawsuit against a foreign State. An end to the matter at its beginning. A clear, final and definitive decision on the question of immunity is therefore needed, which cannot in the nature of things be arrived at except through a thorough examination of evidence, and elaborate argumentation and reasoning, with the result that the fight over immunity, which is purportedly a mere preliminary question, assumes in every respect the same intensity and fierceness as in a battle over the merits. With this in mind, one can easily and fully appreciate why Justice Saville said this in *A Company Ltd*:

> It is clear that when a State seeks to rely on the general immunity ... the Court must *finally decide at the outset* whether or not such immunity exists. Thus when a State seeks to discharge a *Mareva* injunction on the grounds that it is immune from the jurisdiction of the Courts of the United Kingdom, the Court cannot allow the injunction to continue on the basis that the plaintiff has a good arguable case that immunity does not exist, for if in truth immunity does exist

PREJUDGMENT MEASURES 377

then the Court simply has no power to continue the injunction ... It follows from the foregoing that where such a challenge to the jurisdiction is made, the parties must be given an opportunity ... to prepare themselves properly to *fight to finality* on the issue *at the outset*, rather than to deal with the matter on an interlocutory basis.[129]

All that can safely be said about the statement 'immunity is a preliminary issue' is that the issue of immunity must be settled before anything else, for immunity, once established, vitiates the whole legal process *ab initio*, including the prejudgment measures. But if what determines the existence or absence of immunity is the nature (or the context) of the acts of the foreign State, then it will always be necessary for the court to consider the merits before reaching a decision, even one on prejudgment measures of constraint. That is to say, in any case concerning foreign State immunity, the court has always to be mindful of two points: first, whether there is an 'arguable' case for prejudgment measures, which is common to all cases; secondly, whether the foreign State would ultimately be immune, which is unique to immunity cases. Accordingly, the question whether a prima facie or arguable case will be needed for a plaintiff successfully to apply for prejudgment measures is not particularly precise or helpful with regard to State immunity. Thus, 'a prima facie or arguable case' in a case where immunity is pleaded is quite different from 'a prima facie or arguable case' in an ordinary case where immunity is not at issue. A prima facie or arguable case in an immunity case will have more content than it does in an ordinary case. Not only must it be shown that the assets of the defendant State may be rendered unavailable for a potential judgment, but it must also be proven that the foreign State would ultimately not be entitled to immunity, either from adjudication or from execution, by virtue of the nature of the activity of that State. In a word, the plaintiff has to prove both the need and justifiability of a prejudgment measure, and the absence of immunity from such measure. In some cases the facts may be so clear-cut that such an arguable case can be established without much difficulty; but in other cases the facts may not be so straightforward, so that by the time the court is satisfied with the categorization of the acts of the foreign State, considerable contestation and deliberation would have already taken place, with the result that the proceedings become in every sense a full-blown process. It is then not inconceivable that, in some cases, the 'case' of the plaintiff for prejudgment measures has to be demonstrated in the same way and to the same extent that their case should be demonstrated for a full judgment in their

378 MEASURES OF CONSTRAINT

favour. In other words, in such cases merely a prima facie or arguable case will not be sufficient, for the simple reason that, by the time the application for prejudgment measures is granted, the plaintiff would have had to show much more than a mere 'prima facie' case.

Interim measures, safeguard measures, attachment for the purpose of establishing jurisdiction, protective attachment, injunctions, and so on, strangely straddle the stages of adjudication and execution. On the one hand, such measures are taken even before the court has decided on the merits; on the other hand, they are forcible measures restricting the foreign State's proprietary rights over its property, and can cause far more interference with the foreign State. Thus they are treated with caution and are granted only under clear guidelines. In this respect, it is certainly inaccurate to say that the foreign State should be treated exactly like a private person.

4.2. The conditions for prejudgment measures

When we put various legal instruments and cases together and compare the conditions for granting prejudgment measures with those for permitting the eventual execution of judgment, three patterns, at least in theory, appear to suggest themselves: prejudgment measures can be taken under the same, more liberal or more stringent conditions in comparison with execution.

4.2.1. Under the same conditions as execution

Generally speaking, civil law jurisprudence does not seem to draw a sharp dividing line between prejudgment attachment and execution. Courts usually speak of prejudgment/interim attachment *and* execution within the same frame of reference and place them under the same conditions. The whole position can be summed up by a statement of the framers of the 1972 European Convention, to the effect that:

Where Article 26 permits execution against the property of a foreign State in the State of the forum conservatory measures may also be taken against such property with a view to ensuring eventual execution of the judgment.[130]

The German Federal Constitutional Court discussed in the same breath 'preventive measures and measures of forced execution against foreign States',[131] or 'execution against the assets of a foreign State on the basis of a [final] judgment on the merits' and 'coercive measures against the assets of a foreign State to protect claims brought by creditors, where such measures are based on a decision rendered in proceedings for interim relief.[132] Thus, in the German practice:

The restrictive immunity of the foreign state which applies to a suit on a debt in Germany applies also to the petition for a preliminary attachment ... If exercise of jurisdiction is permissible, attachment on the local assets of a foreign state is also permissible.[133]

On the other hand:

assets of a foreign State situated or present within the State of the forum cannot be subjected to measures of enforcement or even safeguarding measures without the consent of the foreign State concerned, so long as they serve sovereign purposes of that State.[134]

In Switzerland, the power of the court to impose enforcement measures (including prejudgment attachment as a safeguarding measure), which is regarded as flowing from the power to adjudicate, is allowed with respect to acts *jure gestionis* connected with Swiss territory.[135]

The Italian Court of Cassation, in the case of *Condor*, said:

If immunity from jurisdiction does not apply to activities *jure privatorum*, the same must be true for immunity from the execution of a judgment that has recognized a private claim, where the foreign State does not comply with that judgment ... This argument applies also to provisional measures, which aim at preserving the guarantee of the debt.[136]

The French practice applies exactly the same criteria for both the so-called 'conservatory attachment' (prejudgment attachment for the purposes of guaranteeing payment of a possible judgment debt) and post-judgment execution. In fact, 'conservatory attachment' (*saisie conservatoire*) is so popular in the French legal process that most, if not all, reported French cases deal with this measure, and it is precisely in these cases that the French courts lay down their rules for 'immunity from execution', which thus covers both pre- and post-judgment stages.[137] On the whole, the French courts use the word 'execution' to refer to both conservatory or interim measures and the actual execution of judgments. To avoid confusion, one has to be careful in any particular case whether by the word 'execution' the court means a pre- or a post-judgment measure. Thus, the Court of Appeal of Paris said that:

[This Court] considers that the immunity from execution which applies to the property of a foreign State is not absolute and can be set aside in exceptional cases wherever the property seized is allocated, at the wishes of that State, for the performance of a purely commercial purpose.[138]

380   MEASURES OF CONSTRAINT

It was in a case concerning provisional measures. In that case, in pursuit of claims for compensation following their dismissal, two former pilots of Air Zaire sought to obtain the attachment of aircraft of that company landing at Roissy airport in France, in order to guarantee payment of their debts.

Similarly, the French Court of Cassation declared, in *Creighton*, that:

> an undertaking entered into by a State signing an arbitration clause, to comply with the award in accordance with the provisions of Article 24 of the Arbitration Rules of the International Chamber of Commerce implies waiver by that State of its immunity from execution.[139]

It was actually referring to a conservatory attachment (*saisie conservatoire*) obtained pursuant to an arbitral award, a prejudgment measure which, in its own declared opinion, 'does not involve an examination of the merits of the case'.[140] For this reason, the above declaration of the loss of 'immunity from execution' must be understood in a very limited sense, with the result that it still remains doubtful, in the French judicial practice, whether an arbitration clause would constitute a waiver not only of immunity from adjudication but also of immunity from actual post-judgment execution. This is especially the case with regard to arbitral awards, since, according to the Court of Cassation, an *exequatur* (order of recognition and enforcement) granted by a court for an arbitral award 'does not itself constitute an act of execution of such a nature as to provoke the immunity from execution of the State in question'.[141] With such pronouncements that do more to befuddle than to elucidate, one is compelled to envisage two scenarios. Either the enforcement of arbitral awards is regarded with a most generous attitude by the French courts, with no immunity from execution (because seen as waived) available to foreign States, or more is yet to be considered when it comes to actual attachment of foreign State assets. The latter would appear more likely to be the case; for in *Noga*, where, pursuant to arbitration clauses in two loan agreements with the Soviet Union, Noga, a Swiss company, obtained arbitral awards from the Institute of Arbitration of the Chamber of Commerce of Stockholm, against the Russian Federation as the successor State. The awards were confirmed by Swedish courts. Noga then secured an order for the enforcement of the awards (*exequatur*) from the court of first instance of Paris and an attachment order for the attachment of bank accounts of, in particular, the Russian Embassy and other diplomatic missions. Upon Russia's appeal, the Court of Appeal of Paris held that the bank accounts were covered by immunity, on the ground that the simple statement in the contracts that 'the borrower waives all rights of immunity with regard to the application of the arbitral award rendered against it' did not constitute a waiver of 'diplomatic immunity from execution'.[142]

In Austria, adjudicative jurisdiction (including the taking of interim measures) can be established by the presence of property in Austria. Article 99 of the Jurisdictional Statute (JN) provides:

> Claims concerning property rights or interests against persons having no domicile in Austria may be brought before any Austrian court within whose jurisdiction area are located assets of such persons or the asset actually forming the object of the litigation.[143]

In *Neustein*, where an Austrian university professor, who had been appointed by authority of the Government of Indonesia as professor at an Indonesian university, sued Indonesia for premature termination of his contract of employment, the Austrian Supreme Court, while finding the employment relationship to be of a private law character, based Austrian jurisdiction on the presence of property within the Austrian territory (Indonesia 'or its Legation' had an account with a bank in Vienna). In the Court's opinion, since the contract of employment was a contract under private law, and since a bank credit in Vienna on which a foreign State or its diplomatic representatives abroad might draw was unquestionably an 'asset' in the sense of Article 99:

> Domestic jurisdiction therefore exists for the present dispute and the court has both jurisdiction over the subject matter and local jurisdiction to deal with the claim as well as the application for an interim injunction.[144]

That is to say, the mere fact that the defendant State owns some property in Austria would establish prima facie jurisdiction over the case. The Court pointed out, in particular, that:

> So far as the creation of jurisdiction under Article 99 is concerned it is irrelevant that such an asset may be exempt from execution, for example, on the ground of extraterritoriality.[145]

However, the Supreme Court more recently amended its position by interpreting the 'property' in this requirement as meaning *executable* property. That is to say, even though the foreign State may own property in Austria, Austrian jurisdiction may still not be established where such property, being used for sovereign purposes, cannot be executed upon.[146] Here one finds a most interesting phenomenon, namely that

382 MEASURES OF CONSTRAINT

the possibility or impossibility of execution has a decisive impact on the exercise even of adjudicatory jurisdiction.

In this connection, an illustrative incident may be mentioned. In the *Nuclear Power Plant Injunction Case*, an Austrian national lodged a claim against Czechoslovakia for a mandatory injunction to prevent the construction of a nuclear power plant in that country. He alleged that the installation would seriously contaminate the land which he owned in Austria. The Supreme Court opined that Austrian jurisdiction could be established in the case since 'financial penalties exacted to enforce the claim ... could probably be enforced in Austria and any failure by the defendant to comply with a mandatory court injunction could provide a legal ground for a claim to damages brought by the plaintiff'.[147] Such reliance upon a flimsy ground of the mere possibility of a fine was treated with scorn in the local appellate court, which, in what would be regarded as an act of utmost irreverence in a common law country, reprimanded the Supreme Court for the suggestion of Austrian jurisdiction and declared that the latter's line of reasoning did not 'stand up to closer examination',[148] saying that:

municipal execution by the imposition of a penalty or imprisonment, in order to enforce an order to desist [from certain action] abroad, constitutes a deliberate attempt at trans-frontier judicial interference and is therefore an infringement of foreign sovereignty ... Furthermore no Austrian court has enforcement jurisdiction because the territorial competence of the court levying execution is governed by the law of the place where the order concerning the obligation is to be served ... How an unenforceable judicial order to desist [from certain action] can provide a legal basis for a claim to damages is incomprehensible.[149]

The German courts also adopt an 'executability' test. In the *Garden Contamination Case (2)*, it was declared that, for the purposes of the so-called 'situs jurisdiction', the plaintiff must not only prove that the defendant has property within the area of the court in question by indicating a specific piece of property; but he must also, where embassy property is included within the inventory of the targeted property, show that certain specified property within the Embassy was used for non-sovereign State activity, so as to overcome diplomatic immunity.[150] That is to say, the situs jurisdiction can only be founded where the defendant State has non-immune, i.e. executable property within the jurisdictional area of the court. In other words, whereas, in a case against a private person, only the *situs* of that person's property within the court's area will suffice, in a case against a foreign State, the establishment of the situs jurisdiction requires more: it requires both the *situs* and the *non-immunity* of foreign State property.

By contrast, in *Forth Tugs*, the Scottish Court of Session held that the possession of immovable property (called 'heritage') within the territorial jurisdiction was sufficient to found jurisdiction against a foreigner in the Scottish courts, even though the property in question, the building of the US Consulate-General in Edinburgh, could not be subjected to execution.[151] In other words, even *non-executable* property can establish jurisdiction in Scotland. Besides, the fact that the value of the property within the jurisdiction was insufficient to satisfy the judgment debt did not, for example, oust the jurisdiction of the courts.

4.2.2. Under more liberal conditions

The Australia FSIA, while subjecting executionary measures to more detailed conditions, provides that 'a court may make any order (including an order for interim or final relief) against a foreign State that it may otherwise lawfully make' except for 'an order that a foreign State employ a person or re-instate a person in employment' (section 29).

The drafters thus explain:

a court with jurisdiction over a case should be able to make such orders (including interim or final orders, and orders of a procedural or substantive character) as are appropriate and otherwise within power. This extends to remedies such as injunctions or orders for specific performance against a foreign state ... The basic principle is that, if jurisdiction is permissible, it should in the absence of special circumstances be possible to make it effective.[152]

4.2.3. Under stricter conditions

The 2004 UN Convention treats prejudgment measures separately from post-judgment measures and sets them forth in two separate articles. Article 18, entitled 'State immunity from pre-judgment measures of constraint', provides:

No pre-judgment measures of constraint, such as attachment or arrest, against property of a State may be taken in connection with a proceeding before a court of another State unless and except to the extent that:

(a) the State has expressly consented to the taking of such measures ... or
(b) the State has allocated or earmarked property for the satisfaction of the claim which is the object of that proceeding.

As for 'allocated or earmarked', the drafters of the original article explained:

384   MEASURES OF CONSTRAINT

This should have the effect of preventing extraneous or unprotected claimants from frustrating the intention of the State to satisfy specific claims or to make payment for an admitted liability.[153]

In other words, this is to ensure that property specifically set aside for the definite purpose of satisfying a particular claim should be used for none other than that purpose. It is not possible to envisage such an allocation or earmarking without a conscious and deliberate decision on the part of the defendant State to relinquish any claim of immunity from enforcement with regard to the allocated or earmarked property. This part of the provision can therefore be seen as laying down a scheme whereby a defendant State can *impliedly* give its consent to the taking of prejudgment measures.

This article is to be contrasted with Article 19, entitled 'State immunity from post-judgment measures of constraint':

No post-judgment measures of constraint, such as attachment, arrest or execution, against property of a State may be taken in connection with a proceeding before a court of another State unless and except to the extent that:

(a) the State has expressly consented to the taking of such measures . . . or
(b) the State has allocated or earmarked property for the satisfaction of the claim which is the object of that proceeding; or
(c) it has been established that the property is specifically in use or intended for use by the State for other than government non-commercial purposes and is in the territory of the State of the forum, provided that post-judgment measures of constraint may only be taken against property that has a connection with the entity against which the proceeding was directed.

Article 19(a) and (b) reproduce the provisions of Article 18, while Article 19(c) makes special provisions allowing post-judgment measures where the property is used for commercial purposes. This shows that even *commercial property* cannot be made the subject of prejudgment measures if the conditions in Article 18 are not fulfilled.

The UK SIA likewise imposes more restrictions on prejudgment measures. Section 13 prohibits injunctive relief against a State in the absence of written consent of the State concerned but allows execution either with written consent, or, in the case of commercial property, in the absence of written consent. For this purpose, mere submission to the jurisdiction of the courts is not to be regarded as consent (section 13(2), (3), (4)).

The relevant parts of section 13 read:

> (2) Subject to subsections (3) and (4) below –
>   (a) relief shall not be given against a State by way of injunction or order for specific performance or for the recovery of land or other property; and
>   (b) the property of a State shall not be subject to any process for the enforcement of a judgment or arbitration award or, in an action *in rem*, for its arrest, detention or sale.
> (3) Subsection (2) above does not prevent the giving of any relief or the issue of any process with the written consent of the State concerned; and any such consent (which may be contained in a prior agreement) may be expressed so as to apply to a limited extent or generally; but a provision merely submitting to the jurisdiction of the courts is not to be regarded as a consent for the purposes of this subsection.
> (4) Subsection (2)(b) above does not prevent the issue of any process in respect of property which is for the time being in use or intended for use for commercial purposes.[154]

In the English jurisprudence, prejudgment measures take the form of an injunction, hence the term 'injunctive relief'. The most famed is the so-called *Mareva* injunction,[155] which is an interlocutory order, often granted *ex parte* for the purpose of preventing the defendant from removing his assets from the jurisdiction of the court or otherwise disposing of them so as to frustrate an eventual judgment. It may be granted at any stage in an action or proposed action. To add to its power, the *Mareva* injunction can be used together with an *Anton Piller* order[156] and *ne exeat regno* writ.[157] It is a remedy *in personam* so that non-compliance is punished as contempt of court. In any case, strictly speaking, it is not prejudgment attachment, which operates *in rem*.[158] Under the Civil Procedure Rules 1998 for England and Wales (SI 1998/3132, which came into force on 26 April 1999), these terms have now been replaced by new ones: '*Mareva* injunction' by 'freezing injunction' (rule 25.1(1)(f)), '*Anton Piller* order' by 'search order' (rule 25.1(1)(h)) and '*ex parte*' by 'without notice' (rule 25.3(1)).

The *Mareva* injunction was briefly granted in cases against the Central Bank of Nigeria.[159] However, the enactment of the UK SIA quickly put an end to injunctive relief against a foreign State in the absence of written consent.[160] Consequently, the normally swift and decisive remedy available in cases of private litigation is no longer available when a foreign State is involved. Of course, with the written consent or waiver of immunity of a foreign State, a court can still grant a *Mareva* injunction[161] or some other type of injunction, such as an anti-suit injunction.[162] Besides, since section 13(2)(a) only bans injunctive relief 'against

386 MEASURES OF CONSTRAINT

a *State*', it would seem that *separate entities*, which are not included in the definition of State, are not exempt from such relief even where they can claim immunity. In this connection, it is worth recalling that section 14(1) of the UK SIA defines a 'State' as including references to:

(a) the sovereign or other head of that State in his public capacity;
(b) the government of that State; and (c) any department of that government, but not to any entity (hereafter referred to as a 'separate entity') which is distinct from the executive organs of the government of the State and capable of suing or being sued.

Since the definition of State is confined to the most essential and core organs of the State, the term 'separate entities' is extensive enough to cover the myriad agencies and instrumentalities established by the State to carry out governmental functions, as well as those for commercial or other non-governmental purposes. Thus the possible reach of the injunctive relief is not as restricted as it may first appear. For one thing, since central banks are normally 'distinct from the executive organs of the government of the State and capable of suing or being sued', the *Mareva*/freezing injunction can certainly still be imposed on foreign central banks under the UK SIA.

Just like the UK SIA, the US FSIA imposes stricter conditions for prejudgment attachment than for actual execution. Section 1610(d) stipulates:

(d) The property of a foreign state ... used for a commercial activity in the United States, shall not be immune from attachment prior to the entry of judgment ... if –
(1) the foreign state has explicitly waived its immunity from attachment prior to judgment ... and
(2) the purpose of the attachment is to secure satisfaction of a judgment that has been or may ultimately be entered against the foreign state, and not to obtain jurisdiction.

By contrast, section 1610(a) makes the following provision for post-judgment attachment or execution:

The property in the United States of a foreign state ... used for a commercial activity in the United States, shall not be immune from attachment in aid of execution, or from execution ... if –

(1) the foreign state has waived its immunity from attachment in aid of execution or from execution either explicitly or by implication ... or
(2) the property is or was used for the commercial activity upon which the claim is based.

The greatest difference between immunity from prejudgment attachment and immunity from post-judgment attachment and execution is that immunity from prejudgment attachment must be explicitly waived[163] while immunity from execution can be waived either explicitly or implicitly. Furthermore, while immunity from prejudgment attachment cannot be denied without an explicit waiver, immunity from execution can be denied in a number of situations besides waiver. The reason for more limitations on prejudgment or provisional measures is that such measures are, because they are normally granted *ex parte* before a full exploration of issues in a case, too 'disruptive' or 'harassing' to be 'freely granted' without incurring 'potential foreign policy implications'.[164]

This over-strict approach to prejudgment attachment has led to much criticism over the years and to a series of (unsuccessful) amendment efforts during the 1980s.[165] Before the enactment of the FSIA, attachment of foreign State property to establish jurisdiction (attachment *ad fundandam jurisdictionem*) used to be a popular way of starting lawsuits in the US. In 1959, the State Department even went so far as to assert that jurisdiction 'could not be obtained otherwise'.[166] However, as pointed out by the drafters of the FSIA:

Attachments for jurisdictional purposes have been criticized as involving U.S. courts in litigation not involving any significant U.S. interest or jurisdictional contacts, apart from the fortuitous presence of property in the jurisdiction ... Such attachments can also give rise to serious friction in United States' foreign relations.[167]

The US FSIA therefore places prejudgment attachment under three important restrictions: first, the property must be 'used for a commercial activity in the United States'; secondly, the foreign State must have 'explicitly waived its immunity from attachment prior to judgment'; and thirdly, the purpose of the attachment must be 'to secure satisfaction of a judgment[168] that has been or may ultimately be entered against the foreign state, and not to obtain jurisdiction'.

Thus, in order for a prejudgment attachment order to stand, not only must the relevant property be used for a commercial activity in the US (that is, having a territorial nexus apart from serving a commercial purpose) but there also has to be an explicit waiver, and the attachment must only serve a limited, judgment-related purpose. An explicit waiver itself does not necessarily lead to the upholding of a prejudgment attachment order unless the property is used for a commercial activity and is

388   MEASURES OF CONSTRAINT

located within the US.[169] Moreover, that certain property is commercial property does not mean that that property is attachable, if a judgment in the plaintiff's favour is not ultimately obtainable. Mere presence of certain property in the US is not enough.[170] Briefly, in granting prejudgment attachment, three requirements have to be satisfied: (1) there must be an explicit waiver; (2) the targeted property must be or must have been used by the foreign State in the US for commercial purposes; and (3) the purpose of the attachment is to obtain security, not jurisdiction, i.e. to secure satisfaction of a judgment which the court already has competence to render.[171] We can sum up the essence of these restrictions in four words: explicitness, commerciality, territoriality and specificity:

(1) explicitness: the waiver must be explicit;
(2) commerciality: the property in question must be or must have been used by the foreign State for a commercial activity;
(3) territoriality: the property must be in the US; and
(4) specificity: the waiver must be made specifically for prejudgment attachment; and the attachment must be judgment-specific.

The most decisive factor is the waiver, for in the absence of an explicit waiver, no prejudgment attachment can take place, even with regard to commercial property. Much of the case law thus centres on the notion of an 'explicit waiver'. It is not disputed that waiver of immunity from prejudgment attachment must be explicit.[172] It is also generally agreed that an explicit waiver means that the waiver must be clear, unequivocal, unambiguous and unmistakable.[173] Where a contractual clause expressly waives 'immunity from attachment before/prior to judgment', that is naturally such an explicit waiver.[174] Waiver of immunity 'with respect to any attachment' is also an explicit waiver of immunity from prejudgment attachment.[175] The word 'attachment', without qualification, has even been held capable of explicitly waiving immunity from both pre- and post-judgment attachment.[176]

What is in dispute is whether a waiver by a foreign State, where it is indeed explicit, in the sense that it is clear and unmistakable, must mention 'prejudgment attachment' for it to be an explicit waiver of immunity from prejudgment attachment. The now standard position of the US judiciary is that, even though an exact intonation of 'prejudgment attachment' is not necessary, the waiver has nonetheless to be unambiguous enough for the court to reach a conclusion in favour of prejudgment attachment. In the leading case of *Libra Bank*, the court held that the purpose of section 1610(d)(1) was to preclude unintended, inadvertent, implied, or constructive waiver in cases where the intent of the foreign State was equivocal or ambiguous. The provision did not require verbatim recitation, or express reference to, or express enumeration of immunity from prejudgment attachment as one of the waived immunities. If the waiver was clear and unambiguous, then it was explicit. So when the defendant foreign State entity in promissory notes 'irrevocably and unconditionally waives any right or immunity from legal proceedings including suit judgment and execution on grounds of sovereignty which it or its property may now or hereafter enjoy', that evinced a clear and unambiguous intent to waive all claims of immunity in all legal proceedings, including prejudgment attachment, which is a form of 'legal proceedings'.[177]

An explicit waiver can also be obtained through a less direct route. The case of *Banco de Seguros* concerned the power of an arbitrator to order a letter of credit as security against a possible final award. According to the Second Circuit, although the 'Umbrella Agreements' in dispute did not explicitly authorize the arbitrator to do so, their arbitration clause, by stating that the arbitrators 'are relieved of all judicial formalities and may abstain from following the strict rules of law', endowed them with wide discretion to order remedies they might deem appropriate, including the power to require a posting of pre-hearing security. Therefore, the foreign State entity in this case had explicitly waived its immunity from prejudgment attachment.[178]

By contrast, waiver of immunity merely from 'other liability', in a waiver clause under which the defendant 'shall not claim or enjoy immunity from suit, execution of judgment, or other liability',[179] does not constitute an explicit waiver of immunity from prejudgment attachment.[180] Nor is immunity from prejudgment attachment explicitly waived by a 'Service of Suit Clause' in reinsurance treaties which provides that the reinsurers 'will submit to the jurisdiction of any Court of competent jurisdiction within the United States and will comply with all requirements necessary to give such Court jurisdiction and all matters arising hereunder shall be determined in accordance with the law and practice of such Court'.[181]

There arises another question. Since section 1610(d) only refers to prejudgment *attachment*, it may be asked whether the FSIA permits the granting of a preliminary or interim *injunction* preventing foreign States from transferring assets abroad, or indeed any other measures, such as finding a contempt of court.[182] The standard position is that the term 'prejudgment attachment' includes an injunction, so that where a foreign State is not entitled to immunity from prejudgment attachment, it can also be subjected to injunction.[183] On the other hand, where a foreign State is indeed protected from prejudgment attachment, then the court cannot grant an injunction, or 'any other means to effect the same result', on the ground that, literally, the FSIA mentions no 'immunity from injunction', since:

> The FSIA would become meaningless if courts could eviscerate its protections merely by denominating their restraints as injunctions against the negotiation or use of property rather than as attachments of that property ... [C]ourts in this context may not grant, by injunction, relief which they may not provide by attachment.[184]

5. The conditions for measures of constraint

The conditions for measures of constraint are of considerable practical importance, since these are really the operative rules that determine whether or not measures of constraint will be granted. These conditions are either laid down by statutes or have evolved through case law. As such, some of them indeed tend to be more closely connected to the practice of particular States, whereas others would be of more general applicability.

5.1. Waiver

Because of the prevalent disinclination for, even aversion to, forcible measures against a foreign State and its property, even if such measures are but a rightful exercise of territorial jurisdiction, absolute immunity dies hard with respect to enforcement measures. Consent of the defendant State, a hallmark of the era of absolutism, has survived the vicissitudes of history and remains pivotal in activating measures of constraint, even when it has been decided, through the adjudicative process, that the foreign State is or, for the purposes of interim measures, may most probably be liable. Thus, unlike in the case of immunity from adjudication, waiver emerges as the most important condition for the taking of measures of constraint, especially in the States with immunity legislation. As a matter of practical necessity, at the very least there will be no need to decide the awkward issue of public/private purpose so long as a waiver, whether explicit or implicit, can be or has been obtained from the defendant State. The first question is whether a waiver of immunity from adjudication extends equally to immunity from measures of constraint. As noted previously, the prevailing position now is that waiver of immunity from suit does not automatically mean waiver of immunity from measures of constraint.

The next question is the manner in which waiver is to be effected. On this point current instruments display some diversity, though the general tenor remains constant. The US FSIA stipulates explicit or implicit waiver for execution (section 1610(a)(1) and (b)(1)), but requires explicit waiver for prejudgment attachment (section 1610(d)(1)) and for execution on foreign central bank property (section 1611(b)(1)). Likewise, the Canada SIA permits execution in case of explicit or implicit waiver (section 12(1)(a)) but allows injunctive relief only in case of 'consent in writing' (section 11(1)). The UK SIA requires 'written consent of the State concerned' (i.e. explicit waiver) for both injunctive relief and execution (section 13(3)).[185] This is in line with the 1972 European Convention, Article 23 of which provides that:

No measures of execution or preventive measures against the property of a Contracting State may be taken in the territory of another Contracting State except where and to the extent that the State has expressly consented thereto in writing in any particular case.

Similarly, Articles 18(a) and 19(a) of the 2004 UN Convention prescribe exactly the same manner for a defendant State to consent to prejudgment and post-judgment measures of constraint, that is:

the State has expressly consented to the taking of such measures as indicated:

   (i) by international agreement;
  (ii) by an arbitration agreement or in a written contract; or
 (iii) by a declaration before the court or by a written communication after a dispute between the parties has arisen.

The Australia FSIA merely says that a foreign State 'may at any time by agreement' waive immunity from execution (section 31(1)) without specifying whether it should be explicit or implicit. However, the legislative intent seems to be that this has to be a *written* agreement. Not only does section 31(4) provide that:

A waiver does not apply in relation to property that is diplomatic property or military property unless *a provision in the agreement* expressly designates the property as property to which the waiver applies (emphasis added)

but the drafters also stated in unequivocal terms that:

Unlike immunity from jurisdiction, there should be no scope for waiver of immunity from execution arising by implication. In particular it should not be implied from a waiver of immunity from jurisdiction that immunity from execution has thereby been waived.[186]

One also finds waivers subjected to certain qualifications in some instruments. Under Article 23 of the European Convention, measures of execution or preventive measures against the property of a Contracting State can only be taken 'to the extent that the State has expressly consented thereto in writing in any particular case'. Under the UK SIA a waiver 'may be expressed so as to apply to a limited extent or generally' (section 13(3));[187] the Canada SIA stipulates that 'the relief granted shall not be greater than that consented to by the state' (section 11(1)); while the Australia FSIA says that 'the waiver may be subject to specified limitations' (section 31(2)).

Under some instruments waiver may not be withdrawn except in accordance with its terms.[188]

5.2. The 'purpose' test

The 'purpose' test at the enforcement stage, which plays a largely complementary role to the requirement of consent/waiver, is a carry-over of the time-honoured *jure imperii / jure gestionis* dichotomy from the adjudicative stage. Having dismissed the purpose or motive behind a particular act as indecisive or even irrelevant for the purpose of exercising adjudicative jurisdiction, courts now, without remorse, refer to the uses or purposes of foreign State property as the determinative criterion for the attachability of that property. This volte-face at the interface of two stages of the judicial process is a vivid condensation of the whole history of State immunity as a series of practical adjustments in complete disregard of doctrinal consistency and coherence. It reflects the realization or concession that the 'nature' test, which, by assimilating the State in its commercial garb to a private individual, has proved so effective in holding a foreign State liable for its debt, is now unworkable, not because it all of a sudden ceases to be tenable theoretically, but because disastrous consequences would ensue should one insist on applying it to the property of a foreign State upon which execution is to be levied. If you put the embassy of a foreign State out of operation by forcibly seizing its bank accounts, your embassy in that State would be closed down too, with or without a court judgment. It is that simple. True, the 'nature' test is most useful; but what test can be so dear as to be purchased at the price of a cessation of diplomatic relations?

As has been shown previously, current State practice is remarkably unanimous in treating the 'purpose' of the property as a foremost condition for measures of constraint. According to the universally accepted position, the purpose or use for which the property is destined determines whether the property can be levied upon in a particular case. A distinction is thus drawn between two types of property. On the one hand, the property used or designated for governmental, public, non-commercial or sovereign purposes or functions will be immune from enforcement measures, even if the original claim may have been based on *jure gestionis* activities of the foreign State; on the other hand, the property used or intended for use for non-governmental, private or commercial purposes or activities will be subjected to execution. Such an approach immediately leads to a characterization problem, namely, how to ascertain whether the particular property against which execution is sought is devoted to commercial or non-commercial purposes. Since the property used for a commercial or private-law activity will not be immune from enforcement, it becomes imperative again to consider what is a commercial activity at the enforcement stage. This brings back the whole lot of the complicated and perplexing issues concerning the criteria for distinguishing between *acta jure imperii* and *acta jure gestionis* during the adjudicative proceedings. The court, having just overcome the difficulty in characterizing activities as *jure imperii* and *jure gestionis*, and having just decided that there is indeed a commercial activity for which the foreign State does not enjoy immunity, must now consider the issue anew for the purposes of enforcement measures.

What is more, it bears reiterating that, at the adjudicatory stage, many courts tend to discredit the 'purpose' test by declaring that the 'nature' of the act of the foreign State is the sole criterion for deciding the issue of immunity. The inadequacy of the 'nature' test is nowhere more acutely felt than in the area of enforcement measures. As we have seen, the essence of the 'nature' test is to place a foreign State and a private individual on an equal footing: if something can be done by a private person, then that is an act *jure gestionis*; that, in doing it, the foreign State also sought to achieve some sovereign objective is irrelevant. Such a test tends to be unworkable with regard to enforcement measures. Since, in most cases, the property (such as a building or a bank account) held by a foreign State is by *nature* no different from that held by a private person (a private person can also own buildings and bank accounts), a rule that would place a foreign State and a private person on absolute parity and would thus preclude the purpose served by the property (the building being used to house a diplomatic mission, or the account being used for the functioning of such a mission) would subject almost any foreign State property to enforcement or executory measures. Such a scenario will be as undesirable as it is disastrous.

Given the ever-present problem of the distinction between *acta jure imperii* and *acta jure gestionis*, which has been reintroduced into the execution stage by the notion of public purposes, it seems only too natural to expect, as does the UN Convention, that the foreign State would allocate or earmark certain funds for the purpose of satisfying any judgment that might be rendered against it in the future with regard to commercial or non-public dealings with private individuals or companies (as contemplated in Articles 18 and 19 of the UN Convention). In any event, allocation or earmarking will no doubt save the trouble of ascertaining the public or private purpose/use of the property concerned, thereby giving both the court and the private litigant a great measure of certainty.

5.3. Separate entity ownership

A separate entity is an entity, incorporated or otherwise, which is separate from the State and has an independent legal personality, can possess and dispose of property and is capable of suing and being sued. While it is always difficult to ascertain the public or private purpose of foreign State property, the fact that certain property is owned or operated by a separate entity engaged in commercial activities provides strong evidence that the particular property is used for commercial purposes. Furthermore, execution against separate entity property would be the least offensive since, in theory at least, the property of the State itself is untouched. Consequently, courts seldom hesitate to attach or seize the property of a separate entity to satisfy a judgment. The primary concern is, of course, that there should be a clear distinction between the State and the entity.

5.3.1. Legal instruments

In one way or another, current legal instruments treat a foreign State and its separate entities separately.

The US FSIA affords exactly the same protection to a foreign State and its agencies and instrumentalities as regards prejudgment attachment, but draws a clear distinction between the property of a foreign State and the property of an agency or instrumentality of a foreign State in relation to post-judgment attachment. It does this, though, in a somewhat convoluted manner. Leaving aside the provisions on waiver and others, the relevant parts of section 1610 read:

(a) The property in the United States of a foreign state, as defined in section 1603(a) ... used for a commercial activity in the United States, shall not be immune from attachment in aid of execution, or from execution ... if –
  (2) the property is or was used for the commercial activity upon which the claim is based,
(b) In addition to subsection (a), any property in the United States of an agency or instrumentality of a foreign state engaged in commercial activity in the United States shall not be immune from attachment in aid of execution, or from execution ... if –
  (2) the judgment relates to a claim for which the agency or instrumentality is not immune ... regardless of whether the property is or was involved in the act upon which the claim is based.
  ...
(d) The property of a foreign state, as defined in section 1603(a) ... used for a commercial activity in the United States, shall not be immune from attachment prior to the entry of judgment ... if –
  (1) the foreign state has explicitly waived its immunity from attachment prior to judgment ... and
  (2) the purpose of the attachment is to secure satisfaction of a judgment that has been or may ultimately be entered against the foreign state, and not to obtain jurisdiction.

The first thing to note is that the concept of 'foreign State' in section 1610 is 'as defined in section 1603(a)'; and section 1603(a) provides that a '"foreign state" ... includes a political subdivision of a foreign state or an *agency or instrumentality* of a foreign state' (emphasis added). Thus the starting point is that an agency or instrumentality of a foreign State, such as a State-owned enterprise, is given the same protection as the State in respect of both prejudgment and post-judgment attachment, as the term 'foreign State' in section 1610(a) and (d), by virtue of section 1603(a), must include an agency or instrumentality. This conclusion is supported by the legislative report.[189] That explains the necessity of the phrase 'in addition to subsection (a)' in section 1610(b), which, in defiance of section 1603(a), purports to treat agencies and instrumentalities of a foreign State differently from the foreign State itself with regard to post-judgment attachment. Still, in this connection, the FSIA becomes self-contradictory, for it demands two diametrically opposed attitudes of the reader: when you read section 1610(a) and (d), you must think of a 'foreign State' as *including* its agencies and instrumentalities; but, when you come to section 1610(b), you must consider a 'foreign State' as *minus* its agencies and instrumentalities.

Be that as it may, the different treatment of a foreign State and its agencies and instrumentalities consists in this: for the purposes of 'attachment in aid of execution, or from execution', i.e. post-judgment attachment, it is enough that an agency or instrumentality of a foreign State is engaged in commercial activity in the US. By virtue of section 1610(b)(2), so long as 'the judgment relates to a claim for which the agency or instrumentality is not immune' under the FSIA, then execution can be levied upon 'any property, commercial and non-commercial, of the agency or instrumentality',[190] 'regardless of whether the property is or was involved in the act upon which the claim is based'. By contrast, for the property of the foreign State itself to be levied upon, the property must be or have been 'used for a commercial activity in the United States', and it must be or have been 'used for the commercial activity upon which the claim is based'. In other words, in the case of a foreign State (narrowly defined), the targeted property must not only be commercial property; it must also be commercial property with a specific connection with the proceedings. Two main differences in the treatment of a foreign State and its agencies or instrumentalities can be summed up here: first, while the property of a foreign State can be executed upon only if it is 'used for a commercial activity', '*any* property of an agency or instrumentality of a foreign State' (emphasis added) can be attached, regardless of its use; secondly, whereas the attachable property of a foreign State must not only be commercial but must also be or have been 'used for the commercial activity upon which the claim is based', the property of an agency or instrumentality can be attached 'regardless of whether the property is or was involved in the act upon which the claim is based'.[191] All that matters is that the agency or instrumentality should be 'engaged in commercial activity in the United States'. Thus, there is a shift of focus from the *use of the property* in the case of a foreign State to the *engagement in commercial activity* where an agency or instrumentality is sued. In the latter case, the use of the property becomes irrelevant.

The separateness and distinctness between a foreign State and its entities also means that a judgment against a foreign State cannot be enforced against a State entity, and vice versa. In *Hercaire*, the Court of Appeals vacated a district court's order attaching the aircraft of the Argentine national airline company (Aerolineas) for the purpose of providing security for a judgment against Argentina;[192] and in *Letelier*,

THE CONDITIONS FOR MEASURES OF CONSTRAINT   397

an attempt to seize the property of the Chilean national airline to execute a judgment against Chile arising from an assassination in the US was rejected for the same reason.[193]

Under the UK SIA, a 'separate entity' 'which is distinct from the executive organs of the government of the State and capable of suing or being sued', is not included in the definition of a 'State' (section 14(1)). Such an entity is immune only with respect to 'anything done by it in the exercise of sovereign authority' (section 14(2)). Section 14(3) goes on to provide:

If a separate entity (not being a State's central bank or other monetary authority) submits to the jurisdiction in respect of proceedings in the case of which it is entitled to immunity by virtue of subsection (2) above, subsections (1) to (4) of section 13 above shall apply to it in respect of those proceedings as if references to a State were references to that entity.

That is to say, where a separate entity is immune from adjudicative proceedings, it enjoys exactly the same immunity from enforcement as a foreign State; and a submission to adjudicative jurisdiction is not a submission to enforcement jurisdiction.[194] On the other hand, if such an entity is not immune, then its property will be attachable regardless of its uses. This format is in accord with that of the European Convention, under which 'the expression "Contracting State" shall not include any legal entity of a Contracting State which is distinct therefrom and is capable of suing or being sued, even if that entity has been entrusted with public functions' (Article 27(1)), and a separate entity is protected only 'in respect of acts performed by the entity in the exercise of sovereign authority (*acta jure imperii*)' (Article 27(2)).

Like the UK SIA, the Canada SIA also adopts a presumption of non-immunity for 'an agency of a foreign state', but manages to import the self-contradiction in the US FSIA. On the one hand, under section 2 of the SIA, the term 'foreign state' includes 'any agency of the foreign state' that is 'an organ of the foreign state but that is separate from the foreign state';[195] but, on the other hand, in the provision concerning enforcement jurisdiction, it excludes 'an agency of a foreign State' from the protection enjoyed by a foreign State, that is, by a foreign State *minus* its 'agency'. An 'agency of a foreign State' is *not*, like the State, protected against injunctive relief (section 11(3)), attachment, execution, arrest, detention, seizure and forfeiture (section 12(2)), and penalty or fine (section 13(2)). Whereas the Canada SIA provides that no injunctive relief 'may be granted against a foreign state' (section 11(1)), that 'property of a

398   MEASURES OF CONSTRAINT

foreign state' is immune from attachment and execution (section 12(1)), and that 'no penalty or fine may be imposed against a foreign state' (section 13(1)), the reader is expected, when reading these references, to construe them as *not including* an 'agency of a foreign State', despite the clear and unambiguous provisions of section 2.

5.3.2.   The practice of the States without immunity legislation

The same rule allowing attachment and execution against the property of separate entities also emerges from those States without immunity legislation. Thus, in the *NIOC Revenues Case*, the Germany Federal Constitutional Court, after an arduous journey through various cases and writings, upheld enforcement measures because the funds attached were held in accounts standing in the name of the company instead of the State. This very fact, according to the Court, meant that it was not necessary for the Court further to decide if the property was that of a foreign *State*: it was not, because it stood in the name of the company.[196] The general rule thus was:

The commercial undertakings of a foreign State which had the status of independent legal persons did not enjoy any immunity according to old-established German case law and legal doctrine.[197]

The French courts have since very early times sought to distinguish between the foreign State and its separate entities. At a time when absolute immunity was granted to the foreign State itself, the French courts upheld attachment and garnishee orders in cases against the Soviet Trade Delegation, on the ground that the transaction out of which the dispute had arisen was purely commercial in nature and that the property was in the possession of a separate entity instead of the Soviet State itself.[198]

The rule was further consolidated in the era of restrictive immunity. As declared by the Court of Cassation in *Société Sonatrach*:

a distinction is to be drawn [between two types of assets]. The assets of a foreign State are, in principle, not subject to seizure, subject to exceptions in particular where they have been allocated for an economic or commercial activity under private law which is at the origin of the title of the attaching debtor. On the other hand, the assets of public entities, whether personalized or not, which are distinct from the foreign State, may be subjected to attachment by all debtors of that entity, of whatever type, where the assets form part of a body of funds which that entity has allocated for a principal activity governed by private law.[199]

In this connection, the fact that the shares of the separate entity may be owned by the foreign State, or that the foreign State exercises supervision or control over the entity, or that the entity performs a devolved public service function, does not make that entity an emanation or a part of the State, or otherwise assimilated to it.[200] That is to say, being a separate entity means that the entity in question cannot partake of the immunity enjoyed by the State itself.

5.4. The 'connection' requirement

In some instances a particular connection is required before measures of constraint can be taken. These include a subject-matter connection, a territorial connection and an entity connection.

5.4.1. Subject-matter connection

Under section 1610(a)(2) of the US FSIA, execution can be levied upon the property of a foreign State if the property 'is or was used for the commercial activity upon which the claim is based'. One can at once see that this provision is patterned on the 'based upon' criterion found in the context of a 'commercial activity' in section 1605(a)(2). Whatever the original policy considerations for such a formula,[201] it has been persistently subjected to criticism.[202] In particular, even though section 1605(a)(5) of the FSIA allows action against a foreign State for personal injury or death, and damage to or loss of property occurring in the US, the plaintiff cannot have his judgment enforced unless it is covered by an insurance claim, which is often unavailable. Thus, while the plaintiff in *Letelier* successfully obtained a judgment against Chile with regard to the murder of former Chilean foreign minister in Washington by the secret service of Chile,[203] no property with a sufficient nexus with the assassination (which, besides, was not a 'commercial activity') could be found to enforce the judgment. The Second Circuit was compelled to draw the conclusion that, by legislating in this way, the Congress created 'a right without a remedy'.[204]

Apart from some occasional, inadvertent remarks,[205] courts in other countries seem to be quite unaware of such an issue.

5.4.2. Territorial connection – *Binnenbeziehung*

The requirement of *Binnenbeziehung* has been discussed elsewhere in this book.[206] Here I shall only examine its impact on the taking of enforcement measures. As noted previously, the seemingly relaxed rule of applying the same criteria to both adjudication and enforcement in the Swiss courts is circumscribed by two stringent restrictions: (1) sovereign/public purpose; and (2) territorial connection. Foreign State property reserved for sovereign purposes is not subject to enforcement or execution. Moreover, the fact that a particular transaction has a private-law character, though necessary, is insufficient for the levying of enforcement measures. There must also be a connection between the legal relationship in question and the Swiss territory. In other words, the Swiss courts apply a twofold test of *jus gestionis* and territorial nexus in the determination of immunity, including both immunity from adjudication and immunity from execution. Attachment of the property of a foreign State will be permissible only when (1) the claim arises out of a transaction of a private law nature and (2) the place of performance is in Switzerland or there otherwise exists a connection with the Swiss territory.

The rule of territorial connection dates back to the *Dreyfus* case, where the Swiss Federal Tribunal upheld an order of arrest against Austria because the claim arose from a debt relationship established within the Swiss territory: Austria had offered the litigated loan for subscription in Switzerland, and performance in Switzerland was explicitly provided for in the conditions of the loan.[207] The territorial connection requirement was later stated as follows:

In order to consider the debt out of which arose the claims for attachment as one established in Swiss territory, it should have been either originated, concluded, or performed here by the debtor, or there should have been at least such acts performed by the debtor for which he must have designated a place of performance in Switzerland.[208]

The absence of a territorial connection will be conclusive of the case. In *LIAMCO*, the Federal Tribunal found it unnecessary to determine whether Libya had acted *jure gestionis* or, by an arbitration clause, had waived its immunity, since Swiss law did not permit proceedings against a foreign State unless there was a close connection between the subject matter and Switzerland. In the present case, although the arbitration had taken place in Geneva, it had only done so because the Sole Arbitrator had so decided. That decision did not create a sufficient legal relationship with Switzerland where, as here, the subject matter at issue in the arbitration had no connection with Switzerland. The Tribunal said:

The Federal Court [*Bundesgericht*] does not permit court or enforcement proceedings against a foreign State when it is merely established that the foreign State is acting as possessor of private and not of sovereign rights. The Federal Court demands, in addition, that the legal relationship involved have a sufficient domestic relationship to the territory of Switzerland [*eine genügende Binnenbeziehung zum schweizerischen Staatsgebiet*].[209]

However, despite the ever-strict application of the requirement, its precise rationale has never been clearly articulated by the Swiss courts. It would seem that such a requirement has more to do with practical considerations of Swiss national interests, such as the 'concern for foreign governmental depositors in Swiss banks and the problem of having their assets attached',[210] and the need, given 'Switzerland's unique position as a banking centre', to prevent the Swiss courts from becoming 'a collecting agency for claims against foreign States all over the world'.[211] In the words of the Federal Tribunal:

> It is therefore – even if the legal dispute is based on a non-sovereign action of the foreign State – necessary that circumstances exist which tie the legal relationship to such an extent to Switzerland that it is justified to bring the foreign State before Swiss authorities, as there is no reason, and does not substantively make any sense, to permit legal actions against foreign States if a somewhat intensive domestic relationship is lacking [*wenn eine einigermassen intensive Binnenbeziehung fehlt*]. The interests of Switzerland do not require such a procedure; they could, on the contrary, easily cause political and other difficulties.[212]

5.4.3. The entity connection

The provision on execution in the 2004 UN Convention contains an entity connection requirement. Article 19(c) provides:

> No post-judgment measures of constraint, such as attachment, arrest or execution, against property of a State may be taken in connection with a proceeding before a court of another State unless and except to the extent that: (c) it has been established that the property is specifically in use or intended for use by the State for other than government non-commercial purposes and is in the territory of the State of the forum, provided that post-judgment measures of constraint may only be taken against property that has *a connection with the entity against which the proceeding was directed*. (Emphasis added.)

The term 'entity' is not defined in the Convention. However, the Annex to the Convention, which by virtue of Article 25 'forms an integral part of the Convention', contains an understanding regarding Article 19:

> The expression 'entity' in subparagraph (c) means the State as an independent legal personality, a constituent unit of a federal State, a subdivision of a State, an agency or instrumentality of a State or other entity, which enjoys independent legal personality.

402   MEASURES OF CONSTRAINT

The words 'property that has a connection with the entity' in subparagraph (c) are to be understood as broader than ownership or possession.

Article 19 does not prejudge the question of 'piercing the corporate veil', questions relating to a situation where a State entity has deliberately misrepresented its financial position or subsequently reduced its assets to avoid satisfying a claim, or other related issues.

Thus to a certain extent, with the word 'connection' undefined, Article 19(c) may permit the levying of execution upon the property of a State to satisfy a judgment against a State entity, or vice versa, provided some kind of connection can be shown. Compare this with the original 1991 ILC draft Article 18(c):

the property is specifically in use or intended for use by the State for other than government non-commercial purposes and is in the territory of the State of the forum and has a connection with the claim which is the object of the proceeding or with the agency or instrumentality against which the proceeding was directed.

One can see that, under the 2004 Convention, the scope of executable property is significantly broadened.

5.5.   The territorial presence requirement

Article 19(c) of the 2004 UN Convention contains a territorial presence requirement, that is, one of the conditions for post-judgment measures of constraint is that the targeted foreign State property must be 'in the territory of the State of the forum'.[213] This seems to owe its inspiration to section 1610(a)(1) and (2) of the US FSIA, which provides:

(a)   The property in the United States of a foreign state … used for a commercial activity in the United States, shall not be immune from attachment in aid of execution, or from execution … if –

(1)   the foreign state has waived its immunity from attachment in aid of execution or from execution either explicitly or by implication … or

(2)   the property is or was used for the commercial activity upon which the claim is based.

The chapeau of this subsection makes it abundantly clear that, even when a foreign State has completely waived its immunity from execution, the US courts still may execute only against 'property in the United States' that is 'used for a commercial activity in the United States'.[214] Two repetitions in this subsection attest to the peculiarity of the US FSIA: first, the repetition of the phrase 'used for a/the commercial activity', which means that not only must the property be used for a commercial activity, but the commercial activity must form the basis for the claim;[215] secondly, the awkward repetition of the phrase 'in the United States' in 'the property in the United States of a foreign state … used for a commercial activity in the United States', which amounts to a stringent, *double territoriality* requirement: in order for execution to be granted, the property must be both physically located *in the US* and used for a commercial activity *in the US*.[216]

Thus the *situs* of the property of a foreign State becomes a determinative test in US law because a court can only attach a foreign State's property if that property is in the US.[217] This strict territorial presence requirement means that every time a US court orders attachment or execution, it must ascertain whether the targeted property is 'in the United States'. Bad luck for the plaintiff if the assets are found to be located outside the US.[218] The process of assigning a location to particular property is replete with practical difficulties, especially in the case of intangible property, such as the obligation to pay royalties[219] or a letter of credit,[220] which has no physical existence and no actual situs, and whose situs therefore is only a 'legal fiction'.[221] The practical solution, naturally, is that 'the debt follows the debtor': the situs of a debt obligation is that of the debtor.[222]

Once it can be established that the foreign State has waived its immunity from execution, and that the targeted property has been used for commercial purposes, there is still the issue of *when* the property has to be in the US in order for the execution to be permissible. The issue is conveniently dubbed as the '§ 1610(a) situs snapshot', or the 'situs snapshot'.[223]

In *FG Hemisphere*, the Fifth Circuit considered the 'applicable time period during which the [royalty] obligations [against which garnishment is sought] must be in the United States for § 1610(a) purposes';[224] that is, whether the 'situs snapshot' should be taken when the writs of garnishment were issued (as the Congo defendants contended), or whether the situs determination should be made either when the suit commenced or when the garnishees received notice of the garnishment action against them (as argued by the plaintiff). The court held that, since the FSIA does not use the words 'was' or 'has been in the US', for the purposes of section 1610(a), 'the situs snapshot is taken when the court makes the § 1610(a) situs determination'; that is, stated differently, the foreign State's property must be in the US when the court authorizes execution. Such a result prevents 'garnishing

404   MEASURES OF CONSTRAINT

property that *was* in the United States but is now exclusively in a foreign country'.[225] To make it clearer:

tangible property that was in the United States at the onset of litigation, or when notice of the litigation was received, but was not there when a writ of garnishment was requested, issued, or served would not be considered 'property in the United States' for purposes of garnishment ... [T]he § 1610(a) situs of tangible property is its location when the court determines whether it is immune from execution. Similarly ... the situs of intangible property is the location of the garnishee when the immunity determination is made.[226]

5.6. *Executive oversight or authorization*

In a number of countries, chief among which are Italy[227] and Greece,[228] the executive branch retains a significant role in overseeing or even authorizing measures of constraint against foreign States.[229] The exact implications of such practice are yet to be fully assessed; but we can at least remark here that this shows an awareness on the part of these States that the issue of State immunity cannot be regarded as a purely judicial matter: there are political aspects involved that might better be dealt with by the political organs.

6. Categories of property under special protection

It is now the time to complete the list of hurdles a plaintiff must overcome before the execution against the property of a foreign State can become a reality. Certain categories of property are regarded as so sensitive that they are under special protection and absolutely immune from execution; that is, they cannot be subjected to execution without express consent of the foreign State concerned.

6.1. *Diplomatic property*

Here the term 'diplomatic property' is intended to be a generic term covering movable and immovable property of a foreign diplomatic or consular mission, or any other mission enjoying diplomatic privileges and immunities. Copious statements have been made by various courts, which it is neither possible, for lack of space, nor really necessary to cite here,[230] on the protection of diplomatic property (including embassy premises and bank accounts) from measures of constraint. They boil down to this: since the operation of embassies and other diplomatic/ consular missions is a quintessentially sovereign activity, diplomatic

CATEGORIES OF PROPERTY UNDER SPECIAL PROTECTION   405

property must be shielded from judicial processes, so as to ensure an unimpeded and unimpaired functioning of such missions (*ne impediatur legatio*) which is vital to the friendly relations between States and their – or rather their peoples' – well-being. Thus diplomatic property is absolutely immune from enforcement and execution unless the State concerned has explicitly, i.e. clearly and unequivocally, waived that immunity. In this regard, a simple statement that the foreign State 'waives all rights of immunity with regard to the application of the arbitral award rendered against it in relation to this contract' does not constitute an unequivocal waiver of immunity from execution of embassy bank accounts.[231]

This is the most prominent category of property under special protection, as can be seen from various statements on the 'purpose' test regarding enforcement measures, which often refer to bank accounts, premises and other property of embassies as the primary example of foreign State property used for sovereign purposes and therefore exempt from measures of constraint. The legal basis for this immunity actually extends beyond the immediate perimeter of the law of State immunity, and is to be found primarily in the treaties and customary international law relating to diplomatic and consular immunities.[232] The law of State immunity, however, has extended the scope of protection to cover items not specifically mentioned in the Vienna Conventions, such as embassy bank accounts, and has been especially generous in the protection of diplomatic property. When in doubt, grant immunity (*in dubio pro immunitate*); and an *abstract danger* that embassy functions might be hampered is sufficient to stop short any attempt to levy attachment and execution. This is, broadly speaking, the position of the law at present. The rule is now universally accepted that all diplomatic property, movable and immovable, is immune from attachment, arrest, seizure or any other form of forcible execution. Article 21(1)(a) of the 2004 UN Convention thus provides:

> property, including any bank account, which is used or intended for use in the performance of the functions of the diplomatic mission of the State or its consular posts, special missions, missions to international organizations or delegations to organs of international organizations or to international conferences ... shall not be considered as property specifically in use or intended for use by the State for other than government non-commercial purposes.[233]

6.1.1.   Diplomatic premises

The inviolability of diplomatic and consular premises has long been established in international law.[234] Section 1610(a)(4)(B) of the US FSIA protects the immovable property of a foreign State in the US that is 'used for purposes of maintaining a diplomatic or consular mission or the residence of the Chief of such mission'. According to the legislative report, such property includes 'embassies and *related buildings*'.[235] Thus in *S & S Machinery*, the court held that a Romanian Consulate building was immune from attachment. In the court's opinion, the term 'mission' was not restricted to the premises occupied, but meant a group of people sent by one State to another. The premises occupied by such personnel, such as the building in question in the present case, enjoyed the same inviolability as the mission's primary premises, i.e. its embassy, even if the persons working in such offices might not enjoy the same immunity.[236] From this it is but a small step towards holding that the term 'diplomatic premises' extended to the living quarters of the members of the mission. In *US* v. *Arlington*, the court had to consider whether the provision of section 1610(a)(4)(B) should be interpreted to include a building used by the embassy of the Democratic Republic of Germany exclusively for the housing of members of the mission and their families. The court upheld the immunity for the building on the ground that, because the property was owned by a foreign State, and was presently used exclusively by its diplomatic and consular staff and their families, it was not operated for profit as a commercial venture but served a public function. The court added that, although the purchase of the property was a commercial act, the commercial acquisition of the property could not indelibly stamp the use of the property as a commercial activity.[237]

There are also some interesting cases about the relevant time during which the diplomatic property can be immune from execution. In the *Hungarian Embassy Case*, the German Federal Supreme Court held that the immunity of embassy property from execution extended only so far as performance of the duties of the diplomatic mission required. The test was whether satisfaction of a claim by execution would interfere with the functioning of the mission. Where immovable property used for the purposes of the mission ceased to be so used, its immunity from execution automatically ended.[238] The English High Court is also of the view that State immunity only applies to premises currently used for the purposes of a diplomatic mission and does not apply to premises which have ceased to be used for diplomatic purposes.[239] Former consulate premises now used for rental will no longer be exempt from execution.[240]

On the other hand, a building which, although in the process of being sold and no longer used as an embassy residence, was still regularly used

CATEGORIES OF PROPERTY UNDER SPECIAL PROTECTION   407

by embassy staff for meetings and conferences, was regarded as still being used for sovereign purposes and therefore continued to be protected by immunity from execution.[241] Besides, diplomat premises are also immune from eviction orders.[242]

6.1.2. Embassy bank accounts

In contrast to diplomatic buildings, whose undisputed sovereign functions and purposes put them beyond the reach of enforcement measures, bank accounts, because of their fungible character, possible commercial uses to which they may be put, and the fact that in many cases they represent the only visible assets that a plaintiff may find of a foreign State, have been a popular target over the years. And yet courts have remained adamantly opposed to the taking of forcible measures against foreign embassy bank accounts, and have generally erred on the side of being over-cautious and over-protective. This should also apply to bank accounts of consulates and other missions.

The first point to note is that the protection for embassy bank accounts is nowhere mentioned in the 1961 Vienna Convention on Diplomatic Relations. As Article 22(3) of the Vienna Convention expressly protects 'the premises of the mission, their furnishings and other property *thereon*' (emphasis added), it might be argued that, since embassy bank accounts cannot possibly be physically *on* the premises of the embassy (they are *in* the bank – well, even this may be disputed under modern circumstances), then they cannot be protected by the provisions of Article 22(3). However, this point has rarely been urged in practice, and when it was, it was, unsurprisingly, rejected straightaway.[243] In general practice, therefore, it has simply been taken for granted that embassy bank accounts enjoy absolute immunity from execution. In the US, for example, even though the US FSIA only expressly protects the immovable property of an embassy,[244] embassy accounts have nonetheless been repeatedly held immune from attachment.[245]

The leading case concerning embassy bank accounts is the *Philippine Embassy Bank Account Case*, decided by the German Federal Constitutional Court, which laid down strict rules prohibiting execution against the bank accounts of a foreign embassy:

Claims against a general current bank account of the embassy of a foreign State which exists in the State of the forum and the purpose of which is to cover the embassy's costs and expenses are not subject to forced execution by the State of the forum.[246]

408 MEASURES OF CONSTRAINT

The principle of international law *ne impediatur legatio* precludes such measures where they might impair the exercise of diplomatic duties.[247]

... preventive measures or measures of execution against a foreign State may not, under international law, be levied on property which at the relevant time was being used by its diplomatic mission for the performance of its official functions ... Because of the difficulties of delimitation involved in judging whether that ability to function is endangered, and because of the potential for abuse, general international law makes the area of protection enjoyed by the foreign State very wide and refers to the typical *abstract danger*, but not to the specific threat to the ability of the diplomatic mission to function posed by measures on the part of the receiving State.[248]

The financial settlement of the costs and expenses of an embassy through a general current account of the sending State maintained with a bank in the receiving State pertains directly to the continued discharge of the diplomatic functions of the sending State, notwithstanding the fact that some transactions through such an account may, as regards relations with the bank or with third parties, be effected in the context of legal relationships or forms of activity which can, by their legal nature, be termed acts *iure gestionis*. Claims of the sending State on the bank arising out of such an account therefore enjoy, under general international law, at least the immunity afforded to diplomatic missions in respect of measures of execution. Taking any other view of the matter would mean that the executing authorities of the receiving State might have to ascertain the existence of funds in such an account and the purposes for which the sending State intended such funds or parts of them to be used. In the case of a general current account, it may be doubtful ... whether criteria for determining that some of the assets may be liable to attachment can be arrived at in this way.[249]

Moreover, for the executing authorities of the receiving State to require the sending State, without its consent, to provide details concerning the existence or the past, present or future purposes of funds in such an account would constitute interference, contrary to international law, in matters within the exclusive competence of the sending State.[250]

As for the exemption from the duty to provide evidence, the German Federal Supreme Court further elaborated:

The debtor, as a sovereign State, is however not required to disclose details of its sovereign activity, in particular the exercise of official functions by its diplomatic service. The taking of evidence in that regard would lead to the disclosure of internal matters (for example, the frequency with which the residency was used by members of the mission or by delegations, the number of persons, precise details of the purpose of the meetings), knowledge and review of which would infringe the principle of non-intervention in the exercise of another State's sovereign powers (*ne impediatur legatio*). It would, as a rule, exceed what

CATEGORIES OF PROPERTY UNDER SPECIAL PROTECTION   409

is permissible under international law if other States were required fully to prove the purposes of use establishing the obligation to grant immunity.[251]

The German jurisprudence on this issue has been widely regarded as authoritative. Courts in other countries, for their part, added further refinements. According to the Austrian Supreme Court in *Leasing West*:

> Claims against a general bank account of the embassy of a foreign State held in the State of the forum, which is also allocated *partly* [but not exclusively] to cover the embassy's costs and expenses, are therefore not subject to enforcement proceedings in the State of the forum without the consent of the foreign State concerned. Consequently, enforcement against a bank account of a foreign embassy, held within the jurisdiction of the forum State, will generally be excluded unless it can be shown ... that the account over which attachment in execution is sought serves *exclusively* private law purposes and therefore *exceptionally* is subject to enforcement. In the absence of such proof, an application for enforcement must be rejected.[252]

In a similar vein, Lord Diplock said in *Alcom*:

> The debt owed by the bank to the foreign sovereign state and represented by the credit balance in the current account kept by the diplomatic mission of that state as a possible subject matter of the enforcement jurisdiction of the court is, however, *one and indivisible*; it is not susceptible of anticipatory dissection into the various uses to which moneys drawn upon it might have been put in the future if it had not been subjected to attachment by garnishee proceedings. Unless it can be shown by the judgment creditor who is seeking to attach the credit balance by garnishee proceedings that the bank account was earmarked by the foreign state *solely* (save for de minimis exceptions) for being drawn upon to settle liabilities incurred in commercial transactions, as for example by issuing documentary credits in payment of the price of goods sold to the state, it cannot, in my view, be sensibly brought within the crucial words of the exception [to immunity from execution] for which section 13(4) provides.[253]

The general rule now is that embassy bank accounts enjoy absolute immunity from execution because of the peculiar character of such accounts. They enjoy immunity because they are used for the maintenance and functioning of the diplomatic mission; that is, they are destined for a public or sovereign purpose. In this respect, it is precisely this sovereign *purpose* that endows these accounts with a sovereign *nature*. Thus, even though a private person may also keep a bank account, the bank account kept by a foreign State for the maintenance of a diplomatic mission, by virtue of that sovereign purpose, is now different from the bank account of a private person, to such an extent that it can even be asserted that an embassy bank account has an intrinsically sovereign nature, which, in the eyes of the law, must shield it from enforcement measures. Once it is accepted that it is the inherent *nature* of the account itself that entitles it to special protection, then this account should always enjoy immunity as of its own right. It then becomes irrelevant that the debt the defendant foreign State or the embassy owes to the private litigant arose from an act *jure gestionis*, or otherwise from a private law relationship. Thus, once it is established that the funds in question are destined for the diplomatic or consular service, then such funds are immune from enforcement or execution even though the debt giving rise to the claim may be of a private law nature, such as payment of overdue rent for diplomatic premises.[254] In other words, even though an embassy is normally expected to pay the rent for its premises out of the embassy bank accounts, when the embassy refuses to pay the rent, the landlord cannot force the embassy to do so by seizing its bank accounts. If the plaintiff cannot find a *commercial* bank account of the foreign State, then no *judicial* remedy will be available.

It then also becomes imperative to know what the courts generally understand by the 'maintenance and functioning of the diplomatic mission'. From the cases that specifically address the issue one finds that funds used for the following are regarded as being used for public/sovereign purposes: the provision of accommodation for diplomatic personnel;[255] repair and maintenance of non-commercial real estate;[256] payment of salaries, wages, allowances and travel and other expenses for diplomatic personnel;[257] and the 'day-to-day running of the diplomatic mission'.[258]

6.2. Central bank property

Central banks and other monetary authorities frequently keep accounts with foreign banks for various purposes, such as foreign exchange reserves and funds for currency-regulating purposes. Conceivably, an attachment of such funds will cause serious financial problems, and with them damage to the friendly relations between States. Therefore it is little wonder that, in the practice of some States, special considerations apply to the immunity of foreign central banks.[259] In these States the property of foreign central banks is accorded absolute or near-absolute immunity from execution.

6.2.1. The US FSIA

The US FSIA affords special protection to the assets of foreign central banks. Section 1611(b)(1) stipulates:

CATEGORIES OF PROPERTY UNDER SPECIAL PROTECTION 411

Notwithstanding the provisions of section 1610 ... the property of a foreign state shall be immune from attachment and from execution, if the property is that of a foreign central bank or monetary authority held for its own account, unless such bank or authority, or its parent foreign government, has explicitly waived its immunity from attachment in aid of execution, or from execution.[260]

The term 'foreign central bank' or 'monetary authority' is not defined in the FSIA; however, such bank or authority must first of all qualify as an 'agency or instrumentality' of the foreign State, which is an easy and relatively straightforward exercise.[261] If a central bank is an 'agency or instrumentality' of the foreign State, then it is included in the definition of 'foreign State' under section 1603(a); thus the property of a central bank is property of a 'foreign State'. This explains why section 1611(b)(1) uses the formula 'the property of a foreign state ... is that of a foreign central bank or monetary authority'.

The mention of the property of a foreign central bank in section 1611 in relation to 'attachment in aid of execution or execution', but not in section 1610 with respect to 'attachment prior to the entry of judgment', gives rise to the question whether immunity enjoyed by the property of a foreign central bank from *prejudgment* attachment can be waived. A careful examination of the FSIA itself, the legislative report, and the relevant case law indicates that this still seems to be a moot point. To start with, section 1610(d)(1) stipulates that:

The property of a foreign state ... used for a commercial activity in the United States, shall not be immune from attachment prior to the entry of judgment ... if the foreign state has explicitly waived its immunity from attachment prior to judgment.

As discussed above, the phrase 'property of a foreign state', by virtue of section 1603(a), includes the 'property of a foreign central bank', thus it seems possible that immunity from prejudgment attachment enjoyed by the property of a foreign central bank can indeed be waived under section 1610(d)(1), provided, of course, that such property is or can be regarded as property 'used for a commercial activity in the United States'. The question then becomes whether the property of a foreign central bank can be so regarded. The FSIA itself is ambiguous on this point: it all depends on how one interprets the phrase, the 'property of a foreign central bank or monetary authority held for its own account'. On the one hand, according to the legislative report:

Section 1611(b)(1) provides for the immunity of central bank funds from attachment or execution. It applies to funds of a foreign central bank or monetary

412   MEASURES OF CONSTRAINT

authority which are deposited in the United States and 'held' for the bank's or authority's 'own account' – i.e., funds used or held in connection with central banking activities, as distinguished from funds used solely to finance the commercial transactions of other entities or of foreign states. If execution could be levied on such finds without an explicit waiver, deposit of foreign funds in the United States might be discouraged. Moreover, execution against the reserves of foreign states could cause significant foreign relations problems.[262]

This distinction between two types of accounts, that of the central bank 'for its own account' and that for the financing of commercial activities clearly envisages, in the words of the Second Circuit, the possibility that 'foreign central banks might be engaged in commercial activity in the United States while managing reserves and engaging in financial transactions'.[263] If that is the case, then one has every reason to assert that foreign central banks may also possess commercial property that is subject to attachment, whether pre- or post-judgment. By drawing the aforegoing distinction, however, the legislators seem to suggest that the 'property of a foreign central bank *held for its own account*' is not, or should not be regarded as, property 'used for a commercial activity'. One then wonders why the legislators did not expressly say so, either in the FSIA or in the legislative report. At any rate, if that is indeed what they intended when enacting the FSIA, then the 'property of a foreign central bank held for its own account', not being property 'used for a commercial activity', is not covered at all by section 1610, with the result that the provision on waiver does not apply to such property. That is to say, the immunity from prejudgment attachment, enjoyed by the 'property of a foreign central bank *held for its own account*', cannot be waived, because the FSIA does not provide for, or contemplate, such a waiver.[264] The correlative conclusion is that the property of a foreign central bank, used for a commercial activity in the US, in contrast to property held in its own account, *can* be subjected to both pre- and post-judgment attachment. In general terms, this means that only *part* of the property of a foreign central bank is absolutely immune.

On the other hand, since section 1611(b)(1) starts with the expression 'notwithstanding the provisions of section 1610', and section 1610 provides that the property of a foreign State/central bank does not enjoy immunity if it is 'used for a commercial activity', then it is not difficult to conclude that '§ 1611(b)(1), in other words, is an exception to § 1610, providing for immunity from attachment that would otherwise be allowed by § 1610', and from this further to conclude that:

CATEGORIES OF PROPERTY UNDER SPECIAL PROTECTION   413

Property used for commercial activity and property of a central bank held for its own account are not mutually exclusive categories. Rather, as the structure of the FSIA makes clear, property of a central bank held for its own account is a category of property used for commercial activity.[265]

If that is the case, then there is no reason why, as the court held in this case, the property of a central bank held for its own account should be shielded from prejudgment attachment.[266] Nevertheless, the case buttresses the point that funds belonging to a foreign central bank and used for commercial purposes can be subject to execution.[267]

As far as post-judgment attachment is concerned, since section 1611 immunizes the 'property a foreign central bank held for its own account', it becomes imperative to know what is meant by 'held for its own account'. The legislative report equates 'held for its own account' with 'held in connection with central banking activities'.[268] According to one court:

Funds are considered to be 'held for a central bank's own account' if they are used to perform functions that are normally understood to be the functions of a nation's central bank, and are not utilized in commercial activities.[269]

Unfortunately, however, there is no standard list of what are 'normally understood to be' the functions or activities of a central bank. These may include, for example: formulating and administering monetary policies; issuing and regulating currency; establishing interest rates; maintaining monetary stability; purchasing and selling financial instruments; monitoring external debt; keeping custody of and administering monetary reserves (including cash reserves collected from commercial banks, and gold and foreign currency/exchange reserves) for the central government; as well as performing general banking and agency services for the government (that is, acting as the banker and fiscal agent for the government).[270]

Additionally, since section 1611 exempts foreign central bank property 'from attachment and from execution', it can be asked if other coercive measures, which may usually not be regarded as attachment or execution, fall outside the proscription of section 1611 and can therefore be allowed. This question was answered in the affirmative in the case of *Riggs*, where the court allowed *set-off* against the funds held in the name of a foreign central bank, on the ground that section 1611 provides for immunity from attachment and execution, not immunity from set-off. Besides, the deposit in question had been placed to guarantee loans. In other words, it was placed to finance the commercial transactions of other entities, not as part of central banking activities.[271]

414   MEASURES OF CONSTRAINT

One last issue of importance remains to be noted. If a central bank is seen as an 'agency or instrumentality' of a foreign State, it may be asked whether the doctrine of 'piercing the corporate veil' can be applied as between a foreign State and its central bank, as sometimes takes place with respect to other entities of a foreign State. In practice, the US courts display an even greater aversion to such a suggestion and apply the principle of respect for separate legal personality in a more rigorous and exacting manner in cases against foreign central banks. As a consequence, a foreign State cannot waive the immunity from execution on behalf of its central bank unless the bank is expressly mentioned *by name*;[272] and the property of a foreign central bank held for its own account cannot be executed upon to satisfy a judgment against the foreign State[273] or another agency or instrumentality of that State.[274] Moreover, even though a foreign State may have indeed waived the immunity of its central bank, such as when that State has 'irrevocably' waived, on behalf of itself and 'any Governmental Agency', 'any immunity from jurisdiction of any court or from any legal process under any laws ... whether through service or notice, attachment prior to judgment, attachment in aid of execution, execution or otherwise, with respect to itself or its property',[275] such a waiver does not automatically render a central bank liable for a judgment entered against its parent government.[276]

Thus, the assets of or held by a foreign central bank in the US enjoy three layers of protection: (1) the requirement of an explicit waiver of immunity from enforcement; (2) the presumption of separate personality of the central bank, which insulates it from claims against the parent foreign State or that State's other agencies or instrumentalities; and (3) unavailability for execution of funds held in the central bank's 'own account'. Conversely, three conditions must be satisfied before any funds held by a foreign central bank in the US can be attached: (1) the claim is against the central bank itself and is one for which only the central bank is answerable; (2) the immunity from attachment has been waived; and (3) the funds are not held for the central bank's own account.

6.2.2.   The UK SIA

At common law, foreign central banks did not enjoy any special status or protection. Thus if a foreign central bank was not immune from adjudication, its funds could not be immune from seizure either.[277] This situation was quickly terminated by the UK SIA, which largely superseded the common law on foreign State immunity. Now, even though a foreign central bank is still considered a separate entity[278] and can therefore be sued and can enjoy immunity from suit only when it has acted in the exercise of sovereign authority (section 14(1)(2)),[279] the UK SIA affords absolute protection to foreign central bank property. Section 13(4) of the UK SIA provides that execution is permissible in respect of property of a foreign State 'which is for the time being in use or intended for use for commercial purposes'; and section 14(3) extends this provision to a separate entity which enjoys immunity from jurisdiction but which has waived that immunity. That is, if a separate entity, which is otherwise entitled to immunity, submits to the adjudicative jurisdiction of the UK courts, then the property of that separate entity used for commercial purposes can be subject to enforcement measures. A central bank, in this connection, is distinguished from other separate entities, for section 14(4) provides that:

Property of a State's central bank or other monetary authority shall not be regarded for the purposes of [section 13(4)] as in use or intended for use for commercial purposes; and where any such bank or authority is a separate entity [section 13(1) to (3)] shall apply to it as if references to a State were references to the bank or authority.[280]

Not only is the same immunity enjoyed by a foreign State from measures of constraint also given to a central bank, but the property of a central bank shall not be treated as being used for commercial purposes. In a case against a foreign central bank, the court is thus precluded from considering whether all or part of the property of a foreign central bank is used for commercial purposes and therefore executable under section 13(4), as the court is empowered to do to other separate entities. Thus the property of a foreign central bank is immune from measures of constraint regardless of its uses. This means that, unlike the property of a foreign State itself or that of any other separate entity, the property of a central bank is not subject to enforcement or execution even if it is actually being used for commercial purposes. Particularly notable is the use of the term 'property of a central bank' without any further qualifier or distinction between the funds 'held for the central bank's own account' and funds 'used to finance commercial activities', as can be found in the US practice under the US FSIA. Under the UK SIA, therefore, *any and all the property* of a foreign central bank is under protection. In a word, short of written consent by the central bank or its parent State (section 13(3)), the

416 MEASURES OF CONSTRAINT

property of a foreign central bank is *completely and absolutely* immune from enforcement in the UK. This effectively forecloses the recurrence of *Trendtex* types of cases.

This conclusion is supported by statements from the legislature and the courts. Thus, the property of a foreign central bank is immune 'irrespective of whether the central bank is a separate entity or is acting in the exercise of sovereign authority'.[281] This means that, where a foreign central bank is not a separate entity, and where therefore the moneys of that central bank actually belong to the foreign State, such moneys, simply by virtue of the fact that they are held in the name of the central bank, are 'immune from execution irrespective of the source of the funds in the account or the use of the account or the purpose for which the account is maintained'.[282] Where a central bank is a separate entity, it 'differs from other such entities in two respects: (a) even if not immune from suit, its property will normally be immune from execution because its property is not regarded as in use or intended for use for commercial purposes; and (b) it is specifically provided that such a separate entity is entitled to immunity from injunctive relief and execution as if it were a state. Accordingly ... the property of a central bank will only be liable to process of execution if it has waived in writing its immunity from execution'.[283] So long as a bank remains the central bank of a foreign State, all of its property is immune from execution[284] or any other type of enforcement measure.[285] This is a 'complete immunity from the enforcement process in the UK courts', so that even if 'the central bank has an interest in the property concerned, and the state of the central bank has another interest in the same property, the relevant property is immune from enforcement in respect of a judgment against that State, whether the property concerned is in use or intended for use for commercial purposes or not'.[286]

6.2.3. The Australia FSIA

By contrast, the Australia FSIA simply applies the provisions concerning immunity from execution of foreign States to foreign central banks (section 35(1)). The ALRC did not think that Australia should adopt either the US or the UK approach since both their provisions 'were at least partly motivated by a desire to protect the positions of New York and London respectively as investment centres for foreign state reserves. Australia has at present no similar interest.'[287]

6.3. Military property

Obviously, property in the possession or control of a military authority cannot be regarded as in use or intended for use for commercial purposes. The immunity of warships, for example, is well established in international law.[288] Thus, some instruments provide immunity for military property of a foreign State, though they are not at all uniform in the particular formula for granting such immunity.

Section 1611(b)(2) of the US FSIA classifies as military the property that 'is, or is intended to be, used in connection with a military activity and (A) is of a military character, or (B) is under the control of a military authority or defence agency'.[289] According to the legislative report, this provision is designed to protect both property of a military character, such as 'weapons, ammunition, military transport, warships, tanks, communications equipment', and 'other military property, such as food, clothing, fuel and office equipment which although not of a military character, is essential to military operations'; and the overall condition is that 'property will be immune only if its present or future use is military (e.g., surplus military equipment withdrawn from military use would not be immune)'.[290]

The Australia FSIA stipulates a general immunity for 'military property' in section 31(4) and section 32(3)(a), and it defines military property in section 3(1) as:

(a) a ship of war, a Government yacht, a patrol vessel, a police or customs vessel, a hospital ship, a defence force supply ship or an auxiliary vessel, being a ship or vessel that, at the relevant time, is operated by the foreign State concerned (whether pursuant to requisition or under a charter by demise or otherwise); or

(b) property (not being a ship or vessel) that is –
    (i) being used in connection with a military activity; or
    (ii) under the control of a military authority or defence agency for military or defence purposes.

According to the draftsmen, the protection extends to 'military material sold in Australia for export ... while in packing cases on the wharf awaiting shipment'.[291]

In this connection, a distinction must be drawn between the goods in actual possession or control of a military authority and the transaction to procure such goods. That is, whilst purchase of military equipment is regarded as a commercial activity,[292] such equipment, once bought and placed in the possession of military authorities, shall be immune from enforcement.

418   MEASURES OF CONSTRAINT

6.4. *Other types of public property*

In practice, immunity from enforcement has also been extended to other types of public property, such as buildings for the purposes of establishing an educational and cultural centre,[293] registration fees and other taxes due to the foreign government,[294] overflight charges,[295] antiquities in the possession of a university and museums,[296] and works of art.[297]

Article 21(1) of the 2004 UN Convention provides:

> The following categories, in particular, of property of a State shall not be considered as property specifically in use or intended for use by the State for other than government non-commercial purposes under article 19, subparagraph (c): (d) property forming part of the cultural heritage of the State or part of its archives and not placed or intended to be placed on sale; (e) property forming part of an exhibition of objects of scientific, cultural or historical interest and not placed or intended to be placed on sale.

However, in view of the scant practice in this regard, it is advisable to leave the matter at that and refrain from drawing any conclusion of a general nature.

7. Mixed accounts and accounts without definite destination

Bank accounts have been particularly popular targets of attachment and execution. The majority of the cases involving measures of constraint concern bank accounts. Apparently they are often the first or the only objects that the plaintiffs can lay their hands on. Fungible in character and easily transferable, they are often the most readily available objects to satisfy a claim. On the other hand, it is precisely owing to this fungible and transferable nature that bank accounts can pose the most difficult problems of characterization. Invariably the purpose or use of the bank accounts in a particular case is not quite certain: they may be used indiscriminately for both public and private purposes or simply not assigned for any definite destination. In fact, these two kinds are closely related, because accounts currently 'lying idle' have the obvious possibility of being destined for exclusively public or purely private purposes or for a combination of both.

7.1. *Mixed accounts*

'Mixed accounts' are those accounts maintained in the name of a diplomatic mission but occasionally used for payment, for instance, for supply of goods or services to the mission itself (which is regarded as a commercial activity by most courts). In a word, mixed accounts are those that are used simultaneously for public and commercial purposes. The problem often arises as to how the specific purposes of the accounts can be ascertained.

The UK case that merits special attention is *Alcom*, where the Court of Appeal opined:

> The purpose of money in a bank account can never be 'to run an embassy'. It can only be to pay for goods and services or to enter into other transactions which enable the embassy to be run.[298]

But, under section 13(4) of the UK SIA, enforcement measures are allowable against 'property which is for the time being in use or intended for use for commercial purposes'. Under section 17(1), '"commercial purposes" means purposes of such transactions or activities as are mentioned in section 3(3)', under which, in turn, 'commercial transaction' includes 'any contract for the supply of goods or services' (section 3(3)(a)).

The above reasoning of the Court of Appeal would subject any and all foreign embassy accounts in the UK to attachment and execution; for, once embassy bank accounts are seen as simply containing money 'to pay for goods and services or to enter into other transactions', then the combined effect of sections 3(3)(a), 13(4) and 17(1) will mean that such accounts are property used for commercial purposes and therefore outside the scope of protection afforded by the UK SIA. The House of Lords reversed this decision by holding that an embassy bank account was 'one and indivisible' and that:

> The onus of proving that the balance standing to the credit of the diplomatic mission's current bank account falls within the exception created by the crucial words in section 13(4) lies upon the judgment creditor.[299]

In this case the Colombian Ambassador's certificate that the funds were not used (or intended for use) for commercial purposes was given 'conclusive' effect by the House of Lords,[300] since section 13(5) of the UK SIA provides that:

> for the purposes of [section 13(4)], [the] certificate [of the head of a State's diplomatic mission in the UK] to the effect that any property is not in use or intended for use by or on behalf of the State for commercial purposes shall be accepted as sufficient evidence of that fact unless the contrary is proved.[301]

The important principle established by *Alcom* is that, in cases of mixed accounts in the name of an embassy, immunity should be presumed

420   MEASURES OF CONSTRAINT

unless commercial uses can be proved by the judgment creditor. In most, if not all, cases this would be an impossible task to accomplish.[302] Unbelievable as it may sound, this conforms to the general rule of absolute immunity of embassy bank accounts in current law on State immunity and represents the position adopted by the courts which have had occasion to pronounce upon this issue. The current law of State immunity regards a general current account of a diplomatic mission as one and indivisible, i.e. not to be divided into parts serving respectively private and public purposes, even though some parts of such an account may indeed be or have been devoted to commercial acts or transactions. That is, even if such an account is allocated only partly but not exclusively to cover the embassy's costs and expenses, it is still immune from enforcement; and the foreign State has only to allege an abstract danger to the functioning of the diplomatic mission for that immunity to be available, but is not required to provide evidence as to the uses and purposes of the funds in question. The onus is on the plaintiff seeking enforcement to prove that the account serves exclusively private law purposes.[303]

In *LETCO*, a US court thus stated:

The Court presumes that some portion of the funds in the bank accounts may be used for commercial activities in connection with running the Embassy, such as transactions to purchase goods or services from private entities ... The Court, however, declines to order that if any portion of a bank account is used for a commercial activity then the entire account loses its immunity. On the contrary ... funds used for commercial activities which are 'incidental' or 'auxiliary', not denoting the essential character of the use of the funds in question, would not cause the entire bank account to lose its mantle of sovereign immunity. Indeed, a diplomatic mission would undergo a severe hardship if a civil judgment creditor were permitted to freeze bank accounts used for the purposes of a diplomatic mission for an indefinite period of time until exhaustive discovery had taken place to determine the precise portion of the bank account used for commercial activities.[304]

The Spanish Constitutional Court expressed the same opinion:

The fact that funds held in an account to cover the day-to-day functioning of diplomatic and consular missions may also be used for commercial purposes does not justify the exclusion of such funds from immunity against execution, and hence from attachment. This follows both from the single and indivisible nature of the funds and from the impossibility, in the case of an account operated by a diplomatic mission, of investigating the transactions, flow of funds and purposes to which such funds are applied. Such an investigation would involve an interference with the mission's activity, in breach of the rules of public international law.[305]

As did the Italian Court of Cassation:

Therefore any attempt to check if such funds are effectively used in whole or in part for those purposes would inevitably result in an undue interference in the affairs of the diplomatic mission … In the presence of mixed uses, the magistrate cannot be obliged to try and identify that portion of assets not used for sovereign purposes. Such intervention would be inadmissible as it would intrude into the exercise of sovereignty. Unless a non-sovereign use emerges clearly from the investigation and the evidence, the concept of immunity must prevail and be maintained.[306]

7.2. Accounts without definite destination

A related problem to mixed accounts is that of accounts with no current use or to which a definite use cannot be assigned, especially those accounts held not only in the name of public bodies but also in the ownership of various separate entities. For such accounts attachment and execution are usually allowed unless the contrary can be shown by the foreign State.[307] A possible future use for public purposes is not sufficient to provide a basis for immunity.[308]

The Australia FSIA 1985 is the only national statute that addresses the situation of what the framers call 'property lying idle'.[309] It provides that:

property that is apparently vacant or apparently not in use shall be taken to be being used for commercial purposes unless the court is satisfied that it has been set aside otherwise than for commercial purposes. (Section 32(3)(b).)

Conclusion

Measures of constraint are the most obvious manifestations of the court's power forcibly to enforce its rulings and decisions against a party to the legal proceedings against its will. Because such measures affect the property owned, possessed or operated by a foreign State in the territory of the State of the forum and therefore impinge upon crucial national interests of the foreign State, they have always been regarded as forming the most sensitive part of the law of State immunity. Over the years courts have displayed remarkable caution and restraint with respect to enforcement and execution against foreign State property, and even those most liberal in exercising their jurisdiction of adjudication have treated the issue with circumspection, and have taken meticulous care to ensure that measures of constraint are allowed only in the most indisputable cases where the least possible hassle and hindrance is caused to the defendant foreign State

422 MEASURES OF CONSTRAINT

in performing its public functions. Thus three principles have emerged on which there is now little dissension: first, a distinction must be drawn between immunity from adjudication and immunity from execution, so that a loss of immunity at the adjudicative stage does not mean an automatic loss of immunity at the stage of enforcement and execution, for which a separate determination is necessary; secondly, even where a foreign State is found not to be immune, execution is permissible only as against the property used for commercial or private purposes but not as against property used for sovereign or public purposes; and, thirdly, certain categories of State property, such as diplomatic and consular property and military property, enjoy absolute immunity from execution. In some States, notably the UK and the US, foreign central bank property is also given special protection. The divergence in State practice concerns mainly the actual manner in which these principles are implemented.

The current law of State immunity imposes a number of conditions and limitations on measures of constraint against foreign States, particularly as regards the manner in which the measures of constraint are taken and the property on which execution may be levied. It is now universally agreed that the purpose of the property is the decisive test: property used for public or sovereign purposes is immune from enforcement, while property used for commercial or private purposes is not. It is also universally agreed that immunity from measures of constraint is distinct from immunity from adjudication, so that the fact that a court may be competent to exercise jurisdiction, either because of a waiver of immunity from adjudication or with regard to the non-immune activities of a foreign State, does not necessarily mean that it can authorize measures of constraint against any property of that State situated in the territory of the State of the forum. As regards prejudgment measures, State practice is far from uniform. In some countries, such as the UK and the US, even more restrictions are imposed on prejudgment attachment, injunctions or other measures; whereas in others, especially the civil law countries, the same conditions apply to both pre- and post-judgment measures of constraint.

In most cases, the judicial process against a foreign State stops short at the close of the adjudicatory stage. It almost seems as if the regime of State immunity is simply to declare a foreign State liable but leaves the enforcement of that liability to chance and the goodwill of the defendant State. Thus courts freely handing down judgments against foreign States without little prospect of enforcement will remain a constant feature of the law and practice on State immunity.

10 State immunity and human rights violations

Speaking of 'State immunity and human rights violations' begs the question, for one has to explain at the outset what is meant by 'human rights' and their 'violations', and, because one implies the question to be whether a State should enjoy immunity from litigation concerning such violations, what type(s) of litigation one has in mind. More importantly, because immunity basically means exemption from *territorial* jurisdiction of the forum State, one has to specify *where* the alleged wrongdoings took place. For the sake of simplicity and space, I shall focus only on the issues of immunity, leaving such things as 'human rights' and their 'violations' to common understanding. The jurisdiction of the court will be indisputable where the alleged violations took place within the territory of the forum State. With regard to the question of immunity, insofar as a human rights claim concerns money damages for intentional infliction of bodily injury within the territory of the State of the forum, it is already subject to the tort exception to immunity under current law. A criminal action against the individual perpetrator of such an offence (that is, one committed within the territory of the State of the forum) is also covered by current law on human rights or ordinary criminal law. The problems herein considered arise where human rights litigation is instituted against an alleged perpetrator when that person remains outside the territory of the forum State, and/or with respect to human rights violations committed outside that territory. Thus, the crux of the matter, when it comes to immunity with regard to human rights violations, is the exercise of *extraterritorial jurisdiction* and the exemption therefrom. As international law currently stands, there are insuperable obstacles to an ideally unhampered exercise of jurisdiction (and denial of immunity) over human rights violations committed abroad.

1. Territorial jurisdiction

It is only when the jurisdiction is established that it becomes necessary, or meaningful, to speak of exemption from that jurisdiction, i.e. immunity. Thus the issue of jurisdiction logically precedes that of immunity. The absence of discussion of the existence of jurisdiction in State immunity cases, where courts usually proceed directly to the issue of immunity, is due to the fact that, in these cases, there is no doubt about jurisdiction. In other words, with only rare exceptions which will be discussed below, traditional cases of immunity involve matters that either occurred within the territorial limits of, or otherwise bear a close territorial nexus to, the forum State. The issue of territorial jurisdiction has thus remained largely in the background, and, being to a great extent obscured by the discussion of immunity that dominates these cases, is easily overlooked. Since its existence is accepted as a given premise without the necessity of proof, territorial jurisdiction can be, and often is, elided; it then becomes possible to discuss the issue of immunity without having to establish jurisdiction. Where the subject matter of the case arose within the territorial limits of the forum State, this may not pose any difficulty; but where the court is called upon to judge a case which requires an exercise of extraterritorial jurisdiction, this will lead to a conflation of the issues of jurisdiction and immunity, so that the court will commit the error of equating the denial of immunity to the establishment of jurisdiction. That is to say, the court will assert its jurisdiction when that jurisdiction in fact does not exist. This is so because the court will simply forget that it should have jurisdiction before it can discuss the issue of immunity. Since the traditional law of State immunity has been confined to dealing with matters arising within the territorial limits of the forum States, there has been no need to view the possibility of elision as a serious problem; but the rapid development of international human rights law, in which the notion of extraterritorial jurisdiction plays a crucial role, and with it the increasing number of claims based on events taking place far beyond the national boundaries of the forum State, mean that it has now become a practical necessity for courts to discuss the issue of jurisdiction before they can embark on a decision on immunity.

Immunity means exemption from an otherwise existent and exercisable jurisdiction. The issue of immunity can, and often is, decided upon the assumption that territorial jurisdiction exists. That is, in practical terms, it is often decided without consideration as to whether or not the court has jurisdiction. This might seem trite or even trivial; and indeed, as we have seen, it often tends to be obscured or rendered nugatory or otiose by the actual existence of territorial jurisdiction in the case in question; however, in some cases this may have significant implications. For sometimes the minds of the judges would be so carried away by the assumption of jurisdiction that, once the point of immunity is decided in the negative, they would actually be taken in by their own assumption and would proceed under the delusion that jurisdiction had in reality existed in the first place.

The pitfall lies in the fact that normally State immunity issues arise within the territorial jurisdiction; so the issue whether or not the court has jurisdiction is often superfluous and of little practical import: the court simply *has* jurisdiction by virtue of the territoriality principle. In the context of human rights litigation, however, the claimant in many cases has to argue for extraterritorial jurisdiction, which may or may not exist. State immunity is a preliminary issue, in that it may disable an otherwise exercisable jurisdiction; that is why in an ordinary case of State immunity it is often only secondary to prove jurisdiction, though the issue of jurisdiction logically precedes that of immunity; for, in the event of immunity being proven then the previous efforts of establishing jurisdiction would be pointless. Thus it is more sensible simply to assume jurisdiction in the first place and to see if the court would have to grant immunity even though the court has jurisdiction; it is this assumption of jurisdiction that can prove treacherous. For in a human rights proceeding, there is always the danger of conflating the issue of State immunity and that of jurisdiction, so that, once immunity can be shown not to be available the court would proceed as if it already had jurisdiction over the case, quite unaware that that jurisdiction is only an assumption.

It is therefore necessary to treat jurisdiction and immunity as two separate issues, both of which will have to be settled by a domestic court before it can assert jurisdiction over matters occurring in foreign countries. As the International Court of Justice rightly stated in the *Arrest Warrant* case:

the rules governing the jurisdiction of national courts must be carefully distinguished from those governing jurisdictional immunities: jurisdiction does not imply absence of immunity, while absence of immunity does not imply jurisdiction.[1]

Thus, although 'lack of jurisdiction' and 'immunity' are often used interchangeably as terms of convenience, it will be erroneous doctrinally to treat them as identical; for, more accurately speaking, 'immunity' in fact affirms jurisdiction by being exemption from it. In other words, immunity signifies the *presence* of jurisdiction rather than the *absence* or *lack* of it. To say that there is immunity in a case does not mean that jurisdiction does not exist in this case; it only means that the court has jurisdiction but cannot exercise it: immunity precludes the exercise of an otherwise exercisable jurisdiction.

The territoriality of State immunity law means that, if violation takes place in the State of the forum then jurisdiction can be exercised in one way or another; but if it takes place outside the forum State, then jurisdiction cannot be established on the ground of illegality alone and must be demonstrated in accordance with rules and principles of international law allowing extraterritorial jurisdiction. Where no jurisdiction can be shown to exist, the question of immunity does not arise in the first place. Important as the issue of extraterritorial jurisdiction is for international human rights litigation, current international law, however, is far from settled on this matter; further exploration is therefore highly necessary.[2]

2. State immunity and criminal proceedings

Extraterritorial jurisdiction is indeed contemplated by international human rights law; but, because of a crucial discrepancy between that law and the law of State immunity, such a jurisdiction cannot easily be translated into a viable basis for the denial of immunity.

Current international law on State immunity consists of a general presumption of immunity and a number of specified exceptions, which have been formulated almost exclusively in a commercial and trading context. That is, apart from a limited number of allowable lawsuits sounding in contract or tort, State immunity remains intact.

Article 15 of the 1972 European Convention provides:

A Contracting State shall be entitled to immunity from the jurisdiction of the courts of another Contracting State if the proceedings do not fall within Articles 1 to 14.

Since Articles 1 to 14 concern only civil matters and do not contain a criminal law exception to immunity, it can be concluded that, under the European Convention, States enjoy complete immunity with regard to criminal proceedings. This general pattern, i.e. immunity plus exceptions in respect of *civil* proceedings, is the one followed by all current national statutes on State immunity,[3] by texts prepared by international bodies,[4] and by the ILC 1991 Draft and the 2004 UN Convention.[5] Some national statutes specifically state that they do not apply to criminal proceedings.[6] The ILC declared in the commentary that its 1991 Draft Articles do not cover criminal proceedings.[7] This was further affirmed by the Ad Hoc Committee on State Immunity.[8] The UN General Assembly, in its resolution finally adopting the 2004 UN Convention, declared that the Convention 'does not cover criminal proceedings'.[9]

Thus one can safely assert that, under current international law, States qua States still enjoy absolute immunity from criminal proceedings, even if the alleged offence should have taken place within the territory of the forum State.[10]

In this connection it is worth noting that the notion of a crime committed by a State does not exist in international law. The ILC in Article 19 of its 1976 Draft Articles on State Responsibility proposed a category of 'international crimes', comprising serious breaches of international obligations 'of essential importance', as opposed to 'international delicts', i.e. all other cases of internationally wrongful acts;[11] but it later abandoned the idea in its 2001 Draft Articles, on the ground that: 'There has been ... no development of penal consequences for States of breaches of these fundamental norms.'[12]

On the other hand, current international law on human rights dates from the UN Charter and the 1948 Universal Declaration of Human Rights,[13] and has evolved chiefly through international conventions. These conventions speak of violations of human rights largely in criminal law terms; and indeed their very titles reveal the *penal* nature of the remedies envisaged.[14] To be sure, some of the treaties currently in force do contain provisions on civil remedies (such as compensation). For example, Article 14(1) of the Torture Convention provides that:

Each State Party shall ensure in its legal system that the victim of an act of torture obtains redress and has an enforceable right to fair and adequate compensation, including the means for as full rehabilitation as possible. In the event of the death of the victim as a result of an act of torture, his dependants shall be entitled to compensation.

However, without carefully crafted parameters of application, such as can be found in relation to the exercise of criminal jurisdiction (e.g. Articles 5 to 13 of the Torture Convention), this isolated stipulation proves to be vague and controversial, and its exact implications are yet to be worked out.[15] To put it simplistically and crudely, the main concern of current international human rights law is to prevent and punish, not to compensate.

Because most, if not all, of the human rights cases involve an exercise of extraterritorial jurisdiction, the first task for the court is to ascertain that such jurisdiction does exist in a particular case. Recourse must invariably be had to international law, but international law on human rights is largely couched in terms of criminal law, whereas the rules and principles of State immunity have been developed almost exclusively in a civil (as opposed to criminal) context, focusing as it has done on commercial activities in particular. This discrepancy precludes any claim for money damages but on the other hand provides some possibility to sue individual violators of human rights (as opposed to State violators) for criminal liability, when immunity they formerly may have enjoyed becomes unavailable and where there exist jurisdictional links requisite for an exercise of extraterritorial jurisdiction (such as the presence of the defendant in the territory of the State of the forum).

In any case, the fact remains that there is a significant incongruity between the urgent need for the international protection of human rights and the utter absence of rules and precedents regarding the issue of State immunity in cases alleging violations of human rights. Human rights advocates are thus confronted with the awkward task of transposing rules and principles prohibiting violations of human rights from the field of criminal law to the regime of State immunity, which knows no criminal proceedings. The necessity of recasting prohibitive rules found in general international law in the image of a perceived human rights exception to immunity has led international lawyers to resort to all sorts of ingenious arguments, chief among which is the one based on the notion of *jus cogens*.

3. State immunity and *jus cogens*

The relationship between State immunity and the notion of *jus cogens* is one of the most intensely debated topics in current international law doctrine.[16] Human rights advocates have utilized the notion of *jus cogens* precisely to overcome the difficulty of having to argue for a denial of immunity within a legal framework that contains no exception to immunity with respect to human rights violations. Such a method has been shown to be fraught with difficulties and has been generally unsuccessful before various courts which have had occasion to consider the matter.[17]

The *jus cogens* hypothesis comes in two forms: override and waiver. It has been suggested that certain norms for the protection of human rights (such as that prohibiting torture) have attained the status of *jus cogens* and have by virtue of this exalted status acquired a higher hierarchical position from whence they override any and all norms inferior in stature.[18] Alternatively, it has been asserted that a violation of a *jus cogens* human rights norm constitutes a waiver of immunity before a foreign national court.[19]

So far, these arguments have been rejected by the courts.[20] Nonetheless, in a few cases, *jus cogens* was indeed referred to by the courts in their reasoning when denying immunity. A closer examination of these cases, however, discloses that *jus cogens* was employed by the courts as a reinforcement of more traditional grounds for exercising jurisdiction, rather than a separate and independent ground itself. Thus, in the case of *Distomo*, even though the court took the view that Germany had impliedly waived its immunity when its soldiers engaged in a massacre in a Greek village during the Second World War, it is obvious that the court based its jurisdiction on the existence of *territorial jurisdiction*, rather than on a *jus cogens* norm prohibiting the killing of a civilian population.[21] The *Ferrini* case, decided by the Italian Court of Cassation, relied likewise on the *territorial jurisdiction* (the plaintiff had been captured in Italy by the German occupation forces and deported to Germany for forced labour during the Second World War).[22] Given the indispensable role of territorial jurisdiction,[23] the *Ferrini* case offers nothing new from *Distomo*, and furnishes no support for a denial of immunity in respect of acts committed outside the forum State.[24] In the *Pinochet* case, though their Lordships had little difficulty in accepting that the prohibition of torture had acquired a *jus cogens* character,[25] their ultimate rationale for denying Pinochet's immunity was predicated on the fact that both Chile, which was claiming immunity on Pinochet's behalf, and the UK were States parties to the Torture Convention. Because Chile was obligated by the Torture Convention not to object to the exercise of *criminal* jurisdiction over its nationals arrested in UK territory, it was prevented from blocking that jurisdiction by claiming for Pinochet any immunity with respect to criminal proceedings (in this case extradition proceedings).[26] In other words, it was a treaty obligation, rather than *jus cogens*, that displaced immunity.

The question whether *jus cogens* can automatically vitiate immunity is closely bound up with a long-standing, overarching dispute among international lawyers, namely, whether the notion of *jus cogens*, originating as it did in the context of the law of treaties,[27] can be extended to counteract other, customary rules of international law. Apart from those who are either sceptical or openly scornful of the idea of *jus cogens*,[28] there are scholars who maintain that the effects of *jus cogens* cannot go beyond the law of treaties.[29] The now prevailing authorities, however, seem to incline towards a wider role for *jus cogens*. According to Crawford:

it is difficult to accept that a rule should be sacrosanct in one context and freely derogable in another ... If agreements of States can be invalid as contravening fundamental norms, so too can their other transactions.[30]

In *Prosecutor* v. *Furundzija*, the ICTY held that a *jus cogens* norm enjoys:

a higher rank in the international hierarchy than treaty law and even 'ordinary' customary rules. The most conspicuous consequence of this higher rank is that the principle at issue cannot be derogated from by States through international treaties or local or special customs or even general customary rules not endowed with the same normative force.[31]

Article 40 of the 2001 ILC Draft Articles on State Responsibility refers to 'international responsibility which is entailed by a serious breach by a State of an obligation arising under a peremptory norm of general international law' and goes on to define 'serious' as involving 'a gross or systematic failure by the responsible State to fulfill the obligation',[32] without specifying what form such a 'failure' ought to take. It is obvious that, in the opinion of the ILC, a *jus cogens* obligation could be breached by means other than the conclusion of a treaty.[33] More importantly, the ICJ, which traditionally has shunned the notion of *jus cogens*,[34] has recently accepted its existence. In the *Armed Activities* case, the ICJ accepted that the prohibition of genocide was a norm of *jus cogens*, but it nevertheless held that such a finding did not prejudge the question of jurisdiction. It thus perceived:

the relationship between peremptory norms of general international law *(jus cogens)* and the establishment of the Court's jurisdiction: the fact that a dispute relates to compliance with a norm having such a character, which is assuredly the case with regard to the prohibition of genocide, cannot of itself provide a basis for the jurisdiction of the Court to entertain that dispute. Under the Court's Statute that jurisdiction is always based on the consent of the parties.[35]

That is to say, in spite of the fact that a *jus cogens* norm may be at issue, the ICJ's jurisdiction in a case must be established, not by virtue of that *jus cogens* norm, but on the principle that 'its jurisdiction always depends on the consent of the parties':

THE ASSERTION OF EXTRATERRITORIAL JURISDICTION 431

the mere fact that rights and obligations *erga omnes* or peremptory norms of general international law (*jus cogens*) are at issue in a dispute cannot in itself constitute an exception to the principle that its jurisdiction always depends on the consent of the parties.[36]

Transposed onto the plane of national law, this would mean that, even where *jus cogens* norms are involved, the jurisdiction of a domestic court must still be established through traditional means, such as territoriality or nationality: the mere fact that a *jus cogens* norm has been violated cannot of itself secure jurisdiction, if jurisdiction does not otherwise exist under international law. We are back to square one – that is, if the court does not have jurisdiction in the first place, the question of immunity does not arise. We now proceed from the issue of immunity to the issue of extraterritorial jurisdiction.

4. The assertion of extraterritorial jurisdiction

The assertion of extraterritorial jurisdiction, in the absence of a treaty basis to do so, is generally resisted by States. Strong protest from the State concerned is not uncommon.[37] The US Helms-Burton Act is a good example.[38] So is the *Sharon* case.

In the *Sharon* case, criminal prosecution was instituted in Belgium against Ariel Sharon, then Israeli Prime Minister, and other Israeli high officials, for war crimes, crimes against humanity, and genocide in connection with the 1982 massacre of Palestinian and Lebanese civilians in the Sabra and Shatila Palestinian refugee camps in Beirut, Lebanon. The case was brought under the Belgian Law of 10 February 1999 concerning the Punishment of Grave Breaches of International Humanitarian Law, enacted to modify the Law of 16 June 1993 concerning the Punishment of Grave Breaches of the Geneva Conventions of 12 August 1949 and their Additional Protocols I and II of 8 June 1977.[39] The 1993/1999 Belgian Laws are also known as 'Universal Jurisdiction Laws' or 'Anti-Atrocity Laws'. Article 7 of the Law confers on the Belgian courts jurisdiction over these breaches 'irrespective of where such breaches have been committed', while Article 5(3) stipulates: 'The immunity attributed to the official capacity of a person does not prevent the application of the present Act.' The Court of Appeal of Brussels held the proceedings inadmissible on the ground, inter alia, that the defendants were not present on Belgian territory. The Court of Cassation, in partly reversing the decision, drew a distinction between Sharon, who enjoyed immunity under customary international law, and other defendants, who enjoyed no such immunity.[40]

432   STATE IMMUNITY AND HUMAN RIGHTS VIOLATIONS

This attempt to exercise extraterritorial jurisdiction provoked a harsh reaction from Israel and the US. Shortly after the Belgian Court of Cassation's decision, the US initiated the process of enacting a 'Universal Jurisdiction Rejection Bill'.[41] Section 2(1) to (12) makes it abundantly clear that the Bill was designed as a response to the Belgian case against Israeli Prime Minister Ariel Sharon under the 'Anti-Atrocity Laws' of 1993/1999, and section 2(14) sees in the 'very concept of universal jurisdiction' 'a threat to the sovereignty of the United States', for it envisages 'the possibility that foreign courts claiming universal jurisdiction could entertain suits brought by third-country nationals against members of the Armed Forces of the United States and the President and other senior elected and appointed officials of the United States Government'. Section 3 declares:

It is the policy of the United States to reject any claim of universal jurisdiction made by foreign governments and to refuse to render any assistance or support to any foreign government pursuing an investigation or prosecution under a universal jurisdiction act.

It was Belgium that chose to back down. On 23 April 2003, the Belgian Parliament amended the 1993/1999 Laws.[42] Article 5(3) of the 1993/1999 Laws as amended now stipulates that '[i]nternational immunity derived from a person's official capacity does not prevent the application of the present law except under those limits established under international law'; and the new Article 7 requires a strict territorial connection with Belgium. Further amendments on 5 August 2003[43] inserted a new article into the Belgian Code of Criminal Procedure, to the effect that:

In accordance with international law, there shall be no prosecution with regard to: Heads of State, heads of government, and foreign ministers of foreign affairs, during their terms of office.

It should be noted that the Belgian Laws only concerned *criminal prosecution*, not civil remedies such as compensation, the latter being the core of the issue of universal civil jurisdiction, which is currently under intense academic debate.[44] Apart from demonstrating the difficulty in establishing extraterritorial jurisdiction, the *Sharon* case also brings into sharp focus the position of heads of State/government before foreign courts.

5. The State and its officials

The monolithic nature of the immunity enjoyed by States has made it necessary for human rights advocates to adopt the new strategy of suing officials in their individual capacity for criminal liabilities. Because such lawsuits have become frequent only in recent years, the immunity of State officials from foreign criminal jurisdiction is becoming increasingly topical in international law and is in need of urgent reassessment.[45] Traditionally the position of heads of State, heads of government and other senior officials before foreign courts is a complicated matter in international law.[46] As far as current law on State immunity is concerned, it is generally accepted that, where a State enjoys immunity, then that immunity extends to its officials, if they have acted with the authority of the State. In *Propend*, Leggatt LJ opined:

> The protection afforded by the Act of 1978 to States would be undermined if employees, officers ... could be sued as individuals for matters of State conduct in respect of which the State they were serving had immunity. [The SIA] must be read as affording to individual employees or officers of a foreign State protection under the same cloak as protects the State itself.[47]

In *Jones*, Lord Bingham stated pointedly that: 'The foreign state's right to immunity cannot be circumvented by suing its servants or agents.'[48] Lord Hoffmann agreed by holding that the term 'State' in the UK SIA 'must be construed to include any individual representative of the state acting in that capacity ... The official acting in that capacity is entitled to the same immunity as the state itself'.[49]

In the words of Finlayson JA in *Jaffe* v. *Miller*:

> What is the point of the state having immunity if its personnel have none when carrying out their official duties in the host country? ... In the event that the plaintiff recovered judgment, the foreign state would have to respond to it by indemnifying its functionaries, thus, through this indirect route, losing the immunity conferred on it by the Act.[50]

The 2004 UN Convention on State Immunity in its Article 2 defines the word 'State' as including 'representatives of the state acting in that capacity'. Article 6(2)(b) further provides that:

> A proceeding before a court of a state shall be considered to have been instituted against another state if that other state ... (b) is not named as a party to the proceeding but the proceeding in effect seeks to affect the property, rights, interests or activities of that other State.

It now appears generally established that officials acting in their official capacity or in the course of their duties are to be entitled to the same immunity as the States they represent, since their acts are treated as the public/sovereign/governmental acts of the State.[51] Such immunity also extends to individuals and institutions who act at the request of a foreign State in situations where that State would enjoy immunity, such as a commercial bank and its employees who assist a foreign government in a criminal investigation.[52]

Senior officials in particular are treated with especial reverence. With perhaps the rarest of exceptions,[53] lawsuits against incumbent heads of State, heads of government or other high-ranking officials have met with no success.[54] This bears vivid testimony to the tenacity of a traditional rule of international law whereby, according to the ICJ in the *Arrest Warrant* case:

certain holders of high-ranking office in a State, such as the Head of State, Head of Government and Minister for Foreign Affairs, enjoy immunities from jurisdiction in other States, both civil and criminal.[55]

However, in a number of cases against *former* heads of State, immunity has indeed been denied;[56] and these cases merit special attention; for they show that it is now increasingly difficult for a *former* head of State (and by extension a former head of government) to claim immunity,[57] and such immunity can easily be waived by a new government.[58] Needless to say, a self-proclaimed 'head of State' cannot claim immunity on the basis of a future possibility of becoming a real one.[59] It must also be borne in mind that the issue of immunity before national courts does not prejudge the issue of immunity before international courts and tribunals. A head of State or government – even an incumbent one – may well be denied immunity before an international or a quasi-international tribunal.[60]

It is generally agreed that officials acting in their official capacity should be identified with the State. In the leading US case of *Chuidian*, Daza, a Philippine government official, was sued for having, pursuant to an Executive Order, instructed the Philippine National Bank to dishonour a letter of credit issued by the Philippine Government to the plaintiff. The central issue was whether Daza was entitled to immunity for acts committed in his official capacity as a member of the Presidential Commission on Good Government, an executive agency charged with recovering 'ill-gotten wealth' accumulated by the former Philippine President Marcos and his associates. The Ninth Circuit conceded that Congress in enacting the FSIA 'was primarily concerned with *organizations* acting for the foreign state, and may not have expressly contemplated the case of *individuals* acting as sovereign instrumentalities'.[61] However, the court said:

It is generally recognized that a suit against an individual acting in his official capacity is the practical equivalent of a suit against the sovereign directly.[62]

... we cannot infer that Congress, in passing the Act, intended to allow unrestricted suits against individual foreign officials acting in their official capacities. Such a result would amount to a blanket abrogation of foreign sovereign immunity by allowing litigants to accomplish indirectly what the Act barred them from doing directly.[63]

We thus join the majority of courts which have similarly concluded that section 1603(b) can fairly be read to include individuals sued in their official capacity.[64]

The *Chuidian* case thus established the rule that the FSIA applies to foreign officials acting in an official capacity for acts within the scope of their authority.[65] The *Chuidian* holding leads to two further conclusions. First, officers of corporations or other entities considered as foreign States are also protected when they act in their official capacity.[66] Secondly, and more importantly, officials are not entitled to immunity for acts which are not committed in an official capacity (such as selling personal property), and for acts beyond the scope of their authority (such as doing something they are not empowered to do).[67]

It is important, however, to bear in mind that the *Chuidian* holding has no impact on the position of foreign heads of State. According to established US case law, the FSIA does not apply to foreign heads of State.[68] Therefore, the traditional regime of 'suggestion of immunity by the State Department' with regard to foreign heads of State remains unaffected by the FSIA,[69] and the attitude of the Executive Branch, especially a suggestion of immunity, is dispositive of the issue of immunity.[70] The immunity of foreign heads of State is thus treated as an issue *sui generis*, more political than judicial, which it will be more appropriate for the Executive Branch to handle.[71]

The identification of the individual official with the State appeared so entrenched that the American Bar Association even proposed an amendment to apply the FSIA to foreign heads of State and officials.[72] Quite unexpectedly, however, the US Supreme Court took the position, in the case of *Samantar* in 2010, that an individual foreign official sued for conduct undertaken in his official capacity is not a 'foreign State' entitled to immunity from suit within the meaning of the FSIA; in other words, the FSIA does not, and should not, apply to foreign officials.[73] This case abrogates a substantial body of the US case law[74] and runs counter to cases from other countries as discussed above. The impact of this wholly novel holding remains to be assessed in the light of future developments.

6. The *Pinochet* case: a dissection

The *Pinochet* case involved the personal immunity of a former head of State from criminal (extradition) proceedings instituted in a State whose authorities had custody of the person of the defendant. It did not concern the immunity of the Chilean State, nor did it give rise to the complicated issues of jurisdiction *in absentia* (that is, while the defendant remains outside the territory of the forum State, such as happened in the *Arrest Warrant* and the *Sharon* cases). The jurisdiction of the forum State was asserted by virtue of the fact that all the three States concerned (Chile, where the alleged acts of torture had been committed; the UK, where Pinochet was arrested; and Spain, which was seeking Pinochet's extradition from the UK for torture committed against Spanish nationals) were States parties to the Torture Convention, and therefore Chile was precluded from claiming immunity on Pinochet's behalf.[75] However, the denial of immunity turned out to be only a partial (or even symbolic) victory for those endeavouring to bring Pinochet to justice. For the *Pinochet* case, to be more accurate, was only about the *extraditability*, rather than extradition, of Pinochet; that is, the case decided only whether Pinochet *could* be extradited to Spain, but the final decision whether he *should* eventually be extradited remained with the Home Secretary, who decided on 2 March 2000 to release Pinochet on health grounds. Pinochet left the UK the next day.[76]

To the extent that it merely affirmed a treaty-based universal criminal jurisdiction over torture the *Pinochet* case can hardly be considered groundbreaking; nor, in view of what happened to Ferdinand Marcos in the US, was it the first time a former foreign head of State had been denied immunity. However, whereas in Marcos's case the new Philippine Government not only waived his immunity but also actively pursued its own actions against him,[77] Pinochet lost his immunity in spite of vigorous contention for immunity on his behalf by the Chilean Government; and, what is more important, the Torture Convention, at least in its express terms, remains silent on the issue of immunity of heads of States, heads of governments, or other senior officials of a State. For the first time in history a rule has been established that a former head of State shall not enjoy immunity from criminal proceedings in a foreign court for acts of torture committed during his term of office and in his own country, whether or not such acts were committed as or pursuant to State policy. In this sense the *Pinochet* case is without doubt a monumental landmark celebrating the triumphant march of international human rights law over the past half century.[78]

In what can rightly be regarded as a direct response to the *Pinochet* case, the ICJ made this declaration in the *Arrest Warrant* case:

after a person ceases to hold the office of Minister for Foreign Affairs, he or she will no longer enjoy all of the immunities accorded by international law in other States. Provided that it has jurisdiction under international law, a court of one State may try a former Minister for Foreign Affairs of another State in respect of acts committed *prior or subsequent to* his or her period of office, as well as in respect of acts committed during that period of office *in a private capacity*.[79]

Such an unqualified, sweeping statement immunizes everything done by a senior government official *in a public capacity* during the period of office. It will be recalled that in the *Pinochet* case, five of the seven Law Lords were agreed that the acts of torture of which Pinochet stood accused, criminal as they were, were nevertheless committed in an official or governmental or public capacity.[80] Indeed, Article 1(1) of the Torture Convention itself defines torture as any act that is committed 'by or at the instigation of or with the consent or acquiescence of a public official or other person acting in an official capacity'.[81] Thus, contrary to a popular assumption, Pinochet's immunity in this case was denied not on the basis that torture was *not* a public function, nor solely for the reason that torture was a criminal offence, but chiefly on the ground that, by virtue of the Torture Convention, which confers a universal criminal jurisdiction over torture on the courts of the States parties, Chile, as a contracting party to the Torture Convention, had the legal obligation *not* to defeat such universal jurisdiction by claiming immunity for Pinochet before the courts of another contracting party, i.e. the UK.[82] In other words, a claim of immunity would be incompatible with the treaty obligation under the Torture Convention to ensure prosecution of torturers anywhere in the world. Doctrinal difficulties apart, this is what is truly revolutionary about the *Pinochet* case: it created an exception to immunity enjoyed by senior State officials where international law allows universal jurisdiction on a conventional or contractual basis, a development otherwise unthinkable without the rapid advancement of international human rights law over the previous two decades. Strangely oblivious to this important development in international law, the ICJ's pronouncement, without further qualifications, would leave it dubiously open for acts of torture to be exempted from the jurisdictional reach of a foreign court if such acts could be argued as forming part of the State policy at the time of commission, as definitely was the case under Pinochet's regime, and therefore committed in a public capacity and, consequently, covered by immunity.

If the public/private capacity distinction had been used as the only test for immunity, as formulated by the ICJ, then the *Pinochet* case would have been decided five to two in favour of Pinochet. The flaw in the ICJ's decision thus lies in treating the official capacity as the sole criterion for deciding on immunity, whereas the defence of official functions is becoming more and more untenable in the eyes of international human rights law, the most fundamental objective of which is precisely to prevent abuses of public authority.

7. Immunity and legality

Illegality does not make a particular activity private/commercial and therefore non-immune; in some cases, immunity was granted even though the act in question was of doubtful legality or was positively illegal. Generally speaking, the *jure imperii / jure gestionis* distinction is not made by reference to the lawfulness of the act; and the evolution of the restrictive doctrine of State immunity has been predicated on the commerciality, rather than legality, of the act in question. That is to say, the distinction between immune and non-immune activity is not based on the lawfulness or unlawfulness of a particular act but on whether that act can also be performed by a private person in furtherance of a private-law relationship. Sometimes the commercial nature of an act would be asserted in express disregard of its criminality. In US practice, the illegality of an act does not necessarily negate its commercial character. Thus a financial scam can be treated as a commercial activity because the purported act is a commercial activity.[83] Correlatively, even an internationally illegal act might still be regarded as a sovereign act (*jure imperii*) and therefore immune. Thus, in *Herman Grote*, a Dutch court said:

It may safely be said that with regard to *acta imperii*, either lawful or unlawful, whether acts of war or not, a State is not subject to the jurisdiction of the judiciary of another State.[84]

In *Amerada Hess*, the US Supreme Court held the US FSIA to be the 'sole basis for obtaining jurisdiction over a foreign state in [US] courts',[85] and drew 'the plain implication that immunity is granted in those cases involving alleged violations of international law that do not come within one of the FSIA's exceptions'.[86] In *McElhinney*, the plaintiff claimed, inter alia, that the British soldier was *unlawfully present* in Irish territory (he was carried over the UK–Ireland border on the towbar of a truck he was trying to stop at a checkpoint). The Irish Supreme Court seemed unimpressed by this aspect of the case; for it did not even discuss this point but instead proceeded to hold that the soldier, in carrying out his duties, was performing a sovereign or governmental act (act *jure imperii*).[87]

In *Herbage*, a British citizen incarcerated in the US after extradition brought action against various functionaries of the British Government, alleging that they had acted illegally in extraditing him. Following *Amerada Hess*, the court declared:

these men were acting in their official capacities as agents of the British government ... those actions cannot and do not subject them to liability in the courts of the United States. Since the activity complained of is governmental in nature and performed by officials of that government, this Court does not have jurisdiction over a foreign sovereign. The FSIA is absolute in this regard, *no matter how heinous the alleged illegalities.* The Court has no authority to address the legality of the defendants' actions.[88]

Lord Wilberforce said in *I Congreso del Partido*:

It was argued ... that even if ... Cuba might appear to be entitled to plead the state immunity, it should be denied that right [on the ground] that its acts were contrary to international law ... [However,] [t]he whole purpose of the doctrine of state immunity is to prevent such issues being canvassed in the courts of one state as to the acts of another.[89]

The now prevailing position therefore is that even illegal activities can attract immunity, provided they are of a sovereign, public or governmental nature.[90] In the words of Finlayson JA, in *Jaffe* v. *Miller*:

The illegal and malicious nature of the acts alleged do not of themselves move the actions outside the scope of the official duties of the responding defendants ... These were functionaries of a foreign state and whether acting legally or illegally they attract immunity in the same way as the state itself.[91]

The abuse of sovereign power is also regarded as a sovereign act. In *Nelson*, for example, the US Supreme Court found that:

the intentional conduct alleged here (the Saudi Government's wrongful arrest, imprisonment, and torture of Nelson) could not qualify as commercial under the restrictive theory. The conduct boils down to abuse of the power of its police by the Saudi Government, and however monstrous such abuse undoubtedly may be, a foreign state's exercise of the power of its police has long been understood for purposes of the restrictive theory as peculiarly sovereign in nature.[92]

In other words, because the power of the police was 'sovereign', then the *abuse* of that power was also sovereign in nature. More recently, Lord Hoffmann in *Jones* rejected the argument that an act in contravention of *jus cogens* cannot be an official act.[93]

It must be noted that the position that even illegal acts can be immune is due largely to the exclusively civil – and therefore limited – nature of the law of State immunity, which has developed chiefly in the context of commercial and trading disputes. This is a limitation placed on the law by history and, in the face of the rapidly advancing international human rights law, would appear particularly odious and would conceivably be subjected to serious attack.

Conclusion

The core issue concerning the relationship between State immunity and violations of human rights is the existence of extraterritorial jurisdiction (whether over criminal or civil matters). This part of the law is fraught with difficulties, logical, legal and practical. Current law on State immunity does not cover criminal proceedings, making it difficult to rely on current international human rights law, which has developed chiefly as a body of criminal law, as a basis for denying immunity. The fact that the *jure imperii / jure gestionis* distinction is generally drawn not by reference to the legality of the act in question renders it well-nigh impossible to fit a violation of human rights into any of the exceptions evolved largely in commercial and trading contexts. Violations of international law, even of *jus cogens* norms, cannot automatically strip a State of immunity before a foreign domestic court. The principle that immunity may subsist for illegal acts violating human rights, odious though it may be, nonetheless remains the law at the present moment. The matter is further compounded by the fact that officials may in certain circumstances be assimilated to the State and therefore may enjoy the same immunity as does the State. All these signal the unsatisfactory state of the law of State immunity in the face of the advancements made by international human rights law. That the immunity of former high-ranking officials has become less sacrosanct is certainly to be welcomed by human rights advocates.

11 The genesis of the UN Convention

The 2004 United Nations Convention on Jurisdictional Immunities of States and Their Property is an epoch-making document. It marks the final establishment of restrictive immunity as the prevailing doctrine in international law. As is the case with the development of the law of State immunity in general, the evolution of the UN Convention has had its fair share of vicissitudes. It has undergone an exceptionally long period of gestation, thanks to the slow and gradual process, often shot through with controversy, whereby the idea of restrictive immunity has come to be entrenched in international law. The UN Convention embodies all the general principles of restrictive immunity as discussed in this book while at the same time steering clear of various legal issues still in dispute. The culmination of many years of codification efforts at various levels, including deliberations of the International Law Commission, and consultations within the framework of the United Nations General Assembly, it represents the advances and compromises in this field of the law that may prove generally acceptable and will serve as an important basis for harmonizing the practice of different States and for achieving relative uniformity in an area of international law ever plagued with disputes between and among States.

1. Early efforts at codification

The attempt to reduce the customary international law of State immunity to some sort of written formulation designed to be generally applicable is almost as old as the law itself. As early as 1867, Bluntschli proposed a number of principles regarding various immunities enjoyed by (personal) sovereigns.[1] Judged objectively, however, Bluntschli's statute-book style of presenting various purported rules and principles of

441

442   THE GENESIS OF THE UN CONVENTION

international law is more indicative of a personal idiosyncrasy than of a serious possibility of codification, *stricto sensu*, of such rules and principles as binding rules of international law. The Institut de Droit International (IDI) decided to consider the question of 'Compétence des tribunaux dans les procès contre les États ou souverains étrangers' in 1888[2] and produced a set of five draft articles in 1891.[3] This tradition of learned bodies pursuing projects of an academic nature, once originated by the IDI, was carried to an admirable height in 1932 by the Harvard Research in International Law, organized under the auspices of the Faculty of the Harvard Law School, with Philip C. Jessup as Reporter for the subject of 'Competence of Courts in regard to Foreign States'. The final product of the Research, in the form of a draft international convention of twenty-eight articles, accompanied by detailed commentaries,[4] is a monumental document in the history of the codification of State immunity. These articles were the result of studious distillation from a wealth of materials, including especially case law from various countries, and, whether in terms of the abundance of materials examined, the depth of analysis or the range of issues addressed, can be regarded as the culmination of the efforts of previous generations of international lawyers and in many ways remains unsurpassed by subsequent works of the IDI and the International Law Association (ILA). Following its draft of 1891, the IDI found it necessary to renew the codification attempt several times over the years[5] and finally produced a draft in 1954[6] and – not surprisingly – another one in 1991.[7] The ILA, for its part, first noted the issue of immunity in 1926, when Karl Strupp presented a paper entitled 'Réforme et codification du droit international – Projet d'une convention sur l'immunité en droit international'.[8] The paper itself appears rather primitive from today's perspective, since it lumps together and deals indiscriminately with State immunity, head of State immunity, diplomatic and consular immunities, immunity of special envoys, of the judges of the Permanent Court of International Justice, and of the League of Nations officials. In other words, at that time within the ILA there was as yet neither clear conceptualization of, nor conscious differentiation between, these myriad and disparate species of immunity. After that, the topic was dropped and came back many years later, in 1950, only to disappear again in 1960.[9] The ILA resumed its work in 1978[10] and produced a draft in 1982[11] and again a revised draft in 1994.[12]

This intriguing spectacle of repeatedly abandoning and returning to the subject and of discarding and revising what were perceived to be definitively completed projects has been the hallmark of the work on the law of State immunity[13] and, one fears, might cast a gloom over the future prospects of any legal instrument on State immunity intended to be universal in application. Further, and more interestingly, the subject of State immunity has a number of times been considered as sufficiently developed to be susceptible of codification at intergovernmental level, that is, capable of being rendered into a legally binding instrument, but has been quietly abandoned each time for no apparent reason.

The codification of the law of State immunity at intergovernmental level dates back to the times of the League of Nations. On 22 September 1924, the Fifth Assembly of the League of Nations adopted a resolution in which it requested the Council to 'convene a committee of experts', who would have the duty to 'prepare a provisional list of the subjects of international law the regulation of which by international agreement would seem to be most desirable and realisable' and then to report on the questions which were 'sufficiently ripe' for codification, as well as on the procedure to be followed in preparing for conferences for their solution.[14] The Committee of Experts for the Progressive Codification of International Law, chaired by Hjalmar Hammarskjöld, was duly established[15] and discussed the issue of State immunity at its four sessions in 1925–1928.[16] In April 1927, at its Third Session, the Committee decided to include in its list the item 'Competence of the Courts in regard to Foreign States',[17] and requested the opinions of governments on the following question:

Whether and in what cases, particularly in regard to action taken by a State in the exercise of a commercial or industrial activity, a State can be liable to be sued in the courts of another State.[18]

The replies from governments were overwhelmingly encouraging. Of the twenty-four States that replied, twenty-one agreed that codification was 'desirable and realisable'.[19] Thus, on 27 June 1928, the Committee of Experts, in its second report to the Council of the League of Nations, listed 'Competence of the Courts with regard to Foreign States' as 'sufficiently ripe'.[20]

However, one year previously, on the basis of the Committee's first report to the Council,[21] the Eighth Assembly of the League of Nations in its resolution on 27 September 1927 had already decided to convene a diplomatic conference to codify three topics out of those considered as 'ripe' by the Committee.[22] Needless to say, the question of State immunity was not mentioned in the resolution, nor was it on the agenda of the

444   THE GENESIS OF THE UN CONVENTION

Conference for the Codification of International Law, which eventually met at The Hague from 13 March to 12 April 1930.[23] Two years had elapsed between the Committee's second report and the Codification Conference, and the Assembly would have had plenty of time to add State immunity as a further item for codification. Why it did not do so can only be a matter of conjecture. At any rate, even though the work of the Committee of Experts came to no fruition in this respect, the modus operandi established by it,[24] comprising the work of a committee of experts, questionnaires addressed to governments, analyses of the replies, comments and observations received from governments, draft articles as a basis for discussion and, finally, a diplomatic conference, has proved to be of great value and has become the standard procedure for the ILC's work leading to the current UN Convention.

During this time, several international conventions were concluded prior to, or outside the framework of, the League of Nations. The peace treaties concluded after the First World War, collectively known as the Peace of Paris (1919–1920),[25] contain some interesting provisions. Article 281 of the Treaty of Versailles provides:

> If the German Government engages in international trade, it shall not in respect thereof have or be deemed to have any rights, privileges or immunities of sovereignty.

The same provision is repeated in the Treaty of Saint-Germain (Article 233), Treaty of Trianon (Article 216), Treaty of Neuilly (Article 161) and Treaty of Sèvres (Article 268). It must be noted that this provision is expressly directed against the specific governments mentioned by it (i.e. the German, Austrian, Hungarian, Bulgarian, and Turkish Governments). There is no indication in any of these treaties that the Allied and Associated Powers, collectively constituting the other contracting party, would be subjected to the same restriction of immunity. On the contrary, Article 267 of the Treaty of Versailles ensures that:

> Every favour, immunity or privilege in regard to the importation, exportation or transit of goods granted by Germany to any Allied or Associated State or to any other foreign country whatever shall simultaneously and unconditionally, without request and without compensation, be extended to all the Allied and Associated States.[26]

It then becomes obvious that Article 281 enshrines, not a reciprocal obligation undertaken by the parties, but a restriction on State sovereignty imposed by one contracting party on the other, and is clearly intended to be punitive in nature. It furnishes no evidence either that States at that time considered the subject of State immunity suitable for regulation by international convention,[27] or that State immunity ought to be restricted in a general manner.[28]

As far as State immunity is concerned, the first real breakthrough came in 1926. Simultaneously with the deliberations of the Committee of Experts,[29] the International Maritime Committee organized two international conferences to consider the subject of State-owned ships, resulting in the 1926 International Convention for the Unification of Certain Rules relating to the Immunity of State-owned Vessels, concluded at a diplomatic conference held in Brussels. Article 1 of the Convention subjects State-owned or -operated vessels and the States owning or operating them 'to the same rules of liability and to the same obligations as those applicable to private vessels'; under Article 2:

For the enforcement of such liabilities and obligations there shall be the same rules concerning the jurisdiction of tribunals, the same legal actions, and the same procedure as in the case of privately owned merchant vessels and cargoes and of their owners.

Thus, with the exception of warships and other ships used 'exclusively on Governmental and non-commercial service' (Article 3), States and their ships were to be denied immunity regarding both adjudication and execution.[30] This assimilation of the position of State trading vessels to that of private merchant ships was later incorporated in a number of conventions on the law of the sea;[31] and the expression 'government and non-commercial' became a standard formula in these conventions and later in the ILC draft articles, and finally in the 2004 UN Convention.[32] Even though it sought to restrict immunity only within the narrow sphere of State-owned ships, the Brussels Convention was still the most revolutionary instrument at that time, in view of the position of absolute immunity adopted by many States even with regard to State trading vessels. By contrast, the Bustamante Code, adopted at the Sixth Inter-American Conference at Havana in 1928, evinces much caution and provides that national courts shall be incompetent except in cases of express submission or counterclaim (Article 333), real or mixed actions (Article 335) and 'universal causes (*juicios universales*, e.g. distribution of a bankrupt's or decedent's effects)' (Article 336). Given the adherence to it by the American countries,[33] the Code can be regarded as reflective of generally accepted exceptions to immunity at that time.

446   THE GENESIS OF THE UN CONVENTION

The most notable achievement is undoubtedly the conclusion of the European Convention on State Immunity in 1972.[34] It remains the only international convention on State immunity currently in force and has exerted considerable influence over the evolution of the law of State immunity.[35] The Organization of American States produced a draft convention but has not yet turned it into a binding instrument.[36] Provisions on immunity can also be found in international instruments dealing with nuclear liability. Thus, Article 13(e) of the 1960 Paris Convention on Third Party Liability in the Field of Nuclear Energy and Article 14 of the 1963 Vienna Convention on Civil Liability for Nuclear Damage preclude the invocation of jurisdictional immunities (but preserve immunity from measures of execution) before the competent court. Directly relevant to these instruments, Article 29(b) of the 1972 European Convention provides that the Convention 'shall not apply to proceedings concerning damage or injury in nuclear matters', since, according to the drafters, '[o]ther conventions deal with nuclear damage'.[37]

2. The work of the International Law Commission

From the moment of its establishment,[38] the UN International Law Commission (ILC) started considering the law of State immunity for possible codification. In 1948, in preparation for the First Session of the ILC, the UN Secretariat conducted a 'survey of international law' and published a memorandum which sanguinely declared that 'the question – in all its aspects – of jurisdictional immunities of foreign States is capable and in need of codification'.[39] On the basis of the *Survey*, the ILC at its First Session in 1949 proposed the subject of 'Jurisdictional immunities of States and their property' as one of the 'topics selected for codification' without, however, giving it priority.[40] After that, for twenty-eight years, notwithstanding repeated insinuations from the Secretariat, which produced, in particular, another 'survey of international law' in 1971,[41] nothing was done with regard to the subject of State immunity until 1977 when, at its Twenty-ninth Session, the ILC recommended (or rather re-recommended, considering the 1949 selection) the topic of 'Jurisdictional immunities of States and their property' 'for selection in the near future for active consideration'.[42] Following the General Assembly Resolution 32/151 (1977), which invited the ILC, 'at an appropriate time ... to commence work on the topic[] of ... jurisdictional immunities of States and their property',[43] the ILC decided at its Thirtieth Session in 1978, upon recommendation by a Working Group established for the purpose (another ILC Working Group was to be set up again in 1999), to 'include in its current programme of work the topic "Jurisdictional immunities of States and their property"', appointed Sompong Sucharitkul as Special Rapporteur for the topic, and requested the Secretary-General to invite the governments of Member States to submit 'relevant materials on the topic, including national legislation, decisions of national tribunals and diplomatic and official correspondence'.[44] The inclusion of the topic of State immunity was consistently confirmed by the General Assembly in its resolutions over the following years,[45] a fact that demonstrates that the codification of the law of State immunity – along the lines of restrictive immunity, which ought to have become obvious once the ILC started to carve out exceptions to immunity at its Thirty-fifth Session in 1983[46] – has enjoyed considerable support throughout the whole process.

The ILC considered the topic from its Thirty-first to Thirty-eighth and from its Forty-first to Forty-third Sessions, from 1979 to 1986 and from 1989 to 1991.[47] It appointed Motoo Ogiso as the new Special Rapporteur for the topic at its Thirty-ninth Session in 1987. In particular, the ILC considered the reports of the Special Rapporteurs[48] and comments and observations of governments.[49] In 1991, at its Forty-third Session, the ILC finally completed a set of twenty-two Draft Articles and submitted them, together with commentaries, to the General Assembly, recommending the convening of 'an international conference of plenipotentiaries to examine the draft articles on the jurisdictional immunities of States and their property and to conclude a convention on the subject'.[50] The General Assembly duly expressed its 'appreciation ... for the completion of the final draft articles on jurisdictional immunities of States and their property'.[51] More importantly, the General Assembly decided to establish at its Forty-seventh Session an open-ended working group of the Sixth (Legal) Committee to examine:

(a) Issues of substance arising out of the draft articles, in order to facilitate a successful conclusion of a convention through the promotion of general agreement;
(b) The question of the convening of an international conference, to be held in 1994 or subsequently, to conclude a convention on jurisdictional immunities of States and their property.[52]

3. The debate in the General Assembly Sixth Committee

The Sixth Committee Working Group, with Carlos Calero-Rodrigues as Chairman, held two sessions in 1992–1993, followed by 'informal consultations' in 1994, again convened by Calero-Rodrigues.[53] The Working Group considered the following issues of substance: (1) the definition of the terms 'State' and 'commercial transaction', including the question of the criterion for determining whether a contract or transaction is a 'commercial transaction'; (2) the question of the legal distinction between a State and certain of its entities in respect of State immunity; (3) contracts of employment; (4) the question of immunity from measures of constraint. The debate chiefly focused on the criterion for determining a commercial transaction, the separate status of State entities and measures of constraint.[54]

As for 'commercial transaction', views were divided on whether the commercial character of a transaction should be determined on the sole basis of the 'nature' of the transaction or whether the 'purpose' of that transaction should also be taken into account.[55] Briefly put, the dispute was between a 'nature only' position and a 'purpose also' position: some States maintained either that 'nature' should be the only relevant criterion, or that 'purpose' should be relevant only when the State in question has notified the private party of its relevance or, better still, when both parties to the transaction have expressly agreed.[56] At the other end of the spectrum, there were States that insisted on treating purpose as an independent criterion alongside nature; that is, they did not object to 'nature' playing the *main* role, but they took the view that a governmental purpose should also be taken into consideration notwithstanding the apparently commercial nature of a contract or transaction.[57] Still others seemed more flexible and expressed their readiness to accept a role for 'purpose', as drafted by the ILC in draft Article 2(2).[58] It must be pointed out here that the final UN Convention to some extent accommodates the 'purpose also' approach.[59]

In relation to State enterprises/entities, the debate was around whether a State and its enterprises/entities should be mutually liable or whether they should be treated separately.[60] Many States were of the view that a State should be treated separately from its enterprises; that is, they were in favour of the principle of non-liability of the State for the debts of its enterprises and vice versa, as provided for in Article 10 of the 1991 ILC Draft.[61] Other States either pushed for the possibility of 'piercing the corporate veil', which would allow recourse to the assets of the State for the liability of a State enterprise, or questioned the advisability of dealing with what they perceived as an issue of State responsibility/liability within the framework of the draft articles.[62] In between was a position of a semi-separate status for State-owned enterprises, which would concede the separate status for State enterprises but wish to see a joint liability of the State under certain circumstances.[63]

As regards measures of constraint, differences were between the position that measures of constraint could only be taken against commercial State property having a connection with the underlying claim or with the agency or instrumentality concerned, and the position that such a link would be unduly restrictive of the judicial powers of the court in granting remedies and therefore unnecessary and undesirable.[64] Both the demand for a connection[65] and the objection to it[66] were strongly contended and passionately defended, and may well be regarded as the main causes of the long delay in reaching any definitive solution at all. The Chairman of the Working Group proposed that the connection requirement should be removed in cases of post-judgment execution but retained for cases of interim or pre-judgment measures;[67] and this met with some support.[68]

Generally speaking, the States that participated in the Sixth Committee consultations evinced a highly favourable view of the ILC draft articles, considering them to be in the nature of a well-balanced compromise accommodating various positions, and to be capable of serving as a good basis for an international instrument that would bring certainty and uniformity into an otherwise disorderly field.[69] Most significantly, since all the States supported the ILC draft articles, it must follow that none advocated an absolute immunity doctrine. Thus it is safe to conclude that, at the time when the ILC submitted its draft to the UN General Assembly in 1991, the general principle of restrictive immunity had been universally accepted, at least on the international plane, both as an established fact and as established law.

On the other hand, although there was a general consensus that an international instrument was urgently needed, there was yet no agreement as to when an international conference should be held. Some delegations suggested that an international conference should and could be convened at once, possibly without further working group consultations;[70] others felt that it was too early to take a formal decision on the matter; still others could not commit themselves to the idea of a conference.[71] The prevailing opinion was in favour of a diplomatic conference but held that that conference should be convened only when all the outstanding issues of principle had been settled and reasonable consensus reached, thus the consultations should continue (preferably in the form of a working group) for an eventual consensus, since a failed conference might do greater damage to the codification efforts than no

450 THE GENESIS OF THE UN CONVENTION

conference at all.[72] At any rate, the 'international conference' was not held until 2004, thirteen years after the ILC's submission of the draft articles to the General Assembly in 1991.

The topic of 'Convention on jurisdictional immunities of States and their property' remained on the General Assembly's agenda[73] until 1994, when it became evident that the controversies within the Sixth Committee rendered the prospect of convening a diplomatic conference to negotiate a convention increasingly remote, and that a period of further reflection was necessary.[74] Thus, by Resolution 49/61 (1994), the General Assembly decided to leave the matter aside for three years, that is, it would 'resume consideration, at its fifty-second session, of the issues of substance ... and to determine, at its fifty-second or fifty-third session, the arrangements for the conference, including the date and place'.[75]

No progress was made in 1997–1998 at the Fifty-second and Fifty-third Sessions of the General Assembly.[76] In Resolution 53/98 (1998), the General Assembly decided to start all over again at its Fifty-fourth Session to be held in 1999, this time involving not only the General Assembly itself, in the form of an open-ended working group of the Sixth Committee, which would 'consider outstanding substantive issues related to the draft articles on jurisdictional immunities of States and their property', but also the ILC, which was invited to 'present any preliminary comments it may have regarding outstanding substantive issues related to the draft articles by 31 August 1999'.[77]

This decision of the General Assembly brought forth two working groups: the ILC Working Group[78] and the Sixth Committee Working Group,[79] both chaired by Gerhard Hafner. The Sixth Committee Working Group was converted into an Ad Hoc Committee in 2000.

The ILC Working Group decided to concentrate its work on the five main issues identified in the conclusions of the Chairman of the 1994 informal consultations, namely: (1) concept of a State for purposes of immunity; (2) criteria for determining the commercial character of a contract or transaction; (3) concept of a State enterprise or other entity in relation to commercial transactions; (4) contracts of employment; and (5) measures of constraint against State property.[80] For each issue the ILC Working Group's report started from the 1991 draft articles and then proceeded to examine the evolution of the issue, summarizing recent relevant case law, and then to suggest possible ways of resolving the issue.

With regard to the criteria for determining the commercial character of a contract or transaction, the ILC Working Group thought that 'the distinction between the so-called nature and purpose tests might be less significant in practice than the long debate about it might imply', and therefore thought it better to have no criterion at all.[81]

As concerns the separateness of a State enterprise from the State itself, the ILC Working Group suggested that the immunity of a State should not apply to liability claims in relation to a commercial transaction engaged in by a State enterprise or other entity established by that State where: (a) the State enterprise or other entity engages in a commercial transaction as an authorized agent of the State; (b) the State acts as a guarantor of a liability of the State enterprise or other entity.[82] However, the Working Group refused to go any further in the direction of 'piercing the corporate veil'.[83]

In respect of contracts of employment, the ILC Working Group found it advisable to clarify the relevant provisions so that immunity would remain untouched 'if the employee has been recruited to perform functions in the exercise of governmental authority, in particular: (a) diplomatic staff and consular officers, as defined in the Vienna Convention on Diplomatic Relations and the Vienna Convention on Consular Relations, respectively; (b) diplomatic staff of permanent missions to international organizations and of special missions; (c) other persons enjoying diplomatic immunity, such as persons recruited to represent a State in international conferences'.[84]

As for measures of constraint, the ILC Working Group proposed a distinction between prejudgment and post-judgment measures of constraint. Prejudgment measures would be possible only upon consent of the State concerned, or on property designated to satisfy the claim, or under internationally accepted provisions such as ship arrest under the 1952 International Convention relating to the Arrest of Seagoing Ships, or on property of a separate entity, whereas post-judgment measures would be allowed only upon consent of the State concerned, or on property designated to satisfy the claim.[85]

The discussions of the Sixth Committee Working Group, chaired by Gerhard Hafner:

revolved around the following points ... namely: (1) possible form of the outcome of the work on the topic; (2) the five outstanding substantive issues identified in the report of the Working Group of the International Law Commission, namely, (a) concept of a State for purposes of immunity; (b) criteria for determining the commercial character of a contract or transaction; (c) concept of a State enterprise or other entity in relation to commercial transactions; (d) contracts of employment; and (e) measures of constraint against State property; (3) the appendix to the

452   THE GENESIS OF THE UN CONVENTION

report of the Working Group concerning the existence or non-existence of immunity in the case of violation by a State of *jus cogens* norms; and (4) future course of action to be taken with regard to the topic.[86]

The views expressed within the Sixth Committee Working Group, whose debates revolved around the ILC Working Group report, were generally brief, in contrast to – and repetitive of – the deliberations in 1991–1994. Apart from further approval of the 1991 ILC Draft,[87] there was widespread appreciation for the work of the ILC Working Group.[88] Not surprisingly, more discussion was deemed necessary within the Sixth Committee Working Group.[89] With respect to the substantive issues, positions seem to have become even more diversified along the fault lines of old divisions. As regards the criteria for determining commercial transactions, States were divided in their opinions on the suggestions made by the ILC Working Group in its report.[90] In particular, there were those that supported the ILC Working Group report in deleting the references to nature and purpose,[91] as well as those sceptical of the deletion.[92] Moreover, there was still the renewed adherence to a 'nature alone' approach,[93] as opposed to a 'purpose also' stance,[94] as well as the non-committal position that would be happy either way.[95] The same variegated situation persisted with regard to State enterprises/entities[96] and measures of constraint.[97] One finds support for the ILC Working Group's suggestion of a degree of joint State liability,[98] insistence on separateness between the State and its enterprises,[99] and the proposal that such a provision be deleted altogether.[100] As for measures of constraint, however, despite the old division between 'link'[101] and 'no link',[102] it seemed promising that the majority of the States favoured a solution proposed by the ILC Working Group that drew a distinction between pre- and post-judgment measures.[103] Furthermore, disagreement occurred regarding the final form that ought to be taken by the projected international instrument.[104] There was an equal split between those wishing to have a convention[105] and those preferring to see only a 'model law'.[106]

There was general agreement that the divergence of views made further efforts necessary.[107] Not surprisingly, the General Assembly decided that the Sixth Committee Working Group should continue its work in 2000, 'to consider the future form of, and outstanding substantive issues related to, the draft articles on jurisdictional immunities of States and their property'.[108]

In contrast to his report of 1999, the Chairman of the Sixth Committee Working Group submitted a substantial report in 2000, in which he listed a variety of alternative texts for the articles embodying the outstanding substantive issues.[109] An important development occurred in 2000, however, when the General Assembly, in its resolution 55/150, decided to set up an Ad Hoc Committee on Jurisdictional Immunities of States and their Property, scheduled to meet in March 2002, for the purposes of 'elaborating a generally acceptable instrument based on the [1991 ILC] draft articles'.[110]

The establishment of an Ad Hoc Committee, thereby transforming the never-ending and fruitless debate in the Sixth Committee into focused and well-informed deliberation of a group of competent experts, was indeed a most ingenious idea and should be a valuable example for similar undertakings within the UN framework in the future. Following the decision, the volume of those repetitive disputes drastically diminished in 2001.[111]

The Ad Hoc Committee was reconvened on 24–28 February 2003 'to make a final attempt at consolidating areas of agreement and resolving outstanding issues, with a view to elaborating a generally acceptable instrument',[112] and again on 1–5 March 2004, 'with the mandate to formulate a preamble and final clauses, with a view to completing a convention on jurisdictional immunities of States and their property'.[113] In total, the Ad Hoc Committee submitted three reports to the General Assembly.[114]

What is truly remarkable is that, even though the old controversies resurfaced in 2002, when States were called upon to consider the Ad Hoc Committee's report,[115] these controversies miraculously disappeared a year later; and Hafner, Chairman of the Ad Hoc Committee, confidently pronounced that 'all outstanding issues – some of which had been on the agenda of the ILC for 25 years – had been settled'.[116] What is more, States were unanimously agreed that the final form of the international instrument should be a convention.[117]

In its third and final report the Ad Hoc Committee presented the Draft UN Convention,[118] whereupon the General Assembly then adopted the UN Convention on Jurisdictional Immunities of States and Their Property in Resolution A/RES/59/38 of 2 December 2004, thus successfully accomplishing an eventful, long drawn-out codification process.[119] If one considers the year of 1978 as the time when the work on the UN Convention began in earnest in the International Law Commission, then it had taken twenty-six years for that convention finally to come into being – and it is still not yet in force.

4. Universal support for the UN Convention

Already the UN Convention has attracted some favourable remarks from national courts.[120] Another important indicator of the favourable reception of the UN Convention is furnished by the positive attitude now adopted by Asian-African countries in general. Traditionally, apart from chiefly being defendants before foreign courts, Asian-African States have generally made very limited contribution to the development of the law of State immunity.[121] With the exception of only a few countries (Japan, the Philippines, India, Singapore, Pakistan, South Africa, etc.), they do not have a regular case reporting system, nor do their courts deal with many cases in this field. Also compared with other groups of States (EU and Rio Group, for example), Asian-African countries have not shown significant cooperation during the debates on the UN Convention on State Immunity. Nonetheless, Asian-African countries collectively began considering the issue of State immunity at a very early stage. The Asian-African Legal Consultative Committee (AALCC, changed into the Asian-African Legal Consultative Organization (AALCO) in 2001) considered the issue of immunity at its first three sessions in 1957–1960.[122] However, like the codification within the UN framework, nothing happened for the next forty years until the AALCO took up the matter again at its Thirty-ninth Session in 2000, when the topic 'Jurisdictional Immunities of States and their Property' was included in its agenda following a proposal from Japan. The item remained on the agenda from 2000–2005 and the Secretariat presented reports on the developments on the topic at successive sessions of AALCO. The title of the agenda item repeats that of the ILC and later the UN Convention, and therefore reflects a highly positive attitude towards the work within the UN. Indeed, consistent approval and support has been expressed for the work of the UN Ad Hoc Committee on State Immunity and later for the UN Convention.[123] Thus one can safely conclude that Asian-African States in general have now accepted the restrictive immunity doctrine. However, useful materials (especially case reports) from these countries are still hard to come by.[124]

Moreover, the fact that China and Russia, two erstwhile staunchest adherents of absolute immunity, not only actively participated in the consultations held under the auspices of the UN General Assembly Sixth Committee, but also signed the 2004 Convention (China on 14 September 2005; Russia on 1 December 2006), is surely an encouraging sign for the supporters of the Convention in particular and of the restrictive doctrine in general.

5. What the UN Convention enshrines

The UN Convention has already been subjected to voluminous and meticulous scholarly scrutiny – and by some of the most eminent authorities in this field.[125] I shall here attempt only to sketch in broad strokes its most salient features.

The UN Convention encapsulates all the currently accepted general principles on State immunity. These are broadly in line with present national statutes on immunity. These principles include:

(1) States enjoy immunity as a principle of customary international law (preamble, paragraph 1).

(2) In principle States are immune from proceedings before foreign national courts (Article 5) subject to clearly defined exceptions to that immunity (Articles 7–17).

(3) In order to deny immunity, a court must have jurisdiction in the first place. Thus a jurisdictional connection is built into all the articles dealing with the proceedings in which State immunity cannot be invoked. As Hafner and Köhler point out:

> A prerequisite for the question of whether a state enjoys immunity is the existence of jurisdiction of the court. Therefore, Article 10 first requires that the transactions envisaged, in accordance with the rules of private international law, fall within the jurisdiction of a court of another state. Such jurisdiction could be based, *inter alia*, on the place of conclusion of the contract, the place where the obligations arising from the contract are to be performed, or on the basis of the nationality of one of the contracting parties. In this context, Articles 11 until 17 refer to the existence of the jurisdiction of the court by using the formula of the 'court of another state which is otherwise competent' in the relevant proceeding.[126]

> In addition, several articles specifically require a territorial nexus. Article 11 denies immunity with regard to contracts of employment 'for work performed or to be performed, in whole or in part, in the territory of that other State'; Article 12 applies if the tortious 'act or omission occurred in whole or in part in the territory of that other State and if the author of the act or omission was present in that territory at the time of the act or omission'; and Article 19 conditions the execution against State property, in the absence of a waiver or earmarking, on the presence of the property 'in the territory of the State of the forum'.

(4) The immunity enjoyed by a foreign State encompasses two distinct immunities: immunity from jurisdiction and immunity from execution; waiver of immunity from jurisdiction does not mean waiver of immunity from execution, for which a separate waiver is needed.

(5) Accordingly the issue of enforcement is treated separately from the issue of adjudication.

6. What the UN Convention avoids

It is actually easier and simpler to assess the hope of success in terms of what is *not* covered by the UN Convention. The Convention steers clear of such issues as State immunity in respect of human rights violations, the notion of *jus cogens* and its possible effect on State immunity,[127] immunity of State officials with regard to criminal proceedings, extraterritorial jurisdiction, and the status of foreign armed forces.[128] All these issues are subject to intense debate and controversy at present. They are in urgent need of further exploration[129] and States are still far from reaching any consensus. An attempt to place any of these issues within the ambit of a UN Convention on State Immunity would indefinitely put off its completion, if completion can be achieved at all. Thus the fact that the UN Convention stays within the traditional bounds reflects a wise decision to avoid the entanglements that may necessarily result from a discussion of these complicated issues over which international law is just starting to evolve. In brief, the UN Convention has left untouched those aspects of the law that are not yet 'ripe' for codification. Only by concentrating on those areas where consensus is most likely to be achieved can the prospects of winning wide acceptance be assured.

The UN Convention says nothing about the question of immunity with regard to violations of human rights.[130] In particular, the report of the ILC Working Group contains a very brief appendix on 'the question of the existence or non-existence of jurisdictional immunity in actions arising . . . out of violations of *jus cogens* norms'. However, the Working Group chose only to refer the matter to the Sixth Committee.[131] The Sixth Committee Working Group (not to be confused with the ILC Working Group) in its report found that the issue of *jus cogens* did not 'fit into the present draft articles' and, moreover, did not 'seem to be ripe enough for the Working Group to engage in a codification exercise over it'.[132]

On the whole, the UN Convention embodies the crystallization of all the traditional aspects of the law of State immunity but stands – for better or for worse – aloof from recent developments (or thwarted attempts thereat) in other contexts, especially that of transnational human rights litigation. In other words, the UN Convention stays strictly within the traditional bounds, which have been defined and delimited chiefly by cases involving commercial and similar transactions, and are firmly rooted in the fundamental principle of territorial jurisdiction. This may have helped the Convention escape a fate of perpetual gestation with little hope of final conclusion as a binding instrument; but for those wishing to see even greater erosion of State immunity by an extensive, extraterritorial jurisdiction, it will understandably be deplored as something of a disappointment. Still, even the staunchest and the most radical of the advocates of restrictive immunity a century ago could scarcely have imagined the massive scale and the far-reaching implications of the encroachments made – albeit ever so slowly and gradually – over the years on the position of States before foreign national courts, encroachments that are now simply taken for granted. The UN Convention is both the testimony and the culmination of the century-long drama in which restrictive immunity has slowly but surely replaced absolute immunity as *the* governing principle of international law. Seen in this light it is nothing short of a great achievement.

Conclusion

The UN Convention, which lays down a general principle of immunity qualified by a finite number of narrowly defined exceptions, will in effect place the restriction of immunity within currently accepted boundaries, so that further restrictions will become extremely difficult, if not impossible. This means that States are now unanimous in thinking that further erosions of State immunity should be curbed.

The perfect irony is that the variedness of the law makes an international convention urgently necessary for the sake of uniformity, clarity and a reassuring sense of certainty, but at the same time ill-fated for a complete success. Because of its necessarily reductionist outlook an international convention represents at best some expedient compromise catering to the caprices of all while satisfying the needs of none, and might not find wide acceptance in a short span of time – by acceptance I mean not half-hearted encomiums and rhetorical support – a standard feature of the proceedings in the General Assembly, of which one has had more than an earful in the Sixth Committee – but ratifications followed by effective domestic legislative steps to render its provisions binding law for the courts that regularly deal with immunity cases.

The chequered history of the codification efforts leading to the UN Convention vividly testifies to the twists and turns in the development of the current restrictive doctrine. The Convention is an authoritative statement of how far States are now prepared to go in exercising jurisdiction over foreign States and in relinquishing their own immunity. It represents the crystallization of various principles developed in the 'traditional' (i.e. chiefly commercial and trading) areas of the law and marks the final victory of the restrictive immunity doctrine. In its content, however, it remains loyally within the bounds of that doctrine as developed by courts and other tribunals in dealing with mainly commercial disputes between individuals and foreign States. It is a landmark document in a twofold sense: it signifies the end of a century-long antipathy between the doctrine of restrictive immunity and that of (almost) unlimited immunity; and, in solidifying what has been achieved, it indicates those areas where new developments are certainly to be expected. Thus, the history of State immunity has not ended with the UN Convention: it has started anew, on a different front.

General conclusions

State immunity, in the narrow sense as used in this book, is a principle of customary international law, by virtue of which one sovereign State cannot, without its consent, be sued before the national courts of another sovereign State. Put in another way, a sovereign State is exempt from the jurisdiction of foreign national courts. Thus the notion of immunity consists of two elements: an otherwise existing and exercisable jurisdiction and exemption from it. Seen from the perspective of the State of the forum, State immunity means that the courts must refrain from exercising the jurisdiction they may otherwise lawfully exercise if the defendant is not a foreign sovereign State. For this reason State immunity is also referred to as 'jurisdictional immunity' or 'immunity from jurisdiction'. One can at once see that immunity is different from lack or absence of jurisdiction; quite the contrary, for the very idea of immunity actually affirms the existence of jurisdiction by suggesting an exception to or exemption from it. The usual shorthand formula used by courts, namely, 'This court does not have jurisdiction in this case', must then be understood as simply meaning that the court refuses to exercise its jurisdiction.

Therefore, the existence of jurisdiction logically precedes the question of immunity. That is to say, the question of immunity is at once a question of jurisdiction: only when the court already has, or has established, jurisdiction will it become meaningful to speak of immunity or exemption from that jurisdiction. If the court does not have jurisdiction in the first place, then the case must be dismissed, even if the defendant happens to be a private individual. Since the chief legal basis of jurisdiction under international law is territoriality, State immunity has been rightly perceived from the start as an exception to the territorial jurisdiction of the national courts of a foreign State.

459

However, given the now firmly established position of State immunity within the general paradigm of international law, it is more convenient and accurate to regard State immunity as a principle in its own right, rather than simply as an exception to a principle. Current international law on State immunity embodies the doctrine of limited or restrictive immunity, which grants a general blanket of immunity to foreign States subject to a number of exceptional situations in which immunity will be denied. The pattern of immunity plus exceptions means that immunity is always the starting assumption in a case against a foreign State. That is to say, a sovereign State is always presumed immune from the legal proceedings in a foreign national court unless the contrary can be proven. A private litigant against a foreign State thus bears the burden of proving that the defendant foreign State has acted in a way that disentitles it to immunity. The whole history of the practice and doctrine of restrictive immunity centres on the so-called 'exceptions' to the presumption of immunity. In the sense that immunity itself already is actually an exception to the territorial jurisdiction of the court, the situations in which a defendant foreign State should not enjoy immunity constitute, in a manner of speaking, exceptions to an exception.

The evolution of the law of State immunity started from the principle of absolute immunity, which exempted a State from any and all legal proceedings in foreign national courts, whatever the character of the legal relationship involved in a particular case and whatever the nature of the legal proceedings, and has now finally settled on the principle of limited, or relative, or restrictive immunity, pursuant to which a foreign State enjoys immunity only in some cases but not in all of them. As international law currently stands, States enjoy immunity for sovereign, non-commercial, public, or governmental acts (*acta jure imperii*) but not for non-sovereign, commercial, private, or non-governmental acts (*acta jure gestionis*). The transition from absolute to restrictive immunity has been a slow, gradual process, but it also seems to be an irreversible process, in that no State that has moved to restrictive immunity has ever reverted to absolute immunity. It can be seen that the principle of territoriality played a crucial role in the transition. As the most important legal basis of jurisdiction, it provided the strongest rationale for the denial of immunity. The fundamental change in the attitude towards the issue of immunity has been due chiefly to the practical necessity to reconsider the position of foreign States before national courts, presented to lawyers and judges alike by the growing participation of States in commercial and trading activities in foreign countries. Thus the law of State immunity is firmly rooted in and forms a counterpoint to the fundamental principle of territorial jurisdiction. And, from the very beginning, the modern law of restrictive State immunity developed clearly as a response to new realities; and it has remained reactive and of a remarkably haphazard, makeshift and patchwork nature. The academic theory of State immunity, though it may have in some measure boosted the development of the law, has been, and still is, a mere offshoot and reflection of the latter.

The international law on State immunity has been the result of a confluence of the judicial practice of those national courts that have had occasion to decide on the matter. In other words, the law of State immunity has developed largely *from within* the States, rather than *between* them. In fact, the whole history of the law in this field has been a steady movement away from the international plane and into the arena of national judicial practice. As a consequence, one observes two essentially opposing trends in the development of the law: *unification* in general principles and *fragmentation* in technical rules. That is, while States, especially their courts, have come to be increasingly unanimous on the general principles concerning the grant and denial of immunity, the law itself has also undergone and continues to undergo a process of further differentiation, particularization and specialization, with ever more refined domestic legal rules concerning the actual circumstances under which immunity is to be granted or denied.

Now the question of State immunity is rightly regarded as a major concern of international law and of law in general. The fact that the issue of immunity now as a general rule must be contested before the court has revolutionized the thinking and the language of State immunity. An increasingly legalistic discourse has emerged, with the result that the issue of State immunity can be routinely examined in a court with clinical detachment, without much need for doctrinal probe into the legal and philosophical underpinnings, and ostensibly without the necessity to consider possible political implications. This has to a large extent given a – partially false – appearance of technicality to the question of immunity and has therefore obscured or even concealed the tension and sensitivity inherent in bringing a sovereign State before a foreign national court. In other words, the emergence of technicalities also means that granting or denying immunity to a foreign State now seems little more than a mundane exercise of judicial authority for the judge, part of any day's work only; and certain aspects of the issue of State immunity, especially those closely bound up with the State-to-State

462   GENERAL CONCLUSIONS

relations, that is, the political aspects of State immunity, have been rendered less evident by a seemingly technical, i.e. legal, manner in which questions of State immunity are argued before and decided by courts.

There is currently not much controversy on the general principles concerning State immunity; for it is now universally accepted that State immunity can be restricted in certain circumstances. What is in dispute is the actual manner in which that immunity is to be given effect. The courts are not agreed on what exactly constitutes *actum jure imperii* or *actum jure gestionis*, nor are they unanimous as to precisely what criteria must be applied when deciding upon the situations in which immunity can be denied in individual cases. The practice of various national courts regarding foreign State immunity is marked by pragmatism and flexibility. Thus, for example, the 'nature' or its variant 'private person' test, so important for distinguishing 'commercial transactions', comes to be largely discarded by courts in dealing with contracts of employment. A teleological construction is adopted to preserve the immunity of foreign States with regard to certain employment relationships, such as the employment of embassy personnel. The general rule of thumb, i.e. immunity is available to acts *jure imperii* but not to acts *jure gestionis*, has also been subjected to very ingenious reconstruction in relation to tortious liability. And the 'purpose' test, so much discredited in many courts at the adjudicative stage, now re-emerges as the decisive criterion in dealing with enforcement and execution against foreign State property.

We have been repeatedly confronted not only with the inadequacy of the doctrine, and with the crude, patchy and improvisatory nature of the practice of restrictive immunity, but also with the inherent dilemma of the law of State immunity as a whole. With the vast increase of State commercial activities, it is no longer in keeping with justice and fairness to regard all the acts of a State as *acta jure imperii*. In order to exercise jurisdiction over some acts of foreign States within the forum State, a theory is needed that distinguishes between *acta jure imperii* and *acta jure gestionis*; but of course one also needs to avoid characterizing all the acts of a foreign State as *acta jure gestionis*. It is then inevitable that the courts, faced with all and sundry cases involving foreign States, have found it necessary to perform various balancing stunts by modifying the doctrine from time to time in order to accommodate the realities. It is also natural that different courts have different ways of distinguishing *acta jure imperii* from *acta jure gestionis*, while one and the same act might be considered *actum jure imperii* in some courts but *actum jure gestionis* in others. This also means that the attempt to resolve the disputation between the 'purpose' and the 'nature' tests will lead nowhere, since there cannot be, and courts cannot afford to confine themselves to, any single, pure, unalloyed test. Diverse approaches and varied results will continue to characterize the law of State immunity. Ultimately, after all, the law of State immunity is, if anything, but the sum total of various rules and principles that have evolved and accumulated over the years in the actual solving of practical problems. Such rules and principles are more in the nature of makeshift measures and are often remarkably elastic, malleable, even self-contradictory and mutually conflicting. They work best if one actually refrains from questioning their logic, from too much theorizing, and from reducing them to absurdity. The law of State immunity is not, and has never been, an exact, accurate science that can be reasoned, honed, and perfected in the rarefied atmosphere of a law school; it is just a pragmatic tool for dealing with everyday problems. It is a good tool when it solves problems; otherwise it is not and has to be adjusted and readjusted as circumstances may require. For those who use the tool, what is important is that it works; there is little need to worry about its mechanics.

A number of exceptions to the immunity of States before foreign national courts can be found in current legal instruments and case law. While the list may vary from instrument to instrument, and from court to court, there is little dispute concerning the core items, and these include commercial activity, contracts of employment, and personal injury or damage to property. What must be noted, though, is the great diversity in State practice concerning the actual definition of these exceptions and the circumstances in which they apply. Strictly speaking, however, the question of exceptions to immunity from jurisdiction only concerns the immunity of a foreign State from the *adjudicative power* of the court, and does not prejudge the possibility of enforcement of the court's rulings and decisions against either the defendant foreign State or its property. In other words, the question of exceptions to immunity from jurisdiction only concerns whether and in what circumstances a State can be sued before a foreign national court, and does not have any bearing on the question whether the property of the defendant foreign State can be subjected to enforcement measures either to secure guarantee for a probable judgment in favour of the private litigant, or to execute a final judgment. Separate and distinct considerations apply to the process of enforcement and execution. Ultimately, if the judicial power of a court is to be considered as naturally consisting of both the

464 GENERAL CONCLUSIONS

power to hear and determine a case, and the power to enforce its rulings and decisions, then such a dichotomy between the power to decide and the power to enforce appears extremely artificial and poses serious questions about the effectiveness of the judicial remedies for the private litigant.

'International law' with regard to State immunity assumes a double, or ambiguous, character. On the one hand, since courts regularly cross-refer to one another and to 'international law', international law can be seen as playing a pivotal role in shaping the current rules and principles applied by the courts; on the other hand, however, the content of the international law of State immunity represents nothing more than a collection of the lowest common denominators of the practice of various States, and is therefore of limited guidance as to the handling of a particular case in a particular court, for which the lawyer has to be familiar with whatever procedural (and in some cases substantive) rules prevailing in that court. International law in this respect leaves a wide measure of discretion to national courts as concerns the modalities in which the principle of State immunity is to be given effect, resulting in a multitude of ways of dealing with the issue of immunity. State immunity thus becomes, in a deeper sense, the application and interpretation of national law in the name of international law. In a way this is a vivid reflection of the inherent nature of international law, which abounds in primary rules of obligation but lacks secondary rules for their implementation. Such a debilitating aloofness on the part of international law may be remedied by the entry into force of the UN Convention on State Immunity. The main difficulty with the Convention is that, although it is a workable compromise that may hopefully command wide support, when considered in the broader context of State practice it is only one of many patterns, alternately moving close to or away from the practice of a particular State (or group of States) depending on the subject matter at hand, so that no State can be satisfied with the whole of the Convention. But, as noted, the varying positions adopted by States on immunity are of a highly responsive and reactive nature and, more importantly, have not sprung from any unshakable philosophy. Adaptations and adjustments are not only possible: indeed they are most fittingly descriptive of how the law of State immunity has evolved over the years. If that is the case, one cannot see why it is not *legally* possible for a State, whatever its practice now, to subscribe to the UN Convention.

It must also be remembered that the question of immunity is one of procedure only; it concerns the *forum* for the settlement of a dispute but has nothing directly to do with substantive responsibility or guilt. Immunity does not mean impunity. To say that a defendant is immune from current proceedings is not to say that it/he is not guilty or not responsible for the wrong committed; it is simply saying that this court or tribunal is, in the eyes of international law, not the right place to settle that dispute.

Thus it becomes important to know what the dispute is. The same set of substantive facts may give rise to a host of different claims. Depending on how the claim is formulated and pleaded and what type of action is brought before the court, the decision can be vastly different. The court may grant or deny immunity just because, given the plaintiff's claim as presented to the court, the court has to view the facts of the case from a different perspective. Since, as a general principle, it is not for the court of its own accord to amend or make good on behalf of the plaintiff a claim which otherwise has no prospect of being admitted under current procedural rules, it is then imperative for the plaintiff to know intimately what are the circumstances under which a foreign State, together with its emanations and officials, does not enjoy immunity. And who will not say that herein also lies the strategy of defence for the defendant State?

Notes

Foreword

1 GA Res 59/38, Annex, 2 December 2004.

Chapter 1

1 See especially von Bar, *The Theory*; de Visscher, Les gouvernements; Weiss, Compétence; Phillimore, Immunité; Allen, *The Position*; Fitzmaurice, State Immunity; Fawcett, Legal Aspects; Lauterpacht, The Problem; Lalive, L'immunité; Sucharitkul, *State Immunities*, esp. pp. 3–19 and 162–256; Murphy, The American; O'Connell, *International Law*, pp. 841–886; Dunbar, Controversial Aspects; Sucharitkul, Immunities; Sucharitkul, Second Report, pp. 214–228, paras. 65–118 and earlier writers cited there; Sinclair, The Law; Badr, *State Immunity*, esp. pp. 9–19 and 41–62; Trooboff, Foreign State; Marasinghe, The Modern; Dellapenna, Foreign State; Pingel-Lenuzza, *Les immunités*, esp. Première Partie, Titre II, pp. 59–231; Bankas, *The State Immunity Controversy*, chs. 2–5. In order to save space endnotes in this book appear in a skeletal form only. For full citations please refer to the Table of Cases, Legal Instruments and Codification Documents and the Bibliography.
2 *The Schooner Exchange* v. *McFaddon*, US, 11 US (7 Cranch) 116 (1812).
3 See especially his equivocation concerning foreign State-owned trading ships: *The Schooner Exchange*, US, 11 US (7 Cranch) 116, 142 (1812).
4 See Badr, *State Immunity*, pp. 10–14; Sinclair, The Law, 122.
5 See *The Philippine Admiral*, England, 1975, [1977] AC 373, 391–397; 64 ILR 90, 97–103.
6 See, e.g., *The Parlement Belge*, England, (1880) 5 PD 197, 214–215; reversing *The Parlement Belge*, England, (1879) 4 PD 129; *Mighell* v. *Sultan*, England, 1893, [1894] 1 QB 149; *The Jassy*, England, [1906] P 270; *The Broadmayne*, England, [1916] P 64; *The Gagara*, England, [1919] P 95; *The Porto Alexandre*, England, 1919, [1920] P 30; *The Tervaete*, England, [1922] P 259; 1 AD 148; *The Jupiter*, England, [1924] P 236; *Compania Mercantil* v. *US*, England, [1924] 18 Lloyd's Rep 369; 2 AD 138; *Duff* v. *Kelantan*, England, [1924] AC 797; 2 AD 124; *Kahan* v. *Pakistan*, England, [1951] 2

NOTES TO PAGES 9–10   467

KB 1003; 18 ILR 210; *Swiss* v. *Salta*, England, [1972] 1 Lloyd's Rep 497; 55 ILR 411; *Owners* v. *Owners*, Scotland, 1921, (1922) SLT 68, 70; 11 AD 149, 151. See also *Brown* v. *Indochine*, Canada, (1922) CLR, 21 Exchequer, 406; 1 AD 157, 157.

7 *The Cristina*, England, [1938] AC 485, 490; 9 AD 250, 252 (emphasis added). For early criticism see Mann, Immunity. For cases following *The Cristina* see, e.g., *Haile* v. *Cable*, England, [1938] Ch 839; 9 AD 171; *Krajina* v. *Tass*, England, [1949] 2 All ER 274; 16 AD 129; *USA* v. *Dollfus*, England, [1952] AC 582; 19 ILR 163; *Sultan* v. *Abubakar*, England, [1952] AC 318; 19 ILR 182; *Baccus* v. *Servicio*, England, 1956, [1957] 1 QB 438; 23 ILR 160; *Mellenger* v. *New Brunswick*, England, [1971] 1 WLR 604; 52 ILR 322. For early UK practice see Sucharitkul, *State Immunities*, pp. 162–182 and the cases discussed there. See especially *Swiss* v. *Salta*, England, [1972] 1 Lloyd's Rep 497, 502; 55 ILR 411, 420. *The Cristina* was quoted in a number of foreign cases, see, e.g., *Canada* v. *Burke*, Ireland, [1992] 2 IR 484, 495; 95 ILR 467, 476–477; *Australian* v. *Westpac*, Australia, (1988) 17 NSWLR 623, 631; 104 ILR 405, 414.

8 *The Pesaro*, US, 271 US 562, 574 (1926); 3 AD 186. See also *White* v. *Frank Dale*, Canada, (1946) 13 AD 82. But see *Mexico* v. *Hoffman*, US, 324 US 30, 40 (1945); 12 AD 143, 148.

9 *The Navemar*, US, 303 US 68, 74 (1938); 9 AD 176, 179. See also *West* v. *Captain*, Belgium, (1920) 1 AD 152, 154; *The India*, South Africa, [1921] SALR 451, 464; 1 AD 156, 156.

10 See *The India*, South Africa, [1921] SALR 451, 464; 1 AD 156, 156; *The Pesaro*, US, 271 US 562, 574 (1926); 3 AD 186, 187; *Morocco* v. *Laurens*, France, (1930) 5 AD 116, 117; *Austrian* v. *Hungarian*, Austria, (1930) 5 AD 120, 121; *De Froe* v. *Russian*, Netherlands, (1932) 6 AD 170, 171.

11 In the English case law, the term 'plaintiff' has now been replaced by 'claim-ant'. See Lord Woolf, *Access to Justice*, ch. 20, 'The New Rules', para. 13; Civil Procedure Rules 1998, r. 2.3(1). However, the term 'plaintiff' continues to be used in cases in which the claim was brought before the alteration policy, see, e.g., *Johnson* v. *Unisys*, England, [2003] 1 AC 518; [2001] ICR 480; [2001] IRLR 279.

12 *Duff* v. *Kelantan*, England, [1924] AC 797, 822; *The Cristina*, England, [1938] AC 485, 503, 515; *Sultan* v. *Abubakar*, England, [1952] AC 318, 341–343; 19 ILR 182, 188–190; *Lebanon Expropriation Case*, Lebanon, (1926) 3 AD 44, 45; *Saorstat* v. *Rafael*, Ireland, 1944, [1945] IR 291; 12 AD 97, 98; *Republic of China* v. *Chuka*, Japan, (1955) 23 ILR 210, 211; *Pärtsel* v. *Tsentrosojuss*, Estonia, (1934) 8 AD 244, 245; *Peru* v. *SA Sociedad*, Argentina, (1958) 26 ILR 195; *Dessaulles* v. *Poland*, Canada, (1944) 4 DLR 1, 4–5; 12 AD 92, 93.

13 *The Cristina*, England, [1938] AC 485, 515; 9 AD 250; *Chung* v. *The King*, England, 1938, [1939] AC 160; 9 AD 264; *Soviet Trade Delegation* v. *Paulin*, Estonia, (1927) 8 AD 241, 242; *Officina* v. *Domenech*, France, (1938) 9 AD 239, 240; *Turkish Purchases Commission Case*, Germany, (1920) 1 AD 114; *French Shares Case*, Germany, (1928) 4 AD 163, 163; *Morocco* v. *Laurens*, France, (1930) 5 AD 116, 117; affirmed, *Laurens* v. *Morocco*, France, (1934) 7 AD 171; *In re Hanukiew*, France, (1933) 7 AD 174, 174–175; *Crédit Lyonnais* v. *Viel*, France, (1936) 8 AD 228, 228; *Lebanon Expropriation Case*, Lebanon, (1926) 3 AD 44, 45. *De Booy* v. *German*, Netherlands, (1924) 1 AD 124, 128; *NV Limburgsch* v. *German*, Netherlands, (1916) 1 AD 129

468   NOTES TO PAGE 10

note; *Bergverksaktiebolaget* v. *Militär-Liquidierungsamt*, Netherlands, (1921) 1 AD 130, 132; *In re Hoover*, Japan, (1956) 23 ILR 265, 267; *Masatoshi* v. *Tokyo Civilian Open Mess*, Japan, (1957) 24 ILR 226, 227; *Indian* v. *Maux*, India, (1955) 22 ILR 248; *Chateau-Gai* v. *France*, Canada, (1967) 61 DLR (2d) 709, 711; 53 ILR 284, 285; *Ibarra* v. *Captain*, Argentina, (1937) 8 AD 247, 247 and 9 AD 293, 294; *Peru* v. *SA Sociedad*, Argentina, (1958) 26 ILR 195; *Townshend* v. *Office*, Argentina, (1949) 65 ILR 1; *Oppenlander* v. *Embassy*, Argentina, (1951) 65 ILR 2.

14 *Trade* v. *Maurycy*, Poland, (1928) 4 AD 170, 171; *National* v. *Republic of China*, US, 348 US 356, 361–362 (1955); 22 ILR 210, 213–214; *The Cumene*, Germany, (1925) 3 AD 175, 175. Cf. *Belgium* v. *EAG*, Netherlands, (1922) 1 AD 129, 130; *USSR* v. *Belaiew*, England, (1925) 42 TLR 21; 3 AD 172, 173; *French Shares Case*, Germany, (1928) 4 AD 163, 164.

15 *Solon* v. *Gouvernement égyptien*, France, 1847, Dalloz, 1849-I-7; *The Charkieh*, England, (1873) LR 4 A & E 59, 97–98; *The Philippine Admiral*, England, 1975, [1977] AC 373, 392–393; 64 ILR 90, 98–99; *The Ice King*, Germany, (1921) 1 AD 150, 151; *Restitution of Property Case*, Germany, (1951) 18 ILR 221, 222; *Jurisdiction over Yugoslav Military Mission Case*, Germany, 38 ILR 162; *Yugoslav Military Mission Case*, Germany (1969) 65 ILR 108, 109; *Hungarian Embassy Case*, Germany, (1969) 65 ILR 110; *Land Sale Authorisation Case*, Germany, (1973) 65 ILR 122; *Land Purchase Broker's Commission Case*, Germany, (1974) 65 ILR 125; *Foreign States Immunities Case*, Austria, (1928) 4 AD 178, 179; *Petrococchino* v. *Swedish State*, France, (1929) 5 AD 306, 307; *Limbin* v. *Burma*, Japan, (1954) 32 ILR 124, 125; *S* v. *British Treasury*, Poland, (1948) 24 ILR 223, 225; *Enforcement of International Awards*, Czechoslovakia, (1928) 4 AD 174, 176 (but see *Immunity of Legation Buildings Case*, Czechoslovakia, (1929) 4 AD 370, 372; *Nashashibi* v. *Consul-General*, Jordan, (1958) 26 ILR 190, 191–192; *Congo* v. *Syndicat*, France, 2005, 95 RCDIP (2006) 123. See also Lauterpacht, The Problem, 244.

16 See US FSIA, s. 1605(a)(4); UK SIA, s. 6(a); Pakistan SIO, s. 7(1); Singapore SIA, s. 8(1); South Africa FSIA, s. 7(1); Canada SIA, s. 12(c); Australia FSIA 1985, s. 14(1); 1972 European Convention, Art. 9; 2004 UN Convention, Art. 13(a); US House of Representatives, Report No. 94-1487, 1976, p. 20; 1976 USCCAN 6604, 6619. For cases involving s. 1605(a)(4) of US FSIA see *Permanent* v. *New York*, US, 551 US 193 (2007); affirming *New York* v. *Permanent*, US, 446 F.3d 365, 369 (2nd Cir. 2006); affirming *New York* v. *Permanent*, US, 376 F.Supp.2d 429, 432 (S.D.N.Y. 2005); *In re Republic of Philippines*, US, 309 F.3d 1143, 1150 (9th Cir. 2002); *Fagot* v. *Costa Rica*, US, 297 F.3d 1, 11–13 (1st Cir. 2002); affirming *Fagot* v. *Costa Rica*, US, 139 F.Supp.2d 173 (D.P.R. 2001), on reconsideration from *Fagot* v. *Costa Rica*, US, 934 F.Supp. 493, 500–501 (D.P.R. 1996); *767 Third* v. *Consulate*, US, 218 F.3d 152 (2nd Cir. 2000); *MacArthur* v. *Peru*, US, 809 F.2d 918, 920–921 (D.C. Cir. 1987); 107 ILR 196; *City of Englewood* v. *Libya*, US, 773 F.2d 31, 36 (3rd Cir. 1985); *Asociacion* v. *Mexico*, US, 735 F.2d 1517, 1520–1524 (D.C.Cir. 1984); 84 ILR 87; affirming *Asociacion* v. *Mexico*, US, 561 F.Supp. 1190, 1196–1197 (D.D.C. 1983); *Gutch* v. *Germany*, US, 444 F.-Supp.2d 1, 11 (D.D.C. 2006); *Pulaski* v. *India*, US, 212 F.Supp.2d 653, 655 (S.D.Tex. 2002); *Fickling* v. *Australia*, US, 775 F.Supp. 66, 72 (E.D.N.Y. 1991); 103 ILR 447.

17 See 1928 Bustamante Code, Art. 336; Tate Letter, 1952 (see below); *Lariviere* v. *Morgan*, England, (1872) LR 7 Ch 550, 560; reasoning endorsed in *Morgan* v.

NOTES TO PAGES 10–11   469

Lariviére, England, (1875) LR 7 HL 423; *Strousberg v. Costa Rica*, England, (1881) 44 LT 199, 20; *Rahimtoola v. Nizam*, England, 1957, [1958] AC 379, 418, 420–421; 24 ILR 175, 196, 198–199; *Civil Air v. Central Air*, England, 1952, [1953] AC 70, 79–81; 19 ILR 85; *The Philippine Admiral*, England, 1975, [1977] AC 373, 393; 64 ILR 90, 99; *Institute v. Borges*, India, (1958) 27 ILR 111, 114; *Roumania v. Arricastre*, France, (1937) 8 AD 232, 233. Cf. *Roumania v. Aricastre*, France, (1949) 16 AD 138, 140. But see *Municipality v. Fraser-Brace*, Canada, (1958) 13 DLR (2d) 177; 26 ILR 165; partially reversing *Fraser-Brace v. Municipality*, Canada, (1957) 9 DLR (2d) 391; 24 ILR 231.

18 See IDI, Projet, 1891, Art. II-1-1 and II-1-4 (see also Rapport par de Bar, p. 414 at 415); 1928 Bustamante Code, Arts. 333 and 335; Tate Letter, 1952 (see below); *L'Affaire du Département des chemins de fer*, Allemagne, 1905, 34 *JDIP* (1907) 166, 168; *Polish Loan Bank Case*, Germany, (1921) 1 AD 116, 118; *The Ice King*, Germany, (1921) 1 AD 150, 151; *Halig v. Polish*, Germany, (1928) 4 AD 164, 165; Art. IX(2) of the (Austrian) Introductory Act to the Jurisdictional Statute: Seidl-Hohenveldern, State Immunity, 97; *Leasing v. Algeria*, Austria, (1986) 116 ILR 526, 530; duplicate report *sub nom Republic of 'A'*, Austria, (1986) 77 ILR 488, 491, fn. 5; *Neustein v. Indonesia*, Austria, (1958) 65 ILR 3, 9, fn. 3; *Matsuyama v. China*, Japan, (1928) 4 AD 168, 168–169; *Limbin v. Burma*, Japan, (1954) 32 ILR 124, 125; *Pärtsel v. Tsentrosojuss*, Estonia, (1932) 8 AD 242, 243; *S v. British Treasury*, Poland, (1948) 24 ILR 223, 224–225; *French Consulate Case*, Poland, (1958) 26 ILR 178, 179; reaffirmed in *Maria v. Austrian*, Poland, (1987) 82 ILR 1, 4; *Brazilian Embassy Employee Case*, Portugal, (1984) 116 ILR 625, 631; *Ramos v. USA*, Portugal, (1994) 116 ILR 634, 635. For early studies of waiver see Cohn, Waiver; Waring, Waiver.

19 Some of the early cases characterized a commercial activity as a 'waiver' largely because, one suspects, waiver was at that time the only other available exception to immunity apart from immovable property. See *The Charkieh*, England, (1873) LR 4 A & E 59, 99; *Soviet Republic Case*, Greece, (1928) 4 AD 172; *Storelli v. French*, Italy, (1924) 2 AD 129, 130; *Russian Commercial Representation v. Tesini*, Italy, (1925) 3 AD 176, 176–177.

20 As noted in the Tate Letter, 1952, see below.

21 *S v. British Treasury*, Poland, (1948) 24 ILR 223, 224–225. See also *The Charkieh*, England, (1873) LR 4 A & E 59, 98–99.

22 See *The Jassy*, England, [1906] P 270; *The Gagara*, England, [1919] P 95; *The Porto Alexandre*, England, [1920] P 30; *The Jupiter*, England, [1924] P 236; *Rizaeff v. Soviet*, China, (1927) 40 ILR 84; *Compania Mercantil v. US*, England, [1924] 18 Lloyd's Rep 369; 2 AD 138; *The Cristina*, England, [1938] AC 485; 9 AD 250; *The Hanna I*, Norway, (1948) 15 AD 146; *Fredrikstad v. Bertelsens*, Norway, (1949) 17 ILR 167. On early practice involving State ships see also Sucharitkul, *State Immunities*, ch. 3, pp. 51–103.

23 As noted in the Tate Letter, 1952. After the 1958 Geneva Conventions on the Law of the Sea, the denial of immunity of State trading vessels became customary international law. See Sucharitkul, *State Immunities*, ch. 3, esp. pp. 92–103. See also *The Ramava*, Ireland, (1941) 10 AD 91.

24 For comprehensive accounts of the transition from absolute to restrictive immunity see, in particular, Sucharitkul, *State Immunities*, ch. 5, pp. 162–256; Pingel-Lenuzza, *Les immunités*.

470 NOTES TO PAGES 11–13

25 *The Philippine Admiral*, England, 1975, [1977] AC 373, 397, see also 402; 64 ILR 90, 103.
26 Tate Letter, 1952. See also a survey of State practice in *Dralle* v. *Czechoslovakia*, Austria, (1950) 17 ILR 155, 158–161, 164–165.
27 *The Philippine Admiral*, England, 1975, [1977] AC 373, 400; 64 ILR 90, 106. See also Lauterpacht, The Problem, 250–272.
28 *Empire of Iran Case*, Germany, 45 ILR 57, 61 (internal quotation marks omitted).
29 Council of Europe, *Explanatory Reports*, 1972, p. 22, para. 56.
30 *The Philippine Admiral*, England, 1975, [1977] AC 373, 400; 64 ILR 90, 106.
31 Some countries may still have an absolutist streak in their practice. The uncertainty is due largely to the paucity of available materials. This is especially true in the case of Asian-African countries.
32 Lauterpacht *et al.* (eds.), *ILR Consolidated Indexes*, p. 1484.
33 China may have accepted restrictive immunity *internationally* but may still adhere to absolute immunity *internally*. For a discussion of China's position see Chapter 9; for a brief account of Asian-African practice see Chapter 11; for the practice of some other countries not examined in this chapter see the Council of Europe Data Base on State Immunities and its companion volume, Hafner *et al.* (eds.), *State Practice.* Bulgaria in 1993, South Korea in 1994, reported adherence to restrictive immunity: Note verbale of 1993 (Bulgaria to the UN), A/C.6/48/3, para. 3; GAOR, Forty-ninth Session, A/C.6/49/SR.32, para. 35; Suh, Transboundary Civil Litigation in Korea, 188–190 (noting a lower court case in 1994 favouring restrictive immunity). Iran declared its support for restrictive immunity in 1991, GAOR, Forty-sixth Session, A/C.6/46/SR.24, para. 7 (Iran). Cuba supported the UN Convention, GAOR, Fifty-fourth Session, A/C.6/54/SR.28, para. 98 (Cuba). A note verbale in 1993 from Japan to the UN, A/48/464, para. 4, noted Japan's position of absolute immunity (since *Matsuyama* v. *China*, Japan, 4 AD 168 (1928)) in courts even in 1993, and Japanese practice still envisaged only two exceptions to immunity (voluntary appearance and real estate) in 1997, *X* v. *USA*, Japan, 1997, 41 *JAIL* (1998) 91, 91, but accepted the restrictive theory in 1998, *X* v. *USA*, Japan, 1998, 42 *JAIL* (1999) 138, 142; affirmed, *X* v. *USA*, Japan, 2002, 46 *JAIL* (2003) 161, 163; see also *X* v. *Marshall Islands*, Japan, 2000, 45 *JAIL* (2002) 146; Case No. 1231, 100 *AJIL* (2006) 908. The Tokyo High Court drew a distinction between acts *jure imperii* and acts *jure gestionis* in two cases: *X* v. *The Mayor*, Japan, 2007, 51 *JYIL* (2008) 533; *X* v. *Georgia*, Japan, 2008 (quashed by the Supreme Court in 2009), 52 *JYIL* (2009) 658; Hirobe, Immunity; Kono, International Civil, 119–120. Japan accepted on 11 May 2010 the 2004 UN Convention, an indication that it now adheres to the restrictive approach. Swedish case law has generally embraced the distinction between public and private acts but shows a 'decided reluctance to rule against the immunity of states', Mahmoudi, Case note on *Local Authority of Västerås* v. *Iceland*, 195. Swedish Supreme Court has been consistent in upholding immunity: *In re Bolin*, Sweden, (1934) 7 AD 186; *The Rigmor*, Sweden, (1942) 10 AD 240; *The Solgry*, Sweden, (1942) 11 AD 153; *Russian* v. *Carlbom*, Sweden, (1944) 12 AD 112; *Backman* v. *Chinese*, Sweden, (1957) 24 ILR 221; *Västerås* v. *Iceland*, Sweden, (1999) 128 ILR 705, 707. Immunity

was indeed denied by a local court: *Erixon* v. *Bulgaria*, Sweden, (1949) 16 AD 141. Sweden ratified the 2004 UN Convention on 23 December 2009. So far the few reported cases from Chile adhere to absolute immunity: *X* v. *Embassy*, Chile, 1968; *X* v. *Bolivia*, Chile, 1969, *Materials on Jurisdictional Immunities*, pp. 250–251; *X* v. *China*, Chile, (1969) 65 ILR 31 note; and *Senerman* v. *Cuba*, Chile, (1975) 65 ILR 29. In a case concerning Embassy villa rent arrears, the Gabon Supreme Court granted immunity: *Nkoghe* v. *Embassy*, Gabon, (1989) 89 ILR 43. Gautama, International, 95–96 (mainly absolute immunity). The position of Nigeria seems equivocal: *Kramer* v. *Belgium*, Nigeria, 1988, (1989) 1 CLRQ 126; 103 ILR 299; Osinbajo, Sovereign Immunity; Ogunniran, The Successive; Unegbu, Immunity. So far the few reported cases from Poland are of the absolutist strain: *Czechoslovak Republic Case*, Poland, (1926) 3 AD 180; *Trade* v. *Maurycy*, Poland, (1928) 4 AD 170; *German Immunities Case*, Poland, (1937) 8 AD 239; Wyrozumska, The State Immunity. See also *Ministry of Defence* v. *Joel*, Kenya, 1983, (1982–88) KAR 135, 138; (1983) 103 ILR 235, 239. Balaš and Pauknerová, The Czechoslovak Approach; Michalchuk, Filling. In response to a UN questionnaire in 1982 regarding their respective State practice, Czechoslovakia, Ecuador, Hungary, Sudan, Syria, Trinidad and Tobago, USSR and Venezuela said 'absolute'; Egypt, Lebanon, Madagascar, Mexico, Senegal, Togo and Yugoslavia said 'restrictive'; while Kenya, Romania and Tunisia said 'uncertain'. *Materials on Jurisdictional Immunities*, pp. 557–645. In 1988, Bulgaria, Byelorussia, Cameroon, Chile, China, Czechoslovakia, Finland, Iceland, Mexico, Qatar, Thailand, USSR, Venezuela and Yugoslavia provided the ILC with detailed article-by-article comments on the ILC's draft articles, thereby impliedly accepting the restrictive doctrine that underlaid those articles. Comments and observations, 1988, *YILC*, 1988-II-1, p. 45 at pp. 59–61, 62–65, 73, 74–79, 81–84, 90–91. Sucharitkul, Immunity; The Thai Practice. Cases from Estonia are very old: *Soviet* v. *Paulin*, Estonia, (1927) 8 AD 241, 242; *Pärtsel* v. *Tsentrosojuss*, Estonia, (1932) 8 AD 242; *Pärtsel* v. *Tsentrosojuss*, Estonia, (1934) 8 AD 244. Austria, Iran, Japan, Kazakhstan, Lebanon, Norway, Portugal, Romania, Sweden and Switzerland have now ratified, accepted or acceded to the 2004 UN Convention; Belgium, China, the Czech Republic, Denmark, Estonia, Finland, France, Iceland, India, Madagascar, Mexico, Morocco, Paraguay, the Russian Federation, Senegal, Sierra Leone, Slovakia, Timor-Leste and the UK have signed but not ratified the Convention. Since the 2004 Convention is predicated on the restrictive doctrine, the list may serve as a good indication of the move from the absolutist to the relativist position.

34 In some cases jurisdiction was asserted when the court was satisfied that the plaintiff was a national of the forum State. However, these were, after all, minority cases and, moreover, they fulfilled various private international law requirements for the exercise of jurisdiction. See, e.g., *Soviet Republic Case*, Greece, (1935) 8 AD 30; *Société* v. *Chaussois*, France, (1969) 65 ILR 44, 45–46; affirming *Chaussois* v. *La Tabacoop*, France, (1966) 47 ILR 152.

35 For detailed discussion of early Belgian and Italian cases see Allen, *The Position*, pp. 187–264; Sucharitkul, *State Immunities*, pp. 233–251. See also *Empire of Iran Case*, Germany, 45 ILR 57, 63.

472   NOTES TO PAGES 13−15

36 *Rau* v. *Duruty*, Belgium, 1879, 26 *AJIL Supplement* (1932) 612, 613.
37 *Société pour la Fabrication* v. *Ministre*, Belgium, 1888, *Pasicrisie Belge*, 1889-III-62; Allen, *The Position*, p. 193.
38 *Société anonyme Compagnie des chemins de fer Liégeois Limbourgeois* v. *Etat Néerlandais*, Belgium, 1903, 31 *JDIP* (1904) 417, 427−429.
39 *Société Monnoyer* v. *France*, Belgium, (1927) 4 AD 177, 177.
40 *Morellet* v. *Governo Danese*, Italy, 1882, 26 *AJIL Supplement* (1932) 481 at 481−482 and 595 at 596.
41 *Typaldos* v. *Manicomio*, Italy, 1886, 26 *AJIL Supplement* (1932) 623, 623.
42 *Guttieres* v. *Elmilik*, Italy, 1886, 26 *AJIL Supplement* (1932) 622, 622−623. See also *Hamspohn* v. *Bey di Tunisi*, Italy, 1887, 26 *AJIL Supplement* (1932) 480, 481 (the state as a political power (*potere politico*) contrasted with the state as a civil person (*persona civile*)); *Rumania* v. *Trutta*, Italy, 1926, 26 *AJIL Supplement* (1932) 626, 628−629 (private-law capacity (*capacità di diritto privato*) or civil personality (*personalità civile*) in contrast to public-law personality (*persona pubblica*)).
43 *Guttieres* v. *Elmilik*, Italy, 1886, 26 *AJIL Supplement* (1932) 622, 623 (emphasis added). See also *Nobili* v. *Emperor*, Italy, (1921) 1 AD 36; *Bolivia* v. *Italian*, Italy, (1948) 15 AD 133, 135−136; *Campione* v. *Peti-Nitrogenmuvek*, Italy, (1972) 65 ILR 287, 293.
44 *Dreyfus*, Switzerland, (1918) BGE 44 I 49, 54.
45 *Dreyfus*, Switzerland, (1918) BGE 44 I 49, 55. The territorial connection in *Dreyfus* was emphasized in later cases: *Greek Republic* v. *Walder*, Switzerland, (1930) 5 AD 121, 122−123; *Greece* v. *Julius Bär*, Switzerland, (1956) 23 ILR 195, 196−197.
46 See *Greek Republic* v. *Walder*, Switzerland, (1930) 5 AD 121, 122−123; *Greece* v. *Julius Bär*, Switzerland, (1956) 23 ILR 195, 196 and 200; *State Immunity Case*, Switzerland, (1937) 10 AD 230, 231. Further cases will be discussed in other parts of this book.
47 *Soviet Republic Case*, Greece, (1928) 4 AD 172, affirmed by the Areopagus (Supreme Court), No. 29, Themis, Vol. 40, p. 842. See also *Roumanian Legation Case*, Greece, (1949) 16 AD 291.
48 As mentioned in *Dralle* v. *Czechoslovakia*, Austria, (1950) 17 ILR 155, 156.
49 *Immunities Case*, Austria, (1920) 1 AD 118, 119.
50 See the brief history in *Dralle* v. *Czechoslovakia*, Austria, (1950) 17 ILR 155, 157. For cases see *Foreign States Immunities Case*, Austria, (1928) 4 AD 178, 179; *Austrian Bondholders* v. *Hungarian State*, Austria, (1930) 5 AD 120, 121; *German Immunities Case*, Austria, (1935) 8 AD 246, 246. A more detailed history can be found in a fuller English translation of the *Dralle* case: *X* v. *Czechoslovakia*, Austria, 1950, *Materials on Jurisdictional Immunities*, pp. 184−186.
51 *Dralle* v. *Czechoslovakia*, Austria, (1950) 17 ILR 155, 156−157 and 163. Later confirmed by the Supreme Court in *X* v. *Germany*, Austria, (1963) 65 ILR 10, 12 and *Steinmetz* v. *Hungary*, Austria, (1970) 65 ILR 15, 19.
52 For detailed discussion of early French practice see Allen, *The Position*, pp. 149−185; Sucharitkul, *State Immunities*, pp. 202−218; Hamson, Immunity.

NOTES TO PAGES 15-16   473

53 In a case concerning the purchase of army boots: *Gouvernment espagnol* v. *Cassaux*, France, 1849, Sirey, 1849-I-81; Dalloz, 1849-I-5. See Sucharitkul, *State Immunities*, p. 207.

54 See *Officina* v. *Domenech*, France, (1938) 9 AD 239, 241–242, the Editor's note with the cases cited therein.

55 Compare, e.g., *Socifros* v. *USSR*, France, (1938) 9 AD 236, 237 with *Officina* v. *Domenech*, France, (1938) 9 AD 239, 240.

56 *Roumania* v. *Aricastre*, France, (1949) 16 AD 138, 139; *Rossignol* v. *Czechoslovakia*, France, (1949) 16 AD 140, 140.

57 *Roumania* v. *Pascalet*, France, (1924) 2 AD 132, 132. Actually, a 1921 case had already contemplated the political act / business act distinction: *Lakhowsky* v. *Swiss*, France, (1919/1921) 1 AD 122, 123.

58 *Société le Gostrog* v. *Association*, France, (1926) 3 AD 174, 175; affirmed, *USSR* v. *Association*, France, (1929) 5 AD 18; *In re Commercial Representation*, France, (1927) 4 AD 30; *Chaliapine* v. *Russia*, France, (1930) 5 AD 19 note; *Petrococchino* v. *Sweden*, France, (1929) 5 AD 306, 307; *Chaliapine* v. *USSR*, France, (1936) 8 AD 225; *Roumania* v. *Arricastre*, France, (1937) 8 AD 232. Cf. *Morocco* v. *Laurens*, France, (1930) 5 AD 116, 117. See also *Hertzfeld* v. *USSR*, France, (1933) 7 AD 184, 185; *Spanish* v. *Banco*, France, (1937) 8 AD 229, 231–232; *Aget* v. *French*, France, (1939) 11 AD 144, 144; *Russian* v. *Société Française*, France, (1940) 9 AD 245, 246 (but the attachment order was annulled in *Société Française* v. *Russian*, France, (1941) 11 AD 145); *Société Immobilière* v. *USA*, France, (1960) 42 ILR 123, 124; *Société Bauer-Marchal* v. *Gouvernment Turc*, France, (1965) 47 ILR 155, 156.

59 *Morocco* v. *Laurens*, France, (1930) 5 AD 116, 116–117; affirmed, *Laurans* v. *Morocco*, France, (1934) 7 AD 171; *Hertzfeld* v. *USSR*, France, (1933) 7 AD 184, 185 (for facts see 5 AD 114); *Huttinger* v. *Upper Congo*, France, (1934) 7 AD 172, 173; *Larrasquitu* v. *Société*, France, (1937) 8 AD 196, 197; *Société Viajes* v. *Office*, France, (1936) 8 AD 227, 227; *Socifros* v. *USSR*, France, (1938) 9 AD 236; *Roumania* v. *Aricastre*, France, (1949) 16 AD 138, 139; *Rossignol* v. *Czechoslovakia*, France, (1949) 16 AD 140, 140.

60 *USSR* v. *Association*, France, (1929) 5 AD 18, 19; *In re Hanukiew*, France, (1933) 7 AD 174, 174; *Laurans* v. *Morocco*, France, (1934) 7 AD 171; *Guggenheim* v. *Vietnam*, France, (1961) 44 ILR 74; affirming *Guggenheim* v. *Vietnam*, France, (1955) 22 ILR 224, 225. The *Guggenheim* case may be regarded as ambiguous, see *Empire of Iran Case*, Germany, 45 ILR 57, 68. For more recent French practice see Pingel-Lenuzza, *Les immunités*.

61 *Chaliapine* v. *USSR*, France, (1936) 8 AD 225, 225; affirming *Chaliapine* v. *Russia*, France, (1930) 5 AD 19 note; *Procureur* v. *Vestwig*, France, (1946) 13 AD 78, 79.

62 *Administration* v. *Société Levant*, France, (1969) 52 ILR 315; *Englander* v. *Statni*, France, (1969) 52 ILR 335; *Société* v. *Chaussois*, France, (1969) 65 ILR 44, 45–46.

63 In particular, the Tate Letter 'offers no guide-lines or criteria for differentiating between a sovereign's private and public acts': *Victory* v. *Comisaría*, US, 336 F.2d 354, 359 (2nd Cir. 1964); 35 ILR 110.

64 For a concise early explanation of the practice, see *In re Muir*, US, 254 US 522, 532–533 (1921); 1 AD 143, 144. See also Jaffe, *Judicial Aspects*, p. 53.

474   NOTES TO PAGE 16

65 *North East* v. *Pakistan*, US, (S.D.N.Y. 1975); 63 ILR 52; *ADM* v. *Bolivia*, US, 63 ILR 56 (D.D.C. 1975); *Renchard* v. *Humphreys*, US, 381 F.Supp. 382 (D.D.C. 1974); 63 ILR 33; *French* v. *Banco Nacional*, US, 295 N.Y.S. 433, 439 (1968); 66 ILR 6; *Amkor* v. *Bank of Korea*, US, 298 F.Supp. 143, 144 (S.D.N.Y. 1969); 53 ILR 291, 292; *Ocean* v. *Ivory Coast*, US, 269 F.Supp. 703 (E.D.Louis. 1967); 63 ILR 9; *Gonzalez* v. *Industrial*, US, 227 N.Y.S. 2d 456, 458 (1961); 63 ILR 1, 2.

66 *Ex parte Peru*, US, 318 US 578, 589–590 (1943); 10 AD 199, 203–204; *New York* v. *Korea*, US, 132 F.Supp. 684, 685 (S.D.N.Y. 1955); *Hellenic* v. *South*, US, 275 F.Supp. 860 (S.D.N.Y. 1967); 63 ILR 16; *Isbrandtsen* v. *President*, US, 446 F.2d 1198 (2nd Cir. 1971); 57 ILR 147; *Spacil* v. *Crowe*, US, 489 F.2d 614 (5th Cir. 1974); 63 ILR 24; *Southeastern* v. *Stern*, US, 493 F.2d 1223 (1st Cir. 1974); 63 ILR 39; *Greenspan* v. *Crosbie*, US, 63 ILR 67 (S.D.N.Y. 1976); *Logan* v. *Secretary*, US, 553 F.2d 107 (D.C. Cir. 1976); 63 ILR 70.

67 *The Navemar*, US, 303 US 68, 74–75 (1938); 9 AD 176, 179; *Gonzalez* v. *Industrial*, US, 227 N.Y.S. 2d 456, 458 (1961); 63 ILR 1, 2; *Victory* v. *Comisaría*, US, 336 F.2d 354, 358–360 (2nd Cir. 1964); 35 ILR 110, 116; *Flota* v. *Motor*, US, 335 F.2d 619 (4th Cir. 1964); 35 ILR 122; *Heaney* v. *Spain*, US, 445 F.2d 501, 503 (2nd Cir. 1971); 57 ILR 153, 156; *Aerotrade* v. *Haiti*, US, 376 F.Supp. 1281 (S.D.N.Y. 1974); 63 ILR 41; *National* v. *Nigeria*, US, 420 F.Supp. 954 (S.D.N.Y. 1976); 63 ILR 63. For general principle see *Mexico* v. *Hoffman*, US, 324 US 30, 34–35 (1945). The practice of limited autonomy subsists even after the enactment of the FSIA, especially with regard to foreign head-of-State immunity: *Abiola* v. *Abubakar*, US, 267 F.Supp.2d 907, 915 (N.D.Ill. 2003); *In re Doe*, US, 860 F.2d 40, 45 (2nd Cir. 1988); 121 ILR 567. See also Simmonds, The Limits; Bamberger, Determination; Connors, The Foreign.

68 *Mexico* v. *Hoffman*, US, 324 US 30, 35 (1945); 12 AD 143, 145. Quoted with approval in *Alfred Dunhill* v. *Cuba*, US, 425 US 682, 699–700 (1976); 66 ILR 212. See also *Guaranty* v. *US*, US, 304 US 126, 138 (1938); 9 AD 184, 187; *National* v. *Republic of China*, US, 348 US 356, 360 (1955); 22 ILR 210, 212–213; *Ex parte Peru*, US, 318 US 578, 588 (1943); 10 AD 199, 203; *The Navemar*, US, 303 US 68, 75 (1938); 9 AD 176; *US* v. *Lee*, US, 106 US 196, 209 (1882); *Sea* v. *The S/T*, US, 405 F.Supp. 1244 (S.D.N.Y. 1975); 63 ILR 49. For similar practice see UK SIA, s. 21; *Duff* v. *Kelantan*, England, [1924] AC 797, 808–809, 813, 816, 820, 824, 830; *The Arantzazu Mendi*, England, [1939] AC 256, 265; 9 AD 60, 66; *Sultan* v. *Abubakar*, England, [1952] AC 318, 340; 19 ILR 182, 188; *Sayce* v. *Ameer*, England, [1952] 2 QB 390; 19 ILR 212; Canada SIA, s. 14(1); *Old* v. *Minister*, Canada, [1991] 43 FTR 197, 200–201; reversed on other grounds, *Old* v. *Minister*, Canada, [1993] 153 NR 136, 143.

69 *Chuidian* v. *Philippine*, US, 912 F.2d 1095, 1100 (9th Cir. 1990); 92 ILR 480, citing *Ex parte Peru*. The 'suggestion of immunity' has survived to this day, especially regarding the immunity of foreign heads of State and heads of government. See, e.g., *Saltany* v. *Reagan*, US, 702 F.Supp. 319, 320 (D.D.C. 1988); 80 ILR 19; affirmed, *Saltany* v. *Reagan*, US, 886 F.2d 438, 440–1 (D.C.Cir. 1989); 87 ILR 679.

70 *Victory Transport* v. *Comisaría*, US, 336 F.2d 354, 363 (2nd Cir. 1964); 35 ILR 110.

71 US FSIA, Public Law 94-583, October 21, 1976, 90 Stat. 2891, 28 USC Chapter 97.

72 US House of Representatives, Report No. 94-1487, 1976, p. 7; 1976 USCCAN 6604, 6606. See *Gittler* v. *German*, US, 408 N.Y.S. 2d 600, 601 (N.Y.S.C. 1978); 63 ILR 170, 171; *Dames* v. *Regan*, US, 453 US 654, 685 (1981); 72 ILR 270, 288; *American* v. *Iran*, US, 657 F.2d 430, 444 (D.C.Cir. 1981). For discussion see Martin, Sovereign, 436; Brock, The Foreign. However, the Executive Branch still retains an important role in immunity cases, see the Leigh Letter, 1976; and the US Supreme Court reasserted the Executive's entitlement to deference for its 'suggestions of immunity': *Austria* v. *Altmann*, US, 541 US 677, 701–702 (2004).

73 See my discussion in various chapters in this book. For the requirement of various jurisdictional contacts under the FSIA see also Lacroix, The Theory; Pendergast, Strangers; Carter, God Save; Halverson, Is a Foreign; Garbarino, *Adler*; Farr, *BP*.

74 *Empire of Iran Case*, Germany, (1963) 45 ILR 57. See also *Jurisdiction over Yugoslav Military Mission Case*, Germany, (1962) 38 ILR 162. According to Lord Wilberforce, *Empire of Iran* was a case of 'great clarity' and contained 'an instructive review of the law of state immunity over a wide area': *I Congreso del Partido*, England, 1981, [1983] 1 AC 244, 263 and 267; 64 ILR 307, 315 and 318. For history of the German practice see also Oehrle, German.

75 *Empire of Iran Case*, Germany, (1963) 45 ILR 57, 62; Sucharitkul, *State Immunities*, pp. 83–85 and 218–225, and the cases cited there. For early absolute immunity cases see also *L'Affaire du Département*, Germany, 1905, 34 JDIP (1907) 166 (French translation) (perhaps the earliest traceable German case on State immunity); *French Shares Case*, Germany, (1928) 4 AD 163, 163–164; *Polish Loan Bank Case*, Germany, (1921) 1 AD 116, 118; *The Ice King*, Germany, (1921) 1 AD 150, 151; *Halig* v. *Polish State*, Germany, (1928) 4 AD 164, 165; *Immunity of UK Case*, Germany, (1957) 24 ILR 207, 209. Cf. *The Visurgis*, Germany, (1937/1938) 9 AD 284.

76 *In re Danish State Railways*, Germany, (1953) 20 ILR 178, 179. The Court expressly declined to follow the jurisprudence of the Supreme Court (Reichsgericht) between the years 1905 and 1921. See also *Latvia Case*, Germany, (1953) 20 ILR 180, 181; affirmed, *Latvia Case*, Germany, (1955) 22 ILR 230, 231; *In re The Charkow*, Germany, (1959) 65 ILR 100, 105. For a brief history see also *Empire of Iran Case*, Germany, (1963) 45 ILR 57, 62.

77 *Empire of Iran Case*, Germany, (1963) 45 ILR 57, 63–79.

78 *Empire of Iran Case*, Germany, (1963) 45 ILR 57, 79, see also 61–62, 73.

79 *Empire of Iran Case*, Germany, (1963) 45 ILR 57, 61, 79–81.

80 *Empire of Iran Case*, Germany, (1963) 45 ILR 57, 80. For detailed discussion of the test see Chapters 2 and 3.

81 *Empire of Iran Case*, Germany, (1963) 45 ILR 57, 80. Naturally, here the 'municipal law' means the law of the forum State.

82 See *The Charkieh*, England, (1873) LR 4 A & E 59, 99–100; reasoning overruled, *The Parlement Belge*, England, (1880) 5 PD 197, 214–215; reversing *The Parlement Belge*, England, (1879) 4 PD 129. For doubts on absolute immunity see also *The Cristina*, England, [1938] AC 485, 494, 498, 510, 512, and 516–521; *USA* v.

476   NOTES TO PAGES 17–18

Dollfus, England, [1952] AC 582, 607; 19 ILR 163, 170; *Sultan* v. *Abubakar*, England, [1952] AC 318, 343–344; 19 ILR 182, 190–192; *Rahimtoola* v. *Nizam*, England, 1957, [1958] AC 379, 418, 422–424; 24 ILR 175, 196–197. See also Mann, Immunity.

83 *I Congreso del Partido*, England, 1981, [1983] 1 AC 244, 261 per Lord Wilberforce; 64 ILR 307, 312; *Holland* v. *Lampen-Wolfe*, England, [2000] 1 WLR 1573, 1584; 119 ILR 367, 379. The practice of absolute immunity in England can be traced as early as the case of *The Prins Frederik*, England, (1820) 2 Dods. 451: see Sucharitkul, *State Immunities*, p. 4; Sucharitkul, Second Report, *YILC*, 1980-II-1, 199 at 216, para. 68. An interdepartmental committee on the subject (1949–1953) achieved nothing: see Mann, Sovereign Immunity, 186.

84 *Alcom* v. *Colombia*, England, [1984] 1 AC 580, 600; 74 ILR 170, 183.

85 The European Convention has now been ratified by eight States: Austria, Belgium, Cyprus, Germany, Luxembourg, the Netherlands, Switzerland and the UK. Portugal has signed but not ratified it.

86 For background and assessment see Bowett, The State; Shaw, The State; Mann, The State. For supersession of the common law see *I Congreso del Partido*, England, 1981, [1983] 1 AC 244, 257 and 260; 64 ILR 307, 308 and 311; *Alcom* v. *Colombia*, England, [1984] 1 AC 580, 600; 74 ILR 170, 183; *Kuwait Airways* v. *Iraqi Airways*, England, [1995] 1 WLR 1147, 1157; 103 ILR 340, 399; *In re Banco*, England, [2001] 3 All ER 923, 932; [2001] 1 WLR 2039, 2049; 124 ILR 550, 559; *AIC* v. *Nigeria*, England, [2003] EWHC 1357 (QB); (2003) 129 ILR 571, 575, para. 16; *AIG* v. *Kazakhstan*, England, 2005, [2006] 1 WLR 1420, 1429–1430, para. 22; [2006] 1 All ER 284; 129 ILR 589, 599–600; *Argentina* v. *NML*, England, [2010] EWCA Civ 41, para. 48.

87 Bingham, *The Business*, p. 92.

88 *The Philippine Admiral*, England, 1975, [1977] AC 373, 401–402; 64 ILR 90; *Trendtex* v. *Central Bank*, England, [1977] QB 529, 556; 64 ILR 111. On State immunity the common law in Scotland followed that of England: *Forth Tugs* v. *Wilmington*, Scotland, 1985, 1985 SC 317, 327; 1987 SLT 153, 158; 107 ILR 641, 651–652. In fact, an earlier 1975 case would certainly have been decided on the basis of restrictive immunity had the relevant incidents taken place in the UK. *Thai-Europe* v. *Pakistan*, England, [1975] 1 WLR 1485, 1491–1492; 64 ILR 81, 85–86. For a case following *Thai-Europe* see *Uganda* v. *Uganda*, England, 1978, [1979] 1 Lloyd's Rep 481; 64 ILR 209.

89 *Trendtex* v. *Central Bank*, England, [1977] QB 529, 558; 64 ILR 111, 132 (emphasis added); reversing *Trendtex* v. *Central Bank*, England, [1976] 1 WLR 868; 64 ILR 111. *Trendtex was followed in Hispano* v. *Central Bank*, England, [1979] 2 Lloyd's Rep 277; 64 ILR 221. See also *Szczesniak* v. *Backer*, Belgium, (1955) 65 ILR 23, 24.

90 *I Congreso del Partido*, England, 1981, [1983] 1 AC 244, 257; 64 ILR 307, 309. See especially the explanations in *I Congreso del Partido*, England, 1977, [1978] 1 QB 500, 534; 64 ILR 154; *I Congreso del Partido*, England, 1979 [1980] 1 Lloyd's Rep 23, 30; 64 ILR 227; *I Congreso del Partido*, England, 1981, [1983] 1 AC 244, 272; 64 ILR 307, 323. For critical comment see Fox, State Immunity: House of Lord's Decision. *I Congreso* was decided at common law because the relevant facts

NOTES TO PAGE 18   477

had occurred before the coming into force of the UK SIA on 22 November 1978: *I Congreso del Partido*, England, 1981, [1983] 1 AC 244, 257, 260, 272, 276, 278; 64 ILR 307, 308, 311, 323–324, 327, 329. See also *Planmount v. Zaire*, England, [1980] 2 Lloyd's Rep 393, 395; 64 ILR 268, 269. For practice surrounding the 'sister ship' principle see *I Congreso del Partido*, England, 1981, [1983] 1 AC 244, 257; 64 ILR 307, 308–309; *The Eschersheim*, England, [1976] 1 WLR 430; 72 ILR 1; *Coreck v. Sevrybokholodflot*, Scotland, 1993, [1994] SLT 893, 894; 107 ILR 658, 660; *The Rigmor*, Sweden, (1942) 10 AD 240, 243; *Société Paul v. Captain*, France, (1964) 65 ILR 38, 39. In New Zealand, the sister ship jurisdiction is provided in ss. 4 and 5 of the Admiralty Act 1973; see *Reef v. Fua Kavenga*, New Zealand, [1987] 1 NZLR 550, 556–557; 90 ILR 556. For the 'sister ship' jurisdiction in Canadian law see Federal Courts Act 1985, s. 22(2) and Canada SIA, s. 7; *Sarafi v. Ship*, Canada, [1996] 111 FTR 256; [1996] 2 FC 954, paras. 14–17. In South Africa, the 'sister ship' jurisdiction is governed by the Admiralty Jurisdiction Regulation Act 105 of 1983 (as amended by Act 87 of 1992): *The Akademik Fyodorov*, South Africa, 1996 (4) SA 422, esp. 427–429; 131 ILR 460, 463–466. The 1952 International Convention relating to the Arrest of Seagoing Ships, Arts. 1(1), 3(1), 4; repeated in the 1999 International Convention on the Arrest of Ships (not yet in force), Arts. 1, 2, 3.

91 *Harry Lyons v. USA*, Philippines, (1958) 88 ILR 711; *Carried Lumber v. USA*, Philippines, (1974) 64 ILR 661. For absolute immunity cases in the Philippines see *Syquia v. López*, Philippines, (1949) 18 ILR 228; *Philippine Alien v. Castelo*, Philippines, 1951; *Parreño v. McGranery*, Philippines, 1953; *Baer v. Tizon*, Philippines, 1974, *Materials on Jurisdictional Immunities*, pp. 364, 367, 370; *Johnson v. Major-General*, Philippines, (1954) 21 ILR 103. For discussion of the Philippine practice see Bautista, Philippine; Feliciano, The Doctrine,.

92 *NV Cabolent v. National*, Netherlands, (1968) 47 ILR 138 For early tentative endorsement of the restrictive doctrine see *South Moluccas v. Royal*, Netherlands, (1951) 17 ILR 143, 152; *Krol v. Bank*, Netherlands, (1958) 26 ILR 180, 180–181 and *Indonesia v. Van der Haas*, Netherlands, (1958) 26 ILR 181, 182. For a history of early Dutch practice, which was ambivalent but largely absolute, see Sucharitkul, *State Immunities*, pp. 225–232 and the cases cited there.

93 *Société Européenne v. Yugoslavia*, Netherlands, (1972/1973) 65 ILR 356; 1975, 1 YCA (1976) 198. For more recent Dutch practice see Voskuil, State Immunity.

94 *Inter-Science v. Moçambique*, South Africa, 1979, 1980 (2) SA 111, 118–126; 64 ILR 689, 697–706; *Kaffraria v. Zambia*, South Africa, 1980 (2) SA 709; 64 ILR 708. For cases leading up to the change see *Lendalease v. Corporacion*, South Africa, 1975 (4) SA 397, 403–404; 1976 (4) SA 464, 498–499; 64 ILR 675, 682–683, 684; *Prentice v. Bolivia*, South Africa, 1978 (3) SA 938, 940–941; 64 ILR 685, 687–688. South Africa enacted its Foreign States Immunities Act in 1981. For absolute immunity cases in South Africa see *The India*, South Africa, (1921) 1 AD 156; *Ex parte Sulman*, South Africa, (1942) 10 AD 247; *Kavouklis v. Bulgaris*, South Africa, (1943) 12 AD 113; *Parkin v. Congo*, South Africa, (1970) 64 ILR 668; *Leibowitz v. Schwartz*, South Africa, (1973) 64 ILR 672. For discussion of South African practice see Barrie, Sovereign Immunity.

478   NOTES TO PAGE 18

95 By enacting the Singapore State Immunity Act in 1979. For absolute immunity cases in Singapore see *The Hai Hsuan*, Singapore, (1950) 17 ILR 170; *Olofsen v. Malaysia*, Singapore, [1966] 2 MLJ 300, 301–302; (1966) 55 ILR 409.

96 *Qureshi v. USSR*, Pakistan, (1981) 64 ILR 585. A local court in 1970 denied immunity in a case involving a contract for the construction of the Chancery Building of the US Embassy in Karachi: *Secretary v. Gammon-Layton*, Pakistan, (1970) 64 ILR 567. Pakistan enacted its State Immunity Ordinance in 1981.

97 *Marine v. Marshall*, New Zealand, (1981) 64 ILR 539; *Marine v. Marshall*, New Zealand, (1982) 64 ILR 562; *Buckingham v. Aircraft*, New Zealand, [1982] 2 NZLR 738; (1982) 64 ILR 551; *Reef v. Fua Kavenga*, New Zealand, [1987] 1 NZLR 550, 569; 90 ILR 556, 562. The common law in New Zealand follows that of England: *Governor v. Sutton*, New Zealand, 1994, [1995] 1 NZLR 426, 436; 104 ILR 508, 522; *Controller v. Davison*, New Zealand, [1996] 2 NZLR 278, 308; 104 ILR 526, 605.

98 Canada enacted its State Immunity Act in 1982 (modelled on the US FSIA: *Re Canada Labour Code*, Canada, (1992) 91 DLR (4th) 449, 456; 486; 94 ILR 264, 271, 301); however, restrictive immunity had already started to assert itself since the late 1960s, see *Venne v. Congo*, Canada, (1968) 5 DLR (3d) 128, 138; 64 ILR 1, 11; reversed, *Congo v. Venne*, Canada, (1971) 22 DLR (3d) 669, 673; 64 ILR 24; *Penthouse v. Venezuela*, Canada, (1969) 8 DLR (3d) 686; 64 ILR 20; *Smith v. Canadian*, Canada, (1976) 68 DLR (3d) 428; 64 ILR 47; *Zodiac v. Polish*, Canada, (1977) 81 DLR (3d) 656; 64 ILR 51; *Corriveau v. Cuba*, Canada, (1979) 103 DLR (3d) 520; 64 ILR 59; *Re Royal Bank*, Canada, (1980) 117 DLR (3d) 199; 64 ILR 69; *Amanat v. Fredson*, Canada, (1982) 36 OR (2d) 17; 133 DLR (3d) 632; 64 ILR 733. For the position of the Canadian common law see *Cargo v. Lorac*, Canada, (1986) 28 DLR (4th) 309, 315–316; 84 ILR 700, 706–707; affirming *Lorac v. Owners*, Canada, (1984) 9 DLR (4th) 129. For absolute immunity cases in Canada see *Brown v. Indochine*, Canada, (1922) 1 AD 157; *Dessaulles v. Poland*, Canada, (1944) 4 DLR 1; 12 AD 92; *Municipality v. Fraser-Brace*, Canada, (1958) 13 DLR (2d) 177; 26 ILR 165; *Flota v. Cuba*, Canada, (1962) 34 DLR (2d) 628; 42 ILR 125; *Chateau-Gai v. France*, Canada, (1967) 61 DLR (2d) 709; 53 ILR 284. For discussion of early Canadian practice see Molot and Jewett, The State Immunity Act, 79–88.

99 *Embassy v. Jens*, Denmark, (1982) 78 ILR 81; *Den Franske v. Intra*, Denmark, 1992; *Italien v. Amaliegade*, Denmark, 1993; *Pakistans v. Shah*, Denmark, 1999, Council of Europe, Database on State Immunities.

100 *Barker v. Kenya*, Zimbabwe, (1983) (4) SA 817, 821; 84 ILR 18, 23.

101 With the enactment of the Australia Foreign States Immunities Act in 1985, which is the brainchild of Professor Crawford: see Crawford, A Foreign. For absolute immunity cases in Australia see *USA v. Republic of China*, Australia, (1950) 17 ILR 168; *Grunfeld v. USA*, Australia, (1968) 52 ILR 332.

102 *Harbhajan v. India*, India, (1986) 92 ILR 530, 536–537. For earlier indications of the restrictive tendency see *Agarwala v. India*, India, (1980) 118 ILR 421, 423–424; *New v. VEB*, India, (1983) 92 ILR 509, 528 (The Supreme Court did not challenge the restrictive immunity point on appeal in 1993, 5 *Asian YIL*

NOTES TO PAGE 18   479

(1995)). For absolute immunity cases in India see *Indian* v. *Maux*, India, (1955) 22 ILR 248; *UAR* v. *Mirza*, India, (1961) 64 ILR 394; affirmed on different grounds, *Mirza* v. *UAR*, India, (1965) 64 ILR 489; *Royal* v. *Monorama*, India, (1964) 64 ILR 430; *German* v. *Dynamic*, India, (1970) 64 ILR 504; *Union* v. *Chinoy*, India, (1976) 64 ILR 534. The common law in India follows that of England: *UAR* v. *Mirza*, India, (1961) 64 ILR 394, 406, 415–416, 419–420, 422. For discussion of the Indian practice see Vibhute, Transnational.

103 *Emilio* v. *Embassy*, Spain, (1986) 86 ILR 508; *Diana* v. *South Africa*, Spain, (1986) 86 ILR 512. Both judgments mentioned a 1980 Decree (Royal Decree No. 1654/1980 of 11 June 1980 (R. 1856 and 2119)) which stated that the doctrine of absolute immunity had 'reached its final stage' (see 86 ILR 508, 510 and 86 ILR 512, 515). See also an ambiguous case: *Leon* v. *Federal*, Spain, (1982) 88 ILR 687. For discussion of the Spanish practice see Jiménez, The Evolution in Spanish Law.

104 *Représentation commerciale de RDA*, Brazil, 1989, noted in 126 *JDI* (1999) 451, 452. But see also *Syria* v. *Egypt*, Brazil, (1982) 91 ILR 288, 297. For a more recent case see *Consulate* v. *Ribeiro*, Brazil, 2002, noted in *JIBLR*, 2009, 24 (12), N102.

105 *Australia* v. *Midford*, Malaysia, (1990) 86 ILR 640, 650. The common law in Malaysia follows that of England. For an earlier absolutist case see *Village* v. *Her Majesty*, Malaysia, 1987, [1988] 2 MLJ 656; 87 ILR 223.

106 *Canada* v. *Burke*, Ireland, 1991/1992, [1992] 2 IR 484; 95 ILR 467. For absolute immunity cases in Ireland see *Saorstat* v. *Rafael*, Ireland, 1944, [1945] IR 291; 12 AD 97.

107 *Case against South Africa*, Norway, 1992; *Case against the USA*, Norway, 1992; *Case against the USA*, Norway, 2001; noted in 70 *Nordic JIL* (2001) 547, 550–551. Early Norwegian cases mostly involved immunity granted to State-owned vessels used for public purposes and cannot therefore be regarded as conclusive, see *Campuzano* v. *Spanish*, Norway, (1938) 11 AD 68; *The Guernica*, Norway, (1938) 11 AD 139; *The Hanna I*, Norway, (1948) 15 AD 146; *Fredrikstad* v. *Bertelsens*, Norway, (1949) 17 ILR 167. For difficulty in identifying an exact date of adoption of the restrictive doctrine see Fife and Jervell, Norwegian State Practice, 548.

108 *National* v. *Embassy*, Argentina, (1992) 113 ILR 434; *Manauta* v. *Embassy*, Argentina, (1994) 113 ILR 429, 433 (also referring to the Decree Law No. 9015/63 of 1963, under which immunity could be denied if the Executive declared that there was a lack of reciprocity: 432). Argentina promulgated its statute of Immunity of Foreign States in 1995. For absolute immunity cases in Argentina see *Ibarra* v. *Captain*, Argentina, (1937) 8 AD 247 and 9 AD 293; *Peru* v. *SA Sociedad*, Argentina, (1958) 26 ILR 195; *Townshend* v. *Office*, Argentina, (1949) 65 ILR 1; *Oppenlander* v. *Ecuador*, Argentina, (1951) 65 ILR 2.

109 *Her Majesty* v. *Edelson*, Israel, 1997, (1997) 131 ILR 279, 297. Lower courts in Israel embraced restrictive immunity at the start of the 1990s in the cases of *Reinhold* v. *The Queen*, Israel, 1991 and *Rina* v. *South African*, Israel, 1992, noted in 26 *Israel LR* (1992) 559. Israel enacted its Foreign States Immunity Law in 2008.

480　NOTES TO PAGES 18–21

110 *Stukonis* v. *Embassy*, Lithuania, 1998, noted in 2 *Baltic YIL* (2002) 270, 271; *Cudak* v. *Embassy*, Lithuania, 2001, noted in 3 *Baltic YIL* (2003) 320, 320; *Norwegian* v. *Embassy*, Lithuania, 2003, noted in 4 *Baltic YIL* (2004) 351.

111 *X* v. *Israel*, Portugal, (2002) 127 ILR 310. Earlier Portuguese practice, which largely followed that of Spain, tended to be either ambivalent or positively absolutist. See especially *Brazilian Embassy Employee Case*, Portugal, (1984) 116 ILR 625, 628–631; *Ramos* v. *USA*, Portugal, (1994) 116 ILR 634, 635. Portugal has signed (but not ratified) the (restrictive) 1972 European Convention.

112 As noted in *Victory* v. *Comisaría*, US, 336 F.2d 354, 358 (2nd Cir. 1964); 35 ILR 110. See various bilateral treaties cited in *Materials on Jurisdictional Immunities*, pp. 131–150.

113 See Sucharitkul, *State Immunities*, p. 3.

114 The earliest reference to the 'arena' can be traced to *Gouvernement espagnol* v. *Veuve*, France, Dalloz, 1867-II-49 (case note by Royer) ('descend dans l'arène où s'agitent les intérêts privés'). This comment no doubt inspired the observations in, e.g., *Guttieres* v. *Elmilik*, Italy, 1886, 26 *AJIL Supplement* (1932) 622, 622 and *Rahimtoola* v. *Nizam*, England, 1957, [1958] AC 379, 395; 24 ILR 175, 179.

115 *The Charkieh*, England, (1873) LR 4 A & E, 59, 99–100.

116 *Typaldos* v. *Manicomio*, Italy, 26 *AJIL Supplement* (1932) 623, 624.

117 *Guttieres* v. *Elmilik*, Italy, Giurisprudenza Italiana, 1886-I-1-486, 487.

118 See Sucharitkul, *State Immunities*, p. 19.

119 *Dralle* v. *Czechoslovakia*, Austria, (1950) 17 ILR 155, 163.

120 The Tate Letter. The increasing contact between US citizens and foreign States was stressed as an important reason for enacting the US FSIA: US House of Representatives, Report No. 94-1487, 1976, pp. 6–7; 1976 USCCAN 6604, 6605.

121 *Alfred Dunhill* v. *Cuba*, US, 425 US 682, 703 (1976); 66 ILR 212, 225.

122 *Empire of Iran Case*, Germany, (1963) 45 ILR 57, 61 and 63.

123 *Victory Transport* v. *Comisaría*, US, 336 F.2d 354, 357 (2nd Cir. 1964); 35 ILR 110 (emphasis added).

124 *Trendtex* v. *Central Bank*, England, [1977] QB 529, 555; 64 ILR 111, 129; see also 573 and 576; 64 ILR 111, 147 and 150. Quoted with approval in *Inter-Science* v. *Moçambique*, South Africa, 1979, 1980 (2) SA 111, 122; 64 ILR 689, 701; *Reef* v. *Fua Kavenga*, New Zealand, [1987] 1 NZLR 550, 570; 90 ILR 556. See also *I Congreso del Partido*, England, 1981, [1983] 1 AC 244, 262; 64 ILR 307, 313– 314; *Sengupta* v. *India*, England, 1982, [1983] ICR 221, 227; 64 ILR 352, 359; *Alcom* v. *Colombia*, England, [1984] 1 AC 580, 598; 74 ILR 170, 180–181; *Kuwait Airways* v. *Iraqi Airways*, England, [1995] 1 WLR 1147, 1157; 103 ILR 340, 398; *Propend* v. *Sing*, England, (1997) 111 ILR 611, 668; *Forth Tugs* v. *Wilmington*, Scotland, 1985, 1985 SC 317, 327; 1987 SLT 153, 158; 107 ILR 641, 651–652; *Barker* v. *Kenya*, Zimbabwe, (1983) (4) SA 817; (1985) (4) SA 197; 84 ILR 18, 33; *Buckingham* v. *Aircraft*, New Zealand, [1982] 2 NZLR 738, 739; 64 ILR 551; *Reef* v. *Fua Kavenga*, New Zealand, [1987] 1 NZLR 550, 570; 90 ILR 556; *Governor* v. *Sutton*, New Zealand, 1994, [1995] 1 NZLR 426, 435; 104 ILR 508, 520; *Controller* v. *Davison*, New Zealand, [1996] 2 NZLR 278, 300, 311; 104 ILR 526, 570, 613; *Re*

NOTES TO PAGE 21 481

Canada Labour Code, Canada, 1989, [1990] 1 FC 332, 338; 86 ILR 626, 629; *Re Canada Labour Code*, Canada, (1992) 91 DLR (4th) 449, 462; 94 ILR 264, 277; *Reid* v. *Nauru*, Australia, 1992, [1993] 1 VR 251, 252; 101 ILR 193, 194; *Canada* v. *Burke*, Ireland, 1991; [1992] 2 IR 484, 487–488; 95 ILR 467, 469–470; agreed: *Canada* v. *Burke*, Ireland, [1992] 2 IR 484, 500; 95 ILR 467, 481.

125 See *Dralle* v. *Czechoslovakia*, Austria, (1950) 17 ILR 155, 163; *Arrears of Rent Case*, Austria, 2001, 6 *Austrian RIEL* (2001) 313, 314; *Socobelge* v. *Greek State*, Belgium, (1951) 18 ILR 3, 7; *In re Danish State Railways*, Germany, (1953) 20 ILR 178, 179–180; *Latvia Case*, Germany, (1955) 22 ILR 230, 231; *In re The Charkow*, Germany, (1959) 65 ILR 100, 104; *Garden Contamination Case (2)*, Germany, (1987) 80 ILR 377, 381; *Castiglioni* v. *Yugoslavia*, Italy, (1952) 19 ILR 203, 204; *Padri* v. *Nunzi*, Italy, (1957) 24 ILR 214, 215; *Greece* v. *Gamet*, Italy, (1959) 28 ILR 153, 155; *The Ditta* v. *Germany*, Italy, (1960) 40 ILR 64, 65; *Mininni* v. *Bari Institute*, Italy, (1986) 87 ILR 28, 35; *France* v. *Jacuzio*, Italy, (1987) 87 ILR 53, 54; *Banamar-Capizzi* v. *Embassy*, Italy, (1989) 87 ILR 56, 60; *Libya* v. *Rossbeton*, Italy, (1989) 87 ILR 63, 68; *Venne* v. *Congo*, Canada, (1968) 5 DLR (3d) 128, 138; 64 ILR 1, 11; *Re Canada Labour Code*, Canada, 1989, [1990] 1 FC 332, 343; 86 ILR 626, 633; *Re Canada Labour Code*, Canada, (1992) 91 DLR (4th) 449, 462; 94 ILR 264, 277; *Bouzari* v. *Iran*, Canada, (2002) 124 ILR 427, 434; *Manauta* v. *Embassy*, Argentina, (1994) 113 ILR 429, 432; *Secretary* v. *Gammon-Layton*, Pakistan, (1970) 64 ILR 567, 576; *German* v. *Dynamic*, India, (1970) 64 ILR 504, 516; *Zodiac* v. *Polish*, Canada, (1977) 81 DLR (3d) 656, 663; 64 ILR 51, 58; *Société Européenne* v. *Yugoslavia*, Netherlands, (1973) 65 ILR 356, 361; *Inter-Science* v. *Moçambique*, South Africa, 1979, 1980 (2) SA 111, 120; 64 ILR 689, 699; *Qureshi* v. *USSR*, Pakistan, (1981) 64 ILR 585, 634; *Alcom* v. *Colombia*, England, [1984] 1 AC 580, 598; 74 ILR 170, 180; *Littrell* v. *USA (No. 2)*, England, (1992) 100 ILR 438, 446; *Marine* v. *Marshall*, New Zealand, (1981) 64 ILR 539, 549; *X* v. *USA*, Japan, 1998, 42 *JAIL* (1999) 138, 142; affirmed, *X* v. *USA*, Japan, 2002, 46 *JAIL* (2003) 161, 163; *Propend* v. *Sing*, England, (1996) 111 ILR 611, 632; *Governor* v. *Sutton*, New Zealand, 1994, [1995] 1 NZLR 426, 433; 104 ILR 508, 517; *USA* v. *Ruiz*, Philippines, (1985) 102 ILR 122, 125; *The Holy See* v. *Starbright*, Philippines, (1994) 102 ILR 163, 170. See also Sucharitkul, *State Immunities*, esp. pp. 14–19; Higgins, Certain, 265.

126 See *The Cristina*, England, [1938] AC 485, 498, 521; 9 AD 250, 260, 261, quoted in *Mexico* v. *Hoffman*, US, 324 US 30, 41 (1945); 12 AD 143, 148–149; *The Porto Alexandre*, England, 1919, [1920] P 30, 34, 36, 38–39; *Hannes* v. *Kingdom*, US, 20 N.Y.S. 2d 825 (1940); 9 AD 198, 202–203.

127 Badr, *State Immunity*, pp. 9–19. See also *The Philippine Admiral*, England, 1975, [1977] AC 373, 391–402; 64 ILR 90, 97–108.

128 *The Philippine Admiral*, England, 1975, [1977] AC 373, 403; 64 ILR 90, 109; *Trendtex* v. *Central Bank*, England, [1977] QB 529, 553, 556–557, 570; 574, 576; 64 ILR 111, 127, 130–131, 144, 148, 150; *I Congreso del Partido*, England, 1981, [1983] 1 AC 244, 262; 64 ILR 307, 314. See also *Inter-Science* v. *Moçambique*, South Africa, 1979, 1980 (2) SA 111, 120 and 124; 64 ILR 689, 699 and 704; *New Central* v. *VEB*, India, (1983) 92 ILR 509, 528; *Reef* v. *Fua Kavenga*, New

482 NOTES TO PAGES 22–24

Zealand, [1987] 1 NZLR 550, 571; 90 ILR 556, 564–565; *Controller* v. *Davison, New Zealand,* [1996] 2 NZLR 278, 311; 104 ILR 526, 613. Even at the time of absolute immunity, the validity of absolute immunity was already questioned on the basis of 'justice': *The Cristina,* England, [1938] AC 485, 519 and 521; *Rahimtoola* v. *Nizam,* England, 1957, [1958] AC 379, 416 and 420–421; 24 ILR 175, 195, 198.

129 *Inter-Science* v. *Moçambique,* South Africa, 1979, 1980 (2) SA 111, 120; 64 ILR 689, 699. See also *Kaffraria* v. *Zambia,* South Africa, 1980 (2) SA 709, 713; 64 ILR 708, 712.

130 On the other hand, it must be admitted that, in its practical effects on the *internal* political order, complete immunity does invest the State (and those personifying it) with a mysterious aura of unimpeachability, a hallmark of those wielding or advocating unlimited, *absolute* power. It is then no surprise that former communist States were among the most adamant adherents of absolute immunity.

131 A default judgment was entered against the USSR: *Von Dardel* v. *USSR,* US, 623 F.Supp. 246 (D.D.C. 1985); 77 ILR 258.

132 *Von Dardel* v. *USSR,* US, 736 F.Supp. 1, 3 (D.D.C. 1990). For reasoning couched in terms of international law see also the memorandum presented to the ILC by Ushakov, the Soviet member of the ILC. The USSR's defence in terms of international law was the same even under the rule of Stalin: *USSR* v. *Association,* France, (1929) 5 AD 18.

133 *Jackson* v. *China,* US, 794 F.2d 1490, 1494 (11th Cir. 1986); 84 ILR 132, 152.

134 *Jackson* v. *China,* US, 794 F.2d 1490, 1497–1498 (11th Cir. 1986); 84 ILR 132, 155–156; affirming *Jackson* v. *China,* US, 596 F.Supp. 386, 388–389 (N.D.Ala. 1984); 84 ILR 132, 147–148. For earlier stages of the case see *Jackson* v. *China,* US, 550 F.Supp. 869, 873–874 (N.D.Ala. 1982); 84 ILR 132, 138–139; *Jackson* v. *China,* US, 23 ILM 402, 408–410 (N.D.Ala. 1984); 84 ILR 132, 143–144. For criticism of the case see Sgro, China's Stance; Hsu, The Invalidity; Wang, Sovereign; Pax, Old Bonds; Feinerman, Sovereign Immunity.

135 *Morris* v. *China,* US, 478 F.Supp.2d 561, 563 (S.D.N.Y. 2007).

136 *Carl Marks* v. *USSR,* US, 665 F.Supp. 323, 332 (S.D.N.Y. 1987); 84 ILR 158 (citing *Jackson*); affirmed, *Carl Marks* v. *USSR,* US, 841 F.2d 26, 27 (2nd Cir. 1988). For non-retroactivity of the FSIA see also *Slade* v. *Mexico,* US, 617 F.Supp. 351, 356–358 (D.D.C. 1985); affirmed, *Slade* v. *Mexico,* US, 790 F.2d 163 (1986) (Table); *Schmidt* v. *Poland,* US, 742 F.2d 67, 71 (2nd Cir. 1984); affirming *Schmidt* v. *Poland,* US, 579 F.Supp. 23 (S.D.N.Y. 1984); *Djordjevich* v. *Bundesminister,* US, 827 F.Supp. 814, 817 (D.D.C. 1993); *Lin* v. *Japan,* US, 1994 WL 193948, 1994 US Dist. Lexis 6061, p. 2 (D.D.C. 1994); *Hwang* v. *Japan,* US, 332 F.3d 679, 686 (D.C. Cir. 2003); affirming *Hwang* v. *Japan,* US, 172 F.Supp.2d 52 (D.D.C. 2001). (The decision of *Hwang* was later vacated and remanded by the Supreme Court, *Hwang* v. *Japan,* 542 US 901 (2004), but was reaffirmed on the ground of non-justiciable political question: *Hwang* v. *Japan,* US, 413 F.3d 45 (D.C.Cir. 2005).) But the Supreme Court held that the FSIA could be applied retroactively: *Austria* v. *Altmann,* US, 541 US 677, 700 (2004), noted in Brower, Case

NOTES TO PAGE 25   483

note. For cases following *Altmann* see *Abrams* v. *Société Nationale*, US, 389 F.3d 61, 63 (2nd Cir. 2004); *Cruz* v. *US*, US, 387 F.Supp.2d 1057, 1060–1061 (N.D.Cal. 2005); *Garb* v. *Poland*, US, 440 F.3d 579, 581–582 (2nd Cir. 2006); affirming *Garb* v. *Poland*, US, 207 F.Supp.2d 16 (E.D.N.Y. 2002). For discussion on retroactivity see Mortara, The Case; DuCaine, Expectations; Lupu and Risen, Retroactive; Adelman, Sovereign; Wernicke, The 'Retroactive'; Murray, Jurisdiction, 280–283; Goodman, The Destruction; Vázquez, *Altmann*.

137 Although some States may still tend to think in such terms, see the debates in the Asian-African Legal Consultative Organisation (AALCO) from its Thirty-ninth Session, 2000 to Forty-fourth Session, 2005: www.aalco.int/content/annual-session (this is a poorly serviced website, however, and documents (even the whole website itself) may disappear and reappear without notice). Traces of such thinking may also be found in the ILC's commentary to its 1991 draft articles: *YILC*, 1991-II-2, p. 12. Discourse grounded in the developing/developed countries dichotomy was quite common during the 1980s to 1990s and permeated the ILC deliberations, see various annual reports of the ILC on its work on State immunity; Cristy, Amending; McGinty, Opening.

138 *Mwani* v. *Afghanistan*, US, 417 F.3d 1 (D.C.Cir. 2005); *Smith* v. *Afghanistan*, US, 262 F.Supp.2d 217 (S.D.N.Y. 2003).

139 *GE* v. *Albania*, US, 693 F.Supp.2d 132 (D.D.C. 2010).

140 *Banamar-Capizzi* v. *Embassy*, Italy, (1989) 87 ILR 56; *Leasing* v. *Algeria*, Austria, (1986) 116 ILR 526.

141 *First Fidelity* v. *Antigua*, US, 877 F.2d 189 (2nd Cir. 1989); 99 ILR 125.

142 *NML* v. *Argentina*, England, [2009] QB 579; reversed, *Argentina* v. *NML*, England, [2010] EWCA Civ 41; *X* v. *Argentina*, Germany, (1996) 114 ILR 502; *Siderman* v. *Argentina*, US, 965 F.2d 699 (9th Cir. 1992); 103 ILR 454; *Argentina* v. *Weltover*, US, 504 US 607 (1992); 100 ILR 509; *Argentine Republic* v. *Amerada Hess*, US, 488 US 428 (1989); 81 ILR 658.

143 *Singh* v. *Australia*, US, 521 F.Supp.2d 91 (D.D.C. 2007); *Fickling* v. *Australia*, US, 775 F.Supp. 66 (E.D.N.Y. 1991); 103 ILR 447; *Australia* v. *Midford*, Malaysia, (1990) 86 ILR 640; *Yendall* v. *Australia*, England, (1984) 107 ILR 590.

144 *Austria* v. *Altmann*, US, 541 US 677 (2004); *Whiteman* v. *Dorotheum*, US, 431 F.3d 57 (2nd Cir. 2005).

145 *Daventree* v. *Azerbaijan*, US, 349 F.Supp.2d 736, 750 (S.D.N.Y. 2004); *Frontera* v. *State Oil Company*, US, 479 F.Supp.2d 376 (S.D.N.Y. 2007); vacated and remanded, *Frontera* v. *State Oil Company*, US, 582 F.3d 393 (2nd Cir. 2009).

146 *Jayetilleke* v. *High Commission*, England, (1994) 107 ILR 622.

147 *Kramer* v. *Belgium*, Nigeria, 1988, (1989) 1 CLRQ 126; 103 ILR 299.

148 *Shapiro* v. *Bolivia*, US, 930 F.2d 1013 (2nd Cir. 1991); 98 ILR 109; *Practical* v. *Bolivia*, US, 811 F.2d 1543 (D.C.Cir. 1987); 92 ILR 420; *ETI* v. *Bolivia*, England, [2008] EWHC 1689 (Comm), 2008 WL 2697081; affirmed, *ETI* v. *Bolivia*, England, [2008] EWCA Civ 880, [2009] 1 WLR 665.

149 *Carbonar* v. *Magurno*, Italy, (1993) 114 ILR 534; *Brazilian Embassy Employee Case*, Portugal, (1984) 116 ILR 625.

484   NOTES TO PAGE 25

150 *Canada* v. *Cargnello*, Italy, (1998) 114 ILR 559; *Canada* v. *Burke*, Ireland, 1991/
1992, [1992] 2 IR 484; 95 ILR 467; *François* v. *Canada*, Belgium, (1989) 115 ILR
418.

151 *Orascom* v. *Chad*, England, [2008] EWHC 1841 (Comm), [2008] 2 Lloyd's Rep
396.

152 *Jackson* v. *China*, US, 550 F.Supp. 869 (N.D.Ala. 1982); 596 F.Supp. 386 (N.D.
Ala. 1984); 794 F.2d 1490 (11th Cir. 1986); 84 ILR 132; *Morris* v. *China*, US, 478
F.Supp.2d 561 (S.D.N.Y. 2007).

153 *Alcom* v. *Colombia*, England, 1983/1984; [1984] 1 AC 580; 74 ILR 170.

154 *Congo* v. *Venne*, Canada, (1971) 22 DLR (3d) 669; 64 ILR 24; *Zaire* v. *D'Hoop*,
Belgium, (1995) 106 ILR 294; *SA Biocare* v. *Zaire*, Belgium, (1989) 115 ILR 415;
Zaire v. *Duclaux*, Netherlands, (1988) 94 ILR 368; *Planmount* v. *Zaire*, England,
[1980] 2 Lloyd's Rep 393; 64 ILR 268. The Democratic Republic of the Congo
was called the Republic of Zaire from October 1971 to May 1997.

155 *I Congreso del Partido*, England, 1981, [1983] 1 AC 244; 64 ILR 307.

156 *Embassy* v. *Jens*, Denmark, (1982) 78 ILR 81.

157 *Meadows* v. *Dominican Republic*, US, 817 F.2d 517 (9th Cir. 1987); 98 ILR 37.

158 *Weston* v. *Ecuador*, US, 823 F.Supp. 1106 (S.D.N.Y. 1993); *Ecuador* v. *ChevronTexaco Corporation*, US, 376 F.Supp.2d 334 (S.D.N.Y. 2005).

159 *Embassy* v. *Lasheen*, US, 603 F.3d 1166 (9th Cir. 2010); *M* v. *Egypt*, Switzerland,
(1994) 116 ILR 656.

160 *Emilio* v. *Embassy*, Spain, (1986) 86 ILR 508.

161 *Eckert* v. *Fiji*, US, 32 F.3d 77 (4th Cir. 1994); 107 ILR 347.

162 *Giaffreda* v. *French*, Italy, (1992) 114 ILR 558 note; *Gerding* v. *France*, US, 943
F.2d 521 (4th Cir. 1991); 98 ILR 159; *French Consular Employee Claim Case*,
Austria, (1989) 86 ILR 583; *France* v. *Jacuzio*, Italy, (1987) 87 ILR 53.

163 *Paprocki* v. *German*, England, (1995) 104 ILR 684; *Panattoni* v. *Germany*, Italy,
(1987) 87 ILR 42; *LF* v. *Germany*, Netherlands, (1986) 94 ILR 342; *Attorney-
General* v. *Germany*, Spain, (1983) 88 ILR 679; *The Ditta* v. *Germany*, Italy,
(1960) 40 ILR 64.

164 *Rush-Presbyterian* v. *Hellenic*, US, 877 F.2d 574 (7th Cir. 1989); 101 ILR 509.

165 *The Holy See* v. *Starbright*, Philippines, (1994) 102 ILR 163; *Doe* v. *Holy See*, US,
557 F.3d 1066 (9th Cir. 2009); partly affirming, partly reversing and
remanding *Doe* v. *Holy See*, US, 434 F.Supp.2d 925 (D.Or. 2006); *O'Bryan* v. *Holy
See*, US, 556 F.3d 361 (6th Cir. 2009); affirming *O'Bryan* v. *Holy See*, US, 471
F.Supp.2d 784 (W.D.Ky. 2007); *Doe* v. *Holy See*, US, 434 F.Supp.2d 925 (D.Or.
2006), noted in Mason, A New. See also Martinez, Sovereign.

166 *Phaneuf* v. *Indonesia*, US, 106 F.3d 302 (9th Cir. 1997).

167 *Cicippio* v. *Iran*, US, 30 F.3d 164 (D.C.Cir. 1994); 107 ILR 296; *Ministry* v. *Société
Framatome*, France, (1990) 113 ILR 452; *Foremost-McKesson* v. *Iran*, US, 905 F.2d
438 (D.C.Cir. 1990); 101 ILR 536; *Iran* v. *Société Eurodif*, France, (1989) 89 ILR 31.

168 *Agrocomplect* v. *Iraq*, US, 524 F.Supp.2d 16 (D.D.C. 2007); *Iraq* v. *Dumez*,
Belgium, (1995) 106 ILR 284 and *R* v. *Iraq*, Switzerland, (1994) 116 ILR 664.

169 *Gilson* v. *Ireland*, US, 682 F.2d 1022 (D.C.Cir.1982); 92 ILR 374; *Gibbons* v. *Ireland*,
US, 532 F.Supp. 668 (D.D.C. 1982); 86 ILR 75.

NOTES TO PAGE 25 485

170 *Chalabi* v. *Jordan*, US, 503 F.Supp.2d 267, 272–273 (D.D.C. 2007); affirmed, *Chalabi* v. *Jordan*, US, 543 F.3d 725 (D.C.Cir. 2008).

171 *AIG* v. *Kazakhstan*, England, 2005, [2006] 1 WLR 1420; [2006] 1 All ER 284; 129 ILR 589.

172 *Barker* v. *Kenya*, Zimbabwe, (1983) (4) SA 817; (1985) (4) SA 197; 84 ILR 18.

173 *Al-Adsani* v. *Kuwait*, England, (1994) 100 ILR 465; *Al-Adsani* v. *Kuwait*, England, (1995) 103 ILR 420; *Al-Adsani* v. *Kuwait*, England, (1996) 107 ILR 536.

174 *American* v. *Lebanon*, US, 408 F.Supp.2d 409, 413 (E.D.Mich. 2005); affirmed, *American* v. *Lebanon*, US, 501 F.3d 534 (6th Cir. 2007).

175 *LETCO*, US, 650 F.Supp. 73 (S.D.N.Y. 1986); 89 ILR 355; *LETCO*, US, 659 F.Supp. 606 (D.D.C. 1987); 89 ILR 360.

176 *Smith* v. *Libya*, US, 101 F.3d 239 (2nd Cir. 1996); 113 ILR 534; *Libya* v. *Trobbiani*, Italy, (1990) 114 ILR 520; *Libya* v. *Rossbeton*, Italy, (1989) 87 ILR 63; *Libya* v. *SpA*, Italy, (1983) 87 ILR 11.

177 *Svenska* v. *Lithuania (No. 2)*, England, [2006] EWCA Civ 1529, [2007] QB 886; affirming *Svenska* v. *Lithuania (No. 2)*, England, [2005] EWHC 2437 (Comm), [2006] 1 Lloyd's Rep 181.

178 *Marine* v. *Marshall*, New Zealand, (1981) 64 ILR 539; *Marine* v. *Marshall*, New Zealand, (1982) 64 ILR 562.

179 *Olsen* v. *Mexico*, US 729 F.2d 641 (9th Cir. 1984); 84 ILR 96; *Asociacion* v. *Mexico*, US, 561 F.Supp. 1190 (D.D.C. 1983); affirmed, *Asociacion* v. *Mexico*, US, 735 F.2d 1517 (D.C.Cir. 1984); 84 ILR 87.

180 *Morocco* v. *DR*, Belgium, (1989) 115 ILR 421 and *Stichting* v. *Morocco*, Netherlands, (1984/1986) 94 ILR 355.

181 *Inter-Science* v. *Moçambique*, South Africa, (1979) 64 ILR 689;

182 *Reid* v. *Nauru*, Australia, (1992) 101 ILR 193.

183 *AIC* v. *Nigeria*, England, [2003] EWHC 1357 (QB), 129 ILR 571; *Adler* v. *Nigeria*, US, 219 F.3d 869 (9th Cir. 2000); *Adler* v. *Nigeria*, US, 107 F.3d 720 (9th Cir. 1997); *Antares* v. *Nigeria*, US, 999 F.2d 33 (2nd Cir. 1993); 107 ILR 225; *Texas Trading* v. *Nigeria*, US, 647 F.2d 300 (2nd Cir. 1981); 63 ILR 552; *Trendtex* v. *Central Bank*, England, [1977] QB 529. See also Nwogugu, Immunity.

184 *Norwegian* v. *Quattri*, Italy, (1991) 114 ILR 525; *Risk* v. *Halvorsen*, US, 936 F.2d 393 (9th Cir. 1991); 98 ILR 125.

185 *Sabah* v. *Pakistan*, England, [2002] EWCA Civ 1643, [2003] 2 Lloyd's Rep 571.

186 *Amorrortu* v. *Peru*, US, 570 F.Supp.2d 916 (S.D.Tex. 2008); *MacArthur* v. *Peru*, US, 809 F.2d 918 (D.C.Cir. 1987); 107 ILR 196.

187 *Walter* v. *Philippines*, US, 965 F.2d 1375 (5th Cir. 1992); 103 ILR 503.

188 *Garb* v. *Poland*, US, 440 F.3d 579 (2nd Cir. 2006).

189 *De Queiroz* v. *Portugal*, Belgium, (1992) 115 ILR 430; *Portugal* v. *Algemene*, Netherlands, (1982) 94 ILR 315; *Portugal* v. *De Sousa*, Netherlands, (1981) 94 ILR 314.

190 *Creighton* v. *Minister*, France, (2000) 127 ILR 154; *Creighton* v. *Qatar*, US, 181 F.3d 118 (D.C.Cir. 1999).

191 *UNC* v. *Saudi Arabia*, US, 581 F.3d 210 (5th Cir. 2009); *Moran* v. *Saudi Arabia*, US, 27 F.3d 169 (5th Cir. 1994); 107 ILR 303; *Saudi Arabia* v. *Nelson*, US, 507 US 349

486 NOTES TO PAGE 25

(1993); 100 ILR 544; *Zedan* v. *Saudi Arabia*, US, 849 F.2d 1511 (D.C.Cir. 1988); 92 ILR 462; *Jones* v. *Saudi Arabia*, England, 2003/2004/2006, [2005] QB 699; [2007] 1 AC 270; 129 ILR 629.

192 *Société Ouest* v. *Senegal*, France, (1989/1991) 113 ILR 440; *Senghor* v. *International Bank*, France, (1990) 113 ILR 460.

193 *Philipp Brothers* v. *Sierra Leone*, England, 1993/1995, [1994] 1 Lloyd's Rep 111; [1995] 1 Lloyd's Rep 289; 107 ILR 517.

194 *Transamerican* v. *Somalia*, US, 590 F.Supp. 968 (D.D.C. 1984); 767 F.2d 998 (D.C. Cir. 1985); 86 ILR 55.

195 *Oster* v. *South Africa*, US, 530 F.Supp.2d 92 (D.D.C. 2007); *Martin* v. *South Africa*, US, 836 F.2d 91 (2nd Cir. 1987); 92 ILR 448; *Diana* v. *South Africa*, Spain, (1986) 86 ILR 512.

196 *Carl Marks* v. *USSR*, US, 665 F.Supp. 323 (S.D.N.Y. 1987); 84 ILR 158; *USSR* v. *ICC*, Netherlands, (1981/1987) 87 ILR 103; *Von Dardel* v. *USSR*, US, 623 F.Supp. 246 (D.D.C. 1985); 77 ILR 258; *Von Dardel* v. *USSR*, US, 736 F.Supp. 1 (D.D.C. 1990). See also Boguslavsky, Foreign State Immunity.

197 *Allen* v. *Russian Federation*, US, 522 F.Supp.2d 167 (D.D.C. 2007).

198 *Cassirer* v. *Spain*, US, 580 F.3d 1048 (9th Cir. 2009); partly affirming, partly reversing and remanding *Cassirer* v. *Spain*, US, 461 F.Supp.2d 1157 (C.D.Cal. 2006).

199 *Travel Associates* v. *Swaziland*, US, 107 ILR 219 (D.D.C. 1990).

200 *Gates* v. *Syria*, US, 580 F.Supp.2d 53 (D.D.C. 2008); *Wyatt* v. *Syria*, US, 362 F.Supp.2d 103 (D.D.C. 2005); *Syria* v. *Jajodia*, India, 2004.

201 *Reef* v. *Fua Kavenga*, New Zealand, (1987) 90 ILR 556.

202 *MK* v. *Turkey*, Netherlands, (1985) 94 ILR 350.

203 *Uganda Co.* v. *Uganda*, England, 1978, [1979] 1 Lloyd's Rep 481; 64 ILR 209.

204 *UAE* v. *Abdelghafar*, England, (1995) 107 ILR 626.

205 *Moore* v. *UK*, US, 384 F.3d 1079 (9th Cir. 2004); *Ministry of Defence* v. *Joel*, Kenya, 1983, (1982–88) KAR 135; 103 ILR 235; *Bulli* v. *FCO*, Italy, (1981) 65 ILR 343.

206 *Mills* v. *USA*, England, (2000) 120 ILR 612; *USA* v. *Friedland*, Canada, (1998) 40 OR (3d) 747; (1999) 182 DLR (4th) 614; 120 ILR 417; *Barrandon* v. *USA*, France, 1992/1995, 113 ILR 464; *Barrandon* v. *USA*, France, (1998) 116 ILR 622; *Muller* v. *USA*, Germany, (1998) 114 ILR 512; *USA* v. *Perières*, France, (1997) 113 ILR 494; *Hicks* v. *USA*, England, (1995) 120 ILR 606; *X* v. *USA*, Switzerland, (1995) 116 ILR 668; *USA* v. *Lo Gatto*, Italy, (1995) 114 ILR 555; *Ramos* v. *USA*, Portugal, (1994) 116 ILR 634; *Littrell* v. *USA (No. 2)*, England, 1992/1993, [1995] 1 WLR 82; 100 ILR 438; *Seidenschmidt* v. *USA*, Austria, (1992) 116 ILR 530; *Re Canada Labour Code*, Canada, (1992) 91 DLR (4th) 449; 94 ILR 264; *USA* v. *Guinto*, *USA* v. *Ceballos*, *USA* v. *Rodrigo*, Philippines, (1990) 102 ILR 132; *Van der Hulst* v. *US*, Netherlands, (1989) 94 ILR 373; *Tritt* v. *USA*, Canada, (1989) 68 OR (2d) 284; 94 ILR 260; *Landano* v. *USA*, Switzerland, (1987) 116 ILR 636; *Forth* v. *Wilmington*, Scotland, 1985, 1985 SC 317; 1987 SLT 153; 107 ILR 641; *USA* v. *Ruiz*, Philippines, (1985) 102 ILR 122; *Carrato* v. *USA*, Canada, (1982) 141 DLR (3d) 456; 90 ILR 229; *Harry Lyons* v. *USA*, Philippines, (1958) 88 ILR 711.

207 *Arias* v. *Venezuela*, Netherlands, (1998) 128 ILR 684.

208 *S & Davis* v. *Yemen*, US, 218 F.3d 1292 (11th Cir. 2000); *Mouracade* v. *Yemen*, France, (1991) 113 ILR 462.

209 *Donegal* v. *Zambia*, England, [2007] EWHC 197 (Comm), [2007] 1 Lloyd's Rep 397; *An International* v. *Zambia*, England, (1997) 118 ILR 602; *Kaffraria* v. *Zambia*, South Africa, (1980) 64 ILR 708.

210 See especially Fox, *The Law of State Immunity*, Part II, pp. 173–412; Fox, International Law and Restraints, pp. 346–349; Gong, *A Comparative Study*, ch. 3; Pingel, *Droit des immunités*, pp. 7–11; Pingel-Lenuzza, *Les immunités*, pp. 239–263; Schreuer, *State Immunity*, pp. 2–6; Sucharitkul, Preliminary Report, *YILC*, 1979-II-1, p. 227 at pp. 231–237, paras. 22–45; Sucharitkul, *State Immunities*, pp. 1–2.

211 See, e.g., Harvard Research; *Materials on Jurisdictional Immunities*; Comments and observations received from Governments, A/CN.4/410 and Add.l-5, *YILC*, 1988-II-1, p. 45; Dickinson *et al.* (eds.), *State Immunity*; Council of Europe Database on State Immunities and its companion volume, Hafner *et al.* (eds.), *State Practice*.

212 See *X* v. *Germany*, Austria, (1963) 65 ILR 10, 12; *UAR* v. *Mirza*, India, (1961) 64 ILR 394, 401, 406; *Iran* v. *Société Eurodif*, France, (1984) 77 ILR 513, 515; *Société* v. *Migeon*, France, (1985) 77 ILR 525, 527; *Secretary* v. *Gammon-Layton*, Pakistan, (1970) 64 ILR 567, 579; *Olofsen* v. *Malaysia*, Singapore, [1966] 2 MLJ 300, 301–302; (1966) 55 ILR 409, 410–411; *X* v. *Germany*, Austria, (1963) 65 ILR 10, 12; *Senerman* v. *Cuba*, Chile, (1975) 65 ILR 29, 30. In Australia, cases of State immunity are officially reported either under the headnote 'Private International Law' (e.g. *Victoria* v. *US*, Australia, [2005] VSCA 76, 190 FLR 351; *Pan* v. *Bo*, Australia, [2008] NSWSC 961, 220 FLR 271) or 'Public International Law' (e.g. *Thor* v. *Al Duhail*, Australia, [2008] FCA 1842, 252 ALR 20; 173 FCR 524; 140 ILR 530).

213 See 1928 Bustamante Code, Arts. 333–338.

214 This is the consensus of leading scholars of major jurisdictions. See Collins (gen. ed.), *Conflict of Laws*, pp. 273–293, Rule 19; Fawcett *et al.*, *Private International Law*, pp. 491–502; Anton and Beaumont, *Private International Law*, pp. 107–120; Kropholler, *Internationales Privatrecht*, pp. 581–584; Monéger, *Droit international privé*, pp. 180–182; Courbe, *Droit international privé*, p. 138; Gutmann, *Droit international privé*, pp. 236–8. Publicists would concede as much, see Sucharitkul, Third Report, *YILC*, 1981-II-1, p. 125 at pp. 134–135, paras. 22–24. Indeed, the case of State immunity stands as living proof to Jennings' observation that 'the old well-defined boundaries between public international law, private international law and municipal law are no longer boundaries but grey areas', Jennings, The Judiciary, 102 ILR ix, xiii. For an interesting case study see Davies, Kuwait Airways.

215 See *Manauta* v. *Embassy*, Argentina, (1994) 113 ILR 429, 433; *Wright* v. *Cantrell*, Australia, (1943) 12 AD 133, 135, 137, 140; *Chow* v. *The King*, Australia, (1948) 15 AD 147, 158, 160–161, 164–167, 171; *USA* v. *Republic of China*, Australia, (1950) 17 ILR 168, 169; *Kubacz* v. *Shah*, Australia, 1983, [1984] WAR 156, 160–161; 118 ILR 293, 297–298; *Australian* v. *Westpac*, Australia, (1988) 17 NSWLR

488   NOTES TO PAGE 28

623, 629–633; 104 ILR 405, 412–417; *Reid* v. *Nauru*, Australia, 1992, [1993] 1 VR 251, 252–254, 256; 101 ILR 193, 194–197, 199–200; *Victoria* v. *US*, Australia, [2005] VSCA 76, 190 FLR 351, 356, 359–360; *Thor Shipping* v. *Al Duhail*, Australia, [2008] FCA 1842, 252 ALR 20; 173 FCR 524, 540–544; 140 ILR 530, 551–557; *Dralle* v. *Czechoslovakia*, Austria, (1950) 17 ILR 155, 158–161, 164–165; *Republic of 'A'*, Austria, (1986) 77 ILR 488, 492–493; *Leasing West* v. *Algeria*, Austria, (1986) 116 ILR 526, 528–529; *Reference re Exemption*, Canada, [1943] SCR 483, 498, 509–510, 514–517, 524–526; 12 AD 124, 127, 129–133; *Dessaulles* v. *Poland*, Canada, (1944) 4 DLR 1, 3, 6–7; 12 AD 92, 93–95; *White* v. *Frank Dale*, Canada, (1946) 13 AD 82, 83; *Municipality* v. *Fraser-Brace*, Canada, (1958) 13 DLR (2d) 177, 181–184, 190–193; 26 ILR 165, 168, 169, 171, 174–176; *Flota* v. *Cuba*, Canada, [1962] SCR 598, 603–608; 42 ILR 125, 130–134; *Congo* v. *Venne*, Canada, (1971) 22 DLR (3d) 669, 675, 677, 679, 681–688; 64 ILR 24, 30, 32, 34, 36–43; *Amanat* v. *Fredson*, Canada, (1982) 133 DLR (3d) 632, 634–635; (1982) 36 OR 17, 19–20; 64 ILR 733, 735–736; *Cargo* v. *Lorac*, Canada, (1986) 28 DLR (4th) 309, 315; 84 ILR 700, 706; *Re Canada Labour Code*, Canada, 1989, [1990] 1 FC 332, 337–338, 345–348; 86 ILR 626, 629, 635–638; *Re Canada Labour Code*, Canada, (1992) 91 DLR (4th) 449, 458–459, 462–465, 468, 471–473, 475, 483–485, 490; 94 ILR 264, 273–274, 277–280, 283, 286–288, 290, 298–300, 305; *Jaffe* v. *Miller*, Canada, (1993) 103 DLR (4th) 315; 13 OR (3d) 745, 752–753, 758, 761; 95 ILR 446, 452–453, 458, 461; *USA* v. *Friedland*, Canada, (1998) 40 OR (3d) 747, 759; 120 ILR 417, 428–429; *Schreiber* v. *Germany*, Canada, (2001) 196 DLR (4th) 281, 295–296, 297; *Bouzari* v. *Iran*, Canada, (2002) 124 ILR 427, 435, 442–444; *Roxford* v. *Cuba*, Canada, (2003) 124 ACWS (3d) 294; [2003] 236 FTR 1, [2003] 2003 FCT 763; [2003] 4 FC 1182, paras. 30–34; *Manuel* v. *Ministère Public*, Egypt, (1943) 12 AD 154, 157, 160; *The Parlement Belge*, England, (1880) 5 PD 197, 206, 208, 212, 216, 220; *The Cristina*, England, [1938] AC 485, 508–509, 510, 518–519; 9 AD 250, 258, 260, 262; *Chung* v. *The King*, England, 1938, [1939] AC 160, 168–171; *Thai-Europe* v. *Pakistan*, England, [1975] 1 WLR 1485, 1490, 1491; 64 ILR 81, 84, 86; *The Philippine Admiral*, England, 1975, [1977] AC 373, 391, 394, 396, 397–401, 403; 64 ILR 90, 97, 100, 102, 103–107, 109; *Trendtex* v. *Central Bank*, England, [1977] QB 529, 555–559, 562–563, 566, 570, 572; 64 ILR 111, 129–133, 136–137, 140, 144, 146; *Planmount* v. *Zaire*, England, 1980, [1981] 1 All ER 1110, 1114; 64 ILR 268, 272; *I Congreso del Partido*, England, 1979, [1981] 1 All ER 1092, 1102, 1106–1107; [1980] 1 Lloyd's Rep 23, 30, 33–34; 64 ILR 227, 234, 238–239; *I Congreso del Partido*, England, 1981, [1983] 1 AC 244, 263–267, 276; 64 ILR 307, 314–315, 317–319, 327; *Sengupta* v. *India*, England, 1982, [1983] ICR 221, 226, 229–230; 64 ILR 352, 358, 362; *Alcom* v. *Colombia*, England, [1984] 1 AC 580, 598–599; 74 ILR 170, 181–182; *R* v. *Inland Revenue*, England, 1989, [1990] 1 WLR 191, 201; 103 ILR 327, 336–337; *Kuwait Airways* v. *Iraqi Airways*, England, 1992/1993/1995, [1995] 1 Lloyd's Rep 25; [1995] 1 WLR 1147, 1160, 1173; 103 ILR 340, 354, 373–374, 375, 382, 385, 401–402, 417; *Egypt* v. *Gamal-Eldin*, England, 1995, [1996] 2 All ER 237, 247; 104 ILR 673, 682; *Al-Adsani* v. *Kuwait*, England, (1995) 103 ILR 420, 429–431; *Al-Adsani* v. *Kuwait*, England, (1996) 107 ILR 536, 542–543, 546–548; *Propend* v. *Sing*, England, (1997) 111 ILR 611, 667–669; *Jones* v. *Saudi Arabia*,

England, [2006] 2 WLR 1424, 1430, 1448; [2007] 1 AC 270, 281, 299, paras. 10 and 67; 129 ILR 629, 717, 740; *Orascom* v. *Chad*, England, [2008] EWHC 1841 (Comm), [2008] 2 Lloyd's Rep 396, 406–407; *Empire of Iran Case*, Germany, (1963) 45 ILR 57, 62–73; *Spanish Consular Bank Accounts Case*, Germany, (1971) 65 ILR 114, 116–117; *Philippine Embassy Bank Account Case*, Germany, (1977) 65 ILR 146, 164–175, 189–190; *NIOC Revenues Case*, Germany, (1983) 65 ILR 215, 229–236, 239–241, 244–245; *Indian National* v. *Maux*, India, (1955) 22 ILR 248, 250–252; *UAR* v. *Mirza*, India, (1961) 64 ILR 394, 416; *Royal Nepal* v. *Monorama*, India, (1964) 64 ILR 430, 456; *New Central* v. *VEB*, India, (1983) 92 ILR 509, 517, 527–529; *Harbhajan* v. *India*, India, (1986) 92 ILR 530, 534–535, 538; *The Ramava*, Ireland, (1941) 10 AD 91, 93–95; *Saorstat* v. *Rafael*, Ireland, (1944) 12 AD 97, 98, 100; *Canada* v. *Burke*, Ireland, [1992] 2 IR 484, 491, 493–495, 498–500; 95 ILR 467, 472, 474–476, 479–481; *Fusco* v. *O'Dea*, Ireland, [1994] 2 ILRM 389, 392; 103 ILR 318, 321; *McElhinney* v. *Williams*, Ireland, 1995, [1996] 1 ILRM 276, 283–289; 104 ILR 691, 697–703; *Her Majesty* v. *Edelson*, Israel, (1997) 131 ILR 279, 293–296, 300–306; *Libya* v. *Rossbeton*, Italy, (1989) 87 ILR 63, 66; *Condor* v. *Minister of Justice*, Italy, (1992) 101 ILR 394, 401–402; *Ferrini* v. *Germany*, Italy, (2004) 128 ILR 658, 667, 670–674; *Ministry* v. *Joel*, Kenya, (1983) 103 ILR 235, 237–238, 241–242; *Village* v. *Her Majesty*, Malaysia, (1987) 87 ILR 223, 232, 234, 236–238; *Australia* v. *Midford*, Malaysia, (1990) 86 ILR 640, 644–647, 650–651; *Marine* v. *Marshall*, New Zealand, (1981) 64 ILR 539, 542–545, 549–550; *Buckingham* v. *Aircraft*, New Zealand, [1982] 2 NZLR 738, 739–744; (1982) 64 ILR 551, 552–560; *Marine* v. *Marshall*, New Zealand, (1982) 64 ILR 562, 565–566; *Reef* v. *Fua Kavenga*, New Zealand, [1987] 1 NZLR 550, 568–572; 90 ILR 556, 561–566; *Governor* v. *Sutton*, 1994, [1995] 1 NZLR 426, 428–429, 434–438; 104 ILR 508, 510–511, 519–524; *Controller* v. *Davison*, New Zealand, [1996] 2 NZLR 278, 288–290, 299–301, 303, 305–306, 308, 318; 104 ILR 526, 537–540, 568–571, 574, 577–578, 605, 622; *Kramer* v. *Belgium*, Nigeria, (1988) 103 ILR 299, 301, 303–310; *Secretary* v. *Gammon-Layton*, Pakistan, (1970) 64 ILR 567, 578; *Qureshi* v. *USSR*, Pakistan, (1981) 64 ILR 585, 591, 601–602, 641–648; *Brazilian Embassy Employee Case*, Portugal, (1984) 116 ILR 625, 630, 632; *X* v. *Israel*, Portugal, (2002) 127 ILR 310, 312; *Parkin* v. *Congo*, South Africa, 1970, 1971 (1) SA 259, 261; 64 ILR 668, 670–671; *Leibowitz* v. *Schwartz*, South Africa, 1973, 1974 (2) SA 661, 662; 64 ILR 672, 674; *Lendalease* v. *Corporacion*, South Africa, 1975 (4) SA 397, 402–404; 1976 (4) SA 464, 499; 64 ILR 675, 681–683, 684; *Prentice* v. *Bolivia*, South Africa, 1978 (3) SA 938, 941–942; 64 ILR 685, 687–689; *Inter-Science* v. *Moçambique*, South Africa, 1979, 1980 (2) SA 111, 119–125; 64 ILR 689, 698–705; *Kaffraria* v. *Zambia*, South Africa, 1980 (2) SA 709, 712–715; 64 ILR 708, 711–714; *Banco* v. *Inter-Science*, South Africa, 1982 (3) SA 330, 335, 339–342, 344; 87 ILR 239, 244, 248–252, 253; *The Akademik Fyodorov*, South Africa, 1996 (4) SA 422, 447; 131 ILR 460, 488; *Abbott* v. *South Africa*, Spain, (1992) 113 ILR 411, 421–424; *Dreyfus*, Switzerland, (1918) BGE 44 I 49, 54; *UAR* v. *Mrs X*, Switzerland, (1960) 65 ILR 385, 389–390; *Italian* v. *Beta*, Switzerland, (1966) 65 ILR 394, 398, 401; *Banque Centrale* v. *Weston*, Switzerland, (1978) 65 ILR 417, 421; *Libya* v. *LIAMCO*,

490   NOTES TO PAGES 28–30

Switzerland, (1980) 62 ILR 228, 233; *S* v. *India*, Switzerland, (1984) 82 ILR 13, 19–20; *Spain* v. *Company X*, Switzerland, (1986) 82 ILR 38, 41; *Landano* v. *USA*, Switzerland, (1987) 116 ILR 636, 638–641; *Nicoud* v. *USA*, Switzerland, (1994) 116 ILR 650, 655; *X* v. *USA*, Switzerland, (1995) 116 ILR 668, 671–672, 675; *In re Muir*, US, 254 US 522, 533 (1921); 1 AD 143; *Mexico* v. *Hoffman*, US, 324 US 30, 41 (1945); 12 AD 143, 148–149; *Barker* v. *Kenya*, Zimbabwe, (1983/1985) 84 ILR 18, 21–26, 29–37. For lack of space the exact citations of the cases referred to are omitted here. See also Sucharitkul, Preliminary Report, *YILC*, 1979-II-1, p. 227 at p. 233, paras. 28–30; Siewert, Reciprocal.

216 See *Dralle* v. *Czechoslovakia*, Austria, (1950) 17 ILR 155, 157–158; *The Cristina*, England, [1938] AC 485, 497; 9 AD 250, 260; *The Philippine Admiral*, England, 1975, [1977] AC 373, 391; 64 ILR 90, 97; *Trendtex* v. *Central Bank*, England, [1977] QB 529, 552, 555–556; 575; 64 ILR 111, 126; 129–130, 149; *I Congreso del Partido*, England, 1977, [1978] 1 QB 500, 529; 64 ILR 154, 180; *I Congreso del Partido*, England, 1981, [1983] 1 AC 244, 265; 64 ILR 307, 316; *Sengupta* v. *India*, England, 1982, [1983] ICR 221, 229; 64 ILR 352, 362; *Empire of Iran Case*, Germany, (1963) 45 ILR 57, 61–62; *Philippine Embassy Case*, Germany, (1977) 65 ILR 146, 166–167, Ground C.I.3.; *Distomo Massacre Case*, Greece, (2000) 129 ILR 513, 516; *The Ramava*, Ireland, 1941, [1942] IR 148, 161; 10 AD 91, 93; *Saorstat* v. *Rafael*, Ireland, 1944, [1945] IR 291, 298; 12 AD 97, 97; *Canada* v. *Burke*, Ireland, [1992] 2 IR 484, 496; 95 ILR 467, 477; *Kramer* v. *Belgium*, Nigeria, (1988) 103 ILR 299, 307; *Abbott* v. *South Africa*, Spain, (1992) 113 ILR 411, 418–419; *M* v. *Egypt*, Switzerland, (1994) 116 ILR 656, 658, Ground 2.

217 See such references in, e.g., *Pinochet No. 3*, England, 1999, [2000] 1 AC 147; 119 ILR 135; *Holland* v. *Lampen-Wolfe*, England, [2000] 1 WLR 1573; 119 ILR 367; *Jones* v. *Saudi Arabia*, England, 2004, [2005] QB 699; 2006, [2007] 1 AC 270; 129 ILR 629.

218 *Arrest Warrant*, *ICJ Reports* 2002, p. 3 at p. 21, para. 51 (emphases added); 128 ILR 1, 76.

219 In the words of Lord Browne-Wilkinson, for instance, 'The foreign state is entitled to procedural *immunity* from the *processes* of the forum state. This *immunity* extends to both criminal and civil liability.' *Pinochet No. 3* [2000] 1 AC 147, 201; 119 ILR 135. Emphases added.

220 See, e.g., *Trendtex* v. *Central Bank*, England, [1977] QB 529; 64 ILR 111; *The Philippine Admiral*, England, 1975, [1977] AC 373; 64 ILR 90; *Thai-Europe* v. *Pakistan*, England, [1975] 1 WLR 1485; 64 ILR 81; *Rahimtoola* v. *Nizam*, England, 1957, [1958] AC 379; 24 ILR 175; *The El Condado*, Scotland, (1937) 59 Lloyd's Rep 119; *The El Condado*, Scotland, (1939) 63 Lloyd's Rep 330; *Spain* v. *National*, Scotland, 1939 SC 413; *Venne* v. *Congo*, Canada, (1968) 64 ILR 1; *Congo* v. *Venne*, Canada, (1971) 64 ILR 24; *Re Royal Bank*, Canada, (1980) 64 ILR 69; *Amanat* v. *Fredson*, Canada, (1982) 64 ILR 733; *Cargo* v. *Lorac*, Canada, (1986) 84 ILR 700; *Royal* v. *Monorama*, India, (1964) 64 ILR 430; *Marine* v. *Marshall*, New Zealand, (1981) 64 ILR 539; *Marine* v. *Marshall*, New Zealand, (1982) 64 ILR 562; *Reef* v. *Fua Kavenga*, New Zealand, [1987] 1 NZLR 550, 568–573; 90 ILR 556, 561–566; *Governor* v. *Sutton*, New Zealand, (1994) 104 ILR 508; *Qureshi* v. *USSR*, Pakistan,

NOTES TO PAGE 30   491

(1981) 64 ILR 585; *Inter-Science* v. *Moçambique*, South Africa, (1979) 64 ILR 689; *Kaffraria* v. *Zambia*, South Africa, (1980) 64 ILR 708; *Barker* v. *Kenya*, Zimbabwe, (1983) 84 ILR 18; *Australia* v. *Midford*, Malaysia, (1990) 86 ILR 640; *Schmidt* v. *Home Secretary*, Ireland, [1997] 2 IR 121. But see *USA* v. *Dollfus*, England, [1952] AC 582, 605–606; 19 ILR 163, 169.

221 See, e.g., *I Congreso del Partido*, England, 1981, [1983] 1 AC 244; 64 ILR 307; *Maclaine* v. *Department*, England, [1988] 3 WLR 1033, 1101, 1103; 80 ILR 47, 116, 118; *Sabah* v. *Pakistan*, England, [2002] EWCA Civ 1643, [2003] 2 Lloyd's Rep 571; *Svenska* v. *Lithuania (No. 2)*, England, [2006] EWCA Civ 1529, [2007] QB 886; *Ministry* v. *Tsavliris*, England, [2008] EWHC 612 (Comm), [2008] 2 Lloyd's Rep 90; *Forth* v. *Wilmington*, Scotland, 1985, 1985 SC 317; 1987 SLT 153; 107 ILR 641. This mixture, interestingly, can also be found in earlier case law. See *USA* v. *Dollfus*, England, [1952] AC 582, 605–606; 19 ILR 163, 169. Notably, in *Alcom*, 'sovereign immunity' was used despite the application of the UK SIA: *Alcom* v. *Colombia*, England, [1984] 1 AC 580; 74 ILR 170.

222 See, e.g., *Jaffe* v. *Miller*, Canada, (1990) 87 ILR 197; *Jaffe* v. *Miller*, Canada, (1993) 95 ILR 446; *Re Canada Labour Code*, Canada, (1989) 86 ILR 626; *Re Canada Labour Code*, Canada, (1992) 94 ILR 264; *Bouzari* v. *Iran*, Canada, (2004) 128 ILR 586; *Canada* v. *Burke*, Ireland, (1991/1992) 95 ILR 467; *Village* v. *Her Majesty*, Malaysia, (1987) 87 ILR 223; *Australia* v. *Midford*, Malaysia, (1990) 86 ILR 640; *Buckingham* v. *Aircraft*, New Zealand, [1982] 2 NZLR 738; (1982) 64 ILR 551; *Reef* v. *Fua Kavenga*, New Zealand, (1987) 90 ILR 556; *Controller* v. *Davison*, New Zealand, (1996) 104 ILR 526; *Barker* v. *Kenya*, Zimbabwe, (1983) 84 ILR 18.

223 See, e.g., *Russian Federation Payment Case*, Germany, (2005) VII ZB 9/05; *Claim against the Kenyan Embassy Case*, Germany, (2003) IXa ZB 19/03; *Distomo Massacre Case*, Germany, (2003) III ZR 245/98; 129 ILR 556; *Former Syrian Ambassador*, Germany, (1997) BVerfGE 96, 68; 115 ILR 595; *NIOC Revenues Case*, Germany, (1983) BVerfGE 64, 1; (1983) 65 ILR 215; *Philippine Embassy Case*, Germany, (1977) BverfGE 46, 342; (1977) 65 ILR 146; *Empire of Iran Case*, Germany, (1963) BVerfGE 16, 27; (1963) 45 ILR 57; *Jurisdiction over Yugoslav Military Mission Case*, Germany, (1962) BVerfGE 15, 25; 38 ILR 162.

224 See, e.g., *Claim against the Kenyan Embassy Case*, Germany, (2003) IXa ZB 19/03.

225 See, e.g., *National Iranian* v. *Pipeline*, France, 1990, 80 RCDIP (1991) 140; (1990) 113 ILR 446; *Kuwait* v. *Parrott*, France, 1990, 80 RCDIP (1991) 142; (1990) 113 ILR 457; *Senghor* v. *International Bank*, France, 1990, 80 RCDIP (1991) 341; (1990) 113 ILR 460; *Mouracade* v. *Yemen*, France, 1991, 119 JDI (1992) 398; (1991) 113 ILR 462; *Barrandon* v. *USA*, France 1992/1995; 123 JDI (1996) 102; (1992/1995) 113 ILR 464; *Mobutu* v. *Société Logrine*, France, 1994, 122 JDI (1995) 641; (1994) 113 ILR 481; *Saignie* v. *Embassy*, France, 1997, 86 RCDIP (1997) 332; (1997) 113 ILR 492; *X* v. *Saudi School*, France, 2003, 130 JDI (2003) 1124; 92 RCDIP (2003) 647; (2003) 127 ILR 163; *Cotigny* v. *Suarez*, France, 2004, 94 RCDIP (2005) 75; (2004) 127 ILR 168. The Italian courts use 'immunity from civil jurisdiction' or 'jurisdictional immunity'. See, e.g., *Presidenza* v. *Federazione*, Italy, 2000, RDI 2000, 1155 ('l'immunità della giurisdizione civile' and 'l'immunità giurisdizionale').

492   NOTES TO PAGES 30-31

226 See, e.g., *A* v. *B*, Switzerland, (2003) ATF 130 III 136; *Banque Bruxelles* v. *Paraguay*, Switzerland, (1998) ATF 124 III 382; *Greece* v. *Julius Bär*, Switzerland, (1956) ATF 82 I 75; 23 ILR 195; *UAR* v. *Mrs X*, Switzerland, (1960) ATF 86 I 23; 65 ILR 385.

227 See, e.g., *Banque* v. *Weston*, Switzerland, Federal Tribunal, (1978) BGE 104 Ia 367; 65 ILR 417.

228 See *Soviet Distillery Case*, Austria, (1954) 21 ILR 101, 102–103; *Neustein* v. *Indonesia*, Austria, (1958) 65 ILR 3, 9, fn. 3; Art. IX of the Austrian Introductory Act, cited in *Collision Case*, Austria, (1961) 40 ILR 73, 78; *Private Servant Case*, Austria, (1971) 71 ILR 546, 547, fn. 3; *Leasing West* v. *Algeria*, Austria, (1986) 116 ILR 526, 530; *Mighell* v. *Sultan*, England, [1894] 1 QB 149, Headnote; *Gouvernement espagnol* v. *Cassaux*, France, 1849, Sirey, 1849-I-81; *Petrococchino* v. *Swedish*, France, (1929) 5 AD 306, 307; *Restitution of Property Case*, Germany, (1951) 18 ILR 221, 222; *Latvia Case*, Germany, (1955) 22 ILR 230, 231; *Import of Cigarettes Case*, Germany, (1955) 22 ILR 233, 234; *Dreyfus*, Switzerland, (1918) BGE 44 I 49, 53. See also Westlake, *A Treatise*, pp. 211–219; Kelsen, *Principles*, pp. 228–235.

229 See *Neustein* v. *Indonesia*, Austria, (1958) 65 ILR 3, 7, 9, 9, fn. 3; *Private Servant Case*, Austria (1971) 71 ILR 546, 547, fn. 3; *Republic of 'A' Case*, Austria, (1986) 77 ILR 488, 491; *Leasing* v. *Algeria*, Austria, (1986) 116 ILR 526, 528, 530; *Congo* v. *Venne*, Canada, (1971) 22 DLR (3d) 669, 685; 64 ILR 24, 40; *Embassy* v. *Jens*, Denmark, (1982) 78 ILR 81, 82–83; *Clerget* v. *Représentation*, France, (1967) 48 ILR 145, 148; *Foreign State Garnishment Case*, Germany, (1966) 57 ILR 152, 153; *Hungarian Embassy Case*, Germany, (1969) 65 ILR 110, 112–113; *Conrades* v. *UK*, Germany, (1981) 65 ILR 205, 207; *Distomo Massacre Case*, Greece, (2000) 129 ILR 513, 516, 519, 521, 524; *Poortensdijk* v. *Latvia*, Holland, (1941/1942) 11 AD 142, 142, 143; *In re Savini*, Italy, (1927) 4 AD 166, 167; *Harrie* v. *Steinmann*, Italy, (1927) 4 AD 364, 364; *In re Polimeni*, Italy, (1935) 8 AD 248, 248; *In re Bolin*, Sweden, (1934) 7 AD 186, 186.

230 Even though the word 'extraterritoriality' is commonly understood to mean exemption or immunity from jurisdiction, it is sometimes used to refer to exactly the opposite, that is, the assertion (and the effects) of extraterritorial jurisdiction, i.e. jurisdiction aimed at regulating conduct in foreign territory. See Rosenthal and Knighton, *National Laws*.

231 See, e.g., IDI, Projet; Harvard Research.

232 See, generally, Shortell, *Rights*; Durchslag, *State Sovereign Immunity*; Guittari, *The American Law*; Krent, Reconceptualizing; Siegel, The Hidden; Rutherglen, Sovereign; Bohannan, Beyond; Bandes, Treaties; Rispin, Cooperative.

233 See, e.g., *Gomez-Perez* v. *Potter*, US, 128 S.Ct. 1931, 1942–1943 (2008); *Sosa* v. *Alvarez-Machain*, US, 542 US 692, 698–700 (2004); 159 L.Ed.2d 718, 733–734 (2004); 127 ILR 691, 770–771, quoting *Richards* v. *US*, US, 369 US 1, 6 (1962); *Scarborough* v. *Principi*, US, 541 US 401, 419–423 (2004); *Flatow* v. *Iran*, US, 74 F.Supp.2d 18, 20–22 (D.D.C. 1999); *Saltany* v. *Reagan*, US, 702 F.Supp. 319, 321 (D.D.C. 1988); 80 ILR 19; affirmed, *Saltany* v. *Reagan*, US, 886 F.2d 438, 440–441 (D.C.Cir. 1989); 87 ILR 679; *Sanchez-Espinoza* v. *Reagan*, US, 770 F.2d 202, 207

NOTES TO PAGE 31   493

(D.C.Cir. 1985); 80 ILR 586; *Flatow* v. *Iran*, US, 74 F.Supp.2d 18, 20–22 (D.D.C. 1999).

234 See, e.g., *Tennessee* v. *Lane*, US, 541 US 509, 517–522 (2004); *Tennessee* v. *Hood*, US, 541 US 440, 446–455 (2004); *Lapides* v. *Board*, US, 535 US 613, 618–624 (2002); *College* v. *Florida*, US, 527 US 666, 669–670 (1999).

235 See, e.g., *City* v. *Oneida*, US 125 S.Ct. 1478, 1489 (2005); *C* v. *Citizen*, US, 532 US 411 (2001); *Kiowa* v. *Manufacturing*, US, 523 US 751 (1998); *Ingrassia* v. *Chicken*, US, 676 F.Supp.2d 953 (E.D.Cal. 2009); *Allen* v. *Gold*, US, 464 F.3d 1044, 1047–1048 (9th Cir. 2006). See also Clement, Strengthening; Borchert, Tribal.

236 See, e.g., *Alig* v. *Trust*, (1967) 61 ILR 88; *People* v. *US*, US, 356 F.Supp. 645, 659 (D. Haw. 1973); affirmed, *People* v. *US*, US, 502 F.2d 90 (9th Cir. 1974); 61 ILR 113; *Temengil* v. *Trust*, US, 881 F.2d 647 (9th Cir. 1989); 96 ILR 32. For other instances see, e.g., *Porto Rico* v. *Rosaly*, US, 227 US 270 (1913), *People* v. *Shell*, US, 302 US 253 (1952); *Harris* v. *Boreham*, US, 233 F.2d 110 (3rd Cir. 1956) and *Harris* v. *Municipality*, US, 212 F.2d 323 (3rd Cir. 1954). But see *Sablan* v. *Pacific*, US, 526 F.Supp. 135 (1981); 87 ILR 546; *Morgan* v. *Palau*, US, 924 F.2d 1237 (2nd Cir. 1991); 87 ILR 590; vacating *Morgan* v. *Palau*, US, 639 F.Supp. 706 (S.D.N.Y. 1986); 87 ILR 590; noted in Hendricks, Birth; later 971 F.2d 917 (2nd Cir. 1992); and *Marine* v. *Marshall*, New Zealand, (1981) 64 ILR 539, 545–548; *Marine* v. *Marshall*, New Zealand, (1982) 64 ILR 562, 565.

237 See, e.g., *Bouchard* v. *JL*, Canada, (1984) 45 OR (2d) 792; 92 ILR 658, 661; *Western* v. *Elk*, Canada, (1985) 23 DLR (4th) 464.

238 See, e.g., Fox, *The Law of State Immunity*; Dickinson *et al.* (eds.), *State Immunity*; Lewis, *State and Diplomatic Immunity*; Schreuer, *State Immunity*, 1988; Badr, *State Immunity*. But cf. Sucharitkul, *State Immunities*.

239 See, e.g., the US cases against Palestine, which the US does not recognize as a State: *Ungar* v. *Palestinian Authority*, US, 613 F.Supp.2d 219 (DRI 2009); *Sokolow* v. *PLO*, US, 583 F.Supp.2d 451 (S.D.N.Y. 2008); *Gilmore* v. *Palestinian Authority*, US, 422 F.Supp.2d 96, 100–101 (D.D.C. 2006); *Biton* v. *Palestinian Authority*, US, 510 F.Supp.2d 144, 147 (D.D.C. 2007); *Biton* v. *Palestinian Authority*, US, 412 F.Supp.2d 1, 4–5 (D.D.C. 2005); *Ungar* v. *PLO*, US, 402 F.3d 274, 288–292 (1st Cir. 2005); *Ungar* v. *Palestinian Authority*, US, 153 F.Supp.2d 76, 89 (D.R.I. 2001); *Ungar* v. *Palestinian Authority*, US, 315 F.Supp.2d 164, 186–187 (D.R.I. 2004); *Ungar* v. *Palestinian Authority*, US, 325 F.Supp.2d 15, 28 (D.R.I. 2004); *Knox* v. *PLO*, US, 306 F.Supp.2d 424, 438–48 (S.D.N.Y. 2004); *Klinghoffer* v. *Achille*, US, 937 F.2d 44, 47–48 (2nd Cir. 1991); 96 ILR 68; *Tel-Oren* v. *Libya*, US, 517 F.Supp. 542, 549, fn. 3 (D.D.C. 1981); affirmed, *Tel-Oren* v. *Libya*, US, 726 F.2d 774, 775 (D.C.Cir. 1984); 77 ILR 192. See also *Re Arafat*, Italy, 1985, 7 *Italian YIL* (1986–87) 287, 297; *European* v. *Piette*, Italy, 1999, 9 *Italian YIL* (1999) 155.

240 *Pocket* v. *Safenames*, England, [2009] EWHC 2529 (Ch), paras. 9–24; *Diepreye* v. *Crown Prosecution Service*, England, [2005] EWHC 2704 (Admin), paras. 48, 56 (noted in Walker, Sovereign); *South Africa* v. *Herman*, Netherlands, (1921) 1 AD 22, 23; *Ceara* v. *Dorr*, France (1928) 4 AD 39, 39–40; *Céara* v. *D'Archer*, France, (1932) 6 AD 162, 163; *Dumont* v. *Amazonas*, France, (1948) 15 AD 140, 141; *Neger* v. *Hesse*, France, (1969) 52 ILR 329, 331; *Commissioner* v. *Bahadur*, India, (1965) 64

494   NOTES TO PAGE 31

ILR 482; *Colonel* v. *Commissioner*, India, (1971) 64 ILR 523. Cf. *Maharaja* v. *Assam*, India, (1948) 22 ILR 64. Notably, the 2004 UN Convention grants immunity to the 'constituent units of a federal State or political subdivisions of the State' under certain conditions (Art. 2(1)(ii)). By contrast, Art. 28 of the 1972 European Convention denies immunity to 'the constituent States of a Federal State' unless otherwise arranged under the Convention. By the State Immunity Order 1979 and the State Immunity Order 1993, the UK extended immunity to the 'constituent territories' of Austria and Germany.

241   *Céara* v. *D'Archer*, France, (1932) 6 AD 162, 163; *Neger* v. *Hesse*, France, (1969) 52 ILR 329, 331; *Dumont* v. *Amazonas*, France, (1948) 15 AD 140, 141; *Roumania* v. *Aricastre*, France, (1949) 16 AD 138, 139; *Commissioner* v. *Bahadur*, India, (1965) 64 ILR 482; *Colonel* v. *Commissioner*, India, (1971) 64 ILR 523.

242   The most prominent example is the status enjoyed by the Sovereign Order of Malta in the Italian courts: *Nanni* v. *Pace*, Italy, (1935) 8 AD 2; *Sovereign* v. *Soc*, Italy, (1954) 22 ILR 1, 2; *Scarfò* v. *Sovereign*, Italy, (1957) 24 ILR 1; *Association* v. *Piccoli*, Italy, (1974) 65 ILR 308, 309; *Ministry* v. *Association*, Italy, (1978) 65 ILR 320, 323; *Association* v. *Guidetti*, Italy, 1999, 9 *Italian YIL* (1999) 154. Cf. *Bacchelli* v. *Comune*, Italy, (1978) 77 ILR 621, 624. See also the immunity status accorded to the Vatican City: *Pontificia* v. *Inps*, Italy, (1979) 65 ILR 333; *Special* v. *Pieciukiewicz*, Italy, (1982) 78 ILR 120, 121; *Re Marcinkus*, Italy, (1987) 87 ILR 48; *Re Marcinkus*, Vatican City, (1987) 100 ILR 603; *Banque* v. *Chambre*, Switzerland, (1987) 82 ILR 50; *The Holy See* v. *Starbright*, Philippines, (1994) 102 ILR 163; *Doe* v. *Holy See*, US, 557 F.3d 1066 (9th Cir. 2009); partly affirming, partly reversing and remanding *Doe* v. *Holy See*, US, 434 F.Supp.2d 925 (D.Or. 2006); *O'Bryan* v. *Holy See*, US, 556 F.3d 361 (6th Cir. 2009); affirming *O'Bryan* v. *Holy See*, US, 471 F.Supp.2d 784 (W.D.Ky. 2007); *Dale* v. *Colagiovanni*, US, 443 F.3d 425 (5th Cir. 2006); partly affirming and partly reversing *Dale* v. *Colagiovanni*, US, 337 F.Supp.2d 825 (S.D.Miss. 2004); *Doe* v. *Holy See*, US, 434 F.Supp.2d 925 (D.Or. 2006); *Baronci* v. *Ospedale*, Italy, (1956) 24 ILR 215; *JRS* v. *Glendinning*, Canada, (2000) 191 DLR (4th) 750, 753; *The Holy See* v. *Starbright*, Philippines, (1994) 102 ILR 163. For earlier examples see Sucharitkul, Second Report, *YILC*, 1980-II-1, p. 199 at pp. 208–209, para. 40 and Sucharitkul, Third Report, *YILC*, 1981-II-1, p. 125 at p. 137, paras. 33–35 and the cases cited there. A colony having a distinct personality from the metropolis was treated separately with regard to immunity: *Montefiore* v. *Colony*, France, (1961) 44 ILR 72. See also *LM* v. *Netherlands*, Netherlands, (1998) 128 ILR 681, 682. *Olofsen* v. *Malaysia*, Singapore, [1966] 2 MLJ 300, 301–302; (1966) 55 ILR 409.

243   *KPMG* v. *Davison*, New Zealand, [1996] 2 NZLR 278, 288, 310; 104 ILR 526, 537, 611; *Ter* v. *Netherlands*, Netherlands, (1951) 18 ILR 223, 224; *Laurens* v. *Morocco*, France, (1934) 7 AD 171, 172; affirming *Morocco* v. *Laurens*, France, (1930) 5 AD 116, 116–117. See also *Governor* v. *Sutton*, New Zealand, 1994, [1995] 1 NZLR 426, 428; 104 ILR 508, 509.

244   *Duff* v. *Kelantan*, England, [1924] AC 797, 814; 2 AD 124, 127; *Morocco* v. *Laurens*, France, (1930) 5 AD 116, 116–117; *Laurens* v. *Morocco*, France, (1934) 7 AD 171, 172.

NOTES TO PAGES 31–35   495

245 *Saez* v. *Pinillos*, Belgium, (1938/1939) 9 AD 289, 290; *Duff* v. *Kelantan*, England, [1924] AC 797, 820; *The Rita Garcia*, England, (1937) 59 Ll L Rep 140, 142; 9 AD 272, 273; *The Cristina*, England, [1938] AC 485, 503, 516, 518; 9 AD 250, 254–255; *The Arraiz*, England, (1938) 61 Ll L Rep 39; 9 AD 273; *Maclaine* v. *Department*, England, 1988, [1989] Ch 72, 200; 80 ILR 47, 125; *Bank* v. *Price*, England, 1996, [1997] 4 All ER 108, 110; 111 ILR 604, 606; *The Condado*, Scotland, (1939) 63 Ll L Rep 83, 87; (1939) 63 Ll L Rep 330, 334; 9 AD 225; *Socifros* v. *USSR*, France, (1938) 9 AD 236, 237–238; *Aget* v. *French*, France, (1939) 11 AD 144, 144; *In re Savini*, Italy, (1927) 4 AD 166, 167; *Consorzio* v. *Federazione*, Italy, (1966) 65 ILR 265, 266; *Campuzano* v. *Spanish*, Norway, (1938) 11 AD 68, 72; *In re Bolin*, Sweden, (1934) 7 AD 186, 186; *Guaranty* v. *US*, US, 304 US 126, 137 (1938); 9 AD 184, 187; *US* v. *Lumumba*, US, 741 F.2d 12, 15 (2nd Cir. 1984); 88 ILR 37. For some courts it makes no difference whether the recognition is de jure or de facto: *German* v. *Dynamic*, India, (1970) 64 ILR 504, 518–519; *Old HW-GW* v. *Minister*, Canada, [1991] 43 FTR 197, 200; reversed on other grounds, *Old HW-GW* v. *Minister*, Canada, [1993] 153 NR 136, 143. But see *Weber* v. *USSR*, Holland, (1942) 11 AD 140, 141–142. Recognition may also impinge on the standing of a State to be a plaintiff: *Campuzano* v. *Spanish*, Norway, (1938) 11 AD 68, 72; *In re Muir*, US, 254 US 522, 532 (1921); 1 AD 143, 144. Non-recognition, however, does not prevent an entity from being made a defendant: *Klinghoffer* v. *Achille*, US, 937 F.2d 44, 48 (2nd Cir. 1991); 96 ILR 68; *Civil* v. *Singapore*, Singapore, [2004] 1 SLR 570; 133 ILR 371; *Parent* v. *Singapore*, Canada, (2003) 133 ILR 264. Some national statutes provide for the Executive branch to certify the status of a foreign entity: UK SIA, s. 21; Canada SIA, s. 14; Australia FSIA, s. 40; Pakistan SIO, s. 18; Singapore SIA, s. 18; South Africa FSIA, s. 17. For discussions see Hines, Why; Smith, State; Movsesian, The Persistent. But see *Clerget* v. *Banque*, France, (1971) 65 ILR 54, 56; affirming *Clerget* v. *Banque*, France, (1969) 52 ILR 310, 311–312, 313, which in its turn affirmed *Clerget* v. *Représentation*, France, (1967) 48 ILR 145, 149; *South Moluccas* v. *Royal*, Netherlands, (1951) 17 ILR 143, 151; *Limbin* v. *Burma*, Japan, (1954) 32 ILR 124, 124; *Re Honecker*, Germany, (1984) 80 ILR 365 (citing *Re Treaty*, Germany, (1973) 78 ILR 149, 165–166). The US law gives Taiwan a special status despite the lack of formal recognition: Taiwan Relations Act, Public Law 96–8, 93 Stat. 14, April 10, 1979, 22 USC § 3303(b)(1): *Millen* v. *Coordination*, US, 855 F.2d 879, 883 (D.C.Cir. 1988); 98 ILR 61; *Kao* v. *China*, US, 816 F.Supp. 910, 914, fn. 5 (S.D.N.Y. 1993).

Chapter 2

1 See *The Schooner Exchange* v. *McFaddon*, US, 11 US (7 Cranch) 116, 136–137 (1812); *Blanchet* v. *Gouvernement d'Haïti*, France, 1827, Dalloz, 1849-I-6; Sirey, 1849-I-83; *Gouvernment espagnol* v. *Cassaux*, France, 1849, Sirey, 1849-I-81, 93; *Société* v. *Syndicat*, Belgium, 1840, Pas 1841-II-33, 52–53; *De Haber* v. *The Queen*, England, (1851) 17 QB 171/204, 207; *The Parlement Belge*, England, (1880) 5 PD 197, 205, 207, 214–215.

496   NOTES TO PAGE 35

2 *Ibarra* v. *Captain*, Argentina, (1937) 8 AD 247, 247 and 9 AD 293, 294 (reported twice in AD); *Manauta* v. *Embassy*, Argentina, (1994) 113 ILR 429, 431, 432–433; *Foreign States Immunities Case*, Austria, (1928) 4 AD 178, 179; *Dralle* v. *Czechoslovakia*, Austria, (1950) 17 ILR 155, 157–158, 163, 166; *Soviet Distillery Case*, Austria, (1954) 21 ILR 101, 102; *X* v. *Germany*, Austria, (1963) 65 ILR 10, 12, fn. 3; *Private Servant of Diplomat Case*, Austria, (1971) 71 ILR 546, 549; *Embassy Interpreter Dismissal Case*, Austria, (1985) 77 ILR 485, 488; *Leasing* v. *Algeria*, Austria, (1986) 116 ILR 526, 528–529; *Nuclear Power Plant Injunction Case (No. 1)*, Austria, (1988) 86 ILR 575, 577; *French Consular Employee Claim Case*, Austria, (1989) 86 ILR 583, 585; *Case against the Foreign Minister*, Austria, 2001, 6 *Austrian RIEL* (2001) 288, 294; *Syria* v. *Egypt*, Brazil, (1982) 91 ILR 288, 298; *City of Ottawa*, Canada, (1943) 2 DLR 481, 488, 500–501, 502–503, 508, 519; 10 AD 337; *Reference re Exemption*, Canada, (1943) 4 DLR 11, 14, 32, 35, 44; 12 AD 124; *Dessaulles* v. *Poland*, Canada, (1944) 4 DLR 1, 3; 12 AD 92, 93; *Re Canada Labour Code*, Canada, (1992) 91 DLR (4th) 449, 451, 461; 94 ILR 264, 267, 276; *Schreiber* v. *Germany*, Canada, (2002) 216 DLR (4th) 513, 518, 522–524, 543; *X* v. *China*, Chile, (1969) 65 ILR 31 note; *Senerman* v. *Cuba*, Chile, (1975) 65 ILR 29, 30; *Embassy* v. *Jens*, Denmark, (1982) 78 ILR 81, 83; *Den Franske* v. *Intra*, Denmark, 1992; *Pakistans* v. *Shah*, Denmark, 1999; *The Cristina*, England, [1938] AC 485, 490, 497–498, 502, 509; 9 AD 250, 252, 254, 258–259, 260; *Chung* v. *The King*, England, 1938, [1939] AC 160, 167; 9 AD 264, 266; *The Arantzazu Mendi*, England, [1939] AC 256, 265; 9 AD 60, 66; *Sultan* v. *Abubakar*, England, [1952] AC 318, 342–343; 19 ILR 182, 190; *USA* v. *Dollfus*, England, [1952] AC 582, 605; 613; 19 ILR 163, 169, 174; *Juan* v. *Indonesia*, England, 1954, [1955] AC 72, 86; 21 ILR 95, 96; *The Philippine Admiral*, England, 1975, [1977] AC 373, 395–396; 64 ILR 90, 101–102; *I Congreso del Partido*, England, 1981, [1983] 1 AC 244, 257, 260, 265, 278; 64 ILR 307, 308, 311, 316, 329; *Alcom* v. *Colombia*, England, [1984] 1 AC 580; 74 ILR 170 (*passim*, esp. [1984] 1 AC 580, 597–598, 598–599, 600, 602–603, 603–604; 74 ILR 170, 180–181, 182–183, 185–186, 187); *Kuwait Airways* v. *Iraqi Airways*, England, [1995] 1 WLR 1147, 1156, 1159; 103 ILR 340, 397, 400–401; *Pinochet No. 3*, England, 1999, [2000] 1 AC 147, 201, 210, 220, 251, 268–269; 119 ILR 135, 152, 162, 172, 204, 221–222, 223; *Holland* v. *Lampen-Wolfe*, England, [2000] 1 WLR 1573, 1577–1578, 1580, 1583, 1588; 119 ILR 367, 372, 374, 378, 384; *Matthews* v. *Ministry*, UK, [2003] 1 AC 1163, 1196; *Jones* v. *Saudi Arabia*, England, 2006, [2007] 1 AC 270, 278, 281, 283, 292–293, 296, 298, 306; 129 ILR 629, 713, 718, 720, 731–733, 737, 739, 748; *Pärtsel* v. *Tsentrosojuss (No. 1)*, Estonia, (1932) 8 AD 242, 243; *General* v. *Société Marseille*, France, (1986) 77 ILR 530, 532; *Société* v. *Lao*, France, (1987) 80 ILR 688, 690; *Creighton* v. *Minister*, France, (2000) 127 ILR 154, 154, 155; *X* v. *Saudi*, France, (2003) 127 ILR 163, 166; *Congo* v. *Syndicat*, France, 2005, 95 *RCDIP* (2006) 123, 124; *L'Affaire du Département*, Germany, 1905, 34 *JDIP* (1907) 166, 168 (French translation); *Empire of Iran Case*, Germany, (1963) 45 ILR 57, 58, 61–62, 73, 79; *Philippine Embassy Bank Account Case*, Germany, (1977) 65 ILR 146 (*passim*); *Church of Scientology Case*, Germany, (1978) 65 ILR 193, 195–196; *NIOC Revenues Case*, Germany, (1983) 65 ILR 215 (*passim*); *Re Honecker*, Germany, (1984) 80 ILR 365, 365; *Kenyan Diplomatic Residence Case*, Germany, (2003) 128 ILR 632, 635, 636; *Distomo*

Massacre Case, Germany, (2003) 129 ILR 556, 559–560, Ground B.I.2(a); *Distomo Massacre Case*, Greece, (2000) 129 ILR 513, 516; *Margellos* v. *Germany*, Greece, (2002) 129 ILR 525, 532–533; *Mirza* v. *UAR*, India, 1965, [1966] 1 SCR 319, 325–326, 333; 64 ILR 489, 494, 502; *Agarwala* v. *India*, India, (1980) 118 ILR 421, 423–424; *Saorstat* v. *Rafael*, Ireland, 1944, [1945] IR 291; 12 AD 97, 97; *Canada* v. *Burke*, Ireland, [1992] 2 IR 484, 490, 491–492, 498; 95 ILR 467, 471, 472–473, 479; *McElhinney* v. *Williams*, Ireland, 1995, [1996] 1 ILRM 276, 284; 104 ILR 691, 698; *Her Majesty* v. *Edelson*, Israel, (1997) 131 ILR 279, 287, para. 12; 291–297, paras. 15–21; *Typaldos* v. *Manicomio*, Italy, 1886, 26 *AJIL Supplement* (1932) 623, 623; *Nanni* v. *Pace*, Italy, (1935) 8 AD 2, 4; *Greece* v. *Gamet*, Italy, (1957) 24 ILR 209, 210; *Pauer* v. *Hungarian*, Italy, (1956) 24 ILR 211, 212; *Greece* v. *Gamet*, Italy, (1959) 28 ILR 153, 155; *Hungarian* v. *Hungarian*, Italy, (1960) 40 ILR 59, 61; *Campione* v. *Peti-Nitrogenmuvek*, Italy, (1972) 65 ILR 287, 292; *Luna* v. *Romania*, Italy, (1974) 65 ILR 313, 314; *Ministry of Finance* v. *Association*, Italy, (1978) 65 ILR 320, 321–322; *Danish* v. *Hansen*, Italy, (1979) 65 ILR 325, 326; *Banco* v. *Credito*, Italy, (1984) 87 ILR 15, 17; *Cristiani* v. *Italian*, Italy, (1985) 87 ILR 20, 23, 26; *Panattoni* v. *Germany*, Italy, (1987) 87 ILR 42, 45; *France* v. *Jacuzio*, Italy, (1987) 87 ILR 53, 54, 55; *Banamar-Capizzi* v. *Embassy*, Italy, (1989) 87 ILR 56, 59, 62; *Libya* v. *Rossbeton*, Italy, (1989) 87 ILR 63, 65, 66; *British* v. *Toglia*, Italy, (1989) 101 ILR 379, 382; *Libya* v. *Trobbiani*, Italy, (1990) 114 ILR 520, 522–523; *Norwegian* v. *Quattri*, Italy, (1991) 114 ILR 525, 527; *Condor* v. *Minister*, Italy, (1992) 101 ILR 394, 403, 405; *Zambian* v. *Sendanayake*, Italy, (1992) 114 ILR 532, 533; *Carbonar* v. *Magurno*, Italy, (1993) 114 ILR 534, 535; *Perrini* v. *Académie*, Italy, (1994) 114 ILR 536, 538; *Nacci* v. *Bari*, Italy, (1994) 114 ILR 539, 551; *USA* v. *Lo Gatto*, Italy, (1995) 114 ILR 555, 557; *Ecole* v. *Guadagnino*, Italy, 1997, 9 *Italian YIL* (1999) 152, 153; *Canada* v. *Cargnello*, Italy, (1998) 114 ILR 559, 565; *FILT-CGIL* v. *USA*, Italy, (2000) 128 ILR 644, 647; *Ferrini* v. *Germany*, Italy, (2004) 128 ILR 658, 663–664; *Borri* v. *Repubblica*, Italy, 2005, 88 *RDI* (2005) 856, 858; *Matsuyama* v. *China*, Japan, (1928) 4 AD 168, 169; *X* v. *USA*, Japan, 2002, 46 *JAIL* (2003) 161, 163; *Cudak* v. *Embassy*, Lithuania, 2001, noted in 3 *Baltic YIL* (2003) 320, 320; *De Booy* v. *German*, Netherlands, (1924) 1 AD 124, 128; *Société Européenne* v. *Yugoslavia*, Netherlands, (1973) 65 ILR 356, 361; *MK* v. *State*, Netherlands, (1986) 94 ILR 357, 359; *Governor* v. *Sutton*, New Zealand, 1994, [1995] 1 NZLR 426, 428, 432–433; 104 ILR 508, 510, 516; *Controller* v. *Davison*, New Zealand, [1996] 2 NZLR 278, 288, 300, 308, 310, 314; 104 ILR 526, 537, 570, 605, 612, 616; *The Guernica*, Norway, (1938) 11 AD 139, 139; *Qureshi* v. *USSR*, Pakistan, PLD 1981 SCt 377, 397–402; 64 ILR 585, 597–602; *Parreño* v. *McGranery*, Philippines, 1953, *Materials on Jurisdictional Immunities*, p. 367; *USA* v. *Guinto*; *USA* v. *Ceballos*; *USA* v. *Rodrigo*, Philippines, (1990) 102 ILR 132, 138–139; *French Consulate in Cracow Case*, Poland, (1958) 26 ILR 178, 179; *Brazilian Embassy Employee Case*, Portugal, (1984) 116 ILR 625, 627, 628, 631; *X* v. *Israel*, Portugal, (2002) 127 ILR 310, 310; *Parkin* v. *Congo*, South Africa, 1970, 1971 (1) SA 259, 262; 64 ILR 668, 672; *Leibowitz* v. *Schwartz*, South Africa, 1973, 1974 (2) SA 661, 661; 64 ILR 672, 673; *Lendalease* v. *Corporacion*, South Africa, 1975, 1975 (4) SA 397, 403–404; 64 ILR 675, 682–683; *Inter-Science* v. *Moçambique*, South Africa, 1979, 1980 (2) SA 111, 120, 124; 64 ILR 689, 699, 704; *Kaffraria* v. *Zambia*, South Africa, 1980 (2) SA 709,

498   NOTES TO PAGE 35

712, 715; 64 ILR 708, 711, 714; *Emilio* v. *Embassy*, Spain, (1986) 86 ILR 508, 510, 511; *Diana* v. *South Africa*, (1986) 86 ILR 512, 516; *Abbott* v. *South Africa*, Spain, (1992) 113 ILR 411 (*passim*, esp. 417, 418–419, 422–425); *In re Bolin*, Sweden, (1934) 7 AD 186, 186; *Västerås* v. *Iceland*, Sweden, (1999) 128 ILR 705, 706; *Dreyfus*, Switzerland, (1918) BGE 44 I 49, 53; *Italian* v. *Beta*, Switzerland, (1966) 65 ILR 394, 398; *Libya* v. *LIAMCO*, Switzerland, (1980) 62 ILR 228, 233, Ground 3(a); *Universal* v. *Iran*, Switzerland, (1981) 65 ILR 436, 437, Ground 4; *Italian* v. *X*, Switzerland, (1985) 82 ILR 23, 25, Ground 3; 27, Ground 4b; *Libya* v. *Actimon*, Switzerland, (1985) 82 ILR 30, 32, Ground 4; *Swissair* v. *X*, Switzerland, (1985) 82 ILR 36, 37; *Spain* v. *Company X*, Switzerland, (1986) 82 ILR 38, 44, Ground 5a; *S* v. *Romania*, Switzerland, (1987) 82 ILR 45, 47, Ground 1; *Z* v. *Geneva*, Switzerland, (1990) 102 ILR 205, 207, Ground 2b; *M* v. *Egypt*, Switzerland, (1994) 116 ILR 656, 658, Ground 2; *Barker* v. *Kenya*, Zimbabwe, (1983) (4) SA 817, 819, 823; 84 ILR 18, 20.

3 The lower court cases recognizing the international law principle of State immunity are legion. Cited here is a selection of leading and representative cases from a variety of jurisdictions. See *British Embassy Driver Case*, Austria, (1978) 65 ILR 20, 22; *Brasseur* v. *Greece*, Belgium, (1933) 6 AD 164, 167; *Saez* v. *Pinillos*, Belgium, (1938/1939) 9 AD 289, 290, 293; *De Decker* v. *USA*, Belgium, (1956) 23 ILR 209, 209; *Rousseau* v. *Upper Volta*, Belgium, (1983) 82 ILR 118, 120; *Iraq* v. *Vinci*, Belgium, (2002) 127 ILR 101, 109; *Chateau-Gai* v. *Le Gouvernement*, Canada, (1967) 61 DLR (2d) 709, 713; 53 ILR 284, 287; *Jaffe* v. *Miller*, Canada, (1993) 103 DLR (4th) 315; 13 OR (3d) 745, 752; 95 ILR 446, 452; *Bouzari* v. *Iran*, Canada, (2002) 124 ILR 427, 433; affirmed, *Bouzari* v. *Iran*, Canada, (2004) 243 DLR (4th) 406, 418; 128 ILR 586, 596; *Roxford* v. *Cuba*, Canada, [2003] 236 FTR 1, [2003] 2003 FCT 763; [2003] 4 FC 1182, para. 28; *Rizaeff* v. *Soviet*, China, (1927) 40 ILR 84, 85; *Italien* v. *Amaliegade*, Denmark, 1993; *Trendtex* v. *Central Bank*, England, [1977] QB 529; 64 ILR 111 (*passim*); *Sengupta* v. *India*, England, 1982, [1983] ICR 221, 229; 64 ILR 352, 362; *UAE* v. *Abdelghafar*, England, 1994, [1995] ICR 65, 73; 104 ILR 647, 655; *Propend* v. *Sing*, England, (1996) 111 ILR 611, 632; *Roumania* v. *Pascalet*, France, (1924) 2 AD 132, 132; *Ceara* v. *Dorr*, France, (1928) 4 AD 39, 39; *Hertzfeld* v. *USSR*, France, (1933) 7 AD 184, 185; *Socifros* v. *USSR*, France, (1938) 9 AD 236, 237–238; *Roumania* v. *Aricastre*, France, (1949) 16 AD 138, 139; *Salabert* v. *US*, France, (1956) 23 ILR 192, 193; *Société Bauer-Marchal* v. *Ministre*, France, (1957) 24 ILR 204, 204; *Statni* v. *Englander*, France, (1966) 47 ILR 157, 161–162; *Clerget* v. *Banque*, France, (1969) 52 ILR 310, 312; affirmed, *Clerget* v. *Banque*, France, (1971) 65 ILR 54, 56; *Russian* v. *Noga*, France, (2000) 127 ILR 156, 159, 160; *Polish Loan Bank Case*, Germany, (1921) 1 AD 116, 118; *Halig* v. *Polish*, Germany, (1928) 4 AD 164, 165; *Economic Agreement Case*, Germany, (1933) 7 AD 175, 177; *Restitution of Property Case*, Germany, (1951) 18 ILR 221, 223; *In re Danish State Railways*, Germany, (1953) 20 ILR 178, 179; *Latvia Case*, Germany, (1953) 20 ILR 180, 181; affirmed, *Latvia Case*, Germany, (1955) 22 ILR 230, 231; *In re The Charkow*, Germany, (1959) 65 ILR 100, 103–105; *Spanish Consular Bank Accounts Case*, Germany, (1971) 65 ILR 114, 117; *Central Bank of Nigeria Case*, Germany, (1975) 65 ILR 131, 134–136; *Spanish State Tourist Office Case*, Germany, (1977) 65 ILR 140,

141; *NIOC Legal Status Case*, Germany, (1980) 65 ILR 199, 202; *Conrades* v. *UK*, Germany, (1981) 65 ILR 205, 207; *NIOC Pipeline Contracts Case*, Germany, (1982) 65 ILR 212, 213–214; *Garden Contamination Case (1)*, Germany, (1987) 80 ILR 367, 372; *X* v. *Argentina*, Germany, (1996) 114 ILR 502, 504–505, 507; *Muller* v. *USA*, Germany, (1998) 114 ILR 512, 516; *Roumanian Legation (Greece) Case*, Greece, (1949) 16 AD 291; *Purchase of Embassy Staff Residence Case*, Greece, (1967) 65 ILR 255, 255; *UAR* v. *Mirza*, India, (1961) 64 ILR 394, 416, 419–420, 430; *German* v. *Dynamic*, India, (1970) 64 ILR 504, 512–515, 517, 519, 521, 523; *New* v. *VEB*, India, (1983) 92 ILR 509, 528; *The Ramava*, Ireland, (1941) 10 AD 91, 97; *McElhinney* v. *Williams*, Ireland, [1994] 2 ILRM 115, 120; 103 ILR 311, 316–317; *Harrie* v. *Steinmann*, Italy, (1927) 4 AD 364, 364; *Castiglioni* v. *Yugoslavia*, Italy, (1952) 19 ILR 203, 209–210; *Hungarian* v. *Hungarian*, Italy, (1957) 24 ILR 218, 219; *Francischiello* v. *USA*, Italy, (1959) 28 ILR 158, 160; *US* v. *Bracale*, Italy, (1968) 65 ILR 273, 274; *Limbin* v. *Burma*, Japan, (1954) 32 ILR 124, 125; *Republic of China* v. *Chuka*, Japan, (1955) 23 ILR 210, 211; *In re Hoover*, Japan, (1956) 23 ILR 265, 267; *Ryuichi* v. *The State*, Japan, (1963) 32 ILR 626, 638; 8 *JAIL* (1964) 212; *X* v. *USA*, Japan, 1997, 41 *JAIL* (1998) 91, 91; *NV Limburgsch* v. *German*, Netherlands, (1916) 1 AD 129 note; *Bergverksaktiebolaget* v. *Militär-Liquidierungsamt*, Netherlands, (1921) 1 AD 130, 131–132; *Advokaat* v. *Schuddinck*, Netherlands, (1923) 2 AD 133, 133; *The Garbi*, Netherlands, (1938) 11 AD 155, 155; *Poortensdijk* v. *Latvia*, Netherlands, (1941/1942) 11 AD 142, 142–143; *Nederlandse* v. *Mühlig*, Netherlands, (1947) 14 AD 77, 78; *South Moluccas* v. *Royal*, Netherlands, (1951) 17 ILR 143, 152; *NV Exploitatie-Maatschappij* v. *Bank*, Netherlands, (1963) 65 ILR 348, 352–353; *Portugal* v. *De Sousa*, Netherlands, (1981) 94 ILR 314, 315; *Portugal* v. *Algemene*, Netherlands, (1982) 94 ILR 315, 317; *LF* v. *Germany*, Netherlands, (1986) 94 ILR 342, 347; *MK* v. *Turkey*, Netherlands, (1985) 94 ILR 350, 352–353; *Edwards* v. *BV Bureau*, Netherlands, (1987) 94 ILR 361, 364; *Zaire* v. *Duclaux*, Netherlands, (1988) 94 ILR 368, 369; *Netherlands* v. *Azeta*, Netherlands, (1998) 128 ILR 688, 689; *Ramos* v. *USA*, Portugal, (1994) 116 ILR 634, 635; *Owners* v. *Owners*, Scotland, 1921, (1922) SLT 68, 70; 11 AD 149, 151; *Landano* v. *USA*, Switzerland, (1987) 116 ILR 636, 638; *Siderman* v. *Argentina*, US, 965 F.2d 699, 718 (9th Cir. 1992); 103 ILR 454; *Ungar* v. *Palestinian*, US, 315 F.Supp.2d 164, 175 (D.R.I. 2004); *Borgships* v. *Macarena*, US, 1993 WL 278453, p. 2 (E.D.La. 1993); *International* v. *OPEC*, US, 477 F.Supp. 553, 565 (C.D.Cal. 1979); 63 ILR 284; *Jet* v. *Marsa*, US, 462 F.Supp. 1165, 1168 (D.Md. 1978); 63 ILR 214.

4 The 1972 European Convention on State Immunity, Preamble, para. 2; Council of Europe, *Explanatory Reports*, 1972, p. 5, para. 1; 2004 UN Convention on Jurisdictional Immunities of States and Their Property, Preamble, para. 1.

5 See *Arrest Warrant*, ICJ, *ICJ Reports* 2002, 3 at 20–22, paras. 51–53; 24–25, paras. 58–59; 25, para. 61; 29–30, paras. 70–72; 31, para. 75; 128 ILR 1, 76–78, 80–81, 81–82, 85–87, 87–88; *Al-Adsani* v. *UK*, ECHR, 2001, (2002) 34 EHRR 11, para. 54; 123 ILR 24, 40; *Fogarty* v. *UK*, ECHR, 2001, (2002) 34 EHRR 12, para. 34; 123 ILR 53, 65; *McElhinney* v. *Ireland*, ECHR, 2001, (2002) 34 EHRR 13, para. 35; 123 ILR 73, 84; *Kalogeropoulou* v. *Greece*, ECHR, (2002) 129 ILR 537, 546; *Saudi Arabia* v. *ARAMCO*, Arbitration Tribunal, (1958) 27 ILR 117, 155–156, cited in *Texaco* v.

500   NOTES TO PAGE 35

Libya, (1977) 53 ILR 389, 433–434; *SPP* v. *Egypt*, International Chamber of Commerce, (1983) 86 ILR 434, 460–461; ILC, Reports, 1978–1991, 1999; ILA, Reports of the Committee on State Immunity, 1982, 1992, 1994.

6 See US FSIA, s. 1602; US House of Representatives, Report No. 94–1487, 1976, p. 8; 1976 USCCAN 6604, 6606, see also pp. 9/6608, 14/6613; ALRC, Report No. 24, *Foreign State Immunity*, 1984, pp. 24–25, para. 40.

7 See Aust, *Handbook*, ch. 7, p. 145; Fox, *The Law of State Immunity* (*passim*; esp. pp. 18–19); Hafner *et al.* (eds.), *State Practice* (*passim*); Gong, *A Comparative Study* (*passim*); Bankas, *The State Immunity Controversy* (*passim*; esp. pp. 28–31); Dickinson *et al.* (eds.), *State Immunity* (*passim*); Vibhute, *International Commercial Arbitration* (*passim*); Pingel-Lenuzza, *Les immunités* (*passim*); Cosnard, *La soumission des États* (*passim*); Schreuer, *State Immunity* (*passim*); ALI, *Third Restatement*, Vol. 1, pp. 390 and 396, s. 451; Badr, *State Immunity* (*passim*); Centres de Droit International, *L'Immunité* (*passim*); Sucharitkul, *State Immunities* (*passim*; esp. p. 3); Aust, The Law, 255; Hafner and Lange, La Convention, 45; Trooboff, Foreign State; Sinclair, The Law; Sucharitkul, Immunities; Dunbar, Controversial; Lalive, L'immunité; Phillimore, Immunité; Evans (ed.), *International Law*, ch. 12 (by Fox); Daillier *et al.*, *Droit international public*, p. 497; Brownlie, *Principles*, ch. 16; Shaw, *International Law*, ch. 13; Dixon, *Textbook*, ch. 7; Lowe, *International Law*, pp. 184–186; Cassese, *International Law*, ch. 6; Higgins, *Problems and Process*, ch. 5; Jennings and Watts (eds.), *Oppenheim's International Law*, pp. 341–363; Lauterpacht (ed.), *Oppenheim's International Law*, pp. 264–267; Hackworth, *Digest*, Vol. II, ch. VII, p. 393, para. 169; *Halsbury's Laws of England*, p. 794, para. 1548, quoted in *Pinochet No. 3*, [2000] 1 AC 147, 251–252; 119 ILR 135, 204–205; Collins (gen. ed.), *Conflict of Laws*, p. 273, Rule 19, para. 10.002; Kropholler, *Internationales Privatrecht*, p. 581.

8 *French Consular Employee Case*, Austria, (1989) 86 ILR 583, 585; *Case against the Foreign Minister*, Austria, 2001, 6 *Austrian RIEL* (2001) 288, 294; *Brasseur* v. *Greece*, Belgium, (1933) 6 AD 164, 167; *Iraq* v. *Vinci*, Belgium, (2002) 127 ILR 101, 109; *Jaffe* v. *Miller*, Canada, (1993) 103 DLR (4th) 315; 13 OR (3d) 745, 752; 95 ILR 446, 452; *Schreiber* v. *Germany*, Canada, (2002) 216 DLR (4th) 513, 518; *Bouzari* v. *Iran*, Canada, (2002) 124 ILR 427, 433; affirmed, *Bouzari* v. *Iran*, Canada, (2004) 243 DLR (4th) 406, 418; 128 ILR 586, 596; *Roxford* v. *Cuba*, Canada, [2003] 236 FTR 1, [2003] 2003 FCT 763; [2003] 4 FC 1182, para. 28; *The Parlement Belge*, England, (1880) 5 PD 197, 205; *Propend* v. *Sing*, England, (1996) 111 ILR 611, 632–633; *Holland* v. *Lampen-Wolfe*, England, [2000] 1 WLR 1573, 1583, 1588; 119 ILR 367, 378, 384; *Matthews* v. *Ministry*, England, [2003] 1 AC 1163, 1196; *Passelaigues* v. *Mortgage*, France, (1955) 22 ILR 227, 229; *Salabert* v. *USA*, France, (1956) 23 ILR 192, 193; *Barrandon* v. *USA*, France, (1992/1995) 113 ILR 464, 465, 468; *Russian* v. *Noga*, France, (2000) 127 ILR 156, 159; *In re Danish State Railways*, Germany, (1953) 20 ILR 178, 179; *In re The Charkow*, Germany, (1959) 65 ILR 100, 103; *Jurisdiction Case*, Germany, (1962) 38 ILR 162, 163–164; *Empire of Iran Case*, Germany, (1963) 45 ILR 57, 61; *Spanish Consular Bank Accounts Case*, Germany, (1971) 65 ILR 114, 117; *Spanish State Tourist Office Case*, Germany, (1977) 65 ILR 140, 141; *Philippine Embassy Bank Account Case*, Germany, (1977) 65 ILR 146,

passim, esp. 150, 164, 184; *NIOC Revenues Case*, Germany, (1983) 65 ILR 215, 227; *Shooting Range Extension Case*, Germany, (1984) 86 ILR 532, 534; *X* v. *Argentina*, Germany, (1996) 114 ILR 502, 504–505; *Muller* v. *USA*, Germany, (1998) 114 ILR 512, 517; *Kenyan Diplomatic Residence Case*, Germany, (2003) 128 ILR 632, 635; *Distomo Massacre Case*, Germany, (2003) 129 ILR 556, 560, Ground B.I.2(a); *Distomo Massacre Case*, Greece, (2000) 129 ILR 513, 516; *Her Majesty* v. *Edelson*, Israel, (1997) 131 ILR 279, 287, para. 12; 291–297, paras. 15–21; *Nanni* v. *Pace*, Italy, (1935) 8 AD 2, 4; *Bolivia* v. *Italian*, Italy, (1948) 15 AD 133, 133–135; *Castiglioni* v. *Yugoslavia*, Italy, (1952) 19 ILR 203, 207–209; *Sovereign* v. *Soc*, Italy, (1954) 22 ILR 1, 4; *Padri* v. *Nunzi*, Italy, (1957) 24 ILR 214, 215; *Hungarian* v. *Hungarian*, Italy, (1957) 24 ILR 218, 219; *Greece* v. *Gamet*, Italy, (1959) 28 ILR 153, 155; *Francischiello* v. *USA*, Italy, (1959) 28 ILR 158, 160; *The Ditta* v. *Germany*, Italy, (1960) 40 ILR 64, 65; *US* v. *Bracale*, Italy, (1968) 65 ILR 273, 274; *Campione* v. *Peti-Nitrogenmuvek*, Italy, (1972) 65 ILR 287, 292; *Mallaval* v. *French*, Italy, (1974) 65 ILR 303, 305; *Association* v. *Piccoli*, Italy, (1974) 65 ILR 308, 309; *Luna* v. *Romania*, Italy, (1974) 65 ILR 313, 314; *Bruno* v. *US*, Italy, (1977) 65 ILR 316, 318; *Bari* v. *Jasbez*, Italy, (1977) 77 ILR 602, 604, 607; *Ministry* v. *Association*, Italy, (1978) 65 ILR 320, 321–322; *Danish* v. *Hansen*, Italy, (1979) 65 ILR 325, 326; *Libya* v. *SpA*, Italy, (1979) 78 ILR 90, 92; *Italian* v. *US*, Italy, (1981) 65 ILR 338, 340; *Special* v. *Pieciukiewicz*, Italy, (1982) 78 ILR 120, 121; *Banco* v. *Credito*, Italy, (1984) 87 ILR 15, 17; *Cristiani* v. *Italian*, Italy, (1985) 87 ILR 20, 23, 26; *Panattoni* v. *Germany*, Italy, (1987) 87 ILR 42, 45; *France* v. *Jacuzio*, Italy, (1987) 87 ILR 53, 54, 55; *Banamar-Capizzi* v. *Embassy*, Italy, (1989) 87 ILR 56, 59, 62; *Libya* v. *Rossbeton*, Italy, (1989) 87 ILR 63, 65, 66, 67; *British* v. *Toglia*, Italy, (1989) 101 ILR 379, 382; *Libya* v. *Trobbiani*, Italy, (1990) 114 ILR 520, 522–523; *Giamahiria* v. *Condor*, Italy, 1990, n. 8568, 74 RDI (1991) 679; *Giamahiria* v. *Riunione*, Italy, 1990, n. 5091, 74 RDI (1991) 990; *Norwegian* v. *Quattri*, Italy, (1991) 114 ILR 525, 527; *Condor* v. *Minister*, Italy, (1992) 101 ILR 394, 403; *Nacci* v. *Bari*, Italy, (1994) 114 ILR 539, 551; *USA* v. *Lo Gatto*, Italy, (1995) 114 ILR 555, 557; *Ecole* v. *Guadagnino*, Italy, 1997, 9 *Italian YIL* (1999) 152, 153; *Regno* v. *Chiesa*, Italy, 1997, n. 3957, 80 RDI (1997) 1163; *Canada* v. *Cargnello*, Italy, (1998) 114 ILR 559, 565; *FILT-CGIL* v. *USA*, Italy, (2000) 128 ILR 644, 647; *Ferrini* v. *Germany*, Italy, (2004) 128 ILR 658, 663–664; *Borri* v. *Repubblica*, Italy, 2005, 88 RDI (2005) 856, 858; *Republic of China* v. *Chuka*, Japan, (1955) 23 ILR 210, 211; *X* v. *USA*, Japan, 2002, 46 *JAIL* (2003) 161, 163; *De Booy* v. *German*, Netherlands, (1924) 1 AD 124, 128; *NV Cabolent* v. *National*, Netherlands, (1968) 47 ILR 138, 144; *MK* v. *State*, Netherlands, (1986) 94 ILR 357, 359; *Arias* v. *Venezuela*, Netherlands, (1998) 128 ILR 684, 685–686, paras. 4.3–4.4; *Netherlands* v. *Azeta*, Netherlands, (1998) 128 ILR 688, 689; *Qureshi* v. *USSR*, Pakistan, PLD 1981 SCt 377, 397–402; 64 ILR 585, 597–602; *USA* v. *Guinto*; *USA* v. *Ceballos*; *USA* v. *Rodrigo*, Philippines, (1990) 102 ILR 132, 140; *German Immunities Case*, Poland, (1937) 8 AD 239, 240; *French Consulate Case*, Poland, (1958) 26 ILR 178, 179; *Brazilian Embassy Employee Case*, Portugal, (1984) 116 ILR 625, 627, 629, 631; *X* v. *Israel*, Portugal, (2002) 127 ILR 310, 310–311; *Kaffraria* v. *Zambia*, South Africa, 1980 (2) SA 709, 715; 64 ILR 708, 714; *Emilio* v. *Embassy*, Spain, (1986) 86 ILR 508, 510; *Banque* v. *Weston*, Switzerland, (1978) 65 ILR 417, 418–419, Ground 2a; *Libya* v. *LIAMCO*, Switzerland,

502   NOTES TO PAGE 35

(1980) 62 ILR 228, 233, Ground 3; *Universal* v. *Iran*, Switzerland, (1981) 65 ILR 436, 437, Ground 4; *Italian* v. *X*, Switzerland, (1985) 82 ILR 23, 25, Ground 3; 27, Ground 4b; *Libya* v. *Actimon*, Switzerland, (1985) 82 ILR 30, 32, Ground 4; *Swissair* v. *X*, Switzerland, (1985) 82 ILR 36, 37; *Spain* v. *Company X*, Switzerland, (1986) 82 ILR 38, 40–41, Grounds 3 and 4a; *S* v. *Romania*, Switzerland, (1987) 82 ILR 45, 47, Ground 1; 48, Ground 2; *M* v. *Egypt*, Switzerland, (1994) 116 ILR 656, 658, Ground 2.

9 See, e.g., the Constitution of Austria, Art. 9(1); Basic Law of Germany, Art. 25; Constitution of Greece, Art. 28(1); Constitution of Ireland, Art. 29(3); Constitution of Italy, Art. 10; Constitution of Japan, Art. 98; Constitution of Portugal, Art. 8(1). See *Soviet Distillery Case*, Austria, (1954) 21 ILR 101, 102; *Philippine Embassy Bank Account Case*, Germany, (1977) 65 ILR 146, 150, 164, Ground C; *Kenyan Diplomatic Residence Case*, Germany, (2003) 128 ILR 632, 635; *Distomo Massacre Case*, Greece, (2000) 129 ILR 513, 516; *Saorstat* v. *Rafael*, Ireland, 1944, [1945] IR 291, 298; 12 AD 97, 97–98; *Canada* v. *Burke*, Ireland, 1992, [1992] 2 IR 484, 490, 491, 498; 95 ILR 467, 471, 472, 479; *Borri* v. *Repubblica*, Italy, 2005, 88 RDI (2005) 856, 858; *Ferrini* v. *Germany*, Italy, (2004) 128 ILR 658, 663–664; *FILT-CGIL* v. *USA*, Italy, (2000) 128 ILR 644, 647, 651; *Canada* v. *Cargnello*, Italy, (1998) 114 ILR 559, 567; *USA* v. *Lo Gatto*, Italy, (1995) 114 ILR 555, 557; *Nacci* v. *Bari*, Italy, (1994) 114 ILR 539, 551; *Perrini* v. *Académie*, Italy, (1994) 114 ILR 536, 538; *Carbonar* v. *Magurno*, Italy, (1993) 114 ILR 534, 535; *Condor* v. *Minister*, Italy, (1992) 101 ILR 394, 403–405; *Norwegian* v. *Quattri*, Italy, (1991) 114 ILR 525, 527; *Libya* v. *Trobbiani*, Italy, (1990) 114 ILR 520, 523; *Banamar-Capizzi* v. *Embassy*, Italy, (1989) 87 ILR 56, 61–62; *Libya* v. *Rossbeton*, Italy, (1989) 87 ILR 63, 66; *France* v. *Jacuzio*, Italy, (1987) 87 ILR 53, 54; *Panattoni* v. *Germany*, Italy, (1987) 87 ILR 42, 45; *Cristiani* v. *Italian*, Italy, (1985) 87 ILR 20, 26; *Banco* v. *Credito*, Italy, (1984) 87 ILR 15, 17; *Italian* v. *US*, Italy, (1981) 65 ILR 338, 340; *Danish* v. *Hansen*, Italy, (1979) 65 ILR 325, 326; *Ministry* v. *Association*, Italy, (1978) 65 ILR 320, 322; *Luna* v. *Romania*, Italy, (1974) 65 ILR 313, 314; *Association* v. *Piccoli*, Italy, (1974) 65 ILR 308, 309; *Campione* v. *Peti-Nitrogenmuvek*, Italy, (1972) 65 ILR 287, 292; *Ciniglio* v. *Indonesian*, Italy, (1966) 65 ILR 268, 268; *Greece* v. *Gamet*, Italy, (1959) 28 ILR 153, 155; *Greece* v. *Gamet*, Italy, (1957) 24 ILR 209, 210; *Pauer* v. *Hungarian*, Italy, (1956) 24 ILR 211, 212–213; *Nanni* v. *Pace*, Italy, (1935) 8 AD 2, 4; *Brazilian Embassy Employee Case*, Portugal, (1984) 116 ILR 625, 628. In England, Blackstone stated in 1769 that 'the law of nations ... is here adopted in its full extent by the common law, and is held to be a part of the law of the land': Blackstone, *Commentaries*, p. 67; for a leading English case endorsing the doctrine of automatic incorporation of customary international law into domestic law see *Trendtex* v. *Central Bank*, [1977] QB 529, 553–554, 566–572; 64 ILR 111, 127–128; 140–146. Lord Wilberforce considered the English common law rules on State immunity 'part of the corpus of international law': *I Congreso del Partido*, England, 1981, [1983] 1 AC 244, 257, 265; 64 ILR 307, 308, 316. The US jurisprudence regards customary international law as part of federal common law, despite the silence of the US Constitution on this point: *The Nereide*, US, 13 US (9 Cranch) 388, 422 (1815); *The Paquete Habana*, US, 175 US

NOTES TO PAGES 35-38   503

677, 700 (1900); *Filartiga v. Pena-Irala*, US, 630 F.2d 876, 886–887 (2nd Cir. 1980); 77 ILR 169. See also Dickinson, The Law; Brilmayer, International; Bradley, The Status; Kedian, Customary. Israel and South Africa follow the Anglo–US approach: *Her Majesty v. Edelson*, Israel, (1997) 131 ILR 279, 287–289, para. 12; 297, para. 21; *South v. Buchan*, South Africa, 1970, 1971 (1) SA 234, 238; 55 ILR 1, 5; *Inter-Science v. Moçambique*, South Africa, 1979, 1980 (2) SA 111, 124; 64 ILR 689, 704–705; *Kaffraria v. Zambia*, South Africa, 1980 (2) SA 709, 715; 64 ILR 708, 714. In Switzerland, customary international law and the jurisprudence of the Federal Tribunal are considered identical: *Banque v. Weston*, Switzerland, (1978) 65 ILR 417, 419, Ground 2a; *Libya v. LIAMCO*, Switzerland, (1980) 62 ILR 228, 233–234, Ground 3a; *Italian v. X*, Switzerland, (1985) 82 ILR 23, 25, Ground 3; *Spain v. Company X*, Switzerland, (1986) 82 ILR 38, 40, Ground 3b; *S v. Romania*, Switzerland, (1987) 82 ILR 45, 48, Ground 2; *Landano v. USA*, Switzerland, (1987) 116 ILR 636, 638; *M v. Egypt*, Switzerland, (1994) 116 ILR 656, 661, Ground 3d. See also *Parreño v. McGranery*, Philippines, 1953, *Materials on Jurisdictional Immunities*, p. 367; *Barker v. Kenya*, Zimbabwe, (1983) (4) SA 817, 821; 84 ILR 18, 23.

10 See especially the US and Israeli protest over Belgium's assertion of jurisdiction in the *Sharon* case, and Germany's case against Italy before the International Court of Justice, discussed in Chapter 10.

11 The 1972 European Convention, Arts. 1–14 (exceptions) and Art. 15 (immunity); ILC 1991 Draft and 2004 UN Convention, Art. 5 (general principle of State immunity) and Arts. 10–17 (exceptions to immunity); US FSIA, s. 1604 ('Immunity of a foreign state from jurisdiction') and s. 1605 ('General exceptions to the jurisdictional immunity of a foreign state'); UK SIA, s. 1 ('General immunity from jurisdiction') and ss. 2–11 ('Exceptions from immunity'); Canada SIA, s. 3 (general immunity) and ss. 4–8 (exceptions); Australia FSIA, s. 9 ('General immunity from jurisdiction') and ss. 10–21 (exceptions); Pakistan SIO, s. 3 ('General immunity from jurisdiction') and ss. 4–12 ('Exceptions from immunity'); Singapore SIA, s. 3 ('Immunity from jurisdiction') and ss. 4–13 ('Exceptions from immunity'); South Africa FSIA, s. 2 (general immunity) and ss. 3–12 (exceptions); Argentina immunity statute, Art. 1 (general immunity) and Art. 2 (exceptions); Israel Immunity Law, Chapter Two, Part One: 'Immunity of the Foreign State' and Part Two: 'Exceptions to Immunity', ILA, Drafts, Art. II (general immunity) and Art. III (exceptions); OAS Draft, 1983, Art. 1 and Arts. 4–7. The IDI's 1991 Draft is an interesting document in this respect, for it purports to list both the 'criteria indicative of the competence of the relevant organs of the forum State to determine the substance of the claim' and the 'criteria indicative of the incompetence of the organs of the forum State to determine the substance of the claim' (Art. 2(2) and (3)), while declaring that each case is to be 'characterised in the light of ... the relevant criteria, both of competence and incompetence', and that 'no presumption is to be applied concerning the priority of either group of criteria' (Art. 2(1)). Such a formula may not contemplate a presumption of immunity, but then it does not suggest a presumption of non-immunity either.

504 NOTES TO PAGES 38-39

12 US House of Representatives, Report No. 94-1487, 1976, p. 17; 1976 USCCAN 6604, 6616.

13 *Rex v. Compania*, US, 660 F.2d 61, 72, 74 (3rd Cir. 1981); 72 ILR 93.

14 *Gibbons v. Udaras*, US, 549 F.Supp. 1094, 1106 (S.D.N.Y. 1982); 86 ILR 81.

15 *Alberti v. Empresa*, US, 705 F.2d 250, 256 (7th Cir. 1983); 92 ILR 392; *Von Dardel v. USSR*, US, 623 F.Supp. 246, 253 (D.D.C. 1985); 77 ILR 258; *Baglab v. Johnson*, US, 665 F.Supp. 289, 294 (S.D.N.Y. 1987); *Carl v. USSR*, US, 665 F.Supp. 323, 333 (S.D.N.Y. 1987); 84 ILR 158; *West v. Multibanco*, US, 807 F.2d 820, 824 (9th Cir. 1987); 84 ILR 187; *Meadows v. Dominican*, US, 817 F.2d 517, 522–523 (9th Cir. 1987); 98 ILR 37; *Joseph v. Office*, US, 830 F.2d 1018, 1021 (9th Cir. 1987); 101 ILR 485; *Gregorian v. Izvestia*, US, 871 F.2d 1515, 1528, fn. 11 (9th Cir. 1989); 98 ILR 76; *Security v. Derderian*, US, 872 F.2d 281, 285 (9th Cir. 1989); *First v. Antigua*, US, 877 F.2d 189, 195 (2nd Cir. 1989); 99 ILR 125; *Laroque v. Qantas*, US, 900 F.2d 263 (9th Cir. 1990) (Table); *Bahsoon v. Pezetel*, US, 768 F.Supp. 507, 511 (E.D.N.C. 1991); *Siderman v. Argentina*, US, 965 F.2d 699, 708, fn. 9 (9th Cir. 1992); 103 ILR 454; *Walter v. Philippines*, US, 965 F.2d 1375, 1380 (5th Cir. 1992); 103 ILR 503.

16 *Saudi Arabia v. Nelson*, US, 507 US 349, 355 (1993); 123 L.Ed.2d 47, 58; 100 ILR 544, 550. Emphasis added. Later reaffirmed in *Permanent Mission v. New York*, US, 551 US 193, 197; 127 S.Ct. 2352, 2355 (2007); affirming *New York v. Permanent Mission*, US, 446 F.3d 365, 369 (2nd Cir. 2006); affirming *New York v. Permanent Mission*, US, 376 F.Supp.2d 429, 432 (S.D.N.Y. 2005). Two earlier Supreme Court cases affirmed the gist of the rule without using the expression: *Argentine Republic v. Amerada Hess*, US, 488 US 428, 443 (1989); 102 L.Ed.2d 818, 834; 81 ILR 658, 669; *Verlinden v. Central Bank*, US, 461 US 480, 488 (1983); 79 ILR 548, 554. See also *Austria v. Altmann*, US, 541 US 677, 726 (2004) per Justice Kennedy, with whom the Chief Justice and Justice Thomas joined, dissenting.

17 See *Orient v. Bank*, US, 506 F.3d 980, 991 (10th Cir. 2007); *New York v. Permanent Mission*, US, 446 F.3d 365, 369 (2nd Cir. 2006); *BP v. Jiangsu*, US, 420 F.3d 810, 816 (8th Cir. 2005); *Globe v. AO*, US, 376 F.3d 282, 285 (4th Cir. 2004); *Southway v. Central Bank*, US, 328 F.3d 1267, 1271 (10th Cir. 2003); *Price v. Libya*, US, 294 F.3d 82, 87 (D.C.Cir. 2002); *BP v. Jiangsu*, US, 285 F.3d 677, 681–682 (8th Cir. 2002); *Corzo v. Banco*, US, 243 F.3d 519, 522 (9th Cir. 2001); *Adler v. Nigeria*, US, 219 F.3d 869, 874 (9th Cir. 2000); *S v. Yemen*, US, 218 F.3d 1292, 1300 (11th Cir. 2000); *Transatlantic v. Shanghai*, US, 204 F.3d 384, 388 (2nd Cir. 2000); *Adler v. Nigeria*, US, 107 F.3d 720, 728 (9th Cir. 1997); *Phaneuf v. Indonesia*, US, 106 F.3d 302, 306 (9th Cir. 1997); *Holden v. Canadian*, US, 92 F.3d 918, 920 (9th Cir. 1996); *Brown v. Valmet-Appleton*, US, 77 F.3d 860, 862 (5th Cir. 1996); *Gates v. Victor*, US, 54 F.3d 1457, 1459 (9th Cir. 1995); 107 ILR 371; *Federal v. Richard*, US, 12 F.3d 1270, 1285 (3rd Cir. 1993). Because the cases are too numerous (over 150 of them), this is but a sample from various circuit courts only; and the cases that merely quote from other cases are not cited. District court cases are not cited.

18 *Case against the Foreign Minister*, Austria, 2001, 6 *Austrian RIEL* (2001) 288, 295; *Jaffe v. Miller*, Canada, (1993) 103 DLR (4th) 315; 13 OR (3d) 745, 755; 95 ILR 446, 455; *Walker v. Bank*, Canada, (1994) 111 DLR (4th) 186, 191; 104 ILR

277, 282; *USA* v. *Friedland*, Canada, (1999) 182 DLR (4th) 614, 617, 619; 120 ILR 417, 455, 457; *Schreiber* v. *Attorney*, Canada, (2000) 187 DLR (4th) 146, 158; affirmed, *Schreiber* v. *Germany*, Canada, (2001) 196 DLR (4th) 281, 287; affirmed, *Schreiber* v. *Germany*, Canada, (2002) 216 DLR (4th) 513, 518, 524; *Bouzari* v. *Iran*, Canada, (2002) 124 ILR 427, 433; affirmed, *Bouzari* v. *Iran*, Canada, (2004) 243 DLR (4th) 406, 419, 421–422; 128 ILR 586, 597, 599; *Arar* v. *Syria*, Canada, [2005] OJ No. 752, paras. 10–11; *I Congreso del Partido*, England, 1981, [1983] 1 AC 244, 260; 64 ILR 307, 311; *Alcom* v. *Colombia*, England, [1984] 1 AC 580, 600; 74 ILR 170, 183; *Kuwait Airways* v. *Iraqi Airways*, England, (1992) 103 ILR 340, 353; 1993, [1995] 1 Lloyd's Rep 25, 28; 1995, [1995] 1 WLR 1147, 1157; 103 ILR 340, 370; 399; *Saudi Arabia* v. *Ahmed*, England, (1993) 104 ILR 629, 632; affirmed, *Ahmed* v. *Saudi Arabia*, England, 1995, [1996] 2 All ER 248, 250; [1996] ICR 25, 28; 104 ILR 629, 640; *An International* v. *Zambia*, England, (1997) 118 ILR 602, 607–608, 615–619; *Mills* v. *USA*, England, (2000) 120 ILR 612, 616; affirmed, *Mills* v. *Embassy*, England, 2000; *AIG* v. *Kazakhstan*, England, 2005, [2006] 1 WLR 1420, 1437–1438, para. 42; 129 ILR 589, 610; *Svenska* v. *Lithuania (No. 2)*, England, 2006, [2007] QB 886, 924, para. 113; affirming *Svenska* v. *Lithuania (No. 2)*, England, 2005, [2006] 1 Lloyd's Rep 181, 193, para. 38; *Ministry* v. *Tsavliris*, England, [2008] 2 Lloyd's Rep 90, 99, para. 52; *ETI* v. *Bolivia*, England, 2008, [2009] 1 WLR 665, 689, para. 110; 693, para. 128; *Argentina* v. *NML*, England, [2010] EWCA Civ 41, para. 49; *Governor* v. *Sutton*, New Zealand, 1994, [1995] 1 NZLR 426, 438; 104 ILR 508, 525; *Forth* v. *Wilmington*, Scotland, 1985, 1985 SC 317, 324–325, 327, 331–332; 1987 SLT 153, 157, 158, 161; 107 ILR 641, 648–649, 652, 657–658.

19 *Svenska* v. *Lithuania (No. 2)*, England, 2005, [2006] 1 Lloyd's Rep 181, 193, para. 38; affirmed, *Svenska* v. *Lithuania (No. 2)*, England, 2006, [2007] QB 886, 924, para. 113; *Ministry* v. *Tsavliris*, England, 2008, [2008] 2 Lloyd's Rep 90, 99, para. 52; *Governor* v. *Sutton*, New Zealand, 1994, [1995] 1 NZLR 426, 438; 104 ILR 508, 525. See also; *Iraq* v. *Vinci*, Belgium, (2002) 127 ILR 101, 106.

20 Originally, Arts. 6(1), 8(4) and 21(1)(c) in the 1991 ILC Draft Articles. For commentary see ILC, Report, *YILC*, 1991-II-2, p. 12 at 24, 30, 61.

21 Article 15. See also Council of Europe, *Explanatory Reports*, 1972, p. 22, para. 57.

22 US FSIA, s. 1608(e); UK SIA, s. 1(2); Pakistan SIO, s. 3(2); Singapore SIA, s. 3(2); South Africa FSIA, s. 2(2); Canada SIA, 1982, s. 3(2); Australia FSIA, 1985, s. 27(1); Israel Immunity Law, s. 14.

23 *Mauritius* v. *Wong*, England, 2008 WL 4963091, paras. 53–54.

24 *Verlinden* v. *Central Bank*, US, 461 US 480, 493, fn. 20 (1983); 79 ILR 548, 557; see also 485, fn. 5, 488, 489; 79 ILR 548, 551–552, 554; reiterated in *Argentine Republic* v. *Amerada Hess*, US, (1989) 488 US 428, 434–435 (1989); 102 L.Ed.2d 818, 828; 81 ILR 658, 663; *Austria* v. *Altmann*, US, 541 US 677, 691 (2004). See also *Von Dardel* v. *USSR*, US, 736 F.Supp. 1, 4 (D.D.C. 1990); overruling *Von Dardel* v. *USSR*, US, 623 F.Supp. 246, 252–253 (D.D.C. 1985); 77 ILR 258; *Practical* v. *Bolivia*, US, 811 F.2d 1543, 1547 (D.C.Cir. 1987); 92 ILR 420; *Frolova* v. *USSR*, US, 761 F.2d 370, 378 (7th Cir. 1985); 85 ILR 236; *MOL* v. *Bangladesh*, US, 736 F.2d 1326, 1328 (9th Cir. 1984); 80 ILR 583.

506   NOTES TO PAGE 40

25 *I Congreso del Partido*, England, 1981, [1983] 1 AC 244, 260; 64 ILR 307, 311; *Sengupta* v. *India*, England, 1982, [1983] ICR 221; 64 ILR 352; *Alcom* v. *Colombia*, England, [1984] 1 AC 580, 600; 74 ILR 170, 183; *Banai* v. *Canadian*, England, (1990) 107 ILR 600, 603; *Paprocki* v. *German*, England, (1995) 104 ILR 684; *UAE* v. *Abdelghafar*, England, 1994, [1995] ICR 65, 73–74; 104 ILR 647, 655; affirmed, *UAE* v. *Abdelghafar*, England, (1995) 107 ILR 626, 630; *Egypt* v. *Gamal-Eldin*, England, 1995, [1996] 2 All ER 237, 242–243; 104 ILR 673, 678; *Malaysian* v. *Jeyasingham*, England, 1997, [1998] ICR 307, 315; *Holland* v. *Lampen-Wolfe*, England, [2000] 1 WLR 1573, 1575, 1584; 119 ILR 367, 369, 379; *Yemen* v. *Aziz*, England, [2005] ICR 1391, 1407–1408, paras. 59–60; *Mauritius* v. *Wong*, England, 2008 WL 4963091, paras. 39, 47, 50. For UK position prior to the SIA see *Duff* v. *Kelantan*, England, [1924] AC 797, 817; 2 AD 124; *Chung* v. *The King*, England, 1938, [1939] AC 160, 175; 9 AD 264, 270–271.

26 *Pan* v. *Bo*, Australia, 2008, 220 FLR 271, 275–277; *Jaffe* v. *Miller*, Canada, (1993) 103 DLR (4th) 315; 13 OR (3d) 745, 765; 95 ILR 446, 465; *Kaffraria* v. *Zambia*, South Africa, 1980 (2) SA 709; 64 ILR 708; *Jose* v. *Namibia*, South Africa, noted in 19 *SAYIL* (1993–94) 157, 161.

27 *De Queiroz* v. *Portugal*, Belgium, (1992) 115 ILR 430; *Iraq* v. *Vinci*, Belgium, (2002) 127 ILR 101, 106; *Hanna* v. *Turkish*, Finland, 1993, 5 *Finnish YIL* (1994) 408; *Clerget* v. *Représentation*, France, (1967) 48 ILR 145 and later (1969) 52 ILR 310; affirmed, *Clerget* v. *Banque*, France, (1971) 65 ILR 54; *Société* v. *Lao*, France, (1983) 80 ILR 430, 432; affirmed, *Société* v. *Lao*, France, (1987) 80 ILR 688, 690; *General* v. *Société*, France, (1986) 77 ILR 530, 531–532; *National* v. *Pipeline*, France, (1990) 113 ILR 446; *Barrandon* v. *USA*, France, (1992/1995) 113 ILR 464; *Philippine Embassy Bank Account Case*, Germany, (1977) 65 ILR 146, 160, Ground B.2(a)(b); *Canada* v. *Burke*, Ireland, 1992, [1992] 2 IR 484; 95 ILR 467; *Canada* v. *Cargnello*, Italy, (1998) 114 ILR 559, 561; *NV Limburgsch* v. *German*, Netherlands, (1916) 1 AD 129 note; *De Froe* v. *The Russian*, Netherlands, (1932) 6 AD 170; *JPH* v. *Indonesian*, Netherlands, (1979) 65 ILR 379 note; *LF* v. *Germany*, Netherlands, (1986) 94 ILR 342; *Maria* v. *Austrian*, Poland, (1987) 82 ILR 1, 2; *In re Bolin*, Sweden, (1934) 7 AD 186; *Tsakos* v. *USA*, Switzerland, (1972) 75 ILR 78; *K* v. *Vietnam*, Switzerland, (1981) 75 ILR 122; *Champel* v. *Geneva*, Switzerland, (1984) 102 ILR 180; *Nicoud* v. *USA*, Switzerland, (1994) 116 ILR 650, 653; *X* v. *USA*, Switzerland, (1995) 116 ILR 668.

28 *Cargill* v. *Pavel Dybenko*, US, 991 F.2d 1012, 1016 (2nd Cir. 1993); 103 ILR 572. See also *Virtual* v. *South Africa*, US, 300 F.3d 230, 241 (2nd Cir. 2002); *Drexel* v. *Committee*, US, 12 F.3d 317, 325 (2nd Cir. 1993). This apparently was adapted from a statement in the legislative report, the slightly different nuances of which will, for lack of space, not be explored here. See US House of Representatives, Report No. 94-1487, 1976, p. 17; 1976 USCCAN 6604, 6616. The exact passage from the legislative report was quoted in *Gerding* v. *France*, US, 943 F.2d 521, 525 (4th Cir. 1991); 98 ILR 159; *Gould* v. *Pechiney*, US, 853 F.2d 445, 451, fn. 5 (6th Cir. 1988); 98 ILR 136; *Meadows* v. *Dominican*, US, 817 F.2d 517, 522 (9th Cir. 1987); 98 ILR 37; and *Alberti* v. *Empresa*, US, 705 F.2d 250, 255 (7th Cir. 1983); 92 ILR 392.

29 *Youming* v. *Ministry*, US, 475 F.Supp.2d 54, 61 (D.D.C. 2007). For further US cases on the burden of proof see *FG* v. *Congo*, US, 447 F.3d 835, 842 (D.C.Cir. 2006); *Kilburn* v. *Libya*, US, 376 F.3d 1123, 1131–1133 (D.C. Cir. 2004); *Virtual* v. *South Africa*, US, 300 F.3d 230, 241 (2nd Cir. 2002); *International* v. *Caja*, US, 293 F.3d 392, 397 (7th Cir. 2002); *Robinson* v. *Malaysia*, US, 269 F.3d 133, 141 (2nd Cir. 2001); *Phoenix* v. *Angola*, US, 216 F.3d 36, 40 (D.C.Cir. 2000); *Aquamar* v. *Del*, US, 179 F.3d 1279, 1290 (11th Cir. 1999); *Randolph* v. *Budget*, US, 97 F.3d 319, 324 (9th Cir. 1996); *Gates* v. *Victor*, US, 54 F.3d 1457, 1463 (9th Cir. 1995); 107 ILR 371; *Moran* v. *Saudi Arabia*, US, 27 F.3d 169, 172 (5th Cir. 1994); 107 ILR 303; *Princz* v. *Germany*, US, 26 F.3d 1166, 1171 (D.C.Cir. 1994); 103 ILR 594; *General* v. *Grossman*, US, 991 F.2d 1376, 1382 (8th Cir. 1993); *Walter* v. *Philippines*, US, 965 F.2d 1375, 1383 (5th Cir. 1992); 103 ILR 503; *Stena* v. *Comision*, US, 923 F.2d 380, 390, fn. 14 (5th Cir. 1991); 103 ILR 433; *Forsythe* v. *Saudi*, US, 885 F.2d 285, 289, fn. 6 (5th Cir. 1989); *Joseph* v. *Office*, US, 830 F.2d 1018, 1021 (9th Cir. 1987); 101 ILR 485; *Transamerican* v. *Somali*, US, 767 F.2d 998, 1002 (D.C.Cir. 1985); 86 ILR 55; *Letelier* v. *Chile*, US, 748 F.2d 790, 795 (2nd Cir. 1984); 79 ILR 561; *Vencedora* v. *Compagnie*, US, 730 F.2d 195, 199 (5th Cir. 1984); 87 ILR 520; *Alberti* v. *Empresa*, US, 705 F.2d 250, 253, 255–256 (7th Cir. 1983); 92 ILR 392; *Arango* v. *Guzman*, US, 621 F.2d 1371, 1378 (5th Cir. 1980); 63 ILR 467; *Elbasir* v. *Saudi Arabia*, US, 468 F.Supp.2d 155, 160 (D.D.C. 2007); *Filler* v. *Hanvit*, US, 247 F.Supp.2d 425, 428 (S.D.N.Y. 2003); *Daliberti* v. *Iraq*, US, 97 F.Supp.2d 38, 42 (D.D.C. 2000); *El-Hadad* v. *Embassy*, US, 69 F.Supp.2d 69 (D.D.C. 1999); *Drexel* v. *Committee*, US, 810 F.Supp. 1375, 1380–1381 (S.D.N.Y. 1993); 103 ILR 532; *Baglab* v. *Johnson*, US, 665 F.Supp. 289, 293–294 (S.D.N.Y. 1987). Cf. US House of Representatives, Report No. 94-1487, 1976, p. 17; 1976 USCCAN 6604, 6616.

30 *Iraq* v. *Vinci*, Belgium, (2002) 127 ILR 101, 106.

31 US House of Representatives, Report No. 94-1487, 1976, pp. 12, 13, 14; 1976 USCCAN 6604, 1610, 1611, 1613 (emphases added).

32 *Ruggiero* v. *Compania*, US, 639 F.2d 872, 875, 878 (2nd Cir. 1981); 63 ILR 540.

33 *Williams* v. *Shipping*, US, 653 F.2d 875, 878, 881 (4th Cir. 1981); 63 ILR 639.

34 *Rex* v. *Compania*, US, 660 F.2d 61, 62 (3rd Cir. 1981); 72 ILR 93. See also *Goar* v. *Compania*, US, 688 F.2d 417, 421 (5th Cir. 1982); *McKeel* v. *Iran*, US, 722 F.2d 582, 585–586 (9th Cir. 1983); 81 ILR 543; *Asociacion* v. *United*, US, 735 F.2d 1517, 1520 (D.C.Cir.1984); 84 ILR 87; *First* v. *Kaufman*, US, 593 F.Supp. 1189, 1191, 1192 (N.D.Ala. 1984); *Jackson* v. *China*, US, 596 F.Supp. 386, 387 (N.D.Ala. 1984); affirmed, *Jackson* v. *China*, US, 794 F.2d 1490 (11th Cir. 1986); 84 ILR 132; *Frolova* v. *USSR*, US, 761 F.2d 370, 372 (7th Cir. 1985); 85 ILR 236; *Slade* v. *Mexico*, US, 617 F.Supp. 351, 355 (D.D.C. 1985); *Tote* v. *Iberia*, US, 649 F.Supp. 41, 42 (E.D.Pa. 1986); *Carl* v. *USSR*, US, 665 F.Supp. 323, 328, 333, 335 (S.D.N.Y. 1987); 84 ILR 158; *English* v. *Thorne*, US, 676 F.Supp. 761, 764 (S.D.Miss. 1987); *Concepcion* v. *VEB*, US, 120 FRD 482, 484 (D.N.J. 1988).

35 *Verlinden* v. *Central Bank*, US, 461 US 480, 488 (1983); 79 ILR 548, 554.

36 *Verlinden*, 461 US 480, 493–494 (1983); 79 ILR 548, 557. For the comprehensiveness of the FSIA see also *Argentina* v. *Weltover*, US, 504 US 607, 610 (1992); 119 L.Ed.2d 394, 402; 100 ILR 509, 512; *Austria* v. *Altmann*, US, 541 US 677, 691, 699

508   NOTES TO PAGES 42–43

(2004); *Samantar* v. *Yousuf*, US, 130 S.Ct. 2278, 2291 (2010); *Chuidian* v. *Philippine*, US, 912 F.2d 1095, 1102 (9th Cir. 1990); 92 ILR 480.

37 *Verlinden*, 461 US 480, 489 (1983); 79 ILR 548, 554.

38 *Argentine Republic* v. *Amerada Hess*, US, 488 US 428, 437 (1989); 102 L.Ed.2d 818, 830; 81 ILR 658, 665; see also 435, fn. 3 and 438; 102 L.Ed.2d 818, 828, 830; 81 ILR 658, 663, 665.

39 *Argentine Republic* v. *Amerada Hess*, US, 488 US 428, 434, 439, 443 (1989); 102 L.Ed.2d 818, 828, 831, 834; 81 ILR 658, 663, 666, 669. Later reaffirmed in *Argentina* v. *Weltover*, US, 504 US 607, 610–611 (1992); 119 L.Ed.2d 394, 402–403; 100 ILR 509, 512–513; *Saudi Arabia* v. *Nelson*, US, 507 US 349, 355 (1993); 123 L.Ed.2d 47, 58; 100 ILR 544, 550; *Austria* v. *Altmann*, US, 541 US 677, 691, 699 (2004); *Permanent Mission* v. *New York*, US, 551 US 193, 197; 127 S.Ct. 2352, 2355 (2007); *Samantar* v. *Yousuf*, US, 130 S.Ct. 2278, 2285–2286 (2010).

40 Lower court cases adhering to this decision are too numerous (over 270 reported cases as at the time of writing) to be cited exhaustively. For more recent Circuit Court cases see *Guirlando* v. *TC*, US, 602 F.3d 69, 74 (2nd Cir. 2010); *Anglo-Iberia* v. *PT*, US, 600 F.3d 171, 174–175 (2nd Cir. 2010); *UNC* v. *Saudi Arabia*, US, 581 F.3d 210, 215 (5th Cir. 2009); *Cassirer* v. *Spain*, US, 580 F.3d 1048, 1055 (9th Cir. 2009); *Matar* v. *Dichter*, US, 563 F.3d 9, 12 (2nd Cir. 2009); *O'Bryan* v. *Holy See*, US, 556 F.3d 361, 374 (6th Cir. 2009); *Yousuf* v. *Samantar*, US, 552 F.3d 371, 376 (4th Cir. 2009); *In re Terrorist*, US, 538 F.3d 71, 80 (2nd Cir. 2008); *American* v. *Lebanon*, US, 501 F.3d 534, 538 (6th Cir. 2007); *Nemariam* v. *Ethiopia*, US, 491 F.3d 470, 474 (D.C. Cir. 2007); 135 ILR 679; *Gupta* v. *Thai*, US, 487 F.3d 759, 763 (9th Cir. 2007); *Af-Cap* v. *Congo*, US, 462 F.3d 417, 428 (5th Cir. 2006); *FG* v. *Congo*, US, 455 F.3d 575, 584 (5th Cir. 2006); *New York* v. *Permanent Mission*, US, 446 F.3d 365, 369 (2nd Cir. 2006); *Dale* v. *Colagiovanni*, US, 443 F.3d 425, 427–428 (5th Cir. 2006); *Mwani* v. *bin Laden*, US, 417 F.3d 1, 14–15 (D.C. Cir. 2005); *Peterson* v. *Saudi Arabia*, US, 416 F.3d 83, 86 (D.C. Cir. 2005); *Calzadilla* v. *Banco*, US, 413 F.3d 1285, 1286 (11th Cir. 2005); *Ministry* v. *Cubic*, US, 385 F.3d 1206, 1217 (9th Cir. 2004); *Filler* v. *Hanvit*, US, 378 F.3d 213, 216 (2nd Cir. 2004); *Velasco* v. *Indonesia*, US, 370 F.3d 392, 397 (4th Cir. 2004); *Gulf* v. *Congo*, US, 370 F.3d 65, 70 (D.C. Cir. 2004); *Hwang* v. *Japan*, US, 332 F.3d 679, 682 (D.C. Cir. 2003); *Southway* v. *Central*, US, 328 F.3d 1267, 1271 (10th Cir. 2003); *EIE* v. *Long*, US, 322 F.3d 635, 639 (9th Cir. 2003); *Altmann* v. *Austria*, US, 317 F.3d 954, 962 (9th Cir. 2002); affirming *Altmann* v. *Austria*, US, 142 F.Supp.2d 1187, 1197 (C.D. Cal. 2001); *Flatow* v. *Iran*, US, 308 F.3d 1065, 1069 (9th Cir. 2002); *World* v. *Kazakhstan*, US, 296 F.3d 1154, 1161 (D.C. Cir. 2002); *Jordan* v. *Layale*, US, 272 F.3d 264, 270 (5th Cir. 2001); *McKesson* v. *Iran*, US, 271 F.3d 1101, 1105 (D.C. Cir. 2001); *Robinson* v. *Malaysia*, US, 269 F.3d 133, 138 (2nd Cir. 2001); *Corzo* v. *Banco*, US, 243 F.3d 519, 522 (9th Cir. 2001); *Reiss* v. *Société*, US, 235 F.3d 738, 746–747 (2nd Cir. 2000); *S* v. *Yemen*, US, 218 F.3d 1292, 1300 (11th Cir. 2000); *Phoenix* v. *Angola*, US, 216 F.3d 36, 39–40 (D.C. Cir. 2000); *Kelly* v. *Syria*, US, 213 F.3d 841, 845 (5th Cir. 2000); *Sun* v. *Taiwan*, US, 201 F.3d 1105, 1107 (9th Cir. 2000). Thus, 'immunity remains the rule rather than the exception', *MacArthur* v. *Peru*, US, 809 F.2d 918, 919 (D.C. Cir. 1987); 107 ILR 196, citing *Gibbons* v. *Ireland*, US, 532 F.Supp. 668, 671 (D.D.C. 1982); 86 ILR 75.

41 *Alcom* v. *Colombia*, England, [1984] 1 AC 580, 600; 74 ILR 170, 183; quoted in *Al-Adsani* v. *Kuwait*, England, (1996) 107 ILR 536, 542, 548; *Forth* v. *Wilmington*, Scotland, 1985, 1985 SC 317, 324–325; 1987 SLT 153, 157; 107 ILR 641, 648–649.

42 *Pinochet No. 3*, England, 1999, [2000] 1 AC 147, 209; 119 ILR 135, 160.

43 *Al-Adsani* v. *Kuwait*, England, (1996) 107 ILR 536, 542.

44 *Bouzari* v. *Iran*, Canada, (2002) 124 ILR 427, 433; affirmed, *Bouzari* v. *Iran*, Canada, (2004) 243 DLR (4th) 406, 419; 128 ILR 586, 597. See also *Schreiber* v. *Germany*, Canada, (2002) 216 DLR (4th) 513, 524.

45 From the perspective of national law, whether rules and principles of *customary international law* (in contradistinction to treaty rules, which go through a different process) can be directly applied by a domestic court is primarily a question of *constitutional law*; and international law on this point is at best unsettled. For general discussion on the application of customary international law in domestic courts see also Stirling-Zanda, *L'application judiciaire*.

46 US House of Representatives, Report No. 94-1487, 1976, pp. 8, 9, 14; 1976 USCCAN 6604, 6606, 6608, 6613. See *Siderman* v. *Argentina*, US, 965 F.2d 699, 718 (9th Cir. 1992); 103 ILR 454; *Ungar* v. *Palestinian*, US, 315 F.Supp.2d 164, 175 (D.R.I. 2004); *Borgships* v. *Macarena*, US, 1993 WL 278453, p. 2 (E.D. La. 1993); *International* v. *OPEC*, US, 477 F.Supp. 553, 565 (C.D. Cal. 1979); 63 ILR 284; *Jet* v. *Marsa*, US, 462 F.Supp. 1165, 1168 (D. Md. 1978); 63 ILR 214.

47 The expression 'immunity in the courts' is used here advisedly and to simplify the matter. In its broad sense, however, the word 'immunity' is capable of covering every situation in which a State (together with its various emanations) enjoys exemption from all manifestations of sovereign authority of another State, whether legislative, administrative, or judicial. For example, the word 'immunity' can be used to refer to exemption from various forms of taxation: *Gobierno* v. *Consejo*, Argentina, (1940) 10 AD 196; *Municipality* v. *Fraser-Brace*, Canada, (1958) 13 DLR (2d) 177; 26 ILR 165; partially reversing *Fraser-Brace* v. *Municipality*, Canada, (1957) 9 DLR (2d) 391; 24 ILR 231; *In Re D*, France, (1966) 47 ILR 57; *Maharaja* v. *Assam*, India, (1948) 22 ILR 64; *Commissioner* v. *HEH*, India, (1965) 64 ILR 482; *Colonel* v. *Commissioner*, India, (1971) 64 ILR 523; *Ministry* v. *Association*, Italy, (1978) 65 ILR 320; *Attorney-General* v. *Germany*, Spain, (1983) 88 ILR 679; UK SIA, s. 16(5) (excluding 'any proceedings relating to taxation other than those mentioned in section 11') and s. 11 (no immunity from value added tax, customs duties, and rates for commercial premises); *R* v. *Inland Revenue*, England, 1989, [1990] 1 WLR 191, 200–201; 103 ILR 327, 336–337; *US* v. *Arlington*, US, 669 F.2d 925 (4th Cir. 1982); 72 ILR 652; a fine: *In re Commercial*, France, (1927) 4 AD 30; or some other fees/charges: *Congo* v. *Syndicat*, France, 2005, 95 RCDIP (2006) 123 (condominium (or co-ownership or maintenance) charges (charges de copropriété)). See also *Soviet Distillery Case*, Austria, (1954) 21 ILR 101 (concerning immunity from a decree ordering confiscation of spirits); *Import of American Cigarettes Case*, Germany, (1955) 22 ILR 233 (concerning immunity from customs officers' boarding of a ship); *Jurisdiction over Yugoslav Military Mission Case*, Germany, (1962) 38 ILR 162

510   NOTES TO PAGES 44–46

(rectification of the land register in respect of embassy premises); *Fusco* v. *O'Dea*, Ireland, [1994] 2 ILRM 389; 103 ILR 318 (immunity from third party discovery); *Nanni* v. *Pace*, Italy, (1935) 8 AD 2 (exemption from the necessity of obtaining the permission from the government for the acquisition of immovable property). The question of immunity may also be decided by various specialized tribunals (such as employment/labour tribunals), administrative courts, or even executive organs: *Soviet Distillery Case*, Austria, Administrative Court, (1954) 21 ILR 101, 102; *Embassy Interpreter Dismissal Case*, Austria, Administrative Court, (1985) 77 ILR 485; *Novopharm* v. *USA*, Canada, Commissioner of Patents, 18 CPR (3d) 26 (1987); *In Re D*, France, Conseil d'État, (1966) 47 ILR 57; *Minister* v. *Burgat*, France, Conseil d'Etat, (1976) 74 ILR 277; *Syndicat des Copropriétaires*, France, Administrative Court of Appeal of Paris (Third Chamber), (1992) 113 ILR 470; *Shooting Range Extension Case*, Germany, Supreme Administrative Court of Kassel, (1984) 86 ILR 532; *Indian Foreign Minister Case*, Germany, Federal Administrative Court, (1988) 90 ILR 408; *French Consulate Disabled Employee Case*, Germany, Administrative Court (VG) of Mainz, (1988) 114 ILR 507; *MK* v. *State Secretary*, Netherlands, Council of State, (1986) 94 ILR 357. For labour/employment tribunals see Chapter 4.

48 *Chung* v. *The King*, England, 1938, [1939] AC 160, 168 per Lord Atkin. See an interesting article by Siewert, Reciprocal. *The Schooner Exchange* has also been called the 'fountain-head' of the law of State immunity: *Wright* v. *Cantrell*, Australia, (1943) 12 AD 133, 140 per Jordan CJ. Chief Justice Marshall himself said that he was 'exploring an unbeaten path': *The Schooner Exchange* v. *McFaddon*, US, 11 US (7 Cranch) 116, 136 (1812).

49 *The Schooner Exchange* v. *McFaddon*, US, 11 US (7 Cranch) 116, 136–137 (1812).

50 *Immunities Case*, Austria, (1920) 1 AD 118, 119; *Soviet Distillery Case*, Austria, (1954) 21 ILR 101, 102; *X* v. *Germany*, Austria, (1963) 65 ILR 10, 12; *Steinmetz* v. *Hungarian*, Austria, (1970) 65 ILR 15, 19; *Rau* v. *Duruty*, Belgium, 1879, 26 *AJIL* Supplement (1932) 612, 613; *Ministère* v. *Tsoukharis*, Egypt, (1943) 12 AD 150, 150; *The Tervaete*, England, [1922] P 259, 268–269; *Duff* v. *Kelantan*, England, [1924] AC 797, 822; *Société le Gostrog* v. *Association*, France, (1926) 3 AD 174, 175; *Procureur* v. *Vestwig*, France, (1946) 13 AD 78, 79; *Société Bauer-Marchal* v. *Ministre*, France, (1957) 24 ILR 204, 204; *Congo* v. *Syndicat*, France, 2005, 95 RCDIP (2006) 123, 124; *Roumanian Legation Case*, Greece, (1949) 16 AD 291; *German* v. *Dynamic*, India, (1970) 64 ILR 504, 517, 519, 523; *Rumania* v. *Trutta*, Italy, 1926, 26 *AJIL* Supplement (1932) 626, 628; *Little* v. *Riccio*, Italy, (1933/1934) 7 AD 177, 177; *Borga* v. *Russian*, Italy, (1953) 22 ILR 235, 235; *Consorzio* v. *Federazione*, Italy, (1966) 65 ILR 265, 266; *Mallaval* v. *French*, Italy, (1974) 65 ILR 303, 306; *Mininni* v. *Bari*, Italy, (1986) 87 ILR 28, 34–35; *Weber* v. *USSR*, Netherlands, (1942) 11 AD 140, 140; *Krol* v. *Bank*, Netherlands, (1958) 26 ILR 180, 180–181; *Owners* v. *Owners*, Scotland, 1921, (1922) SLT 68, 70; 11 AD 149, 151; *The Rigmor*, Sweden, (1942) 10 AD 240, 246.

51 *Urrutia* v. *Martiarena*, Belgium, (1937) 8 AD 237, 238; *Jaffe* v. *Miller*, Canada, (1993) 103 DLR (4th) 315; 13 OR (3d) 745, 752; 95 ILR 446, 452; *Duke of Brunswick* v. *King*, England, (1848) 6 Beav 1, 50; *Haile* v. *Cable (No. 1)*, England, [1938] Ch

NOTES TO PAGE 46 511

839, 844; 9 AD 171, 173; *Kahan v. Pakistan*, England, [1951] 2 KB 1003, 1011; 18 ILR 210, 213; *Sultan v. Abubakar*, England, [1952] AC 318, 340, 342–343; 19 ILR 182, 188, 190; *Gouvernment espagnol v. Cassaux*, France, 1849, Sirey, 1849-I-81, 93; *Lakhowsky v. Swiss*, France, (1921) 1 AD 122, 123; *Morocco v. Laurens*, France, (1930) 5 AD 116, 116; *In re Hanukiew*, France, (1933) 7 AD 174, 174; *Huttinger v. Upper*, France, (1934) 7 AD 172, 173; *Roumanian State v. Arricastre*, France, (1937) 8 AD 232, 233; *Rossignol v. Czechoslovakia*, France, (1949) 16 AD 140, 140; *Guttieres v. Elmilik*, Italy, 26 *AJIL Supplement* (1932) 622, 622; *Pauer v. Hungarian*, Italy, (1956) 24 ILR 211, 212; *Greece v. Gamet*, Italy, (1959) 28 ILR 153, 155; *Czechoslovak Republic Case*, Poland, (1926) 3 AD 180, 180; *Diana v. South Africa*, Spain, (1986) 86 ILR 512, 514; *In re Bolin*, Sweden, (1934) 7 AD 186, 186; *Västerås v. Iceland*, Sweden, (1999) 128 ILR 705, 706.

52 *Brasseur v. Greece*, Belgium, (1933) 6 AD 164, 167; *Senerman v. Cuba*, Chile, (1975) 65 ILR 29, 30; *Matthews v. Ministry*, England, [2003] 1 AC 1163, 1196; *French Consulate Disabled Employee Case*, Germany, (1988) 114 ILR 507, 510; *Stukonis v. Embassy*, Lithuania, 1998, noted in 2 *Baltic YIL* (2002) 270, 270; *Cudak v. Embassy*, Lithuania, 2001, noted in 3 *Baltic YIL* (2003) 320, 322; *South Moluccas v. Royal*, Netherlands, (1951) 17 ILR 143, 152; *S v. British*, Poland, (1948) 24 ILR 223, 224.

53 *The Charkieh*, England, (1873) LR 4 A & E 59, 97; *Juan v. Indonesia*, England, 1954, [1955] AC 72, 86; 21 ILR 95, 96; *Buttes v. Hammer (No. 2)*, England, 1974, [1975] QB 557, 573; 57 ILR 33, 39; *Ex parte Peru*, US, 318 US 578, 586–587, 588 (1943); 10 AD 199, 202, 203; *Mexico v. Hoffman*, US, 324 US 30, 35–36 (1945); 12 AD 143, 145; *Saudi Arabia v. ARAMCO*, Arbitration Tribunal, (1958) 27 ILR 117, 155; cited in *Texaco v. Libya*, Arbitral Tribunal, (1977) 53 ILR 389, 433;. However, according to the Italian Court of Cassation, the 'dignity of a State' may have been more in accord with 'the old conception of the absolute State', implying that 'dignity' might be out of place in modern times: *Borga v. Russian*, Italy, (1953) 22 ILR 235, 237–238. See also *The Cristina*, England, [1938] AC 485, 521; 9 AD 250, 261.

54 *Walker v. Bank*, Canada, (1994) 111 DLR (4th) 186, 190; 104 ILR 277, 282; *Schreiber v. Attorney*, Canada, (2000) 187 DLR (4th) 146, 158; *Duff v. Kelantan*, England, [1924] AC 797, 820; *The El Neptuno*, England, (1938) 62 Ll L Rep 7, 9; 9 AD 279, 281; *Buck v. Attorney-General*, England, 1964, [1965] Ch 745, 770; 42 ILR 11, 22; *Trendtex v. Central Bank*, England, [1977] QB 529, 576; 64 ILR 111, 150; *Westland v. Arab*, England, 1994, [1995] QB 282, 293; 108 ILR 564, 575; *An International v. Zambia*, England, (1997) 118 ILR 602, 616; *The Ramava*, Ireland, (1941) 10 AD 91, 97; *Masatoshi v. Tokyo*, Japan, (1957) 24 ILR 226, 227; *Australia v. Midford*, Malaysia, [1990] 1 Curr LJ 878, 885; 86 ILR 640, 651; *Forth v. Wilmington*, Scotland, 1985, 1985 SC 317, 327; 1987 SLT 153, 158; 107 ILR 641, 651; *Guaranty v. US*, US, 304 US 126, 134 (1938); 9 AD 184, 185; *Ulen v. Bank*, US, 24 N.Y.S.2d 201 (1940); 9 AD 213, 215; *Victory v. Comisaría*, US, 336 F.2d 354, 360 (2nd Cir. 1964); 35 ILR 110; *First National v. Banco*, US, 406 US 759, 762, 765 (1972); 66 ILR 102, 105, 106; *Verlinden v. Central Bank*, US, 461 US 480, 486 (1983); 79 ILR 548, 552; *West v. Multibanco*, US, 807 F.2d 820, 823 (9th Cir. 1987); 84 ILR 187;

512   NOTES TO PAGE 46

Corzo v. Banco, US, 243 F.3d 519, 524 (9th Cir. 2001); *Sampson v. Germany*, US, 250 F.3d 1145, 1149, fn. 3 (7th Cir. 2001); *Connecticut v. Congo*, US, 309 F.3d 240, 250 (5th Cir. 2002); *Dole Food v. Patrickson*, US, 538 US 468, 479 (2003); *Abiola v. Abubakar*, US, 267 F.Supp.2d 907, 916 (N.D. Ill. 2003); *Austria v. Altmann*, US, 541 US 677, 689 (2004); *Malewicz v. Amsterdam*, US, 362 F.Supp.2d 298, 309 (D.D.C. 2005); *Philippines v. Pimentel*, US, 128 S.Ct. 2180, 2190 (2008).

55 *Immunity of UK Case*, Germany, (1957) 24 ILR 207, 209; *Village v. Her Majesty*, Malaysia, (1987) 87 ILR 223, 237; *German Immunities Case*, Poland, (1937) 8 AD 239, 240; *S v. British*, Poland, (1948) 24 ILR 223, 224–225; repeated verbatim in *French Consulate Case*, Poland, (1958) 26 ILR 178, 179–180; *Maria v. Austrian*, Poland, (1987) 82 ILR 1, 4. See also Glannon and Atik, Politics, 691. Diametrically opposed is the position adopted by two local German courts, which held that reciprocity, i.e. readiness to accord immunity to Germany, did not constitute a sufficient ground for granting immunity: *Central Bank of Nigeria Case*, Germany, (1975/1976) 65 ILR 131, 136 and *Spanish State Tourist Office Case*, Germany, (1977) 65 ILR 140, 141. See also *UAR v. Mirza*, India, (1961) 64 ILR 394, 409–410, where Lahiri CJ expressed strong doubts about reciprocity being a basis for immunity.

56 *Ibarra v. Captain*, Argentina, (1937) 8 AD 247, 248 and 9 AD 293, 294; *Re Canada Labour Code*, Canada, (1992) 91 DLR (4th) 449, 476; 94 ILR 264, 291; *Socifros v. USSR*, France, (1938) 9 AD 236, 236 (notice the different rationale (independence and sovereignty) given by the Court of Appeal of Aix in the same case at 237–238); *Re Honecker*, Germany, (1984) 80 ILR 365, 366; *Harry v. USA*, Philippines, (1958) 88 ILR 711, 711; *In re Muir*, US, 254 US 522, 533 (1921); 1 AD 143, 144; *Heaney v. Spain*, US, 445 F.2d 501, 503 (2nd Cir. 1971); 57 ILR 153; *Isbrandtsen v. President*, US, 446 F.2d 1198, 1200 (2nd Cir. 1971); 57 ILR 147; *Segni v. Commercial*, US, 835 F.2d 160, 162 (7th Cir. 1987); 98 ILR 55; *In re Texas*, US, 15 F.3d 1230, 1239 (3rd Cir. 1994); *Pullman v. US*, US, 23 F.3d 1166, 1169 (7th Cir. 1994); *Pere v. NuovoPignone*, US, 150 F.3d 477, 480, 481 (5th Cir. 1998); *In re Ski*, US, 198 F.Supp.2d 420, 426 (S.D.N.Y. 2002); *USX v. Adriatic*, US, 345 F.3d 190, 207, 208, 209 (3rd Cir. 2003); *Murphy v. Korea*, US, 421 F.Supp.2d 627, 640 (S.D.N.Y. 2005). See also *Al-Adsani v. UK*, ECHR, 2001, (2002) 34 EHRR 11, para. 54; 123 ILR 24, 40; *Fogarty v. UK*, ECHR, 2001, (2002) 34 EHRR 12, para. 34; 123 ILR 53, 65; *McElhinney v. Ireland*, ECHR, 2001, (2002) 34 EHRR 13, para. 35; 123 ILR 73, 85.

57 *The Schooner Exchange* is the exemplar of such a combination, see above (sovereignty, independence, equality and dignity, etc.). See also *Manauta v. Embassy*, Argentina, (1994) 113 ILR 429, 431–432; *Australian v. Westpac*, Australia, (1988) 17 NSWLR 623, 631; 104 ILR 405, 414; *Reid v. Nauru*, Australia, 1992, [1993] 1 VR 251, 253; 101 ILR 193, 195; *De Roover v. States*, Belgium, (1920) 1 AD 120, 121; *West v. Captain*, Belgium, (1920) 1 AD 152, 153; *Portugal v. Sauvage*, Belgium, (1921) 1 AD 154, 155; *Urrutia v. Martiarena*, Belgium, (1937) 8 AD 237, 238, 239; *Saez v. Pinillos*, Belgium, (1938/1939) 9 AD 289, 290; *Socobelge v. Greek*, Belgium, (1951) 18 ILR 3, 7–8; *De Decker v. USA*, Belgium, (1956) 23 ILR 209, 209; *Castanheira v. Commercial*, Belgium, (1980) 82 ILR 100, 102; *Rousseau v. Upper Volta*, Belgium, (1983) 82 ILR 118, 120; *Dessaulles v. Poland*, Canada, (1944) 4 DLR

1, 7, 8; 12 AD 92, 95, 96; *Municipality* v. *Fraser-Brace*, Canada, (1958) 13 DLR (2d) 177, 181–182, 191, 192–193; 26 ILR 165, 168, 170, 174, 176; *Cargo* v. *Lorac*, Canada, (1986) 28 DLR (4th) 30, 315; 84 ILR 700, 707; *Re Canada Labour Code*, Canada, 1989, [1990] 1 FC 332, 337; 86 ILR 626, 629; *Schreiber* v. *Germany*, Canada, (2001) 196 DLR (4th) 281, 290; affirmed, *Schreiber* v. *Germany*, Canada, (2002) 216 DLR (4th) 513, 523, 526; *Bouzari* v. *Iran*, Canada, (2002) 124 ILR 427, 433; affirmed, *Bouzari* v. *Iran*, Canada, (2004) 243 DLR (4th) 406, 418; 128 ILR 586, 596; *Arar* v. *Syrian*, Canada, [2005] OJ No. 752, para. 21; *The Parlement Belge*, England, (1880) 5 PD 197, 206, 207, 214–215, 220; *The Porto Alexandre*, England, 1919, [1920] P 30, 36; *The Cristina*, England, [1938] AC 485, 497, 498, 502, 509, 515, 518–519; 9 AD 250, 254, 258, 259, 260; *The Arantzazu Mendi*, England, [1939] AC 256, 265; 9 AD 60, 66; *USA* v. *Dollfus*, England, [1952] AC 582, 605, 621; 19 ILR 163, 169, 181; *Rahimtoola* v. *Nizam*, England, 1957, [1958] AC 379, 395–396; 404; 417; 24 ILR 175, 179, 186, 196; *Trendtex* v. *Central Bank*, England, [1977] QB 529, 561, 576; 64 ILR 111, 135, 150; *I Congreso del Partido*, England, 1977, [1978] 1 QB 500, 527, 528; 64 ILR 154, 178, 179; *I Congreso del Partido*, England, 1981, [1983] 1 AC 244, 262; 64 ILR 307, 314; *Propend* v. *Sing*, England, (1996) 111 ILR 611, 632; *Pinochet No. 3*, England, 1999, [2000] 1 AC 147, 265, 268, 269, 284; 119 ILR 135, 219, 221, 222, 223, 238; *Holland* v. *Lampen-Wolfe*, England, [2000] 1 WLR 1573, 1580, 1581, 1588; 119 ILR 367, 374, 376, 384; *Matthews* v. *Ministry*, England, [2003] 1 AC 1163, 1196; *Jones* v. *Saudi Arabia*, England, 2004, [2005] QB 699, 754, para. 104; 129 ILR 629, 704; *Roumania* v. *Pascalet*, France, (1924) 2 AD 132, 132; *Ceara* v. *Dorr*, France, (1928) 4 AD 39, 39; *Hertzfeld* v. *USSR*, France, (1933) 7 AD 184, 185; *Spanish* v. *Banco*, France, (1937) 8 AD 229, 231; *Roumanian* v. *Arricastre*, France, (1937) 8 AD 232, 233; *Socifros* v. *USSR*, France, (1938) 9 AD 236, 237–238; *Officina* v. *Domenech*, France, (1938) 9 AD 239, 240; *Roumania* v. *Aricastre*, France, (1949) 16 AD 138, 139; *Guggenheim* v. *Vietnam*, France, (1955) 22 ILR 224, 225; *USA* v. *Perignon*, France, (1962) 44 ILR 76, 76; *Chaussois* v. *La Tabacoop*, France, (1966) 47 ILR 152, 154; affirmed, *Société* v. *Chaussois*, France, (1969) 65 ILR 44; *Statni* v. *Englander*, France, (1966) 47 ILR 157, 161–162; *Red* v. *Mrs Cavaillé*, France, (1968) 65 ILR 41, 42; *Clerget* v. *Banque*, France, (1969) 52 ILR 310, 312; 315; affirmed, *Clerget* v. *Banque*, France, (1971) 65 ILR 54, 56; *Procureur* v. *SA Ipitrade*, France, (1978) 65 ILR 75, 76; *Procureur* v. *LIAMCO*, France, (1979) 65 ILR 78, 80; *Yugoslavia* v. *Société*, France, (1985) 82 ILR 58, 73; *L'Affaire du Département*, Germany, 1905, 34 *JDIP* (1907) 166, 167 (French translation); *In re Danish*, Germany, (1953) 20 ILR 178, 179; *Latvia Case*, Germany, (1953) 20 ILR 180, 181; affirmed, *Latvia Case*, Germany, (1955) 22 ILR 230; *X* v. *Argentina*, Germany, (1996) 114 ILR 502, 506; *Purchase of Embassy Staff Residence Case*, Greece, (1967) 65 ILR 255, 255, 257; *Margellos* v. *Germany*, Greece, (2002) 129 ILR 525, 532; *UAR* v. *Mirza*, India, (1961) 64 ILR 394, 401–402, 415–416; *Harbhajan* v. *India*, India, (1986) 92 ILR 530, 538; *Fusco* v. *O'Dea*, Ireland, [1994] 2 ILRM 389, 393; 103 ILR 318, 321; *Guttieres* v. *Elmilik*, Italy, 1886, 26 *AJIL Supplement* (1932) 622, 622; *Typaldos* v. *Manicomio*, Italy, 1886, 26 *AJIL Supplement* (1932) 623, 623; *Storelli* v. *French*, Italy, (1924) 2 AD 129, 129; *Harrie* v. *Steinmann*, Italy, (1927) 4 AD 364, 364; *Castiglioni* v. *Yugoslavia*, Italy, (1952) 19

514   NOTES TO PAGES 46–47

ILR 203, 206, 209, 210; *Borga* v. *Russian*, Italy, (1953) 22 ILR 235, 237–238; *Sovereign* v. *Soc*, Italy, (1954) 22 ILR 1, 4; *Francischiello* v. *USA*, Italy, (1959) 28 ILR 158, 160; *Ministry* v. *Association*, Italy, (1978) 65 ILR 320, 321, 322; *Libya* v. *SpA* Italy, (1979) 78 ILR 90, 92; *Italian* v. *US*, Italy, (1981) 65 ILR 338, 341; *France* v. *Jacuzio*, Italy, (1987) 87 ILR 53, 54–55; *USA* v. *Lo Gatto*, Italy, (1995) 114 ILR 555, 557; *Advokaat* v. *Schuddinck*, Netherlands, (1923) 2 AD 133, 133; *Poortensdijk* v. *Latvia*, Netherlands, (1941) 11 AD 142, 142; *Governor* v. *Sutton*, New Zealand, 1994, [1995] 1 NZLR 426, 428; 104 ILR 508, 509, 510; *USA* v. *Ruiz*, Philippines, (1985) 102 ILR 122, 124–125; *Trade* v. *Maurycy*, Poland, (1928) 4 AD 170, 171; *Leibowitz* v. *Schwartz*, South Africa, (1973) 64 ILR 672, 673; *Abbott* v. *South Africa*, Spain, (1992) 113 ILR 411, 417, 419, 422, 424; *Dreyfus*, Switzerland, (1918) BGE 44 I 49, 54; *S* v. *India*, Switzerland, (1984) 82 ILR 13, 18, Ground 3; *Ex parte Peru*, US, 318 US 578, 587 (1943); 10 AD 199, 202; *National* v. *Republic of China*, US, 348 US 356, 359, 362 (1955); 22 ILR 210, 211, 214; *Nevada* v. *Hall*, US, 440 US 410, 416 (1979); *Ruggiero* v. *Compania*, US, 639 F.2d 872, 878 (2nd Cir. 1981); 63 ILR 540; *Arango* v. *Guzman*, US, 761 F.2d 1527, 1534 (11th Cir. 1985); *Callejo* v. *Bancomer, SA*, US, 764 F.2d 1101, 1112 (5th Cir. 1985); *General* v. *Grossman*, US, 991 F.2d 1376, 1381 (8th Cir. 1993); *Borgships* v. *Macarena*, US, 1993 WL 278453, pp. 3–4 (E.D. La. 1993); *Gates* v. *Victor*, US, 54 F.3d 1457, 1466 (9th Cir. 1995); 107 ILR 371; *Belgrade* v. *Sidex*, US, 2 F.Supp.2d 407, 412 (S.D.N.Y. 1998); *Garb* v. *Poland*, US, 440 F.3d 579, 585 (2nd Cir. 2006); *Wahba* v. *National*, US, 457 F.Supp.2d 721, 729 (E.D. Tex. 2006); *Philippines* v. *Pimentel*, US, 128 S.Ct. 2180, 2189–2190 (2008); *Prosecutor* v. *Taylor*, Special Court for Sierra Leone, (2004) 128 ILR 239, 264, para. 51.

58 *Halsbury's Laws of England*, p. 794, para. 1548 (emphases added), quoted by Lord Hutton in *Pinochet No. 3*, England, 1999, [2000] 1 AC 147, 251–252; 119 ILR 135, 204–205 and referred to in *Governor* v. *Sutton*, New Zealand, 1994, [1995] 1 NZLR 426, 433; 104 ILR 508, 516–517. The proposition in the *Halsbury's* passage can be traced to, among others, Lord Reid's pronouncement in *Rahimtoola* v. *Nizam*, England, 1957, [1958] AC 379, 404; 24 ILR 175, 186. Lord Reid was quoted in *Controller* v. *Davison*, New Zealand, [1996] 2 NZLR 278, 304; 104 ILR 526, 576.

59 *Controller* v. *Davison*, New Zealand, [1996] 2 NZLR 278, 300 per Richardson J; 313 per Thomas J; 104 ILR 526, 570, 616 (emphases added).

60 *Distomo Massacre Case*, Greece, (2000) 129 ILR 513, 516 (emphases added).

61 See *Socobelge* v. *Greek*, Belgium, (1951) 18 ILR 3, 7–8; *Congo* v. *Venne*, Canada, (1971) 22 DLR (3d) 669, 684–685; 64 ILR 24, 39–40 per Laskin J, dissenting. For doubts on reciprocity see *USA* v. *Dollfus*, England, [1952] AC 582, 613; 19 ILR 163, 174; *Spanish State Tourist Office Case*, Germany, (1977) 65 ILR 140, 141; *UAR* v. *Mirza*, India, (1961) 64 ILR 394, 409–410; *McElhinney* v. *Williams*, Ireland, 1995, [1996] 1 ILRM 276, 289; 104 ILR 691, 703.

62 *Borga* v. *Russian*, Italy, (1953) 22 ILR 235, 237.

63 *Rahimtoola* v. *Nizam*, England, 1957, [1958] AC 379, 418 per Lord Denning; 24 ILR 175, 196–197.

NOTES TO PAGES 47–48   515

64 *I Congreso del Partido*, England, 1981, [1983] 1 AC 244, 262 per Lord Wilberforce; 64 ILR 307, 313–314. See also *Reid* v. *Nauru*, Australia, 1992, [1993] 1 VR 251, 252; 101 ILR 193, 194; *Re Canada Labour Code*, Canada, 1989, [1990] 1 FC 332, 338; 86 ILR 626, 629; *Re Canada Labour Code*, Canada, (1992) 91 DLR (4th) 449, 462; 94 ILR 264, 277; *Alcom* v. *Colombia*, England, [1984] 1 AC 580, 598; 74 ILR 170, 180–181; *Kuwait Airways* v. *Iraqi Airways*, England, [1995] 1 WLR 1147, 1157; 103 ILR 340, 398; *Buckingham* v. *Aircraft*, New Zealand, [1982] 2 NZLR 738, 739; 64 ILR 551; *Reef* v. *Fua Kavenga*, New Zealand, [1987] 1 NZLR 550, 570; 90 ILR 556; *Governor* v. *Sutton*, New Zealand, 1994, [1995] 1 NZLR 426, 435; 104 ILR 508, 520; *Controller* v. *Davison*, New Zealand, [1996] 2 NZLR 278, 300; 104 ILR 526, 570; *Forth* v. *Wilmington*, Scotland, 1985, 1985 SC 317, 327; 1987 SLT 153, 158; 107 ILR 641, 651–652; *Barker* v. *Kenya*, Zimbabwe, (1983/1985) 84 ILR 18, 33. On dignity see also *Trendtex* v. *Central Bank*, England, [1977] QB 529, 576; 64 ILR 111, 150; *Mariam* v. *Aziz*, England, [2007] Fam Law 1047, paras. 62–98; *Controller* v. *Davison*, New Zealand, [1996] 2 NZLR 278, 318; 104 ILR 526, 623.

65 *Holland* v. *Lampen-Wolfe*, England, [2000] 1 WLR 1573, 1583 per Lord Millett; 119 ILR 367, 378.

66 *USA* v. *Ruiz*, Philippines, (1985) 102 ILR 122, 128 per Makasiar J, dissenting.

67 *Barker* v. *Kenya*, Zimbabwe, (1983) (4) SA 817, 820 per Georges JA; 84 ILR 18, 22. See also *Purchase of Embassy Staff Residence Case*, Greece, (1967) 65 ILR 255, 257; *Her Majesty* v. *Edelson*, Israel, (1997) 131 ILR 279, 298.

68 The Declaration on Principles of International Law concerning Friendly Relations and Co-operation among States in accordance with the Charter of the United Nations, GA Resolution 2625 (XXV) of 24 October 1970, Annex, Principle 6, 'Sovereign equality of States'. The UN Charter uses 'sovereign equality' instead of 'sovereignty' (Arts. 2(1) and 78).

69 Jennings and Watts (eds.), *Oppenheim's International Law*, p. 339; Daillier *et al.*, *Droit international public*, p. 472.

70 Arbitrator Huber, *Island of Palmas Case*, (1928) 2 RIAA 829, 838; *Municipality* v. *Fraser-Brace*, Canada, (1958) 13 DLR (2d) 177, 181; 26 ILR 165, 168; Lauterpacht (ed.), *Oppenheim's International Law*, p. 286; Starke, *Introduction*, p. 100; Shearer, *Starke's International Law*, pp. 90–91. Cf. *Duff* v. *Kelantan*, England, [1924] AC 797, 814; 2 AD 124, 127 (complete independence not necessary for sovereignty).

71 *Société anonyme Compagnie des chemins de fer Liégeois Limbourgeois* v. *Etat Néerlandais*, Belgium, 1903, 31 *JDIP* (1904) 417, 427; *Rousseau* v. *Upper Volta*, Belgium, (1983) 82 ILR 118, 120; *Roumania* v. *Pascalet*, France, (1924) 2 AD 132, 132; *Dumont* v. *Amazonas*, France, (1948) 15 AD 140, 141.

72 *Duff* v. *Kelantan*, England, [1924] AC 797, 814; 2 AD 124, 127; *The Arantzazu Mendi*, England, [1938] P 233, 248; 9 AD 60, 62; Dupuy and Kerbrat, *Droit international public*, p. 31.

73 *UAR* v. *Mirza*, India, (1961) 64 ILR 394, 402 and 406; Daillier *et al.*, *Droit international public*, pp. 466–467; Shaw, *International Law*, p. 211.

74 *Margellos* v. *Germany*, Greece, (2002) 129 ILR 525, 532.

516   NOTES TO PAGES 48-52

75 Jennings and Watts, *Oppenheim's International Law*, p. 125. See also the Declaration on Principles of International Law, Principle 6, 'Sovereign equality of States'.

76 *The Parlement Belge*, England, (1880) 5 PD 197, 206, 207, 209; *Municipality v. Fraser-Brace*, Canada, (1958) 13 DLR (2d) 177, 191; 26 ILR 165, 174.

77 Note that this is very much a simplistic description for the sake of clarity of argument. The actual practice is much more complex and tends to show that the imposition of an external will that may restrict sovereignty is highly possible. Article 2(6) of the UN Charter, for example, provides that the UN 'shall ensure that states which are not Members of the United Nations act in accordance with these Principles so far as may be necessary for the maintenance of international peace and security'. However, even if that be the case, it does not affect the conclusion here about the nature of immunity as doctrinally approached.

78 Council of Europe, *Explanatory Reports*, p. 5, para. 1.

79 *Al-Adsani v. UK*, ECHR, 2001, (2002) 34 EHRR 11, para. 54; 123 ILR 24, 40; *Fogarty v. UK*, ECHR, 2001, (2002) 34 EHRR 12, para. 34; 123 ILR 53, 65; *McElhinney v. Ireland*, ECHR, 2001, (2002) 34 EHRR 13, para. 35; 123 ILR 73, 84–85; *Kalogeropoulou v. Greece*, ECHR, (2002) 129 ILR 537, 546.

80 See *Prosecutor v. Blåskić*, ICTY, (1997) 110 ILR 607, 710, para. 41; *Prosecutor v. Krstić*, ICTY, 2003, Case IT-98-33-A, para. 25; *Arrest Warrant*, ICJ, Joint Separate Opinion of Judges Higgins, Kooijmans and Buergenthal, para. 72; Dissenting Opinion of Judge Al-Khasawneh, para. 7; Dissenting Opinion of Judge van den Wyngaert, para. 23; 2002 *ICJ Reports* 3, 84, 98, 151; 128 ILR 1, 140, 153, 204; *Lechouritou v. Dimosio*, ECJ, Case C-292/05, [2007] ILPr 14, 216 at 234–235, Advocate General's Opinion, para. 76.

81 See ILC, Report, 1978, Annex to Chapter VIII-D, Report of the Working Group on jurisdictional immunities of States and their property, *YILC*, 1978-II-2, p. 153 ('Thus, State immunity is sometimes expressed in the maxim *par in parem imperium non habet.*').

82 Dinstein, Par, 408–409. Dinstein argues that State immunity cannot in theory stem from the *par* principle.

83 Recent studies hold it more likely that Dante quoted his maxim from the Accursian *Gloss* rather than directly from Pope Innocent III's decretal, see Kantorowicz, *The King's*, p. 452, fn. 4 (also enumerating some variants of the axiom).

84 Dante, *Monarchy*, Book I, 10, Nicholl (trans.), p. 14. The original Latin text can be found at http://www.greatdante.net/texts.html. For another English translation see Dante, *Monarchy*, Shaw (trans.), 1996.

85 See Dante, *Monarchy*, Book I, 5–15, Nicholl (trans.), pp. 9–26. Although we must take the word 'mankind' with a grain of salt, for it is clear from the context that 'mankind' here refers only to those living under the Roman Empire, to the exclusion of, say, those in the Far East, who were living under another vast empire at that time. See Book I, 16, p. 26. However, this hardly undermines Dante's thesis of bringing mankind under one mammoth world

government headed by a monarch who alone is 'the purest incarnation of justice' (Book I, 11, p. 17).

86 See, e.g., Locke, *Two Treatises*, pp. 269, 272, 277, 280, ch. II, paras. 4, 7, 14 and ch. III, para. 19.

87 It seems that the first *lawyer* to cite this maxim was Bartolus de Saxoferrato (1313–1357), in his *Tractatus Represaliarum* (1354), Questio I/3, para. 10: see Badr, *State Immunity*, p. 89, where Bartolus is identified as the *author* of this maxim. The idea that Bartolus is the *originator* of the maxim can be traced to Verdross, see Lowenfeld, Claims, 930, fn. 85 (citing Verdross, *Völkerrecht*); Mesch, Jurisdictional, 1228, fn. 17 and Martin, Sovereign, 431, fn. 11. See also Steinberger, State Immunity, pp. 615, 616.

88 Hartmann, De la Compétence, 426 (*Par in parem non habet judicium*), cited in Dinstein, Par, 410–411, fn. 17.

89 Von Bar explained this adage as signifying that 'l'idée de la souveraineté ne permet pas qu'une souveraineté soit soumise à l'autre'. This is to say, it is another way of stating the sovereignty principle. The other three grounds were: (1) traditional jurisprudence; (2) the impossibility of enforcing a judgment against a foreign State or foreign sovereign; and (3) the fear that international relations might be disturbed. Von Bar, Report, 414. He further pointed out that the 'traditional jurisprudence' did not exist. *Ibid.*, p. 415. The enumeration at once of several grounds for immunity became a pattern for later authorities. Starke, for example, lists five grounds: (1) *Par in parem non habet imperium*; (2) reciprocity or comity; (3) unenforceability of domestic judgments against a foreign State; (4) implied concession not to exercise territorial jurisdiction; and (5) foreign policy considerations. Shearer, *Starke's International Law*, p. 192.

90 Von Bar, Report, 415. See also von Bar, *Theorie und Praxis*, pp. 660 *et seq.* In an ancient English case, the maxim '*Par in parem non habet imperium*' appeared as a principle of international law denoting that 'One justice of the peace cannot commit another justice of the peace, for breach of the peace.' *Anonymous*, 3 H 7 (1487), 145 ER 115. For a modern example of *par in parem* being invoked in criminal proceedings see *Attorney-General* v. *Eichmann*, Israel, (1961) 36 ILR 5, 45–46, para. 28.

91 *US* v. *Mora*, US, 821 F.2d 860, 866, fn. 5 (1st Cir. 1987) (concerning the admissibility of evidence obtained through wiretapping).

92 *Texas Trading* v. *Nigeria*, US, 647 F.2d 300, 302 (2nd Cir. 1981); 63 ILR 552, 553.

93 For early scholars who referred to the *par* axiom see the authors cited by Dinstein, Par, 410–411, fn. 17.

94 *Al-Adsani* v. *UK*, ECHR, 2001, (2002) 34 EHRR 11, para. 54; 123 ILR 24, 40; *Fogarty* v. *UK*, ECHR 2001, (2002) 34 EHRR 12, para. 34; 123 ILR 53, 65; *McElhinney* v. *Ireland*, ECHR, 2001, (2002) 34 EHRR 13, para. 35; 123 ILR 73, 84; *Kalogeropoulou* v. *Greece*, ECHR, 2002, Decision on Admissibility, 'The Law', para. 1, Section D.1.(a); *City of Ottawa*, Canada, (1943) 2 DLR 481, 501; 10 AD 337, 345; *Yin-Tso* v. *Toronto*, Canada, (1950) 4 DLR 209, 215; 17 ILR 153; *Schreiber* v. *Germany*, Canada, (2002) 216 DLR (4th) 513, 523; *The Cristina*, England, [1938] AC 485,

518   NOTES TO PAGE 54

502; 9 AD 250, 254; *Pinochet No. 3*, England, 1999, [2000] 1 AC 147, 210, 222, 268; 119 ILR 135, 162, 174, 222; *Holland* v. *Lampen-Wolfe*, England, [2000] 1 WLR 1573, 1580, 1583; 119 ILR 367, 374, 378; *Matthews* v. *Ministry*, England, [2003] 1 AC 1163, 1196; *Jones* v. *Saudi Arabia*, England, 2006, [2007] 1 AC 270, 283, para. 14; 129 ILR 629, 720; *Margellos* v. *Germany*, Greece, (2002) 129 ILR 525, 530; *UAR* v. *Mirza*, India, (1961) 64 ILR 394, 401, 416; *Canada* v. *Burke*, Ireland, [1992] 2 IR 484, 495; 95 ILR 467, 476; *Harrie* v. *Steinmann*, Italy, (1927) 4 AD 364, 364; *Bolivia* v. *Italian*, Italy, (1948) 15 AD 133, 136; *Castiglioni* v. *Yugoslavia*, Italy, (1952) 19 ILR 203, 206, 209; *Greece* v. *Gamet*, Italy, (1957) 24 ILR 209, 210; *Hungarian* v. *Hungarian*, Italy, (1960) 40 ILR 59, 62; *US* v. *Bracale*, Italy, (1968) 65 ILR 273, 274; *Italian* v. *US*, Italy, (1981) 65 ILR 338, 340; *Air* v. *Director*, New Zealand, [2002] 3 NZLR 796, para. 56; *USA* v. *Guinto; USA* v. *Ceballos; USA* v. *Rodrigo*, Philippines, (1990) 102 ILR 132, 139; *Abbott* v. *South Africa*, Spain, (1992) 113 ILR 411, 419. In two English cases concerning diplomatic immunities the maxim was also cited, an indication that State immunity and diplomatic immunities are sometimes treated as of kindred origin: *Ghosh* v. *D'Rozario*, England, 1962, [1963] 1 QB 106, 116; 33 ILR 361; *Radwan* v. *Radwan*, England, 1972, [1973] Fam 24, 31; 55 ILR 579.

95 *Manauta* v. *Embassy*, Argentina, (1994) 113 ILR 429, 431; *Syria* v. *Egypt*, Brazil, (1982) 91 ILR 288, 298, 302; *Harbhajan* v. *India*, India, (1986) 92 ILR 530, 538; *Slomnitzky* v. *Trade*, Italy, (1932) 6 AD 169, 169; *Tani* v. *Russian*, Italy, (1947) 15 AD 141, 144; *Scarfò* v. *Sovereign*, Italy, (1957) 24 ILR 1, 4; *Francischiello* v. *USA*, Italy, (1959) 28 ILR 158, 160, 162; *Mallaval* v. *French*, Italy, (1974) 65 ILR 303, 306; *Association* v. *Piccoli*, Italy, (1974) 65 ILR 308, 309; *Bruno* v. *US*, Italy, (1977) 65 ILR 316, 317; *Bari* v. *Jasbez*, Italy, (1977) 77 ILR 602, 604; *Ministry* v. *Association*, Italy, (1978) 65 ILR 320, 321; *HAFSE* v. *Sindicato*, Italy, (1978) 77 ILR 630, 633; *Danish* v. *Hansen*, Italy, (1979) 65 ILR 325, 326; *Libya* v. *SpA*, Italy, (1979) 78 ILR 90, 92; *Special* v. *Pieciukiewicz*, Italy, (1982) 78 ILR 120, 121; *Food* v. *INPDAI*, Italy, (1982) 87 ILR 1, 7; *Cristiani* v. *Italian*, Italy, (1985) 87 ILR 20, 23, 24, 26; *Mininni* v. *Bari*, Italy, (1986) 87 ILR 28, 34–35; *France* v. *Jacuzio*, Italy, (1987) 87 ILR 53, 54; *Norwegian* v. *Quattri*, Italy, (1991) 114 ILR 525, 527; *Perrini* v. *Académie*, Italy, (1994) 114 ILR 536, 538; *Nacci* v. *Bari*, Italy, (1994) 114 ILR 539, 551; *USA* v. *Lo Gatto*, Italy, (1995) 114 ILR 555, 557; *Canada* v. *Cargnello*, Italy, (1998) 114 ILR 559, 567; *European* v. *Piette*, Italy, 1999, 9 *Italian YIL* (1999) 155, 156; *FILT-CGIL* v. *USA*, Italy, (2000) 128 ILR 644, 647; *Borri* v. *Repubblica*, Italy, 2005, 88 RDI (2005) 856, 857; *Indonesia* v. *Van der Haas*, Netherlands, (1958) 26 ILR 181, 181; *Brazilian Embassy Employee Case*, Portugal, (1984) 116 ILR 625, 627; *Libya* v. *LIAMCO*, Switzerland, (1980) 62 ILR 228, 233, Ground 3(a); *Swissair* v. *X*, Switzerland, (1985) 82 ILR 36, 37; *A* v. *B*, Switzerland, (2003) BGE 130 III 136, 141; *Saudi Arabia* v. *ARAMCO*, Arbitration, (1958) 27 ILR 117, 155; *Texaco* v. *Libya*, Arbitration, (1977) 53 ILR 389, 433.

96 *Philippine Embassy Bank Account Case*, Germany, (1977) 65 ILR 146, 157, Ground A.II.2; *S* v. *British*, Poland, (1948) 24 ILR 223, 224.

97 *Zucca* v. *Fondazione*, Italy, (1969) 65 ILR 280, 281.

98 *I Congreso del Partido*, England, 1981, [1983] 1 AC 244, 262; 64 ILR 307, 313; *Maclaine* v. *Department*, England, [1989] Ch 72, 199–200; [1988] 3 WLR 1033; 80 ILR 47, 125; *Holland* v. *Lampen-Wolfe*, England, [2000] 1 WLR 1573, 1579; 119 ILR 367, 373; *Reef* v. *Fua Kavenga*, New Zealand, [1987] 1 NZLR 550, 570; 90 ILR 556, 563; *Reid* v. *Nauru*, Australia, 1992, [1993] 1 VR 251, 252; 101 ILR 193, 194; *Arrest Warrant*, ICJ, Dissenting Opinion of Judge van den Wyngaert, para. 23, 2002 *ICJ Reports* 3, 151; 128 ILR 1, 204.

99 See *The Ditta* v. *Germany*, Italy, (1960) 40 ILR 64, 66: 'since in international law *par in parem non habet imperium*, it follows that … *par in parem non habet judicium*'.

100 Harvard Research, 527; *Philippine Embassy Bank Account Case*, Germany, (1977) 65 ILR 146, 157, Ground A.II.2.

101 *The Cristina*, England, [1938] AC 485, 502; 9 AD 250, 254; *Ghosh* v. *D'Rozario*, England, 1962, [1963] 1 QB 106, 116; 33 ILR 361; *I Congreso del Partido*, England, 1981, [1983] 1 AC 244, 262; 64 ILR 307, 313; *Maclaine* v. *Department*, England, 1988, [1989] Ch 72, 199; 80 ILR 47, 125; *Slomnitzky* v. *Trade*, Italy, (1932) 6 AD 169, 169; *Bolivia* v. *Italian*, Italy, (1948) 15 AD 133, 136; *Scarfò* v. *Sovereign*, Italy, (1957) 24 ILR 1, 4; *Greece* v. *Gamet*, Italy, (1957) 24 ILR 209, 211; *Hungarian* v. *Hungarian*, Italy, (1960) 40 ILR 59, 62; *The Ditta* v. *Germany*, Italy, (1960) 40 ILR 64, 66; *Mallaval* v. *French*, Italy, (1974) 65 ILR 303, 306; *Danish* v. *Hansen*, Italy, (1979) 65 ILR 325, 326; *Italian* v. *US*, Italy, (1981) 65 ILR 338, 340; *Mininni* v. *Bari*, Italy, (1986) 87 ILR 28, 34–35; *France* v. *Jacuzio*, Italy, (1987) 87 ILR 53, 54; *USA* v. *Lo Gatto*, Italy, (1995) 114 ILR 555, 557; *Reid* v. *Nauru*, Australia, 1992, [1993] 1 VR 251, 252; 101 ILR 193, 194; *Reef* v. *Fua Kavenga*, New Zealand, [1987] 1 NZLR 550, 570; 90 ILR 556, 563; *Swissair* v. *X*, Switzerland, (1985) 82 ILR 36, 37.

102 *UAR* v. *Mirza*, India, (1961) 64 ILR 394, 416; *Harbhajan* v. *India*, India, (1986) 92 ILR 530, 538; *Harrie* v. *Steinmann*, Italy, (1927) 4 AD 364, 364; *S* v. *British*, Poland, (1948) 24 ILR 223, 224; *Texas Trading* v. *Nigeria*, US, 647 F.2d 300, 303, fn. 1 (2nd Cir. 1981); 63 ILR 552, 554; *US* v. *Mora*, US, 821 F.2d 860, 866, fn. 5 (1st Cir. 1987).

103 *Brazilian Embassy Employee Case*, Portugal, (1984) 116 ILR 625, 627.

104 *Ministry* v. *Association*, Italy, (1978) 65 ILR 320, 321.

105 *Schreiber* v. *Germany*, Canada, [2002] 3 SCR 269, 280; (2002) 216 DLR (4th) 513, 523; *Castiglioni* v. *Yugoslavia*, Italy, (1952) 19 ILR 203, 206; *Francischiello* v. *USA*, Italy, (1959) 28 ILR 158, 160; *USA* v. *Guinto*; *USA* v. *Ceballos*; *USA* v. *Rodrigo*, Philippines, (1990) 102 ILR 132, 139; *Abbott* v. *South Africa*, Spain, (1992) 113 ILR 411, 419. See also ILC, Report, 1991, *YILC*, 1991-II-2, p. 12 at 56.

106 *Libya* v. *SpA*, Italy, (1979) 78 ILR 90, 92.

107 Daillier *et al.*, *Droit international public*, p. 497; Brownlie, *Principles*, p. 325; Pingel-Lenuzza, *Les immunités*, pp. 38–39; Cosnard, *La soumission des États*, p. 76; Jennings and Watts (eds.), *Oppenheim's*, p. 341; ALI, *Third Restatement*, p. 438; Centres de Droit International, *L'Immunité*, p. 120; Lauterpacht (ed.), *Oppenheim's*, p. 264; Kelsen, *Principles*, p. 235; Hafner and Köhler, The United Nations, 4; Hafner and Lange, La Convention, 45; Prevost, Does Immunity,

520   NOTES TO PAGES 55–60

119; Sucharitkul, Immunities, 117; Lalive, L'Immunité, 213; Kropholler, *Internationales Privatrecht*, p. 581.

108 Steinberger, State Immunity, pp. 615, 616; Von Bar, Report, 414.

109 Fox, *The Law of State Immunity*, p. 57.

110 Dupuy and Kerbrat, *Droit international public*, p. 142; Fox, *The Law*, p. 57; Chamlongrasdr, *Foreign State Immunity*, p. 66; Cassese, *International Law*, p. 98; Bankas, *The State Immunity*, p. 7; Vibhute, *International Commercial Arbitration*, p. 3; Shearer, *Starke's*, p. 192; quoted in *Canada* v. *Burke*, Ireland, 1992, [1992] 2 IR 484, 495; 95 ILR 467, 476; Sinclair, The Law, 198; Harvard Research, 527.

111 Stewart, The UN, 195; Lalive, Quelques, p. 369; Badr, *State Immunity*, p. 89; Martin, Sovereign, 431, fn. 11; Lowenfeld, Claims, 930; Collins (gen. ed.), *Conflict of Laws*, p. 273, Rule 19, para. 10.002.

112 Compare *City of Ottawa*, Canada, (1943) 2 DLR 481, 501; 10 AD 337, 345 (independence) and *Yin-Tso* v. *Toronto*, Canada, (1950) 4 DLR 209, 215 with *Schreiber* v. *Germany*, Canada, (2002) 216 DLR (4th) 513, 523 (equality).

113 *UAR* v. *Mirza*, India, (1961) 64 ILR 394, 401 per Lahiri CJ (sovereignty), 416 per Bachawa J (equality).

114 *I Congreso del Partido*, England, 1981, [1983] 1 AC 244, 262; 64 ILR 307, 313. See also *Holland* v. *Lampen-Wolfe*, England, [2000] 1 WLR 1573, 1579, 1580; 119 ILR 367, 373, 374; *Air* v. *Director*, New Zealand, [2002] 3 NZLR 796, para. 56.

115 *Pinochet No. 3*, England, 1999, [2000] 1 AC 147, 210; 119 ILR 135, 162.

116 *Pinochet No. 3*, England, 1999, [2000] 1 AC 147, 268; 119 ILR 135, 222; *Holland* v. *Lampen-Wolfe*, England, [2000] 1 WLR 1573, 1583; 119 ILR 367, 378; *Matthews* v. *Ministry*, UK, [2003] 1 AC 1163, 1196.

117 US House of Representatives, Report No. 94-1487, 1976, p. 31; 1976 USCCAN 6604, 6630; cited as a 'more compelling reason' for granting immunity in *All* v. *Cuartel*, US, 818 F.Supp. 1552, 1556 (S.D. Fla. 1993).

118 In 1997, such an order was made to deny immunity to legal entities not majority-owned by the US government or a political subdivision of the US: Order Restricting Certain Immunity in Relation to the United States, SOR/ 97-121, PC 1997-242, February 18, 1997. For similar provisions see UK SIA, s. 15(1); Singapore SIA, s. 17; Pakistan SIO, s. 16; South Africa FSIA, s. 16; Australia FSIA, s. 42. See also the Australia Foreign States Immunities Amendment Act 2009.

119 See *Emilio* v. *Embassy*, Spain, (1986) 86 ILR 508, 511 and *Diana* v. *South Africa*, Spain, (1986) 86 ILR 512, 516, where reciprocity was treated as a basis of execution.

120 See *USA* v. *Dollfus*, England, [1952] AC 582, 613; 19 ILR 163, 174; *McElhinney* v. *Williams*, Ireland, 1995, [1996] 1 ILRM 276, 288–289; 104 ILR 691, 703; *Central Bank of Nigeria Case*, Germany, (1975/1976) 65 ILR 131, 136; *Spanish State Tourist Office Case*, Germany, (1977) 65 ILR 140, 141.

121 *The Schooner Exchange* v. *M'Faddon*, US, 11 US (7 Cranch) 116, 123 (1812).

122 Royer, case note on *Gouvernement espagnol* v. *Veuve*, Dalloz, 1867-II-49. This remark no doubt inspired the observations in, e.g., *Guttieres* v. *Elmilik*, Italy,

NOTES TO PAGES 60–62   521

1886, 26 *AJIL Supplement* (1932) 622, 622 and *Rahimtoola* v. *Nizam*, England, 1957, [1958] AC 379, 395 per Viscount Simonds ('descend into the arena'); 24 ILR 175, 179.

123 *Morellet* v. *Governo Danese*, Italy, 1882, 26 *AJIL Supplement* (1932) 481 at 481–482, see also 595 at 596.

124 *Guttieres* v. *Elmilik*, Italy, 1886, 26 *AJIL Supplement* (1932) 622, 622. For the 'private person' test in the Italian courts see also *Rumania* v. *Trutta*, Italy, 1926, 26 *AJIL Supplement* (1932) 626, 628–629; *Russian* v. *Kazmann*, Italy, (1933) 7 AD 178, 178; *Tani* v. *Russian*, Italy, (1947) 15 AD 141, 144; *Padri* v. *Nunzi*, Italy, (1957) 24 ILR 214, 215; *Ciniglio* v. *Indonesian*, Italy, (1966) 65 ILR 268, 269; *Ministry* v. *Federici*, Italy, (1968) 65 ILR 275, 278; *Luna* v. *Romania*, Italy, (1974) 65 ILR 313, 314; *Borri* v. *Repubblica*, Italy, 2005, 88 RDI (2005) 856, 858.

125 *Société* v. *Ministre*, Belgium, 1888, Pasicrisie Belge, 1889-III-62; Allen, *Position*, p. 193; Sucharitkul, *State Immunities*, pp. 244–245.

126 *Société anonyme Compagnie des chemins de fer Liégeois Limbourgeois* v. *Etat Néerlandais*, Belgium, 1903, 31 *JDIP* (1904) 417, 427 (emphases added). For subsequent cases see *Société* v. *Belgian*, Belgium, (1925) 3 AD 169, 170; *Société Monnoyer* v. *France*, Belgium, (1927) 4 AD 177, 177–178; *Brasseur* v. *Greece*, Belgium, (1933) 6 AD 164, 169; *Socobelge* v. *Greek*, Belgium, (1951) 18 ILR 3, 6; *De Decker* v. *USA*, Belgium, (1956) 23 ILR 209, 210; *Castanheira* v. *Commercial*, Belgium, (1980) 82 ILR 100, 102; *Rousseau* v. *Upper Volta*, Belgium, (1983) 82 ILR 118, 120; *SA Biocare* v. *Gécamines*, Belgium, (1989) 115 ILR 415, 418; *François* v. *Canada*, Belgium, (1989) 115 ILR 418, 419; *Morocco* v. *DR*, (1989) 115 ILR 421, 421; *De Queiroz* v. *Portugal*, Belgium, (1992) 115 ILR 430, 433–434; *Rafidain* v. *Consarc*, Belgium, (1993) 106 ILR 274, 277; *Iraq* v. *Dumez*, Belgium, (1995) 106 ILR 284, 291; *Iraq* v. *Vinci*, Belgium, (2002) 127 ILR 101, 105–106.

127 *Empire of Iran Case*, Germany, (1963) 45 ILR 57, 80 (emphasis added). See also *In re Danish*, Germany, (1953) 20 ILR 178, 179; *Latvia Case*, Germany, (1955) 22 ILR 230, 231–232; *Conrades* v. *UK*, Germany, (1981) 65 ILR 205, 207.

128 *Steinmetz* v. *Hungarian*, Austria, (1970) 65 ILR 15, 19.

129 US House of Representatives, Report No. 94-1487, 1976, p. 14; 1976 USCCAN 6604, 6613. See also p. 16/6615.

130 *Texas Trading.* v. *Nigeria*, US, 647 F.2d 300, 309 (2nd Cir. 1981); 63 ILR 552. See also *International* v. *OPEC*, US, 649 F.2d 1354, 1357 (9th Cir. 1981); 66 ILR 413; *Velidor* v. *L/P/G*, US, 653 F.2d 812, 817 n. 7 (3rd Cir. 1981); 63 ILR 622; *Letelier* v. *Chile*, US, 748 F.2d 790, 797 (2nd Cir. 1984); 79 ILR 561; *Callejo* v. *Bancomer*, US, 764 F.2d 1101, 1108, fn. 6, 1109, 1110, 1116 (5th Cir. 1985); 84 ILR 106; *De Sanchez* v. *Banco*, US, 770 F.2d 1385, 1394 (5th Cir. 1985); 88 ILR 75; *West* v. *Multibanco*, US, 807 F.2d 820, 825 (9th Cir. 1987); 84 ILR 187; *Practical* v. *Bolivia*, US, 811 F.2d 1543, 1549 (D.C. Cir. 1987); 92 ILR 420; *Meadows* v. *Dominican*, US, 817 F.2d 517, 523 (9th Cir. 1987); 98 ILR 37; *Joseph* v. *Office*, US, 830 F.2d 1018, 1024 (9th Cir. 1987); 101 ILR 485; *Segni* v. *Commercial*, US, 835 F.2d 160, 164 (7th Cir. 1987); 98 ILR 55; *Gould* v. *Pechiney*, US, 853 F.2d 445, 452 (6th Cir. 1988); 98 ILR 136.

131 *Rush-Presbyterian* v. *Hellenic*, US, 877 F.2d 574, 578 (7th Cir. 1989); 101 ILR 509 (emphasis in the original).

522   NOTES TO PAGES 62-63

132 *Alfred Dunhill* v. *Cuba*, US, 425 US 682, 704 (1976); 66 ILR 212, 225; later quoted in *Argentina* v. *Weltover*, US, 504 US 607, 614 (1992); 119 L.Ed.2d 394, 405 (1992); 100 ILR 509, 515 and *Saudi Arabia* v. *Nelson*, US, 507 US 349, 360 (1993); 123 L.Ed.2d 47, 61; 100 ILR 544, 553.

133 *Argentina* v. *Weltover*, US, 504 US 607, 614 (1992); 119 L.Ed.2d 394, 405 (1992); 100 ILR 509, 515 (emphasis in the original). See also *Saudi Arabia* v. *Nelson*, US, 507 US 349, 360–361 (1993); 123 L.Ed.2d 47, 60–61 (1993); 100 ILR 544, 553 (quoting *Alfred Dunhill* and *Weltover*); ALI, *Third Restatement*, p. 396. Cf. US FSIA, s. 1606: 'As to any claim for relief with respect to which a foreign state is not entitled to immunity under section 1605 or 1607 of this chapter, the foreign state shall be liable in the same manner and to the same extent as a private individual under like circumstances.' See *Verlinden* v. *Central Bank*, US, 461 US 480, 488–489 (1983); 79 ILR 548, 554. The numerous lower courts' decisions enthusiastically following the Supreme Court are not cited here. For commentary see Thomas, Two Faces; Orlando, *Republic*; Schano, The Scattered; Leacock, The Joy; Morrissey, Simplifying. See also *USA* v. *Ruiz*, Philippines, (1985) 102 ILR 122, 126.

134 *I Congreso del Partido*, England, 1977, [1978] 1 QB 500, 528; 64 ILR 154, 179. Lord Goff later repeated his proposition in *Kuwait Airways* v. *Iraqi Airways*, England, [1995] 1 WLR 1147, 1160; 103 ILR 340, 401. See also *Planmount* v. *Zaire*, England, [1980] 2 Lloyd's Rep 393; 64 ILR 268, 271–272.

135 *I Congreso del Partido*, England, 1981, [1983] 1 AC 244, 262; ILR 307, 314; quoted in *Reid* v. *Nauru*, Australia, 1992, [1993] 1 VR 251, 252; 101 ILR 193, 194; *Controller* v. *Davison*, New Zealand, [1996] 2 NZLR 278, 300; 104 ILR 526, 570; *Governor* v. *Sutton*, New Zealand, 1994, [1995] 1 NZLR 426, 435; 104 ILR 508, 520. See also *Alcom* v. *Colombia*, England, [1984] 1 AC 580, 597–598; 74 ILR 170, 180.

136 *Kuwait Airways* v. *Iraqi Airways*, England, [1995] 1 WLR 1147, 1160; 103 ILR 340, 401; quoted in *Ministry* v. *Tsavliris*, England, 2008, [2008] 2 Lloyd's Rep 90, 105, para. 79. See also *A Company* v. *Republic of X*, England, 1989, [1990] 2 Lloyd's Rep 520, 523; 87 ILR 412, 415; *Kuwait Airways* v. *Iraqi Airways*, England, 1993, [1995] 1 Lloyd's Rep 25, 29, 33, 35; 1995, [1995] 1 WLR 1147, 1160, 1173; 103 ILR 340, 372, 381, 385, 401, 417; *A Limited* v. *B Bank*, England, 1996, [1997] FSR 165, 171; 111 ILR 590, 596–597; *Propend* v. *Sing*, England, (1997) 111 ILR 611, 667; *Holland* v. *Lampen-Wolfe*, England, [2000] 1 WLR 1573, 1579; 119 ILR 367, 374; *In re Banco*, England, [2001] 3 All ER 923, 934; [2001] 1 WLR 2039, 2051; 124 ILR 550, 561; *Kuwait Airways* v. *Iraqi Airways*, England, [2003] 1 Lloyd's Rep 448, 468, para. 150; 126 ILR 758, 798; *Svenska* v. *Lithuania (No. 2)*, England, 2006, [2007] QB 886, 929, para. 132; *Bouzari* v. *Iran*, Canada, (2002) 124 ILR 427, 435; *Governor* v. *Sutton*, New Zealand, 1994, [1995] 1 NZLR 426, 435; 104 ILR 508, 520; *Controller* v. *Davison*, New Zealand, [1996] 2 NZLR 278, 288, 289, 301, 311, 312; 104 ILR 526, 537, 538, 571, 612, 613, 614.

137 See *Représentation Commerciale*, Brazil, 1989, noted in 126 *JDI* (1999) 451, 452; *Petrococchino* v. *Swedish*, France, (1929) 5 AD 306, 307; *Roumanian* v. *Arricastre*, France, (1937) 8 AD 232, 233; *Officina* v. *Domenech*, France, (1938) 9 AD 239,

240; *Salabert* v. *USA*, France, (1956) 23 ILR 192, 194; *Société Immobilière* v. *USA*, France, (1960) 42 ILR 123, 124; *Société Bauer-Marchal* v. *Gouvernement*, France, (1965) 47 ILR 155, 156; *Spanish* v. *Société*, France, (1973) 65 ILR 61, 62; *Société Européenne* v. *World Bank*, France, (1984) 82 ILR 58, 65; *Mouracade* v. *Yemen*, France, (1991) 113 ILR 462, 463; *Congo* v. *Syndicat*, France, 2005, 95 *RCDIP* (2006) 123, 125; *Soviet Republic Case*, Greece, (1928) 4 AD 172, 172 (affirmed by the Areopagus (Supreme Court) on appeal: Areopagus, No. 29, Themis, Vol. 40, p. 842); *Purchase of Embassy Staff Residence Case*, Greece, (1967) 65 ILR 255, 257; *Distomo Massacre Case*, Greece, (2000) 129 ILR 513, 517; *Her Majesty* v. *Edelson*, Israel, (1997) 131 ILR 279, 306; *Société Européenne* v. *Yugoslavia*, Netherlands, (1973) 65 ILR 356, 361; *ICC* v. *USSR*, Netherlands, (1976) 65 ILR 368, 369; *Parsons* v. *Malta*, Netherlands, (1977) 65 ILR 371, 372; *Morocco* v. *Stichting*, Netherlands, (1978) 65 ILR 375, 376; *De Sousa* v. *Portugal*, Netherlands, (1979) 65 ILR 378, 379; affirmed, *Portugal* v. *De Sousa*, Netherlands, (1981) 94 ILR 314, 315; *JPH* v. *Indonesian*, Netherlands, (1979) 65 ILR 379 note; *MK* v. *Turkey*, Netherlands, (1985) 94 ILR 350, 353; *LF* v. *Germany*, Netherlands, (1986) 94 ILR 342, 347–348; *Russian* v. *Pied-Rich*, Netherlands, 1992, 24 *NYIL* (1993) 346, 350; *Buckingham* v. *Aircraft*, New Zealand, [1982] 2 NZLR 738, 739; 64 ILR 551; *Harry* v. *USA*, Philippines, (1958) 88 ILR 711, 712; *Carried* v. *USA*, Philippines, (1974) 64 ILR 661, 665; *USA* v. *Ruiz*, Philippines, (1985) 102 ILR 122, 126; *Diana* v. *South Africa*, Spain, (1986) 86 ILR 512, 514; *Abbott* v. *South Africa*, Spain, (1992) 113 ILR 411, 426.

138 Article 7(1), emphasis added. See also Arts. 26 and 27(2); Council of Europe, *Explanatory Reports*, pp. 17–18, para. 37, commentary to Art. 7; 36, para. 105, commentary to Art. 26.

139 This perhaps explains why some judges regarded immunity as a principle of 'private international law'. See *UAR* v. *Mirza*, India, (1961) 64 ILR 394, 401, 406 per Lahiri CJ; *Olofsen* v. *Malaysia*, Singapore, (1966) 55 ILR 409, 411 per Ambrose J. Issues surrounding immunity may simply shift between public and private international law. See *Saez* v. *Pinillos*, Belgium, (1938/1939) 9 AD 289, 292–293. See also *X* v. *Germany*, Austria, (1963) 65 ILR 10, 12 and the express reference to 'United Kingdom rules of private international law' in s. 19(3) of the UK SIA and 'applicable rules of private international law' in Art. 10(1) of the 2004 UN Convention (for commentary see *YILC*, 1991-II-2, p. 12 at 34, paras. (2)–(5)).

140 *The Schooner Exchange* v. *McFaddon*, US, 11 US (7 Cranch) 116, 135 (1812) (emphasis added).

141 *The Schooner Exchange* v. *McFaddon*, US, 11 US (7 Cranch) 116, 136–137 (1812) (emphases added).

142 See also *National* v. *Republic of China*, US, 348 US 356, 362 (1955); 22 ILR 210, 214. At the time, *The Schooner Exchange* was unmistakably understood by Wheaton to be about exceptions to *territorial* jurisdiction: Wheaton, *Elements*, pp. 129–134. For immunity as derogation from jurisdiction see also *Victory Transport* v. *Comisaría*, US, 336 F.2d 354, 360 (2nd Cir. 1964); 35 ILR 110.

143 *The Schooner Exchange*, 11 US (7 Cranch) 116, 146 (1812).

524   NOTES TO PAGES 66–68

144 *The Charkieh*, England, (1873) LR 4 A & E 59, 88. The *Charkieh* reasoning was overruled by *The Parlement Belge*, England, (1880) 5 PD 197.

145 *The Parlement Belge*, England, (1880) 5 PD 197, 214–215 (emphases added); see also 217. For absolute immunity cases decided by English courts expressly mentioning territorial jurisdiction see also *The Cristina*, England, [1938] AC 485, 494, 496–497, 502; 9 AD 250, 254, 259; *Haile* v. *Cable (No. 1)*, England, [1938] Ch 839, 844; 9 AD 171, 173; *Chung* v. *The King*, England, 1938, [1939] AC 160, 175–176; 9 AD 264, 270–271; *USA* v. *Dollfus*, England, [1952] AC 582, 620. For similar cases in other countries see *Advokaat* v. *Schuddinck*, Netherlands, (1923) 2 AD 133, 133; *Soviet* v. *JV*, Estonia, (1927) 8 AD 241, 242; *Restitution of Property Case*, Germany, (1951) 18 ILR 221, 222; *Syquia* v. *López*, Philippines, (1949) 18 ILR 228, 232 per Perfecto J, dissenting; *Limbin* v. *Burma*, Japan, (1954) 32 ILR 124, 125; *Municipality* v. *Fraser-Brace*, Canada, (1958) 13 DLR (2d) 177, 181, 193; 26 ILR 165, 168, 176; *UAR* v. *Mirza*, India, (1961) 64 ILR 394, 407, 415–416.

146 *Rahimtoola* v. *Nizam*, England, 1957, [1958] AC 379, 418; 24 ILR 175, 196–197.

147 *Rahimtoola*, [1958] AC 379, 422; 24 ILR 175, 200; quoted in *Thai-Europe* v. *Pakistan*, England, [1975] 1 WLR 1485, 1492–1493; 64 ILR 81; *I Congreso del Partido*, England, 1979, [1980] 1 Lloyd's Rep 23, 30, 33; [1981] 1 All ER 1092, 1102, 1106; 64 ILR 227, 234, 238.

148 *Thai-Europe* v. *Pakistan*, England, [1975] 1 WLR 1485, 1491–1492; 64 ILR 81, 85–86. Immunity was granted because the transactions were 'as far off as the moon' from England (at 1492/86). See also Scarman LJ at 1494/89.

149 *Trendtex* v. *Central Bank*, England, [1977] QB 529, 558; 64 ILR 111, 132. For later affirmation of the territorial principle see also *I Congreso del Partido*, England, 1981, [1983] 1 AC 244, 262, 276; 64 ILR 307, 313, 327; *A Limited* v. *B Bank*, England, 1996, [1997] FSR 165, 171; 111 ILR 590, 597; *AIC* v. *Nigeria*, England, (2003) 129 ILR 571, 579–580, para. 30 per Stanley Burnton J (citing Lord Denning in *Rahimtoola*, *Thai-Europe* and *Trendtex*).

150 *Controller* v. *Davison*, New Zealand, [1996] 2 NZLR 278, 314–315; 104 ILR 526, 618.

151 See, e.g., *Restitution of Property Case*, Germany, (1951) 18 ILR 221, 222. See also *Limbin* v. *Burma*, Japan, (1954) 32 ILR 124, 125; *S* v. *British*, Poland, (1948) 24 ILR 223, 225.

152 IDI, Projet, 436–437 (emphases added). Note that the word 'territoire' appears in all but (4), which deals with voluntary submission to the court's jurisdiction. For some unknown reason the numbering of the articles was changed and the wording slightly varied in a later collection of completed projects, see IDI, *Tableau Général*, p. 344. Article II as quoted here became Art. 4 in the 1919 collection.

153 *Tani* v. *Russian*, Italy, (1947) 15 AD 141, 144; *Francischiello* v. *USA*, Italy, (1959) 28 ILR 158, 160; *Mallaval* v. *French*, Italy, (1974) 65 ILR 303, 305. *Tani* was quoted with approval in the *Empire of Iran Case*, Germany, (1963) 45 ILR 57, 63. See also *The Schooner Exchange* v. *McFaddon*, US, 11 US (7 Cranch) 116, 145 (1812).

NOTES TO PAGES 68–69   525

154 *Guttieres* v. *Elmilik*, Italy, 1886, 26 *AJIL Supplement* (1932) 622, 622–623. For subsequent cases see *Nobili* v. *Emperor*, Italy, (1921) 1 AD 36; *Storelli* v. *French*, Italy, (1924) 2 AD 129, 129–130; *Russian* v. *Tesini*, Italy, (1925) 3 AD 176, 177; *French* v. *Serra*, Italy, (1925) 3 AD 178, 178; *Società Riunite* v. *US*, Italy, (1925) 3 AD 179 note; *Roumanian* v. *Gabriele*, Italy, (1926) 3 AD 179 note; *Perrucchetti* v. *Puig*, Italy, (1928) 4 AD 365, 366; *French* v. *Banca*, Italy, (1932) 6 AD 36, 37; *Slomnitzky* v. *Trade*, Italy, (1932) 6 AD 169, 169–170; *Russian* v. *De Castro*, Italy, (1934/1935) 7 AD 179, 180; *De Semenoff* v. *Railway*, Italy, (1936) 8 AD 234, 234; *Tani* v. *Russian*, Italy, (1947) 15 AD 141, 144–145; *Bolivia* v. *Italian*, Italy, (1948) 15 AD 133, 135–136; *Castiglioni* v. *Yugoslavia*, Italy, (1952) 19 ILR 203, 208.
155 *Borga* v. *Russian*, Italy, (1953) 22 ILR 235, 238.
156 See *Sovereign* v. *Soc An*, Italy, (1954) 22 ILR 1, 5; *La Mercantile* v. *Greece*, Italy, (1955) 22 ILR 240, 241–242; *Hungarian* v. *Onori*, Italy, (1956) 23 ILR 203, 204–205; *Baronci* v. *Ospedale*, Italy, (1956) 24 ILR 215, 217; *Greece* v. *Gamet*, Italy, (1957) 24 ILR 209, 210–211; *Novaco* v. *US*, Italy, (1957) 24 ILR 219, 220; *Greece* v. *Gamet*, Italy, (1959) 28 ILR 153, 154–155; *Hungarian* v. *Hungarian*, Italy, (1960) 40 ILR 59, 62; *The Ditta* v. *Germany*, Italy, (1960) 40 ILR 64, 65; *US* v. *IRSA*, Italy, (1963) 65 ILR 262, 263; *US* v. *Bracale*, Italy, (1968) 65 ILR 273, 274; *Campione* v. *Peti-Nitrogenmuvek*, Italy, (1972) 65 ILR 287, 292; *Mallaval* v. *French*, Italy, (1974) 65 ILR 303, 305; *Association* v. *Piccoli*, Italy, (1974) 65 ILR 308, 309; *Ministry* v. *Association*, Italy, (1978) 65 ILR 320, 322; *Libya* v. *SPA Records*, Italy, (1983) 87 ILR 11, 13–14; *Banco* v. *Credito*, Italy, (1984) 87 ILR 15, 17; *Panattoni* v. *Germany*, Italy, (1987) 87 ILR 42, 45; *Norwegian* v. *Quattri*, Italy, (1991) 114 ILR 525, 528.
157 *Dralle* v. *Czechoslovakia*, Austria, (1950) 17 ILR 155, 156–157 (citing *Immunities Case*, Austria, (1920) 1 AD 118, 119). For subsequent cases see *Soviet Distillery Case*, Austria, (1954) 21 ILR 101, 102–103; *Collision Case*, Austria, (1961) 40 ILR 73, 77–78; *X* v. *Germany*, Austria, (1963) 65 ILR 10, 12; *French Consular Employee Claim Case*, Austria, (1989) 86 ILR 583, 586; *Seidenschmidt* v. *USA*, Austria, (1992) 116 ILR 530, 532; *Arrears of Rent Case*, Austria, 2001, 6 *Austrian RIEL* (2001) 313, 314.
158 Harvard Research, 456–457, 597, Draft Convention, Art. 11. Emphases added.
159 See discussion in Chapter 3.
160 *R* v. *Iraq*, Switzerland, (1994) 116 ILR 664, 666, Ground 5a. See also *UAR* v. *Mrs X*, Switzerland, (1960) 65 ILR 385, 390, Ground 2; 390–391, Ground 3; *Italian* v. *Beta*, Switzerland, (1966) 65 ILR 394, 398, Ground 5; 401, Ground 7a; *Banque* v. *Weston*, Switzerland, (1978) 65 ILR 417, 420, Ground 2c; 423, Ground 4a; *Egypt* v. *Cinetelevision*, Switzerland, (1979) 65 ILR 425, 431–432, Ground 5a; *Libya* v. *LIAMCO*, Switzerland, (1980) 62 ILR 228, 233, Ground 3a; 234, Ground 3b; *S* v. *India*, Switzerland, (1984) 82 ILR 13, 17–18, 19, Ground 3; *Italian* v. *X*, Switzerland, (1985) 82 ILR 23, 26, Ground 4a; *Libya* v. *Actimon*, Switzerland, (1985) 82 ILR 30, 33, Ground 4; 34, Ground 5b; *Swissair* v. *X*, Switzerland, (1985) 82 ILR 36, 37; *Spain* v. *Company X*, Switzerland, (1986) 82 ILR 38, 40–41, Ground 3b; *S* v. *Romania*, Switzerland, (1987) 82 ILR 45, 48–49, Ground 2; *Landano* v. *USA*, Switzerland, (1987) 116 ILR 636, 639; *M* v. *Egypt*, Switzerland, (1994) 116 ILR 656, 662, Ground 4a; *Société* v. *Pakistan*, Switzerland, 2000, 11

526   NOTES TO PAGES 70–72

RSDIE (2001) 587, 587–588; *République Y* v. *X*, Switzerland, 2000, 11 *RSDIE* (2001) 589, 590; *République de Y* v. *Office*, Switzerland, 2001, 12 *RSDIE* (2002) 607, 608; *République X* v. *A*, Switzerland, 2003, 130 *JDI* (2003) 1125, 1126.

161 *Dreyfus*, Switzerland, (1918) BGE 44 I 49, 54–55.

162 *Greek Republic* v. *Walder*, Switzerland, (1930) BGE 56 I 237, 251; 5 AD 121, 122–123.

163 *Greece* v. *Julius Bär*, Switzerland, (1956) ATF 82 I 75, 85, Ground 7; 23 ILR 195, 196.

164 *Greece* v. *Julius Bär*, (1956) ATF 82 I 75, 86, Ground 7; 23 ILR 195, 196–197.

165 *Greece* v. *Julius Bär*, (1956) ATF 82 I 75, 92, Ground 11; 23 ILR 195, 200–201. For early cases see also *State Immunity Case*, Switzerland, (1937) 10 AD 230, 231; *State Immunity (No. 2) Case*, Switzerland, (1939/1940) 10 AD 235, 236.

166 See, e.g., *Société* v. *Pakistan*, Switzerland, 2000, 11 *RSDIE* (2001) 587, 587–588; *République de Y* v. *Office*, Switzerland, 2001, 12 *RSDIE* (2002) 607, 608–609.

167 See *M* v. *Egypt*, Switzerland, (1994) ATF 120 II 400, 406–407, Ground 4b ('*certains liens avec le territoire suisse ('Binnenbeziehung')*'); 116 ILR 656, 662; *R* v. *Iraq*, Switzerland, (1994) ATF 120 II 408, 411, Ground 5c ('*certains liens avec le territoire suisse ('Binnenbeziehung')*'); 116 ILR 664, 667; *État du Koweit* v. *X.S.A.*, Switzerland, 1994, 5 *RSDIE* (1995) 593, 594 ('*Binnenbeziehung*'); *Banque Bruxelles* v. *Paraguay*, Switzerland, (1998) ATF 124 III 382, 388, Considérant 4a ('*rattaché de manière suffisante au territoire suisse ('Binnenbeziehung')*'); *République X* v. *A*, Switzerland, 2003, 130 *JDI* (2003) 1125, 1126 ('*rattaché de manière suffisante au territoire suisse – Binnenbeziehung*'). See also Circulaire du Département fédéral de justice et police, 8 July 1986, 43 *ASDI* (1987) 162, 163–164 (*Binnenbeziehung*); Note de la Direction du droit international public du Département fédéral des affaires étrangères, 28 August 1990, 1 *RSDIE* (1991) 519, 520 (*Binnenbeziehung*).

168 *UAR* v. *Mrs X*, Switzerland, (1960) ATF 86 I 23, 27–28, Ground 2; 65 ILR 385, 389 (citing *Julius Bär*; see also ATF 86 I 23, 30, Grounds 3 and 4; 32, Ground 5; 65 ILR 385, 391, 393). This was more fully stated in *S* v. *Romania*, Switzerland, (1987) ATF 113 Ia 172, 175, Ground 2 ('*rattaché au territoire de ce pays*'); 82 ILR 45, 48. See also *Italian* v. *Beta*, Switzerland, (1966) 65 ILR 394, 398–399, Ground 5; 401, Ground 7b; *Tsakos* v. *USA*, Switzerland, (1972) 75 ILR 78, 79–80; *Egypt* v. *Cinetelevision*, Switzerland, (1979) 65 ILR 425, 430, Ground 4a; 432, Ground 5b; *Swissair* v. *X*, Switzerland, (1985) 82 ILR 36, 37.

169 *Banque Centrale* v. *Weston*, Switzerland, (1978) BGE 104 Ia 367, 373–374, Ground 4; 65 ILR 417, 423; see also 376, Ground 4d; 65 ILR 424–425. See also *Libya* v. *LIAMCO*, Switzerland, (1980) BGE 106 Ia 142, 148–149, Ground 3b ('*eine genügende Binnenbeziehung zum schweizerischen Staatsgebiet*'); 62 ILR 228, 234; *Banco* v. *Banco Cattolica*, Switzerland, (1984) BGE 110 Ia 43, 44, Ground 4a ('*eine Binnenbeziehung zur Schweiz*'); 82 ILR 10, 12; *S* v. *India*, Switzerland, (1984) BGE 110 II 255, 264, Ground 5 ('*Binnenbeziehung zum schweizerischen Staatsgebiet*'); 82 ILR 13, 23; *Italian* v. *X*, Switzerland, (1985) BGE 111 Ia 52, 58, Ground 4a ('*eine genügende Binnenbeziehung zur Schweiz*'); 82 ILR 23, 26; *Libya* v. *Actimon*, Switzerland, (1985) BGE 111 Ia 62; 82 ILR 30, 33, Ground 4; 34, Ground 5b;

NOTES TO PAGES 72–76   527

Spain v. *Company X*, Switzerland, (1986) BGE 112 Ia 148, 150, Ground 3b ('*eine ausreichende Binnenbeziehung zur Schweiz*'); 82 ILR 38, 40; *Landano* v. *USA*, Switzerland, (1987) 116 ILR 636, 639. Puzzlingly, the earliest appearance of the term '*Binnenbeziehung*' in connection with immunity seems to be in a Dutch case: *NV Cabolent* v. *National*, Netherlands, (1968) 47 ILR 138, 144.

170 *Banque Centrale* v. *Weston*, Switzerland, (1978) 65 ILR 417, 420, Ground 2c.

171 *M* v. *Egypt*, Switzerland, (1994) ATF 120 II 400, 406–407, Ground 4b; 116 ILR 656, 662. The case was then decided mainly by virtue of the fact that the place where the plaintiff was employed was Geneva. The pronouncement was repeated verbatim in *R* v. *Iraq*, Switzerland, (1994) ATF 120 II 408, 411, Ground 5c; 116 ILR 664, 667. See also *Nicoud* v. *USA*, Switzerland, (1994) 116 ILR 650, 652–653; *X* v. *USA*, Switzerland, (1995) 116 ILR 668, 673; *État du Koweit* v. *X*, Switzerland, 1994, 5 *RSDIE* (1995) 593, 594; *Banque Bruxelles* v. *Paraguay*, Switzerland, (1998) ATF 124 III 382, 388, Considérant 4a; *République X* v. *A*, Switzerland, 2003, 130 *JDI* (2003) 1125, 1126; Circulaire du Département fédéral de justice et police, 8 July 1986, 43 *ASDI* (1987) 162, 163–164; Note de la Direction du droit international public du Département fédéral des affaires étrangères, 28 August 1990, 1 *RSDIE* (1991) 519, 520.

172 *UAR* v. *Mrs X*, Switzerland, (1960) 65 ILR 385, 390, Ground 2 (emphases added). See also *Banque Centrale* v. *Weston*, Switzerland, (1978) 65 ILR 417, 420, Ground 2c; *S* v. *India*, Switzerland, (1984) 82 ILR 13, 17–18, Ground 3; 22, Ground 4; *S* v. *Romania*, Switzerland, (1987) 82 ILR 45, 49, Ground 2; *République Y* v. *X*, Switzerland, 2000, 11 *RSDIE* (2001) 589, 590; *République de Y* v. *Office*, Switzerland, 2001, 12 *RSDIE* (2002) 607, 608.

173 *Libya* v. *LIAMCO*, Switzerland, (1980) 62 ILR 228, 235, Ground 4.

174 Trooboff and Schreuer think that Swiss courts apply such a strict territorial nexus requirement in order to maintain the unique position of Switzerland as a banking centre of the world: Trooboff, Foreign State, 388; Schreuer, State Immunity, p. 36.

Chapter 3

1 The 1972 European Convention, Art. 7(1); 2004 UN Convention, Art. 10(1); US FSIA, s. 1605(a)(2); UK SIA, s. 3(1); Pakistan SIO, s. 5(1); Singapore SIA, s. 5(1); South Africa FSIA, s. 4(1); Canada SIA, s. 5; Australia FSIA, s. 11(1); Argentina Law of 1995, Art. 2 (c); Israeli Law of 2008, s. 3; OAS Draft, 1983, Art. 5; ILA Drafts, 1982/1994, Art. III(B); IDI Draft, 1991, Art. 2(2)(a).

2 European Convention, Art. 7(1).

3 US FSIA, s. 1603(d); ILA Drafts, Art. I(C).

4 Canada SIA, s. 2.

5 OAS Draft, Art. 5.

6 UK SIA, s. 3(3)(a); Pakistan SIO, s. 5(3)(a); Singapore SIA, s. 5(3)(a); South Africa FSIA, s. 4(3)(a); Australia FSIA, s. 11(3)(a); Israeli Law of 2008, s. 1; UN Convention, Art. 2(1)(c)(i); ILA Drafts, Art. I(C)(1); 1991 IDI Draft, Art. 2(2)(b).

528   NOTES TO PAGES 76-77

7 UK SIA, s. 3(3)(b); Pakistan SIO, s. 5(3)(b); Singapore SIA, s. 5(3)(b); South Africa FSIA, s. 4(3)(b); Australia FSIA, s. 11(3)(b)(c); Israeli Law of 2008, s. 1; UN Convention, Art. 2(1)(c)(ii); ILA Drafts, Art. I(C)(2); IDI Draft, Art. 2(2)(b).

8 *Servaas* v. *Iraq*, US, 686 F.Supp.2d 346, 356 (S.D.N.Y. 2010); *Agudas* v. *Russian*, US, 528 F.3d 934, 948 (D.C. Cir. 2008); *Hilaturas* v. *Iraq*, US, 573 F.Supp.2d 781, 794 (S.D.N.Y. 2008); *Samco* v. *Arita*, US, 395 F.3d 1212, 1216 (11th Cir. 2005); *Gulf* v. *Congo*, US, 276 F.Supp.2d 20, 25 (D.D.C. 2003); *S & Davis* v. *Yemen*, US, 218 F.3d 1292, 1302–1303 (11th Cir. 2000); *Vermeulen* v. *Renault*, US, 985 F.2d 1534, 1544 (11th Cir. 1993); *Walter* v. *Philippines*, US, 965 F.2d 1375, 1384 (5th Cir. 1992); 103 ILR 503; *Rush-Presbyterian* v. *Hellenic*, US, 877 F.2d 574, 578 (7th Cir. 1989); 101 ILR 509; *Segni* v. *Commercial*, US, 835 F.2d 160, 163 (7th Cir. 1987); 98 ILR 55; *Practical* v. *Bolivia*, US, 811 F.2d 1543, 1549 (D.C. Cir. 1987); 92 ILR 420; *Texas* v. *Nigeria*, US, 647 F.2d 300, 309–310 (2nd Cir. 1981); 63 ILR 552; *A Company* v. *Republic of X*, England, 1989, [1990] 2 Lloyd's Rep 520, 523; 87 ILR 412, 415; *British* v. *Toglia*, Italy, (1989) 101 ILR 379, 382.

9 *Reichler* v. *Liberia*, US, 484 F.Supp.2d 1, 2 (D.D.C. 2007); *Adler* v. *Nigeria*, US, 219 F.3d 869, 875 (9th Cir. 2000); *Enron* v. *Titan*, US, 82 F.Supp.2d 602, 612 (W.D. La. 1999); *Honduras* v. *Honduras*, US, 129 F.3d 543, 547–548 (11th Cir. 1997); affirming *Honduras* v. *Honduras*, US, 883 F.Supp. 685 (S.D. Fla. 1995) and superseding *Honduras* v. *Honduras*, US, 119 F.3d 1530 (11th Cir. 1997); *Sealift* v. *Armenia*, US, 965 F.Supp. 81, 85 (D.D.C. 1997); *Eckert* v. *Fiji*, US, 834 F.Supp. 167, 170 (E.D. Va. 1993); *Practical* v. *Bolivia*, US, 811 F.2d 1543, 1548–1549 (D.C. Cir. 1987); 92 ILR 420. But see *Joseph* v. *Office*, US, 830 F.2d 1018, 1024 (9th Cir. 1987); 101 ILR 485. In the practice of the US and South Africa a contract of employment is classified as a contract for services: *Segni* v. *Commercial*, US, 835 F.2d 160, 164–165 (7th Cir. 1987); 98 ILR 55; affirming *Segni* v. *Commercial*, US, 650 F.Supp. 1042 (N.D. Ill. 1986); *Inter-Science* v. *Moçambique*, South Africa, 1979, 1980 (2) SA 111, 126; 64 ILR 689, 706.

10 *Wasserstein* v. *Formosa*, US, 2002 US Dist. Lexis 12012, p. 25 (S.D.N.Y. 2002); *Commercial* v. *Rafidain*, US, 15 F.3d 238, 241 (2nd Cir. 1994); 107 ILR 261, 265; *Morgan* v. *Palau*, US, 693 F.Supp. 1479, 1494 (S.D.N.Y. 1988); 87 ILR 590; *Meadows* v. *Dominican*, US, 817 F.2d 517, 523 (9th Cir. 1987); 98 ILR 37; affirming *Meadows* v. *Dominican*, US, 628 F.Supp. 599, 604 (N.D. Cal. 1986); *Maclaine* v. *Department*, England, [1988] 3 WLR 1033, 1104; 80 ILR 47; *Banque* v. *Weston*, Switzerland, (1978) 65 ILR 417, 423, Ground 4a. Repayment of loans to the World Bank is also considered a commercial activity: *Orascom* v. *Chad*, England, [2008] 2 Lloyd's Rep 396, 403, paras. 20, 23.

11 This, however, does not mean that military property can be subjected to attachment or execution. See Chapter 9.

12 US House of Representatives, Report No. 94-1487, 1976, p. 16; 1976 USCCAN 6604, 6615.

13 *Argentina* v. *Weltover*, US, 504 US 607, 614–615 (1992); 119 L.Ed.2d 394, 405 (1992); 100 ILR 509, 515 (citing *Rumania* v. *Trutta*, Italy, 1926). But of course the earliest 'army boots case' (though one of absolute immunity) seems to be *Gouvernement espagnol* v. *Cassaux*, France, 1849, Sirey 1849-I-81; Dalloz 1849-I-5; discussed

NOTES TO PAGE 77   529

in Sucharitkul, *State Immunities*, pp. 9–10, 207–208, 323 and Dunbar, Controversial, 205–209 (sub nom *Gouvernement espagnol* v. *Lambège*). For the earliest cases denying immunity see *Société* v. *Ministre*, Belgium, 1888, Pasicrisie Belge, 1889-III-62 (purchase of bullets; no immunity); *Rumania* v. *Trutta*, Italy, 1926, 26 *AJIL Supplement* (1932) 626 (purchase of army boots; no immunity); 3 AD 179 note. But cf., *Romania* v. *Guaranty*, US, 250 F. 341, 345 (2nd Cir. 1918) (purchase of army shoes a sovereign act). See also *Gerber* v. *Gerber*, England, [2002] EWHC 428, [2002] ETMR 77, paras. 38–40 (selling baby food at a USAF base was not a sovereign activity).

14 *Guevara* v. *Peru*, US, 468 F.3d 1289, 1300 (11th Cir. 2006); *Samco* v. *Arita*, US, 395 F.3d 1212, 1216 (11th Cir. 2005); *Ministry* v. *Cubic*, US, 385 F.3d 1206, 1219–1220 (9th Cir. 2004); *Globe* v. *AO*, US, 376 F.3d 282, 289 (4th Cir. 2004); *Park* v. *Shin*, US, 313 F.3d 1138, 1145 (9th Cir. 2002); *Virtual* v. *Moldova*, US, 133 F.Supp.2d 1, 4 (D.D.C. 1999); *Joseph* v. *Office*, US, 830 F.2d 1018, 1023 (9th Cir. 1987); 101 ILR 485; *McDonnell* v. *Iran*, US, 758 F.2d 341, 349 (8th Cir. 1985); *Texas* v. *Nigeria*, US, 647 F.2d 300, 309 (2nd Cir. 1981); 63 ILR 552; *Victory* v. *Comisaría*, US, 336 F.2d 354, 359 (2nd Cir. 1964); 35 ILR 110; *Reid* v. *Nauru*, Australia, 1992, [1993] 1 VR 251, 253; 101 ILR 193, 195; *Rafidain* v. *Consarc*, Belgium, (1993) 106 ILR 274, 277; *Trendtex* v. *Central Bank*, England, [1977] QB 529, 558; 64 ILR 111, 132; *A Limited* v. *B Bank*, England, 1996, [1997] FSR 165, 170, 176; 111 ILR 590, 595, 603; *US* v. *IRSA*, Italy, (1963) 65 ILR 262, 263–264. But cf. *Guggenheim* v. *Vietnam*, France, (1955) 22 ILR 224, 225; affirmed, *Guggenheim* v. *Vietnam*, France, (1961) 44 ILR 74; *Société* v. *Pakistan*, France, (1966) 47 ILR 150.

15 UK SIA, s. 3(3)(c); Pakistan SIO, s. 5(3)(c); Singapore SIA, s. 5(3)(c); South Africa FSIA, s. 4(3)(c); Israeli Law of 2008, s. 1; UN Convention, Art. 2(1)(c)(iii); ILA Drafts, Art. I(C). According to the Annex to the UN Convention (which by virtue of Art. 25 forms an integral part of the Convention), as far as arbitration agreements (in Art. 17) are concerned, the expression 'commercial transaction' includes investment matters.

16 IDI Draft, Art. 2(2)(b).

17 Australia FSIA, s. 11(3). Interestingly, although this subsection uses the phrases 'into which the foreign State *has entered*' and 'in which the State *has engaged*', it has been held that 'it would be an unusual result if *future transactions* did not fall within the ambit of that exception'. *Adeang* v. *Nauru*, Australia, 1992, 14 *AYIL* (1993) 340, 341. Emphases added.

18 US FSIA, s. 1603(d); ILA Drafts, Art. I(C).

19 UK SIA, s. 3(3)(c); Pakistan SIO, s. 5(3)(c); Singapore SIA, s. 5(3)(c); South Africa FSIA, s. 4(3)(c); Israeli Law of 2008, s. 1; ILA Drafts, Art. I(C). However, after examining case law, Fox concludes that s. 3 of the UK SIA has actually enabled English courts to 'remove immunity for acts performed in the exercise of sovereign authority'. Fox, A 'Commercial Transaction', 194.

20 For pertinent remarks see *Joseph* v. *Office*, US, 830 F.2d 1018, 1023 (9th Cir. 1987) (the US FSIA 'tautologically' defines 'commercial activity'); 101 ILR 485; *Re Canada Labour Code*, Canada, (1992) 91 DLR (4th) 449, 461 (the Canada SIA defines 'commercial activity' 'in circuitous fashion'); 94 ILR 264, 276.

530 NOTES TO PAGE 77

21 *Pradhan* v. *Al-Sabah*, US, 299 F.Supp.2d 493, 498 (D. Md. 2004); *Fagot* v. *Costa Rica*, US, 297 F.3d 1, 6 (1st Cir. 2002); affirming *Fagot* v. *Costa Rica*, US, 139 F.Supp.2d 173, 192 (D.P.R. 2001); *Berdakin* v. *Consulado*, US, 912 F.Supp. 458, 462–463 (C.D. Cal. 1995); *Saunders* v. *Consulate*, US, 1995 U.S.Dist.Lexis 14893, p. 3 (D. Mass. 1995); *767* v. *Permanent*, US, 988 F.2d 295 (2nd Cir. 1993); 99 ILR 194; partly affirming and reversing *767* v. *Permanent*, US, 787 F.Supp. 389 (S.D.N.Y. 1992); *Joseph* v. *Office*, US, 830 F.2d 1018, 1024 (9th Cir. 1987); 101 ILR 485; *National* v. *Embassy*, Argentina, (1992) 113 ILR 434; *Tasita* v. *Papua*, Australia, [1991] 34 NSWLR 691, 697; *Leasing* v. *Algeria*, Austria, (1986) 116 ILR 526; *Arrears of Rent Case*, Austria, 2001, 6 *Austrian RIEL* (2001) 313, 314; *Zaire* v. *D'Hoop*, Belgium, (1995) 106 ILR 294; *Planmount* v. *Zaire*, England, [1980] 2 Lloyd's Rep 393; [1981] 1 All ER 1110; 64 ILR 268; *Euroéquipement* v. *Centre*, France, (1991) 89 ILR 37, 39; *Société* v. *Guinée Bissau*, France, 2006, 110 *RGDIP* (2006) 971; *Empire of Iran Case*, Germany, (1963) 45 ILR 57; *Land Purchase Broker's Commission Case*, Germany, (1974) 65 ILR 125; *Philippine Embassy Bank Account Case*, Germany, (1977) 65 ILR 146; *Purchase of Embassy Staff Residence Case*, Greece, (1967) 65 ILR 255, 257; *Her Majesty* v. *Edelson*, Israel, (1997) 131 ILR 279, 304–306; *US* v. *Bracale*, Italy, (1968) 65 ILR 273, 274; *Embassy* v. *Società Immobiliare*, Italy, (1979) 65 ILR 331, 332–333; *Nashashibi* v. *Consul-General*, Jordan, (1958) 26 ILR 190; *UAR* v. *Mrs X*, Switzerland, (1960) 65 ILR 385, 390–391, Ground 3; *K* v. *Vietnam*, Switzerland, (1981) 75 ILR 122, 124, Ground 1b; *Z* v. *Geneva*, Switzerland, (1990) 102 ILR 205, 206. But see *Nkoghe* v. *Embassy*, Gabon, (1989) 89 ILR 43.

22 *Spain* v. *Company X*, Switzerland, (1986) 82 ILR 38, 41, Ground 3b.

23 *Argentina* v. *Weltover*, US, 504 US 607 (1992); 100 ILR 509; *Morris* v. *China*, US, 478 F.Supp.2d 561, 567 (S.D.N.Y. 2007); *Velasco* v. *Indonesia*, US, 370 F.3d 392, 398 (4th Cir. 2004); *Global* v. *Mkapa*, US, 290 F.Supp.2d 108, 112 (D.D.C. 2003); *Turkmani* v. *Bolivia*, US, 193 F.Supp.2d 165, 175 (D.D.C. 2002); *Shapiro* v. *Bolivia*, US, 930 F.2d 1013, 1018 (2nd Cir. 1991); 98 ILR 109, 115; *Carl* v. *USSR*, US, 841 F.2d 26, 27 (2nd Cir. 1988); *West* v. *Multibanco*, US, 807 F.2d 820, 825 (9th Cir. 1987); 84 ILR 187; *Braka* v. *Bancomer*, US, 589 F.Supp. 1465, 1469–1470 (S.D.N.Y. 1984); affirmed, *Braka* v. *Bancomer*, US, 762 F.2d 222 (2nd Cir. 1985); *Allied* v. *Banco*, US, 566 F.Supp. 1440, 1443 (S.D.N.Y. 1983); reversed on other grounds, *Allied* v. *Banco*, US, 757 F.2d 516 (2nd Cir. 1985); *Central Bank* v. *Cardinal*, England, 2000, [2001] Lloyd's Rep Bank 1, paras. 11; affirming *Cardinal* v. *Central Bank*, England, 2000, 2000 WL 699384. Guaranteeing a promissory note is also a commercial activity: *Falcon* v. *Venezuela*, US, 2001 WL 584346, p. 2 (D. Kan. 2001).

24 *US Fidelity* v. *Petroleo*, 1999 U.S.Dist.Lexis 7235, pp. 15–16 (S.D.N.Y. 1999) and *US Fidelity* v. *Braspetro*, 1999 U.S.Dist.Lexis 7236, pp. 39–40 (S.D.N.Y. 1999); affirmed, *US Fidelity* v. *Braspetro*, US, 199 F.3d 94 (2nd Cir. 1999); jurisdiction further asserted, *US Fidelity* v. *Braspetro*, US, 379 F.Supp.2d 487, 490 (S.D.N.Y. 2005).

25 *Société Bauer-Marchal* v. *Gouvernment Turc*, France, (1965) 47 ILR 155, 156.

26 *Daly* v. *Castro*, US, 30 F.Supp.2d 407, 418 (S.D.N.Y. 1998); *Chalabi* v. *Jordan*, US, 503 F.Supp.2d 267, 272–273 (D.D.C. 2007); affirmed, *Chalabi* v. *Jordan*, US, 543

NOTES TO PAGES 77–78 531

F.3d 725 (D.C. Cir. 2008). See also *L'Europeenne* v. *Venezuela*, US, 700 F.Supp. 114, 119–120 (S.D.N.Y. 1988); 98 ILR 100 note; criticized in Day, *L'Europeenne*.

27 *Hanil* v. *PT*, US, 148 F.3d 127, 131 (2nd Cir. 1998); affirming *Hanil* v. *PT*, US, 1997 U.S.Dist.Lexis 10450 (S.D.N.Y. 1997); *Verlinden* v. *Central Bank*, US, 461 US 480 (1983); 79 ILR 548; reversing *Verlinden* v. *Central Bank*, US, 488 F.Supp. 1284 (S.D. N.Y. 1980); 63 ILR 390 and *Verlinden* v. *Central Bank*, US, 647 F.2d 320 (2nd Cir. 1981); 63 ILR 573; *Trendtex* v. *Central Bank*, England, [1977] QB 529; 64 ILR 111; *Hispano* v. *Central Bank*, England, [1979] 2 Lloyd's Rep 277; 64 ILR 221; *Central Bank of Nigeria Case*, Germany, (1975/1976) 65 ILR 131, 135; *Banco* v. *Credito*, Italy, (1984) 87 ILR 15, 17–18.

28 *Cameroons* v. *Société*, France, (1986) 77 ILR 532, 533.

29 Though the issuance of currency in the territory of the issuing State is a sovereign activity: *A Limited* v. *B Bank*, England, 1996, [1997] FSR 165, 170–171, 176; 111 ILR 590, 595–597, 603; *Camdex* v. *Bank*, England, [1997] 1 WLR 632, 636F–G.

30 *Wolf* v. *Banco*, US, 739 F.2d 1458, 1460 (9th Cir. 1984); 92 ILR 413.

31 *Robert* v. *Air France*, US, 712 F.Supp. 688, 690 (N.D. Ill. 1989); *Kaffraria* v. *Zambia*, South Africa, 1980 (2) SA 709, 715; 64 ILR 708, 715; *ICC* v. *USSR*, Netherlands, (1976) 65 ILR 368, 369.

32 *Bowers* v. *Transportes*, US, 719 F.Supp. 166, 168 (S.D.N.Y. 1989).

33 *Reef* v. *Fua Kavenga*, New Zealand, [1987] 1 NZLR 550, 572–573; 90 ILR 556, 566.

34 *Reef* v. *Fua Kavenga*, New Zealand, [1987] 1 NZLR 550, 572; 90 ILR 556, 565.

35 *In re Air Crash*, US, 716 F.Supp. 84, 86 (E.D.N.Y. 1989); *Burke* v. *Compagnie*, US, 699 F.Supp. 1016, 1019 (D.P.R. 1988).

36 *Diaz-Aguasviva* v. *Iberia*, US, 902 F.Supp. 314, 317 (D.P.R. 1995).

37 *State Immunity (Denmark) Case*, Denmark, 69 NYIL (2000) 338.

38 *Schoenberg* v. *Exportadora*, US, 930 F.2d 777 (9th Cir. 1991); 98 ILR 118.

39 *Novopharm* v. *USA*, Canada, 18 CPR (3d) 26 (1987), para. 29. See also European Convention, Art. 8; UN Convention, Art. 14; UK SIA 1978, s. 7; Pakistan SIO, s. 8; Singapore SIA, s. 9; South Africa FSIA, s. 8; Australia FSIA, s. 15; ILA Drafts, Art. III(E); IDI Draft 1991, Art. 2.

40 *Intel* v. *Commonwealth*, US, 455 F.3d 1364, 1369–1370 (Fed. Cir. (Cal.) 2006).

41 *Phillips* v. *Hatsujou*, US, 57 F.3d 1051, 1054 (Fed. Cir. (Wis.) 1995) (though this case was not decided under the US FSIA).

42 *Gould* v. *Mitsui*, US, 947 F.2d 218, 221 (6th Cir. 1991); 98 ILR 136, 156; *Gould* v. *Pechiney*, US, 853 F.2d 445, 452 (6th Cir. 1988); 98 ILR 136.

43 *US Fidelity* v. *Braspetro*, US, 1999 U.S.Dist.Lexis 7236, p. 41 (S.D.N.Y. 1999); affirmed *US Fidelity* v. *Braspetro*, US, 199 F.3d 94, 98 (2nd Cir. 1999).

44 *NIOC Pipeline Contracts Case*, Germany, (1982) 65 ILR 212, 214.

45 *Collavino* v. *Yemen*, Canada, [2007] AJ No. 531, para. 135.

46 *Hester* v. *Nigeria*, US, 681 F.Supp. 371, 383 (N.D. Miss. 1988); affirmed, *Hester* v. *Nigeria*, US, 879 F.2d 170 (5th Cir. 1989); 90 ILR 604.

47 *Libya* v. *Actimon*, Switzerland, (1985) 82 ILR 30, 34, Ground 5b.

48 *Sieniecki* v. *Shea*, Canada, 4 ACWS (3d) 244 (1987).

49 *Spain* v. *Company X*, Switzerland, (1986) 82 ILR 38, 41, Ground 3b.

532 NOTES TO PAGES 78-79

50 *Theo* v. *Marshall*, US, 174 F.3d 969, 973–974 (9th Cir. 1998); superseding *Theo* v. *Marshall*, US, 161 F.3d 550, 553 (9th Cir. 1998).

51 *Reiss* v. *Société*, US, 235 F.3d 738, 747 (2nd Cir. 2000).

52 *American* v. *Lebanon*, US, 408 F.Supp.2d 409, 413 (E.D.Mich. 2005); affirmed, *American* v. *Lebanon*, US, 501 F.3d 534 (6th Cir. 2007).

53 *Rush-Presbyterian* v. *Hellenic*, US, 877 F.2d 574, 581 (7th Cir. 1989); 101 ILR 509, 516; affirming *Rush-Presbyterian* v. *Hellenic*, US, 690 F.Supp. 682 (N.D.Ill., 1988).

54 *Leutwyler* v. *Office*, US, 184 F.Supp.2d 277, 291, 297 (S.D.N.Y. 2001).

55 *WMW* v. *Werkzeugmaschinenhandel*, US, 960 F.Supp. 734, 740 (S.D.N.Y. 1997).

56 *Ampac* v. *Honduras*, US, 797 F.Supp. 973, 977 (S.D.Fla. 1992); *In re Banco Nacional*, England, [2001] 3 All ER 923, 934–935; [2001] 1 WLR 2039, 2052–2053, paras. 27–28; 124 ILR 550, 562–563.

57 *Daventree* v. *Azerbaijan*, US, 349 F.Supp.2d 736, 750 (S.D.N.Y. 2004).

58 *Stena* v. *Comision*, US, 923 F.2d 380, 387, fn. 9 (5th Cir. 1991); 103 ILR 433.

59 *National* v. *BP*, US, 319 F.Supp.2d 352, 370 (S.D.N.Y. 2004).

60 *World* v. *Nammo*, US, 51 Fed.Appx. 403, 406 (4th Cir. 2002).

61 *Tonoga* v. *Ministry*, US, 135 F.Supp.2d 350, 356 (N.D.N.Y. 2001).

62 *Condor* v. *Minister*, Italy, (1992) 101 ILR 394, 401–402;

63 *Walter* v. *Philippines*, US, 965 F.2d 1375, 1386 (5th Cir. 1992); 103 ILR 503; *Weltover* v. *Argentina*, US, 941 F.2d 145, 151 (2nd Cir. 1991); affirmed, *Argentina* v. *Weltover*, US, 504 US 607 (1992); 100 ILR 509; *Trans-Orient* v. *Star*, US, 736 F.Supp. 1281, 1283 (S.D.N.Y. 1990). See also *Chisholm* v. *Bank*, US, 643 F.Supp. 1393, 1400 (S.D.Fla. 1986); 121 ILR 487.

64 *Tifa* v. *Ghana*, US, 692 F.Supp. 393, 401 (DNJ 1988).

65 *Rafidain* v. *Consarc*, Belgium, (1993) 106 ILR 274, 277.

66 *Supra* v. *McGonigle*, US, 955 F.Supp. 374, 380 (E.D. Pa. 1997).

67 *Murphy* v. *Korea*, US, 421 F.Supp.2d 627, 647 (S.D.N.Y. 2005).

68 *Siderman* v. *Argentina*, US, 965 F.2d 699, 708–709 (9th Cir. 1992); 103 ILR 454.

69 *Lord Day* v. *Vietnam*, US, 134 F.Supp.2d 549, 559 (S.D.N.Y. 2001); *Caribbean* v. *Nigerian*, US, 1993 WL 541236, p. 7 (S.D.N.Y. 1993).

70 *Foreign Trade Institute Case*, Germany, (1981) 65 ILR 209, 210.

71 *Altmann* v. *Austria*, US, 142 F.Supp.2d 1187, 1204–1205 (C.D.Cal. 2001); affirmed, *Altmann* v. *Austria*, US, 317 F.3d 954, 969 (9th Cir. 2002); affirmed, *Austria* v. *Altmann*, US, 541 US 677 (2004).

72 *Malewicz* v. *Amsterdam*, US, 362 F.Supp.2d 298, 314 (D.D.C. 2005).

73 *Egypt* v. *Cinetelevision*, Switzerland, (1979) 65 ILR 425, 431–432, Ground 5a.

74 *Dominican* v. *Dominican*, US, 903 F.Supp. 1507, 1513 (MC Fla. 1995).

75 *USA* v. *Guinto*, Philippines, (1990) 102 ILR 132, 146.

76 *Ferguson* v. *Arctic*, Canada, [1995] 101 FTR 16, paras. 5–6; [1995] 3 FC 656, 660.

77 *Embassy* v. *Lasheen*, US, 603 F.3d 1166, 1171 (9th Cir. 2010).

78 *Los Angeles* v. *Conus*, US, 969 F.Supp. 579, 586 (C.D.Cal. 1997); *Bryks* v. *Canadian*, US, 906 F.Supp. 204, 207–208 (S.D.N.Y. 1995).

79 *Edwards* v. *BV*, Netherlands, (1987) 94 ILR 361, 365.

80 *Nuclear Power Plant Injunction Case (No. 1)*, Austria, (1988) 86 ILR 575, 577.

NOTES TO PAGES 79–80   533

81 *Iran* v. *Société Eurodif*, France, (1989) 89 ILR 31, 34–35; *Ministry* v. *Société Framatome*, France, (1990) 113 ILR 452, 456.

82 *Antares* v. *Nigeria*, US, 999 F.2d 33, 35 (2nd Cir. 1993); 107 ILR 225; see also *Antares* v. *Nigeria*, US, 948 F.2d 90, 94 (2nd Cir. 1991); 107 ILR 225 (vacated by the Supreme Court).

83 *Keller* v. *Central*, US, 277 F.3d 811, 817 (6th Cir. 2002). This was actually one of a number of cases involving the so-called '419 scam' (an advance fee fraud scam so dubbed by reference to Chapter 77, section 419 of the Nigerian Criminal Code, which outlaws such scams). Other cases in this group include: *Adler* v. *Nigeria*, US, 219 F.3d 869, 875 (9th Cir. 2000); noted in Garbarino, *Adler*; *Southway* v. *Central Bank*, US, 198 F.3d 1210, 1217 (10th Cir. 1999); affirming *Southway* v. *Central Bank*, US, 994 F.Supp. 1299, 1308–1309 (D. Colo. 1998); *Intercontinental* v. *Nigeria*, US, 1999 WL 219909 (S.D.N.Y. 1999). The *Southway* case was later dismissed because the scam had actually been committed by private individuals impersonating Nigerian government officials: *Southway* v. *Central Bank*, US, 149 F.Supp.2d 1268 (D.Colo. 2001); affirmed, *Southway* v. *Central Bank*, US, 328 F.3d 1267 (10th Cir. 2003). See also *Tolliver* v. *Nigeria*, US, 265 F.Supp.2d 873, 877 (W.D.Mich. 2003) and *US* v. *Scott-Emuakpor*, US, 2000 WL 288443, p. 1 (W.D.Mich. 2000) for a description of the 'Nigerian advance fee fraud'. For other schemes see *American* v. *Compagnie*, US, 653 F.Supp. 861, 864 (N.D.Ill. 1987); *Rosner* v. *Bank*, US, 528 F.Supp.2d 419, 424 (S.D.N.Y. 2007).

84 *Dale* v. *Colagiovanni*, US, 337 F.Supp.2d 825, 839 (S.D.Miss. 2004); this part affirmed, *Dale* v. *Colagiovanni*, US, 443 F.3d 425, 429 (5th Cir. 2006). But see *MCI* v. *Alhadhood*, US, 82 F.3d 658, 663 (5th Cir. 1996).

85 *Empire of Iran Case*, Germany, (1963) 45 ILR 57, 81; quoted in *I Congreso del Partido*, England, 1981, [1983] 1 AC 244, 264; 64 ILR 307, 315.

86 *Rahimtoola* v. *Nizam*, England, 1957, [1958] AC 379, 422; 24 ILR 175, 200. See also *Buttes* v. *Hammer*, England, 1974, [1975] QB 557, 573; 57 ILR 33, 39; set aside by *Buttes* v. *Hammer*, England, 1981, [1982] AC 888; 64 ILR 331.

87 *Empire of Iran Case*, Germany, (1963) 45 ILR 57, 81; quoted in *Propend* v. *Sing*, England, (1997) 111 ILR 611, 667.

88 *Société* v. *Banque*, Belgium, (1963) 45 ILR 85, 87.

89 *Victory* v. *Comisaría*, US, 336 F.2d 354, 360 (2nd Cir. 1964); 35 ILR 110, 116.

90 *République Y* v. *X*, Switzerland, 2000, 11 *RSDIE* (2001) 589, 590; *République de Y* v. *Office*, Switzerland, 2001, 12 RSDIE (2002) 607, 608.

91 For rare exceptions see, e.g., the trial of the Lockerbie case by the Scottish High Court of Justiciary at Camp Zeist, the Netherlands: UN Security Council Resolution S/RES/1192 (1998); the 1998 UK–Netherlands Agreement, 38 ILM 926 (1999); *Advocate* v. *Megrahi*, 2001 WL 14966; *Megrahi* v. *Advocate*, 2002 JC 99; and the requisition of a ship in the harbour of Greenock, Scotland, by the Government of the Republic of Spain during the Spanish Civil War: *The El Condado*, Scotland, (1937) 59 Ll L Rep 119; 9 AD 277; *The Condado* Scotland, (1939) 63 Ll L Rep 83; (1939) 63 Ll L Rep 330; 9 AD 225; *Spain* v. *National Bank*, Scotland, 1939 SC 413.

534   NOTES TO PAGES 81–83

92 *Saudi Arabia* v. *Nelson*, US, 507 US 349, 361–362 (1993); 123 L.Ed.2d 47, 61–62;
100 ILR 544, 553–554; reversing *Nelson* v. *Saudi Arabia*, US, 923 F.2d 1528 (11th
Cir. 1991); 88 ILR 189. See also *Bao* v. *Li*, US, 201 F.Supp.2d 14, 24 (D.D.C.
2000); *Daliberti* v. *Iraq*, US, 97 F.Supp.2d 38, 47 (D.D.C. 2000); *Aguasviva* v.
Iberia, US, 937 F.Supp. 141, 143–144 (D.P.R. 1996) (*Aguasviva* v. *Iberia*, US, 902
F.Supp. 314, 317 (D.P.R. 1995) vacated in part); *Herbage* v. *Meese*, US, 747 F.
Supp. 60, 67 (D.D.C. 1990); 98 ILR 101; affirmed, *Herbage* v. *Meese*, US, 946 F.2d
1564 (D.C.Cir. 1991)(Table). US commentators are divided on the assessment
of the *Nelson* case. For criticism see Bodoh, The Routine; Brockbank, The
Sovereign; Whelan, The Commercial; McCarthy, The Commercial; Fastiggi,
A Jurisdictional; Hoek, Foreign. For favourable views see Patchett, *Nelson*;
McIntyre, *Nelson*; Johnson, *Saudi*. For cases in other countries immunizing
uses and abuses of police and associated powers see *Carrato* v. *USA*, Canada,
(1982) 141 DLR (3d) 456, 459; 90 ILR 229, 232; *Tritt* v. *USA*, Canada, (1989) 68
OR (2d) 284, 287; 94 ILR 260, 263; affirmed, *Tritt* v. *USA*, Canada, (1994) 45
ACWS (3d) 1140; *Jaffe* v. *Miller*, Canada, (1990) 73 DLR (4th) 420, 424; 87 ILR
197, 201; affirmed, *Jaffe* v. *Miller*, Canada, (1993) 103 DLR (4th) 315; 13 OR (3d)
745, 759–760; 95 ILR 446, 459–460; *Bouzari* v. *Iran*, Canada, (2002) 124 ILR 427,
435; affirmed, *Bouzari* v. *Iran*, Canada, (2004) 243 DLR (4th) 406, 420–421; 128
ILR 586, 598–599; *Propend* v. *Sing*, England, (1997) 111 ILR 611, 670.
93 *Youming* v. *Ministry*, US, 557 F.Supp.2d 131, 141–142 (D.D.C. 2008). For an
earlier action see *Youming* v. *Ministry*, US, 475 F.Supp.2d 54 (D.D.C. 2007).
94 *Doe I* v. *Israel*, US, 400 F.Supp.2d 86, 106 (D.D.C. 2005).
95 *First* v. *Argentina*, US, 190 F.Supp.2d 1336, 1338–1339 (S.D.Fla. 2002).
96 *Braka* v. *Bancomer*, US, 762 F.2d 222, 225 (2nd Cir. 1985).
97 *Kline* v. *Kaneko*, US, 685 F.Supp. 386, 391 (S.D.N.Y. 1988); 101 ILR 497.
98 *EAL* v. *European*, US, 107 ILR 318, 330 (D. Del. 1994).
99 *Peterson* v. *Saudi Arabia*, US, 332 F.Supp.2d 189, 199–200 (D.D.C. 2004);
affirmed, *Peterson* v. *Saudi Arabia*, US, 416 F.3d 83 (D.C.Cir. 2005).
100 *Rahimtoola* v. *Nizam*, England, 1957, [1958] AC 379, 422; 24 ILR 175; *Barker* v.
Kenya, Zimbabwe, (1983) (4) SA 817; (1985) (4) SA 197; 84 ILR 18, 24. This also
includes a *promise* to enact legislation and to enter into an international
agreement with another State: *Wolf* v. *Germany*, US, 95 F.3d 536, 543–544 (7th
Cir. 1996). See also *Hirsh* v. *Israel*, US, 962 F.Supp. 377, 382–383 (S.D.N.Y. 1997);
113 ILR 543; *Cicippio* v. *Iran*, US, 30 F.3d 164, 168–169 (D.C.Cir. 1994); 107 ILR
296.
101 *Elbasir* v. *Saudi Arabia*, US, 468 F.Supp.2d 155, 161 (D.D.C. 2007).
102 *Fickling* v. *Australia*, US, 775 F.Supp. 66, 71 (E.D.N.Y. 1991); 103 ILR 447.
103 *Controller* v. *Davison*, New Zealand, [1996] 2 NZLR 278, 301; 104 ILR 526, 571.
104 *Butters* v. *Vance*, US, 225 F.3d 462, 465 (4th Cir. 2000).
105 See *Yang* v. *Liaoning*, US, 452 F.3d 883, 890 (D.C.Cir. 2006); affirming *Yang* v.
Liaoning, US, 362 F.Supp.2d 83 (D.D.C. 2005); *Garb* v. *Poland*, US, 440 F.3d 579,
586 (2nd Cir. 2006); affirming *Garb* v. *Poland*, US, 207 F.Supp.2d 16, 31–32
(E.D.N.Y. 2002); *Beg* v. *Pakistan*, US, 353 F.3d 1323, 1326–1327 (11th Cir. 2003);
Anderman v. *Austria*, US, 256 F.Supp.2d 1098, 1107 (C.D.Cal. 2003); *Shakour* v.

Germany, US, 199 F.Supp.2d 8, 13 (E.D.N.Y. 2002); *Haven* v. *Rzeczpospolita*, US, 68 F.Supp.2d 947, 954 (N.D.Ill. 1999); affirmed, *Haven* v. *Rzeczpospolita* US, 215 F.3d 727 (7th Cir. 2000); *Pena-Perez* v. *Procuraduria*, US, 1997 WL 122823, p. 2 (S.D.N.Y. 1997); *Baglab* v. *Johnson*, US, 665 F.Supp. 289, 294 (S.D.N.Y. 1987); *Alberti* v. *Empresa*, US, 705 F.2d 250, 254 (7th Cir. 1983); 92 ILR 392; *Carey* v. *National*, US, 453 F.Supp. 1097, 1102 (S.D.N.Y. 1978); 63 ILR 164; affirmed, *Carey* v. *National*, US, 592 F.2d 673 (1979); 63 ILR 232; *Mexico* v. *Ashley*, US, 556 S.W.2d 784, 786 (1977); 63 ILR 95, 98; *SA Biocare* v. *Gécamines*, Belgium, (1989) 115 ILR 415, 417; *Corporacion* v. *Braden*, France, (1972) 65 ILR 57, 60; *Société Algérienne* v. *Sempac*, France, (1978) 65 ILR 73, 75; *Société* v. *Lao*, France, (1987) 80 ILR 688, 690; affirming *Société* v. *Lao*, France, (1983) 80 ILR 430, 432; *Oder-Neisse Property Expropriation Case*, Germany, (1975) 65 ILR 127, 129; *Inter-Science* v. *Moçambique*, South Africa, 1979, 1980 (2) SA 111, 118, 126; 64 ILR 689, 697, 706; *S* v. *Romania*, Switzerland, (1987) 82 ILR 45, 49–50, Ground 3. However, follow-up activities after the expropriation may be a commercial activity: *Siderman* v. *Argentina*, US, 965 F.2d 699, 708–709 (9th Cir. 1992); 103 ILR 454.

106 *Garb* v. *Poland*, US, 440 F.3d 579, 582 (2nd Cir. 2006); affirming *Garb* v. *Poland*, US, 207 F.Supp.2d 16 (E.D.N.Y. 2002); *First* v. *Argentina*, US, 190 F.Supp.2d 1336, 1338–1339 (S.D.Fla. 2002); *Libya* v. *SpA*, Italy, (1979) 78 ILR 90, 93.

107 *Chisholm* v. *Bank*, US, 643 F.Supp. 1393, 1400 (S.D.Fla. 1986); 121 ILR 487.

108 *NV* v. *Bank Indonesia*, Netherlands, (1963) 65 ILR 348, 353.

109 *Aristocrat* v. *National*, Canada, [2001] 107 ACWS (3d) 595; [2001] OTC 523, para. 16.

110 *Anglo-Iberia* v. *PT*, US, 600 F.3d 171, 178 (2nd Cir. 2010).

111 *Indian Foreign Minister Case*, Germany, (1988) 90 ILR 408, 410–411.

112 *Allianz* v. *USA*, France, (1999) 127 ILR 148, 152–153.

113 *USA* v. *Ruiz*, Philippines, (1985) 102 ILR 122, 126.

114 *National Iranian* v. *Pipeline*, France, (1990) 113 ILR 446, 447.

115 *Yugoslavia* v. *Société*, France, (1985) 82 ILR 58, 73.

116 *Montanez* v. *Banco*, US, 973 F.Supp. 89, 94 (D.P.R. 1997).

117 *Italian* v. *X*, Switzerland, (1985) 82 ILR 23, 26, Ground 4a.

118 *Hirsh* v. *Israel*, US, 962 F.Supp. 377, 382–383 (S.D.N.Y. 1997); 113 ILR 543; affirmed, *Hirsh* v. *Israel*, US, 133 F.3d 907 (2nd Cir. 1997); *Sampson* v. *Germany*, US, 975 F.Supp. 1108, 1116–1117 (N.D.Ill. 1997); affirmed, *Sampson* v. *Germany*, 250 F.3d 1145 (7th Cir. 2001); *Wolf* v. *Germany*, US, 95 F.3d 536, 543–544 (7th Cir. 1996).

119 *Alcom* v. *Colombia*, England, [1984] 1 AC 580, 599; 74 ILR 170, 182.

120 *Fagot* v. *Costa Rica*, US, 934 F.Supp. 493, 500 (D. P. R. 1996); *Karabulut* v. *Allegro*, Canada, [2003] OJ No. 5748; [2003] 130 ACWS (3d) 921, para. 4.

121 *MacArthur* v. *Peru*, US, 809 F.2d 918, 920 (D.C.Cir. 1987); 107 ILR 196.

122 *Teitelbaum* v. *Israel*, Canada, 2008 CarswellQue 12119.

123 *Australia* v. *Midford*, Malaysia, [1990] 1 Curr LJ 878, 884–885; 86 ILR 640, 651.

124 *In Re D*, France, (1966) 47 ILR 57, 57–58.

125 *Zucca* v. *Fondazione*, Italy, (1969) 65 ILR 280, 281–282.

536   NOTES TO PAGES 83-86

126 *Senghor* v. *International*, France, (1990) 113 ILR 460, 461.
127 *Case against the Foreign Minister of Belgium*, Austria, 2001, 6 *Austrian RIEL* (2001) 288, 296.
128 *Västerås* v. *Iceland*, Sweden, (1999) 128 ILR 705, 707; *X* v. *Germany*, Austria, (1963) 65 ILR 10, 12–13.
129 *Victoria* v. *US*, Australia, [2005] VSCA 76, [2005] 218 ALR 640; [2005] 190 FLR 351, 357–358; affirming *Wells* v. *Victoria*, Australia, [2004] VSC 262; 185 FLR 48 and *Wells* v. *Victoria*, Australia, [2004] VSC 341.
130 *Duvalier* v. *Haiti*, France, (1990) 113 ILR 448, 449; *Hilao* v. *Marcos*, US, 94 F.3d 539, 546 (9th Cir. 1996).
131 *EM* v. *Argentina*, US, 473 F.3d 463, 482–484 (2nd Cir. 2007).
132 *Kato* v. *Ishihara*, US, 360 F.3d 106, 111–112 (2nd Cir. 2004).
133 *Virtual Countries* v. *South Africa*, US, 148 F.Supp.2d 256, 264–265 (S.D.N.Y. 2001); affirmed, *Virtual Countries* v. *South Africa*, US, 300 F.3d 230, 232 (2nd Cir. 2002).
134 *Aschenbrenner* v. *Conseil*, US, 851 F.Supp. 580, 585 (S.D.N.Y. 1994) (emphases added).
135 *Intercontinental* v. *De Gruyter*, US, 822 F.Supp. 662, 675–676 (C.D. Cal. 1993). But see *Sun* v. *Taiwan*, US, 201 F.3d 1105, 1108–1109 (9th Cir. 2000) for a criticism of this case.
136 *Hwang* v. *Japan*, US, 172 F.Supp.2d 52, 63 (D.D.C. 2001); affirmed on other grounds, *Hwang* v. *Japan*, US, 332 F.3d 679, 686 (D.C.Cir. 2003). The decision in *Hwang* was later vacated and remanded by the Supreme Court, *Hwang* v. *Japan*, US, 542 US 901 (2004), but was reaffirmed on the ground of non-justiciability, *Hwang* v. *Japan*, US, 413 F.3d 45 (D.C.Cir. 2005).
137 *Kline* v. *Kaneko*, US, 685 F.Supp. 386, 391 (S.D.N.Y. 1988); 101 ILR 497. See also *In re Terrorist*, US, 349 F.Supp.2d 765, 793 (S.D.N.Y. 2005).
138 *Cicippio* v. *Iran*, US, 30 F.3d 164, 168 (D.C.Cir. 1994); 107 ILR 296, 301 (emphasis added). See also *Mwani* v. *bin Laden*, US, 417 F.3d 1, 17 (D.C.Cir. 2005).
139 *In re Terrorist*, US, 349 F.Supp.2d 765, 793 (S.D.N.Y. 2005).
140 *Letelier* v. *Chile*, US, 748 F.2d 790, 797–798 (2nd Cir. 1984); 79 ILR 561.
141 *LF* v. *Germany*, Netherlands, (1986) 94 ILR 342, 347–348. For a similar case see *Schmidt* v. *Home Secretary*, Ireland, (1994) 103 ILR 322; 1997, [1997] 2 IR 121.
142 *Cicippio* v. *Iran*, US, 30 F.3d 164, 168 (D.C.Cir. 1994); 107 ILR 296, 301 (emphasis added).
143 *Practical Concepts* v. *Bolivia*, US, 613 F.Supp. 863, 869 (D.D.C. 1985).
144 *Practical Concepts* v. *Bolivia*, US, 615 F.Supp. 92, 93 (D.D.C. 1985).
145 *Practical Concepts* v. *Bolivia*, US, 811 F.2d 1543, 1550 (D.C.Cir. 1987); 92 ILR 420, 428; vacating *Practical Concepts* v. *Bolivia*, US, 615 F.Supp. 92 (D.D.C. 1985).
146 See Crawford, International Law, 94–102; Badr, *State Immunity*, pp. 63–70; Schreuer, *State Immunity*, pp. 42–43.
147 Crawford, International Law, 114.
148 *Société anonyme Compagnie des chemins de fer Liégeois Limbourgeois* v. *Etat Néerlandais*, Belgium, 1903, 31 *JDIP* (1904) 417, 428. See also *Société* v. *Banque Centrale*, Belgium, (1963) 45 ILR 85, 86–87; *Rousseau* v. *Upper Volta*, Belgium,

NOTES TO PAGES 86–87   537

(1983) 82 ILR 118, 120; *De Queiroz* v. *Portugal*, Belgium, (1992) 115 ILR 430, 433; *Rafidain* v. *Consarc*, Belgium, (1993) 106 ILR 274, 277.

149 *Rafidain* v. *Consarc*, Belgium, (1993) 106 ILR 274, 277.

150 *Collision Case*, Austria, (1961) 40 ILR 73, 76. See also *Hunting Rights Case*, Austria, (1987) 86 ILR 564, 569; *French Consular Employee Claim Case*, Austria, (1989) 86 ILR 583, 586; *Payroll Taxes Case*, Austria, 2001, 6 *Austrian RIEL* (2001) 304, 308; *Arrears of Rent Case*, Austria, 2001, 6 *Austrian RIEL* (2001) 313, 314.

151 *Empire of Iran Case*, Germany, (1963) 45 ILR 57, 80; quoted in *I Congreso del Partido*, England, 1977, [1978] 1 QB 500, 530; 64 ILR 154, 181; *I Congreso del Partido*, England, 1979 [1980] 1 Lloyd's Rep. 23, 30, 34; [1981] 1 All ER 1092, 1102, 1107; 64 ILR 227, 234, 239; *I Congreso del Partido*, England, 1981, [1983] 1 AC 244, 263–264, 276; 64 ILR 307, 315, 327; *Kuwait Airways* v. *Iraqi Airways*, England, 1993, [1995] 1 Lloyd's Rep 25, 29, 34, 36; [1995] 1 WLR 1147, 1173; 103 ILR 340, 374, 382, 385, 417; *Propend* v. *Sing*, England, (1997) 111 ILR 611, 667; *Cargo* v. *Lorac*, Canada, (1986) 28 DLR (4th) 309, 315; 84 ILR 700, 706; *Her Majesty* v. *Edelson*, Israel, (1997) 131 ILR 279, 301. For German cases see also *Arms Sales Case*, Germany, (1972) 65 ILR 119, 121; *Spanish State Tourist Office Case*, Germany, (1977) 65 ILR 140, 143–144; *Conrades* v. *UK*, Germany, (1981) 65 ILR 205, 207; *Foreign Trade Institute Case*, Germany, (1981) 65 ILR 209, 210; *X* v. *Argentina*, Germany, (1996) 114 ILR 502, 505; *Muller* v. *USA*, Germany, (1998) 114 ILR 512, 516–517.

152 *Central Bank of Nigeria Case*, Germany, (1975) 65 ILR 131, 135–136. See also *Segni* v. *Commercial*, US, 835 F.2d 160, 164–165 (7th Cir. 1987); 98 ILR 55, 59–60.

153 *UAR* v. *Mrs X*, Switzerland, (1960) 65 ILR 385, 390, Ground 2; *Italian* v. *Beta*, Switzerland, (1966) 65 ILR 394, 398, Ground 5; 401, Ground 7; *Banque* v. *Weston*, Switzerland, (1978) 65 ILR 417, 420, Ground 2c; 423, Ground 4a; *Egypt* v. *Cinetelevision*, Switzerland, (1979) 65 ILR 425, 431, Ground 5a; *S* v. *India*, Switzerland, (1984) 82 ILR 13, 19, Ground 3; *Italian* v. *X*, Switzerland, (1985) 82 ILR 23, 26, Ground 4a; *Libya* v. *Actimon*, Switzerland, (1985) 82 ILR 30, 33–34 Ground 5b; *S* v. *Romania*, Switzerland, (1987) 82 ILR 45, 48–49, Ground 2; *M* v. *Egypt*, Switzerland, (1994) 116 ILR 656, 662, Ground 4a; *R* v. *Iraq*, Switzerland, (1994) 116 ILR 664, 666, Ground 5a; *République Y* v. *X*, Switzerland, 2000, 11 *RSDIE* (2001) 589, 590; *République de Y* v. *Office*, Switzerland, 2001, 12 *RSDIE* (2002) 607, 608.

154 *Italian* v. *Beta*, Switzerland, (1966) 65 ILR 394, 401, Ground 7a. See also *République Y* v. *X*, Switzerland, 2000, 11 *RSDIE* (2001) 589, 590; *République de Y* v. *Office*, Switzerland, 2001, 12 *RSDIE* (2002) 607, 608.

155 *Russian Federation* v. *Pied-Rich*, Netherlands, 1993, 41 *NILR* (1994) 116, 118; *Portugal* v. *De Sousa*, Netherlands, (1981) 94 ILR 314, 315; *Société Européenne* v. *Yugoslavia*, Netherlands, (1973) 65 ILR 356, 361.

156 *Distomo Massacre Case*, Greece, (2000) 129 ILR 513, 516.

157 *UK* v. *Joel*, Kenya, (1983) 103 ILR 235, 239.

158 *Kramer* v. *Belgium*, Nigeria, (1988) 103 ILR 299, 310.

159 *X* v. *Israel*, Portugal, (2002) 127 ILR 310, 313. But see *Brazilian Embassy Employee Case*, Portugal, (1984) 116 ILR 625.

538   NOTES TO PAGES 87–89

160 *The Akademik Fyodorov*, South Africa, 1996 (4) SA 422, 447; 131 ILR 460, 488; *KJ v. Oscar Jupiter*, South Africa, 1997, 1998 (2) SA 130, 136; 131 ILR 529, 535–536. However, in view of the close affinity between the South African practice with that of the UK, one would suspect that a strictly 'nature' position might not be rigorously adhered to.

161 *Barker v. Kenya*, Zimbabwe, (1983/1985) 84 ILR 18, 25–26, 36.

162 US House of Representatives, Report No. 94-1487, 1976, p. 16; 1976 USCCAN 6604, 6615.

163 Report No. 94-1487, 1976, p. 16/6615 (emphasis added).

164 *De Sanchez v. Banco*, US, 770 F.2d 1385, 1393 (5th Cir. 1985); 88 ILR 75, 85. For sympathetic opinions see *Segni v. Commercial*, US, 835 F.2d 160, 164 (7th Cir. 1987); 98 ILR 55; *Joseph v. Office*, US, 830 F.2d 1018, 1023 (9th Cir. 1987); 101 ILR 485; *Rush-Presbyterian v. Hellenic*, US, 877 F.2d 574, 577 (7th Cir. 1989); 101 ILR 509; *Mukaddam v. Permanent*, US, 111 F.Supp.2d 457, 462 (S.D.N.Y. 2000). See Benjamin, *De Sanchez*, 736–741; Kaiden, *Millen*, 203–209.

165 *Rush-Presbyterian v. Hellenic*, US, 877 F.2d 574, 577 (7th Cir. 1989); 101 ILR 509; quoted in *Re Canada Labour Code*, Canada, (1992) 91 DLR (4th) 449, 465; 94 ILR 264, 280.

166 *Segni v. Commercial*, US, 835 F.2d 160, 164 (7th Cir. 1987); 98 ILR 55 (emphases in the original).

167 *Argentina v. Weltover*, US, 504 US 607, 614 (1992); 119 L.Ed.2d 394, 405; 100 ILR 509, 515 (emphasis in the original). The Supreme Court later quoted itself in *Saudi Arabia v. Nelson*, US, 507 US 349, 360–361 (1993); 123 L.Ed.2d 47, 61; 100 ILR 544, 553. See also *Berdakin v. Consulado*, US, 912 F.Supp. 458, 462 (C.D.Cal. 1995); *Voest-Alpine v. Bank*, US, 142 F.3d 887, 892 (5th Cir. 1998); *First v. Argentina*, US, 190 F.Supp.2d 1336, 1338 (S.D.Fla. 2002); *Anderman v. Austria*, US, 256 F.Supp.2d 1098, 1107 (C.D.Cal. 2003); *Ministry v. Cubic*, US, 385 F.3d 1206, 1219–1220 (9th Cir. 2004); *Cruz v. US*, US, 387 F.Supp.2d 1057, 1064, fn. 4 (N.D.Cal. 2005).

168 *Argentina v. Weltover*, US, 504 US 607, 615, 616 (1992); 119 L.Ed.2d 394, 405, 406 (1992); 100 ILR 509, 515, 516.

169 *Argentina v. Weltover*, US, 504 US 607, 617 (1992); 119 L.Ed.2d 394, 406–407; 100 ILR 509, 516–517 (emphases in the original).

170 *El-Hadad v. UAE*, US, 496 F.3d 658, 668 (D.C.Cir. 2007) (emphasis in the original).

171 *Saudi Arabia v. Nelson*, US, 507 US 349, 360 (1993); 123 L.Ed.2d 47, 61; 100 ILR 544, 553.

172 *Dale v. Colagiovanni*, US, 337 F.Supp.2d 825, 839 (S.D.Miss. 2004); this part affirmed, *Dale v. Colagiovanni*, US, 443 F.3d 425, 429 (5th Cir. 2006). But cf. *In re Terrorist*, US, 349 F.Supp.2d 765, 793 (S.D.N.Y. 2005); *Burnett v. Al Baraka*, US, 292 F.Supp.2d 9, 18 (D.D.C. 2003).

173 For adoption of the expression see also *Globe v. AO*, US, 376 F.3d 282, 289 (4th Cir. 2004); *First v. Argentina*, US, 190 F.Supp.2d 1336, 1338 (S.D.Fla. 2002); *Supra v. McGonigle*, US, 955 F.Supp. 374, 380 (E.D.Pa. 1997); *Caribbean v. Nigerian*, US, 1993 WL 541236, p. 7 (S.D.N.Y. 1993).

NOTES TO PAGES 89–90   539

174 *Los Angeles* v. *Conus*, US, 969 F.Supp. 579, 586 (C.D.Cal. 1997); *Bryks* v. *Canadian*, US, 906 F.Supp. 204, 207–208 (S.D.N.Y. 1995).

175 US House of Representatives, Report No. 94-1487, 1976, pp. 20–21; 1976 USCCAN 6604, 6619–6620.

176 This is actually a criticism by a number of US courts, including the Supreme Court. See *Argentina* v. *Weltover*, US, 504 US 607, 612 (1992); 119 L.Ed.2d 394, 404; 100 ILR 509, 514; *Saudi Arabia* v. *Nelson*, US, 507 US 349, 359 (1993); 123 L.Ed.2d 47, 60; 100 ILR 544, 552; *Texas* v. *Nigeria*, US, 647 F.2d 300, 308–309 (2nd Cir. 1981); 63 ILR 552; *Callejo* v. *Bancomer*, US, 764 F.2d 1101, 1108, fn. 6 (5th Cir. 1985); 84 ILR 106; *Practical* v. *Bolivia*, US, 811 F.2d 1543, 1549 (D.C.Cir. 1987); 92 ILR 420; *Segni* v. *Commercial*, US, 835 F.2d 160, 163 (7th Cir. 1987); 98 ILR 55; *Tifa* v. *Ghana*, US, 692 F.Supp. 393, 400 (D.N.J. 1988); *Rush-Presbyterian* v. *Hellenic*, US, 877 F.2d 574, 577 (7th Cir. 1989); 101 ILR 509; *Stena* v. *Comision*, US, 923 F.2d 380, 387, fn. 9 (5th Cir. 1991); 103 ILR 433; *S & S* v. *Masinexport-import*, US, 802 F.Supp. 1109, 1111–1112 (S.D.N.Y. 1992); 107 ILR 239; *Zveiter* v. *Brazilian*, US, 833 F.Supp. 1089, 1092 (S.D.N.Y. 1993); *Elliott* v. *British*, US, 986 F.Supp. 189, 193 (S.D.N.Y. 1997); *El-Hadad* v. *UAE*, US, 216 F.3d 29, 34 (D.C.Cir. 2000); *Hansen* v. *Danish*, US, 147 F.Supp.2d 142, 150 (E.D.N.Y. 2001); *El-Hadad* v. *Embassy*, US, 2006 WL 826098, p. 7 (D.D.C. 2006).

177 US House of Representatives, Report No. 94-1487, 1976, p. 16; 1976 USCCAN 6604, 6615. On Congress's deliberate omission see *Segni* v. *Commercial*, US, 835 F.2d 160, 163 (7th Cir. 1987); 98 ILR 55; *Practical* v. *Bolivia*, US, 811 F.2d 1543, 1549 (D.C.Cir. 1987); 92 ILR 420; *Transamerican* v. *Somalia*, US, 767 F.2d 998, 1002 (D.C.Cir. 1985); 86 ILR 55; *Velidor* v. *L/P/G*, US, 653 F.2d 812, 817, n. 7 (3rd Cir. 1981); 63 ILR 622.

178 *Argentina* v. *Weltover*, US, 504 US 607, 612–613 (1992); 119 L.Ed.2d 394, 404; 100 ILR 509, 514; *Saudi Arabia* v. *Nelson*, US, 507 US 349, 359 (1993); 123 L.Ed.2d 47, 60; 100 ILR 544, 552.

179 *Saudi Arabia* v. *Nelson*, US, 507 US 349, 359–360 (1993); 123 L.Ed.2d 47, 60; 100 ILR 544, 552.

180 *Walter* v. *Philippines*, US, 965 F.2d 1375, 1384 (5th Cir. 1992) (citing *Callejo*); 103 ILR 503 (emphasis added). This was reiterated in *MCI* v. *Alhadhood*, US, 82 F.3d 658, 663 (5th Cir. 1996). See also *US* v. *Moats*, US, 961 F.2d 1198, 1205 (5th Cir. 1992); 103 ILR 480; *Callejo* v. *Bancomer*, US, 764 F.2d 1101, 1108, fn. 6 (5th Cir. 1985); 84 ILR 106. In fact, there is good evidence that courts in other circuits would also look for a profit motive. See *Tolliver* v. *Nigeria*, US, 265 F.Supp.2d 873, 881 (W.D.Mich. 2003); *World* v. *Nammo*, US, 51 Fed.Appx. 403, 406 (4th Cir. 2002); affirming *World* v. *Nammo*, US, No. 00-1992-A, Mem. Op. at 1–6 (E.D. Va. 2002); *Sun* v. *Taiwan*, US, 201 F.3d 1105, 1108 (9th Cir. 2000); *Intercontinental* v. *De Gruyter*, US, 822 F.Supp. 662, 675–676 (C.D.Cal. 1993); *Schoenberg* v. *Exportadora*, US, 930 F.2d 777, 780 (9th Cir. 1991); 98 ILR 118; *Gould* v. *Pechiney*, US, 853 F.2d 445, 452 (6th Cir. 1988); 98 ILR 136; *LeDonne* v. *Gulf*, US, 700 F.Supp. 1400, 1409 (E.D.Va. 1988); *Kline* v. *Kaneko*, US, 685 F.Supp. 386, 391 (S.D.N.Y. 1988); 101 ILR 497; *Letelier* v. *Chile*, US, 748 F.2d 790, 797 (2nd Cir. 1984); 79 ILR 561; *US* v. *Arlington*, US, 702 F.2d 485, 488 (4th Cir. 1983); *International* v. *OPEC*, US,

540   NOTES TO PAGES 90-96

649 F.2d 1354, 1357–1358 (9th Cir. 1981); 66 ILR 413; affirming *International* v. *OPEC*, US, 477 F.Supp. 553, 566–569 (C.D.Cal. 1979); 63 ILR 284.

181 US House of Representatives, Report No. 94-1487, 1976, p. 16; 1976 USCCAN 6604, 6615 (emphasis added).

182 *Sun* v. *Taiwan*, US, 201 F.3d 1105, 1108 (9th Cir. 2000). For cases where the expression 'private parties' is used without the expression 'for profit' see *Leutwyler* v. *Office*, US, 184 F.Supp.2d 277, 291 (S.D.N.Y. 2001); *Mukaddam* v. *Permanent*, US, 111 F.Supp.2d 457, 462 (S.D.N.Y. 2000).

183 *Malewicz* v. *Amsterdam*, US, 362 F.Supp.2d 298, 314 (D.D.C. 2005) (emphasis added); motion to dismiss denied, *Malewicz* v. *Amsterdam*, US, 517 F.Supp.2d 322 (D.D.C. 2007).

184 *Doe* v. *Holy See*, US, 434 F.Supp.2d 925, 941 (D.Or. 2006) (emphases in the original).

185 *Doe*, 434 F.Supp.2d 925, 941 (D.Or. 2006).

186 *Doe*, 434 F.Supp.2d 925, 941–942, fn. 4 (D.Or. 2006).

187 *Doe*, 434 F.Supp.2d 925, 942 (D.Or. 2006).

188 *Joseph* v. *Office*, US, 830 F.2d 1018, 1024 (9th Cir. 1987) (emphasis in the original); 101 ILR 485. See also *Siderman* v. *Argentina*, US, 965 F.2d 699, 708 (9th Cir. 1992); 103 ILR 454.

189 *Rush-Presbyterian* v. *Hellenic*, US, 877 F.2d 574, 578, fn. 4 (7th Cir. 1989); 101 ILR 509.

190 US House of Representatives, Report No. 94-1487, 1976, p. 16; 1976 USCCAN 6604, 6615. Emphases added.

191 *Letelier* v. *Chile*, US, 748 F.2d 790, 797 (2nd Cir. 1984); 79 ILR 561. See also *Guevara* v. *Peru*, US, 468 F.3d 1289, 1303 (11th Cir. 2006) ('private yet non-commercial activities').

192 *MCI* v. *Alhadhood*, US, 82 F.3d 658, 663 (5th Cir. 1996).

193 *Rush-Presbyterian* v. *Hellenic*, US, 877 F.2d 574, 578–579 (7th Cir. 1989); 101 ILR 509 (emphasis in the original).

194 *Dominican* v. *Dominican*, US, 903 F.Supp. 1507, 1513 (M.C.Fla. 1995).

195 *Argentina* v. *Weltover*, US, 504 US 607, 614 (1992); 119 L.Ed.2d 394, 405; 100 ILR 509, 515.

196 *Argentina* v. *Weltover*, US, 504 US 607, 616 (1992); 119 L.Ed.2d 394, 406; 100 ILR 509, 516. See also *Guevara* v. *Peru*, US, 468 F.3d 1289, 1303 (11th Cir. 2006).

197 *Saudi Arabia* v. *Nelson*, US, 507 US 349, 360 (1993); 123 L.Ed.2d 47, 61; 100 ILR 544, 553; quoting *Argentina* v. *Weltover*, US, 504 US 607, 614 (1992); 119 L.Ed.2d 394, 405 (1992); 100 ILR 509, 515 and *Alfred Dunhill* v. *Cuba*, US, 425 US 682, 704 (1976); 66 ILR 212, 225.

198 US House of Representatives, Report No. 94-1487, 1976, p. 16; 1976 USCCAN 6604, 6615.

199 *Argentina* v. *Weltover*, US, 504 US 607, 612–613 (1992); 119 L.Ed.2d 394, 404; 100 ILR 509, 514.

200 *Argentina* v. *Weltover*, US, 504 US 607, 615–616 (1992); 119 L.Ed.2d 394, 406; 100 ILR 509, 516. For the ambivalence towards the contextual approach see

NOTES TO PAGES 96–101   541

also *Cruz* v. *US*, US, 387 F.Supp.2d 1057, 1063–1064 (N.D.Cal. 2005). Cf. *Globe* v. *AO*, US, 376 F.3d 282, 287 (4th Cir. 2004).

201 *Intercontinental Dictionary Series* v. *De Gruyter*, US, 822 F.Supp. 662, 676 (C.D.Cal. 1993).

202 *EM* v. *Argentina*, US, 473 F.3d 463, 482–484 (2nd Cir. 2007).

203 *USA* v. *Ruiz*, Philippines, (1985) 102 ILR 122, 126 (emphases added).

204 *The Holy See* v. *Starbright*, Philippines, (1994) 102 ILR 163, 171–172.

205 For a pre-SIA case embracing the 'nature' test see *Cargo* v. *Lorac*, Canada, (1986) 28 DLR (4th) 309, 315; 84 ILR 700, 706–707.

206 *Re Canada Labour Code*, Canada, 1989, [1990] 1 FC 332, 338–339, 344, 349; 86 ILR 626, 630, 634, 638.

207 *Re Canada Labour Code*, Canada, (1992) 91 DLR (4th) 449, 460–474; 94 ILR 264, 275–289; reversing *Re Canada Labour Code*, Canada, 1989, [1990] 1 FC 332; 86 ILR 626. See also *Embassy Eviction Case*, Greece, (1965) 65 ILR 248, 250; *Lovell* v. *New Zealand*, Canada, [1992] ACWSJ Lexis 38241, p. 4, paras. 12–14; *Smith* v. *Chin*, Canada, [2006] OJ No. 4091; 152 ACWS (3d) 149, paras. 38, 44–47.

208 *Re Canada Labour Code*, Canada, (1992) 91 DLR (4th) 449, 461; 94 ILR 264, 276. Note the striking similarity with the *De Sanchez* decision. For favourable comment see Hornby, *Re Canada*, 314. See also *Her Majesty* v. *Edelson*, Israel, [1997] IsrLR 403; 131 ILR 279, 303.

209 *Re Canada Labour Code*, Canada, (1992) 91 DLR (4th) 449, 461, 463; 94 ILR 264, 276, 278.

210 *Re Canada Labour Code*, Canada, (1992) 91 DLR (4th) 449, 463; 94 ILR 264, 278.

211 *Re Canada Labour Code*, Canada, (1992) 91 DLR (4th) 449, 483 per Cory J, dissenting; 94 ILR 264, 298.

212 *Congo* v. *Venne*, Canada, (1971) 22 DLR (3d) 669, 673; 64 ILR 24, 28. For critical comment see *Barker* v. *Kenya*, Zimbabwe, (1983) (4) SA 817, 822; 84 ILR 18, 25.

213 See *Rumania* v. *Trutta*, Italy, 1926, 26 *AJIL Supplement* (1932) 626, 629; *US* v. *IRSA*, Italy, (1963) 65 ILR 262, 264; *Consorzio* v. *Federazione*, Italy, (1966) 65 ILR 265, 267; *US* v. *Bracale*, Italy, (1968) 65 ILR 273, 275.

214 *Scarfò* v. *Sovereign*, Italy, (1957) 24 ILR 1, 3–4.

215 *Francischiello* v. *USA*, Italy, (1959) 28 ILR 158, 161. See also *Parravincini* v. *Commercial*, Italy, (1969) 65 ILR 282, 283.

216 *De Ritis* v. *US*, Italy, (1971) 65 ILR 283, 284–285.

217 *Association* v. *Piccoli*, Italy, (1974) 65 ILR 308, 311. See also *Church* v. *Ferraino*, Italy, (1986) 101 ILR 370, 374–375.

218 *Luna* v. *Romania*, Italy, (1974) 65 ILR 313, 314–315.

219 *Danish* v. *Hansen*, Italy, (1979) 65 ILR 325, 328.

220 *Velloso* v. *Borla*, Italy, (1979) 65 ILR 328, 330.

221 *Bulli* v. *UK*, Italy, (1981) 65 ILR 343, 345–346.

222 *Panattoni* v. *Germany*, Italy, (1987) 87 ILR 42, 46–47.

223 *France* v. *Jacuzio*, Italy, (1987) 87 ILR 53, 55.

224 *Libya* v. *Trobbiani*, Italy, (1990) 114 ILR 520, 522.

225 *Norwegian* v. *Quattri*, Italy, (1991) 114 ILR 525, 527–528.

226 *Perrini* v. *Académie*, Italy, (1994) 114 ILR 536, 538–539.

542 NOTES TO PAGES 101–104

227 *Canada* v. *Cargnello*, Italy, (1998) 114 ILR 559, 565–566.
228 *Pontificia* v. *Inps*, Italy, (1979) 65 ILR 333, 336–337.
229 *Rubin* v. *Consul*, Italy, (1977) 77 ILR 593, 596.
230 *Special* v. *Pieciukiewicz*, Italy, (1982) 78 ILR 120, 122.
231 *Libya* v. *SpA*, Italy, (1979) 78 ILR 90, 92; *Embassy* v. *Società*, Italy, (1979) 65 ILR 331, 332–333; *Ministry* v. *Association*, Italy, (1978) 65 ILR 320, 322–323; *Nanni* v. *Pace*, Italy (1935) 8 AD 2, 4.
232 *Argentina* v. *Weltover*, US, 504 US 607, 614–620 (1992); 119 L.Ed.2d 394, 405–409; 100 ILR 509, 515–519; affirming *Weltover* v. *Argentina*, US, 753 F.Supp. 1201 (S.D.N.Y. 1991) and *Weltover* v. *Argentina*, US, 941 F.2d 145 (2nd Cir. 1991).
233 'This is because, while the acts of issuing and placing on the international market of the bonds concerned have an undeniably private-law character, the subsequent measures of moratorium, adopted by the Argentine Government, and the consequent failure of that State to fulfil its obligations, do not have an equally analogous nature.' *Borri* v. *Repubblica Argentina*, Italy, 2005, 88 *RDI* (2005) 856, 859, para. 4.
234 'Such measures ... clearly demonstrate the sovereign power of the State. This is ... above all, because of the *evidently public purposes*, pursued for the regulation of finance for the protection of the primary needs of the economic survival of the population in a historical context of a serious national emergency.' *Borri*, Italy, 2005, 88 *RDI* (2005) 856, 859, para. 4.2, emphasis added. For another case concerning a foreign State's restructuring of its external debt see *Condor* v. *Minister*, Italy, (1992) 101 ILR 394, 400–401.
235 *Libya* v. *SpA*, Italy, (1979) 78 ILR 90, 92 (emphases added).
236 *Administration* v. *Société*, France, (1969) 52 ILR 315, 316. See also *Montefiore* v. *Congo*, France, (1955) 22 ILR 226, 227; *Société* v. *Gouvernement Turc*, France, (1965) 47 ILR 155, 156; *Spanish* v. *Société*, France, (1973) 65 ILR 61, 62–63; *Iran* v. *Société Eurodif*, France, (1984) 77 ILR 513, 516; further confirmed, *Iran* v. *Société Eurodif*, France, (1989) 89 ILR 31; *Coco* v. *Argentina*, France, (1996) 113 ILR 491, 492.
237 *Clerget* v. *Banque*, France, (1969) 52 ILR 310, 313; affirmed, *Clerget* v. *Banque*, France, (1971) 65 ILR 54. See also *Entreprise* v. *États-Unis*, France (1964) 45 ILR 82, 83; *Mouracade* v. *Yemen*, France, (1991) 113 ILR 462, 463.
238 *Société* v. *World Bank*, France, (1984) 82 ILR 58, 64–65.
239 *Euroéquipement* v. *Centre*, France, (1991) 89 ILR 37, 39. See also *Société* v. *Gauthier*, France, (1984) 77 ILR 510, 511.
240 *X* v. *Saudi*, France, (2003) 127 ILR 163, 166 (emphasis added).
241 *Trendtex* v. *Central Bank*, England, [1977] QB 529, 558; 64 ILR 111, 132 (emphasis added); see also [1977] QB 529, 566, 579; 64 ILR 111, 140, 153. Lord Denning was quoted in *Reef* v. *Fua Kavenga*, New Zealand, [1987] 1 NZLR 550, 572; 90 ILR 556, 565; *Reid* v. *Nauru*, Australia, 1992, [1993] 1 VR 251, 253; 101 ILR 193, 195. For an earlier statement of Lord Denning proposing the 'nature' test see *Rahimtoola* v. *Nizam*, England, 1957, [1958] AC 379, 422; 24 ILR 175, 200.

NOTES TO PAGES 104–106   543

242 *I Congreso del Partido*, England, 1977, [1978] 1 QB 500, 528; 64 ILR 154, 179. Quoted by Lord Wilberforce as the 'ultimate test': *I Congreso del Partido*, England, 1981, [1983] 1 AC 244, 269; 64 ILR 307, 320.

243 *I Congreso del Partido*, England, 1979, [1981] 1 All ER 1092, 1102; 64 ILR 227, 234.

244 *Kuwait Airways* v. *Iraqi Airways*, England, [1995] 1 WLR 1147, 1160; 103 ILR 340, 401–402. See also *Kuwait Airways* v. *Iraqi Airways*, England, 1993, [1995] 1 Lloyd's Rep 25, 29–30, 33–34, 36; 103 ILR 340, 373–374, 381–382, 386–387; *In re Banco Nacional*, England, [2001] 3 All ER 923, 934; [2001] 1 WLR 2039, 2052; 124 ILR 550, 561; *Svenska* v. *Lithuania (No. 2)*, England, 2006, [2007] QB 886, 929, para. 132; *Ministry* v. *Tsavliris*, England, 2008, [2008] 2 Lloyd's Rep. 90, 104–105, paras. 78–79.

245 *I Congreso del Partido*, England, 1981, [1983] 1 AC 244, 262; 64 ILR 307, 313.

246 *I Congreso*, [1983] 1 AC 244, 263–264; 64 ILR 307, 315.

247 *I Congreso*, [1983] 1 AC 244, 267; 64 ILR 307, 318.

248 *I Congreso*, [1983] 1 AC 244, 267; 64 ILR 307, 318 (emphasis added). This 'contextual' approach, though evolved at common law, can be of great guidance for deciding those cases not adequately addressed by the UK SIA, especially the cases falling under s. 3(3)(c). Lord Wilberforce's contextual formula has been religiously cited and followed by the English courts, though sometimes with surprising results. The references in the courts are so great in number as to defy enumeration. See especially *Littrell* v. *USA (No. 2)*, England, (1992) 100 ILR 438, 447; 1993, [1994] 4 All ER 203, 212, 216; [1995] 1 WLR 82, 90, 94; 100 ILR 438, 458–459, 463; *Kuwait Airways* v. *Iraqi Airways*, England, 1993, [1995] 1 Lloyd's Rep 25, 35; 1995, [1995] 1 WLR 1147, 1157, 1173; 103 ILR 340, 385, 398, 416; *In re Banco Nacional*, England, [2001] 3 All ER 923, 932; [2001] 1 WLR 2039, 2049; 124 ILR 550, 559; *Kuwait Airways* v. *Iraqi Airways*, England, [2003] 1 Lloyd's Rep 448, 468–469, para. 153; 126 ILR 758, 799.

249 *I Congreso*, England, 1981, [1983] 1 AC 244, 272; 64 ILR 307, 323. Quoted in *Re Canada Labour Code*, Canada, (1992) 91 DLR (4th) 449, 463; 94 ILR 264, 277. See also *Kuwait Airways* v. *Iraqi Airways*, England, (1992) 103 ILR 340, 354.

250 *Littrell* v. *USA (No. 2)*, England, 1993, [1995] 1 WLR 82, 91, 94–95; [1994] 4 All ER 203, 213, 216–217; 100 ILR 438, 459–460, 463–464. For comments see Collier, Municipal; Fox, Access, 14.

251 *Holland* v. *Lampen-Wolfe*, England, [2000] 1 WLR 1573, 1577, 1578, 1580–1581, 1587; 119 ILR 367, 371–372, 375–376, 383.

252 *Holland*, [2000] 1 WLR 1573, 1577, 1579, 1581, 1587; 119 ILR 367, 371–372, 373, 375–376, 383.

253 See Yang, State Immunity (2001).

254 *Hicks* v. *USA*, England, (1995) 120 ILR 606, 610–611 (emphases added).

255 See *Reid* v. *Nauru*, Australia, 1992, [1993] 1 VR 251, 253; 101 ILR 193, 195; *Victoria* v. *US*, Australia, [2005] 190 FLR 351, 357–358; affirming *Wells* v. *Victoria*, Australia, [2004] VSC 262; 185 FLR 48 and *Wells* v. *Victoria (No. 2)*, Australia, [2004] VSC 341; Crawford, A Foreign, 84; *Re Canada Labour Code*, Canada, (1992) 91 DLR (4th) 449, 463, 484–485; 94 ILR 264, 278, 299–300;

544   NOTES TO PAGES 106–109

Canada v. *Burke*, Ireland, [1992] 2 IR 484, 491, 499; 95 ILR 467, 472–473, 480; *McElhinney* v. *Williams*, Ireland, 1995, [1996] 1 ILRM 276, 284–285; 104 ILR 691, 699; *Her Majesty* v. *Edelson*, Israel, (1997) 131 ILR 279, 303; *Australia* v. *Midford*, Malaysia, [1990] 1 Curr LJ 878, 884–885; 86 ILR 640, 651; *Buckingham* v. *Aircraft*, New Zealand, [1982] 2 NZLR 738, 740; 64 ILR 551; *Reef* v. *Fua Kavenga*, New Zealand, [1987] 1 NZLR 550, 570; 90 ILR 556; *Governor* v. *Sutton*, New Zealand, 1994, [1995] 1 NZLR 426, 428; 104 ILR 508, 510; *Controller* v. *Davison*, New Zealand, [1996] 2 NZLR 278, 288, 301, 308, 312, 313; 104 ILR 526, 537, 571, 605, 606, 614, 615–616.

256 *Controller* v. *Davison*, New Zealand, [1996] 2 NZLR 278, 289, 308–309, 312–313; 104 ILR 526, 538–539, 605–606, 615–616.

257 *Reid* v. *Nauru*, Australia, 1992, [1993] 1 VR 251, 253; 101 ILR 193, 195–196.

258 *Västerås* v. *Iceland*, Sweden, (1999) 128 ILR 705, 707. For criticism see Mahmnoudi, *Local Authority*, 195–197.

259 *Stena* v. *Comision*, US, 923 F.2d 380, 386 (5th Cir. 1991) (emphasis added); 103 ILR 433. For connected cases in the same court see *US* v. *Moats*, US, 961 F.2d 1198, 1205 (5th Cir. 1992); 103 ILR 480; *Arriba* v. *Petroleos*, US, 962 F.2d 528, 533 (5th Cir. 1992); 103 ILR 490; *Tubular* v. *Petroleos*, US, 977 F.2d 180, 184–185 (5th Cir. 1992). See also *Evans* v. *Pemex*, US, 390 F.Supp.2d 587, 590 (S.D.Tex. 2005); *Good* v. *Aramco*, US, 971 F.Supp. 254, 257 (S.D.Tex. 1997); *Gerding* v. *France*, US, 943 F.2d 521, 527 (4th Cir. 1991); 98 ILR 159, 165; *Maritime* v. *Guinea*, US, 693 F.2d 1094, 1109 (D.C.Cir. 1982); 72 ILR 152.

260 *Soudavar* v. *Iran*, US, 186 F.3d 671, 674 (5th Cir. 1999). See also *Haven* v. *Rzeczpospolita*, US, 215 F.3d 727, 736 (7th Cir. 2000); affirming *Haven* v. *Rzeczpospolita*, US, 68 F.Supp.2d 947 (N.D.Ill. 1999); *Anderman* v. *Austria*, US, 256 F.Supp.2d 1098 (C.D.Cal. 2003).

261 For the meaning of 'based upon' see *Saudi Arabia* v. *Nelson*, US, 507 US 349, 356–358 (1993); 123 L.Ed.2d 47, 58–59; 100 ILR 544, 550–551; *Murphy* v. *Korea*, US, 421 F.Supp.2d 627, 648 (S.D.N.Y. 2005); *Transatlantic* v. *Shanghai*, US, 204 F.3d 384, 390–391 (2nd Cir. 2000); *Byrd* v. *Corporacion*, US, 182 F.3d 380, 389–390 (5th Cir. 1999); *Voest-Alpine* v. *Bank*, US, 142 F.3d 887, 892 (5th Cir. 1998); *Holden* v. *Canadian*, US, 92 F.3d 918, 920 (9th Cir. 1996); *Gates* v. *Victor*, US, 54 F.3d 1457, 1463 (9th Cir. 1995); 107 ILR 371; *Stena* v. *Comision*, US, 923 F.2d 380, 386–387 (5th Cir. 1991); 103 ILR 433; *Filus* v. *Lot*, US, 907 F.2d 1328, 1333 (2nd Cir. 1990); *Joseph* v. *Office*, US, 830 F.2d 1018, 1023 (9th Cir. 1987); 101 ILR 485; Born, *International Civil Litigation*, p. 257. See also *Teledyne* v. *Kone*, US, 892 F.2d 1404, 1411 (9th Cir. 1989); *Orient* v. *Bank*, US, 506 F.3d 980, 994–996 (10th Cir. 2007).

262 Since by the express terms of s. 1605(a)(2) the commercial activity must be 'by/of the foreign State', *apparent* authority has been held insufficient to attribute the acts of an agent to a foreign State; *actual* authority is required: *Phaneuf* v. *Indonesia*, US, 106 F.3d 302, 308 (9th Cir. 1997). See also *Dale* v. *Colagiovanni*, US, 443 F.3d 425, 428–429 (5th Cir. 2006); on this point reversing *Dale* v. *Colagiovanni*, US, 337 F.Supp.2d 825, 837–839 (S.D.Miss. 2004); *Velasco* v. *Indonesia*, US, 370 F.3d 392, 400 (4th Cir. 2004); *Tolliver* v. *Nigeria*,

NOTES TO PAGES 109–110 545

US, 265 F.Supp.2d 873, 881 (W.D.Mich. 2003). But see *Transamerica* v. *Republica*, US, 200 F.3d 843, 850, 853 (D.C.Cir. 2000); *First* v. *Antigua*, US, 877 F.2d 189, 193 (2nd Cir. 1989); 99 ILR 125; *Storr* v. *National*, US, 1997 WL 633405, p. 3 (S.D.N.Y. 1997). See also Wydeven, The Foreign; Evanoff, Direct. In keeping with this, it has been held that the property of a foreign State shall be subject to execution only if that *State itself* has made commercial use of the property within the US: *Rubin* v. *Iran*, US, 456 F.Supp.2d 228, 233–234 (D.Mass. 2006).

263 *Stena* v. *Comision*, US, 923 F.2d 380, 386 (5th Cir. 1991); 103 ILR 433; reiterated in *Walter* v. *Philippines*, US, 965 F.2d 1375, 1384 (5th Cir. 1992); 103 ILR 503. See also *Vencedora* v. *Compagnie*, US, 730 F.2d 195, 199–202 (5th Cir. 1984); 87 ILR 520; *US* v. *Moats*, US, 961 F.2d 1198, 1205 (5th Cir. 1992); 103 ILR 480; *Arriba* v. *Petroleos*, US, 962 F.2d 528, 533 (5th Cir. 1992); 103 ILR 490; *Tubular* v. *Petroleos*, US, 977 F.2d 180, 184 (5th Cir. 1992); *Coleman* v. *Alcolac*, US, 888 F. Supp. 1388, 1401 (S.D.Tex. 1995); *Good* v. *Aramco*, US, 971 F.Supp. 254, 257 (S. D.Tex. 1997); *Elixir* v. *Perusahaan*, US, 267 F.Supp.2d 659, 663 (S.D.Tex. 2003).

264 *Federal* v. *Richard*, US, 12 F.3d 1270, 1286 (3rd Cir. 1993). See also *Sugarman* v. *Aeromexico*, US, 626 F.2d 270, 272 (3rd Cir. 1980); 63 ILR 446; *Velidor* v. *L/P/G*, US, 653 F.2d 812, 820 (3rd Cir. 1981); 63 ILR 622; *Tote* v. *Iberia*, US, 649 F.Supp. 41, 42 (E.D.Pa. 1986); *Obenchain* v. *Corporation*, US, 656 F.Supp. 435, 439 (W.D.Pa. 1987); *Tifa* v. *Ghana*, US, 692 F.Supp. 393, 402 (D.N.J. 1988); *Supra* v. *McGonigle*, US, 955 F.Supp. 374, 380 (E.D.Pa. 1997). For other circuits see *Raccoon* v. *Navoi*, US, 244 F. Supp.2d 1130 (D.Colo. 2002); *Mann* v. *Hanil*, US, 900 F.Supp. 1077, 1088–1092 (E.D.Wis. 1995); *Gerding* v. *France*, US, 943 F.2d 521, 526 (4th Cir. 1991); 98 ILR 159; *Shapiro* v. *Bolivia*, US, 930 F.2d 1013, 1018 (2nd Cir. 1991); 98 ILR 109; *Casalino* v. *Ente*, US, 779 F.Supp. 338, 341 (S.D.N.Y. 1991); *Bahsoon* v. *Pezetel*, US, 768 F.Supp. 507, 510–511 (E.D.N.C. 1991); *America* v. *GPA*, US, 877 F.2d 793, 796 (9th Cir. 1989); 92 ILR 454; *Rush-Presbyterian* v. *Hellenic*, US, 877 F.2d 574, 577 (7th Cir. 1989); 101 ILR 509; *Robert* v. *Air France*, US, 712 F.Supp. 688, 690 (N.D.Ill. 1989); *Kramer* v. *Boeing*, US, 705 F.Supp. 1392, 1395 (D.Minn. 1989); *Compania* v. *US*, US, 859 F.2d 1354, 1360 (9th Cir. 1988); 98 ILR 69; *Kline* v. *Kaneko*, US, 685 F.Supp. 386, 390–391 (S.D.N.Y. 1988); 101 ILR 497; *Lasagne* v. *Divi*, US, 685 F.Supp. 88, 90 (S.D.N.Y. 1988); *Barkanic* v. *General*, US, 822 F.2d 11, 13 (2nd Cir. 1987); 98 ILR 44; *Barnett* v. *Iberia*, US, 660 F.Supp. 1148, 1151 (N.D.Ill. 1987); *Magnus* v. *Argentine*, US, 637 F.Supp. 487, 492 (N.D.Ill. 1986).

265 *Saudi Arabia* v. *Nelson*, US, 507 US 349 (1993); 100 ILR 544. See also *Good* v. *Aramco*, US, 971 F.Supp. 254, 258–60 (S.D.Tex. 1997).

266 According to the Supreme Court, the 'substantial contact' requirement is to prevent the US courts from turning into 'international courts of claims': *Verlinden* v. *Central Bank*, US, 461 US 480, 490 (1983); 79 ILR 548, 555.

267 *Saudi Arabia* v. *Nelson*, US, 507 US 349, 356 (1993); 123 L.Ed.2d 47, 58; 100 ILR 544, 550.

268 *Shapiro* v. *Bolivia*, US, 930 F.2d 1013, 1018 (2nd Cir. 1991); 98 ILR 109. See also *Filetech* v. *France*, US, 212 F.Supp.2d 183, 191 (S.D.N.Y. 2001) (upon remand from *Filetech* v. *France*, US, 157 F.3d 922 (2nd Cir. 1998), which vacated *Filetech* v. *France*, US, 978 F.Supp. 464 (S.D.N.Y. 1997)); affirmed, *Filetech* v. *France*, US,

546 NOTES TO PAGE 110

304 F.3d 180 (2nd Cir. 2002); *NYSA-ILA* v. *Garuda*, US, 7 F.3d 35, 38 (2nd Cir. 1993); *America* v. *GPA*, US, 877 F.2d 793, 796 (9th Cir. 1989); 92 ILR 454; *Colonial* v. *Compagnie*, US, 645 F.Supp. 1457, 1463 (S.D.N.Y. 1986); 98 ILR 26; *Ministry* v. *Universe*, US, 708 F.2d 80, 84 (2nd Cir. 1983); 98 ILR 13. Where there is no commercial activity whatever in the US, there is of course no jurisdiction under the first clause: *Four* v. *Turbomeca*, US, 677 F.Supp. 1096, 1099 (D.Colo. 1988).

269 *Saudi Arabia* v. *Nelson*, US, 507 US 349, 357 (1993); 123 L.Ed.2d 47, 59; 100 ILR 544, 551. See also *El-Hadad* v. *UAE*, US, 496 F.3d 658, 663 (D.C.Cir. 2007); *Hansen* v. *Danish*, US, 147 F.Supp.2d 142, 149 (E.D.N.Y. 2001); *Santos* v. *Compagnie*, US, 934 F.2d 890, 893 (7th Cir. 1991); 98 ILR 131; *Millen* v. *Coordination*, US, 855 F.2d 879, 885 (D.C.Cir. 1988); 98 ILR 61; *Callejo* v. *Bancomer*, US, 764 F.2d 1101, 1109 (5th Cir. 1985); 84 ILR 106; *Texas* v. *Nigeria*, US, 647 F.2d 300, 308 (2nd Cir. 1981); 63 ILR 552; Donoghue, Taking, 500.

270 *Saudi Arabia* v. *Nelson*, US, 507 US 349, 358 (1993); 123 L.Ed.2d 47, 59; 100 ILR 544, 551. See also *Tonoga* v. *Ministry*, US, 135 F.Supp.2d 350 (N.D.N.Y. 2001). Naturally, the first task in a commercial activity case is for the court to identify the conduct upon which the lawsuit is based. See *Saudi Arabia* v. *Nelson*, US, 507 US 349, 356 (1993); 123 L.Ed.2d 47, 58; 100 ILR 544, 550; *Globe* v. *AO*, US, 376 F.3d 282, 286 (4th Cir. 2004). According to the Fourth Circuit, in identifying the conduct that forms the basis of the lawsuit, the court must focus on the 'specific claim' and the 'elements of that claim' that, if proven, would entitle the plaintiff to relief. *Globe* v. *AO*, US, 376 F.3d 282, 287 (4th Cir. 2004). See also *Weltover* v. *Argentina*, US, 941 F.2d 145, 150 (2nd Cir. 1991); affirmed, *Argentina* v. *Weltover*, US, 504 US 607 (1992); 100 ILR 509.

271 *NYSA-ILA* v. *Garuda*, US, 7 F.3d 35, 38 (2nd Cir. 1993) (emphasis added). See also *Daventree* v. *Azerbaijan*, US, 349 F.Supp.2d 736, 749 (S.D.N.Y. 2004); *BPA* v. *Sweden*, US, 281 F.Supp.2d 73, 81–82 (D.D.C. 2003); *Leutwyler* v. *Office*, US, 184 F.Supp.2d 277, 292, 293, 295 (S.D.N.Y. 2001); *Tonoga* v. *Ministry*, US, 135 F.Supp.2d 350, 356 (N.D.N.Y. 2001); *Reiss* v. *Société*, US, 235 F.3d 738, 747 (2nd Cir. 2000); *Haven* v. *Rzeczpospolita*, US, 215 F.3d 727, 736 (7th Cir. 2000); *Byrd* v. *Corporacion*, US, 182 F.3d 380, 389 (5th Cir. 1999); *In re Tamimi*, US, 176 F.3d 274, 280 (4th Cir. 1999); *Elliott* v. *British*, US, 986 F.Supp. 189, 194 (S.D.N.Y. 1997); affirmed, *Elliott* v. *British*, US, 172 F.3d 37 (2nd Cir. 1999) (Table); *Gates* v. *Victor*, US, 54 F.3d 1457, 1463 (9th Cir. 1995); 107 ILR 371; *Goodman* v. *Rafidain*, US, 26 F.3d 1143, 1146 (D.C.Cir. 1994); *Siderman* v. *Argentina*, US, 965 F.2d 699, 709 (9th Cir. 1992); 103 ILR 454; *Gould* v. *Mitsui*, US, 947 F.2d 218, 221 (6th Cir. 1991); 98 ILR 136; *Gerding* v. *France*, US, 943 F.2d 521, 526 (4th Cir. 1991); 98 ILR 159; *Santos* v. *Compagnie*, US, 934 F.2d 890, 892 (7th Cir. 1991); 98 ILR 131; *Darby* v. *Compagnie*, US, 769 F.Supp. 1255, 1265 (S.D.N.Y. 1991); *America* v. *GPA*, US, 877 F.2d 793, 796–797 (9th Cir. 1989); 92 ILR 454; *Rush-Presbyterian* v. *Hellenic*, US, 877 F.2d 574, 582 (7th Cir. 1989); 101 ILR 509; *Gould* v. *Pechiney*, US, 853 F.2d 445, 452 (6th Cir. 1988); 98 ILR 136; *Joseph* v. *Office*, US, 830 F.2d 1018, 1023 (9th Cir. 1987); 101 ILR 485; *Barkanic* v. *General*, US, 822 F.2d 11, 12 (2nd Cir. 1987); 98 ILR 44; *De Sanchez* v. *Banco*, US, 770 F.2d 1385, 1391 (5th Cir.

NOTES TO PAGES 110–111   547

1985); 88 ILR 75; *Vencedora* v. *Compagnie*, US, 730 F.2d 195, 202 (5th Cir. 1984); 87 ILR 520; *Arango* v. *Guzman*, US, 621 F.2d 1371, 1379 (5th Cir. 1980); 63 ILR 467.

272 *Darby* v. *Compagnie*, US, 769 F.Supp. 1255, 1265 (S.D.N.Y. 1991); *Kramer* v. *Boeing*, US, 705 F.Supp. 1392, 1395–1396 (D.Minn. 1989); *Castillo* v. *Shipping*, US, 606 F.Supp. 497, 501 (S.D.N.Y. 1985); *Harris* v. *VAO*, US, 481 F.Supp. 1056, 1061 (E.D.N.Y. 1979); 63 ILR 318.

273 *Compania* v. *US*, US, 859 F.2d 1354, 1360 (9th Cir. 1988); 98 ILR 69. See also *Barnett* v. *Iberia*, US, 660 F.Supp. 1148, 1152 (N.D.Ill. 1987).

274 *Callejo* v. *Bancomer*, US, 764 F.2d 1101, 1109 (5th Cir. 1985); 84 ILR 106; cited with approval in *Saudi Arabia* v. *Nelson*, US, 507 US 349, 357 (1993); 123 L.Ed.2d 47, 59; 100 ILR 544, 551. See also *Doe* v. *Holy See*, US, 434 F.Supp.2d 925, 940 (D.Or. 2006); *Leutwyler* v. *Office*, US, 184 F.Supp.2d 277, 292 (S.D.N.Y. 2001); *Santos* v. *Compagnie*, US, 934 F.2d 890, 893 (7th Cir. 1991); 98 ILR 131; *Millen* v. *Coordination*, US, 855 F.2d 879, 885 (D.C.Cir. 1988); 98 ILR 61.

275 *Leutwyler* v. *Office*, US, 184 F.Supp.2d 277, 292 (S.D.N.Y. 2001).

276 *Stena* v. *Comision*, US, 923 F.2d 380, 387–388 (5th Cir. 1991); 103 ILR 433. See also *Doe* v. *Holy See*, US, 434 F.Supp.2d 925, 943 (D.Or. 2006); *World* v. *Nammo*, US, 51 Fed.Appx. 403, 406 (4th Cir. 2002); *Nazarian* v. *Compagnie*, US, 989 F.Supp. 504, 508–509 (S.D.N.Y. 1998); *Coleman* v. *Alcolac*, US, 888 F.Supp. 1388, 1401 (S.D.Tex. 1995).

277 *Stena* v. *Comision*, US, 923 F.2d 380, 387–388 (5th Cir. 1991); 103 ILR 433. See also *Croesus* v. *Brazil*, US, 212 F.Supp.2d 30, 33–35 (D.D.C. 2002); *Kelly* v. *Syria*, US, 213 F.3d 841, 853 (5th Cir. 2000); *Soudavar* v. *Iran*, US, 186 F.3d 671, 674 (5th Cir. 1999); *Voest-Alpine* v. *Bank*, US, 142 F.3d 887, 892 (5th Cir. 1998); *Randolph* v. *Budget*, US, 97 F.3d 319, 324 (9th Cir. 1996); reversing *Randolph* v. *Budget*, US, 878 F.Supp. 162 (C.D.Cal. 1995); *Walter* v. *Philippines*, US, 965 F.2d 1375, 1384 (5th Cir. 1992); 103 ILR 503; *Arriba* v. *Petroleos*, US, 962 F.2d 528, 533 (5th Cir. 1992); 103 ILR 490; *US* v. *Moats*, US, 961 F.2d 1198, 1205 (5th Cir. 1992); 103 ILR 480; *Gould* v. *Pechiney*, US, 853 F.2d 445, 450 (6th Cir. 1988); 98 ILR 136; *Joseph* v. *Office*, US, 830 F.2d 1018, 1023 (9th Cir. 1987); 101 ILR 485; *Vencedora* v. *Compagnie*, US, 730 F.2d 195, 200 (5th Cir. 1984); 87 ILR 520; *Arango* v. *Guzman*, US, 621 F.2d 1371, 1379 (5th Cir. 1980); 63 ILR 467.

278 *Tonoga* v. *Ministry*, US, 135 F.Supp.2d 350, 356–357 (N.D.N.Y. 2001). See also *Gibbons* v. *Udaras*, US, 549 F.Supp. 1094, 1113 (S.D.N.Y. 1982).

279 *Corzo* v. *Banco*, US, 243 F.3d 519, 524 (9th Cir. 2001).

280 *Callejo* v. *Bancomer*, US, 764 F.2d 1101, 1109 (5th Cir. 1985); 84 ILR 106.

281 *Millen* v. *Coordination*, US, 855 F.2d 879, 885 (D.C.Cir. 1988); 98 ILR 61. See also *Saudi Arabia* v. *Nelson*, US, 507 US 349, 358, fn. 4 (1993); 123 L.Ed.2d 47, 59; 100 ILR 544, 551; *Texas* v. *Nigeria*, US, 647 F.2d 300, 307 (2nd Cir. 1981); 63 ILR 552.

282 *Honduras Aircraft Registry* v. *Honduras*, US, 129 F.3d 543, 547–548 (11th Cir. 1997); affirming *Honduras* v. *Honduras*, US, 883 F.Supp. 685 (S.D.Fla. 1995) and superseding *Honduras* v. *Honduras*, US, 119 F.3d 1530 (11th Cir. 1997). For a similar case though decided under the third clause of s. 1605(a)(2) see *McKesson* v. *Iran*, US, 271 F.3d 1101, 1105–1106 (D.C.Cir. 2001); *McKesson* v.

548   NOTES TO PAGES 111–113

Iran, US, 52 F.3d 346, 350–351 (D.C.Cir. 1995); *Foremost-McKesson* v. *Iran*, US, 905 F.2d 438, 449–450 (D.C.Cir. 1990); 101 ILR 536.

283 *Guevara* v. *Peru*, US, 468 F.3d 1289, 1298–1299, 1301–1302 (11th Cir. 2006); reversed on other grounds, *Guevara* v. *Peru*, US, 608 F.3d 1297 (11th Cir. 2010).

284 *Saudi Arabia* v. *Nelson*, US, 507 US 349, 358, fn. 4 (1993); 123 L.Ed.2d 47, 59; 100 ILR 544, 551; *Siderman* v. *Argentina*, US, 965 F.2d 699, 709, fn. 10 (9th Cir. 1992); 103 ILR 454.

285 *Santos* v. *Compagnie*, US, 934 F.2d 890, 893 (7th Cir. 1991); 98 ILR 131. See also *TermoRio* v. *Electrificadora*, US, 421 F.Supp.2d 87, 94 (D.D.C. 2006); *BP* v. *Jiangsu*, US, 420 F.3d 810, 816 (8th Cir. 2005); *BP* v. *Jiangsu*, US, 285 F.3d 677, 682 (8th Cir. 2002); reversing *BP* v. *Jiangsu*, US, 144 F.Supp.2d 1140 (E.D.Mo. 2001); *Lord Day* v. *Vietnam*, US, 134 F.Supp.2d 549, 559 (S.D.N.Y. 2001); *Sun* v. *Taiwan*, US, 201 F.3d 1105, 1109 (9th Cir. 2000); *Goodman* v. *Rafidain*, US, 26 F.3d 1143, 1146 (D.C.Cir. 1994); *Sugimoto* v. *Exportadora*, US, 19 F.3d 1309, 1311 (9th Cir. 1994).

286 *Santos* v. *Compagnie*, US, 934 F.2d 890, 894 (7th Cir. 1991); 98 ILR 131.

287 *Santos* v. *Compagnie*, US, 934 F.2d 890, 892–894 (7th Cir. 1991); 98 ILR 131. For a similar case see *Seisay* v. *Air France*, US, 1997 WL 431084, p. 6 (S.D.N.Y. 1997). See also *TermoRio* v. *Electrificadora*, US, 421 F.Supp.2d 87, 94–95 (D.D.C. 2006); *Sun* v. *Taiwan*, US, 201 F.3d 1105, 1110 (9th Cir. 2000); further confirmed upon remand, *Sun* v. *Taipei*, US, 34 Fed.Appx. 529 (9th Cir. 2002).

288 *Kirkham* v. *Air France*, US, 429 F.3d 288, 291–293 (D.C.Cir. 2005). For a similar case see *Nazarian* v. *Air France*, US, 989 F.Supp. 504, 509 (S.D.N.Y. 1998). But cf. *In re Air Crash*, US, 716 F.Supp. 84, 86 (E.D.N.Y. 1989). Conversely, if the air tickets were bought in a foreign country, the claim would fail. See *Coyle* v. *PT*, US, 363 F.3d 979, 994 (9th Cir. 2004); reversing *Coyle* v. *PT*, US, 180 F.Supp.2d 1160 (D.Or. 2001); *Casalino* v. *Ente*, US, 779 F.Supp. 338, 341 (S.D.N.Y. 1991); *Tote* v. *Iberia*, US, 649 F.Supp. 41, 43 (E.D.Pa. 1986).

289 *Saudi Arabia* v. *Nelson*, US, 507 US 349, 358 (1993); 123 L.Ed.2d 47, 59; 100 ILR 544, 551.

290 *Globe* v. *AO*, US, 376 F.3d 282, 291–292 (4th Cir. 2004).

291 *Shapiro* v. *Bolivia*, US, 930 F.2d 1013, 1019–1020 (2nd Cir. 1991); 98 ILR 109. See Jay, United States.

292 *US Fidelity* v. *Braspetro*, US, 1999 U.S.Dist.Lexis 7236, pp. 40–41 (S.D.N.Y. 1999); affirmed, *US Fidelity* v. *Braspetro*, US, 199 F.3d 94 (2nd Cir. 1999).

293 *Turkmani* v. *Bolivia*, US, 193 F.Supp.2d 165, 176 (D.D.C. 2002).

294 *Lempert* v. *Kazakstan*, US, 223 F.Supp.2d 200, 203 (D.D.C. 2002); *In re Papandreou*, US, 139 F.3d 247, 253 (D.C.Cir. 1998); *Morgan* v. *Novokrivorogsky*, US, 57 F.Supp.2d 863, 872 (N.D.Cal. 1998); *Zedan* v. *Saudi Arabia*, US, 849 F.2d 1511, 1513 (D.C.Cir. 1988); 92 ILR 462; *Lasagne* v. *Divi*, US, 685 F.Supp. 88, 90 (S.D.N.Y. 1988); *Falcoal* v. *Turkiye*, US, 660 F.Supp. 1536, 1540 (S.D.Tex. 1987). But see *In re Papandreou*, US, 139 F.3d 247, 253 (D.C.Cir. 1998); *Obenchain* v. *Corporation*, US, 656 F.Supp. 435, 440 (W.D.Pa. 1987). Conversely, see *Janini* v. *Kuwait*, US, 43 F.3d 1534, 1536 (D.C.Cir. 1995); 107 ILR 367.

295 *Fargo* v. *Jamaica*, US, 790 F.Supp. 272, 276 (S.D.Fla. 1992).

296 *Sun* v. *Taiwan*, US, 201 F.3d 1105, 1109–1110 (9th Cir. 2000). See also *Sugimoto* v. *Exportadora*, US, 19 F.3d 1309, 1311 (9th Cir. 1994).

297 *Theo* v. *Marshall Islands*, US, 174 F.3d 969, 973–974 (9th Cir. 1998).

298 *Soudavar* v. *Iran*, US, 186 F.3d 671, 674 (5th Cir. 1999); *Stena* v. *Comision*, US, 923 F.2d 380, 389, fn. 11 (5th Cir. 1991); 103 ILR 433. Cf. *Hester* v. *Nigeria*, US, 681 F.Supp. 371, 384 (N.D.Miss. 1988).

299 *Lempert* v. *Kazakstan*, US, 223 F.Supp.2d 200, 203–204 (D.D.C. 2002); *Morgan* v. *Novokrivorogsky*, US, 57 F.Supp.2d 863, 872 (N.D.Cal. 1998); *Casalino* v. *Ente*, US, 779 F.Supp. 338, 341 (S.D.N.Y. 1991); *Darby* v. *Compagnie*, US, 769 F.Supp. 1255, 1265 (S.D.N.Y. 1991); *Zedan* v. *Saudi Arabia*, US, 849 F.2d 1511, 1514 (D.C.Cir. 1988); 92 ILR 462; *Barnett* v. *Iberia*, US, 660 F.Supp. 1148, 1152–1153 (N.D.Ill. 1987); *Harris* v. *VAO*, US, 481 F.Supp. 1056, 1061 (E.D.N.Y. 1979); 63 ILR 318. In this respect, 'failure to warn' of product defects (such as unairworthiness of plane engines), is not an 'act': *In re Air Crash*, US, 716 F.Supp. 84, 87 (E.D.N.Y. 1989); *Four* v. *Turbomeca*, US, 677 F.Supp. 1096, 1099 (D.Colo. 1988); *Falcoal* v. *Turkiye*, US, 660 F.Supp. 1536, 1540 (S.D.Tex. 1987); *Tucker* v. *Whitaker*, US, 620 F.Supp. 578, 586 (E.D.Pa. 1985); affirmed, *Tucker* v. *Whitaker*, US, 800 F.2d 1140 (3rd Cir. 1986) (Table).

300 *Dewhurst* v. *Telenor*, US, 83 F.Supp.2d 577, 587–590 (D.Md. 2000).

301 US House of Representatives, Report No. 94-1487, 1976, p. 19; 1976 USCCAN 6604, 6617–6618. Emphases added.

302 See *Santos* v. *Compagnie*, US, 934 F.2d 890, 892, fn. 1 (7th Cir. 1991); 98 ILR 131; *Schmidt* v. *Polish*, US, 579 F.Supp. 23, 27, fn. 10 (S.D.N.Y. 1984); *Texas* v. *Nigeria*, US, 647 F.2d 300, 311, fn. 30 (2nd Cir. 1981); 63 ILR 552.

303 See *Santos* v. *Compagnie*, US, 934 F.2d 890, 892, fn. 1 (7th Cir. 1991); 98 ILR 131.

304 *Supra* v. *McGonigle*, US, 955 F.Supp. 374, 380 (E.D.Pa. 1997). But cf. *Voest-Alpine* v. *Bank*, US, 142 F.3d 887, 892 and fn. 5 (5th Cir. 1998); *Byrd* v. *Corporacion*, US, 182 F.3d 380, 390 (5th Cir. 1999).

305 *Saudi Arabia* v. *Nelson*, US, 507 US 349, 358, fn. 4 (1993); 123 L.Ed.2d 47, 59; 100 ILR 544, 551. See also *Foremost-McKesson* v. *Iran*, US, 905 F.2d 438, 450 (D.C.Cir. 1990); 101 ILR 536; *Millen* v. *Coordination*, US, 855 F.2d 879, 885 (D.C.Cir. 1988); 98 ILR 61.

306 *Hanil* v. *PT*, US, 148 F.3d 127, 131 (2nd Cir. 1998); affirming *Hanil* v. *PT*, US, 1997 U.S.Dist.Lexis 10450 (S.D.N.Y. 1997). See also *Wasserstein* v. *Formosa*, US, 2002 U.S.Dist.Lexis 12012, p. 25 (S.D.N.Y. 2002); *Kern* v. *Oesterreichische*, US, 178 F.Supp.2d 367 (S.D.N.Y. 2001); *Parex* v. *Russian*, US, 116 F.Supp.2d 415, 420 (S.D.N.Y. 2000); *US Fidelity* v. *Braspetro*, US, 199 F.3d 94, 98 (2nd Cir. 1999); *Adler* v. *Nigeria*, US, 107 F.3d 720, 726 (9th Cir. 1997); *Federal* v. *Richard*, US, 12 F.3d 1270, 1289–1291 (3rd Cir. 1993).

307 *Pere* v. *Nuovo*, US, 150 F.3d 477, 482 (5th Cir. 1998). See also *Los Angeles* v. *Conus*, US, 969 F.Supp. 579, 586 (C.D.Cal. 1997); *Siderman* v. *Argentina*, US, 965 F.2d 699, 709 (9th Cir. 1992); 103 ILR 454.

308 *Compania* v. *US*, US, 859 F.2d 1354, 1360 (9th Cir. 1988); 98 ILR 69.

309 *Stena* v. *Comision*, US, 923 F.2d 380, 388 (5th Cir. 1991); 103 ILR 433.

310 *US Fidelity* v. *Petroleo*, US, 1999 U.S.Dist.Lexis 7235, p. 24 (S.D.N.Y. 1999); affirmed, *US Fidelity* v. *Braspetro*, US, 199 F.3d 94 (2nd Cir. 1999).

550   NOTES TO PAGES 115–123

311 *Lyon* v. *Agusta*, US, 252 F.3d 1078, 1082 (9th Cir. 2001).
312 *Argentina* v. *Weltover*, US, 504 US 607, 611 (1992); 119 L.Ed.2d 394, 403; 100 ILR 509, 513.
313 *Weltover*, 504 US 607, 612, 615–620 (1992); 119 L.Ed.2d 394, 405–409; 100 ILR 509, 515–519.
314 *Weltover*, 504 US 607, 616 (1992); 119 L.Ed.2d 394, 406; 100 ILR 509, 516.
315 *MOL* v. *Bangladesh*, US, 736 F.2d 1326, 1329 (9th Cir. 1984); 80 ILR 583.
316 *MOL*, 736 F.2d 1326, 1329 (9th Cir. 1984); 80 ILR 583.
317 *Doe I* v. *Unocal*, US, 395 F.3d 932, 958 (9th Cir. 2002) (emphasis in the original); reversing *Doe* v. *Unocal*, US, 963 F.Supp. 880, 888 (C.D.Cal. 1997).
318 US House of Representatives, Report No. 94–1487, 1976, p. 19; 1976 USCCAN 6604, 6618. Emphasis added.
319 The text of s. 18 is quoted in *America* v. *GPA*, US, 877 F.2d 793, 798 (9th Cir. 1989); 92 ILR 454, 459.
320 *Garb* v. *Poland*, US, 440 F.3d 579, 586–588 (2nd Cir. 2006) (emphasis added).
321 *Yang Rong* v. *Liaoning*, US, 452 F.3d 883, 888 (D.C.Cir. 2006).
322 *Yang Rong*, 452 F.3d 883, 890 (D.C.Cir. 2006).
323 *Yang Rong*, US, 452 F.3d 883, 888–891 (D.C.Cir. 2006); affirming *Yang Rong* v. *Liaoning*, US, 362 F.Supp.2d 83, 92–97 (D.D.C. 2005).
324 *Beg* v. *Pakistan*, US, 353 F.3d 1323, 1325 (11th Cir. 2003).
325 *Beg*, 353 F.3d 1323, 1326–1327 (11th Cir. 2003).
326 *Beg*, 353 F.3d 1323, 1328 (11th Cir. 2003).
327 *Drexel* v. *Committee*, US, 12 F.3d 317, 330 (2nd Cir. 1993); reversing *Drexel* v. *Committee*, US, 810 F.Supp. 1375 (S.D.N.Y. 1993); 103 ILR 532. See also *Foremost-McKesson* v. *Iran*, US, 905 F.2d 438 (D.C.Cir. 1990); 101 ILR 536.
328 See also *Zappia* v. *Abu Dhabi*, US, 215 F.3d 247, 251 (2nd Cir. 2000).
329 See *Garb* v. *Poland*, US, 440 F.3d 579, 586 (2nd Cir. 2006).
330 *Beg* v. *Pakistan*, US, 353 F.3d 1323 (11th Cir. 2003).
331 *Garb* v. *Poland*, US, 440 F.3d 579 (2nd Cir. 2006); *Yang* v. *Liaoning*, US, 362 F.Supp.2d 83, 92–97 (D.D.C. 2005); affirmed, *Yang* v. *Liaoning*, US, 452 F.3d 883, 888–891 (D.C.Cir. 2006).
332 *Corzo* v. *Banco*, US, 243 F.3d 519, 524–526 (9th Cir. 2001).
333 *Corzo*, 243 F.3d 519, 524 (9th Cir. 2001).
334 *Corzo*, 243 F.3d 519, 525 (9th Cir. 2001). Cf. *Daliberti* v. *Iraq*, US, 97 F.Supp.2d 38, 47–48 (D.D.C. 2000).
335 *Aldy* v. *Valmet*, US, 74 F.3d 72, 75 (5th Cir. 1996). See also *Ohntrup* v. *Firearms*, US, 516 F.Supp. 1281, 1287 (E.D.Pa. 1981); 63 ILR 632; affirmed, *Ohntrup* v. *Firearms*, US, 760 F.2d 259 (3rd Cir. 1985) (Table).
336 *Poddar* v. *State Bank*, US, 235 F.R.D. 592, 596–597 (S.D.N.Y. 2006) (emphasis added).
337 *Magness* v. *Russian Federation*, US, 54 F.Supp.2d 700, 705 (S.D.Tex. 1999).
338 *Magness*, 54 F.Supp.2d 700, 704 (S.D.Tex. 1999). See also *Siderman* v. *Argentina*, US, 965 F.2d 699, 708–710 (9th Cir. 1992); 103 ILR 454.
339 See *Reichler* v. *Liberia*, US, 484 F.Supp.2d 1, 2 (D.D.C. 2007); *Velasco* v. *Indonesia*, US, 370 F.3d 392, 398 (4th Cir. 2004); *IT* v. *Pakistan*, US, 351 F.3d 1184, 1186 (D.C.Cir. 2003); *BPA* v. *Sweden*, US, 281 F.Supp.2d 73, 80 (D.D.C. 2003); *Gulf* v.

Congo, US, 276 F.Supp.2d 20, 25 (D.D.C. 2003); *Atlantic* v. *Inter-American*, US, 251 F.Supp.2d 126, 134 (D.D.C. 2003); *Filler* v. *Hanvit*, US, 247 F.Supp.2d 425, 429 (S.D.N.Y. 2003); *Connecticut* v. *Congo*, US, 309 F.3d 240, 255 (5th Cir. 2002); *Parex* v. *Russian*, US, 116 F.Supp.2d 415, 420 (S.D.N.Y. 2000); *Mukaddam* v. *Permanent*, US, 111 F.Supp.2d 457, 462 (S.D.N.Y. 2000); *Byrd* v. *Corporacion*, US, 182 F.3d 380, 390 (5th Cir. 1999); *Voest-Alpine* v. *Bank*, US, 142 F.3d 887, 893 (5th Cir. 1998); *Los Angeles* v. *Conus*, US, 969 F.Supp. 579, 587 (C.D.Cal. 1997); *Supra* v. *McGonigle*, US, 955 F.Supp. 374, 380 (E.D.Pa. 1997); *Coleman* v. *Alcolac*, US, 888 F.Supp. 1388, 1401–1402 (S.D.Tex. 1995); *Reed* v. *Donau*, US, 866 F.Supp. 750, 754 (S.D.N.Y. 1994); *Boykin* v. *Bergesen*, US, 835 F.Supp. 274, 287, fn. 20 (E.D.Va. 1993); *Kao* v. *China*, US, 816 F.Supp. 910, 917 (S.D.N.Y. 1993); *Wilk* v. *Creditanstalt*, US, 1993 WL 97259, p. 3 (S.D.N.Y. 1993); *Caribbean* v. *Nigerian*, US, 1993 WL 541236, pp. 7–8 (S.D.N.Y. 1993); *Walter* v. *Philippines*, US, 965 F.2d 1375, 1384–1387 (5th Cir. 1992); 103 ILR 503; *Stena* v. *Comision*, US, 923 F.2d 380, 390 (5th Cir. 1991); 103 ILR 433; *Fickling* v. *Australia*, US, 775 F.Supp. 66, 71, fn. 2 (E.D.N.Y. 1991); 103 ILR 447; *Bahsoon* v. *Pezetel*, US, 768 F.Supp. 507, 510 (E.D.N.C. 1991); *Kramer* v. *Boeing*, US, 705 F.Supp. 1392, 1396 (D.Minn. 1989); *Sudano* v. *Federal*, US, 699 F.Supp. 824, 826 (D.Haw. 1988); *Tifa* v. *Ghana*, US, 692 F.Supp. 393, 402 (D.N.J. 1988); *Four* v. *Turbomeca*, US, 677 F.Supp. 1096, 1100 (D.Colo. 1988); *Hatzlachh* v. *Savannah*, US, 649 F.Supp. 688, 690 (S.D.N.Y. 1986); *Callejo* v. *Bancomer*, US, 764 F.2d 1101, 1111 (5th Cir. 1985); 84 ILR 106; *Harris* v. *National*, US, 691 F.2d 1344, 1351 (11th Cir. 1982); 72 ILR 172.

340 *Morris* v. *China*, US, 478 F.Supp.2d 561, 567 (S.D.N.Y. 2007).

341 *In re Air Crash*, US, 392 F.Supp.2d 461, 468–469 (E.D.N.Y. 2005). See also *Dumont* v. *Saskatchewan*, US, 258 F.3d 880, 884, fn. 6 (8th Cir. 2001).

342 *US Fidelity* v. *Braspetro*, US, 199 F.3d 94, 98–99 (2nd Cir. 1999).

343 *Dominican* v. *Dominican*, US, 903 F.Supp. 1507, 1512 (M.C.Fla. 1995).

344 *Saudi* v. *Exxonmobil*, US, 194 F.Supp.2d 378, 405 (D.N.J. 2002).

345 *US Titan* v. *Guangzhou*, US, 16 F.Supp.2d 326, 334 (S.D.N.Y. 1998); affirmed, *US Titan* v. *Guangzhou*, US, Court of Appeals, 241 F.3d 135 (2nd Cir. 2001).

346 *Siderman* v. *Argentina*, US, 965 F.2d 699, 710 (9th Cir. 1992); 103 ILR 454.

347 *Argentina* v. *Weltover*, US, 504 US 607, 609–610 (1992); 119 L.Ed.2d 394, 401–402 (1992); 100 ILR 509, 511–512; affirming *Weltover* v. *Argentina*, US, 941 F.2d 145 (2nd Cir. 1991) and *Weltover* v. *Argentina*, US, 753 F.Supp. 1201 (S.D.N.Y. 1991).

348 *Voest-Alpine* v. *Bank*, US, 142 F.3d 887, 893 (5th Cir. 1998) (quoting *Callejo*, US, 764 F.2d 1101, 1111 (5th Cir. 1985), 84 ILR 106, which in its turn was quoting *Texas* v. *Nigeria*, US, 647 F.2d 300, 312 (2nd Cir. 1981); 63 ILR 552). See also *United* v. *Mangyshlakneft*, US, 33 F.3d 1232, 1237 (10th Cir. 1994).

349 US House of Representatives, Report No. 94-1487, 1976, p. 19; 1976 USCCAN 6604, 6618. For constitutional law difficulties associated with applying s. 28 to 'direct effect' see Pell, The Foreign, esp. 108–110.

350 See *Nordmann* v. *Thai*, US, 112 F.3d 517 (9th Cir. 1997) (Table); *Siderman* v. *Argentina*, US, 965 F.2d 699, 710 (9th Cir. 1992); 103 ILR 454; *Stena* v. *Comision*,

552   NOTES TO PAGE 125

US, 923 F.2d 380, 390–391 (5th Cir. 1991); 103 ILR 433; *Foremost-McKesson* v. *Iran*, US, 905 F.2d 438, 451 (D.C.Cir. 1990); 101 ILR 536 (confirmed, *McKesson* v. *Iran*, US, 52 F.3d 346, 350–351 (D.C.Cir. 1995); further confirmed, *McKesson* v. *Iran*, US, 271 F.3d 1101, 1105–1106 (D.C.Cir. 2001)); *America* v. *GPA*, US, 877 F.2d 793, 798–800 (9th Cir. 1989); 92 ILR 454; *Gregorian* v. *Izvestia*, US, 871 F.2d 1515, 1527 (9th Cir. 1989); 98 ILR 76; *Zedan* v. *Saudi Arabia*, US, 849 F.2d 1511, 1514, 1515 (D.C.Cir. 1988); 92 ILR 462; *Sudano* v. *Federal*, US, 699 F.Supp. 824, 826 (D.Haw. 1988); *Four* v. *Turbomeca*, US, 677 F.Supp. 1096, 1101 (D.Colo. 1988); *Zernicek* v. *Brown*, US, 826 F.2d 415, 417–419 (5th Cir. 1987); 92 ILR 442; *Transamerican* v. *Somalia*, US, 767 F.2d 998, 1004 (D.C.Cir. 1985); 86 ILR 55; partly affirming *Transamerican* v. *Somalia*, US, 590 F.Supp. 968 (D.D.C. 1984); 86 ILR 55; *Berkovitz* v. *Iran*, US, 735 F.2d 329, 332 (9th Cir. 1984); 81 ILR 552; *Maritime* v. *Guinea*, US, 693 F.2d 1094, 1110–1111 (D.C.Cir. 1982); 72 ILR 152; *Ohntrup* v. *Firearms*, US, 516 F.Supp. 1281, 1286 (E.D.Pa. 1981); 63 ILR 632; affirmed, *Ohntrup* v. *Firearms*, 760 F.2d 259 (3rd Cir. 1985) (Table); *Decor* v. *Nigeria*, US, 497 F.Supp. 893, 904–905 (S.D.N.Y. 1980); 63 ILR 480; affirmed, *Texas* v. *Nigeria*, US, 647 F.2d 300 (2nd Cir. 1981); 63 ILR 552 (which reversed *Texas* v. *Nigeria*, US, 500 F.Supp. 320 (S.D.N.Y. 1980); 63 ILR 459).

351 *Texas Trading* v. *Nigeria*, US, 647 F.2d 300, 311 and fn. 32 (2nd Cir. 1981); 63 ILR 552. See also *International* v. *Rafidain*, US, 893 F.2d 8, 11 (2nd Cir. 1989); 98 ILR 93; *Shapiro* v. *Bolivia*, US, 930 F.2d 1013, 1019 (2nd Cir. 1991); 98 ILR 109; *Security* v. *Derderian*, US, 872 F.2d 281, 286 (9th Cir. 1989); *Meadows* v. *Dominican*, US, 817 F.2d 517, 523 (9th Cir. 1987); 98 ILR 37; affirming *Meadows* v. *Dominican*, US, 628 F.Supp. 599, 604 (N.D.Cal. 1986).

352 *Argentina* v. *Weltover*, US, 504 US 607, 618 (1992); 119 L.Ed.2d 394, 407; 100 ILR 509, 517 (here the Supreme Court also found that s. 18 'obviously deals with jurisdiction to *legislate* rather than jurisdiction to *adjudicate*' (emphasis in the original)); quoting and affirming *Weltover* v. *Argentina*, US, 941 F.2d 145, 152 (2nd Cir. 1991). See also *Orient* v. *Bank*, US, 506 F.3d 980, 997 (10th Cir. 2007); *California* v. *NRG*, US, 391 F.3d 1011, 1024 (9th Cir. 2004); *Strach* v. *Casino*, US, 351 F.Supp.2d 641, 643 (E.D.Mich. 2004); *US Fidelity* v. *Braspetro*, US, 199 F.3d 94, 98 (2nd Cir. 1999); *Hanil* v. *PT*, US, 148 F.3d 127, 131 (2nd Cir. 1998); *Voest-Alpine* v. *Bank*, US, 142 F.3d 887, 896 (5th Cir. 1998); *Princz* v. *Germany*, US, 26 F.3d 1166, 1172 (D.C.Cir. 1994); 103 ILR 594; *Vermeulen* v. *Renault*, US, 985 F.2d 1534 (11th Cir. 1993); *Upton* v. *Iran*, US, 459 F.Supp. 264, 266 (D.D.C. 1978); 63 ILR 211. The *Weltover* case generated considerable debate among US commentators. For criticism see McGuire, Direct; Schano, The Scattered; Ruccolo, The Foreign; Gohlke, Clearing; Baker, Whither; Dellapenna, Refining; ABA, Reforming, 557–563; ABA, Report, 2002, 1261, 1262, 1270. For support see Orlando, *Republic*; Ashe, The Flexible; Fornaro, *Republic*; Sweet, The Foreign; Delaume, The Foreign; Lew, *Republic*. For further discussion see Papajohn, Effects; Abrams, The Foreign, 234–240; Coulson, 'Toto', 448–456; Bensen, The All; Frostestad, *Voest-Alpine*.

353 *Argentina* v. *Weltover*, US, 504 US 607, 618–619 (1992); 119 L.Ed.2d 394, 407–408; 100 ILR 509, 517–518. See also *Wasserstein* v. *Formosa*, 2000 U.S.Dist.Lexis

NOTES TO PAGES 125–126   553

6416 (S.D.N.Y. 2000); *US Fidelity v. Braspetro*, US, 199 F.3d 94, 98–99 (2nd Cir. 1999); *Hanil v. PT*, US, 148 F.3d 127 (2nd Cir. 1998); *Commercial v. Rafidain*, US, 15 F.3d 238, 241 (2nd Cir. 1994); 107 ILR 261.

354 *Virtual Countries v. South Africa*, US, 300 F.3d 230, 237–238 (2nd Cir. 2002); affirming *Virtual Countries v. South Africa*, US, 148 F.Supp.2d 256 (S.D.N.Y. 2001). See also *General v. Grossman*, US, 991 F.2d 1376, 1386 (8th Cir. 1993).

355 *Lyon v. Agusta*, US, 252 F.3d 1078, 1083 (9th Cir. 2001). See also *Doe I v. Israel*, US, 400 F.Supp.2d 86, 107 (D.D.C. 2005); *Bao v. Li*, US, 201 F.Supp.2d 14, 25 (D. D.C. 2000); *Aldy v. Valmet*, US, 74 F.3d 72, 75 (5th Cir. 1996); *Princz v. Germany*, US, 26 F.3d 1166, 1172 (D.C.Cir. 1994); 103 ILR 594; *United v. Mangyshlakneft*, US, 821 F.Supp. 1405, 1409 (D.Colo. 1993); affirmed, *United v. Mangyshlakneft*, US, 33 F.3d 1232 (10th Cir. 1994); *Vermeulen v. Renault*, US, 985 F.2d 1534, 1545 (11th Cir. 1993); *Four v. Turbomeca*, US, 677 F.Supp. 1096, 1101 (D.Colo. 1988).

356 *Voest-Alpine v. Bank*, US, 142 F.3d 887, 894–895, fn.10 (5th Cir. 1998).

357 *United v. Mangyshlakneft*, US, 33 F.3d 1232, 1238 (10th Cir. 1994).

358 *Samco v. Arita*, US, 395 F.3d 1212, 1217 (11th Cir. 2005).

359 *Virtual Countries v. South Africa*, US, 300 F.3d 230, 236 (2nd Cir. 2002). See also *Princz v. Germany*, US, 26 F.3d 1166, 1172 (D.C.Cir. 1994); 103 ILR 594; reversing *Princz v. Germany*, US, 813 F.Supp. 22 (D.D.C. 1992); *Siderman v. Argentina*, US, 965 F.2d 699, 710 (9th Cir. 1992); 103 ILR 454; *Sudano v. Federal*, US, 699 F.Supp. 824, 826 (D.Haw. 1988); *Lasagne v. Divi*, US, 685 F.Supp. 88, 90 (S.D.N.Y. 1988).

360 *Security Pacific v. Derderian*, US, 872 F.2d 281, 286 (9th Cir. 1989).

361 *Gosain v. State*, US, 689 F.Supp.2d 571, 580–581 (S.D.N.Y. 2010); *Big v. Sichuan*, US, 533 F.3d 1183, 1191 (10th Cir. 2008); *Kensington v. Itoua*, US, 505 F.3d 147, 158 (2nd Cir. 2007); *Global v. Mkapa*, US, 290 F.Supp.2d 108, 115 (D.D.C. 2003); *BPA v. Sweden*, US, 281 F.Supp.2d 73 (D.D.C. 2003); *Gulf v. Congo*, US, 276 F.Supp.2d 20, 27 (D.D.C. 2003); *Filler v. Hanvit*, US, 247 F.Supp.2d 425, 429 (S.D.N.Y. 2003); *Filetech v. France*, US, 212 F.Supp.2d 183, 198 (S.D.N.Y. 2001); affirmed, *Filetech v. France*, US, 304 F.3d 180 (2nd Cir. 2002); *Croesus v. Brazil*, US, 212 F.Supp.2d 30, 37, fn. 5 (D.D.C. 2002); *Falcon v. Venezuela*, US, 2001 WL 584346, p. 6 (D.Kan. 2001); *Alpha v. Nippon*, US, 199 F.3d 1078, 1086 (9th Cir. 1999); *Adler v. Nigeria*, US, 107 F.3d 720, 726–727 (9th Cir. 1997); *Dominican v. Dominican*, US, 903 F.Supp. 1507, 1515 (M.D.Fla. 1995); *United v. Mangyshlakneft*, US, 33 F.3d 1232, 1239 (10th Cir. 1994); affirming *United v. Mangyshlakneft*, US, 821 F.Supp. 1405 (D.Colo. 1993); *Antares v. Nigeria*, US, 999 F.2d 33, 36–37 (2nd Cir. 1993); 107 ILR 225; *Gabay v. Mostazafan*, US, 151 F.R.D. 250, 255, fn. 8 (S.D.N.Y. 1993); 107 ILR 242; *Maizus v. Weldor*, US, 820 F.Supp. 101, 104 (S.D.N.Y. 1993); *Siderman v. Argentina*, US, 965 F.2d 699, 710 (9th Cir. 1992); 103 ILR 454; *International v. Rafidain*, US, 893 F.2d 8, 11 (2nd Cir. 1989); 98 ILR 93; *America v. GPA*, US, 877 F.2d 793, 799–800 (9th Cir. 1989); 92 ILR 454; *Rush-Presbyterian v. Hellenic*, US, 877 F.2d 574, 581–582 (7th Cir. 1989); 101 ILR 509; *Gregorian v. Izvestia*, US, 871 F.2d 1515, 1527 (9th Cir. 1989); 98 ILR 76; *Zedan v. Saudi Arabia*, US, 849 F.2d 1511, 1514–1515 (D.C.Cir. 1988); 92 ILR 462; *Colonial v. Compagnie*, US, 645 F.Supp. 1457, 1464–1465 (S.D.N.Y. 1986); 98 ILR 26.

554   NOTES TO PAGES 126–127

362 *Virtual Countries* v. *South Africa*, US, 300 F.3d 230, 240 (2nd Cir. 2002).

363 *Allen* v. *Russian*, US, 522 F.Supp.2d 167, 190 (D.D.C. 2007); *Wahba* v. *National*, US, 457 F.Supp.2d 721, 733–734 (E.D.Tex. 2006); *Elixir* v. *Perusahaan*, US, 267 F.Supp.2d 659, 665 (S.D.Tex. 2003); *Stena* v. *Comision*, US, 923 F.2d 380, 390 (5th Cir. 1991); 103 ILR 433; *Zedan* v. *Saudi Arabia*, US, 849 F.2d 1511, 1515 (D. C.Cir. 1988); 92 ILR 462.

364 *Doe I* v. *Unocal*, US, 395 F.3d 932, 958 (9th Cir. 2002).

365 *American* v. *Lebanon*, US, 408 F.Supp.2d 409, 415 (E.D.Mich. 2005); affirmed, *American* v. *Lebanon*, US, 501 F.3d 534 (6th Cir. 2007).

366 *Daventree* v. *Azerbaijan*, US, 349 F.Supp.2d 736, 751 (S.D.N.Y. 2004); *Saudi* v. *Exxonmobil*, US, 194 F.Supp.2d 378, 406 (D.N.J. 2002); *World* v. *Nammo*, US, 51 Fed.Appx. 403, 407 (4th Cir. 2002); *Voest-Alpine* v. *Bank*, US, 142 F.3d 887, 897 (5th Cir. 1998); *Caribbean* v. *Nigerian*, US, 1993 WL 541236, p. 8 (S.D.N.Y. 1993); *Walter* v. *Philippines*, US, 965 F.2d 1375, 1387 (5th Cir. 1992); 103 ILR 503; *Ampac* v. *Honduras*, US, 797 F.Supp. 973, 977 (S.D.Fla. 1992); *Tifa* v. *Ghana*, US, 692 F.Supp. 393, 403 (D.N.J. 1988); *Falcoal* v. *Turkiye*, US, 660 F.Supp. 1536, 1540–1541 (S.D.Tex. 1987); *Obenchain* v. *Corporation*, US, 656 F.Supp. 435, 440 (W.D.Pa. 1987); *Crimson* v. *Electronum*, US, 629 F.Supp. 903, 907 (S.D.N.Y. 1986); *Hatzlachh* v. *Savannah*, US, 649 F.Supp. 688, 690–691 (S.D.N.Y. 1986); *Callejo* v. *Bancomer*, US, 764 F.2d 1101, 1111–1112 (5th Cir. 1985); 84 ILR 106; accorded, *Grass* v. *Credito*, US, 797 F.2d 220, 221 (5th Cir. 1986);

367 *Texas* v. *Nigeria*, US, 647 F.2d 300, 312 (2nd Cir. 1981); 63 ILR 552.

368 *Gould* v. *Pechiney*, US, 853 F.2d 445, 453 (6th Cir. 1988); 98 ILR 136.

369 *Cruise* v. *Attorney*, US, 600 F.3d 661, 664–665 (D.C.Cir. 2010); reversing *Cruise* v. *Attorney*, US, 634 F.Supp.2d 86 (D.D.C. 2009).

370 *Doe I* v. *Israel*, US, 400 F.Supp.2d 86, 107 (D.D.C. 2005). See also *Gulf* v. *Congo*, US, 276 F.Supp.2d 20, 27 (D.D.C. 2003); *Virtual* v. *South Africa*, US, 300 F.3d 230, 236–237 (2nd Cir. 2002); *Voest-Alpine* v. *Bank*, US, 142 F.3d 887, 894–895, fn. 10 (5th Cir. 1998); *United* v. *Mangyshlakneft*, US, 33 F.3d 1232, 1238 (10th Cir. 1994).

371 *Strach* v. *Casino*, US, 351 F.Supp.2d 641, 643 (E.D.Mich. 2004); *Abrams* v. *Société*, US, 175 F.Supp.2d 423, 430 (E.D.N.Y. 2001); vacated on other grounds, *Abrams* v. *Société*, US, 332 F.3d 173 (2nd Cir. 2003); *Soudavar* v. *Iran*, US, 186 F.3d 671, 674 (5th Cir. 1999); *Nordmann* v. *Thai*, US, 112 F.3d 517 (9th Cir. 1997) (Table); *Good* v. *Aramco*, US, 971 F.Supp. 254, 260 (S.D.Tex. 1997); *Coleman* v. *Alcolac*, US, 888 F.Supp. 1388, 1402 (S.D.Tex. 1995); *Princz* v. *Germany*, US, 26 F.3d 1166, 1173 (D.C.Cir. 1994); 103 ILR 594; *Antares* v. *Nigeria*, US, 999 F.2d 33, 36 (2nd Cir. 1993); 107 ILR 225; *Djordjevich* v. *Bundesminister*, US, 827 F.Supp. 814, 817 (D.D.C. 1993); *United* v. *Mangyshlakneft*, US, 821 F.Supp. 1405, 1409 (D.Colo. 1993); affirmed, *United* v. *Mangyshlakneft*, US, 33 F.3d 1232 (10th Cir. 1994); *Kao* v. *China*, US, 816 F.Supp. 910, 918 (S.D.N.Y. 1993); *Casalino* v. *Ente*, US, 779 F.Supp. 338, 342 (S.D.N.Y. 1991); *Fickling* v. *Australia*, US, 775 F.Supp. 66, 71, fn. 2 (E.D.N.Y. 1991); 103 ILR 447; *Darby* v. *Compagnie*, US, 769 F.Supp. 1255, 1265–1266 (S.D.N.Y. 1991); *Kramer* v. *Boeing*, US, 705 F.Supp. 1392, 1396 (D. Minn. 1989); *Compania* v. *US*, US, 859 F.2d 1354, 1360 (9th Cir. 1988); 98 ILR 69; *Sudano* v. *Federal*, US, 699 F.Supp. 824, 827 (D.Haw. 1988); *Lasagne* v. *Divi*,

US, 685 F.Supp. 88, 90 (S.D.N.Y. 1988); *Zernicek* v. *Brown*, US, 826 F.2d 415, 418 (5th Cir. 1987); 92 ILR 442; *Martin* v. *South Africa*, US, 836 F.2d 91, 94 (2nd Cir. 1987); 92 ILR 448; *Tucker* v. *Whitaker*, US, 620 F.Supp. 578, 586 (E.D.Pa. 1985); affirmed, *Tucker* v. *Whitaker*, US, 800 F.2d 1140 (3rd Cir. 1986) (Table); *Close* v. *American*, US, 587 F.Supp. 1062, 1064–1065 (S.D.N.Y. 1984); *Sugarman* v. *Aeromexico*, US, 626 F.2d 270, 272 (3rd Cir. 1980); 63 ILR 446; *Upton* v. *Iran*, US, 459 F.Supp. 264, 266 (D.D.C. 1978); 63 ILR 211.

372 *Reers* v. *Deutsche*, US, 320 F.Supp.2d 140, 148–149 (S.D.N.Y. 2004); *Zernicek* v. *Brown*, US, 826 F.2d 415, 419 (5th Cir. 1987); 92 ILR 442; *Keller* v. *Transportes*, US, 601 F.Supp. 787, 789–790 (D.D.C. 1985); *Australian* v. *Lynne*, US, 743 F.2d 672, 675 (9th Cir. 1984); 98 ILR 22; *Berkovitz* v. *Iran*, US, 735 F.2d 329, 332 (9th Cir. 1984); 81 ILR 552; *Harris* v. *VAO*, US, 481 F.Supp. 1056, 1062 (E.D.N.Y. 1979); 63 ILR 318; *Upton* v. *Iran*, US, 459 F.Supp. 264, 266 (D.D.C. 1978); 63 ILR 211.

373 *Doe I* v. *Israel*, US, 400 F.Supp.2d 86, 107 (D.D.C. 2005).

374 *Alpha* v. *Nippon*, US, 199 F.3d 1078 (9th Cir. 1999). See also *Berkovitz* v. *Iran*, US, 735 F.2d 329, 332 (9th Cir. 1984); 81 ILR 552.

375 *Wasserstein* v. *Formosa*, US, 2002 U.S.Dist.Lexis 12012, pp. 25–28 (S.D.N.Y. 2002). See also *Shapiro* v. *Bolivia*, US, 930 F.2d 1013, 1018–1020 (2nd Cir. 1991); 98 ILR 109; *Walpex* v. *Yacimientos*, US, 712 F.Supp. 383, 388–390 (S.D. N.Y. 1989).

376 *Dumont* v. *Saskatchewan*, US, 258 F.3d 880, 884, fn. 6 (8th Cir. 2001). See also *In re Air Crash*, US, 392 F.Supp.2d 461, 468–469 (E.D.N.Y. 2005).

377 *TermoRio* v. *Electrificadora*, US, 421 F.Supp.2d 87, 95, 96 (D.D.C. 2006).

378 *Atlantic* v. *Inter-American*, US, 251 F.Supp.2d 126, 134 (D.D.C. 2003) (emphasis in the original). This also applies to an implied contract: *Chisolm* v. *Bank*, US, 643 F.Supp. 1393 (S.D.Fla. 1986).

379 *Pons* v. *China*, US, 666 F.Supp.2d 406, 413–414 (S.D.N.Y. 2009); *Hilaturas* v. *Iraq*, US, 573 F.Supp.2d 781, 795 (S.D.N.Y. 2008); *Agrocomplect* v. *Iraq*, US, 524 F.Supp.2d 16, 26–32 (D.D.C. 2007); *IT* v. *Pakistan*, US, 351 F.3d 1184, 1186 (D.C.Cir. 2003); *Global* v. *Mkapa*, US, 290 F.Supp.2d 108, 113 (D.D.C. 2003); *Virtual* v. *South Africa*, US, 300 F.3d 230, 239–240 (2nd Cir. 2002); *Keller* v. *Central*, US, 277 F.3d 811, 818 (6th Cir. 2002); *Lempert* v. *Kazakstan*, US, 223 F.Supp.2d 200, 204 (D.D.C. 2002); *Croesus* v. *Brazil*, US, 212 F.Supp.2d 30, 36 (D.D.C. 2002); *Hanil* v. *PT*, US, 148 F.3d 127, 132 (2nd Cir. 1998); affirming *Hanil* v. *PT*, US, 1997 U.S.Dist.Lexis 10450 (S.D.N.Y. 1997); *Voest-Alpine* v. *Bank*, US, 142 F.3d 887, 896 (5th Cir. 1998); *Adler* v. *Nigeria*, US, 107 F.3d 720, 727 (9th Cir. 1997); *Commercial* v. *Rafidain*, US, 15 F.3d 238, 241 (2nd Cir. 1994); 107 ILR 261; *Reed* v. *Donau*, US, 866 F.Supp. 750, 754–755 (S.D.N.Y. 1994); *Antares* v. *Nigeria*, US, 999 F.2d 33, 36 (2nd Cir. 1993); 107 ILR 225; *Walter* v. *Philippines*, US, 965 F.2d 1375, 1387 (5th Cir. 1992); 103 ILR 503; *Siderman* v. *Argentina*, US, 965 F.2d 699, 710 (9th Cir. 1992); 103 ILR 454; *Gregorian* v. *Izvestia*, US, 871 F.2d 1515, 1527 (9th Cir. 1989); 98 ILR 76; *Zedan* v. *Saudi Arabia*, US, 849 F.2d 1511, 1515, fn. 2 (D.C.Cir. 1988); 92 ILR 462; *Meadows* v. *Dominican*, US, 817 F.2d 517, 523 (9th Cir. 1987); 98 ILR 37; *Harris* v. *National*, US, 691 F.2d 1344, 1351 (11th Cir. 1982); 72 ILR 172; *Texas* v. *Nigeria*, US, 647 F.2d 300, 312 (2nd Cir. 1981); 63 ILR 552.

556   NOTES TO PAGE 128

380 *Dominican v. Dominican*, US, 903 F.Supp. 1507, 1514–1515 (M.C.Fla. 1995).

381 *Morris v. China*, US, 478 F.Supp.2d 561, 570–571 (S.D.N.Y. 2007); *Broadfield v. Ministry*, US, 99 F.Supp.2d 403, 406 (S.D.N.Y. 2000); *Millicom v. Costa Rica*, US, 995 F.Supp. 14, 22 (D.D.C. 1998); *United v. Mangyshlakneft*, US, 33 F.3d 1232, 1237 (10th Cir. 1994). See also *RSM v. Petroleos*, US, 338 F.Supp.2d 1208, 1214 (D.Colo. 2004).

382 *Argentina v. Weltover*, US, 504 US 607, 618–619 (1992); 119 L.Ed.2d 394, 408; 100 ILR 509, 518.

383 *Keller v. Central*, US, 277 F.3d 811, 818 (6th Cir. 2002); *Parex v. Russian*, US, 116 F.Supp.2d 415, 421 (S.D.N.Y. 2000); *Voest-Alpine v. Bank*, US, 142 F.3d 887, 896 (5th Cir. 1998); *Hanil v. PT*, US, 148 F.3d 127, 132 (2nd Cir. 1998); affirming *Hanil v. PT*, US, 1997 U.S.Dist.Lexis 10450 (S.D.N.Y. 1997); *Adler v. Nigeria*, US, 107 F.3d 720, 727 (9th Cir. 1997) (factual findings changed on remand, *Adler v. Nigeria*, US, 219 F.3d 869 (9th Cir. 2000); *Commercial v. Rafidain*, US, 15 F.3d 238, 241 (2nd Cir. 1994); 107 ILR 261; *Reed v. Donau*, US, 866 F.Supp. 750, 754–755 (S.D.N.Y. 1994); *L'Europeenne v. Venezuela*, US, 700 F.Supp. 114, 121 (S.D.N.Y. 1988); 98 ILR 100 note.

384 *Hanil v. PT*, US, 148 F.3d 127, 132 (2nd Cir. 1998); affirming *Hanil v. PT*, 1997 U.S.Dist.Lexis 10450 (S.D.N.Y. 1997); *Voest-Alpine v. Bank*, US, 142 F.3d 887, 896 (5th Cir. 1998); *US Fidelity v. Petroleo*, US, 1999 U.S.Dist.Lexis 7235, pp. 27–28 (S.D.N.Y. 1999); affirmed, *US Fidelity v. Braspetro*, US, 199 F.3d 94 (2nd Cir. 1999); *Adler v. Nigeria*, US, 107 F.3d 720, 729 (9th Cir. 1997).

385 *IT v. Pakistan*, US, 351 F.3d 1184, 1187, 1189–1191 (D.C.Cir. 2003); *Meadows v. Dominican*, US, 817 F.2d 517, 523 (9th Cir. 1987); 98 ILR 37; affirming *Meadows v. Dominican*, US, 628 F.Supp. 599, 605 (N.D.Cal. 1986).

386 *Hanil v. PT*, US, 148 F.3d 127 (2nd Cir. 1998); affirming *Hanil v. PT*, 1997 U.S. Dist.Lexis 10450 (S.D.N.Y. 1997). See also *Adler v. Nigeria*, US, 107 F.3d 720, 729 (9th Cir. 1997).

387 *Barkanic v. General*, US, 822 F.2d 11, 13 (2nd Cir. 1987); 98 ILR 44.

388 *US Fidelity v. Braspetro*, US, 1999 U.S.Dist.Lexis 7236, p. 45 (S.D.N.Y. 1999); affirmed, *US Fidelity v. Braspetro*, 199 F.3d 94 (2nd Cir. 1999).

389 *Poddar v. State*, US, 235 F.R.D. 592, 597 (S.D.N.Y. 2006); *Peterson v. Saudi Arabia*, US, 416 F.3d 83, 91 (D.C.Cir. 2005); affirming *Peterson v. Saudi Arabia*, US, 332 F.Supp.2d 189, 201 (D.D.C. 2004); *Samco v. Arita*, US, 395 F.3d 1212, 1218 (11th Cir. 2005); *Murphy v. Korea*, US, 421 F.Supp.2d 627, 647, fn. 16 (S.D.N.Y. 2005); *Doe I v. Israel*, US, 400 F.Supp.2d 86, 107 (D.D.C. 2005); *Global v. Mkapa*, US, 290 F.Supp.2d 108, 113–116 (D.D.C. 2003); *Croesus v. Brazil*, US, 212 F.Supp.2d 30, 36–37 (D.D.C. 2002); *Filetech v. France*, US, 212 F.Supp.2d 183, 197 (S.D.N.Y. 2001); affirmed, *Filetech v. France*, US, 304 F.3d 180 (2nd Cir. 2002); *Dewhurst v. Telenor*, US, 83 F.Supp.2d 577, 591 (D.Md. 2000); *Dar v. Iraq*, US, 79 F.Supp.2d 374, 382–385 (S.D.N.Y. 2000); *Goodman v. Rafidain*, US, 26 F.3d 1143, 1146–1147 (D.C.Cir. 1994); *Stena v. Comision*, US, 923 F.2d 380, 390 (5th Cir. 1991); 103 ILR 433.

390 *Global v. Mkapa*, US, 290 F.Supp.2d 108, 115 (D.D.C. 2003); *Falcon v. Venezuela*, US, 2001 WL 584346, p. 6 (D.Kan. 2001); *United v. Mangyshlakneft*, US, 33 F.3d 1232, 1238 (10th Cir. 1994).

NOTES TO PAGES 129–134   557

391 *Guirlando* v. *TC*, US, 602 F.3d 69, 75–79 (2nd Cir. 2010); *Gosain* v. *State*, US, 689 F.Supp.2d 571, 580–581 (S.D.N.Y. 2010); *Morris* v. *China*, US, 478 F.Supp.2d 561, 567 (S.D.N.Y. 2007); *Gulf* v. *Congo*, US, 276 F.Supp.2d 20, 26–27 (D.D.C. 2003); *Virtual* v. *South Africa*, US, 300 F.3d 230, 240–241 (2nd Cir. 2002); *Lyon* v. *Agusta*, US, 252 F.3d 1078, 1083 (9th Cir. 2001); *Falcon* v. *Venezuela*, US, 2001 WL 584346, p. 6 (D.Kan. 2001); *Bao* v. *Li*, US, 201 F.Supp.2d 14, 25 (D.D.C. 2000); *Parex* v. *Russian*, US, 116 F.Supp.2d 415, 421 (S.D.N.Y. 2000); *Alpha* v. *Nippon*, US, 199 F.3d 1078, 1086 (9th Cir. 1999); *US Fidelity* v. *Braspetro*, 1999 U.S.Dist.Lexis 7236, pp. 45–46 (S.D.N.Y. 1999); affirmed, *US Fidelity* v. *Braspetro*, US, 199 F.3d 94 (2nd Cir. 1999); *Filetech* v. *France*, US, 157 F.3d 922, 931 (2nd Cir. 1998); *Hanil* v. *PT*, US, 148 F.3d 127, 133 (2nd Cir. 1998); affirming *Hanil* v. *PT*, 1997 U.S.Dist.Lexis 10450 (S.D.N.Y. 1997); *Morgan* v. *Novokrivorogsky*, US, 57 F.Supp.2d 863, 872 (N.D.Cal. 1998); *Adler* v. *Nigeria*, US, 107 F.3d 720, 726–727 (9th Cir. 1997); *Doe* v. *Unocal*, US, 963 F.Supp. 880, 888 (C.D.Cal. 1997); *United* v. *Mangyshlakneft*, US, 33 F.3d 1232, 1239 (10th Cir. 1994); affirming *United* v. *Mangyshlakneft*, US, 821 F.Supp. 1405, 1409 (D.Colo. 1993); *Antares* v. *Nigeria*, US, 999 F.2d 33, 34–35 (2nd Cir. 1993); 107 ILR 225 and *Antares* v. *Nigeria*, US, 948 F.2d 90, 95 (2nd Cir. 1991); 107 ILR 225; *General* v. *Grossman*, US, 991 F.2d 1376, 1385 (8th Cir. 1993); *Kao* v. *China*, US, 816 F.Supp. 910, 918 (S.D.N.Y. 1993); *Gabay* v. *Mostazafan*, US, 151 F.R.D. 250, 255, fn. 8 (S.D.N.Y. 1993); 107 ILR 242; *Weltover* v. *Argentina*, US, 941 F.2d 145, 152–153 (2nd Cir. 1991); affirmed, *Argentina* v. *Weltover*, US, 504 US 607 (1992); 100 ILR 509; *International* v. *Rafidain*, US, 893 F.2d 8, 11, fn. 3 (2nd Cir. 1989); 98 ILR 93; *Rush-Presbyterian* v. *Hellenic*, US, 877 F.2d 574, 581–582 (7th Cir. 1989); 101 ILR 509; *Zedan* v. *Saudi Arabia*, US, 849 F.2d 1511, 1515 (D.C.Cir. 1988); 92 ILR 462.
392 *Keller* v. *Central*, US, 277 F.3d 811, 818 (6th Cir. 2002); *Saudi* v. *Exxonmobil*, US, 194 F.Supp.2d 378, 406 (D.N.J. 2002); *Voest-Alpine* v. *Bank*, US, 142 F.3d 887, 894–895 (5th Cir. 1998).

Chapter 4

1 See, e.g., *Vaessen* v. *American*, Belgium, (1997) 115 ILR 435, 441; *X* v. *Y1*, Japan, 1990; 35 *JAIL* (1992) 151, 154–155; *Yendall* v. *Australia*, England, (1984) 107 ILR 590; *Morocco* v. *Stichting*, Netherlands, (1978) 65 ILR 375, 376; *De Sousa* v. *Portugal*, Netherlands, (1979) 65 ILR 378, 379; affirmed, *Portugal* v. *De Sousa*, Netherlands, (1981) 94 ILR 314; *Stichting* v. *Morocco*, Netherlands, (1984/1986) 94 ILR 355, 356; *Stichting* v. *Morocco*, Netherlands, (1991/1994) 128 ILR 676, 680; *USA* v. *Rodrigo*, Philippines, (1990) 102 ILR 132, 146; *USA* v. *Ceballos*, Philippines, (1990) 102 ILR 132, 144; *Nicoud* v. *USA*, Switzerland, (1994) 116 ILR 650, 654–655; *X* v. *USA*, Switzerland, (1995) 116 ILR 668, 674; *Ghawanmeh* v. *Islamic*, US, 672 F.Supp.2d 3, 13–20 (D.D.C. 2009). For other examples of failing on the merits see *Harry* v. *USA*, Philippines, (1958) 88 ILR 711, 713–714; *Société* v. *Banque Centrale*, Belgium, (1963) 45 ILR 85, 87–90.

558 NOTES TO PAGES 134-135

2 See, e.g., *Yendall* v. *Australia*, England, (1984) 107 ILR 590; *USA* v. *Rodrigo*, Philippines, (1990) 102 ILR 132, 146; *Vaessen* v. *American*, Belgium, (1997) 115 ILR 435, 441.

3 See, e.g., *Clerget* v. *Représentation*, France, (1967) 48 ILR 145 and later *Clerget* v. *Banque*, France, (1969) 52 ILR 310; affirmed, *Clerget* v. *Banque*, France, (1971) 65 ILR 54; *Banamar-Capizzi* v. *Embassy*, Italy, (1989) 87 ILR 56; *Kenyan Diplomatic Residence Case*, Germany, (2003) 128 ILR 632; *MK* v. *State Secretary*, Netherlands, (1986) 94 ILR 357; *Zaire* v. *Duclaux*, Netherlands, (1988) 94 ILR 368; *Diana* v. *South Africa*, Spain, (1986) 86 ILR 512, 516; *Abbott* v. *South Africa*, Spain, (1992) 113 ILR 411; *State Immunity Case*, Switzerland, (1939/1940) 10 AD 235.

4 See, e.g., s. 230(2) of the UK Employment Rights Act 1996. According to the draftsmen of the European Convention, 'the expression "contract of employ- ment" (in French: *contrat de travail*) [in Article 5] ... is to be understood in a wide sense, comprising the contracts with manual workers as well as con- tracts with other employees'. Council of Europe, *Explanatory Reports*, 1972, p. 15, para. 30.

5 See *Italy* v. *BV*, Netherlands, 1993, 26 NYIL (1995) 338, 340; *Saudi Arabia* v. *Ahmed*, England, (1993/1995) 104 ILR 629.

6 For a detailed and illuminating analysis of the difficulties surrounding the concept of 'contract of employment' in the UK law see Brodie, *The Employment Contract*, esp. pp. 1-24. See also Freedland, *The Personal Employment Contract*; Bowers, *A Practical Approach*, pp. 15-22; Sargeant and Lewis, *Employment Law*, pp. 46-51; Selwyn, *Law of Employment*, pp. 39-47; Honeyball, *Textbook on Employment Law*, pp. 23-29; Deakin and Morris, pp. 121-144; Pitt, *Employment Law*, pp. 82-87; Cavalier and Upex, The Concept.

7 See also s. 295(1) of the Trade Union and Labour Relations (Consolidation) Act 1992. Under s. 53 (1) of the Health and Safety at Work etc. Act 1974, a 'contract of employment' means 'a *contract of employment* or apprenticeship' (emphasis added). In Austrian law it seems that a contract of employment is also called a 'contract of service under private law': *Neustein* v. *Indonesia*, Austria, (1958) 65 ILR 3, 6.

8 As pointed out by scholars, it was chiefly in the context of vicarious liability, i.e. the liability of an employer to a third party for the torts of an employee, that the concept of a contract of service/employment was first formulated. See Bowers, *A Practical Approach*, pp. 17-18; Honeyball, *Textbook on Employment Law*, pp. 21-24; Pitt, *Employment Law*, pp. 82-83; and the cases cited there. See also Deakin and Morris, *Labour Law*, pp. 133-135 for other situations and the cases cited there.

9 The term 'employee' is defined by reference to the contract of employment, that is, 'an individual who has entered into or works under (or, where the employment has ceased, worked under) a contract of employment' (s. 230(1), ERA). See Bowers, *A Practical Approach*, pp. 15-16; Sargeant and Lewis, *Employ- ment Law*, pp. 41-42; Selwyn, *Law of Employment*, p. 40; Honeyball, *Textbook on Employment Law*, pp. 21-22; Deakin and Morris, *Labour Law*, pp. 121-123; Pitt, *Employment Law*, p. 82. By contrast, US law seems to classify a contract of

NOTES TO PAGES 135–137   559

employment as a 'contract for services': *Segni* v. *Commercial Office*, US, 835 F.2d 160, 164–165 (7th Cir. 1987); 98 ILR 55; affirming *Segni* v. *Commercial*, US, 650 F.Supp. 1042 (N.D.Ill. 1986).

10 For convenient lists of rights reserved only to employees see Bowers, *A Practical Approach*, p. 16; Sargeant and Lewis, *Employment Law*, p. 45. See also Selwyn, *Law of Employment*, p. 47; Honeyball, *Textbook on Employment Law*, pp. 21–22; Deakin and Morris, *Labour Law*, pp. 123–125; Pitt, *Employment Law*, p. 81. Section 191(4)(a) of the ERA further extends the references to a contract of employment to the terms of employment of a person in Crown employment for the purposes of statutory protection whereas, in theory, such a person is a 'servant of the Crown' under a letter of appointment regulated by the Royal Prerogative instead of a contract of employment. For detailed analysis of Crown employment see Fredman and Morris, *The State as Employer*.

11 Under s. 235 of the Trade Union and Labour Relations (Consolidation) Act 1992 (TULRCA), as regards the requirement to ballot before industrial action by a trade union, 'references to a contract of employment include any contract under which one person personally does work or performs services for another'. Now if, in the same Act, 'employee' means 'an individual who has entered into or works under (or, where the employment has ceased, worked under) a contract of employment' (s. 295(1), TULRCA), it is obvious that, in this particular context relating to industrial action, an 'independent contractor' is, in the eyes of the law, also an 'employee'. For expansive definitions of 'employee' see also ss. 51(A) and 53(1) of the Health and Safety at Work etc. Act 1974 and s. 163(1) of the Social Security Contributions and Benefits Act 1992.

12 For example, in *Prentice* v. *Bolivia*, South Africa, (1978) (3) SA 938, 940; 64 ILR 685, 687, the court regarded the appointment of quantity surveyors as 'employment', whereas in England such surveyors would most likely be viewed as 'independent contractors' instead of 'employees'.

13 See the leading cases of *Ready Mixed* v. *Minister*, England, [1968] 2 QB 497; *Market Investigations* v. *Minister*, England, [1969] 2 QB 173; *O'Kelly* v. *Trusthouse*, England, [1984] QB 90; *Short* v. *J*, UK, [1946] SC (HL) 24, 33–34; [1946] SLT 230, 233–234.

14 *Ferguson* v. *Dawson*, England, [1976] 1 WLR 1213, 1222–1223, citing *Addiscombe* v. *Crabbe*, England, 1957, [1958] 1 QB 513, 527–528.

15 *Massey* v. *Crown*, England, 1977, [1978] ICR 590, 594.

16 *Montgomery* v. *Johnson*, England, [2001] ICR 819, 830.

17 See *Montgomery* v. *Johnson*, England, [2001] ICR 819; *Stephenson* v. *Delphi*, England, 2002, [2003] ICR 471; *Dacas* v. *Brook*, England, [2004] IRLR 358; [2004] ICR 1437; *Bunce* v. *Postworth*, England, [2005] IRLR 557.

18 *Prentice* v. *Bolivia*, South Africa, (1978) (3) SA 938; 64 ILR 685; *Tsakos* v. *USA*, Switzerland, (1972) 75 ILR 78.

19 In Italy, for example, the first instance employment cases are normally handled by the Examining Magistrate (*Pretore*) sitting as a labour judge. See, e.g., *Danish* v. *Hansen*, Italy, (1979) 65 ILR 325, 325; *Italian* v. *US*, Italy, (1981) 65

560 NOTES TO PAGE 137

ILR 338; *Rubin* v. *Consul*, Italy, (1977) 77 ILR 593; *Panattoni* v. *Germany*, Italy, (1987) 87 ILR 42; *Banamar-Capizzi* v. *Embassy*, Italy (1989) 87 ILR 56, 57; *British Consulate-General* v. *Toglia*, Italy, (1989) 101 ILR 379, 381; *Libya* v. *Trobbiani*, Italy, (1990) 114 ILR 520, 521; *Norwegian Embassy* v. *Quattri*, Italy, (1991) 114 ILR 525, 526–527, 531; *Zambian Embassy* v. *Sendanayake*, Italy, (1992) 114 ILR 532, 532; *Carbonar* v. *Magurno*, Italy, (1993) 114 ILR 534, 534; *Perrini* v. *Académie*, Italy, (1994) 114 ILR 536, 537; *USA* v. *Lo Gatto*, Italy, (1995) 114 ILR 555, 556; *Canada* v. *Cargnello*, Italy, (1998) 114 ILR 559, 561.

20 See *Embassy Interpreter Dismissal Case*, Austria, (1985) 77 ILR 485; *François* v. *Canada*, Belgium, (1989) 115 ILR 418; *Morocco* v. *DR*, Belgium, (1989) 115 ILR 421; *De Queiroz* v. *Portugal*, Belgium, (1992) 115 ILR 430; *Vaessen* v. *American*, Belgium, (1997) 115 ILR 435; *Collée* v. *Gécamines*, Belgium, (1990) 115 ILR 435 note; *Conrades* v. *UK*, Germany, (1981) 65 ILR 205; *X* v. *Argentina*, Germany, (1996) 114 ILR 502, 503–506; *Muller* v. *USA*, Germany, (1998) 114 ILR 512, 514–519; *Brazilian Embassy Employee Case*, Portugal, (1984) 116 ILR 625, 626; *Ramos* v. *USA*, Portugal, (1994) 116 ILR 634, 635; *Tsakos* v. *USA*, Switzerland, (1972) 75 ILR 78; *Landano* v. *USA*, Switzerland, (1987) 116 ILR 636; *Nicoud* v. *USA*, Switzerland, (1994) 116 ILR 650; *R* v. *Iraq*, Switzerland, (1994) 116 ILR 664, 665; *X* v. *USA*, Switzerland, (1995) 116 ILR 668. In France, the first instance employment cases are heard by the so-called 'Conseil de Prud'hommes'. See mentioned in *Clerget* v. *Représentation*, France, (1967) 48 ILR 145 and later *Clerget* v. *Banque*, France, (1969) 52 ILR 310; affirmed, *Clerget* v. *Banque*, France, (1971) 65 ILR 54; *Robert* v. *Procureur*, France, (1990) 113 ILR 450, 451; *Kuwait News* v. *Parrott*, France, (1990) 113 ILR 457, 458–459; *Barrandon* v. *USA*, France, (1992/1995) 113 ILR 464, 466, 468; *USA* v. *Perières*, France, (1997) 113 ILR 494, 495, 497.

21 For example, in the UK, an Employment Tribunal or Employment Appeal Tribunal consists of a legally qualified chairman and two lay members representing employers and workers respectively. One thus will be justified to regard an employment tribunal as a merely quasi-judicial organ. See the Employment Tribunals Act 1996 (initially known as the 'Industrial Tribunals Act'), the Employment Rights (Dispute Resolution) Act 1998, Parts I and II and the Employment Tribunals (Constitution and Rules of Procedure) Regulations 2004, SI 2004/1861, esp. regs. 8 and 9. For general information see www. employmenttribunals.gov.uk. In France, the first instance labour court is a *Conseil de Prud'Hommes*, which is of long-established tradition, with its members (judges) elected on a five-year basis, half of its members by employees and half by employers. There is no requirement that the members be legally qualified. See www.travail-solidarite.gouv.fr. In Germany, there are three levels of labour court: (1) *Arbeitsgerichte* (Labour Courts: first instance); (2) *Landesarbeitsgerichte* (Provincial Labour Courts: courts of appeal); and (3) *Bundesarbeitsgericht* (Federal Labour Court: final court of appeal). Each court consists of a mixture of professional and lay judges, normally one professional judge (*Berufsrichter*) and two lay members (or 'honorary judges' (*ehrenamtliche Richter*)) drawn from both sides of industry. See www.arbeitsrecht. de. See, e.g., *Kenyan Diplomatic Residence Case*, Germany, (2003) 128 ILR 632. By

NOTES TO PAGES 137–140   561

contrast, there are no special employment tribunals in the US, where employment law cases are heard in state or federal courts. However, the National Labor Relations Board (NLRB) deals with collective issues such as collective bargaining and union representation. See, e.g., *British Rail*, US, 163 NLRB 721 (1967); 63 ILR 5; *AGIP*, US, 196 NLRB 1144 (1972); 63 ILR 18; *State Bank*, US, 229 NLRB 838 (1977); 63 ILR 81; *SK Products*, US, 230 NLRB 1211 (1977); 63 ILR 647; *German School*, US, 260 NLRB 1250 (1982); *Goethe House*, US, 288 NLRB 257 (1988). The NLRB calls itself a 'quasi-judicial body', see www.nlrb.gov. See also *Argentine Airlines* v. *Ross*, US, 408 N.Y.S.2d 831 (1978); 63 ILR 195 (appeal from a decision of the New York Unemployment Insurance Appeal Board).

22 For the balancing of interests in employment and other immunity cases see ILC, Report, *YILC*, 1991-II-2, p. 12 at 41–42, commentary to Art. 11, paras. (2)–(5); reaffirmed in Report of the [ILC] Working Group, 1999, *YILC*, 1999-II-2, Annex, p. 149 at 165, para. 85; ALRC, Report No. 24, 1984, p. 55, para. 94; Pingel-Lenuzza, Autonomie; *Victory* v. *Comisaría*, US, 336 F.2d 354, 360, 363 (2nd Cir. 1964); 35 ILR 110; quoted with approval in *I Congreso del Partido*, England, 1981, [1983] 1 AC 244, 265–266; 64 ILR 307, 317; Broadbent v. OAS, US, 628 F.2d 27, 33 (D.C.Cir. 1980); 63 ILR 337; *De Sanchez* v. *Banco*, US, 770 F.2d 1385, 1394 (5th Cir. 1985); 88 ILR 75; *Butters* v. *Vance*, US, 225 F.3d 462, 465 (4th Cir. 2000); *S* v. *India*, Switzerland, (1984) 82 ILR 13, 18, Ground 3; *S* v. *Romania*, Switzerland, (1987) 82 ILR 45, 49, Ground 2; *Landano* v. *USA*, Switzerland, (1987) 116 ILR 636, 642; *M* v. *Egypt*, Switzerland, (1994) 116 ILR 656, 662, Ground 4a; *R* v. *Iraq*, Switzerland, (1994) 116 ILR 664, 666, Ground 5a; *Francischiello* v. *USA*, Italy, (1959) 28 ILR 158, 164; *Libya* v. *Rossbeton*, Italy, (1989) 87 ILR 63, 67; *British* v. *Toglia*, Italy, (1989) 101 ILR 379, 384; *Norwegian* v. *Quattri*, Italy, (1991) 114 ILR 525, 529; *Manauta* v. *Embassy*, Argentina, (1994) 113 ILR 429, 434; *Controller* v. *Davison*, New Zealand, [1996] 2 NZLR 278, 319; 104 ILR 526, 624.

23 *Sengupta* v. *India*, England, 1982, [1983] ICR 221, 228–229; 64 ILR 352, 360–361; quoted with approval in *Reid* v. *Nauru*, Australia, 1992, [1993] 1 VR 251, 257; 101 ILR 193, 199; *Governor* v. *Sutton*, New Zealand, 1994, [1995] 1 NZLR 426, 436; 104 ILR 508, 521; *UAE* v. *Abdelghafar*, England, (1995) 107 ILR 626, 637.

24 *Sengupta* v. *India*, England, 1982, [1983] ICR 221, 228; 64 ILR 352, 360; quoted in *Hicks* v. *USA*, England, (1995) 120 ILR 606, 609.

25 *Scarfò* v. *Sovereign*, Italy, (1957) 24 ILR 1, 4 (emphases added). See also *Church* v. *Ferraino*, Italy, (1986) 101 ILR 370, 374–375. But cf. *Baronci* v. *Ospedale*, Italy, (1956) 24 ILR 215, 217.

26 *Association* v. *Piccoli*, Italy, (1974) 65 ILR 308, 311–312.

27 *Re Canada Labour Code*, Canada, 1989, [1990] 1 FC 332, 339 per Iacobucci CJ; 86 ILR 626, 630; see also [1990] 1 FC 332, 349 per Mahoney JA; 86 ILR 626, 638.

28 *Re Canada Labour Code*, Canada, 1989, [1990] 1 FC 332, 340; 86 ILR 626, 631 per Iacobucci CJ.

29 *Congo* v. *Venne*, Canada, (1971) 22 DLR (3d) 669, 673; 64 ILR 24, 28; reversing *Venne* v. *Congo*, Canada, (1968) 5 DLR (3d) 128; 64 ILR 1. For a critical opinion see *Barker* v. *Kenya*, Zimbabwe, (1983) (4) SA 817, 822; 84 ILR 18, 25.

562 NOTES TO PAGES 140–148

30 *Carrato* v. *USA*, Canada, [1982] 40 OR (2d) 459, 461; (1982) 141 DLR (3d) 456, 459 per Steele J; 90 ILR 229, 231–232 (citing *Congo* v. *Venne*).

31 *X* v. *Argentina*, Germany, (1996) 114 ILR 502, 504–506. See also *French Consulate Disabled Employee Case*, Germany, (1988) 114 ILR 507, 510–511.

32 *Muller* v. *USA*, Germany, (1998) 114 ILR 512, 517. See also *Kato* v. *Ishihara*, US, 360 F.3d 106, 111–112 (2nd Cir. 2004) (engaging in the *promotion of commerce* is not engaging in *commerce*: 'The promotion abroad of the commerce of domestic firms is a basic – even quintessential – governmental function'); affirming, on different grounds, *Kato* v. *Ishihara*, US, 239 F.Supp.2d 359 (S.D.N.Y. 2002).

33 *Canada* v. *Cargnello*, Italy, (1998) 114 ILR 559, 567.

34 In this chapter the terms 'wrongful dismissal' and 'unfair dismissal' are used indiscriminately according to how they appear in various case reports and/or their headnotes. Such case reports emanate from a variety of countries and often contain scanty information on the act of dismissal itself or circumstances surrounding the dismissal. It is crucial to bear in mind that under, for example, the UK employment law, there is a strict distinction between 'wrongful dismissal' (i.e. termination of employment in breach of the contractual or statutory notice period, giving rise chiefly to a contractual claim) and 'unfair dismissal' (i.e. termination of employment on grounds other than those permissible by law, leading mainly to a statutory claim under the Employment Rights Act 1996 – see esp. s. 98 of that Act). Such a distinction results in, among other things, two distinct regimes of compensation. However, since we are here concerned solely with the procedural aspect of whether a foreign State should be immune from proceedings handling a claim of dismissal, the substantive distinction between the two types of dismissal is of little, if any, critical importance.

35 *M* v. *Egypt*, Switzerland, (1994) 116 ILR 656, 662, Ground 4a. The pronouncement was repeated verbatim in *R* v. *Iraq*, Switzerland, (1994) 116 ILR 664, 666, Ground 5a. See also *Landano* v. *USA*, Switzerland, (1987) 116 ILR 636, 642.

36 For the avoidance of confusion the masculine pronoun is used throughout the discussion, though I would much prefer to use more polite forms such as 'he/she', 's/he', 'they', etc.

37 According to the draftsmen, '"Habitual residence" is to be understood as a question of fact.' Council of Europe, *Explanatory Reports*, 1972, p. 15, para. 30. This implies that the person in question does not have to be officially – and, by the logic of it, legally – 'habitually resident', that is, he does not need to have 'permanent residence', 'indefinite leave to remain', 'settlement', 'green card', or some other status that normally requires a formal application process after completing a certain number of years' residence in a country.

38 Garnett, State Immunity (1997), 122; Fox, Employment, 143, 147, 170–172 and 176.

39 Council of Europe, *Explanatory Reports*, p. 15, para. 30.

40 For the unsuitability of the test of place of performance for certain sorts of employment see Fox, Employment, 143.

41 Council of Europe, *Explanatory Reports*, p. 15, para. 30.

NOTES TO PAGES 148–154   563

42 Thus the labour law principle that the employee should be entitled to the most favourable law is incorporated into conflict of law rules. This is essentially the same principle as embodied in Art. 6 of the 1980 Rome Convention, which the Regulation replaces. For comments on Art. 6 see Gamillscheg and Franzen, Conflicts of Laws, 171–173.

43 The Pakistan SIO (s. 6 (save 'citizen' instead of 'national' in s. 6(2)(b)) and Singapore SIA (s. 6 (same as Pakistan SIO)) reproduce verbatim the UK provision. The South Africa FSIA (s. 5) differs in wording, but not in substance, from the UK SIA, except that its s. 5(2)(b) reproduces the substance of s. 16(1)(a) of the UK SIA. For the prevention of a person suing his State of nationality under s. 4(2)(a), UK SIA, see *Sengupta v. India*, England, 1982, [1983] ICR 221, 224; 64 ILR 352, 355.

44 See the Pakistan SIO, s. 5(2); Singapore SIA, s. 5(1). Under s. 4(3) of the South Africa FSIA and s. 11(3) of the Australia FSIA, the term 'commercial transaction' does not include a contract of employment.

45 For explanations see, e.g., Collins, *Conflict of Laws*, pp. 168–171, Rule 16, paras. 6.125–6.130; Lewis, *State and Diplomatic Immunity*, p. 50.

46 *Egypt v. Gamal-Eldin*, England, 1995, [1996] 2 All ER 237, 247; [1996] ICR 13, 24–25; 104 ILR 673, 683.

47 For similar provisions see the Pakistan SIO, s. 6(4); Singapore SIA, s. 6(4).

48 See ss. 203(1) and 204(1) of the UK Employment Rights Act 1996. See, e.g., Deakin and Morris, *Labour Law*, p. 130, para. 3.23; Collins, *Conflict of Laws*, pp. 521, 538–539, Rule 32, paras. 12.096 and 12.130. See also UK SIA 1978, s. 4(4).

49 ALRC, Report No. 24, p. 58, para. 99. The draftsmen also noted the 'range of factors' that ought to be taken into account: p. 55, para. 95.

50 The draftsmen regard such a distinction as 'not exact', 'arbitrary as well as complex'. ALRC, Report No. 24, p. 56, para. 96.

51 'On balance it is sufficient to refer only to the time when the contract is made, both because it is simpler and because that is the time when the intention of the parties is formed. The employee may change status without reference to his employer and, to take the worst case, might even do so simply in order to take advantage of a greater opportunity to sue his employer.' ALRC, Report No. 24, p. 56, para. 96.

52 ALRC, Report No. 24, pp. 57–58, para. 97.

53 ALRC, Report No. 24, p. 58, para. 99.

54 See, e.g., *Reid v. Nauru*, Australia, 1992, [1993] 1 VR 251; 101 ILR 193 (nationality of the plaintiff not mentioned in the court's decision).

55 The 1982 and the 1994 Drafts are identical except for the savings clause.

56 For explanation for these two changes see ILC, Report, 1999, Annex, Report of the Working Group, YILC, 1999-II-2, p. 149 at 167, paras. 104 and 106. The reason for deleting Art. 11(2)(c) was that that paragraph 'could not be reconciled with the principle of non-discrimination based on nationality' (para. 106). However, as has been demonstrated earlier, the original provision does not necessarily preclude a national of the third State from bringing legal action. Greig regards the deleted provision as 'outdated' in face of dual

564 NOTES TO PAGES 154–158

nationality or close connections with States other than the State of nationality, which are quite common in the present-day world. Greig, Specific Exceptions, 565.

57 ILC, Report, *YILC*, 1991-II-2, p. 12 at 43, commentary to Art. 11, para. (10).

58 ILC, Report, 1999, Annex, Report of the Working Group, *YILC*, 1999-II-2, p. 149 at 166, para. 101.

59 ILC, *YILC*, 1991-II-2, p. 12 at 42, commentary to Art. 11, para. (4).

60 *Banai* v. *Canadian*, England, (1990) 107 ILR 600, 603–604.

61 *Sengupta* v. *India*, England, 1982, [1983] ICR 221, 224–225; 64 ILR 352, 355–356.

62 1972 European Convention, Art. 5(1) ('if the proceedings relate to a *contract of employment*'); ILC 1991 Draft Articles and 2004 UN Convention, Article 11 'Contracts of employment' ('in a proceeding which relates to a *contract of employment*'); UK SIA, s. 4(1) ('proceedings relating to a *contract of employment*'); Pakistan SIO, s. 6 'Contracts of employment' ('proceedings relating to a *contract of employment*'); Singapore SIA, s. 6(1) ('proceedings relating to a *contract of employment*'); South Africa FSIA, s. 5(1) ('proceedings relating to a *contract of employment*'); Australian FSIA, s. 12(1) 'Contracts of employment' ('under a *contract of employment*'); Argentina Law of 1995, Art. 2(d) ('relating to a *contract of employment*'); ILA Drafts, Art. III(C) ('Where the foreign State enters into a *contract for employment*'); IDI 1991 Draft, Art. 2(c)('proceedings concerning *contracts of employment*'). Emphases added. The Israeli Law of 2008 is a bit confusing. Section 4 allows an 'applicant for employment' to sue, and yet s. 4 is entitled 'Contract of employment'. It is difficult to see how an applicant can have a contract. Since this is a new piece of legislation, one must wait for clarification by case law in the future.

63 For our purposes Ms Fogarty's fresh claim for sex discrimination during the job application stage (i.e. no contract of employment yet) should be distinguished from her previous successful claim for sex discrimination in her dismissal (i.e. termination of an existing contract).

64 Section 16(1)(a) provides that 'section 4 [the employment contract exception] . . . does not apply to proceedings concerning the employment of the members of a [diplomatic] mission . . . or of the members of a consular post'.

65 *Fogarty* v. *UK*, ECHR, 2001, (2002) 34 EHRR 12, para. 38; 123 ILR 53, 65–66.

66 ILC, Report, *YILC*, 1991-II-2, p. 12 at 42, commentary to Art. 11. Emphases added.

67 ILC, Report, *YILC*, 1991-II-2, p. 12 at 43, commentary to Art. 11(2)(b), para. (10). No further illustrations of possible actions are given.

68 Judge Luocaides (dissenting) would prefer to see Fogarty's case as 'a claim for damages for sex discrimination': *Fogarty* v. *UK*, ECHR, 2001, (2002) 34 EHRR 12; 123 ILR 53, 72.

69 The Canada SIA, which is 'patterned after the American model' (*Re Canada Labour Code*, Canada, (1992) 91 DLR (4th) 449, 456; 94 ILR 264, 271), contains no specific provision on contracts of employment either. Thus an employment case has also to be brought under the 'commercial activity' exception (ss. 2 and 5). For discussion of the US practice see Garnett, The Perils.

NOTES TO PAGES 158–160   565

70 US House of Representatives, Report No. 94-1487, 1976, p. 16; 1976 USCCAN 6604, 6615. The word 'employment' in the legislative report is understood to encompass 'hiring and firing': *Elliott v. British*, US, 986 F.Supp. 189, 193 (S.D.N.Y. 1997); affirmed, *Elliott v. British*, US, 172 F.3d 37 (2nd Cir. 1999) (Table). Note that the report does not define 'civil service', as pointed out in *Kato v. Ishihara*, US, 360 F.3d 106, 110 (2nd Cir. 2004). However, the absence of definition of 'civil service' in either the FSIA or the legislative report has not deterred US courts from granting immunity for employment for 'civil service': *Kato v. Ishihara*, US, 360 F.3d 106, 111–112 (2nd Cir. 2004); affirming, on other grounds, *Kato v. Ishihara*, US, 239 F.Supp.2d 359, 363 (S.D.N.Y. 2002); *El-Hadad v. UAE*, US, 216 F.3d 29, 34 (D.C.Cir. 2000) (citing *Broadbent v. OAS*, US, 628 F.2d 27, 34–36 (D.C.Cir. 1980); 63 ILR 337); *Holden v. Canadian Consulate*, US, 92 F.3d 918, 921 (9th Cir. 1996). Some courts have treated the US civil service system as providing the benchmarks for judging foreign civil service: *Holden v. Canadian Consulate*, US, 92 F.3d 918, 921 (9th Cir. 1996); *Kato v. Ishihara*, US, 239 F.Supp.2d 359, 363 (S.D.N.Y. 2002); *Mukaddam v. Permanent Mission*, US, 111 F.Supp.2d 457, 463 (S.D.N.Y. 2000). By contrast, the Second Circuit held that the term 'civil service' should be interpreted to include the broad range of civil service employment relationships used by countries other than the US: *Kato v. Ishihara*, US, 360 F.3d 106, 112–114 (2nd Cir. 2004).
71 See *Elliott v. British*, US, 986 F.Supp. 189, 193 (S.D.N.Y. 1997).
72 US House of Representatives, Report No. 94-1487, 1976, pp. 16, 19; 1976 USCCAN 6604, 6615, 6617–18.
73 *Broadbent v. OAS*, US, 628 F.2d 27, 34 (D.C.Cir. 1980); 63 ILR 337; *Segni v. Commercial*, US, 835 F.2d 160, 165, fn. 7 (7th Cir. 1987); 98 ILR 55; *Zveiter v. Brazilian*, US, 833 F.Supp. 1089, 1093 (S.D.N.Y. 1993); *Elliott v. British*, US, 986 F.Supp. 189, 194 (S.D.N.Y. 1997); affirmed, *Elliott v. British*, US, 172 F.3d 37 (2nd Cir. 1999) (Table).
74 *El-Hadad v. Embassy*, US, 69 F.Supp.2d 69, 75–76 (D.D.C. 1999).
75 *El-Hadad v. UAE*, US, 216 F.3d 29, 33 (D.C.Cir. 2000); partly reversing and remanding *El-Hadad v. Embassy*, US, 69 F.Supp.2d 69 (D.D.C. 1999).
76 *El-Hadad v. Embassy*, US, No. 96-1943 (D.D.C. 2001).
77 *El-Hadad v. Embassy*, US, 2006 WL 826098 (D.D.C. 2006).
78 *El-Hadad v. UAE*, US, 496 F.3d 658, 661, 667–668 (D.C.Cir. 2007); affirming *El-Hadad v. Embassy*, US, 2006 WL 826098 (D.D.C. 2006).
79 *El-Hadad v. UAE*, US, 216 F.3d 29, 34 (D.C.Cir. 2000); *El-Hadad v. UAE*, US, 496 F.3d 658, 665–667 (D.C.Cir. 2007).
80 *Mukaddam v. Permanent Mission*, US, 111 F.Supp.2d 457, 463 (S.D.N.Y. 2000) (citing *Holden*, US, 92 F.3d 918, 921 (9th Cir. 1996) and *El-Hadad*, US 216 F.3d 29, 34 (D.C.Cir. 2000)).
81 *Mukaddam v. Permanent Mission*, US, 111 F.Supp.2d 457, 464 (S.D.N.Y. 2000).
82 *Mukaddam v. Permanent Mission*, US, 111 F.Supp.2d 457, 466 (S.D.N.Y. 2000).
83 ALI, *Third Restatement*, Vol. I, s. 453, p. 407, Reporters' Note 7. See *Segni v. Commercial*, US, 835 F.2d 160, 165, fn. 7 (7th Cir. 1987); 98 ILR 55.
84 *Verlinden v. Central Bank*, US, 461 US 480, 490–491 (1983); 79 ILR 548.

566 NOTES TO PAGES 160–162

85 Cf. *Hijazi* v. *Permanent Mission*, US, 689 F.Supp.2d 669 (S.D.N.Y. 2010) (Jordanian citizen employed by Saudi Arabia Permanent Mission to the UN; immunity upheld); *Hansen* v. *Danish*, US, 147 F.Supp.2d 142 (E.D.N.Y. 2001) (Danish citizen employed by the Danish Tourist Board in New York; immunity denied).

86 See *Bailey* v. *Grand*, US, 805 F.2d 1097 (2nd Cir. 1986); partly affirming *Bailey* v. *Grand*, US, 609 F.Supp. 48 (D.C.Vt. 1984).

87 *Hijazi* v. *Permanent Mission of Saudi Arabia to United Nations*, US, 689 F.Supp.2d 669, 674 (S.D.N.Y. 2010).

88 *Hijazi* v. *Permanent Mission*, US, 689 F.Supp.2d 669, 674, 674–675 (S.D.N.Y. 2010) (citing *Kato* v. *Ishihara*, US, 360 F.3d 106 (2nd Cir. 2004)).

89 *Hijazi* v. *Permanent Mission*, US, 689 F.Supp.2d 669, 675 (S.D.N.Y. 2010).

90 In *Gates* v. *Victor*, US, 54 F.3d 1457, 1465–1466 (9th Cir. 1995); 107 ILR 371 (employment claim unrelated to commercial activity). For substantive employment law issues involved in *Gates* see Geller, The Interplay. See also *Saudi Arabia* v. *Nelson*, US, 507 US 349, 358 (1993); 123 L.Ed.2d 47, 59; 100 ILR 544, 551 (personal injury claim unrelated to the contract of employment).

91 In *Zedan* v. *Saudi Arabia*, US, 849 F.2d 1511 (D.C.Cir. 1988); 92 ILR 462, a US citizen had been recruited in the US by a Saudi Arabian organization to work as an engineer on a construction project in Saudi Arabia. His claim for breach of contract was rejected because the construction project and the breach of contract took place in Saudi Arabia, while mere recruitment in the US was not enough to establish a substantial contact with the US.

92 *French Consular Employee Claim Case*, Austria, (1989) 86 ILR 583; *Castanheira* v. *Commercial*, Belgium, (1980) 82 ILR 100; *De Queiroz* v. *Portugal*, Belgium, (1992) 115 ILR 430; *Kenyan Diplomatic Residence Case*, Germany, (2003) 128 ILR 632; *Mallaval* v. *French*, Italy, (1974) 65 ILR 303; *De Sousa* v. *Portugal*, Netherlands, (1979) 65 ILR 378, 379; affirmed, *Portugal* v. *De Sousa*, Netherlands, (1981) 94 ILR 314; *M* v. *Egypt*, Switzerland, (1994) 116 ILR 656, 663, Ground 4b; *République X* v. *A*, Switzerland, 2003, 130 JDI (2003) 1125, 1126.

93 *X* v. *Argentina*, Germany, (1996) 114 ILR 502; *Danish* v. *Hansen*, Italy, (1979) 65 ILR 325. See also the pre-UK SIA case, *Sengupta* v. *India*, England, 1982, [1983] ICR 221; 64 ILR 352.

94 *Morocco* v. *DR*, Belgium, (1989) 115 ILR 421; *Zambian Embassy* v. *Sendanayake*, Italy, (1992) 114 ILR 532, 533; *MHC* v. *Cuba*, Netherlands, 1992, 27 NYIL (1996) 319; *Emilio* v. *Embassy*, Spain, (1986) 86 ILR 508; *S* v. *India*, Switzerland, (1984) 82 ILR 13, 19; *Nicoud* v. *USA*, Switzerland, (1994) 116 ILR 650, 652–653; *R* v. *Iraq*, Switzerland, (1994) 116 ILR 664, 667–668; *Segni* v. *Commercial*, US, 835 F.2d 160, 165, fn. 7 (7th Cir. 1987); 98 ILR 55; affirming *Segni* v. *Commercial*, US, 650 F.Supp. 1042 (N.D.Ill. 1986).

95 *MDDA* v. *Australian Embassy*, Netherlands, 1986, 19 NYIL (1988) 438, note 27. But see *Arias* v. *Venezuela*, Netherlands, (1998) 128 ILR 684, 686, paras. 4.5–4.6.

96 See *Manauta* v. *Embassy*, Argentina, (1994) 113 ILR 429; *Reid* v. *Nauru*, Australia, 1992, [1993] 1 VR 251; 101 ILR 193; *Embassy Interpreter Dismissal Case*, Austria, (1985) 77 ILR 485; *De Decker* v. *USA*, Belgium, (1956) 23 ILR 209; *François* v. *Canada*, Belgium, (1989) 115 ILR 418; *Yendall* v. *Australia*, England, (1984) 107

ILR 590; *UAE* v. *Abdelghafar*, England, (1995) 107 ILR 626; *Saudi Arabia* v. *Nasser*, England, (2000) Transcript; *Barrandon* v. *USA*, France, (1992/1995) 113 ILR 464; *Coco* v. *Argentina*, France, (1996) 113 ILR 491; *Saignie* v. *Embassy*, France, (1997) 113 ILR 492; *French Consulate Disabled Employee Case*, Germany, (1988) 114 ILR 507; *Hungarian* v. *Onori*, Italy, (1956) 23 ILR 203; *Scarfò* v. *Sovereign*, Italy, (1957) 24 ILR 1; *Parravicini* v. *Commercial*, Italy, (1969) 65 ILR 282; *Association* v. *Piccoli*, Italy, (1974) 65 ILR 308; *Bari* v. *Jasbez*, Italy, (1977) 77 ILR 602; *Pontificia* v. *Inps*, Italy, (1979) 65 ILR 333; *Special* v. *Pieciukiewicz*, Italy, (1982) 78 ILR 120; *Church* v. *Ferraino*, Italy, (1986) 101 ILR 370; *Libya* v. *Trobbiani*, Italy, (1990) 114 ILR 520; *Norwegian Embassy* v. *Quattri*, Italy, (1991) 114 ILR 525; *Carbonar* v. *Magurno*, Italy, (1993) 114 ILR 534; *Perrini* v. *Académie*, Italy, (1994) 114 ILR 536, 539; *Morocco* v. *Stichting*, Netherlands, (1978) 65 ILR 375; *Stichting* v. *Morocco*, Netherlands, (1984/1986) 94 ILR 355; *Van der Hulst* v. *US*, Netherlands, (1989) 94 ILR 373; *Stichting* v. *Morocco*, Netherlands, 1991; *Morocco* v. *Stichting*, Netherlands, (1994) 128 ILR 676, 680; *BV* v. *Instituto*, Netherlands, 1990, 23 *NYIL* (1992) 447; *BV* v. *Instituto*, Netherlands, 1991, 24 *NYIL* (1993) 341; *G* v. *USA*, Netherlands, 1992, 27 *NYIL* (1996) 320; *FLM* v. *Public Prosecutions*, Netherlands, 1993, 25 *NYIL* (1994) 527; *Italy* v. *BV*, Netherlands, 1993, 26 *NYIL* (1995) 338; *USA* v. *Ceballos*, Philippines, (1990) 102 ILR 132; *X* v. *Israel*, Portugal, (2002) 127 ILR 310; *Diana* v. *South Africa*, Spain, (1986) 86 ILR 512; *Tsakos* v. *USA*, Switzerland, (1972) 75 ILR 78; *X* v. *USA*, Switzerland, (1995) 116 ILR 668; *Janini* v. *Kuwait University*, US, 43 F.3d 1534 (D.C.Cir. 1995); 107 ILR 367; *Gates* v. *Victor*, US, 54 F.3d 1457 (9th Cir. 1995); 107 ILR 371.

97 See *Gittler* v. *German*, US, 408 N.Y.S.2d 600 (N.Y.S.C. 1978); 63 ILR 170; *Velloso* v. *Borla*, Italy, (1979) 65 ILR 328.

98 See *Morocco* v. *Stichting*, Netherlands, (1978) 65 ILR 375; *Stichting* v. *Morocco*, Netherlands, (1984/1986) 94 ILR 355; *Stichting* v. *Morocco*, Netherlands, 1991; *Morocco* v. *Stichting*, Netherlands, (1994) 128 ILR 676.

99 *M* v. *Egypt*, Switzerland, (1994) 116 ILR 656, 663, Ground 4b.

100 See *Re Canada Labour Code*, Canada, (1992) 91 DLR (4th) 449; 94 ILR 264; reversing *Re Canada Labour Code*, Canada, 1989, [1990] 1 FC 332; 86 ILR 626; *Italian Trade Union* v. *US*, Italy, (1981) 65 ILR 338; *Sindacato* v. *Bari*, Italy, (1986) 87 ILR 37.

101 *State Bank of India Case*, US, 229 NLRB 838, 842–843 (1977); 63 ILR 81, 91; overruling *British Rail*, US, 163 NLRB 721, 722 (1967); 63 ILR 5, 7 and *AGIP*, US, 196 NLRB 1144, 1144 (1972); 63 ILR 18; *SK Products*, US, 230 NLRB 1211, 1213 (1977); 63 ILR 647, 651–653; *German School Society*, US, 260 NLRB 1250 (1982); *State Bank* v. *National*, US, 808 F.2d 526 (7th Cir. 1986) (upholding NLRB orders (*State Bank of India*, 273 NLRB 264 (1984) and 273 NLRB 267 (1984)).

102 *Goethe House*, US, 288 NLRB 257, 261 (1988). The case later came before federal courts but was confirmed in *Goethe House* v. *National*, US, 869 F.2d 75 (2nd Cir. 1989); reversing *Goethe House* v. *National*, US, 685 F.Supp. 427 (S.D.N.Y. 1988).

103 *Goethe House*, US, 288 NLRB 257, 260 (1988).

104 For impositions associated with a successful certification process in Canada see *Re Canada Labour Code*, Canada, 1989, [1990] 1 FC 332, 348; 86 ILR 626, 637–638.

568   NOTES TO PAGES 164–166

105 *Italian Trade Union* v. *US*, Italy, (1981) 65 ILR 338, 342; quoted with approval in *Re Canada Labour Code*, Canada, (1992) 91 DLR (4th) 449, 471; 94 ILR 264. See also *Camera* v. *Bari*, Italy, (1979) 78 ILR 86, 89.

106 *Re Canada Labour Code*, Canada, 1989, [1990] 1 FC 332, 339, 348–349; 86 ILR 626, 630, 638.

107 *Re Canada Labour Code*, Canada, 1992, (1992) 91 DLR (4th) 449, 474; 94 ILR 264, 289. For an earlier remark about those contracts of employment that have both commercial and sovereign aspects see Crawford, International Law, 92, fn. 66.

108 *De Queiroz* v. *Portugal*, Belgium, (1992) 115 ILR 430, 434. See also *Portugal* v. *De Sousa*, Netherlands, (1981) 94 ILR 314; affirming *De Sousa* v. *Portugal*, Netherlands, (1979) 65 ILR 378; *Neustein* v. *Indonesia*, Austria, (1958) 65 ILR 3, 6–7.

109 *Collée* v. *Gécamines*, Belgium, (1990) 115 ILR 435 note.

110 *Castanheira* v. *Commercial Office*, Belgium, (1980) 82 ILR 100, 103. Strangely, the judgment of the court – deliberately or otherwise – omitted to mention the job title of the plaintiff (see p. 102). For similar cases concerning other types of commercial entities in Italy see *Slomnitzky* v. *Trade*, Italy, (1932) 6 AD 169, 169 (for historical interest, cf. *Russian* v. *Kazmann*, Italy, (1933) 7 AD 178; *Tani* v. *Russian*, Italy, (1947) 15 AD 141, 142–144; and *Russian* v. *Sakharoff*, France, (1933) 7 AD 170); *De Semenoff* v. *Railway*, Italy, (1936) 8 AD 234, 235. Cf. *Époux* v. *Canada*, Belgium, (1934) 9 AD 249, 249. Also compare *Little* v. *Riccio*, Italy, (1933/1934) 7 AD 177 with *Vaessen* v. *American*, Belgium, (1997) 115 ILR 435, 441.

111 *Castanheira* v. *Commercial Office*, Belgium, (1980) 82 ILR 100, 102. See also *Rousseau* v. *Upper Volta*, Belgium, (1983) 82 ILR 118, 119; *Emilio* v. *Embassy*, Spain, (1986) 86 ILR 508, 509; *Diana* v. *South Africa*, Spain, (1986) 86 ILR 512, 514; *Mukaddam* v. *Permanent*, US, 111 F.Supp.2d 457, 464 (S.D.N.Y. 2000).

112 *Rousseau* v. *Upper Volta*, Belgium, (1983) 82 ILR 118, 120. See also *British Embassy Driver Case*, Austria, (1978) 65 ILR 20, 22.

113 *USA* v. *Perières*, France, (1997) 113 ILR 494, 497. See also *François* v. *Canada*, Belgium, (1989) 115 ILR 418, 419.

114 *MK* v. *Turkey*, Netherlands, (1985) 94 ILR 350, 353. See also *Morocco* v. *Stichting*, Netherlands, (1978) 65 ILR 375, 376; *Stichting* v. *Morocco*, Netherlands, (1984) 94 ILR 355, 356; *Stichting* v. *Morocco*, Netherlands, 1991; *Morocco* v. *Stichting*, Netherlands, (1994) 128 ILR 676, 678, 680.

115 *Seidenschmidt* v. *USA*, Austria, (1992) 116 ILR 530, 532 (it is not clear what functions the plaintiff had performed: he was vaguely referred to as an 'official').

116 *French Consular Employee Claim Case*, Austria, (1989) 86 ILR 583, 586. Cf. *X* v. *Argentina*, Germany, (1996) 114 ILR 502.

117 *De Sousa* v. *Portugal*, Netherlands, (1979) 65 ILR 378, 378–379; affirmed, *Portugal* v. *De Sousa*, Netherlands, (1981) 94 ILR 314, 315.

118 *Mukaddam* v. *Permanent*, US, 111 F.Supp.2d 457, 466 (S.D.N.Y. 2000). See also *Brewer* v. *Iraq*, US, 890 F.2d 97, 101 (8th Cir. 1989); *Good* v. *Aramco*, US, 971 F.Supp. 254, 257 (S.D.Tex. 1997).

119 *Société Air Zaire* v. *Gauthier*, France, (1984) 77 ILR 510, 512; *Reid* v. *Nauru*, Australia, 1992, [1993] 1 VR 251; 101 ILR 193, 200.

NOTES TO PAGES 166–172   569

120 *Zambian Embassy* v. *Sendanayake*, Italy, (1992) 114 ILR 532, 533. See also *Carbonar* v. *Magurno*, Italy, (1993) 114 ILR 534, 535; *Parravicini* v. *Commercial*, Italy, (1969) 65 ILR 282, 283.
121 *R* v. *Iraq*, Switzerland, (1994) 116 ILR 664, 667, Ground 5c.
122 *M* v. *Egypt*, Switzerland, (1994) 116 ILR 656, 662, Ground 4b. See also *S* v. *India*, Switzerland, (1984) 82 ILR 13, 20, Ground 4; *Landano* v. *USA*, Switzerland, (1987) 116 ILR 636, 641–642; *X* v. *USA*, Switzerland, (1995) 116 ILR 668, 670–672; *République X* v. *A*, Switzerland, 2003, 130 *JDI* (2003) 1125, 1126.
123 *Coco* v. *Argentina*, France, (1996) 113 ILR 491, 492. The phrase 'special responsibilities' seems to be a standard formula used by the Court of Cassation. See also *Kuwait News* v. *Parrott*, France, (1990) 113 ILR 457, 459; *Saignie* v. *Embassy*, France, (1997) 113 ILR 492, 493. Cf. *Robert* v. *Procureur*, France, (1990) 113 ILR 450.
124 *X* v. *Israel*, Portugal, (2002) 127 ILR 310, 313.
125 *Segni* v. *Commercial*, US, 835 F.2d 160, 165 (7th Cir. 1987); 98 ILR 55.
126 *Holden* v. *Canadian*, US, 92 F.3d 918, 921 (9th Cir. 1996); noted in Mulvaney, *Holden*.
127 *Holden* v. *Canadian*, US, 92 F.3d 918, 922 (9th Cir. 1996).
128 *Saudi Arabia* v. *Nelson*, US, 507 US 349, 356–357 (1993); 123 L.Ed.2d 47, 58–59 (1993); 100 ILR 544, 550–551; *El-Hadad* v. *UAE*, US, 496 F.3d 658, 663 (D.C.Cir. 2007); affirming *El-Hadad* v. *Embassy*, US, 2006 WL 826098 (D.D.C. 2006).
129 *Elliott* v. *British*, US, 986 F.Supp. 189, 194 (S.D.N.Y. 1997); affirmed, *Elliott* v. *British*, US, 172 F.3d 37 (2nd Cir. 1999) (Table). For another case concerning age discrimination see *Starrett* v. *Iberia*, US, 756 F.Supp. 292, 293, fn. 1 (S.D.Tex. 1989).
130 *Shih* v. *Taipei*, US, 693 F.Supp.2d 805, 811 (N.D.Ill. 2010).
131 *Governor* v. *Sutton*, New Zealand, 1994, [1995] 1 NZLR 426, 431 per Cooke P; 437 per Richardson J; 104 ILR 508, 514, 522–523. For holdings that a secretary, etc., is 'in a position of trust' see also *Libya* v. *Trobbiani*, Italy, (1990) 114 ILR 520, 522; *Norwegian* v. *Quattri*, Italy, (1991) 114 ILR 525, 530; *Perrini* v. *Académie*, Italy, (1994) 114 ILR 536, 538–539. See also *MacFarlane* v. *US*, Canada, 1987 CarswellOnt 2859, para. 4.
132 *USA* v. *Rodrigo*, Philippines, (1990) 102 ILR 132, 145. See also *Société* v. *Chaussois*, France, (1969) 65 ILR 44, 45–46; affirming *Chaussois* v. *La Tabacoop*, France, (1966) 47 ILR 152, 154.
133 *Novaco* v. *US*, Italy, (1957) 24 ILR 219, 220.
134 *Kuwait* v. *Parrott*, France, (1990) 113 ILR 457, 458–459.
135 See the discussion in Chapter 6.
136 *Zveiter* v. *Brazilian*, US, 833 F.Supp. 1089, 1093–1094 (S.D.N.Y. 1993); *Zveiter* v. *Brazilian*, US, 841 F.Supp. 111 (S.D.N.Y. 1993). See also *Mukaddam* v. *Permanent*, US, 111 F.Supp.2d 457, 466 (S.D.N.Y. 2000);
137 *Janini* v. *Kuwait University*, US, 43 F.3d 1534, 1537 (D.C.Cir. 1995); 107 ILR 367, 370.
138 *Hansen* v. *Danish*, US, 147 F.Supp.2d 142, 151 (E.D.N.Y. 2001).
139 *US* v. *Gereschi*, Italy, (1977) 77 ILR 598, 600–601; *Bruno* v. *US*, Italy, (1977) 65 ILR 316, 318–320.

570 NOTES TO PAGES 172-175

140 *Department* v. *Savellini*, Italy, (1955) 23 ILR 201, 202. See also *Francischiello* v. *USA*, Italy, (1959) 28 ILR 158, 161.

141 *Piha* v. *Belgium*, Belgium, (1982) 82 ILR 109, 114. Certainly, the civilian employees themselves should not enjoy immunity from local jurisdiction: *X* v. *Y1*, Japan, 1990, 35 *JAIL* (1992) 151. It is also possible to envisage another category of persons, who are neither 'military personnel' or 'civilian component', nor locally recruited workers. These are so-called 'international civilian personnel', who may be nationals of the receiving State but whose contracts of employment are not subject to the legislation of the receiving State: *Devos* v. *Supreme*, Belgium, (1985) 91 ILR 242, 248.

142 *Tsakos* v. *USA*, Switzerland, (1972) 75 ILR 78, 79-80.

143 *M* v. *Egypt*, Switzerland, (1994) ATF 120 II 400, 407, Ground 4b; 116 ILR 656, 663; repeated verbatim in *R* v. *Iraq*, Switzerland, (1994) ATF 120 II 408, 411, Ground 5c; 116 ILR 664, 667. See also *S* v. *India*, Switzerland, (1984) BGE 110 II 255, 264, Ground 5 ('*Binnenbeziehung der Streitsache zum schweizerischen Staatsgebiet*' ('connection between the subject of the litigation and Swiss territory')); 82 ILR 13, 23; *Landano* v. *USA*, Switzerland, (1987) 116 ILR 636, 639 ('*Binnenbeziehung*').

144 *S* v. *India*, Switzerland, (1984) 82 ILR 13, 19-20, Ground 4; *M* v. *Egypt*, Switzerland, (1994) 116 ILR 656, 662, Ground 4a; *R* v. *Iraq*, Switzerland, (1994) 116 ILR 664, 666, Ground 5b; *Tsakos* v. *USA*, Switzerland, (1972) 75 ILR 78, 79-80; *Landano* v. *USA*, Switzerland, (1987) 116 ILR 636, 639-642 (see also the cases cited at p. 640); *Nicoud* v. *USA*, Switzerland, (1994) 116 ILR 650, 653; *X* v. *USA*, Switzerland, (1995) 116 ILR 668, 673; *République X* v. *A*, Switzerland, 2003, 130 *JDI* (2003) 1125, 1126. Contrast, for example, *Brazilian Embassy Employee Case*, Portugal, (1984) 116 ILR 625; *Ramos* v. *USA*, Portugal, (1994) 116 ILR 634, where immunity was granted with regard to locally recruited embassy employees. These two cases, however, may have lost their validity after *X* v. *Israel*, Portugal, (2002) 127 ILR 310.

145 *De Sousa* v. *Portugal*, Netherlands, (1979) 65 ILR 378, 378-379; affirmed, *Portugal* v. *De Sousa*, Netherlands, (1981) 94 ILR 314, 315; *JPH* v. *Indonesia*, Netherlands, (1979) 65 ILR 379 note; *MK* v. *Turkey*, Netherlands, (1985) 94 ILR 350, 353; *H. 't Hooft* v. *France*, Netherlands, 1986, 19 *NYIL* (1988) 438, note 27; *BV* v. *Instituto*, Netherlands, 1990, 23 *NYIL* (1992) 447; *MHC* v. *Cuba*, Netherlands, 1992, 27 *NYIL* (1996) 319. See also *Consulate-General of Italy Case*, Netherlands, (1979) 65 ILR 380 note.

146 *Diana* v. *South Africa*, Spain, (1986) 86 ILR 512, 516; *Emilio* v. *Embassy*, Spain, (1986) 86 ILR 508, 510.

147 *French Consular Employee Claim Case*, Austria, (1989) 86 ILR 583, 586; *Seidenschmidt* v. *USA*, Austria, (1992) 116 ILR 530, 532.

148 *USA* v. *Perières*, France, (1997) 113 ILR 494, 497.

149 *Morocco* v. *DR*, Belgium, (1989) 115 ILR 421, 422.

150 *Bayerischer* v. *Schiavetti*, Italy, (1987) 87 ILR 38, 40-41.

151 *Diana* v. *South Africa*, Spain, (1986) 86 ILR 512, 514.

152 *François* v. *Canada*, Belgium, (1989) 115 ILR 418, 419.

153 *Landano* v. *USA*, Switzerland, (1987) 116 ILR 636, 642.
154 *Ghawanmeh* v. *Islamic*, US, 672 F.Supp.2d 3, 9–10 (D.D.C. 2009).
155 *MHC* v. *Cuba*, Netherlands, 1992, 27 *NYIL* (1996) 319.
156 *MK* v. *Turkey*, Netherlands, (1985) 94 ILR 350, 353.
157 *USA* v. *FEWH*, Netherlands, 2002, 35 *NYIL* (2004) 447, 449.
158 *Seidenschmidt* v. *USA*, Austria, (1992) 116 ILR 530, 532.
159 *Nicoud* v. *USA*, Switzerland, (1994) 116 ILR 650, 653. The court asserted jurisdiction over the claim for unlawful dismissal even though the pre-amble of the plaintiff's contract stated that 'Swiss laws and regulations relating to … compensation, termination … do not govern your employ-ment' (p. 651). But see *Landano* v. *USA*, Switzerland, (1987) 116 ILR 636, 642, where the same court said that the employer State could have agreed with the employee that foreign law should be applicable.
160 A claim concerning the 'purely financial aspects of the employment rela-tionship' would be one 'for payment of sums due in respect of remuneration whose amounts are not in dispute, or for additional amounts on account of late payment of sums whose exact amounts are known', *Libya* v. *Trobbiani*, Italy, (1990) 114 ILR 520, 524. See also *Norwegian* v. *Quattri*, Italy, (1991) 114 ILR 525, 531 (payment of various allowances).
161 *British* v. *Toglia*, Italy, (1989) 101 ILR 379, 384–385; *Banamar-Capizzi* v. *Embassy*, Italy, (1989) 87 ILR 56; *Libya* v. *Trobbiani*, Italy, (1990) 114 ILR 520, 522; *Norwegian* v. *Quattri*, Italy, (1991) 114 ILR 525, 529–531; *Zambian* v. *Sendan-ayake*, Italy, (1992) 114 ILR 532, 533; *Carbonar* v. *Magurno*, Italy, (1993) 114 ILR 534, 535–536. See also *Kenyan Diplomatic Residence Case*, Germany, (2003) 128 ILR 632; *PAvH* v. *USA*, Netherlands, (1977) 65 ILR 374 note; *Argentine* v. *Ross*, US, 408 N.Y.S.2d 831 (N.Y.S.C. 1978); 63 ILR 195.
162 *Manauta* v. *Embassy*, Argentina, (1994) 113 ILR 429, 433.
163 *Re Canada Labour Code*, Canada, (1992) 91 DLR (4th) 449, 468–474; 94 ILR 264, 283–289.
164 *Lovell* v. *New Zealand Tourism Board*, Canada, [1992] ACWSJ Lexis 38241, paras. 15 and 18. See also *Seidenschmidt* v. *USA*, Austria, (1992) 116 ILR 530, 532–533.
165 See *Butcher* v. *Saint Lucia*, Canada, [1998] 79 ACWS (3d) 815; [1998] 61 OTC 208, paras. 11–21, esp. para. 16; affirmed, *Butcher* v. *Saint Lucia*, Canada, [1999] 87 ACWS (3d) 800; 1999 OAC Lexis 99; *Smith* v. *Chin*, Canada, [2006] OJ No. 4091, paras. 38–46.
166 *Société Air Zaire* v. *Gauthier*, France, (1984) 77 ILR 510, 512. See also *Société Sonatrach* v. *Migeon*, France, (1985) 77 ILR 525.
167 See *Canada* v. *Cargnello*, Italy, (1998) 114 ILR 559, 566; *USA* v. *Lo Gatto*, Italy, (1995) 114 ILR 555, 557–558; *Perrini* v. *Académie*, Italy, (1994) 114 ILR 536, 539; *Giaffreda* v. *French*, Italy, (1992) 114 ILR 558 note; *Norwegian* v. *Quattri*, Italy, (1991) 114 ILR 525, 531; *British* v. *Toglia*, Italy, (1989) 101 ILR 379, 384–385 (contrast this case with *Rubin* v. *Consul*, Italy, (1977) 77 ILR 593); *France* v. *Jacuzio*, Italy, (1987) 87 ILR 53. See also *Paradiso* v. *Bari*, Italy, (1986) 87 ILR 38 note; *Nacci* v. *Bari*, Italy, (1994) 114 ILR 539. But see *Mallaval* v. *French*, Italy, (1974) 65 ILR 303; *Bayerischer* v. *Schiavetti*, Italy, (1987) 87 ILR 38.

572   NOTES TO PAGES 177–181

168 See *Diana* v. *South Africa*, Spain, (1986) 86 ILR 512, 516; *Emilio* v. *Embassy*, Spain, (1986) 86 ILR 508, 511.

169 *MHC* v. *Cuba*, Netherlands, 1992, 27 NYIL (1996) 319.

170 *MK* v. *Turkey*, Netherlands, (1985) 94 ILR 350, 353. However, it seems that the plaintiff was awarded compensation rather than reinstatement: *MK* v. *State*, Netherlands, (1986) 94 ILR 357.

171 *BV* v. *Instituto*, Netherlands, 1990, 23 NYIL (1992) 447, 448–449.

172 *BV* v. *Instituto*, Netherlands, 1991, 24 NYIL (1993) 341, 345–346.

173 *Italy* v. *BV*, Netherlands, 1993, 26 NYIL (1995) 338, 340. See also *De Sousa* v. *Portugal*, Netherlands, (1979) 65 ILR 378, 379.

174 *François* v. *Canada*, Belgium, (1989) 115 ILR 418, 420.

175 *Morocco* v. *DR*, Belgium, (1989) 115 ILR 421, 423. See also s. 98 of the UK Employment Rights Act 1996, under which the employer is required to show the reason for the dismissal, and a 'fair reason' would be one related to, among others, the capability or conduct of the employee.

176 *Nicoud* v. *USA*, Switzerland, (1994) 116 ILR 650, 655; *X* v. *USA*, Switzerland, (1995) 116 ILR 668, 675.

177 *X* v. *USA*, Switzerland, (1995) 116 ILR 668, 675.

178 See, e.g., the statutory compensation regime under ss. 118–123 of the UK Employment Rights Act 1996.

179 This despite that fact that, under UK employment law, once unfair dismissal is established, reinstatement is one of the remedies statutorily available to the complainant (s. 114, Employment Rights Act 1996).

180 The European Convention, Art. 32; UN Convention, Art. 3(1); US FSIA, s. 1604; UK SIA, s. 16(1); Pakistan SIO, s. 17(1); Singapore SIA, s. 19(1); South Africa FSIA, s. 5(2)(b); Canada SIA, s. 16; Australia FSIA, s. 6; Argentina Law 1995, Art. 6; Israeli Law 2008, s. 21; ILC Draft, Art. 3(1); IDI Draft, Art. 7; ILA Drafts, Art. IX.

181 It has been held that, when the foreign State itself is sued, the Vienna Conventions would be of no assistance except in excluding certain property allocated for diplomatic/consular use from forced execution: *Abbott* v. *South Africa*, Spain, (1992) 113 ILR 411, 422.

182 US House of Representatives, Report No. 94-1487, 1976, p. 16; 1976 USCCAN 6604, 6615.

183 See also Pakistan SIO, s. 17(1)(a); Singapore SIA, s. 19(1); South Africa FSIA, s. 5(2)(b).

184 ILC, Report, 1999, Annex, Report of the Working Group, YILC, 1999-II-2, p. 127 at 128, para. 484 and p. 149 at 167, para. 105.

185 *Sengupta* v. *India*, England, 1982, [1983] ICR 221, 228–229; 64 ILR 352, 360–361.

186 *Sengupta*, [1983] ICR 221, 227, 229; 64 ILR 352, 359, 361; quoted with approval in *Egypt* v. *Gamal-Eldin*, England, 1995, [1996] 2 All ER 237, 246; 104 ILR 673, 681.

187 *Sengupta*, [1983] ICR 221, 225; 64 ILR 352, 357; quoted with approval in *Ahmed* v. *Saudi Arabia*, England, 1995, [1996] 2 All ER 248, 252; 104 ILR 629, 643 and

NOTES TO PAGES 181–183   573

UAE v. *Abdelghafar*, England, (1995) 107 ILR 626, 636–637. See generally Garnett, The Precarious.

188 *Mills* v. *USA*, England, (2000) 120 ILR 612, 613; affirmed, *Mills* v. *Embassy*, England, 2000, unreported.

189 *Saudi Arabia* v. *Ahmed*, England, 1993, Transcript; affirmed, *Ahmed* v. *Saudi Arabia*, England, 1995, [1996] 2 All ER 248, 251–252, 256; 104 ILR 629, 636–637, 642–643, 646. See also *Kuwait* v. *Fevzi*, England, 1999, 1999 WL 1425695.

190 The medical office was held to be part of the mission. *Egypt* v. *Gamal-Eldin*, England, 1995, [1996] 2 All ER 237, 245–246; 104 ILR 673, 681. It was declared that 'Drivers form part of the administrative and technical staff' ([1996] 2 All ER 237, 246; 104 ILR 673, 681); see also *Saudi Arabia* v. *Nasser*, England, (2000) Transcript. This can be contrasted with a Dutch case holding that a chauffeur at the Mexican Embassy was not immune from criminal jurisdiction because he belonged to the *service staff* of the mission, instead of the *administrative and technical staff*. *LFLM* v. *Public Prosecutions*, Netherlands, 1993, 25 NYIL (1994) 527.

191 *Jayetilleke* v. *High Commission*, England, (1994) 107 ILR 622, 624.

192 *UAE* v. *Abdelghafar*, England, (1995) 107 ILR 626, 636–638 (the Medical Office was considered 'part of the administrative and technical service of the Embassy', so the claimants were 'part of the administrative and technical staff of that mission').

193 *Military* v. *Caramba-Coker*, England, 2003 WL 1610407, paras. 14, 25.

194 *Saudi Arabia* v. *Ahmed*, England, 1993, Transcript; affirmed, *Ahmed* v. *Saudi Arabia*, England, 1995, [1996] 2 All ER 248, 251–252; 104 ILR 629, 637–638, 642–643; *Egypt* v. *Gamal-Eldin*, England, 1995, [1996] 2 All ER 237, 246; 104 ILR 673, 681; *UAE* v. *Abdelghafar*, England, (1995) 107 ILR 626, 636, 640. As for attaching no importance to the plaintiff's lack of diplomatic immunities see also *Bulli* v. *Foreign*, Italy, (1981) 65 ILR 343, 346. Of course, if the plaintiff did enjoy diplomatic status, that would certainly be a ground for upholding the immunity of the employer State: *Arias* v. *Venezuela*, Netherlands, (1998) 128 ILR 684, 686–687, para. 4.7.

195 *Canada* v. *Burke*, Ireland, 1991/1992, [1992] 2 IR 484, 500; 95 ILR 467, 481.

196 *Gootjes* v. *Belgium*, Netherlands, (1978) 65 ILR 372, 373. But see a different judgment by the same court in a case concerning employment in the administrative service: *PAvH* v. *USA*, Netherlands, (1977) 65 ILR 374 note, possibly because the plaintiff only claimed unemployment benefit in the latter case.

197 *Hanna* v. *Turkish*, Finland, 1993, 5 *Finnish YIL* (1994) 408, 409.

198 *Prentice* v. *Bolivia*, South Africa, (1978) (3) SA 938; 64 ILR 685.

199 *Gittler* v. *German*, US, 408 N.Y.S.2d 600, 602 (N.Y.S.C. 1978); 63 ILR 170, 172.

200 *Nicoud* v. *USA*, Switzerland, (1994) 116 ILR 650, 654–655; *X* v. *USA*, Switzerland, (1995) 116 ILR 668, 674–675.

201 *Conrades* v. *UK*, Germany, (1981) 65 ILR 205, 208.

202 *X* v. *Argentina*, Germany, (1996) 114 ILR 502, 506.

203 *French Consulate Disabled Employee Case*, Germany, (1988) 114 ILR 507, 511.

574   NOTES TO PAGES 184–186

204 *Muller* v. *USA*, Germany, (1998) 114 ILR 512, 518–519.

205 *X* v. *Argentina*, Germany, (1996) 114 ILR 502, 504–506; *French Consulate Disabled Employee Case*, Germany, (1988) 114 ILR 507, 510–511; *Muller* v. *USA*, Germany, (1998) 114 ILR 512, 517. See similar opinions in *Luna* v. *Romania*, Italy, (1974) 65 ILR 313, 314–315; *Gootjes* v. *Belgium*, Netherlands, (1978) 65 ILR 372, 373; *Van der Hulst* v. *US*, Netherlands, (1989) 94 ILR 373.

206 *Seidenschmidt* v. *USA*, Austria, (1992) 116 ILR 530, 532–533.

207 *Yendall* v. *Australia*, England, (1984) 107 ILR 590, 595–598.

208 *Van der Hulst* v. *US*, Netherlands, (1989) 94 ILR 373, 376–377.

209 *USA* v. *FEWH*, Netherlands, 2002, 35 *NYIL* (2004) 447, 450. The court nevertheless held that, even though, in keeping with *Van der Hulst*, it may not assess the alleged security risk, it was still entitled to review whether the result required by the US could not have been other than dismissal; the court concluded that the dismissal in the case was unreasonable.

210 According to the understanding in the Annex to the Convention, which pursuant to Art. 25 'forms an integral part of the Convention': 'The reference ... to the "security interests" of the employer State is intended primarily to address matters of national security and the security of diplomatic missions and consular posts.'

211 *Scarfò* v. *Sovereign*, Italy, (1957) 24 ILR 1, 4. See also *Francischiello* v. *USA*, Italy, (1959) 28 ILR 158, 161; *Parravincini* v. *Commercial*, Italy, (1969) 65 ILR 282, 283.

212 *De Ritis* v. *US*, Italy, (1971) 65 ILR 283, 284–285.

213 *Association* v. *Piccoli*, Italy, (1974) 65 ILR 308, 311. See also *Church* v. *Ferraino*, Italy, (1986) 101 ILR 370, 374–375.

214 *Luna* v. *Romania*, Italy, (1974) 65 ILR 313, 314–315. See also *Norwegian* v. *Quattri*, Italy, (1991) 114 ILR 525, 527–528.

215 *Danish* v. *Hansen*, Italy, (1979) 65 ILR 325, 328.

216 *Velloso* v. *Borla*, Italy, (1979) 65 ILR 328, 330 (emphasis added).

217 *Pontificia* v. *Inps*, Italy, (1979) 65 ILR 333, 336–337.

218 *Bulli* v. *Foreign*, Italy, (1981) 65 ILR 343, 345–346.

219 *Rubin* v. *Consul*, Italy, (1977) 77 ILR 593, 597. See similar judgments in *Hurwitz* v. *Consul*, Italy, (1977) 77 ILR 598 note and *Consul-General* v. *Esposito*, Italy, (1986) 101 ILR 376, 376. Contrast *Rubin* with *Toglia*, 101 ILR 379, below.

220 *Panattoni* v. *Germany*, Italy, (1987) 87 ILR 42, 46–47. Cf. *Embassy Interpreter Dismissal Case*, Austria, (1985) 77 ILR 485; *S* v. *India*, Switzerland, (1984) 82 ILR 13 and *Rousseau* v. *Upper Volta*, Belgium, (1983) 82 ILR 118. The Italian Court of Cassation has repeatedly stressed its distinction between menial/manual/auxiliary duties and more important duties, see, e.g., *Velloso* v. *Borla*, Italy, (1979) 65 ILR 328, 330; *British* v. *Toglia*, Italy, (1989) 101 ILR 379, 384; *Norwegian* v. *Quattri*, Italy, (1991) 114 ILR 525, 529–530. The Court denied immunity in a case brought by a kitchen/scullery boy/dishwasher employed by the US Armed Forces stationed in Italy (Case No. 4671/1964) and one by a canteen waitress/charwoman hired by the Venezuelan Navy (Case No. 3160/1959), both cited in *De Ritis* v. *US*, Italy, (1971) 65 ILR 283, 284; *Association* v. *Piccoli*,

NOTES TO PAGES 186–191   575

Italy, (1974) 65 ILR 308, 312; *Velloso* v. *Borla*, Italy, (1979) 65 ILR 328, 330 and *Panattoni* v. *Germany*, Italy, (1987) 87 ILR 42, 46.

221 *France* v. *Jacuzio*, Italy, (1987) 87 ILR 53, 55. Contrast an opposite decision in *Mallaval* v. *French*, Italy, (1974) 65 ILR 303, 306.

222 *British* v. *Toglia*, Italy, (1989) 101 ILR 379, 383.

223 *Toglia*, (1989) 101 ILR 379, 384.

224 *Toglia*, (1989) 101 ILR 379, 384–385. Note that the cases of *Rubin* (77 ILR 593) and *Toglia* (101 ILR 379), both involving a so-called 'grade II consular employee', can only be distinguished by a thin and artificial line, namely that in *Toglia* the claimant brought her claim upon retirement.

225 *Libya* v. *Trobbiani*, Italy, (1990) 114 ILR 520, 522. 'A position of trust' was repeated in *Norwegian* v. *Quattri*, Italy, (1991) 114 ILR 525, 530.

226 *Libyan* v. *Trobbiani*, Italy, (1990) 114 ILR 520, 523–524.

227 *Trobbiani*, (1990) 114 ILR 520, 524.

228 *Norwegian* v. *Quattri*, Italy, (1991) 114 ILR 525, 527–528 (emphases added). See also *Perrini* v. *Académie*, Italy, (1994) 114 ILR 536, 539, where the court found irrelevant the fact that the employment was governed by the terms of a standard collective contract.

229 *Norwegian* v. *Quattri*, Italy, (1991) 114 ILR 525, 530–531.

230 *USA* v. *Lo Gatto*, Italy, (1995) 114 ILR 555, 557–558. See also *Giaffreda* v. *French Republic*, Italy, (1992) 114 ILR 558 note; *Perrini* v. *Académie*, Italy, (1994) 114 ILR 536, 538–539.

231 As for 'inserted into the organisation' see the same language in *Rubin* v. *Consul*, Italy, (1977) 77 ILR 593, 597; *British* v. *Toglia*, Italy, (1989) 101 ILR 379, 383; *USA* v. *Lo Gatto*, Italy, (1995) 114 ILR 555, 558. See also very similar language in *Governor* v. *Sutton*, New Zealand, 1994, [1995] 1 NZLR 426, 431, 437; 104 ILR 508, 514, 522–523. For reasons for dismissal cf. the UK law of unfair dismissal, where the employer is required by law to furnish a reason/reasons for the dismissal and failure to do so would result in a decision of unfair dismissal; ss. 94 and 98, Employment Rights Act 1996.

232 *Canada* v. *Cargnello*, Italy, (1998) 114 ILR 559, 565–566. See also *Bari* v. *Chirico*, Italy, (1985) 87 ILR 19, 20.

233 See *Danish* v. *Hansen*, Italy, (1979) 65 ILR 325, 326; *Pontificia* v. *Inps*, Italy, (1979) 65 ILR 333, 336; *Panattoni* v. *Germany*, Italy, (1987) 87 ILR 42, 46; *France* v. *Jacuzio*, Italy, (1987) 87 ILR 53, 55; *British* v. *Toglia*, Italy, (1989) 101 ILR 379, 382; *Norwegian* v. *Quattri*, Italy, (1991) 114 ILR 525, 527–528.

234 *Special* v. *Pieciukiewicz*, Italy, (1982) 78 ILR 120, 121–122 (emphases added).

235 *Pieciukiewicz*, (1982) 78 ILR 120, 123.

236 *MDDA* v. *Australian*, Netherlands, 1986, 19 *NYIL* (1988) 438, note 27.

237 *Robert* v. *Procureur*, France, (1990) 113 ILR 450, 452. Cf. *Barrandon* v. *USA*, France, (1992/1995) 113 ILR 464; *Coco* v. *Argentina*, France, (1996) 113 ILR 491; *Saignie* v. *Embassy*, France, (1997) 113 ILR 492.

238 *Tabion* v. *Mufti*, US, 73 F.3d 535, 538–539 (4th Cir. 1996); 107 ILR 452; affirming *Tabion* v. *Mufti*, US, 877 F.Supp. 285, 291 (E.D.Va. 1995). See also

576   NOTES TO PAGES 191–194

Sabbithi v. *KH*, US, 605 F.Supp.2d 122, 128–129 (D.D.C. 2009); *Gonzalez* v. *Vila*, US, 479 F.Supp.2d 187 (D.D.C. 2007).

239 The personal immunities of diplomats were also confirmed obiter in e.g., *Emilio* v. *Embassy*, Spain, (1986) 86 ILR 508, 510 and *Diana* v. *South Africa*, Spain, (1986) 86 ILR 512, 516. Cf. *Syndicat*, France, (1992) 113 ILR 470, 471–472 (holding that the Vienna Convention only concerns diplomatic agents and has no bearing in a case where the foreign State itself is sued).

240 *Swarna* v. *Al-Awadi*, US, 607 F.Supp.2d 509, 524–525 (S.D.N.Y. 2009).

241 In this connection the question also arises whether it is the embassy or the foreign State proper that should be sued. While courts in some countries regard the embassy as possessing no independent legal personality and therefore incapable of being sued in its own name: *Embassy Interpreter Dismissal Case*, Austria, (1985) 77 ILR 485, 487; *Cavallucci* v. *Hungarian*, Italy, (1967) 71 ILR 238, 239; *Barrandon* v. *USA*, France, (1992) 113 ILR 464, 466; others have reached an opposite conclusion: *Embassy* v. *Jens*, Denmark, (1982) 78 ILR 81, 83. The safest way thus seems to be to sue the foreign State proper, treating the embassy as a mere representative office, see *Barrandon* v. *USA*, France, (1992/1995) 113 ILR 464, 466–468.

242 *Carbonar* v. *Magurno*, Italy, (1993) 114 ILR 534. See also *Mallaval* v. *French*, Italy, (1974) 65 ILR 303, 307.

243 *X* v. *Israel*, Portugal, (2002) 127 ILR 310, 313.

244 *Park* v. *Shin*, US, 313 F.3d 1138, 1145 (9th Cir. 2002).

245 European Convention, Art. 31; US FSIA, s. 1604; UK SIA, s. 16(2); Pakistan SIO, s. 17(2)(a); Singapore SIA, s. 19(2)(a); Canada SIA, s. 15; Australia FSIA, s. 6; Israeli Law 2008, s. 22; ILA 1994 Revised Draft, Art. III(C)(4).

246 See *Re Canada Labour Code*, Canada, 1992, (1992) 91 DLR (4th) 449; 94 ILR 264.

247 See, e.g., 1951 NATO Status of Forces Agreement.

248 See *USA* v. *Ceballos*, Philippines, (1990) 102 ILR 132, 143–144; *Sanders* v. *Veridiano*, Philippines, (1988) 102 ILR 148 note; *Larkins* v. *National*, Philippines, (1995) 102 ILR 148 note; *G* v. *USA*, Netherlands, 1992, 27 *NYIL* (1996) 320.

249 See my discussion on Art. IX(4) of SOFA, above, and Garnett, State Immunity, 108.

250 *Hicks* v. *USA*, England, (1995) 120 ILR 606, 610.

251 *UNC* v. *Saudi Arabia*, US, 581 F.3d 210, 216 (5th Cir. 2009).

252 See *Hungarian* v. *Onori*, Italy, (1956) 23 ILR 203, 204–205; *De Ritis* v. *US*, Italy, (1971) 65 ILR 283, 286–287; *Special* v. *Pieciukiewicz*, Italy, (1982) 78 ILR 120, 123; *Perrini* v. *Académie*, Italy, (1994) 114 ILR 536, 538–539; *Ecole* v. *Guadagnino*, Italy, 1997, 9 *Italian YIL* (1999) 152, 153.

253 See *Époux* v. *Canada*, Belgium, (1934) 9 AD 249, 249; *De Decker* v. *USA*, Belgium, (1956) 23 ILR 209, 210; *De Ritis* v. *US*, Italy, (1971) 65 ILR 283, 284–285; *Danish* v. *Hansen*, Italy, (1979) 65 ILR 325, 327–328; *Church* v. *Ferraino*, Italy, (1986) 101 ILR 370, 374–375; *France* v. *Jacuzio*, Italy, (1987) 87 ILR 53, 55 (but cf. *Mallaval* v. *French*, Italy, (1974) 65 ILR 303, 306); *Perrini* v. *Académie*, Italy, (1994) 114 ILR 536, 538; *Maria* v. *Austrian*, Poland, (1987) 82 ILR 1, 4–5.

254 See *De Decker* v. *USA*, Belgium, (1956) 23 ILR 209, 210; *Danish* v. *Hansen*, Italy, (1979) 65 ILR 325, 328; *Perrini* v. *Académie*, Italy, (1994) 114 ILR 536, 539.

255 See *De Ritis* v. *US*, Italy, (1971) 65 ILR 283, 285; *Association* v. *Piccoli*, Italy, (1974) 65 ILR 308, 311; *Danish* v. *Hansen*, Italy, (1979) 65 ILR 325, 328; *Pontificia* v. *Inps*, Italy, (1979) 65 ILR 333, 336–337; *Special* v. *Pieciukiewicz*, Italy, (1982) 78 ILR 120, 121, 123; *Cristiani* v. *Italian*, Italy, (1985) 87 ILR 20, 28; *Galasso* v. *Italian*, Italy, (1986) 87 ILR 28 note; *Mininni* v. *Bari*, Italy, (1986) 87 ILR 28, 36; *Paradiso* v. *Bari*, Italy, (1986) 87 ILR 37 note; *France* v. *Jacuzio*, Italy, (1987) 87 ILR 53, 55; *Libya* v. *Trobbiani*, Italy, (1990) 114 ILR 520, 522; *Perrini* v. *Académie*, Italy, (1994) 114 ILR 536, 539; *Nacci* v. *Bari*, Italy, (1994) 114 ILR 539.

256 See *Libya* v. *Trobbiani*, Italy, (1990) 114 ILR 520, 524; *Sindacato* v. *Bari*, Italy, (1986) 87 ILR 37, 37–38; *Paradiso* v. *Bari*, Italy, (1986) 87 ILR 38 note. It should be noted that the Italian cases involving the Bari Institute concerned jurisdictional immunity of international organizations. They are cited here as illustrations of analogous reasoning that courts may, and do, apply to foreign States.

257 This modifies Art. 11(2)(a) of the 1991 ILC Draft, which reads: 'the employee has been recruited to perform functions closely related to the exercise of governmental authority'. At its 1999 session the ILC suggested that the words 'closely related to' be deleted in order to restrict the scope of the subparagraph to 'persons performing functions in the exercise of governmental authority'. ILC, Report, 1999, Annex, Report of the Working Group, *YILC*, 1999-II-2, p. 149 at 167, para. 104.

258 It seems that the same effect can also be achieved by the ILA Drafts. Article III(C) of the 1982 ILA Draft 1982 provides that immunity will remain 'in respect of employees appointed under the public (administrative) law of the foreign State'. The 1994 ILA Draft amends it as: 'The employer was appointed under the public (administrative) law of the foreign State, such as, inter alia, members of the mission, diplomatic, consular or military staff' (Art. III(C)(4)).

259 *Barrandon* v. *USA*, France, (1992) 113 ILR 464, 466.

260 *Barrandon* v. *USA*, France, (1995) 113 ILR 464, 469.

261 *Barrandon* v. *USA*, France, (1998) 116 ILR 622, 624. See also *Coco* v. *Argentina*, France, (1996) 113 ILR 491, 491–492; *Saignie* v. *Embassy*, France, (1997) 113 ILR 492, 493. A Dutch case went through similarly conflicting decisions. *BV* v. *Instituto*, Netherlands, 1990, 23 *NYIL* (1992) 447; *BV* v. *Instituto*, Netherlands, 1991, 24 *NYIL* (1993) 341; *Italy* v. *BV*, Netherlands, 1993, 26 *NYIL* (1995) 338.

262 *Canada* v. *Burke*, Ireland, 1991, [1992] 2 IR 484, 488; 95 ILR 467, 470.

263 *Canada* v. *Burke*, Ireland, 1992, [1992] 2 IR 484, 500; 95 ILR 467, 481; see also [1992] 2 IR 484, 490, 491; 95 ILR 467, 471, 473.

264 See *R* v. *Iraq*, Switzerland, (1994) 116 ILR 664; *X* v. *Israel*, Portugal, (2002) 127 ILR 310; *X* v. *Saudi*, France, (2003) 127 ILR 163.

265 *Governor* v. *Sutton*, New Zealand, 1994, [1995] 1 NZLR 426, 435; 104 ILR 508, 520.

266 *Governor* v. *Sutton*, New Zealand, 1994, [1995] 1 NZLR 426, 431, 437; 104 ILR 508, 514, 523.

578   NOTES TO PAGE 196

267 See, e.g., *Rubin* v. *Consul*, Italy, (1977) 77 ILR 593 (immunity); *British* v. *Toglia*, Italy, (1989) 101 ILR 379 (no immunity); *Libya* v. *Trobbiani*, Italy, (1990) 114 ILR 520 (immunity).

268 Immunity granted in: *Egypt* v. *Gamal-Eldin*, England, 1995, [1996] 2 All ER 237; 104 ILR 673; *Saudi Arabia* v. *Nasser*, England, (2000) Transcript; *Canada* v. *Burke*, Ireland, (1991/1992), [1992] 2 IR 484; 95 ILR 467; *Crum* v. *Saudi Arabia*, US, 2005 WL 3752271, pp. 3–4 (E.D.Va. 2005). Immunity denied in: *British Embassy Driver Case*, Austria, (1978) 65 ILR 20; *Rousseau* v. *Upper Volta*, Belgium, (1983) 82 ILR 118; *Morocco* v. *DR*, Belgium, (1989) 115 ILR 421; *Zambian* v. *Sendanayake*, Italy, (1992) 114 ILR 532; *Emilio* v. *Embassy*, Spain, (1986) 86 ILR 508; *Nicoud* v. *USA*, Switzerland, (1994) 116 ILR 650; *M* v. *Egypt*, Switzerland, (1994) 116 ILR 656.

269 Immunity granted in: *UAE* v. *Abdelghafar*, England, (1995) 107 ILR 626; *Saudi Arabia* v. *Nasser*, England, (2000) Transcript; *Hanna* v. *Turkish*, Finland, 1993, 5 *Finnish YIL* (1994) 408; *Conrades* v. *UK*, Germany, (1981) 65 ILR 205; *Rubin* v. *Consul*, Italy, (1977) 77 ILR 593; *Special* v. *Pieciukiewicz*, Italy, (1982) 78 ILR 120. Immunity denied in: *Embassy Interpreter Dismissal Case*, Austria, (1985) 77 ILR 485; *Novaco* v. *US*, Italy, (1957) 24 ILR 219; *Zambian* v. *Sendanayake*, Italy, (1992) 114 ILR 532; *S* v. *India*, Switzerland, (1984) 82 ILR 13; *R* v. *Iraq*, Switzerland, (1994) 116 ILR 664. A simultaneous interpreter could be seen as merely performing 'the mechanical repetition in a foreign language of words spoken or written by others', a duty unconnected with the public function of the employer: *Bari* v. *Jasbez*, Italy, (1977) 77 ILR 602, 609; *Special* v. *Pieciukiewicz*, Italy, (1982) 78 ILR 120, 123; but a simultaneous interpreter with some additional duties such as the supervision of postgraduate students and the coordination of the activities of other interpreters was regarded as 'integrated into the organizational structure' of the employer: *Bari* v. *Chirico*, Italy, (1985) 87 ILR 19, 20.

270 Immunity granted in: *Saudi Arabia* v. *Ahmed*, England, 1993/1995, [1996] 2 All ER 248; 104 ILR 629; *Kuwait* v. *Fevzi*, England, 1999, 1999 WL 1425695; *Hanna* v. *Turkish*, Finland, 1993, 5 *Finnish YIL* (1994) 408; *Conrades* v. *UK*, Germany, (1981) 65 ILR 205; *Association* v. *Piccoli*, Italy, (1974) 65 ILR 308; *Luna* v. *Romania*, Italy, (1974) 65 ILR 313; *Danish* v. *Hansen*, Italy, (1979) 65 ILR 325; *Consul-General* v. *Esposito*, Italy, (1986) 101 ILR 376; *Libya* v. *Trobbiani*, Italy, (1990) 114 ILR 520; *Norwegian* v. *Quattri*, Italy, (1991) 114 ILR 525; *Cudak* v. *Embassy*, Lithuania, 2001, 3 *Baltic YIL* (2003) 320; *Van der Hulst* v. *US*, Netherlands, (1989) 94 ILR 373; *Arias* v. *Venezuela*, Netherlands, (1998) 128 ILR 684. Immunity denied in: *Barrandon* v. *USA*, France, (1998) 116 ILR 622; *Norwegian* v. *Quattri*, Italy, (1991) 114 ILR 525; *MK* v. *Turkey*, Netherlands, (1985) 94 ILR 350; *Zaire* v. *Duclaux*, Netherlands, (1988) 94 ILR 368; *Diana* v. *South Africa*, Spain, (1986) 86 ILR 512; *Zveiter* v. *Brazilian*, US, 833 F.Supp. 1089, 1093–1094 (S.D.N.Y. 1993); *Shih* v. *Taipei*, US, 693 F.Supp.2d 805, 811 (N.D.Ill. 2010).

271 Immunity granted in: *Mills* v. *USA*, England, (2000) 120 ILR 612; affirmed, *Mills* v. *Embassy*, England, 2000, unreported; *Conrades* v. *UK*, Germany, (1981) 65 ILR 205; *Luna* v. *Romania*, Italy, (1974) 65 ILR 313; *Velloso* v. *Borla*, Italy,

NOTES TO PAGE 196   579

(1979) 65 ILR 328; *Libya* v. *Trobbiani*, Italy, (1990) 114 ILR 520; *Giaffreda* v. *French Republic*, Italy, (1992) 114 ILR 558 note; *Perrini* v. *Académie*, Italy, (1994) 114 ILR 536; *USA* v. *Lo Gatto*, Italy, (1995) 114 ILR 555. Immunity denied in: *Coco* v. *Argentina*, France, (1996) 113 ILR 491; *Carbonar* v. *Magurno*, Italy, (1993) 114 ILR 534; *S* v. *India*, Switzerland, (1984) 82 ILR 13; *Landano* v. *USA*, Switzerland, (1987) 116 ILR 636; *X* v. *USA*, Switzerland, (1995) 116 ILR 668.

272 *Pontificia* v. *Inps*, Italy, (1979) 65 ILR 333 (immunity); *Piha* v. *Belgium*, Belgium, (1982) 82 ILR 109 (no immunity).

273 Immunity granted in: *De Decker* v. *USA*, Belgium, (1956) 23 ILR 209 (assistant librarian); *Sengupta* v. *India*, England, 1982, [1983] ICR 221; 64 ILR 352 (low-level clerk); *Yendall* v. *Australia*, England, (1984) 107 ILR 590 (machine operator); *Francischiello* v. *USA*, Italy, (1959) 28 ILR 158 (lift attendant and messenger); *De Ritis* v. *US*, Italy, (1971) 65 ILR 283 (assistant librarian); *Special* v. *Pieciukiewicz*, Italy, (1982) 78 ILR 120 (radio announcer); *Gootjes* v. *Belgium*, Netherlands, (1978) 65 ILR 372 (typist); *Governor* v. *Sutton*, New Zealand, 1994, [1995] 1 NZLR 426; 104 ILR 508 (typist/clerk); *Maria* v. *Austrian*, Poland, (1987) 82 ILR 1 (librarian). Immunity denied in: *Saignie* v. *Embassy*, France, (1997) 113 ILR 492 (caretaker); *Barrandon* v. *USA*, France, (1998) 116 ILR 622, 624 (nurse and medical secretary); *Hungarian* v. *Onori*, Italy, (1956) 23 ILR 203 (general domestic duties); *Novaco* v. *US*, Italy, (1957) 24 ILR 219 (cashier, interpreter, clerk and bookkeeper); *X* v. *Israel*, Portugal, (2002) 127 ILR 310 (catering assistant and cleaner).

274 *M* v. *Egypt*, Switzerland, (1994) 116 ILR 656, 662, Ground 4b; *République X* v. *A*, Switzerland, 2003, 130 *JDI* (2003) 1125, 1126 ('un chauffeur, un portier, un jardinier ou un cuisinier') (in this case a 'femme de ménage'). See also *Consulate* v. *Ribeiro*, Brazil, 2002, 24 *JIBLR* (2009), N102 (laundry services).

275 *Governor* v. *Sutton*, New Zealand, 1994, [1995] 1 NZLR 426, 436–437; 104 ILR 508, 522. See also *Rubin* v. *Consul*, Italy, (1977) 77 ILR 593, 596.

276 *Hijazi* v. *Permanent*, US, 689 F.Supp.2d 669, 675 (S.D.N.Y. 2010).

277 *MacFarlane* v. *US*, Canada, 1987 CarswellOnt 2859, para. 4. See also *Panattoni* v. *Germany*, Italy, (1987) 87 ILR 42, 46

278 Immunity granted in: *France* v. *Jacuzio*, Italy, (1987) 87 ILR 53; *Consulate-General of Italy Case*, Netherlands, (1979) 65 ILR 380 note. Immunity denied in: *Neustein* v. *Indonesia*, Austria, (1958) 65 ILR 3; *De Queiroz* v. *Portugal*, Belgium, (1992) 115 ILR 430; *X* v. *Saudi*, France, (2003) 127 ILR 163; *Mallaval* v. *French*, Italy, (1974) 65 ILR 303; *Portugal* v. *De Sousa*, Netherlands, (1981) 94 ILR 314; affirming *De Sousa* v. *Portugal*, Netherlands, (1979) 65 ILR 378; *Ghawanmeh* v. *Islamic*, US, 672 F.Supp.2d 3 (D.D.C. 2009).

279 Scholars are unanimous that no uniform rules can be identified, much less rules of customary international law. See Pingel, Immunité, 1122–1124; Yang, State Immunity in the ECHR, 403–404; Garnett, State Immunity (2002), 370; Garnett, State Immunity (1997), 85–86, 124; Fox, Employment, 98; Greig, Specific, 560. See also ILC, Report, 1999, Annex, Report of the Working Group, A/54/10, *YILC*, 1999-II-2, p. 149 at 166, para. 96.

Chapter 5

1 The word does appear in various commentaries and explanatory notes accompanying these instruments. See also Art. 6(e) of the OAS Draft, 1983, where the word 'tort' is used in the commercial context.

2 The term 'non-commercial torts' is borrowed from US House of Representatives, Report No. 94-1487, 1976, pp. 20–21; 1976 USCCAN 6604, 6619–6620; and Sucharitkul, Fifth Report, *YILC*, 1983-II-1, p. 25 at 38, para. 63; 42, paras. 84 and 85.

3 In fact, the word 'tort' in this context might be a very misleading one, given its very broad (and oftentimes indefinite) scope in municipal legal systems. See Fox, State Responsibility, 12–13 and 22.

4 The Pakistan SIO does not contain a provision on non-commercial torts. The reason for the absence is unclear. See, however, criticism of the tort provisions in the US and UK statutes by a Pakistani scholar: Masud, Immunity, 65.

5 1972 European Convention, Art. 11 ('injury to the person'). It is unclear why the European Convention covers only personal *injury* whilst all other instruments mention personal injury *or death* (unless 'injury' is broadly construed as including 'death').

6 US FSIA, s. 1605(a)(5).

7 UK SIA, s. 5(a); Singapore SIA, s. 7(a); ILA, Drafts, Art. III(F).

8 Canada SIA, s. 6(a).

9 2004 UN Convention, Art. 12.

10 Australia FSIA, s. 13(a); IDI, Draft, 1991, Art. 2(2)(e).

11 South Africa FSIA, s. 6(a).

12 US FSIA, s. 1605(a)(5); Canada SIA, s. 6(b); ILA, Drafts, Art. III(F).

13 UK SIA, s. 5(b); Singapore SIA, s. 7(b); South Africa FSIA, s. 6(b); 2004 UN Convention, Art. 12.

14 Australian FSIA, s. 13(b); IDI, Draft, 1991, Art. 2(2)(e).

15 1972 European Convention, Art. 11.

16 *USA* v. *Friedland*, Canada, (1999) 182 DLR (4th) 614, 622; 120 ILR 417, 460; *Gascon* v. *Paradis*, Canada, [1991] 26 ACWS (3d) 722, para. 17. For a similar position see *Case against the Foreign Minister*, Austria, 2001, 6 *Austrian RIEL* (2001) 288, 294.

17 *Castle* v. *US*, Canada, [2006] OJ No. 4897, para. 5.

18 See *Carey* v. *National*, US, 453 F.Supp. 1097, 1102 (S.D.N.Y. 1978); 63 ILR 164; affirmed, *Carey* v. *National*, US, 592 F.2d 673 (1979); 63 ILR 232.

19 *Military* v. *Caramba-Coker*, England, 2003 WL 1610407, para. 16.

20 On the other hand, *psychiatric harm* is usually treated as a species of personal/physical injury: *Military* v. *Caramba-Coker*, England, 2003 WL 1610407, paras. 16, 17 and 20.

21 Economic loss can be recovered only where it is 'parasitic on physical injury'. ALRC, Report No. 24, 1984, p. 68, para. 115.

22 See Council of Europe, *Explanatory Reports*, p. 20, para. 48; Crawford, International Law, 111; Sucharitkul, Fifth Report, *YILC*, 1983-II-1, p. 25 at 38, para. 63; 39, para. 64; 40, para. 75; 44, para. 90; ALRC, Report No. 24, 1984, p. 68,

para. 115; 59, para. 101; ILC, Report, *YILC*, 1991-II-2, p. 12 at 45, commentary to Art. 12, paras. (4)–(5); *Case against the Foreign Minister*, Austria, 2001, 6 *Austrian RIEL* (2001) 288, 294.

23 See *Fagan* v. *Deutsche Bundesbank*, US, 438 F.Supp.2d 376, 388 (S.D.N.Y. 2006); *Calzadilla* v. *Banco*, US, 413 F.3d 1285, 1288 (11th Cir. 2005); *Blaxland* v. *Commonwealth*, US, 323 F.3d 1198, 1203–1206, 1209 (9th Cir. 2003); *Leutwyler* v. *Office*, US, 184 F.Supp.2d 277, 293–294 (S.D.N.Y. 2001); *Adler* v. *Nigeria*, US, 219 F.3d 869, 880 (9th Cir. 2000); *Alpha* v. *Nippon*, US, 199 F.3d 1078, 1087, fn. 1 (9th Cir. 1999); *Cabiri* v. *Ghana*, US, 165 F.3d 193, 200 (2nd Cir. 1999); *Whitehead* v. *Luxembourg*, 1998 US App. LEXIS 22307, pp. 16–17 (4th Cir. 1998); *Ortega* v. *Banco*, US, 17 F.Supp.2d 1340 (S.D.Fla. 1998); *Intercontinental* v. *De Gruyter*, US, 822 F.Supp. 662, 677 (C.D.Cal. 1993); *Travel Associates* v. *Swaziland*, US, 107 ILR 219, 223–224 (D.D.C. 1990); *Von Dardel* v. *USSR*, US, 736 F.Supp. 1, 7 (D.D.C. 1990); *Gregorian* v. *Izvestia*, US, 871 F.2d 1515 (9th Cir. 1989); 98 ILR 76; partly affirming *Gregorian* v. *Izvestia*, US, 658 F.Supp. 1224 (C.D.Cal. 1987); *De Sanchez* v. *Banco*, US, 770 F.2d 1385, 1398 (5th Cir. 1985); 88 ILR 75; *Yessenin-Volpin* v. *Novosti*, US, 443 F.Supp. 849, 855 (S.D.N.Y. 1978); 63 ILR 127. Moreover, if the plaintiff's claim resides in a taking of property in violation of international law, then the claim can only be brought under s. 1605(a)(3), but cannot be repackaged as a tort claim under s. 1605(a)(5): *Gutch* v. *Germany*, US, 444 F.Supp.2d 1, 11–12 (D.D.C. 2006); *Chuidian* v. *Philippine*, US, 912 F.2d 1095, 1106 (9th Cir. 1990); 92 ILR 480; *De Sanchez* v. *Banco*, US, 770 F.2d 1385, 1398 (5th Cir. 1985); 88 ILR 75.

24 A word of caution. I here use the phrase 'based on, or closely connected with, a commercial activity' as a rather loose indicator of a logical possibility and as a general summary of what has been attempted in a number of cases. As a matter of fact, certain conditions must be fulfilled before a claim can be held as 'based on' a commercial activity, while in most cases a mere 'connection' is not enough. See discussion in Chapter 3 and, especially, *Saudi Arabia* v. *Nelson*, US, 507 US 349, 357–358 (1993); 123 L.Ed.2d 47, 59 (1993); 100 ILR 544, 551.

25 See *Fagan* v. *Deutsche Bundesbank*, US, 438 F.Supp.2d 376, 389 and 390 (S.D.N.Y. 2006); *Dale* v. *Colagiovanni*, US, 337 F.Supp.2d 825, 841 (S.D.Miss. 2004); *Leutwyler* v. *Office*, US, 184 F.Supp.2d 277, 294–296 (S.D.N.Y. 2001); *El-Hadad* v. *UAE*, US, 216 F.3d 29, 35–36 (D.C.Cir. 2000); affirming *El-Hadad* v. *Embassy*, US, 69 F.Supp.2d 69 (D.D.C. 1999); in further proceedings: *El-Hadad* v. *UAE*, US, 496 F.3d 658, 663 (D.C.Cir. 2007); affirming *El-Hadad* v. *Embassy*, US, 2006 WL 826098, pp. 14–18 (D.D.C. 2006); *Mukaddam* v. *Permanent Mission*, US, 111 F.Supp.2d 457, 474 (S.D.N.Y. 2000); *Southway* v. *Central Bank*, US, 198 F.3d 1210, 1219 (10th Cir. 1999); affirming *Southway* v. *Central Bank*, US, 994 F.Supp.2d 1299, 1310 (D.Colo. 1998); *WMW* v. *Werkzeugmaschinenhandel*, US, 960 F.Supp. 734, 742 (S.D.N.Y. 1997); *Yucyco* v. *Slovenia*, US, 984 F.Supp. 209, 224 (S.D.N.Y. 1997); *Export* v. *Reef*, US, 54 F.3d 1466, 1473–1477 (9th Cir. 1995); 107 ILR 393, 404; *Carnival* v. *Oy*, US, 159 B.R. 984, 1002 (S.D.Fla. 1993); *Foremost-McKesson* v. *Iran*, US, 759 F.Supp. 855, 859 (D.D.C. 1991); *LeDonne* v. *Gulf*, US, 700 F.Supp. 1400, 1410–1411 (E.D.Va. 1988); *Tifa* v. *Ghana*, US, 692 F.Supp. 393, 404 (D.N.J. 1988); *Letelier* v. *Chile*, US, 748 F.2d 790, 795 (2nd Cir. 1984); 79 ILR 561;

582   NOTES TO PAGES 201–203

Gilson v. *Ireland*, US, 682 F.2d 1022, 1028, fn. 27 (D.C.Cir. 1982); 92 ILR 374; *United Euram* v. *USSR*, US, 461 F.Supp. 609, 612 (S.D.N.Y. 1978); 63 ILR 228; *Yessenin-Volpin* v. *Novosti*, US, 443 F.Supp. 849, 855 (S.D.N.Y. 1978); 63 ILR 127. For discussion see Havkin, The Foreign Sovereign; Lovell, *Export Group*, 463–465. The ABA proposed, but failed to secure, an amendment to the FSIA explicitly allowing claims of misrepresentation, deceit, malicious prosecution and defamation to be brought under the commercial activity exception: ABA, Reforming, 571–573, 601; ABA, Report, 2002, 1262, 1271; Dellapenna, Refining.

26 FTCA, 1946/1948, 28 USC Chapter 171.

27 See US House of Representatives, Report No. 94-1487, 1976, p. 21; 1976 USCCAN 6604, 6620.

28 See *Art Metal* v. *US*, US, 753 F.2d 1151, 1156 (D.C.Cir. 1985); *Hoesl* v. *US*, US, 451 F.Supp. 1170, 1178–1180 (N.D.Cal. 1978); affirmed, *Hoesl* v. *US*, US, 629 F.2d 586 (9th Cir. 1980). Even libel claims of a clearly commercial nature are barred: *Bosco* v. *US Army*, US, 611 F.Supp. 449, 452–453 (D.C.Tex. 1985); *Gregorian* v. *Izvestia*, US, 658 F.Supp. 1224, 1233 (C.D.Cal. 1987). See also Roufail, *Gregorian*.

29 *Gregorian* v. *Izvestia*, US, 658 F.Supp. 1224, 1233–1234 (C.D.Cal. 1987) (holding that foreign governments were also immune from libel); affirmed, *Gregorian* v. *Izvestia*, US, 871 F.2d 1515, 1522 n. 4 (9th Cir. 1989); 98 ILR 76; *Bryks* v. *CBC*, 906 F.Supp. 204, 209 (S.D.N.Y. 1995). But see *Export* v. *Reef*, US, 54 F.3d 1466, 1472–1473 (9th Cir. 1995); 107 ILR 393.

30 ILC, Report, *YILC*, 1991-II-2, p. 12 at 45, commentary to Art. 12, para. (4) (emphases added). See also ILC, Report, *YILC*, 1983-II-2, p. 17 at 19, paras. 87 and 89; ILC, Report, *YILC*, 1984-II-2, p. 58 at 66, commentary to then Art. 14, para. (4); Sucharitkul, Fifth Report, *YILC*, 1983-II-1, p. 25 at 40, para. 73; Sucharitkul, Sixth Report, *YILC*, 1984-II-1, p. 5 at 11, para. 17; 14, para. 36.

31 ALRC, Report No. 24, 1984, pp. 68–69, para. 115.

32 *Letelier* v. *Chile*, US, 488 F.Supp. 665 (D.D.C. 1980); 63 ILR 378; noted in Singer, Terrorism. See ILC, Report, *YILC*, 1984-II-2, p. 58 at 66, commentary to then Art. 14 (on tort), para. (4) and footnote 225; ILC, Report, *YILC*, 1991-II-2, p. 12 at 45, commentary to Art. 12, para. (4) and footnote 149; Sucharitkul, Fifth Report, *YILC*, 1983-II-1, p. 25 at 43, para. 85.

33 US House of Representatives, Report No. 94-1487, 1976, pp. 20–21; 1976 USCCAN 6604, 6619–6620 (emphasis added). See also *Argentine Republic* v. *Amerada Hess*, US, (1989) 488 US 428, 439–440 (1989); 102 L.Ed.2d 818, 831 (1989); 81 ILR 658, 666.

34 *McElhinney* v. *Ireland*, ECHR, 2001, (2002) 34 EHRR 13; (2001) 123 ILR 73, 85, para. 38. However, the word 'insurable' was not used in the national proceedings: *McElhinney* v. *Williams*, Ireland, [1994] 2 ILRM 115; 103 ILR 311; affirmed, *McElhinney* v. *Williams*, Ireland, 1995, [1996] 1 ILRM 276; 104 ILR 691.

35 *Margellos* v. *Germany*, Greece, (2002) 129 ILR 525, 531.

36 *Distomo Massacre Case*, Germany, (2003) 129 ILR 556, 560, Ground B.I.2(b).

37 US House of Representatives, Report No. 94-1487, 1976, p. 21; 1976 USCCAN 6604, 6620. For discussion see Yee, The Discretionary.

38 *Dalehite* v. *US*, US, 346 US 15, 36 (1953).

NOTES TO PAGES 204–206   583

39 *Berkovitz v. US*, US, 486 US 531, 536 (1988).

40 *US v. SA Empresa*, US, 467 US 797, 814 (1984).

41 *Berkovitz v. US*, US, 486 US 531, 537 (1988).

42 See *In re Terrorist Attacks*, US, 392 F.Supp.2d 539, 554 (S.D.N.Y. 2005); affirmed, *In re Terrorist Attacks*, US, 538 F.3d 71 (2nd Cir. 2008); *Rendall-Speranza v. Nassim*, US, 942 F.Supp. 621, 627 (D.D.C. 1996); reversed on other grounds, *Rendall-Speranza v. Nassim*, US, 107 F.3d 913 (D.C.Cir. 1997); *Risk v. Halvorsen*, US, 936 F.2d 393, 395 (9th Cir. 1991); 98 ILR 125, 128. See also *Alicog v. Saudi Arabia*, 860 F.Supp. 379, 382 (S.D.Tex. 1994); 113 ILR 509, 512; *Liu v. Republic of China*, US, 892 F.2d 1419, 1431 (9th Cir. 1989); 101 ILR 519, 532; *MacArthur Area v. Peru*, US, 809 F.2d 918, 922 (D.C.Cir. 1987); 107 ILR 196, 200; vacated on other grounds, *MacArthur Area v. Peru*, US, 823 F.2d 606 (D.C.Cir. 1987).

43 *In re Terrorist Attacks*, US, 392 F.Supp.2d 539, 555–556 (S.D.N.Y. 2005); affirmed, *In re Terrorist Attacks*, US, 538 F.3d 71 (2nd Cir. 2008). See also *In re Terrorist Attacks*, US, 349 F.Supp.2d 765, 802–804 (S.D.N.Y. 2005); affirmed, *In re Terrorist Attacks*, US, 538 F.3d 71 (2nd Cir. 2008); *Burnett v. Al Baraka*, US, 292 F.Supp.2d 9, 20–21 (D.D.C. 2003).

44 *Alicog v. Saudi Arabia*, US, 860 F.Supp. 379, 382 (S.D.Tex. 1994); 113 ILR 509, 512.

45 *Risk v. Halvorsen*, US, 936 F.2d 393, 395–396 (9th Cir. 1991); 98 ILR 125, 128–129; affirming *Risk v. Norway*, US, 707 F.Supp. 1159, 1166–1167 (N.D.Cal. 1989).

46 *Travel Associates v. Swaziland*, US, 107 ILR 219, 223 (D.D.C. 1990). See also *English v. Thorne*, US, 676 F.Supp. 761, 763–764 (S.D.Miss. 1987).

47 *Matter of Sedco*, US, 543 F.Supp. 561, 567 (S.D.Tex. 1982); 72 ILR 110, 115.

48 *Fagot v. Costa Rica*, US, 297 F.3d 1, 10–11 (1st Cir. 2002); affirming *Fagot v. Costa Rica*, US, 139 F.Supp.2d 173 (D.P.R. 2001). See also *MacArthur Area v. Peru*, US, 809 F.2d 918, 922 (D.C.Cir. 1987); 107 ILR 196, 200; *Risk v. Norway*, US, 707 F.Supp. 1159, 1166 (N.D.Cal. 1989).

49 *Joseph v. Office*, US, 830 F.2d 1018, 1027 (9th Cir. 1987); 101 ILR 485.

50 *Gerritsen v. Miguel*, US, 819 F.2d 1511, 1518 (9th Cir. 1987); 101 ILR 476. See also *Rendall-Speranza v. Nassim*, US, 942 F.Supp. 621, 627 (D.D.C. 1996) and *Rendall-Speranza v. Nassim*, US, 932 F.Supp. 19, 24–25 (D.D.C. 1996); reversed on other grounds, *Rendall-Speranza v. Nassim*, US, 107 F.3d 913 (D.C.Cir. 1997).

51 *Doe v. Holy See*, US, 434 F.Supp.2d 925, 956 (D.Or. 2006); partly affirmed/reversed/remanded, *Doe v. Holy See*, US, 557 F.3d 1066 (9th Cir. 2009). But see *English v. Thorne*, US, 676 F.Supp. 761, 763–764 (S.D.Miss. 1987). Cf. *Swarna v. Al-Awadi*, US, 607 F.Supp.2d 509, 525–526 (S.D.N.Y. 2009).

52 *O'Bryan v. Holy See*, US, 556 F.3d 361, 387 (6th Cir. 2009); affirming *O'Bryan v. Holy See*, US, 471 F.Supp.2d 784 (W.D.Ky. 2007).

53 See Fox, State Responsibility, 27.

54 *Olsen v. Mexico*, US, 729 F.2d 641, 645 (9th Cir. 1984) (emphasis added); 84 ILR 96. See also the case cited above where the courts rejected the argument of discretionary function.

55 *Olsen v. Mexico*, US, 729 F.2d 641, 647 (9th Cir. 1984), 84 ILR 96 (citing *Lindgren v. US*, US, 665 F.2d 978, 980 (9th Cir. 1982); *Thompson v. US*, US, 592 F.2d 1104,

584 NOTES TO PAGES 206–207

1111 (9th Cir. 1979); *Driscoll* v. *US*, US, 525 F.2d 136, 138 (9th Cir. 1975)); noted in Miranda, Sovereign Immunity, 289–292.

56 *Olsen* v. *Mexico*, US, 729 F.2d 641, 647 (9th Cir. 1984); 84 ILR 96.

57 *Olsen* v. *Mexico*, US, 729 F.2d 641, 647 (9th Cir. 1984); 84 ILR 96.

58 See *In re Terrorist Attacks*, US, 392 F.Supp.2d 539, 554 (S.D.N.Y. 2005); *In re Terrorist Attacks*, US, 349 F.Supp.2d 765, 802–804 (S.D.N.Y. 2005); affirmed, *In re Terrorist Attacks*, US, 538 F.3d 71 (2nd Cir. 2008); *Marchisella* v. *Japan*, US, 2004 WL 307248, p. 2 (S.D.N.Y. 2004); *Napolitano* v. *Tishman*, US, 1998 WL 102789, p. 4 (E.D.N.Y. 1998); *Olson* v. *Singapore*, US, 636 F.Supp. 885, 886 (D.D.C. 1986).

59 *Letelier* v. *Chile*, US, 488 F.Supp. 665, 673 (D.D.C. 1980); 63 ILR 378, 388. See Collums, The *Letelier* Case, 267.

60 *Liu* v. *Republic of China*, US, 892 F.2d 1419, 1431 (9th Cir. 1989); 101 ILR 519, 532.

61 *Pulaski* v. *India*, US, 212 F.Supp.2d 653, 656 (S.D.Tex. 2002).

62 *Letelier* v. *Chile*, US, 488 F.Supp. 665 (D.D.C. 1980); 63 ILR 378.

63 *Liu* v. *Republic of China*, US, 892 F.2d 1419 (9th Cir. 1989); 101 ILR 519.

64 Fox, State Responsibility, 29.

65 See below.

66 See European Convention, Art. 32; UK SIA, s. 16(1); Australia FSIA, s. 6. See also US House of Representatives, Report No. 94-1487, 1976, p. 21; 1976 USCCAN 6604, 6620. But see Art. 43(2)(b) of the 1963 Vienna Convention on Consular Relations, under which consular officers and consular employees shall not be immune in respect of a civil action 'by a third party for damage arising from an accident in the receiving State caused by a vehicle, vessel or aircraft'.

67 See Art. 12 of the 1991 ILC Draft and of the 2004 UN Convention. See also ILC, Report, *YILC*, 1991-II-2, p. 12 at 45, commentary to Art. 12, para. (8) and footnote 152.

68 For example, damage or injury in nuclear matters: European Convention, Art. 29(b) and UK SIA, s. 16 (3). Section 10(6) of the UK SIA also excludes certain admiralty proceedings from the scope of the tort exception.

69 Section 1605(a)(5) of the US FSIA limits the action to 'money damages'; while Art. 12 of the 1991 ILC Draft and of the 2004 UN Convention contemplates only recovery of 'pecuniary compensation'. See ILC, Report, *YILC*, 1991-II-2, p. 12 at 46, commentary to Art. 12, para. (10); Sucharitkul, Sixth Report, *YILC*, 1984-II-1, p. 5 at 11, para. 17. This will preclude non-pecuniary remedies such as injunctions.

70 Council of Europe, *Explanatory Reports*, p. 38, para. 113.

71 Sucharitkul, Fifth Report, *YILC*, 1983-II-1, p. 25 at 39, para. 67; 39–40, para. 69. See also pp. 39–40, paras. 68–75; 41, para. 77. The reasoning was adopted by the ILC. See ILC, Report, *YILC*, 1984-II-2, p. 58 at 67, commentary to then Art. 14, paras. (6) and (8); ILC, Report, *YILC*, 1991-II-2, p. 12 at 45, commentary to Art. 12, paras. (6) and (8). See also ILA, Second Report, 1992, p. 290 at 317.

72 ALRC, Report No. 24, 1984, p. 66, para. 113 (emphasis in the original).

73 ALRC, Report No. 24, 1984, pp. 67, para. 113 and 68–69, para. 115.

74 ALI, *Third Restatement*, Vol. 1, s. 454 ('Claims in Tort'), Comments a and b, p. 408 (though the ALI bases its conclusion on the nature/purpose test in the context of commercial activities).

75 *Letelier* v. *Chile*, US, 488 F.Supp. 665, 671 (D.D.C. 1980); 63 ILR 378, 386. For s. 1605(a)(5) jurisdiction over political assassinations see also *Liu* v. *Republic of China*, US, 892 F.2d 1419 (9th Cir. 1989); 101 ILR 519.

76 Crawford, International Law, 111. The *Rainbow Warrior* case, involving the destruction of a Greenpeace vessel in Auckland harbour, New Zealand, by members of the French armed forces under orders from the French Ministry of Defence, provides a germane example. *The Rainbow Warrior Case*, New Zealand, (1985/1986) 74 ILR 241; *Rainbow Warrior*, Arbitration Tribunal, (1990) 82 ILR 499.

77 *Walker* v. *Bank*, Canada, (1993) 15 OR (3d) 596, 601.

78 *Walker* v. *Bank*, Canada, (1994) 111 DLR (4th) 186, 191–192; 104 ILR 277, 282.

79 *Schreiber* v. *Germany*, Canada, (2002) 216 DLR (4th) 513, 528–530. For commentary see Yee, Foreign.

80 *Ferrini* v. *Germany*, Italy, (2004) 128 ILR 658, 671–672, para. 10.1; noted in Focarelli, Denying, 954–955.

81 See, e.g., *Belgian State* v. *Dahlen*, Belgium, (1985) 91 ILR 239, 241; *Hunting Rights Case*, Austria, (1987) 86 ILR 564, 569; *Nuclear Power Plant Case*, Austria, (1988) 86 ILR 575, 577; *Garden Contamination Case*, Germany, (1987) 80 ILR 377, 381–382.

82 *Collision Case*, Austria, (1961) 40 ILR 73, 77–78. See also ALI, *Third Restatement*, Vol. 1, s. 454, Comment a, p. 408.

83 *Ciniglio* v. *Indonesian Embassy*, Italy, (1966) 65 ILR 268, 269. But the claim was dismissed because it had been brought against the Indonesian Embassy rather than the Indonesian State, even though the plaintiff sued the insurance company of the Embassy as well.

84 *Morocco* v. *Stichting*, Netherlands, (1978) 65 ILR 375, 376; *Stichting* v. *Morocco*, Netherlands, (1984/1986) 94 ILR 355, 356; *Stichting* v. *Morocco*, Netherlands, 1991; *Morocco* v. *Stichting*, Netherlands, (1994) 128 ILR 676, 680. The final conclusion was that Morocco did not owe a duty of care to the caretaker to insure him and his family against medical expenses.

85 *Ministry* v. *Federici*, Italy, (1968) 65 ILR 275, 277–279.

86 *Church of Scientology* v. *Herold*, Netherlands, (1980) 65 ILR 380, 381.

87 *Schmidt* v. *Home Secretary*, Ireland, 1994, [1995] ILRM 301, 304; 103 ILR 322, 324; affirmed, *Schmidt* v. *Home Secretary*, Ireland, [1997] 2 IR 121.

88 *McElhinney* v. *Williams*, Ireland, 1994, [1994] 2 ILRM 115, 119–120; 103 ILR 311, 316; affirmed, *McElhinney* v. *Williams*, Ireland, 1995, [1996] 1 ILRM 276, 288; 104 ILR 691, 702–703.

89 *McElhinney* v. *Ireland*, ECHR, 2001, (2002) 34 EHRR 13; (2001) 123 ILR 73, 85, para. 38.

90 1972 European Convention, Art. 31; UK SIA, s. 16(2); Canada SIA, s. 16 (originally s. 15); Australia FSIA, s. 6; Pakistan SIO, s. 17(2)(a); Singapore SIA, s. 19(2)(a).

91 US House of Representatives, Report No. 94-1487, Sept. 9, 1976, p. 17; 1976 USCCAN 6604, 6616.

586 NOTES TO PAGES 213–217

92 *Holland* v. *Lampen-Wolfe*, England, [2000] 1 WLR 1573, 1577, 1578–1579, 1580–1581, 1586–1587; 119 ILR 367, 371–372, 372–373, 375–376, 382.

93 *Littrell* v. *USA (No. 2)*, England, 1993, [1995] 1 WLR 82, 91, 95, 95–96; 100 ILR 438, 451–452, 459–460, 464. Noted by Collier, Municipal Law. See also *Cotigny* v. *Suarez*, France, (2004) 127 ILR 168, 172.

94 Bantekas, *Voiotia* v. *Germany*; affirmed, *Distomo Massacre Case*, Greece, (2000) 129 ILR 513, noted by Gavouneli and Bantekas, *Voiotia* v. *Germany*.

95 *Margellos* v. *Germany*, Greece, (2002) 129 ILR 525, 533. The proceedings before the European Court of Human Rights were unsuccessful: *Kalogeropoulou* v. *Greece and Germany*, ECHR, (2002) 129 ILR 537. See also the reaction of the German Supreme Court: *Distomo Massacre Case*, Germany, (2003) 129 ILR 556.

96 See Born, *International Civil Litigation*, p. 272.

97 See, e.g., *FILT-CGIL* v. *USA*, Italy, (2000) 128 ILR 644; *USA* v. *Eemshaven*, Netherlands, (1999) 127 ILR 225, 229; *Yamaguchi* v. *US*, Japan, 2002, noted by Mizushima, *Yamaguchi* v. *United States*; *Airport Linz* v. *US*, Austria, 2003, noted by Wittich, *Airport Linz* v. *United States*; *USA* v. *Havenschap*, Netherlands, 2003, 36 *NYIL* (2005) 436.

98 ILC, Report, *YILC*, 1991-II-2, p. 12 at 45, commentary to Art. 12, para. (8), reproducing ILC, Report, *YILC*, 1984-II-2, p. 58 at 67, commentary to then Art. 14, para. (8).

99 See Sucharitkul, Fifth Report, *YILC*, 1983-II-1, p. 25 at 44, para. 91; 39, para. 67; 45, para. 99; Schreuer, *State Immunity*, p. 44; Fox, Private Law Damages, 113; Steinberger, State Immunity, p. 626; *Jaffe* v. *Miller*, Canada, (1993) 103 DLR (4th) 315; 13 OR (3d) 745, 756, 764–766; 95 ILR 446, 456, 464–466; *Walker* v. *Bank*, Canada, (1993) 15 OR (3d) 596, 601; reversed on other grounds, *Walker* v. *Bank*, Canada, (1994) 111 DLR (4th) 186, 191–192; 104 ILR 277, 282–283; *Schreiber* v. *Germany*, Canada, (2001) 196 DLR (4th) 281, 292–293; affirmed, *Schreiber* v. *Germany*, Canada, (2002) 216 DLR (4th) 513, 528; *Bouzari* v. *Iran*, Canada, (2002) 124 ILR 427, 436.

100 Schreuer, *State Immunity*, p. 61.

101 See Crawford, A Foreign State Immunities Act?, 92; ALRC, Report No. 24, 1984, pp. 66–67, paras. 113–114; Sucharitkul, Fifth Report, *YILC*, 1983-II-1, p. 25 at 39–40, para. 69; 41, para. 77.

102 See also Singapore SIA, s. 7; South Africa FSIA, s. 6.

103 *Al-Adsani* v. *Kuwait*, England, (1995) 103 ILR 420, 429; affirmed, *Al-Adsani* v. *Kuwait*, England, (1996) 107 ILR 536, 549–550; noted in Marks, Torture; *Al-Adsani* v. *UK*, ECHR, 2001, (2002) 34 EHRR 11; (2001) 123 ILR 24.

104 *Jones* v. *Saudi Arabia*, England, 2003 WL 22187644, para. 13; *Jones* v. *Saudi Arabia*, England, 2004, [2005] QB 699; *Jones* v. *Saudi Arabia*, England, 2006, [2007] 1 AC 270; 129 ILR 629.

105 See *Tokic* v. *Yugoslavia*, Australia, 1991, 13 *AYIL* (1990–1991) 258 and 14 *AYIL* (1992) 335; *Costa Vraca* v. *Bell*, Australia, [2003] FCA 65 (Transcript).

106 ALRC, Report No. 24, 1984, p. 67, para. 114.

107 ILC, Report, *YILC*, 1991-II-2, p. 12 at 45, commentary to Art. 12, para. (6); ILC, Report, *YILC*, 1984-II-2, p. 58 at 67, commentary to then Art. 14, para. (6).

NOTES TO PAGES 217-220   587

108 ILC, Report, *YILC*, 1991-II-2, p. 12 at 45, commentary to Art. 12, para. (7) (emphasis added), reproducing (but deleting 'letter-bomb'), ILC, Report, *YILC*, 1984-II-2, p. 58 at 67, commentary to then Art. 14, para. (7). See also Sucharitkul, Sixth Report, *YILC*, 1984-II-1, p. 5 at 11, para. 17 ('transboundary torts or letter-bomb cases').

109 According to the drafters, the 'author' does not necessarily mean the 'person' liable. 'For example, when a vehicle belonging to a State is involved in a traffic accident, then, provided the driver of the vehicle was present, the State as owner or possessor of the vehicle may be sued, even though the plaintiff does not seek to establish the personal liability of the driver.' Council of Europe, *Explanatory Reports*, 1972, p. 21, para. 49.

110 *Garden Contamination Case (1)*, Germany, (1987) 80 ILR 367, 372. In particular, the *situs* jurisdiction of the Bonn court was found to be lacking: 80 ILR 367, 372–373 and *Garden Contamination Case (2)*, Germany, (1987) 80 ILR 377, 380–381.

111 See, e.g., Lewis, *State and Diplomatic Immunity*, pp. 53–54.

112 The words 'or bodily' did not appear in the original SIA. They have been inserted perhaps to underscore the case law requirement of *physical*, as opposed to *mental*, injury.

113 '. . . such as a claim arising out of a sale of defective products manufactured abroad'. ALI, *Third Restatement*, Vol. 1, s. 454, p. 410, Reporters' Note, 1.

114 That is, 'when the act and the result are separated in space and time', such as where a nuclear accident in one country causes radioactive damage in another: *Garden Contamination Case (2)*, Germany, (1987) 80 ILR 377, 383–385; or 'where the act causing damage produces its effects in a different location from the place where it was committed', such as where objects from an upstream State cause damage in a downstream State: *Municipality v. Deutsche*, Austria, (1981) 86 ILR 542, 544–545. See also *Hunting Rights Case*, Austria, (1987) 86 ILR 564, 566 (claim against the Soviet Union for damage arising from the accident at the Chernobyl nuclear reactor in April 1986).

115 *Municipality v. Deutsche*, Austria, (1981) 86 ILR 542, 544–545.

116 *Jaffe v. Miller*, Canada, (1993) 103 DLR (4th) 315; 13 OR (3d) 745, 764–767; 95 ILR 446, 464–467; affirming *Jaffe v. Miller*, Canada, [1990] 75 OR (2d) 133; (1990) 73 DLR (4th) 420, 427; 87 ILR 197, 204. See also *Castle v. US*, Canada, [2006] OJ No. 4897, paras. 2 and 7. For non-retroactivity of the SIA see also *Carrato v. USA*, Canada, [1982] 40 OR (2d) 459; (1982) 141 DLR (3d) 456, 459; 90 ILR 229, 232; *Tritt v. USA*, Canada, (1989) 68 OR (2d) 284, 287; 94 ILR 260, 262; *Cargo v. Lorac*, Canada, (1986) 28 DLR (4th) 309, 316–317; 84 ILR 700, 707–708; *Re Canada Labour Code*, Canada, (1992) 91 DLR (4th) 449, 463–464; 94 ILR 264, 278–279.

117 *Walker v. Bank*, Canada, (1994) 111 DLR (4th) 186, 192; 104 ILR 277, 283; reversing *Walker v. Bank*, Canada, (1993) 15 OR (3d) 596, 602–603. See also *Gascon v. Paradis*, Canada, [1991] 26 ACWS (3d) 722, para. 15; *Ritter v. Donell*, Canada, [2005] AJ No. 958, para. 27. But see *University v. Colorado*, Canada, [1995] 179 AR 81, 90 (defamation).

588   NOTES TO PAGES 220-223

118 *USA* v. *Friedland*, Canada, (1999) 182 DLR (4th) 614, 621-622; 120 ILR 417, 460; cited with approval in *Schreiber* v. *Attorney General*, Canada, (2000) 187 DLR (4th) 146, 156-157; *Schreiber* v. *Germany*, Canada, (2001) 196 DLR (4th) 281, 294; *Schreiber* v. *Germany*, Canada, (2002) 216 DLR (4th) 513, 530-531; *Castle* v. *US*, Canada, [2006] OJ No. 4897, para. 4.

119 *Schreiber* v. *Germany*, Canada, (2002) 216 DLR (4th) 513, 531-533; 543-544; affirming *Schreiber* v. *Germany*, Canada, (2001) 196 DLR (4th) 281, 294-298 (puzzlingly, Doherty JA also said: 'If this were a matter of first impression, I might be disposed to interpret "personal injury" as including non-physical injuries' - p. 295); affirming *Schreiber* v. *Attorney General*, Canada, (2000) 187 DLR (4th) 146, 157-158.

120 *Schreiber* v. *Germany*, Canada, (2002) 216 DLR (4th) 513, 531. See also *P* v. *Westwood*, Canada, [2003] BCJ N. 1944, para. 22.

121 *Schreiber* v. *Germany*, Canada, (2002) 216 DLR (4th) 513, 543.

122 *Bouzari* v. *Iran*, Canada, (2002) 124 ILR 427, 436; affirmed, *Bouzari* v. *Iran*, Canada, (2004) 243 DLR (4th) 406, 419-420; 128 ILR 586, 597-598; application for leave to appeal dismissed, *Bouzari* v. *Iran*, Canada, (2005)122 CRR (2d) 376 (note).

123 *Castle* v. *US*, Canada, [2006] OJ No. 4897, para. 7.

124 US House of Representatives, Report No. 94-1487, 1976, p. 21; 1976 USCCAN 6604, 6619.

125 ALI, *Third Restatement*, Vol. 1, s. 454 ('Claims in Tort'), p. 409, Comment e and Reporters' Note 1. Emphasis added.

126 *Letelier* v. *Chile*, US, 488 F.Supp. 665, 674 (D.D.C. 1980); 63 ILR 378, 389 (emphasis added).

127 *Persinger* v. *Iran (No. 2)*, US, 729 F.2d 835, 842 (D.C.Cir. 1984); 90 ILR 586 and *Asociacion* v. *Mexico*, US, 735 F.2d 1517, 1524-1525 (D.C.Cir. 1984); 84 ILR 87. District Judge Robertson in the *Burnett* case held that it was sufficient if the *injury or death* had occurred in the US: *Burnett* v. *Al Baraka*, US, 292 F.Supp.2d 9, 19, fn. 4 (D.D.C. 2003). Of course, he was reading only the FSIA itself without reference to the legislative report, and he was citing the *lower court's* reasoning in the *Letelier* case as authority without seeming to be aware of its rejection by the higher court.

128 *Argentine Republic* v. *Amerada Hess*, US, 488 US 428, 439-441 (1989); 102 L.Ed.2d 818, 831-832 (1989); 81 ILR 658, 666-667; reversing *Amerada Hess* v. *Argentine Republic*, US, 830 F.2d 421 (2nd Cir. 1987); 79 ILR 1.

129 *Amorrortu* v. *Peru*, US, 570 F.Supp.2d 916, 925 (S.D.Tex. 2008); *Gutch* v. *Germany*, US, 444 F.Supp.2d 1, 11 (D.D.C. 2006); *Abur* v. *Sudan*, US, 437 F.Supp.2d 166, 174-175 (D.D.C. 2006); *Doe I* v. *Israel*, US, 400 F.Supp.2d 86, 108 (D.D.C. 2005); *Abrams* v. *Societe Nationale*, US, 175 F.Supp.2d 423, 431 (E.D.N.Y. 2001) (vacated and remanded on other grounds, *Abrams* v. *Societe Nationale*, US, 332 F.3d 173 (2nd Cir. 2003)); *Alpha* v. *Nippon*, US, 199 F.3d 1078, 1087 (9th Cir. 1999); *Cabiri* v. *Ghana*, US, 981 F.Supp. 129, 132 (E.D.N.Y. 1997); affirmed, *Cabiri* v. *Ghana*, US, 165 F.3d 193, 200 (2nd Cir. 1999); *Sampson* v. *Germany*, US, 975 F.Supp. 1108, 1117-1119 (N.D.Ill. 1997); *Hirsh* v. *Israel*, US, 962 F.Supp. 377, 384 (S.D.

N.Y. 1997); 113 ILR 543; *Smith* v. *Libya*, US, 101 F.3d 239, 246 (2nd Cir. 1996); 113 ILR 534; affirming *Smith* v. *Libya*, US, 886 F.Supp. 306, 312–314 (E.D.N.Y. 1995); 107 ILR 382; *Wolf* v. *Germany*, US, 95 F.3d 536, 542 (7th Cir. 1996); *Greenpeace* v. *France*, US, 946 F.Supp. 773, 784–787 (C.D.Cal. 1996); *Ratnaswamy* v. *Air Afrique*, US, No. 95-CV-7670, 1996 WL 507267, p. 10 (N.D.Ill. 1996); *Coleman* v. *Alcolac*, US, 888 F.Supp. 1388, 1403 (S.D.Tex. 1995); *Cicippio* v. *Iran*, US, 30 F.3d 164, 169 (D.C.Cir. 1994); 107 ILR 296; *Intercontinental* v. *De Gruyter*, US, 822 F.Supp. 662, 677 (C.D.Cal. 1993); *Jones* v. *Petty-Ray*, US, 954 F.2d 1061, 1065 (5th Cir. 1992); *Siderman* v. *Argentina*, US, 965 F.2d 699, 714 (9th Cir. 1992); 103 ILR 454; *Street* v. *Quebec*, US, 1992 US App. Lexis 5591, p. 4 (1st Cir. 1992); *Fickling* v. *Australia*, US, 775 F.Supp. 66, 72 (E.D.N.Y. 1991); 103 ILR 447; *Von Dardel* v. *USSR*, US, 736 F.Supp. 1, 7–8 (D.D.C. 1990); *Security Pacific* v. *Derderian*, US, 872 F.2d 281, 285 n. 8 (9th Cir. 1989); *Kline* v. *Kaneko*, US, 685 F.Supp. 386, 391 (S.D.N.Y. 1988); 101 ILR 497; *Four Corners* v. *Turbomeca*, US, 677 F.Supp. 1096, 1102 (D.Colo. 1988); *English* v. *Thorne*, US, 676 F.Supp. 761, 764 (S.D.Miss. 1987); *Frolova* v. *USSR*, US, 761 F.2d 370, 379 (7th Cir. 1985); 85 ILR 236; affirming *Frolova* v. *USSR*, US, 558 F.Supp. 358 (N.D.Ill. 1983); *Tucker* v. *Whitaker*, US, 620 F.Supp. 578, 584, fn. 5 (E.D.Pa. 1985); *Ledgerwood* v. *Iran*, US, 617 F.Supp. 311, 314–315 (D.D.C. 1985); *Kline* v. *El Salvador*, US, 603 F.Supp. 1313, 1315–1316 (D.D.C. 1985); *Berkovitz* v. *Iran*, US, 735 F.2d 329, 331 (9th Cir. 1984); 81 ILR 552, 554; *Persinger* v. *Iran (No. 2)*, US, 729 F.2d 835, 842 (D.C.Cir. 1984); 90 ILR 586; vacating *Persinger* v. *Iran*, US, 72 ILR 132, 141 (D.C.Cir. 1982); noted in Smith, *Persinger*; *Asociacion* v. *Mexico*, US, 735 F.2d 1517, 1524–1525 (D.C.Cir. 1984); 84 ILR 87, 94–95; affirming *Asociacion* v. *Mexico*, US, 561 F.Supp. 1190 (D.D.C. 1983); *Tel-Oren* v. *Libya*, US, 517 F.Supp. 542, 549, fn. 3 (D.D.C. 1981); affirmed, *Tel-Oren* v. *Libya*, US, 726 F.2d 774, 775 (D.C.Cir. 1984); 77 ILR 192; *McKeel* v. *Iran*, US, 722 F.2d 582, 587–588, 589, fn. 10 (9th Cir. 1983); 81 ILR 543; *Matter of Sedco*, US, 543 F.Supp. 561, 567 (S.D.Tex. 1982); 72 ILR 110; *Perez* v. *The Bahamas*, US, 652 F.2d 186, 188–189 (D.C.Cir 1981); 63 ILR 601; affirming *Perez* v. *The Bahamas*, US, 482 F.Supp. 1208, 1210–1211 (D.D.C. 1980); 63 ILR 350; *Chicago* v. *Iran*, US, 506 F.Supp. 981, 990 (N.D.Ill. 1980); 63 ILR 511. For early practice see Abbott, The Noncommercial.

130 *Olsen* v. *Mexico*, US, 729 F.2d 641, 645–646 (9th Cir. 1984); 84 ILR 96, 100; noted in Miranda, Sovereign Immunity, 292–294. The ABA proposed, but failed to secure, an amendment to allow claims where a 'substantial portion of the tortious act or omission occurs in the United States', without regard to the place of injury or damage. ABA, Reforming, 566–569, 573, 601; ABA, Report, 2002, 1262, 1270; Dellapenna, Refining.

131 Section-by-section analysis of the 1994 Revised ILA Draft, ILA, Final Report, 1994, p. 452 at 495.

132 For targeted torts see Schreuer, *State Immunity*, pp. 61–62.

133 See the relevant discussion in Chapter 3.

134 *Argentine Republic* v. *Amerada Hess*, US, 488 US 428, 441 (1989); 102 L.Ed.2d 818, 832 (1989); 81 ILR 658, 667; reversing *Amerada Hess* v. *Argentine Republic*, US, 830 F.2d 421 (2nd Cir. 1987); 79 ILR 1.

590   NOTES TO PAGES 224-225

135 *Red Nacional* v. *Mrs Cavaillé*, France, (1968) 65 ILR 41; *Hunting Rights Case*, Austria, (1987) 86 ILR 564; *Radiation Contamination Claim Case*, Austria, (1988) 86 ILR 571; *Nuclear Power Plant Case*, Austria, (1989) 86 ILR 578 (in dismissing the claim the court launched into a scathing critique (86 ILR 578, 581) of the Supreme Court's decision granting the injunction application (*Nuclear Power Plant Case*, Austria, (1988) 86 ILR 575).

136 Some instruments contain an express provision to the effect that they apply only to those acts or omissions attributable to the foreign State. Section 1605 (a)(5) of the US FSIA provides that the envisaged injury/damage must be 'caused by the tortious act or omission of that foreign state or of any official or employee of that foreign state while acting within the scope of his office or employment'. See Engle, Choosing Law. Article 2(2)(e) of the 1991 IDI Draft requires the injury to be 'attributable to activities of a foreign State and its agents'. Under Art. 12 of the 1991 ILC Draft it suffices that the injury is 'caused by an act or omission which is *alleged* to be attributable to the State' (emphasis added). See also Sucharitkul, Fifth Report, *YILC*, 1983-II-1, p. 25 at 38, para. 63; 39, para. 67.

137 See *Blaxland* v. *Commonwealth*, US, 323 F.3d 1198, 1204-1206 (9th Cir. 2003), where the plaintiff sued Australia for, inter alia, false imprisonment, but the court found that he had actually been imprisoned by the US authorities upon Australia's extradition request, but not by Australian officials.

138 See *Burnett* v. *Al Baraka*, US, 292 F.Supp.2d 9, 20 (D.D.C. 2003).

139 *Robinson* v. *Malaysia*, US, 269 F.3d 133, 145-146 (2nd Cir. 2001).

140 *Randolph* v. *Budget*, US, 97 F.3d 319, 326-327 (9th Cir. 1996); reversing *Randolph* v. *Budget*, US, 878 F.Supp. 162 (C.D.Cal. 1995). See also *Howland* v. *Hertz*, US, 431 F.Supp.2d 1238, 1241-1244 (M.D.Fla. 2006); *MCI* v. *Alhadhood*, US, 82 F.3d 658, 664 (5th Cir. 1996); *Moran* v. *Saudi Arabia*, US, 27 F.3d 169, 173-174 (5th Cir. 1994); 107 ILR 303; *Castro* v. *Saudi Arabia*, US, 510 F.Supp. 309 (W.D. Tex. 1980); 63 ILR 419.

141 *Guzel* v. *Kuwait*, US, 818 F.Supp. 7, 10-12 (D.D.C. 1993); *Skeen* v. *Brazil*, US, 566 F.Supp. 1414, 1418 (D.D.C. 1983); 121 ILR 481. But cf. *Doe* v. *Holy See*, US, 434 F.Supp.2d 925, 950 (D.Or. 2006).

142 *Liu* v. *Republic of China*, US, 892 F.2d 1419, 1425 (9th Cir. 1989); 101 ILR 519, 526; *Joseph* v. *Office*, US, 830 F.2d 1018, 1025 (9th Cir. 1987); 101 ILR 485, 493.

143 *Al-Adsani* v. *Kuwait*, England, (1995) 103 ILR 420, 431-432; affirmed, *Al-Adsani* v. *Kuwait*, England, (1996) 107 ILR 536, 544-545, 550-551.

144 AEDPA, Public Law 104-132, April 24, 1996, 110 Stat. 1241, Section 221; 36 ILM 759 (1997). See Cooper-Hill, *The Law of Sovereign Immunity and Terrorism*; Brookes, *Frolova*; Beresovski, A Proposal; Wuebbels, Commercial; Dellapenna, Has the Time Come?; Leung, *Cicippio*; Tan, Protecting; MacKusick, Human Rights; McKay, A New Take; Roht-Arriaza, The Foreign; Jacobson, Trying; Zinman, Holding; Early, *Flatow*; Sealing, 'State Sponsors' (2000); Vadnais, The Terrorism; Reitz, Raising; Micco, Putting; Vitrano, Hell-Bent;

NOTES TO PAGE 225   591

Baletsa, The Cost; Caplan, The Constitution; Diaz, A Critique; Murphy, US Judgments; Gartenstein-Ross, A Critique; Defeis, The Foreign; Taylor, Another Front; Sealing, 'State Sponsors' (2003); Sealing, Cuba; Kim, Making; Deutsch, Suing.

145 '... a plaintiff need not establish that the material support or resources provided by a foreign state for a terrorist act contributed directly to the act from which his claim arises ... Sponsorship of a terrorist group which causes the personal injury or death of a United States national alone is sufficient to invoke jurisdiction.' *Flatow v. Iran*, US, 999 F.Supp. 1, 18 (D.D.C. 1998); 121 ILR 618. However, a plaintiff does have to establish 'a legally sufficient evidentiary basis' of the injury in question. *Ungar v. Iran*, US, 211 F.Supp.2d 91, 98 (D.D.C. 2002).

146 See *Oveissi v. Iran*, US, 573 F.3d 835 (D.C.Cir. 2009); reversing and remanding *Oveissi v. Iran*, US, 498 F.Supp.2d 268 (D.D.C. 2007); *Brewer v. Iran*, US, 664 F.Supp.2d 43 (D.D.C. 2009); *Wachsman v. Iran*, US, 603 F.Supp.2d 148 (D.D.C. 2009); *Wachsman v. Iran*, US, 537 F.Supp.2d 85 (D.D.C. 2008); *Massie v. DPRK*, US, 592 F.Supp.2d 57 (D.D.C. 2008); *Wagner v. Iran*, US, 172 F.Supp.2d 128, 134, n. 7 (D.D.C. 2001); *Daliberti v. Iraq*, US, 97 F.Supp.2d 38, 43 (D.D.C. 2000); *Cicippio v. Iran*, US, 18 F.Supp.2d 62, 68–69 (D.D.C. 1998); *Flatow v. Iran*, US, 999 F.Supp. 1, 13–14 (D.D.C. 1998); 121 ILR 618; *Alejandre v. Cuba*, US, 996 F.Supp. 1239, 1247, fn. 4 (S.D.Fla. 1997); 121 ILR 603. The vast majority of the cases decided under the AEDPA involved acts occurring before its enactment. See *Acosta v. Iran*, US, 574 F.Supp.2d 15 (D.D.C. 2008); *Bakhtiar v. Iran*, US, 571 F.Supp.2d 27 (D.D.C. 2008); *Fisher v. Libya*, US, 541 F.Supp.2d 46 (D.D.C. 2008); *Ben-Rafael v. Iran*, US, 540 F.Supp.2d 39 (D.D.C. 2008); *Pugh v. Libya*, US, 530 F.Supp.2d 216 (D.D.C. 2008); *Levin v. Iran*, US, 529 F.Supp.2d 1 (D.D.C. 2007); *Valore v. Iran*, US, 478 F.Supp.2d 101 (D.D.C. 2007); *La Reunion v. Libya*, US, 477 F.Supp.2d 131 (D.D.C. 2007); affirmed, *La Reunion v. Libya*, US, 533 F.3d 837 (D.C. Cir. 2008); *Hurst v. Libya*, US, 474 F.Supp.2d 19 (D.D.C. 2007); *Nikbin v. Iran*, US, 517 F.Supp.2d 416 (D.D.C. 2007); *Nikbin v. Iran*, US, 471 F.Supp.2d 53 (D.D.C. 2007); *Reed v. Iran*, US, 439 F.Supp.2d 53 (D.D.C. 2006); reconsideration partly granted, *Reed v. Iran*, US, 242 F.R.D. 125 (D.D.C. 2007); *Bodoff v. Iran*, US, 424 F.Supp.2d 74 (D.D.C. 2006); *Prevatt v. Iran*, US, 421 F.Supp.2d 152 (D.D.C. 2006); *Haim v. Iran*, US, 425 F.Supp.2d 56 (D.D.C. 2006); *Beecham v. Libya*, US, 245 F.R.D. 1 (D.D.C. 2007); *Beecham v. Libya*, US, 424 F.3d 1109 (D.C.Cir. 2005); *Hegna v. Iran*, US, 402 F.3d 97 (2nd Cir. 2005); *Wyatt v. Syria*, US, 362 F.Supp.2d 103 (D.D.C. 2005); *Simpson v. Libya*, US, 362 F.Supp.2d 168 (D.D.C. 2005); *Dammarell v. Iran*, US, 404 F.Supp.2d 261 (D.D.C. 2005); *Salazar v. Iran*, US, 370 F.Supp.2d 105 (D.D.C. 2005); *Collett v. Libya*, US, 362 F.Supp.2d 230 (D.D.C. 2005); *Price v. Libya*, US, 389 F.3d 192 (D.C.Cir. 2004); *Kilburn v. Libya*, US, 376 F.3d 1123 (D.C.Cir. 2004); affirming *Kilburn v. Iran*, US, 277 F.Supp.2d 24 (D.D.C. 2003); *Regier v. Iran*, US, 281 F.Supp.2d 87 (D.D.C. 2003); *Tracy v. Iran*, US, Civ. No. 01-2517, slip op. (D.D.C. 2003); *Acree v. Iraq*, US, 271 F.Supp.2d 179 (D.D.C. 2003); *Peterson v. Iran*, US, 515 F.Supp.2d 25 (D.D.C. 2007); *Peterson v. Iran*, US, 264 F.Supp.2d 46 (D.D.C. 2003); *Kerr v. Iran*, US, 245 F.Supp.2d 59 (D.D.C.

2003); *Cronin* v. *Iran*, US, 238 F.Supp.2d 222 (D.D.C. 2002); *Surette* v. *Iran*, US, 231 F.Supp.2d 260 (D.D.C. 2002); *Turner* v *Iran*, US, 2002 U.S.Dist.Lexis 26730 (D.D.C. 2002); *Weinstein* v. *Iran*, US, 184 F.Supp.2d 13 (D.D.C. 2002); *Eisenfeld* v. *Iran*, US, 172 F.Supp.2d 1 (D.D.C. 2000); *Mousa* v. *Iran*, US, 238 F.Supp.2d 1 (D.D.C. 2001); *Hill* v. *Iraq*, US, 175 F.Supp.2d 36 (D.D.C. 2001); *Polhill* v. *Iran*, US, 2001 U.S.Dist.Lexis 15322 (D.D.C. 2001); *Jenco* v. *Iran*, US, 154 F.Supp.2d 27 (D.D.C. 2001); *Sutherland* v. *Iran*, US, 151 F.Supp.2d 27 (D.D.C. 2001). But see *Roeder* v. *Iran*, US, 195 F.Supp.2d 140, 144–146 (D.D.C. 2002) (the 1980 US–Iran Algiers Accords and implementing regulations prohibited lawsuits arising out of the 1979–1980 Tehran hostage crisis); affirmed, *Roeder* v. *Iran*, US, 333 F.3d 228, 235–239 (D.C.Cir. 2003); Anonymous, D.C. Circuit Holds, esp. 749–750. A ten-year statute of limitations was imposed in 2008 by s. 1605A(b) of the FSIA (see also s. 1605A note).

147 Civil Liability for Acts of State Sponsored Terrorism, enacted as part of the Omnibus Consolidated Appropriations Act of 1997, Public Law No. 104-208, 30 September 1996, 110 Stat. 3009-172, Section 589, 28 USC § 1605 note. Noted at 36 ILM 759 (1997). The defendant foreign State can be held liable for acts of its agents: *Alejandre* v. *Cuba*, US, 42 F.Supp.2d 1317, 1322 (S.D.Fla. 1999) (but this judgment was vacated on the ground that certain debts owed to a Cuban telecommunications company could not be garnished for judgments against Cuba: *Alejandre* v. *Telefonica*, US, 183 F.3d 1277, 1282–1290 (11th Cir. 1999)); *Flatow* v. *Iran*, US, 999 F.Supp. 1, 27 (D.D.C. 1998); 121 ILR 618; *Alejandre* v. *Cuba*, US, 996 F.Supp. 1239, 1249 (S.D.Fla. 1997); 121 ILR 603; *Jenco* v. *Iran*, US, 154 F.Supp.2d 27, 34–35 (D.D.C. 2001); *Sutherland* v. *Iran*, US, 151 F.Supp.2d 27, 48–50 (D.D.C. 2001). See also Christopher, State Responsibility.

148 *Flatow* v. *Iran*, US, 999 F.Supp. 1, 12–14 (D.D.C. 1998); 121 ILR 618; *Flatow* v. *Iran*, US, 308 F.3d 1065, 1067 (9th Cir. 2002).

149 But note that the Flatow Amendment does not mention 'foreign States'. See *Cicippio-Puleo* v. *Iran*, US, 353 F.3d 1024, 1033–1036 (D.C.Cir. 2004). This effectively abrogated a number of decisions by the DC District Court: *Cronin* v. *Iran*, US, 238 F.Supp.2d 222, 231 (D.D.C. 2002); *Regier* v. *Iran*, US, 281 F.Supp.2d 87, 98–99 (D.D.C. 2003); *Kilburn* v. *Iran*, US, 277 F.Supp.2d 24, 36–37 (D.D.C. 2003). See also *Price* v. *Libya*, US, 294 F.3d 82, 87 (D.C.Cir. 2002). In 1998, s. 1610 of the US FSIA was further amended to expand the categories of property subject to attachment/execution. In particular, s. 1606 of the US FSIA was amended to permit punitive damages to be awarded against a foreign State in any action under s. 1605(a)(7). Omnibus Consolidated and Emergency Supplemental Appropriations Act of 1999, Public Law 105–277, 21 October 1998, 112 Stat. 2681-491, Section 117, codified at 28 USC § 1610(f) (1)(A)(B)(2)(A)(B)). Cited in full in *Alejandre* v. *Cuba*, US, 42 F.Supp.2d 1317, 1323–1324 (S.D.Fla. 1999). Punitive damages were awarded against Iran: *Eisenfeld* v. *Iran*, US, 172 F.Supp.2d 1, 9 (D.D.C. 2000). The punitive damages provision was soon repealed by Victims of Trafficking and Violence Protection Act of 2000, Public Law 106-386, 28 October 2000, 114 Stat. 1543, Section 2002(f)(2). Thus, for a period, as previously provided for under

s. 1606 of the US FSIA, a foreign State (but not its agencies or instrumentalities) was exempt from punitive damages, before punitive damages were restored by the 2008 enactment. The case law on punitive damages seems to have developed almost without regard to the statutory law. See *Estate of Heiser* v. *Iran*, US, 659 F.Supp.2d 20, 31 (D.D.C. 2009); *Estate of Heiser* v. *Iran*, US, 605 F.Supp.2d 248, 249 (D.D.C. 2009); *Gates* v. *Syria*, US, 580 F.Supp.2d 53, 75 (D.D.C. 2008); *Rimkus* v. *Iran*, US, 575 F.Supp.2d 181, 198 (D.D.C. 2008); *Acosta* v. *Iran*, US, 574 F.Supp.2d 15 (D.D.C. 2008); *Fisher* v. *Libya*, US, 541 F.Supp.2d 46, 53–54 (D.D.C. 2008); *Estate of Bayani* v. *Iran*, US, 530 F.Supp.2d 40, 46 (D.D.C. 2007); *Hurst* v. *Libya*, US, 474 F.Supp.2d 19, 28 (D.D.C. 2007); *Estate of Heiser* v. *Iran*, US, 466 F.Supp.2d 229, 270 (D.D.C. 2006); *Blais* v. *Iran*, US, 459 F.Supp.2d 40, 60–61 (D.D.C. 2006); *Greenbaum* v. *Iran*, US, 451 F.Supp.2d 90, 105 (D.D.C. 2006); *Stethem* v. *Iran*, US, 201 F.Supp.2d 78, 92, n. 21 (D.D.C. 2002); *Weinstein* v. *Iran*, US, 184 F.Supp.2d 13, 24, n. 1 (D.D.C. 2002); *Hill* v. *Iraq*, US, 175 F.Supp.2d 36, 48 (D.D.C. 2001); *Wagner* v. *Iran*, US, 172 F.Supp.2d 128, 134, n. 9 (D.D.C. 2001); *Polhill* v. *Iran*, US, 2001 U.S.Dist.Lexis 15322 (D.D.C. 2001), p. 17, n. 5; *Elahi* v. *Iran*, US, 124 F.Supp.2d 97, 114 (D.D.C. 2000); *Anderson* v. *Iran*, US, 90 F.Supp.2d 107, 114 (D.D.C. 2000); *Alejandre* v. *Cuba*, US, 996 F.Supp. 1239, 1253–1254 (S.D.Fla. 1997); 121 ILR 603. In a number of cases, punitive damages were awarded despite the 2000 statute: *Stern* v. *Iran*, US, 271 F.Supp.2d 286, 302 (D.D.C. 2003); *Cronin* v. *Iran*, US, 238 F.Supp.2d 222, 236 (D.D.C. 2002); *Surette* v. *Iran*, US, 231 F.Supp.2d 260, 274 (D.D.C. 2002); *Stethem* v. *Iran*, US, 201 F.Supp.2d 78, 93 (D.D.C. 2002); *Weinstein* v. *Iran*, US, 184 F.Supp.2d 13, 25 (D.D.C. 2002); *Mousa* v. *Iran*, US, 238 F.Supp.2d 1, 13 (D.D.C. 2001); *Wagner* v. *Iran*, US, 172 F.Supp.2d 128, 138 (D.D.C. 2001); *Jenco* v. *Iran*, US, 154 F.Supp.2d 27, 40 (D.D.C. 2001); *Sutherland* v. *Iran*, US, 151 F.Supp.2d 27, 53 (D.D.C. 2001); *Elahi* v. *Iran*, US, 124 F.Supp.2d 97, 114 (D.D.C. 2000); *Eisenfeld* v. *Iran*, US, 172 F.Supp.2d 1, 11 (D.D.C. 2000); *Anderson* v. *Iran*, US, 90 F.Supp.2d 107, 114 (D.D.C. 2000); *Flatow* v. *Iran*, US, 999 F.Supp. 1, 5 (D.D.C. 1998); 121 ILR 618; *Higgins* v. *Iran*, US, 2000 WL 33674311, p. 9 (D.D.C. 2000); *Acree* v. *Iraq*, US, 271 F.Supp.2d 179, 224 (D.D.C. 2003); vacated on other grounds, *Acree* v. *Iraq*, US, 370 F.3d 41, 58–60 (D.C.Cir. 2004); attempt to reinstate the judgment under the NDAA failed: *Acree* v. *Iraq*, US, 661 F.Supp.2d 1 (D.D.C. 2009); *Hill* v. *Iraq*, US, 175 F.Supp.2d 36, 48 (D.D.C. 2001); reversed and remanded on other grounds, *Hill* v. *Iraq*, US, 328 F.3d 680 (D.C.Cir. 2003). For detailed analysis of how damages are awarded under s. 1605(a)(7) see Karnezis, Annotation, Award of Damages. The Flatow Amendment has now been replaced by s. 1605A(c) and (d), which added that the foreign State shall be vicariously liable for the acts of its officials, employees or agents. So far as international law is concerned, the authoritative position is that awarding punitive damages 'is not a suitable remedy in international law': Gray, *Judicial Remedies*, 1987, p. 28.

150 NDAA, Public Law 110-181, January 28, 2008, 122 Stat. 338, s. 1083.

151 Section 1605A(a)(1). Section 1605A does not automatically apply retroactively to cases pending under s. 1605(a)(7); a re-filing is needed: *Baumel* v.

594   NOTES TO PAGE 226

Syria, US, 667 F.Supp.2d 39, 45–47 (D.D.C. 2009); *Simon* v. *Iraq*, US, 529 F.3d 1187, 1192 (D.C.Cir. 2008); reversing and remanding *Vine* v. *Republic of Iraq*, US, 459 F.Supp.2d 10 (D.D.C. 2006); overruled on other grounds, *Iraq* v. *Beaty*, US, 129 S.Ct. 2183, 173 L.Ed.2d 1193 (2009); *Rux* v. *Sudan*, US, 672 F.Supp.2d 726 (E.D.Va. 2009); on remand from *Rux* v. *Sudan*, US, No. 07–1835 (4th Cir. 2009); *Gates* v. *Syria*, US, 646 F.Supp.2d 79, 89–90 (D.D.C. 2009); *Saludes* v. *Cuba*, US, 655 F.Supp.2d 1290, 1296–1297 (S.D.Fla. 2009); *Kirschenbaum* v. *Iran*, US, 572 F.Supp.2d 200, 204, fn. 1, 214 (D.D.C. 2008); *Bakhtiar* v. *Iran*, US, 571 F.Supp.2d 27, 37–38 (D.D.C. 2008); *Stethem* v. *Iran*, US, 568 F.Supp.2d 1, 2 (D.D.C. 2008); *Haim* v. *Iran*, US, 567 F.Supp.2d 146, 147 (D.D.C. 2008); *Prevatt* v. *Iran*, US, 567 F.Supp.2d 144, 145–146 (D.D.C. 2008); *Bodoff* v. *Iran*, US, 567 F.Supp.2d 141, 142 (D.D.C. 2008); *Higgins* v. *Iran*, US, 545 F.Supp.2d 122, 123 (D.D.C. 2008); *Holland* v. *Iran*, US, 545 F.Supp.2d 120, 121–122 (D.D.C. 2008); *Welch* v. *Iran*, US, 545 F.Supp.2d 118, 119 (D.D.C. 2008); *Beer* v. *Iran*, US, 574 F.Supp.2d 1, 14 (D.D.C. 2008).

152 It must also be pointed out that the threshold requirement for invoking s. 1610(a)(7), as in other cases of execution, is that the targeted property be 'used for a commercial activity'. Thus embassy premises and bank accounts not used for commercial activities are not subject to execution: *Flatow* v. *Iran*, US, 76 F.Supp.2d 16, 22–25 (D.D.C. 1999); *Hegna* v. *Iran*, US, 287 F.Supp.2d 608, 610 (D.Md. 2003); affirmed, *Hegna* v. *Iran*, US, 376 F.3d 226 (4th Cir. 2004). See also *Rubin* v. *Iran*, US, 456 F.Supp.2d 228, 233–234 (D.Mass. 2006). A 'Bill to Modify the Enforcement of Certain Anti-Terrorism Judgments, and for Other Purposes', s. 1796, § 1(3)(A), 106th Cong. (1999), which would otherwise have amended s. 1610, FSIA, to permit the attachment of the property of foreign diplomatic missions used for non-diplomatic purposes such as rental property, as well as any rental proceeds, was rejected, as mentioned in *Flatow* v. *Iran*, US, 76 F.Supp.2d 16, 28 (D.D.C. 1999).

153 See also *Weininger* v. *Castro*, US, 462 F.Supp.2d 457, 485 (S.D.N.Y. 2006) (holding that the 2002 Terrorism Risk Insurance Act could override the *Bancec* considerations). For the issue of separate status see *First National* v. *Bancec*, US, 462 US 611 (1983); 80 ILR 566; *Alejandre* v. *Telefonica*, US, 183 F.3d 1277, 1282–1290 (11th Cir. 1999).

154 See *Price* v. *Libya*, US, 294 F.3d 82, 89–90 (D.C.Cir. 2002), pp. 15–18. See also Caplan, *The Constitution*, 406–408; Glannon and Atik, *Politics*, 681–682.

155 Iraq's designation as a 'State sponsor of terrorism' was officially rescinded on 20 October 2004. See US Secretary of State, *Country Reports on Terrorism 2004*, Chapter 5B. Even several months before the announcement, it was already impossible to sue Iraq under the AEDPA: *Acree* v. *Iraq*, US, 370 F.3d 41, 58–60 (D.C.Cir. 2004); vacating *Acree* v. *Iraq*, US, 271 F.Supp.2d 179 (D.D.C. 2003). The terrorism exception was suspended altogether with respect to Iraq by the National Defense Authorization Act for Fiscal Year 2008, Public Law 110-181, div. A, title X, s. 1083(d), 28 January 2008, 122 Stat. 343, and Determination of the President of the United States, No. 2008-9, 28 January 2008, 73 F.R. 6571. See *Iraq* v. *Beaty*, US, 129 S.Ct. 2183 (2009); abrogating *Acree*

NOTES TO PAGES 226–227   595

v. *Iraq*, US, 370 F.3d 41 (D.C.Cir. 2004) and reversing *Beaty* v. *Iraq*, US, 480 F.Supp.2d 60 (D.D.C. 2007).

156 Libya's designation was rescinded on 30 June 2006. See US Secretary of State, *Country Reports on Terrorism 2006*, Chapter 2. But see *La Reunion* v. *Libya*, US, 477 F.Supp.2d 131, 138 (D.D.C. 2007); affirmed, *La Reunion* v. *Libya*, US, 533 F.3d 837 (D.C.Cir. 2008). Private claims against Libya under the terrorism exception were finally settled (and extinguished) by the Libyan Claims Resolution Act (LCRA), Public Law 110-301, 4 August 2008, 122 Sta. 2999, and the Executive Order No. 13477, 31 October 2008, 73 F.R. 65965. For cases dismissing claims under LCRA see *Certain Underwriters* v. *Libya*, US, 677 F.Supp.2d 270 (D.D.C. 2010); *McDonald* v. *Libya*, US, 666 F.Supp.2d 50 (D.D.C. 2009); *Harris* v. *Libya*, US, 620 F.Supp.2d 1 (D.D.C. 2009); *Clay* v. *Libya*, US, 614 F.Supp.2d 21 (D.D.C. 2009).

157 North Korea's designation was rescinded on 11 October 2008. See US Secretary of State, *Country Reports on Terrorism 2008*, Chapter 3.

158 For the most current list see the official website: www.state.gov/j/ct/c14151.htm. See also *Daliberti* v. *Iraq*, US, 97 F.Supp.2d 38, 44, fn. 3 (D.D.C. 2000); *Flatow* v. *Iran*, US, 999 F.Supp. 1, 12, fn. 4 (D.D.C. 1998); 121 ILR 618; *Estates of Yaron* v. *Palestinian Authority*, US, 153 F.Supp.2d 76, 93, fn. 4 (D.R.I. 2001).

159 *Saludes* v. *Cuba*, US, 655 F.Supp.2d 1290 (S.D.Fla. 2009); *Saludes* v. *Cuba*, US, 577 F.Supp.2d 1243, 1251–1255 (S.D.Fla. 2008); *Alejandre* v. *Cuba*, US, 42 F.Supp.2d 1317, 1322 (S.D.Fla. 1999); *Alejandre* v. *Cuba*, US, 996 F.Supp. 1239 (S.D.Fla. 1997); 121 ILR 603.

160 *Estate of Botvin* v. *Iran*, US, 684 F.Supp.2d 34 (D.D.C. 2010); *Oveissi* v. *Iran*, US, 573 F.3d 835 (D.C.Cir. 2009); reversing and remanding *Oveissi* v. *Iran*, US, 498 F.Supp.2d 268 (D.D.C. 2007); *Belkin* v. *Iran*, US, 667 F.Supp.2d 8 (D.D.C. 2009); *Brewer* v. *Iran*, US, 664 F.Supp.2d 43 (D.D.C. 2009); *Estate of Heiser* v. *Iran*, US, 659 F.Supp.2d 20, 31 (D.D.C. 2009); *Estate of Heiser* v. *Iran*, US, 605 F.Supp.2d 248, 249 (D.D.C. 2009); *Wachsman* v. *Iran*, US, 603 F.Supp.2d 148 (D.D.C. 2009); *Rimkus* v. *Iran*, US, 575 F.Supp.2d 181 (D.D.C. 2008); *Acosta* v. *Iran*, US, 574 F.Supp.2d 15 (D.D.C. 2008); *Beer* v. *Iran*, US, 574 F.Supp.2d 1 (D.D.C. 2008); *Kirschenbaum* v. *Iran*, US, 572 F.Supp.2d 200 (D.D.C. 2008); *Bakhtiar* v. *Iran*, US, 571 F.Supp.2d 27 (D.D.C. 2008); *Ben-Rafael* v. *Iran*, US, 540 F.Supp.2d 39 (D.D.C. 2008); *Wachsman* v. *Iran*, US, 537 F.Supp.2d 85 (D.D.C. 2008); *Estate of Bayani* v. *Iran*, US, 530 F.Supp.2d 40 (D.D.C. 2007); *Levin* v. *Iran*, US, 529 F.Supp.2d 1 (D.D.C. 2007); *Nikbin* v. *Iran*, US, 517 F.Supp.2d 416 (D.D.C. 2007); *Peterson* v. *Iran*, US, 515 F.Supp.2d 25 (D.D.C. 2007); *Bennett* v. *Iran*, US, 507 F.Supp.2d 117 (D.D.C. 2007); *Valore* v. *Iran*, US, 478 F.Supp.2d 101 (D.D.C. 2007); *Nikbin* v. *Iran*, US, 471 F.Supp.2d 53 (D.D.C. 2007); *Estate of Heiser* v. *Iran*, US, 466 F.Supp.2d 229 (D.D.C. 2006); *Blais* v. *Iran*, US, 459 F.Supp.2d 40 (D.D.C. 2006); *Greenbaum* v. *Iran*, US, 451 F.Supp.2d 90 (D.D.C. 2006); *Sisso* v. *Iran*, US, 448 F.Supp.2d 76 (D.D.C. 2006); *Bodoff* v. *Iran*, US, 424 F.Supp.2d 74 (D.D.C. 2006); *Prevatt* v. *Iran*, US, 421 F.Supp.2d 152 (D.D.C. 2006); *Haim* v. *Iran*, US, 425 F.Supp.2d 56 (D.D.C. 2006); *Hegna* v. *Iran*, US, 402 F.3d 97 (2nd Cir. 2005); *Salazar* v. *Iran*, US, 370 F.Supp.2d 105 (D.D.C. 2005); *Bettis* v. *Iran*, US, 315 F.3d

596   NOTES TO PAGE 227

325 (D.C.Cir. 2003); affirming *Jenco* v. *Iran*, US, 154 F.Supp.2d 27 (D.D.C. 2001); *Campuzano* v. *Iran*, US, 281 F.Supp.2d 258 (D.D.C. 2003); *Dammarell* v. *Iran*, US, 281 F.Supp.2d 105 (D.D.C. 2003); vacated on other grounds but later redecided, *Dammarell* v. *Iran*, US, 404 F.Supp.2d 261 (D.D.C. 2005); *Regier* v. *Iran*, US, 281 F.Supp.2d 87 (D.D.C. 2003); *Kilburn* v. *Iran*, US, 277 F.Supp.2d 24 (D. D.C. 2003); *Stern* v. *Iran*, US, 271 F.Supp.2d 286 (D.D.C. 2003); *Peterson* v. *Iran*, US, 264 F.Supp.2d 46 (D.D.C. 2003); *Kerr* v. *Iran*, US, 245 F.Supp.2d 59 (D.D.C. 2003); *Tracy* v. *Iran*, US, Civ. No. 01-2517, slip op. (D.D.C. 2003); *Cronin* v. *Iran*, US, 238 F. Supp.2d 222 (D.D.C. 2002); *Surette* v. *Iran*, US, 231 F.Supp.2d 260 (D.D.C. 2002); *Stethem* v. *Iran*, US, 201 F.Supp.2d 78 (D.D.C. 2002); *Weinstein* v. *Iran*, US, 184 F. Supp.2d 13 (D.D.C. 2002); *Turner* v. *Iran*, US, 2002 U.S.Dist.Lexis 26730 (D.D.C. 2002); *Wagner* v. *Iran*, US, 172 F.Supp.2d 128 (D.D.C. 2001); *Sutherland* v. *Iran*, US, 151 F.Supp.2d 27 (D.D.C. 2001); *Polhill* v. *Iran*, US, 2001 U.S.Dist.Lexis 15322 (D.D.C. 2001); *Eisenfeld* v. *Iran*, US, 172 F.Supp.2d 1 (D.D.C. 2000); *Elahi* v. *Iran*, US, 124 F.Supp.2d 97 (D.D.C. 2000); *Flatow* v. *Iran*, US, 76 F.Supp.2d 16 (D.D.C. 1999); *Flatow* v. *Iran*, US, 999 F.Supp. 1 (D.D.C. 1998); 121 ILR 618; *Cicippio* v. *Iran*, US, 18 F.Supp.2d 62 (D.D.C. 1998).

161 *Smith* v. *Afghanistan*, US, 262 F.Supp.2d 217 (S.D.N.Y. 2003); *Acree* v. *Iraq*, US, 271 F.Supp.2d 179 (D.D.C. 2003) (but later vacated, *Acree* v. *Iraq*, US, 370 F.3d 41, 58–60 (D.C.Cir. 2004)); *Hill* v. *Iraq*, US, 175 F.Supp.2d 36 (D.D.C. 2001) (reversed and remanded on other grounds, *Hill* v. *Iraq*, US, 328 F.3d 680 (D.C.Cir. 2003)); *Daliberti* v. *Iraq*, US, 146 F.Supp.2d 19 (D.D.C. 2001); *Daliberti* v. *Iraq*, US, 97 F.Supp.2d 38 (D.D.C. 2000).

162 *Fisher* v. *Libya*, US, 541 F.Supp.2d 46 (D.D.C. 2008); *Pugh* v. *Libya*, US, 530 F.Supp.2d 216 (D.D.C. 2008); *Hurst* v. *Libya*, US, 474 F.Supp.2d 19 (D.D.C. 2007); *Price* v. *Libya*, US, District Court, 384 F.Supp.2d 120 (D.D.C. 2005); *Collett* v. *Libya*, US, 362 F.Supp.2d 230 (D.D.C. 2005); *Price* v. *Libya*, US, 389 F.3d 192 (D.C.Cir. 2004); affirming *Price* v. *Libya*, US, 274 F.Supp.2d 20 (D.D.C. 2003) (earlier: *Price* v. *Libya*, US, 110 F.Supp.2d 10 (D.D.C. 2000); reversed in part and remanded, *Price* v. *Libya*, US, 294 F.3d 82 (D.C.Cir. 2002)); *Kilburn* v. *Libya*, US, 376 F.3d 1123 (D.C.Cir. 2004); affirming *Kilburn* v. *Iran*, US, 277 F.Supp.2d 24 (D.D.C. 2003); *Simpson* v. *Libya*, US, 180 F.Supp.2d 78 (D.D.C. 2001); affirmed in part and remanded, *Simpson* v. *Libya*, US, 326 F.3d 230 (D.C.Cir. 2003); further decided, *Simpson* v. *Libya*, US, 362 F.Supp.2d 168 (D.D.C. 2005); affirmed and remanded, *Simpson* v. *Libya*, US, 470 F.3d 356 (D.C.Cir. 2006); *Rein* v. *Libya*, US, 995 F.Supp. 325 (E.D.N.Y. 1998); affirmed, *Rein* v. *Libya*, US, 162 F.3d 748 (2nd Cir. 1998).

163 *Massie* v. *DPRK*, US, 592 F.Supp.2d 57 (D.D.C. 2008).

164 *Owens* v. *Sudan*, US, 531 F.3d 884 (D.C.Cir. 2008); affirming and remanding *Owens* v. *Sudan*, US, 412 F.Supp.2d 99 (D.D.C. 2006); *Rux* v. *Sudan*, US, 495 F.Supp.2d 541 (E.D.Va. 2007), upon denial of Sudan's motion to dismiss in *Rux* v. *Sudan*, US, 461 F.3d 461 (4th Cir. 2006); affirming *Rux* v. *Sudan*, US, 2005 WL 2086202 (E.D.Va. 2005); *Abur* v. *Sudan*, US, 437 F.Supp.2d 166 (D.D.C. 2006); *Owens* v. *Sudan*, US, 412 F.Supp.2d 99 (D.D.C. 2006); *Owens* v. *Sudan*, US, 374 F.Supp.2d 1 (D.D.C. 2006).

NOTES TO PAGE 227   597

165 *Gates* v. *Syria*, US, 580 F.Supp.2d 53 (D.D.C. 2008); *Wyatt* v. *Syria*, US, 362 F.Supp.2d 103 (D.D.C. 2005).

166 See *Peterson* v. *Iran*, US, 515 F.Supp.2d 25 (D.D.C. 2007); *Bennett* v. *Iran*, US, 507 F.Supp.2d 117 (D.D.C. 2007); *Valore* v. *Iran*, US, 478 F.Supp.2d 101 (D.D.C. 2007); *Estate of Heiser* v. *Iran*, US, 466 F.Supp.2d 229 (D.D.C. 2006); *Abur* v. *Sudan*, US, 437 F.Supp.2d 166 (D.D.C. 2006); *Haim* v. *Iran*, US, 425 F.Supp.2d 56 (D.D.C. 2006); *Bodoff* v. *Iran*, US, 424 F.Supp.2d 74 (D.D.C. 2006); *Prevatt* v. *Iran*, US, 421 F.Supp.2d 152 (D.D.C. 2006); *Salazar* v. *Iran*, US, 370 F.Supp.2d 105 (D. D.C. 2005); *Campuzano* v. *Iran*, US, 281 F.Supp.2d 258 (D.D.C. 2003); *Dammarell* v. *Iran*, US, 281 F.Supp.2d 105 (D.D.C. 2003); *Regier* v. *Iran*, US, 281 F.Supp.2d 87 (D.D.C. 2003); *Kilburn* v. *Iran*, US, 277 F.Supp.2d 24 (D.D.C. 2003); *Stern* v. *Iran*, US, 271 F.Supp.2d 286 (D.D.C. 2003); *Acree* v. *Iraq*, US, 271 F.Supp.2d 179 (D.D.C. 2003); *Peterson* v. *Iran*, US, 264 F.Supp.2d 46 (D.D.C. 2003); *Smith* v. *Afghanistan*, US, 262 F.Supp.2d 217 (S.D.N.Y. 2003); *Kerr* v. *Iran*, US, 245 F.Supp.2d 59 (D.D.C. 2003); *Tracy* v. *Iran*, US, Civ. No. 01-2517, slip op. (D.D.C. 2003); *Cronin* v. *Iran*, US, 238 F.Supp.2d 222 (D.D.C. 2002); *Surette* v. *Iran*, US, 231 F.Supp.2d 260 (D.D.C. 2002); *Ungar* v. *Iran*, US, 211 F.Supp.2d 91 (D.D.C. 2002); *Stethem* v. *Iran*, US, 201 F.Supp.2d 78 (D.D.C. 2002); *Roeder* v. *Iran*, US, 195 F.Supp.2d 140 (D.D.C. 2002); *Weinstein* v. *Iran*, US, 184 F.Supp.2d 13 (D.D.C. 2002); *Turner* v. *Iran*, 2002 U.S.Dist.Lexis 26730 (D.D.C. 2002); *Hill* v. *Iraq*, US, 175 F.Supp.2d 36 (D.D.C. 2001); *Wagner* v. *Iran*, US, 172 F.Supp.2d 128 (D.D.C. 2001); *Jenco* v. *Iran*, US, 154 F.Supp.2d 27 (D.D.C. 2001); *Sutherland* v. *Iran*, US, 151 F.Supp.2d 27 (D.D.C. 2001); *Daliberti* v. *Iraq*, US, 146 F.Supp.2d 19 (D.D.C. 2001); *Polhill* v. *Iran*, US, 2001 U.S.Dist.Lexis 15322 (D.D.C. 2001); *Eisenfeld* v. *Iran*, US, 172 F.Supp.2d 1 (D.D.C. 2000); *Alejandre* v. *Cuba*, US, 42 F.Supp.2d 1317 (S.D.Fla. 1999); *Flatow* v. *Iran*, US, 999 F.Supp. 1 (D.D.C. 1998); 121 ILR 618; *Cicippio* v. *Iran*, US, 18 F.Supp.2d 62 (D.D.C. 1998); *Alejandre* v. *Cuba*, US, 996 F.Supp. 1239 (S.D.Fla. 1997); 121 ILR 603.

167 This is manifested by a minatory remark by a US court in a case arising out of the Lockerbie Incident of 1998: 'Any foreign state would know that the United States has substantial interests in protecting its flag carriers and its nationals from terrorist activities and should reasonably expect that if these interests were harmed, it would be subject to a variety of potential responses, including civil actions in United States courts.' *Rein* v. *Libya*, US, 995 F.Supp. 325, 330 (E.D.N.Y. 1998). See also *Sutherland* v. *Iran*, US, 151 F.Supp.2d 27, 53 (D.D.C. 2001) ('those who intentionally harm United States nationals will be held accountable for that harm in United States courts').

168 See *Singh* v. *Australia*, US, 521 F.Supp.2d 91, 93 (D.D.C. 2007); *Mwani* v. *Afghanistan*, US, 417 F.3d 1, 15, fn. 15 (D.C.Cir. 2005); *In re Terrorist Attacks*, US, 349 F.Supp.2d 765, 794 (S.D.N.Y. 2005); affirmed, *In re Terrorist Attacks*, US, 538 F.3d 71 (2nd Cir. 2008); *Burnett* v. *Al Baraka*, US, 292 F.Supp.2d 9, 16, fn. 3 (D.D.C. 2003); *Abrams* v. *Société*, US, 175 F.Supp.2d 423, 433 (E.D.N.Y. 2001) (vacated on other grounds, *Abrams* v. *Société*, US, 332 F.3d 173 (2nd Cir. 2003)); *Moses* v. *Air Afrique*, US, No. 99-CV-541, 2000 WL 306853, p. 5 (E.D.N.Y. 2000).

598   NOTES TO PAGE 227

169 See *Kalasho v. Iraqi Government*, 2001 U.S.Dist.Lexis 7504, pp. 5–6 (W.D.Mich. 2001).

170 See *Abur v. Sudan*, US, 437 F.Supp.2d 166, 174–179 (D.D.C. 2006) (rejecting claims by Kenyan nationals but admitting those by US nationals against the Sudan and Iran for bombings of US embassies in Tanzania and Kenya in 1998). Originally, the AEDPA applied only if both the claimant and the victim were US nationals when the act upon which the claim was based occurred (s. 1605(a)(7)(B)(ii)); but this provision was amended in 1997 to allow suit if either the claimant or the victim was a US national when the tortious act occurred. Public Law 105-11, 25 April 1997, 36 ILM 760 (1997). For the purposes of suits under AEDPA, the term 'US national' covers not only a US citizen but also a person whose circumstances (including the length of residence in the US) indicate a 'permanent allegiance to the United States'. See US Immigration and Nationality Act, 1952, 8 USC § 1101(a)(22); *Asemani v. Iran*, US, 266 F.Supp.2d 24, 25–27 (D.D.C. 2003); on appeal, *In re Asemani*, US, 455 F.3d 296, 297–298 (D.C.Cir. 2006). The protection was extended in 2008 by s. 1605A of FSIA to certain non-US nationals, such as 'employee[s] of the Government of the United States, or of an individual performing a contract awarded by the United States Government' (s. 1605A(a)(2)(A)(ii)(III) and (c)).

171 See Bianchi, Immunity, 266, fn. 130; Bradley and Goldsmith, *Pinochet*, 2157; Gergen, Human Rights, 766, 797–798.

172 See Glannon and Atik, Politics, 699–703.

173 See Damrosch, Enforcing, 175; Glannon and Atik, Politics, 701; Gergen, Human Rights, 797. For the role of the Executive see also Brock, The Foreign; Chorazak, Clarity; Ketchel, Deriving.

174 US House of Representatives, Report No. 94-1487, 1976, pp. 12, 45; 1976 USCCAN 6604, 6610, 6634. See *Cargill v. Pavel Dybenko*, US, 991 F.2d 1012, 1016 (2nd Cir. 1993); 103 ILR 572; *Dames v. Regan*, US, 453 US 654, 685 (1981); 72 ILR 270, 288; *American v. Iran*, US, 657 F.2d 430, 444 (D.C.Cir. 1981). See also *Tachiona v. Mugabe*, US, 169 F.Supp.2d 259, 271–272 (S.D.N.Y. 2001).

175 *Price v. Libya*, US, 294 F.3d 82, 89 (D.C.Cir. 2002). See also *Cicippio-Puleo v. Iran*, US, 353 F.3d 1024, 1035 (D.C.Cir. 2004); Murphy, Civil Liability, 35–39.

176 See Vadnais, The Terrorism, 216–218; Vitrano, Hell-Bent. For a comprehensive analysis of, in particular, the background and difficult issues such as the actual compensation under this statute see Elsea, *Suits against Terrorist States*.

177 For the damages (compensatory and punitive) involved see (in US dollars): *Belkin v. Iran*, US, 667 F.Supp.2d 8, 24 (D.D.C. 2009) (over 10.38 million); *Estate of Heiser v. Iran*, US, 659 F.Supp.2d 20, 31 (D.D.C. 2009) (336.658 million); *Saludes v. Cuba*, US, 655 F.Supp.2d 1290, 1297–1298 (S.D.Fla. 2009) (27.5 million); *Wachsman v. Iran*, US, 603 F.Supp.2d 148, 160–162 (D.D.C. 2009) (22.5 million); *Massie v. DPRK*, US, 592 F.Supp.2d 57, 77 (D.D.C. 2008) (65.85 million); *Gates v. Syria*, US, 580 F.Supp.2d 53, 75 (D.D.C. 2008) (412.91 million); *Rimkus v. Iran*, US, 575 F.Supp.2d 181, 198 (D.D.C. 2008) (5 million); *Acosta v. Iran*, US, 574

F.Supp.2d 15 (D.D.C. 2008) (335.2 million); *Beer* v. *Iran*, US, 574 F.Supp.2d 1, 14 (D.D.C. 2008) (13 million); *Kirschenbaum* v. *Iran*, US, 572 F.Supp.2d 200, 213 (D. D.C. 2008) (10 million); *Bakhtiar* v. *Iran*, US, 571 F.Supp.2d 27 (D.D.C. 2008) (12 million); *Ben-Rafael* v. *Iran*, US, 540 F.Supp.2d 39, 60 (D.D.C. 2008) (62.44 million); *Pugh* v. *Libya*, US, 530 F.Supp.2d 216, 262–274 (D.D.C. 2008) (108 million); *Estate of Bayani* v. *Iran*, US, 530 F.Supp.2d 40, 46 (D.D.C. 2007) (407 million); *Levin* v. *Iran*, US, 529 F.Supp.2d 1 (D.D.C. 2007) (28.8 million); *Nikbin* v. *Iran*, US, 517 F.Supp.2d 416, 429 (D.D.C. 2007) (2.6 million); *Peterson* v. *Iran*, US, 515 F.Supp.2d 25, 60 (D.D.C. 2007) (2,657 million); *Bennett* v. *Iran*, US, 507 F.Supp.2d 117, 130 (D.D.C. 2007) (12.5 million); *Rux* v. *Sudan*, US, 495 F.Supp.2d 541 (E.D.Va. 2007) (8 million); *Estate of Heiser* v. *Iran*, US, 466 F.Supp.2d 229, 356 (D.D.C. 2006) (254.4 million); *Blais* v. *Iran*, US, 459 F.Supp.2d 40 (D.D.C. 2006) (28.8 million); *Greenbaum* v. *Iran*, US, 451 F.Supp.2d 90 (D.D.C. 2006) (19.88 million); *Stern* v. *Iran*, US, 271 F.Supp.2d 286, 302 (D.D.C. 2003) (313 million); *Cronin* v. *Iran*, US, 238 F.Supp.2d 222, 236 (D.D.C. 2002) (301.2 million); *Wagner* v. *Iran*, US, 172 F.Supp.2d 128, 138 (D.D.C. 2001) (over 316 million); *Jenco* v. *Iran*, US, 154 F.Supp.2d 27, 40 (D.D.C. 2001) (nearly 315 million); *Sutherland* v. *Iran*, US, 151 F.Supp.2d 27, 53 (D.D.C. 2001) (over 353 million); *Eisenfeld* v. *Iran*, US, 172 F.Supp.2d 1, 10–11 (D.D.C. 2000) (326.1 million); *Elahi* v. *Iran*, US, 124 F.Supp.2d 97, 115 (D.D.C. 2000) (over 311 million); *Anderson* v. *Iran*, US, 90 F.Supp.2d 107, 114 (D.D.C. 2000) (over 341 million).

178 *Flatow* v. *Iran*, US, 76 F.Supp.2d 16, 28 (D.D.C. 1999). Flatow obtained a default judgment against Iran for over US$ 247.5 million in compensatory and punitive damages for the death of his daughter killed in a suicide bomber attack on a tourist bus in Israel. *Flatow* v. *Iran*, US, 999 F.Supp. 1, 5 (D.D.C. 1998); 121 ILR 618. Flatow's attempts to collect the judgment were unsuccessful: *Flatow* v. *Iran*, US, 308 F.3d 1065 (9th Cir. 2002); *Flatow* v. *Iran*, US, 76 F.Supp.2d 28 (D.D.C. 1999); *Flatow* v. *Iran*, US, 76 F.Supp.2d 16 (D.D.C. 1999) (US Government intervening); *Flatow* v. *Iran*, US, 74 F.Supp.2d 18 (D.D.C. 1999). Subsequently, the Victims of Trafficking and Violence Protection Act of 2000, Public Law No. 106-386, 114 Stat 1464 (28 October 2000) (Victims Protection Act) afforded certain victims of terrorist acts an opportunity to recover funds from the US Government to satisfy their outstanding judgments (See especially ss. 2002(a)(1) and 2002(a)(2)(C)(D), reproduced and explained in *Flatow* v. *Iran*, US, 305 F.3d 1249, 1250–1251, fns. 2–3 (D.C.Cir. 2002)). Flatow later applied and obtained from the US Treasury over US$ 26 million, representing the compensatory damages award and post-judgment interest on that portion of the judgment. As an important condition of receiving funds from the US Government, Flatow was required to relinquish 'all rights to execute against or attach property [that is, property of Iran] that is ... subject to section 1610(f)(1)(A) of title 28, United States Code [i.e. FSIA]': *Flatow* v. *Iran*, US, 305 F.3d 1249, 1250–1251 (D.C.Cir. 2002); *Flatow* v. *Iran*, US, 308 F.3d 1065, 1069, fn. 6 (9th Cir. 2002); *Ministry* v. *Cubic*, US, 236 F.Supp.2d 1140, 1146–1148 (S.D.Cal. 2002); affirmed, *Ministry* v. *Cubic*, US, 385

600   NOTES TO PAGES 228–233

F.3d 1206, 1213–1217 (9th Cir. 2004). For relinquishment of rights under the Victims Protection Act see also *Hegna* v. *Iran*, US, 299 F.Supp.2d 229, 230 (S.D. N.Y. 2004); affirmed, *Hegna* v. *Iran*, US, 376 F.3d 226 (4th Cir. 2004); cf. *Ministry* v. *Cubic*, US, 495 F.3d 1024, 1030–1034 (9th Cir. 2007). For the epithet 'Pyrrhic victory' see also *Eisenfeld* v. *Iran*, US, 172 F.Supp.2d 1, 9 (D.D.C. 2000). For the difficulty in enforcing the judgments see also the *Rubin*, the *Weinstein*, and the *Smith* cases: *Rubin* v. *Iran*, US, 456 F.Supp.2d 228 (D.Mass. 2006); *Rubin* v. *Iran*, US, 408 F.Supp.2d 549 (N.D.Ill. 2005); *Rubin* v. *Iran*, US, 349 F.Supp.2d 1108 (N.D.Ill. 2004); *Rubin* v. *Iran*, US, 281 F.Supp.2d 258 (D.D.C. 2003) (371.5 million); *Weinstein* v. *Iran*, US, 299 F.Supp.2d 63 (E.D.N.Y. 2004); *Weinstein* v. *Iran*, US, 274 F.Supp.2d 53 (D.D.C. 2003); *Weinstein* v. *Iran*, US, 184 F.Supp.2d 13, 22–26 (D.D.C. 2002) (over 183 million); *Smith* v. *Federal*, US, 280 F.Supp.2d 314 (S.D.N.Y. 2003); *Smith* v. *Afghanistan*, US, 262 F.Supp.2d 217, 240–241 (S.D. N.Y. 2003) (63 million). For a succinct summary of the US Congress' legislative efforts to facilitate enforcement see Murphy, Contemporary Practice. For discussions on the difficulty of recovery see also Cooper-Hill, *The Law of Sovereign Immunity and Terrorism*, pp. 167–180; Atherton, Compensating; Gartenstein-Ross, Resolving; Gartenstein-Ross, A Critique, 898–902; Murphy, Satisfaction; Murphy, *Flatow* Case; Zaffuto, A 'Pirate's Victory'.

179 *In re Iran*, US, 659 F.Supp.2d 31, 37 (D.D.C. 2009).
180 *In re Iran*, US, 659 F.Supp.2d 31, 38 (D.D.C. 2009).

Chapter 6

1 The 'contracting-out' of prisons to private companies in the UK is a salient example. See UK House of Commons Home Affairs Committee, Second Report.
2 *NV* v. *Bank*, Netherlands, (1963) 65 ILR 348, 353.
3 *Arango* v. *Guzman*, US, 621 F.2d 1371, 1379 (5th Cir. 1980); 63 ILR 467; quoted with approval in *Kuwait* v. *Iraqi*, England, [1995] 1 WLR 1147, 1160; 103 ILR 340, 402. Further proceedings in *Arango* v. *Guzman*, US, 761 F.2d 1527, 1529, 1532–1533 (11th Cir. 1985).
4 See *Moses* v. *Air Afrique*, US, No. 99-CV-541, 2000 WL 306853, p. 5 (E.D.N.Y. 2000); *In re Air Crash*, US, 96 F.3d 932, 939 (7th Cir. 1996); *In re Hashim*, US, 188 B.R. 633, 645 (D.Ariz. 1995); 107 ILR 405; *Mangattu* v. *Ibn Hayyan*, US, 35 F.3d 205, 207–209 (5th Cir. 1994); *EAL* v. *European*, US, 107 ILR 318 (D.Del. 1994); *LeDonne* v. *Gulf*, US, 700 F.Supp. 1400 (E.D.Va. 1988); *Arab* v. *Hashim (No. 3)*, England, 1991, [1991] 2 AC 114; *Rios* v. *Marshall*, US, 530 F.Supp. 351, 371 (S.D.N.Y. 1981). See also discussion of 'pooling', below.
5 See *Trendtex* v. *Central Bank*, England, [1977] QB 529, 559, 572–573; 64 ILR 111, 133, 146–147; *Mellenger* v. *New Brunswick*, England, [1971] 1 WLR 604, 609; 52 ILR 322; *Baccus* v. *Servicio*, England, 1956, [1957] 1 QB 438; 23 ILR 160. See also *Coreck* v. *Sevrybokholodflot*, Scotland, 1993, [1994] SLT 893, 896–897; 107 ILR 658, 665–666.
6 *Trendtex* v. *Central Bank*, England, [1977] QB 529, 560; 64 ILR 111, 134 (emphases added).

NOTES TO PAGES 233-239   601

7 *Trendtex* [1977] QB 529, 560; 64 ILR 111, 134.
8 *Trendtex* [1977] QB 529, 563–565; 64 ILR 111, 137–139.
9 *Trendtex* [1977] QB 529, 573; 64 ILR 111, 147 (emphasis added).
10 *Trendtex* [1977] QB 529, 573–575; 64 ILR 111, 147–149. The same elaborate assessment, to a lesser extent, was also conducted in *C. Czarnikow* v. *Rolimpex*, England, 1977, [1978] QB 176, 195; 1978, [1979] AC 351, 364, 367, 369; 64 ILR 195, 201, 207, 208. See also *I Congreso del Partido*, England, 1981, [1983] 1 AC 244, 258 per Lord Wilberforce; 64 ILR 307, 310.
11 Dickinson *et al.*, *State Immunity*, p. 403, paras. 4.101 and 4.102; quoted with approval in *Ministry* v. *Tsavliris*, England, [2008] 2 Lloyd's Rep. 90, 102, para. 64.
12 Moorthy, The Malaysian, 640–641.
13 See reproductions in the Pakistan SIO, s. 15(1) and (2); Singapore SIA, s. 16(1) and (2); South Africa FSIA, ss. 1(2)(c)(i) and 15(1). See also the ILA Drafts, Art. I(B). The UK SIA here implements Art. 27 of the European Convention (with a slightly different wording). A constituent territory of a federal State not the subject of an Order in Council under s. 14(5) of the UK SIA according it the immunities of an independent State is regarded as a 'separate entity' within the meaning of s. 14(2)(3). *Bank* v. *Price*, England, 1996, [1997] 4 All ER 108, 112; 111 ILR 604, 608.
14 *Ministry* v. *Tsavliris*, England, [2008] 2 Lloyd's Rep. 90, 102–104, paras. 67, 70–74.
15 *Tsavliris*, p. 104, para. 71.
16 *Tsavliris*, pp. 104–105, paras. 78–80, citing *Kuwait Airways* v. *Iraqi Airways*, England, [1995] 1 WLR 1147, 1159–1160; 103 ILR 340, 400–402.
17 *Wilhelm Finance* v. *Ente*, England, [2009] 1 CLC 867, 884, para. 52 per Teare J (emphasis added); for the consideration of these factors see pp. 872–884, paras. 12–51.
18 Mann, The State, 48.
19 *Propend* v. *Sing*, England, (1996) 111 ILR 611, 646.
20 *Propend* v. *Sing*, England, (1997) 111 ILR 611, 667, 669.
21 *Kuwait Airways* v. *Iraqi Airways*, England, 1992/1993/1995, [1995] 1 Lloyd's Rep 25; [1995] 1 WLR 1147; 103 ILR 340. See Fox, A 'Commercial'; Marks, State; Talmon, War; Fox, The Commerciality; Evans, When; Davies, Kuwait Airways.
22 *Kuwait Airways*, England, High Court, 1992, 103 ILR 340, 352; Court of Appeal, 1993, [1995] 1 Lloyd's Rep 25, 26, 34; 103 ILR 340, 368, 383; House of Lords, 1995, [1995] 1 WLR 1147, 1158, 1174; 103 ILR 340, 383, 400, 417.
23 *Kuwait Airways*, (1992) 103 ILR 340, 352–356. For criticism of the over-emphasis on the commercial purposes see Fox, A 'Commercial', 198–199. In an earlier case, Iraqi Airways was held to be a commercial enterprise, even though it was a State-owned body. *Re Rafidain Bank*, England, (1991) 101 ILR 332, 336.
24 *Kuwait Airways*, 1993, [1995] 1 Lloyd's Rep 25, 29–30, 33–34, 36; 103 ILR 340, 372–374, 380–382, 386–388.
25 *Kuwait Airways*, 1993, [1995] 1 Lloyd's Rep 25, 37; 103 ILR 340, 388.
26 *Kuwait Airways* [1995] 1 WLR 1147, 1163, 1168, 1172, 1175; 103 ILR 340, 405–406, 411, 416, 419. It was later discovered that, as regards the period

602 NOTES TO PAGES 239-243

between 9 August and 17 September 1990, the factual basis for the decision of the House of Lords depended upon false and perjured evidence deployed by the IAC. In a separate action, it was established that, during that period, the IAC was so much involved in preparing the aircraft for commercial flights between Iraq and Kuwait (including changing the aircraft livery, re-registering them, insuring them and employing maintenance personnel) that its acts were not acts *jure imperii*. Thus the basis for denying immunity in respect of the period after 17 September applied with equal force to the interim period: *Kuwait Airways* v. *Iraqi Airways (No. 2)*, England, 2000, [2001] 1 WLR 429; *Kuwait Airways* v. *Iraqi Airways ('Perjury Action')*, England, [2003] 1 Lloyd's Rep 448, 468, paras. 149–152; 126 ILR 758, 798–799.

27 *Kuwait Airways* [1995] 1 WLR 1147, 1163, 1168, 1175; 103 ILR 340, 405–406, 411, 419, Lord Mustill and Lord Slynn of Hadley dissenting.

28 *Kuwait Airways* [1995] 1 WLR 1147, 1160; 103 ILR 340, 401–402; cited in *Ministry* v. *Tsavliris*, England, [2008] 2 Lloyd's Rep. 90, 105, para. 79.

29 *I Congreso*, England, [1983] 1 AC 244, 267, 272; 64 ILR 307, 318, 323.

30 *Kuwait Airways* [1995] 1 WLR 1147, 1163; 103 ILR 340, 405.

31 *Kuwait Airways*, 1993, [1995] 1 Lloyd's Rep 25, 29–30, 33–34, 36; 103 ILR 340, 372–374, 380–382, 386–388; *Kuwait Airways* [1995] 1 WLR 1147, 1172, 1174–1175; 103 ILR 340, 415, 418–419.

32 The exclusion of US citizens covers, for example, 'a corporation organized and incorporated under the laws of the State of New York but owned by a foreign state'. US House of Representatives, Report No. 94-1487, 1976, p. 15; 1976 USCCAN 6604, 6614. See *Flatow* v. *Iran*, US, 67 F.Supp.2d 535, 538 (D.Md. 1999); *Rimsat* v. *Hilliard*, US, 207 B.R. 964, 968 (D.D.C. 1997); *Matter of Rimsat*, US, 98 F.3d 956, 963 (7th Cir. 1996); *Gould* v. *Aerospatiale*, US, 40 F.3d 1033, 1034 (9th Cir. 1994); *Bahsoon* v. *Pezetel*, US, 768 F.Supp. 507, 510 (E.D.N.C. 1991).

33 For entities created under the laws of third countries see *In re Air Crash*, US, 96 F.3d 932, 938 (7th Cir. 1996); *Mangattu* v. *Ibn Hayyan*, US, 35 F.3d 205, 209 (5th Cir. 1994); *Mobil* v. *Abeille*, US, 984 F.2d 664, 665, fn. 1 (5th Cir. 1993); *Coastal* v. *Gustav Sule*, US, 942 F.Supp. 1082, 1084–1085 (E.D.La. 1996); *Borgships* v. *Macarena*, US, 1993 WL 278453, p. 3 (E.D.La. 1993); *LeDonne* v. *Gulf*, US, 700 F.Supp. 1400, 1406 (E.D.Va. 1988).

34 See especially *Taff* v. *Amalgamated*, England, [1901] AC 426; Trade Union and Labour Relations (Consolidation) Act 1992, s. 10.

35 US House of Representatives, Report No. 94-1487, Sept. 9, 1976, p. 15; 1976 USCCAN 6604, 6614.

36 *In re Ski*, US, 198 F.Supp.2d 420, 423 (S.D.N.Y. 2002); *Kern* v. *Oesterreichische*, US, 178 F.Supp.2d 367, 373 (S.D.N.Y. 2001); *Zveiter* v. *Brazilian*, US, 833 F.Supp. 1089, 1091–1092 (S.D.N.Y. 1993); *Schoenberg* v. *Exportadora*, US, 930 F.2d 777, 778, 779, fn. 1 (9th Cir. 1991); 98 ILR 118.

37 *In re Air Crash*, US, 96 F.3d 932, 938 (7th Cir. 1996).

38 *Gupta* v. *Thai*, US, 487 F.3d 759, 767, fn. 12 (9th Cir. 2007); *US Fidelity* v. *Braspetro*, US, 219 F.Supp.2d 403, 411 (S.D.N.Y. 2002); *Crédit* v. *Getty*, US, 876 F. Supp. 517, 520 (S.D.N.Y. 1995); *Kern* v. *Jeppesen*, US, 867 F.Supp. 525, 531 (S.D.

NOTES TO PAGES 243–244   603

Tex. 1994); *Linton v. Airbus*, US, 794 F.Supp. 650, 652, 653 (S.D.Tex. 1992); appeal dismissed, *Linton v. Airbus*, US, 30 F.3d 592 (5th Cir. 1994); *Kramer v. Boeing*, US, 705 F.Supp. 1392, 1394 (D.Minn. 1989).

39 *International v. Caja*, US, 293 F.3d 392, 399 (7th Cir. 2002).

40 *In re Aircrash*, US, 987 F.Supp. 975, 978 (E.D.Mich. 1997); *Wilk v. Creditanstalt*, US, 1993 WL 97259, pp. 1–2 (S.D.N.Y. 1993). See also *Balentine v. Union*, US, 795 F.Supp. 266, 269 (N.D.Ill. 1992); *Canadian v. Compania*, US, 727 F.2d 274 (2nd Cir. 1984); 101 ILR 470; affirming *Canadian v. Compania*, US, 528 F.Supp. 1337 (S.D.N.Y. 1982); cf. *Coreck v. Sevrybokholodflot*, Scotland, 1993, [1994] SLT 893, 896; 107 ILR 658, 665.

41 US House of Representatives, Report No. 94-1487, Sept. 9, 1976, pp. 15–16; 1976 USCCAN 6604, 6614.

42 *Coyle v. PT*, US, 363 F.3d 979 (9th Cir. 2004); *In re Tamimi*, US, 176 F.3d 274, 278 (4th Cir. 1999); *Randolph v. Budget*, US, 97 F.3d 319, 324 (9th Cir. 1996); *Brink's v. South African*, US, 93 F.3d 1022, 1026, n. 4 (2nd Cir. 1996); *Forsythe v. Saudi*, US, 885 F.2d 285, 287, n. 1 (5th Cir. 1989); *America v. GPA*, US, 877 F.2d 793, 796 (9th Cir. 1989); 92 ILR 454; *Compania v. US District*, US, 859 F.2d 1354, 1359 (9th Cir. 1988); 98 ILR 69; *Arango v. Guzman*, US, 761 F.2d 1527, 1529, 1532–1533 (11th Cir. 1985); *Arango v. Guzman*, US, 621 F.2d 1371, 1374 (5th Cir. 1980); 63 ILR 467. See Collier, The Foreign.

43 *Argentina v. Weltover*, US. 504 US 607, 611, n. 1 (1992); 119 L.Ed.2d 394, 403, fn. 1; 100 ILR 509, 513; *Verlinden v. Central*, US, 461 US 480, 482 (1983); 79 ILR 548, 550; *Peterson v. Iran*, US, 563 F.Supp.2d 268, 275 (D.D.C. 2008); *Chalabi v. Jordan*, US, 503 F.Supp.2d 267, 269 (D.D.C. 2007); *Olympic v. Ministry*, US, 134 F.Supp.2d 528, 534 (S.D.N.Y. 2001); *LNC v. Nicaragua*, US, 115 F.Supp.2d 358 (S.D.N.Y. 2000); affirmed, *LNC v. Banco*, US, 228 F.3d 423 (2nd Cir. 2000); *Adler v. Nigeria*, US, 107 F.3d 720, 723 (9th Cir. 1997); *Commercial v. Rafidain*, US, 15 F.3d 238, 239 (2nd Cir. 1994); 107 ILR 261; *Gadsby v. Romania*, US, 698 F.Supp. 483, 485 (S.D.N.Y. 1988); *S & S v. Masinexportimport*, US, 706 F.2d 411, 414 (2nd Cir. 1983); 72 ILR 183.

44 *Orient v. Bank*, US, 506 F.3d 980 (10th Cir. 2007); *Voest-Alpine v. Bank*, US, 142 F.3d 887, 890 (5th Cir. 1998); *Commercial v. Rafidain*, US, 15 F.3d 238, 239 (2nd Cir. 1994); 107 ILR 261; *Barragan v. Banco*, US, 188 Cal.App.3d 283, 295; 232 Cal. Rptr. 758 (1986).

45 *Los Angeles v. Conus*, US, 969 F.Supp. 579, 585 (C.D.Cal. 1997).

46 *Gang v. China*, US, 320 Fed.Appx. 71, 73, 2009 WL 932578.

47 *Karaha v. Perusahaan*, US, 313 F.3d 70, 75–76 (2nd Cir. 2002).

48 *World v. Kazakhstan*, US, 296 F.3d 1154 (D.C.Cir. 2002).

49 *Globe v. AO*, US, 376 F.3d 282 (4th Cir. 2004); *S & S v. Masinexportimport*, US, 802 F.Supp. 1109, 1110 (S.D.N.Y. 1992); 107 ILR 239; *S & S v. Masinexportimport*, US, 706 F.2d 411 (2nd Cir. 1983); 72 ILR 183; *Ferrostaal v. SS*, US, 652 F.Supp. 420, 422 (S.D.N.Y. 1987).

50 *Raccoon v. Navoi*, US, 244 F.Supp.2d 1130 (D.Colo. 2002).

51 *US Titan v. Guangzhou*, US, 16 F.Supp.2d 326 (S.D.N.Y. 1998); affirmed, *US Titan v. Guangzhou*, US, 241 F.3d 135 (2nd Cir. 2001).

52 *Abrams v. Société*, US, 175 F.Supp.2d 423 (E.D.N.Y. 2001); affirmed, *Abrams v. Société*, US, 389 F.3d 61 (2nd Cir. 2004).

604   NOTES TO PAGES 244–245

53 *Fabe* v. *Aneco*, US, 784 F.Supp. 448, 450–451 (S.D.Ohio 1991).

54 *Vermeulen* v. *Renault*, US, 985 F.2d 1534, 1542 (11th Cir. 1993).

55 *Hijazi* v. *Permanent*, US, 689 F.Supp.2d 669, 670 (S.D.N.Y. 2010); *Berdakin* v. *Consulado*, US, 912 F.Supp. 458, 466 (C.D.Cal. 1995); *Gerritsen* v. *Miguel*, US, 819 F.2d 1511, 1517 (9th Cir. 1987); 101 ILR 476; *Gray* v. *Permanent*, US, 443 F.Supp. 816, 819 (S.D.N.Y. 1978); 63 ILR 121; affirmed, *Gray* v. *Permanent*, US, 580 F.2d 1044 (2nd Cir. 1978) (Table).

56 *EOTT* v. *Winterthur*, US, 257 F.3d 992, 997 (9th Cir. 2001); *Patrickson* v. *Dole*, US, 251 F.3d 795, 808 (9th Cir. 2001); *Risk* v. *Norway*, US, 707 F.Supp. 1159, 1167 and fn. 12 (N.D.Cal. 1989); *California* v. *Powerex*, US, 533 F.3d 1087 (9th Cir. 2008).

57 *Gates* v. *Victor*, US, 54 F.3d 1457, 1460 (9th Cir. 1995); 107 ILR 371; reiterated in *EIE* v. *Long*, US, 322 F.3d 635, 640 (9th Cir. 2003) and quoted in *USX* v. *Adriatic*, US, 345 F.3d 190, 206 (3rd Cir. 2003).

58 *Saudi Arabia* v. *Nelson*, US, 507 US 349, 355 (1993); 123 L.Ed.2d 47, 58; 100 ILR 544, 550. The Supreme Court, however, was only confirming a long-standing principle laid down by the FSIA and consistently adhered to by the US courts. Since all the cases concerning foreign State entities contain some declaration to this effect, I shall not bore the reader with superfluous citations. The pre-FSIA rule seems to have been the exact reverse; that is, entities with separate legal personalities used to be presumed not to enjoy immunity, see Hoffman, *The Separate*, 542–565.

59 *First National* v. *Bancec*, US, 462 US 611, 624 (1983); 80 ILR 566, 574–575.

60 *Powerex* v. *Reliant*, US, 551 US 224; 127 S.Ct. 2411, 2414 (2007); *Kensington* v. *Itoua*, US, 505 F.3d 147, 154 (2nd Cir. 2007); *Wahba* v. *National*, US, 457 F.Supp.2d 721, 730 (E.D.Tex. 2006); *Howland* v. *Hertz*, US, 431 F.Supp.2d 1238, 1241 (M.D.Fla. 2006); *BP* v. *Jiangsu*, US, 420 F.3d 810, 816 (8th Cir. 2005); *Globe* v. *AO*, US, 376 F.3d 282, 285 (4th Cir. 2004); *Coyle* v. *PT*, US, 363 F.3d 979, 982, fn. 2 (9th Cir. 2004); *National* v. *BP*, US, 319 F.Supp.2d 352, 369–370 (S.D.N.Y. 2004); *Elixir* v. *Perusahaan*, US, 267 F.Supp.2d 659, 662 (S.D.Tex. 2003); *Karaha* v. *Perusahaan*, US, 313 F.3d 70, 75–76 (2nd Cir. 2002); *World* v. *Kazakhstan*, US, 296 F.3d 1154, 1157–1158, 1167 (D.C.Cir. 2002); *BP* v. *Jiangsu*, US, 285 F.3d 677, 682 (8th Cir. 2002); *Raccoon* v. *Navoi*, US, 244 F.Supp.2d 1130, 1137–1138 (D. Colo. 2002); *US Titan* v. *Guangzhou*, US, 241 F.3d 135, 150 (2nd Cir. 2001); affirming *US Titan* v. *Guangzhou*, US, 16 F.Supp.2d 326, 333 (S.D.N.Y. 1998); *Abrams* v. *Société*, US, 175 F.Supp.2d 423 (E.D.N.Y. 2001); vacated and remanded, *Abrams* v. *Société*, US, 332 F.3d 173 (2nd Cir. 2003); vacated and remanded, *Société* v. *Abrams*, US, 124 S.Ct. 2834 (2004); 542 US 901 (2004); affirmed, *Abrams* v. *Société*, US, 389 F.3d 61 (2nd Cir. 2004); *Space Systems*, US, 164 F.Supp.2d 397, 401 (S.D.N.Y. 2001); *LNC* v. *Nicaragua*, US, 115 F.Supp.2d 358, 364 (S.D.N.Y. 2000); affirmed, *LNC* v. *Banco*, US, 228 F.3d 423 (2nd Cir. 2000); *In re Tamimi*, US, 176 F.3d 274, 278 (4th Cir. 1999); *Enron* v. *Titan*, US, 82 F.Supp.2d 602, 606–607 (W.D.La. 1999); *HSMV* v. *ADI*, US, 72 F.Supp.2d 1122, 1126 (C.D.Cal 1999); *First City* v. *Rafidain*, US, 150 F.3d 172, 174 (2nd Cir. 1998); *Mendenhall* v. *Saudi*, US, 991 F.Supp. 856, 857–858 (S.D.Tex. 1998); *Doty* v. *Magnum*, US, 994 F.Supp. 894, 896–897 (N.D.Ohio 1997); *Elliott* v. *British*, US, 986 F.Supp. 189, 190, 192 (S.D.

N.Y. 1997); *Good* v. *Aramco*, US, 971 F.Supp. 254, 256 (S.D.Tex. 1997); *Los Angeles* v. *Conus*, US, 969 F.Supp. 579, 585 (C.D.Cal. 1997); *Randolph* v. *Budget*, US, 97 F.3d 319, 324 (9th Cir. 1996); reversing on other grounds *Randolph* v. *Budget*, US, 878 F.Supp. 162, 164 (C.D.Cal. 1995); *Brink's* v. *South African*, US, 93 F.3d 1022, 1026, fn. 4 (2nd Cir. 1996); *Seramur* v. *Saudi*, US, 934 F.Supp. 48, 51 (E. D.N.Y. 1996); *Bryks* v. *Canadian*, US, 906 F.Supp. 204, 206 (S.D.N.Y. 1995); *Coleman* v. *Alcolac*, US, 888 F.Supp. 1388, 1400 (S.D.Tex. 1995); *Commercial* v. *Rafidain*, US, 15 F.3d 238, 239 (2nd Cir. 1994); 107 ILR 261; *NYSA-ILA* v. *Garuda*, US, 7 F.3d 35, 38 (2nd Cir. 1993); *Vermeulen* v. *Renault*, US, 985 F.2d 1534, 1537, 1542 (11th Cir. 1993); *S & S* v. *Masinexportimport*, US, 802 F.Supp. 1109, 1110 (S.D.N.Y. 1992); 107 ILR 239; *Bahsoon* v. *Pezetel*, US, 768 F.Supp. 507, 511 (E.D.N.C. 1991); *Forsythe* v. *Saudi*, US, 885 F.2d 285, 287, fn. 1 (5th Cir. 1989); *Hester* v. *Nigeria*, US, 879 F.2d 170, 176, fn. 5 (5th Cir. 1989); 90 ILR 604; *America* v. *GPA*, US, 877 F.2d 793, 796 (9th Cir. 1989); 92 ILR 454; *Branko* v. *Saudi*, US, 704 F.Supp. 386, 387 (S.D. N.Y. 1989); affirmed, *Branko* v. *Saudi*, US, 880 F.2d 1318 (2nd Cir. 1989) (Table); *Compania* v. *US District*, US, 859 F.2d 1354, 1359 (9th Cir. 1988); 98 ILR 69; *Gadsby* v. *Romania*, US, 698 F.Supp. 483, 485 (S.D.N.Y. 1988); *Campbell* v. *Canadian*, US, 684 F.Supp. 14, 15 (D.Me. 1988); *Ferrostaal* v. *SS*, US, 652 F.Supp. 420, 422 (S.D. N.Y. 1987); *Bailey* v. *Grand*, US, 805 F.2d 1097, 1100–1101 (2nd Cir. 1986); *Colonial* v. *Compagnie*, US, 645 F.Supp. 1457, 1459 (S.D.N.Y. 1986); 98 ILR 26; *Arango* v. *Guzman*, US, 761 F.2d 1527, 1529, 1532–1533 (11th Cir. 1985); *Castillo* v. *Shipping*, US, 606 F.Supp. 497, 500 and fn. 4 (S.D.N.Y. 1985); *Exchange* v. *Empresa*, US, 595 F.Supp. 502, 503–504 (S.D.N.Y. 1984); *Banque* v. *Banco*, US, 583 F.Supp. 320, 321 (S.D.N.Y. 1984); 92 ILR 399; *S & S* v. *Masinexportimport*, US, 706 F.2d 411, 414–415 (2nd Cir. 1983); 72 ILR 183; *Goar* v. *Compania*, US, 688 F.2d 417, 419, 421 (5th Cir. 1982); *Rio Grande*, US, 516 F.Supp. 1155, 1158 (S.D.N.Y. 1981); 63 ILR 604; *Sugarman* v. *Aeromexico*, US, 626 F.2d 270, 271 (3rd Cir. 1980); 63 ILR 446; *Arango* v. *Guzman*, US, 621 F.2d 1371, 1374 (5th Cir. 1980); 63 ILR 467; *Corporacion* v. *Vintero*, US, 477 F.Supp. 615, 619 (S.D.N.Y. 1979); 63 ILR 299.

61 *Gupta* v. *Thai*, US, 487 F.3d 759, 761, fn. 2, 767 (9th Cir. 2007); *Telcordia* v. *Telkom*, US, 458 F.3d 172, 175, fn. 4 (3rd Cir. 2006); *TermoRio* v. *Electrificadora*, US, 421 F.Supp.2d 87, 89 (D.D.C. 2006); affirmed, *TermoRio* v. *Electranta*, US, 487 F.3d 928, 930 (D.C.Cir. 2007); *Commonwealth* v. *Bulgartabac*, US, 360 F.Supp.2d 791, 794 (E.D.Va. 2005); *Concesionaria* v. *International*, US, 307 F.Supp.2d 553, 558, fn. 2 (S.D.N.Y. 2004); *Bayer* v. *Gambia*, US, 283 F.Supp.2d 1, 4 (D.D.C. 2003); *Chukwu* v. *Air France*, US, 218 F.Supp.2d 979, 983–984 (N.D.Ill. 2002); *Saudi* v. *Exxonmobil*, US, 194 F.Supp.2d 378, 384, 401 (D.N.J. 2002); *Kern* v. *Oesterreichische*, US, 178 F.Supp.2d 367, 373 (S.D.N.Y. 2001); *Venus* v. *CVG*, US, 210 F.3d 1309, 1311 (11th Cir. 2000); *Abbott* v. *A-Best*, US, 122 F.Supp.2d 688, 690 (N.D.W.V. 2000); *Brenntag* v. *Norddeutsche* US, 9 F.Supp.2d 331, 333, fn. 1 (S.D.N.Y. 1998); *Nazarian* v. *Compagnie*, US, 989 F.Supp. 504, 507 (S.D.N.Y. 1998); *Koirala* v. *Thai*, US, 126 F.3d 1205, 1208, fn. 2 (9th Cir. 1997); *Seisay* v. *Air France*, US, 1997 WL 431084, p. 4 (S.D.N.Y. 1997); *Diaz-Aguasviva* v. *Iberia*, US, 902 F.Supp. 314, 316 (D.P.R. 1995); *Nationsbank* v. *Banco*, US, 867 F.Supp. 167, 174 (S.D.N.Y. 1994); *Zveiter* v. *Brazilian*, US, 833 F.Supp. 1089, 1091–1092 (S.D.N.Y. 1993); *Kao* v. *China*, US, 816

606   NOTES TO PAGE 245

F.Supp. 910, 914 (S.D.N.Y. 1993); *Carnival* v. *Oy*, US, 159 B.R. 984, 1000 (S.D.Fla. 1993); *In re Surinam*, US, 974 F.2d 1255, 1258 (11th Cir. 1992); *Santos* v. *Compagnie*, US, 934 F.2d 890, 891 (7th Cir. 1991); 98 ILR 131; *Schoenberg* v. *Exportadora*, US, 930 F.2d 777, 778, 779, fn. 1 (9th Cir. 1991); 98 ILR 118; *Darby* v. *Compagnie*, US, 769 F.Supp. 1255, 1265 (S.D.N.Y. 1991); *Chuidian* v. *Philippine*, US, 912 F.2d 1095, 1098 (9th Cir. 1990); 92 ILR 480; *Cimino* v. *Raymark*, US, 751 F.Supp. 649, 659 (E.D.Tex. 1990); *Atwood* v. *Petroleo*, US, 875 F.2d 1174, 1176 (5th Cir. 1989); *Kramer* v. *Boeing*, US, 705 F.Supp. 1392, 1394 (D.Minn. 1989); *Burke* v. *Compagnie*, US, 699 F.Supp. 1016, 1019 (D.P.R. 1988); *Tote* v. *Iberia*, US, 649 F.Supp. 41 (E.D.Pa. 1986); *Kalamazoo* v. *Provisional*, US, 616 F.Supp. 660, 664 (W.D.Mich. 1985); 90 ILR 596; *Keller* v. *Transportes*, US, 601 F.Supp. 787, 788 (D.D.C. 1985); *Exchange* v. *Empresa*, US, 595 F.Supp. 502, 503–504 (S.D.N.Y. 1984); *Lonon* v. *Companhia*, US, 85 F.R.D. 71, 72 (E.D.Pa. 1979); 63 ILR 329.

62 *Saudi Arabia* v. *Nelson*, US, 507 US 349, 356 (1993); 123 L.Ed.2d 47, 58; 100 ILR 544, 550; *Argentina* v. *Weltover*, US, 504 US 607, 612, fn. 1 (1992); 119 L.Ed.2d 394, 403; 100 ILR 509, 513; *Guirlando* v. *TC*, US, 602 F.3d 69, 72 (2nd Cir. 2010); *In re Potash*, US, 686 F.Supp.2d 816, 820 (N.D.Ill. 2010); *Freund* v. *France*, US, 592 F.Supp.2d 540 (S.D.N.Y. 2008); *Orient* v. *Bank*, US, 506 F.3d 980 (10th Cir. 2007); *Kensington* v. *Société*, US, 2006 WL 846351, p. 6 (S.D.N.Y. 2006); this point upheld in the reversing decision of *Kensington* v. *Itoua*, US, 505 F.3d 147, 154 (2nd Cir. 2007); *Poddar* v. *State*, US, 235 F.R.D. 592, 596 (S.D.N.Y. 2006); *In re Air Crash*, US, 392 F.Supp.2d 461, 467 (E.D.N.Y. 2005); *Malewicz* v. *Amsterdam*, US, 362 F.Supp.2d 298, 306 (D.D.C. 2005); *Ministry* v. *Cubic*, US, 385 F.3d 1206, 1218, fn. 13 (9th Cir. 2004); *Kato* v. *Ishihara*, US, 360 F.3d 106, 108, fn. 1 (2nd Cir. 2004); affirming *Kato* v. *Ishihara*, US, 239 F.Supp.2d 359, 362, fn. 2 (S.D.N.Y. 2002); *Peterson* v. *Saudi Arabia*, US, 332 F.Supp.2d 189, 198 (D.D.C. 2004); affirmed, *Peterson* v. *Saudi Arabia*, US, 416 F.3d 83 (D.C.Cir. 2005); *Reers* v. *Deutsche*, US, 320 F.Supp.2d 140, 147 (S.D.N.Y. 2004); *National* v. *BP*, US, 319 F.Supp.2d 352, 369–370 (S.D.N.Y. 2004); *World* v. *Kazakhstan*, US, 296 F.3d 1154, 1161, fn. 8 (D.C.Cir. 2002); *US Fidelity* v. *Braspetro*, US, 219 F.Supp.2d 403, 473 (S.D.N.Y. 2002); *Corzo* v. *Banco*, US, 243 F.3d 519, 521 (9th Cir. 2001); *Hansen* v. *Danish*, US, 147 F.Supp.2d 142, 149 (E.D.N.Y. 2001); *Empresa* v. *Culbro*, US, 123 F.Supp.2d 203, 212, fn. 6 (S.D.N.Y. 2000); *World* v. *Kazakhstan*, US, 116 F.Supp.2d 98, 102 (D.D.C. 2000); *Mukaddam* v. *Permanent*, US, 111 F.Supp.2d 457, 461–462 (S.D.N.Y. 2000); *Broadfield* v. *Ministry*, US, 99 F.Supp.2d 403, 406 (S.D.N.Y. 2000); *Moses* v. *Air Afrique*, US, 2000 WL 306853, p. 2 (E.D.N.Y. 2000); *Byrd* v. *Corporacion*, US, 182 F.3d 380, 388 (5th Cir. 1999); *Aquamar* v. *Del*, US, 179 F.3d 1279, 1290 (11th Cir. 1999); *Hanil* v. *PT*, US, 148 F.3d 127, 130 (2nd Cir. 1998); *Voest-Alpine* v. *Bank*, US, 142 F.3d 887, 890 (5th Cir. 1998); *Morgan* v. *Novokrivorogsky*, US, 57 F.Supp.2d 863, 869 (N.D.Cal. 1998); *Daly* v. *Castro*, US, 30 F.Supp.2d 407, 417 (S.D.N.Y. 1998); *Ortega* v. *Banco*, US, 17 F.Supp.2d 1340, 1342 (S.D.Fla. 1998); *Pravin* v. *Banco*, US, 9 F.Supp.2d 300, 301 (S.D.N.Y. 1998); *Millicom* v. *Costa Rica*, US, 995 F.Supp. 14, 18, fn. 5 (D.D.C. 1998); *Phaneuf* v. *Indonesia*, US, 106 F.3d 302, 306, fn. 1 (9th Cir. 1997); *Commercial* v. *Corporacion*, US, 980 F.Supp. 710, 712 (S.D.N.Y. 1997); *Aldy* v. *Valmet*, US, 74 F.3d 72, 75 (5th Cir. 1996); *Fidelity* v. *Philippine*, US,

921 F.Supp. 1113, 1117 (S.D.N.Y. 1996); *Bybee v. Oper*, US, 899 F.Supp. 1217, 1220 (S.D.N.Y. 1995); *ICC v. Industrial*, US, 886 F.Supp. 1, 1 (S.D.N.Y. 1995); *Reed v. Donau*, US, 866 F.Supp. 750, 754 (S.D.N.Y. 1994); *Drexel v. Committee*, US, 12 F.3d 317, 324 (2nd Cir. 1993); *Eaglet v. Banco*, US, 839 F.Supp. 232, 233 (S.D. N.Y. 1993); *Zveiter v. Brazilian*, US, 833 F.Supp. 1089, 1092 (S.D.N.Y. 1993); *Maizus v. Weldor*, US, 820 F.Supp. 101, 104 (S.D.N.Y. 1993); *Tennessee v. Continental*, US, 814 F.Supp. 1302, 1306 (M.D.La. 1993); *Gabay v. Mostazafan*, US, 151 F.R.D. 250, 252 (S.D.N.Y. 1993); 107 ILR 242; *S & S v. Masinexportimport*, US, 802 F.Supp. 1109, 1110 (S.D.N.Y. 1992); 107 ILR 239; *Stena v. Comision*, US, 923 F.2d 380, 386, fn. 7 (5th Cir. 1991); 103 ILR 433; *Casalino v. Ente*, US, 779 F.Supp. 338, 340 (S.D.N.Y. 1991); *Fickling v. Australia*, US, 775 F.Supp. 66, 68 (E.D.N.Y. 1991); 103 ILR 447; *America v. GPA*, US, 877 F.2d 793, 796 (9th Cir. 1989); 92 ILR 454; *Starrett v. Iberia*, US, 756 F.Supp. 292, 293 (S.D.Tex. 1989); *Bowers v. Transportes*, US, 719 F.Supp. 166, 168 (S.D.N.Y. 1989); *National v. Ashland*, US, 716 F.Supp. 268, 270 (S.D.Miss. 1989); *Robert v. Air France*, US, 712 F.Supp. 688, 689 (N.D.Ill. 1989); *Sudano v. Federal*, US, 699 F.Supp. 824, 826 (D.Haw. 1988); *Tifa v. Ghana*, US, 692 F.Supp. 393, 407 (D.N.J. 1988); *Goethe v. NLRB*, US, 685 F.Supp. 427, 428 (S.D.N.Y. 1988); *Four v. Turbomeca*, US, 677 F.Supp. 1096, 1098 (D.Colo. 1988); *Goethe House*, US, 288 NLRB 257, 260 (1988); *Barkanic v. General*, US, 822 F.2d 11, 12 (2nd Cir. 1987); 98 ILR 44; *West v. Multibanco*, US, 807 F.2d 820, 823 (9th Cir. 1987); 84 ILR 187; *Crimson v. Electronum*, US, 629 F.Supp. 903, 906 (S.D.N.Y. 1986); *Walpex v. Yacimientos*, US, 109 F.R.D. 692, 693 and fn. 2 (S.D.N.Y. 1986); *National v. DuBois*, US, 605 F.Supp. 1206, 1211 and fn. 18 (W.D.Pa. 1985); *Keller v. Transportes*, US, 601 F.Supp. 787, 788 (D.D.C. 1985); *Banque v. Banco*, US, 583 F.Supp. 320, 321 (S.D. N.Y. 1984); 92 ILR 399; *Wyle v. Bank*, US, 577 F.Supp. 1148, 1155 (N.D.Cal. 1983); *Libra v. Banco*, US, 676 F.2d 47, 49 (2nd Cir. 1982); 72 ILR 119; *In re Disaster*, US, 540 F.Supp. 1141, 1150 (D.D.C. 1982); *Alifieris v. American*, US, 523 F.Supp. 1189, 1190 (E.D.N.Y. 1981); *Chicago v. Iran*, US, 506 F.Supp. 981, 983 (N.D.Ill. 1980); 63 ILR 511; *Decor v. Nigeria*, US, 497 F.Supp. 893, 904 (S.D.N.Y. 1980); 63 ILR 480; *American v. Iran*, US, 493 F.Supp. 522, 523 (D.D.C. 1980); 63 ILR 452; *Behring v. Imperial*, US, 475 F.Supp. 383, 388 (D.N.J. 1979); 63 ILR 261.

63 See *Kensington v. Itoua*, US, 505 F.3d 147, 154 (2nd Cir. 2007); *Gupta v. Thai*, US, 487 F.3d 759, 761, fn. 2 (9th Cir. 2007); *Globe v. AO*, US, 376 F.3d 282, 285 (4th Cir. 2004); *In re Ski*, US, 198 F.Supp.2d 420, 423 (S.D.N.Y. 2002); *Saudi v. Exxonmobil*, US, 194 F.Supp.2d 378, 401 (D.N.J. 2002); *Kern v. Oesterreichische*, US, 178 F.Supp.2d 367, 373 (S.D.N.Y. 2001); *Alejandre v. Telefonica*, US, 183 F.3d 1277, 1283 (11th Cir. 1999); *Bank v. State Bank*, US, 46 F.Supp.2d 231, 234 (S.D.N. Y. 1999); *Hanil v. PT*, US, 148 F.3d 127, 130 (2nd Cir. 1998); *In re Air Crash*, US, 987 F.Supp. 975, 978 (E.D.Mich. 1997); *In re Air Crash*, US, 96 F.3d 932, 937 (7th Cir. 1996); affirming *In re Air Crash*, US, 909 F.Supp. 1083, 1097 (N.D.Ill. 1995); *Mangattu v. Ibn Hayyan*, US, 35 F.3d 205, 206–207 (5th Cir. 1994); *Kern v. Jeppesen*, US, 867 F.Supp. 525, 531 (S.D.Tex. 1994); *Wilk v. Creditanstalt*, US, 1993 WL 97259, p. 2 (S.D.N.Y. 1993); *America v. GPA*, US, 877 F.2d 793, 796 (9th Cir. 1989); 92 ILR 454; *Kramer v. Boeing*, US, 705 F.Supp. 1392, 1394

608 NOTES TO PAGES 247–249

(D.Minn. 1989); *In re Disaster*, US, 540 F.Supp. 1141, 1150 (D.D.C. 1982); *Sugarman* v. *Aeromexico*, US, 626 F.2d 270 (3rd Cir. 1980); 63 ILR 446.

64 *Trans Chemical*, US, 978 F.Supp. 266, 276–289; 290 (S.D.Tex. 1997); affirmed, *Trans Chemical* v. *China*, US, 161 F.3d 314, 319 (5th Cir. 1998). For a similar case concerning another Chinese State-owned corporation see *Richmark* v. *Timber*, US, 747 F.Supp. 1409, 1411–1412 (D.Or. 1990).

65 US House of Representatives, Report No. 94-1487, 1976, p. 15; 1976 USCCAN 6604, 6614. For cases see *Hyatt* v. *Stanton*, US, 945 F.Supp. 675, 681, 683–690 (S.D.N.Y. 1996); *Gates* v. *Victor*, US, 54 F.3d 1457, 1460 (9th Cir. 1995); 107 ILR 371; *Intercontinental* v. *De Gruyter*, US, 822 F.Supp. 662, 672 (C.D.Cal. 1993); *Bowers* v. *Transportes*, US, 719 F.Supp. 166, 170 (S.D.N.Y. 1989); *Unidyne* v. *Aerolineas*, US, 590 F.Supp. 398, 400 (E.D.Va. 1984).

66 *Segni* v. *Commercial*, US, 650 F.Supp. 1040, 1041–1042 (N.D.Ill. 1986).

67 *Transaero* v. *La Fuerza*, US, 30 F.3d 148, 152 (D.C.Cir. 1994); 107 ILR 308.

68 *Transaero* v. *La Fuerza*, US, 30 F.3d 148, 151–152 (D.C.Cir. 1994); 107 ILR 308.

69 *Transaero*, US, 30 F.3d 148, 153 (D.C.Cir. 1994); 107 ILR 308.

70 *Roeder* v. *Iran*, US, 333 F.3d 228, 234–235 (D.C.Cir. 2003). For the 'core functions' test see also *TMR* v. *State*, US, 411 F.3d 296, 300 (D.C.Cir. 2005); *Baumel* v. *Syria*, US, 550 F.Supp.2d 110, 113 (D.D.C. 2008); *Karaha* v. *Perusahaan*, US, 313 F.3d 70, 75 (2nd Cir. 2002); *Garb* v. *Poland*, US, 440 F.3d 579, 594 (2nd Cir. 2006); affirming *Garb* v. *Poland*, US, 207 F.Supp.2d 16, 35 (E.D.N.Y. 2002); *Compagnie* v. *Russian*, US, 361 F.3d 676, 688 (2nd Cir. 2004); *Velasco* v. *Indonesia*, US, 370 F.3d 392, 398 (4th Cir. 2004); *Magness* v. *Russian*, US, 247 F.3d 609, 613, fn. 7 (5th Cir. 2001).

71 See *Regier* v. *Iran*, US, 281 F.Supp.2d 87, 103 (D.D.C. 2003); *Dammarell* v. *Iran*, US, 281 F.Supp.2d 105, 201 (D.D.C. 2003); vacated on other grounds, *Dammarell* v. *Iran*, US, 404 F.Supp.2d 261, 274 (D.D.C. 2005); *Tracy* v. *Iran*, US, Civ. No. 01-2517, slip op. at 17 (D.D.C. 2003); *Letelier* v. *Chile*, US, District Court, 502 F.Supp. 259, 266–267 (D.D.C. 1980). But see *Kilburn* v. *Iran*, US, 277 F.Supp.2d 24, 44 (D. D.C. 2003). For pre-*Roeder* award of punitive damages see Chapter 5. For punitive damages being an unsuitable remedy in international law see Gray, *Judicial Remedies*, pp. 26–28; Wittich, Punitive Damages, pp. 667–675.

72 *Ministry of Defense of Iran* v. *Cubic*, US, 29 F.Supp.2d 1168 (S.D.Cal. 1998).

73 *Elahi* v. *Iran*, US, 124 F.Supp.2d 97, 114–115 (D.D.C. 2000).

74 *Ministry of Defense of Iran* v. *Cubic*, US, 236 F.Supp.2d 1140 (S.D.Cal. 2002).

75 *Ministry of Defense of Iran* v. *Cubic*, US, 385 F.3d 1206 (9th Cir. 2004).

76 *Ministry of Defense of Iran* v. *Elahi*, US, 546 US 450, 451–452 (2006); vacating and remanding *Ministry of Defense of Iran* v. *Cubic*, US, 236 F.Supp.2d 1140 (S.D.Cal. 2002) and *Ministry of Defense and Support of Iran* v. *Cubic*, US, 385 F.3d 1206 (9th Cir. 2004).

77 *Ministry of Defense of Iran* v. *Elahi*, US, 546 US 450, 453 (2006), citing *Transaero* v. *La Fuerza*, US, 30 F.3d 148, 153 (D.C.Cir. 1994); 107 ILR 308.

78 *Ministry of Defense of Iran* v. *Cubic*, US, 495 F.3d 1024, 1035 (9th Cir. 2007); reversed in respect of enforcement, *Ministry of Defense of Iran* v. *Elahi*, US, 129 S.Ct. 1732 (2009).

NOTES TO PAGES 249–253 609

79 See *Kelly* v. *Syria*, US, 213 F.3d 841, 847 (5th Cir. 2000); *Alpha* v. *Nippon*, US, 199 F.3d 1078, 1084 (9th Cir. 1999); *Supra* v. *McGonigle*, US, 955 F.Supp. 374, 378–379 (E.D.Pa. 1997).
80 *US Fidelity* v. *Braspetro*, US, 1999 WL 307666, pp. 5–6 (S.D.N.Y. 1999).
81 *US Fidelity* v. *Braspetro*, 1999 WL 307666, p. 8 (S.D.N.Y. 1999).
82 *US Fidelity* v. *Braspetro*, 1999 WL 307666, p. 9 (S.D.N.Y. 1999).
83 *US Fidelity* v. *Braspetro*, US, 1999 WL 307666, p. 11 (S.D.N.Y. 1999); affirmed, *US Fidelity* v. *Braspetro*, US, 199 F.3d 94 (2nd Cir. 1999); confirmed again, *US Fidelity* v. *Braspetro*, US, 219 F.Supp.2d 403, 473 (S.D.N.Y. 2002).
84 *Gates* v. *Victor*, US, 54 F.3d 1457, 1460–1461 (9th Cir. 1995); 107 ILR 371.
85 The court did paraphrase the legislative report as meaning 'that a "state trading company" and "an export association" can be "organs" of a foreign state': *Gates* v. *Victor*, US, 54 F.3d 1457, 1461 (9th Cir. 1995); 107 ILR 371.
86 *Gates* v. *Victor*, US, 54 F.3d 1457, 1462 (9th Cir. 1995); 107 ILR 371.
87 Petroleos Mexicanos (Pemex) controlled all petroleum production, manufacturing, transportation, distribution, and commercialization in Mexico from 1938 until 1992, when it was restructured by the Mexican Government to create four subsidiaries, each of which was responsible for a separate part of the Mexican petroleum business. One of the subsidiaries was Pemex-Refining: *Corporacion Mexicana* v. *Respect*, US, 89 F.3d 650, 654 (9th Cir. 1996). See also *Tubular* v. *Petroleos*, US, 977 F.2d 180 (5th Cir. 1992)
88 *Corporacion Mexicana* v. *Respect*, US, 89 F.3d 650, 654 (9th Cir. 1996) (emphases in the original); quoting *Gates* v. *Victor*, US, 54 F.3d 1457, 1461 (9th Cir. 1995); 107 ILR 371; reiterated in *EIE* v. *Long*, US, 322 F.3d 635, 639 (9th Cir. 2003).
89 *Mexicana*, 89 F.3d 650, 655 (9th Cir. 1996) (emphasis added).
90 *Mexicana*, 89 F.3d 650, 655 (9th Cir. 1996).
91 *Patrickson* v. *Dole*, US, 251 F.3d 795, 807 (9th Cir. 2001); affirmed for other reasons, *Dole* v. *Patrickson*, US, 538 US 468 (2003). Repeated in *EOTT* v. *Winterthur*, US, 257 F.3d 992, 997 (9th Cir. 2001); *EIE* v. *Long*, US, 322 F.3d 635, 640 (9th Cir. 2003) and *California* v. *NRG*, US, 391 F.3d 1011, 1026 (9th Cir. 2004). For parties and the underlying dispute in *EOTT* see *Enron* v. *Walbrook*, US, 132 F.3d 526 (9th Cir. 1997). The passage was quoted with approval in *USX* v. *Adriatic*, US, 345 F.3d 190, 206 (3rd Cir. 2003). See also *Alpha* v. *Nippon*, US, 199 F.3d 1078, 1084 (9th Cir. 1999).
92 *Intercontinental Dictionary Series* v. *De Gruyter*, US, 822 F.Supp. 662, 672 (C.D.Cal. 1993).
93 *Intercontinental Dictionary Series*, 822 F.Supp. 662, 673 (C.D.Cal. 1993).
94 *Supra Medical* v. *McGonigle*, US, 955 F.Supp. 374, 379 (E.D.Pa. 1997) (citing *Corporacion Mexicana*, 89 F.3d 650, 654–655). Quoted with approval in *Peninsula* v. *Hankook*, US, 476 F.3d 140, 143 (2nd Cir. 2007); *Filler* v. *Hanvit*, US, 378 F.3d 213, 217 (2nd Cir. 2004); *Murphy* v. *Korea*, US, 421 F.Supp.2d 627, 641 (S.D.N.Y. 2005); *In re Terrorist*, US, 392 F.Supp.2d 539, 552 (S.D.N.Y. 2005); *In re Terrorist*, US, 349 F.Supp.2d 765, 791 (S.D.N.Y. 2005); *US Fidelity* v. *Braspetro*, US, 1999 WL 307666, p. 5 (S.D.N.Y. 1999); *Glencore* v. *Chase*, US, 1998 WL 74294, p. 3 (S.D.N.Y. 1998).

610   NOTES TO PAGES 253-258

95 *Supra Medical* v. *McGonigle*, US, 955 F.Supp. 374, 379 (E.D.Pa. 1997).
96 *Alpha* v. *Nippon*, US, 199 F.3d 1078, 1084-1085 (9th Cir. 1999); withdrawn on other grounds *sub nom Alpha* v. *Nippon*, US, 237 F.3d 1007 (9th Cir. 2001).
97 *Kelly* v. *Syria*, US, 213 F.3d 841, 848-849 (5th Cir. 2000). Cf. *Ebrahim* v. *Shell*, US, 847 F.Supp. 65, 67 (S.D.Tex. 1994), where Al Furat was determined to be a Syrian agency or instrumentality.
98 *Kelly* v. *Syria*, US, 213 F.3d 841, 847 (5th Cir. 2000) (emphasis in the original). Both the *Supra* factors and the *Kelly* caveat were quoted with approval in *Board* v. *Nippon*, US, 478 F.3d 274, 279 (5th Cir. 2007); *USX* v. *Adriatic*, US, 345 F.3d 190, 206-207 (3rd Cir. 2003).
99 *Board of Regents* v. *Nippon*, US, 478 F.3d 274, 279-280 (5th Cir. 2007).
100 *Filler* v. *Hanvit*, US, 378 F.3d 213, 217 (2nd Cir. 2004); approving *Filler* v. *Hanvit*, US, 247 F.Supp.2d 425, 428 (S.D.N.Y. 2003).
101 *Filler* v. *Hanvit*, US, 378 F.3d 213, 217 (2nd Cir. 2004).
102 *Peninsula* v. *Hankook*, US, 476 F.3d 140, 143-144 (2nd Cir. 2007); affirming *Peninsula* v. *Hankook*, US, 2005 WL 3046284 (S.D.N.Y. 2005).
103 *Peninsula* v. *Hankook*, US, 476 F.3d 140, 142-143 (2nd Cir. 2007).
104 *Murphy* v. *Korea*, US, 421 F.Supp.2d 627, 640 (S.D.N.Y. 2005).
105 *Murphy*, 421 F.Supp.2d 627, 640 (S.D.N.Y. 2005), citing *EIE* v. *Long*, US, 322 F.3d 635, 640 (9th Cir. 2003).
106 *Murphy*, 421 F.Supp.2d 627, 641 (S.D.N.Y. 2005).
107 *USX* v. *Adriatic*, US, 345 F.3d 190, 207-208 (3rd Cir. 2003) (Emphases added). The Ninth Circuit likewise found its decision on 'organ' unaffected by *Dole Food*: *EIE* v. *Long*, US, 322 F.3d 635, 639, fn. 3 (9th Cir. 2003).
108 *USX* v. *Adriatic*, US, 345 F.3d 190, 208 (3rd Cir. 2003). See also *Shirobokova* v. *CSA*, US, 335 F.Supp.2d 989, 991 (D.Minn. 2004).
109 *USX* v. *Adriatic*, US, 345 F.3d 190, 209 (3rd Cir. 2003) (referring to *EOTT, Patrickson, Gates* and *Kelly*). The seven factors were quoted in *RSM* v. *Petroleos*, US, 338 F.Supp.2d 1208, 1215 (D.Colo. 2004), and were studiously adhered to in *URS* v. *Lebanese*, US, 512 F.Supp.2d 199, 211-215 (D.Del. 2007).
110 *USX* v. *Adriatic*, US, 345 F.3d 190, 209, fn. 17 (3rd Cir. 2003).
111 *USX*, 345 F.3d 190, 209-214 (3rd Cir. 2003).
112 *Murphy* v. *Korea*, US, 421 F.Supp.2d 627, 642-645 (S.D.N.Y. 2005).
113 *EIE* v. *Long*, US, 322 F.3d 635, 640-642, 642 (9th Cir. 2003); noted with approval in *USX*, 345 F.3d 190, 214-215 (3rd Cir. 2003).
114 See *In re Terrorist*, US, 392 F.Supp.2d 539, 552-553 (S.D.N.Y. 2005); *RSM* v. *Petroleos*, US, 338 F.Supp.2d 1208, 1215-1216 (D.Colo. 2004); *Siderman* v. *Argentina*, US, 965 F.2d 699, 712 (9th Cir. 1992); 103 ILR 454.
115 *Procter* v. *Viskoza-Loznica*, US, 33 F.Supp.2d 644, 654 (W.D.Tenn. 1998). See also *Corporacion Mexicana* v. *Respect*, US, 89 F.3d 650, 655 (9th Cir. 1996); *Gates* v. *Victor*, US, 54 F.3d 1457, 1460-1461 (9th Cir. 1995); 107 ILR 371; *Intercontinental* v. *De Gruyter*, US, 822 F.Supp. 662, 673 (C.D.Cal. 1993); *Rios* v. *Marshall*, US, 530 F.Supp. 351, 371 (S.D.N.Y. 1981); *Yessenin-Volpin* v. *Novosti*, US, 443 F.Supp. 849, 852-854 (S.D.N.Y. 1978); 63 ILR 127; *Edlow* v. *Nuklearna*, US, 441 F.Supp. 827, 832 (D.D.C. 1977); 63 ILR 100.

NOTES TO PAGES 258–262 611

116 *Patrickson* v. *Dole*, US, 251 F.3d 795, 808 (9th Cir. 2001); reaffirmed in *California* v. *NRG*, US, 391 F.3d 1011, 1026 (9th Cir. 2004).
117 See Yang, Together.
118 See Dellapenna, *Suing*, p. 88.
119 *Linton* v. *Airbus*, US, 794 F.Supp. 650, 652 (S.D.Tex. 1992) (emphasis added); quoted in *Gardiner* v. *Iberia*, US, 896 F.Supp. 125, 131 (S.D.N.Y. 1995) and *Mangattu* v. *Ibn Hayyan*, US, 35 F.3d 205, 208 (5th Cir. 1994).
120 Dellapenna, *Suing*, pp. 88–89.
121 *In re Air Crash*, US, 96 F.3d 932, 938 (7th Cir. 1996).
122 Dellapenna, *Suing*, p. 89.
123 Hardy, Wipe Away, 1153–1155.
124 *Linton* v. *Airbus*, US, 794 F.Supp. 650, 652–653 (S.D.Tex. 1992) (pooling was nevertheless disallowed in this case); appeal dismissed for lack of jurisdiction to review the appeal, *Linton* v. *Airbus*, US, 30 F.3d 592 (5th Cir. 1994).
125 *Linton* v. *Airbus*, US, 30 F.3d 592, 598, fn. 29 (5th Cir. 1994), citing *LeDonne* v. *Gulf*, US, 700 F.Supp. 1400, 1405–1406 (E.D.Va. 1988); *Rios* v. *Marshall*, US, 530 F.Supp. 351, 371 (S.D.N.Y. 1981); and *International* v. *OPEC*, US, 477 F.Supp. 553, 568–569 (C.D.Cal. 1979); 63 ILR 284; affirmed on other grounds, *International* v. *OPEC*, US, 649 F.2d 1354 (9th Cir. 1981); 66 ILR 413.
126 *LeDonne* v. *Gulf*, US, 700 F.Supp. 1400, 1406 (E.D.Va. 1988). See also *Rios* v. *Marshall*, US, 530 F.Supp. 351, 371 (S.D.N.Y. 1981); *International* v. *OPEC*, US, 477 F.Supp. 553, 568–569 (C.D.Cal. 1979); 63 ILR 284; *Aboujdid* v. *Singapore*, US, 18 Avi.Cas. (CCH) No. 18,059, No. 18,060 (N.Y.Sup.Ct. 1984); reversed in part on other grounds, *Aboujdid* v. *Singapore*, US, 67 N.Y.2d 450, 503 N.Y.S.2d 555, 494 N.E.2d 1055 (N.Y.Ct.App. 1986).
127 *Mangattu* v. *Ibn Hayyan*, US, 35 F.3d 205, 207–208 (5th Cir. 1994).
128 *Mangattu*, 35 F.3d 205, 208 (5th Cir. 1994). See also *Kern* v. *Jeppesen*, US, 867 F.Supp. 525, 530–531 (S.D.Tex. 1994) (Airbus Industries, jointly majority-owned by France and Spain (later by Germany as well)).
129 *In re Air Crash Disaster*, US, 96 F.3d 932, 938–939 (7th Cir. 1996); affirming *In re Air Crash Disaster*, US, 909 F.Supp. 1083, 1090–1097 (N.D.Ill. 1995).
130 *Dole Food* v. *Patrickson*, US, 538 US 468, 473–477 (2003).
131 *In re Air Crash Disaster*, US, 96 F.3d 932, 936 (7th Cir. 1996) (emphasis added), see also p. 938.
132 *In re Air Crash Disaster*, 96 F.3d 932, 935, 938 (7th Cir. 1996).
133 *In re Air Crash Disaster*, 96 F.3d 932, 938 (7th Cir. 1996) (emphasis added). For instances of 'suits against commercial entities controlled by foreign governments' the court cited *Arango* v. *Guzman*, US, 761 F.2d 1527, 1534 (11th Cir. 1985) and *Goar* v. *Compania*, US, 688 F.2d 417, 419, 421 (5th Cir. 1982), but the *Arango* case involved a suit against the Dominicana Airlines, the Dominican national airline wholly and *directly* owned by the Dominican Government; and the *Goar* case likewise involved Compania Peruana de Vapores, S.A. (CPV), a corporation wholly owned by Peru, and its insurer.
134 *Moses* v. *Air Afrique*, US, 2000 WL 306853, p. 2 (E.D.N.Y. 2000); *Ratnaswamy* v. *Air Afrique*, US, 1996 WL 507267, p. 3 (N.D.Ill. 1996).

612   NOTES TO PAGES 262–266

135 *Linton* v. *Airbus*, US, 794 F.Supp. 650, 652 (S.D.Tex. 1992). But cf. *Kern* v. *Jeppesen*, US, 867 F.Supp. 525, 530–531 (S.D.Tex. 1994), where Airbus Industrie was held to be a 'sovereign entity'. According to the *Kern* court, the *Linton* case had focused on the construction of Airbus in 1989, not 1977, when France owned 47.80 per cent and Spain 2.76 per cent of Airbus Industrie, or 1987, when Airbus Industrie was 37.88 per cent owned by France, 3.03 per cent by Spain and 16.97 per cent by Germany.

136 *Gardiner* v. *Iberia*, US, 896 F.Supp. 125, 131–132 (S.D.N.Y. 1995); *Sea* v. *Industries*, US, 411 F.Supp.2d 386, 392 (S.D.N.Y. 2006).

137 *LeDonne* v. *Gulf*, US, 700 F.Supp. 1400, 1406 (E.D.Va. 1988).

138 *Mangattu* v. *Ibn Hayyan*, US, 35 F.3d 205, 209 (5th Cir. 1994).

139 *LeDonne* v. *Gulf*, US, 700 F.Supp. 1400, 1406 (E.D.Va. 1988).

140 *Linton* v. *Airbus*, US, 794 F.Supp. 650, 652–653 (S.D.Tex. 1992).

141 *In re Air Crash Disaster*, US, 96 F.3d 932, 938 (7th Cir. 1996).

142 *In re Air Crash Disaster*, US, 96 F.3d 932, 937 (7th Cir. 1996); *Linton* v. *Airbus*, US, 794 F.Supp. 650, 652–653 (S.D.Tex. 1992); appeal dismissed, *Linton* v. *Airbus*, US, 30 F.3d 592 (5th Cir. 1994). See also *LeDonne* v. *Gulf*, US, 700 F.Supp. 1400, 1405 (E.D.Va. 1988); *Gardiner* v. *Iberia*, US, 896 F.Supp. 125, 129 (S.D.N.Y. 1995). For scholarly comments see Dellapenna, *Suing*, pp. 88–90; Hardy, Wipe Away, 1152–1155.

143 For cases disallowing pooling see *Linton* v. *Airbus*, US, 794 F.Supp. 650, 652 (S.D. Tex. 1992); *Gardiner* v. *Iberia*, US, 896 F.Supp. 125, 131–132 (S.D.N.Y. 1995); *Sea* v. *Industries*, US, 411 F.Supp.2d 386, 392 (S.D.N.Y. 2006).

144 *Parex* v. *Russian*, US, 81 F.Supp.2d 506, 507 (S.D.N.Y. 2000).

145 *Gates* v. *Victor*, US, 54 F.3d 1457, 1462 (9th Cir. 1995); 107 ILR 371; quoted in *Gardiner* v. *Iberia*, US, 896 F.Supp. 125, 130 (S.D.N.Y. 1995). For policy considerations against tiering, see Hardy, Wipe Away, 1128–1152 and Hoffman, The Separate, 569–571. See also Dellapenna, *Suing*, pp. 83–88; Yang, A State-owned; Griggs, The Foreign. Contrast Harjani, Litigating, 185–187.

146 *Aluminum Distributors* v. *Gulf*, US, 1989 WL 64174, p. 1 (N.D.Ill. 1989).

147 *Aluminum Distributors*, 1989 WL 64174, p. 2 (N.D.Ill. 1989).

148 *Aluminum Distributors*, 1989 WL 64174, p. 1 (N.D.Ill. 1989).

149 This seems to be the understanding of the *Linton* court when it commented that: 'In [*Aluminum Distributors*] more than 50% of the defendant's shares were owned by entities *which were themselves foreign states*.' *Linton* v. *Airbus*, US, 794 F.Supp. 650, 653, fn. 5 (S.D.Tex. 1992) (emphasis in the original). For a similar case to *Aluminum Distributors* see *Crédit* v. *Getty*, US, 876 F.Supp. 517, 519–520 (S.D.N.Y. 1995) (allowing both pooling and tiering and holding that Crédit Lyonnais, 48.5 per cent owned by the French State and 8.67 per cent owned by another French corporation 99.97 per cent owned by France, was a 'foreign State').

150 *In re Air Crash Disaster*, US, 96 F.3d 932, 939 (7th Cir. 1996) (emphases in the original); affirming and quoting *In re Air Crash Disaster*, US, 909 F.Supp. 1083, 1093–1094 (N.D.Ill. 1995). Also variously called the 'infinite looping': *Millicom* v. *Costa Rica*, US, 995 F.Supp. 14, 18, fn. 5 (D.D.C. 1998); the 'transitive' theory:

NOTES TO PAGES 266–268   613

Filler v. *Hanvit*, US, 378 F.3d 213, 218 (2nd Cir. 2004); or the 'linguistic argument': *Musopole* v. *South*, US, 172 F.Supp.2d 443, 445 (S.D.N.Y. 2001). For the looping theory see also *Bank* v. *NBM*, US, 2002 WL 1072235, 3 (S.D.N.Y. 2002); *Lehman* v. *Minmetals*, US, 169 F.Supp.2d 186, 190 (S.D.N.Y. 2001); *Parex* v. *Russian*, US, 81 F.Supp.2d 506, 507 (S.D.N.Y. 2000).

151 *Ocasek* v. *Flintkote Co*, US, 796 F.Supp. 362, 365 (N.D.Ill. 1992).

152 See, e.g., *Kensington* v. *Itoua*, US, 505 F.3d 147, 154 (2nd Cir. 2007); *Gupta* v. *Thai*, US, 487 F.3d 759, 761, fn.2 (9th Cir. 2007); *Globe* v. *AO*, US, 376 F.3d 282, 285, (4th Cir. 2004); *In re Air Crash Disaster*, US, 96 F.3d 932, 937 (7th Cir. 1996); affirming *In re Air Crash Disaster*, US, 909 F.Supp. 1083, 1097 (N.D.Ill. 1995); *Mangattu* v. *Ibn Hayyan*, US, 35 F.3d 205, 206–207, (5th Cir. 1994); *Saudi* v. *Exxonmobil*, US, 194 F.Supp.2d 378, 401 (D.N.J. 2002); *Kern* v. *Oesterreichische*, US, 178 F.Supp.2d 367, 373 (S.D.N.Y. 2001); *Crédit* v. *Getty*, US, 876 F.Supp. 517, 519–520 (S.D.N.Y. 1995); *Aluminum Distributors* v. *Gulf*, US, 1989 WL 64174, p. 2 (N.D.Ill. 1989).

153 *In re Air Crash Disaster*, US, 96 F.3d 932, 935–936 (7th Cir. 1996). The court had to draw a diagram of the complicated ownership patterns as between the various intermediaries, see p. 948 Appendix A.

154 *In re Air Crash Disaster*, US, 96 F.3d 932, 941 (7th Cir. 1996); affirming *In re Air Crash Disaster*, US, 909 F.Supp. 1083, 1090–1097 (N.D.Ill. 1995).

155 *Gates* v. *Victor*, US, 54 F.3d 1457, 1462–1463 (9th Cir. 1995); 107 ILR 371. The Ninth Circuit reaffirmed this position in *EOTT* v. *Winterthur*, US, 257 F.3d 992, 997 (9th Cir. 2001); *Patrickson* v. *Dole*, US, 251 F.3d 795, 805 (9th Cir. 2001) and *Corporacion* v. *Respect*, US, 89 F.3d 650, 655 (9th Cir. 1996). But the Seventh Circuit disagreed. See *In re Air Crash Disaster*, US, 96 F.3d 932, 939–941 (7th Cir. 1996).

156 See *Patrickson* v. *Dole*, US, 251 F.3d 795, 806–807 (9th Cir. 2001); *Corporacion* v. *Respect*, US, 89 F.3d 650, 655 (9th Cir. 1996).

157 *Jackson* v. *Resolution*, US, 136 F.3d 1130, 1132 (7th Cir. 1998); *In re Air Crash Disaster*, US, 96 F.3d 932, 941 (7th Cir. 1996); affirming *In re Air Crash Disaster*, US, 909 F.Supp. 1083, 1090–1097 (N.D.Ill. 1995); *Allendale* v. *Bull*, US, 10 F.3d 425, 426–427 (7th Cir. 1993); *State* v. *NLRB*, US, 808 F.2d 526, 530, 535 (7th Cir. 1986).

158 *World* v. *Nammo*, US, 51 Fed.Appx. 403, 404–405 (4th Cir. 2002); *Alejandre* v. *Telefonica*, US, 183 F.3d 1277, 1283 (11th Cir. 1999); vacating but on this point agreeing with *Alejandre* v. *Cuba*, US, 42 F.Supp.2d 1317 (S.D.Fla. 1999); *Antoine* v. *Atlas*, US, 66 F.3d 105, 109 (6th Cir. 1995); *Trump* v. *Costruzioni*, US, 958 F.2d 365 (3rd Cir. 1992) (Table); affirming *Trump* v. *Costruzioni*, US, 761 F.Supp. 1143, 1149–1150 (D.N.J. 1991); *JJ* v. *Rhone*, US, 863 F.2d 315, 317 (4th Cir. 1988); *Gould* v. *Pechiney*, US, 853 F.2d 445, 450 (6th Cir. 1988); 98 ILR 136; *ONE* v. *Flota*, US, 830 F.2d 449, 450 (2nd Cir. 1987); *O'Connell* v. *Americana*, US, 734 F.2d 115, 116–117 (2nd Cir. 1984); 81 ILR 539; affirming *O'Connell* v. *Americana*, US, 566 F.Supp. 1381 (S.D.N.Y. 1983); *Gilson* v. *Ireland*, US, 682 F.2d 1022, 1026 (D.C.Cir. 1982); 92 ILR 374.

159 See *Straub* v. *AP*, US, 38 F.3d 448, 451 (9th Cir. 1994); 107 ILR 359; *America* v. *GPA*, US, 877 F.2d 793, 796–800 (9th Cir. 1989); 92 ILR 454.

614 NOTES TO PAGES 268–271

160 For cases permitting tiering see *Musopole* v. *South*, US, 172 F.Supp.2d 443, 445–447 (S.D.N.Y. 2001); *Lehman* v. *Minmetals*, US, 169 F.Supp.2d 186, 190–191 (S.D.N.Y. 2001); *Parex* v. *Russian*, US, 81 F.Supp.2d 506 (S.D.N.Y. 2000); *In re Clearsky*, US, 1999 WL 1021825, pp. 3–5 (E.D.La. 1999); *US Fidelity* v. *Braspetro*, US, 1999 WL 307666, pp. 8–11 (S.D.N.Y. 1999); *Daly* v. *Castro*, US, 30 F.Supp.2d 407, 415–417 (S.D.N.Y. 1998); *Millicom* v. *Costa Rica*, US, 995 F.Supp. 14, 18, fn. 5 (D.D.C. 1998); *Mann* v. *Hanil*, US, 900 F.Supp. 1077, 1084, fn. 2 (E.D.Wis. 1995); *Crédit* v. *Getty*, US, 876 F.Supp. 517, 519–520 (S.D.N.Y. 1995); *New York* v. *State Bank*, US, 1994 WL 369406, p. 2 (S.D.N.Y. 1994); *Talbot* v. *Saipem*, US, 835 F.Supp. 352, 353 and fn. 2 (S.D.Tex. 1993); *Borgships* v. *Macarena*, US, 1993 WL 278453, p. 3 (E.D.La. 1993); *Ocasek* v. *Flintkote*, US, 796 F.Supp. 362, 365 (N.D.Ill. 1992); *Trump* v. *Costruzioni*, US, 761 F.Supp. 1143, 1149–1150 (D.N.J. 1991); affirmed, *Trump* v. *Costruzioni*, US, 958 F.2d 365 (3rd Cir. 1992) (Table); *Rutkowski* v. *Occidental*, US, 1988 WL 107342, p. 1 (N.D.Ill. 1988); *Ford* v. *Johns-Manville*, US, 662 F.Supp. 930, 934 (S.D.Ind. 1987); *Great* v. *Alsthom*, US, 1987 WL 4766, p. 3 (E.D.La. 1987). For cases disallowing tiering see *Sea* v. *Industries*, US, 411 F.Supp.2d 386, 392 (S.D.N.Y. 2006); *In re Ski*, US, 198 F.Supp.2d 420, 424–427 (S.D.N.Y. 2002); *Bank* v. *NBM*, US, 2002 WL 1072235, p. 6 (S.D.N.Y. 2002); *Dewhurst* v. *Telenor*, US, 83 F.Supp.2d 577, 592–595 (D.Md. 2000); *Southern* v. *Holt*, US, 1997 WL 539763, p. 5 and fn. 9 (E.D.Pa. 1997); *Hyatt* v. *Stanton*, US, 945 F.Supp. 675, 685–690 (S.D.N.Y. 1996); *Martinez* v. *Dow*, US, 1996 WL 502461, p. 2 (E.D.La. 1996); *Gardiner* v. *Iberia*, US, 896 F.Supp. 125, 130–131 (S.D. N.Y. 1995).
161 *Delgado* v. *Shell*, US, 231 F.3d 165, 175 (5th Cir. 2000).
162 *Delgado* v. *Shell*, US, 231 F.3d 165, 176 (5th Cir. 2000); affirming *Delgado* v. *Shell*, US, 890 F.Supp. 1315, 1319 (S.D.Tex. 1994). See also *Kelly* v. *Syria*, US, 213 F.3d 841, 848–849 (5th Cir. 2000); *Linton* v. *Airbus*, 30 F.3d 592, 598, fn. 29 (5th Cir. 1994); affirming *Linton* v. *Airbus*, US, 794 F.Supp. 650 (S.D.Tex. 1992). But cf. *Kern* v. *Jeppesen*, US, 867 F.Supp. 525, 530–531 (S.D.Tex. 1994).
163 *Patrickson* v. *Dole*, US, 251 F.3d 795, 808 (9th Cir. 2001).
164 *Dole Food* v. *Patrickson*, US, 538 US 468, 471 (2003).
165 *Dole Food* v. *Patrickson*, US, 538 US 468, 473 (2003); affirming *Patrickson* v. *Dole Food*, US, 251 F.3d 795, 806–808 (9th Cir. 2001).
166 *Dole Food* v. *Patrickson*, US, 538 US 468, 473–474 (2003).
167 *Dole Food*, 538 US 468, 474 (2003).
168 *Dole Food*, 538 US 468, 474 (2003) (emphasis added). See also *California* v. *NRG*, US, 391 F.3d 1011, 1026 (9th Cir. 2004).
169 *Dole Food*, 538 US 468, 474 (2003).
170 *Dole Food*, 538 US 468, 475 (2003).
171 *Dole Food*, 538 US 468, 475 (2003).
172 *Dole Food*, 538 US 468, 477 (2003); affirming *Patrickson* v. *Dole Food*, US, 251 F.3d 795, 806–808 (9th Cir. 2001). For pre-*Dole Food* comments against tiering see Loewenstein, The Foreign, 353; Shaul, Tiered, 1820; Hardy, Wipe Away, 1124; Hoffman, The Separate, 569–571. For opinion critical of *Dole Food* see Lang and Bales, The Immunity. In *Reers*, a district court held that 'mere

NOTES TO PAGES 271–273   615

departments' – as opposed to 'subsidiaries' – of a foreign State instrumentality (in this case Deutsche Bahn, the nationally owned rail operator of Germany) shared the immunity of that instrumentality, an issue, in the opinion of the court, not addressed by *Dole Food*. *Reers* v. *Deutsche*, US, 320 F.Supp.2d 140, 151 (S.D.N.Y. 2004).

173 For the impact of *Dole Food* on *Delgado* see *Delgado* v. *Shell*, US, 322 F.Supp.2d 798, 802–803, 816 (S.D.Tex. 2004).

174 *Filler* v. *Hanvit*, US, 378 F.3d 213, 218 (2nd Cir. 2004).

175 *Filler*, 378 F.3d 213, 218 (2nd Cir. 2004) (emphasis in the original).

176 *Filler*, 378 F.3d 213, 219 (2nd Cir. 2004) (emphases in the original); affirming *Filler* v. *Hanvit*, US, 2003 WL 21729978, 2003 U.S.Dist.Lexis 12836 (S.D.N.Y. 2003) and *Baker* v. *Hanvit*, US, 2003 WL 21729962, 2003 U.S.Dist.Lexis 12837 (S.D.N.Y. 2003), which revised and vacated *Filler* v. *Hanvit*, US, 247 F.Supp.2d 425, 429 (S.D.N.Y. 2003). See also *Murphy* v. *Korea*, US, 421 F.Supp.2d 627, 640, fn. 12 (S.D.N.Y. 2005); *In re Terrorist*, US, 349 F.Supp.2d 765, 790 (S.D.N.Y. 2005); *Allen* v. *Russian*, US, 522 F.Supp.2d 167, 184–185 (D.D.C. 2007); *Ocean* v. *China*, US, 578 F.Supp.2d 621, 625–627 (S.D.N.Y. 2008).

177 *Dole Food* v. *Patrickson*, US, 538 US 468, 471 (2003).

178 *Dole Food*, 538 US 468, 478 (2003), citing *Keene* v. *US*, US, 508 US 200, 207 (1993); affirming *Patrickson* v. *Dole Food*, US, 251 F.3d 795, 806 (9th Cir. 2001). For cases following this see *USX* v. *Adriatic*, US, 345 F.3d 190, 208, fn. 16 (3rd Cir. 2003). See also *Telcordia* v. *Telkom*, US, 458 F.3d 172, 175, fn. 4 (3rd Cir. 2006). Before *Dole Food* there was confusion over the temporal dimension of the instrumentality status. Some courts thought that the status should be determined at the time of suit: *In re Ski*, US, 198 F.Supp.2d 420, 422, fn. 2 (S.D. N.Y. 2002); *Straub* v. *AP*, US, 38 F.3d 448, 451 (9th Cir. 1994); 107 ILR 359; *Jones* v. *Petty-Ray*, US, 954 F.2d 1061, 1065 (5th Cir. 1992); *Ocasek* v. *Flintkote*, US, 796 F.Supp. 362, 365 (N.D.Ill. 1992); *West* v. *Multibanco*, US, 807 F.2d 820, 823 (9th Cir. 1987); 84 ILR 187; *Morgan* v. *Palau*, US, 639 F.Supp. 706, 712 (S.D.N.Y. 1986); 87 ILR 590; vacated on other grounds, *Morgan* v. *Palau*, US, 924 F.2d 1237, 1245 (2nd Cir. 1991); 87 ILR 590; *Wolf* v. *Banco*, US, 739 F.2d 1458, 1460 (9th Cir. 1984); 92 ILR 413. Other courts opined that the proper time for the determination should be the time of the alleged wrongdoing: *Pere* v. *Nuovo*, US, 150 F.3d 477, 480–481 (5th Cir. 1998); *Trans Chemical*, US, 978 F.Supp. 266, 277 (S.D.Tex. 1997); affirmed, *Trans Chemical* v. *China*, US, 161 F.3d 314, 319 (5th Cir. 1998); *In re Aircrash*, US, 987 F.Supp. 975, 978 (E.D.Mich. 1997); *Delgado* v. *Shell*, US, 890 F.Supp. 1324, 1340, fn. 33 (S.D.Tex. 1995); *Kern* v. *Jeppesen*, US, 867 F.Supp. 525, 530–531 (S.D.Tex. 1994); *General* v. *Grossman*, US, 991 F.2d 1376, 1381–1382 (8th Cir. 1993); *Gould* v. *Pechiney*, US, 853 F.2d 445, 450 (6th Cir. 1988); 98 ILR 136. Still others assumed an ambiguous position: *Belgrade* v. *Sidex*, US, 2 F.Supp.2d 407, 414 (S.D.N.Y. 1998); *Gardiner* v. *Iberia*, US, 896 F.Supp. 125, 129–130 (S.D.N.Y. 1995); *Cargill* v. *Pavel Dybenko*, US, 991 F.2d 1012, 1115–1116 (2nd Cir. 1993); 103 ILR 572; *In re Chase*, US, 835 F.2d 1341, 1347–1348 (11th Cir. 1988); reversed on other grounds, *Granfinanciera* v. *Nordberg*, US, 492 US 33 (1989); *LeDonne* v. *Gulf*, US, 700 F.Supp. 1400, 1406

616 NOTES TO PAGES 273-274

(E.D.Va. 1988). For discussion of the issue of timing see also Dellapenna, *Suing*, pp. 90–95; Narver, Putting; Simmons, Nationalized. However, in *Altmann*, the district court relied on the time when the relevant events occurred: *Altmann* v. *Austria*, US, 142 F.Supp.2d 1187, 1204 (C.D.Cal. 2001). Neither the Court of Appeals nor the Supreme Court voiced any objection.

179 *Dole Food* v. *Patrickson*, US, 538 US 468, 480 (2003).

180 The Canadian courts face the same issues owing to the similarity of the Canadian provision on State entities. See *Croteau* v. *USA*, Canada, [2005] OJ No. 6222; reversed, *Croteau* v. *USA*, Canada, [2006] OJ No. 158 (service of process).

181 *Granfinanciera* v. *Nordberg*, US, 492 US 33, 38–39 (1989); *Olympia* v. *Linee*, US, 437 F.Supp.2d 780 (N.D.Ill. 2006); petition denied, *In re Linee*, US, 469 F.3d 638 (7th Cir. 2006); *Bank* v. *NBM*, US, 2002 WL 1072235 (S.D.N.Y. 2002); *Lehman* v. *Minmetals*, US, 169 F.Supp.2d 186 (S.D.N.Y. 2001); *In re Air Crash*, US, 96 F.3d 932, 943–947 (7th Cir. 1996); affirming *In re Air Crash*, US, 909 F.Supp. 1083, 1104–1114 (N.D.Ill. 1995); *Gould* v. *Aerospatiale*, US, 40 F.3d 1033, 1034 (9th Cir. 1994); *Cimino* v. *Raymark*, US, 751 F.Supp. 649, 659 (E.D.Tex. 1990); *Aluminum* v. *Gulf*, US, 1989 WL 64174 (N.D.Ill. 1989); *Burke* v. *Compagnie*, US, 699 F.Supp. 1016, 1019 (D.P.R. 1988); *Campbell* v. *Canadian*, US, 684 F.Supp. 14, 15 (D.Me. 1988); *Bailey* v. *Grand*, US, 805 F.2d 1097, 1100–1101 (2nd Cir. 1986); *Arango* v. *Guzman*, US, 761 F.2d 1527 (11th Cir. 1985); *Goar* v. *Compania*, US, 688 F.2d 417 (5th Cir. 1982); affirming *Goar* v. *Compania*, US, 510 F.Supp. 737 (E.D.La. 1981); *Rex* v. *Compania*, US, 660 F.2d 61 (3rd Cir. 1981); 72 ILR 93; reversing and remanding *Rex* v. *Compania*, US, 493 F.Supp. 459 (E.D.Pa. 1980); 63 ILR 435; *Williams* v. *Shipping*, US, 653 F.2d 875 (4th Cir. 1981); 63 ILR 639; *Ruggiero* v. *Compania*, US, 639 F.2d 872 (2nd Cir. 1981); 63 ILR 540; *Lonon* v. *Companhia*, US, 85 F.R.D. 71 (E.D.Pa. 1979); 63 ILR 329. It has been noted that the jurisdiction under FSIA is 'original but not exclusive': *In re Air Crash*, US, 96 F.3d 932, 936 (7th Cir. 1996). See also Groobey, The Foreign; New York Bar Association, A Foreign-State; Abir, Foreign.

182 *Ecuador* v. *ChevronTexaco*, US, 376 F.Supp.2d 334, 346 (S.D.N.Y. 2005); *EOTT* v. *Winterthur*, US, 257 F.3d 992, 996–997 (9th Cir. 2001); *Dewhurst* v. *Telenor*, US, 83 F.Supp.2d 577, 595–596 (D.Md. 2000); *In re Hashim*, US, 188 B.R. 633, 640–641 (D.Ariz. 1995); 107 ILR 405; *General* v. *Grossman*, US, 991 F.2d 1376, 1380–1382 (8th Cir. 1993); *Gabay* v. *Mostazafan*, US, 151 F.R.D. 250, 258 (S.D.N.Y. 1993); 107 ILR 242; *LeDonne* v. *Gulf*, US, 700 F.Supp. 1400 (E.D.Va. 1988); *Bailey* v. *Grand*, US, 805 F.2d 1097, 1100–1101 (2nd Cir. 1986); *Lonon* v. *Companhia*, US, 85 F.R.D. 71 (E.D.Pa. 1979); 63 ILR 329.

183 *Shirobokova* v. *CSA*, US, 335 F.Supp.2d 989, 991 (D.Minn. 2004).

184 *Powerex* v. *Reliant*, US, 551 US 224 (2007); *Dole Food* v. *Patrickson*, US, 538 US 468 (2003); partly affirming *Patrickson* v. *Dole Food*, US, 251 F.3d 795 (9th Cir. 2001); *Kully* v. *Aircraft*, US, 662 F.Supp.2d 259 (E.D.N.Y. 2009); *Board* v. *Nippon*, US, 478 F.3d 274 (5th Cir. 2007); *Poddar* v. *State*, US, 235 F.R.D. 592 (S.D.N.Y. 2006); *Commonwealth* v. *Bulgartabac*, US, 360 F.Supp.2d 791, 793–794 (E.D.Va. 2005); *California* v. *NRG*, US, 391 F.3d 1011, 1025–1026 (9th Cir. 2004); *USX* v. *Adriatic*,

NOTES TO PAGE 274   617

US, 345 F.3d 190 (3rd Cir. 2003); *EIE v. Long*, US, 322 F.3d 635, 642–649 (9th Cir. 2003); *EOTT v. Winterthur*, US, 257 F.3d 992 (9th Cir. 2001); *Musopole v. South*, US, 172 F.Supp.2d 443 (S.D.N.Y. 2001); *Delgado v. Shell*, US, 231 F.3d 165, 175–176 (5th Cir. 2000); affirming *Delgado v. Shell*, US, 890 F.Supp. 1315, 1319 (S.D.Tex. 1994); *Parex v. Russian*, US, 81 F.Supp.2d 506 (S.D.N.Y. 2000); *In re Clearsky*, US, 1999 WL 1021825 (E.D.La. 1999); *Jackson v. Resolution*, US, 136 F.3d 1130, 1132 (7th Cir. 1998); *Doe v. Bolkiah*, US, 74 F.Supp.2d 969, 971 (D.Haw. 1998); *Belgrade v. Sidex*, US, 2 F.Supp.2d 407, 411–415 (S.D.N.Y. 1998); *In re Air Crash*, US, 987 F.Supp. 975, 977–978 (E.D.Mich. 1997); *In re Air Crash*, US, 96 F.3d 932, 941–943 (7th Cir. 1996); affirming *In re Air Crash*, US, 909 F.Supp. 1083, 1097–1104 (N.D.Ill. 1995); *Hyatt v. Stanton*, US, 945 F.Supp. 675, 690–692 (S.D.N.Y. 1996); *Martinez v. Dow*, US, 1996 WL 502461, p. 2 (E.D.La. 1996); *Gould v. Aerospatiale*, US, 40 F.3d 1033, 1034 (9th Cir. 1994); *Kern v. Jeppesen*, US, 867 F.Supp. 525, 529–531 (S.D.Tex. 1994); *Mobil v. Abeille*, US, 984 F.2d 664 (5th Cir. 1993); *Talbot v. Saipem*, US, 835 F.Supp. 352, 353 (S.D.Tex. 1993); *In re Surinam*, US, 974 F.2d 1255 (11th Cir. 1992); *Jones v. Petty-Ray*, US, 954 F.2d 1061, 1061 (5th Cir. 1992); *Balentine v. Union*, US, 795 F.Supp. 266, 268–269 (N.D.Ill. 1992); *Linton v. Airbus*, US, 794 F.Supp. 650 (S.D.Tex. 1992); appeal dismissed, *Linton v. Airbus*, US, 30 F.3d 592 (5th Cir. 1994); *Fabe v. Aneco*, US, 784 F.Supp. 448 (S.D. Ohio 1991); *Trump v. Costruzioni*, US, 761 F.Supp. 1143, 1149–1150 (D.N.J. 1991); affirmed, *Trump v. Costruzioni*, US, 958 F.2d 365 (3rd Cir. 1992) (Table); *Chuidian v. Philippine*, US, 912 F.2d 1095, 1098–1099 (9th Cir. 1990); 92 ILR 480; *Forsythe v. Saudi*, US, 885 F.2d 285, 287 (5th Cir. 1989); *Arango v. Guzman*, US, 761 F.2d 1527, 1531–1533 (11th Cir. 1985); *Alifieris v. American*, US, 523 F.Supp. 1189 (E. D.N.Y. 1981). See also Thornton and Ares, Foreign.

185 Section 1606 provides that 'a foreign state except for an agency or instrumentality thereof shall not be liable for punitive damages'. Thus the US FSIA does not permit the award of punitive damages against a foreign State, but allows such damages against an 'agency or instrumentality' of the foreign State. *Regier v. Iran*, US, 281 F.Supp.2d 87, 101 (D.D.C. 2003); *Weinstein v. Iran*, US, 184 F.Supp.2d 13, 24, fn. 1 (D.D.C. 2002); *Letelier v. Chile*, US, District Court, 502 F.Supp. 259, 266–267 (D.D.C. 1980). See also Chapter 5.

186 *Baumel v. Syria*, US, 550 F.Supp.2d 110 (D.D.C. 2008); *Magness v. Russian*, US, 247 F.3d 609, 612–614 (5th Cir. 2001); *Procter v. Viskoza-Loznica*, US, 33 F.Supp.2d 644, 664–667 (W.D.Tenn. 1998); *Daly v. Castro*, US, 30 F.Supp.2d 407, 415–416 (S.D.N.Y. 1998); *Doty v. Magnum*, US, 994 F.Supp. 894, 895–897 (N.D.Ohio 1997); *Hyatt v. Stanton*, US, 945 F.Supp. 675, 680–683 (S.D.N.Y. 1996); *Seramur v. Saudi*, US, 934 F.Supp. 48, 50–52 (E.D.N.Y. 1996); *Antoine v. Atlas*, US, 66 F.3d 105, 108–111 (6th Cir. 1995); *Straub v. AP*, US, 38 F.3d 448, 452–455 (9th Cir. 1994); 107 ILR 359; *Transaero v. La Fuerza*, US, 30 F.3d 148, 153–154 (D. C.Cir. 1994); 107 ILR 308; *Sherer v. Construcciones*, US, 987 F.2d 1246 (6th Cir. 1993); *Bowers v. Transportes*, US, 719 F.Supp. 166, 169–170 (S.D.N.Y. 1989); *LeDonne v. Gulf*, US, 700 F.Supp. 1400, 1411–1414 (E.D.Va. 1988); *Great v. Alsthom*, US, 1987 WL 4766, p. 3 (E.D.La. 1987); *Segni v. Commercial*, US, 650 F.Supp. 1040, 1041 (N.D.Ill. 1986); *International v. Iran*, US, 505 F.Supp. 178 (D.

618   NOTES TO PAGES 274-277

N.J. 1981); 63 ILR 550. See also Bradley, Service; Hayes, The ABCs, 282–287. For the issue of service of process based on the status of the entity see also *Sarrio* v. *Kuwait*, England, 1995, [1996] 1 Lloyd's Rep 650, 653; *Sarrio* v. *Kuwait*, England, 1996, [1997] 1 Lloyd's Rep 113, 125; *ABCI* v. *Banque*, England, 2001, [2002] 1 Lloyd's Rep 511, 534; *ABCI* v. *Banque*, England, [2003] 2 Lloyd's Rep 146, 157–158.

187 *Peninsula* v. *Hankook*, US, 476 F.3d 140 (2nd Cir. 2007); partly affirming *Peninsula* v. *Hankook*, US, 2005 WL 3046284 (S.D.N.Y. 2005).

188 See, e.g., *Ministry* v. *Cubic*, US, 236 F.Supp.2d 1140 (S.D.Cal. 2002); affirmed, *Ministry* v. *Cubic*, US, 385 F.3d 1206 (9th Cir. 2004); vacated and remanded, *Ministry* v. *Elahi*, US, 546 US 450 (2006). See Chapter 9.

189 See, e.g., *In re Air Crash*, US, 96 F.3d 932 (7th Cir. 1996); affirming *In re Air Crash Disaster*, US, 909 F.Supp. 1083 (N.D.Ill. 1995).

190 In *Walker*, an appellate court held that the word 'organ' was broad enough to cover 'individuals and institutions who act at the request of a foreign state in situations where that state would enjoy sovereign immunity'. *Walker* v. *Bank*, Canada, (1994) 111 DLR (4th) 186, 190–191; 104 ILR 277, 282.

191 *D & J* v. *Cia*, Canada, [1990] 48 FTR 161, 163, 165, paras. 8, 12. The academic view is the same: Molot and Jewett, The State, 107–108.

192 *Collavino* v. *Yemen*, Canada, [2007] AJ No. 531, para. 105.

193 As noted in *Collavino*, [2007] AJ No. 531, paras. 118–119.

194 *D & J* v. *Cia*, Canada, [1990] 48 FTR 161, para. 9, quoting Williams and de Mestral, *An Introduction to International Law*, pp. 149–150. See also Molot and Jewett, The State, 107–108.

195 *Croteau* v. *USA*, Canada, [2006] OJ No. 158, para. 5.

196 *TMR* v. *State*, Canada, 2003 FC 1517, para. 113 (citing *Trendtex*); quoted in *Collavino* v. *Yemen*, Canada, [2007] AJ No. 531, para. 106.

197 *Ferranti-Packard* v. *Cushman*, Canada, (1981) 30 O.R. (2d) 194; affirmed, (1981) 31 O.R. (2d) 799 (C.A.); 64 ILR 93.

198 *Ferguson* v. *Arctic*, Canada, [1995] 3 FC 656, 665–668; [1995] 101 FTR 16, 18–24.

199 *University of Calgary* v. *Colorado School of Mines*, Canada, [1995] 179 AR 81, 89, para. 22 per Kent J.

200 *University of Calgary*, [1995] 179 AR 81, 89–90, paras. 23–26.

201 *Roxford* v. *Cuba*, Canada, [2003] 236 FTR 1, [2003] 2003 FCT 763; [2003] 4 FC 1182, paras. 35–38.

202 *Collavino* v. *Yemen*, Canada, [2007] AJ No. 531, paras. 71–72, 90–100, 109–114.

203 *Roxford* v. *Cuba*, Canada; [2003] 236 FTR 1, [2003] 2003 FCT 763; [2003] 4 FC 1182, paras. 35–41 (citing *Bancec*, US, 462 US 611 (1983); 80 ILR 566 and *Hercaire* v. *Argentina*, US, 821 F.2d 559 (11th Cir. 1987); 98 ILR 48); *Collavino* v. *Yemen*, Canada, [2007] AJ No. 531, paras. 105–121 (citing *Roxford*; *Bridas* v. *Turkmenistan*, US, 447 F.3d 411 (5th Cir. 2006) and *S* v. *Yemen*, US, 218 F.3d 1292 (11th Cir. 2000)).

204 See, e.g., *Kuwait Airways* v. *Iraqi Airways*, England, [1995] 1 WLR 1147, 1160–1161, 1163, 1168, 1172, 1175; 103 ILR 340, 402–403, 405–406, 411, 415, 418–419; *In re Banco*, England, [2001] 1 WLR 2039, 2051–2052; [2001] 3 All ER 923, 933–934; 124 ILR 550, 560–562, paras. 23–25.

NOTES TO PAGES 278–286   619

205 Sucharitkul, Second Report, *YILC*, 1980-II-1, p. 199 at 209, para. 41. See also Sucharitkul, Third Report, *YILC*, 1981-II-1, p. 125 at 138–139, para. 38.

206 As insightfully noted in ALRC, Report No. 24, 1984, pp. 38–39, para. 71.

207 See the US House of Representatives, Report No. 94-1487, 1976, p.7; 1976 USCCAN 6604, 6605. The long title of the UK SIA states that it was designed to 'make new provision with respect to proceedings in the United Kingdom by or against other States'. See *Alcom* v. *Colombia*, England, [1984] 1 AC 580, 600; 74 ILR 170, 183. In point of historical fact, the UK SIA was enacted shortly after a significant shift at common law in the landmark cases of *The Philippine Admiral*, England, 1975, [1977] AC 373; 64 ILR 90; and *Trendtex* v. *Central Bank*, England, [1977] QB 529; 64 ILR 111, where jurisdiction was for the first time asserted over a foreign State or its property pursuant to the doctrine of restrictive immunity.

208 ALRC, Report No. 24, p. 38, para. 71.

209 See, e.g., *Adeang* v. *Nauru*, Australia, 1992, 14 *AYIL* (1993) 340.

210 *Central Bank of Nigeria Case*, Germany, (1975/1976) 65 ILR 131, 134. The same Provincial Court in the *NIOC Revenues* case again held that 'legally independent organisations' of a foreign State did not enjoy any immunity. The German Constitutional Court, although finding it unnecessary to decide whether the immunity of undertakings of foreign States with their own legal personalities ought to be decided in the same way as for their 'mother State', affirmed the decision of the Provincial Court without in any way questioning the latter's reasoning. See *NIOC Revenues Case*, Germany, (1983) 65 ILR 215, 219, 229.

211 See *NIOC Pipeline Contracts Case*, Germany, (1982) 65 ILR 212, 213.

212 See *NIOC Legal Status Case*, Germany, (1980) 65 ILR 199, 202–203; *Foreign Trade Institute Bank Account Case*, Germany, (1981) 65 ILR 209, 210–211.

213 *Central Bank of Nigeria Case*, Germany, (1975/1976) 65 ILR 131, 134.

214 *Garden Contamination Case (2)*, Germany, (1987) 80 ILR 377, 384–386.

215 *Central Bank of Nigeria Case*, Germany, (1975/1976) 65 ILR 131, 134–137; *Spanish State Tourist Office Case*, Germany, (1977) 65 ILR 140, 143–144.

216 *NIOC Legal Status Case*, Germany, (1980) 65 ILR 199, 202; *NIOC Pipeline Contracts Case*, Germany, (1982) 65 ILR 212, 213.

217 *NIOC Pipeline Contracts Case*, Germany, (1982) 65 ILR 212, 213–214.

218 *National Iranian Gas Corporation* v. *Pipeline Services*, France, (1990) 113 ILR 446. See also *Caisse d'Assurance* v. *Caisse Nationale*, France, (1977) 65 ILR 70; *Blagojevic* v. *Bank*, France, (1976) 65 ILR 63; *Société* v. *Chaussois*, France, (1969) 65 ILR 44; affirming *Chaussois* v. *La Tabacoop*, France, (1966) 47 ILR 152; *Red* v. *Mrs Cavaillé*, France, (1968) 65 ILR 41.

219 *Kuwait News Agency* v. *Parrott*, France, (1990) 113 ILR 457, 458–459. See also *Office* v. *Société Bec*, France, (1995) 113 ILR 485. Earlier cases of the Court of Cassation display the same structure/particular act analysis. *Société Sonatrach* v. *Migeon*, France, (1985) 77 ILR 525; *Société Nationale* v. *Compagnie Algérienne*, France, (1979) 65 ILR 83, 85.

220 *Euroéquipment* v. *Centre Européen*, France, (1991) 89 ILR 37.

620   NOTES TO PAGES 286–289

221 *Banque Centrale* v. *Weston*, Switzerland, (1978) 65 ILR 417, 422–423, Ground 3.

222 *Banco de la Nacion Lima* v. *Banco Cattolica*, Switzerland, (1984) 82 ILR 10, 11, Ground 4a and 13, Ground 4b. See also *Greek Republic* v. *Walder*, Switzerland, (1930) 5 AD 121; *Greece* v. *Julius*, Switzerland, (1956) 23 ILR 195, 198; *Libya* v. *LIAMCO*, Switzerland, (1980) 62 ILR 228, 233, Ground 3; *UAR* v. *Mrs X*, Switzerland, (1960) 65 ILR 385, 390; *Banque Centrale* v. *Weston*, Switzerland, (1978) 65 ILR 417, 419, Ground 2.

223 *Consorzio* v. *Federazione*, Italy, (1966) 65 ILR 265.

224 *Vaessen* v. *American*, Belgium, (1997) 115 ILR 435, 440.

225 See *Brinkhof* v. *NV Nederlandse*, Netherlands, (1969) 65 ILR 354, 355; *NV Exploitatie-Maatschappij* v. *Bank*, Netherlands, (1963) 65 ILR 348, 352–353.

226 *Banco* v. *First National*, US, 505 F.Supp. 412, 427–428 (S.D.N.Y. 1980); reversed, *Banco* v. *First National*, US, 658 F.2d 913 (2nd Cir. 1981).

227 *First National* v. *Bancec*, US, 462 US 611, 626–627 (1983); 80 ILR 566, 576–577; quoted in *Dole Food* v. *Patrickson*, US, 538 US 468, 475 (2003).

228 *First National* v. *Bancec*, US, 462 US 611, 627 (1983) (emphasis added); 80 ILR 566, 577. For the presumption of independent status see also *EM* v. *Argentina*, US, 473 F.3d 463, 478 (2nd Cir. 2007); *Dale* v. *Colagiovanni*, US, 443 F.3d 425, 429 (5th Cir. 2006); *California* v. *NRG*, US, 391 F.3d 1011, 1025 (9th Cir. 2004); *Bayer* v. *Gambia*, US, 283 F.Supp.2d 1, 5–6 (D.D.C. 2003); *Flatow* v. *Iran*, US, 308 F.3d 1065, 1070 (9th Cir. 2002); *S* v. *Yemen*, US, 218 F.3d 1292, 1298 (11th Cir. 2000); *LNC* v. *Nicaragua*, US, 115 F.Supp.2d 358, 363 (S.D.N.Y. 2000); affirmed, *LNC* v. *Banco*, US, 228 F.3d 423 (2nd Cir. 2000); *Alejandre* v. *Telefonica*, US, 183 F.3d 1277, 1284–1287 (11th Cir. 1999); *Flatow* v. *Iran*, US, 67 F.Supp.2d 535, 538 (D.Md. 1999); *Foremost-McKesson* v. *Iran*, US, 905 F.2d 438, 446 (D.C.Cir. 1990); 101 ILR 536; *Hester* v. *Nigeria*, US, 879 F.2d 170, 176 (5th Cir. 1989); 90 ILR 604; *Hercaire* v. *Argentina*, US, 821 F.2d 559, 565 (11th Cir. 1987); 98 ILR 48; *Letelier* v. *Chile*, US, 748 F.2d 790, 794–795 (2nd Cir. 1984); 79 ILR 561.

229 US House of Representatives, Report No. 94-1487, 1976, pp. 28, 29–30; 1976 USCCAN 6604, 6627, 6628–6629. For the voicing of a similar concern in Canada see *Roxford* v. *Cuba*, Canada, [2003] 236 FTR 1, [2003] 2003 FCT 763; [2003] 4 FC 1182, para. 39.

230 *First National* v. *Bancec*, US, 462 US 611, 628 (1983); 80 ILR 566, 577.

231 *Bancec*, 462 US 611, 629 (1983); 80 ILR 566, 578, quoting *Taylor* v. *Standard*, US, 306 US 307, 322 (1939).

232 *Bancec*, 462 US 611, 614 (1983); 80 ILR 566, 568.

233 *Bancec*, 462 US 611, 617 (1983); 80 ILR 566, 570–571, quoting *Banco* v. *First National*, US, 505 F.Supp. 412, 427 (S.D.N.Y. 1980).

234 *Bancec*, 462 US 611, 632 (1983); 80 ILR 566, 580.

235 *Bancec*, 462 US 611, 633–634 (1983); 80 ILR 566, 580–581.

236 See *Foremost-McKesson* v. *Iran*, US, 905 F.2d 438, 448 (D.C.Cir. 1990); 101 ILR 536; *Hester* v. *Nigeria*, US, 879 F.2d 170, 181 (5th Cir. 1989); 90 ILR 604; *Hercaire* v. *Argentina*, US, 821 F.2d 559, 565 (11th Cir. 1987); 98 ILR 48.

237 *Peterson* v. *Saudi Arabia*, US, 332 F.Supp.2d 189, 198 (D.D.C. 2004); affirmed, *Peterson* v. *Saudi Arabia*, US, 416 F.3d 83 (D.C.Cir. 2005); *Bayer* v. *Gambia*, US,

283 F.Supp.2d 1 (D.D.C. 2003); *Flatow* v. *Iran*, US, 308 F.3d 1065, 1073 (9th Cir. 2002); *Transamerica* v. *Venezuela*, US, 200 F.3d 843, 848–854 (D.C.Cir. 2000); *LNC* v. *Nicaragua*, US, 115 F.Supp.2d 358, 363, 365 (S.D.N.Y. 2000); affirmed, *LNC* v. *Banco*, US, 228 F.3d 423 (2nd Cir. 2000); *Alejandre* v. *Telefonica*, US, 183 F.3d 1277, 1284 (11th Cir. 1999); *McKesson* v. *Iran*, US, 52 F.3d 346, 351–352 (D.C. Cir. 1995); *Walter* v. *Philippines*, US, 965 F.2d 1375, 1381 (5th Cir. 1992); 103 ILR 503; *Foremost-McKesson* v. *Iran*, US, 905 F.2d 438, 440, 447–448 (D.C.Cir. 1990); 101 ILR 536; *Hester* v. *Nigeria*, US, 879 F.2d 170, 181 (5th Cir. 1989); 90 ILR 604; affirming *Hester* v. *Nigeria*, US, 681 F.Supp. 371, 375–381 (N.D.Miss. 1988); *Hercaire* v. *Argentina*, US, 821 F.2d 559, 565 (11th Cir. 1987); 98 ILR 48; partly reversing *Hercaire* v. *Argentina*, US, 642 F.Supp. 126, 130 (S.D.Fla. 1986); *Kalamazoo* v. *Provisional*, US, 616 F.Supp. 660, 666 (W.D.Mich. 1985); 90 ILR 596; *Letelier* v. *Chile*, US, 748 F.2d 790, 794 (2nd Cir. 1984); 79 ILR 561. See also Goekjian, Jurisdiction; Bowling and Cohen, When.

238 *Pravin* v. *Banco*, US, 9 F.Supp.2d 300, 306 (S.D.N.Y. 1998); *Minpeco* v. *Hunt*, US, 686 F.Supp. 427, 435 (S.D.N.Y. 1988); *Baglab* v. *Johnson*, US, 665 F.Supp. 289, 294–297 (S.D.N.Y. 1987); *Letelier* v. *Chile*, US, 748 F.2d 790 (2nd Cir. 1984); 79 ILR 561.

239 *Transamerica* v. *Venezuela*, US, 200 F.3d 843, 848–849 (D.C.Cir. 2000); remanding *Transamerica* v. *Venezuela*, US, 21 F.Supp.2d 47 (D.D.C. 1998).

240 *Hercaire* v. *Argentina*, US, 821 F.2d 559, 565 (11th Cir. 1987); 98 ILR 48; partly reversing *Hercaire* v. *Argentina*, US, 642 F.Supp. 126, 130 (S.D.Fla. 1986). See also *Hester* v. *Nigeria*, US, 879 F.2d 170, 181 (5th Cir. 1989); 90 ILR 604; affirming *Hester* v. *Nigeria*, US, 681 F.Supp. 371, 375–381 (N.D.Miss. 1988); *Flatow* v. *Iran*, US, 67 F.Supp.2d 535, 539–542 (D.Md. 1999); affirmed, *Flatow* v. *Alavi*, US, 225 F.3d 653 (4th Cir. 2000) (Table).

241 *S & Davis* v. *Yemen*, US, 218 F.3d 1292, 1298–1300 (11th Cir. 2000).

242 *S & Davis*, 218 F.3d 1292, 1299 (11th Cir. 2000).

243 *LNC* v. *Nicaragua*, US, 115 F.Supp.2d 358, 364–365 (S.D.N.Y. 2000); affirmed, *LNC* v. *Banco*, US, 228 F.3d 423 (2nd Cir. 2000); *Flatow* v. *Iran*, US, 67 F.Supp.2d 535, 539, 540–542 (D.Md. 1999); affirmed, *Flatow* v. *Alavi*, US, 225 F.3d 653 (4th Cir. 2000) (Table); *Gabay* v. *Mostazafan*, US, 968 F.Supp. 895, 898–899, 900 (S.D. N.Y. 1997); affirmed, *Gabay* v. *Mostazafan*, US, 152 F.3d 918 (2nd Cir. 1998) (Table); *McKesson* v. *Iran*, US, 52 F.3d 346, 352 (D.C.Cir. 1995); *Gabay* v. *Mosta-zafan*, US, 151 F.R.D. 250, 257 (S.D.N.Y. 1993); 107 ILR 242; *Hester* v. *Nigeria*, US, 879 F.2d 170, 178–180 (5th Cir. 1989); 90 ILR 604; *Baglab* v. *Johnson*, US, 665 F.Supp. 289, 294–297 (S.D.N.Y. 1987).

244 *Dole Food* v. *Patrickson*, US, 538 US 468, 477 (2003).

245 It must be noted that the word 'agency' in 'agency relationship' is different from that in 'agency or instrumentality of a foreign State'. In short, being an 'agency of a foreign State' does not necessarily mean that there is an 'agency relationship' between the 'agency' and the foreign State, for which more is needed. See, e.g., *Trans Chemical*, US, 978 F.Supp. 266, 276, fn. 37 (S.D.Tex. 1997).

246 The exact location of the incident seems to have been in dispute. The US claimed that the plane had been shot down over *international waters*,

622   NOTES TO PAGES 291-293

meaning that Cuba had overstepped the limits permitted by the principle that every State has complete and exclusive sovereignty over the airspace above its *territory* (see 1944 Chicago Convention, Article 1). On the other hand, according to the UN Security Council Resolution 1067 (1996) concerning the incident, Cuba had violated 'the principle that States must refrain from the use of weapons against civil aircraft in flight' (see para. 2), but not the principle of (territorial) airspace sovereignty.

247 The judgment was rendered in *Alejandre* v. *Cuba*, US, 996 F.Supp. 1239, 1253–1254 (S.D.Fla. 1997); 121 ILR 603, where the court awarded compensatory damages of circa $50 million against Cuba and the Cuban Air Force and punitive damages of $137.7 million against the Cuban Air Force. The case was decided under the AEDPA, a statute peculiar to the US. See Chapter 5.

248 The 'State instrumentality' status of the ETECSA, which was only *indirectly* owned by the Cuban Government, should now be reconsidered in the light of *Dole Food*. See the discussion of 'tiering' in this chapter. On the other hand, if the ETECSA were a private entity, there would be more reason that its assets could not be garnished to satisfy a judgment against Cuba.

249 *Alejandre* v. *Cuba*, US, 42 F.Supp.2d 1317, 1339 (S.D.Fla. 1999).

250 *Alejandre* v. *Telefonica*, US, 183 F.3d 1277, 1286–1287 (11th Cir. 1999); vacating *Alejandre* v. *Cuba*, US, 42 F.Supp.2d 1317 (S.D.Fla. 1999).

251 *Bridas* v. *Turkmenistan*, US, 447 F.3d 411, 416 (5th Cir. 2006), citing *In re Multiponics*, US, 622 F.2d 709, 724–725 (5th Cir. 1980) and *Bridas* v. *Turkmenistan*, US, 345 F.3d 347, 359 (5th Cir. 2003).

252 *Bridas* v. *Turkmenistan*, US, 447 F.3d 411, 417, 419–420 (5th Cir. 2006).

253 *Bridas*, 447 F.3d 411, 420 (5th Cir. 2006).

254 *Transamerica* v. *Venezuela*, US, 200 F.3d 843, 854 (D.C.Cir. 2000); remanding *Transamerica* v. *Venezuela*, US, 21 F.Supp.2d 47 (D.D.C. 1998); *Pravin* v. *Banco*, US, 9 F.Supp.2d 300, 305 (S.D.N.Y. 1998).

255 *Transamerica* v. *Venezuela*, US, 200 F.3d 843, 854 (D.C.Cir. 2000); remanding *Transamerica* v. *Venezuela*, US, 21 F.Supp.2d 47 (D.D.C. 1998).

256 *Pravin* v. *Banco*, US, 9 F.Supp.2d 300, 306 (S.D.N.Y. 1998); *Banco* v. *Chemical*, US, 782 F.2d 377, 380 (2nd Cir. 1986); *Minpeco* v. *Hunt*, US, 686 F.Supp. 427, 432 (S.D.N.Y. 1988).

257 *LNC* v. *Nicaragua*, US, 115 F.Supp.2d 358, 366 (S.D.N.Y. 2000); affirmed, *LNC* v. *Banco*, US, 228 F.3d 423 (2nd Cir. 2000).

258 See *US Fidelity* v. *Braspetro*, US, 219 F.Supp.2d 403, 473 (S.D.N.Y. 2002); *US Fidelity* v. *Braspetro*, US, 1999 WL 307666, p. 11 (S.D.N.Y. 1999); *Gabay* v. *Mostazafan*, US, 968 F.Supp. 895, 898–899, 900 (S.D.N.Y. 1997); affirmed, *Gabay* v. *Mostazafan*, US, 152 F.3d 918 (2nd Cir. 1998) (Table).

259 *First City* v. *Rafidain*, US, 150 F.3d 172, 176 (2nd Cir. 1998).

260 For a succinct summary of this principle see ALI, *Third Restatement*, Vol. 1, pp. 399–401. For earlier cases see *Gilson* v. *Ireland*, US, 682 F.2d 1022 (D.C.Cir. 1982); 92 ILR 374; *Gibbons* v. *Ireland*, US, 532 F.Supp. 668, 671 (D.D.C. 1982); 86 ILR 75.

261 *US Fidelity* v. *Braspetro*, US, 1999 U.S.Dist.Lexis 7236, p. 35 (S.D.N.Y. 1999).

NOTES TO PAGES 293–295   623

262 *Transamerica* v. *Venezuela*, US, 200 F.3d 843, 848 (D.C.Cir. 2000); *Foremost-McKesson* v. *Iran*, US, 905 F.2d 438, 446–447 (D.C.Cir. 1990); 101 ILR 536; *Hester* v. *Nigeria*, US, 879 F.2d 170, 176, 181 (5th Cir. 1989); 90 ILR 604; *Gilson* v. *Ireland*, US, 682 F.2d 1022, 1026, fn. 16, 1029–1030 (D.C.Cir. 1982); 92 ILR 374; ALI, *Third Restatement*, Vol. 1, p. 400, s. 452, Comment c.

263 *Karaha* v. *Perusahaan*, US, 313 F.3d 70, 90–92 (2nd Cir. 2002) (with the exception of a 5 per cent 'retention', which was within the company's control and therefore validly subject to attachment: p. 92).

264 *Bayer* v. *Gambia*, US, 283 F.Supp.2d 1, 4 (D.D.C. 2003); *Pravin* v. *Banco*, US, 9 F.Supp.2d 300, 304–307 (S.D.N.Y. 1998); *Letelier* v. *Chile*, US, 748 F.2d 790, 794–795 (2nd Cir. 1984); 79 ILR 561; reversing *Letelier* v. *Chile*, US, 567 F.Supp. 1490 (S.D.N.Y. 1983) and *Letelier* v. *Chile*, US, 575 F.Supp. 1217 (S.D.N.Y. 1983).

265 US House of Representatives, Report No. 94-1487, 1976, pp. 29–30; 1976 USCCAN 6604, 6628–6629; quoted in *Bancec*, US, 462 US 611, 627–628 (1983); 80 ILR 566, 577. See also *NYSA-ILA* v. *Garuda*, US, 7 F.3d 35, 38–39 (2nd Cir. 1993); *Gates* v. *Victor*, US, 54 F.3d 1457, 1465 (9th Cir. 1995); 107 ILR 371. Cf. *Banco* v. *Riggs*, US, 919 F.Supp. 13, 16 (D.D.C. 1994).

266 *Dole Food* v. *Patrickson*, US, 538 US 468, 475 (2003). For rejection of the separate juridical personality under the Terrorism Risk Insurance Act (TRIA) see *US* v. *Holy Land*, US, 445 F.3d 771, 787 (5th Cir. 2006); *Weininger* v. *Castro*, US, 462 F.Supp.2d 457, 485 (S.D.N.Y. 2006); *Ungar* v. *Palestinian*, US, 304 F.Supp.2d 232, 241 (D.R.I. 2004); *Smith* v. *Federal*, US, 280 F.Supp.2d 314, 319 (S.D.N.Y. 2003); affirmed, *Smith* v. *Federal*, US, 346 F.3d 264 (2nd Cir. 2003); *Hill* v. *Iraq*, US, 2003 WL 21057173, p. 2 (D.D.C. 2003).

267 See *Flatow* v. *Iran*, US, 308 F.3d 1065, 1069–1071 (9th Cir. 2002); *Arriba* v. *Petroleos*, US, 962 F.2d 528 (5th Cir. 1992); 103 ILR 490; *Gregorian* v. *Izvestia*, US, 871 F.2d 1515 (9th Cir. 1989); 98 ILR 76; *Dayton* v. *Czechoslovak*, US, 834 F.2d 203 (D.C.Cir. 1987); 79 ILR 590; *Hercaire* v. *Argentina*, US, 821 F.2d 559 (11th Cir. 1987); 98 ILR 48; *Baglab* v. *Johnson*, US, 665 F.Supp. 289 (S.D.N.Y. 1987); *Letelier* v. *Chile*, US, 748 F.2d 790 (2nd Cir. 1984); 79 ILR 561.

268 *Roxford* v. *Cuba*, Canada, [2003] 236 FTR 1, [2003] 2003 FCT 763; [2003] 4 FC 1182, paras. 30 and 33 per Prothonotary Lefreniere.

269 *Roxford*, para. 23.

270 *Roxford*, paras. 35–41.

271 *Roxford*, para. 40. The *Roxford* test, together with the elaborate examination of evidence, was closely followed in *Collavino* v. *Yemen*, Canada, [2007] AJ No. 531, paras. 75, 105, 107, 109–117, 121, 140, 142. See also *Karabulut* v. *Allegro*, Canada, [2003] OJ No. 5748, para. 5.

272 *Banco de Moçambique* v. *Inter-Science*, South Africa, 1982 (3) SA 330, 332–333, 335–345, 347; 87 ILR 239, 241, 244–255, 256. For the earlier action see *Inter-Science* v. *Moçambique*, South Africa, 1979, 1980 (2) SA 111; 64 ILR 689.

273 *C. Czarnikow* v. *Rolimpex*, England, 1977, [1978] QB 176; 1978, [1979] AC 351; 64 ILR 195; *Empresa* v. *Industria*, England, (1982) 64 ILR 368.

274 *Société Algérienne* v. *Sempac*, France, (1978) 65 ILR 73, 75; *Ministry* v. *Société Framatome*, France, (1990) 113 ILR 452, 455; *Castanheira* v. *Commercial*,

624   NOTES TO PAGES 295–299

Belgium, (1980) 82 ILR 100, 102; *Brinkhof* v. *NV Nederlandse*, Netherlands, (1969) 65 ILR 354, 355.

275 *Vaessen* v. Belgium, (1997) 115 ILR 435, 440; *Rafidain* v. *Consarc*, Belgium, (1993) 106 ILR 274, 278–279; *Mobutu* v. *SA Cotoni*, Belgium, (1988) 91 ILR 259, 262; *Dumez* v. *Iraq*, France, (1999) 127 ILR 144, 146–147; *Office* v. *Société Bec*, France, (1995) 113 ILR 485, 486; *Senghor* v. *International*, France, (1990) 113 ILR 460, 461; *Benvenuti* v. *Banque*, France, (1987) 82 ILR 91, 92; *Egypt* v. *Southern*, France, (1984/1987) 86 ILR 474, 483–489; *Garden Contamination Case (2)*, Germany, (1987) 80 ILR 377, 384–386; *NIOC Revenues Case*, Germany, (1983) 65 ILR 215, 228–229, Ground B.III.2; *NIOC Pipeline Contracts Case*, Germany, (1982) 65 ILR 212, 213; *NIOC Legal Status Case*, Germany, (1980) 65 ILR 199, 203; *USSR* v. *ICC*, Netherlands, (1987) 87 ILR 103, 105.

276 *NIOC Revenues Case*, Germany, (1983) 65 ILR 215, 219, Ground A.I; *Garden Contamination Case (2)*, Germany, (1987) 80 ILR 377, 386; *Benvenuti* v. *Banque*, France, (1987) 82 ILR 91, 92; *Office* v. *Société Bec*, France, (1995) 113 ILR 485, 486; *Dumez* v. *Iraq*, France, (1999) 127 ILR 144, 146–147.

Chapter 7

1 *Greek Republic* v. *Walder*, Switzerland, (1930) 5 AD 121, 122–123; *Hertzfeld* v. *USSR*, France, (1933) 7 AD 184, 185; affirmed, *Hertzfeld* v. *USSR*, France, (1938) 9 AD 243, 245; *General National* v. *Société Marseille*, France, (1986) 77 ILR 530, 532; *In re Bolin*, Sweden, (1934) 7 AD 186, 186–187; *Brasseur* v. *Greece*, Belgium, (1933) 6 AD 164, 167–168; *Petroleum Companies Case*, Belgium, (1939) 8 AD 239 note; *The Kabalo*, England, (1940) 67 Ll L Rep 572; 9 AD 281; *Cantieri* v. *Gdynia-Ameryka*, Canada, 1939, (1940) 1 DLR 102, 104; 9 AD 282, 283; *Poortensdijk* v. *Latvia*, Netherlands, (1941/1942) 11 AD 142; *Indonesia* v. *Van der Haas*, Netherlands, (1958) 26 ILR 181, 182; *Underhill* v. *Hernandez*, US, 168 US 250, 252 (1897); *Victory Transport* v. *Comisaría*, US, 336 F.2d 354, 360 (2nd Cir. 1964); 35 ILR 110, 116; *Mexico* v. *Ashley*, US, 556 S.W.2d 784, 786 (1977); 63 ILR 95, 98; *Hunt* v. *Mobil*, US, 550 F.2d 68, 73 (2nd Cir. 1977); 66 ILR 288, 292; *Germany* v. *Elicofon*, US, 536 F.Supp. 813, 825–826 (E.D.N.Y. 1978); 94 ILR 133, 151–152; *Oder-Neisse Property Expropriation Case*, Germany, (1975) 65 ILR 127, 130; *Pauer* v. *Hungary*, Italy, (1956) 24 ILR 211, 213; *Greece* v. *Gamet*, Italy, (1957) 24 ILR 209, 211; *Greece* v. *Gamet*, Italy, (1959) 28 ILR 153, 155; *Campione* v. *Peti-Nitrogenmuvek*, Italy, (1972) 65 ILR 287, 301–302; *Libya* v. *SpA Imprese*, Italy, (1979) 78 ILR 90, 92. A great number of cases involved the requisition of Spanish ships in foreign waters by both the Nationalist and the Republic Governments of Spain during the Spanish Civil War (1936–1939): *Larrasquitu* v. *Société Cementos*, France, (1937) 8 AD 196, 197; *Urrutia* v. *Martiarena*, Belgium, (1937) 8 AD 237, 238–239; *Ibarra* v. *Captain*, Argentina, (1937) 8 AD 247 and 9 AD 293, 294; *The Rita Garcia*, England, (1937) 59 Ll L Rep 140, 142; 9 AD 272, 273; *The Arraiz*, England, (1938) 61 Ll L Rep 39; 9 AD 273; *The El Neptuno*, England, (1938) 62 Ll L Rep 7; 9 AD 279; *Saez* v. *Pinillos*, Belgium, (1938/1939) 9 AD 289, 290–291; *The Guernica*, Norway, (1938) 11

AD 139; *The Garbi*, Netherlands, (1938) 11 AD 155, 155–156. For history see Preuss, State Immunity. Cf. *The Jupiter (No. 3)*, England, [1927] P 122; *S* v. *Romania*, Switzerland, (1987) 82 ILR 45, 49–50, Ground 3.

2 *The Navemar*, US, 18 F.Supp. 153 (E.D.N.Y. 1937); 90 F. 673 (2nd Cir. 1937); 303 US 68 (1938); 24 F.Supp. 495 (E.D.N.Y. 1938); 102 F. 444 (2nd Cir. 1939); 9 AD 176; *The Cristina*, England, [1938] AC 485; 9 AD 250 (see esp. AC 485, 508–509; AD 250, 258–259); *The Arantzazu Mendi*, England, [1938] P 233; [1939] P 37; [1939] AC 256; 9 AD 60.

3 *Ervin* v. *Quintanilla*, US, 99 F. 935 (5th Cir. 1938); 9 AD 219, 223–224; *The Rigmor*, Sweden, (1942) 10 AD 240; *The Solgry*, Sweden, (1942) 11 AD 153, 154.

4 *The El Condado*, Scotland, (1937) 59 Ll L Rep 119, 121; 9 AD 277, 279; *The Condado*, Scotland, (1939) 63 Ll L Rep 83, 86–88; (1939) 63 Ll L Rep 330, 333–334; 9 AD 225, 227, 228–230, 231–233; *Spain* v. *National*, Scotland, 1939 SC 413.

5 *Russian* v. *Carlbom (No. 1)*, Sweden, (1944) 12 AD 61, 62. However, execution was refused on the ground that the ship was in the possession of the Soviet Union, even though the ship could not be considered the property of the Soviet Union: *Russian* v. *Carlbom (No. 2)*, Sweden, (1944) 12 AD 112, 113.

6 *SA Biocare* v. *Gécamines*, Belgium, (1989) 115 ILR 415, 417.

7 *S* v. *Romania*, Switzerland, (1987) 82 ILR 45, 48, Ground 2 and 49–50, Ground 3. See also *Campione* v. *Peti-Nitrogenmuvek*, Italy, (1972) 65 ILR 287, 301–302.

8 *Société* v. *Sempac*, France, (1978) 65 ILR 73, 75. The same decision was later repeated in *Société* v. *Lao*, France, (1987) 80 ILR 688, 690; affirming *Société* v. *Lao*, France, (1983) 80 ILR 430, 432. See also *Kuwait Airways* v. *Iraqi Airways*, England, [1995] 1 WLR 1147, 1163; 103 ILR 340, 405. However, the UK SIA does not have a provision on expropriation.

9 *Société Nationale* v. *Compagnie Algérienne*, France, (1979) 65 ILR 83, 85.

10 *Russian* v. *Société Française*, France, (1940) 9 AD 245, 246. See also *Corporacion* v. *Braden*, France, (1972) 65 ILR 57, 60.

11 *Banco Nacional* v. *Sabbatino*, US, 376 US 398, 428 (1964); 35 ILR 2. See also *Carl Zeiss* v. *VEB*, US, 293 F.Supp. 892 (S.D.N.Y. 1968); affirmed, *Carl Zeiss* v. *VEB*, US, 433 F.2d 686 (2nd Cir. 1970); 61 ILR 35. For development of the 'act of State doctrine' in US case law see, especially, *Alfred Dunhill* v. *Cuba*, US, 425 US 682 (1976); 66 ILR 212; *Kirkpatrick* v. *Environmental*, US, 493 US 400 (1990); 88 ILR 93. The so-called 'Second Hickenlooper Amendment' (Public Law No. 89-171, 79 Stat. 653 (1964), codified at 22 USC § 2370(e)(2)), under which 'no court in the United States shall decline on the ground of the federal act of state doctrine to make a determination ... in a case ... based upon ... a confiscation or other taking ... in violation of the principles of international law, including the principles of compensation', can be regarded as a legislative response designed to lessen the effects of *Sabbatino*, and is thus a precursor to the expropriation exception in the FSIA. For narrow construction of Hickenlooper see *Mexico* v. *Ashley*, US, 556 S.W.2d 784, 786–787 (1977); 63 ILR 95, 98–99; *Menendez* v. *Saks*, US, 485 F.2d 1355, 1364, 1372 (2nd Cir. 1973); reversed on other grounds, *Alfred Dunhill* v. *Cuba*, US, Supreme Court, 425 US 682 (1976); 66 ILR 212; *Banco Nacional* v. *First National*, US, 431 F.2d 394, 399–402 (2nd Cir.

626   NOTES TO PAGES 302–304

1970); 42 ILR 45; vacated, *First National* v. *Banco Nacional*, US, 400 US 1019 (1971); on remand, *Banco Nacional* v. *First National*, US, 442 F.2d 530 (2nd Cir. 1971); reversed, *First National* v. *Banco Nacional*, US, 406 US 759 (1972); 66 ILR 102; *French* v. *Banco*, US, 23 N.Y.2d 46 (1968).

12 *Campione* v. *Peti-Nitrogenmuvek*, Italy, (1972) 65 ILR 287, 302.

13 *Kuwait Airways* v. *Iraqi Airways*, England, 1993, [1995] 1 Lloyd's Rep 25, 29, 36–37; 103 ILR 340, 372–373, 386–388; [1995] 1 WLR 1147, 1156–1160, 1163; 103 ILR 340, 397–402, 405.

14 *Kuwait Airways* v. *Iraqi Airways*, England, [1995] 1 WLR 1147, 1163; 103 ILR 340, 397–402, 405–406.

15 *Kuwait Airways* v. *Iraqi Airways*, England, 1998, [1999] CLC 31, 73–83; 116 ILR 534, 591–606; affirmed, *Kuwait Airways* v. *Iraqi Airways (Nos. 4 and 5)*, England, 2000, [2001] 3 WLR 1117, 1219–1220, paras. 379 and 382; [2002] 2 AC 883, 988–989, paras. 379 and 382; affirmed, *Kuwait Airways* v. *Iraqi Airways (Nos. 4 and 5)*, England, [2002] 2 AC 883, 1081–1083, paras. 28–36; 1101–1103, paras. 113–116; 1105, para. 125; 1107, 1109, 1110–1111, 1114–1115, 1116, paras. 134, 140, 144–149, 160–161 and 166–170; *Kuwait Airways* v. *Iraqi Airways*, England, [2003] 1 Lloyd's Rep 448, 453, 467–469; 126 ILR 758, 767–768, 797–800, paras. 32–34, 146–154.

16 ILC, Report, *YILC*, 1986-II-2, p. 7 at 11 and 17. For the initial version see ILC, Report, *YILC*, 1984-II-2, p. 58 at 59, fn. 200. See also Sucharitkul, Eighth Report, *YILC*, 1986-II-1, p. 21 at 29.

17 Comments and Observations, *YILC*, 1988-II-1, p. 45 at 55 (Australia: removal), 56 (Austria: welcome), 64 (Czechoslovakia: deletion), 69 (Germany Democratic Republic: deletion), 72 (Federal Republic of Germany: appropriate), 76 (Mexico: confusing), 82 (Thailand: no objection), 83 (USSR: misleading). See also Ogiso, Preliminary Report, *YILC*, 1988-II-1, p. 96 at 116, para. 204; GAOR, A/C.6/46/SR.23, para. 96 (China: deletion).

18 See ILC, Report, *YILC*, 1989-II-2, p. 97 at 116, paras. 567–568; ILC, Report, *YILC*, 1990-II-2, p. 31 at 39, para. 215; Ogiso, Preliminary Report, *YILC*, 1988-II-1, p. 96 at 116, para. 208; Ogiso, Second Report, *YILC*, 1989-II-1, p. 59 at 71, para. 41; Ogiso, Third Report, *YILC*, 1990-II-1, p. 3 at 17, comments to Art. 20.

19 Occasionally, claims involving foreign expropriation are brought – unsuccessfully – under s. 1605(a)(5) (tortious liability exception), see *Chuidian* v. *Philippine*, US, 912 F.2d 1095, 1105–1106 (9th Cir. 1990); 92 ILR 480; *Asociacion* v. *Mexico*, US, 561 F.Supp. 1190 (D.D.C. 1983); affirmed, *Asociacion* v. *Mexico*, US, 735 F.2d 1517 (D.C.Cir. 1984); 84 ILR 87; or under s. 1605(a)(2) (commercial activity exception), see *Garb* v. *Poland*, US, 207 F.Supp.2d 16, 31–32 (E.D.N.Y. 2002); affirmed, *Garb* v. *Poland*, US, 440 F.3d 579, 586 (2nd Cir. 2006); *Beg* v. *Pakistan*, US, 353 F.3d 1323 (11th Cir. 2003); *Haven* v. *Rzeczpospolita*, US, 68 F.Supp.2d 947 (N.D.Ill. 1999); affirmed, *Haven* v. *Rzeczpospolita*, US, 215 F.3d 727 (7th Cir. 2000); *Baglab* v. *Johnson*, US, 665 F.Supp. 289 (S.D.N.Y. 1987); *Alberti* v. *Empresa*, US, 705 F.2d 250 (7th Cir. 1983); 92 ILR 392. Sometimes a claim would be brought under both s. 1605(a)(2) and (3): *Wahba* v. *National Bank*, US, 457 F.Supp.2d 721 (E.D.Tex. 2006). Article III (G) of the 1982 ILA Montreal Draft

NOTES TO PAGES 304–305   627

copies almost verbatim the provisions of s. 1605(a)(3). The 1994 ILA Revised Draft retains the provision. According to the ILA, the provision is based on s. 1605(a)(3) of the US FSIA. See ILA, *Report*, 1982, p. 5 at 8 and p. 325 at 332–333; ILA, *Report*, 1994, p. 21 at 25 and p. 452 at 491.

20 US House of Representatives, Report No. 94–1487, 1976, p. 19; 1976 USCCAN 6604, 6618.

21 See *Austria* v. *Altmann*, US, 541 US 677, 685 (2004); affirming *Altmann* v. *Austria*, US, 317 F.3d 954, 967 (9th Cir. 2002); affirming *Altmann* v. *Austria*, US, 142 F.Supp.2d 1187, 1202 (C.D.Cal. 2001); *Cassirer* v. *Spain*, US, 580 F.3d 1048, 1056 (9th Cir. 2009); *Nemariam* v. *Ethiopia*, US, 491 F.3d 470, 474 (D.C.Cir. 2007); 135 ILR 679; affirming *Nemariam* v. *Ethiopia*, US, 400 F.Supp.2d 76, 81 (D.D.C. 2005); *Allen* v. *Russia*, US, 522 F.Supp.2d 167, 185–187 (D.D.C. 2007); *Chalabi* v. *Jordan*, US, 503 F.Supp.2d 267 (D.D.C. 2007); *Wahba* v. *National Bank*, US, 457 F.Supp.2d 721, 730 (E.D.Tex. 2006); *Gutch* v. *Germany*, US, 444 F.Supp.2d 1, 10–11 (D.D.C. 2006); *Yang* v. *Liaoning*, US, 452 F.3d 883, 887 and fns. 4 and 5 (D.C.Cir. 2006); affirming *Yang* v. *Liaoning*, US, 362 F.Supp.2d 83, 98, 100 (D.D.C. 2005); *Peterson* v. *Saudi Arabia*, US, 416 F.3d 83, 87–88 (D.C.Cir. 2005); affirming *Peterson* v. *Saudi Arabia*, US, 332 F.Supp.2d 189, 196–197 (D.D.C. 2004); *Alperin* v. *Vatican Bank*, US, 410 F.3d 532, 553 (9th Cir. 2005); *Daventree* v. *Azerbaijan*, US, 349 F.Supp.2d 736, 749, 751 (S.D.N.Y. 2004); *Anderman* v. *Austria*, US, 256 F.Supp.2d 1098, 1105, 1109–1111 (C.D.Cal. 2003); *Garb* v. *Poland*, US, 207 F.Supp.2d 16, 32 (E.D.N.Y. 2002); *Lord Day* v. *Vietnam*, US, 134 F.Supp.2d 549, 560 (S.D.N.Y. 2001); *Zappia* v. *Abu Dhabi*, US, 215 F.3d 247, 250–252 (2nd Cir. 2000); affirming *Zappia* v. *Abu Dhabi*, US, 1996 WL 413680, p. 6 (S.D.N.Y. 1996); *Millicom* v. *Costa Rica*, US, 995 F.Supp. 14, 18, 22–23 (D.D.C. 1998); *Gabay* v. *Mostazafan*, US, 968 F.Supp. 895, 897–898 (S.D.N.Y. 1997); *Gabay* v. *Mostazafan*, US, 151 F.R.D. 250, 252, 254 (S.D.N.Y. 1993); 107 ILR 242; *Antares* v. *Nigeria*, US, 948 F.2d 90, 96–97 (2nd Cir. 1991); 107 ILR 225; vacated on other grounds, *Antares* v. *Nigeria*, US, 505 US 1215 (1992); and affirmed on rehearing, *Antares* v. *Nigeria*, US, 999 F.2d 33 (2nd Cir. 1993); 107 ILR 225; *Brewer* v. *Iraq*, US, 890 F.2d 97, 101 (8th Cir. 1989); *Friedar* v. *Israel*, US, 614 F.Supp. 395, 399 (S.D.N.Y. 1985); *Vencedora* v. *Compagnie*, US, 730 F.2d 195, 197, 202 (5th Cir. 1984); 87 ILR 520.

22 See *Freund* v. *France*, US, 592 F.Supp.2d 540 (S.D.N.Y. 2008); *Garb* v. *Poland*, US, 440 F.3d 579, 588 (2nd Cir. 2006); affirming *Garb* v. *Poland*, US, 207 F.Supp.2d 16, 20–21 (E.D.N.Y. 2002); *Greenpeace* v. *France*, US, 946 F.Supp. 773, 782 (C.D.Cal. 1996); *Fagot* v. *Costa Rica*, US, 934 F.Supp. 493, 500 (D. P. R. 1996); *Intercontinental* v. *De Gruyter*, US, 822 F.Supp. 662, 678 (C.D.Cal. 1993); *Siderman* v. *Argentina*, US, 965 F.2d 699, 708, 711–712 (9th Cir. 1992); 103 ILR 454; *Chuidian* v. *Philippine*, US, 912 F.2d 1095, 1103 (9th Cir. 1990); 92 ILR 480; *Kline* v. *Kaneko*, US, 685 F.Supp. 386, 391 (S.D.N.Y. 1988); 101 ILR 497; *West* v. *Multibanco*, US, 807 F.2d 820, 826 (9th Cir. 1987); 84 ILR 187.

23 *Freund* v. *France*, US, 592 F.Supp.2d 540, 556–559 (S.D.N.Y. 2008).

24 *Allen* v. *Russian Federation*, US, 522 F.Supp.2d 167, 186–187 (D.D.C. 2007); *Nemariam* v. *Ethiopia*, US, 491 F.3d 470, 475 (D.C.Cir. 2007); 135 ILR 679; affirming *Nemariam* v. *Ethiopia*, US, 400 F.Supp.2d 76, 81, 84 (D.D.C. 2005);

628   NOTES TO PAGES 305–306

Garb v. *Poland*, US, 440 F.3d 579, 588 (2nd Cir. 2006); *Peterson* v. *Saudi Arabia*, US, 416 F.3d 83, 86–87 (D.C.Cir. 2005); affirming *Peterson* v. *Saudi Arabia*, US, 332 F.Supp.2d 189, 196, 197–198 (D.D.C. 2004); *Yang* v. *Liaoning*, US, 362 F.Supp.2d 83, 97–98 (D.D.C. 2005); affirmed, *Yang* v. *Liaoning*, US, 452 F.3d 883 (D.C.Cir. 2006); *Malewicz* v. *Amsterdam*, US, 362 F.Supp.2d 298, 306 (D.D.C. 2005); *Daventree* v. *Republic*, US, 349 F.Supp.2d 736, 749 (S.D.N.Y. 2004); *Altmann* v. *Austria*, US, 317 F.3d 954, 968–969 (9th Cir. 2002); affirming *Altmann* v. *Austria*, US, 142 F.Supp.2d 1187, 1202–1205 (C.D.Cal. 2001); *Lord Day* v. *Vietnam*, US, 134 F.Supp.2d 549, 560 (S.D.N.Y. 2001); *Zappia* v. *Abu Dhabi*, US, 215 F.3d 247, 251 (2nd Cir. 2000); *Greenpeace* v. *France*, US, 946 F.Supp. 773, 784 (C.D.Cal. 1996); *De Sanchez* v. *Banco*, US, 770 F.2d 1385, 1395, fn. 12 (5th Cir. 1985); 88 ILR 75; *Kalamazoo* v. *Ethiopia*, US, 616 F.Supp. 660, 663 (W.D.Mich. 1985); 90 ILR 596; *National* v. *DuBois*, US, 605 F.Supp. 1206, 1210 (W.D.Pa. 1985). The Austrian Supreme Court would also deny immunity to a foreign State acting 'as the owner of a nationalized enterprise': *Steinmetz* v. *Hungaria*, Austria, (1970) 65 ILR 15, 19.

25 *Garb* v. *Poland*, US, 440 F.3d 579, 590 (2nd Cir. 2006); *Yang* v. *Liaoning*, US, 362 F.Supp.2d 83, 101 (D.D.C. 2005); affirmed, *Yang* v. *Liaoning*, US, 452 F.3d 883 (D.C. Cir. 2006); *West* v. *Multibanco*, US, 807 F.2d 820, 833 (9th Cir. 1987); 84 ILR 187.

26 *Lord Day* v. *Vietnam*, US, 134 F.Supp.2d 549, 561, 563 (S.D.N.Y. 2001).

27 *Siderman* v. *Argentina*, US, 965 F.2d 699, 712 (9th Cir. 1992); 103 ILR 454. See Lieberman, Expropriation, 521–532.

28 *Gutch* v. *Germany*, US, 444 F.Supp.2d 1, 10 (D.D.C. 2006); *Nemariam* v. *Ethiopia*, US, 400 F.Supp.2d 76, 81–84 (D.D.C. 2005); *Yang* v. *Liaoning*, US, 362 F.Supp.2d 83, 101 (D.D.C. 2005); affirmed, *Yang* v. *Liaoning*, US, 452 F.3d 883 (D.C.Cir. 2006); *Daventree* v. *Azerbaijan*, US, 349 F.Supp.2d 736, 749, 751 (S.D.N.Y. 2004); *Peterson* v. *Saudi Arabia*, US, 332 F.Supp.2d 189, 197 (D.D.C. 2004); affirmed, *Peterson* v. *Saudi Arabia*, US, 416 F.3d 83, 87–89 (D.C.Cir. 2005); *Leutwyler* v. *Office*, US, 184 F.Supp.2d 277, 289 fn. 13 (S.D.N.Y. 2001); *Lord Day* v. *Vietnam*, US, 134 F.Supp.2d 549, 560 (S.D.N.Y. 2001); *Sampson* v. *Germany*, US, 975 F.Supp. 1108, 1117 (N.D.Ill. 1997); affirmed, *Sampson* v. *Germany*, US, 250 F.3d 1145 (7th Cir. 2001); *Hirsh* v. *Israel*, US, 962 F.Supp. 377, 383 (S.D.N.Y. 1997); 113 ILR 543; *Zappia* v. *Abu Dhabi*, US, 1996 WL 413680, p. 8 (S.D.N.Y. 1996); affirmed on other grounds, *Zappia* v. *Abu Dhabi*, US, 215 F.3d 247, 251 (2nd Cir. 2000); *Intercontinental* v. *De Gruyter*, US, 822 F.Supp. 662, 678 (C.D.Cal. 1993); *Brewer* v. *Iraq*, US, 890 F.2d 97, 101 (8th Cir. 1989); *De Sanchez* v. *Banco*, US, 770 F.2d 1385, 1395 (5th Cir. 1985); 88 ILR 75; *Friedar* v. *Israel*, US, 614 F.Supp. 395, 399 (S.D.N.Y. 1985); *Canadian* v. *Compania*, US, 528 F.Supp. 1337, 1346 (S.D.N.Y. 1982); affirmed, *Canadian* v. *Compania*, US, 727 F.2d 274 (2nd Cir. 1984).

29 *Peterson* v. *Saudi Arabia*, US, 332 F.Supp.2d 189, 198 (D.D.C. 2004); affirmed, *Peterson* v. *Saudi Arabia*, US, 416 F.3d 83 (D.C.Cir 2005).

30 *Altmann* v. *Austria*, US, 317 F.3d 954, 968 (9th Cir. 2002); affirmed, *Austria* v. *Altmann*, US, 541 US 677 (2004); see Murray, Stolen; Murray, Jurisdiction. See also *Yang* v. *Liaoning*, US, 362 F.Supp.2d 83, 100 (D.D.C. 2005); affirmed, *Yang* v. *Liaoning*, US, 452 F.3d 883 (D.C.Cir. 2006).

NOTES TO PAGES 306–309   629

31 *Kalamazoo* v. *Ethiopia*, US, 616 F.Supp. 660, 663 (W.D.Mich. 1985); 90 ILR 596. The 'controlling interest' has been understood by other courts as 'akin to physical assets': *Peterson* v. *Saudi Arabia*, US, 332 F.Supp.2d 189, 197, fn. 2 (D.D.C. 2004); affirmed, *Peterson* v. *Saudi Arabia*, US, 416 F.3d 83, 87–88 (D.C.Cir. 2005); *Yang* v. *Liaoning*, US, 362 F.Supp.2d 83, 100 (D.D.C. 2005); affirmed, *Yang* v. *Liaoning*, US, 452 F.3d 883 (D.C.Cir. 2006). *Kalamazoo* has been cited with approval in *Gutch* v. *Germany*, US, 444 F.Supp.2d 1, 10 (D.D.C. 2006); *Yang* v. *Liaoning*, US, 362 F.Supp.2d 83, 100–101 (D.D.C. 2005); affirmed, *Yang Rong* v. *Liaoning*, US, 452 F.3d 883 (D.C.Cir. 2006); *Nemariam* v. *Ethiopia*, US, 400 F.Supp.2d 76, 83, fn. 3 (D.D.C. 2005); *Peterson* v. *Saudi Arabia*, US, 332 F.Supp.2d 189, 197, fn. 2 (D.D.C. 2004); affirmed, *Peterson* v. *Saudi Arabia*, US, 416 F.3d 83, 87–88 (D.C.Cir. 2005); *Lord Day* v. *Vietnam*, US, 134 F.Supp.2d 549, 560 (S.D.N.Y. 2001). Cf. *West* v. *Multibanco*, US, 807 F.2d 820, 830 (9th Cir. 1987) ('the rights arising from a certificate of deposit are "rights to property" capable of being expropriated by foreign states'); 84 ILR 187. However, the relevant observation in *West* concerns the 'Second Hickenlooper Amendment', outside the context of the FSIA: see *Peterson* v. *Saudi Arabia*, US, 332 F.Supp.2d 189, 197, fn. 2 (D.D.C. 2004); affirmed, *Peterson* v. *Saudi Arabia*, US, 416 F.3d 83, 87–88 (D.C.Cir. 2005).

32 *Intercontinental* v. *De Gruyter*, US, 822 F.Supp. 662, 678 (C.D.Cal. 1993).

33 *Nemariam* v. *Ethiopia*, US, 400 F.Supp.2d 76, 81–84 (D.D.C. 2005) (the quotation is from p. 83).

34 *Nemariam* v. *Ethiopia*, US, 491 F.3d 470, 479–480 (D.C.Cir. 2007); 135 ILR 679; affirming, on other grounds *Nemariam* v. *Ethiopia*, US, 400 F.Supp.2d 76 (D.D.C. 2005).

35 *Cassirer* v. *Spain*, US, 580 F.3d 1048, 1056 (9th Cir. 2009); partly affirming, partly reversing and remanding *Cassirer* v. *Spain*, US, 461 F.Supp.2d 1157 (C.D.Cal. 2006).

36 ALI, *Third Restatement*, Vol. 2, s. 712, p. 196. See *West* v. *Multibanco*, US, 807 F.2d 820, 831–832 (9th Cir. 1987); 84 ILR 187; *Siderman* v. *Argentina*, US, 965 F.2d 699, 711–712 (9th Cir. 1992); 103 ILR 454; *Crist* v. *Turkey*, US, 995 F.Supp. 5, 10 (D.D.C. 1998); *Altmann* v. *Austria*, US, 317 F.3d 954, 968 (9th Cir. 2002); affirming *Altmann* v. *Austria*, US, 142 F.Supp.2d 1187, 1202–1203 (C.D.Cal. 2001); *Wahba* v. *National Bank*, US, 457 F.Supp.2d 721, 731 (E.D.Tex. 2006). Christie, What Constitutes, 331–332.

37 *West* v. *Multibanco*, US, 807 F.2d 820, 831 (9th Cir. 1987); 84 ILR 187.

38 *West* v. *Multibanco*, US, 807 F.2d 820, 832 (9th Cir. 1987); 84 ILR 187.

39 *Zappia* v. *Abu Dhabi*, US, 215 F.3d 247, 252 (2nd Cir. 2000); *First Fidelity* v. *Antigua*, US, 877 F.2d 189, 193 (2nd Cir. 1989); 99 ILR 125.

40 *Greenpeace* v. *France*, US. 946 F.Supp. 773, 783 (C.D.Cal. 1996).

41 US House of Representatives, Report No. 94-1487, 1976, pp. 19–20; 1976 USCCAN 6604, 6618.

42 ALI, *Third Restatement*, Vol. 2, s. 712 and Comments c and d, pp. 196–198. See also Amerasinghe, Assessment.

43 Apparently, up to now, in only three cases has the formula 'prompt, adequate and effective compensation' been mentioned as the *sole* standard of

630   NOTES TO PAGES 309–310

compensation: *Zappia* v. *Abu Dhabi*, US, 215 F.3d 247, 251 (2nd Cir. 2000); *Alberti* v. *Empresa*, US, 705 F.2d 250, 255 (7th Cir. 1983); 92 ILR 392; *De Sanchez* v. *Banco*, US, 515 F.Supp. 900, 910, fn. 10 (E.D.La. 1981); 63 ILR 584.

44 *Crist* v. *Turkey*, US, 995 F.Supp. 5, 10 (D.D.C. 1998); *Millicom* v. *Costa Rica*, US, 995 F.Supp. 14, 23 (D.D.C. 1998); *Greenpeace* v. *France*, US, 946 F.Supp. 773, 783 (C.D. Cal. 1996); *Foremost-McKesson* v. *Iran*, US, 905 F.2d 438, 452, fn. 16 (D.C.Cir. 1990); 101 ILR 536; *West* v. *Multibanco*, US, 807 F.2d 820, 832–833 (9th Cir. 1987); 84 ILR 187; *Gibbons* v. *Udaras*, US, 549 F.Supp. 1094, 1107, fn. 4 (S.D.N.Y. 1982).

45 *Banco Nacional* v. *Chase*, US, 658 F.2d 875, 892 (2nd Cir. 1981) (for detailed analysis of various positions see pp. 887–893).

46 *Siderman* v. *Argentina*, US, 965 F.2d 699, 711–712 (9th Cir. 1992); 103 ILR 454; *West* v. *Multibanco*, US, 807 F.2d 820, 832–833 (9th Cir. 1987); 84 ILR 187.

47 See, e.g., 1997 Treaty for the Encouragement and Reciprocal Protection of Investment between the US and Estonia, Art. III; 1983 Treaty between the United States of America and the Republic of Haiti concerning the Reciprocal Encouragement and Protection of Investment, Art. 3(1)(e). See also 1955 US–Iran Treaty of Amity, Economic Relations and Consular Rights, Art. IV(2).

48 See, e.g., 1988 Agreement concerning the Encouragement and Reciprocal Protection of Investment between China and Japan, Art. 5(2) and (3). See also UNGA Resolution 1803 (XVII)(1962), para. 4 ('appropriate compensation') and UNGA Resolution 3281 (XXIX)(1974), 'Charter of Economic Rights and Duties of States', Art. 2(2)(c) ('appropriate compensation').

49 Emphasis added. The best way to access the report is by searching through the 'Documents and Reports' section on the official website of the World Bank, 'Publications' page: www.worldbank.org/reference, using the title 'Guidelines on the Treatment of Foreign Direct Investment' or report number '11415'. The document is listed as 'Legal Framework for the Treatment of Foreign Investment', Vol. 2, 'Guidelines', dated 1 January 1992, Report No. 11415.

50 *Wahba* v. *National Bank*, US, 457 F.Supp.2d 721, 731–732 (E.D.Tex. 2006); *Yang* v. *Liaoning*, US, 362 F.Supp.2d 83, 101–103 (D.D.C. 2005); affirmed, *Yang* v. *Liaoning*, US, 452 F.3d 883 (D.C.Cir. 2006); *Beg* v. *Pakistan*, US, 353 F.3d 1323, 1328, fn. 3 (11th Cir. 2003); *Altmann* v. *Austria*, US, 317 F.3d 954, 968 (9th Cir. 2002); *Fogade* v. *ENB*, US, 263 F.3d 1274, 1294 (11th Cir. 2001); *Siderman* v. *Argentina*, US, 965 F.2d 699, 711 (9th Cir. 1992); 103 ILR 454; *Chuidian* v. *Philippine*, US, 912 F.2d 1095, 1105 (9th Cir. 1990); 92 ILR 480; *De Sanchez* v. *Banco*, US, 770 F.2d 1385, 1395, 1397–1398 (5th Cir. 1985); 88 ILR 75; reversing *De Sanchez* v. *Banco*, US, 515 F.Supp. 900 (E.D.La. 1981); 63 ILR 584. See also *US* v. *Belmont*, US, 301 US 324, 332 (1937); *Palicio* v. *Brush*, US, 256 F.Supp. 481, 487 (S.D.N.Y. 1966).

51 This was made especially poignant in *Siderman*, where Jose Siderman could not claim under the expropriation exception but his daughter, Susana, could, because, at the time of the alleged expropriation, Jose was an Argentine national whereas Susana was a US citizen. *Siderman* v. *Argentina*, US, 965 F.2d 699, 711 (9th Cir. 1992); 103 ILR 454.

52 *Siderman* v. *Argentina*, US, 965 F.2d 699, 711 (9th Cir. 1992); 103 ILR 454.

NOTES TO PAGES 310–312   631

53 See *Greenpeace v. France*, US, 946 F.Supp. 773, 783 (C.D.Cal. 1996); *Millicom v. Costa Rica*, US, 995 F.Supp. 14, 23 (D.D.C. 1998). See also *Austria v. Altmann*, US, 541 US 677, 714 (2004); *Interhandel Case, ICJ Reports* 1959, p. 6 at 26–27. However, the 'exhaustion' requirement does not apply where 'such remedies are clearly sham or inadequate, or their application is unreasonably prolonged', or 'when the claim is for injury for which the respondent state firmly denies responsibility'. ALI, *Third Restatement*, Vol. 2, s. 713, p. 219. See *Malewicz v. Amsterdam*, US, 362 F.Supp.2d 298, 307 (D.D.C. 2005); *Millicom v. Costa Rica*, US, 995 F.Supp. 14, 23 (D.D.C. 1998); *McKesson v. Iran*, US, 1997 WL 361177, p. 15, fn. 25 (D.D.C. 1997); *Crimson v. Electronum*, US, 629 F.Supp. 903, 909 (S.D.N.Y. 1986); *Mills v. Aetna*, US, 511 A.2d 8, 13 (D.C.App. 1986).

54 But see *I Congreso del Partido*, England, 1979, [1981] 1 All ER 1092, 1103 per Lord Denning; 64 ILR 227, 235 ('confiscation or expropriation by a foreign government of the property of aliens resident there, without compensation, is contrary to international law; and the foreign government have no immunity in respect of it'). For criticism of this opinion see Schreuer, *State Immunity*, p. 56.

55 For a case brought under the commercial activity exception see *Carey v. National Oil*, US, 453 F.Supp. 1097, 1102 (S.D.N.Y. 1978); 63 ILR 164; affirmed, *Carey v. National Oil*, US, 592 F.2d 673 (1979); 63 ILR 232.

56 See *Altmann v. Austria*, US, 317 F.3d 954, 968 (9th Cir. 2002); affirming *Altmann v. Austria*, US, 142 F.Supp.2d 1187, 1202 (C.D.Cal. 2001); *Crist v. Turkey*, US, 995 F.Supp. 5, 11 (D.D.C. 1998); *Siderman v. Argentina*, US, 965 F.2d 699, 711 (9th Cir. 1992); 103 ILR 454; *West v. Multibanco*, US, 807 F.2d 820, 826 (9th Cir. 1987); 84 ILR 187.

57 *American v. Iran*, US, 493 F.Supp. 522, 524 (D.D.C. 1980); 63 ILR 452; *Kalamazoo v. Ethiopia*, US, 616 F.Supp. 660 (W.D.Mich. 1985); 90 ILR 596.

58 *Haven v. Rzeczpospolita*, US, 68 F.Supp.2d 947, 956 (N.D.Ill. 1999); *Gabay v. Mostazafan*, US, 151 F.R.D. 250, 253 (S.D.N.Y. 1993); 107 ILR 242.

59 *Jafari v. Iran*, US, 539 F.Supp. 209, 211–212 (N.D.Ill. 1982); 72 ILR 124.

60 *Greenpeace v. France*, US, 946 F.Supp. 773, 784 (C.D.Cal. 1996).

61 *Anderman v. Austria*, US, 256 F.Supp.2d 1098, 1110 (C.D.Cal. 2003); *Dewhurst v. Telenor*, US, 83 F.Supp.2d 577, 592 (D.Md. 2000); *Haven v. Rzeczpospolita*, US, 68 F.Supp.2d 947, 957 (N.D.Ill. 1999); *Fagot v. Costa Rica*, US, 934 F.Supp. 493, 500 (D. P. R. 1996); *Intercontinental v. De Gruyter*, US, 822 F.Supp. 662, 678 (C.D.Cal. 1993); *Security v. Derderian*, US, 872 F.2d 281, 285, fn. 8 (9th Cir. 1989); *Kline v. Kaneko*, US, 685 F.Supp. 386, 391 (S.D.N.Y. 1988); 101 ILR 497; *National v. DuBois*, US, 605 F.Supp. 1206, 1211 (W.D.Pa. 1985).

62 *Garb v. Poland*, US, 440 F.3d 579, 582 (2nd Cir. 2006); affirming *Garb v. Poland*, US, 207 F.Supp.2d 16 (E.D.N.Y. 2002); *Lord Day v. Vietnam*, US, 134 F.Supp.2d 549, 560–561 (S.D.N.Y. 2001); *Haven v. Rzeczpospolita*, US, 68 F.Supp.2d 947, 957 (N.D.Ill. 1999); *Crist v. Turkey*, US, 995 F.Supp. 5, 10 (D.D.C. 1998); *Hirsh v. Israel*, US, 962 F.Supp. 377, 383 (S.D.N.Y. 1997); 113 ILR 543; *Greenpeace v. France*, US, 946 F.Supp. 773, 784 (C.D.Cal. 1996); *Intercontinental v. De Gruyter*, US, 822 F.Supp. 662, 678 (C.D.Cal. 1993); *Fickling v. Australia*, US, 775 F.Supp. 66, 71–72

632   NOTES TO PAGES 312-314

(E.D.N.Y. 1991); 103 ILR 447; *Kline* v. *Kaneko*, US, 685 F.Supp. 386, 391 (S.D.N.Y. 1988); 101 ILR 497.

63 Pursuant to 22 USC § 2459. See *Malewicz* v. *Amsterdam*, US, 362 F.Supp.2d 298, 310–312 (D.D.C. 2005).

64 *Kalamazoo* v. *Ethiopia*, US, 616 F.Supp. 660, 664 (W.D.Mich. 1985); 90 ILR 596; *Gibbons* v. *Udaras*, US, 549 F.Supp. 1094, 1107, fn. 4 (S.D.N.Y. 1982); *De Sanchez* v. *Banco*, US, 515 F.Supp. 900, 910–912 (E.D.La. 1981); 63 ILR 584.

65 *Garb* v. *Poland*, US, 207 F.Supp.2d 16, 33 (E.D.N.Y. 2002); affirmed, *Garb* v. *Poland*, US, 440 F.3d 579 (2nd Cir. 2006).

66 *Dayton* v. *Czechoslovak*, US, 672 F.Supp. 7, 10 (D.D.C. 1986); 79 ILR 590; affirmed, *Dayton* v. *Czechoslovak*, US, 834 F.2d 203, 206 (D.C.Cir. 1987); 79 ILR 590; *Vencedora* v. *Compagnie*, US, 730 F.2d 195, 204 (5th Cir. 1984); 87 ILR 520, 530.

67 *Altmann* v. *Austria*, US, 142 F.Supp.2d 1187, 1204 (C.D.Cal. 2001); affirmed, *Altmann* v. *Austria*, US, 317 F.3d 954 (9th Cir. 2002).

68 *Vencedora* v. *Compagnie*, US, 730 F.2d 195, 204 (5th Cir. 1984); 87 ILR 520, 530; *Greenpeace* v. *France*, US, 946 F.Supp. 773, 784 (C.D.Cal. 1996); *Nemariam* v. *Ethiopia*, US, 400 F.Supp.2d 76, 84–86 (D.D.C. 2005).

69 *Nemariam* v. *Ethiopia*, US, 491 F.3d 470, 480–481 (D.C.Cir. 2007); 135 ILR 679; on this point overruling *Nemariam* v. *Ethiopia*, US, 400 F.Supp.2d 76, 84–86 (D.D.C. 2005). See also *Anderman* v. *Austria*, US, 256 F.Supp.2d 1098, 1110–1111 (C.D. Cal. 2003), where the court implied that to 'own' meant to be 'in possession'.

70 *Vencedora* v. *Compagnie*, US, 730 F.2d 195, 204 (5th Cir. 1984); 87 ILR 520, 530.

71 *Antares* v. *Nigeria*, US, 948 F.2d 90, 97 (2nd Cir. 1991); 107 ILR 225; vacated on other grounds, *Antares* v. *Nigeria*, US, 505 US 1215 (1992); and affirmed on rehearing, *Antares* v. *Nigeria*, US, 999 F.2d 33 (2nd Cir. 1993); 107 ILR 225.

72 *Gabay* v. *Mostazafan*, US, 151 F.R.D. 250, 253–255 (S.D.N.Y. 1993); 107 ILR 242.

73 *Gabay* v. *Mostazafan*, US, 968 F.Supp. 895, 898–900 (S.D.N.Y. 1997); affirmed, *Gabay* v. *Mostazafan*, US, 152 F.3d 918 (2nd Cir. 1998) (Table).

74 The Cuban Liberty and Democratic Solidarity (Libertad) Act of 1996 (Helms-Burton Act), Public Law 104-114, 12 March 1996, 35 ILM 357 (1996). Title III of the Act, entitled 'Protection of Property Rights of United States Nationals', encompasses ss. 301 through 306.

75 European Union: Demarches.

76 European Union: Council Regulation (EC) No. 2271/96. See especially, Arts. 1, 4, 5, 6 and Annex. At the same time, the EU affirmed that it was 'not European Union policy to try to bring about change by coercive measures'. European Union: Council of Ministers Common Position on Cuba.

77 See, e.g., Canada, Foreign Extraterritorial Measures Act; Mexico, Act to Protect Trade, 1996; OAS, Inter-American Juridical Committee Opinion, 1996; Cuba, Reaffirmation of Cuban Dignity and Sovereignty Act. For scholarly opinions in the US contrast, e.g., Lowenfeld, Congress, 434 ('unlawful and unwise'), with Clagett, Title III, 440 (lawful). For criticism of the Helms-Burton Act see also Busby, Jurisdiction; van den Brink, Helms-Burton; Weerts and Chaïbi, Le Titre III.

78 The suspension is made in the form of a letter addressed by the US President, twice a year in January and July, to the Chairmen and Ranking Members of

NOTES TO PAGES 314–317   633

the House and Senate Committees on Appropriations, the House Committee on Foreign Affairs, and the Senate Committee on Foreign Relations. See United States: Statement by the President on Suspending Title III of the Helms-Burton Act, 3 January 1997, 36 ILM 216 (1997). That is to say, this part of the Helms-Burton Act has been suspended, continuously on a six-month basis, ever since the Act itself came into force.

79 See, e.g., EU–US Memorandum of Understanding, whereby the EU agreed to suspend proceedings of the WTO panel, on condition that the US should continue to suspend Title III. For comment see Smis and van der Borght, The EU–US Compromise.

80 See, especially, *Argentine Republic* v. *Amerada Hess*, US, 488 US 428, 434, 439, 443 (1989); 102 L.Ed.2d 818, 828, 831, 834; 81 ILR 658, 663, 666, 669.

Chapter 8

1 For the sake of simplicity these terms are used interchangeably in this book but as juridical concepts they may have different connotations. For an exposition of their nuances see Sucharitkul, Third Report, *YILC*, 1981-II-1, p. 125 at 141–50, paras. 45–92.

2 See *Ministry* v. *Cubic*, US, 385 F.3d 1206, 1218 (9th Cir. 2004); *Ministry* v. *Cubic*, US, 29 F.Supp.2d 1168 (S.D.Cal. 1998); *Philippines* v. *Westinghouse*, US, 43 F.3d 65 (3rd Cir. 1994/1995); *Panama* v. *Air*, US, (S.D.Fla. 1988); 96 ILR 43; *Ministry* v. *Gould*, US, 887 F.2d 1357 (9th Cir. 1989); 969 F.2d 764 (9th Cir. 1992); 96 ILR 1; *Germany* v. *Elicofon*, US, 536 F.Supp. 813 (E.D.N.Y. 1978); 94 ILR 133; *Philippines* v. *Marcos (No. 2)*, US, 818 F.2d 1473 (9th Cir. 1987); 862 F.2d 1355 (9th Cir. 1988); 81 ILR 608; *Philippines* v. *Marcos (No. 1)*, US, 806 F.2d 344 (2nd Cir. 1986); 81 ILR 581; *Iran* v. *Pahlavi*, US, 464 N.Y.S.2d 487 (1983); 478 N.Y.S.2d 597 (1984); 81 ILR 557; *Argentina* v. *New York*, US, 25 N.Y.2d 252 (1969); 53 ILR 544. The only qualification is that an unrecognized State cannot sue in a foreign court, but then this does not prevent an unrecognized State from being made a defendant. See *Banco Nacional* v. *Sabbatino*, US, 376 US 398, 410–411 (1964); 35 ILR 2; *Guaranty* v. *US*, US, 304 US 126, 137 (1938); 9 AD 184; *Vietnam* v. *Pfizer*, US, 556 F.2d 892, 894 (8th Cir. 1977); 94 ILR 199; *National* v. *Stolt Sheaf*, US, 860 F.2d 551, 554–555 (2nd Cir. 1988); 87 ILR 583; reversing *National* v. *Stolt Sheaf*, US, 671 F.Supp. 1009 (S.D.N.Y. 1987); *Klinghoffer* v. *Achille Lauro*, US, 937 F.2d 44, 48 (2nd Cir. 1991); 96 ILR 68; *Liberia* v. *Bickford*, US, 787 F.Supp. 397 (S.D.N.Y. 1992); 96 ILR 90; *Haiti* v. *Duvalier*, England, 1988, [1990] QB 202; 107 ILR 490; *French Consulate Case*, Germany, (1988) 114 ILR 507; *Republic of China* v. *Chuka*, Japan, (1955) 23 ILR 210, 211; *USA* v. *Republic of China*, Australia, (1950) 17 ILR 168; *Indian National* v. *Maux*, India, (1955) 22 ILR 248.

3 This formula appears in ss. 1605(a)(1), 1610(a)(1), 1610(b)(1), 1610(d)(1), and 1611(b)(1).

4 US House of Representatives, Report No. 94-1487, 1976, p. 18; 1976 USCCAN 6604, 6617.

634   NOTES TO PAGES 317–319

5 ALI, *Third Restatement*, Vol. 1, s. 456(3), p. 416.
6 *Aquamar v. Del Monte*, US, 179 F.3d 1279, 1287, n. 18 (11th Cir. 1999).
7 *Aquamar v. Del Monte*, US, 179 F.3d 1279, 1294 (11th Cir. 1999). See Hulbig, *Aquamar*; McCoy, Broadening; Pittman, Ambassadorial.
8 *Aquamar v. Del Monte*, US, 179 F.3d 1279, 1291–1292 (11th Cir. 1999).
9 *Maritime v. Caribbean*, US, 722 F.Supp. 1032, 1037–1038 (S.D.N.Y. 1989); confirming *Maritime v. Caribbean*, US, 689 F.Supp. 1340, 1351 (S.D.N.Y. 1988).
10 *Aquamar v. Del Monte*, US, 179 F.3d 1279, 1299 (11th Cir. 1999).
11 *First Fidelity v. Antigua*, US, 877 F.2d 189, 193–196 (2nd Cir. 1989); 99 ILR 125.
12 US House of Representatives, Report No. 94-1487, 1976, p. 18; 1976 USCCAN 6604, 6617.
13 *Chuidian v. Philippine*, US, 912 F.2d 1095, 1103–1104 (9th Cir. 1990); 92 ILR 480. Of course the immunity of a State entity cannot be waived by a foreign corporation: *Coleman v. Alcolac*, US, 888 F.Supp. 1388, 1403 (S.D.Tex. 1995).
14 *Hercaire v. Argentina*, US, 821 F.2d 559, 563–565 (11th Cir. 1987); 98 ILR 48; partly reversing *Hercaire v. Argentina*, US, 642 F.Supp. 126 (S.D.Fla. 1986).
15 *Foremost-McKesson v. Iran*, US, 905 F.2d 438, 452 (D.C.Cir. 1990); 101 ILR 536; *Berkovitz v. Iran*, US, 735 F.2d 329, 333 (9th Cir. 1984); 81 ILR 552; *S & S v. Masinexportimport*, US, 706 F.2d 411, 417 (2nd Cir. 1983); 72 ILR 183; *Jafari v. Iran*, US, 539 F.Supp. 209, 211 (N.D.Ill. 1982); 72 ILR 124; *Harris v. National*, US, 691 F.2d 1344, 1350 (11th Cir. 1982); 72 ILR 172; *Security v. Iran*, US, 513 F.Supp. 864, 880, fn. 23 (C.D.Cal. 1981); *Mashayekhi v. Iran*, US, 515 F.Supp. 41, 43 (D. D.C. 1981). For similar decisions concerning a virtually identical provision, Art. XV(3) of the 1950 US–Ireland Treaty of Friendship, Commerce and Navigation, see *Gibbons v. Udaras*, US, 549 F.Supp. 1094, 1107–1108, fn. 4 (S.D.N.Y. 1982) and *Gibbons v. Ireland*, US, 532 F.Supp. 668, 672 (D.D.C. 1982); 86 ILR 75. For other instances of the State waiving immunity for enterprises see *Ferrostaal v. SS Lash*, US, 652 F.Supp. 420, 423 (S.D.N.Y. 1987); *Gadsby v. Romania*, US, 698 F.Supp. 483, 485 (S.D.N.Y. 1988).
16 See US House of Representatives, Report No. 94-1487, 1976, p. 18; 1976 USCCAN 6604, 6617.
17 *LNC v. Nicaragua*, US, 115 F.Supp.2d 358, 361 (S.D.N.Y. 2000) (emphasis added).
18 *LNC v. Nicaragua*, US, 115 F.Supp.2d 358, 362 (S.D.N.Y. 2000) (citing *Bancec*, US, 462 US 611, 620 (1983); affirmed, *LNC v. Banco*, US, 228 F.3d 423 (2nd Cir. 2000).
19 US House of Representatives, Report No. 94-1487, 1976, p. 18; 1976 USCCAN 6604, 6617.
20 See, e.g., *International v. Caja*, US, 293 F.3d 392, 399–400 (7th Cir. 2002).
21 *Enron v. Titan*, US, 82 F.Supp.2d 602, 611 (W.D.La. 1999).
22 *Maritime v. Guinea*, US, 693 F.2d 1094, 1100, fn. 10 (D.C.Cir. 1982); 72 ILR 152; reversing *Maritime v. Guinea*, US, 505 F.Supp. 141 (D.D.C. 1981); 63 ILR 535. For the specificity of waiver see below.
23 *Gutch v. Germany*, US, 444 F.Supp.2d 1, 8 (D.D.C. 2006); *Walker v. Congo*, US, 395 F.3d 229, 234 (5th Cir. 2004); *Good v. Aramco*, US, 971 F.Supp. 254, 261 (S.D.Tex. 1997); *Castro v. Saudi Arabia*, US, 510 F.Supp. 309, 312 (W.D.Tex. 1980); 63 ILR 419.

NOTES TO PAGES 319–320   635

24 *Capital* v. *Argentina*, US, 552 F.3d 289, 294 (2nd Cir. 2009); *EM* v. *Argentina*, US, 473 F.3d 463, 485, fn. 22 (2nd Cir. 2007); *Kensington* v. *Congo*, US, 461 F.3d 238, 243 (2nd Cir. 2006); *Gutch* v. *Germany*, US, 444 F.Supp.2d 1, 9 (D.D.C. 2006); *Ungar* v. *Palestinian Authority*, US, 325 F.Supp.2d 15, 27 (D.R.I. 2004); *Banco* v. *Mutual Marine*, US, 344 F.3d 255, 261 (2nd Cir. 2003); *Hwang* v. *Japan*, US, 172 F.Supp.2d 52, 59 (D.D.C. 2001); affirmed, *Hwang* v. *Japan*, US, 332 F.3d 679 (D.C. Cir. 2003); *World Wide* v. *Kazakhstan*, US, 296 F.3d 1154, 1162 (D.C.Cir. 2002); *Saudi Basic* v. *Exxonmobil*, US, 194 F.Supp.2d 378, 402 (D.N.J. 2002); *Wasserstein* v. *Formosa*, US, 2000 WL 573231, p. 4 (S.D.N.Y. 2000); *Aquamar* v. *Del Monte*, US, 179 F.3d 1279, 1292 (11th Cir. 1999); *Aguinda* v. *Texaco*, US, 175 F.R.D. 50, 52 (S.D.N.Y. 1997); vacated on other grounds *sub nom Jota* v. *Texaco*, US, 157 F.3d 153 (2nd Cir. 1998); *Commercial* v. *Corporacion*, US, 980 F.Supp. 710, 712–713 (S.D.N.Y. 1997); *Eaglet* v. *Banco*, US, 839 F.Supp. 232, 234 (S.D.N.Y. 1993); *S & S* v. *Masinexportimport*, US, 706 F.2d 411, 416 (2nd Cir. 1983); 72 ILR 183; *Libra Bank* v. *Banco*, US, 676 F.2d 47, 49 (2nd Cir. 1982); 72 ILR 119.

25 *Gutch* v. *Germany*, US, 444 F.Supp.2d 1, 9 (D.D.C. 2006).

26 *Hwang* v. *Japan*, US, 172 F.Supp.2d 52, 59 (D.D.C. 2001) (Japan did not waive immunity by accepting the Potsdam Declaration); affirmed, *Hwang* v. *Japan*, US, 332 F.3d 679 (D.C.Cir. 2003).

27 *Argentine Republic* v. *Amerada Hess*, US, 488 US 428, 442 (1989); 102 L.Ed.2d 818, 833 (1989); 81 ILR 658, 668. See also *Haven* v. *Rzeczpospolita*, US, 215 F.3d 727, 733–734 (7th Cir. 2000); affirming *Haven* v. *Rzeczpospolita*, US, 68 F.Supp.2d 947 (N.D.Ill. 1999); *Greenpeace* v. *France*, US, 946 F.Supp. 773, 781 (C.D.Cal. 1996); *Travel* v. *Swaziland*, US, 107 ILR 219, 222 (D.D.C. 1990); *Von Dardel* v. *USSR*, US, 736 F.Supp. 1, 7 (D.D.C. 1990); overruling *Von Dardel* v. *USSR*, US, 623 F.Supp. 246, 255–256; 77 ILR 258; *Colonial Bank* v. *Compagnie*, US, 645 F.Supp. 1457, 1460–1461 (S.D.N.Y. 1986); 98 ILR 26; *Frolova* v. *USSR*, US, 761 F.2d 370, 376 (7th Cir. 1985); 85 ILR 236; affirming *Frolova* v. *USSR*, US, 558 F.Supp. 358 (N.D.Ill. 1983).

28 *Reers* v. *Deutsche Bahn*, US, 320 F.Supp.2d 140, 147–148 (S.D.N.Y. 2004).

29 *Smith* v. *Libya*, US, 101 F.3d 239, 245–246 (2nd Cir. 1996); 113 ILR 534.

30 *Eaglet* v. *Banco*, US, 839 F.Supp. 232, 234 (S.D.N.Y. 1993); affirmed, *Eaglet* v. *Banco*, US, 23 F.3d 641 (2nd Cir. 1994).

31 *Gulf* v. *Congo*, US, 370 F.3d 65, 71–74 (D.C.Cir. 2004); reversing *Gulf* v. *Congo*, US, 276 F.Supp.2d 20 (D.D.C. 2003); *Kern* v. *Oesterreichische*, US, 178 F.Supp.2d 367, 373–374 (S.D.N.Y. 2001). Even more caution is needed where a third party attempts to benefit from an implied waiver: *Pere* v. *Nuovo*, US, 150 F.3d 477, 482 (5th Cir. 1998); *Cargill* v. *Pavel Dybenko*, US, 991 F.2d 1012, 1017 (2nd Cir. 1993); 103 ILR 572; *Raccoon* v. *Navoi*, US, 244 F.Supp.2d 1130, 1139 (D.Colo. 2002); *Kern* v. *Oesterreichische*, US, 178 F.Supp.2d 367, 374–375 (S.D.N.Y. 2001); *Zernicek* v. *Petroleos*, US, 614 F.Supp. 407, 411 (S.D.Tex. 1985); affirmed, *Zernicek* v. *Brown*, US, 826 F.2d 415, 419 (5th Cir. 1987); 92 ILR 442.

32 *Anderman* v. *Austria*, US, 256 F.Supp.2d 1098, 1106 (C.D.Cal. 2003).

33 *World Wide* v. *Kazakhstan*, US, 296 F.3d 1154, 1162–1164 (D.C.Cir. 2002); partly affirming *World Wide* v. *Kazakhstan*, US, 116 F.Supp.2d 98 (D.D.C. 2000).

636   NOTES TO PAGES 320–323

34 *Aquamar* v. *Del Monte*, US, 179 F.3d 1279, 1293 (11th Cir. 1999).
35 *World Wide* v. *Kazakhstan*, US, 296 F.3d 1154, 1162 (D.C.Cir. 2002); *Af-Cap* v. *Chevron*, US, 475 F.3d 1080, 1087 (9th Cir. 2007); *Gutch* v. *Germany*, US, 444 F.Supp.2d 1, 8 (D.D.C. 2006); *Ungar* v. *Palestinian Authority*, US, 325 F.Supp.2d 15, 27 (D.R.I. 2004); *Atlantic* v. *Inter-American*, US, 251 F.Supp.2d 126, 133 (D.D.C. 2003); *Fickling* v. *Australia*, US, 775 F.Supp. 66, 70 (E.D.N.Y. 1991); 103 ILR 447.
36 *Kensington* v. *Congo*, US, 461 F.3d 238, 243 (2nd Cir. 2006).
37 *Capital* v. *Argentina*, US, 552 F.3d 289, 293–294 (2nd Cir. 2009).
38 *National* v. *Congo*, US, 729 F.Supp. 936, 940 (S.D.N.Y. 1989).
39 *International* v. *Embassy*, US, 131 F.Supp.2d 248, 252 (D.D.C. 2001).
40 *Ferrostaal* v. *SS Lash*, US, 652 F.Supp. 420, 423 (S.D.N.Y. 1987); *Gadsby* v. *Romania*, US, 698 F.Supp. 483, 485 (S.D.N.Y. 1988).
41 *Karaha* v. *Perusahaan*, US, 313 F.3d 70, 82–83 (2nd Cir. 2002).
42 *Atwood* v. *Petroleo*, US, 875 F.2d 1174, 1177 (5th Cir. 1989) (emphasis in the original); cited with approval in *Walker* v. *Congo*, US, 395 F.3d 229, 234 (5th Cir. 2004).
43 *Walker* v. *Congo*, US, 395 F.3d 229, 234 (5th Cir. 2004).
44 *Proyecfin* v. *Banco*, US, 760 F.2d 390, 393 (2nd Cir. 1985) (emphasis in the original); 87 ILR 538.
45 *Coyle* v. *PT*, US, 363 F.3d 979, 984 (9th Cir. 2004). Such a permit no doubt constitutes an explicit waiver of immunity and it also extends to the liability insurer of the permit holder: *In re Air Crash*, US, 392 F.Supp.2d 461, 466, fn. 3 and 469 (E.D.N.Y. 2005). 'International transportation' is defined by Art. 1(2) of the 1929 Warsaw Convention. See *Lee* v. *China*, US, 669 F.Supp.979, 980 (C.D. Cal. 1987). Previously, such permits were issued by the Civil Aeronautics Board, and were equally effective as indicating an express waiver: *Argentine* v. *Ross*, US, 408 N.Y.S.2d 831, 832 (N.Y.S.C. 1978); 63 ILR 195, 196.
46 *Coyle* v. *PT*, US, 363 F.3d 979, 989–993 (9th Cir. 2004); reversing *Coyle* v. *PT*, US, 180 F.Supp.2d 1160 (D.Or. 2001). See also *Compania* v. *US District*, US, 859 F.2d 1354, 1359 (9th Cir. 1988); 98 ILR 69 (between points in Mexico); *Barkanic* v. *General*, US, 822 F.2d 11, 12 (2nd Cir. 1987); 98 ILR 44 (between destinations in China).
47 *Trajano* v. *Marcos*, US, 978 F.2d 493, 498, fn. 11 (9th Cir. 1992); 103 ILR 521.
48 *Libra Bank* v. *Banco*, US, 676 F.2d 47, 49–50 (2nd Cir. 1982) (emphases added); 72 ILR 119. See also *Banco* v. *Mutual*, US, 344 F.3d 255, 261 (2nd Cir. 2003); *Kensington* v. *Congo*, US, 461 F.3d 238, 243 (2nd Cir. 2006).
49 *S & S Machinery* v. *Masinexportimport*, US, 706 F.2d 411, 416 (2nd Cir. 1983); 72 ILR 183, quoted in *Banco* v. *Mutual*, US, 344 F.3d 255, 261 (2nd Cir. 2003) and *Kensington* v. *Congo*, US, 461 F.3d 238, 243 (2nd Cir. 2006).
50 *S & S Machinery*, US, 706 F.2d 411, 417 (2nd Cir. 1983); 72 ILR 183. For the decision that waiver of immunity from 'other liability' does not constitute a waiver of immunity from prejudgment attachment see also *Security* v. *Iran*, US, 513 F.Supp. 864, 879–880 (C.D.Cal. 1981); *New England* v. *Iran*, US, 502 F.Supp. 120, 126–127 (S.D.N.Y. 1981); 63 ILR 497; remanded on other grounds, *New England* v. *Iran*, 646 F.2d 779 (2nd Cir. 1981); *E-Systems* v. *Iran*, US, 491

F.Supp. 1294, 1300–1302 (N.D.Tex. 1980); 63 ILR 424; *Reading* v. *National*, US, 478 F.Supp. 724, 728 (S.D.N.Y. 1979); 63 ILR 305; *Behring*. v. *Imperial*, US, 475 F.Supp. 383, 392–393 (D.N.J. 1979); 63 ILR 261.

51 *ICC* v. *Industrial*, US, 886 F.Supp. 1, 2 (S.D.N.Y. 1995).

52 US House of Representatives, Report No. 94-1487, 1976, p. 18; 1976 USCCAN 6604, 6617. This list forms the core of the US jurisprudence on implied waiver. See *Af-Cap* v. *Congo*, US, 462 F.3d 417, 426 (5th Cir. 2006); *Gutch* v. *Germany*, US, 444 F.Supp.2d 1, 9 (D.D.C. 2006); *Abur* v. *Sudan*, US, 437 F.Supp.2d 166, 178 (D.D.C. 2006); *Poddar* v. *State Bank*, US, 235 F.R.D. 592, 598 (S.D.N.Y. 2006); *Calzadilla* v. *Banco*, US, 413 F.3d 1285, 1287 (11th Cir. 2005); *Elixir* v. *Perusahaan*, US, 267 F.Supp.2d 659, 666 (S.D.Tex. 2003); *Anderman* v. *Austria*, US, 256 F.Supp.2d 1098, 1106 (C.D.Cal. 2003); *In re Philippines*, US, 309 F.3d 1143, 1151 (9th Cir. 2002); *World Wide* v. *Kazakhstan*, US, 296 F.3d 1154, 1161, fn. 11 (D.C.Cir. 2002); *World Wide* v. *Nammo*, US, 51 Fed.Appx. 403, 405 (4th Cir. 2002); *Saudi Basic* v. *Exxonmobil*, US, 194 F.Supp.2d 378, 402 (D.N.J. 2002); *Sampson* v. *Germany*, US, 250 F.3d 1145, 1154 (7th Cir. 2001); *Kern* v. *Oesterreichische*, US, 178 F.Supp.2d 367, 374 (S.D.N.Y. 2001); *Abrams* v. *Société*, US, 175 F.Supp.2d 423, 431 (E.D.N.Y. 2001); *Alpha* v. *Nippon*, US, 199 F.3d 1078, 1085 (9th Cir. 1999); *Aquamar* v. *Del Monte*, US, 179 F.3d 1279, 1291, fn. 24 (11th Cir. 1999); *In re Tamimi*, US, 176 F.3d 274, 278 (4th Cir. 1999); *Cabiri* v. *Ghana*, US, 165 F.3d 193, 201, fn. 5 (2nd Cir. 1999); *Enron* v. *Titan*, US, 82 F.Supp.2d 602, 608, 611 (W.D.La. 1999); *HSMV* v. *ADI*, US, 72 F.Supp.2d 1122, 1127 (C.D.Cal 1999); *Trans Chemical*, US, 978 F.Supp. 266, 291, fn. 119 (S.D.Tex. 1997); affirmed, *Trans Chemical* v. *China*, US, 161 F.3d 314, 319 (5th Cir. 1998); *Pere* v. *Nuovo*, US, 150 F.3d 477, 482 (5th Cir. 1998); *Commercial* v. *Corporacion*, US, 980 F.Supp. 710, 712, fn. 1 (S.D.N.Y. 1997); *Good* v. *Aramco*, US, 971 F.Supp. 254, 261 (S.D.Tex. 1997); *Smith* v. *Libya*, US, 101 F.3d 239, 243 (2nd Cir. 1996); 113 ILR 534; *Hilao* v. *Marcos*, US, 94 F.3d 539, 546 (9th Cir. 1996); *Corporacion* v. *Respect*, US, 89 F.3d 650, 655 (9th Cir. 1996); *Coastal* v. *Gustav Sule*, US, 942 F.Supp. 1082, 1086–1087 (E.D.La. 1996); *Gates* v. *Victor*, US, 54 F.3d 1457, 1465 (9th Cir. 1995); 107 ILR 371; *Coleman* v. *Alcolac*, US, 888 F.Supp. 1388, 1403 (S.D.Tex. 1995); *Eckert* v. *Fiji*, US, 32 F.3d 77, 79 (4th Cir. 1994); 107 ILR 347; *Princz* v. *Germany*, US, 26 F.3d 1166, 1174 (D.C. Cir. 1994); 103 ILR 594; *Rodriguez* v. *Transnave*, US, 8 F.3d 284, 287 (5th Cir. 1993); *Drexel* v. *Committee*, US, 12 F.3d 317, 325 (2nd Cir. 1993); *Cargill* v. *Pavel Dybenko*, US, 991 F.2d 1012, 1017 (2nd Cir. 1993); 103 ILR 572; *Eaglet* v. *Banco*, US, 839 F.Supp. 232, 234 (S.D.N.Y. 1993); *Kao Hwa* v. *China Steel*, US, 816 F.Supp. 910, 916 (S.D.N.Y. 1993); *Siderman* v. *Argentina*, US, 965 F.2d 699, 721 (9th Cir. 1992); 103 ILR 454; *Shapiro* v. *Bolivia*, US, 930 F.2d 1013, 1017 (2nd Cir. 1991); 98 ILR 109; *Fickling* v. *Australia*, US, 775 F.Supp. 66, 70 (E.D.N.Y. 1991); 103 ILR 447; *Von Dardel* v. *USSR*, US, 736 F.Supp. 1, 6 (D.D.C. 1990); *Joseph* v. *Office*, US, 830 F.2d 1018, 1022 (9th Cir. 1987); 101 ILR 485; *Colonial Bank* v. *Compagnie*, US, 645 F.Supp. 1457, 1461 (S.D.N.Y. 1986); 98 ILR 26; *Frolova* v. *USSR*, US, 761 F.2d 370, 377 (7th Cir. 1985); 85 ILR 236; *Zernicek* v. *Petroleos*, US, 614 F.Supp. 407, 411 (S.D. Tex. 1985); affirmed, *Zernicek* v. *Brown*, US, 826 F.2d 415 (5th Cir. 1987); 92 ILR 442; *Maritime* v. *Guinea*, US, 693 F.2d 1094, 1102 (D.C.Cir. 1982); 72 ILR 152; *Ohntrup* v.

638   NOTES TO PAGE 324

Firearms, US, 516 F.Supp. 1281, 1284–1285 (E.D.Pa. 1981); 63 ILR 632; affirmed, *Ohntrup* v. *Firearms*, US, 760 F.2d 259 (3rd Cir. 1985) (Table); *Castro* v. *Saudi Arabia*, US, 510 F.Supp. 309, 312 (W.D.Tex. 1980); 63 ILR 419; *Harris* v. *VAO*, US, 481 F.Supp. 1056, 1158 (E.D.N.Y. 1979); 63 ILR 318.

53 *In re Tamimi*, US, 176 F.3d 274, 278 (4th Cir. 1999). See also *World Wide* v. *Nammo*, US, 51 Fed.Appx. 403, 405 (4th Cir. 2002).

54 *Af-Cap* v. *Congo*, US, 462 F.3d 417, 427 (5th Cir. 2006); *Gutch* v. *Germany*, US, 444 F.Supp.2d 1, 9 (D.D.C. 2006); *Abur* v. *Sudan*, US, 437 F.Supp.2d 166, 177 (D.D.C. 2006); *Poddar* v. *State Bank*, US, 235 F.R.D. 592, 598 (S.D.N.Y. 2006); *Calzadilla* v. *Banco*, US, 413 F.3d 1285, 1287 (11th Cir. 2005); *Doe I* v. *Israel*, US, 400 F.Supp.2d 86, 105 (D.D.C. 2005); *Blaxland* v. *Commonwealth*, US, 323 F.3d 1198, 1206 (9th Cir. 2003); *Elixir* v. *Perusahaan*, US, 267 F.Supp.2d 659, 666 (S.D.Tex. 2003); *In re Philippines*, US, 309 F.3d 1143, 1151 (9th Cir. 2002); *World Wide* v. *Kazakhstan*, US, 296 F.3d 1154, 1161, fn. 11 (D.C.Cir. 2002); *Raccoon* v. *Navoi*, US, 244 F. Supp.2d 1130, 1139 (D.Colo. 2002); *Saudi Basic* v. *Exxonmobil*, US, 194 F.Supp.2d 378, 402 (D.N.J. 2002); *Sampson* v. *Germany*, US, 250 F.3d 1145, 1156 (7th Cir. 2001); *Corzo* v. *Banco*, US, 243 F.3d 519, 523 (9th Cir. 2001); *Kern* v. *Oesterreichische*, US, 178 F.Supp.2d 367, 374 (S.D.N.Y. 2001); *Lord Day* v. *Vietnam*, US, 134 F.Supp.2d 549, 558 (S.D.N.Y. 2001); *S & Davis* v. *Yemen*, US, 218 F.3d 1292, 1301 (11th Cir. 2000); *Transatlantic* v. *Shanghai*, US, 204 F.3d 384, 391 (2nd Cir. 2000); *Daliberti* v. *Iraq*, US, 97 F.Supp.2d 38, 48, fn. 5 (D.D.C. 2000); *Alpha* v. *Nippon*, US, 199 F.3d 1078, 1085 (9th Cir. 1999); *Creighton* v. *Qatar*, US, 181 F.3d 118, 122 (D.C.Cir. 1999); *In re Tamimi*, US, 176 F.3d 274, 278 (4th Cir. 1999); *Cabiri* v. *Ghana*, US, 165 F.3d 193, 201 (2nd Cir. 1999); *Mendenhall* v. *Saudi*, US, 991 F. Supp. 856, 858 (S.D.Tex. 1998); *Commercial* v. *Corporacion*, US, 980 F.Supp. 710, 712, fn. 1 (S.D.N.Y. 1997); *Trans Chemical*, US, 978 F.Supp. 266, 291, fn. 119 (S.D. Tex. 1997); affirmed, *Trans Chemical* v. *China*, US, 161 F.3d 314, 319 (5th Cir. 1998); *Pere* v. *Nuovo*, US, 150 F.3d 477, 482 (5th Cir. 1998); *Hirsh* v. *Israel*, US, 962 F.Supp. 377, 380 (S.D.N.Y. 1997); 113 ILR 543; *Smith* v. *Libya*, US, 101 F.3d 239, 243 (2nd Cir. 1996); 113 ILR 534; *Hilao* v. *Marcos*, US, 94 F.3d 539, 546 (9th Cir. 1996); *Corporacion* v. *Respect*, US, 89 F.3d 650, 655 (9th Cir. 1996); *Greenpeace* v. *France*, US, 946 F.Supp. 773, 781 (C.D.Cal. 1996); *Coastal* v. *Gustav Sule*, US, 942 F. Supp. 1082, 1087 (E.D.La. 1996); *Gates* v. *Victor*, US, 54 F.3d 1457, 1465 (9th Cir. 1995); 107 ILR 371; *Coleman* v. *Alcolac*, US, 888 F.Supp. 1388, 1403 (S.D.Tex. 1995); *Drexel* v. *Committee*, US, 12 F.3d 317, 325 (2nd Cir. 1993); *Rodriguez* v. *Transnave*, US, 8 F.3d 284, 287 (5th Cir. 1993); *Cargill* v. *Pavel Dybenko*, US, 991 F.2d 1012, 1017 (2nd Cir. 1993); 103 ILR 572; *Seetransport* v. *Navimpex*, US, 989 F.2d 572, 577 (2nd Cir. 1993); 103 ILR 559; *Eaglet* v. *Banco*, US, 839 F.Supp. 232, 235 (S.D.N.Y. 1993); *Kao Hwa* v. *China Steel*, US, 816 F.Supp. 910, 916 (S.D.N.Y. 1993); *Siderman* v. *Argentina*, US, 965 F.2d 699, 720 (9th Cir. 1992); 103 ILR 454; *Shapiro* v. *Bolivia*, US, 930 F.2d 1013, 1017 (2nd Cir. 1991); 98 ILR 109; *Foremost-McKesson* v. *Iran*, US, 905 F.2d 438, 444 (D.C.Cir. 1990); 101 ILR 536; *L'Europeenne* v. *Venezuela*, US, 700 F.Supp. 114, 123 (S.D.N.Y. 1988); 98 ILR 100 note; *Joseph* v. *Office*, US, 830 F.2d 1018, 1022 (9th Cir. 1987); 101 ILR 485; *Colonial Bank* v. *Compagnie*, US, 645 F.Supp. 1457, 1461 (S.D.N.Y. 1986); 98 ILR 26; *Zernicek* v. *Petroleos*, US, 614 F.Supp. 407, 411

NOTES TO PAGES 324–325 639

(S.D.Tex. 1985); affirmed, *Zernicek v. Brown*, US, 826 F.2d 415 (5th Cir. 1987); 92 ILR 442; *Frolova v. USSR*, US, 761 F.2d 370, 377 (7th Cir. 1985); 85 ILR 236.

55 *Af-Cap* v. *Congo*, US, 462 F.3d 417, 426 (5th Cir. 2006); *Gutch* v. *Germany*, US, 444 F.Supp.2d 1, 9 (D.D.C. 2006); *Calzadilla* v. *Banco*, US, 413 F.3d 1285, 1287–1288 (11th Cir. 2005); *In re Philippines*, US, 309 F.3d 1143, 1151–1152 (9th Cir. 2002); *Saudi Basic* v. *Exxonmobil*, US, 194 F.Supp.2d 378, 402 (D.N.J. 2002); *Abrams* v. *Société*, US, 175 F.Supp.2d 423, 431 (E.D.N.Y. 2001); *Aquamar* v. *Del Monte*, US, 179 F.3d 1279, 1291, fn. 24 (11th Cir. 1999); *In re Tamimi*, US, 176 F.3d 274, 278–279 (4th Cir. 1999); *Mendenhall* v. *Saudi Aramco*, US, 991 F.Supp. 856, 858 (S.D. Tex. 1998); *Commercial* v. *Corporacion*, US, 980 F.Supp. 710, 712, fn. 1 (S.D.N.Y. 1997); *Good* v. *Aramco*, US, 971 F.Supp. 254, 261 (S.D.Tex. 1997); *Corporacion* v. *Respect*, US, 89 F.3d 650, 655 (9th Cir. 1996); *Coleman* v. *Alcolac*, US, 888 F.Supp. 1388, 1403 (S.D.Tex. 1995); *Eaglet* v. *Banco*, US, 839 F.Supp. 232, 234 (S.D.N.Y. 1993); *Rodriguez* v. *Transnave*, US, 8 F.3d 284, 287 (5th Cir. 1993); *Kao Hwa* v. *China Steel*, US, 816 F.Supp. 910, 916 (S.D.N.Y. 1993); *Shapiro* v. *Bolivia*, US, 930 F.2d 1013, 1017 (2nd Cir. 1991); 98 ILR 109; *Fickling* v. *Australia*, US, 775 F.Supp. 66, 70 (E.D.N.Y. 1991); 103 ILR 447; *Joseph* v. *Office*, US, 830 F.2d 1018, 1022 (9th Cir. 1987); 101 ILR 485; *Zernicek* v. *Petroleos*, US, 614 F.Supp. 407, 411 (S.D.Tex. 1985); affirmed, *Zernicek* v. *Brown*, US, 826 F.2d 415 (5th Cir. 1987); 92 ILR 442; *Colonial Bank* v. *Compagnie*, US, 645 F.Supp. 1457, 1461 (S.D.N.Y. 1986); 98 ILR 26; *Frolova* v. *USSR*, US, 761 F.2d 370, 377 (7th Cir. 1985); 85 ILR 236. See also *Poddar* v. *State Bank*, US, 235 F.R.D. 592, 597–598 (S.D.N.Y. 2006) (a forum selection clause is not one of the three examples and therefore not an implied waiver).

56 *Frolova* v. *USSR*, US, 761 F.2d 370, 377 (7th Cir. 1985); 85 ILR 236; *Fickling* v. *Australia*, US, 775 F.Supp. 66, 70 (E.D.N.Y. 1991); 103 ILR 447.

57 *Princz* v. *Germany*, US, 26 F.3d 1166, 1174 (D.C.Cir. 1994); 103 ILR 594; reversing *Princz* v. *Germany*, US, 813 F.Supp. 22 (D.D.C. 1992); 103 ILR 594; *Cabiri* v. *Ghana*, US, 981 F.Supp. 129, 133–134 (E.D.N.Y. 1997); implicitly affirmed, *Cabiri* v. *Ghana*, US, 165 F.3d 193, 201 (2nd Cir. 1999). See also *Sampson* v. *Germany*, US, 250 F.3d 1145, 1150–1151 (7th Cir. 2001); affirming *Sampson* v. *Germany*, US, 975 F.Supp. 1108 (N.D.Ill. 1997); *Doe I* v. *Israel*, US, 400 F.Supp.2d 86, 105 (D. D.C. 2005); but cf. *Smith* v. *Libya*, US, 101 F.3d 239, 245 (2nd Cir. 1996) (declaring its decision not based 'on reading a subjective "intentionality" requirement into section 1605(a)(1)'); 113 ILR 534.

58 *Frolova* v. *USSR*, US, 761 F.2d 370, 377 (7th Cir. 1985); 85 ILR 236. The 'rarely find' pronouncement has been repeated in: *Af-Cap* v. *Congo*, US, 462 F.3d 417, 427 (5th Cir. 2006); *Sampson* v. *Germany*, US, 250 F.3d 1145, 1150 (7th Cir. 2001); *Alpha* v. *Nippon*, US, 199 F.3d 1078, 1085 (9th Cir. 1999); *Creighton* v. *Qatar*, US, 181 F.3d 118, 122 (D.C.Cir. 1999); *Cabiri* v. *Ghana*, US, 165 F.3d 193, 201 (2nd Cir. 1999); *Corporacion* v. *Respect*, US, 89 F.3d 650, 655 (9th Cir. 1996); *Princz* v. *Germany*, US, 26 F.3d 1166, 1174 (D.C.Cir. 1994); 103 ILR 594; *Rodriguez* v. *Transnave*, US, 8 F.3d 284, 287 (5th Cir. 1993); *Foremost-McKesson* v. *Iran*, US, 905 F.2d 438, 444 (D.C.Cir. 1990); 101 ILR 536; *Gutch* v. *Germany*, US, 444 F.Supp.2d 1, 9 (D.D.C. 2006); *Elixir* v. *Perusahaan*, US, 267 F.Supp.2d 659, 666 (S.D.Tex. 2003); *Coastal* v. *Gustav Sule*, US, 942 F.Supp. 1082, 1087 (E.D.La. 1996);

640   NOTES TO PAGES 325–327

Coleman v. *Alcolac*, US, 888 F.Supp. 1388, 1403 (S.D.Tex. 1995); *Zernicek* v. *Petroleos*, US, 614 F.Supp. 407, 411 (S.D.Tex. 1985); affirmed, *Zernicek* v. *Brown*, US, 826 F.2d 415 (5th Cir. 1987); 92 ILR 442. The 'reluctant to stray beyond' part has also been quoted with approval in *World Wide* v. *Kazakhstan*, US, 296 F.3d 1154, 1161, fn. 11 (D.C.Cir. 2002); *Abrams* v. *Société*, US, 175 F.Supp.2d 423, 432 (E.D.N.Y. 2001); *In re Tamimi*, US, 176 F.3d 274, 278 (4th Cir. 1999); *Coleman* v. *Alcolac*, US, 888 F.Supp. 1388, 1403 (S.D.Tex. 1995); *Rodriguez* v. *Transnave*, US, 810 F.Supp. 194, 197 (S.D.Tex. 1993); *L'Europeenne* v. *Venezuela*, US, 700 F.Supp. 114, 123, fn. 9 (S.D.N.Y. 1988); 98 ILR 100 note.

59 *Frolova* v. *USSR*, US, 761 F.2d 370, 378 (7th Cir. 1985); 85 ILR 236; *Von Dardel* v. *USSR*, US, 736 F.Supp. 1, 7 (D.D.C. 1990); overruling *Von Dardel* v. *USSR*, US, 623 F.Supp. 246, 255–256 (D.D.C 1985); 77 ILR 258. For comments on the 1985 case see Merrell, *Von Dardel*; Vardiman, The Foreign.

60 *Maritime* v. *Caribbean*, US, 689 F.Supp. 1340, 1351 (S.D.N.Y. 1988); quoted with approval in *Cargill* v. *Pavel Dybenko*, US, 991 F.2d 1012, 1017 (2nd Cir. 1993); 103 ILR 572 and *Seetransport* v. *Navimpex*, US, 989 F.2d 572, 577 (2nd Cir. 1993); 103 ILR 559. For an earlier warning see *Verlinden* v. *Central Bank*, US, 488 F.Supp. 1284, 1302 (S.D.N.Y. 1980); 63 ILR 390.

61 *Enron* v. *Titan*, US, 82 F.Supp.2d 602, 612 (W.D.La. 1999); *HSMV* v. *ADI*, US, 72 F.Supp.2d 1122, 1127 (C.D.Cal 1999); *Trans Chemical*, US, 978 F.Supp. 266, 291, fn. 119 (S.D.Tex. 1997); affirmed, *Trans Chemical* v. *China*, US, 161 F.3d 314, 319 (5th Cir. 1998); *Maritime* v. *Caribbean*, US, 689 F.Supp. 1340, 1351 (S.D.N.Y. 1988); *Birch* v. *Embassy*, US, 507 F.Supp. 311, 312 (D.D.C. 1980); 63 ILR 524. For a pre-FSIA case to the same effect see *Premier* v. *Embassy*, US, 336 F.Supp. 507, 509 (S.D.N.Y. 1971); 57 ILR 328, 330.

62 *Cargill* v. *Pavel Dybenko*, US, 991 F.2d 1012, 1017 (2nd Cir. 1993); 103 ILR 572; *Frolova* v. *USSR*, US, 761 F.2d 370, 377 (7th Cir. 1985); 85 ILR 236; *Maritime* v. *Guinea*, US, 693 F.2d 1094, 1103–1104 (D.C.Cir. 1982); 72 ILR 152; reversing *Maritime* v. *Guinea*, US, 505 F.Supp. 141 (D.D.C. 1981); 63 ILR 535; *Ohntrup* v. *Firearms*, US, 516 F.Supp. 1281, 1285 (E.D.Pa. 1981); 63 ILR 632; affirmed, *Ohntrup* v. *Firearms*, 760 F.2d 259 (3rd Cir. 1985) (Table); *Verlinden* v. *Central Bank*, US, 488 F.Supp. 1284, 1300–1302 (S.D.N.Y. 1980); 63 ILR 390.

63 *Seetransport* v. *Navimpex*, US, 989 F.2d 572, 578–579 (2nd Cir. 1993); 103 ILR 559; reversing *Seetransport* v. *Navimpex*, US, 793 F.Supp. 444 (S.D.N.Y. 1992). See also *Frontera* v. *State Oil*, US, 479 F.Supp.2d 376, 379–380 (S.D.N.Y. 2007); *Monegasque* v. *Nak*, US, 311 F.3d 488, 494 (2nd Cir. 2002); *MBL* v. *Trinidad*, US, 725 F.Supp. 52, 55–56 (D.D.C. 1989); *Ipitrade* v. *Nigeria*, US, 465 F.Supp. 824, 826 (D.D.C. 1978); 63 ILR 196. See Luzzatto, International Commercial, 93.

64 *S & Davis* v. *Yemen*, US, 218 F.3d 1292, 1301 (11th Cir. 2000).

65 Section 1605(a)(6) was inserted into the FSIA by Public Law 100-669, 16 November 1988, 102 Stat. 3969, 28 ILM 398 (1989).

66 Section 1605(a)(6) does not apply to an action that does not seek to enforce an arbitration agreement or to confirm an arbitration award: *Hirsh* v. *Israel*, US, 962 F.Supp. 377, 384–385 (S.D.N.Y. 1997); 113 ILR 543; nor does it apply to an action to *vacate* an arbitration award: *HSMV* v. *ADI*, US, 72 F.Supp.2d 1122,

1127, fn. 7 (C.D.Cal. 1999). For a history of this provision see Rothstein, Recognizing; Kahale, New Legislation.

67 *S & Davis* v. *Yemen*, US, 218 F.3d 1292, 1302 (11th Cir. 2000). For a similar case see *Creighton* v. *Qatar*, US, 181 F.3d 118, 123 (D.C.Cir. 1999).

68 *Cargill* v. *Pavel Dybenko*, US, 991 F.2d 1012, 1018 (2nd Cir. 1993); 103 ILR 572; quoted with approval in *Creighton* v. *Qatar*, US, 181 F.3d 118, 123–124 (D.C.Cir. 1999); *S & Davis* v. *Yemen*, US, 218 F.3d 1292, 1302 (11th Cir. 2000); *Trans Chemical*, US, 978 F.Supp. 266, 291 (S.D.Tex. 1997); affirmed, *Trans Chemical* v. *China*, US, 161 F.3d 314, 319 (5th Cir. 1998); *TMR* v. *State Property*, US, 411 F.3d 296, 299 (D.C.Cir. 2005); *Continental* v. *Nigeria*, US, 697 F.Supp.2d 46, 56 (D.D.C. 2010); *GE* v. *Albania*, US, 693 F.Supp.2d 132, 136 (D.D.C. 2010).

69 *Transatlantic* v. *Shanghai*, US, 204 F.3d 384, 391 (2nd Cir. 2000); reversing *Transatlantic* v. *Shanghai*, 1998 WL 799671 (S.D.N.Y. 1998).

70 *TermoRio* v. *Electrificadora*, US, 421 F.Supp.2d 87, 93–94 (D.D.C. 2006); affirmed, *TermoRio* v. *Electranta*, US, 487 F.3d 928 (D.C.Cir. 2007); *TMR* v. *State Property*, US, 411 F.3d 296, 299 (D.C.Cir. 2005); *US Titan* v. *Guangzhou*, US, 16 F.Supp.2d 326, 334 (S.D.N.Y. 1998); affirmed, *US Titan* v. *Guangzhou*, US, 241 F.3d 135, 151 (2nd Cir. 2001); *Trans Chemical*, US, 978 F.Supp. 266, 292–297 (S.D.Tex. 1997); affirmed, *Trans Chemical* v. *China*, US, 161 F.3d 314, 319 (5th Cir. 1998); *Chromalloy*, US, 939 F.Supp. 907, 909 (D.D.C. 1996); *Cargill* v. *Pavel Dybenko*, US, 991 F.2d 1012, 1018–1020 (2nd Cir. 1993); 103 ILR 572; *Bergesen* v. *Joseph*, US, 710 F.2d 928, 932–933 (2nd Cir. 1983); affirming *Bergesen* v. *Joseph*, US, 548 F.Supp. 650 (S.D.N.Y. 1982).

71 *International* v. *Caja*, US, 293 F.3d 392, 397 (7th Cir. 2002); *Banco* v. *Mutual Marine*, US, 230 F.Supp.2d 362, 367 (S.D.N.Y. 2002); *Employers* v. *Banco*, US, 199 F.3d 937, 941 (7th Cir. 1999); affirming *Employers* v. *Banco*, US, 34 F.Supp.2d 1115, 1119 (E.D.Wis. 1999); *Trans Chemical*, US, 978 F.Supp. 266, 291 (S.D.Tex. 1997); affirmed, *Trans Chemical* v. *China*, US, 161 F.3d 314, 319 (5th Cir. 1998).

72 *Ministry* v. *Gould*, US, 887 F.2d 1357, 1362 (9th Cir. 1989); 969 F.2d 764 (9th Cir. 1992); 96 ILR 1; quoted with approval in *Cargill* v. *Pavel Dybenko*, US, 991 F.2d 1012, 1018 (2nd Cir. 1993); 103 ILR 572.

73 *LETCO*, US, 650 F.Supp. 73, 76 (S.D.N.Y. 1986); 89 ILR 355. For the arbitration award see *LETCO* v. *Liberia*, ICSID, (1986) 89 ILR 313.

74 *Berdakin* v. *Consulado*, US, 912 F.Supp. 458, 461 (C.D.Cal. 1995) (the premises were located in Los Angeles, California, USA).

75 *Marlowe* v. *Argentine*, US, 604 F.Supp. 703, 708–709 (D.D.C. 1985).

76 *Resource* v. *General*, US, 593 F.Supp. 572, 575 (N.D.Ga. 1984).

77 *World Wide* v. *Nammo*, US, 51 Fed.Appx. 403, 405–406 (4th Cir. 2002).

78 *Ghawanmeh* v. *Islamic*, US, 672 F.Supp.2d 3, 9–10 (D.D.C. 2009).

79 *Kramer* v. *Boeing*, US, 705 F.Supp. 1392, 1395 (D.Minn. 1989).

80 *Compagnie Noga* v. *Russian*, US, 361 F.3d 676, 679, 698–690 (2nd Cir. 2004).

81 *Joseph* v. *Office*, US, 830 F.2d 1018, 1022 (9th Cir. 1987) (emphasis in the original); 101 ILR 485.

82 *Pere* v. *Nuovo*, US, 150 F.3d 477, 482 (5th Cir. 1998).

83 *Eckert* v. *Fiji*, US, 32 F.3d 77, 80 (4th Cir. 1994); 107 ILR 347.

642   NOTES TO PAGES 328–330

84 *Eckert* v. *Fiji*, US, 32 F.3d 77, 82 (4th Cir. 1994); 107 ILR 347; affirming *Eckert* v. *Fiji*, US, 834 F.Supp. 167, 170 (E.D.Va. 1993).

85 *Atlantic* v. *Inter-American*, US, 251 F.Supp.2d 126, 133 (D.D.C. 2003); *Kao Hwa* v. *China Steel*, US, 816 F.Supp. 910, 917 (S.D.N.Y. 1993); *Eaglet* v. *Banco*, US, 839 F.Supp. 232, 234–236 (S.D.N.Y. 1993); *Colonial Bank* v. *Compagnie*, US, 645 F.Supp. 1457, 1461–1462 (S.D.N.Y. 1986); 98 ILR 26. *Zernicek* v. *Brown*, US, 826 F.2d 415, 419 (5th Cir. 1987); 92 ILR 442; affirming *Zernicek* v. *Petroleos*, US, 614 F.Supp. 407 (S.D.Tex. 1985).

86 *Pere* v. *Nuovo*, US, 150 F.3d 477, 482 (5th Cir. 1998).

87 *Falcoal* v. *Turkiye*, US, 660 F.Supp. 1536, 1538–1539 (S.D.Tex. 1987).

88 *Arriba* v. *Petroleos*, US, 962 F.2d 528, 538–539 (5th Cir. 1992); 103 ILR 490.

89 *Dayton* v. *Czechoslovakia*, US, 834 F.2d 203, 205 (D.C.Cir. 1987); 79 ILR 590; affirming *Dayton* v. *Czechoslovakia*, US, 672 F.Supp. 7 (D.D.C. 1986); 79 ILR 590; *Intercontinental* v. *De Gruyter*, US, 822 F.Supp. 662, 679 (C.D.Cal. 1993).

90 *Good* v. *Aramco*, US, 971 F.Supp. 254, 260–261 (S.D.Tex. 1997).

91 *Saudi Basic* v. *Exxonmobil*, US, 194 F.Supp.2d 378, 403 (D.N.J. 2002); *Belgrade* v. *Sidex*, US, 2 F.Supp.2d 407, 419 (S.D.N.Y. 1998).

92 *Canadian Overseas* v. *Compania*, US, 727 F.2d 274, 277–278 (2nd Cir. 1984); 101 ILR 470; affirming *Canadian Overseas* v. *Compania*, US, 528 F.Supp. 1337 (S.D.N.Y. 1982); *Ungar* v. *Palestinian Authority*, US, 315 F.Supp.2d 164, 173 (D.R.I. 2004).

93 *Fargo* v. *Jamaica*, US, 790 F.Supp. 272, 275 (S.D.Fla. 1992).

94 *Gutch* v. *Germany*, US, 444 F.Supp.2d 1, 9 (D.D.C. 2006); *Ungar* v. *Palestinian Authority*, US, 315 F.Supp.2d 164, 173 (D.R.I. 2004); *World Wide* v. *Nammo*, US, 51 Fed.Appx. 403, 405, fn. 2 (4th Cir. 2002); *Fargo* v. *Jamaica*, US, 790 F.Supp. 272, 275 (S.D.Fla. 1992); *Canadian Overseas* v. *Compania*, US, 727 F.2d 274, 277–278 (2nd Cir. 1984); 101 ILR 470; affirming *Canadian Overseas* v. *Compania*, US, 528 F.Supp. 1337 (S.D.N.Y. 1982).

95 *Rodriguez* v. *Transnave*, US, 8 F.3d 284, 288–289 (5th Cir. 1993); reversing *Rodriguez* v. *Transnave*, US, 810 F.Supp. 194 (S.D.Tex. 1993).

96 *Haven* v. *Rzeczpospolita*, US, 215 F.3d 727, 732–733 (7th Cir. 2000); affirming *Haven* v. *Rzeczpospolita*, US, 68 F.Supp.2d 947 (N.D.Ill. 1999); *Hirsh* v. *Israel*, US, 962 F.Supp. 377, 380 (S.D.N.Y. 1997); 113 ILR 543.

97 *Coastal Cargo* v. *Gustav Sule*, US, 942 F.Supp. 1082, 1087 (E.D.La. 1996); *Borgships* v. *Macarena*, US, 1993 WL 408342, p. 3 (E.D.La. 1993).

98 *Rio Grande*, US, 516 F.Supp. 1155, 1159 (S.D.N.Y. 1981); 63 ILR 604.

99 *Gupta* v. *Thai*, US, 487 F.3d 759, 761–762 (9th Cir. 2007).

100 *Hirsh* v. *Israel*, US, 962 F.Supp. 377, 380 (S.D.N.Y. 1997); 113 ILR 543; *Drexel* v. *Committee*, US, 12 F.3d 317, 326 (2nd Cir. 1993); reversing *Drexel* v. *Committee*, US, 810 F.Supp. 1375 (S.D.N.Y. 1993); 103 ILR 532.

101 *Frolova* v. *USSR*, US, 761 F.2d 370, 378 (7th Cir. 1985); 85 ILR 236; *Kao Hwa* v. *China Steel*, US, 816 F.Supp. 910, 917 (S.D.N.Y. 1993).

102 *Canadian Overseas* v. *Compania*, US, 727 F.2d 274, 277–278 (2nd Cir. 1984); 101 ILR 470; affirming *Canadian Overseas* v. *Compania*, US, 528 F.Supp. 1337 (S.D.N.Y. 1982).

103 *Foremost-McKesson* v. *Iran*, US, 905 F.2d 438, 443 (D.C.Cir. 1990); 101 ILR 536.

104 *Talbot* v. *Saipem*, US, 835 F.Supp. 352, 354 (S.D.Tex. 1993).

105 *Bank of Credit* v. *State Bank*, US, 46 F.Supp.2d 231, 234 (S.D.N.Y. 1999).

106 *HSMV* v. *ADI*, US, 72 F.Supp.2d 1122, 1127 (C.D.Cal 1999).

107 *Lord Day* v. *Vietnam*, US, 134 F.Supp.2d 549, 558–559 (S.D.N.Y. 2001). See also *Sotheby's* v. *Garcia*, US, 802 F.Supp. 1058, 1063 (S.D.N.Y. 1992).

108 *Canadian Overseas* v. *Compania*, US, 727 F.2d 274, 276–278 (2nd Cir. 1984); 101 ILR 470; affirming *Canadian Overseas* v. *Compania*, US, 528 F.Supp. 1337 (S.D. N.Y. 1982); *Rodriguez* v. *Transnave*, US, 8 F.3d 284, 289–290 (5th Cir. 1993); reversing *Rodriguez* v. *Transnave*, US, 810 F.Supp. 194 (S.D.Tex. 1993).

109 *Siderman* v. *Argentina*, US, 965 F.2d 699, 721 (9th Cir. 1992); 103 ILR 454. See also *Cabiri* v. *Ghana*, US, 165 F.3d 193, 201, fn. 5 (2nd Cir. 1999); *Smith* v. *Libya*, US, 101 F.3d 239, 244 (2nd Cir. 1996); 113 ILR 534; *Hilao* v. *Marcos*, US, 94 F.3d 539, 546 (9th Cir. 1996).

110 *Joseph* v. *Office*, US, 830 F.2d 1018, 1022 (9th Cir. 1987); 101 ILR 485.

111 *Joseph* v. *Office*, US, 830 F.2d 1018, 1023 (9th Cir. 1987); 101 ILR 485; quoted with approval in *Siderman* v. *Argentina*, US, 965 F.2d 699, 721 (9th Cir. 1992); 103 ILR 454 and *Greenpeace* v. *France*, US, 946 F.Supp. 773, 781 (C.D. Cal. 1996).

112 *Siderman* v. *Argentina*, US, 965 F.2d 699, 721–722 (9th Cir. 1992); 103 ILR 454.

113 *Siderman* v. *Argentina*, US, 965 F.2d 699, 722 (9th Cir. 1992); 103 ILR 454. See also *Sampson* v. *Germany*, US, 250 F.3d 1145, 1154 (7th Cir. 2001); *Hilao* v. *Marcos*, US, 94 F.3d 539, 547 (9th Cir. 1996).

114 *Hilao* v. *Marcos*, US, 94 F.3d 539, 547 (9th Cir. 1996) (emphasis in the original).

115 *Hilao*, 94 F.3d 539, 547 (9th Cir. 1996).

116 *Gates* v. *Victor*, US, 54 F.3d 1457, 1466 (9th Cir. 1995); 107 ILR 371. See also *Keller* v. *Transportes*, US, 601 F.Supp. 787, 789 (D.D.C. 1985) (waiver of immunity in a Credit Agreement with banks to finance the cost of an aircraft did not constitute a waiver in a wrongful death action based on the aircraft's crash, the plaintiff not being party to the Credit Agreement).

117 *Blaxland* v. *Commonwealth*, US, 323 F.3d 1198, 1206–1207, 1209 (9th Cir. 2003). On extradition as an executive process see, e.g., *Barapind* v. *Reno*, US, 225 F.3d 1100, 1105 (9th Cir. 2000); *Lopez-Smith* v. *Hood*, US, 121 F.3d 1322, 1326 (9th Cir. 1997); *Martin* v. *Warden*, US, 993 F.2d 824, 828 (11th Cir. 1993). For a similar case in Canada concerning extradition see *Schreiber* v. *Germany*, Canada, (2002) 216 DLR (4th) 513, 526; affirming *Schreiber* v. *Germany*, Canada, (2001) 196 DLR (4th) 281.

118 *Autotech* v. *Integral*, US, 499 F.3d 737, 743 (7th Cir. 2007).

119 *Aguinda* v. *Texaco*, US, 175 F.R.D. 50, 52 (S.D.N.Y. 1997); vacated on other grounds *sub nom Jota* v. *Texaco*, US, 157 F.3d 153 (2nd Cir. 1998); *Shapiro* v. *Bolivia*, US, 930 F.2d 1013, 1017 (2nd Cir. 1991); 98 ILR 109; *Drexel* v. *Committee*, US, 12 F.3d 317, 325 (2nd Cir. 1993); *Hirsh* v. *Israel*, US, 962 F.Supp. 377, 380 (S.D. N.Y. 1997); 113 ILR 543; *In re Tamimi*, US, 176 F.3d 274, 278–279 (4th Cir. 1999).

120 See *Anderman* v. *Austria*, US, 256 F.Supp.2d 1098, 1105 (C.D.Cal. 2003); *Corzo* v. *Banco*, US, 243 F.3d 519, 523 (9th Cir. 2001); *Aguinda* v. *Texaco*, US, 175 F.R.D.

644 NOTES TO PAGES 333-335

50, 52 (S.D.N.Y. 1997); vacated on other grounds *sub nom Jota* v. *Texaco*, US, 157 F.3d 153 (2nd Cir. 1998).

121 *Frolova* v. *USSR*, US, 761 F.2d 370, 377–378 (7th Cir. 1985); 85 ILR 236; *Joseph* v. *Office*, US, 830 F.2d 1018, 1023 (9th Cir. 1987); 101 ILR 485; *Foremost-McKesson* v. *Iran*, US, 905 F.2d 438, 443–444 (D.C.Cir. 1990); 101 ILR 536; *Von Dardel* v. *USSR*, US, 736 F.Supp. 1, 7 (D.D.C. 1990); overruling *Von Dardel* v. *USSR*, US, 623 F.Supp. 246, 255–256 (D.D.C 1985); 77 ILR 258; *Fickling* v. *Australia*, US, 775 F.Supp. 66, 70 (E.D.N.Y. 1991); 103 ILR 447; *Rodriguez* v. *Transnave*, US, 8 F.3d 284, 287 (5th Cir. 1993); *Drexel* v. *Committee*, US, 12 F.3d 317, 327 (2nd Cir. 1993); *Princz* v. *Germany*, US, 26 F.3d 1166, 1174 (D.C.Cir. 1994); 103 ILR 594; *Pere* v. *Nuovo*, US, 150 F.3d 477, 482 (5th Cir. 1998); *Cabiri* v. *Ghana*, US, 165 F.3d 193, 202 (2nd Cir. 1999); on this point affirming *Cabiri* v. *Ghana*, US, 981 F.Supp. 129, 133–134 (E.D.N.Y. 1997); *In re Tamimi*, US, 176 F.3d 274, 279 (4th Cir. 1999); *Alpha* v. *Nippon*, US, 199 F.3d 1078, 1085 (9th Cir. 1999); *Haven* v. *Rzeczpospolita*, US, 215 F.3d 727, 733 (7th Cir. 2000); *Anderman* v. *Austria*, US, 256 F.Supp.2d 1098, 1106 (C.D.Cal. 2003); *Ungar* v. *Palestinian Authority*, US, 325 F.Supp.2d 15, 27 (D.R.I. 2004).

122 *Maritime* v. *Guinea*, 693 F.2d 1094, 1100, fn. 10 (D.C.Cir. 1982); 72 ILR 152; reversing *Maritime* v. *Guinea*, US, 505 F.Supp. 141 (D.D.C. 1981); 63 ILR 535; *Libra* v. *Banco, SA*, US, 676 F.2d 47, 49 (2nd Cir. 1982); 72 ILR 119.

123 *General Electric* v. *Grossman*, US, 991 F.2d 1376, 1386 (8th Cir. 1993).

124 *Joseph* v. *Office*, US, 830 F.2d 1018, 1022 (9th Cir. 1987) (emphasis in the original); 101 ILR 485.

125 *Keller* v. *Transportes*, US, 601 F.Supp. 787, 789 (D.D.C. 1985); *Siderman* v. *Argentina*, US, 965 F.2d 699, 722 (9th Cir. 1992); 103 ILR 454; *Gates* v. *Victor*, US, 54 F.3d 1457, 1466 (9th Cir. 1995); 107 ILR 371; *Hilao* v. *Marcos*, US, 94 F.3d 539, 547 (9th Cir. 1996); *Smith* v. *Libya*, US, 101 F.3d 239, 243–244 (2nd Cir. 1996); 113 ILR 534; *Sampson* v. *Germany*, US, 250 F.3d 1145, 1154 (7th Cir. 2001).

126 *In re Tamimi*, US, 176 F.3d 274, 279–280 (4th Cir. 1999).

127 *Colonial Bank* v. *Compagnie*, US, 645 F.Supp. 1457, 1462 (S.D.N.Y. 1986); 98 ILR 26.

128 *Gates* v. *Victor*, US, 54 F.3d 1457, 145–166 (9th Cir. 1995); 107 ILR 371; *Keller* v. *Transportes*, US, 601 F.Supp. 787, 789 (D.D.C. 1985); *Paterson* v. *Compania*, US, 493 F.Supp. 621, 624 (S.D.N.Y. 1980); 63 ILR 354.

129 *In re Terrorist*, US, 392 F.Supp.2d 539, 553 (S.D.N.Y. 2005); *Friedar* v. *Israel*, US, 614 F.Supp. 395, 398 (S.D.N.Y. 1985).

130 *Ohntrup* v. *Firearms*, US, 516 F.Supp. 1281, 1285 (E.D.Pa. 1981); 63 ILR 632; affirmed, *Ohntrup* v. *Firearms*, 760 F.2d 259 (3rd Cir. 1985) (Table).

131 *Elixir* v. *Perusahaan*, US, 267 F.Supp.2d 659, 666–667 (S.D.Tex. 2003).

132 *Saudi Basic* v. *Exxonmobil*, US, 194 F.Supp.2d 378, 403–404 (D.N.J. 2002).

133 *Commercial* v. *Corporacion*, US, 980 F.Supp. 710, 712–713 (S.D.N.Y. 1997).

134 *Libya* v. *Miski*, US, 683 F.Supp.2d 1, 7–9 (D.D.C. 2010); *In re Oil Spill*, US, 491 F.Supp. 161, 168 (N.D.Ill. 1979); 63 ILR 310. See also *Corporacion* v. *Respect*, US, 89 F.3d 650, 656 (9th Cir. 1996); *Lord Day* v. *Vietnam*, US, 134 F.Supp.2d 549, 557–558 (S.D.N.Y. 2001). For pre-FSIA cases see: *French Republic* v. *Inland*, US, 263

NOTES TO PAGES 335–337   645

F. 410 (E.D.Mo. 1920); *Republic of China* v. *American*, US, 195 F.2d 230 (2 Cir. 1952); 19 ILR 192; *Hungarian* v. *Cecil*, US, 118 F.Supp. 954 (S.D.N.Y. 1953); 20 ILR 176; *National City* v. *Republic of China*, US, 348 US 356, 361–365 (1955); 22 ILR 210, 213–215. See also *USSR* v. *Belaiew*, England, (1925) 42 TLR 21; 3 AD 172.

135 *Germany* v. *Elicofon*, US, 536 F.Supp. 813, 826, fn. 18 (E.D.N.Y. 1978); 94 ILR 133; affirmed, *Kunstsammlungen* v. *Elicofon*, US, 678 F.2d 1150, 1160 (2nd Cir. 1982); 94 ILR 133; *Shapiro* v. *Republic of Bolivia*, US, 930 F.2d 1013, 1017–1018 (2nd Cir. 1991); 98 ILR 109.

136 *Allendale* v. *Bull*, US, 10 F.3d 425, 432 (7th Cir. 1993).

137 *Cabiri* v. *Ghana*, US, 165 F.3d 193, 198 (2nd Cir. 1999); on this point reversing *Cabiri* v. *Ghana*, US, 981 F.Supp. 129, 132 (E.D.N.Y. 1997).

138 *Cabiri* v. *Ghana*, US, 165 F.3d 193, 198–199 (2nd Cir. 1999); on this point affirming *Cabiri* v. *Ghana*, US, 981 F.Supp. 129, 132 (E.D.N.Y. 1997).

139 See near-reproductions or very similar provisions in the Pakistan SIO, ss. 4 and 10; Singapore SIA, ss. 4 and 11; South Africa FSIA, ss. 3 and 10; Canada SIA, s. 4 (with the notable absence of arbitration; but see *Collavino* v. *Yemen*, Canada, [2007] AJ No. 531, para. 139 (agreement to arbitration constituted waiver of immunity from enforcement of the arbitral award)); Australia FSIA, ss. 10, 17 and 37; Argentina Law of 1995, Art. 2(h); UN Convention, Arts. 7, 8, 9, and 17.

140 *Argentina* v. *NML*, England, [2010] EWCA Civ 41, para. 100 per Aikens LJ; see also para. 104. See also *Svenska* v. *Lithuania (No. 2)*, England, 2005, [2006] 1 Lloyd's Rep. 181, 193, para. 37 per Gloster J; affirmed, *Svenska* v. *Lithuania (No. 2)*, England, 2006, [2007] QB 886, 928, para. 128.

141 See *Duff* v. *Kelantan*, England, [1924] AC 797; 2 AD 124; *Kahan* v. *Pakistan*, England, [1951] 2 KB 1003; 18 ILR 210; *A Company* v. *Republic of X*, England, 1989, [1990] 2 Lloyd's Rep 520, 524; 87 ILR 412, 416; but see Mann, Waiver, 364 (calling this 'an English aberration'). This is also the position of the Canadian courts: *Congo* v. *Venne*, Canada, (1971) 22 DLR (3d) 669, 679, 681; 64 ILR 24, 34, 36; *Jaffe* v. *Miller*, Canada, (1993) 103 DLR (4th) 315, 332; 13 OR (3d) 745, 763; 95 ILR 446, 463; affirming *Jaffe* v. *Miller*, Canada, 1990, (1991) 73 DLR (4th) 420; 87 ILR 197.

142 See, e.g., *Svenska*, where 'waiver' is unqualified but 'submission' is followed by 'to the jurisdiction of the English court/courts': *Svenska* v. *Lithuania (No. 2)*, England, 2005, [2006] 1 Lloyd's Rep. 181, 193, para. 37 per Gloster J; affirmed, *Svenska* v. *Lithuania (No. 2)*, England, 2006, [2007] QB 886, 928, para. 128.

143 *Argentina* v. *NML*, England, [2010] EWCA Civ 41, paras. 99–105, 108 and Appendix 3; on point of waiver reversing *NML* v. *Argentina*, England, [2009] QB 579, 591–592, paras. 36–38. The High Court case is noted in Fox, Enforcement. However, the Supreme Court reversed the decision of the Court of Appeal on the ground that Argentina had indeed waived its immunity from the proceedings for the enforcement of a New York judgment in the English courts by agreeing elsewhere in the bonds that a 'related judgment', i.e. the New York judgment, could be 'enforced in any specified court or in any

646 NOTES TO PAGES 337-339

other courts to the jurisdiction of which the republic is or may be subject by a suit upon such judgment'. *NML v. Argentina*, England, [2011] 2 AC 495, 518–519, 542, paras. 59–64, 127–130.

144 *Donegal v. Zambia*, England, [2007] 1 Lloyd's Rep 397, 402–403, para. 17 and 478, para. 500.

145 *Svenska v. Lithuania (No. 2)*, England, 2005, [2006] 1 Lloyd's Rep. 181, 193, para. 35.

146 *Svenska v. Lithuania (No. 2)*, England, 2006, [2007] QB 886, 928, para. 128; affirming *Svenska v. Lithuania (No. 2)*, England, 2005, [2006] 1 Lloyd's Rep. 181, 193, para. 35.

147 *A Company Ltd v. Republic of X*, England, 1989, [1990] 2 Lloyd's Rep 520, 522–523; 87 ILR 412, 414–416; noted in Mann, Waiver. Parties later identified in: *Philipp Brothers v. Sierra Leone*, England, [1995] 1 Lloyd's Rep 289; 107 ILR 517.

148 *Sabah v. Pakistan*, England, 2002, [2003] 2 Lloyd's Rep 571, 577; noted in Wilkes, Enforcing.

149 *Svenska v. Lithuania (No. 2)*, England, 2006, [2007] QB 886, 924–927, paras. 115–123; affirming *Svenska v. Lithuania (No. 2)*, England, 2005, [2006] 1 Lloyd's Rep. 181. An arbitration clause was regarded as voluntary submission to the jurisdiction of the arbitrators and the supervision of them by the courts even during the time of absolute immunity: *Thai-Europe v. Pakistan*, England, [1975] 1 WLR 1485, 1491; 64 ILR 81, 85 (citing *President v. Metcalfe*, England, [1970] 1 QB 289).

150 *Ministry v. Tsavliris*, England, 2008, [2008] 2 Lloyd's Rep. 90, 100–101, paras. 55–59.

151 *Mills v. USA*, England, (2000) 120 ILR 612, 614–616; affirmed, *Mills v. Embassy*, England, 2000, Transcript. See also *USA v. Friedland*, Canada, (1999) 182 DLR (4th) 614, 618; 120 ILR 417, 456 ('clear and unequivocal' and 'cannot be presumed'); on point of waiver reversing *USA v. Friedland*, Canada, (1998) 40 OR (3d) 747; 120 ILR 417.

152 *Saudi Arabia v. Ahmed*, England, (1993) 104 ILR 629, 635–636; affirmed, *Ahmed v. Saudi Arabia*, England, 1995, [1996] 2 All ER 248, 254–255; [1996] ICR 25, 33–34; 104 ILR 629, 645.

153 *Kuwait Airways v. Iraqi Airways*, England, (1992) 103 ILR 340, 355–356; affirmed, 1993, [1995] 1 Lloyd's Rep 25, 31–32, 34, 37–38; affirmed, [1995] 1 WLR 1147, 1164; 103 ILR 340, 378–379, 382; 389–390; 406.

154 *Egypt v. Gamal-Eldin*, England, 1995, [1996] 2 All ER 237, 244–245; [1996] ICR 13, 21–22; 104 ILR 673, 680.

155 *Paprocki v. German State*, England, (1995) 104 ILR 684, 689, 690; *Westminster v. Iran*, England, [1986] 1 WLR 979, 984; 108 ILR 557, 563. For similar practice in other States see *Kubacz v. Shah*, Australia, 1983, [1984] WAR 156, 160; 118 ILR 293, 297–298; *Robinson v. Kuwait*, Australia, (1997) 145 ALR 68, 77; *Reef v. Fua Kavenga*, New Zealand, [1987] 1 NZLR 550, 568; 90 ILR 556, 561; *USA v. Friedland*, Canada, (1999) 182 DLR (4th) 614, 619–621; 120 ILR 417, 457–459; on point of waiver reversing *USA v. Friedland*, Canada, (1998) 40 OR (3d) 747; 120 ILR 417; *Schreiber v. Attorney General*, Canada, (2000) 187 DLR (4th) 146, 152–

153; affirmed, *Schreiber* v. *Germany*, Canada, (2001) 196 DLR (4th) 281, 290; affirmed, *Schreiber* v. *Germany*, Canada, (2002) 216 DLR (4th) 513, 526.

156 *London Branch* v. *Bastians*, England, 1994, [1995] ICR 358, 365–366; 107 ILR 613, 620–621.

157 *Propend* v. *Sing*, England, (1997) 111 ILR 611, 671; *Ahmed* v. *Saudi Arabia*, England, 1995, [1996] 2 All ER 248, 255; 104 ILR 629, 646; affirming *Saudi Arabia* v. *Ahmed*, England, (1993) 104 ILR 629; *Egypt* v. *Gamal-Eldin*, England, 1995, [1996] 2 All ER 237, 244; [1996] ICR 13, 21; 104 ILR 673, 679; *Malaysian* v. *Jeyasingham*, England, 1997, [1998] ICR 307, 315; *Yemen* v. *Aziz*, England, [2005] ICR 1391, 1405; reversing *Aziz* v. *Embassy of Yemen*, England, [2004] All ER (D) 347.

158 *Egypt* v. *Gamal-Eldin*, England, 1995, [1996] 2 All ER 237, 244; [1996] ICR 13, 21; 104 ILR 673, 679.

159 *Yendall* v. *Australia*, England, (1984) 107 ILR 590, 598–599.

160 *Rousseau* v. *Upper Volta*, Belgium, (1983) 82 ILR 118, 120; *Burundi* v. *Landau*, Belgium, (2002) 127 ILR 98, 100; *Procureur* v. *Ipitrade*, France, (1978) 65 ILR 75, 77; *Iran* v. *Société Eurodif*, France, (1982) 65 ILR 93, 98; *Caisse* v. *Société Midland*, France, (1983) 77 ILR 524, 525; *Russian Federation* v. *Noga*, France, (2000) 127 ILR 156, 160; *Embassy Eviction Case*, Greece, (1965) 65 ILR 248, 251; *Ramos* v. *USA*, Portugal, (1994) 116 ILR 634, 635; *Västerås* v. *Iceland*, Sweden, (1999) 128 ILR 705, 707. For express waiver see also Art. 7 of the 2004 UN Convention.

161 *Marcos* v. *Federal Department*, Switzerland, (1989) 102 ILR 198, 204, Ground 5d.

162 *West* v. *Captain*, Belgium, (1920) 1 AD 152, 154; *Brasseur* v. *Greece*, Belgium, (1933) 6 AD 164, 167; *Ramos* v. *USA*, Portugal, (1994) 116 ILR 634, 635; *Arab Organization* v. *Westland*, Switzerland, (1987/1988) 80 ILR 622, 644.

163 *West* v. *Captain*, Belgium, (1920) 1 AD 152, 154; *Church of Scientology Case*, Germany, (1978) 65 ILR 193, 199; *Larkins* v. *National*, Philippines, (1995) 102 ILR 148 note. See also Art. 8(2)(3)(4) of the 2004 UN Convention.

164 *'Atlantic'* v. *USSR*, Netherlands, (1979) 65 ILR 377, 377; *Portugal* v. *Algemene*, Netherlands, (1982) 94 ILR 315, 317; *Crédit Lyonnais* v. *Viel*, France, (1936) 8 AD 228, 228. See also Art. 8(1) of the 2004 UN Convention.

165 *Yugoslavia* v. *Société Européenne*, France, (1970) 65 ILR 46, 48 (the award reported at *Société Européenne* v. *Yugoslavia*, Arbitrators, (1956) 24 ILR 761); *Société Européenne* v. *World Bank*, France, (1984) 82 ILR 58, 65; affirmed, *Société Européenne* v. *France*, France, (1986) 82 ILR 58, 74; *Malagasy* v. *Société*, France, (1971) 65 ILR 51, 52; *Procureur* v. *Ipitrade*, France, (1978) 65 ILR 75; *Iran* v. *Société Eurodif*, France, (1984) 77 ILR 513, 515–516; *Société Européenne* v. *France*, France, (1986) 82 ILR 58, 74; *Guinea* v. *Atlantic Triton*, France, (1984/1986) 82 ILR 75, 84; *Iran* v. *Société Eurodif*, France, (1989) 89 ILR 31, 35; *Ministry* v. *Société Framatome*, France, (1990) 113 ILR 452; *Société Ouest* v. *Senegal*, France, (1991) 113 ILR 440, 445; *Creighton* v. *Minister*, France, (2000) 127 ILR 154, 155; noted in Moury, L'Incidence; Zeyen, Immunities (but see *Société Transshipping* v. *Pakistan*, France, (1966) 47 ILR 150, 151); *NV Cabolent* v. *National*, Netherlands, (1968) 47 ILR 138, 144; *Libya* v. *LIAMCO*, Switzerland, (1980) 62 ILR 228, 235, Ground 4; *Arab Organization* v. *Westland*, Switzerland, (1987/1988) 80 ILR 622,

648   NOTES TO PAGES 340-341

644–645, 659–661; *SPP* v. *Egypt*, International Chamber of Commerce, (1983) 86 ILR 434, 461 (however, the award was set aside on the ground that Egypt was not a party to the arbitration agreement: *Egypt* v. *Southern Pacific*, France, (1984/1987) 86 ILR 474, 483–489 (see especially p. 487)). For scholarly comments on arbitration see Chamlongrasdr, *Foreign State Immunity*; Vibhute, *International Commercial Arbitration*; Schreuer, *State Immunity*, Chapter 4; Fox, State Immunity and Enforcement; Fox, States; Lalive, Quelques Observations; Booysen, The Municipal; Blane, Sovereign; Chukwumerije, ICSID. See also Art. 17 of the 2004 UN Convention.

166 *Embassy of Czechoslovakia* v. *Jens*, Denmark, (1982) 78 ILR 81, 83–84.

167 *Universal* v. *Iran*, Switzerland, (1981) 65 ILR 436, 438, Ground 4. See also Art. 9 of the 2004 UN Convention.

168 *Sogerfin* v. *Yugoslavia*, Switzerland, (1938) 10 AD 232, 234; but cf. *State Immunity Case*, Switzerland, (1939/1940) 10 AD 235.

169 See *Corzo* v. *Banco*, US, 243 F.3d 519, 524 (9th Cir. 2001); *Atlantic* v. *Inter-American*, US, 251 F.Supp.2d 126, 133 (D.D.C. 2003); *Fickling* v. *Australia*, US, 775 F.Supp. 66, 70 (E.D.N.Y. 1991); 103 ILR 447; *Perez* v. *The Bahamas*, US, 482 F.Supp. 1208, 1209–1210 (D.D.C. 1980); 63 ILR 350.

170 See *Princz* v. *Germany*, US, 26 F.3d 1166, 1184 per Wald J, dissenting (D.C.Cir. 1994); 103 ILR 594; *Smith* v. *Libya*, US, 101 F.3d 239, 244 (2nd Cir. 1996); 113 ILR 534.

171 *Argentine Republic* v. *Amerada Hess*, US 488 US 428, 434, 436 (1989); 102 L.Ed.2d 818, 828, 829 (1989); 81 ILR 658, 663, 664.

172 *Siderman* v. *Argentina*, US, 965 F.2d 699, 718–719 (9th Cir. 1992); 103 ILR 454; *Smith* v. *Libya*, US, 101 F.3d 239, 242 (2nd Cir. 1996); 113 ILR 534; affirming *Smith* v. *Libya*, US, 886 F.Supp. 306 (E.D.N.Y. 1995); 107 ILR 382; *Sampson* v. *Germany*, US, 250 F.3d 1145, 1156 (7th Cir. 2001); affirming *Sampson* v. *Germany*, US, 975 F.Supp. 1108 (N.D.Ill. 1997); *Wei* v. *Jiang*, US, 383 F.3d 620, 627 (7th Cir. 2004); affirming *Plaintiffs* v. *Jiang*, US, 282 F.Supp.2d 875, 883 (N. D.Ill. 2003); *Boshnjaku* v. *Yugoslavia*, US 2002 WL 1575067, p. 3 (N.D.Ill. 2002); *Doe* v. *Liu*, US, 349 F.Supp.2d 1258, 1284 (N.D.Cal. 2004); *Doe I* v. *Israel*, US, 400 F.Supp.2d 86, 105 (D.D.C. 2005).

173 *Princz* v. *Germany*, US, 26 F.3d 1166, 1174 (D.C.Cir. 1994); 103 ILR 594; reversing *Princz* v. *Germany*, US, 813 F.Supp. 22 (D.D.C. 1992); 103 ILR 594; see Zimmermann, Sovereign; *Smith* v. *Libya*, US, 101 F.3d 239, 245 (2nd Cir. 1996); 113 ILR 534; affirming *Smith* v. *Libya*, US, 886 F.Supp. 306 (E.D.N.Y. 1995); 107 ILR 382; *Hirsh* v. *Israel*, US, 962 F.Supp. 377, 381–382 (S.D.N.Y. 1997); 113 ILR 543; *Cabiri* v. *Ghana*, US, 981 F.Supp. 129, 133–134 (E.D.N.Y. 1997); implicitly affirmed, *Cabiri* v. *Ghana*, US, 165 F.3d 193, 201 (2nd Cir. 1999); *Daliberti* v. *Iraq*, US, 97 F.Supp.2d 38, 48, fn. 5 (D.D.C. 2000); *Sampson* v. *Germany*, US, 250 F.3d 1145, 1150–1151 (7th Cir. 2001); affirming *Sampson* v. *Germany*, US, 975 F.Supp. 1108 (N.D.Ill. 1997); *Garb* v. *Poland*, US, 207 F.Supp.2d 16, 38–39 (E.D.N.Y. 2002); *Hwang* v. *Japan*, US, 332 F.3d 679, 686–687 (D.C.Cir. 2003); affirming *Hwang* v. *Japan*, US, 172 F.Supp.2d 52, 60–61 (D. D.C. 2001) (the *Hwang* decision was later vacated and remanded by the

NOTES TO PAGES 344-346   649

Supreme Court, *Hwang* v. *Japan*, US, 542 US 901 (2004), but was reaffirmed on the ground of non-justiciability: *Hwang* v. *Japan*, US, 413 F.3d 45 (D.C.Cir. 2005)); *Doe I* v. *Israel*, US, 400 F.Supp.2d 86, 105 (D.D.C. 2005). See also *Jones* v. *Saudi Arabia*, England, [2007] 1 AC 270, 297–298, paras. 59–63; 129 ILR 629, 737–739; *Ferrini* v. *Germany*, Italy, (2004) 128 ILR 658, 668, para. 8.2; noted in Bianchi, *Ferrini*, 243 and fn. 13; and in Focarelli, Denying, 957.

Chapter 9

1 See Loi n° 91-650 of 1991; *Iran* v. *Eurodif*, France, (1989) 89 ILR 31, 35; 79 *RCDIP* (1990) 346, 348; *Guinea* v. *Atlantic*, France, (1984/1986) 82 ILR 75, 84; 114 *JDI* (1987) 125, 126.

2 See *Szczesniak* v. *Backer*, Belgium, (1955) 65 ILR 23, 26.

3 See *Rafidain* v. *Consarc*, Belgium, (1993) 106 ILR 274, 277.

4 See *NIOC Revenues Case*, Germany, (1983) BVerfGE 64, 1 at 22, 36, 40; 65 ILR 215, 228, 239, 242.

5 See *Philippine Embassy Case*, Germany, (1977) BVerfGE 46, 342; 65 ILR 146 (*passim*); *NIOC Revenues Case*, Germany, (1983) BVerfGE 64, 1 at 40–41, 44; 65 ILR 215, 242, 244. Or '*Maßnahmen der Sicherung und der Zwangsvollstreckung*' (preventive measures and measures of forced execution), *Philippine Embassy Case*, Germany, (1977) BVerfGE 46, 342 at 347; 65 ILR 146, 166.

6 US FSIA, s. 1610.

7 UK SIA, s. 13.

8 ILC, Report, *YILC*, 1985-II-2, p. 51 at 55, para. 230. For further explanation see ILC, Report, *YILC*, 1991-II-2, p. 12 at 55–56, commentary to Part IV, para. (2). The term 'measures of constraint' is used in Art. 18 of the 1991 ILC Draft and Arts. 18 and 19 of the 2004 UN Convention, and is also adopted by IDI in its 1991 Draft (Art. 4).

9 See *National Iranian* v. *Pipeline*, France, 1990, 80 *RCDIP* (1991) 140; (1990) 113 ILR 446; *Kuwait News* v. *Parrott*, France, 1990, 80 *RCDIP* (1991) 142; (1990) 113 ILR 457; *Senghor* v. *International*, France, 1990, 80 *RCDIP* (1991) 341; (1990) 113 ILR 460; *Mouracade* v. *Yemen*, France, 1991, 119 *JDI* (1992) 398; (1991) 113 ILR 462; *Barrandon* v. *USA*, France, 1992/1995; 123 *JDI* (1996) 102; (1992/1995) 113 ILR 464; *Mobutu* v. *Société Logrine*, France, 1994, 122 *JDI* (1995) 641; (1994) 113 ILR 481; *Saignie* v. *Embassy*, France, 1997, 86 *RCDIP* (1997) 332; (1997) 113 ILR 492; *X* v. *Saudi School*, France, 2003, 130 *JDI* (2003) 1124; 92 *RCDIP* (2003) 647; (2003) 127 ILR 163; *Cotigny* v. *Suarez*, France, 2004, 94 *RCDIP* (2005) 75; (2004) 127 ILR 168.

10 See *Société Ouest* v. *Senegal*, France, 1989/1991, 117 *JDI* (1990) 141; 118 *JDI* (1991) 1005; (1989/1991) 113 ILR 440; *Dumez* v. *Iraq*, France, 1999, 127 *JDI* (2000) 45; (1999) 127 ILR 144; *Creighton* v. *Qatar*, France, 127 *JDI* (2000) 1054; (2000) 127 ILR 154; *Russian* v. *Noga*, France, 2000, 128 *JDI* (2001) 116; (2000) 127 ILR 156; *Federal* v. *Republics*, France, 1999, 127 *JDI* (2000) 1036; (1999) 128 ILR 627.

11 See *Rafidain* v. *Consarc*, Belgium, (1993) 106 ILR 274, 277–278 (seeking *exequatur* for a US judgment (*Consarc* v. *Iraqi Ministry*, US, 27 F.3d 695 (D.C.Cir. 1994); 106 ILR 408)).

650   NOTES TO PAGES 346-349

12 See *Société Ouest* v. *Senegal*, France, (1991) 113 ILR 440, 445; *Benvenuti* v. *Congo*, France, (1981) 65 ILR 88, 91; *Yugoslavia* v. *Société Européenne*, France, (1970) 65 ILR 46, 49.

13 See *Argentina* v. *NML*, England, [2010] EWCA Civ 41, paras. 51, 55–56, 58, 93, 103, 107; *AIC* v. *Nigeria*, England, (2003) 129 ILR 571, 576–577, paras. 18–22.

14 See *Republic of Ghana Case*, Switzerland, (1973) 65 ILR 404, 405–406.

15 See *Oltmans* v. *Surinam*, Netherlands, 1990, 23 *NYIL* (1992) 442, 446–447; *Zaire* v. *Duclaux*, Netherlands, (1988) 94 ILR 368, 368–369.

16 See *Fusco* v. *O'Dea*, Ireland, [1994] 2 ILRM 389, 392–394; 103 ILR 318, 320–321. See also US House of Representatives, Report No. 94-1487, 1976, p. 23; 1976 USCCAN 6604, 6621–6622.

17 See also Pakistan SIO, s. 14(1); Singapore SIA, s. 15(1); Canada SIA, s. 13(1); Australia FSIA, s. 34; the Israeli Immunity Law 5769-2008, s. 15(b). For the unenforceability of a fine against a foreign State see also US House of Representatives, Report No. 94-1487, 1976, p. 22; 1976 USCCAN 6604, 6621; ALRC, Report No. 24, 1984, p. 84, para. 137.

18 According to the drafters: 'Under current international practice, punitive damages are usually not assessed against foreign states.' US House of Representatives, Report No. 94-1487, 1976, p. 22; 1976 USCCAN 6604, 6621. For punitive damages being an unsuitable remedy in international law see Gray, *Judicial Remedies*, pp. 26–28; Wittich, Punitive Damages, pp. 667–675.

19 See Sinclair, The Law, 220; Lalive, L'Immunité, 273.

20 The lengths earlier courts would go to in disproving an alleged general rule of customary international law banning execution are little short of amazing. See, e.g., *Philippine Embassy Case*, Germany, (1977) 65 ILR 146, 164–184, Ground C.I.; *NIOC Revenues Case*, Germany, (1983) 65 ILR 215, 228–245, Ground B.III.

21 Blackstone, *Commentaries*, Book I, 1765, Chapter 7, p. 235.

22 See *Dreyfus*, Switzerland, (1918) BGE 44 I 49, 54–55; *Greek Republic* v. *Walder*, Switzerland, (1930) 5 AD 121, 122–123; *Greece* v. *Julius Bär*, Switzerland, (1956) 23 ILR 195, 196, Ground 7; *UAR* v. *Mrs X*, Switzerland, (1960) 65 ILR 385, 389, Ground 2; *Italian* v. *Beta*, Switzerland, (1966) 65 ILR 394, 398, Ground 5; *Banque Commerciale Case*, Switzerland, (1977) 65 ILR 412, 414–415, Ground 1; *Banque Centrale* v. *Weston*, Switzerland, (1978) 65 ILR 417, 419–420, Grounds 2c, 4 and 4d; *Egypt* v. *Cinetelevision*, Switzerland, (1979) 65 ILR 425, 430, Ground 4; *Libya* v. *LIAMCO*, Switzerland, (1980) 62 ILR 228, 233–234, Grounds 3a and 3b; *Italian* v. *X*, Switzerland, (1985) 82 ILR 23, 26, Ground 4a; *Libya* v. *Actimon*, Switzerland, (1985) 82 ILR 30, 32–33, Ground 4; *Swissair* v. *X*, Switzerland, (1985) 82 ILR 36, 37; *Spain* v. *Company X*, Switzerland, (1986) 82 ILR 38, 40, Ground 3b; *S* v. *Romania*, Switzerland, (1987) 82 ILR 45, 48, Ground 2; *Landano* v. *USA*, Switzerland, (1987) 116 ILR 636, 639.

23 *Greece* v. *Julius Bär*, Switzerland, (1956) 23 ILR 195, 198, Ground 10.

24 *UAR* v. *Mrs X*, Switzerland, (1960) 65 ILR 385, 391, Ground 4.

25 *Egypt* v. *Cinetelevision*, Switzerland, (1979) 65 ILR 425, 430, Ground 4b; citing *UAR* v. *Mrs X*, Switzerland, (1960) 65 ILR 385, 391, Ground 4 and *Greece* v. *Julius*

NOTES TO PAGES 349–356   651

Bär, Switzerland, (1956) 23 ILR 195, 198–199, Ground 10. Notice the important proviso at the end. See also *République Y* v. *X*, Switzerland, 2000, 11 *RSDIE* (2001) 589, 590.

26 See *NV* v. *National Iranian*, Netherlands, (1968) 47 ILR 138, 147.

27 *Duff* v. *Kelantan*, England, [1924] AC 797, 834–835 per Lord Carson, dissenting; *Trendtex* v. *Central Bank*, England, [1977] QB 529, 561; 64 ILR 111, 135; *Hispano* v. *Central Bank*, England, [1979] 2 Lloyd's Rep 277; 64 ILR 221. Traditionally, the common law held otherwise, see Lewis, *State and Diplomatic Immunity*, p. 77.

28 See *Central Bank of Nigeria Case*, Germany, (1975/1976) 65 ILR 131, 135.

29 *Banamar-Capizzi* v. *Embassy*, Italy, (1989) 87 ILR 56, 60; *Libya* v. *Rossbeton*, Italy, (1989) 87 ILR 63, 67; *Condor* v. *Minister*, Italy, (1992) 101 ILR 394, 401.

30 *Abbott* v. *South Africa*, Spain, (1992) 113 ILR 411, 415–416, 419–420, 422.

31 See especially Council of Europe, *Explanatory Reports*, 1972, pp. 33–34, paras. 96–98, commentary to Article 24, and p. 36, paras. 104–105, commentary to Article 26.

32 Council of Europe, *Explanatory Reports*, p. 33, para. 92, commentary to Art. 23.

33 ILR, Report, *YILC*, 1991-II-2, p. 12 at 56.

34 For pre-FSIA practice along the same lines see *Dexter* v. *Kunglig*, US, 43 F.2d 705 (2nd Cir. 1930); 5 AD 109, 110; *New York* v. *Korea*, US, 132 F.Supp. 684 (1955); 22 ILR 220; *Weilamann* v. *Chase*, US, 192 N.Y.S.2d 469 (1959); 28 ILR 165; *State* v. *Dekle*, US, 137 So.2d 581 (Fla. 1962); 33 ILR 181; *City* v. *Ghana*, US, 255 N.Y.S.2d 178 (1964); 35 ILR 129. See also Metzger, *Immunity*; Delaume, *The Foreign*, 266–277.

35 *FG Hemisphere* v. *Congo*, US, 455 F.3d 575, 589 (5th Cir. 2006), quoting *Connecticut* v. *Congo*, US, 309 F.3d 240, 252 (5th Cir. 2002).

36 US House of Representatives, Report No. 94-1487, 1976, pp. 8 and 27; 1976 USCCAN 6604, 6606 and 6626. Emphases added.

37 *Letelier* v. *Chile*, US, 748 F.2d 790, 799 (2nd Cir. 1984); 79 ILR 561; reversing *Letelier* v. *Chile*, US, 567 F.Supp. 1490 (S.D.N.Y. 1983) and *Letelier* v. *Chile*, US, 575 F.Supp. 1217 (S.D.N.Y. 1983). See also *Connecticut* v. *Congo*, US, 309 F.3d 240, 252 (5th Cir. 2002).

38 *Ministry of Defense* v. *Cubic*, US, 385 F.3d 1206, 1219 (9th Cir. 2004). For pre-FSIA US cases that confirmed the principle see *Flota* v. *Motor*, US, 335 F.2d 619, 626 (4th Cir. 1964); *Rich* v. *Naviera*, US, 197 F.Supp. 710, 722–723 (E.D.Va. 1961); 32 ILR 127; *Dexter* v. *Kunglig*, US, 43 F.2d 705, 708 (2nd Cir. 1930).

39 ALI, *Third Restatement*, Vol. 1, s. 456(1)(b) ('Waiver of Immunity'), pp. 415–416.

40 Emphasis added. See near-reproductions or very similar provisions in the Pakistan SIO, ss. 3 and 14; Singapore SIA, ss. 3 and 15; South Africa FSIA, ss. 2 and 14; Canada SIA, ss. 3, 11 and 12; Australia FSIA, Part II and Part IV, see especially ss. 9, 30 and 31(1); ALRC, Report No. 24, p. 71, para. 119 and p. 72, para. 121; Israel Immunity Law, Chapter Two and Chapter Three, see especially ss. 2, 15 and 17(c). The Argentina Immunity Law does not contain any provision on enforcement but instead provides a general immunity for foreign States subject only to exceptions which lie within the realm of adjudication. If this Law can be taken at its face value, then Argentina seems to adhere to absolute immunity from execution.

652 NOTES TO PAGES 356-359

41 *Alcom* v. *Colombia*, England, [1984] 1 AC 580, 600; 74 ILR 170, 183. See also *Forth* v. *Wilmington*, Scotland, 1985, 1985 SC 317, 324–325, 327; 1987 SLT 153, 157–158, 158, 161; 107 ILR 641, 648–651, 652, 657; *Al-Adsani* v. *Kuwait*, England, (1996) 107 ILR 536, 542, 548; *AIC* v. *Nigeria*, England, (2003) 129 ILR 571, 575–576, paras. 16–17; *AIG* v. *Kazakhstan*, England, 2005, [2006] 1 WLR 1420, 1434, para. 29(3); 1438, para. 42; 1439, paras. 47–48; 1440, para. 54; 129 ILR 589, 606, 610, 611–612, 613; *Svenska* v. *Lithuania (No. 2)*, England, 2006, [2007] QB 886, 930, para. 135; *ETI* v. *Bolivia*, England, 2008, [2009] 1 WLR 665, 693, paras. 127–128; *Argentina* v. *NML*, England, [2010] EWCA Civ 41, paras. 49, 51, 103.

42 *AIC* v. *Nigeria*, England, (2003) 129 ILR 571, 575–576, para. 17.

43 For pre-SIA UK practice along the same lines see Higgins, Execution.

44 *Argentina* v. *NML*, England, [2010] EWCA Civ 41, paras. 107 per Aikens LJ (see also paras. 51, 55–56, 58, 93, 103); *AIC* v. *Nigeria*, England, (2003) 129 ILR 571, 576–577, paras. 18–22.

45 *AIC* v. *Nigeria*, England, (2003) 129 ILR 571, 578–580, paras. 24–30.

46 *Svenska* v. *Lithuania (No. 2)*, England, 2006, [2007] QB 886, 925, para. 117; affirming *Svenska* v. *Lithuania (No. 2)*, England, 2005, [2006] 1 Lloyd's Rep. 181, 202, para. 69. See also *ETI* v. *Bolivia*, England, 2008, [2009] 1 WLR 665, 690, para. 114.

47 *ETI* v. *Bolivia*, England, 2008, [2009] 1 WLR 665, 690, para. 113; affirming *ETI* v. *Bolivia*, England, [2008] EWHC 1689 (Comm), 2008 WL 2697081; noted in Charles, Section 44.

48 *Mitchell* v. *Al-Dali*, England, [2005] EWCA Civ 720, paras. 1–3.

49 *Argentina* v. *NML*, England, [2010] EWCA Civ 41, para. 103.

50 *West* v. *Captain*, Belgium, (1920) 1 AD 152, 153–154; *Portugal* v. *Sauvage*, Belgium, (1921) 1 AD 154, 155; *Brasseur* v. *Greece*, Belgium, (1933) 6 AD 164, 167; Sucharitkul, *State Immunities*, p. 87 and cases cited there. For more recent Belgian practice see d'Argent, Jurisprudence belge.

51 *Socobelge* v. *Greek State*, Belgium, (1951) 18 ILR 3, 6. However, *Socobelge* has been viewed as a departure from the usual Belgian practice. See Colliard, *Socobelge*; Suy, Immunity, 684; Vennemann, L'Immunité, in Centres de Droit International, *L'Immunité*, pp. 143–145; Verhoeven, Jurisprudence, 645.

52 See *British* v. *Guerrato*, Italy, (1959) 28 ILR 156, 158; *Prefect* v. *Federici*, Italy, (1968) 65 ILR 270, 271; *Campione* v. *Peti-Nitrogenmuvek*, Italy, (1972) 65 ILR 287, 293; *Banamar-Capizzi* v. *Embassy*, Italy, (1989) 87 ILR 56, 61; *Libya* v. *Rossbeton*, Italy, (1989) 87 ILR 63, 66–67; *Condor* v. *Minister*, Italy, (1992) 101 ILR 394, 400.

53 *Banamar-Capizzi* v. *Embassy*, Italy, (1989) 87 ILR 56, 62; *Libya* v. *Rossbeton*, Italy, (1989) 87 ILR 63, 66–67; *Condor* v. *Minister*, Italy, (1992) 101 ILR 394, 403–406.

54 *Banamar-Capizzi* v. *Embassy*, Italy, (1989) 87 ILR 56, 59. For distinction between 'jurisdiction' and 'execution' see also *Mininni* v. *Bari*, Italy, (1981) 78 ILR 112, 114–115.

55 *Soviet Republic Case*, Greece, (1928) 4 AD 172; affirmed by the Areopagus (Supreme Court) on appeal: Areopagus, No. 29, Themis, Vol. 40, p. 842.

56 See *Sale of British Embassy Building Case*, Greece (1962) 65 ILR 247, 247; *Embassy Eviction Case*, Greece, (1965) 65 ILR 248, 251–252; *Purchase of Embassy Staff*

NOTES TO PAGES 359-361   653

Residence Case, Greece, (1967) 65 ILR 255, 256. For a more recent example of the refusal of ministerial authorization see the *Distomo* case: *Distomo Massacre Case*, Greece, (2000) 129 ILR 513; *Kalogeropoulou* v. *Greece*, ECHR, (2002) 129 ILR 537.

57 *Embassy Eviction Case*, Greece, (1965) 65 ILR 248, 251.

58 See the Swiss Government ordinance of 12 July 1918 prohibiting arrest and execution directed against the property of foreign States, noted in *Greek Republic* v. *Walder*, Switzerland, (1930) 5 AD 121, 122, fn. 2; and the Swiss Federal Council Decree of 24 October 1939 subjecting execution to the consent of the Federal Council, noted in *State Immunity Case*, Switzerland, (1939/1940) 10 AD 235, 238-239.

59 *Dralle* v. *Czechoslovakia*, Austria, (1950) 17 ILR 155.

60 *Garnishee Order Case*, Austria, (1952) 19 ILR 211.

61 *British Embassy Driver Case*, Austria, (1978) 65 ILR 20.

62 *Neustein* v. *Indonesia*, Austria, (1958) 65 ILR 3, 9.

63 *Neustein* v. *Indonesia*, Austria, (1958) 65 ILR 3, 9, fn. 3. For text see also *Leasing* v. *Algeria*, Austria, (1986) 116 ILR 526, 530; duplicate report *sub nom Republic of 'A' Case*, Austria, (1986) 77 ILR 488, 491, fn. 5; Seidl-Hohenveldern, State Immunity, 97.

64 *Leasing* v. *Algeria*, Austria, (1986) 116 ILR 526, 528-529; duplicate report *sub nom Republic of 'A' Case*, Austria, (1986) 77 ILR 488.

65 See especially *Administration* v. *Société Levant*, France, (1969) 52 ILR 315.

66 *Société* v. *Gouvernement Turc*, France, (1965) 47 ILR 155; *Clerget* v. *Représentation*, France, (1967) 48 ILR 145; *Clerget* v. *Banque*, France, (1969) 52 ILR 310; affirmed, *Clerget* v. *Banque*, France, (1971) 65 ILR 54, 56; but cf. *Englander* v. *Statni*, France, (1969) 52 ILR 335, 336; quashing *Statni* v. *Englander*, France, (1966) 47 ILR 157; *Société* v. *Captain Serdjuk*, France, (1964) 65 ILR 38, 39.

67 *Procureur* v. *SA Ipitrade*, France, (1978) 65 ILR 75, 77.

68 *Corporacion* v. *Braden*, France, (1972) 65 ILR 57, 60.

69 *Yugoslavia* v. *Société Européenne*, France, (1970) 65 ILR 46, 49; *Malagasy* v. *Société*, France, (1971) 65 ILR 51, 54; *Iran* v. *Société Eurodif*, France, (1982) 65 ILR 93, 97; *Caisse* v. *Société Midland*, France, (1983) 77 ILR 524, 525 note; *Russian* v. *Noga*, France, (2000) 127 ILR 156, 160.

70 *Empire of Iran Case*, Germany, (1963) 45 ILR 57.

71 *Philippine Embassy Bank Account Case*, Germany, (1977) 65 ILR 146, 150, 164. For earlier cases see *In re The Charkow*, Germany, (1959) 65 ILR 100, 104-105; *Spanish Consular Bank Accounts Case*, Germany, (1971) 65 ILR 114, 117-118; *Central Bank of Nigeria Case*, Germany, (1975/1976) 65 ILR 131, 135-136.

72 See *Philippine Embassy Bank Account Case*, Germany, (1977) 65 ILR 146, 190, Ground C.II.4(d); *NIOC Revenues Case*, Germany, (1983) 65 ILR 215, 226-227.

73 *NIOC Revenues Case*, Germany, (1983) 65 ILR 215, 226-229. See also *NIOC Legal Status Case*, Germany, (1980) 65 ILR 199; *NIOC Pipeline Contracts Case*, Germany, (1982) 65 ILR 212.

74 *Philippine Embassy Case*, Germany, (1977) 65 ILR 146, 160, Ground B(a); *Kenyan Diplomatic Residence Case*, Germany, (2003) 128 ILR 632, 638-639.

75 *Emilio* v. *Embassy*, Spain, (1986) 86 ILR 508, 510; *Diana* v. *South Africa*, Spain, (1986) 86 ILR 512, 515.

654   NOTES TO PAGES 361–364

76 *Emilio* v. *Embassy*, Spain, (1986) 86 ILR 508, 511; *Diana* v. *South Africa*, Spain, (1986) 86 ILR 512, 516.

77 *Abbott* v. *South Africa*, Spain, (1992) 113 ILR 411, 422, 425–426.

78 Fox, *The Law of State Immunity* Chapter 18; Fox, International Law, in Evans (ed.), *International Law*, 361–362; Chamlongrasdr, *Foreign State Immunity*, p. 59; Gong, *A Comparative Study*, Chapter 7; Pingel, *Droit des immunités*; Verhoeven, *Le droit international*, pp. 36–42; Pingel-Lenuzza, *Les immunités* (see esp. pp. 74–91, 92–99, 100–136, 136–158, 161–173, 174–180, 281–291, 339–360, 360–376); Cosnard, *La soumission des États*, pp. 95–142, 143–202; Schreuer, *State Immunity*, Chapter 6; Badr, *State Immunity*, pp. 115–127, 129–132; ILA, Drafts (1982 and 1994), Articles II and VII; IDI, Draft, 1991, Articles 2 and 4; Green, A General; Crawford, Execution, 820; Sucharitkul, Second Report, *YILC*, 1980-II-1, p. 199 at 206, para. 31; Sinclair, The Law, 242; Bouchez, The Nature, 17–25; Centres de Droit International, *L'Immunité*; Schaumann and Habscheid, *Die Immunität*, p. 304; Boguslavsky, *Staatliche Immunität*, p. 152; Daillier *et al.*, *Droit international public*, pp. 498–503; Brownlie, *Principles*, pp. 342–343; Shaw, *International Law*, pp. 744–748; Cassese, *International Law*, pp. 109–110; Dupuy and Kerbrat, *Droit international public*, pp. 143–147; Steinberger, State Immunity, pp. 615, 624–630; Higgins, *Problems and Process*, p. 85; Bedjaoui, *Droit international*, pp. 361–362; Rousseau, *Droit international public*, p. 16; Sørensen, *A Manual*, p. 440; Kropholler, *Internationales Privatrecht*, pp. 582–583; Courbe, *Droit international privé*, p. 138; Monéger, *Droit international privé*, p. 181; Gutmann, *Droit international privé*, p. 238; Martiny *et al.*, *Handbuch*, pp. 261–262.

79 ILC, Report, *YILC*, 1991-II-2, p. 12 at 56, commentary to Art. 18. See also Sucharitkul, Seventh Report, *YILC*, 1985-II-1, p.21 at 30, para. 40; Ostrander, The Last Bastion.

80 *Philippine Embassy Case*, Germany, (1977) 65 ILR 146, 166, Ground C.I.2. See also *Embassy Eviction Case*, Greece, (1965) 65 ILR 248, 251. For concurring scholarly opinions see especially, Schreuer, *State Immunity*, p. 126; Sinclair, The Law, 219–220, 223; Bouchez, The Nature, 19; Sinclair, The European, 273; Lalive, L'Immunité, 273; Lauterpacht, The Problem, 243.

81 ILC, Report, *YILC*, 1991-II-2, p. 12 at 58, commentary to Art. 18(1)(c), para. 11.

82 See, e.g., *FG Hemisphere* v. *Congo*, US, 455 F.3d 575, 592–594 (5th Cir. 2006); *AfCap* v. *Congo*, US, 383 F.3d 361 (5th Cir. 2004) (*passim*); *Connecticut* v. *Congo*, US, 309 F.3d 240, 251–258 (5th Cir. 2002).

83 US House of Representatives, Report No. 94-1487, 1976, p. 28; 1976 USCCAN 6604, 6627.

84 *City of Englewood* v. *Libya*, US, 773 F.2d 31, 36–37 (3rd Cir. 1985) (emphasis added); quoted with approval in *Connecticut* v. *Congo*, US, 309 F.3d 240, 253, fn. 4 (5th Cir. 2002).

85 For definition of 'garnishment' in the US law see *Shaffer* v. *Heitner*, US, 433 US 186, 199, fn. 17 and 212, fn. 38 (1977); *FG Hemisphere* v. *Congo*, US, 455 F.3d 575, 589 (5th Cir. 2006); *Westex*, US, 950 F.2d 1187, 1192, fn. 7 (5th Cir. 1992); *Stena* v. *Comision*, US, 923 F.2d 380, 391 (5th Cir. 1991); 103 ILR 433.

NOTES TO PAGES 364–367   655

86 See especially *Connecticut* v. *Congo*, US, 309 F.3d 240 (5th Cir. 2002); *Af-Cap* v. *Congo*, US, 383 F.3d 361 (5th Cir. 2004); *FG Hemisphere* v. *Congo*, US, 455 F.3d 575 (5th Cir. 2006); *Af-Cap* v. *Congo*, US, 462 F.3d 417 (5th Cir. 2006); *Af-Cap* v. *Chevron*, US, 475 F.3d 1080 (9th Cir. 2007).

87 The waiver clause was quoted in full in the concurring/dissenting opinion of Circuit Judge Dennis in *Connecticut* v. *Congo*, US, 309 F.3d 240, 261 (5th Cir. 2002). See also *Connecticut* v. *Congo*, US, 309 F.3d 240, 247 (5th Cir. 2002); *Af-Cap* v. *Congo*, US, 383 F.3d 361, 364 (5th Cir. 2004); *Af-Cap* v. *Chevron*, US, 475 F.3d 1080, 1084, 1087 (9th Cir. 2007).

88 *Connecticut* v. *Congo*, US, 309 F.3d 240, 247, 251 (5th Cir. 2002). See also *Af-Cap* v. *Chevron*, US, 475 F.3d 1080, 1087 (9th Cir. 2007); *Atwood* v. *Petroleo*, US, 875 F.2d 1174, 1176–1177 (5th Cir. 1989).

89 *Connecticut* v. *Congo*, US, 309 F.3d 240, 251 (5th Cir. 2002); quoted with approval in *Af-Cap* v. *Chevron*, US, 475 F.3d 1080, 1087 (9th Cir. 2007). See also *Walker* v. *Congo*, US, 395 F.3d 229, 235–236 (5th Cir. 2004).

90 *Connecticut* v. *Congo*, US, 309 F.3d 240, 254 (5th Cir. 2002); see also *Af-Cap* v. *Chevron*, US, 475 F.3d 1080, 1084, 1087, 1091–1095 (9th Cir. 2007).

91 *Connecticut* v. *Congo*, US, 309 F.3d 240, 259 (5th Cir. 2002).

92 *Af-Cap* v. *Congo*, US, 383 F.3d 361, 369–370 (5th Cir. 2004). See also *Af-Cap* v. *Chevron*, US, 475 F.3d 1080, 1091 (9th Cir. 2007).

93 *Af-Cap* v. *Chevron*, US, 475 F.3d 1080, 1091, 1094 (9th Cir. 2007) (emphases in the original), citing *Connecticut* v. *Congo*, US, 309 F.3d 240 (5th Cir. 2002). This was reiterated in *Ministry* v. *Cubic*, US, 495 F.3d 1024, 1036 (9th Cir. 2007) (on remand from *Ministry* v. *Elahi*, US, 546 US 450 (2006), which vacated and remanded *Ministry* v. *Cubic*, US, 236 F.Supp.2d 1140 (S.D.Cal. 2002) and *Ministry* v. *Cubic*, US, 385 F.3d 1206 (9th Cir. 2004); the court nonetheless affirmed the judgment of the district court by holding that *Elahi* could attach the *Cubic* judgment under the Terrorism Risk Insurance Act (TRIA), 495 F.3d 1024, 1031–1034).

94 *Connecticut* v. *Congo*, US, 309 F.3d 240, 254–257 (5th Cir. 2002). The court refrained from expressing any opinion on *when* the property must be used for a commercial activity in the US. *Ibid.*, 257–258. Agreed, *Af-Cap* v. *Chevron*, US, 475 F.3d 1080, 1089–1090 (9th Cir. 2007).

95 *Connecticut* v. *Congo*, US, 309 F.3d 240, 256, fn. 5 (5th Cir. 2002) (emphasis in the original), citing *Flatow* v. *Iran*, US, 76 F.Supp.2d 16, 21–23 (D.D.C. 1999). Agreed: *Af-Cap* v. *Chevron*, US, 475 F.3d 1080, 1090–1091 (9th Cir. 2007).

96 *Connecticut* v. *Congo*, US, 309 F.3d 240, 252 (5th Cir. 2002).

97 See, e.g., *Flatow* v. *Iran*, US, 76 F.Supp.2d 16, 21–24 (D.D.C. 1999).

98 See the same or very similar provisions in the Pakistan SIO, s. 14(2)(b); Singapore SIA, s. 15(4); South Africa FSIA, s. 14(3); Canada SIA, s. 12(1)(b). Because of the words 'for the time being', 'the relevant time ... is the time of the issue of the process for the attachment of the property, whatever its use or intended use at any other time may have been'. *The Akademik Fyodorov*, South Africa, 1996 (4) SA 422, 447; 131 ILR 460, 487–488. See also *KJ* v. *Oscar Jupiter*, South Africa, 1997, 1998 (2) SA 130, 136; 131 ILR 529, 535–536.

656   NOTES TO PAGES 369-371

99 In *Orascom*, the judge when deciding on the issue of execution only considered whether the property in question was 'for the time being in use or
intended for use for the purposes of a contract for the supply of goods or
services, or of a loan or other transaction for the provision of finance':
Orascom v. *Chad*, England, [2008] 2 Lloyd's Rep 396, 400, para. 15. That is,
for the definition of 'commercial transaction' the judge only considered
s. 3(3)(a) and (b) and left out s. 3(3)(c).

100 See *Alcom* v. *Colombia*, England, [1984] 1 AC 580, 604–605 (holding that a
certificate given by the Colombian Ambassador to the effect that the funds
in question were 'not in use nor intended for use for commercial purposes
but only to meet the expenditure necessarily incurred in the day to day
running of the Diplomatic Mission' was 'conclusive'); 74 ILR 170, 187–188;
AIC v. *Nigeria*, England, (2003) 129 ILR 571, 586–587, paras. 52–53 (accepting a
certificate by the Nigerian High Commissioner). Cf. *Orascom* v. *Chad*, England,
[2008] 2 Lloyd's Rep 396, 403–404, para. 24 (refusing to accept a certificate by
the ambassador of Chad on the ground that the contrary had been proved).
See similar provisions in the Pakistan SIO, s. 14(4); Singapore SIA, s. 15(5);
Australia FSIA, s. 41.

101 This despite the drafters' criticism of the 'commercial purposes' test under
the UK SIA: ALRC, Report No. 24, p. 76, para. 125.

102 *Philippine Embassy Case*, Germany, (1977) 65 ILR 146, 150; 164, Ground
C (emphases added); see also 65 ILR 146, 181, Ground C.I.6; 184, Ground
C.II.1. See also *NIOC Revenues Case*, Germany, (1983) 65 ILR 215, 226, Ground
B.III.1; 241–242, Ground B.III.2(d); *Kenyan Diplomatic Residence Case*, Germany,
(2003) 128 ILR 632, 636, Ground II.3b. Lord Diplock found this case 'particu-
larly helpful' on the issue of embassy accounts: *Alcom* v. *Colombia*, England,
[1984] 1 AC 580, 599; 74 ILR 170, 182. Also cited with approval in *Leasing* v.
Algeria, Austria, (1986) 116 ILR 526, 528.

103 *Empire of Iran Case*, Germany, (1963) 45 ILR 57, 80.

104 *NIOC Revenues Case*, Germany, (1983) 65 ILR 215, 242, Ground B.III.2(d)
(emphases added); see also 65 ILR 215, 219, Ground A.I; 243–245, Ground
B.III.2(d)(bb), (2), (e) and (f).

105 *Spanish Consular Case*, Germany, (1971) 65 ILR 114, 118 (emphases added).

106 *Italian* v. *Beta*, Switzerland, (1966) 65 ILR 394, 402, Ground 8. See also *Egypt* v.
Cinetelevision, Switzerland, (1979) 65 ILR 425, 430, Ground 4b; 435, Ground 5c.

107 *Libya* v. *Actimon*, Switzerland, (1985) BGE 111 Ia 62, 65, Ground 7b; 82 ILR 30,
35 (slightly different translation).

108 *Z* v. *Geneva*, Switzerland, (1990) 102 ILR 205, 207, Ground 2b. See also *Greece* v.
Julius Bär, Switzerland, (1956) 23 ILR 195, 198–199, Ground 10; *UAR* v. *Mrs X*,
Switzerland, (1960) 65 ILR 385, 391, Ground 4; 392, Ground 5; *Egypt* v.
Cinetelevision, Switzerland, (1979) 65 ILR 425, 430, Ground 4b; *Griessen*, Switz-
erland, (1982) 82 ILR 5, 7, Ground 1; *Libya* v. *Actimon*, Switzerland, (1985) 82
ILR 30, 36, Ground 7b; *Guinée* v. *M*, Switzerland, 1985, 42 *ASDI* (1986) 69, 71;
Spain v. *Company X*, Switzerland, (1986) 82 ILR 38, 41, Ground 4a; 44, Ground
5a; *République Y* v. *X*, Switzerland, 2000, 11 *RSDIE* (2001) 589, 590.

NOTES TO PAGES 371–374 657

109 *Italian* v. *Beta*, Switzerland, (1966) 65 ILR 394, 402, Ground 8; repeated verbatim in *Egypt* v. *Cinetelevision*, Switzerland, (1979) 65 ILR 425, 435, Ground 5c. See also *Banque Commerciale Arabe Case*, Switzerland, (1977) 65 ILR 412, 414–415, Ground 1.

110 *Libya* v. *Actimon*, Switzerland, (1985) 82 ILR 30, 35, Ground 7b. For similar categorizations see *Spanish Consular Case*, Germany, (1971) 65 ILR 114, 118; *NIOC Revenues Case*, Germany, (1983) 65 ILR 215, 244, Ground B.III.2(d)(bb)(2)); *Embassy Eviction Case*, Greece, (1965) 65 ILR 248, 250. But see *État C* v. *Dame X*, Switzerland, 8 *RSDIE* (1998) 643, 643–648 ('indivisible').

111 *Neustein* v. *Indonesia*, Austria, (1958) 65 ILR 3, 9.

112 *Leasing West* v. *Algeria*, Austria, (1986) 116 ILR 526, 528 (emphasis in the original) (citing *Neustein*, Austria, (1958) 65 ILR 3 and *Philippine Embassy Case*, Germany, (1977) 65 ILR 146); duplicate report *sub nom Republic of 'A' Case*, Austria, (1986) 77 ILR 488. See also *British Embassy Driver Case*, Austria, (1978) 65 ILR 20, 22; *Foreign State Bank Account Case*, Austria, (1986) 86 ILR 570 note; *Radiation Contamination Claim Case*, Austria, (1988) 86 ILR 571, 573.

113 *Hamspohn* v. *Bey*, Italy, 1887, 26 *AJIL Supplement* (1932) 713, 713; *Rumania* v. *Trutta*, Italy, 1926, 26 *AJIL Supplement* (1932) 711, 712.

114 *Banamar-Capizzi* v. *Embassy*, Italy, (1989) 87 ILR 56, 60, 62. See also *Libya* v. *Rossbeton*, Italy, (1989) 87 ILR 63, 66, 67, 68; *Condor* v. *Minister*, Italy, (1992) 101 ILR 394, 402, 403, 404.

115 *Iran* v. *Société Eurodif*, France, (1984) 77 ILR 513, 515 (quashing *Iran* v. *Société Eurodif*, France, (1982) 65 ILR 93); repeated and further confirmed, *Iran* v. *Société Eurodif*, France, (1989) 89 ILR 31, 34–35; again repeated in a parallel case, *Ministry* v. *Société Framatome*, France, (1990) 113 ILR 452, 456. See also *Société Air Zaire* v. *Gauthier*, France, (1984) 77 ILR 510, 511–512; *Yugoslavia* v. *Société Européenne*, France, (1985/1986) 82 ILR 58, 72–73;

116 *Société Sonatrach* v. *Migeon*, France, (1985) 77 ILR 525, 527.

117 *Abbott* v. *South Africa*, Spain, (1992) 113 ILR 411, 419–420, 423. See also pp. 425 and 426.

118 *NV Filmpartners*, Belgium, (1971) 65 ILR 26, 28. See also *Iraq* v. *Vinci*, Belgium, (2002) 127 ILR 101, 105, 107.

119 *Embassy Eviction Case*, Greece, (1965) 65 ILR 248, 250.

120 *NV Cabolent* v. *National*, Netherlands, (1968) 47 ILR 138, 148; *MK* v. *State*, Netherlands, (1986) 94 ILR 357, 360; *Netherlands* v. *Azeta*, Netherlands, (1998) 128 ILR 688, 689.

121 See *Szczesniak* v. *Backer*, Belgium, (1955) 65 ILR 23; *NV Filmpartners*, Belgium, (1971) 65 ILR 26; *Caisse* v. *Société Midland*, France, (1983) 77 ILR 524 note; *Société Air Zaire* v. *Gauthier*, France, (1984) 77 ILR 510; *Iran* v. *Société Eurodif*, France, (1984) 77 ILR 513, 516; *Société Sonatrach* v. *Migeon*, France, (1985) 77 ILR 525; *Guinea* v. *Atlantic*, France, (1984/1986) 82 ILR 75, 84; *Iran* v. *Société Eurodif*, France, (1989) 89 ILR 31, 35; *Ministry* v. *Société Framatome*, France, (1990) 113 ILR 452, 454; *UAR* v. *Mrs X*, Switzerland, (1960) 65 ILR 385, 391, Ground 4.

658   NOTES TO PAGES 374–376

122 See *Alcom* v. *Colombia*, England, [1984] 1 AC 580; 74 ILR 170; *Philipp Brothers* v. *Sierra Leone*, England, 1993/1994, [1994] 1 Lloyd's Rep 111; [1995] 1 Lloyd's Rep 289; 107 ILR 517; *Yugoslavia* v. *Société Européenne*, France, (1985) 82 ILR 58.

123 See *Trendtex* v. *Central Bank*, England, [1977] QB 529; 64 ILR 111; *Atwood* v. *Petroleo*, US, 875 F.2d 1174 (5th Cir. 1989); *Brenntag* v. *Bank*, US, 175 F.3d 245, 252–254 (2nd Cir. 1999); affirming *Brenntag* v. *Norddeutsche*, US, 9 F.Supp.2d 331, 346–347 (S.D.N.Y. 1998).

124 See *In re Estate of Ferdinand Marcos*, US, 94 F.3d 539, 548 (9th Cir. 1996).

125 For a pre-FSIA case see *New York* v. *Korea*, US, 132 F.Supp. 684, 687, fn. 7 (S.D. N.Y. 1955); 22 ILR 220, 223.

126 *ETI* v. *Bolivia*, England, 2008, [2009] 1 WLR 665, 693, para. 128. Section 13 of the UK SIA prohibits injunctive relief against a *State* in the absence of written consent.

127 *Libya* v. *SpA Imprese*, Italy, (1979) 78 ILR 90, 91, citing *Greece* v. *Gamet*, Italy, (1957) 24 ILR 209. See also *Tani* v. *Russian*, Italy, (1947) 15 AD 141, 142; *Greece* v. *Gamet*, Italy, (1959) 28 ILR 153, 154; *Parravincini* v. *Commercial*, Italy, (1969) 65 ILR 282, 283; *Mallaval* v. *French*, Italy, (1974) 65 ILR 303, 305; *Association* v. *Piccoli*, Italy, (1974) 65 ILR 308; *Rubin* v. *Consul*, Italy, (1977) 77 ILR 593; *US* v. *Gereschi*, Italy, (1977) 77 ILR 598; *Bari* v. *Jasbez*, Italy (1977) 77 ILR 602, 603; *Special* v. *Pieciukiewicz*, Italy, (1982) 78 ILR 120; *Libya* v. *SPA Records*, Italy, (1983) 87 ILR 11, 12; *Banco* v. *Credito Varesino*, Italy, (1984) 87 ILR 15, 16; *Sindacato* v. *Bari*, Italy, (1986) 87 ILR 37, 37; *Church* v. *Ferraino*, Italy, (1986) 101 ILR 370; *Bayerischer* v. *Schiavetti*, Italy, (1987) 87 ILR 38, 39; *France* v. *Jacuzio*, Italy, (1987) 87 ILR 53, 54; *Banamar-Capizzi* v. *Embassy*, Italy, (1989) 87 ILR 56, 58; *Libya* v. *Rossbeton*, Italy, (1989) 87 ILR 63, 64; *British* v. *Toglia*, Italy, (1989) 101 ILR 379, 381; *Libya* v. *Trobbiani*, Italy, (1990) 114 ILR 520, 521; *Norwegian* v. *Quattri*, Italy, (1991) 114 ILR 525, 527; *Zambian* v. *Sendanayake*, Italy, (1992) 114 ILR 532, 533; *Giaffreda* v. *French*, Italy, (1992) 114 ILR 558 note; *Carbonar* v. *Magurno*, Italy, (1993) 114 ILR 534, 535; *Perrini* v. *Académie*, Italy, (1994) 114 ILR 536, 537; *USA* v. *Lo Gatto*, Italy, (1995) 114 ILR 555, 556; *FILT-CGIL* v. *USA*, Italy, (2000) 128 ILR 644, 646–647. For cases in other countries see *Private Servant of Diplomat Case*, Austria, (1971) 71 ILR 546, 549; *SA Biocare* v. *Gécamines*, Belgium, (1989) 115 ILR 415, 417; *Schreiber* v. *Germany*, Canada, (2001) 196 DLR (4th) 281, 288; affirmed, *Schreiber* v. *Germany*, Canada, (2002) 216 DLR (4th) 513, 524; *Trendtex* v. *Central Bank*, England, [1977] QB 529, 549; 64 ILR 111, 123; *Maclaine* v. *Department*, England, 1988, [1989] Ch 72, 194, 252; [1988] 3 WLR 1033; 80 ILR 47; *Ahmed* v. *Saudi Arabia*, England, 1995, [1996] 2 All ER 248, 250; 104 ILR 629, 640; *London* v. *Bastians*, England, 1994, [1995] ICR 358, 362; 107 ILR 613, 617; *Egypt* v. *Gamal-Eldin*, England, 1995, [1996] 2 All ER 237, 239; 104 ILR 673, 674; *Paprocki* v. *German*, England, (1995) 104 ILR 684, 686, 690; *UAE* v. *Abdelghafar*, England, (1995) 107 ILR 626, 632; *Re P (No. 2)*, England, [1998] 1 FLR 1027, 1028, 1035, 1036, 1039; 114 ILR 485, 489, 496, 497, 501; *Mills* v. *USA*, England, (2000) 120 ILR 612, 614, 616; affirmed, *Mills* v. *Embassy*, England, 2000, unreported; *In re Banco*, England, [2001] 3 All ER 923, 932; [2001] 1 WLR 2039, 2049; 124 ILR 550, 559; *Kuwait Airways* v. *Iraqi Airways*, England, [2003] 1

Lloyd's Rep 448, 449; 126 ILR 758, 760; *ETI* v. *Bolivia*, England, 2008, [2009] 1 WLR 665, 689, para. 110; 693, para. 128; *Mauritius* v. *Wong*, England, 2008 WL 4963091, para. 47; *Argentina* v. *NML*, England, [2010] EWCA Civ 41, para. 58; *Forth* v. *Wilmington*, Scotland, 1985, 1985 SC 317, 319, 322; 1987 SLT 153, 154, 161; 107 ILR 641, 643, 658; *Cameroons* v. *Société*, France, (1986) 77 ILR 532, 534; *Iran* v. *Société Eurodif*, France, (1989) 89 ILR 31, 35; *German* v. *Dynamic*, India, (1970) 64 ILR 504, 510–511; *New* v. *VEB*, India, (1983) 92 ILR 509, 528; *Governor* v. *Sutton*, New Zealand, 1994, [1995] 1 NZLR 426, 428; 104 ILR 508, 509; *The Holy See* v. *Starbright*, Philippines, (1994) 102 ILR 163, 172; *Västerås* v. *Iceland*, Sweden, (1999) 128 ILR 705, 708; *Italian* v. *X*, Switzerland, (1985) 82 ILR 23, 26, Ground 4a; *Barker* v. *Kenya*, Zimbabwe, (1983) (4) SA 817, 823–824; 84 ILR 18, 26.

128 *Maclaine Watson* v. *Department*, England, [1988] 3 WLR 1033, 1103–1104, 1157–1158; 80 ILR 47, 118–119, 179–180; affirmed, *JH Rayner* v. *Department*, England, 1989, [1990] 2 AC 418; [1989] 3 WLR 969; 81 ILR 670. See also *A Company* v. *Republic of X*, England, 1989, [1990] 2 Lloyd's Rep 520, 524–525; 87 ILR 412, 417; *Schreiber* v. *Germany*, Canada, (2001) 196 DLR (4th) 281, 288; affirmed, *Schreiber* v. *Germany*, Canada, (2002) 216 DLR (4th) 513, 524.

129 *A Company Ltd* v. *Republic of X*, England, 1989, [1990] 2 Lloyd's Rep 520, 524–525 (emphases added); 87 ILR 412, 417 (citing *Maclaine Watson*, [1988] 3 WLR 1033; 80 ILR 47). Mann finds the non-disclosure of the names of both parties in this case 'contrary to practice and principle': Mann, Waiver, 362. The parties' identities were eventually revealed in *Philipp* v. *Sierra Leone*, England, 1993/1995, [1994] 1 Lloyd's Rep 111; [1995] 1 Lloyd's Rep 289; 107 ILR 517.

130 Council of Europe, *Explanatory Reports*, p. 36, para. 106, commentary to Art. 26. See also p. 33, para. 93, commentary to Art. 23. The UK SIA, which gives effect to the European Convention, departs from this position. See below.

131 *Philippine Embassy Case*, Germany, (1977) 65 ILR 146, 167, 181, Ground C.I.4 and 6; 185, Ground C.II.3.

132 *NIOC Revenues Case*, Germany, (1983) 65 ILR 215, 239 and 241, Ground B.III.2(c)(d).

133 *Central Bank of Nigeria Case*, Germany, (1975/1976) 65 ILR 131, 135.

134 *NIOC Revenues Case*, Germany, (1983) 65 ILR 215, 242, Ground B.III.2(d).

135 *UAR* v. *Mrs X*, Switzerland, (1960) 65 ILR 385, 391, Ground 4; *Banque* v. *Weston*, Switzerland, (1978) 65 ILR 417, 424–425, Ground 4d.

136 *Condor* v. *Minister*, Italy, (1992) 101 ILR 394, 401, citing *Libya* v. *Rossbeton*, Italy, (1989) 87 ILR 63, 67.

137 See *Procureur* v. *SA Ipitrade*, France, (1978) 65 ILR 75; *Procureur* v. *LIAMCO*, France, (1979) 65 ILR 78; *Société Air* v. *Gauthier*, France, (1984) 77 ILR 510; *Iran* v. *Société Eurodif*, France, (1984) 77 ILR 513; *Caisse* v. *Société Midland*, France, (1983) 77 ILR 524 note; *General* v. *Société Marseille*, France, (1986) 77 ILR 530; *Cameroons* v. *Société*, France, (1986) 77 ILR 532; *Société Européenne* v. *World Bank*, France, 1984; *Yugoslavia* v. *Société Européenne*, France, 1985; *Société Européenne* v. *France*, France, (1986) 82 ILR 58; *Guinea* v. *Atlantic*, France, (1984/1986) 82 ILR 75; *Iran* v. *Société Eurodif*, France, (1989) 89 ILR 31; *Société Ouest* v. *Senegal*, France, (1989/1991) 113 ILR 440; *Ministry* v. *Société Framatome*, France, (1990)

660 NOTES TO PAGES 379-385

113 ILR 452; *Office* v. *Société Bec*, France, (1995) 113 ILR 485; *Dumez* v. *Iraq*, France, (1999) 127 ILR 144; *Creighton* v. *Minister*, France, (2000) 127 ILR 154.

138 *Société Air Zaire* v. *Gauthier*, France, (1984) 77 ILR 510, 511.

139 *Creighton* v. *Minister*, France, (2000) 127 ILR 154, 155.

140 *Iran* v. *Société Eurodif*, France, (1989) 89 ILR 31, 35.

141 *Société Ouest* v. *Senegal*, France, (1991) 113 ILR 440, 445.

142 *Russian Federation* v. *Noga*, France, (2000) 127 ILR 156, 160.

143 *Neustein* v. *Indonesia*, Austria, (1958) 65 ILR 3, 7, fn. 2b; *Hunting Rights Case*, Austria, (1987) 86 ILR 564, 564–565, fn. 1.

144 *Neustein* v. *Indonesia*, Austria, (1958) 65 ILR 3, 7.

145 *Neustein*, (1958) 65 ILR 3, 7. See also *Steinmetz* v. *Hungarian*, Austria, (1970) 65 ILR 15, 19.

146 See *Hunting Rights Case*, Austria, (1987) 86 ILR 564 567–568; *Radiation Contamination Case*, Austria, (1988) 86 ILR 571, 573–574. But cf. *Foreign State Bank Account Case*, Austria, (1986) 86 ILR 570 note.

147 *Nuclear Power Plant Injunction Case (No. 1)*, Austria, (1988) 86 ILR 575, 578.

148 *Nuclear Power Plant Injunction Case (No. 2)*, Austria, (1989) 86 ILR 578, 581.

149 *Nuclear Power Plant Injunction Case (No. 2)*, (1989) 86 ILR 578, 581–582.

150 *Garden Contamination Case (2)*, Germany, (1987) 80 ILR 377, 380–381.

151 *Forth Tugs* v. *Wilmington*, Scotland, 1985, 1987 SLT 153, 155–157, 159–160, 161; 107 ILR 641, 645–648, 652–656, 657–658.

152 ALRC, Report No. 24, 1984, pp.83–84, para. 137. For theoretical underpinnings of this provision see Crawford, Execution, 854.

153 ILC, Report, *YILC*, 1991-II-2, p. 12 at 58, commentary to Art. 18(1)(b), para. 10. The IDI used the same formula in its 1991 Draft Articles (Arts. 4(3)(a) and 5).

154 See near-reproductions or very similar provisions in the Pakistan SIO, s. 14(2), (3); Singapore SIA, s. 15(2), (3), (4); South Africa FSIA, s. 14; Canada SIA, ss. 11 and 12.

155 So named after the case *Mareva* v. *International*, England, [1975] 2 Lloyd's Rep 509, though the very first case in which such an injunction was granted was *Nippon* v. *Karageorgis*, England, [1975] 1 WLR 1093. The power of the High Court to grant a *Mareva* injunction is incorporated in s. 37 of the Supreme Court Act 1981, now called the 'Senior Courts Act 1981', as amended by the Constitutional Reform Act 2005. For *Mareva* injunction see, generally, Gee, *Gee*; Ough, *Mareva*; Courtney, *Mareva*; Hoyle, *Mareva*; Marston, State Immunity, 353.

156 By the *Anton Piller* order (named after the case *Anton Piller* v. *Manufacturing*, England, [1976] Ch 55) the plaintiff is entitled to search for articles which are or may be the subject or evidence of litigation. Now it is incorporated in s. 7 of the Civil Procedure Act 1997.

157 This writ prevents the defendant from leaving the jurisdiction for a short period of time. Literally, 'that he not leave the kingdom'.

158 See *Cretanor* v. *Irish*, England, [1978] 1 WLR 966, 974, 976; *Third* v. *Unimarine*, England, [1979] QB 645, 668–669; *Iraqi* v. *Arcepey*, England, [1980] 1 All ER 480, 486–487; *Derby* v. *Weldon*, England, [1989] 2 WLR 412; [1990] Ch 65; *Ketchum* v. *Group*, England, [1997] 1 WLR 4.

NOTES TO PAGES 385-388 661

159 *Trendtex* v. *Central Bank*, England, [1977] QB 529, 561, 572, 579–580; 64 ILR 111, 135, 146, 153–154; *Hispano* v. *Central Bank*, England, [1979] 2 Lloyd's Rep 277, 279–280; 64 ILR 221, 225.

160 For rationale behind this see Hansard, *Parliamentary Debates*, Series 5, House of Lords, 16 March 1978, Vol. 389, cols. 1527–1528. For similar sentiments in the US legislature see US House of Representatives, Report No. 94-1487, 1976, p. 22; 1976 USCCAN 6604, 6621.

161 *A Company* v. *Republic of X*, England, 1989, [1990] 2 Lloyd's Rep 520; 87 ILR 412.

162 *Sabah* v. *Pakistan*, England, 2002, [2003] 2 Lloyd's Rep 571, 577, para. 23, noted in Wilkes, Enforcing.

163 See *S* v. *Masinexportimport*, US, 706 F.2d 411, 416 (2nd Cir. 1983); 72 ILR 183; *Banco* v. *Mutual*, US, 344 F.3d 255, 261 (2nd Cir. 2003); *Sea* v. *Industries*, US, 411 F.Supp.2d 386, 391 (S.D.N.Y. 2006).

164 *Weston* v. *Ecuador*, US, 823 F.Supp. 1106, 1111 (S.D.N.Y. 1993); *New England* v. *Iran*, US, 502 F.Supp. 120, 126–127 (S.D.N.Y. 1980); 63 ILR 497; petition denied and remanded, *New England* v. *Iran*, US, 646 F.2d 779 (2nd Cir. 1981).

165 See Schreuer, *State Immunity*, p. 166; Atkeson and Ramsey, Proposed; Foresta, Prejudgment; Trooboff, Foreign, 380; Sandrock, Prejudgment; Basham, Prejudgment, 651–652 and Annex A; Nakasian, Proposed, 195, 197, 209–210.

166 Quoted in *Stephen* v. *Zivnostenska*, US, 222 N.Y.S.2d 128, 134 (1961) and *Ocean* v. *Ivory Coast*, US, 269 F.Supp. 703, 705, fn. 8 (E.D.Louis. 1967); 63 ILR 9. But see *Shaffer* v. *Heitner*, US, 433 US 186 (1977) and *Rush* v. *Savchuk*, US, 444 US 320 (1980).

167 US House of Representatives, Report No. 94-1487, 1976, pp. 26–27; 1976 USCCAN 6604, 6625–6626.

168 This includes the provision of security: *Enron* v. *Titan 2*, US, 82 F.Supp.2d 602, 612 (W.D.La. 1999); *Banco* v. *Riggs*, US, 919 F.Supp. 13, 17, fn. 1 (D.D.C. 1994).

169 *Kensington* v. *Congo*, US, 461 F.3d 238, 243 (2nd Cir. 2006).

170 *Venus* v. *CVG*, US, 210 F.3d 1309, 1313 (11th Cir. 2000). The Second Circuit explained that the 'reason for this limitation is to prevent the location of the property from conferring jurisdiction on the court – *i.e.*, to prevent *in rem* and *quasi-in-rem* actions from undermining the general principles codified in the FSIA': *Brenntag* v. *Bank*, US, 175 F.3d 245, 253 (2nd Cir. 1999); affirming *Brenntag* v. *Norddeutsche*, US, 9 F.Supp.2d 331 (S.D.N.Y. 1998).

171 See *Venus* v. *CVG*, US, 210 F.3d 1309, 1311 (11th Cir. 2000); *Stena* v. *Comision*, US, 923 F.2d 380, 392, fn. 18 (5th Cir. 1991); 103 ILR 433; *Atwood* v. *Petroleo*, US, 875 F.2d 1174, 1177 (5th Cir. 1989); *Banco* v. *Mutual*, US, 344 F.3d 255, 261 (2nd Cir. 2003).

172 See *Reading* v. *National*, US, 478 F.Supp. 724, 728–729 (S.D.N.Y. 1979); 63 ILR 305; *New England* v. *Iran*, US, 502 F.Supp. 120, 126–127 (S.D.N.Y. 1980); 63 ILR 497; *Chicago* v. *Iran*, US, 506 F.Supp. 981, 985 (N.D.Ill. 1980); 63 ILR 511; *Moore* v. *National*, US, 143 F.R.D. 526, 536 (S.D.N.Y. 1992); affirmed, *Stephens* v. *National*, US, 69 F.3d 1226 (2nd Cir. 1995); *Mangattu* v. *Ibn Hayyan*, US, 35 F.3d 205, 210 (5th Cir. 1994); *Venus* v. *CVG*, US, 210 F.3d 1309, 1311 (11th Cir. 2000).

662   NOTES TO PAGES 388–390

173 See *Libra* v. *Banco*, US, 676 F.2d 47, 49 (2nd Cir. 1982); 72 ILR 119; *S & S* v. *Masinexportimport*, US, 706 F.2d 411, 416 (2nd Cir. 1983); 72 ILR 183; *Kensington* v. *Congo*, US, 461 F.3d 238, 243 (2nd Cir. 2006); *Banco* v. *Mutual*, US, 344 F.3d 255, 261 (2nd Cir. 2003).

174 *Atwood* v. *Petroleo*, US, 875 F.2d 1174, 1177 (5th Cir. 1989); *Kensington* v. *Congo*, US, 461 F.3d 238, 243–244 (2nd Cir. 2006); affirming *Kensington* v. *Congo*, US, 2005 WL 646086 (S.D.N.Y. 2005).

175 *Sperry* v. *Israel*, US, 532 F.Supp. 901, 908–909 (S.D.N.Y. 1982).

176 *Venus* v. *CVG*, US, 210 F.3d 1309, 1312 (11th Cir. 2000).

177 *Libra Bank* v. *Banco*, US, 676 F.2d 47, 49–50 (2nd Cir. 1982); 72 ILR 119. See also *S & S* v. *Masinexportimport*, US, 706 F.2d 411, 416, 418 (2nd Cir. 1983); 72 ILR 183; *Banque Compafina* v. *Banco*, US, 583 F.Supp. 320 (S.D.N.Y. 1984); 92 ILR 399; *Moore* v. *National*, US, 143 F.R.D. 526, 536 (S.D.N.Y. 1992); *Venus* v. *CVG*, US, 210 F.3d 1309, 1312 (11th Cir. 2000); *Banco* v. *Mutual*, US, 344 F.3d 255, 261 (2nd Cir. 2003); *Kensington* v. *Congo*, US, 461 F.3d 238, 243 (2nd Cir. 2006).

178 *Banco de Seguros* v. *Mutual*, US, 344 F.3d 255, 261–262 (2nd Cir. 2003); affirming *Banco* v. *Mutual*, US, 230 F.Supp.2d 362 (S.D.N.Y. 2002) and *Banco* v. *Mutual*, US, 230 F.Supp.2d 427 (S.D.N.Y. 2002).

179 As in Art. XI(4) of the 1955 US–Iran Treaty of Amity. See Schachter, Prejudgment. Compare this waiver clause with the formula of waiving immunity from 'legal proceedings' in *Libra Bank*.

180 *Reading* v. *National*, US, 478 F.Supp. 724, 728–729 (S.D.N.Y. 1979); 63 ILR 305; *E-Systems* v. *Iran*, US, 491 F.Supp. 1294, 1300–1302 (N.D.Tex. 1980); 63 ILR 424; *New England* v. *Iran*, US, 502 F.Supp. 120, 126–127 (S.D.N.Y. 1980); 63 ILR 497 (however, prejudgment attachment was granted because immunity was held to have been suspended by an Executive Order); remanded, *New England* v. *Iran*, US, 646 F.2d 779 (2nd Cir. 1981); *Chicago* v. *Iran*, US, 506 F.Supp. 981, 985 (N.D.Ill. 1980); 63 ILR 511; *Security* v. *Iran*, US, 513 F.Supp. 864, 879–880 (C.D. Cal. 1981). But see *Behring* v. *Imperial*, US, 475 F.Supp. 383, 395 (D.N.J. 1979); 63 ILR 261. For similar provisions in other treaties see *Libra Bank* v. *Banco*, US, 676 F.2d 47, 50 (2nd Cir. 1982); 72 ILR 119; *S & S* v. *Masinexportimport*, US, 706 F.2d 411, 416–417 (2nd Cir. 1983); 72 ILR 183; *O'Connell* v. *Americana*, US, 566 F.Supp. 1381 (S.D.N.Y. 1983); affirmed, *O'Connell* v. *Americana*, US, 734 F.2d 115 (2nd Cir. 1984); 81 ILR 539.

181 *Moore* v. *National*, US, 143 F.R.D. 526, 535–536 (S.D.N.Y. 1992); affirmed, *Stephens* v. *National*, US, 69 F.3d 1226 (2nd Cir. 1995). See also *In re Delta*, US, 900 F.2d 890, 892–894 (6th Cir. 1990).

182 See *Af-Cap* v. *Congo*, US, 462 F.3d 417, 428–429 (5th Cir. 2006) (finding contempt order barred by the FSIA); *FG* v. *Congo*, US, 603 F.Supp.2d 1, 2 (D.D.C. 2009) (holding the Congo in civil contempt). Cf. the statement by Lord McCluskey in the UK House of Lords, Hansard, *Parliamentary Debates*, Series 5, House of Lords, 16 March 1978, Vol. 389, cols. 1527–1528 ('Clearly the processes for punishing contempt cannot be used against a foreign State.').

183 *American* v. *Iran*, US, 493 F.Supp. 522, 526 (D.D.C. 1980); 63 ILR 452; *Harris* v. *National*, US, 691 F.2d 1344, 1353–1358 (11th Cir. 1982); 72 ILR 172; *Atwood* v.

NOTES TO PAGES 390–398   663

Petroleo, US, 875 F.2d 1174, 1177 (5th Cir. 1989). See also US House of Representatives, Report No. 94-1487, 1976, p. 22; 1976 USCCAN 6604, 6621. For cases holding 'prejudgment security' as equivalent to prejudgment attachment see *Willamette* v. *Compania*, US, 491 F.Supp. 442, 443–444 (E.D. La. 1980); 63 ILR 416; *Bowers* v. *Transportes*, US, 719 F.Supp. 166, 171–172 (S.D. N.Y. 1989); *Caribbean* v. *Nigerian*, US, 948 F.2d 111, 116 (2nd Cir. 1991); *Mangattu* v. *Ibn Hayyan*, US, 35 F.3d 205, 210 (5th Cir. 1994); *Stephens* v. *National*, US, 69 F.3d 1226, 1229 (2nd Cir. 1995); affirming *Stephens* v. *National*, US, 1993 WL 228851 (S.D.N.Y. 1993) and *Moore* v. *National*, US, 143 F.R.D. 526, 535 (S.D.N.Y. 1992); *International* v. *Caja*, US, 293 F.3d 392, 399–400 (7th Cir. 2002); *Banco* v. *Mutual*, US, 344 F.3d 255, 260 (2nd Cir. 2003); *Kensington* v. *Congo*, US, 461 F.3d 238, 243 (2nd Cir. 2006).

184 *S & S Machinery* v. *Masinexportimport*, US, 706 F.2d 411, 418 (2nd Cir. 1983); 72 ILR 183.

185 See reproductions in the Pakistan SIO, s. 14(3); Singapore SIA, s. 15(3); South Africa FSIA, s. 14(2).

186 ALRC, Report No. 24, 1984, p. 72, para. 121.

187 See reproductions in the Pakistan SIO, s. 14(3); Singapore SIA, s. 15(3); South Africa FSIA, s. 14(2).

188 US FSIA 1976, s. 1610(a)(1), (b)(1) and (d)(1), s. 1611(b)(1); Canada SIA 1982, s. 12(1)(a); Australia FSIA 1985, s. 31(3); ILA Drafts, Art. VIII(A)(1).

189 US House of Representatives, Report No. 94-1487, 1976, pp. 28 and 30; 1976 USCCAN 6604, 6627 and 6629.

190 US House of Representatives, Report No. 94-1487, 1976, p. 29; 1976 USCCAN 6604, 6628. See also *Walker* v. *Congo*, US, 395 F.3d 229, 237 (5th Cir. 2004); *Bayer* v. *Gambia*, US, 283 F.Supp.2d 1, 4 (D.D.C. 2003).

191 See *Ministry* v. *Elahi*, US, 546 US 450, 452 (2006); *Letelier* v. *Chile*, US, 748 F.2d 790, 798–799 (2nd Cir. 1984); 79 ILR 561; *Connecticut* v. *Congo*, US, 309 F.3d 240, 252–253 (5th Cir. 2002); *Karaha* v. *Perusahaan*, US, 313 F.3d 70, 82 (2nd Cir. 2002); *EM* v. *Argentina*, US, 473 F.3d 463, 472–473 (2nd Cir. 2007); *Af-Cap* v. *Chevron*, US, 475 F.3d 1080, 1088–1089 (9th Cir. 2007). See also ALI, *Third Restatement*, Vol. 1, p. 435, s. 460, comment b.

192 *Hercaire* v. *Argentina*, US, 821 F.2d 559, 565 (11th Cir. 1987); 98 ILR 48; partly reversing *Hercaire* v. *Argentina*, US, 642 F.Supp. 126 (S.D.Fla. 1986).

193 *Letelier* v. *Chile*, US, 748 F.2d 790, 794–795 (2nd Cir. 1984); 79 ILR 561; reversing *Letelier* v. *Chile*, US, 575 F.Supp. 1217 (S.D.N.Y. 1983).

194 See similar provisions in the Pakistan SIO, s. 15(1)(2)(3); Singapore SIA, s. 16(1)(2)(3); South Africa FSIA, ss. 1(2) and 15(1)(2). Australia FSIA contains a similar provision (s. 35).

195 In this respect the Canada SIA's definition of a State 'agency' is narrower than the 'agency' under the US FSIA, which includes not only an 'organ' of the foreign State, but also an enterprise majority-owned by the State.

196 *NIOC Revenues Case*, Germany, (1983) 65 ILR 215, 219, Ground A.I.

197 *NIOC Revenues Case*, Germany, (1983) 65 ILR 215, 221, Ground A.I; see also 226–229, Ground B.III.1 and 2. See also *NIOC Legal Status Case*, Germany, (1980) 65

664 NOTES TO PAGES 398-401

ILR 199; *Foreign Trade Institute Case*, Germany, (1981) 65 ILR 209, 210–211; *NIOC Pipeline Contracts Case*, Federal Germany, (1982) 65 ILR 212; *NV Cabolent v. National*, Netherlands, (1968) 47 ILR 138, 144–147.

198 *Société le Gostrog v. Association*, France, (1926) 3 AD 174, 175; *USSR v. Association*, France, (1929) 5 AD 18, 19. See also similar cases in Italy: *Russian v. De Castro*, Italy, (1934/1935) 7 AD 179; *Società v. Russian*, Italy, (1938) 9 AD 247.

199 *Société Sonatrach v. Migeon*, France, (1985) 77 ILR 525, 527. See also *Caisse d'Assurance v. Caisse Nationale*, France, (1977) 65 ILR 70, 73; *Société Air Zaire v. Gauthier*, France, (1984) 77 ILR 510, 511–512.

200 *NIOC Revenues Case*, Germany, (1983) 65 ILR 215, 219, Ground A.I; *Office v. Société Bec*, France, (1995) 113 ILR 485, 486; *Dumez v. Iraq*, France, (1999) 127 ILR 144, 146–147.

201 The legislative report provides no clue in this respect.

202 See Atkeson and Ramsey, Proposed; Feldman, Amending; Delaume, Sovereign, 815–819; Dellapenna, Has the Time; Dorsey, Reflections, 268–271; Dellapenna, Refining; ABA, Reforming, 588, 612–613; ABA, Report, 2002, 1262, 1272–1274. See also ALRC, Report No. 24, p. 76, para. 125. Note that in 1988 s. 1610(a) was amended by adding a new paragraph that abolished the connection requirement with regard to arbitral awards. Section 1610(a)(6), Public Law 100–669, 16 November 1988, 102 Stat. 3969–3970, 28 ILM (1989) 396, 398.

203 *Letelier v. Chile*, US, 488 F.Supp. 665 (D.D.C. 1980); 63 ILR 378.

204 *Letelier v. Chile*, US, 748 F.2d 790, 798–799 (2nd Cir. 1984); 79 ILR 561. See also Feldman, Foreign, 43. It must also be pointed out that, in a number of situations such a subject-matter connection is expressly *not* required by the US FSIA. These include judgments involving the expropriation exception, succession or gift, immovable property, indemnity obligations, arbitral awards, acts of a 'State sponsor of terrorism', and an agency or instrumentality of a foreign State (s. 1610(a)(3)(4)(5)(6)(7) and (b)(2)).

205 See *Société Sonatrach v. Migeon*, France, (1985) 77 ILR 525, 527; *Abbott v. South Africa*, Spain, (1992) 113 ILR 411, 425–426.

206 See Chapter 2.

207 *Dreyfus*, Switzerland, (1918) BGE 44 I 49, 54–55.

208 *Greek Republic v. Walder*, Switzerland, (1930) 5 AD 121, 123. See also *State Immunity (No. 1) Case*, Switzerland, (1937) 10 AD 230, 231–232; *State Immunity (No. 2) Case*, Switzerland, (1939/1940) 10 AD 235, 235–236; *Greece v. Julius Bär*, Switzerland, (1956) 23 ILR 195, 196–197, 200.

209 *Libya v. LIAMCO*, Switzerland, (1980) BGE 106 Ia 142, 148, Ground 3b; 62 ILR 228, 234. See also *UAR v. Mrs X*, Switzerland, (1960) 65 ILR 385, 389, Ground 2; 391, Grounds 3 and 4; *Italian v. Beta*, Switzerland, (1966) 65 ILR 394, 398–399, Ground 5; 401, Ground 7b; *Banque v. Weston*, Switzerland, (1978) 65 ILR 417, 419–420, Ground 2c; 423, Ground 4; 424–425, Ground 4d; *Egypt v. Cinetelevision*, Switzerland, (1979) 65 ILR 425, 430, Ground 4a; 432, Ground 5b; *Banco v. Banco Cattolica*, Switzerland, (1984) 82 ILR 10, 11–12, Ground 4a; *Libya v. Actimon*, Switzerland, (1985) 82 ILR 30, 32–33, Ground 4; 34, Ground 5b;

NOTES TO PAGES 401-404 665

Swissair v. *X*, Switzerland, (1985) 82 ILR 36, 37; *Spain* v. *Company X*, Switzerland, (1986) 82 ILR 38, 40, Ground 3b; *S* v. *Romania*, Switzerland, (1987) 82 ILR 45, 48, Ground 2.

210 Trooboff, Foreign, 388.

211 Schreuer, *State Immunity*, p. 36.

212 *Libya* v. *LIAMCO*, Switzerland, (1980) BGE 106 Ia 142, 148, Ground 3b; 62 ILR 228, 234.

213 See also Canada SIA, s. 12(1); ILA Drafts, Art. VIII(A).

214 *LETCO*, US, 659 F.Supp. 606, 609 (D.D.C. 1987); 89 ILR 360; *Philippine* v. *Chuidian*, US, 218 Cal.App.3d 1058, 1096; 267 Cal.Rptr. 457, 478 (1990); *Connecticut* v. *Congo*, US, 309 F.3d 240, 247, 251 (5th Cir. 2002); *Af-Cap* v. *Congo*, US, 383 F.3d 361, 367 (5th Cir. 2004); *Walker* v. *Congo*, US, 395 F.3d 229, 234 (5th Cir. 2004); *FG* v. *Congo*, US, 455 F.3d 575, 585 (5th Cir. 2006); *Kensington* v. *Congo*, US, 461 F.3d 238, 243 (2nd Cir. 2006).

215 See *Sesostris* v. *Transportes*, US, 727 F.Supp. 737, 744 (D.Mass. 1989).

216 *Petroleos* v. *Crawford*, US, 643 F.Supp. 370, 381-382 (S.D.Tex. 1986); *Philippine* v. *Chuidian*, US, 218 Cal.App.3d 1058, 1093-1099; 267 Cal.Rptr. 457, 477-481 (1990); *Richmark* v. *Timber*, US, 959 F.2d 1468, 1477 (9th Cir. 1992); *Fidelity* v. *Philippine*, US, 921 F.Supp. 1113, 1118-1119 (S.D.N.Y. 1996); *Fidelity* v. *First*, US, 58 F.Supp.2d 52, 53-54 (S.D.N.Y. 1997).

217 *Af-Cap* v. *Congo*, US, 462 F.3d 417, 429, fn. 10 (5th Cir. 2006); *Af-Cap* v. *Congo*, US, 383 F.3d 361, 371 (5th Cir. 2004).

218 See *Walters* v. *China*, US, 672 F.Supp.2d 573, 575 (S.D.N.Y. 2009).

219 *Connecticut* v. *Congo*, US, 309 F.3d 240, 257-259, 261-262, 265-266 (5th Cir. 2002); *Af-Cap* v. *Congo*, US, 383 F.3d 361, 364, 368-373 (5th Cir. 2004); *FG* v. *Congo*, US, 455 F.3d 575, 585-590, 592-593, 595, fn. 4, (5th Cir. 2006).

220 *Atwood* v. *Petroleo*, US, 875 F.2d 1174 (5th Cir. 1989).

221 *FG* v. *Congo*, US, 455 F.3d 575, 590 (5th Cir. 2006).

222 *Rush* v. *Savchuk*, US, 444 US 320, 330 (1980); *Af-Cap* v. *Congo*, US, 383 F.3d 361, 371 (5th Cir. 2004); *Walker* v. *Congo*, US, 395 F.3d 229, 235 (5th Cir. 2004); *FG* v. *Congo*, US, 455 F.3d 575, 586 (5th Cir. 2006).

223 *FG Hemisphere* v. *Congo*, US, 455 F.3d 575, 586, 588-590, 593-594 (5th Cir. 2006).

224 *FG Hemisphere* v. *Congo*, US, 455 F.3d 575, 586 (5th Cir. 2006).

225 *FG*, 455 F.3d 575, 588-589 (5th Cir. 2006) (emphasis in the original).

226 *FG*, 455 F.3d 575, 589-590 (5th Cir. 2006).

227 Law No. 1263 of 15 July 1926.

228 Article 923 of the Code of Civil Procedure.

229 See Art. IX (3) of the Austrian Introductory Act to the Jurisdictional Statute (*EGJN*): *Neustein* v. *Indonesia*, Austria, (1958) 65 ILR 3, 9, fn. 3; *Private Servant of Diplomat Case*, Austria, (1971) 71 ILR 546, 547, fn. 3; *Leasing* v. *Algeria*, Austria, (1986) 116 ILR 526, 530; duplicate report *sub nom Republic of 'A' Case*, Austria, (1986) 77 ILR 488, 491, fn. 5; Art. 13(4) of the Bailiff's Regulations in the Netherlands: *MK* v. *State*, Netherlands, (1986) 94 ILR 357, 357, fn. 3; *Emilio* v. *Embassy*, Spain, (1986) 86 ILR 508, 511; *Diana* v. *South Africa*, Spain, (1986) 86

666   NOTES TO PAGES 404–406

ILR 512, 516; the Swiss Government ordinance of 12 July 1918, noted in *Greek Republic* v. *Walder*, Switzerland, (1930) 5 AD 121, 122, fn. 2; the Swiss Federal Council Decree of 24 October 1939, noted in *State Immunity (No. 2) Case*, Switzerland, (1939/1940) 10 AD 235, 238–239; s. 1610(f)(3) of the US FSIA (which gives the US President the power to disapply the provisions of s. 1610(f)(1) concerning execution of the property of a foreign State that is not immune under s. 1605(a)(7) (later s. 1605A)); *Dames* v. *Regan*, US, 453 US 654, 685 (1981); 72 ILR 270; For comments and criticism see Bouchez, The Nature, 28–30; Seidl-Hohenveldern, State Immunity, 97; Schreuer, *State Immunity*, p. 136; Reinisch, European, 813–817.

230 See, nevertheless, *Leasing* v. *Algeria*, Austria, (1986) 116 ILR 526, 528; duplicate report *sub nom Republic of 'A' Case*, Austria, (1986) 77 ILR 488; partly overruling *Neustein* v. *Indonesia*, Austria, (1958) 65 ILR 3, 9; *Radiation Contamination Claim Case*, Austria, (1988) 86 ILR 571, 573; *Burundi* v. *Landau*, Belgium, (2002) 127 ILR 98, 99; *Iraq* v. *Vinci*, Belgium, (2002) 127 ILR 101, 105–107; quashing *Iraq* v. *Dumez*, Belgium, (1995) 106 ILR 284; *Alcom* v. *Colombia*, England, [1984] 1 AC 580, 597, 599, 603–604; 74 ILR 170, 180, 182, 187; *Russian* v. *Noga*, France, (2000) 127 ILR 156, 160; *Philippine Embassy Bank Account Case*, Germany, (1977) 65 ILR 146, 185–186, 187–189, 190–191, Ground C.II.2, 3, 4(a), 5; *Kenyan Diplomatic Residence Case*, Germany, (2003) 128 ILR 632, 635, 636, 638, Ground II.3; *Abbott* v. *South Africa*, Spain, (1992) 113 ILR 411, 423–424; *UAR* v. *Mrs X*, Switzerland, (1960) 65 ILR 385, 392, Ground 5; *Italian* v. *Beta*, Switzerland, (1966) 65 ILR 394, 402, Ground 8; *Griessen*, Switzerland, (1982) 82 ILR 5, 7, Ground 1; *Spain* v. *Company X*, Switzerland, (1986) 82 ILR 38, 41, Ground 4a.

231 *Russian* v. *Noga*, France, (2000) 127 ILR 156, 160.

232 See especially the provisions on the inviolability and protection of diplomatic and consular premises, property and archives in the 1961 Vienna Convention on Diplomatic Relations (Arts. 22, 23, 24, 30, 45) and the 1963 Vienna Convention on Consular Relations (Arts. 27, 31, 32, 33, 59, 60, 61).

233 See similar protection under US FSIA, ss. 1610(a)(4)(B) and 1611(c); UK SIA, s. 16(1); Pakistan SIO, s. 17(1); Singapore SIA, s. 19(1); Australia FSIA, ss. 6, 31 (4), 33(3)(a); 1972 European Convention, Art. 32; ILA Drafts, Art. VIII(C)(1); IDI Draft 1991, Art. 4(2)(a). The Australia FSIA 1985 not only provides for immunity for diplomatic property (s. 31(4) and s. 32(3)(a)), but also puts forward a definition of diplomatic property as 'property that, at the relevant time, is in use predominantly for the purpose of establishing or maintaining a diplomatic or consular mission, or a visiting mission, of a foreign State to Australia' (s. 3(1)).

234 See especially the 1961 Vienna Convention, Art. 22; 1963 Vienna Convention, Art. 31.

235 US House of Representatives, Report No. 94-1487, 1976, p. 29; 1976 USCCAN 6604, 6628 (emphasis added). A 'Bill to Modify the Enforcement of Certain Anti-Terrorism Judgments, and for Other Purposes', S.1796, § 1(3)(A), 106th Cong. (1999), which would otherwise have amended s. 1610, FSIA, to permit

the attachment of the property of foreign diplomatic missions used for non-diplomatic purposes such as rental property, as well as any rental proceeds, was rejected: *Flatow* v. *Iran*, US, 76 F.Supp.2d 16, 28 (D.D.C. 1999).

236 *S & S Machinery* v. *Masinexportimport*, US, 802 F.Supp. 1109, 1110–1111 (S.D.N.Y. 1992); 107 ILR 239, 240–241. See also *Gerritsen* v. *Escobar*, US, 688 F.Supp. 556, 559 (C.D.Cal. 1988). But cf. *Intpro* v. *Sauvel*, England, [1983] QB 1019, 1031–1032, 1033, 1034; 64 ILR 384 (holding that on its true construction the phrase 'used for the purposes of a diplomatic mission' in s. 16(1)(b) of the UK SIA refers to premises used for the professional diplomatic purposes of such a mission and does not include a diplomatic agent's private residence albeit that the diplomatic agent occasionally carried out official social obligations there); reversing *Intpro* v. *Sauvel*, England, [1983] QB 1019; 64 ILR 363.

237 *US* v. *Arlington*, US, 669 F.2d 925, 934 (4th Cir. 1982) (citing *US* v. *Kostadinov*, US, 734 F.2d 905, 908 (2nd Cir. 1984)); 72 ILR 652 (also reported at 98 ILR 1); further confirmed, *US* v. *Arlington*, US, 702 F.2d 485 (4th Cir. 1983).

238 *Hungarian Embassy Case*, Germany, (1969) 65 ILR 110, 112.

239 *Westminster* v. *Iran*, England, [1986] 1 WLR 979; 108 ILR 557.

240 *Lab* v. *Rasheed*, Canada, [2003] 127 ACWS (3d) 757. Cf. *Bennett* v. *Iran*, US, 604 F.Supp.2d 152, 170 (D.D.C. 2009) (former diplomatic properties immune).

241 *Kenyan Diplomatic Residence Case*, Germany, (2003) 128 ILR 632, 635, 636, 638, Ground II.3.

242 *Embassy Eviction Case*, Greece, (1965) 65 ILR 248, 252; *Champel* v. *Geneva*, Switzerland, (1984) 102 ILR 180, 182; *Gray* v. *Permanent*, US, 443 F.Supp. 816, 822, fn. 6 (S.D.N.Y. 1978); 63 ILR 121.

243 *Russian* v. *Noga*, France, (2000) 127 ILR 156, 161; *Abbott* v. *South Africa*, Spain, (1992) 113 ILR 411, 423. See also *Philippine Embassy Case*, Germany, (1977) 65 ILR 146, 185, Ground C.II.2 ('partially codified in the Vienna Convention'). See also *Iraq* v. *Vinci*, Belgium, (2002) 127 ILR 101, 106–107 (bank statements constitute 'archives and documents of the mission' protected by Art. 24 of the 1961 Vienna Convention); quashing *Iraq* v. *Dumez*, Belgium, (1995) 106 ILR 284.

244 See *New York* v. *Permanent*, US, 446 F.3d 365, 370 (2nd Cir. 2006) (citing s. 1610(a)(4)(B)); affirming *New York* v. *Permanent*, US, 376 F.Supp.2d 429 (S.D.N.Y. 2005); *Af-Cap* v. *Congo*, US, 326 F.Supp.2d 128, 130–131 (D.D.C. 2004); *Hegna* v. *Iran*, US, 287 F.Supp.2d 608, 610 (D.Md. 2003); affirmed, *Hegna* v. *Iran*, US, 376 F.3d 226 (4th Cir. 2004); *S & S* v. *Masinexportimport*, US, 802 F.Supp. 1109, 1110–1112 (S.D.N.Y. 1992); 107 ILR 239; *Gerritsen* v. *Escobar*, US, 688 F.Supp. 556, 559 (C.D.Cal. 1988).

245 *Flatow* v. *Iran*, US, 76 F.Supp.2d 16, 22–24 (D.D.C. 1999); *Foxworth* v. *Permanent*, US, 796 F.Supp. 761, 763 (S.D.N.Y. 1992); 99 ILR 138; *LETCO*, US, 659 F.Supp. 606, 610–611 (D.D.C. 1987); 89 ILR 360.

246 *Philippine Embassy Bank Account Case*, Germany, (1977) 65 ILR 146, 150 and 164, Ground C. Cited in *Leasing* v. *Algeria*, Austria, (1986) 116 ILR 526, 528; *Alcom* v. *Colombia*, England, [1984] 1 AC 580, 599; 74 ILR 170, 182. See also *Spain* v. *Company X*, Switzerland, (1986) 82 ILR 38, 44, Ground 5a.

668 NOTES TO PAGES 408–411

247 *Philippine Embassy Case*, Germany, (1977) 65 ILR 146, 186, Ground C.II.3.

248 *Philippine Embassy Case*, Germany, (1977) 65 ILR 146, 185–186, Ground C.II.3 (emphasis added); see also 190–191, Ground C.II.5. The point on 'abstract danger' was cited in *Kenyan Diplomatic Residence Case*, Germany, (2003) 128 ILR 632, 636, Ground II.3b; *Leasing* v. *Algeria*, Austria, (1986) 116 ILR 526, 528. See also *Procureur* v. *SA Ipitrade*, France, (1978) 65 ILR 75, 77; *Procureur* v. *LIAMCO*, France, (1979) 65 ILR 78, 81.

249 *Philippine Embassy Case*, (1977) 65 ILR 146, 188, Ground C.II.4(a). See also *Spanish Consular Case*, Germany, (1971) 65 ILR 114, 118.

250 *Philippine Embassy Case*, (1977) 65 ILR 146, 189, Ground C.II.4(a). Cited in *Kenyan Diplomatic Residence Case*, Germany, (2003) 128 ILR 632, 638, Ground II.3.c.aa; *Leasing* v. *Algeria*, Austria, (1986) 116 ILR 526, 528–529. Lord Diplock found the reasoning of the German Constitutional Court 'wholly convincing': *Alcom* v. *Colombia*, England, [1984] 1 AC 580, 599; 74 ILR 170, 182. See also *Iraq* v. *Vinci*, Belgium, (2002) 127 ILR 101, 105–106; quashing *Iraq* v. *Dumez*, Belgium, (1995) 106 ILR 284; *Spanish Consular Case*, Germany, (1971) 65 ILR 114, 118; *MK* v. *State*, Netherlands, (1986) 94 ILR 357, 360; *Netherlands* v. *Azeta*, Netherlands, (1998) 128 ILR 688, 690.

251 *Kenyan Diplomatic Residence Case*, Germany, (2003) 128 ILR 632, 638, Ground II.3.c.aa.

252 *Leasing West* v. *Algeria*, Austria, (1986) 116 ILR 526, 529 (emphases in the original); duplicate report *sub nom Republic of 'A' Case*, Austria, (1986) 77 ILR 488.

253 *Alcom* v. *Colombia*, England, [1984] 1 AC 580, 604; 74 ILR 170, 187 (emphases added). Lord Diplock accepted as 'conclusive' a certificate provided by the head of the mission: pp. 604–605 / ILR 187–188. For earlier stages see *Alcom* v. *Colombia*, England, 1983, [1984] 2 Lloyd's Rep 31 and *Alcom* v. *Colombia*, England, [1983] 3 WLR 906; [1984] 1 AC 580; 74 ILR 170. See also *A Company* v. *Republic of X*, England, 1989, [1990] 2 Lloyd's Rep 520, 524–525; 87 ILR 412, 416–417; *Banamar-Capizzi* v. *Embassy*, Italy, (1989) 87 ILR 56, 60–61; *Libya* v. *Rossbeton*, Italy, (1989) 87 ILR 63; *Condor* v. *Minister*, Italy (1992) 101 ILR 394, 402; *Abbott* v. *South Africa*, Spain, (1992) 113 ILR 411, 423–424.

254 *Z* v. *Geneva*, Switzerland, (1990) 102 ILR 205, 206, Ground 1; 207–208, Ground 2c. See also *B* v. *Autorité*, Switzerland, 1990, 2 *RSDIE* (1992) 585. For a similar case see *Re Royal Bank*, Canada, (1980) 117 DLR (3d) 199; 64 ILR 69.

255 *Z* v. *Geneva*, Switzerland, (1990) 102 ILR 205, 207, Ground 2b.

256 *Flatow* v. *Iran*, US, 76 F.Supp.2d 16, 22–24 (D.D.C. 1999).

257 *LETCO*, US, 659 F.Supp. 606, 610–611 (D.D.C. 1987); 89 ILR 360; *Foxworth* v. *Permanent*, US, 796 F.Supp. 761, 763 (S.D.N.Y. 1992); 99 ILR 138.

258 *Alcom* v. *Colombia*, England, [1984] 1 AC 580, 597, 599, 604; 74 ILR 170, 180, 182, 187.

259 See especially Mann, The State, 62; Crawford, International, 117; Schreuer, State Immunity, pp. 156–159; Asiedu-Akrofi, Central; Blair, The Legal; Reinisch, European, 826–827.

260 Of course, a financial institution, such as an insurance and economic development agency, which is not a central bank, is not protected: *Concord*

NOTES TO PAGES 411–414   669

v. *Caja*, US, 1994 WL 86401, p. 2 (S.D.N.Y. 1994). The Canada SIA 1982 provides the same rule but adds one more qualification, namely, that the property must not be 'used or intended for a commercial activity' (s. 12(4)). The ILA Drafts provide that the property must be either 'that of a State central bank held by it for central banking purposes' or 'that of a State monetary authority held by it for monetary purposes' (Art. VIII(C)(3)(4)). The IDI 1991 Draft is a bit vague. The property is defined as that 'of the central bank or monetary authority of the State in use or set aside for use for the purposes of the central bank or monetary authority' (Art. 4(2)(c)). The 2004 UN Convention is even more vague. The property is that 'of the central bank or other monetary authority of the State' (Art. 21(1)(c)). For US practice regarding the execution of foreign central bank property see especially Dellapenna, *Suing*, pp. 756–760; Lee, Central, 375–391; and the literature therein cited.

261 *Olympic* v. *Ministry*, US, 134 F.Supp.2d 528, 534 and fn. 3 (S.D.N.Y. 2001); *LNC* v. *Nicaragua*, US, 115 F.Supp.2d 358, 364–366 (S.D.N.Y. 2000); affirmed, *LNC* v. *Banco*, US, 228 F.3d 423 (2nd Cir. 2000); *Commercial* v. *Rafidain*, US, 15 F.3d 238, 239 (2nd Cir. 1994); 107 ILR 261; *Banco* v. *Riggs*, US, 919 F.Supp. 13, 16 (D.D.C. 1994); *Banque Compafina* v. *Banco*, US, 583 F.Supp. 320, 321 (S.D.N.Y. 1984); 92 ILR 399. See also Lee, Central, 350–351.

262 US House of Representatives, Report No. 94-1487, 1976, p. 31; 1976 USCCAN 6604, 6630.

263 *EM* v. *Argentina*, US, 473 F.3d 463, 473 (2nd Cir. 2007).

264 *Banque Compafina* v. *Banco*, US, 583 F.Supp. 320, 322 (S.D.N.Y. 1984); 92 ILR 399; *Weston* v. *Ecuador*, US, 823 F.Supp. 1106, 1111 (S.D.N.Y. 1993); *Concord* v. *Caja*, US, 1994 WL 86401, p. 2 (S.D.N.Y. 1994).

265 *Weston* v. *Ecuador*, US, 823 F.Supp. 1106, 1112 (S.D.N.Y. 1993).

266 *Weston* v. *Ecuador*, US, 823 F.Supp. 1106, 1111 (S.D.N.Y. 1993). The court did this in reliance on an absence of provision in this regard.

267 *Weston* v. *Ecuador*, US, 823 F.Supp. 1106, 1114 (S.D.N.Y. 1993).

268 US House of Representatives, Report No. 94-1487, 1976, p. 31; 1976 USCCAN 6604, 6630.

269 *Bank of Credit* v. *State Bank*, US, 46 F.Supp.2d 231, 239 (S.D.N.Y. 1999). See also *Banque Compafina* v. *Banco*, US, 583 F.Supp. 320, 323 (S.D.N.Y. 1984); 92 ILR 399; *Weston* v. *Ecuador*, US, 823 F.Supp. 1106, 1113 (S.D.N.Y. 1993); *Olympic* v. *Ministry*, US, 134 F.Supp.2d 528, 534 (S.D.N.Y. 2001).

270 See *EM* v. *Argentina*, US, 473 F.3d 463, 485, fn. 22 (2nd Cir. 2007); *Olympic* v. *Ministry*, US, 134 F.Supp.2d 528, 534 and fn. 3 (S.D.N.Y. 2001); *LNC* v. *Nicaragua*, US, 115 F.Supp.2d 358, 364 (S.D.N.Y. 2000); affirmed, *LNC* v. *Banco*, US, 228 F.3d 423 (2nd Cir. 2000); *Banque Compafina* v. *Banco*, US, 583 F.Supp. 320, 321 (S.D. N.Y. 1984); 92 ILR 399; *Banco Nacional* v. *Chase*, US, 505 F.Supp. 412, 420 (S.D. N.Y. 1980); affirmed, *Banco Nacional* v. *Chase*, US, 658 F.2d 875 (2nd Cir. 1981). See also Patrikis, Foreign, 273–278; Lee, Central, 354–360.

271 *Banco* v. *Riggs*, US, 919 F.Supp. 13, 17 (D.D.C. 1994). See also Mayer and Odorizzi, Foreign.

670 NOTES TO PAGES 414–416

272 However sweeping the terms of the waiver. See *EM* v. *Argentina*, US, 473 F.3d 463, 468, 485, fn. 22, 486 (2nd Cir. 2007) (Argentina 'has irrevocably waived ... immunity to the fullest extent'); *EM* v. *Argentina*, US, 2003 WL 22120745, p. 1 (S.D.N.Y. 2003).

273 *EM* v. *Argentina*, US, 473 F.3d 463, 473–480 (2nd Cir. 2007) (for the judgment against Argentina see *EM* v. *Argentina*, US, 2003 WL 22120745 (S.D.N.Y. 2003); amended, *EM* v. *Argentina*, US, 2003 WL 22454934 (S.D.N.Y. 2003); affirmed, *EM* v. *Argentina*, US, 382 F.3d 291, 292–294 (2nd Cir. 2004)); *LNC* v. *Nicaragua*, US, 115 F.Supp.2d 358, 363–366 (S.D.N.Y. 2000); affirmed, *LNC* v. *Banco*, US, 228 F.3d 423 (2nd Cir. 2000). See also *Olympic* v. *Ministry*, US, 134 F.Supp.2d 528, 530, 534 (S.D.N.Y. 2001).

274 *First City* v. *Rafidain*, US, 150 F.3d 172, 176 (2nd Cir. 1998). See also Lee, Central, 395.

275 *LNC* v. *Nicaragua*, US, 115 F.Supp.2d 358, 361 and fn. 2 (S.D.N.Y. 2000).

276 *LNC* v. *Nicaragua*, US, 115 F.Supp.2d 358, 362–363, 364–366 (S.D.N.Y. 2000); affirmed, *LNC* v. *Banco*, US, 228 F.3d 423 (2nd Cir. 2000).

277 *Trendtex* v. *Central Bank*, England, [1977] QB 529, 561, 572, 579–580; 64 ILR 111, 135, 146, 153–154; reversing *Trendtex* v. *Central Bank*, England, [1976] 1 WLR 868; 64 ILR 111; *Hispano* v. *Central Bank*, England, [1979] 2 Lloyd's Rep 277, 279–280; 64 ILR 221, 225. The Swiss Federal Tribunal also upheld attachment orders against bank deposits of the Turkish Central Bank held in Switzerland: *Banque Centrale* v. *Weston*, Switzerland, (1978) 65 ILR 417.

278 *Koo* v. *Bank*, England, 2007, [2008] QB 717, 733, para. 40; *Central Bank* v. *Cardinal*, England, 2000, [2001] Lloyd's Rep Bank 1, paras. 11, 17; affirming *Cardinal* v. *Central Bank*, England, 2000 WL 699384.

279 *Koo* v. *Bank*, England, 2007, [2008] QB 717, 733, paras. 40–42; *AIG* v. *Kazakhstan*, England, 2005, [2006] 1 WLR 1420, 1441–1442, para. 58; 129 ILR 589, 615.

280 For identical provisions see the Pakistan SIO, s. 15(4); Singapore SIA, s. 16(4); South Africa FSIA, s. 15(3). See also 2004 UN Convention, Art. 21(1)(c). China's 'Law of Immunity of the Property of Foreign Central Banks from Judicial Compulsory Measures', promulgated in 2005, grants absolute immunity from measures of constraint, including pre-judgment attachment and execution, to the property of foreign central banks. The Chinese text can be found at: www.gov.cn/flfg/2005-10/26/content_83865.htm. An English version can be found at: www.npc.gov.cn/englishnpc/Law/2007-12/13/content_1384123. htm. This is a very odd piece of legislation, especially given that China does not have a comprehensive statute, such as the US FSIA and the UK SIA, on the immunity of foreign States or their central banks in general. If even the possibility of *suing* does not or may not exist, why the need for immunity from *execution*? However, this is not the place further to explore the political and legal considerations (particularly regarding the position of Hong Kong as a financial centre) behind such an oddity.

281 Hansard, *Parliamentary Debates*, Series 5, House of Commons, 13 June 1978, Vol. 951, col. 844. See also *AIG* v. *Kazakhstan*, England, 2005, [2006] 1 WLR 1420, 1435, para. 33; 1441, para. 57; 129 ILR 589, 607, 614.

NOTES TO PAGES 416–419 671

282 *AIC* v. *Nigeria*, England, (2003) 129 ILR 571, 586, para. 47. See also *AIG* v. *Kazakhstan*, England, 2005, [2006] 1 WLR 1420, 1435, para. 33; 129 ILR 589, 607, para. 33; Blair, The Legal, 380–381.

283 *In re Banco*, England, [2001] 3 All ER 923, 933–934; [2001] 1 WLR 2039, 2051, para. 23; 124 ILR 550, 561.

284 *In re Banco*, England, [2001] 3 All ER 923, 927; [2001] 1 WLR 2039, 2044, para. 6; 124 ILR 550, 553; *AIG* v. *Kazakhstan*, England, 2005, [2006] 1 WLR 1420, 1441, para. 57; 129 ILR 589, 614.

285 For example, a court cannot order a central bank to re-transfer certain funds: *Banco* v. *Cosmos*, England, 1999, [2000] BCC 910, 916.

286 *AIG* v. *Kazakhstan*, England, 2005, [2006] 1 WLR 1420, 1441, para. 57; 129 ILR 589, 614–615.

287 ALRC, Report No. 24, 1984, p. 81, para. 132.

288 See the 1926 Brussels Convention, Art. 3(1); 1958 Convention on the Territorial Sea, Arts. 18–22; 1958 Convention on the High Seas, Arts. 8–9; 1982 UN Convention on the Law of the Sea, Arts. 29, 32, 95, 96, 236; 1969 International Convention on Civil Liability for Oil Pollution Damage, Art. 11(1); 1973 International Convention for the Prevention of Pollution from Ships, Art. 3(3).

289 Section 12(3) of the Canada SIA provides the same formula. See also 2004 UN Convention, Art. 21(1)(b); ILA Drafts, Art. VIII(C)(2)); IDI 1991 Draft, Art. 4(2)(b)).

290 US House of Representatives, Report No. 94-1487, 1976, p. 31; 1976 USCCAN 6604, 6630. See *All American* v. *Cuartel*, US, 818 F.Supp. 1552, 1556 (S.D.Fla. 1993). See also *State Marine* v. *USA*, Spain, (1999) 128 ILR 701, 703.

291 ALRC, Report No. 24, 1984, p. 80, para. 130.

292 See US House of Representatives, Report No. 94-1487, 1976, p. 16; 1976 USCCAN 6604, 6615; ALRC, Report No. 24, 1984, p. 52, para. 90.

293 *Spain* v. *Company X SA*, Switzerland, (1986) 82 ILR 38, 44–45, Ground 5b.

294 *LETCO*, US, 650 F.Supp. 73, 77–78 (S.D.N.Y. 1986); 89 ILR 355.

295 *Yugoslavia* v. *Société Européenne*, France, (1985) 82 ILR 58, 72–73. The application for an *exequatur* in the Netherlands was unsuccessful: *Société Européenne* v. *Yugoslavia*, Netherlands, (1972/1973) 65 ILR 356, 364 note.

296 *Rubin* v. *Iran*, US, 456 F.Supp.2d 228, 233–234 (D.Mass. 2006).

297 See Diplomatic note from the Egyptian authorities to the Swiss Embassy in Egypt requesting and the latter's response assuring immunity from seizure for Egyptian objects of art to be on exhibition in Switzerland; Weller, Immunity.

298 *Alcom* v. *Colombia*, England, 1983, [1984] 1 AC 580, 588–589; 74 ILR 170, 178.

299 *Alcom* v. *Colombia*, England, [1984] 1 AC 580, 604; 74 ILR 170, 187; noted in Fox, Enforcement; Jones, State.

300 *Alcom* v. *Colombia*, England, [1984] 1 AC 580, 604–605; 74 ILR 170, 187–188.

301 See identical provisions in the Pakistan SIO, s. 14(4); Singapore SIA, s. 15(5). See also *MK* v. *State*, Netherlands, (1986) 94 ILR 357, 360. Cf. Australia FSIA, s. 41(b) (such a certificate is merely 'admissible as evidence'); ALRC, Report No. 24, 1984, pp. 78, para. 127.

672   NOTES TO PAGES 420–427

302 The ILA Drafts follow the opposite approach, i.e., non-immunity should be presumed unless public uses can be shown (Art. VIII(B)); but this is imposing an onus on the foreign State which is absent from current international practice – and law.

303 See *Philippine Embassy Case*, Germany, (1977) 65 ILR 146, 186, Ground C.II.3; 188–189, Ground C.II.4(a); *Kenyan Diplomatic Residence Case*, Germany, (2003) 128 ILR 632, 636, Ground II.3b; *Leasing* v. *Algeria*, Austria, (1986) 116 ILR 526, 528–529; duplicate report *sub nom Republic of 'A' Case*, Austria, (1986) 77 ILR 488; *État C* v. *Dame X*, Switzerland, 8 *RSDIE* (1998) 643; Crawford, Execution, 864. On the other hand, if a bank account stands to the name of an individual, then non-immunity is presumed unless the individual can furnish direct proof of the allocation of his private assets to public uses: *Griessen*, Switzerland, (1982) 82 ILR 5, 7, Ground 1; 9, Ground 2; 10, Ground 4 (a businessman acting as Honorary Consul of Chad in Geneva).

304 *LETCO*, US, 659 F.Supp. 606, 610 (D.D.C. 1987); 89 ILR 360. Cf. *Birch* v. *Embassy*, US, 507 F.Supp.311, 313 (D.D.C. 1980); 63 ILR 524. For US practice see also Smith, Executing.

305 *Abbott* v. *South Africa*, Spain, (1992) 113 ILR 411, 424. For difficulty in isolating public from commercial purposes see also *Statni* v. *Englander*, France, (1966) 47 ILR 157, 161 (but quashed by *Englander* v. *Statni*, France, (1969) 52 ILR 335, 336); *Procureur* v. *LIAMCO*, France, (1979) 65 ILR 78, 81.

306 *Banamar-Capizzi* v. *Embassy*, Italy, (1989) 87 ILR 56, 60–61; citing *Paradiso* v. *Bari*, Italy, (1986) 87 ILR 37 note. See also *Libya* v. *Rossbeton*, Italy, (1989) 87 ILR 63; *Condor* v. *Minister*, Italy (1992) 101 ILR 394, 402.

307 See *Zaire* v. *D'Hoop*, Belgium, (1995) 106 ILR 294, 296 (but see 106 ILR 297 note); *Spanish Consular Case*, Germany, (1971) 65 ILR 114, 118–119; *NIOC Revenues Case*, Germany, (1983) 65 ILR 215, 229, Ground B.III.2(b); *UAR* v. *Mrs X*, Switzerland, (1960) 65 ILR 385, 392, Ground 5; *Libya* v. *Actimon*, Switzerland, (1985) 82 ILR 30, 36, Ground 7b; *Guinée* v. *M*, Switzerland, 1985, 42 *ASDI* (1986) 69; *Banque du Gothard* v. *Chambre*, Switzerland, (1987) 82 ILR 50, 52, Ground 3.

308 *NIOC Revenues Case*, Germany, (1983) 65 ILR 215, 243–245, Ground B.III.2(d)(bb), (2), (e). See also *Morocco* v. *Stichting*, Netherlands, (1978) 65 ILR 375, 376.

309 ALRC, Report No. 24, 1984, p. 78, para. 127.

Chapter 10

1 *Arrest Warrant, ICJ Reports* 2002, p. 3 at 24, para. 59; 128 ILR 1, 80. See also *East Timor, ICJ Reports* 1995, p. 90 at 102, para. 29.

2 The ILC decided in 2006 to include the topic 'Extraterritorial jurisdiction' in its long-term programme of work. See ILC, Report, 2006, A/61/10, paras. 22, 257, 260 and Annex E.

3 See US FSIA, s. 1604 (general immunity) and s. 1605 (exceptions); *US* v. *Hendron*, US, 813 F.Supp. 973, 975 (E.D.N.Y. 1993); UK SIA, s. 1 and ss. 2–11; *Jones* v. *Saudi*

NOTES TO PAGE 427   673

Arabia, England, [2005] QB 699, 713, para. 11; 129 ILR 629, 653; Canada SIA 2, s. 3 and ss. 4–8; Australia FSIA, s. 9 and ss. 10–21; Pakistan SIO, s. 3 and ss. 4–12; Singapore SIA, s. 3 and ss. 4–13; South Africa FSIA, s. 2 and ss. 3–12; Argentina Immunity Law, Art. 1 and Art. 2; Israel Immunity Law, Chapter Two, Part One and Part Two.

4 ILA, Drafts, Art. II (general immunity) and Art. III (exceptions); IDI, Draft, 1991, Art. 2(2) and (3); OAS Draft, 1983, Art. 1 and Arts. 4–7.

5 ILC 1991 Draft and the 2004 UN Convention, Art. 5 (immunity) and Arts. 7–17 (exceptions).

6 See UK SIA, s. 16(4); Singapore SIA, s. 19(2)(b); Pakistan SIO, s. 17(2)(b); South Africa FSIA, s. 2(3); Canada SIA (as amended), s. 18. Section 1330(a) of the US FSIA restricts the application of the statute to 'any nonjury *civil* action against a foreign state' (emphasis added). The Australia FSIA does not contain a similar provision; but the drafters recommended 'the same position'. ALRC, Report No. 24, 1984, p. 100, para. 161.

7 ILC, Report, *YILC*, 1991-II-2, p. 12 at 14, commentary to Art. 2, para. (2). For very brief mentioning of the word 'criminal' see: ILC, Report, *YILC*, 1978-II-2, Chapter VIII-D, Annex, p. 153 at 154, para. 22; ILC, Report, *YILC*, 1983-II-2, p. 17 at 19, para. 86; Sucharitkul, Seventh Report, *YILC*, 1985-II-1, p. 21 at 45, para. 125; Sucharitkul, Eighth Report, *YILC*, 1986-II-1, p. 21 at 31, para. 39; Ogiso, Second Report, *YILC*, 1989-II-1, p. 59 at 66, para. 22.

8 Report of the Ad Hoc Committee, 2003, A/58/22, Annex II, p. 15; Report of the Ad Hoc Committee, 2004, A/59/22, pp. 3 and 4, paras. 11 and 14.

9 UNGA, Resolution A/RES/59/38 of 2 December 2004, para. 2. This originated from a general understanding reached in the Ad Hoc Committee. See Report of the Ad Hoc Committee, 2003, A/58/22, para. 9 and Annex II; Report of the Ad Hoc Committee, 2004, A/59/22, paras. 11 and 14, and Annex II.

10 For further discussion see Yang, State Immunity in the ECHR, 345–355.

11 See ILC, Report, *YILC*, 1976-II-2, p. 69 at 95–122, especially commentary, paras. 6–34.

12 ILC, Report, *YILC*, 2001-II-2, p. 20 at 111, commentary to Chapter III of Part Two, para. (5). The ILC also said: 'Nor does any distinction exist between the "civil" and "criminal" responsibility as is the case in internal legal systems.' *Ibid.*, p. 55, commentary to Art. 12, para. (5). See also *Genocide Convention*, *ICJ Reports* 2007, para. 170; Crawford, International Crimes, pp. 405–414.

13 Adopted and proclaimed by General Assembly Resolution 217 A (III) of 10 December 1948.

14 See, e.g., 1948 Convention on the Prevention and *Punishment* of the *Crime* of Genocide, Art. 1 ('genocide ... is a *crime* under international law'); 1965 International Convention on the Elimination of All Forms of Racial Discrimination, Art. 4(a) ('*an offence punishable by law*'); 1973 International Convention on the Suppression and *Punishment* of the *Crime* of Apartheid, Art. 1(1) ('apartheid is a *crime* against humanity'); 1984 Convention against Torture, Art. 4 (1) ('offences under its *criminal law*'). Emphases added. See generally Macedo, *Universal Jurisdiction*; van Alebeek, *The Immunity*, 2008.

674   NOTES TO PAGES 427-429

15 See generally, Scott, *Torture as Tort.*
16 See, e.g., Yang, *Jus Cogens*; Orakhelashvili, *Peremptory Norms*, Chapter 10; Ora-khelashvili, State Immunity and International Public Order, 255–267; Ora-khelashvili, State Immunity Revisited, 353–363; Eboe-Osuji, State Immunity.
17 For detailed analysis see Yang, *Jus Cogens.*
18 See *Al-Adsani* v. *UK*, ECHR, dissenting opinion of Judge Rozakis *et al.*, paras. 3–4, (2001) 123 ILR 24, 50–51; and of Judge Loucaides, 123 ILR 24, 52; *Arrest Warrant, ICJ Reports* 2002, p. 3, dissenting opinion of Judge Al-Khasawneh, at p. 98, para. 7; and of Judge van den Wyngaert, at pp. 156–157, para. 28; 128 ILR 1, 153, 208–209; *Princz* v. *Germany*, US, 26 F.3d 1166, 1182 per Judge Wald, dissenting (D.C.Cir. 1994); 103 ILR 594, 618; Bianchi, Denying, 222–223; Haffke, The Torture Victim, 1501–1505; Reimann, A Human Rights Exception, 407–408; Gergen, Human Rights, 791; Byers, case note on *Al-Adsani*, 539–540, 542; Bröhmer, *State Immunity*, p. 208; Karagiannakis, State Immunity, 19–20; Kelley, Does Customary, 507, 517–518; Bianchi, Immunity, 262, 265; de Cara, L'Affaire Pinochet, 88; Charney, Progress, 457; Horowitz, *Regina*, 490, 524; van Alebeek, The *Pinochet* Case, 49; Bartsch and Elberling, *Jus Cogens*, 484.
19 See Belsky *et al.*, Implied Waiver, esp. 394–401; Richman, *Siderman*, 978–981; Haffke, The Torture Victim, 1497–1499; Anonymous, Case note on *Princz*, 516–517; Johnson, A Violation, 284–287; Hoops, Retroactivity, 537–539; Bederman, Dead Man's Hand, 272–278; Vivekananthan, The Doctrine, 147; Levy, As Between, 2710; Osofsky, Foreign Sovereign, 44; Karagiannakis, State Immunity, 20–21; Horowitz, *Regina*, 522–523; Bergen, *Princz*; Vournas, *Prefecture of Voiotia*, 635.
20 For cases rejecting the 'override' theory see *Siderman* v. *Argentina*, US, 965 F.2d 699, 718–719 (9th Cir. 1992); 103 ILR 454, 474–475; *Wei* v. *Jiang*, US, 383 F.3d 620, 627 (7th Cir. 2004); affirming *Plaintiffs* v. *Jiang*, US, 282 F.Supp.2d 875, 883 (N.D.Ill. 2003); *Doe* v. *Liu*, US, 349 F.Supp.2d 1258, 1284 (N.D.Cal. 2004); *Belhas* v. *Ya'alon*, US, 515 F.3d 1279, 1286–1288 (D.C.Cir. 2008); *Al-Adsani* v. *Kuwait*, England, (1995) 103 ILR 420, 427–431; affirmed, *Al-Adsani* v. *Kuwait*, England, (1996) 107 ILR 536, 542, 549–550; noted in Marks, Torture; *Al-Adsani* v. *UK*, ECHR, (2001) 123 ILR 24, 42, para. 61; 43, para. 66; *Kalogeropoulou* v. *Greece*, ECHR, (2002) 129 ILR 537, 546–547; *Jones* v. *Saudi Arabia*, England, [2007] 1 AC 270, 288, para. 24; 302, para. 85; 129 ILR 629, 726–727, 744; *Sam* v. *Jiang*, New Zealand, 2006, CIV 2004-404-5843, para. 63; *Bouzari* v. *Iran*, Canada, (2002) 124 ILR 427, 443, para. 63; affirmed, *Bouzari* v. *Iran*, Canada, (2004) 243 DLR (4th) 406, 428–429; 128 ILR 586, 605–606; application for leave to appeal dismissed, *Bouzari* v. *Iran*, Canada, (2005) 122 CRR (2d) 376 (note); Novo-grodsky, Immunity. See also *Schreiber* v. *Germany*, Canada, (2002) 216 DLR (4th) 513, 533–534; *Arar* v. *Syria*, Canada, [2005] OJ No. 752; [2005] 137 ACWS (3d) 823; *République fédérale*, France, 2004, 94 *RCDIP* (2005) 79. For cases rejecting the waiver argument see *Ferrini* v. *Germany*, Italy, (2004) 128 ILR 658, 668, para. 8.2; noted in Bianchi, *Ferrini*, 243 and fn. 13; and in Focarelli, Denying, 957; *Hwang* v. *Japan*, US, 332 F.3d 679, 686–687 (D.C.Cir. 2003); affirming *Hwang* v. *Japan*, US, 172 F.Supp.2d 52, 60–61 (D.D.C. 2001) (the

decision of *Hwang* was later vacated and remanded: *Hwang* v. *Japan*, US, 542 US 901 (2004), but was reaffirmed on the ground of non-justiciable political question: *Hwang* v. *Japan*, US, 413 F.3d 45 (D.C.Cir. 2005)); Park, The Unspeakable Experience; Gotfredsen, Seeking Comfort; Park, Comfort Women; Niekrasz, The Past; *Sampson* v. *Germany*, US, 250 F.3d 1145, 1155–1156 (7th Cir. 2001); *Smith* v. *Libya*, US, 101 F.3d 239, 242–245 (2nd Cir. 1996); 113 ILR 534, 539; affirming *Smith* v. *Libya*, US, 886 F.Supp. 306, 314–315 (E.D.N.Y. 1995); 107 ILR 382; *Princz* v. *Germany*, US, 26 F.3d 1166, 1174 (D.C.Cir. 1994); 103 ILR 594, 610; reversing *Princz* v. *Germany*, US, 813 F.Supp 22 (D.D.C. 1992); *Garb* v. *Poland*, US, 207 F.Supp.2d 16, 38–39 (E.D.N.Y. 2002); *Nexhat* v. *Yugoslavia*, US, 2002 U.S. Dist.Lexis 13763, pp. 10–11 (N.D.Ill. 2002).

21 Bantekas, *Prefecture of Voiotia*, see especially p. 767, Ground f; affirmed, Gavouneli and Bantekas, *Prefecture of Voiotia*, 200; *Distomo Massacre Case*, Greece, (2000) 129 ILR 513. See also Gavouneli, War Reparation. Contrary to the belief of the following authors who think that *jus cogens* was the chief rationale in the case: Horowitz, *Regina*, 510–511, 522; Vournas, *Prefecture of Voiotia*; Bartsch and Elberling, *Jus Cogens*, 483; Caplan, State Immunity, 768–770, 779–780; de Wet, The Prohibition, 106–107. Immunity was granted in *Margellos* v. *Germany*, Greece, (2002) 129 ILR 525, noted in Panezi, Sovereign. For the reaction of the Germany judiciary see *Distomo Massacre Case*, Germany, (2003) 129 ILR 556, noted in Pittrof, Compensation Claims; *Distomo Massacre Case*, Germany, (2006) 135 ILR 186.

22 *Ferrini* v. *Germany*, Italy, (2004) 128 ILR 658, 670–671, para. 10; noted in Bianchi, *Ferrini*. The Italian Court of Cassation confirmed its *Ferrini* judgment in a series of decisions delivered on 29 May 2008 (*Germany* v. *Mantelli*, No. 14201/2008, noted in Focarelli, *Germany* v. *Mantelli*) and in a further judgment of 21 October 2008 (*Milde* v. *Italy*, Cass. sez. I pen. Sentenza n. 1072 ud., noted in Ciampi, The *Civitella* Case).

23 Contrary to De Sena and De Vittor, State Immunity, 95–97, where they suggest that the territorial nexus was only of secondary importance in the *Ferrini* case.

24 See Gattini, War Crimes, esp. 233–241 for a similar view. This is contrary to De Sena and De Vittor, State Immunity, 100–103, and to Focarelli, Denying, 957, who assert an emergent rule based on *jus cogens*.

25 *Pinochet No. 3*, England, [2000] 1 AC 147, 198, 203, 204, 247, 261, 275, 278, 290; 119 ILR 135, 149, 155, 156, 200, 214, 229, 232, 244.

26 *Pinochet No. 3*, England, [2000] 1 AC 147, 204–205, 247, 277–278, 290; 119 ILR 135, 155–157, 200, 231–232, 244–245.

27 See the 1969 Vienna Convention on the Law of Treaties, Arts. 53 and 64. See Aust, *Modern Treaty Law*, pp. 319–320; Corten and Klein, *The Vienna Conventions*.

28 See Schwarzenberger, International *Jus Cogens*, 476, 477–478 (cf. Mann, The Doctrine of *Jus Cogens*, 87); Watson, *Theory & Reality*, p. 44; D'Amato, Human Rights, 57; D'Amato, There Is, 34–35; D'Amato, It's a Bird, 1–2.

29 See, e.g., Hannikainen, *Peremptory Norms*, pp. 293–314.

676   NOTES TO PAGES 430–432

30 Crawford, *The Creation of States*, pp. 102 and 105. See also Suy, The Concept of *Jus Cogens*, p. 75; Rozakis, *The Concept of Jus Cogens*, pp. 16–27; Linderfalk, The Effect; Bianchi, Human Rights.

31 *Prosecutor* v. *Furundzija*, ICTY, (1998) 121 ILR 213, 260–261, para. 153. See also Crawford, *The International Law Commission's Articles*, pp. 54–56. On the idea of hierarchy see generally Meron, On a Hierarchy; Koskenniemi, Hierarchy; Salcedo, Reflections; Koji, Emerging Hierarchy; Paulus, *Jus Cogens*, 319–323; Shelton, Normative Hierarchy.

32 ILC, Report, *YILC*, 2001-II-2, p. 20, Chapter VI. See also Art. 41.

33 See also Art. 26 and its commentary.

34 The ICJ in the past has used the term '*erga omnes*' rather than '*jus cogens*'. See *Barcelona Traction*, *ICJ Reports* 1970, p. 3 at 32, para. 33; *Military and Paramilitary Activities*, *ICJ Reports* 1986, p. 14 at 100–101, para. 190; *East Timor*, *ICJ Reports* 1995, p. 90 at 102, para. 29; *Genocide Convention*, *ICJ Reports* 1996, p. 595 at 616, para. 31; *Armed Activities*, *ICJ Reports* 2002, p. 219 at 245, para. 71; *Wall*, *ICJ Reports* 2004, p. 136 at 172 and 199, paras. 88 and 155–157. In *Nuclear Weapons*, the ICJ opined that the fundamental rules of international humanitarian law constituted 'intransgressible principles of international customary law', but still declined to pronounce on the notion of *jus cogens*: *Nuclear Weapons*, *ICJ Reports* 1996, p. 226, at 257, para. 79 and 258, para. 83. For a criticism of this practice of the ICJ see the separate opinion of Judge ad hoc Dugard in the *Armed Activities* case, especially paras. 10–12. For the relationship between the notions of *jus cogens* and *erga omnes* see ILC, Report, *YILC*, 2001-II-2, p. 20 at 111, commentary to Part Two, Chapter III, para. (7). See also Meron, On a Hierarchy, 11; de Hoogh, *Obligations*, pp. 53–56; Byers, Conceptualising; Ragazzi, *The Concept*, pp. 43–73; Tams, *Enforcing*, pp. 139–153.

35 *Armed Activities*, *ICJ Reports* 2006, p. 6 at 32, para. 64.

36 *Armed Activities*, *ICJ Reports* 2006, p. 6 at 52, para. 125. See also *East Timor*, *ICJ Reports* 1995, p. 90 at 102, para. 29.

37 See, e.g., the angry response from the Chinese Government regarding the hearing by a Spanish court of allegations of genocide in Tibet: www.fmprc. gov.cn/eng/xwfw/s2510/2511/t256872.htm; http://english.gov.cn/2006-06/09/ content_305067.htm.

38 See discussion in Chapter 7.

39 38 ILM 918 (1999) (English translation, where the Law is referred to as 'Act'). For favourable comments see Winants, The *Yerodia* Ruling. For a similar law see Germany: Act to Introduce the Code of Crimes against International Law of 26 June 2002, entered into force 30 June 2002, 42 ILM 998 (2003) (English translation).

40 *Re Sharon and Yaron*, Belgium, (2002/2003) 127 ILR 110, 115–124.

41 US Universal Jurisdiction Rejection Bill, introduced in the House of Representatives, 108th Congress, 1st Session, H.R. 2050, 9 May 2003, available from the US Library of Congress legislative information website http://thomas.loc.gov.

42 42 ILM 749 (2003) (English translation).

43 42 ILM 1258 (2003) (English translation). For an account of the 'life and death of Belgium's universal jurisdiction law' see Ratner, Belgium's.

44 For discussion on universal jurisdiction (including universal criminal and/or civil jurisdiction) see Redress, *Challenging Impunity*; Scott, *Torture as Tort*; Bleimaier, The Private; Lininger, Overcoming; Garnett, The Defence; Garnett, Should Foreign; Zinman, Holding; White, Nowhere; Murphy, Civil Liability; White, Pinochet; Seidl-Hohenveldern, International Immunity; Roht-Arriaza, The Pinochet Precedent; Burr, From Noriega; Cassel, Empowering; Orakhelashvili, State Immunity; Rau, After *Pinochet*; Tams, Well-Protected; Henzelin, La compétence; Orakhelashvili, Restrictive; Thomas and Small, Human Rights; Bates, The Al-Adsani Case; de Oliveira Moll, *Al-Adsani*; O'Keefe, Universal Jurisdiction; Marks, Mending; Fox, State Immunity and the International Crime of Torture. For an early call for the abolition of State immunity see Lauterpacht, The Problem, 247–250.

45 See ILC, Report, 2006, A/61/10, paras. 22, 257, 260 and Annex A; ILC, Report, 2007, A/62/10, paras. 19, 376, 378, 386; ILC, Report, 2008, A/63/10, Chapter X; ILC, Report, 2009, A/64/10, Chapter X; ILC, Report, 2010, A/65/10, Chapter IX.

46 See generally Watts, The Legal Position and Bassiouni, *Crimes against Humanity*, pp. 465–467. See also the 1919 Treaty of Versailles, Art. 227 (the 'special tribunal' envisaged by this article for the purpose of trying the German Emperor never materialized. See, e.g., Scott, The Trial of the Kaiser; Bassiouni, From Versailles, 18–19); 1945 Nuremberg Charter, Art. 7; Charter of the International Military Tribunal for the Far East (Tokyo Charter), Art. 6; ILC's Nuremberg Principles: Principle III, *YILC*, 1950-II, p. 374 at 375; 1998 Rome Statute, Art. 27; Tunks, Diplomats; Singerman, It's Still.

47 *Propend Finance Pty Ltd* v. *Sing*, England, Court of Appeal, (1997) 111 ILR 611, 669 per Leggatt LJ.

48 *Jones* v. *Saudi Arabia*, England, [2006] 2 WLR 1424, 1430; [2007] 1 AC 270, 281, para. 10; 129 ILR 629, 717; cited in *Koo* v. *Bank*, England, 2007, [2008] QB 717, 734, para. 45.

49 *Jones* v. *Saudi Arabia*, England, [2006] 2 WLR 1424, 1448–1449; [2007] 1 AC 270, 298–300, paras. 66, 69, 70; 129 ILR 629, 739–741; reversing *Jones* v. *Saudi Arabia*, England, 2004, [2005] QB 699; 129 ILR 629. See also *Grovit* v. *De Nederlandsche*, England, 2005, [2006] 1 WLR 3323, 3338–3339, paras. 62–67; affirmed, *Grovit* v. *De Nederlandsche*, England, 2007, [2008] 1 WLR 51, 56–57, paras. 16–17. For comments on *Jones* see Orakhelashvili, State Immunity and the Hierarchy of Norms; Bates, State Immunity; Fox, Where Does; Yang, Universal; Seymour, Immunity; Parlett, Immunity; Parlett, Universal; McGregor, Torture; Hall, The Duty; Mizushima, Denying, 745–748; Wright, Retribution.

50 *Jaffe* v. *Miller*, Canada, (1993) 13 OR (3d) 745, 758–759; 95 ILR 446, 458–459.

51 See *Carrato* v. *USA*, Canada, (1982) 141 DLR (3d) 456, 459; 90 ILR 229, 232; *Tritt* v. *USA*, Canada, (1989) 68 OR (2d) 284, 287; 94 ILR 260, 263; affirmed, *Tritt* v. *USA*, Canada, (1994) 45 A.C.W.S. (3d) 1140; *Jaffe* v. *Miller*, Canada, (1990) 73 DLR (4th) 420, 425, 428; 87 ILR 197, 202–203, 205; affirmed, *Jaffe* v. *Miller*, Canada, (1993) 13 OR (3d) 745, 759–760; 95 ILR 446, 459–460; *Walker* v. *Bank*, Canada, (1994)

678　NOTES TO PAGES 433-434

111 DLR (4th) 186, 191; 104 ILR 277, 282; *USA* v. *Friedland*, Canada, (1999) 182 DLR (4th) 614, 622-623; 120 ILR 417, 461; *P* v. *Westwood*, Canada, [2003] BCJ N. 1944, para. 20; *Ritter* v. *Donell*, Canada, [2005] AJ No. 958, paras. 24 and 34; *Smith* v. *Chin*, Canada, [2006] OJ No. 4091, para. 16; *Smith* v. *Canadian*, Canada, (1976) 68 DLR (3d) 428, 432; 64 ILR 47; *Kline* v. *Kaneko*, US, 685 F.Supp. 386, 390 (S.D.N.Y. 1988); 101 ILR 497; *Herbage* v. *Meese*, US, 747 F.Supp. 60 (D.D.C. 1990); 98 ILR 101; affirmed, *Herbage* v. *Meese*, US, 946 F.2d 1564 (D.C.Cir. 1991) (Table); *Re Marcinkus*, Italy, (1987) 87 ILR 48, 52; *Re Marcinkus*, Vatican City, (1987) 100 ILR 603, 608-609; *Church of Scientology Case*, Germany, (1978) 65 ILR 193, 198; *Indian Foreign Minister Case*, Germany, (1988) 90 ILR 408; *Pinochet No. 3*, England, 1999, [2000] 1 AC 147, 269, 285-286; 119 ILR 135, 222, 239-240; *Holland* v. *Lampen-Wolfe*, England, [2000] 1 WLR 1573, 1583; 119 ILR 367, 378; *Schmidt* v. *Home Secretary*, Ireland, 1994, [1995] ILRM 301, 303-304; 103 ILR 322, 323-325; *Schmidt* v. *Home Secretary*, Ireland, [1997] 2 IR 121; *Herron* v. *Ireland*, Ireland, 1997; *Lakhowsky* v. *Swiss Federal*, France, (1919/1921) 1 AD 122, 124; *Agent judiciaire* v. *Malta*, France, 2004, 94 RCDIP (2005) 469; *AXA* v. *Asecna*, France, 2004, 94 RCDIP (2005) 470; *Prosecutor* v. *Bläskić*, ICTY, (1997) 110 ILR 607, 707. See also Sucharitkul, Immunities, 100; Whomersley, Some Reflections; Fitzpatrick, The Claim; Barker, State Immunity; Gully-Hart, The Function; Mizushima, The Individual; Wen, Suing.

52 *Walker* v. *Bank*, Canada, (1994) 111 DLR (4th) 186, 190-191; 104 ILR 277, 281-282.

53 See *Mobutu* v. *Société Logrine*, France, (1994) 113 ILR 481, 483-484; *Kubacz* v. *Shah*, Australia, 1983, [1984] WAR 156, 160; 118 ILR 293, 297-298; *Nobili* v. *Emperor*, Italy, (1921) 1 AD 36.

54 See *Zhang* v. *Jiang*, Australia, (2008) 251 ALR 707; *Garsec* v. *His Majesty*, Australia, (2008) 250 ALR 682; affirming *Garsec* v. *His Majesty*, Australia, (2007) 213 FLR 331; *Pan* v. *Bo*, Australia, (2008) 220 FLR 271; *Thor Shipping* v. *Al Duhail*, Australia, (2008) 252 ALR 20; (2008) 173 FCR 524; 140 ILR 530; noted in Alderton, Immunity; *Davidson* v. *British Columbia*, Canada, [2006] 214 CCC (3d) 373; *Li* v. *Jiang*, New Zealand, 2006, CIV 2004-404-5843; *Sam* v. *Jiang*, New Zealand, 2006, CIV 2004-404-5843, para. 73; *Center* v. *Rumsfeld*, Germany, 2005, 45 ILM 119 (2006); *Center* v. *Rumsfeld*, Germany, 2005, 45 ILM 122 (2006); *Re Honecker*, Germany, (1984) 80 ILR 365, 366; *Re Sharon*, Belgium, (2002/2003) 127 ILR 110; *Gaddafi*, France, (2000/2001) 125 ILR 490; *Village* v. *Her Majesty*, Malaysia, (1987) 87 ILR 223, 238; *RSM* v. *Fridman*, US, 643 F.Supp.2d 382 (S.D. N.Y. 2009); *Collett* v. *Libya*, US, 362 F.Supp.2d 230, 243-244 (D.D.C. 2005); *Wei* v. *Jiang*, US, 383 F.3d 620, 627 (7th Cir. 2004); affirming *Plaintiffs* v. *Jiang*, US, 282 F.Supp.2d 875, 883 (N.D.Ill. 2003); *Zhou* v. *Li*, US, 286 F.Supp.2d 255 (S.D.N.Y. 2003); *Tachiona* v. *Mugabe*, US, 234 F.Supp.2d 401 (S.D.N.Y. 2002); *Tachiona* v. *Mugabe*, US, 216 F.Supp.2d 262 (S.D.N.Y. 2002); *Tachiona* v. *Mugabe*, US, 186 F.Supp.2d 383 (S.D.N.Y. 2002); *Tachiona* v. *Mugabe*, US, 169 F.Supp.2d 259 (S.D.N.Y. 2001); affirmed, *Tachiona* v. *US*, US, 386 F.3d 205, 220-221 (2nd Cir. 2004); *Bao* v. *Li*, US, 201 F.Supp.2d 14 (D.D.C. 2000); *Saltany* v. *Reagan*, US, 702 F.Supp. 319, 320 (D.D.C. 1988); 80 ILR 19; affirmed, *Saltany* v. *Reagan*, US, 886 F.2d 438, 440-441

(D.C.Cir. 1989); 87 ILR 679; *O'Hair* v. *Andrus*; *Wojtyla*, US, 81 ILR 607 (D.D.C. 1979); *Kilroy* v. *Windsor*, US, 81 ILR 605 (N.D.Ohio 1978); *Psinakis* v. *Marcos*, US, 81 ILR 605 (N.D.Cal. 1975); *Chong* v. *Kim*, US, 81 ILR 604 (Hawaii Cir.Ct. 1963); 58 *AJIL* (1964) 186; *Association v France*, ECHR, 2006, unreported but noted in *EHRLR* (2007-1) 93. See also *Mighell* v. *Sultan*, England, 1893, [1894] 1 QB 149; *Sayce* v. *Ameer*, England, [1952] 2 QB 390, 393–394; 19 ILR 212; *Mobutu* v. *Cotoni*, Belgium, (1988) 91 ILR 259, 260; *Bank* v. *Price*, England, 1996, [1997] 4 All ER 108, 111; 111 ILR 604, 607; noted in Hopkins, Immunity; Ruffert, Pinochet; Zappalà, Do Heads; Mundis, *Tachiona*; Warbrick, Immunity. However, such immunity does not give foreign heads of State the privilege to have their immunity claims heard in private: *Harb* v. *His Majesty*, England, [2005] Fam Law 778; 136 ILR 574; *Aziz* v. *Aziz*, England, 2007, [2008] 2 All ER 501; 136 ILR 587.

55 *Arrest Warrant*, *ICJ Reports* 2002, p. 3 at 20–21, para. 51; 128 ILR 1, 76. But contrast this dictum with a remark in Ogiso, Third Report, *YILC*, 1990-II-1, p. 3 at 9. At any rate, Art. 3(2) of the 2004 UN Convention (and of the 1991 ILC Draft) provides: 'The present Convention is without prejudice to privileges and immunities accorded under international law to heads of State *ratione personae*.' Scholars have passed varying verdicts on the *Arrest Warrant* case. See Cassese, When; Orakhelashvili, *Arrest Warrant*; Wirth, Immunity; Spinedi, State Responsibility; Jennings, Jurisdiction; Schreuer and Wittich, Immunity; Yang, Immunity; Turns, The International; Frulli, The ICJ; Rispin, Implications; Zuppi, Immunity; Sands, International Law; Wouters, The Judgment; de Smet, The Immunity; Summers, The International; Carty, *Philosophy of International Law*, pp. 41–46; Summers, Diplomatic; Orakhelashvili, Between; Stern, Can A State. For the immunity of a serving/acting head of State see especially *Pinochet No. 3*, England, 1999, [2000] 1 AC 147, 201–202, 209–210, 240–241, 244–245, 265, 268–269, 280, 285; 119 ILR 135, 152–153, 160–161, 193, 197–198, 219, 222, 234, 239; Lord Hope of Craighead even went so far as to pronounce the '*jus cogens* character of the immunity enjoyed by serving heads of State ratione personae' (p. 244; ILR 197); *Lafontant* v. *Aristide*, US, 844 F.Supp. 128, 131–132 (E.D.N.Y. 1994); 103 ILR 581; *Marcos* v. *Federal*, Switzerland, (1989) 102 ILR 198, 201–203, Ground 5(b)(c); *Prince of X Case*, Austria, (1964) 65 ILR 13. For more recent cases concerning the immunity of high-ranking governmental or military officials see especially *Re Mofaz*, England, (2004) 128 ILR 709; *Tatchell* v. *Mugabe*, England, (2004) 136 ILR 572; *Re Bo Xilai*, England, (2005) 128 ILR 713; cf. *Pinochet No. 3*, England, 1999, [2000] 1 AC 147, 268 per Lord Millett; 119 ILR 135, 222. For further discussion of head-of-State immunity see Bass, Ex-Head; Hickey, The Dictator; Callan, In re Mr. and Mrs. Doe; George, Head-of-State; Fitzgerald, The Pinochet; Stern, Immunities; Toner, Competing; O'Donnell, *Certain Criminal*.

56 For less eminent examples see *Ex-King* v. *Christian Dior*, France, (1957) 24 ILR 228; *Société* v. *Prince Farouk*, France, (1963) 65 ILR 37; *Honecker Prosecution Case*, Germany, (1993) 100 ILR 393, 399–400; *Haiti* v. *Duvalier*, England, 1988, [1990] 1 QB 202, 215; 107 ILR 490, 501; cf. *Duvalier* v. *Haiti*, France, (1990) 113 ILR 448, 449.

680   NOTES TO PAGE 434

57 Notably, a more recent project of the Institut de Droit International draws a distinction between a serving and former head of State / head of government: IDI, Draft, 2001, see especially Arts. 1, 2, 13 and 15. For comments on the project see Fox, The Resolution. But see *Abiola* v. *Abubakar*, US, 267 F.Supp.2d 907, 916 (N.D.Ill. 2003).

58 See *In Re Grand Jury*, US, 817 F.2d 1108, 1111 (4th Cir. 1987); 81 ILR 599; *In re Doe*, US, 860 F.2d 40, 44–45 (2nd Cir. 1988); 121 ILR 567; *Paul* v. *Avril*, US, 812 F.Supp. 207, 210–211 (S.D.Fla. 1993); 103 ILR 553. See also *Iran* v. *Pahlavi*, US, 464 N.Y.S.2d 487, 496 (1983); affirmed, 478 N.Y.S.2d 597, 603–604 (1984), 81 ILR 557.

59 *Kadic* v. *Karadzic*, US, 70 F.3d 232, 248 (2nd Cir. 1995); reversing *Doe* v. *Karadzic*, US, 866 F.Supp. 734 (S.D.N.Y. 1994). See also *US* v. *Noriega*, US, 746 F.Supp. 1506, 1519–1521 (S.D.Fla. 1990); 99 ILR 143; affirmed, *US* v. *Noriega*, US, 117 F.3d 1206, 1212 (11th Cir. 1997); 121 ILR 591; Re *Arafat*, Italy, 1985, 7 *Italian YIL* (1986–1987) 287.

60 See *Arrest Warrant*, *ICJ Reports* 2002, p. 3 at 25–26, para. 61; 128 ILR 1, 81–82; Slobodan Milošević, former President of Yugoslavia, was tried by the ICTY in 2004–2006 before he died in prison, case documents available at www.icty. org. Charles Taylor was the incumbent President of Liberia when he was indicted in 2003 and was denied immunity in 2004, following his resignation, by the Special Court for Sierra Leone, a court jointly established by the UN and the Government of Sierra Leone: *Prosecutor* v. *Taylor*, (2004) 128 ILR 239. For comments see Frulli, The Question; Deen-Racsmány, *Prosecutor*; Nouwen, The Special Court. The Cambodian Government and the UN jointly created the 'Extraordinary Chambers in the Courts of Cambodia for the Prosecution of Crimes Committed during the Period of Democratic Kampuchea' (ECCC), composed of both Cambodian and international judges, to try serious crimes committed during the Khmer Rouge regime 1975–1979. The work of the ECCC began in 2007. See www.eccc.gov.kh. For the trial of former Iraqi leader Saddam Hussein see Bantekas, The Iraqi Special Tribunal. For further discussion on international tribunals see Scharf, The Amnesty; van Alebeek, From Rome; Penrose, It's Good; Brower, International; Johnson, The Extradition; Wirth, Immunities; Popoff, Inconsistency; Zelniker, Towards; Mochochoko, The Agreement; Hasson, Extraterritorial; Akande, International Law; Grosscup, The Trial; Koller, Immunities; Ettari, A Foundation; Frulli, The Question; Bantekas, Head of State; Summers, Immunity; Gaeta, Does; Akande, The Legal Nature; Williams and Sherif, The Arrest Warrant.

61 *Chuidian* v. *Philippine*, US, 912 F.2d 1095, 1101 (9th Cir. 1990) (emphases in the original); 92 ILR 480 (quoting US House of Representatives, Report No. 94-1487, 1976, pp. 15–16; 1976 USCCAN 6604, 6614). See also *Philippines* v. *Marcos*, US, 665 F.Supp. 793, 797 (N.D.Cal. 1987).

62 *Chuidian* v. *Philippine*, US, 912 F.2d 1095, 1101 (9th Cir. 1990); 92 ILR 480, later reiterated in *Hilao* v. *Marcos*, US, 25 F.3d 1467, 1472 (9th Cir. 1994); 104 ILR 119; and in *Park* v. *Shin*, US, 313 F.3d 1138, 1144 (9th Cir. 2002). See also *Doe I* v. *Israel*, US, 400 F.Supp.2d 86, 104 (D.D.C. 2005); *Velasco* v. *Indonesia*, US, 370 F.3d 392, 399 (4th Cir. 2004); *Doe* v. *Liu*, US, 349 F.Supp.2d 1258, 1281 (N.D.Cal. 2004).

NOTES TO PAGE 435   681

63 *Chuidian* v. *Philippine*, US, 912 F.2d 1095, 1102 (9th Cir. 1990); 92 ILR 480. See also *Velasco* v. *Indonesia*, US, 370 F.3d 392, 399 (4th Cir. 2004).

64 *Chuidian* v. *Philippine*, US, 912 F.2d 1095, 1103 (9th Cir. 1990); 92 ILR 480. This was reaffirmed by the Ninth Circuit in *Trajano* v. *Marcos*, US, 978 F.2d 493, 496 (9th Cir. 1992); 103 ILR 521; *Hilao* v. *Marcos*, US, 25 F.3d 1467, 1470, fn. 2 (9th Cir. 1994); 104 ILR 119; *Park* v. *Shin*, US, 313 F.3d 1138, 1144 (9th Cir. 2002). See also *In re Terrorist Attacks*, US, 538 F.3d 71, 81 (2nd Cir. 2008); *Velasco* v. *Indonesia*, US, 370 F.3d 392, 398 (4th Cir. 2004); *Baumel* v. *Syria*, US, 550 F. Supp.2d 110, 113–115 (D.D.C. 2008); *Belhas* v. *Ya'alon*, US, 515 F.3d 1279, 1283–1284 (D.C.Cir. 2008); affirming *Belhas* v. *Ya'alon*, US, 466 F.Supp.2d 127 (D.D.C. 2006); *In re Terrorist Attacks*, US, 392 F.Supp.2d 539, 551, 553 (S.D.N.Y. 2005); *In re Terrorist Attacks*, US, 349 F.Supp.2d 765, 788 (S.D.N.Y. 2005); *Doe* v. *Liu*, US, 349 F.Supp.2d 1258, 1281 (N.D.Cal. 2004); *Pradhan* v. *Al-Sabah*, US, 299 F.Supp.2d 493, 497 (D.Md. 2004); *Kato* v. *Ishihara*, US, 360 F.3d 106, 108, fn. 1 (2nd Cir. 2004); affirming *Kato* v. *Ishihara*, US, 239 F.Supp.2d 359, 362, fn. 2, 363 (S.D.N.Y. 2002); *Leutwyler* v. *Office*, US, 184 F.Supp.2d 277, 286–287 (S.D.N.Y. 2001); *Dewhurst* v. *Telenor*, US, 83 F.Supp.2d 577, 595 (D.Md. 2000); *Byrd* v. *Corporacion*, US, 182 F.3d 380, 388 (5th Cir. 1999); *Jungquist* v. *Sheikh*, US, 115 F.3d 1020, 1027 (D.C.Cir. 1997); reversing, on other grounds, *Jungquist* v. *Sheikh*, US, 940 F.Supp. 312 (D.D.C. 1996); 113 ILR 522; *Supra* v. *McGonigle*, US, 955 F.Supp. 374, 378 (E.D. Pa. 1997); *El-Fadl* v. *Central Bank*, US, 75 F.3d 668, 671 (D.C.Cir. 1996); *Cabiri* v. *Assasie-Gyimah*, US, 921 F.Supp. 1189, 1197 (S.D.N.Y. 1996); *Tannenbaum* v. *Rabin*, US, 1996 WL 75283, p. 2 (E.D.N.Y. 1996); *Bryks* v. *CBC*, US, 906 F.Supp. 204, 210 (S.D.N.Y. 1995); *Intercontinental* v. *De Gruyter*, US, 822 F.Supp. 662, 674 (C.D.Cal. 1993); *Kline* v. *Kaneko*, US, 685 F.Supp. 386, 389 (S.D.N.Y. 1988); 101 ILR 497; *American Bonded* v. *Compagnie*, US, 653 F.Supp. 861, 863 (N.D.Ill. 1987); *Rios* v. *Marshall*, US, 530 F.Supp. 351, 371, 374 (S.D.N.Y. 1981). But see *Enahoro* v. *Abubakar*, US, 408 F.3d 877, 881–882 (7th Cir. 2005); *Philippines* v. *Marcos*, US, 665 F.Supp. 793, 797 (N.D.Cal. 1987).

65 *Chuidian* v. *Philippine*, US, 912 F.2d 1095, 1103, 1106–1107 (9th Cir. 1990); 92 ILR 480; later reaffirmed in *Park* v. *Shin*, US, 313 F.3d 1138, 1144 (9th Cir. 2002). See also *Sanchez-Espinoza* v. *Reagan*, US, 770 F.2d 202, 207 (D.C.Cir. 1985); 80 ILR 586; *Phaneuf* v. *Indonesia*, US, 106 F.3d 302, 306 (9th Cir. 1997); *Jungquist* v. *Sheikh*, US, 115 F.3d 1020, 1027 (D.C.Cir. 1997); *Doe* v. *Liu*, US, 349 F.Supp.2d 1258, 1281 (N.D.Cal. 2004); *Doe I* v. *Israel*, US, 400 F.Supp.2d 86, 104 (D.D.C. 2005); *Chalabi* v. *Jordan*, US, 503 F.Supp.2d 267, 271 (D.D.C. 2007); *Belhas* v. *Ya'alon*, US, 515 F.3d 1279, 1283–1284 (D.C.Cir. 2008); affirming *Belhas* v. *Ya'alon*, US, 466 F.Supp.2d 127 (D.D.C. 2006); *Matar* v. *Dichter*, US, 563 F.3d 9 (2nd Cir. 2009); affirming *Matar* v. *Dichter*, US, 500 F.Supp.2d 284 (S.D.N.Y. 2007). It appears that such immunity also extends to private contractors when they act under the authority of a foreign State and the relevant acts are sovereign in nature: *Butters* v. *Vance*, US, 225 F.3d 462, 466 (4th Cir. 2000); *Alicog* v. *Saudi Arabia*, US, 860 F.Supp. 379 (S.D.Tex. 1994); 113 ILR 509; affirmed, *Alicog* v. *Saudi Arabia*, US, 79 F.3d 1145 (5th Cir. 1996) (Table).

682 NOTES TO PAGE 435

66 *Keller* v. *Central Bank*, US, 277 F.3d 811, 815 (6th Cir. 2002); *Byrd* v. *Corporacion*, US, 182 F.3d 380, 388 (5th Cir. 1999); *El-Fadl* v. *Central Bank*, US, 75 F.3d 668, 671 (D.C.Cir. 1996).

67 *Trajano* v. *Marcos*, US, 978 F.2d 493, 497 (9th Cir. 1992); 103 ILR 521; reaffirming *Chuidian* v. *Philippine*, US, 912 F.2d 1095, 1106 (9th Cir. 1990); 92 ILR 480; reiterated in *Hilao* v. *Marcos*, US, 25 F.3d 1467, 1472 (9th Cir. 1994); 104 ILR 119 and *Phaneuf* v. *Indonesia*, US, 106 F.3d 302, 306 (9th Cir. 1997). See also *Velasco* v. *Indonesia*, US, 370 F.3d 392, 399 (4th Cir. 2004); *Park* v. *Shin*, US, 313 F.3d 1138, 1144 (9th Cir. 2002); *Byrd* v. *Corporacion*, US, 182 F.3d 380, 388–389 (5th Cir. 1999); *Doe* v. *Bolkiah*, US, 74 F.Supp.2d 969, 973–974 (D.Haw. 1998); *Cabiri* v. *Assasie-Gyimah*, US, 921 F.Supp. 1189, 1197–1198 (S.D.N.Y. 1996); *Xuncax* v. *Gramajo*, US, 886 F.Supp. 162, 175–176 (D.Mass. 1995); 104 ILR 165.

68 *US* v. *Noriega*, US, 117 F.3d 1206, 1212 (11th Cir. 1997); 121 ILR 591; *Abiola* v. *Abubakar*, US, 267 F.Supp.2d 907, 914 (N.D.Ill. 2003) (overruling its own reasoning in *Boshnjaku* v. *Yugoslavia*, US, No. 01 C 4608, 2002 WL 1575067, p. 1 (N.D.Ill. 2002)). For comments on the US practice see Mallory, Resolving; Bass, Ex-Head.

69 *La Reunion* v. *Libya*, US, 477 F.Supp.2d 131, 140 (D.D.C. 2007); *Doe* v. *Roman*, US, 408 F.Supp.2d 272, 277–282 (S.D.Tex. 2005); *Collett* v. *Libya*, US, 362 F.Supp.2d 230, 243–244 (D.D.C. 2005); *Plaintiffs* v. *Jiang*, US, 282 F.Supp.2d 875, 881 (N.D. Ill. 2003); *Abiola* v. *Abubakar*, US, 267 F.Supp.2d 907, 915 (N.D.Ill. 2003); *Tachiona* v. *Mugabe*, US, 169 F.Supp.2d 259, 290 (S.D.N.Y. 2001); *US* v. *Noriega*, US, 117 F.3d 1206, 1212 (11th Cir. 1997); 121 ILR 591; *First American* v. *Al-Nahyan*, US, 948 F.Supp. 1107, 1119 (D.D.C. 1996); 121 ILR 577; *Lafontant* v. *Aristide*, US, 844 F.Supp. 128, 137 (E.D.N.Y. 1994); 103 ILR 581; *Kline* v. *Kaneko*, 535 N.Y.S.2d 303, 305 (N.Y.Sup.Ct. 1988).

70 *Wei* v. *Jiang*, US, 383 F.3d 620, 627 (7th Cir. 2004); affirming *Plaintiffs* v. *Jiang*, US, 282 F.Supp.2d 875, 883 (N.D.Ill. 2003); *Leutwyler* v. *Office*, US, 184 F.Supp.2d 277, 280 (S.D.N.Y. 2001); *US* v. *Noriega*, US, 117 F.3d 1206, 1212 (11th Cir. 1997); 121 ILR 591; affirming *US* v. *Noriega*, US, 746 F.Supp. 1506 (S.D.Fla. 1990); 99 ILR 143; *First American* v. *Al-Nahyan*, US, 948 F.Supp. 1107, 1119 (D.D.C. 1996); 121 ILR 577; *Lafontant* v. *Aristide*, US, 844 F.Supp. 128, 139 (E.D.N.Y. 1994); 103 ILR 581; *Alicog* v. *Saudi Arabia*, US, 860 F.Supp. 379, 382 (S.D.Tex. 1994); 113 ILR 509; affirmed, *Alicog* v. *Saudi Arabia*, US, 79 F.3d 1145 (5th Cir. 1996) (Table); *Kline* v. *Kaneko*, US, 535 N.Y.S.2d 303, 304–305 (N.Y.Sup.Ct. 1988). *Saltany* v. *Reagan*, US, 702 F.Supp. 319, 320 (D.D.C. 1988); 80 ILR 19; affirmed, *Saltany* v. *Reagan*, US, 886 F.2d 438, 440–441 (D.C.Cir. 1989); 87 ILR 679. See also *Li* v. *Bo*, US, 568 F.Supp.2d 35 (D.D.C. 2008). US Department of Justice, Suggestion of Immunity for Pope Benedict XVI.

71 See, e.g., *In re Doe*, US, 860 F.2d 40, 45 (2nd Cir. 1988); 121 ILR 567.

72 ABA, Reforming, 531–536, 541, 598; ABA, Report, 2002, 1261, 1268–1269; Dellapenna, Refining.

73 *Samantar* v. *Yousuf*, US, 130 S.Ct. 2278, 2286–2292 (2010); affirming *Yousuf* v. *Samantar*, US, 552 F.3d 371, 378 (4th Cir. 2009).

NOTES TO PAGES 435–437   683

74 Among other cases, *Chuidian* v. *Philippine*, US, 912 F.2d 1095 (9th Cir. 1990); 92 ILR 480; *In re Terrorist Attacks*, US, 538 F.3d 71 (2nd Cir. 2008); *Keller* v. *Central Bank*, US, 277 F.3d 811 (6th Cir. 2002); *Byrd* v. *Corporacion*, US, 182 F.3d 380 (5th Cir. 1999); *El-Fadl* v. *Central Bank*, US, 75 F.3d 668 (D.C.Cir. 1996).

75 *Pinochet No. 3*, England, 1999, [2000] 1 AC 147, 201, 205; 248; 261–262; 266–267; 277–278; 290; 119 ILR 135, 152, 156, 201, 214–215, 220–221, 231–232, 244–245. For detailed discussion see Yang, State Immunity in the ECHR, 355–359.

76 See *Kingdom of Spain* v. *Pinochet*, England (1999) 119 ILR 253; *Regina* v. *Secretary of State*, England, (2000) 119 ILR 261; the Home Secretary's written answer to a Parliamentary Question. For related proceedings in other States see *Pinochet*, Spain, (1998) 119 ILR 331; *Re Pinochet*, Belgium, (1998) 119 ILR 345. See Sands, *Lawless World*, pp. 23–45 for a vivid account of the drama of the *Pinochet* case. See also Johnson, The Case.

77 See *Philippines* v. *Marcos*, US, 806 F.2d 344 (2nd Cir. 1986); 81 ILR 581; *Philippines* v. *Marcos*, US, 818 F.2d 1473 (9th Cir. 1987); 81 ILR 608; reheard en banc, *Philippines* v. *Marcos*, US, 862 F.2d 1355, 1358 (9th Cir. 1988); 81 ILR 608; *Trajano* v. *Marcos*, US, 878 F.2d 1439 (9th Cir. 1989) (Table); *Trajano* v. *Marcos*, US, 978 F.2d 493 (9th Cir. 1992); 103 ILR 521; *Hilao* v. *Marcos*, US, 25 F.3d 1467 (9th Cir. 1994); 104 ILR 119; *Hilao* v. *Marcos*, US, 94 F.3d 539 (9th Cir. 1996); Damiani, The Power. See also *Marcos* v. *Chambre*, Switzerland, (1987) 82 ILR 53; *Marcos* v. *Federal Department*, Switzerland, (1989) 102 ILR 198.

78 The *Pinochet* case has given rise to a gigantic body of – mostly laudatory – literature. See Fox, The Pinochet Case; Barker, The Future; Denza, *Ex parte Pinochet*; Warbrick, Extradition; O'Keefe, The European; Klabbers, The General; Mitchell, Leave; Bhuta, Justice; Dominicé, Quelques Observations; Handl, The Pinochet Case; Bröhmer, Diplomatic Immunity; Davis, Accountability; Nanda, Human Rights; Bradley and Goldsmith, *Pinochet*; Bröhmer, Immunity; Woodhouse, *The Pinochet Case*; Rodley, Breaking; Villalpando, L'Affaire Pinochet; Swain, A Discussion; Turns, Pinochet's Fallout; Seyedin-Noor, The Spanish Prisoner; Pierson, Pinochet; Solé, The Pinochet Case; Byers, The Law; Nicholls, Reflections; Wedgwood, International; Aceves, Liberalism; Sugarman, The Pinochet Case; Powell and Pillay, Revisiting; Murphy, The Pinochet Judgment; McLachlan, *Pinochet* Revisited; Opara, Sovereign. For exploration of further implications of the *Pinochet* case see Boister and Burchill, The Implications; du Plessis, The Pinochet Cases; Taylor, *Pinochet*; Anderson, An Asian; O'Neill, A New.

79 *Arrest Warrant, ICJ Reports* 2002, p. 3 at 25, para. 61; 128 ILR 1, 81. Emphases added.

80 *Pinochet No. 3*, England, [2000] 1 AC 147, 205 per Lord Browne-Wilkinson (torture not a public function), 217 per Lord Goff (dissenting) (governmental function), 242 per Lord Hope (criminal yet governmental), 257 per Lord Hutton (not a governmental function), 266 per Lord Saville ('official torture'); 270 per Lord Millett ('public and official acts'), and 289–290 per Lord Philips (criminal and official); 119 ILR 135, 156–157, 169, 194–195, 211, 220, 224, 244.

684   NOTES TO PAGES 437–439

81 This is also the definition in s. 134(1) of the 1988 UK Criminal Justice Act. See especially the comment by Lord Millett in *Pinochet No. 3*, England, [2000] 1 AC 147, 277; 119 ILR 135, 231.

82 See *Pinochet No. 3*, England, [2000] 1 AC 147, 205, 248, 266–267, 277, 290; 119 ILR 135, 156, 201, 220–221, 231, 244–245.

83 See the group of '419 scam' and other cases discussed in Chapter 3.

84 *South Africa* v. *Herman Grote*, Netherlands, (1921) 1 AD 22, 23. See also *South Moluccas* v. *Royal Packet*, Netherlands, (1951) 17 ILR 143, 152; *Herbillon* v. *Lentz*, Belgium, (1920) 1 AD 120, 120; *German Immunities Case*, Austria, (1935) 8 AD 246, 246; *Ryuichi* v. *The State*, Japan, (1963) 32 ILR 626, 638–640.

85 *Argentine Republic* v. *Amerada Hess*, US, 488 US 428, 434, 439, 443 (1989); 102 L.Ed.2d 818, 828, 831, 834; 81 ILR 658, 663, 666, 669.

86 *Argentine Republic* v. *Amerada Hess*, US, 488 US 428, 436 (1989); 102 L.Ed.2d 818, 829; 81 ILR 658, 664; reversing *Amerada Hess* v. *Argentine Republic*, US, 830 F.2d 421 (2nd Cir. 1987); 79 ILR 1. For comments see Morrison-Sinclair, Foreign; Stitcher, *Amerada*; DiBiagio, Federal; O'Toole, *Amerada*; Webster, *Amerada*; Campisano, Foreign; Morris, Sovereign; Ho, Foreign.

87 *McElhinney* v. *Williams*, Ireland, 1995, [1996] 1 ILRM 276, 288; 104 ILR 691, 702–703; affirming *McElhinney* v. *Williams*, Ireland, 1994, [1994] 2 ILRM 115, 119–120; 103 ILR 311, 316. Cf. *Border Guards Prosecution Case*, Germany, (1992) 100 ILR 364, 372–373 (soldiers prosecuted for killing unarmed fugitive at the Berlin Wall because their State (German Democratic Republic) no longer existed).

88 *Herbage* v. *Meese*, US, 747 F.Supp. 60, 67 (D.D.C. 1990) (emphasis added); 98 ILR 101; affirmed, *Herbage* v. *Meese*, US, 946 F.2d 1564 (D.C.Cir. 1991) (Table). The District Court statement was quoted with approval in *Jaffe* v. *Miller*, Canada, (1993) 13 OR (3d) 745, 761; 95 ILR 446, 461.

89 *I Congreso del Partido*, England, 1981, [1983] 1 AC 244, 272; 64 ILR 307, 323. The argument was dealt with in like manner in *I Congreso del Partido*, England, 1977, [1978] 1 QB 500, 531–532; 64 ILR 154, 182–183; *I Congreso del Partido*, England, 1979, [1980] 1 Lloyd's Rep 23, 36; 64 ILR 227, 241.

90 See *Carrato* v. *USA*, Canada, (1982) 141 DLR (3d) 456, 458–459; 90 ILR 229, 231–232; *Tritt* v. *USA*, Canada, (1989) 68 OR (2d) 284, 287; 94 ILR 260, 263; affirmed, *Tritt* v. *USA*, Canada, (1994) 45 A.C.W.S. (3d) 1140; *Jaffe* v. *Miller*, Canada, (1990) 73 DLR (4th) 420, 428; 87 ILR 197, 205; affirmed, *Jaffe* v. *Miller*, Canada, (1993) 13 OR (3d) 745, 760, 762; 95 ILR 446, 460, 462; *Australia* v. *Midford*, Malaysia, [1990] 1 Curr LJ 878, 884–885; 86 ILR 640, 651; *Herron* v. *Ireland*, Ireland, Case No. 242/1997 (1997); *South Africa* v. *Herman Grote*, Netherlands, (1921) 1 AD 22, 23; *Indonesia* v. *Van der Haas*, Netherlands, (1958) 26 ILR 181, 182; *LF* v. *Germany*, Netherlands, (1986) 94 ILR 342, 348; *Libya* v. *SpA Imprese*, Italy, (1979) 78 ILR 90, 93; *Greece* v. *Gamet*, Italy, (1957) 24 ILR 209, 211; *Greece* v. *Gamet*, Italy, (1959) 28 ILR 153, 155; *The Cristina*, England, [1938] AC 485, 509; 9 AD 250, 258; *German Immunities Case*, Austria, (1935) 8 AD 246, 246. See also discussion in Chapter 3. Cf. *The Rainbow Warrior Case*, New Zealand, (1985/1986) 74 ILR 241 and *Rainbow Warrior*, Arbitration Tribunal, (1990) 82 ILR 499, in which France did not

NOTES TO PAGES 439–442   685

claim immunity for its agents who, acting on orders from the French Ministry of Defence, had sunk a ship belonging to Greenpeace. For an interesting case concerning whether the UN Security Council resolutions can diminish the sovereignty and therefore the immunity of a State see *Dumez* v. *Iraq*, France, (1999) 127 ILR 144; *État d'Irak* v. *Dumez*, France, 2002, 91 *RCDIP* (2002) 746; 107 *RGDIP* (2003) 1008; *État Irakien* v. *Dumez*, France, 2006, 110 *RGDIP* (2006) 950.

91 *Jaffe* v. *Miller*, Canada, (1993) 13 OR (3d) 745, 760; 95 ILR 446, 460; affirming *Jaffe* v. *Miller*, Canada, (1990) 73 DLR (4th) 420, 428; 87 ILR 197, 205. See also *Schreiber* v. *Attorney General*, Canada, (2000) 187 DLR (4th) 146, 154–155.

92 *Saudi Arabia* v. *Nelson*, US, 507 US 349, 361 (1993); 123 L.Ed.2d 47, 61 (2003); 100 ILR 544, 553.

93 *Jones* v. *Saudi Arabia*, England, [2006] 2 WLR 1424, 1452; [2007] 1 AC 270, 302, para. 85 per Lord Hoffmann; 129 ILR 629, 744. See also Cassese, When, 869; Gattini, War, 234, fn. 41; Fox, Where, 355.

Chapter 11

1 Under the rubric 'Exterritorialität', Bluntschli, *Das moderne Völkerrecht* (containing the preface to the first edition in 1867), pp. 121–129, Articles 135–153. For French translation see Lardy, *Le droit international codifié*.

2 With von Bar and Westlake as Rapporteurs. *AIDI*, Vol. 10 (1888), pp. 16 and 295.

3 IDI, Projet. For some unknown reason, the numbering of the articles was changed (into nine articles) and the wording slightly varied in a later collection of completed projects, see IDI, *Tableau Général*, pp. 344–346. The same irregularity can also be observed with regard to the IDI's subsequent and more recent drafts on State immunity. Also compare various texts with those published on the official IDI website: www.idi-iil.org.

4 'Draft Convention on Competence of Courts in regard to Foreign States, with Comment', 26 *AJIL* (1932), Supplement: Research in International Law, pp. 451–738.

5 The IDI's work on State immunity in 1932 and 1939 did not produce any meaningful additions to the 1891 draft; however, the 1952 session did present some drafts. See especially *AIDI*, Vol. 44-I, 1952, L'immunité de juridiction et d'exécution forcée des Etats étrangers, p. 5 at 5–7; p. 36 ('Projet définitif' (containing nine articles)) and p. 39 ('Projet provisoire de convention sur l'immunité de juridiction et d'exécution forcée des Etats étrangers' (containing seventeen articles)).

6 *AIDI*, Vol. 45-II, 1954, p. 293, Résolution III, L'immunité de juridiction et d'exécution forcée des Etats étrangers' (containing five articles) (English translation on p. 301).

7 *AIDI*, Vol. 64-II, 1991, p. 389, Résolution, Contemporary Problems concerning the Immunity of States in Relation to Questions of Jurisdiction and Enforcement (seven articles altogether). For sessions leading to the 1991 draft see *AIDI*,

686   NOTES TO PAGES 442–443

Vol. 62-I, 1987, p. 13 (Brownlie, Preliminary Report); p. 45 (Brownlie, Definitive Report and Draft Set of Resolutions); *AIDI*, Vol. 63-I, 1989, p. 13 (Brownlie, Supplementary Report); *AIDI*, Vol. 64-I, 1991, p. 80 (Brownlie, Memorandum). Though in substance very much in line with other legal instruments, the 1991 IDI draft in its form adopts Brownlie's formula (see Brownlie, *Principles*, Chapter 16.6, 'The modalities of restrictive immunity', pp. 334–335), which envisages immunity and its exceptions as subject to, on the one hand, 'criteria indicative of the competence of the relevant organs of the forum State to determine the substance of the claim' and, on the other, 'criteria indicative of the incompetence of the organs of the forum State to determine the substance of the claim' (Art. 2(2) and (3)). Such a method, however, fails to take account of the fact that the list of exceptions to immunity has always been in flux and must of necessity remain open-ended: what if some situation arises which is not covered by these two groups of criteria?

8 See ILA, *Report*, 1926, p. 426 (in French). The ILA did not establish a committee on State immunity at this conference.

9 See ILA, *Report*, 1950, pp. xxxv and 204; ILA, *Report*, 1952, pp. vi, xxxvi and 210; ILA, *Report*, 1954, p. xxxviii and 395; ILA, *Report*, 1956, p. xxxi; ILA, *Report*, 1958, p. xxxix.

10 ILA, *Report*, 1978, p. 51; ILA, *Report*, 1980, pp. 52 and 208 ('Preliminary Report of the Working Group').

11 ILA, *Report*, 1982, pp. 5 (Resolution on State immunity with nine draft articles to be designated as 'The ILA Montreal Draft Convention on State Immunity') and 325 ('State Immunity: Final Report of the Committee', containing a section-by-section analysis of the Draft Convention).

12 See ILA, *Report*, 1988, pp. 37 (Resolution on State Immunity, requesting the Committee to consider the new developments since the 1982 Montreal Draft, and whether the 1982 Montreal Draft should be amended) and 973 (Interim Report of the Committee on State Immunity, which spoke of the 'Revival of the Committee on State Immunity'); ILA, *Report*, 1990, pp. 14 (Resolution on State Immunity, recommending various issues to be considered by the Committee) and 393 (First Report); ILA, *Report*, 1992, pp. 10 (Resolution on State Immunity, requesting amendments to the Montreal Draft 1982) and 290 (Second Report); ILA, *Report*, 1994, p. 21 (Resolution on State Immunity, containing 'Revised Buenos Aires Draft Convention on State Immunity' (nine articles)) and 452 (Final Report and Proposal for a Revised Draft Convention on State Immunity, with a section-by-section analysis of the Revised Draft Convention).

13 The ILC established a working group in 1999 to reassess its 1991 draft articles. See below. The IDI returned to the issue of immunity again in 2001, this time concerning the immunity of heads of State. See *AIDI*, Vol. 69, 2001, p. 742, Les immunités de juridiction et d'exécution du chef d'Etat et de gouvernement en droit international; p. 743, Immunities from Jurisdiction and Execution of Heads of State and of Government in International Law (English translation).

14 League of Nations, *Official Journal, Special Supplement*, No. 21, p. 10. Rosenne, *League of Nations Committee*, Vol. 1, Minutes, p. vii. In fact, as early as 1907, the

NOTES TO PAGE 443 687

second Hague Peace Conference had already envisaged a 'preparatory committee' charged with 'ascertaining what subjects are ripe for embodiment in an international regulation', thus sowing 'the seed which was ultimately to burgeon forth first as the Committee of Experts for the Progressive Codification of International Law of the League of Nations, and later as the International Law Commission of the United Nations'. *Ibid.*, Introduction, pp. xxix–xxx. The 1924 Resolution can also be found in 22 *AJIL* (1928), Supplement: Codification of International Law, p. v.

15 By a decision of the Council on 11 December 1924, 6 *League of Nations Official Journal* (1925) 143.

16 See Rosenne, *League of Nations Committee*, Vol. 1, Minutes, pp. 31 and 49 (minutes of the First Session, Geneva, 1–8 April 1925, where the committee seemed to think that 'the legal status of Government ships employed in commerce' was more appropriate); pp. 191 and 195–196 (minutes of the Second Session, Geneva, 12–29 January 1926, where the Committee decided that the topic should now be '*Compétence des tribunaux à l'égard des Etats étrangers*', and appointed Matsuda as rapporteur); pp. 246–250 (minutes of the Third Session, Geneva, 22 March–2 April 1927, where Matsuda reported positively on the subject and was generally supported by the Committee); and pp. 316–317 (minutes of the Fourth Session, Geneva, 22–28 June 1928, where the Committee adopted the Rapporteur's conclusion that the competence of courts with regard to foreign States was a matter which could be considered by an international conference). Note that the limited time available for the Committee (about one to two weeks for each session) to address a host of issues including State immunity hardly permitted any extensive study.

17 See Letter dated 2 April 1927, from the Chairman of the Committee to the Secretary-General, Reporting on the Work of the Third Session of the Committee, LN Document C.200.M.74.1927.V, Rosenne, *League of Nations Committee*, Vol. 2, Documents, p. 29. See also 22 *AJIL* (1928), Supplement, p. 1.

18 LN Document A.15.1928.V, Annex I, Questionnaire 11, Rosenne, *League of Nations Committee*, Vol. 2, Documents, p. 371 at 411. The Committee reached its conclusion on the basis of a report by a Sub-Committee on this particular subject, dated 11 October 1926, despite some disagreement within that Sub-Committee. Matsuda, the Rapporteur, maintained that: 'At the present time ... it would be hard to extract ... any definite or precise conclusion which could be used as the basis of a uniform arrangement'; whereas Diena opined that 'the question of the competence of courts with regard to foreign States should be regarded ... as a question concerning which an international agreement is not only desirable but also realisable'. *Ibid.*, at pp. 417 and 419. See also 22 *AJIL* (1928), Supplement, p. 117 at 117, 128 and 132.

19 See the analysis of the replies conducted by the Secretariat, LN Document A.15.1928.V, Annex III, Rosenne, *League of Nations Committee*, Vol. 2, Documents, p. 452 at 455–456. Actually, if one also considers the observations made by the members of the Committee of Experts, three more States, which did not reply to the Questionnaire, may be added to the list of supporters. See

688   NOTES TO PAGES 443-445

Rosenne, *League of Nations Committee*, Vol. 1, Minutes, pp. 316–317, minutes of the Fourth Session, Geneva, 22–28 June 1928. At this time the League of Nations had fifty-six member States. See Walters, *A History*, Vol. I, pp. 64–65. One must also note that, in agreeing to the desirability of an international convention these States expressed diametrically opposed views as to whether immunity should be absolute (see the replies of Brazil and Germany) or restrictive (see those of the Netherlands, Sweden and Switzerland). Rosenne, *League of Nations Committee*, Vol. 2, pp. 425, 432, 439, 446–447 and 450.

20 Committee of Experts, Second Report to the Council of the League of Nations on the Questions Which Appear Ripe for International Regulation, dated 27 June 1928, LN Document A.15.1928.V, Rosenne, *League of Nations Committee*, Vol. 2, Documents, p. 367 at 369.

21 Committee of Experts, Report to the Council of the League of Nations on the Questions Which Appear Ripe for International Regulation, dated 2 April 1927, LN Document C.196.M.70.1927.V, Rosenne, *League of Nations Committee*, Vol. 2, Documents, p. 31. See also 22 *AJIL* (1928), Supplement, p. 4.

22 These were: (1) Nationality; (2) Territorial waters; and (3) Responsibility of States for damage done in their territory to the person or property of foreigners. League of Nations, *Official Journal, Special Supplement*, No. 53, p. 9. Rosenne (ed.), *League of Nations Conference*, 1975 (in four volumes), Vol. 1, p. ix. The resolution of 27 September 1927 can also be found in 23 *AJIL* (1929), Supplement: Codification of International Law, p. 2.

23 See generally Rosenne, *League of Nations Conference*.

24 See Committee of Experts, General Report on Procedure, LN Document C.197. M.71.1927.V (dated 2 April 1927) and Report to the Council of the League of Nations on the Procedure to be Followed in regard to the Question of the Procedure of International Conferences and the Procedure for the Conclusion and Drafting of Treaties, LN Document C.198.M.72.1927.V (dated 2 April 1927), Rosenne, *League of Nations Committee*, Vol. 2, Documents, pp. 311 and 313. See also 22 *AJIL* (1928), Supplement, pp. 39 and 43. The procedure was further formalized and more fully stated by a resolution of the 1930 First Conference for the Codification of International Law and given official approval by a resolution of the Twelfth Assembly of the League of Nations on 25 September 1931. League of Nations, *Official Journal, Special Supplement*, No. 92, p. 9. The texts of both the Hague Conference and the Assembly resolutions can be found in 26 *AJIL* (1932) pp. 137 and 141.

25 These were: the 1919 Treaty of Peace between the Allied and Associated Powers and Germany (Treaty of Versailles); 1919 Treaty of Saint-Germain (Austria); 1919 Treaty of Neuilly (Bulgaria); 1920 Treaty of Trianon (Hungary); and 1920 Treaty of Sèvres (Turkey). Carnegie Endowment, *The Treaties of Peace 1919–1923*, Vol. I, pp. 3, 267 and 461; Vol. II, pp. 653 and 789.

26 See also Treaty of Saint-Germain, Art. 220; Treaty of Trianon, Art. 203; Treaty of Neuilly, Art. 150. For some reason, the Treaty of Sèvres does not contain such a provision.

27 Contrary to the belief expressed in Harvard Research, 26 *AJIL* (1932) 474.

28 Contrary to the belief expressed in *Dralle* v. *Czechoslovakia*, Austria, (1950) 17 ILR 155, 161–162 and *Empire of Iran Case*, Germany, (1963) 45 ILR 57, 73.

29 The Committee of Experts submitted a report, 'Legal Status of Government Ships Employed in Commerce', to the Council of the League of Nations, LN Document C.52.M.29.1926.V (dated 29 January 1926), Rosenne, *League of Nations Committee*, Vol. 2, Documents, pp. 15–24. See also 20 *AJIL* (1926), Supplement, pp. 260–278. At the end of the report the Committee proposed certain amendments to the draft prepared by the International Maritime Committee, but, judging from the provisions of the Convention itself, these proposals were ignored by the Brussels diplomatic conference.

30 It was held that a ship had to be owned, possessed or operated by a State in order to enjoy immunity: *The Visurgis*, Germany, (1937/1938) 9 AD 284, 285, 287–288; *The Rigmor*, Sweden, (1942) 10 AD 240; *Russian* v. *Carlbom*, Sweden, (1944) 12 AD 112, 113. For a negative attitude towards the Brussels Convention see *Weber* v. *USSR*, Holland, (1942) 11 AD 140, 141.

31 As opposed to 'warships and other government ships operated for non-commercial purposes'. See the 1958 Convention on the Territorial Sea and the Contiguous Zone, Arts. 21–23; 1958 Convention on the High Seas, Arts. 8–9; 1982 UN Convention on the Law of the Sea, Arts. 32, 95, 96 and 236.

32 Article 16(2) and (4) of the 2004 UN Convention preserves the special position of 'warships, naval auxiliaries, [and] other vessels owned or operated by a State and used, for the time being, only on government non-commercial service' and their cargo. For other issues see *Odyssey* v. *Unidentified*, US, 675 F.Supp.2d 1126 (M.D.Fla. 2009); Dehner, Vessel-Source Pollution; Vierucci, Le Statut juridique; Harris, Protecting.

33 See, e.g., *Senerman* v. *Cuba*, Chile, (1975) 65 ILR 29, 30.

34 The European Convention has now been ratified by eight States: Austria, Belgium, Cyprus, Germany, Luxembourg, the Netherlands, Switzerland, and the UK. Portugal has signed but not ratified it. See also Council of Europe, *Explanatory Reports*, 1972; Centres de Droit International, *L'immunité*, 1969.

35 For mixed and conflicting views on the status of the European Convention (whether it codifies customary international law) see *Distomo Massacre Case*, Greece, (2000) 129 ILR 513, 517; *Distomo Massacre Case*, Germany, (2003) 129 ILR 556, 561, Ground B.I.2(c)); *Muller* v. *USA*, Germany, (1998) 114 ILR 512, 517; *McElhinney* v. *Williams*, Ireland, 1995, [1996] 1 ILRM 276, 287–288; 104 ILR 691, 701–702; *M* v. *Egypt*, Switzerland, (1994) 116 ILR 656, 659–661, Ground 3b and d and 663, Ground 4b; *S* v. *Romania*, Switzerland, (1987) 82 ILR 45, 48, Ground 2; *Spain* v. *Company X*, Switzerland, (1986) 82 ILR 38, 40, Ground 3a; *Libya* v. *Actimon*, Switzerland, (1985) 82 ILR 30, 33, Ground 4; *Italian* v. *X*, Switzerland, (1985) 82 ILR 23, 25, Ground 3; *S* v. *India*, Switzerland, (1984) 82 ILR 13, 21, Ground 4c; *Banco* v. *Banco Cattolica*, Switzerland, (1984) 82 ILR 10, 13, Ground 4b; *Egypt* v. *Cinetelevision*, Switzerland, (1979) 65 ILR 425, 430–431, Ground 4b and 4c; *Banque Centrale* v. *Weston*, Switzerland, (1978) 65 ILR 417, 419, Ground 2a, 421–422, Ground 2e, and 422–423, Ground 3; *X* v. *USA*, Switzerland, (1995) 116 ILR 668, 675; *Seidenschmidt* v. *USA*, Austria, (1992) 116 ILR 530, 532; *French*

690   NOTES TO PAGE 446

Consular Employee Claim Case, Austria, (1989) 86 ILR 583, 585; *De Queiroz v. Portugal*, Belgium, (1992) 115 ILR 430, 433–434; *Morocco v. DR*, Belgium, (1989) 115 ILR 421, 422; *Abbott v. South Africa*, Spain, (1992) 113 ILR 411, 420–421; *Diana v. South Africa*, Spain, (1986) 86 ILR 512, 514–515; *Norwegian Embassy v. Quattri*, Italy, (1991) 114 ILR 525, 529; *British Consulate-General v. Toglia*, Italy, (1989) 101 ILR 379, 383; *Cristiani v. Italian*, Italy, (1985) 87 ILR 20, 27; *Bari v. Jasbez*, Italy, (1977) 77 ILR 602, 607; *I Congreso del Partido*, England, 1981, [1983] 1 AC 244, 260–261; 64 ILR 307, 312; *Holland v. Lampen-Wolfe*, England, [2000] 1 WLR 1573, 1583; 119 ILR 367, 378; *Sengupta v. India*, England, 1982, [1983] ICR 221, 230; 64 ILR 352, 362; *Arias v. Venezuela*, Netherlands, (1998) 128 ILR 684, 685, para. 4.4; *LM v. Netherlands*, Netherlands, (1998) 128 ILR 681, 682; *LF v. Germany*, Netherlands, (1986) 94 ILR 342, 346–347; *Governor v. Sutton*, New Zealand, 1994, [1995] 1 NZLR 426, 433; 104 ILR 508, 517; *Hanna v. Turkish*, Finland, 1993, noted in 5 *Finnish YIL* (1994) 408, 409; *Case against the USA*, Norway, 2001, noted in 70 *Nordic JIL* (2001) 547, 551; *Stukonis v. Embassy*, Lithuania, 1998, noted in 2 *Baltic YIL* (2002) 270, 270; *Cudak v. Embassy*, Lithuania, 2001, noted in 3 *Baltic YIL* (2003) 320, 320. See also von Hennigs, European Convention.

36 Inter-American Juridical Committee, The Inter-American Draft Convention on Jurisdictional Immunity of States of 1983, 22 ILM 292 (1983).

37 Council of Europe, *Explanatory Reports*, 1972, p. 38, para. 113. 'Other conventions' would no doubt refer to such nuclear liability conventions as the 1960 Paris Convention; 1963 Brussels Convention; 1963 Vienna Convention; 1988 Joint Protocol relating to the Application of the Paris and Vienna Conventions; 1997 Protocol to Amend the Vienna Convention; and the 1997 Convention on Supplementary Compensation for Nuclear Damage (not yet in force). The UK SIA, which gives effect to the European Convention, also excludes nuclear matters from its ambit (s. 16(3)).

38 The ILC was established by GA Resolution 174 (II) (1947) and opened its first annual session on 12 April 1949.

39 Survey of International Law, 1949, p. 31, para. 52. By 'all its aspects' the *Survey* meant 'the entire field of jurisdictional immunities of States and their property, of their public vessels, of their sovereigns, and of their armed forces' (pp. 30–31, para. 50) The 1949 *Survey* was actually the work of Hersch Lauterpacht, as was acknowledged by the UN Secretariat at the 535th meeting of the ILC in 1960, see *YILC*, 1960-I, p. 52, para. 33. The 1949 *Survey* is reproduced in Elihu Lauterpacht, *International Law*, p. 445. See also Briggs, *The International Law Commission*, pp. 169–176. For an interesting discussion of the background to the 1949 *Survey* see Koskenniemi, Hersch Lauterpacht, pp. 648–9.

40 ILC, Report, *YILC*, 1949, p. 277 at 281, paras. 16 and 20. The plan was endorsed by the General Assembly in its Resolution 373 (IV) (1949).

41 See various 'working papers' prepared by the Secretariat: Future Work, *YILC*, 1962-II, p. 84 at 89–90, paras. 50–68, esp. para. 65; Organization of Future Work, *YILC*, 1967-II, p. 337 at 339, para. 12(iii); Review of the Commission's

NOTES TO PAGES 446–447   691

Programme, annexed to the Report of the ILC, *YILC*, 1968-II, p. 226 at 228, para. 5(3); Review of the Commission's Programme, *YILC*, 1970-II, p. 247 at 258–259. paras. 60–63; and Survey of International Law, *YILC*, pp. 18–21, paras. 67–79, esp. paras. 68 and 75.

42 ILC, Report, *YILC*, 1977-II-2, p. 130, para. 110.

43 UNGA Resolution 32/151 (1977), para. 7.

44 ILC, Report, *YILC*, 1978-II-2, Chapter VIII-D, p. 152 at 153, paras. 188 and 190, and Annex to Chapter VIII-D, Report of the Working Group. The call for comments and materials was repeated time and again. See, e.g., ILC, Report, *YILC*, 1979-II-2, Chapter VII, p. 185 at 186, para. 183; ILC, Report, *YILC*, 1987-II-2, Chapter VI (B), p. 53, para. 222.

45 See GA Resolution 33/139 (1978), paras. 3 and 6; Resolution 34/141 (1979), para. 4(e); Resolution 35/163 (1980), para. 4(e); Resolution 36/114 (1981), para. 3(b)(iv); Resolution 37/111 (1982), para. 3; Resolution 38/138 (1983), para. 3; Resolution 39/85 (1984), para. 3; Resolution 40/75 (1985), para. 3; Resolution 41/81 (1986), para. 3; Resolution 42/156 (1987), paras. 3; Resolution 43/169 (1988), para. 3; Resolution 44/35 (1989), para. 2; Resolution 45/41 (1990), para. 2.

46 ILC, Report, *YILC*, 1983-II-2, Chapter III, p. 17 at 22, 25–34 and 36–38. In fact, from the very beginning the ILC indicated its inclination towards the restrictive doctrine: ILC, Report, *YILC*, 1978-II-2, Annex to Chapter VIII-D, Report of the Working Group, pp. 154–155, paras. 27–29 (tentatively suggesting 'limitations' to immunity based on a distinction between '*acta jure imperii*, or acts of sovereign authority, as distinct from *acta jure gestionis* or *jure negotii*'); ILC, Report, *YILC*, 1979-II-2, Chapter VII, p. 185 at 186, paras. 176 and 178; Sucharitkul, Preliminary Report, *YILC*, 1979-II-1, Chapter III-E, p. 227 at 241–243.

47 See the list of ILC reports in 'Legal Instruments and Codification Documents'. For a convenient guide see also the official ILC website: http://untreaty.un. org/ilc/guide/4_1.htm.

48 Eleven reports in total, eight by Sompong Sucharitkul and three by Motoo Ogiso: Sucharitkul, Preliminary Report, *YILC*, 1979-II-1, p. 227; Second Report, *YILC*, 1980-II-1, p. 199; Third Report, *YILC*, 1981-II-1, p. 125; Fourth Report, *YILC*, 1982-II-1, p. 199; Fifth Report, *YILC*, 1983-II-1, p. 25; Sixth Report, *YILC*, 1984-II-1, p. 5; Seventh Report, *YILC*, 1985-II-1, p. 21; Eighth Report, *YILC*, 1986-II-1, p. 21; Ogiso, Preliminary Report, *YILC*, 1988-II-1, p. 96; Second Report, *YILC*, 1989-II-1, p. 59; Third Report, *YILC*, 1990-II-1, p. 3.

49 The General Assembly repeatedly urged all the member States to respond in writing to the requests of the International Law Commission for comments, observations and replies to questionnaires and for materials on topics in its programme of work (including State immunity), see GA Resolution 35/163 (1980), para. 7; Resolution 36/114 (1981), para. 7; Resolution 37/111 (1982), para. 6; Resolution 38/138 (1983), para. 6; Resolution 39/85 (1984), para. 6; Resolution 40/75 (1985), para. 6; Resolution 41/81 (1986), paras. 8–9; Resolution 42/156 (1987), paras. 9–10; Resolution 43/169 (1988), para. 11; Resolution 44/35 (1989), para. 11; Resolution 45/41 (1990), para. 13. Still, only fifty-seven States

692   NOTES TO PAGES 447-448

(Argentina, Australia, Austria, Barbados, Belgium, Brazil, Bulgaria, Burma, Byelorussia, Cameroon, Canada, Chile, China, Colombia, Czechoslovakia, Denmark, Ecuador, Egypt, Finland, France, German Democratic Republic, Federal Republic of Germany, Greece, Hungary, Iceland, Italy, Japan, Kenya, Lebanon, Madagascar, Mexico, Netherlands, Norway, Pakistan, Philippines, Poland, Portugal, Qatar, Romania, Senegal, Singapore, South Africa, Spain, Sudan, Suriname, Sweden, Switzerland, Syria, Thailand, Togo, Trinidad and Tobago, Tunisia, USSR, UK, USA, Venezuela, Yugoslavia) responded, and many of them said that they did not have any relevant domestic practice. Only twenty-seven States actually responded to a questionnaire prepared by the ILC. The information and comments received in 1981 were reproduced in *Materials on Jurisdictional Immunities*, 1982; the comments and observations on the draft articles received in 1988 were reproduced in *YILC*, 1988-II-1, p. 45. The request for information later proved not only necessary but also highly prudential, for it appears that later some criticism was levelled against the ILC for deducing rules from the practice of only a small number of States: see Sucharitkul, Fifth Report, *YILC*, 1983-II-1, p. 25 at 29–30, paras. 16–17 and 22–23, where the Special Rapporteur turned uncharacteristically polemical and defensive, obviously in response to such an accusation. In GA Resolution 46/55 (1991), para. 2, the General Assembly again specifically invited the States to submit their comments and observations on the ILC draft articles.

50 ILC, Report, *YILC*, 1991-II-2, p. 12, Chapter II, paras. 23, 25 and 28. The Draft Articles and Commentaries thereto are contained in Chapter II.D.

51 GA Resolution 46/54 (1991), para. 2; Resolution 46/55 (1991), para. 1.

52 GA Resolution 46/55 (1991), para. 4; re-established for the Forty-eighth Session by GA decision 47/414 (1992). At the Forty-ninth Session, however, the form was changed into informal consultations instead of a working group: GA decision 48/413 (1993). See Report of the Working Group, 3 November 1992, A/C.6/47/L.10, para. 1; Report of the Working Group, 11 November 1993, A/C.6/48/L.4 and Corr. 2, para. 1; Report of the Chairman of the informal consultations held in the Sixth Committee, 4 October 1994, A/C.6/49/L.2, para. 1.

53 See Report of the Working Group, 1992, A/C.6/47/L.10; Report of the Working Group, 1993, A/C.6/48/L.4 and Corr. 2; Report of the Chairman of the informal consultations held in the Sixth Committee, 1994, A/C.6/49/L.2.

54 See Report of the Working Group, 1992, A/C.6/47/L.10, paras. 5, 15–20, 21–25, 31–34; Report of the Working Group, 1993, A/C.6/48/L.4 and Corr. 2, para. 6; GAOR, Forty-eighth Session, SRSC, 15 November 1993, A/C.6/48/SR.29, para. 15; Report of the Chairman of the informal consultations held in the Sixth Committee, 1994, A/C.6/49/L.2, Part II; GAOR, Forty-ninth Session, SRSC, 6 October 1994, A/C.6/49/SR.7, para. 47; GAOR, Forty-ninth Session, SRSC, 11 November 1994, A/C.6/49/SR.32, para. 15.

55 See Report of the Working Group, 3 November 1992, A/C.6/47/L.10, paras. 15–20; Report of the Working Group, 11 November 1993, A/C.6/48/L.4 and Corr. 2, paras. 36–48; Report of the Chairman of the informal consultations held in the Sixth Committee, 4 October 1994, A/C.6/49/L.2, para. 5.

NOTES TO PAGE 448   693

56 For this 'nature only' position see GAOR, Forty-sixth Session, SRSC, 28 October 1991, A/C.6/46/SR.22, para. 67 (Poland); GAOR, Forty-sixth Session, SRSC, 30 October 1991, A/C.6/46/SR.24, para. 15 (US), para. 24 (Uruguay), para. 74 (Belgium); GAOR, Forty-sixth Session, SRSC, 30 October 1991, A/C.6/46/SR.25, para. 5 (Austria), para. 18 (UK); Report of the Working Group, 3 November 1992, A/C.6/47/L.10, para. 15 (Chairman's proposal); Report of the Working Group, 11 November 1993, A/C.6/48/L.4 and Corr. 2, Annex, Proposals C (US), D (Spain), E (Chairman of the Working Group); G (Australia); Note verbale dated 12 August 1993 from the Permanent Representative of Belgium to the United Nations addressed to the Secretary-General, A/48/313, p. 3; GAOR, Forty-eighth Session, SRSC, 15 November 1993, A/C.6/48/SR.29, para. 47 (UK), paras. 55–56 (Germany), para. 63 (Belgium), para. 101 (US); Report of the Chairman on the informal consultations held in the Sixth Committee, 4 October 1994, A/C.6/49/L.2, para. 6 (Chairman's compromise solution); GAOR, Forty-ninth Session, SRSC, 11 November 1994, A/C.6/49/SR.32, para. 7 (Japan, retracting from its previous insistence on purpose); para. 11 (UK), paras. 22–24 (Germany), para. 35 (South Korea), para. 44 (Austria), para. 47 (US), paras. 52–53 (Australia); GAOR, Forty-ninth Session, SRSC, 14 November 1994, A/C.6/49/SR.33, para. 22 (Israel).

57 For this 'purpose also' position see GAOR, Forty-sixth Session, SRSC, 29 October 1991, A/C.6/46/SR.23, para. 32 (France), para. 66 (Japan); GAOR, Forty-sixth Session, SRSC, 30 October 1991, A/C.6/46/SR.24, para. 49 (Madagascar); GAOR, Forty-sixth Session, SRSC, 30 October 1991, A/C.6/46/SR.25, para. 41 (India); GAOR, Forty-sixth Session, SRSC, 1 November 1991, A/C.6/46/SR.27, para. 6 (Colombia), para. 45 (Bahrain); GAOR, Forty-sixth Session, SRSC, 7 November 1991, A/C.6/46/SR.32, para. 75 (Cameroon, implicitly); GAOR, Forty-sixth Session, SRSC, 13 November 1991, A/C.6/46/SR.36, para. 12 (Algeria); GAOR, Forty-sixth Session, SRSC, 13 November 1991, A/C.6/46/SR.37, paras. 9–12 (Philippines); GAOR, Forty-sixth Session, SRSC, 10 November 1992, A/C.6/47/SR.32, para. 9 (Japan); Report of the Working Group, 11 November 1993, A/C.6/48/L.4 and Corr. 2, Annex, Proposal F (France); GAOR, Forty-eighth Session, SRSC, 15 November 1993, A/C.6/48/SR.29, paras. 22–24 (France); para. 67 (Algeria), para. 72 (Japan), para. 84 (China), para. 89 (India); GAOR, Forty-ninth Session, SRSC, 11 November 1994, A/C.6/49/SR.32, para. 18 (China); GAOR, Forty-ninth Session, SRSC, 14 November 1994, A/C.6/49/SR.33, para. 4 (France), para. 10 (India), para. 17 (Algeria). See also Report of the Secretary-General, 19 August 1999, A/54/266, p. 3 (Lebanon), p. 4 (Qatar).

58 See GAOR, Forty-sixth Session, SRSC, 29 October 1991, A/C.6/46/SR.23, para. 7 (Germany); GAOR, Forty-sixth Session, SRSC, 30 October 1991, A/C.6/46/SR.25, para. 45 (Bulgaria, though preferring nature only); GAOR, Forty-sixth Session, SRSC, 7 November 1991, A/C.6/46/SR.33, para. 12 (Indonesia); GAOR, Forty-sixth Session, SRSC, 10 November 1992, A/C.6/47/SR.32, para. 33 (UK); see Note verbale dated 6 October 1993 from the Permanent Mission of the Republic of Bulgaria to the United Nations addressed to the Secretary-General, A/C.6/48/3, para. 5 (while expressing a preference for 'nature'); GAOR, Forty-eighth

694   NOTES TO PAGES 448–449

Session, SRSC, 15 November 1993, A/C.6/48/SR.29, para. 34 (Australia, Canada, New Zealand); GAOR, Forty-ninth Session, SRSC, 11 November 1994, A/C.6/49/SR.32, para. 52 (Australia).

59 For discussion see Chapter 3. The final UN Convention provision on 'purpose' may be traced to Spain's proposal, see Report of the Working Group, 11 November 1993, A/C.6/48/L.4 and Corr. 2, Annex, Proposal H (Spain); to a proposal by a small group composed of Australia, China, France, the Russian Federation and Spain, see Report of the Working Group, 11 November 1993, A/C.6/48/L.4 and Corr. 2, Annex, Proposal I; as well as to a proposal by the Chairman, see Report of the Working Group, 11 November 1993, A/C.6/48/L.4 and Corr. 2, Annex, Proposal J (Chairman).

60 See Report of the Working Group, 3 November 1992, A/C.6/47/L.10, paras. 31–34; Report of the Working Group, 11 November 1993, A/C.6/48/L.4 and Corr. 2, paras. 49–57; Report of the Chairman of the informal consultations held in the Sixth Committee, 4 October 1994, A/C.6/49/L.2, para. 7.

61 GAOR, Forty-sixth Session, SRSC, 29 October 1991, A/C.6/46/SR.23, paras. 15–17 (Czechoslovakia), para. 55 (Belarus), para. 67 (Japan), paras. 92–93 (China), paras. 41–42 (USSR); GAOR, Forty-sixth Session, SRSC, 30 October 1991, A/C.6/46/SR.24, para. 56 (Madagascar); GAOR, Forty-sixth Session, SRSC, 1 November 1991, A/C.6/46/SR.27, para. 47 (Bahrain); GAOR, Forty-sixth Session, SRSC, 7 November 1991, A/C.6/46/SR.33, para. 12 (Indonesia); GAOR, Forty-sixth Session, SRSC, 10 November 1992, A/C.6/47/SR.32, para. 8 (Japan), para. 14 (China), para. 18 (Australia, Canada, New Zealand), para. 41 (Myanmar); Note verbale dated 6 October 1993 from the Permanent Mission of the Republic of Bulgaria to the United Nations addressed to the Secretary-General, A/C.6/48/3, para. 6; Report of the Working Group, 11 November 1993, A/C.6/48/L.4 and Corr. 2, Annex, Proposal O (Russian Federation); GAOR, Forty-eighth Session, SRSC, 15 November 1993, A/C.6/48/SR.29, para. 83 (China), paras. 90 and 97 (India); GAOR, Forty-ninth Session, SRSC, 11 November 1994, A/C.6/49/SR.32, para. 19 (China); GAOR, Forty-ninth Session, SRSC, 14 November 1994, A/C.6/49/SR.33, para. 11 (India). See also Report of the Secretary-General, 19 August 1999, A/54/266, p. 3 (Lebanon), p. 5 (Qatar).

62 See GAOR, Forty-sixth Session, SRSC, 29 October 1991, A/C.6/46/SR.23, para. 9 (Germany); GAOR, Forty-sixth Session, SRSC, 30 October 1991, A/C.6/46/SR.24, para. 16 (US); Report of the Working Group, 11 November 1993, A/C.6/48/L.4 and Corr. 2, Annex, Proposal K (UK); GAOR, Forty-eighth Session, SRSC, 15 November 1993, A/C.6/48/SR.29, para. 49 (UK), para. 58 (France), para. 73 (Japan); GAOR, Forty-ninth Session, SRSC, 11 November 1994, A/C.6/49/SR.32, para. 10 (UK), para. 27 (Germany).

63 See GAOR, Forty-sixth Session, SRSC, 29 October 1991, A/C.6/46/SR.23, para. 2 (Australia); GAOR, Forty-sixth Session, SRSC, 30 October 1991, A/C.6/46/SR.25, para. 20 (UK, demanding clarification); GAOR, Forty-sixth Session, SRSC, 10 November 1992, A/C.6/47/SR.32, para. 32 (UK); Report of the Working Group, 11 November 1993, A/C.6/48/L.4 and Corr. 2, Annex, Proposal L (Australia) (when the State acts as a guarantor of the liability of a State enterprise);

NOTES TO PAGE 449   695

Proposal M (Chairman) (guarantor); Proposal N (US) (guarantor or 'where adhering to the separate juridical status of the State enterprise or other entity would result in fraud or injustice'); Report of the Chairman of the informal consultations held in the Sixth Committee, 4 October 1994, A/C.6/49/L.2, paras. 7–8 (Chairman of the informal consultations) (State enterprise acting as authorized agent of the State; State as guarantor of the enterprise or State committing fraud).

64 See Report of the Working Group, 3 November 1992, A/C.6/47/L.10, paras. 21–25; Report of the Working Group, 11 November 1993, A/C.6/48/L.4 and Corr. 2, paras. 67–80; Report of the Chairman of the informal consultations held in the Sixth Committee, 4 October 1994, A/C.6/49/L.2, para. 11.

65 For the requirement of a connection see GAOR, Forty-sixth Session, SRSC, 29 October 1991, A/C.6/46/SR.23, para. 25 (Czechoslovakia); Note verbale dated 30 September 1993 from the Permanent Representative of Japan to the United Nations addressed to the Secretary-General, A/48/464, para. 10; GAOR, Forty-eighth Session, SRSC, 15 November 1993, A/C.6/48/SR.29, para. 25 (France), para. 68 (Algeria), para. 74 (Japan), para. 85 (China), para. 92 (India); GAOR, Forty-ninth Session, SRSC, 11 November 1994, A/C.6/49/SR.32, para. 8 (Japan), para. 20 (China); GAOR, Forty-ninth Session, SRSC, 14 November 1994, A/C.6/49/SR.33, para. 6 (France), para. 13 (India), para. 18 (Algeria); Report of the Secretary-General, 20 August 1997, A/52/294, Reply from Argentina, para. 29. See also Report of the Secretary-General, 19 August 1999, A/54/266, p. 4 (Lebanon, in support of Arts. 18–19 as drafted by the ILC), p. 5 (Qatar, same).

66 For opposition to the link requirement see GAOR, Forty-sixth Session, SRSC, 30 October 1991, A/C.6/46/SR.25, para. 8 (Austria), para. 19 (UK); GAOR, Forty-sixth Session, SRSC, 10 November 1992, A/C.6/47/SR.32, para. 18 (Australia, Canada, New Zealand); Note verbale dated 12 August 1993 from the Permanent Representative of Belgium to the United Nations addressed to the Secretary-General, A/48/313, p. 6; GAOR, Forty-eighth Session, SRSC, 15 November 1993, A/C.6/48/SR.29, para. 51 (UK), para. 57 (Germany), para. 64 (Belgium); GAOR, Forty-ninth Session, SRSC, 11 November 1994, A/C.6/49/SR.32, para. 12 (UK), paras. 25–26 (Germany), paras. 54–55 (Australia); GAOR, Forty-ninth Session, SRSC, 14 November 1994, A/C.6/49/SR.33, para. 23 (Israel).

67 Report of the Working Group, 3 November 1992, A/C.6/47/L.10, para. 21; Report of the Working Group, 11 November 1993, A/C.6/48/L.4 and Corr. 2, para. 74; Report of the Chairman of the informal consultations held in the Sixth Committee, 4 October 1994, A/C.6/49/L.2, paras. 12–13.

68 See GAOR, Forty-eighth Session, SRSC, 15 November 1993, A/C.6/48/SR.29, para. 34 (Australia, Canada, New Zealand); GAOR, Forty-ninth Session, SRSC, 11 November 1994, A/C.6/49/SR.32, para. 45 (Austria).

69 See GAOR, Forty-sixth Session, SRSC, 28 October 1991, A/C.6/46/SR.22, paras. 63–64 (Brazil), paras. 66, 68 (Poland); GAOR, Forty-sixth Session, SRSC, 29 October 1991, A/C.6/46/SR.23, para. 6 (Australia), para. 7 (Germany), paras. 30–31 and 39 (France), paras. 44 and 48 (Ireland), paras. 52 and 58 (Belarus), para. 73 (Cyprus), paras. 99–101 (Spain), para. 105 (Switzerland); GAOR, Forty-

696   NOTES TO PAGE 449

sixth Session, SRSC, 30 October 1991, A/C.6/46/SR.24, para. 21 (Uruguay), para. 32 (Angola), para. 36 (Venezuela), paras. 40 and 44 (USSR), para. 45 (Madagascar), para. 84 (Italy); GAOR, Forty-sixth Session, SRSC, 30 October 1991, A/C.6/46/SR.25, para. 1 (Iceland, speaking for the Nordic countries), para. 2 (Austria), paras. 15–16 (UK), para. 31 (Morocco), para. 36 (Sri Lanka), paras. 40–42 (India), para. 43 (Bulgaria); GAOR, Forty-sixth Session, SRSC, 1 November 1991, A/C.6/46/SR.27, para. 5 (Colombia), para. 22 (Ukraine), para. 32 (Nigeria), para. 43 (Bahrain); GAOR, Forty-sixth Session, SRSC, 7 November 1991, A/C.6/46/SR.33, para. 12 (Indonesia); GAOR, Forty-sixth Session, SRSC, 11 November 1991, A/C.6/46/SR.34, para. 27 (Turkey); GAOR, Forty-sixth Session, SRSC, 12 November 1991, A/C.6/46/SR.35, para. 4 (Argentina); GAOR, Forty-sixth Session, SRSC, 13 November 1991, A/C.6/46/SR.36, para. 11 (Algeria); GAOR, Forty-sixth Session, SRSC, 10 November 1992, A/C.6/47/SR.32, para. 23 (Russia), para. 38 (Belarus), para. 45 (France); Note verbale dated 12 August 1993 from the Permanent Representative of Belgium to the United Nations addressed to the Secretary-General, A/48/313, para. 1; Note verbale dated 30 September 1993 from the Permanent Representative of Japan to the United Nations addressed to the Secretary-General, A/48/464, paras. 2–3; Note verbale dated 6 October 1993 from the Permanent Mission of the Republic of Bulgaria to the United Nations addressed to the Secretary-General, A/C.6/48/3, para. 1; GAOR, Forty-eighth Session, SRSC, 15 November 1993, A/C.6/48/SR.29, paras. 20–21 (France), para. 30 (Australia, Canada, New Zealand), para. 66 (Algeria), para. 80 (Czech Republic), para. 82 (China), para. 88 (India), para. 98 (Italy); GAOR, Forty-ninth Session, SRSC, 11 November 1994, A/C.6/49/SR.32, para. 5 (Russia), para. 6 (Japan), paras. 17 and 21 (China), para. 31 (Germany), para. 32 (Canada), para. 39 (South Korea), para. 47 (US), para. 50 (Australia); GAOR, Forty-ninth Session, SRSC, 14 November 1994, A/C.6/49/SR.33, para. 2 (France), para. 14 (India), paras. 15–16 and 20 (Algeria), para. 25 (Israel); Report of the Secretary-General, 20 August 1997, A/52/294, Reply from Argentina, para. 1. The approbation of States of the ILC draft articles continued after 1998. See, e.g., Report of the Secretary-General, 19 August 1999, A/54/266, p. 2 (Lebanon) and p. 4 (Qatar).

70 For the position on immediately holding an international conference see GAOR, Forty-sixth Session, SRSC, 29 October 1991, A/C.6/46/SR.23, para. 48 (Ireland), para. 58 (Belarus), para. 73 (Cyprus, without ruling out the possibility of a working group), para. 100 (Spain), para. 105 (Switzerland); GAOR, Forty-sixth Session, SRSC, 30 October 1991, A/C.6/46/SR.24, para. 3 (Guatemala, being averse to the idea of a working group), para. 36 (Venezuela), para. 44 (USSR); GAOR, Forty-sixth Session, SRSC, 30 October 1991, A/C.6/46/SR.25, para. 1 (Iceland, speaking for the Nordic countries), para. 2 (Austria), para. 42 (India); GAOR, Forty-sixth Session, SRSC, 1 November 1991, A/C.6/46/SR.27, para. 35 (Nigeria), para. 43 (Bahrain); GAOR, Forty-sixth Session, SRSC, 6 November 1991, A/C.6/46/SR.30, para. 82 (Malta), para. 87 (Hungary); GAOR, Forty-sixth Session, SRSC, 7 November 1991, A/C.6/46/SR.33, para. 12 (Indonesia); GAOR, Forty-sixth Session, SRSC, 11 November 1991, A/C.6/46/SR.34,

NOTES TO PAGES 449–450   697

para. 27 (Turkey), para. 33 (Egypt, not favouring the creation of a working group); GAOR, Forty-sixth Session, SRSC, 13 November 1991, A/C.6/46/SR.36, para. 72 (Romania); GAOR, Forty-sixth Session, SRSC, 10 November 1992, A/C.6/47/SR.32, paras. 29–30 (India); GAOR, Forty-ninth Session, SRSC, 17 November 1994, A/C.6/49/SR.37, paras. 23–24 (Brazil, introducing Draft Resolution A/C.6/49/L.14, pushing for an earlier diplomatic conference).

71 See Report of the Working Group, 11 November 1993, A/C.6/48/L.4 and Corr. 2, paras. 10–12. Russia also made the minority suggestion that the consultations themselves should be done by a diplomatic conference: GAOR, Forty-ninth Session, SRSC, 11 November 1994, A/C.6/49/SR.32, para. 5 (Russia).

72 For the position that an international conference should be held only after full and fruitful consultations see GAOR, Forty-sixth Session, SRSC, 28 October 1991, A/C.6/46/SR.22, paras. 59, 63–64 (Brazil), para. 65 (Mexico), para. 66 (Poland); GAOR, Forty-sixth Session, SRSC, 29 October 1991, A/C.6/46/SR.23, para. 6 (Australia), para. 69 (Japan); GAOR, Forty-sixth Session, SRSC, 30 October 1991, A/C.6/46/SR.24, para. 13 (Iran), para. 20 (US), para. 21 (Uruguay), para. 33 (Angola), para. 77 (Belgium); GAOR, Forty-sixth Session, SRSC, 30 October 1991, A/C.6/46/SR.25, para. 17 (UK), para. 38 (Sri Lanka); GAOR, Forty-sixth Session, SRSC, 1 November 1991, A/C.6/46/SR.27, para. 7 (Colombia); GAOR, Forty-sixth Session, SRSC, 12 November 1991, A/C.6/46/SR.35, para. 4 (Argentina); GAOR, Forty-sixth Session, SRSC, 10 November 1992, A/C.6/47/SR.32, para. 11 (Japan), para. 18 (Australia, Canada, New Zealand), para. 26 (Russia), para. 31 (UK), para. 35 (Austria), para. 46 (France), paras. 47–48 (Italy); GAOR, Forty-ninth Session, SRSC, 17 November 1994, A/C.6/49/SR.37, para. 25 (Mali); GAOR, Forty-ninth Session, SRSC, 18 November 1994, A/C.6/49/SR.38, paras. 26–27 (UK, introducing Draft Resolution A/C.6/49/L.20); Report of the Working Group, 11 November 1993, A/C.6/48/L.4 and Corr. 2, para. 8; Note verbale dated 12 August 1993 from the Permanent Representative of Belgium to the United Nations addressed to the Secretary-General, A/48/313, para. 2; GAOR, Forty-eighth Session, SRSC, 15 November 1993, A/C.6/48/SR.29, para. 17 (Chairman of the Working Group), para. 28 (France), paras. 31, 40 (Australia, Canada, New Zealand), para. 53 (UK), para. 54 (Germany), paras. 62 and 65 (Belgium), para. 70 (Algeria), para. 79 (Japan), para. 81 (Czech Republic), para. 86 (China), para. 93 (India), para. 100 (Italy), para. 102 (US), para. 105 (Austria); GAOR, Forty-ninth Session, SRSC, 11 November 1994, A/C.6/49/SR.32, paras. 13–14 (UK), para. 16 (Brazil), para. 22 (Germany), para. 33 (Canada), para. 42 (Austria), para. 56 (Australia); GAOR, Forty-ninth Session, SRSC, 14 November 1994, A/C.6/49/SR.33, para. 25 (Israel); GAOR, Forty-ninth Session, SRSC, 14 November 1994, A/C.6/49/SR.33, para. 26 (UK).

73 UNGA, Forty-seventh Session, 1992, Agenda item 130 (Resolution 46/55 (1991), para. 5); Forty-eighth Session, 1993, Agenda item 147 (Decision 47/414 of 25 November 1992, para. (c)); Forty-ninth Session, Agenda item 143 (Decision 48/413 of 9 December 1993).

74 See views on a period of reflection expressed in the Sixth Committee: GAOR, Forty-ninth Session, SRSC, 11 November 1994, A/C.6/49/SR.32, para. 14 (UK),

698   NOTES TO PAGES 450-452

para. 16 (Brazil), para. 22 (Germany), paras. 32–33 (Canada), paras. 42–43 (Austria), para. 49 (US), para. 57 (Australia); GAOR, Forty-ninth Session, SRSC, 14 November 1994, A/C.6/49/SR.33, para. 8 (France); GAOR, Forty-ninth Session, SRSC, 14 November 1994, A/C.6/49/SR.33, para. 27 (UK);

75 UNGA Resolution A/RES/49/61 (1994), para. 3. See also UNGA, Resolution A/RES/52/151 (1997), para. 1.

76 The views expressed at these sessions were mere restatements of various previous positions. See GAOR, Fifty-second Session, SRSC, 11 November 1997, A/C.6/52/SR.26, Agenda item 144; Report of the Secretary-General, 24 August and 14 September 1998, A/53/274 and Add. 1; GAOR, Fifty-third Session, SRSC, A/C.6/53/SR.23 (9 November 1998) and A/C.6/53/SR.35 (24 November 1998), Agenda item 148. The topic of State immunity stayed on the General Assembly's agenda until 2004 (1999, Agenda item 152; 2000, Agenda item 157; 2001, Agenda item 160; 2002, Agenda item 154; 2003, Agenda item 150; 2004, Agenda item 142), when the UN Convention on State Immunity was adopted in GA Resolution 59/38 of 2 December 2004.

77 UNGA, Resolution A/RES/53/98 (1998), paras. 1–2. Thus, on the issue of jurisdictional immunities of States and their property, the ILC has been given two separate but related mandates by the General Assembly, in UNGA Resolution 32/151 (1977) and in GA Resolution 53/98 (1998), respectively. From 1999 onwards, the topic of jurisdictional immunities remained on the General Assembly agenda until the final adoption of the UN Convention: UNGA, Fifty-fourth Session, 1999, Agenda item 152; Fifty-fifth Session, 2000, Agenda item 157; Fifty-sixth Session, 2001, Agenda item 160; Fifty-seventh Session, 2002, Agenda item 154; Fifty-eighth Session, 2003, Agenda item 150; Fifty-ninth Session, 2004, Agenda item 142.

78 See ILC, Report, Annex, Report of the Working Group on Jurisdictional Immunities of States and their Property, *YILC*, 1999-II-2, p. 149.

79 See Report of the Chairman of the (Sixth Committee) Working Group, 12 November 1999, A/C.6/54/L.12.

80 See ILC, Report, Annex, Report of the Working Group on Jurisdictional Immunities of States and their Property, *YILC*, 1999-II-2, p. 149 at 155, para. 7 and Report of the Chairman of the informal consultations held in the Sixth Committee, 4 October 1994, A/C.6/49/L.2, Part II.

81 Report of the [ILC] Working Group on Jurisdictional Immunities of States and their Property, *YILC*, 1999-II-2, p. 149 at 162, para. 60.

82 Report of the [ILC] Working Group, *YILC*, 1999-II-2, p. 149 at 164, para. 80.

83 *YILC*, 1999-II-2, p. 149 at 165, paras. 81–83.

84 *YILC*, 1999-II-2, p. 149 at 167, para. 105.

85 *YILC*, 1999-II-2, p. 149 at 171, paras. 127–128.

86 Report of the Chairman of the (Sixth Committee) Working Group, 12 November 1999, A/C.6/54/L.12, para. 5.

87 See GAOR, Fifty-fourth Session, SRSC, 28 October 1999, A/C.6/54/SR.19, para. 4 (France), para. 13 (Italy); GAOR, Fifty-fourth Session, SRSC, 4 November 1999, A/C.6/54/SR.26, para. 40 (Burkina Faso).

NOTES TO PAGE 452   699

88 See GAOR, Fifty-fourth Session, SRSC, 25 October 1999, A/C.6/54/SR.15, para. 46 (Norway, on behalf of the Nordic countries); GAOR, Fifty-fourth Session, SRSC, 26 October 1999, A/C.6/54/SR.16, para. 1 (Chile); GAOR, Fifty-fourth Session, SRSC, 27 October 1999, A/C.6/54/SR.17, para. 39 (Poland); GAOR, Fifty-fourth Session, SRSC, 27 October 1999, A/C.6/54/SR.18, para. 33 (Mexico); GAOR, Fifty-fourth Session, SRSC, 28 October 1999, A/C.6/54/SR.19, para. 1 (Algeria); GAOR, Fifty-fourth Session, SRSC, 28 October 1999, A/C.6/54/SR.20, para. 2 (Guatemala), para. 11 (India), para. 12 (Australia); GAOR, Fifty-fourth Session, SRSC, 1 November 1999, A/C.6/54/SR.22, para. 19 (Singapore), para. 27 (Slovenia), paras. 43–44 (Indonesia, though, puzzlingly, expressing a belief in absolute immunity); GAOR, Fifty-fourth Session, SRSC, 2 November 1999, A/C.6/54/SR.23, para. 49 (Venezuela); GAOR, Fifty-fourth Session, SRSC, 4 November 1999, A/C.6/54/SR.26, para. 60 (Slovakia), para. 65 (Iran), para. 77 (Cyprus); GAOR, Fifty-fourth Session, SRSC, 4 November 1999, A/C.6/54/SR.27, para. 19 (Austria), para. 35 (Egypt); GAOR, Fifty-fourth Session, SRSC, 5 November 1999, A/C.6/54/SR.28, para. 98 (Cuba); Report of the Secretary-General, 17 August 2000, A/55/298, para. 1 (Chile).

89 For general agreement that further efforts should continue in the form of the Sixth Committee Working Group, to be resumed the following year, see Report of the Chairman of the (Sixth Committee) Working Group, 12 November 1999, A/C.6/54/L.12, paras. 51 and 54; GAOR, Fifty-fourth Session, SRSC, 19 November 1999, A/C.6/54/SR.36, paras. 1–3 (Mexico, on behalf of the Rio Group), para. 12 (Burkina Faso), paras. 13–14 (UK), para. 17 (Germany), para. 19 (Czech Republic), para. 21 (Slovakia), para. 25 (Ukraine); GAOR, Fifty-fourth Session, SRSC, 25 October 1999, A/C.6/54/SR.15, para. 46 (Norway, on behalf of the Nordic countries), para. 48 (Japan), para. 57 (Germany); GAOR, Fifty-fourth Session, SRSC, 27 October 1999, A/C.6/54/SR.18, para. 33 (Mexico), para. 39 (Argentina), para. 51 (Japan); GAOR, Fifty-fourth Session, SRSC, 28 October 1999, A/C.6/54/SR.19, para. 34 (US); GAOR, Fifty-fourth Session, SRSC, 28 October 1999, A/C.6/54/SR.20, para. 11 (India); GAOR, Fifty-fourth Session, SRSC, 29 October 1999, A/C.6/54/SR.21, para. 23 (Spain), para. 40 (France); GAOR, Fifty-fourth Session, SRSC, 2 November 1999, A/C.6/54/SR.23, para. 37 (Brazil).

90 See Report of the Chairman of the (Sixth Committee) Working Group, 12 November 1999, A/C.6/54/L.12, paras. 19–23.

91 For support for the ILC Working Group report in deleting the reference to nature and purpose see GAOR, Fifty-fourth Session, SRSC, 25 October 1999, A/C.6/54/SR.15, para. 54 (Germany); GAOR, Fifty-fourth Session, SRSC, 27 October 1999, A/C.6/54/SR.17, para. 40 (Poland); GAOR, Fifty-fourth Session, SRSC, 27 October 1999, A/C.6/54/SR.18, para. 38 (Argentina, invoking its 1994 legislation); GAOR, Fifty-fourth Session, SRSC, 28 October 1999, A/C.6/54/SR.19, para. 1 (Algeria); GAOR, Fifty-fourth Session, SRSC, 28 October 1999, A/C.6/54/SR.20, para. 12 (Australia); GAOR, Fifty-fourth Session, SRSC, 29 October 1999, A/C.6/54/SR.21, para. 22 (Spain); GAOR, Fifty-fourth Session, SRSC, 1 November 1999, A/C.6/54/SR.22, para. 28 (Slovenia); GAOR, Fifty-fourth Session, SRSC, 2 November 1999, A/C.6/54/SR.23, para. 38 (Brazil, but believing

700   NOTES TO PAGE 452

'nature' should be retained); GAOR, Fifty-fourth Session, SRSC, 5 November 1999, A/C.6/54/SR.28, para. 88 (Kuwait); GAOR, Fifty-fourth Session, SRSC, 19 November 1999, A/C.6/54/SR.36, para. 5 (Japan), para. 15 (Germany); para. 20 (Slovakia); Report of the Secretary-General, 17 August 2000, A/55/298, para. 24 (Chile).

92 For scepticism about the deletion see GAOR, Fifty-fourth Session, SRSC, 27 October 1999, A/C.6/54/SR.17, para. 44 (South Korea); GAOR, Fifty-fourth Session, SRSC, 28 October 1999, A/C.6/54/SR.19, para. 14 (Italy); GAOR, Fifty-fourth Session, SRSC, 28 October 1999, A/C.6/54/SR.20, para. 2 (Guatemala), para. 17 (Tanzania).

93 See GAOR, Fifty-fourth Session, SRSC, 27 October 1999, A/C.6/54/SR.18, para. 43 (Netherlands).

94 See GAOR, Fifty-fourth Session, SRSC, 27 October 1999, A/C.6/54/SR.18, para. 34 (Mexico); GAOR, Fifty-fourth Session, SRSC, 28 October 1999, A/C.6/54/SR.19, para. 4 (France); GAOR, Fifty-fourth Session, SRSC, 28 October 1999, A/C.6/54/SR.20, para. 2 (Guatemala), para. 17 (Tanzania); GAOR, Fifty-fourth Session, SRSC, 4 November 1999, A/C.6/54/SR.26, para. 61 (Slovenia), para. 65 (Iran); GAOR, Fifty-fourth Session, SRSC, 5 November 1999, A/C.6/54/SR.28, para. 100 (Haiti); GAOR, Fifty-fifth Session, SRSC, 16 November 2000, A/C.6/55/SR.31, para. 15 (China).

95 See GAOR, Fifty-fourth Session, SRSC, 27 October 1999, A/C.6/54/SR.18, para. 52 (Japan).

96 Various opinions noted in Report of the Chairman of the (Sixth Committee) Working Group, 12 November 1999, A/C.6/54/L.12, paras. 24–28.

97 Various opinions noted in Report of the Chairman of the (Sixth Committee) Working Group, 12 November 1999, A/C.6/54/L.12, paras. 35–45.

98 See GAOR, Fifty-fourth Session, SRSC, 25 October 1999, A/C.6/54/SR.15, para. 54 (Germany); GAOR, Fifty-fourth Session, SRSC, 27 October 1999, A/C.6/54/SR.18, para. 35 (Mexico), para. 54 (Japan); GAOR, Fifty-fourth Session, SRSC, 28 October 1999, A/C.6/54/SR.19, para. 1 (Algeria); GAOR, Fifty-fourth Session, SRSC, 1 November 1999, A/C.6/54/SR.22, para. 29 (Slovenia); GAOR, Fifty-fourth Session, SRSC, 2 November 1999, A/C.6/54/SR.23, para. 38 (Brazil); GAOR, Fifty-fourth Session, SRSC, 5 November 1999, A/C.6/54/SR.28, para. 88 (Kuwait); GAOR, Fifty-fourth Session, SRSC, 19 November 1999, A/C.6/54/SR.36, para. 16 (Germany).

99 For separateness see GAOR, Fifty-fourth Session, SRSC, 28 October 1999, A/C.6/54/SR.20, para. 13 (Australia); GAOR, Fifty-fourth Session, SRSC, 19 November 1999, A/C.6/54/SR.36, para. 27 (France); GAOR, Fifty-fifth Session, SRSC, 16 November 2000, A/C.6/55/SR.31, para. 16 (China).

100 See GAOR, Fifty-fourth Session, SRSC, 27 October 1999, A/C.6/54/SR.18, para. 44 (Netherlands).

101 For link see GAOR, Fifty-fifth Session, SRSC, 16 November 2000, A/C.6/55/SR.31, para. 17 (China).

102 For no link see GAOR, Fifty-fourth Session, SRSC, 27 October 1999, A/C.6/54/SR.18, para. 47 (Netherlands); GAOR, Fifty-fourth Session, SRSC, 28 October 1999, A/C.6/54/SR.19, para. 15 (Italy).

NOTES TO PAGES 452-453   701

103 For support for the ILC Working Group report in distinguishing pre- and post-judgment see GAOR, Fifty-fourth Session, SRSC, 25 October 1999, A/C.6/54/SR.15, para. 55 (Germany); GAOR, Fifty-fourth Session, SRSC, 27 October 1999, A/C.6/54/SR.18, para. 39 (Argentina), para. 53 (Japan); GAOR, Fifty-fourth Session, SRSC, 28 October 1999, A/C.6/54/SR.19, para. 1 (Algeria), para. 4 (France); GAOR, Fifty-fourth Session, SRSC, 1 November 1999, A/C.6/54/SR.22, para. 30 (Slovenia); GAOR, Fifty-fourth Session, SRSC, 2 November 1999, A/C.6/54/SR.23, para. 39 (Brazil); GAOR, Fifty-fourth Session, SRSC, 5 November 1999, A/C.6/54/SR.28, para. 88 (Kuwait); GAOR, Fifty-fourth Session, SRSC, 19 November 1999, A/C.6/54/SR.36, para. 16 (Germany).

104 Opinions noted in Report of the Chairman of the (Sixth Committee) Working Group, 12 November 1999, A/C.6/54/L.12, paras. 7-12.

105 For convention see GAOR, Fifty-fourth Session, SRSC, 27 October 1999, A/C.6/54/SR.17, para. 39 (Poland); GAOR, Fifty-fourth Session, SRSC, 29 October 1999, A/C.6/54/SR.21, para. 40 (France, though also interested in a 'model law'); GAOR, Fifty-fourth Session, SRSC, 2 November 1999, A/C.6/54/SR.23, para. 36 (Brazil), 49 (Venezuela); GAOR, Fifty-fourth Session, SRSC, 5 November 1999, A/C.6/54/SR.28, para. 98 (Cuba); GAOR, Fifty-fourth Session, SRSC, 19 November 1999, A/C.6/54/SR.36, para. 12 (Burkina Faso), para. 19 (Czech Republic), 21 (Slovakia), 23 (Ukraine), para. 26 (France); GAOR, Fifty-fifth Session, SRSC, 16 November 2000, A/C.6/55/SR.31, para. 17 (China).

106 For model law see GAOR, Fifty-fourth Session, SRSC, 25 October 1999, A/C.6/54/SR.15, para. 57 (Germany); GAOR, Fifty-fourth Session, SRSC, 27 October 1999, A/C.6/54/SR.18, para. 50 (UK); GAOR, Fifty-fourth Session, SRSC, 28 October 1999, A/C.6/54/SR.20, para. 14 (Australia); GAOR, Fifty-fourth Session, SRSC, 1 November 1999, A/C.6/54/SR.22, para. 19 (Singapore); GAOR, Fifty-fourth Session, SRSC, 4 November 1999, A/C.6/54/SR.26, para. 78 (Cyprus); GAOR, Fifty-fourth Session, SRSC, 19 November 1999, A/C.6/54/SR.36, para. 14 (UK), para. 17 (Germany), para. 29 (Netherlands), para. 30 (South Africa).

107 Report of the Chairman of the (Sixth Committee) Working Group, 12 November 1999, A/C.6/54/L.12, paras. 51 and 54. And this was also confirmed by the delegations in the discussion of the Chairman's report: GAOR, Fifty-fourth Session, SRSC, 19 November 1999, A/C.6/54/SR.36, paras. 1-3 (Mexico, on behalf of the Rio Group), para. 12 (Burkina Faso), paras. 13-14 (UK), para. 17 (Germany), para. 19 (Czech Republic), para. 21 (Slovakia), para. 25 (Ukraine).

108 UNGA, Resolution A/RES/54/101 (1999), para. 3.

109 Report of the Chairman of the (Sixth Committee) Working Group, 10 November 2000, A/C.6/55/L.12. For the exchange of views following the Chairman's report see GAOR, Fifty-fifth Session, SRSC, 16 November 2000, A/C.6/55/SR.31, Agenda Item 157.

110 UNGA, Resolution A/RES/55/150 (2000), paras. 3-4. The meeting time was changed to 4-15 February 2002 in UNGA Resolution A/RES/56/78 (2001), para. 1. For details see the Ad Hoc Committee's website: http://www.un.

702   NOTES TO PAGE 453

org/law/jurisdictionalimmunities/index.html. For support for an ad hoc committee see Report of the Secretary-General, 14 August 2001, A/56/291, p. 2 (Antigua and Barbuda); Report of the Secretary-General, 24 October 2001, A/56/291/Add.1, p. 2, para. 3 (Italy); Report of the Secretary-General, 5 November 2001, A/56/291/Add.2, p. 2, para. 2 (Japan).

111 For nature/purpose see Report of the Secretary-General, 24 October 2001, A/56/291/Add.1, p. 3, para. 7 (Italy) (Deletion of criterion); Report of the Secretary-General, 5 November 2001, A/56/291/Add.2, p. 2, para. 6 (Japan) (supporting Chairman's Alternative I in A/C.6/55/L.12); for purpose see Report of the Secretary-General, 14 August 2001, A/56/291, p. 3, paras. 5–6 (China); for State enterprises see Report of the Secretary-General, 14 August 2001, A/56/291, pp. 3–4, paras. 7–9 (China) (separateness); Report of the Secretary-General, 24 October 2001, A/56/291/Add.1, p. 3, para. 8 (Italy) (deletion of provision); Report of the Secretary-General, 5 November 2001, A/56/291/Add.2, p. 2, para. 7 (Japan) (same); for measures of constraint see Report of the Secretary-General, 14 August 2001, A/56/291, p. 4, paras. 11–12 (China, arguing that pre-judgment attachment should not be allowed); Report of the Secretary-General, 24 October 2001, A/56/291/Add.1, p. 3, para. 10 (Italy) (separate treatment of pre- and post-judgment attachment); Report of the Secretary-General, 5 November 2001, A/56/291/Add.2, p. 3, para. 9 (Japan) (same); Report of the Secretary-General, 14 August 2001, A/56/291, pp. 4–5, para. 13 (China) (link); Report of the Secretary-General, 24 October 2001, A/56/291/Add.1, p. 3, para. 11 (Italy) (no link; supporting Chairman's Alternative I in A/C.6/55/L.12 but deleting words in square brackets); for final form of the instrument see Report of the Secretary-General, 14 August 2001, A/56/291, p. 2 (China) (convention); Report of the Secretary-General, 24 October 2001, A/56/291/Add.1, p. 2, para. 4 (model law; saying that although a convention would be ideal).

112 UNGA, Resolution A/RES/57/16 (2002), para. 2.

113 UNGA, Resolution A/RES/58/74 (2003), para. 2.

114 Report of the Ad Hoc Committee on Jurisdictional Immunities of States and their Property, 4–15 February 2002, A/57/22; Report of the Ad Hoc Committee, 24–28 February 2003, A/58/22; Report of the Ad Hoc Committee, 1–5 March 2004, A/59/22.

115 For nature/purpose of commercial transactions see GAOR, Fifty-seventh Session, SRSC, 22 October 2002, A/C.6/57/SR.18, para. 45 (Greece), para. 51 (Portugal); GAOR, Fifty-seventh Session, SRSC, 24 October 2002, A/C.6/57/SR.19, para. 7 (Slovakia) (deletion of criteria); GAOR, A/C.6/57/SR.18, para. 20 (Norway), para. 24 (Germany); GAOR, A/C.6/57/SR.19, para. 2 (US) (nature only); GAOR, A/C.6/57/SR.18, para. 33 (Mexico), para. 63 (South Africa); GAOR, A/C.6/57/SR.19, para. 12 (Russia) (nature and purpose); GAOR, A/C.6/57/SR.18, para. 58 (Australia) (purpose where expressly declared); GAOR, A/C.6/57/SR.18, para. 13 (Japan) (ready for a compromise). For State enterprises see GAOR, A/C.6/57/SR.18, para. 34 (Mexico), para. 46 (Greece); GAOR, A/C.6/57/SR.19, para. 13 (Russia) (separate from the State); GAOR, A/C.6/57/SR.18, para.

21 (Norway), para. 52 (Portugal), para. 59 (Australia), para. 64 (South Africa); GAOR, Fifty-seventh Session, SRSC, A/C.6/57/SR.19, para. 2 (US) (not separate); GAOR, A/C.6/57/SR.18, para. 26 (Germany) (joint liability); GAOR, A/C.6/57/SR.18, para. 14 (Japan) (not including provisions on 'undercapitalisation' or 'piercing the corporate veil'). For measures of constraint see GAOR, A/C.6/57/SR.19, para. 18 (Russia) (link); GAOR, A/C.6/57/SR.18, para. 22 (Norway), para. 29 (Germany), para. 48 (Greece), para. 54 (Portugal), para. 61 (Australia); GAOR, A/C.6/57/SR.19, para. 2 (US) (no link); GAOR, A/C.6/57/SR.18, para. 29 (Germany); GAOR, A/C.6/57/SR.19, para. 16 (Russia) (distinction between pre- and post-judgment measures). For the final form see GAOR, A/C.6/57/SR.18, para. 18 (Japan), para. 19 (Norway), para. 29 (Germany), para. 36 (Mexico), para. 39 (Iran, 'a binding instrument'), para. 49 (Greece), para. 55 (Portugal; but also open to a model law); GAOR, A/C.6/57/SR.19, para. 6 (Slovakia), para. 19 (Russia, though also open to a model law), para. 22 (Indonesia) (convention); GAOR, A/C.6/57/SR.18, para. 43 (UK, no longer insistent upon a model law), para. 62 (Australia, but open to convention), para. 66 (South Africa); GAOR, A/C.6/57/SR.19, para. 5 (Morocco) (model law); GAOR, A/C.6/57/SR.19, para. 2 (US), para. 19 (Hungary) (two-step approach).

116 GAOR, Fifty-seventh Session, SRSC, 21 October 2003, A/C.6/58/SR.12, para. 12 (Hafner).

117 See, in particular, GAOR, Fifty-seventh Session, SRSC, 21 October 2003, A/C.6/58/SR.12, paras. 15–16 (Italy, on behalf of the European Union), para. 20 (Norway), para. 22 (Peru, on behalf of the Rio Group), para. 23 (Australia), para. 25 (Japan), para. 26 (China), para. 29 (South Korea), para. 34 (US, not opposed to convention), para. 35 (Russia). See also GAOR, Fifty-seventh Session, SRSC, 26 October 2004, A/C.6/59/SR.14.

118 Report of the Ad Hoc Committee on Jurisdictional Immunities of States and their Property, 1–5 March 2004, A/59/22, Annex I, 'Draft United Nations Convention on Jurisdictional Immunities of States and Their Property'. The previous two reports of the Ad Hoc Committee used the modest expression 'draft articles', see Report of the Ad Hoc Committee, 4–15 February 2002, A/57/22, Annex, 'Draft Articles on Jurisdictional Immunities of States and their Property' and Report of the Ad Hoc Committee, 24–28 February 2003, A/58/22, Annex I, 'Draft Articles'. For a statement on the successful completion of the work of the Ad Hoc Committee see especially GAOR, Fifty-seventh Session, SRSC, 25 October 2004, A/C.6/59/SR.13, paras. 30, 36, 37 (Hafner).

119 The Convention was opened for signature from 17 January 2005 to 17 January 2007. Up to 8 February 2012, twenty-eight States have signed the Convention, while thirteen have ratified, accepted, approved or acceded to it (Austria, France, Iran, Japan, Kazakhstan, Lebanon, Norway, Portugal, Romania, Saudi Arabia, Spain, Sweden and Switzerland) (information regularly updated at http://treaties.un.org/Home.aspx).

120 See *Jones* v. *Saudi Arabia*, England, 2006, [2007] 1 AC 270, 280, 289, 293, paras. 8, 26, 47; 129 ILR 629, 716–717, 727, 733; *Koo* v. *Bank*, England, [2007] EWCA

704   NOTES TO PAGES 454-455

Civ 1443, [2008] QB 717, 734–735, para. 47; *Svenska* v. *Lithuania (No. 2)*, England, [2006] EWCA Civ 1529, [2007] QB 886, 929, para. 132; *AIG* v. *Kazakhstan*, England, 2005, [2006] 1 WLR 1420, 1446–1447, para. 80; 129 ILR 589, 621–622; *Case against the USA*, Norway, 2001, noted in 70 *Nordic JIL* (2001) 547, 551.

121 See Sucharitkul, Jurisdictional Immunities, on the limited role played by Asian countries, especially during the formation of the law on State immunity. The Asian cases collected in this article provide particularly valuable historical material.

122 As noted in Sucharitkul, Jurisdictional Immunities, 17–18. See also Sucharitkul, Preliminary Report, *YILC*, 1979-II-1, p. 227 at 230, para. 20(a); Whiteman, *Digest of International Law*, pp. 572–574; *Empire of Iran Case*, Germany, (1963) 45 ILR 57, 77 and p. 77 fn. 1; *Philippine Embassy Case*, Germany, (1977) 65 ILR 146, 181.

123 See AALCO's resolutions on the Jurisdictional Immunities of States and their Property at its annual sessions: RES/39/10 (2000); RES/40/6 (2001); RES/41/7 (2002); RES/42/7 (2003); RES/43/S7 (2004); RES/44/S7 (2005); RES/45/S7 (2006); Reports prepared by the AALCO Secretariat to the annual sessions: Report to the Forty-fifth Session (2006), AALCO/45/HEADQUARTERS SESSION (NEW DELHI)/2006/SD/S 7, paras. 33–36; the Forty-fourth Session (2005), AALCO/44/NAIROBI/2005/SD/S 7, paras. 33–36; the Forty-third Session (2004), AALCO/43/BALI/2004/SD/S 7, paras. 34–38; the Forty-second Session (2003), AALCO/XLII/SEOUL/2003/S.7, paras. 58–59. See also summary records of the second general meeting of the Forty-first Session, 2002 and the fourth general meeting of the Forty-second Session, 2003. All these documents are available from AALCO's official website: www.aalco.int. However, as noted in Chapter 1, this website tends to be rather unreliable in keeping the documents constantly available.

124 Despite a repeated call for a compilation of 'national legislation, jurisprudence and practices of the AALCC Member States on this item' (see RES/39/10 (2000), para. 2; RES/40/6 (2001), para. 3; RES/41/7 (2002), para. 3; RES/42/7 (2003), para. 3; RES/43/S7 (2004), para. 3; RES/44/S7 (2005), para. 3; RES/45/S7 (2006), para. 2), nothing seems to have come out of this initiative (the Secretariat has received 'responses' from eight States – Bangladesh, Botswana, Cyprus, Japan, Mauritius, Malaysia, Myanmar and Turkey, see Secretariat Report AALCO/XLII/SEOUL/2003/S.7, para. 61, but we do not yet know what these responses are). Moreover, according to the summary records of the third general meeting, Fortieth Session of AALCO, 2001, South Korea indicated at that meeting that the Korean Supreme Court had upheld the restrictive theory of immunity since 1997, but no case report was provided. This fruitless attempt is to be contrasted with that taken by the Council of Europe, which resulted in an impressive database of State practice regarding State immunity, including materials from Israel and Japan: www.coe.int/t/dlapil/cahdi/State_Immunities/default_en.asp.

125 See Fox, *The Law of State Immunity*, pp. 167–169; 373–412; Hafner and Lange, La Convention; Hafner and Köhler, The United Nations Convention; Hafner, L'Immunité; Grant and Barker, *Parry and Grant*; Pingel, Observations;

NOTES TO PAGES 455–456   705

Bankas, *The State Immunity Controversy*, Chapter 10; Stewart, The UN Convention; Denza, The 2005; Fox, In Defence; Gardiner, UN Convention; Hall, UN Convention; Dickinson, Status; McGregor, State Immunity; Fatima and Patel, State Immunity; Donoho, Minimalist. For scholarly commentary on the 1991 ILC Draft Articles see ABA, Report, 1988; Greig, Forum; Greig, Specific; Morris, The International; Lowe, The International; Kessedjian and Schreuer, Le Projet; Greener, The Commercial; Heß, The International; Donoghue, The Public; Robertson, Comments; Byers, State Immunity; Nedjar, Tendances.

126 Hafner and Köhler, The United Nations Convention, 25–26.
127 Lord Bingham noted the absence of a *jus cogens* exception to immunity: *Jones* v. *Saudi Arabia*, England, 2006, [2007] 1 AC 270, 289, para. 26 per Lord Bingham; 129 ILR 629, 727–728. See also *Sam* v. *Jiang*, New Zealand, CIV 2004-404-5843, 2006, para. 65; Hall, UN Convention; McGregor, State Immunity.
128 See Dickinson, Status.
129 The International Law Commission decided in 2006 to include the topics 'Immunity of State officials from foreign criminal jurisdiction' and 'Extraterritorial jurisdiction' in its long-term programme of work. See ILC, Report, 2006, A/61/10, paras. 22, 257, 260 and Annexes A and E. See, further, ILC, Report, 2008, A/63/10, Chapter X; ILC, Report, 2009, A/64/10, Chapter X; ILC, Report, 2010, A/65/10, Chapter IX.
130 As noted by Hafner and Köhler, The United Nations Convention, 47–48.
131 Report of the Working Group on Jurisdictional Immunities of States and their Property, annexed to the Report of the ILC on the Work of its Fifty-first Session, *YILC*, 1999-II-2, p. 149 at 155, para. 9 and Appendix, at pp. 171–172.
132 Report of the Chairman of the (Sixth Committee) Working Group, 12 November 1999, A/C.6/54/L.12, para. 47.

Bibliography

ABA (Working Group of the American Bar Association), Reforming the Foreign Sovereign Immunities Act, 40 *Columbia Journal of Transnational Law* (2002) 489

ABA, Report, 1988: ABA Committee on Foreign Sovereign Immunity, Report on Foreign State Immunity, 22 *International Lawyer* (1988) 906

Report, 2002: ABA, Section of International Law and Practice, Report to the House of Delegates, 36 *International Lawyer* (2002) 1261

Abbott, Judi L., The Noncommercial Torts Exception to the Foreign Sovereign Immunities Act, 9 *Fordham International Law Journal* (1985–86) 134

Abir, Danny, Foreign Sovereign Immunities Act: The Right to a Jury Trial in Suits against Foreign Government-Owned Corporations, 32 *Stanford Journal of International Law* (1996) 159

Abrams, Renana B., The Foreign Sovereign Immunities Act: Inconsistencies in Application of the Commercial Activity Direct Effect Exception, 5 *Emory International Law Review* (1991) 211

Aceves, William J., Liberalism and International Legal Scholarship: The Pinochet Case and the Move Toward a Universal System of Transnational Law Litigation, 41 *Harvard International Law Journal* (2000) 129

Adelman, Jenny, Sovereign Immunity: Ramifications of Altmann, 11 *ILSA Journal of International and Comparative Law* (2004) 173

Akande, Dapo, International Law Immunities and the International Criminal Court, 98 *American Journal of International Law* (2004) 407

The Legal Nature of Security Council Referrals to the ICC and its Impact on Al Bashir's Immunities, 7 *Journal of International Criminal Justice* (2009) 333

Alderton, Matthew, Immunity for Heads of State Acting in their Private Capacity – *Thor Shipping A/S v. The Ship 'Al Duhail'*, 58 *International and Comparative Law Quarterly* (2009) 702

ALI, *Third Restatement: American Law Institute, Restatement of the Law Third: The Foreign Relations Law of the United States*, St Paul, Minnesota: American Law Institute Publishers, 1987, Vols. 1 and 2

Allen, Eleanor Wyllys, *The Position of Foreign States before National Courts: Chiefly in Continental Europe*, New York: Macmillan Co., 1933

ALRC (Australian Law Reform Commission), *Report No. 24, Foreign State Immunity*, Canberra: Australian Government Publishing Service, 1984, also available at: www.alrc.gov.au/report-24

Amerasinghe, C.F., Assessment of Compensation of Expropriated Foreign Property: Three Critical Problems, in Ronald St John Macdonald (gen. ed.), *Essays in Honour of Wang Tieya*, Dordrecht/London: Martinus Nijhoff Publishers, 1994, p. 55

Anderson, Kent, An Asian Pinochet? Not Likely: The Unfulfilled International Law Promise in Japan's Treatment of Former Peruvian President Alberto Fujimori, 38 *Stanford Journal of International Law* (2002) 177

Anonymous Author, Case note on *Princz*, 108 *Harvard Law Review* (1994) 513

Anonymous Author, D.C. Circuit Holds that an International Agreement Bars Former Hostages' Suit against Iran, despite Legislation Aimed at Aiding the Suit (case note on *Roeder* v. *Islamic Republic of Iran*, 333 F.3d 228 (D.C.Cir. 2003)), 117 *Harvard Law Review* (2003) 743

Anton, A.E., and Beaumont, P.R., *Private International Law*, 2nd edn, Edinburgh: W. Green, 1990

Ashe, Lawrence V., The Flexible Approach to the Foreign Sovereign Immunities Act in *Weltover Inc.* v. *Republic of Argentina*, 23 *University of Miami Inter-American Law Review* (1991–92) 465

Asiedu-Akrofi, Derek, Central Bank Immunity and the Inadequacy of the Restrictive Immunity Approach, 28 *Canadian Yearbook of International Law* (1990) 263

Atherton, Kelly A., Compensating Victims under the 'Terrorism Exception' of the Foreign Sovereign Immunities Act: A State-Sponsored Victim's Compensation Fund, 12 *Willamette Journal of International Law and Dispute Resolution* (2004) 158

Atkeson, Timothy B., and Ramsey, Stephen D., Proposed Amendment of the Foreign Sovereign Immunities Act, 79 *American Journal of International Law* (1985) 770

Aust, Anthony, *Handbook of International Law*, 2nd edn, Cambridge University Press, 2010

Modern Treaty Law and Practice, 2nd edn, Cambridge University Press, 2008

The Law of State Immunity, 53 *International and Comparative Law Quarterly* (2004) 255

Badr, Gamal Moursi, *State Immunity: An Analytical and Prognostic View*, The Hague/Boston/Lancaster: Martinus Nijhoff Publishers, 1984

Baker, Mark B., Whither *Weltover*: Has the U.S. Supreme Court Clarified or Confused the Exceptions Enumerated in the Foreign Sovereign Immunities Act? 9 *Temple International and Comparative Law Journal* (1995) 1

Balaš, Vladimir, and Pauknerová, Monika, The Czechoslovak Approach to the Draft Convention on Jurisdictional Immunities of States and Their Property, 12 *Michigan Journal of International Law* (1991) 874

Baletsa, S. Jason, The Cost of Closure: A Reexamination of the Theory and Practice of the 1996 Amendments to the Foreign Sovereign Immunities Act, 148 *University of Pennsylvania Law Review* (2000) 1247

BIBLIOGRAPHY

Bamberger, Craig S., Determination of Private Activity under Tate Letter in Absence of State Department Suggestion of Immunity, 6 *Harvard International Law Club Journal* (1964–1965) 203

Bandes, Susan, Treaties, Sovereign Immunity and 'The Plan of the Convention', 42 *Virginia Journal of International Law* (2002) 743

Bankas, Ernest K., *The State Immunity Controversy in International Law: Private Suits against Sovereign States in Domestic Courts*, Berlin/Heidelberg: Springer, 2005

Bantekas, Ilias, Head of State Immunity in the Light of Multiple Legal Regimes and Non-Self-Contained System Theories: Theoretical Analysis of ICC Third Party Jurisdiction against the Background of the 2003 Iraq War, 10 *Journal of Conflict & Security Law* (2005) 21

    Prefecture of Voiotia v. *Federal Republic of Germany*, Case No. 137/1997, Court of First Instance of Leivadia, Greece, 1997, 92 *American Journal of International Law* (1998) 765

    The Iraqi Special Tribunal for Crimes against Humanity, 54 *International and Comparative Law Quarterly* (2005) 237

Barker, J. Craig, State Immunity, Diplomatic Immunity and Act of State: A Triple Protection against Legal Action? 47 *International and Comparative Law Quarterly* (1998) 950

    The Future of Former Head of State Immunity after *ex parte Pinochet*, 48 *International and Comparative Law Quarterly* (1999) 937

Barrie, George N., Sovereign Immunity of State: Acts *Iure Imperii* and Acts *Iure Gestionis* – What Is the Distinction? 26 *South African Yearbook of International Law* (2001) 156

Bartsch, Kerstin, and Elberling, Björn, *Jus Cogens* vs. State Immunity, Round Two: The Decision of the European Court of Human Rights in the *Kalogeropoulou et al.* v. *Greece and Germany* Decision, 4 *German Law Journal* (2003) 477

Basham, Jonathan G., Prejudgment Attachment under the United States Foreign Sovereign Immunities Act: A Loophole in Need of Repair, 66 *Oregon Law Review* (1988) 627

Bass, Peter Evan, Ex-Head of State Immunity: A Proposed Statutory Tool of Foreign Policy, 97 *Yale Law Journal* (1987) 299

Bassiouni, M. Cherif, *Crimes against Humanity in International Criminal Law*, Dordrecht/Boston/London: Martinus Nijhoff Publishers, 1992

    From Versailles to Rwanda in Seventy-Five Years: The Need to Establish a Permanent International Criminal Court, 10 *Harvard Human Rights Journal* (1997) 11

Bates, Ed, State Immunity for Torture, 7 *Human Rights Law Review* (2007) 651

    The Al-Adsani Case, State Immunity and the International Legal Prohibition on Torture, 3 *Human Rights Law Review* (2003) 193

Bautista, Antonio R., Philippine Civil Procedure in Transboundary Disputes, 6 *Asian Yearbook of International Law* (1996) 63

Bederman, David J., Dead Man's Hand: Reshuffling Foreign Sovereign Immunities in U.S. Human Rights Litigation, 25 *Georgia Journal of International and Comparative Law* (1995–1996) 255

Bedjaoui, Mohammed, (Réd. gén.), *Droit international – Bilan et perspective, Tome 1*, Paris: UNESCO et Pedone, 1991

Belsky, Adam C., Merva, Mark and Roht-Arriaza, Naomi, Implied Waiver under the FSIA: A Proposed Exception to Immunity for Violations of Peremptory Norms of International Law, 77 *California Law Review* (1989) 365

Benjamin, Doodwin E., *De Sanchez v. Banco Central de Nicaragua*: Too Many Exceptions to the Commercial Activities Exception of the Foreign Sovereign Immunities Act of 1976? 14 *Brooklyn Journal of International Law* (1988) 715

Bensen, Matthew, The All New (International) 'People's Court': The Future of the Direct Effect Clause After *Voest-Alpine Trading USA Corp. v. Bank of China*, 83 *Minnesota Law Review* (1999) 997

Beresovski, Catherine M., A Proposal to Deny Foreign Sovereign Immunity to Nations Sponsoring Terrorism, 6 *American University Journal of International Law and Policy* (1990) 77

Bergen, Joseph G., *Princz v. Federal Republic of Germany*: Why the Courts Should Find that Violating *Jus Cogens* Norms Constitutes an Implied Waiver of Sovereign Immunity, 14 *Connecticut Journal of International Law* (1999) 169

Bhuta, Mehal, Justice without Borders? Prosecuting General Pinochet, 23 *Melbourne University Law Review* (1999) 499

Bianchi, Andrea, Denying State Immunity to Violators of Human Rights, 46 *Austrian Journal of Public and International Law* (1993–94) 195

    Ferrini v. Federal Republic of Germany, Italian Court of Cassation, March 11, 2004, 99 *American Journal of International Law* (2005) 242

    Human Rights and the Magic of *Jus Cogens*, 19 *European Journal of International Law* (2008) 491

    Immunity versus Human Rights: The *Pinochet* Case, 10 *European Journal of International Law* (1999) 237

Bingham, Tom, *The Business of Judging: Selected Essays and Speeches*, Oxford University Press, 2000

Blackstone, Sir William, *Commentaries on the Laws of England*, Oxford: Clarendon Press, Book I, 1765; Book IV, 1769

Blair, William, The Legal Status of Central Bank Investments under English Law, 57 *Cambridge Law Journal* (1998) 374

Blane, Alexis, Sovereign Immunity as a Bar to the Execution of International Arbitral Awards, 41 *New York University Journal of International Law and Politics* (2009) 453

Bleimaier, John Kuhn, The Private Litigant's Right to Damages for an Injury Suffered as a Result of an Act of a Foreign Sovereign: An International Property Right, 4 *Hague Yearbook of International Law* (1991) 171

Bluntschli, Johann Caspar, *Das moderne Völkerrecht der civilisierten Staten als Rechtsbuch dargestellt*, 3. Auflage, Nördlingen, 1878; French translation: C. Lardy, *Le droit international codifié*, 5th edn, Paris: Guillaumin, 1895

Bodoh, Keith D., The Routine Torture Practices of the Saudi Arabian Government as 'Commercial Activity' with the Foreign Sovereign Immunities Act of 1976 in the Wake of *Saudi Arabia* v. *Nelson*, 23 *Georgia Journal of International and Comparative Law* (1993) 559

Boguslavsky, Mark Moisejevič, Foreign State Immunity: Soviet Doctrine and Practice, 10 *Netherlands Yearbook of International Law* (1979) 167

Staatliche Immunität, Berlin: Verl. Spitz, 1965

Bohannan, Christina, Beyond Abrogation of Sovereign Immunity: State Waivers, Private Contracts, and Federal Incentives, 77 *New York University Law Review* (2002) 273

Boister, N., and Burchill, R., The Implications of the Pinochet Decisions for the Extradition or Prosecution of Former South African Heads of State for Crimes Committed under Apartheid, 11 *African Journal of International and Comparative Law* (1999) 619

Booysen, H., The Municipal Enforcement of Arbitration Awards against States in Terms of Arbitration Conventions, with Special Reference to the New York Convention – Does International Law Provide for a Municipal Law Concept of an Arbitrable Act of State? 12 *South African Yearbook of International Law* (1986–87) 73

Borchert, John W., Tribal Immunity through the Lens of the Foreign Sovereign Immunities Act: A Warrant for Codification? 13 *Emory International Law Review* (1999) 247

Born, Gary B., *International Civil Litigation in United States Courts: Commentary & Materials*, 3rd edn, The Hague/Boston/London: Kluwer Law International, 1996

Bouchez, Leo J., The Nature and Scope of State Immunity from Jurisdiction and Execution, 10 *Netherlands Yearbook of International Law* (1979) 3

Bowers, John, *A Practical Approach to Employment Law*, 7th edn, Oxford University Press, 2005

Bowett, D. W., The State Immunity Act 1978, 37 *Cambridge Law Journal* (1978) 193

Bowling, John J., and Cohen, Jeff A., When May a Sovereign Be Held Liable for the Acts of Her Instrumentalities under the Foreign Sovereign Immunities Act? The Effect of the *McKesson* Decision, 1 *Tulsa Journal of Comparative and International Law* (1994) 285

Bradley, Andrew G., Service of Process under the Foreign Sovereign Immunity Act of 1976: The Arguments for Exclusivity, 14 *Cornell International Law Journal* (1981) 357

Bradley, Curtis A., The Status of Customary International Law in U.S. Courts – before and after Erie, 26 *Denver Journal of International Law and Policy* (1998) 807

Bradley, Curtis A., and Goldsmith, Jack L., *Pinochet* and International Human Rights Litigation, 97 *Michigan Law Review* (1999) 2129

Briggs, Herbert W., *The International Law Commission*, Ithaca, New York: Cornell University Press, 1965

Brilmayer, Lea, International Law in American Courts: A Modest Proposal, 100 *Yale Law Journal* (1991) 2277

Brock, Carolyn J., The Foreign Sovereign Immunities Act: Defining a Role for the Executive, 30 *Virginia Journal of International Law* (1990) 795

Brockbank, Dean, The Sovereign Immunity Circle: An Economic Analysis of *Nelson* v. *Saudi Arabia* and the Foreign Sovereign Immunities Act, 2 *George Mason University Law Review* (1994) 1

Brodie, Douglas, *The Employment Contract: Legal Principles, Drafting, and Interpretation*, Oxford University Press, 2005

Bröhmer, Jürgen, Diplomatic Immunity, Head of State Immunity, State Immunity: Misconceptions of a Notorious Human Rights Violator, 12 *Leiden Journal of International Law* (1999) 361

Immunity of a Former Head of State General Pinochet and the House of Lords: Part Three, 13 *Leiden Journal of International Law* (2000) 229

State Immunity and the Violation of Human Rights, The Hague/Boston/London: Martinus Nijhoff Publishers, 1997

Brookes, Lyle, *Frolova* v. *U.S.S.R.*: Towards a Human Rights Exception to the Foreign Sovereign Immunities Act? 13 *Brooklyn Journal of International Law* (1987) 159

Brower, Charles H., II, Case note on *Republic of Austria* v. *Altmann*, 99 *American Journal of International Law* (2005) 236

International Immunities: Some Dissident Views on the Role of Municipal Courts, 41 *Virginia Journal of International Law* (2000) 1

Brownlie, Ian, *Principles of Public International Law*, 7th edn, Oxford University Press, 2008

Burr, Sherri L., From Noriega to Pinochet: Is There an International Moral and Legal Right to Kidnap Individuals Accused of Gross Human Rights Violations? 29 *Denver Journal of International Law and Policy* (2001) 101

Busby, Brett, Jurisdiction to Limit Third-Country Interaction with Sanctioned States: The Iran and Libya Sanctions and Helms-Burton Acts, 36 *Columbia Journal of Transnational Law* (1998) 621

Byers, Michael, Case note on *Al-Adsani* v. *Government of Kuwait*, 67 *British Year Book of International Law* (1996) 537

Conceptualising the Relationship between *Jus Cogens* and *Erga Omnes* Rules, 66 *Nordic Journal of International Law* (1997) 211

State Immunity: Article 18 of the International Law Commission's Draft, 44 *International and Comparative Law Quarterly* (1995) 882

The Law and Politics of the Pinochet Case, 10 *Duke Journal of Comparative and International Law* (2000) 415

Callan, Erin M., In re Mr. and Mrs. Doe: Witnesses before the Grand Jury and the Head of State Immunity Doctrine, 22 *New York University Journal of International Law and Politics* (1989) 117

Campisano, Jami J., Foreign Sovereign Immunities Act Is Exclusive Basis for Exercising Subject Matter Jurisdiction in Suits against Foreign States: *Argentine Republic* v. *Amerada Hess Shipping Corp.*, 13 *Tulane Maritime Law Journal* (1989) 327

Canada, Foreign Extraterritorial Measures Act Incorporating the Amendments Countering the U.S. Helms-Burton Act, October 9, 1996 (came into force on 1 January 1997), 36 ILM 111 (1997)

BIBLIOGRAPHY

Caplan, Lee M., State Immunity, Human Rights and *Jus Cogens*: A Critique of the Normative Hierarchy Theory, 97 *American Journal of International Law* (2003) 741

The Constitution and Jurisdiction over Foreign States: The 1996 Amendment to the Foreign Sovereign Immunities Act in Perspective, 41 *Virginia Journal of International Law* (2001) 369

Carnegie Endowment for International Peace, *The Treaties of Peace 1919–1923*, New York, 1924 (in two volumes)

Carter, Victor A., God Save the King: Unconstitutional Assertions of Personal Jurisdiction over Foreign States in U.S. Courts, 82 *Virginia Law Review* (1996) 357

Carty, Anthony, *Philosophy of International Law*, Edinburgh University Press, 2007

Cassel, Douglas, Empowering United States Courts to Hear Crimes within the Jurisdiction of the International Criminal Court, 35 *New England Law Review* (2001) 421

Cassese, Antonio, *International Law*, 2nd edn, Oxford University Press, 2005

When May Senior State Officials Be Tried for International Crimes? Some Comments on the *Congo* v. *Belgium* Case, 13 *European Journal of International Law* (2002) 853

Cavalier, Georges, and Upex, Robert, The Concept of Employment Contract in European Private Law, 55 *International and Comparative Law Quarterly* (2006) 587

Centres de Droit International, *L'Immunité, 1969: Centres de droit international de l'Institut de Sociologie de l'Université Bruxelles et de l'Université de Louvain, L'Immunité de juridiction et d'exécution des Etats: A propos du projet de Convention du Conseil de l'Europe, Actes du Colloque conjoint des 30 et 31 janvier* 1969, Editions de l'Institut de Sociologie de l'Université Libre de Bruxelles, 1969

Chamlongrasdr, Dhisadee, *Foreign State Immunity and Arbitration*, London: Cameron May, 2007

Charles, Philippa, Section 44, Freezing Injunctions and Foreign Arbitrations: Limitations on Jurisdiction, 12 *International Arbitration Law Review* (2009) 34

Charney, Jonathan I., Progress in International Criminal Law? 93 *American Journal of International Law* (1999) 452

Chorazak, Mark J., Clarity and Confusion: Did *Republic of Austria* v. *Altmann* Revive State Department Suggestions of Foreign Sovereign Immunity? 55 *Duke Law Journal* (2005) 373

Christie, G.C., What Constitutes a Taking of Property under International Law? 38 *British Year Book of International Law* (1962) 307

Christopher, Brent E., State Responsibility and Noncommercial Torts under the Foreign Sovereign Immunities Act: Searching for an Applicable Respondeat Superior Doctrine through *Liu* v. *Republic of China*, 27 *Texas International Law Journal* (1992) 137

Chukwumerije, Okezie, ICSID Arbitration and Sovereign Immunity, 19 *Anglo-American Law Review* (1990) 166

Ciampi, Annalisa, The Italian Court of Cassation Asserts Civil Jurisdiction over Germany in a Criminal Case Relating to the Second World War: The *Civitella* Case, 7 *Journal of International Criminal Justice* (2009) 597

Clagett, Brice M., Title III of the Helms-Burton Act Is Consistent with International Law, 90 *American Journal of International Law* (1996) 434

Clement, Julie A., Strengthening Autonomy by Waiving Sovereign Immunity: Why Indian Tribes Should Be 'Foreign' under the Foreign Sovereign Immunities Act, 14 *Thomas M. Coolie Law Review* (1997) 653

Cohn, E. J., Waiver of Immunity, 34 *British Year Book of International Law* (1958) 260

Colliard, C. A., Case note on *Socobelge*, 41 *Revue critique de droit international privé* (1952) 124

Collier, Alan H., The Foreign Sovereign Immunities Act and its Impact on Aviation Litigation, 69 *Journal of Air Law and Commerce* (2004) 519

Collier, J. G., Municipal Law and International Law Tangle Once More, 54 *Cambridge Law Journal* (1995) 7

Collins, Sir Lawrence, (gen. ed.), *Dicey, Morris and Collins on the Conflict of Laws*, 14th edn, Vol. 1, London: Sweet & Maxwell, 2006

Collums, H. D., The *Letelier* Case: Foreign Sovereign Liability for Acts of Political Assassination, 21 *Virginia Journal of International Law* (1980–81) 251

Connors, Todd, The Foreign Sovereign Immunities Act: Using Separation of Powers Analysis to Guide Judicial Decision-Making, 26 *Law and Policy in International Business* (1994) 203

Cooper-Hill, James, *The Law of Sovereign Immunity and Terrorism*, Oxford: Oceana Publications, 2006

Corten, Olivier, and Klein, Pierre, (eds.), *The Vienna Conventions on the Law of Treaties: A Commentary*, Vol. II, Oxford University Press, 2011, pp. 1224–1233 (Eric Suy) and 1234–1235 (Anne Lagerwall)

Cosnard, Michel, *La soumission des États aux tribunaux internes – Face à la théorie des immunités des États*, Paris: Éditions Pedone, 1996

Coulson, Douglas M., 'Toto, I Have a Feeling We're Not in Kansas Anymore': *Voest-Alpine Trading USA Corp. v. Bank of China*, 7 *Tulane Journal of International and Comparative Law* (1999) 431

Council of Europe Database on State Practice regarding State Immunities (www.coe.int/t/dlapil/cahdi/State_Immunities/default_en.asp)

Council of Europe, *Explanatory Reports on the European Convention on State Immunity and the Additional Protocol*, Strasbourg, 1972, also available at: http://conventions.coe.int (Full list – Nos. 74 and 74A)

Courbe, Patrick, *Droit international privé*, 2nd edn, Paris: Armand Colin, 2003

Courtney, Thomas B., *Mareva Injunctions and Related Interlocutory Orders*, West Sussex: Tottel Publishing, 1998

Crawford, James, A Foreign State Immunities Act for Australia? 8 *Australian Yearbook of International Law* (1978–80) 71

    Execution of Judgments and Foreign Sovereign Immunity, 75 *American Journal of International Law* (1981) 820

    International Crimes of States, in J. Crawford, A. Pellet, S. Olleson and K. Parlett) (eds.), *The Law of International Responsibility*, Oxford University Press, 2010, Chapter 29, p. 405

714 BIBLIOGRAPHY

International Law and Foreign Sovereigns: Distinguishing Immune Transactions, 54 *British Year Book of International Law* (1983) 75

The Creation of States in International Law, 2nd edn, Oxford: Clarendon Press, 2006

The International Law Commission's Articles on State Responsibility, Introduction, Text and Commentaries, Cambridge University Press, 2002

Cristy, J. Thomas, Amending the Foreign Sovereign Immunities Act of 1976 to Better Accommodate Non-Market Economies, 8 *Michigan Yearbook of International Legal Studies* (1987) 159

Cuba, Reaffirmation of Cuban Dignity and Sovereignty Act, Adopted 24 December 1996, 36 ILM 472 (1997)

Daillier, Patrick, Forteau, Mathias, and Pellet, Alain, *Droit international public*, 8th edn, Paris: LGDJ, Lextenso éditions, 2009

D'Amato, Anthony, Human Rights as Part of Customary International Law: A Plea for Change of Paradigms, 25 *Georgia Journal of International and Comparative Law* (1995–96) 47

It's a Bird, It's a Plane, It's *Jus Cogens!* 6 *Connecticut Journal of International Law* (1990) 1

There is No Norm of Intervention or Non-Intervention in International Law, 7 *International Legal Theory* (2001) 33

Damiani, Lisa J., The Power of United States Courts to Deny Former Heads of State Immunity from Jurisdiction, 18 *California Western International Law Journal* (1988) 355

Damrosch, Lori Fisler, Enforcing International Law through Non-Forcible Measures, 269 *Recueil des Cours: Collected Courses of the Hague Academy of International Law* (1997) 9

Dante, *Monarchy*, Donald Nicholl (trans.), London: Weidenfeld and Nicolson, 1954

Monarchy, Prue Shaw (trans.), Cambridge University Press, 1996

d'Argent, Pierre, Jurisprudence belge relative au droit international public (1993–2003): Immunités, 36 *Revue belge de droit international* (2003) 605–612

Davies, Martin, *Kuwait Airways Corp.* v. *Iraqi Airways Co.*: The Effect in Private International Law of a Breach of Public International Law by a State Actor, 2 *Melbourne Journal of International Law* (2001) 523

Davis, Michael P., Accountability and World Leadership: Impugning Sovereign Immunity, *University of Illinois Law Review* (1999) 1357

Day, Charles D., *L'Europeenne de Banque* v. *La Republic de Venezuela*: Unnecessarily Permitting Foreign Plaintiffs to Sue Foreign Governments under the Foreign Sovereign Immunities Act, 17 *Brooklyn Journal of International Law* (1991) 165

de Cara, Jean-Yves, L'Affaire Pinochet devant la Chamre des Lords, 45 *Annuaire français de droit international* (1999) 72

de Hoogh, André, *Obligations Erga Omnes and International Crimes*, The Hague/London/Boston: Kluwer Law International, 1996

de Oliveira Moll, Leandro, *Al-Adsani* v. *United Kingdom*: State Immunity and Denial of Justice with Respect to Violations of Fundamental Human Rights, 4 *Melbourne Journal of International Law* (2003) 561

De Sena, Pasquale, and De Vittor, Francesca, State Immunity and Human Rights: The Italian Supreme Court Decision on the *Ferrini* Case, 16 *European Journal of International Law* (2005) 89

de Smet, Simon, The Immunity of Heads of States in US Courts after the Decision of the International Court of Justice, 72 *Nordic Journal of International Law* (2003) 313

de Visscher, Charles, Les gouvernements étrangers en justice, 3 *Revue de droit international et de législation comparée* (1922) 149 and 300 (in two parts)

de Wet, Erika, The Prohibition of Torture as an International Norm of *Jus Cogens* and its Implications for National and Customary Law, 15 *European Journal of International Law* (2004) 97

Deakin, Simon, and Morris, Gillian S., *Labour Law*, 5th edn, Oxford and Portland, Oregon: Hart Publishing, 2009

Deen-Racsmány, Zsuzsanna, *Prosecutor v. Taylor*: The Status of the Special Court for Sierra Leone and its Implications for Immunity, 18 *Leiden Journal of International Law* (2005) 299

Defeis, Elizabeth, The Foreign Sovereign Immunities Act and the Human Rights Violations, 8 *ILSA Journal of International and Comparative Law* (2002) 363

Dehner, Jeffrey S., Vessel-Source Pollution and Public Vessels: Sovereign Immunity v. Compliance, Implications for International Environmental Law, 9 *Emory International Law Review* (1995) 507

Delaume, Georges R., Sovereign Immunity and Public Debt, 23 *International Lawyer* (1989) 811

The Foreign Sovereign Immunities Act and Public Debt Litigation: Some Fifteen Years Later, 88 *American Journal of International Law* (1994) 257

Dellapenna, Joseph W., Foreign State Immunity in Europe, 5 *New York International Law Review* (1992) 51

Has the Time Come to Revise the Foreign Sovereign Immunities Act? 88 *American Society of International Law Proceedings* (1994) 509

Refining the Foreign Sovereign Immunities Act, 9 *Willamette Journal of International Law and Dispute Resolution* (2001) 57

Suing Foreign Governments and their Corporations, 2nd edn, New York: Transnational Publishers, 2003

Denza, Eileen, *Ex parte Pinochet*: Lacuna or Leap? 48 *International and Comparative Law Quarterly* (1999) 949

The 2005 UN Convention on State Immunity in Perspective, 55 *International and Comparative Law Quarterly* (2006) 395

Deutsch, Ruthanne M., Suing State-Sponsors of Terrorism under the Foreign Sovereign Immunities Act: Giving Life to the Jurisdictional Grant after *Cicippio-Puleo*, 38 *International Lawyer* (2004) 891

Diaz, Ismael, A Critique of Proposals to Amend the Foreign Sovereign Immunities Act to Allow Suits against Foreign Sovereigns for Human Rights Violations, 32 *University of Miami Inter-American Law Review* (2001) 137

DiBiagio, Thomas M., Federal Jurisdiction over Foreign Governments for Violations of International Law: Foreign Sovereign Immunity and the

716   BIBLIOGRAPHY

Alien Tort Statute after *Amerada Hess Shipping Corp.* v. *Argentine Republic*, 12 *Maryland Journal of International Law and Trade* (1988) 153

Dickinson, Andrew, Status of Forces under the UN Convention on State Immunity, 55 *International and Comparative Law Quarterly* (2006) 427

Dickinson, Andrew, Lindsay, Rae, Loonam, James P. (eds.), *State Immunity: Selected Materials and Commentary*, Oxford University Press, 2004

Dickinson, Edwin D., The Law of Nations as Part of the National Law of the United States, 101 *University of Pennsylvania Law Review* (1952) 26

Dinstein, Yoram, Par in Parem Non Habet Imperium, 1 *Israel Law Review* (1966) 407

Diplomatic note from the Egyptian authorities to the Swiss Embassy in Egypt requesting and the latter's response assuring immunity from seizure for Egyptian objects of art to be on exhibition in Switzerland: 14 *Revue suisse de droit international et de droit européen* (2004) 672

Dixon, Martin, *Textbook on International Law*, 6th edn, Oxford University Press, 2007

Dominicé, C., Quelques observations sur l'immunité de juridiction pénale de l'ancien Chef d'Etat, 103 *Revue générale de droit international public* (1999) 297

Donner, Ruth, Some Recent Caselaw concerning State Immunity before National Courts, 5 *Finnish Yearbook of International Law* (1994) 388

Donoghue, Joan E., Taking the 'Sovereign' Out of the Foreign Sovereign Immunities Act: A Functional Approach to the Commercial Activity Exception, 17 *Yale Journal of International Law* (1992) 489

The Public Face of Private International Law: Prospects for a Convention on Foreign State Immunity, 57 *Law and Contemporary Problems* (1994) 305

Donoho, Justin, Minimalist Interpretation of the Jurisdictional Immunities Convention, 9 *Chicago Journal of International Law* (2009) 661

Dorsey, William R., III, Reflections on the Foreign Sovereign Immunities Act after Twenty Years, 28 *Journal of Maritime Law and Commerce* (1997) 257

du Plessis, Max, The Pinochet Cases and South African Extradition Law, 16 *South African Journal on Human Rights* (2000) 669

DuCaine, Danielle, Expectations of Immunity: Removing the Barrier to Retroactive Application of the Foreign Sovereign Immunities Act to Pre-1952 Events, 25 *Loyola of Los Angeles International and Comparative Law Review* (2003) 697

Dunbar, N. C. H., Controversial Aspects of Sovereign Immunity in the Case Law of Some States, 132 *Recueil des Cours: Collected Courses of the Hague Academy of International Law* (1971–I) 177

Dupuy, Pierre-Marie and Kerbrat, Yann, *Droit international public*, 10th edn, Paris: Éditions Dalloz, 2010

Durchslag, Melvyn R., *State Sovereign Immunity: A Reference Guide to the United States Constitution*, Westport: Praeger, 2002

Early, Ethan J., *Flatow* v. *Islamic Republic of Iran* and the Foreign Sovereign Immunities Act: Is Peace of Mind Enough? 14 *Connecticut Journal of International Law* (1999) 203

Eboe-Osuji, Chile, State Immunity, State Atrocities, and Civil Justice in the Modern Era of International Law, 45 *Canadian Yearbook of International Law* (2007) 223

Elsea, Jennifer K., *Suits against Terrorist States by Victims of Terrorism, as a Congressional Research Service Report for US Congress*, updated on 8 August 2008, Order Code RL 31258, available at: www.fas.org/sgp/crs/terror/RL31258.pdf

Engle, Sandra, Choosing Law for Attributing Liability under the Foreign Sovereign Immunities Act: A Proposal for Uniformity, 15 *Fordham International Law Journal* (1991–1992) 1060

Ettari, Samantha V., A Foundation of Granite or Sand? The International Criminal Court and United States Bilateral Immunity Agreements, 30 *Brooklyn Journal of International Law* (2004) 205

European Union, Council of Ministers Common Position on Cuba, 2 December 1996, 36 ILM 213 (1997)

 Council Regulation (EC) No. 2271/96, Protecting against the Effects of the Extraterritorial Application of Legislation Adopted by a Third Country, 22 November 1996, 36 ILM 125 (1997)

 Demarches Protesting the Cuban Liberty and Democratic Solidarity (Libertad) Act, 35 ILM 397 (1996)

EU–US Memorandum of Understanding concerning the U.S. Helms-Burton Act and the U.S. Iran and Libya Sanctions Act, 11 April 1997, 36 ILM 529 (1997); 91 *American Journal of International Law* (1997) 497

Evanoff, Nicolas J., Direct Effect Jurisdiction under the Foreign Sovereign Immunities Act of 1976: Ending the Chaos in the Circuit Courts, 28 *Houston Law Review* (1991) 629

Evans, Malcolm D. (ed.), *International Law*, 3rd edn, Oxford University Press, 2010

 When the State Taketh and the State Giveth, 45 *International and Comparative Law Quarterly* (1996) 401

Farr, Kristen, *BP Chemicals, Ltd* v. *Jiangsu Sopo Corp.*: Foreign Sovereign Immunities Act Makes Foreign States Immune from Due Process, 11 *Tulane Journal of International and Comparative Law* (2003) 399

Fastiggi, Michelle, A Jurisdictional Shield for Foreign Nations and their Accountability for Human Rights Violations: *Saudi Arabia* v. *Nelson*, 12 *Dickinson Journal of International Law* (1994) 387

Fatima, Shaheed, and Patel, Naina, State Immunity and the UN Convention: A Practitioner's View, 13 *International Trade Law & Regulation* (2007) 1

Fawcett, James, Carruthers, Janeen M., and North, Peter, *Cheshire, North & Fawcett: Private International Law*, 14th edn, Oxford University Press, 2008

Fawcett, J. E. S., Legal Aspects of State Trading, 25 *British Year Book of International Law* (1948) 34

Feinerman, J. V., Sovereign Immunity in the Chinese Case and its Implications for the Future of International Law, in Ronald St John Macdonald (gen. ed.), *Essays in Honour of Wang Tieya*, Dordrecht/London: Martinus Nijhoff Publishers, 1994, p. 251

Feldman, Mark B., Amending the Foreign Sovereign Immunities Act: The ABA Position, 20 *International Lawyer* (1986) 1289

 Foreign Sovereign Immunity in the United States Courts 1976–1986, *Vanderbilt Journal of Transnational Law* (1986) 19

Feliciano, F. P., The Doctrine of Sovereign Immunity from Suit in a Developing and Liberalizing Economy: Philippine Experience and Caselaw, 3 *Austrian Review of International and European Law* (1998) 1

Fife, Rolf Einar, and Jervell, Kristian, Norwegian State Practice on State Immunity, 70 *Nordic Journal of International Law* (2001) 547

Fitzgerald, Amber, The Pinochet Case: Head of State Immunity within the United States, 22 *Whittier Law Review* (2001) 987

Fitzmaurice, G. G., State Immunity from Proceedings in Foreign Courts, 14 *British Year Book of International Law* (1933) 101

Fitzpatrick, Joan, The Claim to Foreign Sovereign Immunity by Individuals Sued for International Human Rights Violations, 15 *Whittier Law Review* (1994) 465

Focarelli, Carlo, Denying Foreign State Immunity for Commission of International Crimes: The *Ferrini* Decision, 54 *International and Comparative Law Quarterly* (2005) 951

Federal Republic of Germany v. *Giovanni Mantelli and Others*, 103 *American Journal of International Law* (2009) 122

Foresta, Stephen G., Prejudgment Attachment of Foreign Sovereign Assets under the Proposed Amendments to the Foreign Sovereign Immunities Act, 9 *Fordham International Law Journal* (1986) 295

Fornaro, Susan L., *Republic of Argentina* v. *Weltover Inc.*: The Foreign Sovereign Immunities Act: Commercial Activity and Direct Effect Revisited, 1 *Tulane Journal of International and Comparative Law* (1993) 287

Fox, Hazel, A 'Commercial Transaction' under the State Immunity Act 1978, 43 *International and Comparative Law Quarterly* (1994) 193

Access to Justice and State Immunity, 117 *Law Quarterly Review* (2001) 10

Employment Contracts as an Exception to State Immunity: Is All Public Service Immune? 66 *British Year Book of International Law* (1995) 97

Enforcement Jurisdiction, Foreign State Property and Diplomatic Immunity, 34 *International and Comparative Law Quarterly* (1985) 115

Enforcement of Judgments against Foreign States: '. . . the kind of coherent law we ought to have?' 125 *Law Quarterly Review* (2009) 544

In Defence of State Immunity: Why the UN Convention on State Immunity Is Important, 55 *International and Comparative Law Quarterly* (2006) 399

International Law and Restraints on the Exercise of Jurisdiction by National Courts of States, in Malcolm D. Evans (ed.), *International Law*, 3rd edn, Oxford University Press, 2010, Chapter 12, p. 340

Private Law Damages as a Method of State Accountability: The Tort Exception to State Immunity, *Third World Legal Studies* (1993) 107

State Immunity and Enforcement of Arbitral Awards: Do We Need an UNCITRAL Model Law Mark II for Execution against State Property? 12 *Arbitration International* (1996) 89

State Immunity and the International Crime of Torture, *European Human Rights Law Review* (2006–2) 142

State Immunity: The House of Lord's Decision in *I Congreso Del Partido*, 98 *Law Quarterly Review* (1982) 94

State Responsibility and Tort Proceedings against a Foreign State in Municipal
   Courts, 20 *Netherlands Yearbook of International Law* (1989) 3
States and the Undertaking to Arbitrate, 37 *International and Comparative Law
   Quarterly* (1988) 1
The Commerciality of the Spoils of War, 112 *Law Quarterly Review* (1996) 186
The Law of State Immunity, 2nd edn, Oxford University Press, 2008
The Pinochet Case No. 3, 48 *International and Comparative Law Quarterly* (1999) 687
The Resolution of the Institute of International Law on the Immunities of
   Heads of State and Government, 51 *International and Comparative Law
   Quarterly* (2002) 119
Where Does the Buck Stop? State Immunity from Civil Jurisdiction and
   Torture, 121 *Law Quarterly Review* (2005) 353
Fredman, Sandra, and Morris, Gillian S., *The State as Employer: Labour Law in the
   Public Services*, London/New York: Mansell Publishing Ltd, 1989
Freedland, Mark R., *The Personal Employment Contract*, Oxford University Press, 2003
Frostestad, Heidi L., *Voest-Alpine Trading* v. *Bank of China*: Can a Uniform
   Interpretation of a 'Direct Effect' Be Attained under the Foreign Sovereign
   Immunities Act (FSIA) of 1976? 34 *Valparaiso University Law Review* (2000) 515
Frulli, Micaela, The ICJ Judgement on the *Belgium* v. *Congo* Case (14 February
   2002): A Cautious Stand on Immunity from Prosecution for International
   Crimes, 3 *German Law Journal* (2002), No. 3
The Question of Charles Taylor's Immunity: Still in Search of a Balanced
   Application of Personal Immunities? 2 *Journal of International Criminal Justice*
   (2004) 1118
Gaeta, Paola, Does President Al Bashir Enjoy Immunity from Arrest? 7 *Journal of
   International Criminal Justice* (2009) 315
Gamillscheg, F. and Franzen, M., Conflicts of Laws in Employment Contracts and
   Industrial Relations, in R. Blanpain and C. Engels (eds.), *Comparative Labour
   Law*, 4th and revised edn, 1998, The Hague/London/Boston: Kluwer Law
   International, Chapter 9, p. 161
Garbarino, Nicole S., *Adler* v. *Nigeria*: What Congress Forgot to Say about
   Minimum Contacts and the Criminality of Commercial Activity, 9 *Tulane
   Journal of International and Comparative Law* (2001) 561
Gardiner, Richard, UN Convention on State Immunity: Form and Function, 55
   International and Comparative Law Quarterly (2006) 407
Garnett, Richard, Should Foreign State Immunity Be Abolished? 20 *Australian
   Yearbook of International Law* (1999) 175
State Immunity in Employment Matters, 46 *International and Comparative Law
   Quarterly* (1997) 81
State Immunity Triumphs in the European Court of Human Rights, 118 *Law
   Quarterly Review* (2002) 367
The Defence of State Immunity for Acts of Torture, 18 *Australian Yearbook of
   International Law* (1997) 97
The Perils of Working for a Foreign Government: Foreign Sovereign Immunity
   and Employment, 29 *California Western International Law Journal* (1998) 133

720   BIBLIOGRAPHY

The Precarious Position of Embassy and Consular Employees in the United
Kingdom, 54 *International and Comparative Law Quarterly* (2005) 705

Gartenstein-Ross, Daveed, A Critique of the Terrorism Exception to the Foreign
Sovereign Immunities Act, 34 *New York University Journal of International Law
and Politics* (2002) 887

Resolving Outstanding Judgments under the Terrorism Exception to the
Foreign Sovereign Immunities Act, 77 *New York University Law Review*
(2002) 496

Gattini, Andrea, War Crimes and State Immunity in the *Ferrini* Decision, 3 *Journal
of International Criminal Justice* (2005) 224

Gautama, Sudargo, International Civil Procedure in Indonesia, 6 *Asian Yearbook of
International Law* (1996) 87

Gavouneli, Maria, War Reparation Claims and State Immunity, 50 *Revue hellénique
de droit international* (1997) 595

Gavouneli, Maria, and Bantekas, Ilias, *Prefecture of Voiotia v. Federal Republic
of Germany*, Case No. 11/2000, Areios Pagos (Hellenic Supreme Court), 2000,
95 *American Journal of International Law* (2001) 198

Gee, Stephen, *Gee on Commercial Injunctions: Formerly 'Mareva Injunctions and Anton
Piller Relief'*, 5th edn, London: Sweet & Maxwell, 2004

Geller, Karen, The Interplay between the Foreign Sovereign Immunities Act
and ERISA: The Effects of *Gates* v. *Victor Fine Foods*, 29 *University of Miami
Inter-American Law Review* (1998) 575 (ERISA stands for 'Employee Retirement
Income Security Act')

George, Shobha Varughese, Head-of-State Immunity in the United States Courts:
Still Confused after All These Years, 64 *Fordham Law Review* (1995) 1051

Gergen, Jennifer A., Human Rights and the Foreign Sovereign Immunities Act, 36
Virginia Journal of International Law (1996) 765

Glannon, Joseph W., and Atik, Jeffery, Politics and Personal Jurisdiction; Suing
State Sponsors of Terrorism under the 1996 Amendments to the Foreign
Sovereign Immunities Act, 87 *Georgetown Law Journal* (1999) 675

Goekjian, Lisa D., Jurisdiction over Iran under the FSIA and the Algiers Accord,
A Loose Application: *Foremost-McKesson Inc.* v. *Islamic Republic of Iran*, 59 *George
Washington Law Review* (1991) 1311

Gohlke, David E., Clearing the Air or Muddying the Waters? Defining 'A Direct
Effect in the United States' under the Foreign Sovereign Immunities Act
after *Republic of Argentina* v. *Weltover*, 18 *Houston Journal of International Law*
(1995) 261

Gong, Renren, *A Comparative Study of State Immunity*, 2nd edn, Beijing: Peking
University Press, 2005 (in Chinese)

Goodman, Marla, The Destruction of International Notions of Power and
Sovereignty: The Supreme Court's Misguided Application of Retroactivity
Doctrine to the Foreign Sovereign Immunities Act in *Republic of Austria* v.
Altmann, 93 *Georgetown Law Journal* (2005) 1117

Gotfredsen, Dana R., Seeking Comfort in America: Why an Amendment to the
Foreign Sovereign Immunities Act Is the Most Effective Means of Holding

Foreign Governments Accountable for Gender-Based Crimes, 15 *Emory International Law Review* (2001) 647

Grant, John P., and Barker, J. Craig, (eds.), *Parry and Grant: Encyclopaedic Dictionary of International Law*, 2nd edn, Dobbs Ferry, New York: Oceana Publications, Inc., 2004, p. 469, 'Sovereign Immunity'

Gray, Christine D., *Judicial Remedies in International Law*, Oxford: Clarendon Press, 1987

Green, N. A. Maryan, A General Theory of Immunity, 3 *Hague Yearbook of International Law* (1990) 169

Greener, Gary Jay, The Commercial Exception to Foreign Sovereign Immunity: To Be Immune or Not to Be Immune? That Is the Question: A Look at the International Law Commission's Draft Articles on Jurisdictional Immunities of States and their Property, 15 *Loyola of LA International and Comparative Law Journal* (1992) 173

Greig, D. W., Forum State Jurisdiction and Sovereign Immunity under the International Law Commission's Draft Articles, 38 *International and Comparative Law Quarterly* (1989) 243

Specific Exceptions to Immunity under the International Law Commission's Draft Articles, 38 *International and Comparative Law Quarterly* (1989) 560

Griggs, Jane H., The Foreign Sovereign Immunities Act: Do Tiered Corporate Subsidiaries Constitute Foreign States? 20 *New England Law Review* (1998) 387

Groobey, J. Christopher, The Foreign Defendant's Demand for Jury Trial under the Foreign Sovereign Immunities Act, *University of Chicago Legal Forum* (1990) 511

Grosscup, Scott, The Trial of Slobodan Milosevic: The Demise of Head of State Immunity and the Specter of Victor's Justice, 32 *Denver Journal of International Law and Policy* (2004) 355

Guittari, Theodore R., *The American Law of Sovereign Immunity: An Analysis of Legal Interpretation*, New York: Praeger, 1970

Gully-Hart, Paul, The Function of State and Diplomatic Privileges and Immunities in International Cooperation in Criminal Matters: The Position in Switzerland, 23 *Fordham International Law Journal* (2000) 1334

Gutmann, Daniel, *Droit international privé*, 3rd edn, Paris: Dalloz, 2002

Hackworth, Green Haywood, *Digest of International Law*, Washington DC: US Government Printing Office, 1941

Haffke, Christopher W., The Torture Victim Protection Act: More Symbol Than Substance, 43 *Emory Law Journal* (1994) 1467

Hafner, Gerhard, *L'Immunité d'exécution dans le Projet de Convention des Nations Unies sur les immunités juridictionnelles des Etats et de leurs biens*, in Isabelle Pingel (dir.), *Droit des immunités et exigences du procès équitable*, Paris: Editions Pedone, 2004, p. 85

Hafner, Gerhard, and Köhler, Ulrike, The United Nations Convention on Jurisdictional Immunities of States and Their Property, 35 *Netherlands Yearbook of International Law* (2004) 3

Hafner, Gerhard, and Lange, Leonore, La Convention des Nations Unies sur les Immunités juridictionnelles des États et de leurs Biens, 50 *Annuaire français de droit international* (2004) 45

722 BIBLIOGRAPHY

Hafner, Gerhard, Kohen, Marcelo G., and Breau, Susan (eds.), *State Practice Regarding State Immunities*, Leiden/Boston: Martinus Nijhoff Publishers, 2006, companion volume to the Council of Europe Database on State Practice regarding State Immunities (www.coe.int/t/dlapil/cahdi/State_Immunities/default_en.asp)

Hall, Christopher Keith, The Duty of States Parties to the Convention against Torture to Provide Procedures Permitting Victims to Recover Reparations for Torture Committed Abroad, 18 *European Journal of International Law* (2007) 921

UN Convention on State Immunity: The Need for a Human Rights Protocol, 55 *International and Comparative Law Quarterly* (2006) 411

Halsbury's Laws of England, 4th edn, Vol. 18, London: LexisNexis, 1977

Halverson, Karen, Is a Foreign State a 'Person'? Does it Matter? Personal Jurisdictional, Due Process, and the Foreign Sovereign Immunities Act, 34 *NYU Journal of International Law and Politics* (2001) 115

Hamson, C. J., Immunity of Foreign State: The Practice of the French Courts, 27 *British Year Book of International Law* (1950) 293

Handl, G., The Pinochet Case, Foreign State Immunity and the Changing Constitution of the International Community, in Wolfgang Benedek *et al.* (eds.), *Development and Developing International and European law: Essays in Honour of Konrad Ginther on the Occasion of his 65th Birthday*, Bern: Peter Lang, 1999, p. 59

Hannikainen, Lauri, *Peremptory Norms (Jus Cogens) in International Law: Historical Development, Criteria, Present Status*, Helsinki: Finnish Lawyers' Publishing Company, 1988

Hardy, Joseph W., Jr., Wipe Away the Tiers: Determining Agency or Instrumentality Status under the Foreign Sovereign Immunities Act, 31 *Georgia Law Review* (1997) 1121

Harjani, Sunil R., Litigating Claims over Foreign Government-Owned Corporations under the Commercial Activities Exception to the Foreign Sovereign Immunities Act, 20 *Northwestern Journal of International Law and Business* (1999) 181

Harris, Jason R., Protecting Sunken Warships as Objects Entitled to Sovereign Immunity, 33 *University of Miami Inter-American Law Review* (2002) 101

Hartmann, Adolphe, De la Compétence des Tribunaux dans les Procès contre les États et Souverains Étrangers, 22 *Revue de droit international et de législation comparée* (1890) 425

Harvard Research, 1932: Harvard Law School, Research in International Law: Competence of Courts in Regard to Foreign States, 26 *American Journal of International Law Supplement* (1932) 451

Hasson, Adam Isaac, Extraterritorial Jurisdiction and Sovereign Immunity on Trial: Noriega, Pinochet and Milosevic – Trends in Political Accountability and Transnational Criminal Law, 25 *Boston College International and Comparative Law Review* (2002) 125

Havkin, Stella, The Foreign Sovereign Immunities Act: The Relationship between the Commercial Activity Exception and the Noncommercial Tort Exception in Light of *De Sanchez* v. *Banco Central de Nicaragua*, 10 *Hastings International and Comparative Law Review* (1987) 455

Hayes, Ben J., The ABCs of Service of Process under the Foreign Sovereign Immunities Act, 6 *Florida Journal of International Law* (1991) 255

Hendricks, Mark Christian, Birth of a Nation: The Republic of Palau Is Recognized as a Foreign Sovereign under the Foreign Sovereign Immunities Act of 1976 – *Morgan Guaranty Trust* v. *Republic of Palau*, 639 F.Supp. 706 (S.D.N.Y. 1986), *Brigham Young University Law Review* (1987) 709

Henzelin, Marc, La compétence pénal universelle: une question non resolue par l'arret Yerodia, 106 *Revue générale de droit international public* (2002) 819

Heß, Burkhard, The International Law Commission's Draft Convention on the Jurisdictional Immunities of States and their Property, 4 *European Journal of International Law* (1993) 269

Hickey, Charles E., The Dictator, Drugs and Diplomacy by Indictment: Head-of-State Immunity in *United States* v. *Noriega*, 4 *Connecticut Journal of International Law* (1989) 729

Higgins, R., Certain Unresolved Aspects of the Law of State Immunity, 29 *Netherlands International Law Review* (1982) 265

Higgins, Rosalyn, Execution of State Property: United Kingdom Practice, 10 *Netherlands Yearbook of International Law* (1979) 35

Problems and Process: International Law and How We Use It, Oxford: Clarendon Press, 1994

Hines, Julius H., Why Do Unrecognized Governments Enjoy Sovereign Immunity? A Reassessment of the *Wulfsohn* Case, 31 *Virginia Journal of International Law* (1991) 717

Hirobe, K., Immunity of State Property: Japanese Practice, 10 *Netherlands Yearbook of International Law* (1979) 233

Ho, Pik-Kwan, Foreign Sovereign Immunities Act of 1976 Provides the Sole Basis for Obtaining Jurisdiction over Foreign States in United States Courts: *Argentine Republic* v. *Amerada Hess Shipping Corp.*, 488 U.S. 428 (1989), 56 *Journal of Air Law and Commerce* (1991) 1187

Hoek, Danny A., Foreign Sovereign Immunity and *Saudi Arabia* v. *Nelson*: A Practical Guide, 18 *Hastings International and Comparative Law Review* (1995) 617

Hoffman, William C., The Separate Entity Rule in International Perspective: Should State Ownership of Corporate Shares Confer Sovereign Status for Immunity Purposes? 65 *Tulane Law Review* (1991) 535

Honeyball, Simon, *Honeyball & Bowers' Textbook on Employment Law*, 10th edn, Oxford University Press, 2008

Hoops, Michael W., Retroactivity, Implied Waiver, and the FSIA: Is it Time to Reform the Law on Sovereign Immunity? 24 *Hofstra Law Review* (1995) 515

Hopkins, John, Immunity – Head of Foreign State, 57 *Cambridge Law Journal* (1998) 4

Hornby, Ross, *Re Canada Labour Code*: A Common Sense Solution to the Commercial Activity Exception, 30 *Canadian Yearbook of International Law* (1992) 301

724   BIBLIOGRAPHY

Horowitz, Jodi, *Regina v. Bartle and the Commissioner of Police for the Metropolis and Others ex Parte Pinochet*: Universal Jurisdiction and Sovereign Immunity for *Jus Cogens* Violations, 23 *Fordham International Law Journal* (1999) 489

Hoyle, Mark S. W., *Mareva Injunction and Related Orders*, 3rd edn, London: LLP Professional, 1997

Hsu, Richard Tien-Shi, The Invalidity of the Default Judgment in *Jackson v. People's Republic of China*, 23 *Virginia Journal of International Law* (1983) 569

Hulbig, Adam F., *Aquamar v. Del Monte Fresh Produce*: Expanding the Scope of Ambassador's Rights under the Foreign Sovereign Immunities Act, 25 *North Carolina Journal of International Law and Commercial Regulation* (2000) 597

IDI, Draft, 1991: L'Institut de Droit International, Contemporary Problems concerning the Immunity of States in Relation to Questions of Jurisdiction and Enforcement, 1991, *Annuaire de l'Institut de Droit International*, Vol. 64-II, 1992, p. 388

   2001: L'Institut de Droit International, Les immunités de juridiction et d'exécution du chef d'Etat et de gouvernement en droit international / Immunities from Jurisdiction and Execution of Heads of State and of Government in International Law, *Annuaire de l'Institut de Droit International*, Vol. 69 (2000–2001), Session de Vancouver, 2001, p. 742

IDI, Projet, 1891: Projet de règlement international sur la compétence des tribunaux dans les procès contre les États, souverains ou chefs d'État étrangers (Rapporteurs: L. von Bar and J. Westlake), *Annuaire de l'Institut de Droit International*, Vol. 11, Session de Hambourg, Septembre 1891, pp. 436–438

IDI, *Tableau Général pendant la Période décennale 1904 à 1914*, La Haye/Paris, 1919

ILA, Drafts (1982 and 1994): International Law Association, Montreal Draft Articles for a Convention on State Immunity, *Report of the Sixtieth Conference (Montreal)*, 1982, pp. 5 and 325; Revised Buenos Aires Draft Articles for a Convention on State Immunity, *Report of the Sixty-Sixth Conference (Buenos Aires)*, 1994, pp. 21 and 452

Jacobson, Jeffrey, Trying to Fit a Square Peg into a Round Hole: The Foreign Sovereign Immunities Act and Human Rights Violations, 19 *Whittier Law Review* (1998) 757

Jaffe, Louis L., *Judicial Aspects of Foreign Relations*, Cambridge, MA: Harvard University Press, 1933

Jay, Gregory, United States May Exercise Jurisdiction over a Foreign Sovereign Who Has Issued Promissory Notes to a U.S. Corporation: *Shapiro v. Republic of Bolivia*, 930 F.2d 1013 (2d Cir. 1991), 21 *Georgia Journal of International and Comparative Law* (1991) 539

Jennings, Sir Robert, Jurisdiction and Immunity in the ICJ Decision in the Yerodia Case, 4 *International Law Forum* (2002) 99

   The Judiciary, International and National, and the Development of International Law, 102 *ILR* ix, xiii.

Jennings, Sir Robert, and Watts, Sir Arthur, (eds.), *Oppenheim's International Law*, 9th edn, Vol. I: Peace, Harlow, Essex: Longman, 1992

Jiménez, Alberto Soria, The Evolution in Spanish Law of State Immunity Leading to the Acceptance of the Restrictive Theory, 2 *Spanish Yearbook of International Law* (1992) 45

Johnson, Anita C., The Extradition Proceedings against General Augusto Pinochet: Is Justice Being Met under International Law? 29 *Georgia Journal of International and Comparative Law* (2000) 203

Johnson, Everett C., Jr., *Saudi Arabia* v. *Nelson*: The Foreign Sovereign Immunities Act in Perspective, 16 *Houston Journal of International Law* (1993) 291

Johnson, Kathleen M., The Case of General Augusto Pinochet: A Legal Research Guide, 27 *Brooklyn Journal of International Law* (2002) 519

Johnson, Thora A., A Violation of *Jus Cogens* Norms as an Implicit Waiver of Immunity under the Federal Sovereign Immunities Act, 19 *Maryland Journal of International Law and Trade* (1995) 259

Jones, David Lloyd, State Immunity – Execution against Embassy Bank Account, 43 *Cambridge Law Journal* (1984) 222

Kahale, George, III, New Legislation in the United States Facilitates Enforcement of Arbitral Agreements and Awards against Foreign States, 2 *Journal of International Arbitration* (1989) 57

Kaiden, Jonathan, *Millen Industries Inc.* v. *Coordination Council for North American Affairs*: Unnecessarily Denying American Companies the Right to Sue Foreign Governments under the Foreign Sovereign Immunities Act, 17 *Brooklyn Journal of International Law* (1991) 193

Kantorowicz, Ernst H., *The King's Two Bodies: A Study in Mediaeval Political Theology*, Princeton University Press, 1998

Karagiannakis, Magdalini, State Immunity and Fundamental Human Rights, 11 *Leiden Journal of International Law* (1998) 9

Karnezis, Kristine Cordier, *Annotation, Award of Damages under State-Sponsored Terrorism Exception to Foreign Sovereign Immunities Act (28 U.S.C.A. § 1605(a)(7))*, 182 *A.L.R. Fed. 1, 2002 WL 31628515 (2002)*

Kedian, Kathleen M., Customary International Law and International Human Rights Litigation in United States Courts: Revitalizing the Legacy of the *Paquete Habana*, 40 *William and Mary Law Review* (1999) 1395

Kelley, Garland A., Does Customary International Law Supersede a Federal Statute? 37 *Columbia Journal of Transnational Law* (1999) 507

Kelsen, Hans, *Principles of International Law*, New York: Rinehart & Co. Inc., 1952

Kessedjian, Catherine, and Schreuer, Christoph, Le Projet d'articles de la Commission du Droit International des Nations-Unies sur les immunités des États, 96 *Revue générale de droit international public* (1992) 299

Ketchel, Aron, Deriving Lessons for the Alien Tort Claims Act from the Foreign Sovereign Immunities Act, 32 *Yale Journal of International Law* (2007) 191

Kim, Jeewon, Making State Sponsors of Terrorism Pay: A Separation of Power Discourse under the Foreign Sovereign Immunities Act, 22 *Berkeley Journal of International Law* (2004) 513

Klabbers, Jan, The General, the Lords and the Possible End of State Immunity, 68 *Nordic Journal of International Law* (1999) 85

726 BIBLIOGRAPHY

Koji, Teraya, Emerging Hierarchy in International Human Rights and Beyond: From the Perspective of Non-Derogable Rights, 12 *European Journal of International Law* (2001) 917

Koller, David S., Immunities of Foreign Ministers: Paragraph 61 of the *Yerodia* Judgment as it Pertains to the Security Council and the International Criminal Court, 20 *American University International Law Review* (2004) 7

Kono, Toshiyuki, International Civil Procedure in Japan, 6 *Asian Yearbook of International Law* (1996) 105

Koskenniemi, Martti, Hersch Lauterpacht (1897–1960), in Jack Beatson and Reinhard Zimmermann (eds.), *Jurists Uprooted: German-Speaking Émigré Lawyers in Twentieth-Century Britain*, Oxford University Press, 2004, p. 601
  Hierarchy in International Law: A Sketch, 8 *European Journal of International Law* (1997) 566

Krent, Harold J., Reconceptualizing Sovereign Immunity, 45 *Vanderbilt Law Review* (1992) 1529

Kropholler, Jan, *Internationales Privatrecht*, 5. Auflage, Tübingen: Mohr Siebeck, 2004

Lacroix, Gérard, The Theory and Practice of the Foreign Sovereign Immunities Act, Untying the Gordian Knot, 5 *International Tax and Business Lawyer* (1987) 144

Lalive, Jean-Flavien, L'immunité de juridiction des États et des organisations internationales, 84 *Recueil des Cours: Collected Courses of the Hague Academy of International Law* (1953-III) 205
  Quelques observations sur l'immunité d'exécution des Etats et l'arbitrage international, in Yoram Dinstein (ed.), *International Law at a Time of Perplexity: Essays in Honour of Shabtai Rosenne*, Dordrecht/Boston/London: Martinus Nijhoff Publishers, 1989, p. 369

Lang, Melissa, and Bales, Richard, The Immunity of Foreign Subsidiaries under the Foreign Sovereign Immunities Act, 13 *Minnesota Journal of Global Trade* (2004) 353

Lardy, C., *Le droit international codifié*, 5th edn, Paris: Guillaumin, 1895 (French translation of Bluntschli's *Das moderne Völkerrecht*)

Lauterpacht, Elihu, (ed.), *International Law: Being the Collected Papers of Hersch Lauterpacht*, Vol. I, Cambridge University Press, 1970

Lauterpacht, Sir Elihu, *et al.* (eds.), *International Law Reports Consolidated Indexes Volumes 1–125*, Cambridge University Press, 2004

Lauterpacht, Hersch (ed.), *Oppenheim's International Law*, Vol. I: Peace, 8th edn, London/New York/Toronto: Longmans, Green and Co., 1955
  The Problem of Jurisdictional Immunities of Foreign States, 28 *British Year Book of International Law* (1951) 220

Leacock, Stephen J., The Joy of Access to the Zone of Inhibition: *Republic of Argentina v. Weltover, Inc.* and the Commercial Activity Exception under the Foreign Sovereign Immunities Act of 1976, 5 *Minnesota Journal of Global Trade* (1996) 81

Lee, Paul L., Central Banks and Sovereign Immunity, 41 *Columbia Journal of Transnational Law* (2003) 327

Leung, Kevin, *Cicippio v. Islamic Republic of Iran*: Putting the Foreign Sovereign Immunities Act's Commercial Activities Exception in Context, 17 *Loyola of LA International and Comparative Law Journal* (1995) 701

Levy, Jack Alan, As between *Princz* and King: Reassessing the Law of Foreign Sovereign Immunity as Applied to *Jus Cogens* Violators, 86 *Georgetown Law Journal* (1998) 2703

Lew, Avi, *Republic of Argentina v. Weltover, Inc.*: Interpreting the Foreign Sovereign Immunity Act's Commercial Activity Exception to Jurisdictional Immunity, 17 *Fordham International Law Journal* (1994) 726

Lewis, Charles J., *State and Diplomatic Immunity*, 3rd edn, London: Lloyd's of London Press Ltd, 1990

Lieberman, Philippe, Expropriation, Torture, and *Jus Cogens* under the Foreign Sovereign Immunities Act: *Siderman de Blake v. Republic of Argentina*, 24 *University of Miami Inter-American Law Review* (1993) 503

Linderfalk, Ulf, The Effect of *Jus Cogens* Norms: Whoever Opened Pandora's Box, Did You Ever Think about the Consequences? 18 *European Journal of International Law* (2007) 853

Lininger, Tom, Overcoming Immunity Defenses to Human Rights Suits in U.S. Courts, 7 *Harvard Human Rights Journal* (1994) 177

Locke, John, *Two Treatises of Government*, Peter Laslett ed., Book II (Second Treatise), Cambridge University Press, 1988

Loewenstein, Andrew, The Foreign Sovereign Immunities Act and Corporate Subsidies of Agencies or Instrumentalities of Foreign States, 19 *Berkeley Journal of International Law* (2001) 350

Lovell, Benjamin Eric, *Export Group v. Reef Industries, Inc.*: The Reconciliation of the Foreign Sovereign Immunities Act of 1976, 21 *North Carolina Journal of International Law and Commercial Regulation* (1996) 443

Lowe, L. Weatherly, The International Law Commission's Draft Articles on the Jurisdictional Immunities of States and their Property: The Commercial Contract Exception, 27 *Columbia Journal of Transnational Law* (1989) 657

Lowe, Vaughan, *International Law*, Oxford University Press, 2007

Lowenfeld, Andreas F., Claims Against Foreign States – A Proposal for Reform of United States Law, 44 *New York University Law Review* (1969) 901

    Congress and Cuba: The Helms-Burton Act, 90 *American Journal of International Law* (1996) 419

Lupu, Yonatan, and Risen, Clay, Retroactive Application of the Foreign Sovereign Immunities Act: *Landgraf* Analysis and the Political Question Doctrine, 8 *UCLA Journal of International and Foreign Affairs* (2003) 239

Luzzatto, Riccardo, International Commercial Arbitration and the Municipal Law of States, 157 *Recueil des Cours: Collected Courses of the Hague Academy of International Law* (1977-IV) 9

Macedo, Stephen (ed.), *Universal Jurisdiction: National Courts and the Prosecution of Serious Crimes under International Law*, University of Pennsylvania Press, 2004

MacKusick, David, Human Rights v. Sovereign Rights: The State Sponsored Terrorism Exception to the Foreign Sovereign Immunities Act, 10 *Emory International Law Review* (1996) 741

728　BIBLIOGRAPHY

Mahmnoudi, Said, *Local Authority of Västerås* v. *Republic of Iceland*, Case No.
1999:112, Högsta Domstolen (Supreme Court of Sweden), 1999, 95 *American
Journal of International Law* (2001) 192
Mallory, Jerrold L., Resolving the Confusion over Head of State Immunity:
The Defined Rights of Kings, 86 *Columbia Law Review* (1986) 169
Mann, F. A., Immunity of Sovereign States, 2 *Modern Law Review* (1938) 57
Sovereign Immunity, 18 *Modern Law Review* (1955) 184
The Doctrine of *Jus Cogens* in International Law, in F. A. Mann, *Further Studies in
International Law*, Oxford: Clarendon Press, 1990, p. 84
The State Immunity Act 1978, 50 *British Year Book of International Law* (1979) 43
Waiver of Immunity, 107 *Law Quarterly Review* (1991) 362
Marasinghe, Lakshman, The Modern Law of Sovereign Immunity, 54 *Modern Law
Review* (1991) 664
Marks, Jonathan H., Mending the Web: Universal Jurisdiction, Humanitarian
Intervention and the Abrogation of Immunity by the Security Council, 42
Columbia Journal of Transnational Law (2004) 445
Marks, Susan, State Agencies and Foreign Sovereign Immunity, 53 *Cambridge
Law Journal* (1994) 213
Torture and the Jurisdictional Immunity of Foreign States, 56 *Cambridge Law
Journal* (1997) 8
Marston, Geoffrey, State Immunity – Recent United Kingdom Development, 13
Journal of World Trade Law (1979) 349
Martin, Jeffrey N., Sovereign Immunity – Limits of Judicial Control – the Foreign
Sovereign Immunities Act of 1976, Pub. L. No. 94-583, 90 Stat. 2891, 18
Harvard International Law Journal (1977) 429
Martinez, Lucian C., Jr., Sovereign Impunity: Does the Foreign Sovereign
Immunities Act Bar Lawsuits against the Holy See in Clerical Sexual Abuse
Cases? 44 *Texas International Law Journal* (2008) 123
Martiny, Dieter, Waehler, Jan Peter, and Wolff, Martin K., *Handbuch des Internationalen
Zivilverfahrensrechts, Band III/1*, Tübingen: Mohr Siebeck GmbH & Co. K, 1984
Mason, William Brian, A New Call for Reform: Sex Abuse and the Foreign
Sovereign Immunities Act, 33 *Brooklyn Journal of International Law* (2008) 655
Masud, R, Immunity of Foreign States from the Jurisdiction of Courts with
Special Reference to American and English Legal Systems, 33 *All Pakistan
Legal Decisions* (Journal) (1981) 56
Materials on Jurisdictional Immunities, 1982: *United Nations Legislative Series,
ST/LEG/SER.B/20, Materials on Jurisdictional Immunities of States and their Property,
Sales No. E/F 81.V.10*, New York: United Nations, 1982
Mayer, Frank D., Jr., and Odorizzi, Michele, Foreign Government Deposits:
Attachment and Set-Off, *University of Illinois Law Review* (1982) 289
McCarthy, Amelia L., The Commercial Activity Exception – Justice Demands
Congress Define a Line in the Shifting Sands of Sovereign Immunity, 77
Marquette Law Review (1994) 893
McCoy, Barry L., Broadening the Scope of the Foreign Sovereign Immunities
Act: The Explicit Waiver Provision and Limited Foreign Submissions to

Domestic Litigation in *Aquamar S.A.* v. *Del Monte Fresh Produce, Inc.*, 45 *Villanova Law Review* (2000) 319

McGinty, Kevin M., Opening the Courts to Protect Interests Abroad: The Effect of the Foreign Sovereign Immunities Act on Litigation with Developing Countries, 10 *Boston College Third World Law Journal* (1990) 63

McGregor, Lorna, State Immunity and *Jus Cogens*, 55 *International and Comparative Law Quarterly* (2006) 437

Torture and State Immunity: Deflecting Impunity, Distorting Sovereignty, 18 *European Journal of International Law* (2007) 903

McGuire, Matthew Patrick, Direct Effect Jurisdiction in the 90's: *Weltover, Inc.* v. *Republic of Argentina* and a Broad Interpretation of the Foreign Sovereign Immunities Act of 1976, 17 *North Carolina Journal of International Law and Commercial Regulation* (1992) 383

McIntyre, Karleen, *Nelson* v. *Saudi Arabia* – Subject Matter Jurisdiction under the Foreign Sovereign Immunities Act of 1976, 1 *Journal of Transnational Law and Policy* (1992) 273

McKay, Leslie, A New Take on Antiterrorism: *Smith* v. *Socialist People's Libyan Arab Jamahiriya*, 13 *American University International Law Review* (1997) 439

McLachlan, Campbell, *Pinochet* Revisited, 51 *International and Comparative Law Quarterly* (2002) 959

Meron, Theodor, On a Hierarchy of International Human Rights, 80 *American Journal of International Law* (1986) 1

Merrell, Matthew B., *Von Dardel* v. *Union of Soviet Socialist Republics*: An Expansive Interpretation of the Foreign Sovereign Immunities Act, 12 *North Carolina Journal of International Law and Commercial Regulation* (1987) 315

Mesch, Ferdinand, Jurisdictional Immunities of Foreign States, 23 *DePaul Law Review* (1974) 1225

Metzger, S. D., Immunity of Foreign State Property from Attachment or Execution in the USA, 10 *Netherlands Yearbook of International Law* (1979) 131

Mexico, Act to Protect Trade and Investment from Foreign Norms That Contravene International Law, 23 October 1996 (Entered into force 4 November 1996), 36 ILM 133 (1997)

Micco, Richard T., Putting the Terrorist-Sponsoring State in the Dock: Recent Changes in the Foreign Sovereign Immunities Act and the Individual's Recourse against Foreign Powers, 14 *Temple International and Comparative Law Journal* (2000) 109

Michalchuk, Daniel J., Filling a Legal Vacuum: The Form and Content of Russia's Future State Immunity Law Suggestions for Legislative Reform, 32 *Law and Policy in International Business* (2001) 487

Miranda, Michael A., Sovereign Immunity – An Analysis of the Noncommercial Tort Exception of the Foreign Sovereign Immunities Act 1976 – *Olsen ex rel. Sheldon* v. *Government of Mexico*, 7 *New York Law School Journal of International and Comparative Law* (1986) 281

Mitchell, Andrew D., Leave Your Hat On? Head of State Immunity and Pinochet, 25 *Monash University Law Review* (1999) 225

730   BIBLIOGRAPHY

Mizushima, Tomonori, Denying Foreign State Immunity on the Grounds of the Unavailability of Alternative Means, 71 *Modern Law Review* (2008) 734

The Individual as Beneficiary of State Immunity: Problems of the Attribution of Ultra Vires Conduct, 29 *Denver Journal of International Law and Policy* (2001) 261

Yamaguchi v. United States, 56 Minshū 729, Japan, Supreme Court, 12 April 2002, 97 *American Journal of International Law* (2003) 406

Mochochoko, Phakiso, The Agreement on Privileges and Immunities of the International Criminal Court, 25 *Fordham International Law Journal* (2002) 638

Molot, H. L., and Jewett, M. L., The State Immunity Act of Canada, 20 *Canadian Yearbook of International Law* (1982) 79

Monéger, Françoise, *Droit international privé*, 2nd edn, Paris: Litec/Groupe LexisNexis, 2003

Moorthy, V. K., The Malaysian National Oil Corporation – Is it a Government Instrumentality? 30 *International and Comparative Law Quarterly* (1981) 638

Morris, Virginia, Sovereign Immunity for Military Activities on the High Seas: *Amerada Hess v. Argentine Republic*, 23 *International Lawyer* (1989) 213

The International Law Commission's Draft Convention on the Jurisdictional Immunities of States and their Property, 17 *Denver Journal of International Law and Policy* (1989) 395

Morrison-Sinclair, Jeanne, Foreign Sovereign Immunity after *Amerada Hess Shipping Corp. v. Argentine Republic*: Did It Go Down with the *Hercules*? 11 *Fordham International Law Journal* (1988) 660

Morrissey, Joseph F., Simplifying the Foreign Sovereign Immunities Act: If a Sovereign Acts Like a Private Party, Treat It Like One, 5 *Chicago Journal of International Law* (2005) 675

Mortara, Adam K. A., The Case against Retroactive Application of Foreign Sovereign Immunities Act of 1976, 68 *University of Chicago Law Review* (2001) 253

Moury, Jacques, L'Incidence de la stipulation d'une clause compromissoire sur l'immunité d'exécution de l'Etat étranger, 177 Dalloz (2001) No. 27

Movsesian, Mark L., The Persistent Nation State and the Foreign Sovereign Immunities Act, 18 *Cardozo Law Review* (1996) 1083

Mulvaney, Alice K., *Holden v. Canadian Consulate*: A Correct Affirmation of the Foreign Sovereign Immunities Act? 5 *Tulane Journal of International and Comparative Law* (1997) 535

Mundis, Daryl A., *Tachiona v. Mugabe*: A US Court Bows to Personal Immunities of a Foreign Head of State, 1 *Journal of International Criminal Justice* (2003) 462

Murphy, Daniel T., The American Doctrine of Sovereign Immunity: An Historical Analysis, 13 *Villanova Law Review* (1968) 583

Murphy, John F., Civil Liability for the Commission of International Crimes as an Alternative to Criminal Prosecution, 12 *Harvard Human Rights Journal* (1999) 1

Murphy, Sarah L., The Pinochet Judgment: New Accountability for Old Dictators, 32 *Victoria University Wellington Law Review* (2001) 463

Murphy, Sean D., Contemporary Practice of the United States relating to International Law: Terrorist-State Legislation 2002–03, 97 *American Journal of International Law* (2003) 966

Flatow Case: Suit against Iran for Act of Terrorism, 93 *American Journal of International Law* (1999) 181

Satisfaction of U.S. Judgments against State Sponsors of Terrorism, 94 *American Journal of International Law* (2000) 117

US Judgments against Terrorist States, 95 *American Journal of International Law* (2001) 134

Murray, Michael D., Jurisdiction under the Foreign Sovereign Immunities Act for Nazi War Crimes of Plunder and Expropriation, 7 *New York University Journal of Legislation and Public Policy* (2004) 223

Stolen Art and Sovereign Immunity: The Case of *Altmann* v. *Austria*, 27 *Columbia Journal of Law and the Arts* (2004) 301

Nakasian, Stacey P., Proposed Amendments to the Provisions of the Foreign Sovereign Immunities Act of 1976 Governing Execution of Judgments, 23 *George Washington Journal of International Law and Economics* (1989) 179

Nanda, Ved P., Human Rights and Sovereign and Individual Immunities (Sovereign Immunity, Act of State, Head of State Immunity and Diplomatic Immunity) – Some Reflections, 5 *ILSA Journal of International and Comparative Law* (1999) 467

Narver, Clinton L., Putting the 'Sovereign' Back in the Foreign Sovereign Immunities Act: The Case for a Time of Filing Test for Agency or Instrumentality Status, 19 *Boston University International Law Journal* (2001) 163

Nedjar, Didier, Tendances actuelles du droit international des immunités des Etats, 124 *Journal du droit international* (1997) 59

New York Bar Association, Committee on International Litigation, A Foreign-State Defendant's Right to Trial by Jury under the Foreign Sovereign Immunities Act, 26 *Texas International Law Journal* (1991) 71

Nicholls, Clive, Reflections on Pinochet, 41 *Virginia Journal of International Law* (2000) 140

Niekrasz, Andrzej R., The Past Is Another Country: Against the Retroactive Applicability of the Foreign Immunities Act to Pre-1952 Conduct, 37 *John Marshall Law Review* (2004) 1337

Nouwen, Sarah M. H., The Special Court for Sierra Leone and the Immunity of Taylor: The *Arrest Warrant* Case Continued, 18 *Leiden Journal of International Law* (2005) 645

Novogrodsky, Noah Benjamin, Immunity for Torture: Lessons from *Bouzari* v. *Iran*, 18 *European Journal of International Law* (2007) 939

Nwogugu, E. I., Immunity of State Property – The Central Bank of Nigeria in Foreign Courts, 10 *Netherlands Yearbook of International Law* (1979) 179

O'Connell, D. P., *International Law*, 2nd edn, London: Stevens & Sons, 1970

O'Donnell, Kaitlin R., *Certain Criminal Proceedings in France (Republic of Congo* v. *France)* and Head of State Immunity: How Impenetrable Should the Immunity Veil Remain? 26 *Boston University International Law Journal* (2008) 375

Oehrle, Christopher John, German Sovereign Immunity Defense (Interpretation by the German Courts), 6 *Florida Journal of International Law* (1991) 445

732 BIBLIOGRAPHY

Ogunniran, H., The Successive Demise of the Doctrine of State Immunity from Tort Liability: A Comparative Appraisal with Emphasis on the Nigerian Experience, 4 *African Journal of International and Comparative Law* (1992) 369

O'Keefe, Roger, The European Convention on State Immunity and International Crimes, 2 *Cambridge Yearbook of European Legal Studies* (1999) 507, 517–518.

Universal Jurisdiction: Clarifying the Basic Concept, 2 *Journal of International Criminal Justice* (2004) 735

O'Neill, Kerry Creque, A New Customary Law of Head of State Immunity? Hirohito and Pinochet, 38 *Stanford Journal of International Law* (2002) 289

Opara, Victor Nnamdi, Sovereign and Diplomatic Immunity as Customary International Law: Beyond *R. v. Bow Street Metropolitan Stipendiary Magistrate & Others, ex parte Pinochet Ugarte*, 21 *Wisconsin International Law Journal* (2003) 255

Orakhelashvili, Alexander, Between Impunity and Accountability for Serious International Crimes: Legal and Policy Approaches, 55 *Netherlands International Law Review* (2008) 207

Case note on *Arrest Warrant*, 96 *American Journal of International Law* (2002) 677

Peremptory Norms in International Law, Oxford University Press, 2006

Restrictive Interpretation of Human Rights Treaties in the Recent Jurisprudence of the European Court of Human Rights, 14 *European Journal of International Law* (2003) 529

State Immunity and Hierarchy of Norms: Why the House of Lords Got It Wrong, 18 *European Journal of International Law* (2007) 955

State Immunity and International Public Order, 45 *German Yearbook of International Law* (2002) 227

State Immunity and International Public Order Revisited, 49 *German Yearbook of International Law* (2006) 327

State Immunity in National and International Law: Three Recent Cases before the European Court of Human Rights, 15 *Leiden Journal of International Law* (2002) 703

Organization of American States, Inter-American Juridical Committee Opinion Examining the U.S. Helms-Burton Act, 27 August 1996, 35 ILM 1322 (1996)

Orlando, Kristine M., *Republic of Argentina* v. *Weltover*: Adding Clarity to the Foreign Sovereign Immunities Act Commercial Activities Exception, 6 *Florida Journal of International Law* (1991) 475

Osinbajo, Yemi, Sovereign Immunity in International Commercial Arbitration: The Nigerian Experience and Emerging State Practice, 4 *African Journal of International and Comparative Law* (1992) 1

Osofsky, Hari M., Foreign Sovereign Immunity from Severe Human Rights Violations: New Directions for Common Law Based Approaches, 11 *New York International Law Review* (1998) 35

Ostrander, Jeremy, The Last Bastion of Sovereign Immunity: A Comparative Look at Immunity from Execution of Judgments, 22 *Berkeley Journal of International Law* (2004) 541

O'Toole, Teresa M., *Amerada Hess Shipping Corp.* v. *Argentine Republic*: An Alien Tort Statute Exception to Foreign Sovereign Immunity, 72 *Minnesota Law Review* (1988) 829

Ough, Richard N., *Mareva Injunction and Anton Piller Order*, 3rd edn, London: Butterworths, 2000

Panezi, Maria, Sovereign Immunity and Violation of *Jus Cogens* Norms, 56 *Revue hellénique de droit international* (2003) 199

Papajohn, Christopher J., Effects Jurisdiction under the Foreign Sovereign Immunities Act: How Far Does the Long Arm Reach? 20 *NYU Journal of International Law and Politics* (1988) 463

Park, Byoungwook, Comfort Women during WWII: Are U.S. a Final Resort for Justice? 17 *American University International Law Review* (2002) 403

Park, Kyeyoung, The Unspeakable Experience of Korean Women under Japanese Rule, 21 *Whittier Law Review* (2000) 567

Parlett, Kate, Immunity in Civil Proceedings for Torture: The Emerging Exception, *European Human Rights Law Review* (2006-1) 49

  Universal Civil Jurisdiction for Torture, *European Human Rights Law Review* (2007-4) 385

Patchett, Sidney A., *Nelson* v. *Saudi Arabia*: An Unrestricted Reading of the Restrictive Doctrine of Foreign Sovereign Immunity, 23 *University of Miami Inter-American Law Review* (1991–92) 541

Patrikis, Ernest T., Foreign Central Bank Property: Immunity from Attachment in the United States, *University of Illinois Law Review* (1982) 265

Paulus, Andreas L., *Jus Cogens* in a Time of Hegemony and Fragmentation: An Attempt at a Re-appraisal, 74 *Nordic Journal of International Law* (2005) 297

Pax, Thomas J., Old Bonds and New Law: Misunderstanding Sovereign Immunity in the Chinese Railroad Case, 5 *Connecticut Journal of International Law* (1990) 625

Pell, Terence J., The Foreign Sovereign Immunities Act of 1976: Direct Effects and Minimum Contacts, 14 *Cornell International Law Journal* (1981) 97

Pendergast, David Todd, Strangers in a Strange Land: Personal Jurisdiction Analysis under the Foreign Sovereign Immunities Act, 47 *Washington and Lee Law Review* (1990) 1159

Penrose, Mary Margaret, It's Good to Be the King! Prosecuting Heads of State and Former Heads of State under International Law, 39 *Columbia Journal of Transnational Law* (2000) 193

Phillimore, Georg Grenville, Immunité des États au point de vue de la juridiction ou de l'exécution forcée, 8 *Recueil des Cours: Collected Courses of the Hague Academy of International Law* (1925-III) 343

Pierson, Charles, Pinochet and the End of Immunity: England's House of Lords Hold that a Former Head of State Is Not Immune for Torture, 14 *Temple International and Comparative Law Journal* (2000) 263

734 BIBLIOGRAPHY

Pingel, Isabelle, (dir.), *Droit des immunités et exigences du procès équitable*, Paris: Editions Pedone, 2004

Immunité de juridiction et contrat de travail: du nouveau, 130 *Journal du droit international* (2003) 1115

Observations sur la Convention du 17 janvier 2005 sur les immunités juridictionnelle des États et de leur biens, 132 *Journal du droit international* (2005) 1045

Pingel-Lenuzza, Isabelle, Autonomie Juridictionnelle et Employeur Privilégié: Concilier les Contraires, 104 *Revue générale de droit international public* (2000) 445

Les immunités des États en droit français, 22 *Droit et pratique du commerce international* (1996) 5

Les immunités des Etats en droit international, Brussels: Bruylant, 1997

Pitt, Gwyneth, *Employment Law*, 7th edn, London: Sweet & Maxwell, 2009

Pittman, Andrew B., Ambassadorial Waiver of Foreign State Sovereign Immunity to Domestic Adjudication in United States Courts, 58 *Washington & Lee Law Review* (2001) 645

Pittrof, Sabine, Compensation Claims for Human Rights Breaches Committed by German Armed Forces Abroad During the Second World War: Federal Court of Justice Hands Down Decision in the *Distomo* Case, 5 *German Law Journal* (2004) 15

Popoff, Evo, Inconsistency and Impunity in International Human Rights Law: Can the International Criminal Court Solve the Problems Raised by the Rwanda and Augusto Pinochet Cases, 33 *George Washington International Law Review* (2001) 363

Powell, C. H., and Pillay, A., Revisiting *Pinochet*: The Development of Customary International Criminal Law, 17 *South African Journal on Human Rights* (2001) 477

Preuss, Lawrence, State Immunity and the Requisition of Ships during the Spanish Civil War, 35 *AJIL* (1941) 263 and 36 *AJIL* (1942) 37

Prevost, M. D., Does Immunity Attach to State or its Acts? 21 *South African Yearbook of International Law* (1996) 118

Ragazzi, Maurizio, *The Concept of International Obligations Erga Omnes*, Oxford: Clarendon Press, 1997

Ratner, Steven R., Belgium's War Crimes Statute: A Postmortem, 97 *American Journal of International Law* (2003) 888

Rau, Markus, After *Pinochet*: Foreign Sovereign Immunity in Respect of Serious Human Rights Violations – The Decision of the European Court of Human Rights in the *Al-Adsani* Case, 3 *German Law Journal* (2002), No. 6

Redress, *Challenging Impunity for Torture: A Manual for Bringing Criminal and Civil Proceedings in England and Wales for Torture Committed Abroad*, 2000, Appendix 7, Law Reform: Draft Redress for Torture Bill, at p. 273. This publication (without the appendices) can also be found at Redress's official website: www.redress.org/publications/CHA.pdf

Reimann, Mathias, A Human Rights Exception to Sovereign Immunity: Some Thoughts on *Princz v. Federal Republic of Germany*, 16 *Michigan Journal of International Law* (1995) 403

Reinisch, August, European Court Practice Concerning State Immunity from Enforcement Measures, 17 *European Journal of International Law* (2006) 803

Reitz, Daniel E., Raising a Paper Tiger: Public Law No. 105-277 § 117(D) and the Gutting of the State-Sponsored Terrorism Exception to the Foreign Sovereign Immunities Act, 69 *University of Cincinnati Law Review* (2000) 357

Ress, Georg, Second Report on Developments in the Field of State Immunity since 1982, *ILA Report of the Sixty-Fifth Conference (Cairo)*, 1992, p. 290

Richman, Scott A., *Siderman de Blake* v. *Republic of Argentina*: Can the FSIA Grant Immunity for Violations of *Jus Cogens* Norms? 19 *Brooklyn Journal of International Law* (1993) 967

Rispin, Sarah C., Cooperative Federalism and Constructive Waiver of State Sovereign Immunity, 70 *University of Chicago Law Review* (2003) 1639

Implications of *Democratic Republic of the Congo* v. *Belgium* on the *Pinochet* Precedent: A Set Back for International Human Rights Litigation? 3 *Chicago Journal of International Law* (2002) 527

Robertson, Horace B., Jr, Comments on Professor Joan E. Donoghue's Article, The Public Face of Private International Law: Prospects for a Convention on Foreign State Immunity, 57 *Law and Contemporary Problems* (1994) 323

Rodley, Nigel S., Breaking the Cycle of Impunity for Gross Violations of Human Rights: The Pinochet Case in Perspective, 69 *Nordic Journal of International Law* (2000) 11

Roht-Arriaza, Naomi, The Foreign Sovereign Immunities Act and Human Rights Violations: One Step Forward, Two Steps Back? 16 *Berkeley Journal of International Law* (1998) 71

The Pinochet Precedent and Universal Jurisdiction, 35 *New England Law Review* (2001) 311

Rosenne, Shabtai (ed.), *League of Nations Committee of Experts for the Progressive Codification of International Law (1925–1928)*, New York: Oceana Publications, 1972 (in two volumes)

(ed.), *League of Nations Conference for the Codification of International Law (1930)*, New York: Oceana Publications, 1975 (in four volumes)

Rosenthal, Douglas E., and Knighton, William M., *National Laws and International Commerce: The Problem of Extraterritoriality*, London/Boston/Henley: Routledge & Kegan Paul Ltd, 1982

Rothstein, Amy L., Recognizing and Enforcing Arbitral Agreements and Awards against Foreign States: The Mathias Amendments to the Foreign Sovereign Immunities Act and Title 9, 1 *Emory Journal of International Dispute Resolution* (1986) 101

Roufail, Michael, *Gregorian* v. *Izvestia*: Libel and the Foreign Sovereign Immunities Act, 13 *North Carolina Journal of International Law and Commercial Regulation* (1988) 141

Rousseau, Charles, *Droit international public*, Tome IV, Paris: Editions Sirey, 1980

Royer, Charles, Case note on *Gouvernement espagnol* v. *Veuve Aguado*, Dalloz, Pér., 1867-II-49

Rozakis, Christos L., *The Concept of Jus Cogens in the Law of Treaties*, Amsterdam/New York/Oxford: North-Holland Publishing Company, 1976

BIBLIOGRAPHY

Ruccolo, Sharon D., The Foreign Sovereign Immunities Act: Encouraging Foreign Plaintiffs to Sue Foreign Sovereigns in American Courts, 25 *Rutgers Law Review* (1994) 517

Ruffert, Matthias, Pinochet Follow Up: The End of Sovereign Immunity? 48 *Netherlands International Law Review* (2001) 171

Rutherglen, George, Sovereign Immunity, 31 *Journal of Maritime Law and Commerce* (2000) 317;

Salcedo, Juan Antonio Carrillo, Reflections on the Existence of a Hierarchy of Norms in International Law, 8 *European Journal of International Law* (1997) 583

Sandrock, Otto, Prejudgment Attachments: Securing International Loans or Other Claims for Money, 21 *International Lawyer* (1987) 1

Sands, Philippe, International Law Transformed? From Pinochet to Congo . . . ? 16 *Leiden Journal of International Law* (2003) 37

Lawless World: Making and Breaking Global Rules, London: Penguin Books, 2006

Sargeant, Malcolm, and Lewis, David, *Employment Law*, 3rd edn, Harlow: Pearson Education Ltd, 2006

Schachter, M., Prejudgment Attachment of Iranian Assets in the United States: Waiving Sovereign Immunity, 13 *New York University Journal of International Law and Politics* (1981) 675

Schano, Sarah K., The Scattered Remains of Sovereign Immunity for Foreign States after *Republic of Argentina* v. *Weltover Inc.* – Due Process Protection or Nothing, 27 *Vanderbilt Journal of Transnational Law* (1994) 673

Scharf, Michael P., The Amnesty Exception to the Jurisdiction of the International Criminal Court, 32 *Cornell International Law Journal* (1999) 507

Schaumann, Wilfried, and Habscheid, Walther J., *Die Immunität ausländischer Staaten nach Völkerrecht und deutschem Zivilprozessrecht* (Berichte der Deutschen Gesellschaft für Völkerrecht, Heft 8), Karlsruhe: Verlag C. F. Müller, 1968

Schreuer, Christoph H., *State Immunity: Some Recent Developments*, Cambridge: Grotius Publications Ltd, 1988

Schreuer, Christoph, and Wittich, Stephan, Immunity v. Accountability: The ICJ's Judgment in the *Yerodia* Case, 4 *International Law Forum* (2002) 117

Schwarzenberger, Georg, International *Jus Cogens*? 43 *Texas Law Review* (1965) 455

Scott, Craig (ed.), *Torture as Tort: Comparative Perspectives on the Development of Transnational Human Rights Litigation*, Oxford, Hart Publishing, 2001

Scott, James Brown, The Trial of the Kaiser, in Edward M. House and Charles Seymour (eds.), *What Really Happened at Paris: The Story of the Peace Conference, 1918–1919*, London: Hodder & Stoughton, 1921, p. 242

Sealing, Keith E., Cuba and Democratization: Should Sanctions Be Lifted? Cuba Is No Longer a 'State Sponsor of Terrorism': Why the Foreign Sovereign Immunities Act Failed? 14 *Transnational Law and Contemporary Problems* (2004) 143

'State Sponsors of Terrorism' Are Entitled to Due Process Too: The Amended Foreign Sovereign Immunities Act Is Unconstitutional, 15 *American University International Law Review* (2000) 395

Sealing, Keith, 'State Sponsors of Terrorism' Is a Question, Not an Answer: The Terrorism Amendment to the FSIA Makes Less Sense Now than It Did before 9/11, 38 *Texas International Law Journal* (2003) 119

Seidl-Hohenveldern, I., International Immunity Law and Human Rights, in H. W. Arndt *et al.* (eds.), *Völkerrecht und Deutsches Recht: Festschrift für Walter Rudolph zum 70. Geburtstag*, Munich: Beck, 2001, p. 95

    State Immunity: Austria, 10 *Netherlands Yearbook of International Law* (1979) 97

Selwyn, Norman, *Selwyn's Law of Employment*, 15th edn, Oxford University Press, 2008

Seyedin-Noor, Shahram, The Spanish Prisoner: Understanding the Prosecution of Senator Augusto Pinochet Ugarte, 6 *University of California Davis Journal of International Law and Policy* (2000) 41

Seymour, Jillaine, Immunity for Torture: The State and its Representatives Reunited, 65 *Cambridge Law Journal* (2006) 479

Sgro, Jill A., China's Stance on Sovereign Immunity: A Critical Perspective on *Jackson v. People's Republic of China*, 22 *Columbia Journal of Transnational Law* (1983) 101

Shaul, Kelly, Tiered Entities and Sovereign Privileges under the Foreign Sovereign Immunities Act, 34 *San Diego Law Review* (1997) 1817

Shaw, Malcolm N., *International Law*, 6th edn, Cambridge University Press, 2008

    The State Immunity Act 1978, 128 *New Law Journal* (1978) 1136

Shearer, I. A., *Starke's International Law*, 11th edn, London: Butterworths, 1994

Shelton, Dinah, Normative Hierarchy in International Law, 100 *American Journal of International Law* (2006) 291

Shortell, Christopher, *Rights, Remedies and the Impact of State Sovereign Immunity*, Albany: State University of New York Press, 2008

Siegel, Jonathan R., The Hidden Source of Congress's Power to Abrogate State Sovereign Immunity, 73 *Texas Law Review* (1995) 539

Siewert, Clark C., Reciprocal Influence of British and United States Law: Foreign Sovereign Immunity Law from The Schooner Exchange to the State Immunity Act of 1978, 13 *Vanderbilt Journal of Transnational Law* (1980) 761

Simmonds, K. R., The Limits of Sovereign Jurisdictional Immunity: The Petrol Shipping Corporation and Victory Transport Cases, 11 *McGill Law Journal* (1965) 291

Simmons, Rebecca J., Nationalized and Denationalized Commercial Enterprises under the Foreign Sovereign Immunities Act, 90 *Columbia Law Review* (1990) 2278

Sinclair, Sir Ian, The European Convention on State Immunity, 22 *International and Comparative Law Quarterly* (1973) 254

    The Law of Sovereign Immunity: Recent Developments, 167 *Recueil des Cours: Collected Courses of the Hague Academy of International Law* (1980-II) 113

Singer, Eric H., Terrorism, Extradition and FSIA Relief: The *Letelier* Case, 19 *Vanderbilt Journal of Transnational Law* (1986) 57

Singerman, Daniel M., It's Still Good to Be the King: An Argument for Maintaining the Status Quo in Foreign Head of State Immunity, 21 *Emory International Law Review* (2007) 413

738 BIBLIOGRAPHY

Smis, Stefaan, and van der Borght, Kim, The EU–US Compromise on the Helms-Burton and D'Amato Acts, 93 *American Journal of International Law* (1999) 227

Smith, Eric T., State Recognition under the Foreign Sovereign Immunities Act: Who Decides, the Judiciary or the Executive? *Klinghoffer* v. *Palestine Liberation Organization*, 937 F.2d 44 (2d Cir. 1991), 6 *Temple International and Comparative Law Journal* (1992) 169

Smith, Michael D., Executing Judgments against 'Mixed' Commercial and Non-Commercial Embassy Bank Accounts in the United States: Where Sovereign and Diplomatic Immunities Clash, 10 *University of Pennsylvania Journal of International Business Law* (1988) 707

Smith, Scott Hartwell, *Persinger* v. *Islamic Republic of Iran*: Iran Granted Immunity under the Noncommercial Tort Exception of the Foreign Sovereign Immunities Act of 1976, 10 *North Carolina Journal of International Law and Commercial Regulation* (1985) 285

Solé, Antoni Pigrau, The Pinochet Case in Spain, 6 *ILSA Journal of International and Comparative Law* (2000) 653

Sørensen, Max, *A Manual of Public International Law*, London, Melbourne, Toronto, New York: Macmillan, 1968

Spinedi, Marina, State Responsibility v. Individual Responsibility for International Crimes: *Tertium Non Datur?* 13 *European Journal of International Law* (2002) 895

Starke, J. G., *Introduction to International Law*, 10th edn, London: Butterworths, 1989

Steinberger, Helmut, State Immunity, in Rudolf Bernhardt (ed.), *Encyclopaedia of Public International Law*, Vol. 4, Amsterdam: Elsevier Science Publishers B.V., 2000, p. 615

Stern, Brigitte, Can a State or a Head of State Claim the Benefit of Immunities in Case an International Crime Has Been Committed? 14 *ILSA Journal of International and Comparative Law* (2008) 441

Immunities for Heads of State: Where Do We Stand?, in Mark Lattimer and Philippe Sands (eds.), *Justice for Crimes against Humanity*, Oxford: Hart Publishing, 2003, p. 73

Stewart, David P., The UN Convention on Jurisdictional Immunities of States and Their Property, 99 *American Journal of International Law* (2005) 194

Stirling-Zanda, Simonetta, *L'application judiciaire du droit international coutumier – Étude comparée de la pratique europénne*, Zurich: Schulthess, 2000

Stitcher, Kurt Edward, *Amerada Hess* and Foreign Sovereign Immunity: The Conflict between the Foreign Sovereign Immunities Act and the Alien Tort Claims Act in Establishing Jurisdiction over the Extraterritorial Torts of Foreign States, 24 *Stanford Journal of International Law* (1987–1988) 585

Sucharitkul, Sompong, Immunities of Foreign States before National Authorities, 149 *Recueil des Cours: Collected Courses of the Hague Academy of International Law* (1976-I) 87

Immunity from Attachment and Execution of the Property of Foreign States: Thai Practice, 10 *Netherlands Yearbook of International Law* (1979) 143

Jurisdictional Immunities in Contemporary International Law from Asian
   Perspectives, 4 *Chinese Journal of International Law* (2005) 1
State Immunities and Trading Activities in International Law, London: Stevens &
   Sons Ltd, 1959
Sugarman, David, The Pinochet Case: International Criminal Justice in the
   Gothic Style? 64 *Modern Law Review* (2001) 933
Suh, Chul Won, Transboundary Civil Litigation in Korea, 6 *Asian Yearbook of
   International Law* (1996) 169
Summers, Mark A., Diplomatic Immunity Ratione Personae: Did the
   International Court of Justice Create a New Customary Law Rule in *Congo
   v. Belgium?* 16 *Michigan State Journal of International Law* (2007) 459
   Immunity or Impunity? The Potential Effect of Prosecutions of State Officials
   for Core International Crimes in States Like the United States that Are Not
   Parties to the Statute of the International Criminal Court, 31 *Brooklyn Journal
   of International Law* (2006) 463
   The International Court of Justice's Decision in *Congo v. Belgium*: How Has It
   Affected Development of a Principle of Universal Jurisdiction that Would
   Obligate All States to Prosecute War Criminals? 21 *Boston University
   International Law Journal* (2003) 63
Survey of International Law, Working paper prepared by the Secretary-General,
   A/CN.4/245, *YILC*, 1971-II-2, p. 1
Survey of International Law in Relation to the Work of Codification of the
   International Law Commission, *Memorandum submitted by the Secretary-
   General, UN General Assembly*, A/CN.4/1/Rev.1, Sales No. 1948.V.1(1), New York,
   1949
Suy, Erik, Immunity of States before Belgian Courts and Tribunals, 27 *Zeitschrift
   für ausländisches öffentliches Recht und Völkerrecht* (1967) 660
   The Concept of *Jus Cogens* in Public International Law, in Conference on
   International Law, Lagonissi (Greece), April 3–8, 1966, Papers and
   Proceedings II: The Concept of *Jus Cogens* in International Law, Geneva:
   Carnegie Endowment for International Peace (European Centre),
   1967, p. 17
Swain, Rachel, A Discussion of the Pinochet Case (House of Lords Decision of
   24 March 1999) Noting the Juxtaposition of International Relations and
   International Law Perspectives, 69 *Nordic Journal of International Law*
   (2000) 223
Sweet, Lisa Naomi, The Foreign Sovereign Immunities Act before and after
   Republic of Argentina v. Weltover, 12 *Wisconsin International Law Journal*
   (1993–94) 375
Talmon, Stefan, War Booty of 'Separate Entity' Protected by Sovereign Immunity,
   15 *Oxford Journal of Legal Studies* (1995) 295
Tams, Christian J., *Enforcing Obligations Erga Omnes in International Law*, Cambridge
   University Press, 2005
   Well-Protected Enemies of Mankind – Comment on the ECHR's Judgment in
   Al-Adsani v. United Kingdom, 61 *Cambridge Law Journal* (2002) 246

740 BIBLIOGRAPHY

Tan, Carmela, Protecting U.S. Citizens Abroad: Why Foreign States Should Not Be Immune from Suit in the United States for their Mistreatment of Prisoners, 19 *Loyola of Los Angeles International and Comparative Law Journal* (1996) 223

Taylor, Allison, Another Front in the War on Terrorism? Problems with Recent Changes to the Foreign Sovereign Immunities Act, 45 *Arizona Law Review* (2003) 533

Taylor, Roger H., *Pinochet*, Confusion, and Justice: The Denial of Immunity in U.S. Courts to Alleged Torturers Who Are Former Heads of State, 24 *Thomas Jefferson Law Review* (2001) 101

The Thai Practice, 6 *Asian Yearbook of International Law* (1996) 389–390

Thomas, Katherine Reece, and Small, Joan, Human Rights and State Immunity: Is There Immunity from Civil Liability for Torture? 50 *Netherlands International Law Review* (2003) 1

Thomas, Steve H., Two Faces of the Trader: Guidelines for Distinguishing between Governmental and Commercial Acts under the Foreign Sovereign Immunities Act of 1976, 23 *Texas International Law Journal* (1988) 465

Thornton, J. Thompson, and Ares, Aurora A., Foreign Sovereign Immunities Act of 1976: Misjoinder, Nonjoinder, and Collusive Joinder, 58 *Journal of Air Law and Commerce* (1993) 703

Toner, Paul L., Competing Concepts of Immunity: The (R)evolution of the Head of State Immunity Defense, 108 *Penn State Law Review* (2004) 899

Trooboff, Peter D., Foreign State Immunity: Emerging Consensus on Principles, 200 *Recueil des Cours: Collected Courses of the Hague Academy of International Law* (1986-V) 235

Tunks, Michael A., Diplomats or Defendants? Defining the Future of Head-of-State Immunity, 52 *Duke Law Journal* (2002) 651

Turns, David, Pinochet's Fallout: Jurisdiction and Immunity for Criminal Violations of International Law, 20 *Legal Studies* (2000) 566

The International Court of Justice's Failure to Take a Stand on Universal Jurisdiction, 3 *Melbourne Journal of International Law* (2002) 383

UK, Home Secretary, Written Answer to a Parliamentary Question (regarding the *Pinochet* case), 119 ILR 317

UK, House of Commons Home Affairs Committee, Second Report, *The Management of the Prison Service (Public and Private)*, Vol. I, Section D, Privately Managed Prisons, London: The Stationery Office, 1997

Unegbu, M. O., Immunity of State from Judicial Proceedings: The Current Position in Nigeria, 5 *African Journal of International and Comparative Law* (1993) 869

United States, Statement by the President on Suspending Title III of the Helms-Burton Act, 3 January 1997, 36 ILM 216 (1997)

US Department of Justice, Suggestion of Immunity for Pope Benedict XVI (Sept. 19, 2005), *Doe 1 v. Archdiocese of Galveston-Houston*, Civ. Action No. H-05-1047 (S.D. Tex.), 100 *AJIL* (2006) 219

US House of Representatives, Report No. 94-1487, 1976: United States House of Representatives, Legislative History, Foreign Sovereign Immunities Act of

1976, US House of Representatives, Report (Judiciary Committee) No. 94-1487, 9 September 1976; 1976 USCCAN 6604; 15 ILM 1398 (1976)

Ushakov, Nikolai A., Memorandum presented to the ILC, *YILC*, 1983-II-1, p. 53

Vadnais, Molora, The Terrorism Exception to the Foreign Sovereign Immunities Act: Forward Leaning Legislation or Just Bad Law? 5 *UCLA Journal of International Law and Foreign Affairs* (2000) 199

van Alebeek, Rosanne, From Rome to The Hague: Recent Developments on Immunity Issues in the ICC Statute, 13 *Leiden Journal of International Law* (2000) 485

    The Immunity of States and their Officials in International Criminal Law and International Human Rights Law, Oxford University Press, 2008

    The *Pinochet* Case: International Human Rights Law on Trial, 71 *British Year Book of International Law* (2000) 29

van den Brink, Jens, Helms-Burton: Extending the Limits of US Jurisdiction, 44 *Netherlands International Law Review* (1997) 131

Vardiman, Martha Ruth, The Foreign Sovereign Immunities Act of 1976 Does Not Preclude U.S. Courts from Exercising Jurisdiction over the USSR for Soviet Violations of Diplomatic Immunity – *Von Dardel* v. *USSR*, 623 F.Supp. 246 (D.D.C. 1985), 55 *University of Cincinnati Law Review* (1987) 923

Vázquez, Carlos M., *Altmann* v. *Austria* and the Retroactivity of the Foreign Sovereign Immunities Act, 3 *Journal of International Criminal Justice* (2005) 207

Vennemann, Renaat, L'immunité d'exécution de l'État étranger, in Centres de droit international, *L'immunité de juridiction et d'exécution des Etats: A propos du projet de Convention du Conseil de l'Europe*, Brussels, 1969, p. 117

Verdross, Alfred, *Völkerrecht*, 4th edn, Berlin/Heidelberg: Springer, 1959

Verhoeven, J., Jurisprudence belge relative au droit international, *Revue belge de droit international* (1973) 633

    (dir.), *Le droit international des immunités: contestation ou consolidation?* Brussels: De Boeck & Larcier S.A., 2004

Vibhute, K. I., *International Commercial Arbitration and State Immunity*, New Delhi: Butterworths India, 1999

    Transnational Trade Transactions of a Foreign State and Sovereign Immunity in India: An Appraisal, 3 *Asian Yearbook of International Law* (1993) 47

Vierucci, Luisa, Le Statut juridique des Navires de Guerre ayant coulé dans des Eaux étrangères: Le Cas des Frégates Espagnoles *Juno* et *La Galga* Retrouvées au large des Côtes des Etats-Unis, 105 *Revue générale de droit international public* (2001) 705

Villalpando, Santiago, L'affaire Pinochet: beaucoup de bruit pour rien? 104 *Revue générale de droit international public* (2000) 393

Vitrano, Sean P., Hell-Bent on Awarding Recovery to Terrorism Victims: The Evolution and Application of the Antiterrorism Amendments to the Foreign Sovereign Immunities Act, 19 *Dickinson Journal of International Law* (2000) 213

Vivekananthan, Niranjini, The Doctrine of State Immunity and Human Rights Violations of Foreign States, 8 *Sri Lanka Journal of International Law* (1996) 125

742   BIBLIOGRAPHY

von Bar, Ludwig, Report to the 15th Committee, *Annuaire de l'Institut de Droit International*, Vol. 11, Session de Hambourg, septembre 1891, p. 414
   Theorie und Praxis des internationalen Privatrechts, II, Hannover, 1889
   The Theory and Practice of Private International Law, 2nd edn, G. R. Gillespie trans., Edinburgh: William Green & Sons, 1892
von Hennigs, Reinhard, European Convention on State Immunity and Other International Aspects of Sovereign Immunity, 9 *Willamette Journal of International Law and Dispute Resolution* (2001) 185
Voskuil, C. C. A., State Immunity and the Law of Civil Procedure and Execution in the Netherlands, in Terry D. Gill and Wybo P. Heere (eds.), *Reflections on Principles and Practice of International Law: Essays in Honour of Leo J. Bouchez*, The Hague/London: Martinus Nijhoff Publishers, 2000, p. 223
Vournas, Elena, *Prefecture of Voiotia* v. *Federal Republic of Germany*: Sovereign Immunity and the Exception for *Jus Cogens* Violations, 21 *New York Law School Journal of International and Comparative Law* (2002) 629
Walker, C. P., Sovereign Immunity: Claimant Charged with Money Laundering Offences, *Criminal Law Review* (2006) 669)
Walters, Francis Paul, *A History of the League of Nations*, Oxford University Press, 1952 (in two volumes)
Wang, Houli, Sovereign Immunity: Chinese Views and Practices, 1 *Journal of Chinese Law* (1987) 23
Warbrick, Colin, Extradition Law Aspects of *Pinochet 3*, 48 *International and Comparative Law Quarterly* (1999) 958
   Immunity and International Crimes in English Law, 53 *International and Comparative Law Quarterly* (2004) 769
Waring, M. Chase, Waiver of Sovereign Immunity, 6 *Harvard International Law Club Journal* (1964–1965) 189
Watson, J. Shand, *Theory & Reality in the International Protection of Human Rights*, Ardsley, New York: Transnational Publishers, 1999
Watts, Sir Arthur, The Legal Position in International Law of Heads of States, Heads of Governments and Foreign Ministers, 247 *Recueil des Cours: Collected Courses of the Hague Academy of International Law* (1994-III) 9
Webster, William F., *Amerada Hess Shipping Corp.* v. *Argentine Republic*: Denying Sovereign Immunity to Violators of International Law, 39 *Hastings Law Journal* (1988) 1109
Wedgwood, Ruth, International Criminal Law and Augusto Pinochet, 40 *Virginia Journal of International Law* (2000) 829
Weerts, Laurence and Chaïbi, Denis, Le Titre III de la Législation Helms-Burton et le Droit international, 30 *Revue belge de droit international* (1997) 99
Weiss, A., Compétence ou incompetence des tribunaux a l'égard des États étrangers, 1 *Recueil des Cours: Collected Courses of the Hague Academy of International Law* (1923-I) 521
Weller, Matthias, Immunity for Artworks on Loan? A Review of International Customary Law and Municipal Anti-Seizure Statutes in Light of the Liechtenstein Litigation, 38 *Vanderbilt Journal of Transnational Law* (2005) 997

Wen, Abigail Hing, Suing the Sovereign's Servant: The Implications of Privatization for the Scope of Foreign Sovereign Immunities, 103 *Columbia Law Review* (2003) 1538

Wernicke, Vanessa A., The 'Retroactive' Application of the Foreign Sovereign Immunities Act in Recovering Nazi Looted Art, 72 *University of Cincinnati Law Review* (2004) 1103

Westlake, John, *A Treatise on Private International Law*, London: William Maxwell & Son, 1880

Wheaton, Henry, *Elements of International Law*, 8th edn, Dana, 1866, Oxford: Clarendon Press, 1936

Whelan, Deirdre E., The Commercial Activity Exception in the Foreign Sovereign Immunities Act: *Saudi Arabia* v. *Nelson*, 27 *Creighton Law Review* (1994) 1069

White, Jamison G., Nowhere to Run, Nowhere to Hide: Augusto Pinochet, Universal Jurisdiction, The ICC, and a Wake-Up Call for Former Heads of State, 50 *Case Western Reserve Law Reserve* (1999) 127

White, Melinda, Pinochet, Universal Jurisdiction and Impunity, 7 *Southwestern Journal of Law and Trade in the Americas* (2000) 209

Whiteman, Marjorie M., *Digest of International Law*, Vol. 6, Washington DC: Department of State Publication, 1968

Whomersley, C. A., Some Reflections on the Immunities of Individuals for Official Acts, 41 *International and Comparative Law Quarterly* (1992) 848

Wilkes, Guy, Enforcing Anti-Suit Injunctions against Sovereign States, 53 *International and Comparative Law Quarterly* (2004) 512

Williams, Sarah and Lena Sherif, The Arrest Warrant for President al-Bashir: Immunities of Incumbent Heads of State and the International Criminal Court, 14 *Journal of Conflict & Security Law* (2009) 71

Williams, Sharon Anne and de Mestral, Armand L., *An Introduction to International Law: Chiefly as Interpreted and Applied in Canada*, 2nd edn, Toronto: Butterworths, 1987

Winants, Alain, The *Yerodia* Ruling of the International Court of Justice and the 1993/1999 Belgian Law on Universal Jurisdiction, 16 *Leiden Journal of International Law* (2003) 491

Wirth, Steffen, Immunities, Related Problems, and Article 98 of the Rome Statute, 12 *Criminal Law Forum* (2001) 429

Immunity for Core Crimes? The ICJ's Judgment in the *Congo* v. *Belgium* Case, 13 *European Journal of International Law* (2002) 877

Wittich, Stephan, *Airport Linz* v. *United States*, Oberster Gerichtshof (Supreme Court of Austria), Decision No. 2 Ob 156/03k, August 28, 2003, 99 *AJIL* (2005) 248

Punitive Damages, in Crawford *et al.* (eds.), *The Law of International Responsibility*, Oxford University Press, 2010, Chapter 45, p. 667

Woodhouse, Diana, (ed.), *The Pinochet Case: A Legal and Constitutional Analysis*, Oxford: Hart Publishing, 2000

World Bank, *Legal Framework for the Treatment of Foreign Investment*, Vol. 2, Guidelines on the Treatment of Foreign Direct Investment, dated 1 January 1992, Report No. 11415, available at: www.worldbank.org/reference

744 BIBLIOGRAPHY

Wouters, Jan, The Judgment of the International Court of Justice in the *Arrest Warrant* Case: Some Critical Remarks, 16 *Leiden Journal of International Law* (2003) 253

Wright, Jane, Retribution but No Recompense: A Critique of the Torturer's Immunity from Civil Suit, 30 *Oxford Journal of Legal Studies* (2010) 143

Wuebbels, Margot C., Commercial Terrorism: A Commercial Activity Exception under § 1605(a)(2) of the Foreign Sovereign Immunities Act, 35 *Arizona Law Review* (1993) 1123

Wydeven, Richard, The Foreign Sovereign Immunities Act of 1976: A Contemporary Look at Jurisdiction under the Commercial Activity Exception, 13 *Review of Litigation* (1993) 143

Wyrozumska, Anna, The State Immunity in the Practice of Polish Courts, 24 *Polish Yearbook of International Law* (1999–2000) 77

Yang, Xiaodong, A State-Owned Company's Company is Not a State-Owned Company: The Question of Tiering under the US Foreign Sovereign Immunities Act, 19 *International Company and Commercial Law Review* (2008) 149

Immunity for International Crimes: A Reaffirmation of Traditional Doctrine, 61 *Cambridge Law Journal* (2002) 242

Jus Cogens and State Immunity, 3 *New Zealand Yearbook of International Law* (2006) 131

State Immunity in the European Court of Human Rights: Reaffirmations and Misconceptions, 74 *British Year Book of International Law* (2003) 333

State Immunity outside the State Immunity Act, 60 *Cambridge Law Journal* (2001) 17

Together We Are Immune: The Question of 'Pooling' under the US Foreign Sovereign Immunities Act, 19 *International Company and Commercial Law Review* (2008) 18

Universal Tort Jurisdiction over Torture? 64 *Cambridge Law Journal* (2005) 1

Yee, Sienho, Foreign Sovereign Immunities, *Acta Jure Imperii* and *Acta Jure Gestionis*: A Recent Exposition from the Canadian Supreme Court, 2 *Chinese Journal of International Law* (2003) 649

The Discretionary Function Exception under the Foreign Sovereign Immunities Act: When in America, Do the Romans Do as the Romans Wish? 93 *Columbia Law Review* (1993) 744

Zaffuto, Warren D., A 'Pirate's Victory': President Clinton's Approach to the New FSIA Exception Leaves the Victors Empty-Handed, 74 *Tulane Law Review* (1999) 685

Zappalà, Salvatore, Do Heads of State in Office Enjoy Immunity from Jurisdiction for International Crimes? The *Ghaddafi* Case before the French Cour de Cassation, 12 *European Journal of International Law* (2001) 595

Zelniker, Lindsay, Towards a Functional International Criminal Court: An Argument in Favor of a Strong Privileges and Immunities Agreement, 24 *Fordham International Law Journal* (2001) 988

Zeyen, Gaetan, Immunities of States in Investment Agreements: What's New with the Creighton Decision? 3 *International Business Law Journal* (2006) 333

Zimmermann, Andreas, Sovereign Immunity and Violations of International *Jus Cogens* – Some Critical Remarks, 16 *Michigan Journal of International Law* (1995) 433

Zinman, G. Michael, Holding Foreign Governments Accountable for their Human Rights Abuses: A Proposed Amendment to the Foreign Sovereign Immunities Act of 1976, 21 *Loyola of Los Angeles International and Comparative Law Journal* (1999) 185

Zuppi, Alberto-Luis, Immunity v. Universal Jurisdiction: The *Yerodia Ndombasi* Decision of the International Court of Justice, 63 *Louisiana Law Review* (2003) 309

Index

absolute immunity
  abandonment 3
  commercial activities 7–8
  European Convention (1972) 12
  exceptions to immunity 8, 10–11
  immovable property 8, 67–68
  immunity from adjudication 347–362
  immunity from enforcement/execution
    347–362
  jurisdiction not precluded 21
  nineteenth-century doctrine 3, 7–10
  non-sovereign activities 7–8
  The Cristina case 9
  The Schooner Exchange case 8–9, 11,
    53, 65
  waiver 7, 8, 10–11
  see also State immunity
abuse of police powers
  non-commercial activities 81
  Saudi Arabia 81, 112
  torture 81
accountability
  acts within borders 1–2
  local jurisdiction 2
  non-justiciability 2
  procedural rules 2
acta jure imperii/gestionis
  acts distinguished 14, 16, 17, 19, 23, 34,
    41, 58, 86–87, 207–215
  general principle 34
  local jurisdiction 34
  nature approach 86–87
  non-commercial torts 199, 207–215
  private person test 41
  purpose approach 99
  sovereignty 50
activities
  accountability *see* accountability
  commerce *see* commercial activities

employment contracts 173
  non-commercial *see* non-commercial
    activities
  non-sovereign *see* non-sovereign activities
  sovereign *see* sovereign activities
  trade *see* trading activities
acts
  jure imperii see *acta jure imperii/gestionis*
  legally significant acts 129
  prescribed acts 109
  private acts 68–73
  United States
    direct effect *see under* US Foreign
      Sovereign Immunities Act
    outside 113–115, 116–124
    within 110–113
  within borders, accountability 1–2
adjudication
  State immunity 34, 347–362
  waiver of immunity 34
agencies/instrumentalities
  categorical approach 247–249
  legal characteristics test 247
  legal personality 247–249
  other uses 273–274
  pooling *see* pooling
  presumption of immunity 171
  separate entities 243–244
  status 244–247, 273–274
  tiering 264
  timing 273
American Law Institute 222
arbitration
  freezing injunctions 235–236
  ICSID Convention (1965) 325–327
  waiver of immunity 325–327, 336
Argentina
  bonds 89, 102, 116, 124, 125
  employment contracts 152, 176

747

748 INDEX

Argentina (*cont.*)
  IMF loans 97
  remedies 176
armed forces
  education, service families 105–106
  employee status 172–173
  employer status 170–171
  employment contracts
    see under employment contracts
  insurable risks 203
  military bases 98–100, 172–173
  military hospitals 105
  military property 417
  NATO Status of Forces Agreement
    172–173, 213
  non-commercial torts 212–215
  private person test 94
  recreational facilities 170–171
  Saudi Arabia 193
  savings regime 179, 193
  sovereign activities 98–100
  United Kingdom 193, 213
attribution, non-commercial torts 224–225
Australia
  central bank property 416
  choice of law 152
  commercial property 369
  diplomatic services 180
  employment contracts 150–152
  habitual residence 151
  military property 417
  non-commercial torts 202, 207, 216
  plaintiffs 151
  separate entities 236–237, 280–282
  territorial connection 216
  tortious act/omission only 216
Australian Law Commission
  insurable risks 202
  non-commercial torts 202, 207
Austria
  choice of law 175
  diplomatic security 184
  employment contracts 166, 174,
    175, 184
  injury/damage only 218–221
  measures of constraint 381–382, 360
  nature approach 86
  non-commercial activities 210–211
  non-commercial torts 219
  private person test 61, 69
  restrictive/relative immunity 15
  territorial connection 174, 219
  trading activities 20
aviation
  expropriation 302–303
  separate entities 237–239, 240–241
  speculative injuries 125

Bangladesh, import/export 116
banking
  accounts with definite destination 421
  central bank property 410–416
  embassy accounts 41, 407–410
  measures of constraint 407–416,
    418–421
  mixed accounts 418–421
  remote injury 126
  see also financial instruments
Belgium
  choice of law 174
  diplomatic services 165
  employee status 172–173
  employment contracts 165, 172–174, 178
  expropriation 299
  human rights violation 431–432
  measures of constraint 358, 372
  nature approach 86–87
  non-commercial activities 80
  private person test 61
  remedies 178
  restrictive/relative immunity 13–14
  territorial connection 173–174
Binnenbeziehung 71, 72, 173, 399–401
bonds
  Argentina 89, 102, 116, 124, 125
  bonods 89, 124
  China 23–24
  India 123
  see also financial instruments
Brazil, organ of foreign State 249–259

Canada
  architectural drawings 140
  diplomatic services 168
  employment contracts 139–140,
    168, 177
  injury/damage only 219–221
  non-commercial torts 200, 219–221
  personal injury 209–210
  private person test 139–140
  purpose approach 98–100, 139–140
  reciprocity 56
  remedies 177
  separate entities 274–277, 397–398
  territorial connection 219–221
  trade union certification 98–100, 164
canon law 52
case law
  contradictory findings 194–195
  employment 136–143
  expropriation 118–122
  merits considered 134
  nature approach 87–97
  nature/private person test inadequate
    137–143

INDEX 749

State immunity 4, 6–7, 8–10, 27–29
The Cristina case 9
The Schooner Exchange case 8–9, 11, 53, 65
see also local jurisdiction
Chile
  Pinochet case 429, 436–438
  political assassinations 208–209, 222, 399
  Torture Convention 429
China
  bond default 23–24
  joint ventures 119
  separate entities 246–247
  State assets 119
choice of law
  employment contracts 147–148, 149–150,
    152, 174–175
  European Convention (1972) 147–148
commercial activities
  acts *jure imperii* / *jure gestionis*
    distinguished 14, 16, 17, 19, 23, 34,
    86–87
  air transport 78
  categories 77–79
  commercial undefined 90–94
  construction works 78
  contracts *see* contracts
  definition 89–90, 110
  difficulties 87–98
  double commerciality 114–115, 117, 118,
    120, 121
  employment *see* employment contracts
  exceptions to immunity 75–131
  financial instruments 23–24, 77, 113
  immovable property 77, 118–119
  nature/purpose
    Austria 86
    Belgium 86
    Canada 98–100
    case law 87–97
    context approach 85, 103–107
    debate 85
    difficulties with nature approach
      87–98
    education/culture 91
    France 103
    Germany 86–87
    Holy See 91–92
    Italy 100–103, 139
    nature approach 86–87
    The Philippines 97–98
    private person test 93–94, 95
    for profit 90–91, 92–93, 95–96
    purpose approach 98–103
    purposes distinguished 95–96
    self-contradictory purposes 96–98
    Switzerland 87
    trade and traffic or commerce 89

UN Convention (2004) 103
  United Kingdom 103–106
  United States 87–97
  US FSIA (1976) *see under* US Foreign
    Sovereign Immunities Act
  whole context 105
non-sovereign activities 7–8
patents 78
privatization 78
scope 76–79
shipping 77
terminology 75–76, 101
truly commercial 84–85
UN Convention (2004) 27, 103
United States 77, 81–83, 87–97, 108–129
US FSIA (1976) *see under* US Foreign
  Sovereign Immunities Act
see also non-commercial activities
consent
  local jurisdiction 7
  sovereignty 46
context approach
  commercial activities 85, 103–107
  New Zealand 106–107
  Sweden 107
  United Kingdom 103–107
  whole context 105
contracts
  commercial activities, scope 78, 85
  employment *see* employment contracts
  governing law 327–329
  US FSIA (1976) 111
conventions
  Europe *see* European Convention on State
    Immunity (1972)
  United Nations *see* UN Convention on
    State Immunity (2004)
corporate veil, separate entities 287–295
counterclaims, waiver of immunity
  334–335
criminal law
  human rights violation 426–428
  non-commercial activities 84
customary international law
  codification 441–446
  constitutional principle 35
  general principle 34–37
  State immunity 1, 34–37
  UN Convention (2004) 35
Czechoslovakia, trade marks 15

definitions *see* terminology
denial of immunity
  legal basis 58–73
  private person test 41, 59–64
  see also exceptions to immunity
Denmark, employer acts 171

750 INDEX

diplomatic immunity
  bank accounts 41, 407–410
  diplomatic and consular missions
    179–192, 404–410
  diplomatic premises 405–407
  diplomatic property 404–410
  ILA draft articles 180
  institutional aims 185–191
  national security 184–185
  ne impediatur legatio 182, 183
  procedural rules 2
  proceedings against diplomats 191–192
  UN Convention (2004) 181, 184, 194, 405
  Vienna Conventions 153, 180, 191, 407,
    451
diplomatic services
  Australia 180
  Belgium 165, 166
  Canada 168
  employee duties and functions 166–170
  employment contracts
    see under employment contracts
  Finland 182
  France 167
  Germany 183–184
  immunities *see* diplomatic immunity
  Ireland 182
  Italy 166
  legal proceedings 179–192
  The Netherlands 165, 166, 184
  New Zealand 169–170
  Portugal 167
  proceedings
    against diplomats 191–192
    against foreign State 181–185
    employment 179–192
  savings regime 179–192
  South Africa 182
  Spain 167–168
  Switzerland 166–167, 182
  United Kingdom 155–156, 168, 181–182,
    184
  United States 158–161, 167–169
direct effect
  ILA draft articles 223
  non-commercial torts 223
  territorial connection 115–129, 223
  in United States *see under* US Foreign
    Sovereign Immunities Act
double commerciality 114–115, 117, 118,
  120, 121

education
  nature/purpose 91
  service families 105–106
employee status
  armed forces 172–173

Belgium 172–173
  employment contracts 172–173
  Italy 172–173
employer status
  employment contracts 170–171
  France 171
  Italy 170–171
  Kuwait 171
  United States 170–171
employment
  agency workers 136
  case law
    nature/private person test inadequate
      137–143
    peculiar features 136–143
    specialized tribunals 136–137
  Germany 140–141, 183–184
  Italy 100–102, 139, 166, 170–171, 174,
    175, 185–191
  permanency 136
  social security 101–102
  trade union certification 98–100
employment contracts
  Argentina 152, 176
  armed forces
    employee status 172–173
    employer status 170–171
    recreational facilities 170–171
    Saudi Arabia 193
    savings regime 179, 193
    United Kingdom 193
  Australia 150–152
  Austria 166, 174, 175, 184
  background 134
  Belgium 165, 172–174, 178
  Canada 139–140, 168, 177
  choice of law
    Australia 152
    Austria 175
    Belgium 174
    European Convention (1972) 147–148
    Italy 174
    jurisdiction 174–175
    The Netherlands 175
    Spain 174
    Switzerland 175
    United Kingdom 149–150
    United States 175
  complexity 141–142
  contract of service 135
  contract for services 135
  contradictory findings 194–195
  diplomatic services
    employee duties and functions 166–170
    institutional aims 185–191
    legal proceedings 179–192
    proceedings against diplomats 191–192

proceedings against foreign State
181–185
savings regime 179–192
sex discrimination 155–156
United Kingdom 155–156, 168,
181–182, 184
United States 158–161, 167–169
wrongful dismissal 166
diverse approaches 164–179, 194–196
employees
duties and functions 166–170
employer State nationals 160
employment relationship 165–166
status 172–173
employers
acts 171–172
status 170–171
European Convention (1972) 144–148
Finland 182
France 167, 171, 174, 177, 194–195
Germany 183–184
habitual residence
Australia 151
European Convention (1972) 145–146
United Kingdom 145–146, 149
United States 160
IDI draft articles (1991) 152–153
ILA draft articles 153
individuals 162
institutional aims, diplomatic
immunity 185–191
Ireland 182, 195
Israel 152
Italy 139, 166, 170–171, 174, 175, 185–191
jurisdiction 147–148, 149–150, 174–175
military bases 98–100, 172–173
multifactor inquiry 159–160
multiple-factor test 136
nationality
employer State nationals 160
European Convention (1972) 145, 146
third State nationals 146, 158–161
United Kingdom 145, 146
United States 158–161
nature/private person test inadequate
137–143
The Netherlands 165, 166, 173–174, 175,
177–178, 182, 184
New Zealand 169–170, 177, 195
other instruments 152–154
particular activities, nature 173
personal injury 112
The Philippines 170
place of performance 147
plaintiffs
Australia 151
European Convention (1972) 145–146

United Kingdom 149
United States 162–164
Portugal 165, 166, 167
public institutions, foreign States 194
purpose approach 100, 101–102, 106,
134, 141
remedies
Argentina 176
Belgium 178
Canada 177
double aspect 177
financial/sovereign dichotomy
176–177
France 177
Italy 175
The Netherlands 177–178
New Zealand 177
reinstatement 177–178
Switzerland 178
Saudi Arabia 160–161, 193
savings regime
armed forces 179, 193
diplomatic services 179–192
institutional aims 185–191
proceedings against diplomats
191–192
proceedings against foreign State
181–185
public institutions 194
State practice 179–194
South Africa 182
Spain 167–168, 174
State immunity 198
Switzerland 166–167, 173, 175, 178, 182
terminated for security reasons
184–185
terminology 134–136
territorial connection 173–174
third State nationals 146, 158–161
threshold requirements 152
two models 143–144
UK see under United Kingdom
UN Convention (2004) 156, 184, 194
unfair dismissal 106, 138–139
uniform rules lacking 194–196
United Arab Emirates (UAE) 158–159
USA see under United States
England see United Kingdom
European Convention on State Immunity
(1972)
absolute immunity replaced 12
choice of law 147–148
employment contracts 144–148
habitual residence 145–146
measures of constraint 351–352, 363
nationality 145, 146
non-commercial torts 207, 218

752 INDEX

European Convention on State Immunity (1972) (*cont.*)
  par in parem non habet imperium 51
  place of performance 147
  plaintiffs 145–146
  presumption of immunity 39–40
  private person test 63
  territorial connection 218
  third State nationals 146
  tortious act/omission only 218
  United Kingdom, ratification 18
European Union (EU), Helms-Burton Act 314
exceptions to immunity
  absolute immunity 8, 10–11
  commerce *see* commercial activities
  employment *see* employment contracts
  local jurisdiction 34
  presumption of immunity 37–38
  private persons *see* private person test
  torts *see* non-commercial torts
  US FSIA (1976) 40–41
  see also denial of immunity
execution
  State immunity 34, 347–362
  waiver 34
expropriation
  aviation 302–303
  background 298
  Belgium 299
  case law 118–122
  France 301
  immovable property 118–119, 120–121, 123
  immunity principle 299–301
  International Law Commission (ILC) 303
  Italy 301–302
  legality and immunity 301–303
  Pakistan 120–121
  Poland 118–119
  Russian Federation 123
  shipping 299
  State immunity 298–315
  Sweden 299
  Switzerland 300
  United Kingdom 302–303
  United States 313
  US FSIA (1976) 313
extraterritoriality
  human rights 68, 431–432
  terminology 30
  United States 313

financial instruments
  Argentine bonds 89, 102, 116, 124, 125
  China bond default 23–24
  commercial activities 23–24, 77, 113
  India bond redemption 123
  private bank debt 88

promissory notes 113
Finland, employment contracts 182
foreign national courts
  jurisdiction *see* local jurisdiction
  State immunity 3, 6
foreign State property
  exceptions to immunity 34
  see also immovable property; property
foreign States
  activities
    acts within borders 1–2
    commercial *see* commercial activities
    in foreign State distinguished 80–81
    non-commercial *see* non-commercial activities
    outside United States 113–115, 116–124
    sovereign *see* sovereign activities
    trade *see* trading activities
    in United States 110–113
  direct effect in United States *see under* US Foreign Sovereign Immunities Act
  institutional aims 185–191
  proceedings against foreign State 181–185
  public institutions 194
  US FSIA (1976) *see* US Foreign Sovereign Immunities Act
forum State *see* territory of forum State
France
  commercial leases 103
  contradictory findings 194–195
  diplomatic services 167
  employer status 171
  employment contracts 167, 171, 174, 177, 194–195
  expropriation 301
  measures of constraint 360, 371–372, 379–381, 398
  purpose approach 103
  remedies 177
  restrictive/relative immunity 15
  separate entities 285
  territorial connection 174

Germany
  Binnenbeziehung 72
  diplomatic services 183–184
  embassy bank accounts 407–409
  employment 140–141
  employment contracts 183–184
  measures of constraint 360, 370, 378–379, 398
  nature approach 86–87
  non-commercial activities 79–85
  non-commercial torts 218
  private person test 61, 140–141
  restrictive/relative immunity 12, 17, 20–21
  separate entities 284–285

INDEX 753

territorial connection 218
tortious act/omission only 218
Greece
measures of constraint 359
non-commercial activities 213–214
restrictive/relative immunity 15
sovereignty 47

habitual residence, employment
see under employment contracts
health care
medical profession 139
military hospitals 105
Holy See
commercial activities 91–92
papacy 52
purpose approach 190–191
sexual abuse 204
human rights
employment contracts 155–156
extraterritoriality 68, 431–432
human rights violation
background 423
criminal proceedings 426–428
extraterritorial jurisdiction 431–432
immunity and legality 22–23, 438–440
implied waiver 340–341
jus cogens 428–431
Pinochet case 429, 436–438
State immunity 423
State and officials 432–435
territorial jurisdiction 424–426

ICSID Convention (1965) 325–327
ideologies, irrelevance 23–25
immovable property
commercial activities 77, 118–119
diplomatic premises 405–407
expropriation 118–119, 120–121, 123
local jurisdiction 8, 10–11, 67–68
see also property
immunity
absolute see absolute immunity
adjudication 34, 347–362
diplomatic see diplomatic immunity
exceptions see exceptions to immunity
execution 34, 347–362
presumption see presumption of
immunity
restrictive see restrictive/relative
immunity
terminology see terminology
see also State immunity
India, bond redemption 123
injunctions, freezing injunctions 235–236
injury/damage
Austria 218–221

Canada 219–221
non-commercial torts 218–223
territorial connection 218–221
US FSIA (1976) 221–223
see also personal injury
Institut de Droit International (IDI) draft
articles (1991)
competence criteria 80, 152–153
employment contracts 152–153
non-commercial torts 216–217
separate entities 282–283
territoriality 67–68
tortious act/omission only 216–217
insurable risks
armed forces 203
non-commercial torts 201–203
US FSIA (1976) 202–203
interim measures see measures of
constraint
International Court of Justice (ICJ),
Statute 28
international law
customary see customary international
law
public international law 37
violation, expropriation 307–311
International Law Association (ILA) draft
articles
diplomatic immunity 180
direct effect 223
employment contracts 153
International Law Commission (ILC)
codification 446–453
diverse language 24
expropriation 303
insurable risks 201–203
non-commercial torts 215
par in parem non habet imperium 51
recruitment 156
international organizations, dynamics 2
Ireland
diplomatic services 182, 195
employment contracts 182, 195
non-commercial activities 212–213
Israel
employment contracts 152
tiering 269–271
West Bank settlements 82
Italy
Argentine bonds 102
choice of law 174
diplomatic services 166
embassy bank accounts 421
employee status 172–173
employer status 170–171
employment 100–102, 139, 166, 170–171,
174, 175, 185–191

754   INDEX

Italy (cont.)
  employment contracts 139, 166, 170–171, 174, 175, 185–191
  expropriation 301–302
  institutional aims 185–191
  measures of constraint 358, 371
  medical profession 139
  non-commercial activities 211
  non-commercial torts 210
  private person test 60, 68–69, 139
  purpose approach 100–103, 139
  remedies 175
  restrictive/relative immunity 14
  social security 101–102
  terminology 101
  trade unions 163–164

Japan, organ of foreign State 254
joint ventures, China 119
jurisdiction
  employment contracts 147–148, 149–150, 174–175
  national courts see local jurisdiction
  nexus requirement 108–129
  non-commercial torts 199–229
  personal injury 110
  separate entities 230–297
  territorial see territorial jurisdiction
  US FSIA (1976) 38, 108–129
  waiver of immunity 335–336
jus cogens 428–431

Korea, organ of foreign State 254–255, 257
Kuwait
  employer acts 171
  employer status 171

League of Nations 443–444
legal basis for immunity
  basis questioned 55–58
  denial of immunity 58–73
  general principles 44–58
  par in parem non habet imperium 51–55
  reciprocity 56
  sovereignty 46–51
  United States 44–46
legal personality
  categorical approach 247–249
  legal characteristics test 247
  separate entities 235–236, 247–249
Lithuania, waiver 337
local jurisdiction
  absolute immunity waived 8, 7, 10–11
  accountability 2
  acta jure imperii 34
  consent 7
  exceptions to immunity 34

immovable property 8, 10–11, 67–68
lex rei sitae 8, 10
territory see territory of forum State
see also jurisdiction; territorial jurisdiction

Malaysia, employment contracts 224
measures of constraint
  Austria 360, 381–382
  background 343–344
  bank accounts 410–416, 418–421
  Belgium 358, 372
  conditions
    connection 399–402
    executive oversight 404
    legal instruments 394
    purpose approach 392–394
    scope 390–404
    States without immunity statutes 398–399
    waiver 390–392
  connection requirement
    entity connection 401–402
    scope 399–402
    subject matter 399
    territorial connection 399–401
  European Convention (1972) 351–352, 363
  France 360, 371–372, 379–381, 398
  Germany 360, 370, 378–379, 398
  Greece 359
  immunity from execution 347–362
  immunity from suit 347–362
  Italy 358, 371
  judicial powers 348–350
  other public property 418
  prejudgment measures
    conditions 378–390
    immunities 373–390
    liberal conditions 383
    same conditions as execution 378–383
    stricter conditions 383–390
  preliminary issue 374–378
  property under special protection
    central banks 410–416
    diplomatic property 404–410
    immunities 404–418
    military property 417
  purpose approach 362–373, 392–394
  separate entities 394–399
  Spain 372
  State immunity 343–422
  State practice 358–361
  States without immunity statutes 369–373, 398–399
  Switzerland 359, 370
  terminology 344–346
  territorial presence 402–404

treaties 351–353, 363
two immunities 347–362
UN Convention (2004) 352–353, 363
United Kingdom 356–358, 414–416, 369, 386
universal distinction 350–362
universal rule 361–362
US FSIA (1976) 353–356, 363–367,
386–390, 410–414
Mexico, organ of foreign State 251–252
military *see* armed forces
municipal laws
general principles 34
national courts *see* local jurisdiction
States without immunity statutes 36,
224, 283–286, 369–373, 398–399
United Kingdom 43
United States 42–44

national security, diplomatic immunity
184–185
nationality
employer State nationals 160
employment contracts
see under employment contracts
third State nationals 146, 158–161
NATO, Status of Forces Agreement 172–173,
213
nature, nature/purpose compared
see under commercial activities
nature approach
acta jure imperii/gestionis 86–87
Austria 86
Belgium 86–87
commercial activities 86–87
difficulties with nature approach 87–98
employment contracts 137–143
Germany 86–87
Switzerland 87
United Kingdom 103–106
United States 87–97
US FSIA (1976) 87
The Netherlands
choice of law 175
diplomatic services 165, 166, 184
employment contracts 165, 166, 173–174,
175, 177–178, 182, 184
non-commercial activities 84, 211–212
remedies 177–178
territorial connection 173–174
New York Convention (1958) 325–327
New Zealand
contradictory findings 195
diplomatic services 169–170
employment contracts 169–170, 177, 195
purpose approach 106–107
remedies 177
Nicaragua, private bank debt 88

non-commercial activities
abuse of police powers 81
academic activities 84
Austria 210–211
Belgium 80
categories 83
commercial activities distinguished
79–85
crimes 84
Germany 79–85
governmental activities 81–83
Greece 213–214
hiring of thugs 81–82
Ireland 212–213
Italy 211
kidnapping 84
The Netherlands 84, 211–212
United States 80, 81–83
West Bank settlements 82
see also commercial activities
non-commercial torts
acta jure imperii/gestionis 199, 207–215
armed forces 212–215
attribution 224–225
Australia 202, 207, 216
Austria 219
background 199
Canada 200, 219–221
direct effect 223
discretionary function 203–206
European Convention (1972) 207, 218
Germany 218
IDI draft articles (1991) 216–217
injury/damage only 218–221
instant torts 219
insurable risks 201–203
International Law Commission (ILC)
215
Italy 210
jurisdiction 199–229
personal injury 200, 209–210
personal safety 200
physical injury 200–201
property 200
psychological injury 220–221
split/long-range torts 219
tangible property 200–201
targeted torts 200–207
terminology 199–200
territorial connection 215–224
terrorism 225–228
tortious act/omission and injury/damage
221–223
tortious act/omission only 216–218
United Kingdom 213, 214–215
US FSIA (1976) 201, 208–209, 213,
221–223

756   INDEX

non-sovereign activities
  absolute immunity 7–8
  sovereign activities distinguished 7–8,
    19–23
  trading activities 7–8, 19–23
  see also commercial activities

Pakistan, property expropriation 120–121
par in parem non habet imperium
  adage 53
  axiom 52
  European Convention (1972) 51
  International Law Commission (ILC) 51
  maxim 53
  State immunity 51–55
personal injury
  Canada 209–210
  commercial activities 112
  employment contracts 112
  injury/damage only 218–221
  jurisdiction 110
  non-commercial torts 200, 209–210
  physical injury 200–201
  psychological injury 220–221
  tortious act/omission and injury/damage
    221–223
  US FSIA (1976) 112
Peru, judgment creditors 122
The Philippines
  commercial activities 97–98
  employment contracts 170
  officials 434–435
  waiver 332
Phillimore, Robert 19, 66
Pinochet case 429, 436–438
place of performance
  direct effect 127–128
  employment contracts 147
  European Convention (1972) 147
  US FSIA (1976) 127–128
plaintiffs, employment
    see under employment contracts
Poland, property expropriation 118–119
police
  powers abused *see* abuse of police powers
  separate entities 237
pooling
  indirect ownership 261
  infinite loop 265–267
  shareholdings 259–264
  tiering 264
Portugal
  diplomatic services 167
  employment contracts 165, 166, 167
PRC *see* China
presumption of immunity
  agencies/instrumentalities 171

  burden of proof 41
  European Convention (1972) 39–40
  exceptions to immunity 37–38
  general principle 34, 37–41
  separate entities 244
  UN Convention (2004) 39
  United Kingdom 38
  United States 38, 40–41, 171, 244
  US FSIA (1976) 38, 244
private act plus territoriality
  Switzerland 69–72
  United States 69
private person test
  acta jure imperii/gestionis 41, 132
  armed forces 94
  Austria 61, 69
  Belgium 61
  Canada 139–140
  commercial activities 93–94, 95
  denial of immunity 41
  employment contracts 137–143
  European Convention (1972) 63
  Germany 61, 140–141
  Italy 60, 68–69, 139
  opposite test 81, 84
  private act plus territoriality 69–72
  purchase of bullets 61
  Switzerland 69–72
  territory of forum state 68–73
  unfair dismissal 138–139
  United Kingdom 62, 138–139
  United States 61–62, 69
procedural rules
  accountability 2
  diplomatic immunity 2
product liability 122–123
property
  commercial leases 103
  foreign State property 34
  real *see* immovable property
  special protection *see under* measures of
    constraint
purpose, nature/purpose compared
    see under commercial activities
purpose approach
  acta jure imperii/gestionis 99, 134
  Canada 98–100, 139–140
  commercial activities 98–103
  education, service families 105–106
  employment contracts 100, 101–102, 106,
    141, 134
  France 103
  Holy See 190–191
  Italy 100–103, 139
  measures of constraint 362–373, 392–394
  military bases 100
  military hospitals 105

New Zealand 106–107
purposes distinguished 95–96
resurface 362–373
self-contradictory purposes 96–98
sovereign purpose 98–103, 105–106
tax credits 106–107
terminology 101
UN Convention (2004) 103
unfair dismissal 106, 138–139
United Kingdom 105–106, 138–139

real property *see* immovable property
reciprocity
Canada 56
legal basis for immunity 56
UN Convention (2004) 57
recruitment
employment contracts 156–157
International Law Commission (ILC) 156
remedies, employment
see under employment contracts
residence, habitual *see under* employment
contracts
restrictive/relative immunity
Austria 15
Belgium 13–14
cross-fertilization of judicial practice
27–29
descent of the State 19–23
emergence 19
France 15
Germany 12, 17, 20–21
Greece 15
Italy 14
snowballing 28
Switzerland 14
twentieth-century doctrine 3
UN Convention (2004) 12
United Kingdom 17–18
United States 16
US FSIA (1976) 61–62
see also state immunity
rules
comprehensive rules 42–43
employment contracts 194–196
procedural *see* procedural rules
State immunity 36–37
United States 42–43
Russian Federation
property expropriation 123
see also Soviet Union

Saudi Arabia
abuse of police powers 81, 112
armed forces 193
employment contracts 160–161, 193
separate entities

agencies/instrumentalities 243–244
Australia 236–237, 280–282
aviation 237–239, 240–241
background 230–231
Canada 274–277, 397–398
categorical approach 247–249
China 246–247
comparison/summary 277–280
context principle 239–241
corporate veil 287–295
discretion 234
distinctiveness from executive
organs 236–237
diverse approaches 232–286
France 285
Germany 284–285
IDI draft articles (1991) 282–283
infinite loop 265–267
jurisdiction 230–297
legal characteristics test 247
legal personality 235–236, 247–249
majority ownership 243
measures of constraint 394–399
multifactor test 234–235
organ of foreign State 249–259
other models 280–283
police 237
pooling 259–264
presumption of immunity 244
States without immunity
statutes 283–286
status 244–247, 273–274
Switzerland 286
terminology 231
tiering 264
timing 273
two-step analysis 235
UN Convention (2004) 282
United Kingdom 232–241, 397
United States 242–277, 394–397
shareholdings
infinite loop 265–267
majority ownership 243
pooling 259–264
tiering 264
shipping
expropriation 299
salvage arbitration 235–236
sister ship principle 18
State immunity 6, 11
social security, Italy 101–102
South Africa
diplomatic services 182
employment contracts 182
internet domain names 83–84,
125
trading activities 21–22

758 INDEX

sovereign activities
  acts *jure imperii* see *acta jure imperii/
    gestionis*
  military bases 98–100
  nature/purpose *see under* commercial
    activities
  non-commercial *see* non-commercial
    activities
  non-sovereign activities distinguished
    7–8, 19–23
  sovereign purpose *see* purpose
    approach
  State immunity 8, 98–103
  trading activities 7–8, 19–23
sovereign purpose
  activities 98–103
  scope 98–103
  see also purpose approach
sovereignty
  acta jure imperii/gestionis 50
  affiliated concepts 46–51
  consent 46
  forum State, territory 49–50
  legal basis for immunity 46–51
  public policy 46
  Statehood 48–51
  terminology 48–49
  territorial jurisdiction 49–50
Soviet Union
  collapse 3
  ideology 23
  radioactive contamination 218
Spain
  choice of law 174
  diplomatic services 167–168
  embassy bank accounts 420
  employment contracts 167–168, 174
  measures of constraint 372
  territorial connection 174
State immunity
  absolute *see* absolute immunity
  adjudication 34, 347–362
  background 1–5
  broad/narrow meaning 1–2
  case law 4, 6–7, 8–10, 27–29
  conclusions 459–465
  constraint *see* measures of constraint
  cross-fertilization of judicial practice
    27–29
  customary international law 1, 34
  defendant states 25–26
  denial *see* denial of immunity
  diversity 3–4
  employment contracts 198
  entities *see* separate entities
  exceptions *see* exceptions to immunity
  execution *see* execution

factual developments 22–23
foreign national courts 3, 6
general principles 33–74, 299–301
history 6–32
international sources 36
judicial decision-making 4, 27–29
legal basis *see* legal basis for immunity
limited *see* restrictive/relative immunity
merits of case considered 134
par in parem non habet imperium 51–55
presumption *see* presumption of immunity
rules 36–37
shipping 6, 11
singular/plural form 29–30
sources of law 26, 36
sovereign activities 8, 98–103
statement of principles 34
States without immunity statutes 36,
  224, 283–286, 369–373, 398–399
terminology 29–31
The Schooner Exchange case 8–9, 11, 53, 65
torture 43
waiver *see* waiver
States
  activities
    accountability *see* accountability
    commerce *see* commercial activities
    non-commercial *see* non-commercial
      activities
    non-sovereign *see* non-sovereign activities
    sovereign *see* sovereign activities
    trade *see* trading activities
  acts *see* acts
  descent of the State 19–23
  entities *see* separate entities
  foreign *see* foreign States
  jurisdiction *see* territorial jurisdiction
  territory *see* territory of forum state
  without immunity statutes 36, 224,
    283–286, 369–373, 398–399
status
  agencies/instrumentalities 244–247,
    273–274
  employees *see* employee status
  employers *see* employer status
  separate entities 244–247, 273–274
Sweden
  context approach 107
  expropriation 299
Switzerland
  Binnenbeziehung 71, 72, 173
  choice of law 175
  diplomatic services 166–167, 182
  employment contracts 166–167, 173, 175,
    178, 182
  expropriation 300
  measures of constraint 359, 370

nationality 162
nature approach 87
private act plus territoriality 69–72
remedies 178
restrictive/relative immunity 14
separate entities 286
territorial connection 173

Tate Letter (1952) 12, 16, 23
terminology
  commercial activities
    commercial undefined 90–94
    Italy 101
    term of convenience 75–76
    US FSIA (1976) definition 89–90, 110
  employment contracts 134–136
  extraterritoriality 30
  measures of constraint 344–346
  non-commercial torts 199–200
  purpose approach 101
  separate entities 231
  singular/plural form 29–30
  sovereignty 48–49
  State immunity 29–31
  States 433
territorial connection
  Australia 216
  Austria 174, 219
  Belgium 173–174
  Canada 219–221
  commercial activities 124–125
  direct effect 115–129, 223
  employment contracts 173–174
  European Convention (1972) 218
  France 174
  Germany 218
  injury/damage only 218–221
  measures of constraint 399–402
  The Netherlands 173–174
  non-commercial torts 215–224
  Spain 174
  States without immunity statutes 224
  Switzerland 173
  tortious act/omission and injury/damage 221–223
  tortious act/omission only 216–218
  UN Convention (1976) 124–125
  with United States *see under* US Foreign Sovereign Immunities Act
territorial jurisdiction
  human rights violation 424–426
  IDI draft articles (1991) 67–68
  principle 34, 64–68
  sovereignty 49–50
  United Kingdom 66–67
  United States 65, 69
  see also local jurisdiction

territory of forum state
  activities in foreign State distinguished 80–81
  meaning 59
  private acts 68–73
  sovereignty 49–50
  territorial jurisdiction principle 34, 64–68
  United States, forum jurisdiction 38
  see also local jurisdiction
terrorism, non-commercial torts 225–258
tiering 264
tortious act/omission
  Australia 216
  European Convention (1972) 218
  Germany 218
  IDI draft articles (1991) 216–217
  injury/damage 221–223
  non-commercial torts 216–218, 221–223
  personal injury 221–223
  UN Convention (2004) 217–218
torts
  injury *see* personal injury
  non-commercial *see* non-commercial torts
torture
  abuse of police powers 81
  State immunity 43
  Torture Convention 427, 429, 436, 437
trade unions
  Canada 98–100, 164
  certification 98–100, 164
  employment contracts 162–164
  Italy 163–164
  plaintiffs 162–164
  United States 162–164
  see also employment
trading activities
  acts *jure imperii / jure gestionis* distinguished 14, 16, 17, 19, 23, 34
  Austria 20
  non-sovereign activities 7–8, 19–23
  South Africa 21–22
  United Kingdom 21
  United States 20–21
  see also commercial activities

UN Convention on State Immunity (2004)
  assessment 4
  background 441–458
  commercial activities 27, 103
  customary international law 35
  diplomatic immunity 181, 184, 194, 405
  employment contracts 156, 184, 194
  General Assembly debate 447–453
  genesis 441–458
  matters avoided 456–457
  matters enshrined 455
  measures of constraint 352–353, 363

760 INDEX

UN Convention on State Immunity (2004) (*cont.*)
  non-commercial torts 217–218
  presumption of immunity 39
  purpose approach 103
  reciprocity 57
  recruitment 156
  restrictive/relative immunity 12
  separate entities 282
  territorial connection 217–218
  tortious act/omission only 217–218
  universal support 454
unions *see* trade unions
United Arab Emirates (UAE), employment
    contracts 158–159
United Kingdom
  armed forces 193, 213
  central bank property 414–416
  common law 18
  context approach 103–107
  employment contracts
    armed forces 193
    choice of law 149–150
    commercial purposes 149
    contracts compared 135–136
    diplomatic services 155–156, 168,
      181–182, 184
    habitual residence 145–146, 149
    human rights 155–156
    importance of contract 154–157
    jurisdiction 149–150
    nationality 145, 146
    plaintiffs 149
    recruitment 156–157
    separate category 149
    UK model 143, 144–157
    UK SIA (1978) 148–150
  expropriation 302–303
  measures of constraint 356–358, 369, 386,
    414–416
  municipal laws 43
  nature approach 103–106
  non-commercial torts 213, 214–215
  presumption of immunity 38
  private person test 62, 138–139
  purpose approach 105–106, 138–139
  restrictive/relative immunity 17–18
  separate entities 232–241, 397
  State Immunity Act (1978) 18, 38, 148–150
  territorial jurisdiction 66–67
  trading activities 21
  unfair dismissal 138–139
  waiver 335–339
United States
  Argentine bonds 89, 102, 116, 124, 125
  China bond default 23–24
  choice of law 175

commercial activities 77, 81–83, 87–97,
    108–129
contract governing law 327–329
Department of State 16
employment contracts
  choice of law 175
  commercial activities 157–161
  diplomatic services 158–161,
    167–169
  employer acts 171–172
  employer status 170–171
  habitual residence 160
  individuals 162
  multifactor inquiry 159–160
  nationality 158–161
  plaintiffs 162–164
  third State nationals 158–161
  trade unions 162–164
  two-step inquiry 160–161
  US model 144, 164
expropriation 313, 313
extraterritoriality 313
FSIA *see* US Foreign Sovereign Immunities
    Act (1976)
Helms-Burton Act 313
legal basis for immunity 44–46
litigation participation/involvement
    329–333
municipal laws 42–44
nature approach 87–97
non-commercial activities 80, 81–83
presumption of immunity 38, 40–41,
    171, 244
private act plus territoriality 69
private person test 61–62, 69
separate entities 242–277
Tate Letter (1952) 12, 16, 23
territorial jurisdiction 65, 69
terrorism 225–228
trading activities 20–21
waiver
  arbitration 325–327
  background 317
  clear/unambiguous 322–324
  counterclaims 334–335
  explicit/express 319–322
  implicit as explicit 333
  implicit/implied 324–333
  practice 317–335
  specificity 333–334
  who can waive immunity 317–319
US Foreign Sovereign Immunities Act (1976)
  central bank property 410–414
  commercial activities
    attachment of assets 122
    based upon 110–112
    basis of complaint 111

bond redemption 123
contracts 111
definition 89–90, 110
direct effect 115–129
double commerciality 114–115, 117, 120
double connection 118, 121
employment contracts 157–161
of foreign State elsewhere 113–115, 116–124
jurisdictional requirements 108–129
licensing 116
personal injury 112
prescribed acts 109
product liability 122–123
sovereign elements 111–112
substantial contact 112–113
substantive/material connection 115
territorial connection 124–125
in United States by foreign State 110–113
comprehensive rules 42–43
connection with United States
direct effect 115–129
double connection 118, 121
expropriation 311
immediate consequence 125–127
substantive/material 115
territorial 124–125
direct effect
acts 116–124
commercial activities 115–129
dispositive question 126
financial gain 127
financial loss 126–127
immediate consequence 125–127
legally significant acts 129
payments 128
place of performance 127–128
ripple effect 127
speculative injuries 125–126
territorial connection 115–129, 223–224
discretionary function 203–206
employment contracts
commercial activities 157–161
diplomatic services 158–161, 167–169
multifactor inquiry 159–160
third State nationals 158–161
two-step inquiry 160–161
US model 157–161
exceptions to immunity 40–41
expropriation
background 313

international law violation 307–311
provision 313
rights in property 305–307
territorial connection 311
insurable risks 202–203
jurisdiction
forum 38
nexus requirement 108–129, 311
measures of constraint 353–356, 363–367, 386–390, 410–414
nature approach 87
non-commercial torts 201, 208–209, 213, 221–223, 225–228
organ of foreign State 249–259
pooling 259–264
presumption of immunity 38, 244
restrictive/relative immunity 61–62
separate entities 242–244, 394–397
territorial presence 402–404
terrorism 225–228
tiering 264
tortious act/omission and injury/damage 221–223
waiver 317–335

Vatican *see* Holy See

waiver
absolute immunity 7, 8, 10–11
adjudication 34
arbitration 325–327, 336
background 316
clear/unambiguous 322–324
counterclaims 334–335
execution 34
explicit/express 319–322
general principle 34
human rights violation, implied waiver 340–341
implicit 324–333
implicit as explicit 333
implied 324–333, 340–341
jurisdiction 335–336
measures of constraint 390–392
specificity 333–334
State immunity 316–342
State practice 340
United Kingdom 335–339
United States 317–335
who can waive immunity 317–319

CAMBRIDGE STUDIES IN INTERNATIONAL AND COMPARATIVE LAW

Books in the series

XIAODONG YANG
State Immunity in International Law

CONOR MCCARTHY
Reducing Genocide to Law: Definition, Meaning, and the Ultimate Crime

PAYAM AKHAVAN
Decolonizing International Law: Development, Economic Growth and the
Politics of Universality

SUNDHYA PAHUJA
Complicity and the Law of State Responsibility

HELMUT PHILIPP AUST
State Control over Private Military and Security Companies in Armed Conflict

HANNAH TONKIN
'Fair and Equitable Treatment' in International Investment Law

ROLAND KLÄGER
The UN and Human Rights: Who Guards the Guardians?

GUGLIELMO VERDIRAME
Sovereign Defaults before International Courts and Tribunals

MICHAEL WAIBEL
Making the Law of the Sea: A Study in the Development of International Law

JAMES HARRISON
Science and the Precautionary Principle in International Courts and Tribunals:
Expert Evidence, Burden of Proof and Finality

CAROLINE E. FOSTER
Legal Aspects of Transition from Illegal Territorial Regimes in International Law

YAËL RONEN
Access to Asylum: International Refugee Law and the Globalisation of Migration Control

THOMAS GAMMELTOFT-HANSEN
Trading Fish, Saving Fish: The Interaction between Regimes in International Law

MARGARET YOUNG
The Individual in the International Legal System: State-Centrism, History and Change in International Law

KATE PARLETT
The Participation of States in International Organisations: The Role of Human Rights and Democracy

ALISON DUXBURY
'Armed Attack' and Article 51 of the UN Charter: Evolutions in Customary Law and Practice

TOM RUYS
Science and Risk Regulation in International Law: The Role of Science, Uncertainty and Values

JACQUELINE PEEL
Theatre of the Rule of Law: The Theory, History and Practice of Transnational Legal Intervention

STEPHEN HUMPHREYS
The Public International Law Theory of Hans Kelsen: Believing in Universal Law

JOCHEN VON BERNSTORFF
Vicarious Liability in Tort: A Comparative Perspective

PAULA GILIKER
Legal Personality in International Law

ROLAND PORTMANN
Legitimacy and Legality in International Law: An Interactional Account

JUTTA BRUNNÉE AND STEPHEN J. TOOPE
The Concept of Non-International Armed Conflict in International
Humanitarian Law

ANTHONY CULLEN
The Challenge of Child Labour in International Law

FRANZISKA HUMBERT
Shipping Interdiction and the Law of the Sea

DOUGLAS GUILFOYLE
International Courts and Environmental Protection

TIM STEPHENS
Legal Principles in WTO Disputes

ANDREW D. MITCHELL
War Crimes in Internal Armed Conflicts

EVE LA HAYE
Humanitarian Occupation

GREGORY H. FOX
The International Law of Environmental Impact Assessment: Process, Substance
and Integration

NEIL CRAIK
The Law and Practice of International Territorial Administration: Versailles, Iraq
and Beyond

CARSTEN STAHN
Cultural Products and the World Trade Organization

TANIA VOON
United Nations Sanctions and the Rule of Law

JEREMY FARRALL
National Law in WTO Law: Effectiveness and Good Governance in the World
Trading System

SHARIF BHUIYAN
The Threat of Force in International Law

NIKOLAS STÜRCHLER
Indigenous Rights and United Nations Standards

ALEXANDRA XANTHAKI
International Refugee Law and Socio-Economic Rights

MICHELLE FOSTER
The Protection of Cultural Property in Armed Conflict

ROGER O'KEEFE
Interpretation and Revision of International Boundary Decisions

KAIYAN HOMI KAIKOBAD
Multinationals and Corporate Social Responsibility: Limitations and Opportunities in International Law

JENNIFER A. ZERK
Judiciaries within Europe: A Comparative Review

JOHN BELL
Law in Times of Crisis: Emergency Powers in Theory and Practice

OREN GROSS AND FIONNUALA NÍ AOLÁIN
Vessel-Source Marine Pollution: The Law and Politics of International Regulation

ALAN TAN
Enforcing Obligations Erga Omnes in International Law

CHRISTIAN J. TAMS
Non-Governmental Organisations in International Law

ANNA-KARIN LINDBLOM
Democracy, Minorities and International Law

STEVEN WHEATLEY
Prosecuting International Crimes: Selectivity and the International Law Regime

ROBERT CRYER
Compensation for Personal Injury in English, German and Italian Law: A Comparative Outline

BASIL MARKESINIS, MICHAEL COESTER, GUIDO ALPA, AND AUGUSTUS ULLSTEIN
Dispute Settlement in the UN Convention on the Law of the Sea

NATALIE KLEIN
The International Protection of Internally Displaced Persons

CATHERINE PHUONG
Imperialism, Sovereignty and the Making of International Law

ANTONY ANGHIE
Necessity, Proportionality and the Use of Force by States

JUDITH GARDAM
International Legal Argument in the Permanent Court of International Justice:
The Rise of the International Judiciary

OLE SPIERMANN
Great Powers and Outlaw States: Unequal Sovereigns in the International Legal
Order

GERRY SIMPSON
Local Remedies in International Law

C. F. AMERASINGHE
Reading Humanitarian Intervention: Human Rights and the Use of Force in
International Law

ANNE ORFORD
Conflict of Norms in Public International Law: How WTO Law Relates to Other
Rules of Law

JOOST PAUWELYN
Transboundary Damage in International Law

HANQIN XUE
European Criminal Procedures

EDITED BY MIREILLE DELMAS-MARTY AND JOHN SPENCER
The Accountability of Armed Opposition Groups in International Law

LIESBETH ZEGVELD
Sharing Transboundary Resources: International Law and Optimal Resource Use

EYAL BENVENISTI
International Human Rights and Humanitarian Law

RENÉ PROVOST
Remedies Against International Organisations

KAREL WELLENS
Diversity and Self-Determination in International Law

KAREN KNOP
The Law of Internal Armed Conflict

LINDSAY MOIR
International Commercial Arbitration and African States: Practice, Participation
and Institutional Development

AMAZU A. ASOUZU
The Enforceability of Promises in European Contract Law

JAMES GORDLEY
International Law in Antiquity

DAVID J. BEDERMAN
Money Laundering: A New International Law Enforcement Model

GUY STESSENS
Good Faith in European Contract Law

REINHARD ZIMMERMANN AND SIMON WHITTAKER
On Civil Procedure

J. A. JOLOWICZ
Trusts: A Comparative Study

MAURIZIO LUPOI
The Right to Property in Commonwealth Constitutions

TOM ALLEN
International Organizations Before National Courts

AUGUST REINISCH
The Changing International Law of High Seas Fisheries

FRANCISCO ORREGO VICUÑA
Trade and the Environment: A Comparative Study of EC and US Law

DAMIEN GERADIN
Unjust Enrichment: A Study of Private Law and Public Values

HANOCH DAGAN
Religious Liberty and International Law in Europe

MALCOLM D. EVANS
Ethics and Authority in International Law

ALFRED P. RUBIN
Sovereignty Over Natural Resources: Balancing Rights and Duties

NICO SCHRIJVER
The Polar Regions and the Development of International Law

DONALD R. ROTHWELL
Fragmentation and the International Relations of Micro-States:
Self-Determination and Statehood

JORRI DUURSMA
Principles of the Institutional Law of International Organizations

For EU product safety concerns, contact us at Calle de José Abascal, 56–1°,
28003 Madrid, Spain or eugpsr@cambridge.org.

www.ingramcontent.com/pod-product-compliance
Ingram Content Group UK Ltd.
Pitfield, Milton Keynes, MK11 3LW, UK
UKHW020347060825
461487UK00008B/555